MENU SOLUTIONS

Quantity Recipes for Regular and Special Diets

MENU SOLUTIONS

Quantity Recipes for Regular and Special Diets

Sandra J. Frank

Robert E. Baker

John Wiley & Sons, Inc.

New York   Chichester   Brisbane   Toronto   Singapore

Copyright © 1996 by Sandra J. Frank and Robert E. Baker

Published by John Wiley & Sons, Inc.

Library of Congress Cataloging-in-Publication Data

Frank, Sandra J.
Menu solutions: quantity recipes for regular and special diets /
Sandra J. Frank, Bob Baker.
    p.   cm.
Includes bibliographical references.
ISBN 0-471-55458-8 (cloth : alk. paper)
1. Diet therapy. 2. Quantity cookery. I. Baker, Bob (Robert E.)
II. Title.
RM217.F72 1996
615.8'54—dc20   95-42702

Printed in the United States of America.

10 9 8 7 6 5 4 3 2 1

Contents

CONTENTS

PART FOUR: Menu Planning   481

APPENDIXES

Tables

Introduction

Practically every day, we are confronted by TV commentary or info commercials, ads, publications, and even our friends with the latest food- or disease-related story, theory or opinion, usually about what to eat and what it does to our body. They often relate studies or polls on everything from vitamins, fiber, and cholesterol to diabetes and colon cancer. Endless media horror stories report consumer health dangers posed by food additives, animal injections, spraying, poor food inspections, restaurant food handling, and dietary fads gone haywire—to name only a very few! And how many celebrity- or doctor-recommended or -sponsored, "can't-miss" weight loss programs or products do we all encounter weekly? It is any wonder that countless millions have a confused sense of urgency as to what foods should be eaten?

Adding to the confusion are the contradictory product claims and the massive financial resources, media marketing skills, and political influence available to many corporate food purveyors and individuals. These advantages are formidable and appear to routinely overwhelm and circumvent government guidelines and regulations. A legitimate question arises about whether it is possible for the average person to overcome this confusion or whether we should simply throw up our hands and say, "I give up. Why bother? Who really knows anyway?"

Despite the confusion, change has long been under way. While it has been very slow, it appears inevitable. Since the 1950s, the change to a healthier lifestyle has been resisted at each step of the way by politics, spe-cial-interest groups, lobbyists, food manufacturers, and government regulations or lack thereof. Today, we live in an era of more rapid change, where millions of people are adopting a new, healthier eating style, and others are continuing the older, less healthful habits. This period of change is likely to extend well into the twenty first century, as food purveyors position themselves to sell products to both constituencies. The challenge for individuals is first to become better educated and then to act based on our knowledge and common sense. The alternative is to remain susceptible to the whims of those who market food products that both shorten our life span and create unnecessary financial and health-related hardships during our lives.

Dr. Sandra Frank's extraordinary initial body of work was developed over a period of eight years. It involved the identification, testing, and refinement of over 300 modified quantity recipes (50 portions) and included four-week cycle menus and special monthly holiday recipes and menus. The authors' original plan was to compile these recipes and menus with special related materials in a book for food professionals in health care facilities, schools, correctional facilities, and government agencies. These professionals include food service directors, dietitians, doctors, chefs, consultants, administrators, and school/college program educators. We feel, certainly, that we have accomplished that goal. However, closer evaluation and considerable professional input revealed that this book can also provide valuable source materials for the layperson.

Does this book contain invaluable recipes, diets, menus, and food selection materials that can easily be used in the home? The answer is a resounding yes! For countless millions afflicted with long-standing health problems and requiring information on suitable foods, appropriate ingredients, modified diets, recipes, and menus, this book is an indispensable resource. Dr. Frank has broadened the recipes to include smaller test portions for four to eight people. She has also added over 100 more recipes and menus, particularly for individuals wanting a vegetarian or kosher diet. Special holiday recipes and menus were also developed and included.

Importantly, health care professionals will now have available a book that they can recommend to patients or clients. Individuals needing nutritional information, diet support, food selection and preparation assistance, and recipes and menus to meet their nutritional needs will find this book invaluable. It is strongly recommended and advised that before starting a modified diet, you consult with your physician and a registered dietitian/nutritionist.

The book is divided as follows:

Part One: Basic Guidelines for Healthier Eating. These chapters may be the most important ones for the average person or for the past or current health care patient. They should assist you to quickly become educated and to cut through many of the barriers and mystiques built around subjects such as "nutrition" and "diet." Similarly, subjects such as "shopping right," "reading labels," "eating out or at home," and "food controversies," should become much easier to handle. The intent is to equip you with basic information and tools, to deal with health and eating situations that you may encounter and that are important to you. They should also enhance your understanding of this book, including the different modified diets, recipes, and glossary terminology.

Part Two: Diet Planning. These chapters give an overview of the different diets normally required by professionals or encountered by people at home. Each diet is examined, defined, and identified with problems it can assist. Comprehensive charts illustrate foods, ingredients, or additives that should be allowed or restricted. Handy tips for professionals and consumers are listed to support possible dietary situations.

Part Three: Diet Modified Recipes. This section contains over 400 recipes in quantity (50 portions) and household amounts (four to eight portions). Each recipe contains information on ingredients, method of cooking, portion size, and yield. In addition, this part describes directions for preparing recipes for special dietary needs and contains nutrient analyses.

Part Four: Menu Planning. The menus contained in this part have been designed to meet the needs of individuals with special nutritional considerations. Each menu contains recipe codes and serving sizes. Most of the menus are in a four-week cycle format. The following menus are contained in this section: menus for individuals with special needs; vegetarian menus; menus for health care facilities; senior citizen nutrition programs; and special holiday and theme menus.

Appendixes. The Appendixes contain vital reference information, including: abbreviations; weights and measures; food portion aids; common can sizes; food equivalents; ingredient substitutions; herbs and spices; garnishes; and nutrient analysis of the menus.

Glossary. Contains terms and definitions associated with general health conditions, nutrition, and cooking.

PART I

Basic Guidelines for Healthier Eating

1

The USDA Pyramid and Food Labeling

The Food Guide Pyramid

For decades, the official United States Government position on nutrition was represented by the Basic Four Food Groups. This stance had been widely recognized as hopelessly outdated since before the 1970s.

The long delayed need for revision was more than symbolically important. Practically all food service professionals continually utilized them as the gospel truth, including school food service directors, physicians, and food manufacturers. The fear of legal reprisals and mainstream thinking kept all but a few from straying from Basic Four thinking. Therein can be seen both the importance given to guidelines and their potentially adverse impact upon consumers.

In the 1970s, the U.S. government was motivated by private sector pressure and nutrition reformers, to recognize the urgent need for guideline revisions, toward a diet that would address, delay, or prevent the growing incidence of heart disease, cancer, obesity, and other chronic and degenerative diseases.

The revisions began in 1979 with the release of the first Dietary Goals for the United States, which were seven very specific and politically controversial goals. The 1980 revisions were renamed the Dietary Guidelines for Americans. Suggestions for food choices were similar but less specific and therefore less controversial.

Table 1.1 Dietary Guidelines for Americans

1. Eat a variety of foods for energy, protein, vitamins, minerals, and fiber.
2. Maintain healthy weight to reduce chances of heart disease, high blood pressure, strokes, some cancers, and common kinds of diabetes.
3. Choose a diet low in fat, saturated fat, and cholesterol, since fat contains twice the calories of carbohydrate or protein. Lower fat can help maintain a healthy weight and reduce the risk of heart disease.
4. Choose a diet with plenty of vegetables, fruits, and grain products, which provide vitamins, minerals, fiber, and complex carbohydrates and help lower fat intake.
5. Use sugars only in moderation, as they contain excess calories, few nutrients, and cause tooth decay.
6. Use salt and sodium only in moderation to help reduce the risk of high blood pressure.
7. Only drink alcoholic beverages in moderation, as they contain calories, have few nutrients, and cause health problems and addiction.

Finally, what both the government and consumers really needed, was a simple pictorial representation of these guidelines, to fulfill the adage "a picture is worth a 1,000 words." What eventually evolved, after considerable political lobbying, disputes, and delays was the USDA Food Guide Pyramid (Figure 1.1).

While not perfect, the Pyramid represents a significant and effective road map for improving diets. It calls for eating a variety of foods to obtain the nutrients you need and at the same time the right amount of calories to maintain healthy weight. It focuses on reducing dietary fat, particularly saturated fat and promotes a plant-based diet having less animal products. It encourages you to consume more food from the bottom of the Pyramid than from the top. It contains the recommended number of servings per day for each food group, which is more practical than percentages.

Basically, the Pyramid suggests the following:

1. Cut your fat and saturated-fat intake. (Figure 1.2 lists common items from each food group and the amount of fat in each.)
2. Cut cholesterol, refined grains, sodium, and sugar.
3. Your diet should concentrate on grains, vegetables, and fruits.
4. Your diet should be low in meat and dairy products.

The general goals, associated with the Pyramid, are to obtain:

- 55% or more of your calories from carbohydrates.
- 15% or less of your calories from protein.
- 30% or less of your calories from fat.
- 33% or less saturated fat, from total fat.

Pyramid Related Observations

The Pyramid is intended to be used as an outline, not as an inflexible guide, especially relating to the number of servings per day. For example, the Pyramid uses a

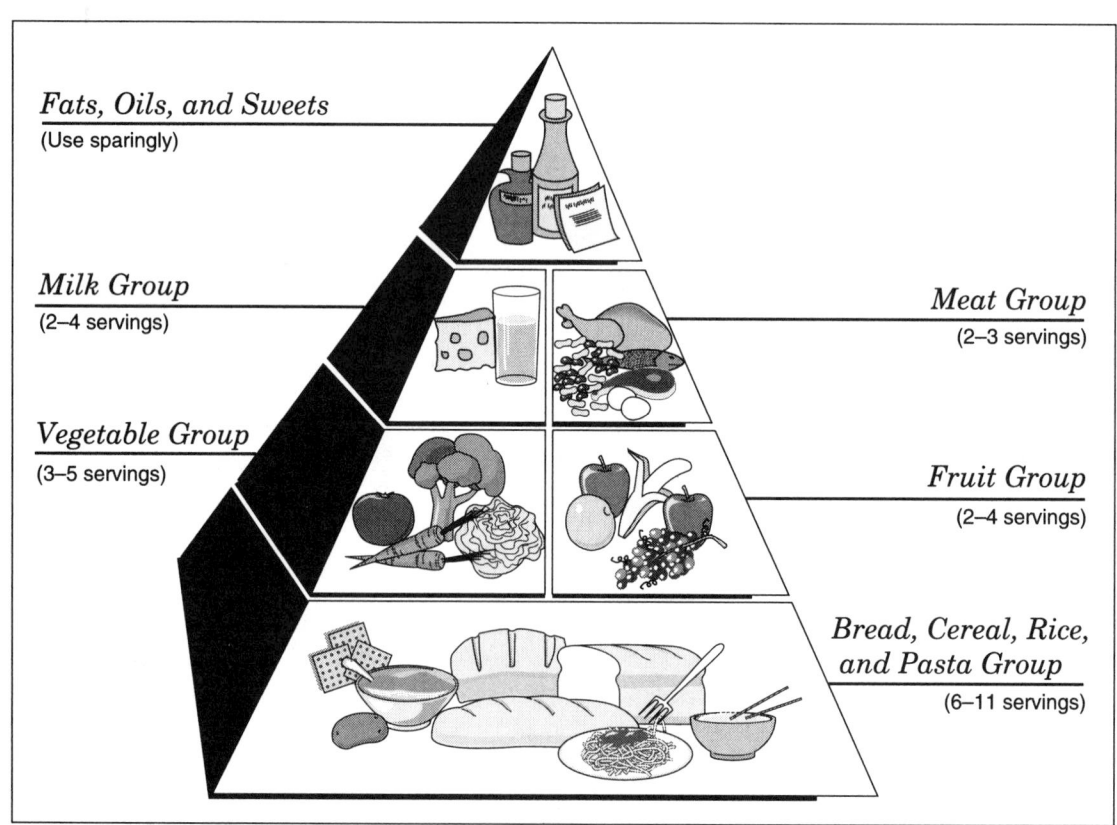

Figure 1.1 **Food Guide Pyramid**

For this amount of food . . .		Count this many . . .

Bread, Cereal, Rice, and Pasta Group

Eat 6 to 11 servings daily	Servings	Grams of fat
Bread, 1 slice	1	1
Hamburger roll, bagel, english muffin, 1	2	2
Tortilla, 1	1	3
Rice, pasta, cooked, 1/2 cup	1	Trace
Plain crackers, small, 3–4	1	3
Breakfast cereal, 1 oz.	1	*
Pancakes, 4" diameter, 2	2	3
Croissant, 1 large (2 oz.)	2	12
Doughnut, 1 medium (2 oz.)	2	11
Danish, 1 medium (2 oz.)	2	13
Cake, frosted, 1/16 average	1	13
Cookies, 2 medium	1	4
Pie, fruit, 2-crust, 1/6 8" pie	2	19

*Check product label

Vegetable Group

Eat 3 to 5 servings daily	Servings	Grams of fat
Vegetables, cooked, 1/2 cup	1	Trace
Vegetables, leafy, raw, 1 cup	1	Trace
Vegetables, nonleafy, raw, chopped, 1/2 cup	1	Trace
Potatoes, scalloped, 1/2 cup	1	4
Potato salad, 1/2 cup	1	8
French fries, 10	1	8

Fruit Group

Eat 2 to 4 servings daily	Servings	Grams of fat
Whole fruit; med. apple, orange, banana	1	Trace
Fruit, raw or canned, 1/2 cup	1	Trace
Fruit juice, unsweetened, 3/4 cup	1	Trace
Avacado, 1/4 whole	1	9

Milk, Yogurt, and Cheese Group

Eat 2 to 3 servings daily	Servings	Grams of fat
Skim milk, 1 cup	1	Trace
Nonfat yogurt, plain, 8 oz.	1	Trace
Lowfat milk, 2 percent, 1 cup	1	5
Whole milk, 1 cup	1	8
Chocolate milk, 2 percent, 1 cup	1	5

For this amount of food . . .		Count this many . . .
Lowfat yogurt, plain, 8 oz.	1	4
Lowfat yogurt, fruit, 8 oz.	1	3
Natural cheddar cheese, 1-1/2 oz.	1	14
Process cheese, 2 oz.	1	18
Mozzarella, part skim, 1-1/2 oz.	1	7
Ricotta, part skim, 1/2 cup	1	10
Cottage cheese, 4 percent fat, 1/2 cup	1/4	5
Ice cream, 1/2 cup	1/3	7
Ice milk, 1/2 cup	1/3	3
Frozen yogurt, 1/2 cup	1/2	2

Meat, Poultry, Fish, Dry Beans, Eggs, and Nuts Group

Eat 5 to 7 oz. daily	Servings	Grams of fat
Lean meat, poultry, fish, cooked	3 oz.*	6
Ground beef, lean, cooked	3 oz.*	16
Chicken, with skin, fried	3 oz.*	13
Bologna, 2 slices	1 oz.*	16
Egg, 1	1 oz.*	5
Dry beans and peas, cooked, 1/2 cup	1 oz.*	Trace
Peanut butter, 2 tbsp.	1 oz.*	16
Nuts, 1/3 cup	1 oz.*	22

*Ounces of lean meat these count as

Fats, Oils, and Sweets

Use sparingly		Grams of fat
Butter, margarine, 1 tsp.	—	4
Mayonnaise, 1 tbsp.	—	11
Salad dressing, 1 tbsp.	—	7
Reduced calorie salad dressing, 1 tbsp.	—	*
Sour cream, 2 tbsp.	—	6
Cream cheese, 1 oz.	—	10
Sugar, jam, jelly, 1 tsp.	—	0
Cola, 12 fl. oz.	—	0
Fruit drink, ade, 12 fl. oz.	—	0
Chocolate bar, 1 oz.	—	9
Sherbet, 1/2 cup	—	2
Fruit sorbet, 1/2 cup	—	0
Gelatin dessert, 1/2 cup	—	0

*Check product label

Figure 1.2 **Daily Food Choices**

range of six to eleven servings per day of the bread and cereal group, reflecting the differences in bigger and smaller eaters. Be aware that shifting your diet to eating more portions of grains, vegetables, fruits, and other less nutrient-dense foods can create much more food than you normally consume. It also becomes harder to over-indulge in high fat and empty calorie food, because you are too full. More informative details about serving sizes are found in the USDA Pyramid booklet.

- Remember that eating three meals per day is not sacred.

- Smaller meals and more frequent snacks allow more room for foods dictated by the Pyramid, which are high in fiber, complex carbohydrate bulk, and water. Between meals, snack on dried or fresh fruits, juices, blender drinks, whole wheat or whole grain bread or pretzels, or air-popped popcorn, which can improve your diet and not spoil your meals.

- The USDA Pyramid booklet notes that "No one food group is more important then another—for your health, you need them all." Despite this statement, it is clear the Pyramid suggests that the core of your diet should be grains, vegetables, and fruits, at the expense of meat and dairy products.

- The positioning of fats and sugars at the top of the pyramid, with the warning "use sparingly," with the meat and dairy group just below, sends a clear and unmistakable message to consumers.

- The single biggest problem with American diets are fatty diets, that cause or significantly contribute to cancer, diabetes, heart disease, and obesity. Each person must become familiar with the fat content of food, to make the best choices, even within each pyramid food group.

- Recognize that only 40% of the consumed fat in average American diets can actually be seen, such as in butter, gravies, margarine, meat fat, oils, and salad dressings. About 60% of the dietary fat can not be seen, such as in bread, cheese, meats, nuts, and convenience foods.

- Remember that fat contains twice the calories of protein or carbohydrates.

  - 1 gram fat = 9 calories
  - 1 gram carbohydrates = 4 calories

- 1 gram protein = 4 calories
- 1 teaspoon butter or margarine = 4 grams fat or 36 calories

Consequently, it's often what you add to foods or cook them with, that adds most of the fat calories.

- The dairy or meat Pyramid groupings do not indicate the vast differences in fat content that exists in each category.

- Use low-fat foods and condiments such as low-fat crackers, desserts, mayonnaise, salad dressings, sour cream, and yogurt.

- The Pyramid is likely to cause food companies to reformulate food products to make them lower in fat and therefore more favorably position that food lower on the Pyramid.

- Use the USDA Food Guide Pyramid and instructional booklet together for optimum results. Write for a free copy to: U.S. Department of Agriculture, Human Nutrition Information Service, 6505 Belcrest Road, Hyattsville, MD 20782.

Food Labeling

According to a former Health and Human Services Secretary, "Consumers need to be linguists, scientists and mind readers to understand the many labels they encounter." Outright deceptive food labeling practices were previously the norm. Today, this is no longer true, as food labeling has undergone a complete revision, resulting in wide, sweeping improvements.

Starting in 1989, the Food and Drug Administration (FDA) and the USDA'S Food Safety and Inspection Service (FSIS) have completed a major overhaul of the system, improving both the format and content of food labels.

A better understanding of the overall "big picture" can be obtained, by first summarizing the various changes. These are:

- Vitamin and mineral labeling emphasis has been replaced by concentration on fat, sodium, cholesterol, carbohydrate (fiber and sugars), protein, and a select few vitamins and minerals. This new emphasis reflects concerns about cancer, diabetes, and heart disease caused by overeating and poor nutrition.

- Nutrition labeling is now mandatory for almost all processed and packaged foods.
- Listing of the new nutrients is required in a specific format.
- Serving sizes for over 130 food categories are now defined and uniform. They are now consistent across product lines and reflect the amounts of food people actually eat.
- Specific acceptable definitions and descriptive words, are now required, when used by food producers, marketers, and consumers and are calculated in common household measures.
- Ingredient labeling is mandatory for previously exempt standardized foods, such as bread, catsup, macaroni, and mayonnaise.
- General requirements are in force for standardized food substitutes, such as butter, cheese, or sour cream regarding acceptable nutrient claims.
- Product health claims regarding the relationship between food nutrients and risk of disease, are now regulated on food labeling.
- Juice beverage regulations are now required, showing the percentage of actual fruit or beverage juice, on all labels.
- Voluntary guidelines have been established, for grocery store displays of over 60 foods, including over 20 of the most frequently consumed raw fruits, vegetables, fish, and poultry.
- A modified form of new nutritional labeling covers vitamin and mineral supplements.

Front of the Package Labeling

The package front has traditionally been used by sellers to get your attention, sometimes with confusing, vague, or inaccurate use of words. Now, approximately 37 new, standard labeling definitions have been mandated for use by the consumer as a quick guide to make purchasing decisions.

There are nine core terms, called "descriptors" or "nutrient content claims," that are FDA definitions used to describe a food, if it meets that definition. The nine terms are:

Free	Source of	Less
Low	Reduced	More
High	Fresh	Light (lite)

These nine terms have also been given specific definitions, when used with certain nutrients, such as low sodium, sugar free, low-fat, or high fiber.

Learning these labeling definition terms will quickly assist consumers to select foods that fit their daily diet. These definitions are listed in Table 1.2.

Back of the Package Labeling

The complete "Nutrition Facts" on the back of most packaged foods helps you select and compare foods for your daily diet. The new panel of redesigned

Nutrition Facts

Serving Size ½ cup (114g)
Servings Per Container 4

Amount Per Serving

Calories 90	Calories from Fat 30
	% Daily Value*
Total Fat 3g	**5%**
Saturated Fat 0g	**0%**
Cholesterol 0mg	**0%**
Sodium 300mg	**13%**
Total Carbohydrate 13g	**4%**
Dietary Fiber 3g	**12%**
Sugars 3g	
Protein 3g	

Vitamin A	80%	•	Vitamin C	60%
Calcium	4%	•	Iron	4%

* Percent Daily Values are based on a 2,000 calorie diet. Your daily values may be higher or lower depending on your calorie needs:

	Calories	2,000	2,500
Total Fat	Less than	65g	80g
Sat Fat	Less than	20g	25g
Cholesterol	Less than	300mg	300mg
Sodium	Less than	2,400mg	2,400mg
Total Carbohydrate		300g	375g
Fiber		25g	30g

Calories per gram:
Fat 9 • Carbohydrate 4 • Protein 4

More nutrients may be listed on some labels.

Figure 1.3 **Back of the Package Label**

Table 1.2   Label Terms and Definitions

Terms	Definitions
calorie free	Fewer than 5 calories per serving.
cholesterol free	Fewer than 2 milligrams cholesterol and 2 grams or less saturated fat per serving.
enriched or fortified	Has been nutritionally altered so that one serving provides at least 10 percent more of the recommended daily amount (daily value) of a nutrient than the comparison food.
extra lean	Fewer than 5 grams fat, 2 grams saturated fat and 95 milligrams of cholesterol per serving and per 100 grams.
fat free	Less than 1/2 gram fat per serving.
fresh	Generally used on food in its raw state. It cannot be used on food that has been frozen or cooked, or on food that contains preservatives.
fresh frozen	Foods that have been quickly frozen while still fresh.
good source	One serving provides 10 to 19 percent of the daily value for a particular nutrient.
good source of fiber	Contains 10 to 19 percent of the daily value for fiber (2.5 to 4.75 grams) per serving. If a food is not "low fat," it must declare the level of total fat per serving and refer to the nutrition panel when a fiber claim is mentioned.
high	One serving provides at least 20 percent of the daily value for a particular nutrient.
high fiber	Contains 20 percent or more of the daily value for fiber (at least 5 grams) per serving. If a food is not "low fat," it must declare the level of total fat per serving and refer to the nutrition panel when a fiber claim is mentioned.
lean	Fewer than 10 grams fat, 4 grams saturated fat and 95 milligrams cholesterol per serving and per 100 grams.
light	At least one-third fewer calories per serving than a comparison food; contains no more than half the fat per serving of a comparison food. If a food derives 50 percent or more of its calories from fat, the reduction must be at least 50 percent of the fat.
texture or color	Explained, such as "light brown sugar."
light meal	A "low fat" or "low calorie" meal, usually using the word "light" in its name such as "Light Delight, a low-fat meal."
light in sodium	At least 50 percent less sodium per serving than a comparison food.
low calorie	40 calories or fewer per serving.
low-calorie meal	120 calories or fewer per 100 grams.
low cholesterol	20 milligrams or less cholesterol and 2 grams or less saturated fat per serving.
low-cholesterol meal	20 milligrams or fewer per 100 grams and no more than 2 grams saturated fat per 100 grams.
low fat	3 grams or less fat per serving.
low-fat meal	3 grams or fewer per 100 grams and 30 percent or less calories from fat.
low saturated fat	1 gram or less per serving and 15 percent or less calories from saturated fat.
low sodium	140 milligrams or less sodium per serving.
low-sodium meal	140 milligrams or less sodium per 100 grams.
more	One serving provides at least 10 percent more of the recommended daily value of a nutrient than the comparison food.

Table 1.2 continued

Terms	Definitions
percent fat free	A claim made on a "low-fat" or "fat-free" product which accurately reflects the amount of fat present in 100 grams of food; a food with 3 grams of fat per 100 grams would be "97 percent fat free."
reduced calorie	At least 25 percent fewer calories per serving than a comparison food.
reduced cholesterol	At least 25 percent less cholesterol and 2 grams or less saturated fat per serving than a comparison food.
reduced fat	At least 25 percent less fat per serving than a comparison food.
reduced sugar	At least 25 percent less sugar per serving than a comparison food.
salt free	Meets requirements for "sodium free."
sodium free	Fewer than 5 milligrams sodium per serving.
sugar free	Less than 0.5 grams of sugars per serving.
very low sodium	35 milligrams or less sodium per serving.
reduced sodium	At least 25 percent less sodium per serving.
unsalted	Has no salt added during processing. To use this term, the product it resembles must normally be processed with salt and the label must note that the food is not a sodium-free food if it does not meet the requirements for "sodium free."

"Nutrition Facts" must always list the nutrients in the proper order. This order reflects the particular importance of fat, cholesterol, sodium, and carbohydrates in modern diets.

The absolute amounts of each nutrient the food product contains, per serving, is given as well as its calories and fat per serving. The percent they each contribute to a healthy daily diet is represented by "**% Daily Value.**"

Optional nutrient components that may be included are:
♦ Calories from saturated fat
♦ Polyunsaturated fat
♦ Mono-unsaturated fat
♦ Potassium
♦ Soluble Fiber
♦ Insoluble Fiber
♦ Sugar alcohol
♦ Other carbohydrate
♦ Other essential vitamins and minerals

Different formats may be utilized for the standard "Nutrition Facts" panel, depending on the package size, the total nutrient content of the food, or both.

Serving sizes must now be consistent and uniform among similar products and provide nutritional information based on standardized serving sizes. These serving sizes are now presented on the label in common household units, such as: g = grams or mg = milligrams. This provides consumers a clear basis to make quick comparisons between similar products.

The "% Daily Value" can indicate precisely if you are getting the proper balance of each nutrient in your diet. The actual "% Daily Value" for each nutrient in the food product is provided opposite each nutrient. Now you can quickly determine if the product provides a large or small amount of a nutrient and choose the other foods you want to eat during the rest of the day. For example, if a nutrient (sodium) provides 50% of the total recommended sodium for the day, you know how to adjust your diet the rest of the day for sodium intake.

Some products may list the total recommended daily values, at the bottom of the nutrition facts panel. These "% Daily Values" are based upon a typical daily 2,000 calorie diet. Be careful to use these comparison values as a guide only, because your own calorie needs will vary, dictating higher or lower daily values.

Remember, the "% Daily Value," is not a rigid, inflexible number, and you can always balance your intake over several days.

More simplified nutritional labeling formats are allowed, when more than one-half of the required nutrients are present in insignificant amounts.

2

Eating at Home and Dining Out

Eating at Home

If eating healthful and nutritious food at home is one of your concerns and objectives, you should develop an organized "game" plan that is tailored to you. It would include meals and menu planning specifics, shopping techniques, and eating at home insights.

Most importantly, you want to keep any plan simple and flexible.

Your plan can now utilize the nutrition knowledge gained from this book and other resources, particularly relating to the "Pyramid," "How to Read Labels," and from the recipes and menus you select.

An absolutely critical question to confront at this point, might well be: Is there someone other than yourself, such as a family member, who is directly involved in your meal and menu planning or shopping? If the answer is yes, this person represents a potential stumbling block to your nutritional objectives.

Since this person may plan your meals and menus, shops for you, and likely eats at home with you, it is best to enroll this person as a partner in assisting you to meet your nutritional objectives. Other than improving your own past nutritional habits, this added factor could potentially be the single biggest problem you encounter.

Meal and Menu Planning

Before shopping, you must begin to think about what foods you want and need to eat together, for each meal day, week, or even month.

Normally, your food choices are dictated by nutritional concerns, habits, available time, personal likes and dislikes, seasonal availability of foods, and other factors. When you add a good dose of menu planning to this equation, you begin to get much better nutritional and health results that can also save time and money.

The following are menu planning suggestions and insights to improve your nutritional status and lay the groundwork for better shopping.

- ◆ It is often difficult, but write out your projected future meals and menus. Incorporating recipes and menus from resources, such as this book, will help this process. Using two- or four-week cycle menus can simplify planning and help you follow it.

- ◆ Use recipes that minimize preparation and cooking time, such as vegetables, stir-fries or potatoes, instead of casseroles or roasted meats.

- ◆ Utilize the Pyramid information to focus on simple nutritional basics, such as avoiding excess calories, enriched foods, fat, sodium, and sugar.

- ◆ Use the Pyramid to determine the number of servings needed from each group and to concentrate on grains, vegetables and fruits, as the basis upon which to build your diet.

- ◆ Menu planning will stimulate your use of different foods to obtain your nutritional requirements.

- ◆ For variety, try new recipes or preparation styles.

- Keep meals attractive and interesting by using different food colors, flavorings, textures, and shapes.

- Menu planning will assist you keeping the necessary foods on hand. This results in fewer supermarket trips and also in fewer convenience store trips, where higher prices, fewer nutritional alternatives, and more temptations are the norm.

- Planning for leftovers, permits less rigid meal and menu schedules and saves time and food costs.

- Prepare pre-cooked excess food as leftovers or as storable meal portions for later use by reheating or re-preparing in another fashion. Good examples are gravies, meat loaf, hamburgers, muffins, pies, rice, sauces, soups, stews, or waffles.

- Use freezing or refrigeration to store pre-cooked and pre-cut portions of chicken, meat, or turkey for future use in casseroles, salads, sandwiches, stir-fries or soups.

Shopping

Once you have started meal and menu planning and hopefully prepared an actual two or four week advance menu, you are ready for shopping.

- Prepare a shopping list to fulfill the menu. Add to this list, any items you have written down on a piece of paper next to the refrigerator.

- Group the listed items by Pyramid nutritional importance and by how a store does it: bread and cereals; fruits and vegetables; beans, nuts, and seeds; meats, fish, and poultry; dairy; oils; and other items.

Where to Shop

- Decide where you want to shop, from the following alternatives.

- Chain supermarkets often represent your habit; good location and check-cashing convenience, better pricing than small stores, and more variety.

- Warehouse stores offer lower prices, fair to good variety, and large bulk-purchasing opportunities.

- Natural food stores often offer goods at slightly higher prices, more healthful choices, less temptation to buy items that should be avoided, and bulk

foods not carried elsewhere, such as grains, nuts, rolled oats, rice, and whole grain foods such as flour and pasta.

- Specialty stores, including bakeries, fruit and vegetable stands or markets, and fish or meat stores often emphasize variety, better quality, and service.

- Local food co-ops, if available, may offer more healthful alternatives, good prices, and high quality.

- Convenience stores normally offer time savings, higher prices, less variety, and emphasis on non-healthful food alternatives.

You should utilize stores that meet your health considerations, even if they are not the cheapest. Careful shopping and purchasing of more healthful food choices will ultimately save you money and protect your health.

Shopping Techniques

Think about and develop a game plan to use when shopping, including:

- Never shop when tired or hungry.

- Put what you have learned about the Pyramid into action and read all labels.

- Keep four things in mind, at all times, when looking at food item labels: 1) fat; 2) salt; 3) sugar; and 4) enriched/refined flour. Armed with a knowledge of avoiding these four things will permit you to master the most common shopping dilemmas.

- In particular, learn to spot words that mean the same as sugar: brown sugar; corn syrup; dextrin; dextrose; fructose; glucose; high fructose corn syrup; honey; invert sugar; jam; jelly; lactose; levulose; maple sugar; maltose; molasses; syrup and turbinado sugar.

Bread, Cereals, and Grains

- Buy unrefined whole grains avoiding enriched white bread and cereals.

- Avoid those products made with eggs, excessive butter, or shortening to reduce fat and cholesterol intake.

- Avoid those brands containing "partially hydrogenated fats."

- Select water bagels, not egg bagels.

- Limit higher fat content products such as biscuits, croissants, puff pastry, or convenience-wrapped foods.

- Avoid packaged cake and dessert mixes, usually made with egg yolks.

- Look for pasta with the "no yolk" noodles, to avoid egg (yolk) noodles. Pasta is normally made from flour and water.

- The culprit in most breakfast cereals is sugar. Those sweetened by fruit juice concentrate or oatmeal and wheat cereals, which are often found in health food stores, are better alternatives.

- Granola bars are normally high in fat, rather than sugar.

Fruits and Vegetables

- Fresh fruits and vegetables should be a cornerstone of your food purchases, as they contain little fat, no cholesterol, and are low in calories. They are also high in vitamins, minerals, and dietary fiber.

- It is increasingly popular to find fruit juice concentrates, as replacements for sugar, in a variety of foods.

- Avocados and olives are high in fat content and calories.

Beans, Nuts, and Seeds

- Buy these as protein and animal fat alternatives, to reduce cholesterol. They include dried beans such as garbanzos, kidneys, lentils, navy, and pinto.

- Use in dips, salads, and soups.

- Oil-roasted nuts are higher in fat than dry-roasted or plain nuts.

- Nuts and seeds contain largely poly- and mono-unsaturated fats, but are higher in total fat and calories.

Meat, Fish, and Poultry

- Reduce your red meat emphasis by switching to turkey and other poultry.

- Buy leaner, less tender meat cuts, with less marbling (fat).

- Buy well-trimmed cuts.

- Avoid high cholesterol organ meats, such as brains, kidney, or liver.

- Replace ground beef with ground turkey, veal, or soy burger substitutes. They all significantly reduce fat content.

- Avoid meats with skin or dark meat to lower fat content.

- White, skinless chicken, particularly breast, is low in cholesterol and can be prepared in many ways.

- Avoid high fat duck or goose.

- Avoid luncheon meats, which are loaded with sodium and fat, such as bologna products and substitute sliced turkey breast.

- Avoid hot dogs by switching to turkey dogs, soy dogs, or lean turkey and reduce the saturated fat, cholesterol, and sodium.

- Avoid bacon and sausage, which contain large amounts of fat and sodium, substituting lower fat Canadian bacon.

- Buy canned tuna or salmon packed in water, not oil, for salads and sandwiches.

- Mackerel, sardines, and salmon are fatty cold water fish, that lower cholesterol levels.

- Scallops are versatile and perhaps the best seafood choice.

- Shrimp is high in cholesterol, as opposed to other shellfish.

- Avoid buying frozen, breaded fish, especially with batters made from egg yolks.

Dairy

- Substitute skim milk for any milk in all recipes.

- Use canned evaporated skim milk or non-fat dry milk in recipes to replace cream.

- Buy non-fat or low-fat cheeses to replace regular cheese in recipes. A low fat cheese has 5 grams fat or less per ounce. Supermarket choices are widespread, including, Borden fat free; Healthy Choice fat free; Kraft Free cheese slices; Polly-O Free, and Sargento low fat.

♦ Buy fat-free cream cheese, available from Alpine Lace, Healthy Choice, Philadelphia, and others.

♦ Buy 1% or non-fat cottage cheese, for regular.

♦ Grated parmesan cheese can be used for higher fat content cheeses such as mozzarella.

♦ Fat free egg substitutes, such as Egg Beaters, can replace eggs. One Egg Beater replaces one egg. Two egg whites can replace one egg.

♦ For baking, replace regular sour cream with fat-free Land O'Lakes, Light N' Lively, or others.

♦ Plain non-fat yogurt can also replace sour cream.

♦ Buy reduced fat or fat-free mayonnaise for regular.

Fats and Oils

It bears repeating: you should keep in mind that in a typical diet, the biggest source of fats are cooking oils and fats. Specifically:

♦ 43% comes from cooking oils and fats

♦ 39% from meats, fish, poultry, and eggs

♦ 11% from dairy

♦ 6% from fruits, vegetables, grains, and beans

Quite accurately, we are often advised that the most important health consideration in using cooking oils, is to reduce saturated fat. This is true, but fats are still fats. It is proper to start looking at reducing both the type and the total amount of cooking oils and fats, by finding substitutes.

♦ While shopping, think about replacing butter, margarine, and oil with substitutes such as applesauce, liquid Butter Buds, Promise Ultra fat-free margarine, Smart Beat low-or non-fat margarine, or Weight Watchers Extra Light margarine.

♦ Rather than buying and using oil, saute meats and vegetables in fat-free chicken or other soup broth, liquid Butter Buds, non-fat cooking spray, salsa, or even wine.

♦ Avoid buying oil products that say "100% vegetable oil," as they may contain coconut, palm, and other saturated fats.

♦ The better cooking oils include canola, safflower, olive, peanut, soybean, and corn.

Snacks

In the last few years, the quality and quantity of available "snack" foods has risen dramatically. Good-sense buying and minor preparation can easily result in food that tastes good and is good for you.

Some of the better and more obvious shopping possibilities include:

♦ Fresh fruit

♦ Canned, sugar-free fruit

♦ Natural fruit jams and jellies

♦ Homemade fruit juice ices

♦ Fruit and yogurt smoothie

♦ Non-fat crackers with non-fat cheese

♦ Matzo crackers

♦ Toasted bagel with non-fat cream cheese

♦ Biscuits, low fat

♦ Frozen waffles, fat free

♦ Non-fat sugar free cereals with skim milk

♦ Pasta (cooked) with non-fat salad dressing

♦ Pasta with low- or non-fat tomato sauce

♦ Baked potato with non-fat sour cream

♦ Rice with seasoning

♦ Vegetables (cut up) with non-fat yogurt onion dip

♦ Plain popcorn

♦ Potato chips and pretzels, fat free

♦ Dips, fat free

♦ Pancakes, low-or non-fat, with natural fruit jam

♦ Pizza, homemade, with low- or non-fat cheese

♦ Low-fat soy burgers or soy hot dogs

♦ Low- or non-fat soups, homemade or commercial

♦ Non-fat cheese sandwich, on low or non-fat bread, with vegetables

♦ Low- or non-fat cookies and muffins

- Salad with non-fat cottage cheese with lemon juice dressing

- Non-fat frozen yogurt

- Non-fat yogurt, with non-fat, sugar-free jam, as sweetener

Dining Out

We all need to realize and deal with a simple fact. Eating out, away from home, is perhaps the most common single pitfall, for the majority of people trying to improve their diet. When eating out, other people are in control of your food preparation, making it especially difficult to recognize and select lower fat and high fiber foods.

While restaurants are the normal place where we eat away from home, we need to also consider the workplace, party or social functions, and vacation and travel, to name a few.

Despite the fact that all of these places are potential dietary stumbling blocks, requiring caution, eating out properly and healthfully, is not impossible.

For starters, most of us need to get away from the habit and routine of repeatedly eating many of the same foods that we usually eat. We need to lower fat, salt, and sugar consumption, while increasing fruits, vegetables and whole grains in our diets.

The good news is that many restaurants increasingly address the public's nutritional concerns. Some are creating new menu food items, while others are changing eating habits by providing the public with a wider selection of more healthful Asian and European cuisines. The variety of new options available can assist you in changing your past meal patterns by offering new food tastes and textures, using food ingredients with far less oil, salt, and sugar.

Establishing Your Ground Rules

How do we develop and implement a long-term plan for eating out? Begin by setting your priorities and ground rules for developing self-responsibility.

First, you must be willing to give up high-fat, "great" tasting foods and exchange them for just as tasty, healthier foods. Eating healthier, doesn't mean eating untasty food. Just learn to combine "healthy" with "tasty." Let's face facts! Fat, saturated fat, cholesterol, sweets, sugar, and sodium stand in the way of establishing healthier eating patterns, of staying well, and avoiding health-threatening diseases, heart attacks, and strokes.

Second, you must obtain the desire and motivation to select healthier foods. This desire could be medically motivated or simply be a desire to eat healthier foods.

Once again, the reality is that most people eat out often. Learning guidelines for eating out will essentially permit you to keep your "special" at-home diet every time you encounter restaurants or other eating-out situations.

It is in your power—if you are "willing" and "wanting."

Develop Restaurant Eating Skills

You can order from virtually any menu in a restaurant, if you are armed with a few facts and realistic guidelines to assist you to make wiser food choices.

Remember, except for a few recommendations and caution flags, the basic rules for healthier restaurant eating are about the same as those for healthier eating at home.

Determine Eating Out Frequency

We already know that eating away from home is more difficult, giving us less control in avoiding temptations.

The more frequently you eat out, the more you need to determine your choices and portions. Cutting back on frequency, may give you a bit more liberty when you dine out.

If you must monitor your fat, cholesterol and sodium intake, due to medical reasons, you must exercise greater control over food choices, fat and portion size. Once you are clear about your health and nutrition goals, it will help determine how frequently you eat out.

No matter what, monitor and limit how often you eat out.

Selecting Restaurants

- Stay away from limited menu restaurants.

- Call the restaurant in advance if you are unfamiliar with the menu. Make sure you ask questions to determine if they:

  — Have healthful specials
  — Accept special requests
  — Serve skim milk or have butter alternatives
  — Omit MSG

— Steam vegetables
— Bake, broil, grill, poach, or steam fish, poultry, and meat
— Offer low-calorie sweeteners
— Leave butter, gravy, and sauces off dishes
— Offer fresh fruit or similar desserts
- When selecting restaurants with a group of people, speak up and be clear, positive, and assertive about your health considerations.

Selecting Menu Choices

- Don't starve or save yourself for the restaurant. You end up rationalizing and selecting foods you would normally avoid, which often results in overeating.

- Select the main item or entree first because it may include a starch and vegetable and that may influence any further ordering. In fast food or simple lunch situations, fewer choices can mean fewer and easier decisions.

- If you are familiar with the menu, plan your order ahead of time and avoid looking at the menu and further tempting yourself.

Minimize Fat Intake

- Restaurants typically use fat (bacon, butter, oil, margarine, sour cream) to enhance taste and flavor, but it's the villain in restaurant menus and it pops up in many items, in many ways. Fat has excess calories, no food volume, and contributes loads of saturated fat and cholesterol.

- Upon arrival beware of and omit bread, butter, cheese, chips, and crackers.

- Fried foods and high-fat appetizers are the norm. Avoid them and select carefully.

- Some entree choices are particularly high in fat, even before adding the fat used to cook the item (such as duck).

- As the meal is served, beware of additional fat from buttered vegetables, salad dressings, melted cheese, and sour cream.

- In most instances, fat and dessert are almost a given combination.

- Pick and choose through the minefield of fatty foods for tasty, healthier, low-fat, and low-calorie items.

- Watch out for menu words which are fat related, such as: "breaded," "fried," "deep fried," and "stuffed."

- Seek out low-fat foods and preparations, by spotting words such as "broiled," "blackened," "steamed," and "stir-fried."

Make Special Requests

- Consider special requests, as virtually a mandatory requirement, to eat healthier. The more you ask, the better off you'll be.

- Ask in a polite, reasonable, friendly, and assertive manner and the request will usually be granted.

- Do not let the server intimidate you. Ask questions and indicate that you are on a special diet or have certain food allergies. Be persistent.

- Restaurants have become used to special requests (even many fast-food outlets), so don't worry about upsetting anyone. Remember, you pay for the meal and they want your business.

- Special requests may include asking the server to withhold adding butter, oil, or salt to dishes; even broiled, sauteed, or seafood dishes.

- Typical requests may include asking for substitutions, such as "mustard, not mayo," "baked potatoes, not fries," or "broiled not sauteed."

- It is OK to say "no potato chips" or "no sour cream" or simply to say, "please cook with as little oil as possible."

- Ask for small portions or items "on the side," such as butter, gravy, sauce, and salad dressing.

- Asking the server to not bring bread, crackers, chips, or cheeses is acceptable. They are often easier to avoid when out of reach.

- Request alternative low-fat cooking methods to replace frying; such as baking, broiling, grilling, poaching, roasting, and steaming.

Control Food Portions

- Without question, most restaurants serve overly abundant portions. Don't overeat food, even if it is good for you.

- Subconsciously, many diners feel they must eat everything served. Resist this temptation.

- The reality is you can likely practice portion control by sharing an order with dining partners, as often occurs at Chinese or pizza restaurants; or by asking the server at order time for a doggie bag, to take excess portions home.

Develop Your Eating Out Plan

Develop a plan, complete with strategies and tactics, that addresses your need to overcome whatever current attitudes and behaviors you have long held. Beginning to change past culinary patterns, by utilizing a new healthier plan, eventually becomes a new routine.

Clearly, you should verbally broadcast your intention to change eating habits, to those around you. Ask for their support. Then, put a plan into action and vigorously follow it.

Changing Your Present Mindset

- Recognize and acknowledge your old ways of thinking, which previously resulted in making poor menu selections or overeating. Resolve to get rid of them once and for all.

- Special occasions bring to mind Christmas, Thanksgiving, weddings, dinner invites, family reunions, anniversaries, vacations, business trips, and restaurant dining in general. Too often, under the cloak of "special occasion," we feel free to eat anything and we disregard health considerations. Do not take a "special occasion" as an excuse for binge dining, because these special times can occur two or three times a week.

- A familiar pattern is eating well at home and "pigging out" in restaurants. Psychologically, food is used by many people as a "reward." It follows that many reward or treat themselves by overeating at a restaurant.

- Celebrating a happy time is often an excuse for overeating, "just this one time," which subsequently becomes a more frequent pattern.

- Stay away from restaurants advertising "all you can eat" or ones with a one price menu, which includes everything in the price.

Establishing Your New Mindset

- Carefully examine and evaluate your old mindset and personally experience its shortcomings.

- In a new mindset, the number one priority is eating healthy and heeding your medical condition, not overeating or eating improperly.

- You need to really believe you can continue to enjoy eating out, while you consume healthier food. You can easily do it, if you so desire. You may become amazed at your new attitude, once you develop and practice the intake of new and different foods that are just as tasty as the old ones.

- Always let your dining partners know about your need and desire to eat healthier foods because it may affect the restaurant of choice.

- Encourage the support of those around you, but don't necessarily expect to always get it.

- Don't let the opinion of others change your plan.

- Steer the dining out focus away from dollars and direct it toward whether you enjoyed your order, feel full, and like the entire eating experience and environment.

Preplanning Your Strategies

- First and foremost, do not starve yourself before going out. Self-created hunger will weaken your resistance and dramatically increase the likelihood of both overeating and rationalizing eating either wrong or extra food.

- Prior to dining out, it's far better to slightly decrease the intake of dietary components, such as calories, cholesterol, saturated fat, or sodium. Later, when dining, you then have a bit more leeway in consuming these components. This concept, often called "calorie banking," is a common weight control method, which teaches users to think about food intake more than one meal or one day, at a time. For example, you might want to limit calories to 1,500/day or 10,000/week and have the choice to consume these calories at your leisure.

- Additional exercise may also assist keeping your calorie bank balanced. As you use more calories (exercise) you can take more in.

- As previously mentioned, preplan what you will order, before eating out, particularly when you know the restaurant offerings. This avoids the temptations of looking at the menu or being enticed by the restaurant smells.

- Order first to avoid being influenced by dining partners.

Change Your Food Intake Patterns

- Curiously, eating more slowly will fill you up much faster, as it takes 20 minutes for stomach signals to tell the brain it's full. Be the last to finish eating!

- Slow your eating pace down by increasing your dining conversation, laying utensils down periodically, or by stopping for more frequent beverage sips.

- Since you know that restaurants serve more food than you need, get into the habit of leaving part of your meal on the plate; offering it to others or asking the server to remove your plate, as soon as possible.

Are You Full?

- Fullness should not be that typical post-holiday meal bloated feeling, which is a sure sign of overeating.

- Clean plates and empty bread baskets may indicate overeating, not fullness.

- Fullness indicators should not be from external signals but from learning to listen to the internal signals your stomach gives you when it feels you have had enough to eat. Translate these signals into a message to put down your utensils and stop overeating.

- Slowing your eating pace, allows you to better determine and recognize fullness.

- Take the time to review and enjoy your meal and it will increase your fullness feelings and counteract overeating.

Observe Your Eating Environment

- The dining out experience is more than just eating.

- Notice the restaurant decor and pictures, enter into and enjoy dining conversation, forget about daily stresses, daydream, enjoy the service, enjoy not cooking or cleaning up, and take a deep breath or two and relax!

- The above will greatly assist you in settling yourself down, help your thought processes, strengthen your resolve, slow down your eating rate, and help limit overeating.

Restaurant Menu Warning Words

- Restaurants typically use certain buzzwords that should be a clue for you to set off an alarm in your mind to check it out, as a potential high-sodium or high-fat item.

High Sodium Buzzwords

Barbecued (BBQ)	Bouillon
Broth	Cocktail Sauce
Cured	Marinated
Pickled	Sauce
Smoked	Soy Sauce
Teriyaki	

High Fat Buzzwords

Alfredo	Au Gratin
Breaded	Butter Sauce (in)
Casserole	Cheesy
Covered In	Creamy (Cream Soups)
Crispy	Crunchy
Flaky	Fried (Deep or Pan Fried)
Fritter	Gravy
Hash	Hors d'Oeuvres
Saucy	Sauteed
Scalloped (escalloped)	Spread
Stewed	

Specific Food and Beverage Options

Developing healthier dining out patterns, ultimately necessitates us to begin to create a basic selection framework, of applicable "dos" and "don'ts."

Table 2.1 permits us to grasp a general, yet specific, look at the meal category options, in terms of what we should normally select or avoid.

Armed with these basics, we will then be ready to more effectively learn about and deal with, the reality of dining out at the many American and ethnic cuisine eating establishments, we are confronted with daily.

Dining Out
Where to Stop, What to Eat

North Americans have an almost limitless variety of dining out experiences available everyday. More often than not, this translates into a great opportunity to overindulge ourselves, from a proper and healthy eating viewpoint. Conversely, it also offers us the opportunity to maintain a healthy eating lifestyle, if we know

Table 2.1   Dining Out Selections

Category	Better Selections	Best to Avoid
Beverage	Request herbal teas; mineral or sparkling water; skim milk; unsweetened fruit juices and occasional decaffeinated diet drinks.	Alcohol; beer; wine; caffeine diet drinks, coffee, or tea; chocolate; cocoa; milk shakes and soft drinks.
Bread	Request whole grains, biscuits, crackers, lavosh, muffins, or pumpernickel.	Glazed cakes; danish; jelly filled or salt covered items; sweet rolls.
Appetizers	Request bouillon, clear broth, or consomme; fresh fruit; fish or meat cocktails; gazpacho; raw or plain vegetables; tomato or vegetable juice; unsweetened fruit juice.	Breaded or fried items; canned fruit; dips; oil marinated or sauce covered items.
Salads	Request fresh fruit; lettuce; tossed or vegetable salad.	Canned fruit; salads with dressings already mixed in.
Fats and Salad Dressings	Request no butter or margarine, or little- or no-fat, low-salt, whipped or soft butter or margarine. Use lemon, vinegar, and mustard in salads or request olive oil. Request oil on the side.	Regular butter, margarine or oils; cream sauce; gravy; salads with mixed-in dressings.
Vegetables	Request boiled, raw, steamed, or stewed.	Au gratin; cheese or sauce covered; creamed, escalloped, fried, or sauteed.
Potatoes and Substitutes	Request baked, boiled, or steamed potatoes; plain pasta or rice.	Creamed, delmonico, escalloped, french-fried, hashed-browned, or mashed potatoes; potato chips and salads.
Meat, Fish, or Poultry	Request meats to be trimmed of fat before it's baked, boiled, broiled, roasted, or stir fried.	Braised, breaded, fried, gravy covered, sauteed, or stewed.
Eggs	Only occasional use of boiled (hard or soft), plain, poached, scrambled, or low-cholesterol substitutes.	Creamed, fried, or oil-cooked omelettes.
Desserts	Request fresh fruit, jello, plain angel food, sponge, or unsweetened fruit filled cake.	Layered cakes, canned fruit, custard, ice cream, pastry, pie, puddings, or any sugar-based item.

enough to avoid the many temptations and choose the better options.

We will first take a look at the different types of typical North American dining places, serving food and beverage, commonly known as "American Cuisine." For each, we will develop a plan to select and avoid items, based upon health considerations.

Secondly, we will examine "Ethnic Cuisines" and develop a similar "select-avoid" game plan.

American Cuisine

Breakfast and Brunch

Only 20% of us eat breakfast out per week, making it the meal least frequently eaten out. It's also the most frequently skipped meal, despite it being the most important meal of the day. We need more fuel for energy earlier in the day and can burn it off more easily, than with a late-night meal. It's best to eat something for breakfast, no matter what healthy foods you select. Nutritionally, however, what's traditional and the most promoted in restaurants, are the worst fat-content foods. Our tendency to rush in the A.M. steers us more and more to fast food, deli, doughnut/bagel, coffee, or waffle-type restaurants. They feature high-fat foods such as eggs, meats, omelettes, buttered toast, sweet rolls, and breakfast potatoes; plus sour cream, syrups, and danish sweet rolls.

Most of them have healthier if not ideal choices, including non-sugar cereals, fresh fruits, yogurt, and

Table 2.2	Breakfast and Brunch Selections
Better Selections	**Best to Avoid**
Order fresh fruit (grapefruit and melon), fruit juice; whole grain cold cereals (shredded or puffed wheat); hot cereals (oat based); dry whole grain breads (toast, bagels, or English muffins); skim milk, poached eggs; fresh fruit on cereals and short stack pancakes or waffles; fresh fruit jams and jellies; whole, unprocessed, non-fried potatoes; herbal teas.	Breakfast meats or lox; excess eggs; omelettes; buttered or creamed entrees; bagels; refined toast, muffins, pancakes, or french toast and waffles; doughnuts; most muffins, croissants, or sweet rolls; regular jam and jellies; syrup; sugar/sodium-based cereals; hash browns, home fries; coffee.

whole wheat breads, served preferably, with real fruit jams. Beware of hidden fat in most "muffins" and request that they and roll breads be served dry. Beware of excess sodium in cold cereals.

Cafeterias

They are typically luncheon oriented. Many working people eat daily in employee cafeterias. They are rapidly becoming a healthier eating alternative, as companies strive to promote keeping employees healthy. If you frequent cafeterias, you know their ups and downs. You often encounter a wide selection of cold or grilled sandwiches, side orders, hot entrees, salad bar, soups, fresh fruit, and yogurt. You can usually special order and make your desires known directly to the manager.

You can also acceptably bring part of your lunch from home, which is particularly important, if the cafeteria does not serve certain healthy items you desire, such as low-cal salad dressing or fresh fruit.

Delicatessen

There are many kosher-style luncheons and some delis that are really sandwich shops. Normally, deli foods are high in fat and sodium, as typified by meats, bagels, cream cheese, and lox. While, it is not the best lunch or dinner choice, some good menu choices are available.

Many deli sandwiches are loaded with meat or tuna/chicken salad. Order extra bread and split the portions of meat with a dining partner or order a half sandwich.

Table 2.3	Delicatessen Selections
Better Selections	**Best to Avoid**
Extra lean corned beef, pastrami, or roast beef, beef brisket, and turkey breast are best; whole wheat or multi-grain breads; chicken or tuna salad; chopped herring; chef salad; fresh fruit plate with cottage cheese; dry bagel; borscht or broth soup; tossed salad, sliced tomatoes, beet salad, or carrot raisin salad.	High-fat meats (regular corn beef, hot pastrami, beef bologna, hot dogs, knockwurst, liverwurst, and salami); potato salad; mayonnaise-based salads; combo sandwiches (Reuben); smoked fish (lox); creamy coleslaw; chopped liver; excess cream cheese and cheese spreads; sauerkraut (high in sodium).

Family Style (American)

These mid-priced lunch/dinner restaurants are typified by Bennigans, Chili's, Denny's, Ground Round, Houlihan's, Ruby Tuesdays, TGI Friday's and many independently owned restaurants. They offer "American" fare similar to the chains—namely burgers, eggs, chicken wings, fries, nachos, pasta, chef salads, and multiple variations of ethnic cuisine—primarily Asian, Italian, Mexican, or American regional

(Cajun). These restaurants fall midway between fast-food offerings and upscale continental cuisine. Generally speaking, the food fare is characterized as high in fat, calories, cholesterol, and sodium and are far from healthy eating. There are often good healthy choices available here, but they are clearly in the minority. Again, fat is your number 1 enemy in selecting suitable choices. Particularly troublesome are many creamy and cheesy soups, most appetizers, green salad

Table 2.4 Family Style (American) Selections

Better Selections	Best to Avoid
Suitable appetizers include vegetable platters (no dip); steamed veggies, peel-and-eat shrimp and raw bar combos; broth-based or gumbo soup. Chef and house salads and combo salads (Cobb, Greek, Spinach), without bacon, cheese, egg and without the fried tortilla shell. Tuna or seafood is OK. Many have a salad and fruit bar. Order low-cal dressing on the side (or bring your own). Stick to sandwiches that are charbroiled or blackened and order chicken, ham, roast beef, or turkey. Burgers with sauteed onions, pepper, mushroom, and tomato are fine. Grilled or stir-fried entrees, often blackened or teriyaki, are good, such as chicken, fresh fish, beef, and fajitas. Good accompaniments include; baked potatoes, rice, steamed, or stir-fried vegetables. Acceptable sauces include BBQ, honey mustard, horse-radish, and teriyaki. Stick to pita bread, rolls, or whole wheat bread.	Appetizers such as chicken wings, nachos, tortilla chips, mozzarella sticks, potato skins, or any with cheese, guacamole, sour cream, or fried. Omit French onion and New England clam chowder, prepared soups, and combo sandwiches on croissants; and items such as club, melts, or Reuben or with avocado, bacon, cheese, mayonnaise, or special (high fat) sauces. Avoid hamburger toppings, french fries, and salad dressings, other than oil, vinegar, and lemon. Request butter and mayonnaise be left off everything from sandwiches to buns.

toppings, hamburger toppings, sandwich combos, most deserts, and, of course, fried foods and other high-fat additions to food, such as mayonnaise, butter, cheese, and sauces. Be assertive and make special requests or substitutions as often as necessary.

Fast Foods

As practically everyone knows, fast-food restaurants are everywhere, and millions dine in them daily, despite their very negative health image. Our health-conscious nation has made some minor inroads into this business which once consisted of burgers, fries, fried chicken, and shakes. In truth there have been some significant changes for the better, particularly in the healthfulness of the original products. The real culprits are the majority of menu choices that are high in calories, saturated fat, and sodium, due to the preparation methods used. Today fast foods also mean ethnic foods, as chains feature items such as egg rolls, pizza, roast beef, salads, and tacos. Our task once again is to avoid the many nutritional roadblocks and emphasize the best selections.

Be aware that:
1. The major problem is fat.
2. Most food is fried and has lots of fat and calories.
3. Pyramid recommended foods are practically non-existent . Whole grains, fruit and vegetables are not commonly included in most menus.

4. Items are heavily covered in bacon, cheese, mayonnaise, sour cream, and several sauces. The more ingredients, the more calories and fat.
5. Sodium food content is often in the 1,000–2,000 milligram range, for a typical meal.
6. Special requests can be difficult and time consuming.
7. Due to employee turnover and poor management, cooking methods often suffer, meaning fat-laden food due to overused cooking oils, excess condiments, or overcooking, often are the rule, not the exception.

If there is a number one rule, it is to try to decide exactly what you want before you enter. This is possible because fast-food outlets are similar coast to coast. Rule number two is to make a special request to leave off all condiments, except lettuce, tomato, onion, and mustard.

Mall or Food Courts

Obviously, this category can mean almost any kind of food. Often, it's the standard American cuisine or fast-food outlets meaning burgers, chicken, fries, hot dogs, subs, salad, potatoes, or popular ethnic fare—from pizza to tacos, fried rice to gyros. Other times, yogurt stands, bakeries, and sushi bars can be found.

The advantage in food courts is you may look at different cuisines and can then quickly pick and choose

Table 2.5   Fast Food Selections

Better Selections	Best to Avoid
Plain burgers; grilled or broiled burgers, chicken or fish; prepared salad or salad bar; oil dressing (bring from home); bean burrito (no lard in cooking); plain baked potato; non-fried (roasted) chicken, without skin; small or regular, plain roast beef sandwich; fruit juice; skim milk; whole wheat bun, if available. Look for small portion words such as children's, junior, single, or small.	Burgers, chicken, roast beef, or fish with bacon, cheese, mayonnaise, pickles, or special sauces; fried chicken and fish sandwiches; french fries; baked potato (loaded or stuffed); salad dressings; shakes; desserts (ice cream, cookies, muffins); caffeine beverages (carbonated, coffee, and tea); avoid large portion words like big, double, extra large, jumbo, super, or triple.

Table 2.6   Mall or Food Court Selections

Better Selections	Best to Avoid
Stick to fresh foods (unadulterated), fruit cups, plain baked potato, or Middle Eastern pita sandwich or Greek salad.	Omit the high-fat, American, or ethnic food fare, common to other eating places.

separately, even if you are with other people who then sit together. However, a big negative is that often so many smells, tastes, and visual stimuli can make you let your guard down. Keep in mind that the enemy is fat and avoid the many fried-food and fast-food pitfalls.

Pizza Parlors

Pizza is the most popular dish we all encounter and can be a decent nutritional choice and a quick, inexpensive meal. Pizza is not only found at fast-food chains, but it has become a mainstay of all types of American family-style restaurants. It is served in many ways from thin to "deep dish" and featured on a menu as plain or gourmet.

Properly ordered, it is a very good nutritional selection, because pizza ingredients are dough, flour, yeast, salt, water, tomato sauce, and less than one ounce of cheese so you are not yet in trouble, until toppings are considered.

Some basic guidelines to consider when ordering pizza:
1. Decide how many pieces you really need to eat to maintain your nutritional goals.
2. Order a salad to help fill you up with lower-calorie, healthy greens.
3. Choose only healthier ingredients and toppings.

Table 2.7   Pizza Parlor Selections

Better Selections	Best to Avoid
You cannot go wrong by ordering extra toppings such as onions, peppers, mushrooms, tomato slices, broccoli and spinach. Even items that are slightly higher in calories, fat, and salt are OK, including black olives, eggplant, feta cheese, artichokes, or pineapples. Other possibilities include chicken, crab meat, or shrimp.	Fat starts with the basic cheese, so avoid extra cheese and in particular mozzarella. Other culprits include bacon, meatballs, pepperoni, sausage, and proscuitto, as well as anchovies.

Salad Bars

Obviously, a salad bar can be a healthful eater's paradise. However, not so obvious is that a tempting salad bar is quite often a nutritional disaster area. Why?

First of all, today salad bars are everywhere, including steak houses, American style, fast-food restaurants, employee cafeterias, and even supermarkets.

The problem is basically that salad bars have evolved from lettuce, raw vegetables, and oil and vinegars, to a bewildering array of additional alternatives—some good but many bad. They have become a perfect place to unconsciously overeat and pig out, as we try to get our money's worth! Especially if you are extremely hungry.

As always, it's best to develop a strategy at salad bars.

1. Think about what you need to order or select before arriving or approaching the salad bar.
2. Use a smaller plate or bowl, if available, and practice portion control.
3. Let a friend get it for you. Specify what you want and avoid temptations.
4. Limit yourself to one trip and don't even think about seconds.
5. Order the pre-packaged salad, if available.
6. Do not use packaged salad dressings, which contain two to four times too much dressing, calories, and fat.
7. Bring your own dressings with you.
8. Use less dressing or dilute it with vinegar, lemon juice, or water.

Table 2.8   Salad Bar Selections

Better Selections	Best to Avoid
Stick to raw, low-calorie, or crunchy vegetables, such as lettuce, broccoli, celery, cucumber, mushrooms, spinach, and sprouts. Next are the layered items which are slightly higher in calorie or carbohydrates but very healthful, such as beets, chick peas, cauliflower, garbanzo beans, green peas, kidney beans, spinach, onions, peppers, and sprouts. Higher-calorie choices include canned artichoke, canned beets, carrots, onions, and tomatoes. Fairly low-calorie, protein choices include plain tuna, cottage cheese, egg, feta cheese, and ham. Higher fat proteins include other cheeses and pepperoni and salads made with tuna, chicken, or seafood. Be careful in selecting breads. Stick to pita and whole wheat. A few marinated salads, in smaller portions, are fine: mixed veggie or mushroom, three bean, coleslaw, and fruit salads. Use low- or reduced-calorie dressing.	Croutons, crackers, etc., are high in sodium and some times fat. Use little oil-based salad mixtures, mayonnaise, or sour cream to keep calories down. Higher calorie items are coleslaw, macaroni, pasta, or potato salad. Higher-fat items include chicken, seafood, or tuna salad and ambrosia fruit salad. Hidden fat calories and sodium are found in salad bar extras such as bacon bits, Chinese dried noodles, nuts, olives, and seeds. Avoid high fat and calorie dressings such as blue cheese, french, italian, russian, and thousand island.

Sandwich Shops

Local sandwich shops, often called coffee shops, typically serve burgers, chicken, tuna salads, and soups. Some are similar to delis, while others double as ice cream chains with sandwiches, such as Friendly's and Swenson's. The newer "nouvelle" sandwich shops generally make healthier choices, served on croissants or baguettes with a variety of mustards, soups, and salads.

Submarine Shops

Subs are often served in small, family-run restaurants or in some large national chains. These long sandwiches originally were filled with high-fat meats and topped with cheese. Today, vegetables, low-fat meats, better breads, and salad offerings have made these shops more acceptable sources to obtain healthier offerings.

Table 2.9 Sandwich Shop Selections

Better Selections	Best to Avoid
Generally, what's between the bread slices, is what's important. Both 100% whole wheat and pita bread are great choices while croissants are high in fat. Good sandwich fillers are grilled chicken breast, ham, roast beef, and turkey breast, while cheese should generally be avoided. Instruct the server not to add butter, margarine, or mayonnaise to the bread and substitute with ketchup, mustard, or horseradish. Remember that salad combos such as tuna, chicken, and crab meat have lots of mayonnaise. If chosen, request no other additions to the bread. Good salad choices include chef, garden, or Greek salads, but remember to ask for low-calorie dressings on the side and to omit egg or cheese. Broth-type soups are good, such as barley, beef, chicken, lentil, split pea, and vegetable noodle. Avoid creamy soups such as chowders or cream of "anything."	Already mentioned are croissants, cheese, additions to bread, excess combos with excess mayonnaise, egg, and creamy soups. Beware of "diet plates" with big burgers and scoops of cottage cheese, which have loads of saturated fat. Omit cheeseburgers, cheese sandwiches, or grilled cheese "melts" over chicken and seafood salads; and cold cuts. Combo sandwiches with meat and cheese and club sandwiches are best avoided due to large portion size.

Table 2.10 Submarine Shop Selections

Better Selections	Best to Avoid
Order the smaller size roll or pita bread. Turkey, smoked turkey, ham, and roast beef are acceptable. Ask the server to go light on the meats, omit the mayonnaise or oil, and generously load up on the shredded lettuce, onion, peppers, pickles, and sliced tomatoes. Choose salads as alternatives when available, such as chef, Greek, or tossed salads with perhaps a scoop of tuna, chicken, or seafood served with Italian or pita bread. Beware again that the dressings are the biggest culprit in salads. Sometimes subs, such as steak and onions, with mushrooms or peppers are OK, or an occasional tuna or chicken salad. Remember that a roast beef sub is better nutritionally, with fewer calories and lower sodium than a tuna fish sub.	Omit meats such as bologna, mortadella (Italian cold cut), salami (hard or Genoa) and sausage, or sausage with veggies. Stay away from cheeses and steak and cheese. Other items to omit include antipasto salads, eggplant (typically fried), chicken cutlet, and chicken or veal parmigiana (all deep fried).

Remember that fat, saturated fat, cholesterol, and sodium are the culprits, all coming between the bread. The bread and toppings, such as lettuce, onions, peppers, pickles, and tomato, are the healthiest part of the sub.

Ethnic Cuisines

North America's unparalleled multi-ethnic diversity has virtually brought all worldwide cuisines to our doorstep. These include some of the world's healthiest cuisines, such as Chinese, Indian, Japanese, Mediterranean, Middle Eastern, and Thai. All have cooking styles and food offerings which we can easily examine to determine the good and poor aspects of each.

The following capsule comments and recommended selections, will quickly prepare you to adopt more healthful dining habits, when dining at any of the eight selected and commonly found ethnic cuisines.

Chinese

More Chinese restaurants are available worldwide, than any other ethnic cuisine. Among the many Chinese regional cuisines, the most popular North American ones are Cantonese, Hunan, Peking, and Szechuan. American Chinese restaurant food is quite different and normally less healthy, than food served in China.

The Chinese use carbohydrates such as noodles or white rice, rather than a protein concentration. Healthwise, it's best to stay with these starches, assorted vegetables, and fruits and omit the high fat, cholesterol, sodium, and hidden sugar used in items such as egg drop soup, pork fried rice, or spicy beef with peanuts and scallions.

Table 2.11 Chinese Selections	
Better Selections	**Best to Avoid**
Order plain steamed rice; boiled, steamed, or stir-fried vegetables (ask for little oil to be used); moderate fish and shellfish; non-fried tofu; skinless poultry and egg roll (insides only).	Anything fried (rice or crispy noodles), or with sweet and sour sauce; egg dishes or soups; salty soups; avoid duck and limit beef, pork, and pickled foods; excess soy sauce; ask chef to leave out MSG and cut down the use of commonly used corn starch, sugar, and salt.

French

French continental style cuisine once defined greatness, in dining out, worldwide. Today, the traditional and classic haute cuisine of French restaurants, with its emphasis on rich sauces, has declined.

It has been replaced by the "newer" French cuisine, called "nouvelle cuisine." It's a lighter and much healthier cooking style that has influenced many other ethnic and American cuisines, including Italian, Cajun, Southwestern, and Californian.

The emphasis is on blackening, grilling, poaching, steaming, and stir-frying. It now avoids the fat from butter, cream, and eggs and creates healthier dishes.

When French Continental restaurant dining is encountered, the patron should beware of fat and excess portions in cheese-covered appetizers, salads, dressings, meat entrees, and, of course, desserts. High-sodium ingredients are prevalent, so let your waitress know of these concerns.

Many of these restaurants are also becoming more health conscious and increasingly offer low-fat and vegetarian items.

Table 2.12 French Selections	
Better Selections	**Best to Avoid**
Order artichoke (no butter); crusty baguettes (no butter); fresh fruit; crepes with fruit or lightly sauteed seafood; salads (dressing on side); steamed vegetables; rack of lamb; sole veronique. Choose cold gazpacho, consomme, vegetables, or onions without au gratin.	Au gratin dishes; butter; cream; eggs; buttery croissants; omelettes; pastries; patés; high fat and salt sauces, such as bearnaise, bechamel, or hollandaise; duck or goose with skin; salads with bacon bits, croutons, and egg; vichyssoise. Beware of high sodium and creamy soups.

Indian

Indian food can vary greatly because of both regional variation and the influence of multiple religions from nearby countries.

Indian menus and dishes can often be confusing. Speak up and ask questions when necessary and learn about common Indian words and the variations in their spellings from restaurant to restaurant.

Table 2.13   Indian Selections

Better Selections	Best to Avoid
Order chutney (except mango); curry sauce (yogurt based); fish (omit butter basting); yogurt with shredded vegetables; basmati rice; biryani (vegetable dish); chapati or papadum bread; masala (chicken or shrimp); tandoori chicken; lentil or mulligatawny soups; Lassi (yogurt beverage).	Creamy or high-salt soups; clarified butter (ghee); deep fried meats; poori or paratha bread; fried samosa or pakora; ask to prepare dishes without excess salt and to omit coconut milk, if possible; omit garnishes with nuts or dried fruit. Beware of appetizers, which are mostly deep fried.

Typically, the use of curry and multiple spices is as common as the use of rice, legumes, and vegetables.

Religious influences are reflected in the de-emphasized use of pork (Moslems) and beef (Hindus) and the popularity of vegetarianism (Buddhists).

Indian food can be quite healthful, with its emphasis on low protein (fish and seafood) and reliance on high-fiber carbohydrates.

Ordering à la carte is a good idea to decrease the portions served. Particularly beware of fat from frying and sauteing and the common use of clarified butter, coconut milk, and excess salt. Unique healthy condiments include "Raita" (rayta), dahl (dall), and onion chutney.

Italian

The second most common restaurant worldwide is perhaps North America's most popular cuisine. Italian dishes are standard fare in most American cuisine restaurants. Italian food runs the gamut from pizza to nouvelle Italian and spaghetti or pasta to scampi. It can be costly or inexpensive.

Italian dishes can be great or poor for your health, so use caution when ordering. Include the strategy of sharing your food with a dining partner to cut down on the often large portions.

Particularly be aware that you want to stay away from the high cholesterol, fat, and sodium in meals. Typical examples are garlic bread with olive oil or butter; cheese covered antipasto with salami; marinated artichokes; fettucini alfredo; deep-fried mozzarella sticks; and heavy sauces.

You would be better off sticking with orders such as minestrone soup; linguine with light sauce; fresh green salads; healthier pastas (angel hair, ziti, or whole wheat or vegetable pasta); marinara and primavera dishes, with clam or tomato sauce.

Regarding pastas, stay away from stuffed or topped with high-fat add-ons, such as bacon, cheese, or cream. Conversely, order pasta when accompanied by words such as garlic, herbs, light sauce, spices, or wine sauce.

The traditional use of olive oil in Italian cooking is an acceptable selection, in moderation. Remember, it is still 100% fat, despite its healthful reputation, when compared to other oils.

Table 2.14   Italian Selections

Better Selections	Best to Avoid
Order antipasto (no oil or excess meats); crusty bread (no oil or butter); broiled or grilled fish, seafood, chicken, and meats; garlic; plain or vegetable pasta; fresh unsalted mozzarella cheese; steamed leafy vegetables (kale and broccoli); salads; fresh tomatoes; zucchini; ices.	Garlic bread; stuffed pastas (ravioli and lasagna); fried eggplant; meatballs or sausage; sauces with butter, cream, oil, and wine base; pesto sauce; cheese-filled or parmesan style dishes; cappuccino; spumoni or tortoni ice cream. Beware of risotto rice; polenta; and high-fat, high-sodium prosciutto ham and pancetta; veal cutlets and caesar salads.

Japanese

Japanese is one of the very healthiest ethnic cuisines. Authentic Japanese food is not typified by the well-known Japanese steak houses. True Japanese cuisine emphasizes rice, seafood, and vegetables and is light on dairy products, fats, and meats.

Healthful and well-known Japanese foods include tofu, a soybean curd, and miso, a soybean paste used in soups and entrees.

Be aware that soy teriyaki and other sauces have high levels of sodium and sugar.

The common methods of Japanese cooking—boil, broil, braise, grill, simmer, and steam—lend themselves to using small amounts of fats.

Raw fish and rice combinations called sushi or sashimi are healthful as appetizers or entrees. Good choices include most salads and entrees and fresh fruits used as dessert options.

Table 2.15   Japanese Selections

Better Selections	Best to Avoid
Order rice; steamed fish; sushi; sashimi; miso soup; raw vegetables; tofu; sukiyaki (stir-fried meat); yakimono (broiled food).	Tempura and other deep-fried food; excess peanut and teriyaki sauce; pickled foods; excess salt and sugar in sauces; excess salt in soy marinades and sauces.

Mediterranean (Middle East)

These ethnic foods come from many countries, including Greece, Turkey, Armenia, Iran, Iraq, Israel, Lebanon, and Syria. Close similarities abound in North Africa, in the countries of Algeria, Egypt, Libya, Morocco, and Tunisia. Be aware that the same food may be spelled or pronounced differently throughout the region and in the menus we use.

Mediterranean–Middle East restaurants are becoming increasingly popular, partly because of their inherent healthful characteristics. The food is often featured in delis, malls, and in American cuisine restaurants as we become more familiar with food names such as couscous, falafel, feta cheese, gyros, hummus, kebabs, pita bread, souvlaki, and tabooli.

There are several important ingredients that dominate this healthful cuisine.

Lamb is the most important protein other than legumes such as chick peas and fava beans, which together make falafel. Eggs are common in pasta dishes, soups, sauces, vegetable pies, and yogurt. Olives and olive oil are standards in cold dishes and salads.

Pita "pockets" are commonly associated with burgers; fillings such as hummus, kibbeh and tabooli, salads and sprouts. Pita is low in fat and calories. Stuffed dishes are a mainstay, usually featuring cabbage, eggplant, grape leaves called dolma, and meat or meatless variations.

Common cuisine items include: couscous, made from cracked wheat; rice pilaf; and tabooli, cold, cracked wheat, marinated with raw vegetables.

Table 2.16   Mediterranean (Middle East) Selections

Better Selections	Best to Avoid
Order couscous, bulgar, and pita bread; legumes such as chickpeas, fava beans, and lentils; hummus; grape leaves; yogurt.	Phyllo (filo or fila) dough dishes for sweet desserts such as baklava; feta and kasseri cheese; excess anchovies and olives; High-sodium foods: feta, olives and sausage; appetizers in general, except salads; excess fat from butter, olive oil, omelettes and tahini.

Mexican

Mexican food is the third most popular cuisine in North American, after Chinese, and Italian. We often encounter it in fast food, Mexican chains, Tex-Mex, or in other full-service Mexican and American cuisine restaurants.

The basics of Mexican cuisine are beans, chilies, and corn, which on their own are nutritionally healthy. When combined with high-fat, high-salt appetizers and entrees, they easily become nutritionally unsound.

Historically, Mexican food is still characterized as hot and spicy, despite its many European and American influences.

Tortillas, the bread of Mexican cuisine is often stuffed with beef, cheese, chicken, and pork and called burritos, enchiladas, and tacos. Common healthy starches are black beans, Mexican rice, and soft, flour tortillas.

The culprits in Mexican cuisine can be numerous and include fried foods, chips, and refried beans, which are often cooked with lard made from rendered hog fat. Chips and cheese and meat stuffing are also high in sodium.

Good entree selections would include beans, chicken, chilies, corn or wheat-based bread, lettuce, onions, peppers, and tomatoes. However, be alert to their accompaniments such as cheese, chips, grated cheese, guacamole, and fried tortilla shells.

Few dairy products are encountered, while coffee is very typical.

In Mexican cuisine, it is essential to make special requests and to ask questions about the food preparation methods and ingredients and to order à la carte, whenever possible.

Table 2.17 Mexican Selections

Better Selections	Best to Avoid
Order soft-shell tacos; burritos; fajitas; salsa; chicken enchilada; black beans or Mexican rice; grilled fish or chicken; salads without chips or shells; moderate corn or flour tortilla, using minimal oil; cerviche (marinated fish); gazpacho; chile con carne soup, with no cheese. Acceptable items include shredded lettuce; spicy meats; diced tomatoes; salsa verde; picante or tomato sauce; use Mexican salads as appetizers, with salsa as the dressing.	Chips, nachos; super nachos; chili con queso; fried taco or tortilla shells; guacamole; sour cream; cheese; refried beans; beef and pork dishes; olives; items such as chilies rellenos, chimichangas, chorizo (sausage), and flautas.

Thai

Thai cuisine is growing rapidly in popularity. Its lighter characteristics make it somewhat healthier than Chinese cooking, to which it is often, and mistakenly compared.

Thai food is rice based, often stir-fried and spicy hot, giving it a taste closer to Indian cuisine. The hot taste comes from various chilies, while the curry flavor comes from blended spices, such as cardamon, cinnamon, coriander, and cumin.

Traditional Thai oils have been coconut oil or lard, but many Thai restaurants now use vegetable oils.

The flavorful but light taste of Thai food comes from the lack of cornstarch or flour as thickening agents.

Typical of many Asian cuisines, Thai food preparation includes deep frying; cream and coconut dishes, excess salt or soy sauce; MSG; nut sauces and sugar.

Since Thai cuisine steams rice, many vegetable dishes are utilized. Usually, consider dishes with curry, rice, cooked vegetables, light sauces, and chicken or seafood entrees.

Salad selections are stressed, unlike other Asian cuisines.

Table 2.18 Thai Selection

Better Selections	Best to Avoid
Order steamed rice; broth-based soups (tom yum koang and pok taek); non-fried proteins, such as chicken, seafood, and tofu; vegetables; satay or steamed mussels; salads with light dressings, made with Thai spices.	Excess sodium; soy sauce and sugar; MSG; coconut milk; coconut oil; cream dishes; high milk and sodium soups; many fried appetizers; curry or curry sauce; fried eggplant; cashew and peanut toppings.

PART II

Diet Planning

In the health care environment, the specific need for a modified diet is dictated solely by the diagnosis of a patient and the prescription, by a physician, to follow a specific diet to treat the disease or injury. Such a diet is often called a "therapeutic diet." **"Diet therapy,"** uses food in the treatment of disease and is the way to change or modify an individuals regular diet to address the patient's diagnosis. It's also called "medical nutrition intervention." A dietitian is a specialist in planning or modifying diets. The dietitian plans the meals to exactly fit the physician's instructions and gives detailed information about foods to utilize or omit. The creation of high-quality and individualized portion recipes and menus, is the foundation of this book, and vital in any consideration of modified diet planning.

An equally important consideration is how to enroll a patient or person to continually utilize, in the short or long term, the modified diet plan. Keep in mind that while the diet plan may start in a health care facility, it may often need to be continued over extended periods of time in the home environment.

A suitable analogy might be to observe the difficulty that millions of people have in following consumer-oriented plans to lose weight in the short term and then maintain the new weight over the long term. Most would agree it's simple in theory, but more difficult in reality.

Diet Therapy

The basis for all "therapeutic" or "modified diet" plans is the "regular diet." The purposes of the regular diet are to:
1. Support and maintain normal nutrition.
2. Provide adequate nutrients for growth or maintenance of normal body function.
3. Maintain optimum body weight.
4. Improve the body's nutrient-using abilities.

Diet Modification

Regular diets are normally modified to influence the following characteristics or categories:
1. Texture and consistency
2. Energy and calorie value
3. Flavor
4. Nutrient levels for carbohydrates, fat, protein, sodium, cholesterol, etc.

Implementation Problems

Many diverse factors work against the success of a modified diet program. Becoming knowledgeable about what they are, can greatly assist the health care team, including the doctor, dietitian, nurse, food server, and homemaker to implement the diet and help the patient to overcome obstacles. These problems include:

1. Illness

- It can affect appetite (e.g., anorexia, gastrointestinal distress, weakness, and exhaustion), cause vomiting, pain or discomfort, and prevent adequate food intake.

- Severe diarrhea may inhibit nutrient absorption, causing dehydration, weight loss, or malnutrition.

- Fever may increase food metabolism, increasing calorie, protein, vitamin, or other needs.

- Metabolic diseases may cause nutrient imbalances.

- The handicapped or elderly may not be able to feed themselves.

2. Medications

- Drugs may produce nausea or vomiting, inhibiting food ingestion.

- Drugs may interfere with enzyme functions, decrease vitamin absorption, or cause diarrhea— all reducing nutrient absorption.

- Drugs may negatively influence the taste of food.

- Conversely, drugs may not mix adequately with food, resulting in poor drug absorption and decreased drug effectiveness.

3. Food Related

- Rejection of new, different, or unfamiliar foods.

- Familiar foods prepared in different ways.

- The diet change cause unappealing food textures or flavors.

- Food portions may be too large or too small.

- Lack of variety of foods from meal to meal.

- Lack of colorful, contrasting, or complimentary food colors.

- Lack of proper food and plate temperature (hot or cold) and food covers.

- Lack of proper tray attractiveness to enhance acceptability, including: cleanliness; arrangement; spotless, non-chipped disks, glassware, or silver;

salt, pepper, and condiments and a colorful garnish.

- Poor attitudes and lack of encouragement; explanation and motivation to accept a new diet; and changing old habits or eating patterns.

4. Cultural and Religious Patterns

- Ethnic groups often have strong attachment to their traditional foods, sometimes making modified diet changes difficult. Possible examples include persons of Chinese, Hispanic, Italian, African American,and Native American Indian heritages.

- Orthodox Jews adhere to dietary laws based on the Bible and tradition. Pork and shellfish are restricted. Animals and poultry are slaughtered according to ritual and the meat undergoes a process called "Koshering." Other food or food preparation restrictions occur on the "Sabbath" and during holidays.

- Muslims do not consume pork or alcoholic beverages. Many fast for one month each year, not eating from dawn until after dark.

- Some Catholics still abstain from eating meat on Friday or other days and periodically refrain from fish and cheese.

- Buddhists and devotees of other religions are vegetarians and consume no flesh from animals, while Seventh-Day Adventists are lacto-ovo vegetarians, and eat no meat but permit eggs, legumes, milk, or nuts as protein.

5. Family Social Patterns

- The family "homemaker," preparing a select few well-liked dishes, over and over, may create habits difficult to change for modified diet users.

- Children may develop early negative attitudes, toward certain foods and carry those opinions long term.

- Foods easily become classified by age group as masculine (e.g., meat and potatoes); feminine (e.g., salad and diet preparations); children (e.g., peanut butter and jelly sandwiches or hamburgers and pizza).

- People develop food value preferences with status, prestige, or poverty connotations, while in fact they are equal in nutrition or taste.

- Food is emotionally linked to feeling of love, happiness, worry, security, and the like, sometimes causing over- or under-eating food consumption problems.

- Some families designate certain meals to be more substantial than others, developing patterns adverse to adapting modified diet plans.

6. Individual Attitudes and Personal Variations

- The individual ability to cooperate sufficiently in diet therapy can be influenced by dissimilar factors such as:

- Institutional or physical confinement.

- Health care financial worries.

- Lack of financial resources to purchase perceived high cost items for prescribed diet.

- Worries about duplicating the new diet plan at home. Particularly, acquiring the new foods, what recipes to follow; what or how much to eat; who will prepare and assist; and how to stick to the diet.

- Physiologic variations for people exist with taste buds, smelling, or feeling abilities or sensitivities. Adults differ from children or babies.

Implementation Process

Despite the numerous problems sometimes encountered, the health care team or at-home support persons are often the source of solutions. These methods or solutions include:

- Recognizing that one on one communication with the modified diet user is essential. After all, we must remember that if the prescribed food is not eaten, the diet is useless and the condition will likely continue. The proper positive attitude of the food server, nurse, or homemaker can encourage or persuade the user to follow the diet. These people can "make or break" the diet process. Cheerfulness, diet explanations and assisting the user to select appropriate diet foods or to overcome food prejudices is often necessary and critical. Simply explaining to the user the basic facts of nutrition and that it will improve health is a useful motivation tool.

- The food server, nurse, or homemaker should pay special attention to addressing the negative possibilities discussed previously under "Food Related" factors. They need to make sure the food looks good, is kept warm or cold, has sufficient positions, and is attractively served on trays or at tables. They can assist in making the environment around the meal, free of interruptions, distractions, and unrelated activities, such as outside visits, TV, group gatherings, or even from laboratory or health facility personnel.

- These same people, the food server, nurse, or homemaker, need to combine their communication skills with the ability to observe, listen, and report. These latter skills will identify problem areas as they arise and permit prompt correction action.

- When the modified diet user refuses to eat certain foods, it may be necessary to use vitamins and minerals or other supplementation as a substitute. The entire health care team starting with the doctor down to the server can assist in that determination.

3

Regular Diet

The regular diet is sometimes referred to as a full, general, house, or normal diet. It is comparable to an average, well-balanced diet. The regular diet is a diet to live by.

The regular diet is utilized for health maintenance. Nonetheless, it has a therapeutic importance. With proper food intake, body tissues are maintained and an individual's chances for repairing the effects of illness are increased. Conversely, a person's failure to eat a regular diet could result in body tissue loss and increased recovery time.

The regular diet follows the guidelines of the Recommended Dietary Allowances, as specified by the National Research Council. This diet plan maintains or achieves the ideal nutritional state. It is normally used for the person or patient who does not have a pre-existing problem or disorder, requiring particular nutrient alterations.

Generally, the regular diet permits all foods. Many health care facilities limit or restrict empty, high-calorie foods, highly seasoned foods or very rich cakes, fried foods, pastries, or even strongly flavored vegetables.

When preparing a regular diet consider the following dietary guidelines:

1. Restrict your intake of alcohol, cholesterol, fat, saturated fat, sugar, and sodium.
2. Consume a variety of foods, particularly fruits, vegetables, starches, and fiber.
3. Maintain proper weight.

The regular diet should be a preventive plan of action that decreases a person's susceptibility to cardiovascular disease, colon cancer, diabetes, hypertension, obesity, and similar disorders.

As a general rule, the regular diet emphasizes a variety of foods, and a caloric intake of 1,800 to 2,500 calories; 65 to 95 grams of protein; 60 to 85 grams of fat; and 250 to 350 grams of carbohydrates.

Table 3.1 Regular Diet

Category	Recommended Daily Servings	Recommended Food Choices	Foods to Limit
Bread, Cereal, Rice, and Pasta	6 to 11 servings.	Enriched or whole grain breads and cereals. Enriched noodles, pasta or rice; bagels, muffins, and tortillas.	Sweetened cereals, chips, crackers, doughnuts, pancakes, pastries.
Fruits	2 to 4 servings (1/2 cup servings); one vitamin C fruit daily.	Fruits, juices, or nectars, unsweetened; canned, dried, fresh, or frozen. Use one vitamin C fruit or juice daily.	Artificially sweetened fruits or juices; avocado or coconut.
Vegetables	3 to 5 servings (1/2 cup servings); include starchy vegetables and one vitamin A.	Vegetables and starch vegetables: fresh, frozen, canned, or dried; potatoes: baked or boiled; vegetable juices; one dark orange-yellow or green leafy vegetable daily.	Highly salted or pickled vegetables or fruits; fried chips or fried vegetables.
Soups	Use as desired.	Fresh ingredients prepared. Low-sodium/salted soups, with fat skimmed; low-fat milk (cream style).	Packaged or commercially prepared soup mixes.
Meats, Fish, Poultry, Dry Beans, Nuts, and Eggs	2 to 3 servings (4 to 6 ounces).	Lean (cut) meats, fish, poultry without skin; shellfish; dried beans and peas; soybeans, tofu; peanut butter.	Fried or fatty fish, meats, or poultry. Omit raw eggs and limit eggs (3/week); Limit nuts.
Milk, Yogurt, and Cheese	2 to 3 servings (2 or more cups), vitamin A and D fortified.	Skim or low-fat milk and yogurt; soy milk; low-fat cheeses (cottage and mozzarella).	Whole milk, yogurt, or ice cream. Higher fat cheeses (processed or cheddar).
Beverages	4 to 6 servings (use as desired to meet calorie and fluid needs).	Water; decaffeinated drinks or unsweetened or non-carbonated soft drinks.	Any alcoholic, caffeine, carbonated or sweetened beverages.
Fats and Oils	3 servings.	Reduced-calorie, low-fat, or non-fat salad dressings and mayonnaise; reduced-calorie margarine; vegetable oil (corn, safflower).	Mayonnaise and salad dressing. Avoid excessive consumption of saturated fats (butter, lard, coconut oil, palm oil, etc.)
Sweets and Desserts	Use occasionally to meet calorie needs.	Fruit-based desserts, angel food cake, puddings made from skim milk; desserts with no sugar, lightly sweetened or low fat.	Cakes, candy, cookies, pastries, pies, puddings (whole milk). Unless in need of additional calories, avoid excessive consumption of concentrated sweets.

4

Liberal Bland Diet

The utilization of a Liberal Bland Diet is closely associated with diseases of the gastrointestinal tract, such as peptic ulcers, hiatal hernia, indigestion, diarrhea, colitis, and diverticulitis.

The Liberal Bland diet closely resembles the Regular Diet. Individual tolerance to certain foods should be noted and those foods avoided on an individual basis.

The Liberal Bland Diet attempts to reduce the excess flow of gastric juices by known irritants. It specifically excludes only a small category of foods and substances. Foods to restrict include caffeine, coffee (including decaffeinated), tea, cocoa, chocolate, alcohol, chili powder, black pepper, cola or carbonated beverages, meat extractives, and broth-based soups.

1. Consider diminishing your food quantity consumption to help decrease excessive expansion of the stomach and excessive acid secretion.

2. Moderately increasing the frequency of meals may be recommended as necessary to meet adequate caloric and nutrient needs. Liberal Bland diets, however, normally do permit three meals per day.

3. Be aware that foods containing high fiber or roughage may initially be difficult to tolerate in the early stages. The reintroduction of fiber foods during the recovery phase is often considered essential in long-term recovery.

4. Eat slowly and chew food well.

5. Use moderation, particularly in selecting and making a food group predominant to the exclusion of others, such as too much milk or high-fiber foods, etc.

6. Stress is a major culprit, so slow down your pace of life.

Table 4.1 **Liberal Bland Diet**

Category	Recommended Daily Servings	Recommended Food Choices	Foods to Restrict
Bread, Cereal, Rice, and Pasta	6 to 11 servings.	Enriched or whole grain breads and cereals. Enriched noodles, pasta or rice; bagels, muffins, and tortillas.	Any not tolerated.
Fruits	2 to 4 servings (1/2 cup servings); one vitamin C fruit daily.	Fruits, juices, or nectars, unsweetened; canned, dried, fresh, or frozen. Use one vitamin C fruit or juice daily.	Any not tolerated.
Vegetables	3 to 5 servings (1/2 cup servings); include starchy vegetables and one vitamin A.	Vegetables and starch vegetables: fresh, frozen, canned, or dried; potatoes: baked or boiled; vegetable juices; one dark orange-yellow or green leafy vegetable daily.	Any not tolerated.
Soups	Use as desired.	Fresh ingredients prepared. Low-sodium/salted soups, with fat skimmed; low-fat milk (cream style).	Packaged or commercially prepared soup mixes with chili powder or black pepper. Consider individual tolerance.
Meats, Fish, Poultry, Dry Beans, Nuts, and Eggs	2 to 3 servings (4 to 6 ounces).	Lean (cut) meats, fish, poultry without skin; shellfish; dried beans and peas; soybeans, tofu; peanut butter.	Any not tolerated.
Milk, Yogurt, and Cheese	2 to 3 servings (2 or more cups), vitamin A and D fortified.	Skim or low-fat milk and yogurt; soy milk; low-fat cheeses (cottage and mozzarella).	Any not tolerated.
Beverages	4 to 6 servings (use as desired to meet calorie and fluid needs).	Water; decaffeinated drinks or unsweetened or non-carbonated soft drinks.	Caffeine or decaffeinated beverages and alcohol.
Fats and Oils	3 servings.	Reduced-calorie, low-fat, or non-fat salad dressings and mayonnaise; reduced-calorie margarine; vegetable oil (corn, safflower).	Salad dressing or sauces made with highly seasoned spices not tolerated.
Sweets and Desserts	Use occasionally to meet calorie needs.	Fruit-based desserts, angel food cake, puddings made from skim milk; desserts with no sugar, lightly sweetened or low fat.	Cocoa.
Miscellaneous	Use as desired.	Flavorings, herbs, salt substitutes, or spices tolerated.	Chili powder, black pepper, and horseradish. Any other spice not tolerated.

5

Sodium-Restricted Diets

Sodium or salt consumption (salt is 40% sodium) can be controlled by a sodium-restricted diet. This diet is typically used to control or reduce hypertension and to prevent, control, or eliminate edema. Importantly, it is also used for cardiovascular disease, or congestive heart failure; impaired liver functions such as cirrhosis; renal therapy; cortisone therapy; kidney diseases or other sodium- or fluid-retaining conditions requiring the promotion of loss of excess fluids or bodily weight.

While this may sound easy, it's best to always remember that sodium (salt) is found in practically all foods, naturally or processed. Dietitians/nutritionists indicate that the proper range for sodium consumption should fall between 1,100–3,300 mg per day. In fact, however, the average person consumes at least 6,000 mg daily. When this excess is not naturally eliminated, causing water and sodium retention, it can lead to kidney, heart, or weight gain disorders. At this point, health care professionals are moved to recommend sodium-restricted diets.

Essentially, a sodium-restricted diet is a "regular diet" with sodium limited to prescribed amounts. Foods are identified and utilized that are naturally low in sodium content and are prepared and served with little or no salt. Foods that are identified as containing high sodium levels are either eliminated completely or used in limited quantities. Keep in mind that a totally sodium / salt-free diet is unlikely to happen as many foods contain it naturally.

Types of Sodium-Restricted Diets

The five variations of the sodium-restricted diet, from most restrictive to most permissive, include ones for 250 mg, 500 mg, 1,000 mg (1 gram), 2,000 mg (2 gram) and 3,000 to 4,000 mg (3 to 4 gram).

For the purpose of this book, a 1,000 to 2,000 milligram (1 to 2 gram) sodium-restricted diet was created. In addition, the 3,000 to 4,000 milligram (3 to 4 gram), also known as a no-added-salt diet is utilized.

Table 5.1 Sodium Restricted Diet: 1,000 to 2,000 mg (1 to 2 grams)

Category	Recommended Daily Servings	Recommended Food Choices	Foods to Restrict
Bread, Cereal, Rice, and Pasta	5 servings.	Regular bread and yeast rolls; cooked cereals, puffed rice or wheat, shredded wheat, muffins, ralston, and low-sodium corn flakes; matzo, unsalted crackers; macaroni, noodles, pasta, rice, and spaghetti (prepared without salt).	Biscuits, cornbread, dry cereals, or hot instant cereals; salted crackers, pretzels, or saltines; breads or rolls made with baking powder, baking soda or self-rising flours; pack aged mixes with cheese, eggs, milk, or salt (sodium) added; snack chips.
Fruits	3 servings (1/2 cup servings); one vitamin C fruit daily.	Fresh, frozen, or canned fruit and fruit juices without added salt or sodium; dried fruits (without sodium sulfate): apples, apricots, peaches, pears, prunes, and raisins. Use one vitamin C fruit or juice daily.	Dried fruits with sodium sulfate or crystallized fruits. Any fruit processed with salt or sodium.
Vegetables	4 to 6 servings (1/2 cup servings); include starchy vegetables and one vitamin A (every other day).	Fresh, canned, or frozen without salt or sodium (except those on restricted list); low-sodium tomato juice; baked, boiled, or mashed white potato (without salt or sodium); sweet potato (1/4 cup). One cup total per week of the following: artichokes, beets, carrots, or celery.	Canned or frozen vegetables prepared with salt or sodium; frozen lima beans, green peas, mixed vegetables; brine or salted sauerkraut or pickles; potatoes prepared with salt or sodium (chips, flakes [dehydrated], mashed with added milk, sweet potatoes in excess of allowed amount); any vegetable prepared with salt or salted meats; packaged mixes with cheese, egg, milk, salt, or sodium. ***Read package labels for salt and/or sodium content.***
Soups	Use as desired.	Homemade soups with allowable foods and without salt added; low-sodium bouillon or low-sodium commercial soups using foods and amounts allowable.	Commercial canned soups, bouillon cubes, instant or dehydrated mixes, stews.
Meats, Fish, Poultry, Dry Beans, Nuts, Cheese, and Eggs	6 ounces (may include one egg daily).	Fresh and unsalted meat, fish, and poultry; unsalted or low-sodium canned meat or fish; unsalted or low-sodium cheese or cottage cheese; dried beans and peas; low-sodium peanut butter; eggs prepared without salt.	Canned, salted, or smoked meats, fish or poultry; bacon, ham, salt pork, and sausage; luncheon meats with sodium additives; frankfurters; bologna, corned beef, kosher meats; soybean meat analogs; shellfish; all other cheeses and spreads (not on allowed list); egg substitutes (frozen or powdered), raw eggs, or eggs above allowed amounts.

Table 5.1 continued

Category	Recommended Daily Servings	Recommended Food Choices	Foods to Restrict
Milk and Yogurt	2 servings (2 cups), vitamin A and D fortified.	Milk (low-fat, whole, skim, evaporated); reconstituted non-fat dry milk solids; yogurt.	Buttermilk, chocolate milk, cocoa, malted, mixes, shakes. Milk in excess of 2 servings per day
Beverages	4 to 6 servings (use as desired to meet calorie and fluid needs).	Carbonated drinks less than 20 mg sodium per serving; coffee or tea; Kool-aid; home-made lemonade.	Low-calorie carbonated drinks with saccharin; frozen or powdered mixes with salt or sodium added. ***Read package labels for salt and/or sodium content.***
Fats and Oils	3 servings (see amounts allowed).	One tsp = 1 serving (regular butter or margarine); 1 1/2 Tbsp = 1 serving (regular salad dressing); 2 Tbsp = 1 serving (may use only one serving per day: cream, sour cream, or cream cheese). May use as desired (unsalted margarine, unsalted butter, oil, cooking spray, unsalted salad dressings).	Bacon, bacon fat; salted nuts. Commercial salad dressings, mayonnaise, cream cheese, or sour cream above allowed amounts.
Sweets and Desserts	Use occasionally to meet calorie needs (limit ice cream to 1/2 cup daily).	Cakes, cookies, pies, or cobblers made without salt, baking powder or baking soda; honey, jam, or jelly; sugar; hard candy; gum drops; jelly beans; marshmallows; low-sodium or flavored gelatin; sherbet; puddings with allowed amounts of milk and eggs.	Any containing salt, baking powder, or baking soda; salted nut candy; chocolate; dutch cocoa; flavored gelatin; commercial frozen desserts and ice cream (above allowed amounts); packaged prepared mixes. ***Read package labels for salt and/or sodium content.***
Miscellaneous	Use as desired.	Flavor extracts; garlic; herbs; spices; pepper; vinegar; dried mustard powder; nuts and popcorn without salt.	Salt; onion salt; celery salt; garlic salt; catsup; lemon pepper; meat sauces and tenderizers; monosodium glutamate; prepared mustard; olives; pickles; soy sauce; tabasco sauce; salted popcorn or any food with salt and/or sodium additives. ***Read package labels for salt and/or sodium content.***

Category	Recommended Daily Servings	Recommended Food Choices	Foods to Restrict
Bread, Cereal, Rice, and Pasta	6 to 11 servings.	Enriched or whole grain breads and cereals. Enriched noodles, pasta, or rice; bagels, muffins, and tortillas.	Salted pretzels; snack chips or snack foods; salted crackers; salted bagels. Do not add salt during cooking or at the table.
Fruits	2 to 4 servings (1/2 cup servings); one vitamin C fruit daily.	Fruits, juices, or nectars, unsweetened; canned, dried, fresh, or frozen. Use one vitamin C fruit or juice daily.	none
Vegetables	3 to 5 servings (1/2 cup servings); include starchy vegetables and one vitamin A.	Vegetables and starch vegetables: fresh, frozen, canned or dried; potatoes: baked or boiled; vegetable juices; one dark orange-yellow or green leafy vegetable daily.	Brine or salted sauerkraut or pickles; olives; relishes.
Soups	Use as desired.	Homemade soups with allowable foods and without salt added; low-sodium bouillon or low-sodium commercial soups using foods and amounts allowable.	Commercial canned soups, bouillon cubes, instant or dehydrated mixes.
Meats, Fish, Poultry, Dry Beans, Nuts, Cheese, and Eggs	2 to 3 servings (4 to 6 ounces) (may include one egg daily).	Fresh and unsalted meat, fish, and poultry; unsalted or low-sodium canned meat or fish; unsalted or low-sodium cheese or cottage cheese; dried beans and peas; low-sodium peanut butter; eggs prepared without salt.	Bacon; bologna; chipped or corned beef; frankfurters; ham; kosher meats; luncheon meats; sausage; salt pork; salted codfish; soybean imitations; any canned, salted, or smoked meats and fish (anchovies, caviar, herring, or sardines); processed cheeses: American, cheese food, or spreads; highly salted natural cheeses (Bleu, Roquefort, feta, Camembert, Gorgonzola, or cottage cheese); TV dinners; dinner mixes.
Milk and Yogurt	2 or more servings (2 cups), vitamin A and D fortified.	Milk (low-fat, whole, skim, evaporated); reconstituted non-fat dry milk solids; yogurt.	none
Beverages	4 to 6 servings (use as desired to meet calorie and fluid needs).	Water; decaffeinated drinks or unsweetened or non-carbonated soft drinks.	none
Fats and Oils	3 servings (see amounts allowed).	Reduced-calorie, low-fat, or non-fat salad dressings and mayonnaise; reduced-calorie margarine; vegetable oil (corn, safflower).	Bacon, bacon fat; salted nuts.

Table 5.2 **Sodium Restricted Diet: 3,000 to 4,000 mg (3 to 4 grams)**

Table 5.2 continued

Category	Recommended Daily Servings	Recommended Food Choices	Foods to Restrict
Sweets and Desserts	Use occasionally to meet calorie needs.	Fruit-based desserts, angel food cake, puddings made from skim milk; desserts with no sugar, lightly sweetened or low fat.	none
Miscellaneous	Use as desired.	Flavor extracts; garlic; herbs; spices; pepper; vinegar; dried mustard powder; nuts and popcorn without salt.	Salt; onion salt; celery salt; garlic salt; catsup; lemon pepper; meat sauces and tenderizers; monosodium glutamate; prepared mustard; olives; pickles; soy sauce; tabasco sauce; chili sauce, salted popcorn; Worcestershire sauce or any food with salt and/or sodium additives. ***Read package labels for salt and/or sodium content.***

6

Consistency- and Texture-Modified Diets

There are five consistency and texture modified diets examined in this chapter. They are the Soft or Surgical Soft; Mechanical Soft; Puree; Low Fiber; and High Fiber diets.

Soft Diet

The soft or surgically soft diet is a nutritionally adequate diet and one of the standard diets used in many health care facilities. It differs from a normal or regular diet only as a result of the modification and reduction in the texture and fiber content of foods, resulting in a soft consistency.

It is used as a transitional diet, after a full liquid diet and before a regular diet; for post-surgical patients with acute infections and fevers, gastrointestinal dis-

turbances or chewing problems. The diet is suitable for acute or chronic conditions that impair the appetite and ability to digest food.

The soft diet includes foods and liquids that have a soft texture and are tender, easily digestible, mildly seasoned, and moderately low in roughage. Generally, foods are not ground or pureed. The diet is often individualized, depending upon the appetite and food tolerance of the patient.

Allowed foods have no tough connective tissue and contain little or no cellulose. Typically, soft diet meats are very tender and often ground or minced. While some fruits on the diet, such as bananas, oranges, or grapefruits are sometimes allowed, most fruits must be cooked. Young, tender-cooked, or pureed vegetables are the norm as are cooked or refined cereals.

Table 6.1 Soft Diet

Category	Recommended Daily Servings	Food Choices	Foods to Restrict
Bread, Cereal, Rice, and Pasta	6 to 11 servings.	Refined and enriched breads; rye bread without seeds; plain rolls and crackers; refined cereals (cooked and dry); rice; plain spaghetti; macaroni; noodles; and pasta.	Bread products containing seeds, nuts, or dried fruit. Coarse whole grain or seasoned breads, rolls, crackers, or snack chips.
Fruits	2 to 4 servings (1/2 cup servings); one vitamin C fruit daily.	Fruits or fruit juices as tolerated: fresh, canned or frozen. Use one vitamin C fruit or juice daily.	Fruits with tough skins or seeds, dried fruit, and any others not tolerated.
Vegetables	3 to 5 servings (1/2 cup servings); include starchy vegetables and one vitamin A.	Cooked vegetables and vegetable juices as tolerated. Potatoes (sweet or white), without frying or skins; creamed or scalloped. At least one vitamin A vegetable every other day.	Raw or fried vegetables. Vegetables not tolerated (consider individual tolerance: broccoli; cabbage; cauliflower; brussel sprouts; onions; corn; dried beans; and peas).
Soups	Use as desired.	Broth; bouillon; lightly seasoned, mild-flavored cream soups containing allowed foods.	Any other soups not tolerated or using restricted foods.
Meats, Fish, Poultry, Dry Beans, Nuts, Cheese and Eggs	2 to 3 servings (4 to 6 ounces).	Recommended cooking methods: baking, broiling, boiling, roasting. Tender and lean beef, pork, veal, liver, poultry, fish; cottage cheese; mild cheeses; smooth peanut butter; eggs (soft, scrambled, poached, hard-boiled).	Fried or tough highly seasoned meat, fish, or poultry; strong flavored cheeses; cold cuts, hot dogs, sausages, ham, corned beef; nuts or dried beans and peas, baked beans; chunky peanut butter; fried or raw eggs.
Milk and Yogurt	2 to 3 servings (2 or more cups), vitamin A and D fortified.	Milk (whole, low-fat, skim, buttermilk); milk drinks (cocoa, pasteurized eggnog; shakes); plain yogurt or yogurt with allowed fruit.	none
Beverages	4 to 6 servings (use as desired to meet calorie and fluid needs).	Water; decaffeinated or caffeinated drinks; coffee, tea, or cereal beverages; carbonated soft drinks.	alcohol
Fats and Oils	3 or more servings.	Margarine; butter; cream; shortening; sour cream; cream cheese; mayonnaise; oil; mildly seasoned cream sauces and gravies; mildly seasoned salad dressings.	Gravies and sauces made from meat fats and salt pork; highly seasoned salad dressing.

Table 6.1 continued

Category	Recommended Daily Servings	Food Choices	Foods to Restrict
Sweets and Desserts	Use occasionally to meet calorie needs.	Sugar; honey; jelly; syrup; hard candies; marshmallows; plain cakes, cookies, and pastries with allowed foods; puddings; custard; ice cream; sherbet with allowable fruits; ices; gelatin desserts.	Desserts or sweets containing coconut, nuts, fruits or any other foods not allowed.
Miscellaneous	Use as desired.	Seasonings, herbs, spices, vinegar, lemon, catsup, cocoa powder.	Pickles; olives; highly seasoned spices; chili powder; mustard; chili sauce; hot sauce; horseradish. Any others not tolerated.

Mechanical Soft Diet

The mechanical soft (dental soft) diet is utilized for persons or patients that have difficulty chewing or swallowing. It differs from the regular (normal) diet only by the fact it is limited to soft foods, for individuals who can't chew properly, due to lack of teeth or poorly fitting dentures. These latter people vary greatly in their ability to chew certain foods, and the diet needs to be individualized to the person/patient, accordingly. Restrictions do not apply to seasonings (use as tolerated) or to method of food preparation.

The mechanical soft diet modifies the regular (normal) diet by:

1. Using chopped meat or poultry that is ground or minced.
2. Using already tender fish.
3. Using sufficiently cooked vegetables, cooked longer to assure softness. Dicing or chopping is utilized, while avoiding raw or tough-skinned vegetables. Chopped lettuce or raw chopped tomatoes are sometimes suitable, if tolerated.
4. Similarly avoiding raw fruits with seeds or tough skins. Permitted are raw fruits that can be softened such as apples, apricots, bananas, berries, citrus sections, grapes, melons, peaches, and pears (diced).
5. Permitting biscuits, bread, or soft rolls, as opposed to crusty breads or crisp rolls.
6. Using desserts from the regular diet that are soft, such as dried fruits, and nuts that are finely chopped or soft cakes, puddings, and pies that have tender crusts.
7. Using broths, gravies, and sauces that promote palpability and enhance food to be moist versus dry.

Food for Thought

An old adage, often quoted, is applicable.

"Don't puree the food if ground will do.
Don't grind the food if chopped will do.
Don't chop the food when whole will do.
Do all you can to make them chew."

Table 6.2 **Mechanical Soft Diet**

Category	Recommended Daily Servings	Food Choices	Foods to Restrict
Bread, Cereal, Rice, and Pasta	6 to 11 servings.	Enriched or whole grain breads and cereals. Enriched noodles, pasta, or rice; bagels, muffins, and tortillas.	Any not tolerated.
Fruits	2 to 4 servings (1/2 cup servings); one vitamin C fruit daily.	Canned, dried, or frozen fruits; banana, melon. Fresh, canned, or frozen juices or nectars. Use one vitamin C fruit or juice daily.	Raw fruits with tough skins and seeds. Any others not tolerated.
Vegetables	3 to 5 servings (1/2 cup servings); include starchy vegetables and one vitamin A.	Vegetables and starch vegetables: cooked (fresh, frozen, canned, or dried); potatoes: baked (without skin) or boiled; vegetable juices.	Raw vegetables, vegetables with tough skins and seeds. Any others not tolerated.
Soups	Use as desired.	Fresh ingredients prepared. Low-sodium/salted soups, with fat skimmed; low-fat milk (cream style).	Any not tolerated.
Meats, Fish, Poultry, Dry Beans, Nuts, and Eggs	2 to 3 servings (4 to 6 ounces).	Lean (cut) meats, fish, poultry without skin; shellfish; dried beans and peas; soybeans, tofu; peanut butter; eggs.	Nuts and any others not tolerated.
Milk, Yogurt, and Cheese	2 to 3 servings (2 or more cups), vitamin A and D fortified.	Skim or low-fat milk and yogurt; soy milk; low-fat cheeses (cottage and mozzarella).	Any not tolerated.
Beverages	4 to 6 servings (use as desired to meet calorie and fluid needs).	Water; decaffeinated drinks or unsweetened or non-carbonated soft drinks.	None.
Fats and Oils	3 servings.	Reduced-calorie, low-fat or non-fat salad dressings and mayonnaise; reduced-calorie margarine; and corn oil.	None.
Sweets and Desserts	Use occasionally to meet calorie needs.	Puddings, ice cream, sherbet, ices, gelatin; sugar, honey, jelly, syrup; cakes, pies, and cookies (if tolerated).	Any dessert containing foods restricted and any others not tolerated.
Miscellaneous	Use as desired.	Flavorings, herbs, or spices.	Any not tolerated.

Puree Diet

The pureed diet is appropriate for individuals or patients experiencing difficulty chewing or swallowing. A pureed diet uses regular food and mechanically alters or changes them to a liquid or semi-solid form.

Several points need to be remembered in administering the puree diet:

1. The diet needs to be carefully prepared to assure adequate nourishment.
2. Do not keep the individual on the pureed diet any longer than is needed.
3. Consult a dietitian/nutritionist if feeding problems develop, continue, or change.
4. Be aware that dental problem individuals, who have difficulty chewing foods, may be better served on a mechanical soft diet.
5. Periodically evaluate individuals to see if they are ready to progress to more solid foods.
6. Establish portion size to ensure nutritional requirements are met in total calories, amount of protein, and other nutrients.
7. Depending upon the person's ability to swallow pureed foods with milk, meat broth, or vegetable broth.
8. Enhance the acceptability of the pureed diet by promoting variety in color, flavor, and temperature.

Dietary Management of Dysphagia

Dysphagia is a neurologic swallowing problem. The person fears choking, resists eating, and therefore is at risk for inadequate food and liquid intake. Evaluation by a speech therapist is required. A speech therapist attempts to observe and evaluate how each person handles foods and food textures, and then assist dysphagic persons to increase their intake of food textures over time.

Dietary management for dysphagic persons include using flavorful, aromatic foods to stimulate swallowing as opposed to dry foods or flavorless liquids. Foods that have texture, hold together and are cold, hot or highly flavored are preferred by dysphagia persons. Some foods should be finely chopped, diced, well cooked, and soft. Caution should particularly be exercised with liquids, since they may spill into the pharynx. Persons with dysphagia often consume fewer liquids. Often liquids are thickened and may be provided in such forms as gelatin desserts, ices, sherbets, and slushes.

Table 6.3   **Puree Diet**

Category	Recommended Daily Servings	Food Choices	Foods to Restrict
Bread, Cereal, Rice, and Pasta	6 to 11 servings.	Cooked cereals; breads as tolerated. Mashed, pureed, or strained noodles, pasta and rice.	Cereals requiring chewing. Bread products not tolerated. Any others not tolerated.
Fruits	2 to 4 servings (1/2 cup servings); one vitamin C fruit daily.	Mashed, pureed, or strained fruits; fruit juices. Use one vitamin C fruit or fruit juice daily.	Whole fruits.
Vegetables	3 to 5 servings (1/2 cup servings); include starchy vegetables and one vitamin A.	Mashed, pureed, or strained vegetables and starch vegetables: vegetable juices. At least one vitamin A vegetable daily.	Raw vegetables.
Soups	Use as desired.	Strained soups with pureed vegetables and/or meats.	Soups requiring chewing.
Meats, Fish, Poultry, Dry Beans, Nuts, Cheese, and Eggs	2 to 3 servings (4 to 6 ounces).	Strained or pureed meat, fish, or poultry; cottage cheese and other cheeses as tolerated; pureed beans; soft poached and scrambled eggs; sieved, hard-cooked eggs; eggs cooked in custards or in commercial eggnogs. (pasteurized).	Nuts and any others not tolerated.
Milk and Yogurt	2 to 3 servings (2 or more cups), vitamin A and D fortified.	Milk (whole, low-fat, skim, buttermilk); milk drinks (cocoa, pasteurized eggnog; shakes); plain or fruit-flavored yogurt.	None.
Beverages	4 to 6 servings (use as desired to meet calorie and fluid needs).	Water; decaffeinated or caffeinated drinks; coffee, tea, or cereal beverages; carbonated soft drinks.	None.
Fats and Oils	4 or more servings.	Margarine, butter, cream, shortening, sour cream, cream cheese, mayonnaise, oil, strained sauces, and gravies.	None.
Sweets and Desserts	Use occasionally to meet calorie needs.	Puddings (not requiring chewing), ice cream, sherbet, ices, gelatin, sugar, honey, jelly, syrup.	Cakes, cookies, pastries, and any dessert requiring chewing.
Miscellaneous	Use as desired.	Seasonings, herbs, spices as tolerated.	Any not tolerated.

Fiber Diets

It is important not to confuse or misuse the words "fiber" and "residue." "Residue" or food residue refers to the part of food the body cannot digest and which is eventually disposed in the feces. Little food residue means little fecal matter to be disposed. Greater food residue increases the fecal matter disposal process.

Increasing food residue is done by eating foods containing large amounts of fiber or roughage (high-fiber diet). Dietary fiber is the indigestible carbohydrate in plants, such as fruits, vegetables, and whole grain cereals, including cellulose. This produces "bulk" or residue in the intestinal tract and stimulates defecation.

It is also noteworthy that all foods have some residue. Milk has no fiber content, but it does increase stool bulk, because the bulk or residue can include dietary fibers, cells split off from intestinal mucosa, intestinal bacteria, or other residues. Therefore, a diet could be low in fiber, without being low in residue.

High-Fiber Diet

A high-fiber diet is actually a normal diet which utilizes foods rich in fiber. It is commonly used in the treatment of constipation, diverticulosis, hemorrhoids, and irritable bowel diarrhea.

Recommended foods, high in fiber, would include bean, corn, or 100% whole wheat and rye cereals, all fruits (cooked or raw), vegetables, and nuts and seeds.

In the earlier acute stages of disorders, such as diverticulosis, tiny sacs or pouches form in the sides of the intestinal walls, often in the colon. They fill with bacteria and food wastes and become infected or inflamed, causing severe pain or perforation. Low-fiber diets over a prolonged period of time contribute to its development.

Treatment during the initial acute stages, includes antibiotics, bed rest, and a clear liquid diet. Later, a low fiber/soft diet is begun and gradually increased until a higher fiber diet takes hold. It may take several weeks for this adjustment to be achieved.

Crude fiber requirements (c.f.) for the average person is thought to be about 8 to 11 grams per day or 30 to 50 grams of dietary fiber. Dietary fiber includes all the indigestible substances in food, while crude fiber is the residue remaining after treatment with alcohol, boiling sulfuric acid, ether, sodium hydroxide, and water.

Dietary fiber is determined by using the following approximate guidelines.

Dietary Fiber = 5 × c.f. breads, cereal grains.
Dietary Fiber = 3.5 × c.f. legumes, nuts, seeds, and vegetables.
Dietary Fiber = 4 × c.f. fruits

According to food selections, it is suggested that a fiber content of 12 to 18 grams of fiber is adequate for a high-fiber diet.

Table 6.4 High-Fiber Diet

Category	Recommended Daily Servings	Recommended Food Choices	Foods to Limit
Bread, Cereal, Rice, and Pasta	6 to 11 servings.	Buckwheat, cracked wheat, rye, or whole wheat breads or coarse-ground biscuits, corn-meal, muffins, or bread from bran, buckwheat, corn meal, rye, or whole wheat flours. Cereals from bran, unprocessed bran, oatmeal, or whole grain (100% bran cereals, Ralston, or Shredded Wheat); brown rice; whole grain pasta and noodles.	Highly refined breads or cereals; crackers, plain muffins, rolls, white bread, cream of rice, cream of wheat; macaroni; noodles; white rice, spaghetti or other refined starches.
Fruits	2 to 4 servings (1/2 cup servings); one vitamin C fruit daily.	Use dried or raw fruit; eat with the peel. Use one vitamin C fruit or juice daily.	Canned or cooked fruit.
Vegetables	3 to 5 servings (1/2 cup servings); include starchy vegetables and one vitamin A.	Raw Vegetables and starch vegetables: fresh or cooked to tender crisp stage; potatoes: baked with skin; one dark orange-yellow or green leafy vegetable daily.	Canned or cooked to tender.
Soups	Use as desired.	Fresh ingredients prepared.	None.
Meats, Fish, Poultry, Dry Beans, Nuts, and Eggs	2 to 3 servings (4 to 6 ounces).	Lean (cut) meats, fish, poultry without skin; shellfish; dried beans and peas; soybeans, tofu; crunchy peanut butter; eggs (no raw).	None.
Milk, Yogurt, and Cheese	2 to 3 servings (2 or more cups), vitamin A and D fortified.	Skim or low-fat milk and yogurt; soy milk; low-fat cheeses (cottage and mozzarella).	None.
Beverages	6 to 8 servings (use as desired to meet calorie and fluid needs).	Water (6 to 8 cups daily); decaffeinated drinks or unsweetened or non-carbonated soft drinks.	None.
Fats and Oils	3 servings.	Reduced-calorie, low-fat or non-fat salad dressings and mayonnaise; reduced-calorie margarine; vegetable oil (corn, safflower).	None.
Sweets and Desserts	Use occasionally to meet calorie needs.	Desserts made from whole grains, fruits, and other high fiber food sources; jams, preserves; pies.	Cakes, candy, cookies, pastries, pies, puddings (whole milk). Unless in need of additional calories, avoid excessive consumption of concentrated sweets.
Miscellaneous	Use as desired.	Nuts, seeds, spices, and herbs.	None.

Low-Fiber Diet

Normally, this diet is devised to provide minimum amounts of fiber and to minimize residue in the intestinal tract. Controlling fiber intake and limiting the fecal matter output, by necessity, limiting foods such as fruits/fruit juices, milk products, and vegetables, all high in crude fiber, cellulose, hemicellulose, and lignin. The diet does allow food and beverages such as bread (white), coffee, desserts (simple), eggs, fish, meats (tender), poultry, soups (clear), and tea.

Persons should also not exceed 15 to 20 grams total dietary fiber (4 gram crude fiber) per day.

This diet is utilized for Crohn's disease, ulcerative colitis, acute diverticular disease, and before/after lower bowel surgery.

A low-fiber food is not necessarily low residue, such as a food is high residue because of its fiber content. The following is a general listing of foods in order of increasing fecal output: Protein, fat, milk, digestible carbohydrate, and carbohydrate without digestible material.

The diet may be reduced in fiber content in the following ways:

- Using tender, young vegetables.

- Puree/strain foods via a sieve.

- Cooking foods.

- Omit foods with seeds, heavy skin, or structural fiber: asparagus, beans, berries, cabbage, celery, corn, and peas.

- Peel skin from fruits and vegetables. Use strained fruit juices, omitting all fruits and vegetables.

- Omit whole grain cereals and breads and replace with refined cereals and white breads.

- Limit milk in low-fiber diets to two cups or less.

Table 6.5 Low-Fiber Diet

Category	Recommended Daily Servings	Recommended Food Choices	Foods to Restrict
Bread, Cereal, Rice, and Pasta	6 to 11 servings.	Enriched, refined flour or fine, whole grain bread; melba toast; cooked or dry refined cereals (corn flakes, plain instant oatmeal or farina, rice crispies, or puffed rice); saltine crackers, rice, spaghetti, macaroni, noodles, and pasta.	Bread and bread products containing seeds, nuts, or dried fruit; coarse whole grain or cracked wheat breads, hard rolls, whole grain crackers, rye crisps; old-fashioned oatmeal.
Fruits	2 or more servings (1/2 cup servings); one vitamin C fruit daily.	Fruits juices; cooked, stewed, or canned fruit without seeds (applesauce, apricots without skin, peaches, pears); citrus fruit sections without membrane. Use one vitamin C fruit or juice daily.	Raw, dried, pickled, or spiced fruits; fruits with tough skins or seeds; pineapple, berries, prune juice.
Vegetables	3 to 5 servings (1/2 cup servings); include starchy vegetables and one vitamin A.	Cooked, tender vegetables; tomato juice; strained puree corn; potatoes (sweet or white), without frying or skins; creamed or scalloped with allowed milk. At least one vitamin A vegetable every other day.	Raw or fried vegetables; strong flavored vegetables (broccoli, cabbage, cauliflower, brussel sprouts, onions); whole kernel corn, dried beans, and peas); fried potatoes or skins; snack chips.
Soups	Use as desired.	Broth; bouillon; lightly seasoned, mild-flavored cream soups (with allowed milk); meat soups with rice and noodles.	Spicy soups or any other soups using restricted foods.
Meats, Fish, Poultry, Dry Beans, Nuts, Cheese, and Eggs	2 to 3 servings (4 to 6 ounces).	Tender and lean beef, pork, ham (if tolerated) veal, liver, poultry, fish (fish, salmon, tuna); cottage cheese; mild cheeses; smooth peanut butter; eggs (soft, scrambled, poached, hard-boiled).	Fried, salted, or highly seasoned meat, fish, or poultry; strong-flavored cheeses; cold cuts, hot dogs, sausages, ham, corned beef; nuts or dried beans and peas, baked beans; chunky peanut butter; fried or raw eggs.
Milk and Yogurt	2 servings (2 cups), vitamin A and D fortified.	Milk (whole, low-fat, skim, buttermilk); nonfat dry milk solids (1/2 cup); milk drinks (pasteurized eggnog; shakes); plain or yogurt with allowed fruit.	Over 2 cups per day as a beverage or in food preparation; cocoa, chocolate milk.
Beverages	4 to 6 servings (use as desired to meet calorie and fluid needs).	Water; decaffeinated or caffeinated drinks; coffee, tea or fruit beverages; carbonated soft drinks.	Alcohol. Milk or milk beverages above 2 cups per day.

Table 6.5 continued

Category	Recommended Daily Servings	Recommended Food Choices	Foods to Restrict
Fats and Oils	3 or more servings.	Margarine; butter; cream; shortening; sour cream; cream cheese; mayonnaise; oil; mildly seasoned cream sauces (with allowed milk); and gravies.	Avocado and any others not tolerated.
Sweets and Desserts	Use occasionally to meet calorie needs	Sugar; honey; jelly; syrup; hard candies; plain cakes, cookies, and pastries with allowed foods; puddings; custard; plain ice cream; sherbet; ices; gelatin desserts. Calculate using allowed milk and use allowed fruit.	Desserts or sweets containing chocolate, coconut, nuts, seeds, jams (with seeds), restricted fruits, or any other foods not allowed.
Miscellaneous	Use as desired.	Mild seasonings and salt.	Pickles; olives; relishes; highly seasoned spices and herbs; barbecue sauce; chili powder; mustard; chili sauce; hot sauce; garlic, vinegar; horseradish. Any others not tolerated.

7

Fat- and Cholesterol-Modified Diets

By definition, this diet attempts to limit the amount of fat and/or cholesterol in the diet. A combined low-fat/low-cholesterol diet assists in the prevention of various types of heart disease and is the beginning recommendation in high blood cholesterol treatment.

Used alone, a low-fat diet (40 to 50 gm) is used in treatment of gall bladder disease, chronic pancreatitis (inflamed pancreas), and fat malabsorption diseases.

Whereas the average daily diet of fat may be in the 150 gram range, the low-fat (or fat restricted) diet limits total daily dietary fat up to 40 to 50 grams. No foods that are high in fat are acceptable. Likewise, foods should be prepared without adding fat. Essentially, visible fat is removed from meat; foods are not fried, and skim milk replaces whole milk. Be aware that, a low-fat diet can seem unpleasant tasting or unpalatable to many persons.

A combination of low fat and low cholesterol is limited to about 30% of the total calories from fat and 300 mg or less of cholesterol daily. The diet varies according to how much your dietitian/nutritionist may prescribe for fat, calories, and cholesterol.

Low cholesterol diets modify the type and amount of allowed fats and is utilized for persons at risk for coronary heart disease. While a necessary part of body cells, cholesterol excess in the blood is associated with atherosclerosis, caused by artery walls becoming thicker and narrower, due to fatty deposits. It may then block or stop blood flow to the heart.

Saturated fat (animal fats) can raise cholesterol, while polyunsaturated fats, liquid at room temperature and derived from plants/fish, can lower it.

Cholesterol-restricted foods typically include animal fats, whole milk, cream- and protein-rich, high-cholesterol content foods such as eggs, organ meats, and shellfish.

Table 7.1 Low-Fat (40 to 50 grams) and Low-Cholesterol Diet

Category	Recommended Daily Servings	Food Choices	Foods to Restrict
Bread, Cereal, Rice, and Pasta	6 servings.	Whole grain and enriched white breads/cereals; plain or graham crackers; matzo; melba toast; yeast rolls (no extra fat); cooked cereal, saltines, rice, barley, noodles, and pasta.	Biscuits, cornbread, dumplings, fritters, granola, muffins, waffles; nutty cereals, crackers with excess fat or spices; chow mein noodles; popcorn (with fat); egg noodles; snack chips, breads with egg and cheese; stuffing.
Fruits	4 servings (1/2 cup servings); one vitamin C fruit daily.	Fruits, juices, or nectars, unsweetened; canned, dried, fresh, or frozen. Use one vitamin C fruit or juice daily.	Avocado in excess amounts. Any causing distress.
Vegetables	4 servings (1/2 cup servings); include starchy vegetables and one vitamin A.	All fresh, frozen, or canned prepared without added fats, oils or fat/cream containing sauces. Include one dark orange-yellow or green leafy vegetable daily.	Buttered, au gratin, creamed, or fried, unless calculated using allowed fat. Any causing problems such as avocado, broccoli, brussel sprouts, cabbage, cauliflower, cucumber, garlic, or olives.
Soups	Use as allowed.	Fat-free broths; fat-free soups, creamed soup made with skim milk; packaged dehydrated soups.	Most store-bought commercial soups; whole-milk based cream soups.
Meats, Fish, Poultry, Dry Beans, and Eggs	6 ounces cooked. Limit eggs to twice a week.	Recommended methods of cooking: broiling, roasting without fat, grilling, or boiling. Lean cuts of beef, lamb, pork, and veal; poultry without skin; fish; egg whites (3); canned fish (water packed); 95% fat-free luncheon meats; legumes cooked without added fat; tofu; egg prepared without added fat (twice a week).	Bacon, capon, cold cuts, corned beef, duck, goose, ham (hocks), luncheon meats, organ meats (liver, kidney); pork, poultry skin, sausage, or spare ribs, or any fatty, fried, or smoked; canned meat or fish (oil based); cheeses; dried beans/peas (if not tolerated); peanut butter; meats prepared with added gravy or sauce prepared; eggs fried in fat or in excess of allowed amounts.
Milk, Cheese, and Yogurt	2 servings (vitamin A and D fortified).	Skim milk and skim milk based buttermilk, evaporated, or yogurt; nonfat dry milk solids. Low-fat, no-cholesterol sour cream and cream cheese. Part-skim and low-fat cheeses; diet cheeses that are less than 55 calories per serving.	Whole, evaporated, or condensed milk; chocolate milk (low-fat or whole); cream, half and half, non-dairy creamer, whipped, or non-dairy whipped cream, eggnog, milk shakes; regular evaporated or whole-milk based yogurt; buttermilk made from whole milk; high-fat cheese (cheddar, American, brie, swiss). Cream cheese and sour cream (in excess of allowed amounts).

Table 7.1 continued

Category	Recommended Daily Servings	Food Choices	Foods to Restrict
Beverages	Use to meet calorie and fluid needs.	Carbonated beverages, decaffeinated or regular coffee, tea, cereal beverages.	Those with ingredients made with whole milk, chocolate, or eggs. Any causing distress.
Fats, Oils, Nuts, Seeds, Salad Dressings, Sauces, and Gravies	3 to 5 servings (approximately 5 grams fat per serving).	Diet or low-calorie margarine or mayonnaise (1 Tbsp); low-calorie salad dressing (2 Tbsp); regular margarine or mayonnaise (1 tsp); regular salad dressing (1 Tbsp). Oil: corn, safflower, soybean, olive, peanut, sunflower (1 tsp). Nuts: almonds (6 whole); cashews (1 Tbsp); pecans (2 whole); peanuts (20 small). Other nuts and seeds (1 Tbsp).	Bacon, bacon fat, butter, lard, saturated oil (coconut, palm); coconuts; mayonnaise; sauces and gravies made with restricted ingredients or in excess of allowed amounts (cream gravies and sauce). Any fat in excess of amounts allowed.
Sweets and Desserts	Use occasionally to meet calorie needs.	Angel food cake; cookies (plain, vanilla wafers, graham crackers); fruit whips, jam or jelly; gelatin; honey, meringues, molasses; fruit ice; plain sugar candy (gumdrops, hard, jellybeans, marshmallows); skim-milk based sherbets, puddings, desserts; sugar; syrup.	Any cakes, candy, and cookies not allowed, chocolate, doughnuts, ice cream, pastries, or pies; dessert containing ingredients such as coconut cream, eggs, fat, nuts, or whole milk.
Miscellaneous	Use as desired.	Catsup; mild spices and herbs (pepper and salt); mustard, pickles, vinegar.	Spices and herbs not tolerated. Nuts and olives in excess amounts. Spicy sauces and gravies not tolerated.

8

Diabetic and Calorie-Controlled Diets

Overview

The Exchange Lists for Meal Planning designed by the American Diabetes Association and The American Dietetic Association is used to control diabetes, a long-term or chronic disorder, causing the body to inadequately produce or utilize insulin.

Insulin is a hormone secreted by the islet of Langerhans in the pancreas. It is needed to change carbohydrates, protein, and fat into energy for daily use. Inadequate supplies of insulin result in the buildup of sugar (glucose) in the blood, which can cause severe complications. Symptoms of untreated diabetes are: appetite or thirst increase; itching skin; increased urine; weakness or loss of weight.

At least two major types of diabetes are recognized:

Insulin-Dependent Diabetes Mellitus (IDDM): Covers about 5% of known cases. Normally, these people have had diabetes for years and it is severe and mandates treatment with insulin (injection) and complete attention to diet management to support and sustain life.

Non-insulin Dependent Diabetes Mellitus (NIDDM): Usually affects the middle-aged or older group, as statistically about 80% of all diabetics are over 40 and 90% are obese. Insulin is not required to sustain life, but it can be treated with insulin, oral medication, or diet therapy alone.

Since most NIDDM (patients) are overweight, the primary goal of diet therapy is controlling the calorie content of their diet. Furthermore, achieving a more ideal (lower) body weight will improve glucose tolerance and reduce hyperglycemia, blood pressure, cholesterol, and triglyceride levels.

When people are not overweight, a major diet therapy concern is the proper spacing of food consumption.

Diabetes Management

The management and balance of diabetes falls within three categories:

- ◆ Food
- ◆ Activity
- ◆ Medication (if required)

Food raises blood-glucose levels. Activity and medications (insulin or oral hypoglycemic agents) lower the blood-glucose levels. Balancing the three areas is a key objective.

Exchange Lists

The Exchange Lists are the basis of a meal planning system designed by a committee of the American Diabetes Association and The American Dietetic Association, Copyright© 1995. While designed primarily for people with diabetes and others who must follow special diets, the Exchange Lists are based on principles of good nutrition that apply to everyone.

Exchange lists are foods listed together because they are alike. Each serving of a food has about the same amount of carbohydrates, protein, fat, and calories as the other foods on that list. That is why any food on a list can be "exchanged" or traded for any other food on the same list. The following are the Foods Groups that makeup the Exchange List.

- Starch List
- Fruit List
- Vegetable List
- Milk List
- Other Carbohydrates List
- Meat and Meat Substitutes List
- Fat List
- Free Foods List
- Combination Foods List
- Fast Foods

The Exchange List provides you with a wide variety of food choices and will control your daily intake of calories, carbohydrates, fats, and protein, thereby balancing insulin and controlling blood-glucose levels. Remember, variety is truly the "spice of life."

Meal Planning

In consultation with a dietitian or nutritionist, construct your own specific meal plan. The meal plan guide will show the number of food choices (exchanges), that you can eat per meal and snack.

You may need to change the way you eat.

- Change habits gradually, setting short-term goals.
- Eat meals at regular times for insulin-sugar balance maintenance.

- Eating the proper portion size is critical to blood-glucose levels and your weight. So measure or weigh your food portions.
- When and if problems arise or adjustments may be necessary, see your registered dietitian or nutritionist.
- Over time, meal plan adjustments may be necessary.
- Learn to read all labels from commercial foods to check for sugar, salts, etc.

No Concentrated Sweets Diet

The No Concentrated Sweets diet is a liberalized approach to treating the controlled diabetic. Patients following this diet should be closely monitored by their physician and/or registered dietitian or nutritionist.

Calorie Distribution

Generally, the calorie distribution within a diabetic meal consists of:

- 50% carbohydrates, with at least 30 to 45% of total calories as starch and other complex carbohydrates.
- 20% protein
- 30% fat, with a minimum of 10% total calories from unsaturated fats.

The diet is given in terms of exchanges rather than particular foods. It is important to follow the meal pattern by choosing the right number of exchanges for each meal.

The Calculated Calorie diets provided in this book are the: 1,200, 1,500, 1,800, 2,000 and 2,200 calorie. Though these diets were designed for persons with diabetes, the 1,200 and 1,500 calorie diets can be used for weight loss.

Table 8.1   No Concentrated Sweets Diet

Category	Recommended Daily Servings	Recommended Food Choices	Foods to Restrict
Bread, Cereal, Rice, and Pasta	6 to 11 servings.	Enriched or whole grain breads and cereals. Enriched noodles, pasta or rice; bagels, muffins, and tortillas,	Sweetened or sugar coated cereals; sweet rolls or sweet breads. ***Read package labels for sugar, sucrose, dextrose, corn syrup, or fructose.***
Fruits	2 to 4 servings (1/2 cup servings); one vitamin C fruit daily.	Fruits, juices, or nectars, unsweetened; canned (water or juice packed), dried, fresh or frozen. Use one vitamin C fruit or juice daily.	Fruits canned in syrups.
Vegetables	3 to 5 servings (1/2 cup servings); include starchy vegetables and one vitamin A.	Vegetables and starch vegetables: fresh, frozen, canned, or dried; potatoes: baked or boiled; vegetable juices; one dark orange-yellow or green leafy vegetable daily.	Pickled vegetables or coleslaw with added sugar.
Soups	Use as desired.	Fresh ingredients prepared. Low sodium/salted soups, with fat skimmed; low-fat milk (cream style).	Soups prepared with sugar. ***Read package labels for sugar, sucrose, dextrose, corn syrup, or fructose.***
Meats, Fish, Poultry, Dry Beans, Nuts, and Eggs	2 to 3 servings (4 to 6 ounces).	Lean (cut) meats, fish, poultry without skin; shellfish; dried beans and peas; soybeans, tofu; peanut butter.	Any prepared with sugar or glazed sauce.
Milk, Yogurt, and Cheese	2 to 3 servings (2 or more cups), vitamin A and D fortified.	Skim or low-fat milk and yogurt; soy milk; low-fat cheeses (cottage and mozzarella).	Chocolate or flavored milk, frappes, eggnogs, instant breakfasts; whole milk; condensed milk; fruit-flavored yogurt.
Beverages	4 to 6 servings (use as desired to meet calorie and fluid needs).	Water; unsweetened drinks or diet carbonated soft drinks.	Alcohol; beverages made with sugar or corn syrup; regular carbonated beverages; punch.
Fats and Oils	3 servings.	Reduced-calorie, low-fat or non-fat salad dressings and mayonnaise; reduced-calorie margarine; vegetable oil (corn, safflower).	Avoid excessive consumption of saturated fats (butter, lard, coconut oil, palm oil, etc.).
Sweets and Desserts	Some foods listed may be used in meal planning, in spite of the sugar and fat content. Consult with a dietitian/nutritionist or physician to work those foods into your meal plan.	Fruit-based desserts, angel food cake, puddings made from skim milk; desserts with no sugar or low fat.	Donuts, frosted cakes, cookies, pastries, and pies; candy, chocolate or candy coated nuts or raisins; sugar; jam; jellies; honey; molasses; corn syrup; regular gelatin desserts; puddings; custards; sherbet; ice cream. Avoid consumption of concentrated sweets.
Miscellaneous	Use as desired.	Flavorings, herbs, spices, salt, or salt substitutes.	Sweet pickle relish. Avoid excessive consumption of salt or salt blends.

Table 8.2 Calculated Diets

Kilocalories, Carbohydrates, Protein, and Fat Distribution

Kilocalories	1,200	1,500	1,800	2,000	2,200
Calculated Kilocalories	1,203	1,513	1,812	2,004	2,201
Carbohydrates (gm)	159	189	219	240	270
Protein (gm)	72	92	98	112	118
Fat (gm)	31	39	55	60	65
Carbohydrates (percentage)	53	51	50	49	50
Protein (percentage)	24	25	22	23	22
Carbohydrates (percentage)	23	24	28	28	28

Number of Servings in Each Exchange Group Per Day

Starch List	5	7	9	10	12
Fruit List	3	3	3	3	3
Vegetable List	3	3	3	3	3
Meat & Meat Substitutes List[1]	5 (2 lean)	7 (3 lean)	7	8	8
Milk List (skim or very low-fat milk)	2	2	2	2 1/2	2 1/2
Fat List	2	2	4	4	5

Suggested Meal Pattern: Number of Servings in Each Exchange Group Per Meal

Breakfast

Starch List	2	2	2	3	3
Fruit List	1	1	1	1	1
Meat & Meat Substitutes List[1]	1	1	1	1	1
Milk List (skim or very low-fat milk)	1	1	1	1	1
Fat List	1	1	1	1	1

Lunch

Starch List	1	2	3	3	4
Fruit List	1	1	1	1	1
Vegetable List	2	2	2	2	2
Meat & Meat Substitutes List[1]	2	3	3	3	3
Milk List (skim or very low-fat milk)	1/2	1/2	1/2	1	1
Fat List	1	1	1	1	2

Dinner

Starch List	1	2	3	3	4
Fruit List	1	1	1	1	1
Vegetable List	1	1	1	1	1
Meat & Meat Substitutes List[1]	2 lean	3 lean	3	3	3
Fat List	0	0	1	1	1

Bedtime Snack

Starch List	1	1	1	1	1
Milk List (skim or very low fat milk)	1/2	1/2	1/2	1/2	1/2
Meat & Meat Substitutes List[1]	0	0	0	1	1
Fat List	0	0	0	1	1

[1]Unless otherwise noted, the medium-fat meat exchange has been used to calculate the meat group. The Exchange Lists for Meal Planning has been designed by the American Diabetes Association and The American Dietetic Association, ©1995.

Table 8.3   **Exchange Lists for Meal Planning**

Table 8.3a   **Starch List**

One starch exchange equals 15 grams of carbohydrate, 3 grams of protein, 0–1 grams fat, and 80 calories.

Cereals, grains, pasta, breads, crackers, snacks, starchy vegetables, and cooked dried beans, peas, and lentils are starches.

In general, one starch is:

♦ 1/2 cup of cereal, grain, pasta, or starchy vegetable.

♦ 1 ounce of a bread product, such as 1 slice of bread.

♦ 3/4 to 1 ounce of most snack foods. (Some snack foods may also have added fat.)

Nutrition Tips

1. Most starch choices are good sources of B vitamins.

2. Foods made from whole grains are good sources of fiber.

3. Dried beans and peas are a good source of protein and fiber.

Selection Tips

1. Choose starches made with little fat as often as you can.

2. Starchy vegetables prepared with fat count as one starch and one fat.

3. Bagels or muffins can be 2, 3, or 4 ounces in size and can, therefore, count as 2, 3, or 4 starch choices. Check the size you eat.

4. Dried beans, peas, and lentils are also found on the Meat and Meat Substitutes list.

5. Regular potato chips and tortilla chips are found on the Other Carbohydrate list.

6. Most of the servings sizes are measured after cooking.

7. Always check Nutrition Facts on the food label.

Breads

Bagel	1/2 (1 oz)
Bread, reduced-calorie	2 sl (1 1/2 oz)
Bread, white, whole-wheat, pumpernickel, rye	1 sl (1 oz)
Bread sticks, crisp, 4 in. long × 1/2 in.	2 (2/3 oz)
English muffin	1/2
Frankfurter or hamburger bun	1/2 (1 oz)
Pita, 6 in. across	1/2
Roll, plain, small	1 (1 oz)
Tortilla, corn, 6 in. across	1
Tortilla, flour, 7–8 in. across	1
Waffle, 4 1/2 in. square, reduced-fat	1

Starchy Vegetables

Baked beans	1/3 cup
Corn	1/2 cup
Corn on cob, medium	1 (5 oz)
Mixed vegetables with corn, peas, or pasta	1 cup
Peas, green	1/2 cup
Plantain	1/2 cup
Potato, baked or boiled	1 small (3 oz)
Potato, mashed	1/2 cup
Squash, winter (acorn, butternut)	1 cup
Yam, sweet potato, plain	1/2 cup

Crackers and Snacks

Animal crackers	8
Graham crackers, 2 1/2 in square	3
Matzoh	3/4 oz
Melba toast	4 sl
Oyster crackers	24
Popcorn (popped, no fat added) or low-fat microwave	3 cups
Pretzels	3/4 oz
Rice cakes, 4 in. across	2
Saltine-type crackers	6
Snack chips, fat-free (tortilla, potato)	15–20 (3/4 oz)
Whole-wheat crackers, no fat added	2–5 (3/4 oz)

Table 8.3a continued

Dry Beans, Peas and Lentils			Puffed cereal	1 1/2 cup

Dry Beans, Peas and Lentils		Puffed cereal	1 1/2 cup
(Count as 1 starch exchange, plus 1 very lean meat exchange.)		Rice milk	1/2 cup
Beans and peas (garbanzo, pinto, kidney, white, split, black-eyed)	1/3 cup	Rice, white or brown	1/3 cup
Lima beans	2/3 cup	Shredded Wheat	1/2 cup
Lentils	1/2 cup	Sugar-frosted cereal	1/2 cup
Miso^s	3 Tbsp	Wheat germ	3 Tbsp

Cereals and Grains		**Starch Foods prepared with Fat**	
Bran cereals	1/2 cup	(Count as 1 starch exchange, plus 1 fat exchange.)	
Bulgur	1/2 cup	Biscuit, 2 1/2 in. across	1
Cereals	1/2 cup	Chow mein noodles	1/2 cup
Cereals, unsweetened, ready-to-eat	1/2 cup	Corn bread, 2 in. cube	1 (2 oz)
Cornmeal (dry)	3 Tbsp	Cracker, round butter type	6
Couscous	1/3 cup	Croutons	1 cup
Flour (dry)	3 Tbsp	French-fried potatoes	16–25 (3 oz)
Granola, low-fat	1/4 cup	Granola	1/4 cup
Grape-Nuts	1/4 cup	Muffin, small	1 (1 1/2 oz)
Grits	1/2 cup	Pancake, 4 in. across	2
Kasha	1/2 cup	Popcorn, microwave	3 cups
Millet	1/4 cup	Sandwich crackers, cheese or peanut butter filling	3
Muesli	1/4 cup	Stuffing, bread (prepared)	1/3 cup
Oats	1/2 cup	Taco shell, 6 in. across	2
Pasta	1/2 cup	Waffle, 4 1/2 in. square	1
		Whole-wheat crackers, fat added	4–6 (1 oz)

^s = 400 mg or more of sodium per serving.

Table 8.3b Fruit List

One fruit contains about 15 grams of carbohydrate, and 60 calories. The weight includes skin, core, seeds, and rind.

Fresh, frozen, canned, and dried fruits and fruit juices are on this list. In general, one fruit exchange is:
• 1 small to medium fresh fruit.

• 1/2 cup of canned or fresh fruit or fruit juice.

• 1/4 cup of dried fruit.

Nutrition Tips

1. Fresh, frozen, and dried fruits have about 2 grams of fiber per choice. Fruit juices contain very little fiber.

2. Citrus fruits, berries, and melons are good sources of vitamin C.

Selection Tips

1. Count 1/2 cup cranberries or rhubarb sweetened with sugar substitutes as free foods.

2. Read the Nutrition Facts on the food label. If one serving has more than 15 grams of carbohydrate, you will need to adjust the size of the serving you eat or drink.

3. Portion sizes for canned fruits are for the fruit and a small amount of juice.

4. Whole fruit is more filling than fruit juice and may be a better choice.

5. Food labels for fruits may contain the words "no sugar added" or "unsweetened." This means that no sucrose (table sugar) has been added.

6. Generally, fruit canned in extra light syrup has the same amount of carbohydrate per serving as the "no sugar added" or the juice pack. All canned fruits on the fruit list are based on one of these three types of pack.

Fruit

Apple, unpeeled, small	1 (4 oz)
Applesauce (unsweetened)	1/2 cup
Apples, dried	4 rings
Apricots, fresh	4 whole (5 1/2 oz)
Apricots	8 halves
Apricots, canned	1/2 cup
Banana, small	1 (4 oz)
Blackberries	3/4 cup
Blueberries	3/4 cup
Cantaloupe, small	1/3 melon (11 oz) or 1 cup cubes
Cherries, sweet, fresh	12 (3 oz)
Cherries, sweet, canned	1/2 cup
Dates	3
Figs, fresh	1 1/2 large or 2 medium (3 1/2 oz)
Figs, dried	1 1/2
Fruit cocktail	1/2 cup
Grapefruit, large	1/2 (11 oz)
Grapefruit, sections, canned	3/4 cup
Grapes (small)	17 grapes (3 oz)
Honeydew melon	1 slice (10 oz) or 1 cup cubes
Kiwi	1 (3 1/2 oz)
Mandarin oranges, canned	3/4 cup
Mango, small	1/2 fruit (5 1/2 oz) or 1/2 cup
Nectarine, small	1 (5 oz)
Orange, small	1 (6 1/2 oz)
Papaya	1/2 fruit (8 oz) or 1 cup cubes
Peach, medium, fresh	1 (6 oz)
Peach, canned	1/2 cup
Pear, large, fresh	1/2 (4 oz)
Pears, canned	1/2 cup
Pineapple, fresh	3/4 cup
Pineapples, canned	1/2 cup
Plums, small	2 (5 oz)
Plums, canned	1/2 cup
Prunes, dried	3
Raisins dried	2 Tbsp
Raspberries	1 cup
Strawberries, whole berries	1 1/4 cup
Tangerines, small	2 (8 oz)
Watermelon	1 slice (13 1/2 oz) or 1 1/4 cup cubes

Fruit Juice

Apple juice/cider	1/2 cup
Cranberry juice cocktail	1/3 cup
Cranberry juice cocktail, reduced-calorie	1/3 cup
Grape juice	1/3 cup
Grapefruit juice	1/2 cup
Orange juice	1/2 cup
Pineapple juice	1/2 cup
Prune juice	1/3 cup

Table 8.3c **Vegetable List**

One vegetable exchange equals 5 grams carbohydrate, 2 grams protein, 0 grams fat, and 25 calories.

Vegetables that contain small amounts of carbohydrates and calories are on this list. Vegetables contain important nutrients. Try to eat at least two to three vegetable choices each day. In general, one vegetable exchange is:

• 1/2 cup of cooked vegetables or vegetable juice.

• 1 cup of raw vegetables.

Nutrition Tips

1. Fresh and frozen vegetables have less added salt than canned vegetables. Drain and rinse canned vegetables if you want to remove some salt.

2. Choose more dark green and dark yellow vegetables, such as spinach, broccoli, romaine, carrots, chilies, and peppers.

3. Broccoli, brussels sprouts, cauliflower, greens, peppers, spinach, and tomatoes are good sources of vitamin C.

4. Vegetables contain 1 to 4 grams of fiber per serving.

Selection Tips

1. A 1-cup portion of broccoli is a portion about the size of a light bulb.

2. Tomato sauce is different from spaghetti sauce, which is on the Other Carbohydrates list.

3. Canned vegetables and juices are available without added salt.

4. If you eat more than 4 cups of raw vegetables, or 2 cups of cooked vegetables at one meal, count them as 1 carbohydrate choice.

5. Starchy vegetable such as corn, peas, winter squash, and potatoes that contain larger amounts of calories and carbohydrates are on the Starch list.

Artichoke
Artichoke hearts
Asparagus
Beans (green, wax, Italian)
Bean sprouts
Beets
Broccoli
Brussels sprouts
Cabbage
Carrots
Cauliflower
Celery
Cucumber
Eggplant
Greens (collard, kale, mustard, turnips)
Kohlrabi
Leeks
Mixed vegetables (without corn, peas, or pasta)
Mushrooms

Okra
Onions
Pea Pods
Peppers (all varieties)
Radishes
Salad greens (endive, escarole, lettuce, romaine, spinach)
Sauerkraut[s]
Spinach
Summer squash
Tomato
Tomatoes, canned
Tomato sauce[s]
Tomato/vegetable juice[s]
Turnips
Water chestnuts
Watercress
Zucchini

   [s] = 400 mg or more of sodium per exchange.

Table 8.3d   Milk List

One milk exchange contains 12 grams of carbohydrate and 8 grams of protein.

Different types of milk and milk products are on this list. Cheeses are on the Meat list and cream and other dairy fats are on the Fat list. Based on the amount of fat they contain, milks are divided into skim/very low-fat, low-fat milk, and whole milk. One choice of these includes:

	Carbohydrates (grams)	Protein (grams)	Fat (grams)	Calories
Skim/very low-fat	12	8	0–3	90
Low-fat	12	8	5	120
Whole	12	8	8	150

Nutrition Tips

1. Milk and yogurt are good sources of calcium and protein. Check the food label.

2. The higher the fat content of milk and yogurt, the greater the amount of saturated fat and cholesterol. Choose lower-fat varieties.

3. For those who are lactose intolerant, look for lactose-reduced or lactose-free varieties of milk.

Selection Tips

1. One cup equals 8 fluid ounces or 1/2 pint.

2. Look for chocolate milk, frozen yogurt, and ice cream on the Other Carbohydrate list.

3. Nondairy creamers are on the Free Foods list.

4. Look for rice milk on the Starch list.

5. Look for soy milk on the Medium-fat Meat list.

Skim and Very Low-fat Milk (0–3 grams fat per serving)

Skim milk	1 cup
1/2% milk	1 cup
1% milk	1 cup
Nonfat or low-fat buttermilk	1 cup
Evaporated skim milk	1/2 cup
Nonfat dry milk	1/3 cup dry
Plain nonfat yogurt	3/4 cup
Nonfat or low-fat fruit-flavored yogurt sweetened with aspartame or with a nonnutritive sweetener	1 cup

Low-fat Milk (5 grams fat per serving)

2% milk	1 cup
Plain low-fat yogurt	3/4 cup
Sweet acidophilus milk	1 cup

Whole Milk (8 grams fat per serving)

Whole milk	1 cup
Evaporated whole milk	1/2 cup
Goat's milk	1 cup
Kefir	1 cup

Table 8.3e **Other Carbohydrates List**

One exchange equals 15 grams carbohydrate, or 1 starch, or 1 fruit, or 1 milk.
Your can substitute food choices from this list for a starch, fruit, or milk choice on your meal plan. Some choices will also count as one or more fat choices.

Nutrition Tips

1. These foods can be substituted in your meal plan, even though they contain added sugar or fat. However, they do not contain as many vitamins and minerals as the choices on the Starch, Fruit, or Milk list.

2. When planning to include these foods in your meal, be sure to include foods from all the lists to eat a balanced meal.

Selection Tips

1. Because many of these foods are concentrated sources of carbohydrate and fat, the portion sizes are often very small.

2. Always check Nutrition Facts on the food label. It will be your most accurate source of information.

3. Many fat-free or reduced products made with fat replacers contain carbohydrate. When eaten in large amounts, they may need to be counted. Talk with your dietitian to determine how to count these in your meal plan.

4. Look for fat-free salad dressings in smaller amounts on the Free Foods list.

Food	Serving Size	Exchanges Per Serving
Angel food cake, unfrosted	1/12th cake	2 carbohydrates
Brownie, small, unfrosted	2 in. square	1 carbohydrate, 1 fat
Cake, unfrosted	2 in. square	1 carbohydrate, 1 fat
Cake, frosted	2 in. square	2 carbohydrates, 1 fat
Cookie, fat-free	2 small	1 carbohydrate
Cookie or sandwich cookie with creme filling	2 in. square	1 carbohydrate, 1 fat
Cupcake, frosted	1 small	2 carbohydrates, 1 fat
Cranberry sauce, jellied	1/4 cup	2 carbohydrates
Doughnut, plain cake	1 medium (1 1/2 oz)	1 1/2 carbohydrates, 2 fats
Doughnut, glazed	3 3/4 in across (2 oz)	2 carbohydrates, 2 fats
Fruit juice bars, frozen, (100%) juice	1 bar (3 oz)	1 carbohydrate
Fruit snacks, chewy (pureed fruit concentrate)	1 roll (3/4 oz)	1 carbohydrate
Fruit spreads, 100% fruit	1 Tbsp	1 carbohydrate
Gelatin, regular	1/2 cup	1 carbohydrate
Gingersnaps	3	1 carbohydrate
Granola bar	1 bar	1 carbohydrate, 1 fat
Granola bar, fat-free	1 bar	2 carbohydrates
Hummus	1/3 cup	1 carbohydrate, 1 fat
Ice cream	1/2 cup	1 carbohydrate, 2 fats
Ice cream, light	1/2 cup	1 carbohydrate, 1 fat
Ice cream, fat-free, no sugar added	1/2 cup	1 carbohydrate
Jam or jelly, regular	1 Tbsp	1 carbohydrate
Milk, chocolate, whole	1 cup	2 carbohydrates, 1 fat
Pie, fruit, 2 crusts	1/6 pie	3 carbohydrates, 2 fats
Pie, pumpkin or custard	1/8 pie	1 carbohydrate, 2 fats
Potato chips	12–18 (1 oz)	1 carbohydrate, 2 fats
Pudding, regular (made with low-fat milk)	1/2 cup	2 carbohydrates
Pudding, sugar-free (made with low-fat milk)	1/2 cup	1 carbohydrate
Salad dressing, fat-free[s]	1/4 cup	1 carbohydrate
Sherbet, sorbet	1/2 cup	2 carbohydrates

Table 8.3e continued

Food	Serving Size	Exchanges Per Serving
Spaghetti or pasta sauce[s]	1/2 cup	1 carbohydrate, 1 fat
Sweet roll or Danish	1 (2 1/2 oz)	2 1/2 carbohydrates, 2 fats
Syrup, light	2 Tbsp	1 carbohydrate
Syrup, regular	1 Tbsp	1 carbohydrate
Syrup, regular	1/4 cup	4 carbohydrates
Tortilla chips	6–12 (1 oz)	1 carbohydrate, 2 fats
Yogurt, frozen, low-fat, fat-free	1/3 cup	1 carbohydrate, 0–1 fat
Yogurt, frozen, fat-free, no sugar added	1/2 cup	1 carbohydrate
Yogurt, frozen, low-fat with fruit	1 cup	3 carbohydrate, 0–1 fat
Vanilla wafers	5	1 carbohydrate, 1 fat

[s] = 400 mg or more of sodium per exchange.

Table 8.3f   Meat and Meat Substitutes List

Meat and meat substitutes that contain both protein and fat are on this list. In general, one meat exchange is:

• 1 ounce meat, fish, poultry, or cheese.

• 1/2 cup dried beans.

Based on the amount of fat they contain, meats are divided into very lean, lean, medium-fat, and high-fat lists. This is done so you can see which ones contain the least amount of fat. One ounce (one exchange) of each of these includes:

	Carbohydrates (grams)	Protein (grams)	Fat (grams)	Calories
Very lean	0	7	0–1	35
Lean	0	7	3	55
Medium-fat	0	7	5	75
High-fat	0	7	8	100

Nutrition Tips

1. Choose very lean and lean meat choices whenever possible. Items from the high-fat group are high in saturated fat, cholesterol, and calories and can raise blood-cholesterol levels.

2. Meats do not have any fiber.

3. Dried beans, peas, and lentils are good sources of fiber.

4. Some processed meats, seafood, and soy products may contain carbohydrate when consumed in large amounts. Check the Nutrition Facts on the label to see if the amount is close to 15 grams. If so, count it as a carbohydrate choice as well as a meat choice.

Selection Tips

1. Weigh meat after cooking and removing bones and fat. Four ounces of raw meat is equal to 3 ounces of cooked meat. Some examples of meat portions are:

   ◆ 1 ounce cheese = 1 meat choice and is about the size of a 1-inch cube.

   ◆ 2 ounces meat = 2 meat choices, such as
       1 small chicken leg or thigh
       1/2 cup cottage cheese or tuna

   ◆ 3 ounces meat = 3 meat choices and is about the size of a deck of cards, such as
       1 medium pork chop
       1 small hamburger
       1/2 of a whole chicken breast
       1 unbreaded fish fillet

2. Limit your choices from the high-fat group to three times per week or less.

3. Most grocery stores stock Select and Choice grades of meat. Select grades of meat are the leanest meats. Choice grades contain a moderate amount of fat, and Prime cuts of meat have the highest amount of fat. Restaurants usually serve Prime cuts of meat.

4. "Hamburger" may contain added seasonings and fat, but ground beef does not.

5. Read labels to find products that are low in fat and cholesterol (5 grams or less of fat per serving).

6. Dried beans, peas, and lentils are also found on the Starch list.

7. Peanut butter, in small amounts, is also found on the Fats list.

8. Bacon, in small amounts, is also found on the Fats list.

Table 8.3f continued

Meal Planning Tips

1. Bake, roast, broil, grill, poach, steam, or boil these foods rather than frying.

2. Place meat on a rack so the fat will drain off during cooking.

3. Use a nonstick spray and a nonstick pan to brown or fry foods.

4. Trim off visible fat before or after cooking.

5. If you add flour, bread crumbs, coating mixes, fat, or marinades when cooking, ask your dietitian how to count it in your meal plan.

Very Lean Meat and Substitutes List

One exchange equals 0 grams carbohydrate, 7 grams protein, 0–1 grams fat, and 35 calories. One very lean meat exchange is equal to any one of the following items.

Poultry: Chicken or turkey (white meat, no skin), Cornish hen (no skin)	1 oz
Fish: Fresh or frozen cod, flounder, haddock, halibut, trout, tuna fresh or canned in water	1 oz
Shellfish: Clams, crab, lobster, scallops, shrimp, imitation shellfish	1 oz
Game: Duck or pheasant (no skin), venison, buffalo, ostrich	1 oz
Cheese with 1 gram or less fat per ounce:	
Nonfat or low-fat cottage cheese	1/4 cup
Fat-free cheese	1 oz
Other: Processed sandwich meats with 1 gram or less fat per ounce, such as deli thin, shaved meats, chipped beef[s], turkey ham	1 oz
Egg whites	2
Egg substitutes, plain	1/4 cup
Hot dogs with 1 gram or less fat per ounce[s]	1 oz
Kidney (high in cholesterol)	1 oz
Sausage with 1 gram or less fat per ounce	1 oz

Count as one very lean meat and one starch exchange:

Dried beans, peas, lentils (cooked)	1/2 cup

Lean Meat and Substitutes List

One exchange equals 0 grams carbohydrate, 7 grams protein, 3 grams fat, and 55 calories. One lean meat exchange is equal to any one of the following items.

Beef: USDA Select or Choice grades of lean beef, such as trimmed of fat, such as round, sirloin, and flank steak; tenderloin; roast (rib, chuck, rump);

steak (T-bone, porterhouse, cubed), ground round	1 oz
Pork: Lean pork, such as fresh ham; canned, cured or boiled ham; Canadian bacon[s]; tenderloin, center loin chop	1 oz
Lamb: Roast, chop, leg	1 oz
Veal: Lean chop, roast	1 oz
Poultry: Chicken, turkey (dark meat, no skin), chicken white meat (with skin), domestic duck or goose (well-drained of fat, no skin)	1 oz
Fish:	
Herring (uncreamed or smoked)	1 oz
Oysters	6 medium
Salmon (fresh or canned), catfish	1 oz
Sardines (canned)	2 medium
Tuna + (canned in oil, drained)	1 oz
Game: Goose (no skin), rabbit	1 oz
Cheese:	
4.5%-fat cottage cheese	1/4 cup
Grated Parmesan	2 Tbsp
Cheeses with 3 grams or less fat per ounce	1 oz
Other:	
Hot dogs with 3 grams or less fat per ounce[s]	1 1/2 oz
Processed sandwich meat with 3 grams or less fat per ounce, such as turkey pastrami or kielbasa	1 oz
Liver (high in cholesterol)	1 oz

Medium-Fat Meat and Substitutes List

One exchange equals 0 grams carbohydrate, 7 grams protein, 5 grams fat, and 75 calories. One medium-fat exchange is equal to any one of the following items.

Beef: Most beef products fall into this category (ground beef, meat loaf, corned beef short ribs, Prime grades of meat trimmed of fat such as prime rib	1 oz

Table 8.3f continued

Medium-Fat Meat and Substitutes List, cont.	High-Fat Meat and Substitutes List
Pork: Top loin, chop, Boston butt, cutlet 1 oz	One exchange equals 0 grams carbohydrate, 7 grams protein, 8 grams fat, and 100 calories. Remember these items are high in saturated fat, cholesterol, and calories and may raise blood cholesterol levels if eaten on a regular basis. One high-fat meat exchange is equal to any one of the following items.
Lamb: Rib roast, ground 1 oz	
Veal: Cutlet (ground or cubed, unbreaded) 1 oz	
Poultry: Chicken dark meat (with skin), ground turkey or ground chicken, fried chicken (with skin) 1 oz	
Fish: Any fried fish product 1 oz	**Pork:** Spareribs, ground pork, pork sausage 1 oz
Cheese: With 5 grams or less fat per ounce	**Cheese:** All regular cheeses, such as American[s], cheddar, Monterey Jack, Swiss 1 oz
Feta or Mozzarella 1 oz	**Other:** Processed sandwich meats with 8 grams or less fat per ounce, such as bologna, pimento loaf, salami 1 oz
Ricotta 1/4 cup (2 oz)	
Other:	Sausage, such as bratwurst, Italian, knockwurst, Polish, smoked 1 oz
Egg (high in cholesterol, limit 3 per week) 1	Hot dog (turkey or chicken)[s] 1 (10/lb)
Sausage with 5 grams or less fat per ounce 1 oz	Bacon (20 slices/lb) 3 slices
Soy milk 1 cup	**Count as one high-fat meat plus one fat exchange:**
Tempeh 1/4 cup	Hot dog (beef, pork, or combination)[s] 1 (10/lb)
Tofu 4 oz (1/2 cup)	Peanut butter (contains unsaturated fat) 2 Tbsp
	[s] = 400 mg or more of sodium per serving.

Table 8.3g **Fat List**

One fat exchange equals 5 grams fat and 45 calories.

Fats are divided into three groups, based on the main type of fat they contain: monounsaturated, polyunsaturated, and saturated. Small amounts of monounsaturated and polyunsaturated fats in the foods we eat are linked with good health benefits. Saturated fats are linked with heart disease and cancer. In general, one fat exchange is:

• 1 teaspoon of regular margarine or vegetable oil.

• 1 tablespoon of regular salad dressing.

Nutrition Tips

1. All fats are high in calories. Limit serving sizes for good nutrition and health.

2. Nuts and seeds contain small amounts of fiber, protein, and magnesium.

3. If blood pressure is a concern, choose fats in the unsalted form to help lower sodium intake, such as unsalted peanuts.

Selection Tips

1. Check the Nutrition Facts on the food labels for serving sizes. One fat exchange is based on a serving size containing 5 grams of fat.

2. When selecting regular margarine, choose those with liquid vegetable oil as the first ingredient. Soft margarines are not as saturated as stick margarines. Soft margarines are healthier choices. Avoid those listing hydrogenated or partially hydrogenated fat as the first ingredient.

3. When selecting low-fat margarines, look for liquid vegetable oil as the second ingredient. Water is usually the first ingredient.

4. When used in smaller amounts, bacon and peanut butter are counted as fat choices. When used in larger amounts, they are counted as high-fat choices.

5. Fat-free salad dressings are on the Other Carbohydrates list and the Free Foods list.

6. See the Free Foods list for nondairy coffee creamers, whipped topping, and fat-free products, such as margarine, salad dressings, mayonnaise, sour cream, cream cheese, and nonstick cooking spray.

Monounsaturated Fats List

Avocado	1/8 (1 oz)
Oil (canola, olive, peanut)	1 tsp
Olives: ripe (black)	8 large
green, stuffed[s]	10 large
Nuts	
Almonds, cashews	6 nuts
Mixed (50% peanuts)	6 nuts
Peanuts	10 nuts
Pecans	4 halves
Peanut Butter, smooth or crunchy	2 tsp
Sesame seeds	1 Tbsp
Tahini paste	2 tsp

Polyunsaturated Fats List

Margarine: stick, tub, or squeeze	1 tsp
lower-fat (30% to 50% vegetable oil)	1 Tbsp
Mayonnaise: regular	1 tsp
reduced-fat	1 Tbsp
Nuts, walnuts, English	4 halves
Oil (corn, safflower, soybean)	1 tsp
Salad dressing, regular[s]	1 Tbsp
reduced-fat	2 Tbsp
Miracle Whip Salad Dressing: regular	2 tsp
reduced-fat	1 Tbsp
Seeds: pumpkin, sunflower	1 Tbsp

Saturated Fats List*

Bacon, cooked (20 slices/lb)	1 slice
Bacon, grease	1 tsp
Butter: stick	1 tsp
whipped	2 tsp
reduced-fat	1 Tbsp
Chitterlings, boiled	2 Tbsp
	(1/2 oz)

Table 8.3g continued

Saturated Fats List*	
Coconut, sweetened, shredded	2 Tbsp
Cream, half and half	2 Tbsp
Cream cheese: regular	1 Tbsp
	(1/2 oz)
reduced-fat	2 Tbsp
	(1 oz)
Fatback or salt pork#	see below
Shortening or Lard	1 tsp
Sour cream: regular	2 Tbsp
reduced-fat	2 Tbsp

*Saturated fats can raise blood cholesterol.

#Use a piece 1 in. × 1 in. ×1/4 in. if you plan to eat the fatback cooked with vegetables. Use a piece 2 in. × 1 in. × 1/2 in. when eating only the vegetables with the fatback removed.

s = 400 mg or more of sodium per exchange.

Table 8.3h Free Foods List

A free food is any food or drink that contains less than 20 calories or less than 5 grams of carbohydrate per serving. Foods with a serving size listed should be limited to three servings per day. Be sure to spread them out throughout the day. If you eat all three servings at one time, it could affect your blood glucose level. Foods listed without a serving size can be eaten as often as you like.

Fat-free or Reduced-fat Foods

Cream cheese, fat-free	1 Tbsp
Creamers, nondairy, liquid	1 Tbsp
Creamers, nondairy, powdered	2 tsp
Mayonnaise, fat-free	1 Tbsp
Mayonnaise, reduced-fat	1 tsp
Margarine, fat-free	4 Tbsp
Margarine, reduced-fat	1 tsp
Miracle Whip®, nonfat	1 Tbsp
Miracle Whip®, reduced-fat	1 tsp
Nonstick cooking spray	
Salad dressing, fat-free	1 Tbsp
Salad dressing, fat-free, Italian	2 Tbsp
Salsa	1/4 cup
Sour cream, fat-free reduced-fat	1 Tbsp
Whipped topping, regular or light	2 Tbsp

Sugar-free or Low-sugar Foods

Candy, hard, sugar-free	1 candy
Gelatin dessert, sugar-free	
Gelatin, unflavored	
Gum, sugar-free	
Jam or jelly, low sugar or light	2 tsp
Sugar substitutes*	
Syrup, sugar-free	2 Tbsp

* Sugar substitutes, alternatives, or replacements that are approved by the Food and Drug Administrative (FDA) are safe to use. Common brand names include:
  Equal® (aspartame)
  Sprinkle Sweet® (saccharin)
  Sweet One® (acesulfame K)
  Sweet-10® (saccharin)
  Sugar Twin® (saccharin)
  Sweet'n Low® (saccharin)

Drinks

Bouillon, broth, consomme[s]	
Bouillon or broth, low-sodium	
Carbonated or mineral water	
Cocoa powder, unsweetened	1 Tbsp
Coffee	
Club soda	
Diet soft drinks, sugar-free	
Drink mixes, sugar-free	
Tea	
Tonic water, sugar-free	

Condiments

Catsup	1 Tbsp
Horseradish	
Lemon juice	
Lime juice	
Mustard	
Pickles, dill[s]	1 1/2 large
Soy sauce, regular or light[s]	
Taco sauce	1 Tbsp
Vinegar	

Seasonings

Be careful with seasonings that contain sodium or are salts, such as garlic or celery salt, and lemon pepper.
Flavoring extracts
Garlic
Herbs, fresh or dried
Pimento
Spices
Tabasco® or hot pepper sauce
Wine, used in cooking
Worcestershire sauce

[s] = 400 mg or more of sodium per exchange.

Table 8.3i **Combination Foods List**

Many of the foods we eat are mixed together in various combinations. These combination foods do not fit into any one exchange list. Often it is hard to tell what is in a casserole dish or prepared food item. This is a list of exchanges for some typical combination foods. This list will help you fit these foods into your meal plan. Ask your dietitian for information about any other combination foods you would like to eat.

Food	Serving Size	Exchanges Per Serving
Entrees		
Tuna noodle casserole, lasagna, spaghetti with meatballs, chili with beans, macaroni and cheese[s]	1 cup (8 oz)	2 carbohydrates, 2 medium-fat meats
Chow mein (without noodles or rice)	2 cups (16 oz)	1 carbohydrate, 2 lean meats
Pizza, cheese, thin crust[s]	1/4 of 10 in. (5 oz)	2 carbohydrates, 2 medium-fat meats, 1 fat
Pizza, meat topping, thin crust[s]	1/4 of 10 in. (5 oz)	2 carbohydrates, 2 medium-fat meats, 2 fats
Pot pie[s]	1 (7 oz)	2 carbohydrates, 1 medium-fat meat, 4 fats
Frozen Entrees		
Salisbury steak with gravy, mashed potato[s]	1 (11 oz)	2 carbohydrates, 3 medium-fat meats, 3–4 fats
Turkey with gravy, mashed potato, dressing[s]	1 (11 oz)	2 carbohydrates, 2 medium-fat meats, 2 fats
Entree with less than 300 calories[s]	1 (8 oz)	2 carbohydrates, 3 lean meats
Soups		
Bean[s]	1 cup	1 carbohydrate, 1 very lean meat
Cream (made with water)[s]	1 cup (8 oz)	1 carbohydrate, 1 fat
Split pea (made with water)[s]	1/2 cup (4 oz)	1 carbohydrate
Tomato (made with water)[s]	1 cup (8 oz)	1 carbohydrate
Vegetable beef, chicken noodle, or other broth-type[s]	1 cup (8 oz)	1 carbohydrate

[s] = 400 mg or more of sodium per exchange.

Table 8.3j **Fast Foods**

Ask at your fast-food restaurant for nutrition information about your favorite fast foods.

Food	Serving Size	Exchanges Per Serving
Burritos with beef[s]	2	4 carbohydrates, 2 medium-fat meats, 2 fats
Chicken nuggets[s]	6	1 carbohydrate, 2 medium-fat meats, 1 fat
Chicken breast and wing, breaded and fried[s]	1 each	1 carbohydrate, 4 medium-fat meats, 2 fats
Fish sandwich/tartar sauce[s]	1	3 carbohydrates, 1 medium-fat meat, 3 fats
French fries, thin	20–25	2 carbohydrates, 2 fats
Hamburger, regular	1	2 carbohydrates, 2 medium-fat meats
Hamburger, large[s]	1	2 carbohydrates, 3 medium-fat meats, 1 fat
Hot dog with bun[s]	1	1 carbohydrate, 1 high-fat meats, 1 fat
Individual pan pizza[s]	1	5 carbohydrates, 3 medium-fat meats, 3 fats
Soft-serve cone	1 medium	2 carbohydrates, 1 fat
Submarine sandwich[s]	1 sub (6 in.)	3 carbohydrates, 1 vegetable, 2 medium-fat meats, 1 fat
Taco, hard shell[s]	1 (6 oz)	2 carbohydrates, 2 medium-fat meats, 2 fats
Taco, soft shell[s]	1 (3 oz)	1 carbohydrate, 1 medium-fat meat, 1 fat

[s] = 400 mg or more of sodium per exchange.

9

Vegetarian Diets

Historically, vegetarianism traces its roots to the 6th century B.C. According to the North American Vegetarian Society, and the International Vegetarian Union, vegetarians include "anyone who lives on the products of the vegetable kingdom, with or without the use of eggs and dairy products, to the entire exclusion of the flesh of all animals (fish, fowl, or meat)."

Today, it is estimated that there are 15 million vegetarians in the United States and about 40 to 50 million Americans who limit their meat consumption.

The number of vegetarians is growing rapidly and polls consistently show that upward of 80% of the U.S. population recognize that vegetarian diets are beneficial to health.

As one might suspect, many vegetarians are aware of the need to add or restrict foods in their diet containing sugar, fat, fiber, and salt.

There are three basic types of vegetarian diets:

Vegan (Total Vegetarian): Foods excluded are meat, fish, poultry, and all dairy products (eggs, butter, milk, and yogurt). About 10% of American vegetarians are vegans.

Lacto Vegetarians: Foods excluded are eggs, meat, fish and poultry. Milk (milk products) are permitted.

Lacto-Ovo Vegetarians: Foods excluded are meat, fish, and poultry. Milk (milk products) and eggs are permitted.

About 90% of American vegetarians follow lacto or lacto-ovo diets.

Not surprisingly, vegetarian diets are closer to the makeup of the U.S. Dietary Guidelines than is the normal diet of Americans.

Meeting nutritive requirements of vegetarian diets is somewhat more difficult for vegan followers, since animal proteins are omitted and plant foods are low in calories. Vegans obtain almost all their nutrients from four basic groups: vegetables, fruits, grains, and bean-nuts, while lacto and lacto-ovo practitioners add dairy products.

When planning vegetarian menus, certain nutrient considerations may be necessary:

Protein: Unlike animal protein, plant proteins need to be combined, preferably at the same meal, to achieve protein completeness. Utilizing a variety of whole grains and legumes such as rice and beans, wheat and beans, or corn and lima beans, form complementary food combinations. Similarly, seeds and legumes such as sesame seeds, peanuts and beans, or sunflower seeds and peanuts, represent good protein completeness.

Calories: When not enough calories are consumed, protein will be utilized by the body to supply energy. This could present possible problems in meeting protein needs.

Vitamin D: Vitamin D enhancement can be provided by small dose supplementation or by ultraviolet rays of the sun. While plant food has no vitamin D, some brands are fortified with it.

Vitamin B-12: Is a component found only in animal sources and before World War I the lack of it was found to sometimes cause nervous disorders, female infertility, and anemia. Today, vitamin B-12 can be obtained for vegans from vitamin supplements or from B-12 fortified food and vegetables. Use of fortified soy milk or meat analogs is satisfactory. Otherwise, use supplements.

Riboflavin: Riboflavin deficiencies are not common but potential. They can be addressed by the intake of green leafy vegetables and fortified soy milk.

Iron: Iron from plant foods is not as well absorbed as iron from animal sources. Therefore, use beans, dried fruit, and certain vegetables containing larger amounts of iron. The iron in eggs is readily absorbed and vitamin C greatly increases the absorption of iron from other foods.

Calcium: In vegetarian diets, calcium may best be obtained from fortified soybean milk. It is also obtained by continual, large servings of plant sources, such as dark leafy, vegetables. Broccoli, collards, greens (mustard and turnips), and kale are good sources for calcium, as are legumes, sesame seeds, and carrageenan (Irish Moss). Adding calcium carbonate to flour (1 teaspoon per pound) is also effective.

Zinc: Vegetarians may receive adequate amounts of zinc from legumes and nuts.

Special Considerations

Children

To receive adequate dietary dosages of nutrients and calories, a larger amount or volume of plant food needs to be consumed daily. For some children, this may pose difficulties. The consumption of fortified soybean milk daily will ensure adequate calories and nutrient absorption. As already discussed, adding vitamin B-12 and D to soy milk or as a separate supplement are possible steps, particularly during winter months for vitamin D. Green leafy vegetables provide calcium and riboflavin and are recommended. Iron-rich foods (beans, dried fruits, some vegetables, and eggs) are good and supplementation is required when children don't take these foods. For adolescent girls, dietary feeding should concentrate on a variety of foods from the applicable basic food groups.

Women

In periods of both pregnancy and lactation, calcium, iron, and vitamin D may need to be added by supplementation, fortified soy bean milk, or from the basic food groups.

Category	Recommended Daily Servings	Food Choices	Foods to Restrict
Bread and Cereal	5 or more servings (increase quantities if additional calories are needed).	Enriched or whole grain breads, cereals, and grains.	Those prepared with eggs, milk, or milk products.
Rice, Pasta, and Potatoes	Use as desired to meet calorie needs.	Potatoes (white, sweet); rice (enriched, brown); enriched, whole wheat, or vegetable-based noodles, spaghetti, macaroni.	Those prepared with eggs, milk, or milk products.
Fruits	4 or more servings (1 cup = 1 serving); include one citrus fruit per meal.	All fresh, dried, canned, or frozen fruits, fruit juices.	None.
Vegetables	1 or more servings (1 cup = 1 serving); include a minimum of one dark green leafy vegetable daily.	All fresh, frozen, canned, or dried vegetables; vegetable juices.	Prepackaged foods prepared with eggs, milk, or milk products.
Soups	Use as desired to meet calorie needs.	Vegetable based.	Meat-based soups, those that contain meat, fish, poultry.
Meat, Fish, Poultry, and Eggs	None.	None.	All.
Meat analogs (combination of grains, legumes, or nuts with the look and taste of comparable meat products)	2 or more servings.	Fortified meat analogs.	Those prepared with eggs, milk, or milk products.
Legumes	2 or more servings (1 cup cooked = 1 serving).	Black beans, butter beans, lima beans, mung beans, pinto beans, red kidney, soybeans, white beans, blackeyed peas, chickpeas, cowpeas, garbanzo beans, lentils.	Prepackaged foods prepared with eggs, milk, or milk products.
Nuts and Seeds	1 or more servings (portion size varies).	Almonds (12–16 nuts), brazil nuts (10 nuts), cashews (12–16 nuts), chestnuts (12–16 nuts), hazelnuts (12–16 nuts), peanuts (2 Tbsp), peanut butter (2 Tbsp), pecans (12–16 nuts), pistachio (1 oz), walnuts (12–16 nuts), pumpkin and squash seeds (2 Tbsp), sesame seeds (3–4 Tbsp).	None.
Milk, Yogurt, and Cheese	2 or more cups, vitamin A and D fortified.	Fortified soy milk, tofu (soy cheese).	All others.

Table 9.1 continued

Category	Recommended Daily Servings	Food Choices	Foods to Restrict
Beverages	4 to 6 servings (use as desired to meet calorie and fluid needs).	Those prepared with allowed foods.	Those prepared with eggs or milk (some vegans restrict the use of beverages containing caffeine: coffee, cola, tea).
Fats and Oils	3 servings (1 tsp = 1 serving).	Fortified margarine, vegetable oils, vegetable shortenings, salad dressings made with allowed foods.	Butter, creams, bacon, meat fats, mayonnaise.
Sweets and Desserts	Use occasionally to meet calorie needs.	Fruits, honey, sugar.	Those prepared with eggs, milk, or milk products, avoid gelatin or any desserts containing animal products, (limit the use of high-calorie, low-nutrient foods).
Miscellaneous	Use as desired.	Herbs, spices, salt, nutritional yeast.	Avoid excessive consumption of salt or salt blends.

Table 9.2 **Lacto-Ovo or Lacto Vegetarian Diet**

Category	Recommended Daily Servings	Food Choices	Foods to Restrict
Bread and Cereal	4 or more servings (increase quantities if additional calories are needed).	Enriched or whole grain breads, cereals, and grains.	Lacto: those prepared with eggs (egg bread).
Rice, Pasta, and Potatoes	Use as desired to meet calorie needs.	Potatoes (white, sweet); rice (enriched, brown); enriched, or whole wheat, or vegetable-based noodles; spaghetti; macaroni.	Lacto: those prepared with eggs.
Fruits	4 or more servings (1 cup = 1 serving); include one citrus fruit per meal.	All fresh, dried, canned, or frozen fruits, fruit juices.	None.
Vegetables	1 or more servings (1 cup = 1 serving); include a minimum of one dark green leafy vegetable daily.	All fresh, frozen, canned, or dried vegetables; vegetable juices.	Lacto: Prepackaged foods prepared with eggs.
Soups	Use as desired to meet calorie needs.	Vegetable based.	Meat-based soups, those that contain meat, fish, or poultry.
Meat, Fish, Poultry, and Eggs	Egg: one or more. Lacto: no eggs.	Eggs (Lacto: no eggs).	Meat, fish, poultry, raw eggs Lacto: no eggs.
Meat analogs (combination of grains, legumes, or nuts with the look and taste of comparable meat products)	Use as desired to meet calorie needs.	Fortified meat analogs.	Lacto: those prepared with eggs.
Legumes	1 or more servings (1 cup cooked = 1 serving).	Black beans, butter beans, lima beans, mung beans, pinto beans, red kidney, soybeans, white beans, black-eyed peas, chickpeas, cow-peas, garbanzo beans, lentils.	Lacto: prepackaged foods prepared with eggs.
Nuts and Seeds	1 or more servings (portion size varies).	Almonds (12–16 nuts), brazil nuts (10 nuts), cashews (12–16 nuts), chestnuts (12–16 nuts), hazelnuts (12–16 nuts), peanuts (2 Tbsp), peanut butter (2 Tbsp), pecans (12–16 nuts), pistachio (1 oz), walnuts (12–16 nuts), pumpkin and squash seeds (2 Tbsp), sesame seeds (3–4 Tbsp).	None.
Milk, Yogurt, and Cheese	2 or more cups, vitamin A and D fortified.	Cheese and cottage cheese; fortified milk, soy milk, yogurt, tofu (soy cheese).	None.

Table 9.2 continued

Category	Recommended Daily Servings	Food Choices	Foods to Restrict
Beverages	4 to 6 servings (use as desired to meet calorie and fluid needs).	Those prepared with allowed foods.	Lacto: those prepared with eggs.
Fats and Oils	3 servings (1 tsp = 1 serving).	Fortified margarine, vegetable oils, vegetable shortenings, salad dressings made with allowed foods.	Butter, creams, bacon, meat fats, mayonnaise Lacto: those prepared with eggs.
Sweets and Desserts	Use occasionally to meet calorie needs.	Fruits, honey, sugar.	Avoid gelatin or any desserts containing animal products, (limit the use of high-calorie, low-nutrient foods). Lacto: those prepared with eggs.
Miscellaneous	Use as desired.	Herbs, spices, salt, nutritional yeast.	Avoid excessive consumption of salt or salt blends.

PART III

Diet-Modified Recipes

The *Standardized Recipe* is a set of instructions for preparing a specific food. Most recipes contain information on ingredients, method of cooking, portion size, and yield. In addition, this book describes directions for preparing modified recipes, yields in quantity and household numbers, and a nutrient analysis.

The *Ingredients* is a list of foods and the amounts needed to prepare the recipe. In this book you will find two set of numbers describing the amount of ingredients needed. One set is to prepare for a large quantity, approximately 50 people. The other set of numbers is for household use, four to eight people.

Method of cooking describes the steps in preparing the recipe. It may include, equipment, cooking temperatures, and cooking time.

Portion size is the amount of food designated for one person. The nutrient analysis is based on one portion.

Yield is the number of portions the recipe will produce. The recipes in this book produce both quantity and household yields. Quantity yields in most cases will be 50 portions and household yields will be four to eight portions. The yield may vary slightly in some recipes.

The *Directions for Diet Preparations* found in each recipe describes how the recipe is made for the different modified diets. In order to modify the recipe a specific ingredient was substituted, a different method of

cooking recommended, and/or a portion size altered. In some cases, the directions for the modified recipe does not differ from the regular and is so stated.

A *Nutrient Analysis* is provided for each recipe. This information is useful in helping plan menus for individuals wanting or needing special nutritional considerations. A comprehensive analysis is provided for the regular recipe. The sodium content is given for the sodium-restricted recipe. For the diabetic instructions the kcalories and exchange list is utilized. The low-fat, low-cholesterol recipe provides nutrient information on fat, cholesterol, saturated fatty acids, and polyunsaturated fatty acids.

Modifying Recipes: A Healthy Alternative

Many people are becoming more aware of their food choices. A healthier lifestyle or medical necessity are the major factors creating this awareness.

Individuals are looking for ways to alter their diet by lowering calories, sodium, fat, cholesterol, and sugar and increasing fiber and other nutrients.

The suggestions that follow can be incorporated into your diet and some of your favorite recipes. Modifying a recipe involves experimenting to achieve the desired outcome. The effort will be worth it.

Table 10.1 Lowering Sodium in the Diet

Avoid	Healthy Alternatives
Bacon	reduced-sodium bacon
Baking powder	low-sodium baking powder
Butter or margarine	low-sodium or unsalted butter or margarine
Breads and crackers	breads and crackers made without salt
Broth, bouillon, soup bases, prepared canned soups	low-sodium broth, low-sodium soup bases, low-sodium prepared canned soups, homemade soups without salt
Catsup, mustard, horseradish	low-sodium catsup, low-sodium mustard, fresh horseradish
Cheese	low-sodium cheese
Cured meats, hot dogs, sausage, ham, luncheon meats	reduced-sodium ham, reduced-sodium luncheon meats, beef, chicken, turkey, veal, fish
Nuts, salted	unsalted nuts
Pretzels, potato chips, popcorn	low-sodium, reduced-sodium or unsalted pretzels, potato chips, popcorn
Salt, MSG, seasoned salt, garlic salt	herbs, spices, low-sodium seasonings, garlic, garlic powder, salt substitutes (with physician's consent)
Soy sauce	low-sodium soy sauce
Tomato sauce, canned tomatoes	low-sodium tomato sauce, low-sodium canned tomatoes, preparing home made tomato sauce without salt, using fresh tomatoes
Tuna and salmon, canned	low-sodium canned tuna and low-sodium canned salmon
Vegetables, canned	low-sodium canned vegetables, fresh vegetables, low-sodium frozen vegetables
Vegetable juices	low-sodium vegetable juices

Table 10.2   Lowering Fat and Cholesterol in the Diet

Avoid	Healthy Alternatives
Butter, margarine, lard	reduced-fat margarine, vegetable cooking spray, using nonstick cookware. If using fat, choose polyunsaturated vegetable oils and margarine (corn, soybean).
Cheese, hard	reduced-fat, low-fat, or part-skim cheese
Cream cheese	imitation, reduced-fat or low-fat cream cheese, low-fat cottage cheese
Desserts: Cakes, pastries	angel food cake, fruit, gelatin
Eggs	cholesterol-free egg substitutes, egg whites
Fish, canned, packed in oil	fish, canned, packed in water
Frying	baking, broiling, boiling, steaming, stewing, stir-frying, using non-stick cookware
Ice cream	ices, sorbet, low-fat or reduced-calorie ice cream, ice milk, sherbet, frozen yogurt
Mayonnaise	low-fat and no-cholesterol mayonnaise, reduced- fat mayonnaise
Meat, high fat (cured meats, hot dogs, sausage, ham, luncheon meats, organ meats, poultry with skin)	lean meat (beef, lamb, pork) poultry without skin, reduced-fat ham, reduced-fat luncheon meats, veal, fish
Milk, whole	skim milk, low-fat milk
Salad dressings	low-fat low cholesterol salad dressings, lemon juice, vinegar
Sour cream	low-fat yogurt, low-fat cottage cheese

Table 10.3 Lowering Sugar and Kcalories in the Diet

Avoid	Healthy Alternatives
Butter, margarine, lard	reduced-fat margarine, vegetable cooking spray, using nonstick cookware.
Cheese, hard	reduced-fat, low-fat, or part-skim cheese
Cream cheese	reduced-fat or low-fat cream cheese, low-fat cottage cheese
Desserts: Cakes, pastries	angel food cake, fresh fruit, canned fruit in water or juice, sugar-free puddings, sugar-free gelatin
Eggs	egg whites
Fish, canned, packed in oil	fish, canned, packed in water
Frying	baking, broiling, boiling, steaming, stewing, stir-frying, using non-stick cookware
Ice cream	ices, sorbet, low-fat or reduced-calorie: ice cream, ice milk, sherbet, frozen yogurt
Jams and jellies	fruit spreads, sugar-free jellies
Juices	unsweetened juices
Mayonnaise	low-fat or reduced fat mayonnaise
Meat, high fat	lean meat (beef, lamb, pork) poultry, reduced-fat ham, reduced fat luncheon meats, without skin, veal, fish
Milk, whole	skim milk, low-fat milk
Salad dressings	low-fat or low-calorie salad dressings, lemon juice, vinegar
Sour cream	imitation sour cream, low-fat yogurt, low-fat cottage cheese
Sugar, granulated	artificial sweeteners (read labels for cooking instructions)
Syrup, maple	light maple syrup, extracts

Beverages

A1 — Grapefruit Cooler

Portion: 6 ounces (3/4 cup)

INGREDIENTS	50 portions		4 portions	
	weights	measures	weights	measures
Grapefruit juice, unsweetened	12 1/2 lb	1 1/2 gal	16 oz	2 cups
Cranberry juice, unsweetened	6 1/4 lb	3 1/8 qt	8 oz	1 cup

Method

1. Combine grapefruit juice and cranberry juice. Chill.
2. Serve over ice.

Directions for Diet Preparations

Sodium Restricted (SR), **Low Fat/Low Cholesterol** (LF): 6 oz, **Diabetic** (DB): 4 oz, and **Mechanical Soft** (SFT): Prepare as directed.

Soft/Low Fiber (SLF) and **Puree** (PUR): Prepare as directed. Strain.

Nutrient Analysis per Serving:

Regular	KCAL	PRO gm	CHO gm	FAT gm	Chol mg	SFA gm	PFA gm	VITA iu	VITC mg	THI mg	RIB mg	NIA mg	CA mg	NA mg	K+ mg	FE mg
	53.8	0.5	12.8	0.1	0.0	0.01	0.02	10.2	51.3	0.05	0.03	0.3	13.0	2.8	185	0.2

Sodium Restricted	NA mg	Diabetic	Kcal	Milk exg	Veg exg	Fruit exg	Bread exg	Meat exg	Fat exg	Low Fat & Low Chol	FAT gm	Chol mg	SFA gm	PFA gm
	2.8		35.8	0.0	0.0	0.6	0.0	0.0	0.0		0.1	0.0	0.01	0.03

Lemonade

Portion: 6 ounces (3/4 cup)

INGREDIENTS	50 portions		4 portions	
	weights	measures	weights	measures
Lemon juice or	2 lb	1 qt	3 oz	1/3 cup
Juice from fresh lemons	6 1/4 lb	25 large	8 1/3 oz	2 large
Water, cold		7 1/2 qt		2 1/2 cups
Sugar, granulated	2 lb	4 1/2 cups	2 2/3 oz	1/3 cup

Method

1. Mix lemon juice and sugar. Add water. Stir until sugar is dissolved.
2. Chill.

Note

[1]May use commercially prepared lemonade. Follow manufacturer's directions. Commercial lemonade is available without sugar.

Directions for Diet Preparations

Sodium Restricted (SR), **Low Fat/Low Cholesterol** (LF): 6 oz, **Mechanical Soft** (SFT), and **Puree** (PUR): Prepare as directed.

Diabetic (DB): 6 oz.

50 portions: Omit granulated sugar, substitute with artificial sweetener equivalent to 2 lb granulated sugar (approximately 5 Tbsp artificial sweetener).

4 portions: Omit granulated sugar, substitute with artificial sweetener equivalent to 1/3 cup granulated sugar (approximately 1 1/4 tsp artificial sweetener).

Soft/Low Fiber (SLF): Strain lemon juice.

Nutrient Analysis per Serving:

Regular	KCAL	PRO gm	CHO gm	FAT gm	Chol mg	SFA gm	PFA gm	VITA iu	VITC mg	THI mg	RIB mg	NIA mg	CA mg	NA mg	K+ mg	FE mg
	75.1	0.1	19.8	0.0	0.0	0.0	0.0	3.9	9.1	0.005	0.002	0.02	4.2	4.7	25.1	0.04

Sodium Restricted	NA mg	Diabetic	Kcal	Milk exg	Veg exg	Fruit exg	Bread exg	Meat exg	Fat exg	Low Fat & Low Chol	FAT gm	Chol mg	SFA gm	PFA gm
	4.7		8.5	0.0	0.0	0.1	0.0	0.0	0.0		0.0	0.0	0.0	0.0

Portion: 8 ounces (1 cup)

INGREDIENTS	50 portions, 3 1/8 gallons		4 portions, 1 quart	
	weights	measures	weights	measures
Nuts (blanched almonds, cashews, or pecans)	3 2/3 lb	3 1/8 qt	4 2/3 oz	1 cup
Water		2 1/3 gal		3 cups
Maple syrup		1/2 cup		2 tsp
Vanilla extract		1/4 cup		1 tsp

Method

1. Grind the nuts in a blender or food processor, until finely powdered.
2. Add the water and blend for 3 minutes.
3. Strain the nut mixture.
4. Add the maple syrup and vanilla; mix well.
5. Serve hot or cold.

Directions for Diet Preparations

Sodium Restricted (SR): Prepare as directed.
Low Fat/Low Cholesterol (LF): Not recommended, use appropriate food alternative.
Diabetic (DB): 1 cup. Omit maple syrup, substitute with unsweetened maple syrup.
Mechanical Soft (SFT): Prepare as directed.
Soft/Low Fiber (SLF): Not recommended, use appropriate food alternative.
Puree (PUR): Prepare as directed.

Nutrient Analysis per Serving:

Regular	KCAL	PRO gm	CHO gm	FAT gm	Chol mg	SFA gm	PFA gm	VITA iu	VITC mg	THI mg	RIB mg	NIA mg	CA mg	NA mg	K+ mg	FE mg
	227	7.5	9.3	19.3	0.0	1.8	4.0	0.0	0.2	0.06	0.25	1.2	94.0	4.0	281	1.4

Sodium Restricted	NA mg	Diabetic	Kcal	Milk exg	Veg exg	Fruit exg	Bread exg	Meat exg	Fat exg	Low Fat & Low Chol	Not recommended
	4.0		220	0.0	0.0	0.0	1.0	0.0	3.2		

Portion: 8 ounces (1 cup)

INGREDIENTS	50 portions		4 portions	
	weights	measures	weights	measures
Orange juice, unsweetened	20 lb	2 1/2 gal	1 2/3 lb	3 1/4 cups
Ice milk, vanilla, low fat	4 3/4 lb	3 1/4 qt	6 oz	1 cup
Cinnamon, ground	1/2 oz	2 Tbsp		1/2 tsp

Method

1. Combine orange juice and ice milk in blender.
2. Cover and blend until smooth and frothy.
3. Pour into chilled glasses.
4. Sprinkle with cinnamon. Serve immediately.

Directions for Diet Preparations

Sodium Restricted (SR), **Low Fat/Low Cholesterol** (LF): 6 oz, **Diabetic** (DB): 6 oz, and **Mechanical Soft** (SFT): Prepare as directed.

Soft/Low Fiber (SLF) and **Puree** (PUR): Strain orange juice.

Nutrient Analysis per Serving:

Regular	KCAL	PRO gm	CHO gm	FAT gm	Chol mg	SFA gm	PFA gm	VITA iu	VITC mg	THI mg	RIB mg	NIA mg	CA mg	NA mg	K+ mg	FE mg
	141.7	3.2	29.7	1.4	3.3	0.7	0.1	402	69.6	0.15	0.19	0.7	89.0	45.3	458	1.1

Sodium Restricted	NA mg	Diabetic	Kcal	Milk exg	Veg exg	Fruit exg	Bread exg	Meat exg	Fat exg	Low Fat & Low Chol	FAT gm	Chol mg	SFA gm	PFA gm
	45.3		106.3	0.2	0.0	1.4	0.0	0.0	0.2		1.1	2.5	0.6	0.1

Passion Punch

Portion: 4 ounces (1/2 cup)

INGREDIENTS	50 portions		4 portions	
	weights	measures	weights	measures
Orange juice, unsweetened	4 1/2 lb	2 1/4 qt	6 oz	3/4 cup
Cranberry juice, unsweetened	8 lb	1 gal	10 2/3 oz	1 1/3 cups

Method

1. Combine orange juice and cranberry juice.
2. Chill.

Directions for Diet Preparations

Sodium Restricted (SR), **Low Fat/Low Cholesterol** (LF): 4 oz, **Diabetic** (DB): 4 oz, and **Mechanical Soft** (SFT): Prepare as directed.

Puree (PUR) and **Soft/Low Fiber** (SLF): Prepare as directed. Strain.

Nutrient Analysis per Serving:

Regular	KCAL	PRO gm	CHO gm	FAT gm	Chol mg	SFA gm	PFA gm	VITA iu	VITC mg	THI mg	RIB mg	NIA mg	CA mg	NA mg	K+ mg	FE mg
	67.0	0.3	16.5	0.2	0.0	0.04	0.02	93.7	51.6	0.05	0.02	0.2	7.4	2.1	105	0.2

Sodium Restricted	NA mg	Diabetic	Kcal	Milk exg	Veg exg	Fruit exg	Bread exg	Meat exg	Fat exg	Low Fat & Low Chol	FAT gm	Chol mg	SFA gm	PFA gm
	2.1		34.9	0.0	0.0	0.6	0.0	0.0	0.0		0.2	0.0	0.04	0.02

Pineapple Punch

Portion: 6 ounces (3/4 cup)

INGREDIENTS	50 portions		4 portions	
	weights	measures	weights	measures
Pineapple juice, unsweetened	14 lb	1 3/4 gal	1 1/8 lb	2 1/4 cups
Cranberry juice, unsweetened	5 lb	2 1/2 qt	6 oz	3/4 cup
Lime juice	12 oz	1 1/2 cup	1 oz	2 Tbsp
Ice cubes	as needed	as needed	as needed	as needed

Method

1. Combine juices. Serve over ice.

Directions for Diet Preparations

Sodium Restricted (SR), Low Fat/Low Cholesterol (LF): 6 oz, **Diabetic** (DB): 4 oz, and **Mechanical Soft (SFT):** Prepare as directed.

Soft/Low Fiber (SLF) and **Puree** (PUR): Prepare as directed. Strain.

Nutrient Analysis per Serving:

Regular	KCAL	PRO gm	CHO gm	FAT gm	Chol mg	SFA gm	PFA gm	VITA iu	VITC mg	THI mg	RIB mg	NIA mg	CA mg	NA mg	K+ mg	FE mg
	81.1	0.4	20.1	0.1	0.0	0.0	0.04	9.3	27.8	0.08	0.03	0.3	26.4	3.8	186	0.4

Sodium Restricted	NA mg	Diabetic	Kcal	Milk exg	Veg exg	Fruit exg	Bread exg	Meat exg	Fat exg	Low Fat & Low Chol	FAT gm	Chol mg	SFA gm	PFA gm
	3.8		54.0	0.0	0.0	0.9	0.0	0.0	0.		0.1	0.0	0.01	0.04

Spicy Vegetable Cocktail (Virgin Mary)

Portion: 4 ounces (1/2 cup)

INGREDIENTS	50 portions		4 portions	
	weights	measures	weights	measures
Tomato juice	12 1/2 lb	6 1/4 qt	16 oz	2 cups
Lemon juice	8 oz	1/2 cup		1 Tbsp
Tabasco sauce		2 tsp		dash

Method

1. Combine all ingredients. Chill.

Directions for Diet Preparations

Sodium Restricted (SR): Use low sodium tomato juice.
Low Fat/Low Cholesterol (LF): 4 oz. Omit tabasco sauce.
Diabetic (DB): 4 oz and **Mechanical Soft** (SFT): Prepare as directed.
Soft/Low Fiber (SLF): Omit tabasco sauce. Strain.
Puree (PUR): Prepare as directed. Strain.

Nutrient Analysis per Serving:

Regular	KCAL	PRO gm	CHO gm	FAT gm	Chol mg	SFA gm	PFA gm	VITA iu	VITC mg	THI mg	RIB mg	NIA mg	CA mg	NA mg	K+ mg	FE mg
	21.9	0.9	5.3	0.07	0.0	0.01	0.03	675.0	23.2	0.06	0.04	0.8	10.8	439	269	0.7

Sodium Restricted	NA mg	Diabetic	Kcal	Milk exg	Veg exg	Fruit exg	Bread exg	Meat exg	Fat exg	Low Fat & Low Chol	FAT gm	Chol mg	SFA gm	PFA gm
	4.1		21.9	0.0	0.8	0.0	0.0	0.0	0.0		0.07	0.0	0.01	0.03

Breakfast Entrees

B1   Hot Cereals: Cream of Wheat, Cream of Rice, Farina, Oatmeal, and Wheatena

Portion: 1/2 cup

INGREDIENTS	50 portions		4 portions	
	weights	measures	weights	measures
Water	2 lb	2 gal		2 cups
Cereal, (whole, flaked cracked, or granular)		varies	2 oz	varies

Method

1. Bring water to a boil. (See package directions for quantities).
2. Stir dry cereal gradually into boiling water. Stir until some thickening takes place. Do not stir excessively.
3. Reduce heat to a slow simmer, cover and cook until desired consistency is reached. (Cooking time varies). Cereal should be thick and creamy, not sticky. Cover until ready to serve.
4. Hold for hot service at 140°F or higher. Serve promptly for the best quality or within 2 hours or less. If held over 2 hours, throw out.

Notes

[1]Granular cereals (farina or cornmeal): Mix with a little cold water before adding boiling water. The cold water must be calculated as part of the total amount of liquid.
[2]If using milk or part milk, calculate as part of the total amount of liquid. Be careful not to scorch.

[3]May purchase commercially prepared cereals. Follow manufacturer's directions.
[4]Variation: Cinnamon Hot Cereal
50 portions: add 1 Tbsp of cinnamon to hot cereal. Mix.
4 portions: add 1/2 tsp cinnamon to hot cereal. Mix.

Directions for Diet Preparations

Sodium Restricted (SR): 1/2 cup. Prepare as directed. Avoid commercially prepared cereals with salt. May use milk in preparation, if able to calculate into daily food plan.

Low Fat/Low Cholesterol (LF): 1/2 cup. Prepare as directed. May use skim milk in preparation.

Diabetic (DB): 1/2 cup. Prepare as directed. Avoid commercially prepared cereals with sugar. May use skim milk in preparation, if able to calculate into daily food plan.

Mechanical Soft (SFT): Prepare as directed.

Soft/Low Fiber (SLF): Use refined cereals.

Puree (PUR): Prepare as directed. Blenderize.

Nutrient Analysis per Serving:

Regular, Sodium Restricted, and Low Fat/Low Cholesterol:

	KCAL	PRO	CHO	FAT	Chol	SFA	PFA	VITA	VITC	THI	RIB	NIA	CA	NA	K+	FE
	gm	gm	gm	mg	gm	gm	iu	mg	mg	mg	mg	mg	mg	mg	mg	mg
Crm Wheat	57.0	1.5	11.0	0.2	0.0	TR	NA	NA	0.0	0.08	0.03	0.6	3	1.0	17	4.0
Crm Rice	63.0	1.0	14.0	0.1	0.0	NA	NA	NA	NA	0.05	0.00	0.5	4	1.0	25	0.02
Farina	58.0	1.7	12.3	0.1	0.0	NA	NA	NA	NA	0.09	0.06	0.6	2	1.0	15	0.6
Oatmeal	55.0	2.0	9.7	1.0	0.0	0.0	0.2	0.0	0.0	0.08	0.02	0.1	9	0.5	50	0.6
Wheatena	67.0	2.5	14.3	0.5	0.0	NA	NA	NA	NA	0.01	0.02	0.7	5	2.5	93	0.7

Diabetic:				Milk	Veg	Fruit	Bread	Meat	Fat
Kcal-same as above				exg	exg	exg	exg	exg	exg
				0.0	0.0	0.0	1.0	0.0	0.0

B2 Grits

Portion: 1/2 cup

INGREDIENTS	50 portions		4 portions	
	weights	measures	weights	measures
Water, boiling		1 3/4 gal		2 1/4 cups
Hominy grits	2 1/8 lb	1 1/2 qt	2 3/4 oz	1/2 cup

Method

1. Add grits gradually to boiling water.
2. Return water to boil. Stir to prevent lumps. Cover.
3. Simmer 30 to 40 minutes.
4. Hold for hot service at 140°F or higher. Serve promptly for the best quality or within 2 hours or less. If held over 2 hours, throw out.

Directions for Diet Preparations

Sodium Restricted (SR), Low Fat/Low Cholesterol (LF): 1/2 cup, Diabetic **(DB): 1/2 cup, and** Mechanical Soft **(SFT): Prepare as directed.**
Soft/Low Fiber (SLF): Not recommended.
Puree (PUR): Prepare as directed. Strain.

Nutrient Analysis per Serving:

Regular	KCAL	PRO gm	CHO gm	FAT gm	Chol mg	SFA gm	PFA gm	VITA iu	VITC mg	THI mg	RIB mg	NIA mg	CA mg	NA mg	K+ mg	FE mg
	72.5	1.7	15.7	0.2	0.0	0.0	0.0	0.0	0.0	0.12	0.07	0.98	0.0	0.0	26.6	0.8

Sodium Restricted	NA mg	Diabetic	Kcal	Milk exg	Veg exg	Fruit exg	Bread exg	Meat exg	Fat exg	Low Fat & Low Chol	FAT gm	Chol mg	SFA gm	PFA gm
	0.0		72.5	0.0	0.0	0.0	1.0	0.0	0.0		0.2	0.0	0.0	0.0

Matzo Cereal

Portion: 3/4 cup

INGREDIENTS	50 portions		4 portions	
	weights	measures	weights	measures
Matzo farfel	5 1/2 lb	2 1/3 gal	7 1/8 oz	3 cups
Milk, skim		1 1/4 gal		1 2/3 cups

Method

1. Add skim milk to farfel.
2. Heat to just before boiling. Stir to prevent burning. Cook until soft.

Directions for Diet Preparations

Sodium Restricted (SR), **Low Fat/Low Cholesterol** (LF): 3/4 cup, **Diabetic** (DB): 1/2 cup, **Mechanical Soft** (SFT), and **Soft/Low Fiber** (SLF): Prepare as directed.
Puree (PUR): Prepare as directed. Blenderize and strain.

Nutrient Analysis per Serving:

Regular	KCAL	PRO gm	CHO gm	FAT gm	Chol mg	SFA gm	PFA gm	VITA iu	VITC mg	THI mg	RIB mg	NIA mg	CA mg	NA mg	K+ mg	FE mg
	167	8.3	35.2	0.8	1.6	0.1	1.2	189	0.9	0.03	0.13	0.08	114	49.1	216	0.04

Sodium Restricted	NA mg	Diabetic	Kcal	Milk exg	Veg exg	Fruit exg	Bread exg	Meat exg	Fat exg	Low Fat & Low Chol	FAT gm	Chol mg	SFA gm	PFA gm
	49.1		111	0.3	0.0	0.0	1.3	0.0	0.0		0.8	1.6	0.1	1.2

Egg Cookery

Portion: 1 egg

Ingredients	50 portions		4 portions	
	weights	measures	weights	measures
Eggs[1]	5 1/2 lb	2 3/4 qt (50 medium)	7 oz	3/4 cup (4 medium)

Method

1. **HARD-BOILED[1]:** Place eggs in cold water. Bring to a boil. Reduce heat and simmer 10 to 20 minutes.
2. **POACHED[1]:** Bring water to a simmer. Break eggs one at a time into a dish or small plate. Carefully shake eggs into water. Simmer 3 1/2 to 5 minutes until whites are coagulated and yolks are soft. Remove eggs with slotted spoon or skimmer.

Notes

[1]Hold for hot service at 140°F or higher. Serve promptly for the best quality or within 2 hours or less. If held over 2 hours, throw out.

Directions for Diet Preparations

Sodium Restricted (SR), **Mechanical Soft** (SFT), and **Soft/Low Fiber** (SLF): Prepare as directed.
Low Fat/Low Cholesterol (LF): Use a commercial egg substitute as per manufacturer's directions.
Diabetic (DB): 1 egg. Prepare as directed.
Puree (PUR): Prepare soft and poached as directed. Sieve or mash hard boiled eggs. Use additional liquid if necessary to obtain desired consistency.

Nutrient Analysis per Serving:

Regular	KCAL	PRO gm	CHO gm	FAT gm	Chol mg	SFA gm	PFA gm	VITA iu	VITC mg	THI mg	RIB mg	NIA mg	CA mg	NA mg	K+ mg	FE mg
	79.0	6.0	0.6	5.5	273	1.67	0.7	259	0.0	0.04	0.13	0.03	28.0	146	65	1.04

Sodium Restricted	NA mg	Diabetic	Kcal	Milk exg	Veg exg	Fruit exg	Bread exg	Meat exg	Fat exg	Low Fat & Low Chol	FAT gm	Chol mg	SFA gm	PFA gm
	146		79.0	0.0	0.0	0.0	0.0	1.0-M	0.0		2.1	0.6	0.4	1.0

B5   Scrambled Egg

Portion: 1 medium egg

INGREDIENTS	50 portions		4 portions	
	weights	measures	weights	measures
Eggs[1]	5 1/2 lb	2 3/4 qt (50 medium)	7 oz	3/4 cup (4 medium)
Milk, skim, hot		1 qt		1/3 cup
Margarine, melted	4 oz	1/2 cup		2 tsp

Method

1. Break eggs into mixing bowl. Beat slightly at medium speed.
2. Add hot milk. Beat until blended.
3. Melt margarine in skillet. Pour in egg mixture.
4. Cook over low heat. Stirring occasionally until desired consistency.
5. Hold for hot service at 140°F or higher. Serve promptly for the best quality or within 2 hours or less. If held over 2 hours, throw out.

Directions for Diet Preparations

Sodium Restricted (SR), **Diabetic** (DB): 1 egg, **Mechanical Soft** (SFT), **Soft/Low Fiber** (SLF), and **Puree** (PUR): Prepare as directed.
Low Fat/Low Cholesterol (LF): Use a commercial egg substitute as per manufacturer's directions.

Notes

[1]May use frozen pasteurized eggs. Prepare as directed by manufacturer.

Nutrient Analysis per Serving:

Regular	KCAL	PRO gm	CHO gm	FAT gm	Chol mg	SFA gm	PFA gm	VITA iu	VITC mg	THI mg	RIB mg	NIA mg	CA mg	NA mg	K+ mg	FE mg
	101.9	6.7	1.6	7.4	274	2.0	1.3	374	0.2	0.05	52.5	0.05	52.5	79.1	98	1.0

Sodium Restricted	NA mg	Diabetic	Kcal	Milk exg	Veg exg	Fruit exg	Bread exg	Meat exg	Fat exg	Low Fat & Low Chol	FAT gm	Chol mg	SFA gm	PFA gm
	79.1		85.9	0.08	0.0	0.0	0.0	1.0	0.5		3.9	1.0	0.7	1.6

Portion: 1 large egg, 2 Tablespoons salsa

INGREDIENTS	50 portions		4 portions	
	weights	measures	weights	measures
Eggs	6 1/4 lb	3 1/8 qt (50 large)	8 oz	1 cup (4 large)
Milk, skim, hot		1 qt		1/3 cup
Margarine, melted, low sodium	4 oz	1/2 cup	1/2 oz	1 Tbsp
Salsa	3 lb	1 1/2 qt	4 oz	1/2 cup

Method

1. Break eggs into mixing bowl. Beat slightly at medium speed.
2. Add hot milk. Beat until blended.
3. Melt margarine in skillet. Pour in egg mixture.
4. Cook over low heat. Stirring occasionally until desired consistency.
5. Serve with a No. 16 scoop.
6. Serve 2 Tbsp salsa over egg.

Directions for Diet Preparations

Sodium Restricted (SR): Use low sodium salsa.
Low Fat/Low Cholesterol (LF): Use a commercial egg substitute as per manufacturer's directions; 2 Tbsp salsa. Omit margarine. Use a non-stick spray.
Diabetic (DB): 1 egg, 2 Tbsp salsa. Omit margarine. Use a non-stick spray.
Mechanical Soft (SFT) and **Puree** (PUR): Use strained salsa.
Soft/Low Fiber (SLF): Omit salsa.

Nutrient Analysis per Serving:

Regular	KCAL	PRO gm	CHO gm	FAT gm	Chol mg	SFA gm	PFA gm	VITA iu	VITC mg	THI mg	RIB mg	NIA mg	CA mg	NA mg	K+ mg	FE mg
	110	7.1	3.4	7.5	273.5	2.1	1.3	637	9.6	0.06	0.19	0.29	60.6	152	175	1.3

Sodium Restricted	NA mg	Diabetic	Kcal	Milk exg	Veg exg	Fruit exg	Bread exg	Meat exg	Fat exg	Low Fat & Low Chol	FAT gm	Chol mg	SFA gm	PFA gm
	83.5		94	0.1	0.3	0.0	0.0	1.0	0.5		3.2	0.9	0.6	1.5

Portion: 1 egg, 1 ounce (2 Tbsp) sauce, 2 ounces spinach

Ingredients	50 portions		4 portions	
	weights	measures	weights	measures
Spinach, chopped, frozen	8 lb	1 gal	10 1/4 oz	1 1/3 cups
Mornay sauce	3 lb	1 1/2 qt	4 oz	1/2 cup
Eggs, poached	6 1/4 lb	3 1/8 qt (50 large)	8 oz	1 cup (4 large)
Parmesan cheese, grated	14 1/3 oz	3 1/8 cups	1 1/8 oz	1/4 cup
Bread crumbs, dry	10 1/2 oz	3 1/8 cups	3/4 oz	1/4 cup

Method

1. Cook spinach as directed on package. Drain.
2. Place spinach in ungreased baking pans. Keep spinach warm.
3. Prepare mornay sauce and poached eggs.
4. Place eggs on spinach. Cover eggs with mornay sauce.
5. Sprinkle parmesan cheese and bread crumbs over eggs.
6. Broil for about 1 minute or until light brown.

Directions for Diet Preparations

Sodium Restricted (SR): 1 medium egg, 1 Tbsp SR mornay sauce, 2 oz spinach. Omit parmesan cheese. Use low sodium bread crumbs.

Low Fat/Low Cholesterol (LF): 2 oz egg substitute, 1 Tbsp SR mornay sauce, 2 oz spinach. Omit poached egg, replace with an egg substitute as per manufacturer's directions. Add spinach to egg substitute mix. Prepare egg substitute as an omelet. Omit parmesan cheese. Cover egg substitute with 1 Tbsp SR mornay sauce. Sprinkle bread crumbs over eggs. Broil for 1 minute or until light brown.

Diabetic (DB): 1 medium egg, 1 Tbsp SR mornay sauce, 2 oz spinach. Omit parmesan cheese.

Mechanical Soft (SFT): Prepare as directed.

Soft/Low Fiber (SLF): Omit mornay sauce and parmesan cheese.

Puree (PUR): Omit bread crumbs. Add additional liquid (i.e. mornay sauce); blenderize to obtain desired consistency.

Nutrient Analysis per Serving:

Regular	KCAL	PRO gm	CHO gm	FAT gm	Chol mg	SFA gm	PFA gm	VITA iu	VITC mg	THI mg	RIB mg	NIA mg	CA mg	NA mg	K+ mg	FE mg
	235	15.9	10.9	14.2	416	4.7	2.1	6224	17.7	0.15	0.39	0.8	253	494	385	3.5

Sodium Restricted	NA mg	Diabetic	Kcal	Milk exg	Veg exg	Fruit exg	Bread exg	Meat exg	Fat exg	Low Fat & Low Chol	FAT gm	Chol mg	SFA gm	PFA gm
	206		130	0.0	0.5	0.0	0.25	1.0	1.0		3.3	1.0	0.6	1.3

B8 French Toast

Portion: 1 slice

INGREDIENTS	50 portions		4 portions	
	weights	measures	weights	measures
Eggs[1]	2 1/4 lb	1 1/8 qt (18 large)	4 oz	1/2 cup (2 large)
Milk, skim		1 1/2 qt		1/2 cup
Cinnamon, ground	1/2 oz	2 Tbsp		2 tsp
Bread	3 1/8 lb	50 slices	4 oz	4 slices

Method

1. Break eggs. Add milk and cinnamon. Mix well.
2. Dip bread into egg mixture. Do not let bread soak in the egg mixture.
3. Fry in deep fat at 360°F or on a well greased griddle until golden brown.
4. Hold for hot service at 140°F or higher. Serve promptly for the best quality or within 2 hours or less. If held over 2 hours, throw out.

Notes

[1]May use frozen pasteurized eggs. Prepare as directed by manufacturer.

Directions for Diet Preparations

Sodium Restricted (SR): 1 slice. Use low sodium bread.
Low Fat/Low Cholesterol (LF): 1 slice.
50 portions: Omit eggs, substitute with 36 egg whites or a commercial egg substitute as per manufacturer's directions. Use non-stick cooking spray.
4 portions: Omit eggs, substitute with 4 egg whites or a commercial egg substitute as per manufacturer's directions. Use non-stick cooking spray.
Diabetic (DB): 1 slice. Use non-stick cooking spray.
Mechanical Soft (SFT) and Soft/Low Fiber (SLF): Prepare as directed.
Puree (PUR): Not recommended.

Nutrient Analysis per Serving:

Regular	KCAL	PRO gm	CHO gm	FAT gm	Chol mg	SFA gm	PFA gm	VITA iu	VITC mg	THI mg	RIB mg	NIA mg	CA mg	NA mg	K+ mg	FE mg
	163	6.1	18.5	7.0	100	1.5	1.5	313	0.4	0.13	0.18	1.1	74.3	208	103	1.4

Sodium Restricted	NA mg	Diabetic	Kcal	Milk exg	Veg exg	Fruit exg	Bread exg	Meat exg	Fat exg	Low Fat & Low Chol	FAT gm	Chol mg	SFA gm	PFA gm
	43.1		128	0.0	0.0	0.0	1.0	0.5	0.5		1.0	1.3	0.3	0.003

Portion: 2 pancakes (each 4-inches diameter)

INGREDIENTS	50 portions		4 portions	
	weights	measures	weights	measures
Flour, all-purpose	4 1/2 lb	4 1/2 qt	6 oz	1 1/2 cups
Baking powder	4 oz	1/2 cup	1/3 oz	2 tsp
Sugar, granulated	12 oz	1 2/3 cups	1 oz	2 1/4 Tbsp
Eggs[1]	1 1/2 lb	3 cups (12 large)	2 oz	1/4 cup (1 large)
Milk, skim		3 1/2 qt		1 1/8 cups
Margarine, low sodium, melted, cooled	12 oz	1 1/2 cups	1 oz	2 Tbsp

Method

1. Combine dry ingredients in mixing bowl.
2. Beat eggs until light.
3. Combine eggs, milk, and margarine. Add to dry ingredients. Mix (low speed) for 30 seconds. If batter is thicker than desired, thin with milk.
4. Use a No. 16 scoop to place batter on a well greased hot griddle (preheat to 350°F).
5. Cook until surface of cake is full of bubbles and golden brown. Turn and finish cooking.
6. Hold for hot service at 140°F or higher. Serve promptly for the best quality or within 2 hours or less. If held over 2 hours, throw out.

Notes

[1]May use frozen pasteurized eggs. Prepare as directed by manufacturer.

Directions for Diet Preparations

Sodium Restricted (SR): Use low sodium baking powder.

Low Fat/Low Cholesterol (LF): 2 pancakes. Omit eggs, replace with a commercial egg substitute as per manufacture's directions. Use reduced calorie margarine. Do not fry, use a non-stick spray.

Diabetic (DB): 2 pancakes.

50 portions: Omit granulated sugar, substitute with an artificial sweetener equal to 12 oz of granulated sugar (approximately 2 Tbsp artificial sweetener). Use reduced-calorie margarine. Do not fry, use a non-stick spray.

4 portions: Omit granulated sugar, substitute with an artificial sweetener equal to 1 oz of granulated sugar (approximately 1/2 tsp artificial sweetener). Use reduced-calorie margarine. Do not fry, use a non-stick spray.

Mechanical Soft (SFT) and Soft/Low Fiber (SLF): Prepare as directed. Consider individual tolerance.

Puree (PUR): Not recommended.

Nutrient Analysis per Serving:

Regular	KCAL	PRO gm	CHO gm	FAT gm	Chol mg	SFA gm	PFA gm	VITA iu	VITC mg	THI mg	RIB mg	NIA mg	CA mg	NA mg	K+ mg	FE mg
	224	6.9	33.1	6.7	51.4	1.7	NA	116.5	0.4	0.23	0.26	1.8	98.0	413	119	1.8

Sodium Restricted	NA mg	Diabetic	Kcal	Milk exg	Veg exg	Fruit exg	Bread exg	Meat exg	Fat exg	Low Fat & Low Chol	FAT gm	Chol mg	SFA gm	PFA gm
	53		124	0.0	0.0	0.0	1.0	0.0	1.0		3.8	1.4	0.6	1.4

Portion: 2 pancakes (each 4-inches diameter)

INGREDIENTS	50 portions		4 portions	
	weights	measures	weights	measures
Flour, all-purpose	4 1/2 lb	4 1/2 qt	6 oz	1 1/2 cups
Baking powder	4 oz	1/2 cup	1/3 oz	2 tsp
Sugar, granulated	12 oz	1 2/3 cups	1 oz	2 1/4 Tbsp
Eggs[1]	1 1/2 lb	3 cups (12 large)	2 oz	1/4 cup (1 large)
Milk, skim		3 1/2 qt		1 1/8 cups
Margarine, low sodium, melted, cooled	12 oz	1 1/2 cups	1 oz	2 Tbsp
Apples, peeled, chopped, cooked	1 lb EP	3 1/2 cups	1 1/3 oz EP	1/3 cup

Method

1. Combine dry ingredients in mixing bowl.
2. Beat eggs until light.
3. Combine eggs, milk, and margarine. Add to dry ingredients. Mix (low speed) for 30 seconds. If batter is thicker than desired, thin with milk.
4. Add cooked apples to batter. Mix in lightly.
5. Use a No. 16 scoop to place batter on a well greased hot griddle (preheat to 350°F).
6. Cook until surface of cake is full of bubbles and golden brown. Turn and finish cooking.
7. Hold for hot service at 140°F or higher. Serve promptly for the best quality or within 2 hours or less. If held over 2 hours, throw out.

Notes

[1]May use frozen pasteurized eggs. Prepare as directed by manufacturer.

Directions for Diet Preparations

Sodium Restricted (SR): Use low sodium baking powder.

Low Fat/Low Cholesterol (LF): 2 pancakes. Omit eggs, replace with a commercial egg substitute as per manufacture's directions. Use reduced calorie margarine. Do not fry, use a non-stick spray.

Diabetic (DB): 2 pancakes.

50 portions: Omit granulated sugar, substitute with an artificial sweetener equal to 12 oz of granulated sugar (approximately 2 Tbsp artificial sweetener). Use reduced-calorie margarine. Do not fry, use a non-stick spray.

4 portions: Omit granulated sugar, substitute with an artificial sweetener equal to 1 oz of granulated sugar (approximately 1/2 tsp artificial sweetener). Use reduced-calorie margarine. Do not fry, use a non-stick spray.

Mechanical Soft (SFT): Cook apples until very soft. Consider individual tolerance.

Soft/Low Fiber (SLF): 2 pancakes.

50 portions: Omit cinnamon. Omit apples, substitute with 1 cup applesauce.

4 portions: Omit cinnamon. Omit apples, substitute with 1 1/2 Tbsp applesauce.

Puree (PUR): Not recommended.

Nutrient Analysis per Serving:

Regular	KCAL	PRO gm	CHO gm	FAT gm	Chol mg	SFA gm	PFA gm	VITA iu	VITC mg	THI mg	RIB mg	NIA mg	CA mg	NA mg	K+ mg	FE mg
	229	6.9	34.2	6.8	51.4	1.7	0.01	120.5	0.4	0.2	0.3	1.8	98.5	413	127	1.9

Sodium Restricted	NA mg	Diabetic	Kcal	Milk exg	Veg exg	Fruit exg	Bread exg	Meat exg	Fat exg	Low Fat & Low Chol	FAT gm	Chol mg	SFA gm	PFA gm
	53		129	0.0	0.0	0.2	1.0	0.0	1.0		3.7	1.4	0.7	1.4

Banana Pancakes

Portion: 3 pancakes

INGREDIENTS	50 portions		6 portions	
	weights	measures	weights	measures
Bananas, peeled, mashed	3 3/4 lb	7 1/4 cups (18 medium)	10 1/4 oz	1 1/4 cups (3 medium)
Flour, whole wheat pastry	2 lb	7 1/4 cups	4 1/3 oz	1 cup
Oats, rolled	2 1/2 lb	7 1/4 cups	5 1/3 oz	1 cup
Cornmeal	2 1/2 lb	7 1/4 cups	5 1/3 oz	1 cup
Baking powder	3 1/2 oz	1/2 cup	1/2 oz	1 Tbsp
Water or milk, soy		2 3/4 qt		1 1/2 cups
Vegetable oil		2/3 cup		1 1/2 Tbsp

Method

1. Mix all ingredients together, except the vegetable oil.
2. Portion 1/4 cup batter per pancake onto oiled heated griddle.
3. Cook over medium heat on both sides until golden brown.
4. Serve with maple syrup, fruit sauce, compote, or jam.

Directions for Diet Preparations

Sodium Restricted (SR): Omit baking powder, substitute with low sodium baking powder as per manufacturer's directions.

Low Fat/Low Cholesterol (LF): 2 pancakes. Prepare as directed.

Diabetic (DB): 2 pancakes. Prepare as directed. Serve with unsweetened maple syrup or unsweetened jam.

Mechanical Soft (SFT): Prepare as directed.

Soft/Low Fiber (SLF): Not recommended. Provide appropriate food substitute.

Puree (PUR): Prepare as directed. Add additional soy milk; blenderize to obtain desired consistency.

Nutrient Analysis per Serving:

Regular	KCAL	PRO gm	CHO gm	FAT gm	Chol mg	SFA gm	PFA gm	VITA iu	VITC mg	THI mg	RIB mg	NIA mg	CA mg	NA mg	K+ mg	FE mg
	229	5.1	43.5	4.3	0.0	0.6	2.2	121	2.9	0.32	0.16	2.1	29.6	296	240	2.5

Sodium Restricted	NA mg	Diabetic	Kcal	Milk exg	Veg exg	Fruit exg	Bread exg	Meat exg	Fat exg	Low Fat & Low Chol	FAT gm	Chol mg	SFA gm	PFA gm
	7.5		152	0.0	0.0	0.0	2.0	0.0	0.2		2.9	0.0	0.4	1.5

Portion: 1 waffle

INGREDIENTS	50 portions		5 portions	
	weights	measures	weights	measures
Flour, all purpose	3 lb	3 qt	5 1/3 oz	1 1/3 cups
Baking powder	3 oz	7 Tbsp	1/3 oz	2 1/4 tsp
Sugar, granulated	3 1/2 oz	1/2 cup	1/3 oz	1 Tbsp
Egg yolks	14 oz	1 3/4 cup (18 medium)	1 1/2 oz	3 1/2 Tbsp (2 medium)
Milk, skim		2 1/4 qt		1 cup
Margarine, low sodium, melted, cooled	1 lb	2 cups	1 3/4 oz	3 1/2 Tbsp
Egg whites	1 1/8 lb	2 1/4 cups (18 medium)	2 oz	1/4 cup (2 medium)

Method

1. Combine dry ingredients in mixing bowl.
2. Combine egg yolks, milk, and margarine. Add to dry ingredients.
3. Mix on low speed just enough to moisten dry ingredients.
4. Beat egg whites until stiff, but not dry. Fold into batter.
5. Use a No. 10 dipper to place batter on preheated waffle iron. Bake about 4 minutes.

Directions for Diet Preparations

Sodium Restricted (SR): Use low sodium baking powder as per manufacturer's directions.

Low Fat/Low Cholesterol (LF): 1 waffle.

50 portions: Omit egg yolks, replace with 1 3/4 cups of a commercial egg substitute. Use reduced-calorie margarine in equal amount specified for regular margarine.

5 portions: Omit egg yolks, replace with 3 1/2 tablespoons (1 1/2 oz) of a commercial egg substitute. Use reduced-calorie margarine in equal amount specified for regular margarine.

Diabetic (DB): 1 waffle.

50 portions: Omit sugar, substitute with an artificial sweetener equivalent to 1/2 cup granulated sugar (approximately 2 tsp artificial sweetener). Use reduced-calorie margarine in equal amount specified for regular margarine.

5 portions: Omit sugar, substitute with an artificial sweetener equivalent to 1 Tbsp granulated sugar (approximately 1/4 tsp artificial sweetener). Use reduced-calorie margarine in equal amount specified for regular margarine.

Mechanical Soft (SFT) and **Soft/Low Fiber** (SLF): Prepare as directed. Consider individual tolerance.

Puree (PUR): Not recommended.

Nutrient Analysis per Serving:

Regular	KCAL	PRO gm	CHO gm	FAT gm	Chol mg	SFA gm	PFA gm	VITA iu	VITC mg	THI mg	RIB mg	NIA mg	CA mg	NA mg	K+ mg	FE mg
	224	6.8	25.7	10.2	127.8	2.0	2.9	536	0.4	0.2	0.2	1.5	91.8	316	124	1.6

Sodium Restricted	NA mg	Diabetic	Kcal	Milk exg	Veg exg	Fruit exg	Bread exg	Meat exg	Fat exg	Low Fat & Low Chol	FAT gm	Chol mg	SFA gm	PFA gm
	46		192	0.0	0.0	0.0	1.25	1.0	1.0		4.2	0.9	0.7	1.5

Portion: 1 waffle

INGREDIENTS	50 portions		4 portions	
	weights	**measures**	**weights**	**measures**
Oatmeal, dry	4 1/8 lb	1 1/2 gal	5 1/3 lb	2 cups
Flour, rice or cornmeal	6 3/4 oz	1 1/2 cups	1/2 oz	2 Tbsp
Sea salt		2 tsp		1/4 tsp
Ginger, ground		2 tsp		1/4 tsp
Cinnamon, ground		2 tsp		1/4 tsp
Soy milk or water		1 1/2 gal		2 cups
Vegetable oil		1 1/2 cups		2 Tbsp
Lemon juice		1/3 cup		1 1/2 tsp
Vanilla extract		3 Tbsp		1 tsp
Apple juice concentrate		1 1/2 cup		2 Tbsp
Blueberries, fresh or frozen	2 lb	1 1/2 qt	2 2/3 oz	1/2 cup
Pecans, chopped	12 1/2 oz	3 1/8 cups	1 oz	1/4 cup

Method

1. Mix the oatmeal, rice flour (or cornmeal), salt, ginger, and cinnamon.
2. Stir in the milk.
3. Combine the oil, lemon juice, vanilla extract, and apple juice concentrate. Stir into the oatmeal mixture. Refrigerate until thick.
4. When ready to cook, fold in the blueberries and pecans.
5. Spoon 1 cup batter onto a preheated waffle iron and cook 7 to 10 minutes.
6. Serve with fruit sauce, maple syrup, or plain yogurt.

Directions for Diet Preparations

Sodium Restricted (SR): Omit sea salt.
Low Fat/Low Cholesterol (LF): 1/2 waffle and **Diabetic** (DB): 1/2 waffle. Omit pecans. Use 1/2 cup batter per serving.
Mechanical Soft (SFT): Omit pecans. Consider individual tolerance.
Soft/Low Fiber (SLF): Not recommended. Provide appropriate food substitute.
Puree (PUR): Prepare waffle without pecans. Add soy milk or apple juice to waffles; blenderize to obtain desired consistency.

Nutrient Analysis per Serving:

Regular	KCAL	PRO gm	CHO gm	FAT gm	Chol mg	SFA gm	PFA gm	VITA iu	VITC mg	THI mg	RIB mg	NIA mg	CA mg	NA mg	K+ mg	FE mg
	298	7.2	36.8	14.3	0.0	1.7	6.1	84.2	3.3	0.33	0.08	0.58	27.3	100	231	2.1

Sodium Restricted	NA mg	Diabetic	Kcal	Milk exg	Veg exg	Fruit exg	Bread exg	Meat exg	Fat exg	Low Fat & Low Chol	FAT gm	Chol mg	SFA gm	PFA gm
	6.2		125	0.0	0.0	0.13	1.0	0.0	1.0		4.6	0.0	0.6	2.4

Cheese and Fruit on Toast

Portion: 1 slice toast, 1/4 cup cottage cheese, 1/4 cup fruit

INGREDIENTS	50 portions		4 portions	
	weights	measures	weights	measures
Bread, lightly toasted	3 1/8 lb	50 slices	4 oz	4 slices
Cottage cheese, low-fat	6 1/4 lb	3 1/8 qt	8 oz	1 cup
Peaches, sliced, drained, unsweetened	6 3/4 lb	3 1/8 qt 1 #10 can	8 3/4 oz	1 cup
Sugar, brown, lightly packed	8 oz	1 1/2 cups	2/3 oz	2 Tbsp
Cinnamon, ground	1/2 oz	2 Tbsp		1/2 tsp

Method

1. Arrange toast on baking pans. Spread each slice with 1/4 cup of cottage cheese.
2. Arrange 4 peach slices on top of cheese.
3. Combine brown sugar and cinnamon. Sprinkle a scant teaspoon over each slice.
4. Bake at 350°F for 5 to 10 minutes, or until hot and bubbly.

Directions for Diet Preparations

Sodium Restricted (SR): Use low sodium bread and low sodium cottage cheese.

Low Fat/Low Cholesterol (LF): 1/4 cup cottage cheese and 1/4 cup fruit on 1 sl toast. Prepare as directed.

Diabetic (DB): 1/4 cup cottage cheese and 1/4 cup unsweetened fruit on 1 sl toast. Omit sugar, use an artificial sweetener as per manufacturer's directions.

Mechanical Soft (SFT): Prepare as directed. Consider individual tolerance in using toast.

Soft/Low Fiber (SLF): Use refined white bread. Do not toast.

Puree (PUR): Omit toast. Use white bread, consider individual tolerance. Puree cottage cheese and fruit. Serve separate from the bread.

Nutrient Analysis per Serving:

Regular	KCAL	PRO gm	CHO gm	FAT gm	Chol mg	SFA gm	PFA gm	VITA iu	VITC mg	THI mg	RIB mg	NIA mg	CA mg	NA mg	K+ mg	FE mg
	171	10.1	28.8	1.6	3.6	0.6	0.04	350	1.9	0.1	0.18	1.5	67.8	400	162	1.5

Sodium Restricted	NA mg	Diabetic	Kcal	Milk exg	Veg exg	Fruit exg	Bread exg	Meat exg	Fat exg	Low Fat & Low Chol	FAT gm	Chol mg	SFA gm	PFA gm
	93		146	0.0	0.0	0.25	1.0	1.0	0.0		1.6	3.6	0.6	0.03

Scrambled Tofu

Portion: 1 cup

INGREDIENTS	50 portions		4 portions	
	weights	**measures**	**weights**	**measures**
Vegetable oil		3 cups		1/4 cup
Green onions, chopped	2 lb EP	1 1/2 qt	2 2/3 oz EP	1/2 cup
Celery, chopped	2 lb EP	1 1/2 qt	2 2/3 oz EP	1/2 cup
Tofu, crumbled	25 lb	3 1/8 gal	2 lb	1 qt
Curry powder		1 1/2 Tbsp		1/2 tsp
Tumeric powder		1 Tbsp		1/4 tsp
Garlic powder		1 Tbsp		1/4 tsp

Method

1. In skillet, sauté green onions and celery in oil.
2. Add tofu and seasonings and mix well.
3. Sauté until well heated.
4. Garnish with fresh parsley.

Directions for Diet Preparations

Sodium Restricted (SR): Prepare as directed.
Low Fat/Low Cholesterol (LF): 3/4 cup and **Diabetic** (DB): 3/4 cup. Sauté vegetables and tofu in 1/3 the amount of vegetable oil specified. Low fat diets should consider individual tolerance to onions and garlic.
Mechanical Soft (SFT): Omit celery and onions.
Soft/Low Fiber (SLF): Omit celery, onions, and seasonings.
Puree (PUR): Prepare as directed. Blenderize. Add additional liquid (i.e. vegetable broth) if necessary to obtain desired consistency.

Nutrient Analysis per Serving:

Regular	KCAL	PRO gm	CHO gm	FAT gm	Chol mg	SFA gm	PFA gm	VITA iu	VITC mg	THI mg	RIB mg	NIA mg	CA mg	NA mg	K+ mg	FE mg
	280	18.7	6.5	21.9	0.0	2.9	12.6	213	2.8	0.2	0.12	0.5	249	29.3	354	12.4

Sodium Restricted	NA mg	Diabetic	Kcal	Milk exg	Veg exg	Fruit exg	Bread exg	Meat exg	Fat exg	Low Fat & Low Chol	FAT gm	Chol mg	SFA gm	PFA gm
	29.3		161	0.0	0.2	0.0	0.0	1.9	1.0		10.9	0.0	1.5	6.2

Soups

C1 — Beef Stock

Portion: 2/3 cup

INGREDIENTS	64 portions, 3 gallons		8 portions, 1 1/2 quarts	
	weights	measures	weights	measures
Beef bones, cracked	15 lb		2 lb	
Beef shank meat, 1-inch pieces	2 1/2 lb	7 1/2 cups	5 1/3 oz	1 cup
Water, hot		5 gal		2 1/2 qt
Celery, chopped	10 1/2 oz	2 cups	1 1/3 oz	1/4 cup
Carrot, chopped	10 1/2 oz	2 cups	1 1/3 oz	1/4 cup
Onions, chopped	1 1/3 lb	1 qt	2 3/4 oz	1/2 cup
Pepper, black		1 tsp		1/8 tsp
Garlic powder		2 tsp		1/4 tsp
Bay leaves		4 leaves		1 leaf
Parsley sprigs		8 sprigs		1 sprig

Method

1. Brown bones and meat at moderate heat in 325°F oven. Stir occasionally.
2. Add water, vegetables, and seasonings. Bring to a boil. Simmer slowly until vegetables are tender, about 3 to 4 hours. Strain stock. Cover.
3. Refrigerate. When cold, remove fat from stock.
4. When ready to serve, bring to a boil. Simmer 15 minutes.

Notes

[1]May use a concentrated beef soup base as a quick beef stock. Prepare as directed by manufacturer.
[2]May be used in soups, gravies, sauces, and entrees.

Variation

Beef consomme:

64 portions: Add eight egg shells and eight large egg whites to clarify broth. Stir constantly until stock comes to a boil. Boil 15 minutes. Strain through cheesecloth or a fine strainer.

8 portions: Add one egg shell and one large egg white to clarify broth. Stir constantly until stock comes to a boil. Boil 15 minutes. Strain through cheesecloth or a fine strainer.

Directions for Diet Preparations

Sodium Restricted (SR): Prepare as directed. May use a low sodium soup base as per manufacturer's directions.
Low Fat/Low Cholesterol (LF): 2/3 cup, **Diabetic** (DB): 2/3 cup, **Mechanical Soft** (SFT), and **Puree** (PUR): Prepare as directed.
Soft/Low Fiber (SLF): Omit black pepper and garlic.

Nutrient Analysis per Serving:

Regular	KCAL	PRO gm	CHO gm	FAT gm	Chol mg	SFA gm	PFA gm	VITA iu	VITC mg	THI mg	RIB mg	NIA mg	CA mg	NA mg	K+ mg	FE mg
	21	2.6	2.1	0.5	0.8	0.25	0.2	1.9	0.0	0.01	0.02	2.1	3.3	35	347	0.6

Sodium Restricted	NA mg	Diabetic	Kcal	Milk exg	Veg exg	Fruit exg	Bread exg	Meat exg	Fat exg	Low Fat & Low Chol	FAT gm	Chol mg	SFA gm	PFA gm
	35		21	0.0	0.0	0.0	0.26	0.0	0.0		0.5	0.8	0.25	0.2

Portion: 2/3 cup

INGREDIENTS	64 portions, 3 gallons		8 portions, 1 1/2 quarts	
	weights	measures	weights	measures
Chicken bones	15 lb		2 lb	
Water, cold		5 gal		2 1/2 qt
Onions, sliced	1 1/3 lb	1 qt	2 3/4 oz	1/2 cup
Celery, chopped	10 1/2 oz	2 cups	1 1/3 oz	1/4 cup
Carrot, chopped	10 1/2 oz	2 cups	1 1/3 oz	1/4 cup
Pepper, black		1 tsp		1/8 tsp
Garlic powder		2 tsp		1/4 tsp
Bay leaves		4 leaves		1 leaf
Parsley sprigs		8 sprigs		1 sprig

Method

1. Combine chicken bones and water.
2. Heat slowly to boiling point.
3. Add vegetables and seasonings. Bring to a boil, remove the scum.
4. Simmer until tender about 3 to 4 hours. Strain stock.
5. Refrigerate. When cold, remove fat from stock
6. When ready to serve, bring to a boil. Simmer 15 minutes.

Notes

[1]May use a concentrated chicken soup base as a quick chicken stock. Prepare as directed by manufacturer.

Variation

Chicken Consomme:

64 portions: Add eight egg shells and eight large egg whites to clarify broth. Stir constantly until stock comes to a boil. Boil 15 minutes. Strain through cheese-cloth or a fine strainer.

8 portions: Add one egg shell and one large egg white to clarify broth. Stir constantly until stock comes to a boil. Boil 15 minutes. Strain through cheesecloth or a fine strainer.

Directions for Diet Preparations

Sodium Restricted (SR): Prepare as directed. May use a low sodium soup base as per manufacturer's directions.
Low Fat/Low Cholesterol (LF): 2/3 cup, **Diabetic** (DB): 2/3 cup, **Mechanical Soft** (SFT), and **Puree** (PUR): Prepare as directed.
Soft/Low Fiber (SLF): Omit black pepper and garlic.

Nutrient Analysis per Serving:

Regular	KCAL	PRO gm	CHO gm	FAT gm	Chol mg	SFA gm	PFA gm	VITA iu	VITC mg	THI mg	RIB mg	NIA mg	CA mg	NA mg	K+ mg	FE mg
	20.3	1.5	1.5	1.0	0.23	0.02	0.67	2.67	0.0	0.02	0.05	1.02	0.0	30.8	337	0.7

Sodium Restricted	NA mg	Diabetic	Kcal	Milk exg	Veg exg	Fruit exg	Bread exg	Meat exg	Fat exg	Low Fat & Low Chol	FAT gm	Chol mg	SFA gm	PFA gm
	30.8		20.3	0.0	0.0	0.0	0.25	0.0	0.0		1.0	0.2	0.02	0.7

Vegetable Stock

Portion: 2/3 cup

INGREDIENTS	64 portions, 3 gallons		8 portions 1 1/2 quarts	
	weights	measures	weights	measures
Onions, thickly sliced	9 lb EP (10 1/4 lb EP)	1 1/8 gal	1 1/8 lb EP (1 1/4 lb AP)	2 1/4 cups
Carrots, chopped	6 lb AP (8 1/2 lb AP)	1 1/4 gal	12 oz EP (1 lb AP)	2 1/2 cups
Tomato, wedges	2 2/3 lb AP	2 1/8 qt	4 7/8 oz AP	1 cup
Bay leaves		8 leaves		1 leaf
Garlic powder		2 tsp		1/4 tsp
Pepper, black		2 tsp		1/4 tsp
Water #1		2 qt		1 cup
Water #2		3 gal		1 1/2 qt

Method

1. Combine all ingredients, except water in roasting pan. Bake at 400°F for 35 minutes. Transfer vegetable mixture to large pot.
2. Add water #1 to the roasting pan to scrape brown particles from the bottom and sides of the pan. Place over moderate heat and bring to a boil.
3. Transfer mixture to pot containing vegetables, add water #2.
4. Simmer about one hour; strain liquid. Discard solids.
5. Refrigerate until ready to use.
6. Serve as a clear vegetable broth at 170°F serving temperature.

Notes

[1]May use a commercially prepared vegetable broth. Prepare as directed by manufacturer. Use a low sodium product for sodium restricted diets.

Directions for Diet Preparations

Sodium Restricted (SR), **Low Fat/Low Cholesterol** (LF): 2/3 cup, **Diabetic** (DB): 2/3 cup, **Mechanical Soft** (SFT), and **Puree** (PUR): Prepare as directed.
Soft/Low Fiber (SLF): Omit garlic and black pepper.

Nutrient Analysis per Serving:

Regular	KCAL	PRO gm	CHO gm	FAT gm	Chol mg	SFA gm	PFA gm	VITA iu	VITC mg	THI mg	RIB mg	NIA mg	CA mg	NA mg	K+ mg	FE mg
	15.2	1.1	1.1	0.0	0.0	0.0	0.0	0.0	0.0	0.01	0.03	0.7	0.0	10.0	0.0	0.5

Sodium Restricted	NA mg	Diabetic	Kcal	Milk exg	Veg exg	Fruit exg	Bread exg	Meat exg	Fat exg	Low Fat & Low Chol	FAT gm	Chol mg	SFA gm	PFA gm
	10.0		15.2	0.0	0.5	0.0	0.0	0.0	0.0		0.0	0.0	0.0	0.0

Portion: 2/3 cup

INGREDIENTS	64 portions, 3 gallons		8 portions, 1 1/2 quarts	
	weights	measures	weights	measures
Dry beans, navy or northern	4 lb	3 qt	8 oz	1 1/2 cups
Water, boiling		3 gal	1 1/4 qt	1 1/4 qt
Ham bones	5 lb		10 oz	
Onions, chopped	1 lb	3 cups	2 oz	1/3 cup
Carrots, diced	10 1/2 oz	2 cups	1 1/3 oz	1/4 cup
Celery, diced	10 1/2 oz	2 cups	1 1/3 oz	1/4 cup
Water		as needed		as needed

Method

1. Wash beans thoroughly in cold water.
2. Cover beans with boiling water; cook 2 minutes. Turn off heat. Let beans stand 1 hour or longer.
3. Simmer beans for 1 hour.
4. Add ham bones, onions, carrots, and celery to the water and beans.
5. Cook covered for 1 1/2 hours or until beans are tender. Mash beans.
6. Add water to equal or bring up to specified yield.
7. Remove ham bones.
8. Hold for hot service at 140°F or higher. Serve promptly for the best quality or within 2 hours or less. If held over 2 hours, throw out.

Directions for Diet Preparations

Sodium Restricted (SR), **Low Fat/Low Cholesterol** (LF): 2/3 cup and **Diabetic** (DB): 2/3 cup. Omit ham bones.
Mechanical Soft (SFT): Prepare as directed.
Soft/Low Fiber (SLF): Not recommended. Use appropriate food substitute.
Puree (PUR): Prepare as directed. Blenderize and strain.
Vegetarian: Omit ham bones.

Nutrient Analysis per Serving:

Regular	KCAL	PRO gm	CHO gm	FAT gm	Chol mg	SFA gm	PFA gm	VITA iu	VITC mg	THI mg	RIB mg	NIA mg	CA mg	NA mg	K+ mg	FE mg
	104	6.4	18.2	0.8	0.4	0.3	0.2	985	2.1	0.19	0.07	0.6	48.2	64.1	357	1.9

Sodium Restricted	NA mg	Diabetic	Kcal	Milk exg	Veg exg	Fruit exg	Bread exg	Meat exg	Fat exg	Low Fat & Low Chol	FAT gm	Chol mg	SFA gm	PFA gm
	8.7		100	0.0	1.0	0.0	1.0	0.0	0.0		0.4	0.0	0.1	0.2

Borscht

Portion: 2/3 cup

Ingredients	64 portions, 3 gallons		8 portions, 1 1/2 quarts	
	weights	measures	weights	measures
Beets, diced, canned with juice	8 lb	1 1/8 gal	1 lb	2 1/4 cups
Water		4 gal		2 qt
Onions, chopped	1 1/3 lb	1 qt	2 2/3 oz	1/2 cup
Sugar, granulated	5 1/3 oz	3/4 cup	3/4 oz	1 1/2 Tbsp
Bay leaves		4 leaves		1 leaf
Lemon juice	8 oz	1 cup	1 oz	2 Tbsp
Sour cream	2 lb	1 qt	4 oz	1/2 cup

Method

1. Combine beet juice, water, and onions in stock pot. Cover. Bring to a boil over low heat.
2. Add beets, sugar, and bay leaves. Simmer 4 minutes.
3. Add lemon juice. Mix. Discard bay leaves.
4. Chill and serve.
5. Garnish with 1 Tbsp sour cream per serving.

Notes

[1]Product is available prepared.

Directions for Diet Preparations

Sodium Restricted (SR): Use low sodium canned beets or raw beets.

Low Fat/Low Cholesterol (LF): 2/3 cup. Prepare as directed. Omit sour cream. Low fat diets should consider individual tolerance to onions.

Diabetic (DB): 2/3 cup.

64 portions: Omit sugar, use artificial sweetener equivalent to 3/4 cup granulated sugar (approx. 1 Tbsp). Omit sour cream.

8 portions: Omit sugar, use artificial sweetener to taste. Omit sour cream.

Mechanical Soft (SFT) and **Soft/Low Fiber** (SLF): Omit onions.

Puree (PUR): Prepare as directed. Blenderize and strain.

Nutrient Analysis per Serving:

Regular	KCAL	PRO gm	CHO gm	FAT gm	Chol mg	SFA gm	PFA gm	VITA iu	VITC mg	THI mg	RIB mg	NIA mg	CA mg	NA mg	K+ mg	FE mg
	62.3	1.1	8.1	3.2	6.4	1.9	0.2	122	5.1	0.02	0.05	0.1	28.3	163	125	1.1

Sodium Restricted	NA mg	Diabetic	Kcal	Milk exg	Veg exg	Fruit exg	Bread exg	Meat exg	Fat exg	Low Fat & Low Chol	FAT gm	Chol mg	SFA gm	PFA gm
	35.8		22.3	0.0	0.8	0.0	0.0	0.0	0.0		0.1	0.0	0.02	0.04

Portion: 2/3 cup

INGREDIENTS	64 portions, 3 gallons		8 portions, 1 1/2 quarts	
	weights	measures	weights	measures
Margarine, melted, low sodium	8 oz	1 cup	1 oz	2 Tbsp
Onions, chopped	8 oz	1 1/2 cups	1 oz	3 Tbsp
Carrots, diced, cooked	1 lb	3 cups	2 oz	1/3 cup
Celery, diced, cooked	1 lb	3 cups	2 oz	1/3 cup
Paprika		1 tsp		1/8 tsp
Pepper, white		1 tsp		1/8 tsp
Milk, skim		1 gal		2 cups
Chicken or vegetable stock[1]		1 1/2 gal		3 cups
Cheddar or american cheese, ground	1 lb	1 qt	2 oz	1/2 cup

Method

1. Sauté onions, carrots, and celery in margarine until lightly browned.
2. Add paprika and pepper. Blend.
3. Add milk and stock slowly; stir to combine. Heat.
4. Remove from heat; stir in cheese.
5. Heat gently to avoid curdling.
6. Hold for hot service at 140°F or higher. Serve promptly for the best quality or within 2 hours or less. If held over 2 hours, throw out.

Notes

[1]May use a concentrated soup base as a quick stock. Prepare as directed by manufacturer.

Directions for Diet Preparations

Sodium Restricted (SR): Use low sodium cheese. May use a low sodium soup base.

Low Fat/Low Cholesterol (LF): 2/3 cup and **Diabetic** (DB): 2/3 cup. Omit margarine, sauté vegetables in a small amount of water. Use a non-stick spray or non-stick cookware. Use low fat cheese. Low fat diets should consider individual tolerance to onions.

Mechanical Soft (SFT): Prepare as directed.

Soft/Low Fiber (SLF): Omit onions and pepper. Use a mild cheese. Consider individual tolerance.

Puree (PUR): Prepare as directed. Blenderize and strain.

Nutrient Analysis per Serving:

Regular	KCAL	PRO gm	CHO gm	FAT gm	Chol mg	SFA gm	PFA gm	VITA iu	VITC mg	THI mg	RIB mg	NIA mg	CA mg	NA mg	K+ mg	FE mg
	85	4.0	4.6	5.5	8.8	2.1	1.0	1284	1.3	0.03	0.13	0.26	135	100	345	0.15

Sodium Restricted	NA mg	Diabetic	Kcal	Milk exg	Veg exg	Fruit exg	Bread exg	Meat exg	Fat exg	Low Fat & Low Chol	FAT gm	Chol mg	SFA gm	PFA gm
	81.7		52	0.3	0.0	0.0	0.38	0.0	0.0		1.7	1.4	0.2	0.03

Beef Noodle (or Rice) Soup

Portion: 2/3 cup

INGREDIENTS	64 portions, 3 gallons		8 portions, 1 1/2 quarts	
	weights	measures	weights	measures
Beef stock[1]		2 1/2 gal	1 1/3 oz	1 1/4 qt
Onions, chopped	10 1/2 oz	2 cups	1 oz	1/4 cup
Celery, chopped	8 oz	1 1/2 cups		3 Tbsp
Pepper, black		2 tsp		1/4 tsp
Beef, cooked, chopped	2 lb	1 1/2 qt	4 oz	3/4 cup
Noodles, uncooked or	2 lb	2 2/3 qt	4 oz	1 1/3 cups
Rice, uncooked	2 lb	1 1/8 qt	4 oz	1/2 cup

Method

1. Prepare beef stock.
2. Combine beef stock and vegetables; cover. Simmer 30 minutes, until vegetables are tender.
3. Add noodles or rice. Simmer 5 to 10 minutes or until noodles (rice) are tender.
4. Hold for hot service at 140°F or higher. Serve promptly for the best quality or within 2 hours or less. If held over 2 hours, throw out.

Notes

[1]May use a concentrated soup base as a quick stock. Prepare as directed by manufacturer.

Directions for Diet Preparations

Sodium Restricted (SR): Prepare as directed. May use a low sodium soup base.

Low Fat/Low Cholesterol (LF): 2/3 cup, **Diabetic** (DB): 2/3 cup, and **Mechanical Soft** (SFT): Prepare as directed. Low fat diets should consider individual tolerance to onions.

Soft/Low Fiber (SLF): Omit onions and pepper.

Puree (PUR): Prepare as directed. Blenderize and strain.

Nutrient Analysis per Serving:

Regular	KCAL	PRO gm	CHO gm	FAT gm	Chol mg	SFA gm	PFA gm	VITA iu	VITC mg	THI mg	RIB mg	NIA mg	CA mg	NA mg	K+ mg	FE mg
Beef Noodle:	103	7.5	12.1	2.6	26.2	0.7	0.01	36.3	0.6	0.15	0.14	2.5	8.7	61.2	82.6	1.7
Beef Rice:	101	6.7	13.6	2.0	12.9	0.5	0.01	5.2	0.6	0.09	0.08	2.2	4.9	60.6	63.3	1.7

Sodium Restricted	NA mg	Diabetic	Kcal	Milk exg	Veg exg	Fruit exg	Bread exg	Meat exg	Fat exg	Low Fat & Low Chol	FAT gm	Chol mg	SFA gm	PFA gm
Beef Noodle:	61.2		103	0.0	0.5	0.0	0.75	0.25	0.5		2.6	26.2	0.7	0.01
Beef Rice:	60.6		101	0.0	0.5	0.0	0.75	0.5	0.1		2.0	12.9	0.5	0.01

C8 — Chicken Noodle (or Rice) Soup

Portion: 2/3 cup

Ingredients	64 portions, 3 gallons weights	64 portions, 3 gallons measures	8 portions, 1 1/2 quarts weights	8 portions, 1 1/2 quarts measures
Chicken stock[1]		2 1/2 gal	1 1/3 oz	1 1/4 qt
Onions, chopped	10 1/2 oz	2 cups	1 oz	1/4 cup
Celery, chopped	8 oz	1 1/2 cups		3 Tbsp
Pepper, black		2 tsp		1/4 tsp
Chicken, cooked, chopped	2 lb	1 1/2 qt	4 oz	3/4 cup
Noodles, uncooked or	2 lb	2 2/3 qt	4 oz	1 1/3 cups
Rice, uncooked	2 lb	1 1/8 qt	4 oz	1/2 cup

Method

1. Prepare chicken stock.
2. Combine chicken stock and vegetables; cover. Simmer 30 minutes, until vegetables are tender.
3. Add noodles or rice. Simmer 5 to 10 minutes or until noodles (rice) are tender.
4. Hold for hot service at 140°F or higher. Serve promptly for the best quality or within 2 hours or less. If held over 2 hours, throw out.

Notes

[1]May use a concentrated soup base as a quick stock. Prepare as directed by manufacturer.

Directions for Diet Preparations

Sodium Restricted (SR): Prepare as directed. May use a low sodium soup base.

Low Fat/Low Cholesterol (LF): 2/3 cup, **Diabetic** (DB): 2/3 cup, and **Mechanical Soft** (SFT): Prepare as directed. Low fat diets should consider individual tolerance to onions.

Soft/Low Fiber (SLF): Omit onions and pepper.

Puree (PUR): Prepare as directed. Blenderize and strain.

Nutrient Analysis per Serving:

Regular	KCAL	PRO gm	CHO gm	FAT gm	Chol mg	SFA gm	PFA gm	VITA iu	VITC mg	THI mg	RIB mg	NIA mg	CA mg	NA mg	K+ mg	FE mg
Chicken Noodle:	103	7.4	12.1	2.7	25.9	0.5	0.2	42.3	0.6	0.15	0.12	3.1	8.9	63.1	70.0	1.3
Chicken Rice:	101	6.7	13.6	2.0	12.6	0.3	0.2	11.1	0.6	0.09	0.07	2.7	5.2	62.6	50.8	1.3

Sodium Restricted	NA mg	Diabetic	Kcal	Milk exg	Veg exg	Fruit exg	Bread exg	Meat exg	Fat exg	Low Fat & Low Chol	FAT gm	Chol mg	SFA gm	PFA gm
Chicken Noodle:	63.1		103.2	0.0	0.3	0.0	0.75	0.75	0.0		2.7	25.9	0.5	0.2
Chicken Rice:	62.6		101.2	0.0	0.2	0.0	0.75	0.75	0.0		2.0	12.6	0.3	0.2

112

SOUPS

Portion: 2/3 cup, 1 matzo ball

INGREDIENTS	64 portions, 3 gallons		8 portions, 1 1/2 quarts	
	weights	measures	weights	measures
Chicken stock[1]		3 gal		1 1/2 qt
Matzo Ball:				
Eggs, beaten	1 3/4 lb	3 1/2 cups (14 large)	3 2/3 oz	1/2 cup (2 medium)
Water, cold	4 oz	3 1/2 cups	1/2 oz	1 Tbsp
Matzo meal	14 oz	3 1/2 cups	2 oz	1/2 cup
Parsley, flakes	1/4 oz	1/3 cup		1 Tbsp
Water, boiling		1 1/2 gal		3 cups

Method

1. Prepare chicken stock.
2. Prepare matzo balls.
   a. Combine eggs with water. Mix well.
   b. Add matzo meal and parsley to egg mixture. Mix thoroughly. Let stand 30 minutes in the refrigerator.
   c. Scoop a level tablespoon of matzo mixture. Form into a ball. Drop into boiling water.
   d. Cover and cook at a slow boil for 20 to 25 minutes. Remove from water.
   e. When ready to serve, place in chicken stock.
3. Bring soup to a boil. Simmer 5 minutes.
4. Hold for hot service at 140°F or higher. Serve promptly for the best quality or within 2 hours or less. If held over 2 hours, throw out.

Notes

[1]May use a concentrated chicken soup base as a quick chicken stock. Prepare as directed by manufacturer.

Directions for Diet Preparations

Sodium Restricted (SR): Prepare as directed. May use a low sodium soup base as per manufacturer's directions.

Low Fat/Low Cholesterol (LF): 2/3 cup, 1 matzo ball.

64 portions: Omit whole eggs, substitute with 25 large egg whites.

8 portions: Omit whole eggs, substitute with 4 medium egg whites.

Diabetic (DB): 2/3 cup, 1 matzo ball, **Mechanical Soft** (SFT), and **Soft/Low Fiber** (SLF): Prepare as directed.

Puree (PUR): Prepare as directed. Blenderize and strain.

Nutrient Analysis per Serving:

Regular	KCAL	PRO gm	CHO gm	FAT gm	Chol mg	SFA gm	PFA gm	VITA iu	VITC mg	THI mg	RIB mg	NIA mg	CA mg	NA mg	K+ mg	FE mg
	74	4.2	8.2	2.7	55.7	0.7	0.2	75.8	0.3	0.03	0.11	1.5	6.1	60.5	528	1.3

Sodium Restricted	NA mg	Diabetic	Kcal	Milk exg	Veg exg	Fruit exg	Bread exg	Meat exg	Fat exg	Low Fat & Low Chol	FAT gm	Chol mg	SFA gm	PFA gm
	60.5		74	0.0	0.0	0.0	1.0	0.0	0.0		1.4	0.0	0.0	0.0

Pureed Cauliflower Soup

Portion: 2/3 cup

INGREDIENTS	64 portions, 3 gallons		8 portions, 1 1/2 quarts	
	weights	measures	weights	measures
Cauliflower, chopped	5 lb EP (8 lb AP)	1 1/4 gal	10 oz EP (1 lb AP)	2 1/2 cups
Onions, diced	1 lb EP (1 1/4 lb AP)	3 cups	2 oz EP (2 1/2 oz AP)	1/3 cup
Pepper, white		2 tsp		1/4 tsp
Chicken or vegetable stock[1]		2 gal		1 qt
Margarine, melted, low sodium	10 oz	1 1/4 cups	1 1/4 oz	2 1/2 Tbsp
Flour, all-purpose	5 oz	1 1/4 cups	2/3 oz	2 1/2 Tbsp
Milk, skim, hot		1 gal		2 cups

Method

1. Combine cauliflower, onions, white pepper, and stock. Bring to a boil. Simmer about 1 hour or until cauliflower is tender.
2. Puree cauliflower and stock mixture.
3. Combine margarine and flour. Simmer and stir 5 minutes. Do not brown.
4. Add hot milk to flour mixture. Whip smooth. Add to cauliflower soup.
5. If soup is too thick add additional stock to obtain desired consistency.
6. Return soup to heat.
7. Hold for hot service at 140°F or higher. Serve promptly for the best quality or within 2 hours or less. If held over 2 hours, throw out.

Directions for Diet Preparations

Sodium Restricted (SR): Prepare as directed. May use a low sodium soup base, instead of the stock. May use if able to calculate into daily food plan.

Low Fat/Low Cholesterol (LF): 2/3 cup and **Diabetic** (DB): 2/3 cup. Use half the amount of margarine and flour specified. Low fat diets should consider individual tolerance when using cauliflower and onions.

Mechanical Soft (SFT): Prepare as directed. Consider individual tolerance.

Soft/Low Fiber (SLF): Not recommended. Provide appropriate food alternative.

Puree (PUR): Prepare as directed. Strain.

Notes

[1]May use a concentrated soup base as a quick stock. Prepare as directed by manufacturer.

Nutrient Analysis per Serving:

Regular	KCAL	PRO gm	CHO gm	FAT gm	Chol mg	SFA gm	PFA gm	VITA iu	VITC mg	THI mg	RIB mg	NIA mg	CA mg	NA mg	K+ mg	FE mg
	126	8.7	12.6	4.5	2.3	0.9	1.4	408	32.7	0.09	0.27	2.2	211	117	519	0.8

Sodium Restricted	NA mg	Diabetic	Kcal	Milk exg	Veg exg	Fruit exg	Bread exg	Meat exg	Fat exg	Low Fat & Low Chol	FAT gm	Chol mg	SFA gm	PFA gm
	117		95.7	0.4	1.0	0.0	0.5	0.0	0.0		1.8	2.3	0.5	0.5

Cream of Celery Soup

Portion: 2/3 cup

INGREDIENTS	64 portions, 3 gallons		8 portions, 1 1/2 quarts	
	weights	measures	weights	measures
Margarine, low sodium	8 oz	1 cup	1 oz	2 Tbsp
Onions, finely chopped	6 oz	1 1/8 cups	3/4 oz	2 1/4 Tbsp
Flour, all-purpose	10 oz	2 1/2 cups	1 1/4 oz	1/3 cup
Pepper, white		2 tsp		1/4 tsp
Milk, skim #1		2 qt		1 cup
Celery, chopped, cooked	2 2/3 lb	2 qt	5 1/3 oz	1 cup
Carrots, diced, cooked	1 lb	3 cups	2 oz	1/3 cup
Milk, skim #2		2 qt		1 cup
Milk, skim, hot		1 1/2 gal		3 cups

Method

1. Add onions to melted margarine sauté until tender.
2. Add flour and pepper to onions. Stir until blended.
3. Add skim milk #1 to seasoned flour and stir until mixture thickens.
4. 64 portions: Set aside 2 cups chopped celery.
   8 portions: Set aside 1/4 cup chopped celery.
5. Puree the remaining celery in skim milk #2. Add chopped celery, diced carrots, and puree celery to cream soup.
6. Stir in hot skim milk. Heat to 170°F.
7. Hold for hot service at 140°F or higher. Serve promptly for the best quality or within 2 hours or less. If held over 2 hours, throw out.

Directions for Diet Preparations

Sodium Restricted (SR) and **Mechanical Soft** (SFT): Prepare as directed.

Low Fat/Low Cholesterol (LF): 2/3 cup and **Diabetic** (DB): 2/3 cup. Use half the amount of margarine and flour specified. Low fat diets should consider individual tolerance to onions.

Soft/Low Fiber (SLF): Omit onions and pepper. Blenderize and strain.

Puree (PUR): Prepare as directed. Blenderize and strain.

Nutrient Analysis per Serving:

Regular	KCAL	PRO	CHO	FAT	Chol	SFA	PFA	VITA	VITC	THI	RIB	NIA	CA	NA	K+	FE
		gm	gm	gm	mg	gm	gm	iu	mg	mg	mg	mg	mg	mg	mg	mg
	102	5.9	12.3	3.2	2.7	0.7	1.0	1924	3.2	0.09	0.24	0.5	200	96.2	327	0.4

Sodium Restricted	NA	Diabetic	Kcal	Milk	Veg	Fruit	Bread	Meat	Fat	Low Fat & Low Chol	FAT	Chol	SFA	PFA
	mg			exg	exg	exg	exg	exg	exg		gm	mg	gm	gm
	96.2		89.2	0.5	0.75	0.0	0.25	0.0	0.25		1.8	2.8	0.5	0.6

Portion: 2/3 cup

INGREDIENTS	64 portions, 3 gallons		8 portions, 1 1/2 quarts	
	weights	measures	weights	measures
Margarine, low sodium	8 oz	1 cup	1 oz	2 Tbsp
Onions, finely chopped	10 1/2 cups	1 1/3 oz	1/4 cup	
Mushrooms, chopped	2 lb	3 qt	4 oz	1 1/2 cups
Flour, all-purpose	10 oz	2 1/2 cups	1 1/4 oz	1/3 cup
Pepper, white		2 tsp		1/4 tsp
Chicken or vegetable stock[1]		1 qt		1/2 cup
Milk, skim, hot		2 1/2 gal		1 1/4 qt

Method

1. Melt margarine. Add onions and mushrooms, sauté until tender. Blenderize until smooth. Return to heat.
2. Add flour and pepper to mushroom mixture. Stir until blended.
3. Combine stock and hot milk. Add gradually to flour. Stir constantly. Cook until thickened.
4. Heat to 170°F.
5. Hold for hot service at 140°F or higher. Serve promptly for the best quality or within 2 hours or less. If held over 2 hours, throw out.

Directions for Diet Preparations

Sodium Restricted (SR) and **Mechanical Soft** (SFT): Prepare as directed.

Low Fat/Low Cholesterol (LF): 2/3 cup and **Diabetic** (DB): 2/3 cup. Use half the amount of margarine and flour specified. Low fat diets should consider individual tolerance to onions.

Soft/Low Fiber (SLF): Omit onions and pepper.

Puree (PUR): Prepare as directed. Blenderize and strain.

Notes

[1]May use a concentrated soup base as a quick stock. Prepare as directed by manufacturer.

Nutrient Analysis per Serving:

Regular	KCAL	PRO gm	CHO gm	FAT gm	Chol mg	SFA gm	PFA gm	VITA iu	VITC mg	THI mg	RIB mg	NIA mg	CA mg	NA mg	K+ mg	FE mg
	107	6.1	13.4	3.3	2.8	0.6	0.9	433	1.8	0.09	0.26	0.7	194	86.3	283	0.4

Sodium Restricted	NA mg	Diabetic	Kcal	Milk exg	Veg exg	Fruit exg	Bread exg	Meat exg	Fat exg	Low Fat & Low Chol	FAT gm	Chol mg	SFA gm	PFA gm
	86.3		85.8	0.5	0.75	0.0	0.2	0.0	0.25		1.8	2.8	0.4	0.5

Cream of Spinach Soup

Portion: 2/3 cup

INGREDIENTS	64 portions, 3 gallons		8 portions, 1 1/2 quarts	
	weights	measures	weights	measures
Margarine, low sodium, melted	8 oz	1 cup	1 oz	2 Tbsp
Onions, finely chopped	6 oz	1 1/8 cups	3/4 oz	2 1/4 Tbsp
Flour, all-purpose	10 oz	2 1/2 cups	1 1/4 oz	1/3 cup
Pepper, white		2 tsp		1 1/4 tsp
Milk, skim #1		2 qt		1 cup
Spinach, chopped, cooked	4 lb	2 1/2 qt	8 oz	1 1/4 cups
Milk, skim #2		2qt		1 cup
Milk, skim, hot		1 1/2 gal		3 cups

Method

1. Add onions to melted margarine sauté until tender.
2. Add flour and pepper to onions. Stir until blended.
3. Add skim milk #1 to seasoned flour and stir until mixture thickens.
4. 64 portions: Set aside 2 cups chopped spinach.
   8 portions: Set aside 1/2 cup chopped spinach.
5. Puree the remaining spinach in skim milk #2. Add chopped spinach and puree spinach to cream soup.
6. Stir in hot skim milk. Heat to 170°F.
7. Hold for hot service at 140°F or higher. Serve promptly for the best quality or within 2 hours or less. If held over 2 hours, throw out.

Directions for Diet Preparations

Sodium Restricted (SR) and **Mechanical Soft** (SFT): Prepare as directed.

Low Fat/Low Cholesterol (LF): 2/3 cup and **Diabetic** (DB): 2/3 cup. Use half the amount of margarine and flour specified. Low fat diets should consider individual tolerance to onions.

Soft/Low Fiber (SLF): Omit onions and pepper.

Puree (PUR): Prepare as directed. Blenderize and strain.

Nutrient Analysis per Serving:

Regular	KCAL	PRO gm	CHO gm	FAT gm	Chol mg	SFA gm	PFA gm	VITA iu	VITC mg	THI mg	RIB mg	NIA mg	CA mg	NA mg	K+ mg	FE mg
	104	6.7	12.3	3.2	2.7	0.7	1.0	2752	4.5	0.11	0.30	0.5	232	101	399	1.3

Sodium Restricted	NA mg	Diabetic	Kcal	Milk exg	Veg exg	Fruit exg	Bread exg	Meat exg	Fat exg	Low Fat & Low Chol	FAT gm	Chol mg	SFA gm	PFA gm
	101		82.7	0.5	0.5	0.0	0.2	0.0	0.3		1.8	2.8	0.4	0.5

Cream of Tomato Soup

Portion: 2/3 cup

INGREDIENTS	64 portions, 3 gallons		8 portions, 1 1/2 quarts	
	weights	measures	weights	measures
Tomato juice		1 1/2 gal		3 cups
Onions, chopped	6 oz	1 1/8 cups	3/4 oz	2 1/4 Tbsp
Bay leaf		4 leaves		1 leaf
Margarine, low sodium, melted	10 oz	1 1/4 cups	1 1/4 oz	2 1/2 Tbsp
Flour, all-purpose	4 oz	1 cup	1/2 oz	2 Tbsp
Pepper, black		2 tsp		1/4 tsp
Milk, skim, hot		1 1/2 gal		3 cups

Method

1. Add onions and bay leaves to tomato juice. Heat to boiling point.
2. Combine margarine, flour, and pepper. Stir until blended.
3. Add milk; continue stirring. Cook until thickened.
4. Just before serving, slowly add hot tomato mixture. Stir.
5. Remove bay leaves before serving.
6. Heat to 170°F.
7. Hold for hot service at 140°F or higher. Serve promptly for the best quality or within 2 hours or less. If held over 2 hours, throw out.

Directions for Diet Preparations

Sodium Restricted (SR): Use low sodium tomato juice.

Low Fat/Low Cholesterol (LF): 2/3 cup and **Diabetic** (DB): 2/3 cup. Use margarine and flour in half the amount specified. Low fat diets should consider individual tolerance to onions.

Mechanical Soft (SFT): Prepare as directed. Consider individual tolerance.

Soft/Low Fiber (SLF): Omit onions and black pepper.

Puree (PUR): Prepare as directed. Blenderize and strain.

Nutrient Analysis per Serving:

Regular	KCAL	PRO gm	CHO gm	FAT gm	Chol mg	SFA gm	PFA gm	VITA iu	VITC mg	THI mg	RIB mg	NIA mg	CA mg	NA mg	K+ mg	FE mg
	92.5	4.0	11.6	3.8	1.7	0.7	1.2	1412	30.1	0.09	0.17	0.8	131	384	350	0.6

Sodium Restricted	NA mg	Diabetic	Kcal	Milk exg	Veg exg	Fruit exg	Bread exg	Meat exg	Fat exg	Low Fat & Low Chol	FAT gm	Chol mg	SFA gm	PFA gm
	58.7		73.6	0.5	1.0	0.0	0.0	0.0	0.25		2.1	1.7	0.4	0.6

Creole Soup

Portion: 2/3 cup

INGREDIENTS	64 portions, 3 gallons		8 portions, 1 1/2 quarts	
	weights	measures	weights	measures
Beef or vegetable stock[1]		2 1/4 gal		4 1/2 cups
Tomatoes, canned, chopped	6 1/2 lb	1 #10 can	14 oz	1 3/4 cups
Green peppers, chopped	1 lb	3 cups	2 oz	1/3 cup
Onions, chopped	10 1/2 oz	2 cups	1 1/3 oz	1/4 cup
Rice, uncooked	1 lb	2 1/4 cups	1 3/4 oz	1/4 cup
Bay leaves		4 leaves		1 leaf
Pepper, black		2 tsp		1/4 tsp

Method

1. Prepare beef or vegetable stock.
2. Add remaining ingredients to the stock. Cook until tender.
3. Remove bay leaves before serving.
4. Heat to 170°F.
5. Hold for hot service at 140°F or higher. Serve promptly for the best quality or within 2 hours or less. If held over 2 hours, throw out.

Notes

[1]May use a concentrated soup base as a quick stock. Prepare as directed by manufacturer.

Directions for Diet Preparations

Sodium Restricted (SR): Use low sodium tomatoes. May use a low sodium soup base as directed by manufacturer.

Low Fat/Low Cholesterol (LF): 2/3 cup, **Diabetic** (DB): 2/3 cup, and **Mechanical Soft** (SFT): Prepare as directed. Low fat diets should consider individual tolerance to onions.

Soft/Low Fiber (SLF): Not recommended. Use appropriate food substitute.

Puree (PUR): Prepare as directed. Blenderize and strain.

Nutrient Analysis per Serving:

Regular	KCAL	PRO gm	CHO gm	FAT gm	Chol mg	SFA gm	PFA gm	VITA iu	VITC mg	THI mg	RIB mg	NIA mg	CA mg	NA mg	K+ mg	FE mg
	56.5	2.3	9.9	1.0	0.0	0.0	0.1	324	13.9	0.07	0.06	1.5	14.9	123	126	1.2

Sodium Restricted	NA mg	Diabetic	Kcal	Milk exg	Veg exg	Fruit exg	Bread exg	Meat exg	Fat exg	Low Fat & Low Chol	FAT gm	Chol mg	SFA gm	PFA gm
	48.6		56.5	0.0	0.75	0.0	0.5	0.0	0.0		1.0	0.0	0.02	0.06

Egg Drop Soup

Portion: 2/3 cup

INGREDIENTS	64 portions, 3 gallons		8 portions, 1 1/2 quarts	
	weights	measures	weights	measures
Chicken or vegetable stock[1]		3 gal		1 1/2 qt
Green onions, diagonally sliced	2 3/4 lb EP (3 1/4 lb AP)	1 1/3 qt	6 1/3 oz EP (7 1/2 oz AP)	3/4 cup
Eggs, slightly beaten	1 lb	2 cups (8 large)	2 oz	1/4 cup (1 large)

Method

1. Prepare chicken or vegetable stock. Bring to a rolling boil.
2. Combine green onions and eggs.
3. Pour egg mixture slowly into stock, stirring constantly with a fork, until the eggs form threads.
4. Hold for hot service at 140°F or higher. Serve promptly for the best quality or within 2 hours or less. If held over 2 hours, throw out.

Notes

[1]May use a concentrated soup base as a quick stock. Prepare as directed by manufacturer.

Directions for Diet Preparations

Sodium Restricted (SR): Prepare as directed. May use a low sodium soup base as directed by manufacturer, instead of the stock.

Low Fat/Low Cholesterol (LF): 2/3 cup. Consider individual tolerance when using onions.

64 portions: Omit whole eggs, substitute with 16 large egg whites.

8 portions: Omit whole eggs, substitute with 2 large egg whites.

Diabetic (DB): 2/3 cup and **Mechanical Soft** (SFT): Prepare as directed.

Soft/Low Fiber (SLF): Omit onions.

Puree (PUR): Prepare as directed. Strain.

Nutrient Analysis per Serving:

Regular	KCAL	PRO gm	CHO gm	FAT gm	Chol mg	SFA gm	PFA gm	VITA iu	VITC mg	THI mg	RIB mg	NIA mg	CA mg	NA mg	K+ mg	FE mg
	39.3	2.6	3.2	1.8	34.1	0.2	0.1	32.5	1.6	0.03	0.07	1.2	8.3	66.1	38.3	1.0

Sodium Restricted	NA mg	Diabetic	Kcal	Milk exg	Veg exg	Fruit exg	Bread exg	Meat exg	Fat exg	Low Fat & Low Chol	FAT gm	Chol mg	SFA gm	PFA gm
	66.1		39.3	0.0	0.5	0.0	0.0	0.5	0.0		1.1	0.0	0.01	0.01

Gazpacho

Portion: 2/3 cup

INGREDIENTS	64 portions, 3 gallons		8 portions, 1 1/2 quarts	
	weights	**measures**	**weights**	**measures**
Tomatoes, fresh, finely chopped	5 3/4 lb EP (6 1/2 lb AP)	3 1/4 qt	11 1/2 oz EP (12 3/4 oz AP)	1 2/3 cups
Green peppers, finely chopped	2 lb EP (2 1/2 lb AP)	6 1/2 cups	3 3/4 oz EP (4 2/3 oz AP)	3/4 cup
Celery, finely chopped	1 3/4 lb EP (2 lb AP)	1 1/4 qt	4 oz EP (4 3/4 oz AP)	3/4 cup
Cucumbers, peeled, finely chopped	1 3/4 lb EP (2 lb AP)	1 1/2 qt	3 1/2 oz EP (4 oz AP)	3/4 cup
Onions, finely chopped	1 3/4 lb EP (2 1/2 lb AP)	6 1/2 cups	3 1/8 oz EP (4 2/3 oz AP)	3/4 cup
Chives, chopped		1/4 cup		1/2 Tbsp
Parsley, chopped		1/3 cup		1 Tbsp
Tarragon wine vinegar		2 3/4 cups		1/3 cup
Tomato juice		1 1/4 gal		2 1/2 cups
Garlic powder		1 Tbsp		1/2 tsp

Method

1. Combine all ingredients. Mix thoroughly.
2. If too thick, add tomato juice.
3. Blenderize for 2 to 5 seconds to obtain desired consistency.
4. Cover and chill.
5. Serve chilled.

Directions for Diet Preparations

Sodium Restricted (SR): Use low sodium tomato juice.
Low Fat/Low Cholesterol (LF): 2/3 cup and **Diabetic** (DB): 2/3 cup. Prepare as directed. Low fat diets should consider individual tolerance to onions and garlic.
Mechanical Soft (SFT) and **Puree** (PUR): Prepare as directed. Blenderize and strain.
Soft/Low Fiber (SLF): Not recommended.

Nutrient Analysis per Serving:

Regular	KCAL	PRO gm	CHO gm	FAT gm	Chol mg	SFA gm	PFA gm	VITA iu	VITC mg	THI mg	RIB mg	NIA mg	CA mg	NA mg	K+ mg	FE mg
	35.2	1.2	8.3	0.2	0.0	0.04	0.1	1476	44.7	0.08	0.05	0.9	22.1	298	335	0.8

Sodium Restricted	NA mg	Diabetic	Kcal	Milk exg	Veg exg	Fruit exg	Bread exg	Meat exg	Fat exg	Low Fat & Low Chol	FAT gm	Chol mg	SFA gm	PFA gm
	20.8		35.2	0.0	1.2	0.0	0.0	0.0	0.0		0.2	0.0	0.04	0.1

Onion Soup

Portion: 2/3 cup

Ingredients	64 portions, 3 gallons		8 portions, 1 1/2 quarts	
	weights	measures	weights	measures
Beef or vegetable stock[1]		2 1/2 gal		1 1/4 qt
Onions, thinly sliced	6 1/2 lb EP	1 1/2 gal	1 lb EP	3 cups
Margarine, low sodium	8 oz	1 cup	1 oz	2 Tbsp
Flour, all-purpose	2 oz	1/2 cup	1/4 oz	1 Tbsp
Worcestershire sauce	1 1/2 oz	3 Tbsp	1/8 oz	1 1/8 tsp
Pepper, black		2 tsp		1/4 tsp

Method

1. Prepare beef or vegetable stock. Bring to a boil.
2. Sauté onions in margarine.
3. Blend flour with onions and margarine.
4. Add worcestershire sauce and pepper to flour and onions. Add to stock. Cook until onions are tender.
5. Heat to 170°F serving.
6. Hold for hot service at 140°F or higher. Serve promptly for the best quality or within 2 hours or less. If held over 2 hours, throw out.

Notes

[1]May use a concentrated soup base as a quick stock. Prepare as directed by manufacturer.

Directions for Diet Preparations

Sodium Restricted (SR): Prepare as directed. May use a low sodium soup base as directed by manufacturer, instead of the stock.

Low Fat/Low Cholesterol (LF): 2/3 cup. and **Diabetic** (DB): 2/3 cup. Use half the amount of margarine and flour specified. Low fat diets should consider individual tolerance to onions.

Mechanical Soft (SFT): Prepare as directed.

Soft/Low Fiber (SLF): Not recommended. Use appropriate food alternative.

Puree (PUR): Blenderize and strain.

Nutrient Analysis per Serving:

Regular	KCAL	PRO gm	CHO gm	FAT gm	Chol mg	SFA gm	PFA gm	VITA iu	VITC mg	THI mg	RIB mg	NIA mg	CA mg	NA mg	K+ mg	FE mg
	69.0	2.2	6.7	3.9	0.0	0.5	1.0	119	6.4	0.06	0.06	1.1	17.1	56.7	102	1.0

Sodium Restricted	NA mg	Diabetic	Kcal	Milk exg	Veg exg	Fruit exg	Bread exg	Meat exg	Fat exg	Low Fat & Low Chol	FAT gm	Chol mg	SFA gm	PFA gm
	56.7		54.6	0.0	1.0	0.0	0.2	0.0	0.25		2.5	0.0	0.2	0.5

Portion: 2/3 cup

INGREDIENTS	64 portions, 3 gallons		8 portions, 1 1/2 quarts	
	weights	measures	weights	measures
Beef or vegetable stock[1]		2 1/2 gal		1 1/4 qt
Onions, thinly sliced	6 1/2 lb EP	1 1/2 gal	1 lb EP	3 cups
Margarine, low sodium	8 oz	1 cup	1 oz	2 Tbsp
Flour, all-purpose	2 oz	1/2 cup	1/4 oz	1 Tbsp
Worcestershire sauce	1 1/2 oz	3 Tbsp	1/8 oz	1 1/8 tsp
Pepper, black		2 tsp		1/4 tsp
Bread, toasted, quartered	1 lb	16 slices	2 oz	2 slices
Parmesan cheese, grated	6 oz	1 1/3 cup	3/4 oz	3 Tbsp

Method

1. Prepare beef or vegetable stock. Bring to a boil.
2. Sauté onions in margarine.
3. Blend flour with onions and margarine.
4. Add worcestershire sauce and pepper to flour and onions. Add to stock. Cook until onions are tender.
5. To serve, pour over toasted bread quarter and sprinkle with 1 tsp parmesan cheese.
6. Hold for hot service at 140°F or higher. Serve promptly for the best quality or within 2 hours or less. If held over 2 hours, throw out.

Notes

[1]May use a concentrated soup base as a quick stock. Prepare as directed by manufacturer.

Directions for Diet Preparations

Sodium Restricted (SR): Use low sodium bread. May use a low sodium soup base as directed by manufacturer, instead of the stock. May use parmesan cheese if able to calculate into daily meal plan.

Low Fat/Low Cholesterol (LF): 2/3 cup. and **Diabetic** (DB): 2/3 cup. Use half the amount of margarine and flour specified. May use parmesan cheese if able to calculate into daily meal plan. Low fat diets should consider individual tolerance to onions.

Mechanical Soft (SFT): Prepare as directed.

Soft/Low Fiber (SLF): Not recommended. Use appropriate food alternative.

Puree (PUR): Omit toasted bread quarters. Blenderize and strain.

Nutrient Analysis per Serving:

Regular	KCAL	PRO	CHO	FAT	Chol	SFA	PFA	VITA	VITC	THI	RIB	NIA	CA	NA	K+	FE
		gm	gm	gm	mg	gm	gm	iu	mg	mg	mg	mg	mg	mg	mg	mg
	98.2	3.6	10.9	4.6	1.5	0.9	1.0	130	6.3	0.08	0.08	1.3	44.0	127	111	1.2

Sodium	NA	Diabetic	Kcal	Milk	Veg	Fruit	Bread	Meat	Fat	Low Fat &	FAT	Chol	SFA	PFA
Restricted	mg			exg	exg	exg	exg	exg	exg	Low Chol	gm	mg	gm	gm
	86.0		72.7	0.0	0.75	0.0	0.5	0.0	0.3		3.1	1.3	0.6	0.5

Portion: 2/3 cup

INGREDIENTS	64 portions, 3 gallons		8 portions, 1 1/2 quarts	
	weights	measures	weights	measures
Beef or vegetable stock[1]		3 gal		1 1/2 qt
Carrots, julienne cut	1 1/3 lb EP (2 lb AP)	1 qt	2 2/3 oz EP (4 oz AP)	1/2 cup
Green beans, cut	1 1/3 lb EP (1 1/2 lb AP)	1 qt	2 2/3 oz EP (3 oz AP)	1/2 cup
Celery, julienne cut	1 lb EP (1 1/4 lb AP)	3 cups	2 oz EP (2 1/2 oz AP)	1/3 cup
Onions, chopped	4 oz	3/4 cup	1/2 oz	1 1/2 Tbsp
Pepper, black		2 tsp		1/4 tsp
Garlic powder		2 tsp		1/4 tsp
Basil, ground		2 tsp		1/4 tsp

Method

1. Prepare beef or vegetable stock. Bring to a boil.
2. Add vegetables and pepper to the stock. Cook until vegetables are tender, about one hour[2].
3. Heat to 170°F.
4. Hold for hot service at 140°F or higher. Serve promptly for the best quality or within two hours or less. If held over two hours, throw out.

Notes

[1]May use a concentrated soup base as a quick stock. Prepare as directed by manufacturer.
[2]Cooking time will be reduced when using canned or frozen vegetables.

Directions for Diet Preparations

Sodium Restricted (SR): Prepare as directed. May use a low sodium soup base as directed by manufacturer, instead of the stock.
Low Fat/Low Cholesterol (LF): 2/3 cup and **Diabetic** (DB): 2/3 cup. Prepare as directed. Low fat diets should consider individual tolerance to onions and garlic.
Mechanical Soft (SFT): Prepare as directed.
Soft/Low Fiber (SLF): Omit celery, onions, pepper, and garlic.
Puree (PUR): Prepare as directed. Blenderize and strain.

Nutrient Analysis per Serving:

Regular	KCAL	PRO gm	CHO gm	FAT gm	Chol mg	SFA gm	PFA gm	VITA iu	VITC mg	THI mg	RIB mg	NIA mg	CA mg	NA mg	K+ mg	FE mg
	30.5	2.0	3.4	1.1	0.0	0.01	0.02	2024	1.9	0.03	0.07	1.2	9.2	64.8	67.7	1.0

Sodium Restricted	NA mg	Diabetic	Kcal	Milk exg	Veg exg	Fruit exg	Bread exg	Meat exg	Fat exg	Low Fat & Low Chol	FAT gm	Chol mg	SFA gm	PFA gm
	64.8		30.5	0.0	1.0	0.0	0.0	0.0	0.05		1.1	0.0	0.01	0.02

Minestrone Soup

Portion: 2/3 cup

INGREDIENTS	64 portions, 3 gallons		8 portions, 1 1/2 quarts	
	weights	measures	weights	measures
Margarine, melted, low sodium	4 oz	1/2 cup	1/2 oz	1 Tbsp
Onions, chopped	12 oz	2 1/4 cups	1 1/2 oz	4 1/2 Tbsp
Beef or vegetable stock[1]		2 gal		1 qt
Bay leaves		4 leaves		1 leaf
Pepper, black		2 tsp		1/4 tsp
Garlic powder		2 tsp		1/4 tsp
Carrots, diced	1 lb	3 cups	2 oz	1/3 cup
Potatoes, raw, chopped	12 oz	2 cups	1 1/2 oz	1/4 cup
Celery, chopped	12 oz	2 cups	1 1/2 oz	1/4 cup
Green beans, cut, canned	1 lb	3 cups	2 oz	1/3 cup
Spinach, chopped	8 oz	1 cup	1 oz	2 Tbsp
Macaroni, uncooked, AP	8 oz	2 cups	1 oz	1/4 cup
Tomatoes, crushed, canned	3 lb	1 1/2 qt	6 oz	3/4 cup
Kidney beans, canned, drained	1 1/3 lb	1 qt	2 2/3 oz	1/2 cup

Method

1. Sauté onions in margarine until tender. Place in large kettle.
2. Prepare beef or vegetable stock.
3. Add stock, bay leaves, pepper, and garlic to onions. Bring to boil.
4. Add vegetables, macaroni, tomatoes, and beans. Simmer 45 minutes.
5. Remove bay leaves before serving.
6. Heat to 170°F.
7. Hold for hot service at 140°F or higher. Serve promptly for the best quality or within 2 hours or less. If held over 2 hours, throw out.

Directions for Diet Preparations

Sodium Restricted (SR): Use low sodium tomatoes. Drain and rinse kidney beans. May use a low sodium soup base as directed by manufacturer, instead of the stock.

Low Fat/Low Cholesterol (LF): 2/3 cup, **Diabetic** (DB): 2/3 cup, and **Mechanical Soft** (SFT): Prepare as directed. Low fat diets should consider individual tolerance to onions and garlic.

Soft/Low Fiber (SLF): Not recommended. Use appropriate food substitute.

Puree (PUR): Prepare as directed. Blenderize and strain.

Notes

[1]May use a concentrated soup base as a quick stock. Prepare as directed by manufacturer.

Nutrient Analysis per Serving:

Regular	KCAL	PRO gm	CHO gm	FAT gm	Chol mg	SFA gm	PFA gm	VITA iu	VITC mg	THI mg	RIB mg	NIA mg	CA mg	NA mg	K+ mg	FE mg
	72.5	3.1	10.5	2.3	0.0	0.2	0.5	1942	5.9	0.09	0.09	1.4	25.8	165	188	1.2

Sodium Restricted	NA mg	Diabetic	Kcal	Milk exg	Veg exg	Fruit exg	Bread exg	Meat exg	Fat exg	Low Fat & Low Chol	FAT gm	Chol mg	SFA gm	PFA gm
	107		72.5	0.0	0.5	0.0	0.5	0.0	0.5		2.3	0.0	0.2	0.5

Mushroom Barley Soup

Portion: 2/3 cup

Ingredients	64 portions, 3 gallons		8 portions, 1 1/2 quarts	
	weights	measures	weights	measures
Barley, uncooked, AP	1 1/4 lb	2 1/2 cups	2 1/2 oz	1/3 cup
Water, boiling		to cover		to cover
Chicken or vegetable stock[1]		2 1/2 gal		1 1/2 qt
Onions, chopped	6 1/2 oz	1 cup	3/4 oz	2 1/2 Tbsp
Carrots, diced	10 1/2 oz	1 1/2 cups	1 1/3 oz	1/4 cup
Mushrooms, sliced, canned	2 1/2 lb	1 qt	6 oz	3/4 cup
Margarine, melted, low sodium	2 1/2 oz	1/3 cup	1/3 oz	1 Tbsp
Pepper, black		2 tsp		1/4 tsp

Method

1. Cook barley in boiling water until tender, about 50 to 60 minutes. Drain.
2. Prepare stock. Bring to a boil.
3. Add onions and carrots to stock. Reduce heat and simmer until the vegetables are just tender.
4. Sauté mushrooms briefly in margarine, without letting them brown.
5. Add mushrooms, barley, and pepper to stock.
6. Simmer about 5 minutes. Degrease soup.
7. Heat to 170°F.
8. Hold for hot service at 140°F or higher. Serve promptly for the best quality or within 2 hours or less. If held over 2 hours, throw out.

Directions for Diet Preparations

Sodium Restricted (SR): Use fresh or low sodium canned mushrooms. May use a low sodium soup base as directed by manufacturer, instead of the stock.

Low Fat/Low Cholesterol (LF): 2/3 cup, **Diabetic** (DB): 2/3 cup, and **Mechanical Soft** (SFT): Prepare as directed. Low fat diets should consider individual tolerance to onions.

Soft/Low Fiber (SLF): Omit onions and black pepper.

Puree (PUR): Prepare as directed. Blenderize and strain.

Notes

[1]May use a concentrated soup base as a quick stock. Prepare as directed by manufacturer.

Nutrient Analysis per Serving:

Regular	KCAL	PRO gm	CHO gm	FAT gm	Chol mg	SFA gm	PFA gm	VITA iu	VITC mg	THI mg	RIB mg	NIA mg	CA mg	NA mg	K+ mg	FE mg
	69.2	2.8	9.4	2.5	0.0	0.2	0.4	991	0.5	0.04	0.07	1.7	4.9	93.3	46.1	1.2

Sodium Restricted	NA mg	Diabetic	Kcal	Milk exg	Veg exg	Fruit exg	Bread exg	Meat exg	Fat exg	Low Fat & Low Chol	FAT gm	Chol mg	SFA gm	PFA gm
	39.7		69.2	0.0	0.5	0.0	0.5	0.0	0.5		2.5	0.0	0.2	0.4

Portion: 2/3 cup

INGREDIENTS	64 portions, 3 gallons		8 portions, 1 1/2 quarts	
	weights	measures	weights	measures
Split peas	3 lb	1 3/4 qt	6 3/4 oz	1 cup
Water		2 gal		1 qt
Ham cubes	1 1/2 lb	4 1/2 cups	2 2/3 oz	1/2 cup
Onions, chopped	5 1/3 oz	1 cup	3/4 oz	2 Tbsp
Carrots, grated	1 lb	3 cups	2 oz	1/3 cup
Potatoes, raw, chopped	1 1/2 lb	4 1/8 cups	3 oz	1/2 cup
Margarine, low sodium	4 oz	1/2 cup	1/2 oz	1 Tbsp
Flour, all-purpose	2 oz	1/2 cup	1/4 oz	1 Tbsp
Chicken or vegetable stock[1]		2 qt		1 cup
Pepper, black		2 tsp		1/4 tsp

Method

1. Wash peas. Add water and bring to a boil for 2 minutes. Turn off heat. Cover and let stand for about 2 hours.
2. Add ham, onions, carrots, and potatoes. Simmer for 1 1/2 hours or until peas are soft.
3. Melt margarine and add flour. Stir until smooth. Cook 5 minutes.
4. Add margarine and flour to stock. Stir and cook until thickened. Add to peas.[2]
5. Season with black pepper.
6. Hold for hot service at 140°F or higher. Serve promptly for the best quality or within 2 hours or less. If held over 2 hours, throw out.

Directions for Diet Preparations

Sodium Restricted (SR): Omit ham. Use a low sodium stock.

Low Fat/Low Cholesterol (LF): 2/3 cup and **Diabetic** (DB): 2/3 cup. Omit ham. Substitute reduced calorie margarine for regular margarine in equal amounts. Low fat diets should consider individual tolerance to onions.

Mechanical Soft (SFT): Prepare as directed.

Soft/Low Fiber (SLF): Not recommended. Use appropriate food substitute.

Puree (PUR): Prepare as directed. Blenderize and strain.

Vegetarian: Omit ham. Use a vegetable stock.

Notes

[1]May use a concentrated soup base as a quick stock. Prepare as directed by manufacturer.

[2]If soup becomes too thick, add hot water to obtain desired consistency. If a smoother soup is preferred, cook and puree peas before adding to ham and vegetables.

Nutrient Analysis per Serving:

Regular	KCAL	PRO gm	CHO gm	FAT gm	Chol mg	SFA gm	PFA gm	VITA iu	VITC mg	THI mg	RIB mg	NIA mg	CA mg	NA mg	K+ mg	FE mg
	130	7.5	16.6	3.9	5.2	0.9	0.8	1560	2.0	0.2	0.08	1.3	16.1	160	295	1.3

Sodium Restricted	NA mg	Diabetic	Kcal	Milk exg	Veg exg	Fruit exg	Bread exg	Meat exg	Fat exg	Low Fat& Low Chol	FAT gm	Chol mg	SFA gm	PFA gm
	15.6		97.7	0.0	0.5	0.0	1.0	0.0	0.25		1.1	0.0	0.2	0.4

Tomato Soup

Portion: 2/3 cup

INGREDIENTS	64 portions, 3 gallons		8 portions, 1 1/2 quarts	
	weights	measures	weights	measures
Beef, chicken, or vegetable stock[1]		2 gal		1 qt
Tomato puree	8 lb	1 gal	1 lb	2 cups
Onions, chopped	2 2/3 oz	1/2 cup	1/3 oz	1 Tbsp
Green pepper, chopped	5 1/3 oz	1 cup	3/4 oz	2 Tbsp
Margarine, low sodium, melted	6 oz	3/4 cup	3/4 oz	1 1/2 Tbsp
Flour, all-purpose	3 oz	3/4 cup	1/2 oz	1 1/2 Tbsp

Method

1. Prepare stock.
2. Add tomato puree to stock. Bring to a boil.
3. Add onions and green peppers. Cook until tender.
4. Combine margarine and flour. Mix until smooth. Add to soup, while stirring.
5. Heat to 170°F.
6. Hold for hot service at 140°F or higher. Serve promptly for the best quality or within 2 hours or less. If held over 2 hours, throw out.

Notes

[1]May use a concentrated soup base as a quick stock. Prepare as directed by manufacturer.

Directions for Diet Preparations

Sodium Restricted (SR): Prepare as directed. May use a low sodium soup base as per manufacturer's directions.
Low Fat/Low Cholesterol (LF): 2/3 cup and **Diabetic** (DB): 2/3 cup. Use half the amount of margarine and flour specified. Low fat diets should consider individual tolerance to onions.
Mechanical Soft (SFT): Prepare as directed.
Soft/Low Fiber (SLF): Omit onions.
Puree (PUR): Prepare as directed. Blenderize and strain.

Nutrient Analysis per Serving:

Regular	KCAL	PRO gm	CHO gm	FAT gm	Chol mg	SFA gm	PFA gm	VITA iu	VITC mg	THI mg	RIB mg	NIA mg	CA mg	NA mg	K+ mg	FE mg
	66.0	2.4	8.7	2.9	0.0	0.3	0.7	958	24.4	0.07	0.08	1.9	10.8	51.5	273	1.2

Sodium Restricted	NA mg	Diabetic	Kcal	Milk exg	Veg exg	Fruit exg	Bread exg	Meat exg	Fat exg	Low Fat& Low Chol	FAT gm	Chol mg	SFA gm	PFA gm
	51.5		56.1	0.0	1.0	0.0	0.4	0.0	0.0		1.9	0.0	0.2	0.4

Portion: 2/3 cup

INGREDIENTS	64 portions, 3 gallons		8 portions, 1 1/2 quarts	
	weights	measures	weights	measures
Beef, chicken, or vegetable stock[1]		2 gal		1 qt
Tomato puree	8 lb	1 gal	1 lb	2 cups
Onions, chopped	2 2/3 oz	1/2 cup	1/3 oz	1 Tbsp
Green pepper, chopped	5 1/3 oz	1 cup	3/4 oz	2 Tbsp
Rice, uncooked	2 lb	1 1/8 qt	3 1/2 oz	1/2 cup
Margarine, low sodium, melted	6 oz	3/4 cup	3/4 oz	1 1/2 Tbsp
Flour, all-purpose	3 oz	3/4 cup	1/2 oz	1 1/2 Tbsp

Method

1. Prepare stock.
2. Add tomato puree to stock. Bring to a boil.
3. Add onions, green peppers, and rice. Cook until tender.
4. Combine margarine and flour. Mix until smooth. Add to soup, while stirring.
5. Heat to 170°F.
6. Hold for hot service at 140°F or higher. Serve promptly for the best quality or within 2 hours or less. If held over 2 hours, throw out.

Directions for Diet Preparations

Sodium Restricted (SR): Prepare as directed. May use a low sodium soup base as per manufacturer's directions.

Low Fat/Low Cholesterol (LF): 2/3 cup and **Diabetic** (DB): 2/3 cup. Use half the amount of margarine and flour specified. Low fat diets should consider individual tolerance to onions.

Mechanical Soft (SFT): Prepare as directed.

Soft/Low Fiber (SLF): Omit onions.

Puree (PUR): Prepare as directed. Blend and strain.

Notes

[1]May use a concentrated soup base as a quick stock. Prepare as directed by manufacturer.

Nutrient Analysis per Serving:

Regular	KCAL	PRO gm	CHO gm	FAT gm	Chol mg	SFA gm	PFA gm	VITA iu	VITC mg	THI mg	RIB mg	NIA mg	CA mg	NA mg	K+ mg	FE mg
	119	3.4	20.4	3.0	0.0	0.3	0.7	958	24.4	0.12	0.08	2.4	11.5	51.6	273	1.6

Sodium Restricted	NA mg	Diabetic	Kcal exg	Milk exg	Veg exg	Fruit exg	Bread exg	Meat exg	Fat	Low Fat & Low Chol	FAT gm	Chol mg	SFA gm	PFA gm
	51.6		109	0.0	1.0	0.0	1.0	0.0	0.2		1.9	0.0	0.2	0.4

Vegetable Beef Soup

Portion: 2/3 cup

Ingredients	64 portions, 3 gallons		8 portions, 1 1/2 quarts	
	weights	measures	weights	measures
Beef stock[1]		3 gal		1 1/2 qt
Carrots, diced	2 lb	1 1/2 qt	4 oz	3/4 cup
Celery, chopped	2 lb	1 1/2 qt	4 oz	3/4 cup
Onions, chopped	1 lb	3 cups	2 oz	1/3 cup
Pepper, black		2 tsp		1/4 tsp
Beef, cooked, chopped	1 lb	3 cups	2 oz	1/3 cup

Method

1. Prepare stock. Bring to boil.
2. Add vegetables and seasoning to beef stock. Cover and simmer about 1 hour. Replace water as necessary.
3. Add meat.
4. Heat to 170°F.
5. Hold for hot service at 140°F or higher. Serve promptly for the best quality or within 2 hours or less. If held over 2 hours, throw out.

Notes

[1]May use a concentrated soup base as a quick stock. Prepare as directed by manufacturer.

Directions for Diet Preparations

Sodium Restricted (SR): Prepare as directed. May use a low sodium soup base as per manufacturer's directions.
Low Fat/Low Cholesterol (LF): 2/3 cup, **Diabetic** (DB): 2/3 cup, and **Mechanical Soft** (SFT): Prepare as directed. Low fat diet should consider individual tolerance when using onions.
Soft/Low Fiber (SLF): Omit onions and black pepper.
Puree (PUR): Prepare as directed. Blend and strain

Nutrient Analysis per Serving:

Regular	KCAL	PRO gm	CHO gm	FAT gm	Chol mg	SFA gm	PFA gm	VITA iu	VITC mg	THI mg	RIB mg	NIA mg	CA mg	NA mg	K+ mg	FE mg
	51.8	3.9	3.7	2.5	6.3	0.5	0.07	2952	2.3	0.04	0.08	1.5	9.7	75.3	103	1.1

Sodium Restricted	NA mg	Diabetic	Kcal exg	Milk exg	Veg exg	Fruit exg	Bread exg	Meat exg	Fat	Low Fat & Low Chol	FAT gm	Chol mg	SFA gm	PFA gm
	75.3		51.8	0.0	1.0	0.0	0.0	0.5	0.0		2.5	6.3	0.5	0.07

Chunky Vegetable Soup

Portion: 2/3 cup

INGREDIENTS	64 portions, 3 gallons		8 portions, 1 1/2 quarts	
	weights	measures	weights	measures
Beef, chicken, or vegetable stock[1]		2 1/2 gal		1 1/2 qt
Carrots, chopped	1 lb	3 cups	2 oz	1/3 cup
Celery, chopped	1 lb	3 cups	2 oz	1/3 cup
Onions, diced	1 lb	3 cups	2 oz	1/3 cup
Potatoes, cubed	1 lb	2 3/4 cups	2 oz	1/3 cup
Green peas, frozen	1 lb	3 cups	2 oz	1/3 cup
Corn, frozen	1 lb	3 cups	2 oz	1/3 cup
Tomatoes, diced, canned	1 1/2 lb	3 1/3 cups	3 2/3 oz	1/2 cup

Method

1. Prepare stock. Bring to a boil.
2. Add celery, carrots, onions, and potatoes. Cover. Simmer about 1 hour. Replace water as necessary.
3. Add peas and corn to soup. Stir to blend. Cook until tender.
4. Add tomatoes.
5. Heat to 170°F.
6. Hold for hot service at 140°F or higher. Serve promptly for the best quality or within 2 hours or less. If held over 2 hours, throw out.

Directions for Diet Preparations

Sodium Restricted (SR): Use fresh tomatoes; crush. May use a low sodium soup base as per manufacturer's directions.

Low Fat/Low Cholesterol (LF): 2/3 cup, **Diabetic** (DB): 2/3 cup, **Mechanical Soft** (SFT): Prepare as directed. Low fat diet should consider individual tolerance to onions.

Soft/Low Fiber (SLF): Not recommended. Use appropriate food substitute.

Puree (PUR): Prepare as directed. Blenderize and strain.

Notes

[1]May use a concentrated soup base as a quick stock. Prepare as directed by manufacturer.

Nutrient Analysis per Serving:

Regular	KCAL	PRO gm	CHO gm	FAT gm	Chol mg	SFA gm	PFA gm	VITA iu	VITC mg	THI mg	RIB mg	NIA mg	CA mg	NA mg	K+ mg	FE mg
	54.1	2.7	9.3	1.1	0.0	0.03	0.07	6048	7.8	0.08	0.08	1.6	21.2	104	215	1.1

Sodium Restricted	NA mg	Diabetic	Kcal exg	Milk exg	Veg exg	Fruit exg	Bread exg	Meat exg	Fat	Low Fat & Low Chol	FAT gm	Chol mg	SFA gm	PFA gm
	83.8		54.1	0.0	1.0	0.0	0.3	0.0	0.0		1.1	0.0	0.03	0.07

French Vegetable Soup

Portion: 2/3 cup

INGREDIENTS	64 portions, 3 gallons		8 portions, 1 1/2 quarts	
	weights	measures	weights	measures
Carrots, sliced, fresh	1 lb EP (1 1/2 lb AP)	3 cups	2 oz EP (3 oz AP)	1/3 cup
Onions, shredded, fresh	1 lb EP (1 1/4 lb AP)	3 cups	2 oz EP (2 1/2 oz AP)	1/3 cup
Cabbage, shredded, fresh	12 oz EP (1 lb AP)	3 cups	1 1/2 oz EP (2 oz AP)	1/3 cup
Tomatoes, canned, diced with juice	1 1/2 lb	3 cups	3 oz	1/3 cup
Green beans, cut, canned	10 2/3 oz	2 cups	1 1/3 oz	1/4 cup
Potatoes, peeled, diced	12 oz EP (1 lb AP)	2 cups	1 1/2 oz EP (2 oz AP)	1/4 cup
Water		2 qt		1 cup
Beef, chicken, or vegetable stock[1]		2 1/2 gal		1 1/4 qt
Thyme, ground		1 Tbsp		1 tsp

Method

1. Combine all vegetables with water and cook in steamer until tender.
2. Prepare stock. Add stock and thyme to vegetables.
3. Simmer about 20 minutes.
4. Hold for hot service at 140°F or higher. Serve promptly for the best quality or within 2 hours or less. If held over 2 hours, throw out.

Notes

[1]May use a concentrated soup base as a quick stock. Prepare as directed by manufacturer.

Directions for Diet Preparations

Sodium Restricted (SR): Use fresh tomatoes; dice. May use a low sodium soup base as per manufacturer's directions.

Low Fat/Low Cholesterol (LF): 2/3 cup, **Diabetic** (DB): 2/3 cup, and **Mechanical Soft** (SFT): Prepare as directed. Low fat diet should consider individual tolerance when using onions and cabbage.

Soft/Low Fiber (SLF): Not recommended. Use appropriate food alternative.

Puree (PUR): Prepare as directed. Blenderize and strain.

Nutrient Analysis per Serving:

Regular	KCAL	PRO gm	CHO gm	FAT gm	Chol mg	SFA gm	PFA gm	VITA iu	VITC mg	THI mg	RIB mg	NIA mg	CA mg	NA mg	K+ mg	FE mg
	34.2	1.9	4.9	1.0	0.0	0.01	0.03	1566	5.9	0.04	0.06	1.2	13.0	81.2	95.8	0.9

Sodium Restricted	NA mg	Diabetic	Kcal exg	Milk exg	Veg exg	Fruit exg	Bread exg	Meat exg	Fat	Low Fat & Low Chol	FAT gm	Chol mg	SFA gm	PFA gm
	50.8		34.2	0.0	1.0	0.0	0.1	0.0	0.0		1.0	0.0	0.01	0.03

Portion: 2/3 cup

INGREDIENTS	64 portions, 3 gallons		8 portions, 1 1/2 quarts	
	weights	measures	weights	measures
Beef or vegetable stock[1]		2 1/2 gal		1 1/4 qt
Carrots, diced	1 lb EP (1 1/2 lb AP)	3 cups	2 oz EP (3 oz AP)	1/3 cup
Onions, chopped	12 oz EP (1 lb AP)	2 1/4 cups	1 1/2 oz EP (2 oz AP)	1/4 cup
Celery, sliced	8 oz EP (10 oz AP)	1 1/2 cups	1 oz EP (1 1/4 oz AP)	3 Tbsp
Potatoes, cubed	1 1/4 lb EP (1 3/4 lb AP)	3 1/2 cups	2 3/4 oz EP (4 oz AP)	1/2 cup
Tomatoes, canned, diced with juice	6 1/4 lb	3 1/8 qt	12 1/2 oz	1 1/2 cups
Pepper, black		2 tsp		1/4 tsp
Beef, cubed, cooked	1 1/2 lb	4 1/2 cups	2 2/3 oz	1/2 cup

Method

1. Prepare stock. Bring to a boil.
2. Add vegetables, pepper, and beef to stock. Cover and simmer until vegetables are tender, begin checking after 20 minutes.
3. Hold for hot service at 140°F or higher. Serve promptly for the best quality or within 2 hours or less. If held over 2 hours, throw out.

Notes

[1]May use a concentrated soup base as a quick stock. Prepare as directed by manufacturer.

Directions for Diet Preparations

Sodium Restricted (SR): Use fresh tomatoes; dice. May use a low sodium soup base as directed by manufacturer, instead of the stock.

Low Fat/Low Cholesterol (LF): 2/3 cup, **Diabetic** (DB): 2/3 cup, and **Mechanical Soft** (SFT): Prepare as directed. Low fat diets should consider individual tolerance when using onions.

Soft/Low Fiber (SLF): Omit onions and black pepper.

Puree (PUR): Prepare as directed. Blenderize and strain.

Vegetarian: Use vegetable stock. Omit beef.

Nutrient Analysis per Serving:

Regular	KCAL	PRO gm	CHO gm	FAT gm	Chol mg	SFA gm	PFA gm	VITA iu	VITC mg	THI mg	RIB mg	NIA mg	CA mg	NA mg	K+ mg	FE mg
	73.7	4.8	7.4	3.0	8.9	0.7	0.1	1772	9.4	0.07	0.09	1.8	18.8	170	230	1.2

Sodium Restricted	NA mg	Diabetic	Kcal exg	Milk exg	Veg exg	Fruit exg	Bread exg	Meat exg	Fat	Low Fat & Low Chol	FAT gm	Chol mg	SFA gm	PFA gm
	60.3		73.7	0.0	1.0	0.0	0.0	0.75	0.1		3.0	8.9	0.7	0.1

Vegetable Chowder

Portion: 2/3 cup

INGREDIENTS	64 portions, 3 gallons		8 portions, 1 1/2 quarts	
	weights	measures	weights	measures
Potatoes, diced	2 lb EP (2 1/2 lb AP)	1 1/3 qt	4 2/3 oz EP (5 3/4 oz AP)	3/4 cup
Carrots, diced	1 lb EP (1 1/2 lb AP)	3 cups	2 oz EP (3 oz AP)	1/3 cup
Margarine, low sodium, melted	8 oz	1 cup	1 oz	2 Tbsp
Onions, finely chopped	4 oz	3/4 cup	1/2 oz	1 1/2 Tbsp
Celery, chopped	5 1/3 oz	1 cup	3/4 oz	2 Tbsp
Green peppers, chopped	5 1/3 oz	1 cup	3/4 oz	2 Tbsp
Flour, all-purpose	12 oz	3 cups	1 1/2 oz	1/3 cup
Chicken or vegetable stock[1]		1 1/2 gal		3 cups
Corn, whole kernel, canned or frozen	3 lb	2 1/4 qt	6 oz	1 1/8 cups
Milk, skim		2 1/2 qt		1 1/4 cups

Method

1. Cook potatoes. Drain. Use promptly or refrigerate.
2. Cook carrots. Drain.
3. Sauté[1] onions, celery, and green peppers in margarine until tender.
4. Add flour to onion mixture. Stir until well blended. Cook for 5 minutes.
5. Add stock, while stirring constantly. Cook until mixture thickens.
6. Add corn, potatoes, and carrots. Heat until hot.
7. Stir milk into chowder.
8. Heat to 170°F.
9. Hold for hot service at 140°F or higher. Serve promptly for the best quality or within 2 hours or less. If held over 2 hours, throw out.

Notes

[1]May use a concentrated soup base as a quick stock. Prepare as directed by manufacturer.

Directions for Diet Preparations

Sodium Restricted (SR): Prepare as directed. May use a low sodium soup base as per manufacturer's directions.

Low Fat/Low Cholesterol (LF): 2/3 cup and **Diabetic** (DB): 2/3 cup. Use half the amount of margarine and flour specified. Low fat diets should consider individual tolerance to onions and corn.

Mechanical Soft (SFT): Prepare as directed. Consider individual tolerance.

Soft/Low Fiber (SLF): Omit onions and corn. Strain.

Puree (PUR): Prepare as directed. Blenderize and strain.

Nutrient Analysis per Serving:

Regular	KCAL	PRO gm	CHO gm	FAT gm	Chol mg	SFA gm	PFA gm	VITA iu	VITC mg	THI mg	RIB mg	NIA mg	CA mg	NA mg	K+ mg	FE mg
	108.3	3.8	15.9	3.7	0.6	0.5	1.1	2072	4.9	0.11	0.13	1.4	55.1	57.6	205	0.9

Sodium Restricted	NA mg	Diabetic	Kcal exg	Milk exg	Veg exg	Fruit exg	Bread exg	Meat exg	Fat	Low Fat & Low Chol		FAT gm	Chol mg	SFA gm	PFA gm
	57.6		85.2	0.2	0.5	0.0	0.75	0.0	0.0			2.2	0.6	0.3	0.6

Beef, Veal, Pork, Lamb, and Variety Meats

D1	Beef Teriyaki

Portion: 3 1/2 ounces cooked (3 ounces edible protein)

INGREDIENTS	50 portions		6 portions	
	weights	measures	weights	measures
Ground beef, lean	12 lb	1 1/2 gal	1 1/2 lb	3 cups
Bread crumbs, dry	8 oz	2 cups	1 oz	1/4 cup
Eggs, beaten	1 lb	2 cups (8 large)	2 oz	1/4 cup (1 large)
Onions, diced	5 1/3 oz	1 cup	3/4 oz	2 Tbsp
Pepper, white		1 tsp		1/8 tsp
Teriyaki Sauce:				
Beef stock[1], low sodium	1 lb	2 cups	2 oz	1/4 cup
Soy sauce	12 oz	1 1/2 cups	1 1/2 oz	3 Tbsp
Pineapple juice, unsweetened	8 oz	1 cup	1 oz	2 Tbsp
Garlic powder		1 Tbsp		1/4 tsp
Ginger, ground		1/2 tsp		pinch

Method

1. Combine beef, bread crumbs, eggs, onions, and pepper. Mix well.
2. Using a No. 8 dipper form into oval shapes.
3. Prepare beef stock.
4. Prepare Teriyaki Sauce:
   a. Combine beef stock, soy sauce, pineapple juice, garlic powder, and ginger. Bring to a boil.
5. Dip each raw patty in sauce and place in sheet pan.
6. Refrigerate and allow to marinate for at least 2 hours.
7. Bake at 325°F for 15 to 20 minutes.

Notes

[1]May use a concentrated beef soup base as a quick stock. Prepare as directed by manufacturer.

Directions for Diet Preparations

Sodium Restricted (SR): Use low sodium soy sauce in half the amount specified for regular soy sauce. May use if able to calculate into daily food plan.

Low Fat/Low Cholesterol (LF): 2 1/2 oz cooked and **Diabetic** (DB): 3 1/2 oz. Omit eggs. Low fat diets should consider individual tolerance to onions and garlic.

Mechanical Soft (SFT): Prepare as directed. Consider individual tolerance.

Soft/Low Fiber (SLF): Omit onions, pepper, and teriyaki sauce. Marinate with beef stock and strained orange juice.

Puree (PUR): Prepare as directed. Add sauce and blenderize to obtain desired consistency.

Nutrient Analysis per Serving:

Regular	KCAL	PRO gm	CHO gm	FAT gm	Chol mg	SFA gm	PFA gm	VITA iu	VITC mg	THI mg	RIB mg	NIA mg	CA mg	NA mg	K+ mg	FE mg
	277	26.0	4.9	16.1	129	6.2	0.7	41.8	0.8	0.08	0.25	5.6	23.0	619	343	2.7

Sodium Restricted	NA mg	Diabetic	Kcal	Milk exg	Veg exg	Fruit exg	Bread exg	Meat exg	Fat exg	Low Fat & Low Chol	FAT gm	Chol mg	SFA gm	PFA gm
	235		277	0.0	0.25	0.0	0.25	3.0-M	0.0		7.3	41.0	2.8	0.3

Portion: 8 ounces (3 ounces edible protein)

INGREDIENTS	50 portions		6 portions	
	weights	measures	weights	measures
Beef, 1-inch cube[1]	12 lb	1 1/2 gal	1 1/2 lb	3 cups
Flour, all-purpose	4 oz	1 cup	1/2 oz	2 Tbsp
Water, hot		3 qt		1 1/2 cups
Carrots, diced	3 lb	2 1/4 qt	6 oz	1 1/8 cups
Onions, chopped	1 lb	3 cups	2 oz	1/3 cup
Potatoes, peeled and cubed	3 1/2 lb	2 1/2 qt	7 oz	1 1/4 cups
Celery, chopped	1 lb	3 cups	2 oz	1/3 cup
Pepper, black		1 Tbsp		1/4 tsp

Method

1. Dredge beef in flour and brown in heavy pan over medium heat, in 325°F oven, or in steam jacketed kettle.
2. Add hot water. Cover. Simmer for 2 1/2 hours, do not boil.
3. Add carrots. Cover and cook for 10 minutes.
4. Add onions, potatoes, celery, and black pepper. Cover. Do not boil. Simmer 30 minutes until beef and vegetables are tender.
5. Heat to 160°F.
6. Hold for hot service at 140°F or higher. Serve promptly for the best quality or within 2 hours or less. If held over 2 hours, throw out.
7. Portion with an 8 oz ladle.

Directions for Diet Preparations

Sodium Restricted (SR), **Low Fat/Low Cholesterol (LF)**: 6 oz and **Diabetic (DB)**: 8 oz. Prepare as directed. Low fat diet consider individual tolerance when using onions.

Mechanical Soft (SFT): Prepare as directed. Consider individual tolerance.

Soft/Low Fiber (SLF): Omit onions and pepper.

Puree (PUR): Prepare as directed. Blenderize. Add additional liquid (i.e. broth) if necessary to obtain desired consistency.

Nutrient Analysis per Serving:

Regular	KCAL	PRO gm	CHO gm	FAT gm	Chol mg	SFA gm	PFA gm	VITA iu	VITC mg	THI mg	RIB mg	NIA mg	CA mg	NA mg	K+ mg	FE mg
	286	22.9	12.1	15.6	71.5	6.2	0.7	6984	4.2	0.14	0.21	3.9	23.5	77.5	529	2.5

Sodium Restricted	NA mg	Diabetic	Kcal	Milk exg	Veg exg	Fruit exg	Bread exg	Meat exg	Fat exg	Low Fat & Low Chol	FAT gm	Chol mg	SFA gm	PFA gm
	77.5		286	0.0	1.0	0.0	0.5	3.0-M	0.0		11.7	53.6	4.7	0.5

Brisket of Beef

Portion: 3 ounces cooked brisket, 2 ounces gravy

INGREDIENTS	50 portions		6 portions	
	weights	measures	weights	measures
Beef brisket, fresh, boneless, well-trimmed	25 lb		3 1/8 lb	
Pepper, black		2 tsp		1/4 tsp
Garlic powder		2 tsp		1/4 tsp
Onions, sliced	1 lb	3 cups	2 oz	1/3 cup
Water		2 qt		1 cup
Gravy:				
Flour, all-purpose	6 oz	1 1/2 cups	3/4 oz	3 Tbsp
Water, cold		1 1/2 cups		3 Tbsp
Pepper, black		1 tsp		1/8 tsp
Tarragon, ground		2 tsp		1/4 tsp

Method

1. Cut meat into 4 to 5 lb pieces.
2. Season meat with pepper and garlic.
3. Place onions on bottom of roasting pan.
4. Put meat into roasting pan at 450°F and brown about 30 minutes.
5. Add water to roasting pan. Cover tightly. Bake at 300°F until meat is no longer pink (about 3 to 5 hours). Add additional water if necessary.
6. Remove meat from pan. Cook 30 minutes before slicing. Slice meat across the grain. Place sliced brisket into stock pot.
7. Prepare gravy:
   a. Mix flour and cold water, stirring until smooth. Add to drippings in pan.
   b. Remove excess fat.
   c. 50 portions: Add water to make one gal of gravy.
      6 portions: Add water to make two cups of gravy.
   d. Add seasonings.
8. Pour gravy over brisket. Bring to a boil, then simmer 1 to 2 hours or until tender.

Directions for Diet Preparations

Sodium Restricted (SR): Prepare as directed.
Low Fat/Low Cholesterol (LF): 2 oz brisket and **Diabetic** (DB): 3 oz. Prepare as directed. Omit gravy. Low fat diet consider individual tolerance when using onions and garlic.
Mechanical Soft (SFT): Omit onions. Chop meat.
Soft/Low Fiber (SLF): Omit black pepper, garlic powder, onions, and gravy.
Puree (PUR): Omit onions. Add gravy to brisket; blenderize to obtain desired consistency.

Nutrient Analysis per Serving:

Regular	KCAL	PRO gm	CHO gm	FAT gm	Chol mg	SFA gm	PFA gm	VITA iu	VITC mg	THI mg	RIB mg	NIA mg	CA mg	NA mg	K+ mg	FE mg
	265	22.6	3.0	17.2	71.5	7.6	0.5	1.5	0.2	0.07	0.16	2.5	10.1	41.9	236	2.6

Sodium Restricted	NA mg	Diabetic	Kcal	Milk exg	Veg exg	Fruit exg	Bread exg	Meat exg	Fat exg	Low Fat & Low Chol	FAT gm	Chol mg	SFA gm	PFA gm
	41.9		213	0.0	0.0	0.0	0.0	3.0-M	0.0		13.0	67.0	5.5	0.4

Portion: 3 ounces cooked brisket, 2 ounces sauce

INGREDIENTS	50 portions		6 portions	
	weights	measures	weights	measures
Beef brisket, fresh, boneless, well-trimmed	25 lb		3 1/8 lb	
Pepper, black		2 tsp		1/4 tsp
Garlic powder		2 tsp		1/4 tsp
Onions, sliced	1 lb	3 cups	2 oz	1/3 cup
Water		2 qt		1 cup
Tomato sauce	8 lb	1 gal	1 lb	2 cups

Method

1. Cut meat into 4 to 5 lb pieces.
2. Season meat with pepper and garlic.
3. Place onions on bottom of roasting pan.
4. Put meat into roasting pan at 450°F and brown about 30 minutes.
5. Add water to roasting pan. Cover tightly. Bake at 300°F until meat is no longer pink (about 3 to 5 hours). Add additional water if necessary.
6. Remove meat from pan. Cook 30 minutes before slicing. Slice meat across the grain. Place sliced brisket into stock pot.
7. Prepare tomato sauce.
8. Pour sauce over brisket. Bring to a boil, then simmer 1 to 2 hours or until tender.

Directions for Diet Preparations

Sodium Restricted (SR): Use low sodium tomato sauce.

Low Fat/Low Cholesterol (LF): 2 oz brisket, 1 oz sauce. Prepare brisket as directed. Consider individual tolerance when using onions. Use low fat tomato sauce. May use sauce if able to calculate into daily food plan.

Diabetic (DB): 3 oz brisket, 1 oz sauce. Use DB tomato sauce. May use sauce if able to calculate into daily food plan.

Mechanical Soft (SFT): Omit onions; chop meat. Use SFT tomato sauce.

Soft/Low Fiber (SLF): Omit black pepper, garlic, and onions. Use SLF tomato sauce.

Puree (PUR): Omit onions. Use SFT tomato sauce. Add sauce to brisket, blenderize. Add additional sauce if necessary to obtain desired consistency.

Nutrient Analysis per Serving:

Regular	KCAL	PRO gm	CHO gm	FAT gm	Chol mg	SFA gm	PFA gm	VITA iu	VITC mg	THI mg	RIB mg	NIA mg	CA mg	NA mg	K+ mg	FE mg
	281	22.9	6.4	17.3	67.0	6.2	1.8	1030	12.6	0.08	0.17	2.9	20.4	223	373	3.0

Sodium Restricted	NA mg	Diabetic	Kcal	Milk exg	Veg exg	Fruit exg	Bread exg	Meat exg	Fat exg	Low Fat & Low Chol	FAT gm	Chol mg	SFA gm	PFA gm
	49.6		236	0.0	0.5	0.0	0.0	3.0-M	0.9		9.8	44.6	3.9	0.7

Corned Beef

Portion: 3 ounces cooked

INGREDIENTS	50 portions		6 portions	
	weights	measures	weights	measures
Corned brisket of beef, boneless	25 lb		3.125 lb	
Cold water	as needed		as needed	

Method

1. Put corned beef in heavy pot. Cover with water. Bring to a boil; cover, reduce heat and simmer 4 to 5 hours (depending on size of the meat).
2. Remove any scum which comes to the surface while beef is cooking.
3. Test each piece after 4 hours and remove any tender pieces. Continue to simmer until all pieces are tender.
4. Let corned beef stand 20 minutes before slicing. (If meat is not to be served right away, it should be refrigerated immediately.)
5. Slice corned beef across grain. The meat will have to be turned several times because the grain runs in different directions.

Directions for Diet Preparations

Sodium Restricted (SR): Not recommended. Use appropriate food alternative.
Low Fat/Low Cholesterol (LF): 2 oz and **Diabetic** (DB): 3 oz. Remove all visible fat.
Mechanical Soft (SFT): Prepare as directed. Chop meat.
Soft/Low Fiber (SLF): Not recommended. Use appropriate food alternative.
Puree (PUR): Prepare as directed. Add liquid (i.e. broth) and blenderize to obtain desired consistency.

Nutrient Analysis per Serving:

Regular	KCAL	PRO gm	CHO gm	FAT gm	Chol mg	SFA gm	PFA gm	VITA iu	VITC mg	THI mg	RIB mg	NIA mg	CA mg	NA mg	K+ mg	FE mg
	213	15.4	0.4	16.1	83.3	5.4	0.5	0.0	13.6	0.02	0.14	2.5	6.8	965	123	1.5

Sodium Restricted	Diabetic	Kcal	Milk exg	Veg exg	Fruit exg	Bread exg	Meat exg	Fat exg	Low Fat & Low Chol	FAT gm	Chol mg	SFA gm	PFA gm
Not recommended		213	0.0	0.0	0.0	0.0	3.0-M	0.25		10.7	55.5	3.5	0.3

Portion: 8 ounces (3 ounces edible protein)

INGREDIENTS	50 portions		6 portions	
	weights	measures	weights	measures
Beef, sirloin, cut into thin strips	12 1/2 lb	1 2/3 gal	1 1/2 lb	3 cups
Margarine, low sodium, melted	8 oz	1 cup	1 oz	2 Tbsp
Onions, chopped	1 lb	3 cups	2 oz	1/3 cup
Beef stock[1]		2 qt		1 cup
Tomatoes, canned, diced	6 1/2 lb	3 1/2 qt	12 3/4 oz	1 3/4 cups
Green peppers, thinly sliced	3 1/4 lb EP (4 lb AP)	2 qt	6 1/2 oz EP (8 oz AP)	1 cup
Cornstarch	2 2/3 oz	1/2 cup	1/3 oz	1 Tbsp
Water, cold		2 1/2 cups		1/3 cup
Soy sauce		1/2 cup		1 Tbsp

Method

1. Brown meat in margarine.
2. Add onions. Cook 5 minutes.
3. Add beef stock and tomatoes to meat. Simmer about 1 hour, until tender, stirring occasionally.
4. Add green pepper. Cook until tender but firm.
5. Mix cornstarch, water, and soy sauce into a smooth paste. Add to meat mixture. Cook 5 minutes.
6. Hold for hot service at 140°F or higher. Serve promptly for the best quality or within 2 hours or less.

Notes

[1]May use a concentrated soup base as a quick stock. Prepare as directed by manufacturer.

Directions for Diet Preparations

Sodium Restricted (SR): Use low sodium beef stock, low sodium tomatoes, and low sodium soy sauce.
Low Fat/Low Cholesterol (LF): 6 oz and **Diabetic** (DB): 8 oz. Omit margarine in step #1. Low fat diets should consider individual tolerance when using onions.
Mechanical Soft (SFT): Prepare as directed. Chop meat and vegetables. Cook vegetables until tender.
Soft/Low Fiber (SLF): Omit onions, green peppers, and soy sauce.
Puree (PUR): Prepare as directed. Add additional beef stock and blend to obtain desired consistency.

Nutrient Analysis per Serving:

Regular	KCAL	PRO gm	CHO gm	FAT gm	Chol mg	SFA gm	PFA gm	VITA iu	VITC mg	THI mg	RIB mg	NIA mg	CA mg	NA mg	K+ mg	FE mg
	305	24.6	6.2	19.8	76.5	7.1	1.9	646	31.8	0.15	0.27	4.2	32.1	344	509	3.4

Sodium Restricted	NA mg	Diabetic	Kcal	Milk exg	Veg exg	Fruit exg	Bread exg	Meat exg	Fat exg	Low Fat & Low Chol	FAT gm	Chol mg	SFA gm	PFA gm
	154		273	0.0	1.0	0.0	0.5	3.0-M	1.0		12.1	57.3	4.9	0.5

Portion: 3 ounces beef without bone, 1 1/2 ounces sauce

INGREDIENTS	50 portions		6 portions	
	weights	measures	weights	measures
Beef short ribs	38 lb		4 3/4 lb	
Barbecue sauce	5 lb	2 1/2 qt	10 oz	1 1/4 cups

Method

1. Remove excess fat from meat.
2. Cut into 7 oz pieces.
3. Place in roasting pan(s). Brown uncovered at 350°F until lightly browned about 30 minutes. Pour off fat.
4. Pour barbecue sauce over ribs. Cover with aluminum foil.
5. Bake at 350°F until meat is tender, about 1 hour.
6. Uncover and bake an additional 25 minutes.

Directions for Diet Preparations

Sodium Restricted (SR): Use low sodium barbecue sauce.

Low Fat/Low Cholesterol (LF): 2 oz beef without bone, 1 1/2 oz sauce. Prepare as directed. Low fat diets should consider individual tolerance when using onions in barbecue sauce.

Diabetic (DB): 3 oz beef without bone, one oz sauce. Use diabetic barbecue sauce.

Mechanical Soft (SFT): Use SFT barbecue sauce. Remove meat from the bone. Chop meat.

Soft/Low Fiber (SLF): Omit barbecue sauce, substitute with broth.

Puree (PUR): Use SFT barbecue sauce. Remove meat from the bone. Combine sauce and beef; blend. Add additional sauce if necessary to obtain desired consistency.

Nutrient Analysis per Serving:

Regular	KCAL	PRO gm	CHO gm	FAT gm	Chol mg	SFA gm	PFA gm	VITA iu	VITC mg	THI mg	RIB mg	NIA mg	CA mg	NA mg	K+ mg	FE mg
	371	19.1	15.8	25.6	73.1	10.8	0.9	621	6.8	0.11	0.18	3.4	20	514	428	2.2

Sodium Restricted	NA mg	Diabetic	Kcal	Milk exg	Veg exg	Fruit exg	Bread exg	Meat exg	Fat exg	Low Fat & Low Chol	FAT gm	Chol mg	SFA gm	PFA gm
	59.7		341	0.0	0.5	0.3	0.0	2.6	3.6		17.1	48.7	7.2	0.6

Portion: 8 ounces (3 ounces edible protein)

INGREDIENTS	50 portions		6 portions	
	weights	measures	weights	measures
Ground beef, lean	10 lb	1 1/4 gal	1 1/4 lb	2 1/2 cups
Onions, chopped	8 oz	1 1/2 cups	1 oz	3 Tbsp
Tomatoes, canned, diced	6 lb	3 qt	12 oz	1 1/2 cups
Tomato puree	2 lb	1 qt	4 oz	1/2 cup
Chili powder	1/2 oz	2 Tbsp		3/4 tsp
Pepper, black		2 tsp		1/4 tsp
Pinto, kidney, or red beans, canned	9 1/2 lb	1 1/2 gal	1 1/4 lb	3 cups
Water		2 qt		1 cup

Method

1. Cook beef and onions until meat loses pink color.
2. Mix tomatoes and seasonings. Add to beef. Cook and blend.
3. Add beans and water. Cover and simmer 1 1/2 to 2 hours.
4. If chili becomes too thick, add water.
5. Serve with an 8 ounce ladle.

Directions for Diet Preparations

Sodium Restricted (SR): Use low sodium canned tomatoes or fresh tomatoes. Rinse kidney beans or prepare dry kidney beans.

Low Fat/Low Cholesterol (LF): 6 oz, **Diabetic** (DB): 8 oz, and **Mechanical Soft** (SFT): Prepare as directed. Low fat diet should consider individual tolerance when using onions and chili powder.

Soft/Low Fiber (SLF): Not recommended. Substitute appropriate food alternative.

Puree (PUR): Prepare as directed. Blend. Add additional liquid if necessary to obtain desired consistency.

Nutrient Analysis per Serving:

Regular	KCAL	PRO gm	CHO gm	FAT gm	Chol mg	SFA gm	PFA gm	VITA iu	VITC mg	THI mg	RIB mg	NIA mg	CA mg	NA mg	K+ mg	FE mg
	287	23.3	25.0	10.6	57.1	4.0	0.6	646	18.5	0.22	0.25	4.8	62.0	625	774	3.5

Sodium Restricted	NA mg	Diabetic	Kcal	Milk exg	Veg exg	Fruit exg	Bread exg	Meat exg	Fat exg	Low Fat & Low Chol	FAT gm	Chol mg	SFA gm	PFA gm
	69.3		287	0.0	1.7	0.0	1.0	3.0	0.0		7.9	42.9	3.0	0.4

Portion: 3 1/2 ounces, one bun (3 ounces edible protein)

INGREDIENTS	50 portions		6 portions	
	weights	measures	weights	measures
Ground beef, lean	12 lb	1 1/2 gal	1 1/2 lb	3 cups
Eggs, beaten	8 oz	1 cup	2 oz	1/4 cup
		(4 large)		(1 large)
Water		2 cups		1/4 cup
Bread crumbs, soft	4 oz	2 cups	1/2 oz	1/4 cup
Pepper, black		2 tsp		1/4 tsp
Onions, chopped	4 oz	3/4 cup	1/2 oz	1 1/2 Tbsp
Hamburger buns		50 buns		6 buns

Method

1. Combine ground beef, eggs, water, bread crumbs, pepper, and onions.
2. Use a No. 10 dipper and shape meat into patties.
3. Place on baking sheets. Bake at 400°F for 15 to 20 minutes or until center is no longer pink.
4. Serve patties on bun.

Directions for Diet Preparations

Sodium Restricted (SR) and **Diabetic** (DB): 3 1/2 oz, 1 bun. Prepare as directed.

Low Fat/Low Cholesterol (LF): 2 1/2 oz, 1 bun. Omit eggs.

Mechanical Soft (SFT): Prepare as directed. Consider individual tolerance when using the bun.

Soft/Low Fiber (SLF): Omit black pepper and onions.

Puree (PUR): Prepare patty as directed. Add broth to hamburger and blend to obtain desired consistency. Omit bun.

Nutrient Analysis per Serving:

Regular	KCAL	PRO gm	CHO gm	FAT gm	Chol mg	SFA gm	PFA gm	VITA iu	VITC mg	THI mg	RIB mg	NIA mg	CA mg	NA mg	K+ mg	FE mg
Hamburger	261	24.9	3.2	15.6	107.8	6.0	0.6	20.9	0.2	0.07	0.23	5.2	18.2	110	313	2.3
with Bun	380	28.2	24.4	17.8	110.2	6.6	0.8	20.9	0.2	0.22	0.32	6.5	47.8	313	351	3.4

Sodium Restricted	NA mg	Diabetic	Kcal	Milk exg	Veg exg	Fruit exg	Bread exg	Meat exg	Fat exg	Low Fat & Low Chol	FAT gm	Chol mg	SFA gm	PFA gm
Hamburger	110		261	0.0	0.25	0.0	0.5	3.0-M	0.0		10.8	61.4	4.2	0.4
with Bun	313		380	0.0	0.25	0.0	2.1	3.0-M	0.0		13.0	63.8	4.7	0.6

Portion: 3 1/2 ounces, one bun (3 ounces edible protein)

INGREDIENTS	50 portions		6 portions	
	weights	measures	weights	measures
Ground beef, lean	10 lb	1 1/4 gal	1 1/4 lb	2 1/2 cups
Eggs, beaten	8 oz	1 cup (4 large)	2 oz	1/4 cup (1 large)
Water		2 cups		1/4 cup
Bread crumbs, soft	4 oz	2 cups	1/2 oz	1/4 cup
Pepper, black		2 tsp		1/4 tsp
Onions, chopped	4 oz	3/4 cup	1/2 oz	1 1/2 Tbsp
Cheese slices	1 1/2 lb	25 slices	3 oz	3 slices
Hamburger buns		50 buns		6 buns

Method

1. Combine ground beef, eggs, water, bread crumbs, pepper, and onions.
2. Use a No. 10 dipper and shape meat into patties.
3. Place on baking sheets. Bake at 400°F for 15 to 20 minutes or until center is no longer pink.
4. Place 1/2 slice cheese on almost done patty. Allow 1/2 minute for cheese to melt.
5. Serve patties on bun.

Directions for Diet Preparations

Sodium Restricted (SR): Use low sodium cheese.
Low Fat/Low Cholesterol (LF): 2 1/2 oz, 1 bun. Use low fat cheese. Omit eggs.
Diabetic (DB): 3 1/2 oz, 1 bun. Prepare as directed.
Mechanical Soft (SFT): Prepare as directed. Consider individual tolerance when using the bun.
Soft/Low Fiber (SLF): Omit black pepper and onions.
Puree (PUR): Prepare patty as directed. Add broth to hamburger and blend to obtain desired consistency. Omit bun.

Nutrient Analysis per Serving:

Regular	KCAL	PRO gm	CHO gm	FAT gm	Chol mg	SFA gm	PFA gm	VITA iu	VITC mg	THI mg	RIB mg	NIA mg	CA mg	NA mg	K+ mg	FE mg
Hamburger	233	20.0	3.4	14.9	92.1	6.7	0.5	185	0.2	0.06	0.21	3.5	98.6	280	236	1.7
with Bun	352	23.2	24.6	17.1	94.5	7.3	0.8	185	0.2	0.21	0.30	4.9	128	482	274	2.8

Sodium Restricted	NA mg	Diabetic	Kcal	Milk exg	Veg exg	Fruit exg	Bread exg	Meat exg	Fat exg	Low Fat & Low Chol	FAT gm	Chol mg	SFA gm	PFA gm
Hamburger	136		233	0.0	0.3	0.0	0.2	3.0-M	0.0		8.5	47.0	3.5	0.3
with Bun	338		352	0.0	0.3	0.0	2.0	3.0-M	0.0		10.7	49.4	4.0	0.5

Portion: 8 ounces (3 ounces edible protein)

INGREDIENTS	48 portions, 2 pans (12 × 20 × 2″) cut 4 × 6		12 portions, 1 pan (13 × 9″) cut 4 × 3	
	weights	measures	weights	measures
Ground beef, lean	5 lb	2 1/2 qt	1 1/4 lb	2 1/2 cups
Onions, finely chopped	8 oz	1 1/2 cups	2 oz	1/3 cup
Tomato sauce	6 lb	3 qt	1 1/2 lb	3 cups
Tomato paste	2 lb	1 qt	8 oz	1 cup
Pepper, black		2 tsp		1/2 tsp
Basil, crumbled		2 tsp		1/2 tsp
Oregano, crumbled		1 Tbsp		1/2 tsp
Noodles, lasagna, uncooked	2 1/2 lb		10 oz	
Water, boiling		2 gal		2 qt
Mozzarella cheese, part skim, shredded	2 1/2 lb	2 1/4 qt	10 oz	2 1/4 cups
Parmesan cheese, grated	6 oz	1 1/3 cups	1 1/2 oz	5 Tbsp
Cottage cheese, dry, low fat, drained	2 1/2 lb	1 1/4 qt	10 oz	1 1/3 cups

Method

1. Cook beef and onions together until the meat has lost its pink color. Drain off excess fat.
2. Add tomato sauce, paste, and seasonings to meat. Continue cooking, about 30 minutes, stirring occasionally.
3. Cook noodles in boiling water until tender, about 10 minutes. Rinse. Drain when ready to use.
4. Combine cheeses.
5. Arrange 1/3 meat sauce; 1/2 lasagna noodles, overlapping; and 1/2 cheeses in baking pan or counter pans. Repeat. Top with remainder of meat sauce.
6. Bake at 350°F for 40 to 45 minutes.
7. Cut in portions specified under the number of servings.
8. Hold for hot service at 140°F or higher. Serve promptly for the best quality or within 2 hours or less.

Directions for Diet Preparations

Sodium Restricted (SR): Use low sodium tomato sauce and low sodium tomato paste. May use if able to calculate into daily food plan.

Low Fat/Low Cholesterol (LF): 6 oz, **Diabetic** (DB): 8 oz, and **Mechanical Soft** (SFT): Prepare as directed.

Soft/Low Fiber (SLF): Omit black pepper and onions.

Puree (PUR): Prepare as directed. Blend. Add additional sauce if necessary to obtain desired consistency.

Nutrient Analysis per Serving:

Regular	KCAL	PRO gm	CHO gm	FAT gm	Chol mg	SFA gm	PFA gm	VITA iu	VITC mg	THI mg	RIB mg	NIA mg	CA mg	NA mg	K+ mg	FE mg
	294	22.8	26.7	10.8	47.6	5.0	0.4	1270	17.1	0.31	0.36	4.8	213	790	580	2.7

Sodium Restricted	NA mg	Diabetic	Kcal	Milk exg	Veg exg	Fruit exg	Bread exg	Meat exg	Fat exg	Low Fat & Low Chol	FAT gm	Chol mg	SFA gm	PFA gm
	288		294	0.0	0.5	0.0	1.0	3.0-M	0.0		7.2	31.7	3.3	0.3

Portion: 8 ounces (3 ounces edible protein)

INGREDIENTS	50 portions		6 portions	
	weights	measures	weights	measures
Onions, chopped	2 lb	1 1/2 qt	4 oz	3/4 cup
Vegetable oil	2 oz	1/4 cup	1/4 oz	1/2 Tbsp
Ground beef, lean	12 lb	1 1/2 gal	1 1/2 lb	3 cups
Tomatoes, diced, canned	8 lb	1 1/3 gal	1 lb	2 2/3 cups
Tomato juice		1 gal		2 cups
Pepper, black		1 Tbsp		1/4 tsp
Oregano, ground		1 1/2 Tbsp		1/2 tsp
Garlic powder		2 tsp		1/4 tsp
Macaroni, cooked	8 1/3 lb	1 1/2 gal	1 lb	3 cups
Cheese, shredded	1 lb	3 1/2 cups	2 1/3 oz	1/2 cup

Method

1. Sauté onions in oil until onions are golden brown.
2. Add beef; cook and stir until meat is well browned. Pour meat into colander, drain off fat. Rinse with water if desired. Discard fat and return to heat.
3. Add diced tomatoes, tomato juice, and seasonings to meat mixture. Blend. Heat to a full boil.
4. Add cooked macaroni and shredded cheese to meat; mix to distribute. Bring to a boil; reduce heat and simmer about 15 minutes or until casserole is heated through.
5. Heat to 170°F.
6. Serve with an 8 oz ladle.

Directions for Diet Preparations

Sodium Restricted (SR): Use low sodium canned tomatoes, low sodium tomato juice, and low sodium cheese.
Low Fat/Low Cholesterol (LF): 6 oz and **Diabetic** (DB): 8 oz. Omit vegetable oil. Sauté onions with ground beef. Use low fat cheese. Low fat diets should consider individual tolerance to onions and garlic.
Mechanical Soft (SFT): Prepare as directed.
Soft/Low Fiber (SLF): Omit onions, pepper, and garlic powder. Use a mild cheese.
Puree (PUR): Prepare as directed. Blend. Add additional liquid (i.e. tomato juice), if necessary to obtain desired consistency.

Nutrient Analysis per Serving:

Regular	KCAL	PRO gm	CHO gm	FAT gm	Chol mg	SFA gm	PFA gm	VITA iu	VITC mg	THI mg	RIB mg	NIA mg	CA mg	NA mg	K+ mg	FE mg
	424	30.1	36.6	16.9	85.7	6.0	1.3	1526	38.3	0.46	0.39	8.6	61.1	525	773	4.2

Sodium Restricted	NA mg	Diabetic	Kcal	Milk exg	Veg exg	Fruit exg	Bread exg	Meat exg	Fat exg	Low Fat & Low Chol	FAT gm	Chol mg	SFA gm	PFA gm
	102		414	0.0	1.5	0.0	1.8	3.0-M	0.0		11.8	64.3	4.4	0.5

Meatballs

Portion: 2, 2 ounce meatballs, cooked (3 ounces edible protein)

INGREDIENTS	50 portions		6 portions	
	weights	measures	weights	measures
Ground beef, lean	12 lb	1 1/2 gal	1 1/2 lb	3 cups
Eggs, beaten[1]	1 lb	2 cups (8 large)	2 oz	1/4 cup (1 large)
Water		1 qt		1/2 cup
Bread crumbs, soft	12 oz	1 1/2 qt	1 1/2 oz	3/4 cup
Pepper, black		1 Tbsp		1/4 tsp
Onions, finely chopped	4 oz	3/4 cup	1/2 oz	1 1/2 Tbsp

Method

1. Combine all ingredients. Blend well.
2. Use a No. 12 dipper and shape meat into balls.
3. Place in pans close together in one layer.
4. Bake at 350°F for 45 minutes or until browned and firm.

Notes

[1]May use frozen pasteurized eggs. Prepare as directed by manufacturer.

Directions for Diet Preparations

Sodium Restricted (SR): Use low sodium bread crumbs.
Low Fat/Low Cholesterol (LF): 3 oz. Omit eggs. Low fat diets should consider individual tolerance when using onions.
Diabetic (DB): 4 oz and **Mechanical Soft** (SFT): Prepare as directed.
Soft/Low Fiber (SLF): Omit black pepper and onions.
Puree (PUR): Prepare as directed. Add liquid (i.e. broth or sauce) and blend to obtain desired consistency.

Nutrient Analysis per Serving:

Regular	KCAL	PRO gm	CHO gm	FAT gm	Chol mg	SFA gm	PFA gm	VITA iu	VITC mg	THI mg	RIB mg	NIA mg	CA mg	NA mg	K+ mg	FE mg
	299	26.4	9.1	16.4	130	6.2	0.7	41.7	0.2	0.10	0.27	5.6	30.2	175	330	2.7

Sodium Restricted	NA mg	Diabetic	Kcal	Milk exg	Veg exg	Fruit exg	Bread exg	Meat exg	Fat exg	Low Fat & Low Chol	FAT gm	Chol mg	SFA gm	PFA gm
	88.3		299	0.0	0.3	0.0	0.8	3.0-M	0.0		11.6	64.8	4.5	0.4

Portion: 3, 1 1/4 ounce meatballs, 2 ounces sauce (3 ounces edible protein)

INGREDIENTS	50 portions		6 portions	
	weights	measures	weights	measures
Ground beef, lean	12 lb	1 1/2 gal	1 1/2 lb	3 cups
Eggs, beaten[1]	1 lb	2 cups (8 large)	2 oz	1/4 cup (1 large)
Water		1 qt		1/2 cup
Bread crumbs, soft	12 oz	1 1/2 qt	1 1/2 oz	3/4 cup
Onions, grated	4 oz	3/4 cup	1/2 oz	1 1/2 Tbsp
Garlic powder		2 tsp		1/4 tsp
Pepper, black		2 tsp		1/4 tsp
Sauce:				
Onion, chopped	8 oz	1 1/2 cups	1 oz	3 Tbsp
Green peppers, chopped	8 oz	1 1/2 cups	1 oz	3 Tbsp
Margarine, low sodium	4 oz	1/2 cup	1/2 oz	1 Tbsp
Vinegar	1 lb	2 cups	2 oz	1/4 cup
Water #1		2 cups		1/4 cup
Sugar, granulated	7 1/4 oz	1 cup	1 oz	2 Tbsp
Soy sauce		3 Tbsp		1 1/8 tsp
Cornstarch	1 1/3 oz	1/4 cup	1/8 oz	1/2 Tbsp
Water, cold #2		1 cup		2 Tbsp
Pineapple tidbits, drained, unsweetened	6 3/4 lb	3 1/8 qt	12 3/4 oz	1 1/2 cup

Method

1. Combine beef, bread crumbs, eggs, onions, garlic, and pepper. Blend well.
2. Measure with No. 16 dipper. Shape into 1 1/4 oz balls.
3. Brown in oven at 350°F for 20 minutes.
4. Prepare sauce.
   a. Sauté onions and green peppers in margarine for 5 minutes. Set aside.
   b. Combine vinegar, water #1, sugar, and soy sauce. Bring to a boil.
   c. Mix cornstarch and water #2 into a smooth paste. Add to hot liquid; stir and cook until clear.
   d. Add vegetables and pineapple to sauce.
5. Pour sauce over meatballs. Bake at 350°F for 15 minutes until warm.

Notes

[1]May use frozen pasteurized eggs. Prepare as directed by manufacturer.

Directions for Diet Preparations

Sodium Restricted (SR): Use low sodium soy sauce and low sodium bread crumbs.

Low Fat/Low Cholesterol (LF): 2 3/4 oz meatballs; 2 oz sauce. Omit eggs. Use reduced-calorie margarine. Consider individual tolerance when using onions and garlic.

Diabetic (DB): 3 3/4 oz meatballs; 2 oz.

50 portions: Use reduced-calorie margarine. Omit sugar, substitute with an artificial sweetener equivalent to 1 cup granulated sugar (approx. 4 tsp artificial sweetener).

6 portions: Use reduced-calorie margarine. Omit sugar, substitute with an artificial sweetener equivalent to 2 Tbsp granulated sugar (approx. 1/2 tsp artificial sweetener).

Mechanical Soft (SFT): Prepare as directed. Consider individual tolerance.

Soft/Low Fiber (SLF): Omit onions, black pepper, and sauce.

Puree (PUR): Prepare as directed. Blend sauce; strain. Add sauce to meatballs and blend to obtain desired consistency.

Nutrient Analysis per Serving:

Regular	KCAL	PRO gm	CHO gm	FAT gm	Chol mg	SFA gm	PFA gm	VITA iu	VITC mg	THI mg	RIB mg	NIA mg	CA mg	NA mg	K+ mg	FE mg
	378	26.9	25.4	18.3	130	6.6	1.3	158	10.8	0.17	0.28	5.9	42.4	239	438	3.1

Sodium Restricted	NA mg	Diabetic	Kcal	Milk exg	Veg exg	Fruit exg	Bread exg	Meat exg	Fat exg	Low Fat & Low Chol	FAT gm	Chol mg	SFA gm	PFA gm
	119		355	0.0	0.25	1.0	0.5	3.0-M	0.5		13.2	69.1	4.9	0.7

Portion: 4 ounces (3 ounces edible protein)

INGREDIENTS	50 portions		6 portions	
	weights	measures	weights	measures
Ground beef, lean	12 lb	1 1/2 gal	1 1/2 lb	3 cups
Eggs, beaten[1]	1 lb	2 cups (8 large)	2 oz	1/4 cup (1 large)
Water		1 qt		1/2 cup
Bread crumbs, soft	12 oz	1 1/2 qt	1 1/2 oz	3/4 cup
Pepper, black		1 Tbsp		1/4 tsp
Onions, finely chopped	4 oz	3/4 cup	1/2 oz	1 1/2 Tbsp
Garlic powder		1 Tbsp		1/4 tsp

Method

1. Combine all ingredients until blended. Do not overmix.
2. Press mixture into loaf pans or counter pans.
3. Bake at 325°F for 1 1/2 to 2 hours.

Notes

[1]May use frozen pasteurized eggs. Prepare as directed by manufacturer.

Directions for Diet Preparations

Sodium Restricted (SR): Use low sodium bread crumbs.

Low Fat/Low Cholesterol (LF): 3 oz. Omit eggs. Consider individual tolerance when using onions and garlic.

Diabetic (DB): 4 oz and **Mechanical Soft** (SFT): Prepare as directed.

Soft/Low Fiber (SLF): Omit black pepper and onions.

Puree (PUR): Prepare as directed. Add liquid (i.e. broth or sauce) and blend to obtain desired consistency.

Nutrient Analysis per Serving:

Regular	KCAL	PRO gm	CHO gm	FAT gm	Chol mg	SFA gm	PFA gm	VITA iu	VITC mg	THI mg	RIB mg	NIA mg	CA mg	NA mg	K+ mg	FE mg
	299	26.4	9.1	16.4	130	6.2	0.7	41.6	0.2	0.10	0.27	5.6	30.1	175	330	2.7

Sodium Restricted	NA mg	Diabetic	Kcal	Milk exg	Veg exg	Fruit exg	Bread exg	Meat exg	Fat exg	Low Fat & Low Chol	FAT gm	Chol mg	SFA gm	PFA gm
	88.7		299	0.0	1.0	0.0	0.5	3.0-M	0.0		11.6	64.7	4.5	0.4

Portion: 4 ounces (3 ounces edible protein)

INGREDIENTS	50 portions		6 portions	
	weights	measures	weights	measures
Ground beef, lean	12 lb	1 1/2 gal	1 1/2 lb	3 cups
Eggs, beaten[1]	1 lb	2 cups (8 large)	2 oz	1/4 cup (1 large)
Water		1 qt		1/2 cup
Bread crumbs, soft	12 oz	1 1/2 qt	1 1/2 oz	3/4 cup
Pepper, black		1 Tbsp		1/4 tsp
Onions, finely chopped	4 oz	3/4 cup	1/2 oz	1 1/2 Tbsp
Garlic powder		1 Tbsp		1/4 tsp
Glaze:				
Sugar, brown	9 2/3 oz	1 1/2 cups	1 1/4 oz	3 Tbsp
Mustard, dry		1 Tbsp		1/4 tsp
Catsup	10 oz	1 1/4 cups	1 1/4 oz	2 1/2 Tbsp

Method

1. Combine all ingredients until blended. Do not overmix.
2. Press mixture into loaf pans or counter pans.
3. Bake at 325°F for 1 1/2 to 2 hours.
4. Prepare glaze.
   a. Combine brown sugar, mustard, and catsup. Spread over loaves for the last 30 minutes of cooking.

Notes

[1]May use frozen pasteurized eggs. Prepare as directed by manufacturer.

Directions for Diet Preparations

Sodium Restricted (SR): Use low sodium bread crumbs and low sodium catsup.

Low Fat/Low Cholesterol (LF): 3 oz. Omit eggs. Low fat diets should consider individual tolerance when using onions and garlic.

Diabetic (DB): 4 oz. Omit brown sugar.

Mechanical Soft (SFT): Prepare as directed.

Soft/Low Fiber (SLF): Omit onion, black pepper, and garlic.

Puree (PUR): Prepare as directed. Add liquid (i.e. broth) and blend to obtain desired consistency.

Nutrient Analysis per Serving:

Regular	KCAL	PRO gm	CHO gm	FAT gm	Chol mg	SFA gm	PFA gm	VITA iu	VITC mg	THI mg	RIB mg	NIA mg	CA mg	NA mg	K+ mg	FE mg
	338	27.1	17.2	16.9	152	6.4	0.7	159.5	1.1	0.11	0.29	5.8	40.3	254	382	3.1

Sodium Restricted	NA mg	Diabetic	Kcal	Milk exg	Veg exg	Fruit exg	Bread exg	Meat exg	Fat exg	Low Fat & Low Chol	FAT gm	Chol mg	SFA gm	PFA gm
	96.2		305	0.0	0.0	0.0	0.75	3.0-M	0.5		11.7	64.8	4.5	0.4

Portion: 4 ounces (3 ounces edible protein), one bun

Ingredients	50 portions		6 portions	
	weights	measures	weights	measures
Ground beef, lean	12 lb	1 1/2 gal	1 1/2 lb	3 cups
Onions, finely chopped	1 lb	3 cups	2 oz	1/3 cup
Margarine, low sodium, melted	4 oz	1/2 cup	1/2 oz	1 Tbsp
Tomato sauce	10 lb	1 1/4 gal	1 1/4 lb	2 1/2 cups
Tomato catsup	1 lb	2 cups	2 oz	1/4 cup
Pepper, black		2 tsp		1/4 tsp
Thyme, ground		2 tsp		1/4 tsp
Basil		1 Tbsp		1/2 tsp
Hamburger buns		50 buns		6 buns

Method

1. Sauté ground beef and onions in melted margarine over moderate heat until meat loses pink color. Stir occasionally to break up beef. Drain fat.
2. Add tomato sauce, catsup, and seasonings to ground beef. Blend. Simmer, uncovered 20 to 25 minutes, stirring frequently.
3. Heat to 160°F.
4. Serve 4 oz meat mixture on bottom half of bun, cover with top half of bun. Serve hot.

Directions for Diet Preparations

Sodium Restricted (SR): Use low sodium tomato sauce and low sodium catsup or may substitute pureed fresh tomatoes for sauce and catsup. May use if able to calculate into daily food plan.

Low Fat/Low Cholesterol (LF): 3 oz meat mixture, one bun and **Diabetic** (DB): 4 oz meat mixture, one bun. Omit margarine. Low fat diets should consider individual tolerance when using onions.

Mechanical Soft (SFT): Prepare as directed. Consider individual tolerance in using the bun.

Soft/Low Fiber (SLF): Omit black pepper and onions.

Puree (PUR): Prepare as directed. Add additional tomato sauce (if necessary) and blend to obtain desired consistency. Omit bun.

Nutrient Analysis per Serving:

Regular	KCAL	PRO gm	CHO gm	FAT gm	Chol mg	SFA gm	PFA gm	VITA iu	VITC mg	THI mg	RIB mg	NIA mg	CA mg	NA mg	K+ mg	FE mg
Without Bun	300	25.6	10.7	17.0	85.7	6.2	1.2	1204	15.4	0.13	0.27	6.4	31.5	790	723	3.0
With Bun	419	28.9	31.9	19.2	88.1	6.7	1.5	1204	15.4	0.29	0.36	7.7	61.1	992	761	4.1

Sodium Restricted	NA mg	Diabetic	Kcal	Milk exg	Veg exg	Fruit exg	Bread exg	Meat exg	Fat exg	Low Fat & Low Chol	FAT gm	Chol mg	SFA gm	PFA gm
Without Bun	100		283	0.0	1.75	0.0	0.0	3.0-M	0.75		11.4	64.3	4.4	0.5
With Bun	302		402	0.0	1.75	0.0	1.75	3.0-M	0.75		13.6	66.7	4.9	0.7

Portion: 4 ounce cabbage roll (3 ounces edible protein), 2 ounces sauce

INGREDIENTS	48 portions		6 portions	
	weights	**measures**	**weights**	**measures**
Cabbage, remove core and discolored leaves	11 1/2 lb EP (13 lb AP)	48 leaves	1 1/2 lb EP (1 2/3 lb AP)	6 leaves
Filling:				
Ground beef, lean	12 lb	1 1/2 gal	1 1/2 lb	3 cups
Rice, cooked	3 1/4 lb (14 oz AP)	2 qt	7 oz EP (1 3/4 oz AP)	1 cup
Onions, chopped	1 lb EP	3 cups	2 oz	1/3 cup
Eggs, beaten	1 lb	2 cups (8 large)	2 oz	1/4 cup (1 large)
Pepper, black		1 Tbsp		1/4 tsp
Garlic powder		1 Tbsp		1/4 tsp
Sauce:				
Onions, diced	8 oz EP	1 1/2 cups	1 oz	3 Tbsp
Margarine, low sodium, melted	2 oz	1/4 cup	1/4 oz	1/2 Tbsp
Beef stock[1]		3 qt		1 1/2 cups
Tomato paste	3 lb	1 1/2 qt	6 oz	3/4 cup
Tomatoes, crushed	1 3/4 lb	1 qt	3 1/2 oz	1/2 cup
Sweet basil		1 Tbsp		1/4 tsp
Pepper, black		1 Tbsp		1/4 tsp

Method

1. Separate cabbage leaves. Blanch 2 or 3 minutes in steamer or boiling water; drain.
2. Combine beef, rice, onions, eggs, and seasonings. Blend well.
3. Using a No. 8 dipper, place 4 oz of filling in center of cabbage leaf. Roll into cylinder, folding in ends. Place seam side down in pan.
4. Prepare sauce.
   a. Saute onions in margarine until tender.
   b. Add stock, paste, tomatoes, and seasonings. Blend. Cover. Simmer 15 minutes.
5. Pour sauce over cabbage rolls.
6. Bake at 350°F for 45 minutes. Baste cabbage rolls with sauce before serving.

Notes

[1]May use a concentrated soup base as a quick stock. Prepare as directed by manufacturer.

Directions for Diet Preparations

Sodium Restricted (SR): Use low sodium beef stock, low sodium tomatoes, and low sodium tomato sauce.

Low Fat/Low Cholesterol (LF): 3 oz cabbage roll. Omit eggs. Place 3 oz of filling in cabbage. Low fat diets should consider individual tolerance when using cabbage, onions, and garlic.

Diabetic (DB): 4 oz cabbage roll, 2 oz sauce. Prepare as directed.

Mechanical Soft (SFT): Prepare as directed. Consider individual tolerance to cabbage.

Soft/Low Fiber (SLF): Not recommended. Use appropriate food alternative.

Puree (PUR): Omit cabbage. Blend sauce, strain. Add sauce to filling and blend. Add additional sauce if necessary to obtain desired consistency.

Nutrient Analysis per Serving:

Regular	KCAL gm	PRO gm	CHO gm	FAT mg	Chol gm	SFA gm	PFA iu	VITA mg	VITC mg	THI mg	RIB mg	NIA mg	CA mg	NA mg	K+ mg	FE
	347	27.5	22.0	16.8	126	6.0	1.2	1134	69.1	0.22	0.34	6.9	89.3	426	937	4.4

Sodium Restricted	NA mg	Diabetic	Kcal	Milk exg	Veg exg	Fruit exg	Bread exg	Meat exg	Fat exg	Low Fat & Low Chol	FAT gm	Chol mg	SFA gm	PFA gm
	143		347	0.0	2.5	0.0	0.5	3.0-M	0.0		13.2	66.7	4.7	0.9

Portion: 3 ounces cooked (3 ounces edible protein), 1 1/2 ounces gravy

INGREDIENTS	50 portions		6 portions	
	weights	**measures**	**weights**	**measures**
Beef round, sliced 3/4 inch thick (4 oz)	12 1/2 lb	50 patties	1 1/2 lb	6 patties
Flour, all-purpose	12 oz	3 cups	1 1/2 oz	1/3 cup
Pepper, black		2 tsp		1/4 tsp
Margarine, hot, low sodium	1 lb	2 cups	2 oz	1/4 cup
Gravy:				
Fat, meat drippings hot	5 oz	2/3 cup	2/3 oz	4 tsp
Flour, all-purpose	5 oz	1 1/4 cups	2/3 oz	2 1/2 Tbsp
Pepper, black		2 tsp		1/4 tsp
Water		2 1/2 qt		1 1/4 cups

Method

1. Cut meat into portions (4 per pound).
2. Mix flour and pepper; pound into meat.
3. Brown meat in margarine. Place meat slightly overlapping in baking or counter pans.
4. Prepare gravy.
   a. Add flour and pepper to fat; blend. Add water gradually, stirring constantly. Cook until smooth and thickened.
5. Add gravy to meat. Cover pans tightly with aluminum foil.
6. Bake at 350°F for 2 to 2 1/2 hours.

Directions for Diet Preparations

Sodium Restricted (SR): Prepare as directed.
Low Fat/Low Cholesterol (LF): 2 oz cooked and **Diabetic** (DB): 3 oz cooked. In step #3 use half the amount of margarine specified. Omit fat, use reduced-calorie margarine in gravy. May use gravy if able to calculate into daily food plan.
Mechanical Soft (SFT): Prepare as directed. Chop meat.
Soft/Low Fiber (SLF): Omit black pepper.
Puree (PUR): Prepare as directed. Blend beef and gravy. Add additional gravy if necessary to obtain desired consistency.

Nutrient Analysis per Serving:

Regular	KCAL	PRO gm	CHO gm	FAT gm	Chol mg	SFA gm	PFA gm	VITA iu	VITC mg	THI mg	RIB mg	NIA mg	CA mg	NA mg	K+ mg	FE mg
	293	25.3	7.7	17.1	72.7	5.1	2.9	304	0.0	0.15	0.23	4.1	8.8	57.2	367	2.7

Sodium Restricted	NA mg	Diabetic	Kcal	Milk exg	Veg exg	Fruit exg	Bread exg	Meat exg	Fat exg	Low Fat & Low Chol	FAT gm	Chol mg	SFA gm	PFA gm
	57.2		245	0.0	0.0	0.0	0.5	3.0-M	0.0		9.1	54.2	2.5	1.6

Portion: 3 1/2 ounces (3 ounces edible protein)

INGREDIENTS	50 portions		6 portions	
	weights	measures	weights	measures
Ground beef, lean	12 lb	1 1/2 gal	1 1/2 lb	3 cups
Bread crumbs, soft	12 oz	1 1/2 qt	1 1/2 oz	3/4 cup
Onions, finely chopped	1 lb	3 cups	2 oz	1/3 cup
Water		3 cups		1/3 cup
Tomato catsup	1 lb	2 cups	2 oz	1/4 cup

Method

1. Combine all ingredients. Mix until blended. Do not over mix.
2. Portion meat with No. 10 dipper. Place on baking sheets, flatten meat slightly.
3. Bake at 350°F for 45 minutes or until firm and center is no longer pink.

Directions for Diet Preparations

Sodium Restricted (SR): Use low sodium bread crumbs and low sodium catsup. May use pureed fresh tomatoes for catsup.

Low Fat/Low Cholesterol (LF): 2 1/2 oz cooked, **Diabetic** (DB): 3 1/2 oz cooked, and **Mechanical Soft** (SFT): Prepare as directed. Low fat diets should consider individual tolerance when using onions.

Soft/Low Fiber (SLF): Omit onions.

Puree (PUR): Prepare as directed. Add liquid (ie. broth or sauce) and blend to obtain desired consistency.

Nutrient Analysis per Serving:

Regular	KCAL	PRO gm	CHO gm	FAT gm	Chol mg	SFA gm	PFA gm	VITA iu	VITC mg	THI mg	RIB mg	NIA mg	CA mg	NA mg	K+ mg	FE mg
	300	25.8	12.3	15.6	86.3	6.0	0.5	155	2.5	0.11	0.25	5.8	29.6	279	370	2.7

Sodium Restricted	NA mg	Diabetic	Kcal	Milk exg	Veg exg	Fruit exg	Bread exg	Meat exg	Fat exg	Low Fat & Low Chol	FAT gm	Chol mg	SFA gm	PFA gm
	79.6		300	0.0	0.8	0.0	0.5	3.0-M	0.0		11.1	61.6	4.3	0.4

D21   Roast Beef

Portion: 3 ounces (3 ounces edible protein)

INGREDIENTS	50 portions		8 portions	
	weights	measures	weights	measures
Beef round or rump, boneless	17 1/4 lb		2 3/4 lb	
Pepper, black		1 Tbsp		1 tsp
Basil, ground		1 Tbsp		1 tsp

Method

1. Rub outside of meat with pepper and basil.
2. Place roast in pan, fat side up. Do not crowd. Do not cover.
3. Insert meat thermometer in center of the thickest part of the meat.
4. Roast at 300°F in oven until thermometer reaches 140°F to 150°F. Use the following table for cooking time.

Cut	Internal Temperature	Approximate Cooking Time (minutes per pound)
Beef Rump, boneless	150°F (medium)	22
	160°F (well)	24
Beef Round, boneless	150°F (medium)	22
	160°F (well)	24

5. Remove meat from pan. Cool 30 minutes. Slice and serve.
6. Drain off fat and make gravy from remaining drippings.

Directions for Diet Preparations

Sodium Restricted (SR): **Low Fat/Low Cholesterol** (LF): 2 oz, **Diabetic** (DB): 3 oz, and **Mechanical Soft** (SFT) and **Soft/Low Fiber** (SLF): Prepare as directed.
Puree (PUR): Prepare as directed. Add liquid (i.e. broth or sauce) and blend to obtain desired consistency.

Nutrient Analysis per Serving:

Regular	KCAL	PRO gm	CHO gm	FAT gm	Chol mg	SFA gm	PFA gm	VITA iu	VITC mg	THI mg	RIB mg	NIA mg	CA mg	NA mg	K+ mg	FE mg
	233	21.7	0.1	15.5	71.5	6.2	0.7	8.7	0.06	0.08	0.18	3.2	8.4	51.1	316	2.1

Sodium Restricted	NA mg	Diabetic	Kcal	Milk exg	Veg exg	Fruit exg	Bread exg	Meat exg	Fat exg	Low Fat & Low Chol	FAT gm	Chol mg	SFA gm	PFA gm
	51.1		233	0.0.	0.0	0.0	0.0	3.0-M	0.0		15.5	71.5	6.2	0.7

Portion: 3 1/2 ounces (3 ounces edible protein)

INGREDIENTS	50 portions		6 portions	
	weights	measures	weights	measures
Veal cutlets, 4 oz each	12 1/2 lb	50 cutlets	1 1/2 lb	6 cutlets
Flour, all-purpose	8 oz	2 cups	1 oz	1/4 cup
Pepper, black		2 tsp		1/4 tsp
Eggs, beaten	12 oz	1 1/2 cups (6 large)	2 oz	1/4 cup (1 large)
Milk, skim or water	12 oz	1 1/2 cups	1 1/2 oz	3 Tbsp
Bread crumbs, fine	1 lb	2 qt	2 oz	1 cup
Margarine, low sodium, melted	2 lb	1 qt	4 oz	1/2 cup

Method

1. Dredge cutlets in mixture of flour and pepper.
2. Combine eggs and milk (or water).
3. Dip cutlets in egg mixture, then roll in bread crumbs.
4. Brown veal in margarine until browned on all sides.
5. Place breaded veal in baking pans. Add 2 cups water to each pan. Cover.
6. Bake at 325°F for about 45 to 60 minutes or until tender.

Notes

[1]May serve with brown gravy, mushroom gravy, or tomato sauce.

Directions for Diet Preparations

Sodium Restricted (SR): Use low sodium bread crumbs.

Low Fat/Low Cholesterol (LF): 2 1/2 oz. Omit eggs, substitute with an equal amount of egg whites or a commercial egg substitute. Omit margarine. Omit step #4. Broil veal until browned on all sides. Bake with broth to moisten.

Diabetic (DB): 3 1/2 oz. Omit margarine. Omit step #4. Broil veal until browned on all sides. Bake with broth to moisten.

Mechanical Soft (SFT): Prepare as directed. Chop meat.

Soft/Low Fiber (SLF): Omit pepper.

Puree (PUR): Prepare as directed. Add liquid (i.e. broth, gravy, or sauce); blend to obtain desired consistency.

Nutrient Analysis per Serving:

Regular	KCAL	PRO gm	CHO gm	FAT gm	Chol mg	SFA gm	PFA gm	VITA iu	VITC mg	THI mg	RIB mg	NIA mg	CA mg	NA mg	K+ mg	FE mg
	355	25.3	15.5	20.5	114.1	7.1	3.4	348	0.01	0.25	0.38	8.4	38.9	206	392	4.2

Sodium Restricted	NA mg	Diabetic	Kcal	Milk exg	Veg exg	Fruit exg	Bread exg	Meat exg	Fat exg	Low Fat & Low Chol	FAT gm	Chol mg	SFA gm	PFA gm
	89.8		286	0.0	0.0	0.0	1.0	3.0-M	0.0		8.6	58.1	4.0	0.5

Veal Chop

Portion: 1 chop, 6 ounces (3 ounces edible protein)

INGREDIENTS	50 portions		6 portions	
	weights	measures	weights	measures
Veal chops, 6 oz each	18 3/4 lb	50 chops	2 1/4 lb	6 chops
Water		3 cups		1/3 cup
Flour, all-purpose	1 lb	1 qt	2 oz	1/2 cup
Pepper, black		2 tsp		1/4 tsp
Margarine, low sodium, melted	2 1/2 lb	1 1/4 qt	5 oz	2/3 cup
Beef stock[1]	1 1/2 gal			3 cups

Method

1. Trim excess fat from chops.
2. Combine flour and pepper. Dip chops in water, then dredge in flour mixture.
3. Heat margarine over moderate heat.
4. Place chops in hot pan (or on griddle or skillet). Cook until browned on both sides.
5. Add beef stock to chops. Simmer 30 minutes at 300°F in oven.

Notes

[1]May use a concentrated soup base as a quick beef stock. Prepare as directed by manufacturer.

Directions for Diet Preparations

Sodium Restricted (SR): Prepare as directed. May use a low sodium soup base as directed by manufacturer, instead of the stock.

Low Fat/Low Cholesterol (LF): 5 oz chop and **Diabetic** (DB): 6 oz chop. Omit margarine and step #3 and #4. Broil until browned on both sides, turn once. Add beef stock to chops. Simmer 30 minutes at 300°F in oven.

Mechanical Soft (SFT): Prepare as directed. Remove veal from bone. Chop meat.

Soft/Low Fiber (SLF): Omit black pepper.

Puree (PUR): Prepare as directed. Remove veal from bone. Combine beef stock with veal. Blend to obtain desired consistency.

Nutrient Analysis per Serving:

Regular	KCAL	PRO gm	CHO gm	FAT gm	Chol mg	SFA gm	PFA gm	VITA iu	VITC mg	THI mg	RIB mg	NIA mg	CA mg	NA mg	K+ mg	FE mg
	306	23.8	7.5	19.3	85.8	6.7	2.6	317	0.01	0.12	0.26	5.2	13.5	67.3	264	3.2

Sodium Restricted	NA mg	Diabetic	Kcal	Milk exg	Veg exg	Fruit exg	Bread exg	Meat exg	Fat exg	Low Fat & Low Chol	FAT gm	Chol mg	SFA gm	PFA gm
	67.3		237	0.0	0.0	0.0	0.75	3.0-L	0.0		7.8	57.2	3.6	0.03

Portion: 3 1/2 ounces veal (3 ounces edible protein), 1/2 cup sauce with vegetables

Ingredients	50 portions		6 portions	
	weights	measures	weights	measures
Veal cutlets, 4 oz each	12 1/2 lb	50 cutlets	1 1/2 lb	6 cutlets
Water		3 cups		1/3 cup
Flour, all-purpose	8 oz	2 cups	1 oz	1/4 cup
Garlic powder		2 tsp		1/4 tsp
Margarine, low sodium, melted	2 lb	1 qt	4 oz	1/2 cup
Sauce:				
Margarine, low sodium, melted	4 oz	1/2 cup	1/2 oz	1 Tbsp
Onions, diced	1 lb	3 cups	2 oz	1/3 cup
Green peppers, cut into strips	1 1/3 lb	1 qt	2 2/3 oz	1/2 cup
Mushrooms, sliced, canned	1 1/2 lb	3 cups	3 oz	1/3 cup
Tomatoes, diced with juice	7 lb	3 1/2 qt	14 oz	1 3/4 cups
Oregano		2 tsp		1/4 tsp
Chicken stock[1]		1 qt		1/2 cup
Flour, all-purpose	4 oz	1 cup	1/2 oz	2 Tbsp
Water, cold		2 cups		1/4 cup

Method

1. Dip cutlets in water, then dredge in mixture of flour and garlic.
2. Brown in margarine. Place in baking pans.
3. Prepare sauce with vegetables.
   a. Sauté onions in margarine. Add green peppers, mushrooms, tomatoes with juice, oregano, and chicken stock.
   b. Mix flour and water. Add to chicken stock mixture. Stir to thicken.
4. Pour sauce with vegetables over veal. Cover.
5. Bake at 325°F for 45 minutes.

Notes

[1]May use a concentrated soup base as a quick chicken stock. Prepare as directed by manufacturer.

Directions for Diet Preparations

Sodium Restricted (SR): Use low sodium tomatoes (or diced fresh tomatoes). Use low sodium chicken broth.

Low Fat/Low Cholesterol (LF): 2 1/2 oz veal, 1/2 cup sauce with vegetables and **Diabetic** (DB): 3 1/2 oz veal, 1/2 cup sauce with vegetables. Omit margarine in steps #2 and #3. Broil veal until browned on all sides. Steam vegetables until tender. Pour sauce and vegetables over veal. Cover. Bake at 325°F for 45 minutes. Low fat diets should consider individual tolerance to garlic powder and onions.

Mechanical Soft (SFT): Prepare as directed. Chop meat. Cook vegetables until tender. Consider individual tolerance.

Soft/Low Fiber (SLF): Omit garlic powder and onions. Cook vegetables until tender.

Puree (PUR): Prepare as directed. Add sauce to veal; blend to obtain desired consistency.

Nutrient Analysis per Serving:

Regular	KCAL	PRO gm	CHO gm	FAT gm	Chol mg	SFA gm	PFA gm	VITA iu	VITC mg	THI mg	RIB mg	NIA mg	CA mg	NA mg	K+ mg	FE mg
	340	25.6	11.9	20.8	85.8	6.8	4.3	867	22.1	0.18	0.31	6.6	38.6	252	431	3.9

Sodium Restricted	NA mg	Diabetic	Kcal	Milk exg	Veg exg	Fruit exg	Bread exg	Meat exg	Fat exg	Low Fat & Low Chol	FAT gm	Chol mg	SFA gm	PFA gm
	93.7		272	0.0	1.25	0.0	0.5	3.0-L	0.0		11.2	73.6	4.7	1.5

Portion: 4 ounces (3 ounces edible protein)

INGREDIENTS	50 portions		6 portions	
	weights	**measures**	**weights**	**measures**
Ground veal, lean	12 lb	1 1/2 gal	1 1/2 lb	3 cups
Bread crumbs, soft	12 oz	1 1/2 qt	1 1/2 oz	3/4 cup
Milk, skim, or water		1 qt		1/2 cup
Eggs, beaten	1 lb	2 cups (8 large)	2 oz	1/4 cup (1 large)
Onion, chopped	4 oz	3/4 cup	1/2 oz	1 1/2 Tbsp
Pepper, black		2 tsp		1/4 tsp
Garlic powder		2 tsp		1/4 tsp

Method

1. Mix all ingredients until blended. Do not over mix.
2. Press mixture into loaf pans or counter pans.
3. Bake at 325°F for 1 1/2 to 2 hours.

Directions for Diet Preparations

Sodium Restricted (SR): Use low sodium bread crumbs.

Low Fat/Low Cholesterol (LF): 3 oz. Omit eggs. Low fat diets should consider individual tolerance to onions and garlic.

Diabetic (DB): 4 oz. Prepare as directed.

Mechanical Soft (SFT): Prepare as directed.

Soft/Low Fiber (SLF): Omit onions and black pepper.

Puree (PUR): Prepare as directed. Add liquid (i.e. broth, gravy, or sauce); blend to obtain desired consistency.

Nutrient Analysis per Serving:

Regular	KCAL	PRO gm	CHO gm	FAT gm	Chol mg	SFA gm	PFA gm	VITA iu	VITC mg	THI mg	RIB mg	NIA mg	CA mg	NA mg	K+ mg	FE mg
	261	26.2	9.1	12.3	130	5.6	1.1	41.6	0.2	0.12	0.31	6.0	30.1	140	223	3.6

Sodium Restricted	NA mg	Diabetic	Kcal	Milk exg	Veg exg	Fruit exg	Bread exg	Meat exg	Fat exg	Low Fat & Low Chol	FAT gm	Chol mg	SFA gm	PFA gm
	54.4		261	0.0	0.25	0.0	1.0	3.0-M	0.0		8.5	64.8	4.0	0.8

Veal Parmesan

Portion: 4 ounces (3 ounces edible protein), 1 ounce sauce

INGREDIENTS	50 portions		6 portions	
	weights	**measures**	**weights**	**measures**
Veal cutlets, 4 oz each	12 1/2 lb	50 cutlets	1 1/2 lb	6 cutlets
Flour, all-purpose	8 oz	2 cups	1 oz	1/4 cup
Garlic powder		2 tsp		1/4 tsp
Eggs, beaten	12 oz	1 1/2 cups (6 large)	2 oz	1/4 cup (1 large)
Milk, skim or water		1 1/2 cups		3 Tbsp
Parmesan cheese, grated	8 oz	1 3/4 cups	1 oz	3 1/2 Tbsp
Bread crumbs, fine	1 lb	2 qt	2 oz	1 cup
Margarine, low sodium, melted	2 lb	1 qt	4 oz	1/2 cup
Tomato sauce	3 1/2 lb	1 3/4 qt	6 oz	3/4 cup
Mozzarella cheese, part skim, shredded	1 1/2 lb	1 1/3 qt	3 oz	2/3 cup

Method

1. Dredge cutlets in mixture of flour and garlic.
2. Combine eggs and milk (or water).
3. Combine parmesan cheese and bread crumbs.
4. Dip cutlets in egg mixture, then roll in bread crumbs mixture.
5. Brown cutlets in margarine until browned on all sides.
6. Place cutlets in baking pans.
7. Pour tomato sauce over cutlets. Top with shredded mozzarella cheese.
8. Bake at 325°F for one hour.

Directions for Diet Preparations

Sodium Restricted (SR): Use low sodium bread crumbs. Omit parmesan cheese. Use low sodium tomato sauce (or puree fresh tomatoes). Use low sodium cheese.

Low Fat/Low Cholesterol (LF): 3 oz veal, 1 oz sauce. Omit eggs, substitute with an equal amount of egg whites or a commercial egg substitute. Omit margarine. Omit step #5. Broil veal until browned on all sides. Pour low fat tomato sauce over cutlets. Top with 1/2 oz low fat low cholesterol cheese per cutlet. Low fat diets should consider individual tolerance to garlic.

Diabetic (DB): 4 oz veal, 1 oz sauce. Omit margarine. Omit step #5. Broil veal until browned on all sides. Pour diabetic tomato sauce over cutlets. Top with 1/2 oz low fat cheese per cutlet.

Mechanical Soft (SFT): Prepare as directed. Chop meat.

Soft/Low Fiber (SLF): Omit garlic and parmesan cheese. Use SLF Tomato Sauce.

Puree (PUR): Prepare as directed. Add sauce; blend to obtain desired consistency.

Nutrient Analysis per Serving:

Regular	KCAL	PRO gm	CHO gm	FAT gm	Chol mg	SFA gm	PFA gm	VITA iu	VITC mg	THI mg	RIB mg	NIA mg	CA mg	NA mg	K+ mg	FE mg
	462	32.6	20.6	26.6	130	9.5	5.0	1224	9.2	0.20	0.41	6.9	189	446	352	4.4

Sodium Restricted	NA mg	Diabetic	Kcal	Milk exg	Veg exg	Fruit exg	Bread exg	Meat exg	Fat exg	Low Fat & Low Chol	FAT gm	Chol mg	SFA gm	PFA gm
	121		366	0.0	1.5	0.0	1.0	3.0-M	0.0		12.5	69.2	6.0	1.3

Veal Patty

Portion: 3 1/2 ounces (3 ounces edible protein)

INGREDIENTS	50 portions		6 portions	
	weights	measures	weights	measures
Ground veal, lean	12 lb	1 1/2 gal	1 1/2 lb	3 cups
Eggs, beaten	8 oz	1 cup (4 large)	2 oz	1/4 cup (1 large)
Water		1 qt		1/2 cup
Bread crumbs, soft	4 oz	2 cups	1/2 oz	1/4 cup
Pepper, black		2 tsp		1/4 tsp
Onions, chopped	4 oz	3/4 cup	1/2 oz	1 1/2 Tbsp

Method

1. Combine all ingredients until blended.
2. Use a No. 10 dipper and shape into patties.
3. Place on baking sheets. Bake at 400°F for 15 to 20 minutes or until center is cooked.

Notes

[1]May grill or broil veal patties.
[2]Serve patty with sauce, gravy, or on a bun.

Directions for Diet Preparations

Sodium Restricted (SR): Use low sodium bread crumbs.
Low Fat/Low Cholesterol (LF): 2 1/2 oz. Omit eggs. Consider individual tolerance when using onions.
Diabetic (DB): 3 1/2 oz and **Mechanical Soft** (SFT): Prepare as directed.
Soft/Low Fiber (SLF): Omit black pepper and onions.
Puree (PUR): Prepare as directed. Add liquid (i.e. broth, sauce, or gravy) and blend to obtain desired consistency.

Nutrient Analysis per Serving:

Regular	KCAL	PRO gm	CHO gm	FAT gm	Chol mg	SFA gm	PFA gm	VITA iu	VITC mg	THI mg	RIB mg	NIA mg	CA mg	NA mg	K+ mg	FE mg
	207	24.0	3.1	10.0	108	4.7	0.6	20.8	0.2	0.07	0.23	4.7	17.2	91.5	273	2.9

Sodium Restricted	NA mg	Diabetic	Kcal	Milk exg	Veg exg	Fruit exg	Bread exg	Meat exg	Fat exg	Low Fat & Low Chol	FAT gm	Chol mg	SFA gm	PFA gm
	62.4		207	0.0	0.0	0.0	0.5	3.0-L	0.0		6.8	61.5	3.2	0.4

D28   Baked Glazed Ham

Portion: 3 ounces (3 ounces edible protein)

INGREDIENTS	50 portions		8 portions	
	weights	**measures**	**weights**	**measures**
Ham, boneless, cooked	15 lb		2 1/2 lb	
Ham Glaze:				
Sugar, brown	8 oz	1 1/2 cups	1 3/4 oz	1/3 cup
Cornstarch		2 Tbsp		1 tsp
Corn syrup		1/4 cup		3/4 Tbsp
Pineapple juice, unsweetened		2 Tbsp		1 tsp

Method

1. Place ham fat side up on rack in roasting pan. Do not cover.
2. Bake at 325°F. Use the following table for cooking times. (Information is based on a fully cooked boneless ham.)

	Weight (in pounds)	Internal Temperature	Approximate Cooking Time (minutes/pound)
Whole	8 to 12 lb	140°F	15 to 18 minutes
Half	4 to 6 lb	140°F	18 to 25 minutes
Portion	3 to 4 lb	140°F	27 to 33 minutes

3. Remove ham from oven about 30 minutes before it is done cooking. Drain fat.
4. Prepare glaze:
   a. Combine ingredients for glaze.
5. Spoon glaze over ham.
6. Return ham to oven. Bake at 325°F until internal temperature reaches 140°F.

Directions for Diet Preparations

Sodium Restricted (SR) and **Soft/Low Fiber** (SLF): Not recommended. Use fresh pork.

Low Fat/Low Cholesterol (LF): 2 oz cooked. Prepare as directed.

Diabetic (DB): 3 oz cooked.

50 portions: Omit glaze. Cover with 2 cups unsweetened pineapple tidbits with juice.

8 portions: Omit glaze. Cover with 1/2 cup unsweetened pineapple tidbits with juice.

Mechanical Soft (SFT): Prepare as directed. Chop meat.

Puree (PUR): Prepare as directed. Add liquid (i.e. gravy or sauce) to ham; blend to obtain desired consistency.

Nutrient Analysis per Serving:

Regular	KCAL	PRO gm	CHO gm	FAT gm	Chol mg	SFA gm	PFA gm	VITA iu	VITC mg	THI mg	RIB mg	NIA mg	CA mg	NA mg	K+ mg	FE mg
	238	18.3	7.9	14.2	52.7	5.1	1.5	0.03	0.3	0.51	0.19	3.8	12.4	1012	267	1.0

Sodium Restricted	Diabetic	Kcal	Milk exg	Veg exg	Fruit exg	Bread exg	Meat exg	Fat exg	Low Fat & Low Chol	FAT gm	Chol mg	SFA gm	PFA gm
Not Recommended		213	0.0	0.0	0.1	0.0	3.0-M	0.0		9.5	35.1	3.3	1.0

Portion: 1 chop, 7 1/2 ounces (3 ounces edible protein)

INGREDIENTS	50 portions		6 portions	
	weights	measures	weights	measures
Pork chops, cut 3 per pound	23 1/2 lb	50 chops	3 lb	6 chops
Flour, all-purpose	12 oz	3 cups	1 1/2 oz	1/3 cup
Pepper, black		1 Tbsp		1/4 tsp
Eggs, beaten	1 lb	2 cups (8 large)	2 oz	1/4 cup (1 large)
Milk, skim or water		3 1/2 cup		1/2 cup
Bread crumbs, dry, ground	1 1/4 lb	1 1/4 qt	2 1/2 oz	2/3 cup
Margarine, low sodium, melted	8 oz	1 cup	1 oz	2 Tbsp
Water		1 qt		1/2 cup

Method

1. Dredge chops in flour/pepper mixture.
2. Combine eggs and milk (or water).
3. Dip chops in egg mixture, then roll in bread crumbs.
4. Place in single layer on greased sheet pans.
5. Pour margarine over chops.
6. Bake at 400°F until browned, about 10 minutes.
7. Remove chops from oven and arrange in counter pans.
8. 50 portions: Add 2 cups water to each pan. Cover pans.
   6 portions: Add 1/2 cup water to pan. Cover pan.
9. Bake at 325°F, about 1 hour or until tender.

Directions for Diet Preparations

Sodium Restricted (SR): Use low sodium bread crumbs.

Low Fat/Low Cholesterol (LF): 2 oz edible cooked portion. Omit eggs, substitute with an equal amount of egg whites or a commercial egg substitute. Omit margarine in step #5. Cover pork chops with chicken broth and continue with step #6.

Diabetic (DB): 3 oz edible cooked portion. Omit margarine in step #5. Cover pork chops with chicken broth and continue with step #6.

Mechanical Soft (SFT): Prepare as directed. Remove from bone. Chop meat.

Soft/Low Fiber (SLF): Omit black pepper.

Puree (PUR): Prepare as directed. Remove from bone. Add liquid (i.e. gravy or broth) to pork; blender to obtain desired consistency.

Nutrient Analysis per Serving:

Regular	KCAL	PRO gm	CHO gm	FAT gm	Chol mg	SFA gm	PFA gm	VITA iu	VITC mg	THI mg	RIB mg	NIA mg	CA mg	NA mg	K+ mg	FE mg
	412	28.0	12.9	26.6	135	8.7	3.9	201	0.2	0.74	0.29	5.9	24.8	130	305	1.6

Sodium Restricted	NA mg	Diabetic	Kcal	Milk exg	Veg exg	Fruit exg	Bread exg	Meat exg	Fat exg	Low Fat & Low Chol	FAT gm	Chol mg	SFA gm	PFA gm
	57.2		380	0.0	0.0	0.0	1.0	3.0-M	1.5		14.7	61.0	5.2	1.7

Portion: 1 chop, 7 1/2 ounces (3 ounces edible protein), 1/4 cup stuffing

INGREDIENTS	50 portions		6 portions	
	weights	measures	weights	measures
Pork chops, cut 3 per pound	23 1/2 lb	50 chops	3 lb	6 chops
Stuffing:				
Onions, chopped	8 oz	1 1/2 cups	1 oz	3 Tbsp
Celery, chopped	8 oz	1 cup	1 oz	2 Tbsp
Margarine, low sodium, melted	6 oz	3/4 cup	3/4 oz	1 1/2 Tbsp
Bread crumbs, soft	12 oz	1 1/2 qt	1 1/2 oz	3/4 cup
Apples, pared, chopped	2 1/4 lb EP (3 lb AP)	2 qt	4 1/2 oz EP (6 oz AP)	1 cup
Poultry seasoning		2 tsp		1/4 tsp
Thyme		2 tsp		1/4 tsp
Chicken stock[1]		1 1/2 qt		3/4 cup

Method

1. Cut a pocket in each pork chop by splitting the meaty part of the chop.
2. Saute onions and celery in margarine. Stir in bread crumbs, apples, and seasonings. Mix well.
3. Fill each pork chop pocket with 1/4 cup (No. 16 dipper) stuffing.
4. Place chops in baking pans.
5. Pour enough chicken stock in each pan to cover bottom of pan about 1/8 inch deep (about 2 cups per pan). Cover pans.
6. Bake at 350°F for about 1 hour or until chops are tender and browned.

Notes

[1]May use a concentrated chicken soup base as a quick chicken stock. Prepare as directed by manufacturer.

Directions for Diet Preparations

Sodium Restricted (SR): Use low sodium bread crumbs and low sodium chicken stock.

Low Fat/Low Cholesterol (LF): 2 oz cooked edible portion; 1/4 cup stuffing and **Diabetic** (DB): 3 oz cooked edible portion; 1/4 cup stuffing. Use reduced-calorie margarine in equal amount specified for regular margarine.

Mechanical Soft (SFT): Prepare as directed. Remove from bone. Chop meat. Consider individual tolerance when using stuffing.

Soft/Low Fiber (SLF): Omit stuffing.

Puree (PUR): Remove pork from bones. Add liquid (i.e. gravy or broth) to pork; blender to obtain desired consistency. Blenderize stuffing. Add additional liquid if necessary to obtain desired consistency.

Nutrient Analysis per Serving:

Regular	KCAL	PRO gm	CHO gm	FAT gm	Chol mg	SFA gm	PFA gm	VITA iu	VITC mg	THI mg	RIB mg	NIA mg	CA mg	NA mg	K+ mg	FE mg
	306	25.5	12.1	16.5	81.5	5.1	2.4	135.7	1.4	0.9	0.4	5.8	25.5	160	468	1.5

Sodium Restricted	NA mg	Diabetic	Kcal	Milk exg	Veg exg	Fruit exg	Bread exg	Meat exg	Fat exg	Low Fat & Low Chol	FAT gm	Chol mg	SFA gm	PFA gm
	74.5		294	0.0	0.0	0.25	0.75	3.0-M	0.0		10.8	54.6	3.4	1.5

Portion: 3 ounces cooked (3 ounces edible protein)

INGREDIENTS	50 portions		8 portions	
	weights	measures	weights	measures
Pork roast, boneless (rolled loin, fresh ham, or shoulder)	18 lb		3 lb	
Pepper, black		1 Tbsp		1 tsp
Basil, ground		1 Tbsp		1 tsp

Method

1. Rub outside of meat with pepper and basil.
2. Place roast in pan. Do not crowd. Do not cover.
3. Insert meat thermometer in center of the thickest part of the meat. Roast at 325°F in oven until thermometer reaches 170°F. Use the following table for cooking time.

Cut	Weight (in pounds)	Internal Temperature	Approximate Cooking Time (minutes per pound)
Loin roast, boneless	3 to 5 lb	170°F	30 to 35 minutes
Shoulder, picnic, boneless	3 to 5 lb	170°F	30 to 35 minutes
Fresh Ham, (leg), whole, boneless	10 to 14 lb	170°F	24 to 28 minutes

4. Remove roast from pan. Cool 30 minutes before slicing.

Directions for Diet Preparations

Sodium Restricted (SR), **Low Fat/Low Cholesterol** (LF): 2 oz cooked and **Diabetic** (DB): 3 oz cooked. Prepare as directed.
Mechanical Soft (SFT): Prepare as directed. Chop meat.
Soft/Low Fiber (SLF): Omit black pepper.
Puree (PUR): Prepare as directed. Add liquid (i.e. gravy or broth) to pork; blender to obtain desired consistency.

Nutrient Analysis per Serving:

Regular	KCAL	PRO gm	CHO gm	FAT gm	Chol mg	SFA gm	PFA gm	VITA iu	VITC mg	THI mg	RIB mg	NIA mg	CA mg	NA mg	K+ mg	FE mg
	278	18.7	0.1	21.8	81.5	7.8	2.4	12.6	0.3	0.45	0.27	3.3	7.6	57.8	261	1.1

Sodium Restricted	NA mg	Diabetic	Kcal	Milk exg	Veg exg	Fruit exg	Bread exg	Meat exg	Fat exg	Low Fat & Low Chol	FAT gm	Chol mg	SFA gm	PFA gm
	57.8		278	0.0	0.0	0.0	0.0	3.0-H	0.0		14.5	54.3	5.2	1.6

Portion: 2 slices

INGREDIENTS	50 portions		6 portions	
	weights	measures	weights	measures
Bacon, sliced (17–20/lb)	6 lb	100 slices	10 1/2 oz	12 slices

Method

1. **Broil:** Place bacon strips on broiling rack 3 inches from heat. Turn once to brown both sides (about 2 minutes on each side).
2. **Bake:** Place bacon strips slightly overlapping in shallow pans. Bake at 350°F for 12 minutes (300°F in convection oven for 8 minutes).
3. **Grill:** Grill at 375°F for 1 to 2 minutes on each side until brown and crisp.

Directions for Diet Preparations

Sodium Restricted (SR), **Low Fat/Low Cholesterol** (LF), **Soft/Low Fiber** (SLF), and **Puree** (PUR): Not recommended.
Diabetic (DB): 1 slice. May use if able to calculate into daily food plan.
Mechanical Soft (SFT): Consider individual tolerance.

Nutrient Analysis per Serving:

Regular	KCAL	PRO gm	CHO gm	FAT gm	Chol mg	SFA gm	PFA gm	VITA iu	VITC mg	THI mg	RIB mg	NIA mg	CA mg	NA mg	K+ mg	FE mg
	72.5	3.8	0.07	6.2	10.7	2.2	NA	0.0	4.2	0.08	0.03	0.92	1.5	201	61.2	0.2

Sodium Restricted	Diabetic	Kcal	Milk exg	Veg exg	Fruit exg	Bread exg	Meat exg	Fat exg	Low Fat & Low Chol	Not Recommended
Not Recommended		36.3	0.0	0.0	0.0	0.0	0.4-H	0.0		

Portion: 2 ounces (1 patty or 2 links)

INGREDIENTS	50 portions		6 portions	
	weights	measures	weights	measures
Sausage, 2 oz patties or	13 1/2 lb	50 patties	1 3/4 lb	6 patties
Links (12 to 16 per pound)	8 lb	100 links	1 lb	12 links

Method

1. **Grill:** Brown both sides on griddle.
2. **Bake:**
   a. Separate sausages. Prick with fork.
   b. Par boil 10 minutes. Drain.
   c. Place sausages close together in baking pan.
   d. Brown 15 minutes in 400°F oven. Remove. Pour off fat.

Directions for Diet Preparations

Sodium Restricted (SR), **Low Fat/Low Cholesterol** (LF), **Soft/Low Fiber** (SLF), and **Puree** (PUR): Not recommended.
Diabetic (DB): 1 oz. May use if able to calculate into daily food plan.
Mechanical Soft (SFT): Prepare as directed. Chop.

Nutrient Analysis per Serving:

Regular	KCAL	PRO	CHO	FAT	Chol	SFA	PFA	VITA	VITC	THI	RIB	NIA	CA	NA	K+	FE
		gm	gm	gm	mg	gm	gm	iu	mg	mg	mg	mg	mg	mg	mg	mg
	190	7.6	0.8	17.2	40.2	6.0	1.8	0.0	10.8	0.1	0.1	1.8	5.7	536	107	0.8

Sodium		Diabetic	Kcal	Milk	Veg	Fruit	Bread	Meat	Fat	Low Fat &	Not Recommended
Restricted				exg	exg	exg	exg	exg	exg	Low Chol	
Not Recommended			95.2	0.0	0.0	0.0	0.0	1.0-H	0.0		

Broiled Lamb Chop

Portion: 1 chop, 6 ounces (3 ounces edible protein)

INGREDIENTS	50 portions		6 portions	
	weights	measures	weights	measures
Lamb chops, 6 oz each	18 3/4 lb	50 chops	2 1/4 lb	6 chops
Basil, ground		1 Tbsp		1 tsp

Method

1. Preheat broiler.
2. Season with basil.
3. Place chops on broiler rack or grid 3 to 5 inches from heat.
4. Broil 6 to 9 minutes on each side, depending on thickness of meat at degree of doneness.

Directions for Diet Preparations

Sodium Restricted (SR), **Low Fat/Low Cholesterol** (LF): 5 oz chop (2 oz edible protein), and **Diabetic** (DB): 6 oz chop (3 oz edible protein). Prepare as directed.
Mechanical Soft (SFT): Remove from bone. Chop meat.
Soft/Low Fiber (SLF): Remove from bone.
Puree (PUR): Remove from bone. Add liquid (i.e. gravy or broth) to lamb; blender to obtain desired consistency.

Nutrient Analysis per Serving:

Regular	KCAL	PRO gm	CHO gm	FAT gm	Chol mg	SFA gm	PFA gm	VITA iu	VITC mg	THI mg	RIB mg	NIA mg	CA mg	NA mg	K+ mg	FE mg
	346	17.0	0.05	30.2	83.2	16.9	0.1	8.5	0.05	0.10	0.17	3.9	9.5	41.8	194	0.9

Sodium Restricted	NA mg	Diabetic	Kcal	Milk exg	Veg exg	Fruit exg	Bread exg	Meat exg	Fat exg	Low Fat & Low Chol	FAT gm	Chol mg	SFA gm	PFA gm
	41.8		346	0.0	0.0	0.0	0.0	3.0-H	1.0		20.1	55.5	11.2	0.07

Portion: 3 ounces (3 ounces edible protein)

INGREDIENTS	50 portions		6 portions	
	weights	measures	weights	measures
Lamb roast, boneless (rolled leg or shoulder)	15 1/3 lb		2 lb	
Tarragon		2 Tbsp		1 tsp
Garlic, finely chopped		4 cloves		1 clove
Garnish:				
Mint jelly	1 1/4 lb	2 1/2 cups	2 oz	1/4 cup

Method

1. Rub outside of roast with tarragon and garlic.
2. Place roast fat side up in roasting pan. Do not cover.
3. Insert meat thermometer in thickest part of meat. Roast in oven at 325°F until meat thermometer registers degree of doneness.
   a. Rolled Leg
      (1) Rare (140°F) 25 to 30 minutes per pound.
      (2) Medium (160°F) 30 to 35 minutes per pound.
      (3) Well-done (175°F) 35 to 40 minutes per pound.
   b. Shoulder, boneless
      (1) Rare (140°F) 30 to 35 minutes per pound.
      (2) Medium (160°F) 35 to 40 minutes per pound.
      (3) Well-done (175°F) 40 to 45 minutes per pound.
4. Remove meat from pan. Cool 20 minutes before slicing.
5. Garnish each serving with 2 tsp of mint jelly.

Directions for Diet Preparations

Sodium Restricted (SR) and **Low Fat/Low Cholesterol** (LF): 2 oz. Prepare as directed. Low fat diets should consider individual tolerance to garlic.

Diabetic (DB): 3 oz. Prepare as directed. Use a sugar free jelly to garnish.

Mechanical Soft (SFT): Prepare as directed. Chop meat.

Soft/Low Fiber (SLF): Omit garlic.

Puree (PUR): Prepare as directed. Add liquid (i.e. gravy or sauce); blender to obtain desired consistency.

Nutrient Analysis per Serving:

Regular	KCAL	PRO gm	CHO gm	FAT gm	Chol mg	SFA gm	PFA gm	VITA iu	VITC mg	THI mg	RIB mg	NIA mg	CA mg	NA mg	K+ mg	FE mg
	318	17.6	0.07	26.9	83.2	15.1	1.8	2.7	0.0	0.10	0.19	3.9	8.4	43.1	199	1.04

Sodium Restricted	NA mg	Diabetic	Kcal	Milk exg	Veg exg	Fruit exg	Bread exg	Meat exg	Fat exg	Low Fat & Low Chol	FAT gm	Chol mg	SFA gm	PFA gm
	43.1		318	0.0	0.0	0.0	0.0	3.0-H	0.25		17.9	55.5	10.0	1.5

Irish Lamb Stew

Portion: 8 ounces (3 ounces edible protein)

Ingredients	50 portions		6 portions	
	weights	measures	weights	measures
Lamb roast, boneless (shank or shoulder), cut into one-inch pieces	15 lb	1 3/8 gal	1 3/8 lb	3 3/4 cups
Water or beef broth, low sodium		1 1/3 gal		3 cups
Tarragon		1 Tbsp		1/2 tsp
Garlic powder		2 tsp		1/4 tsp
Pepper, white		2 tsp		1/4 tsp
Onions, thinly sliced	3 1/2 lb EP (3 3/4 lb AP)	1 1/2 qt	6 1/2 oz EP (7 2/3 oz AP)	3/4 cup
Potatoes, peeled, sliced thin	7 lb EP (9 1/2 lb AP)	5 1/4 qt (28 medium)	14 2/3 oz EP (18 oz AP)	2 3/4 cups (4 medium)
Celery, chopped	1 1/3 lb EP (2 lb AP)	1 qt	2 2/3 oz EP (4 lb AP)	1/2 cup

Method

1. Cut meat into 1- to 1 1/2-inch pieces
2. Bring water to a boil in large pot. Add lamb, seasonings, and fresh vegetables. There should be enough liquid to cover the meat and vegetables. Add more liquid if necessary.
3. Return to boil, reduce heat and simmer (skim scum). Simmer gently for 1 1/2 to 2 hours.
4. Add canned whole potatoes. Return to boil, reduce heat and simmer until potatoes are heated through and meat is tender.

Directions for Diet Preparations

Sodium Restricted (SR), **Low Fat/Low Cholesterol** (LF): 6 oz, **Diabetic** (DB): 8 oz, and **Mechanical Soft** (SFT): Prepare as directed. Low fat diets should consider individual tolerance to garlic and onions.

Soft/Low Fiber (SLF): Omit garlic and onions.

Puree (PUR): Prepare as directed. Add additional gravy if necessary; blender to obtain desired consistency.

Nutrient Analysis per Serving:

Regular	KCAL	PRO gm	CHO gm	FAT gm	Chol mg	SFA gm	PFA gm	VITA iu	VITC mg	THI mg	RIB mg	NIA mg	CA mg	NA mg	K+ mg	FE mg
	348	24.4	15.2	20.5	93.8	8.6	1.7	16.4	7.1	0.17	0.26	7.2	35.5	79.7	535	2.4

Sodium Restricted	NA mg	Diabetic	Kcal	Milk exg	Veg exg	Fruit exg	Bread exg	Meat exg	Fat exg	Low Fat & Low Chol	FAT gm	Chol mg	SFA gm	PFA gm
	79.7		261	0.0	0.75	0.0	0.4	2.25-M	0.75		15.3	70.4	6.4	1.3

Liver and Onions

Portion: 3 ounces liver, 1/4 cup onions

INGREDIENTS	50 portions		6 portions	
	weights	measures	weights	measures
Margarine, low sodium, melted	12 oz	1 1/2 cups	1 1/2 oz	3 Tbsp
Onions, slices	5 lb	3 1/8 qt	10 oz	1 1/2 cups
Liver, chicken or beef, cut 4 per lb	12 1/2 lb	50 pieces	1 1/2 lb	6 pieces
Flour, all-purpose	8 oz	2 cups	1 oz	1/4 cup
Pepper, black		1 Tbsp		1/2 tsp

Method

1. Sauté onions in margarine until browned. Remove from margarine. Set aside and keep warm.
2. Dredge liver in flour/pepper mixture.
3. Oil grill and preheat to 350°F.
4. Brown liver in hot margarine about 2 to 4 minutes on each side.
5. Do not overcook or liver will be tough.

Directions for Diet Preparations

Sodium Restricted (SR) and **Diabetic** (DB): 3 oz cooked liver; 1/4 cup onions. Prepare as directed.
Low Fat/Low Cholesterol (LF): Not recommended for a low cholesterol diet.
Mechanical Soft (SFT): Prepare as directed. Chop meat. Consider individual tolerance when using onions.
Soft/Low Fiber (SLF): Omit black pepper and onions.
Puree (PUR): Prepare as directed. Add liquid to liver and onions and blender to obtain desired consistency.

Nutrient Analysis per Serving:

Regular	KCAL	PRO gm	CHO gm	FAT gm	Chol mg	SFA gm	PFA gm	VITA iu	VITC mg	THI mg	RIB mg	NIA mg	CA mg	NA mg	K+ mg	FE mg
	265	21.7	6.8	16.3	537	3.5	4.7	14400	16.1	0.18	1.5	4.0	24.9	48.1	180	7.5

Sodium Restricted	NA mg	Diabetic	Kcal	Milk exg	Veg exg	Fruit exg	Bread exg	Meat exg	Fat exg	Low Fat & Low Chol		
	48.1		265	0.0	0.25	0.0	0.0	3.0-M	0.5	Not Recommended		

Portion: 2 frankfurters (3 ounces edible protein)

INGREDIENTS	50 portions		4 portions	
	weights	measures	weights	measures
Frankfurters, 10 per lb	10 lb	100 franks	8 oz	8 franks

Method

1. Place in boiling water. Remove from heat. Cover tightly and let simmer 8 minutes.

Directions for Diet Preparations

Sodium Restricted (SR) and **Soft/Low Fiber** (SLF): Not recommended.

Low Fat/Low Cholesterol (LF): 2 oz and **Diabetic** (DB): 3 oz. Prepare as directed.

Mechanical Soft (SFT): Remove skin from frankfurter. Chop.

Puree (PUR): Prepare as directed. Add broth to frankfurter and blender to obtain desired consistency.

Nutrient Analysis per Serving:

Regular	KCAL	PRO gm	CHO gm	FAT gm	Chol mg	SFA gm	PFA gm	VITA iu	VITC mg	THI mg	RIB mg	NIA mg	CA mg	NA mg	K+ mg	FE mg
	268	0.2	1.5	24.2	51.9	10.2	1.2	0.0	20.5	0.04	0.09	2.0	17.0	873	141	1.2

Sodium Restricted	Diabetic	Kcal	Milk exg	Veg exg	Fruit exg	Bread exg	Meat exg	Fat exg	Low Fat & Low Chol	FAT gm	Chol mg	SFA gm	PFA gm
Not Recommended		268	0.0	0.0	0.0	0.0	2.7-H	0.0		16.1	34.5	6.8	0.8

Poultry

E1 — Barbecue Chicken

Portion: 1 leg with thigh or 1/2 breast (3 ounces cooked edible protein)

INGREDIENTS	50 portions		6 portions	
	weights	measures	weights	measures
Chicken, leg with thigh or	20 1/3 lb	50 each	2 1/2 lb	6 each
1/2 breast	18 lb	50 each	2 1/4 lb	6 each
Barbecue sauce, prepared	7 lb	3 1/2 qt	12 oz	1 1/2 cups

Method

1. Brown chicken at 425°F for 20 to 30 minutes.
2. Reduce heat to 325°F.
3. Pour barbecue sauce over chicken.
4. Bake at 325°F for 40 to 45 minutes.

Directions for Diet Preparations

Sodium Restricted (SR): Use low sodium barbecue sauce.

Low Fat/Low Cholesterol (LF): 2 oz cooked edible portion; 2 oz sauce. Remove skin 10 minutes before cooking is completed. Brush chicken with barbecue sauce.

Diabetic (DB): 3 oz cooked edible portion; 2 oz DB barbecue sauce. Remove skin 10 minutes before cooking is completed. Brush chicken with DB barbecue sauce.

Mechanical Soft (SFT): Remove cooked chicken from bone. Chop. Add SFT barbecue sauce to chopped cooked chicken.

Soft/Low Fiber (SLF): Omit barbecue sauce.

Puree (PUR): Remove cooked chicken from bone. Add SFT barbecue sauce to chicken; blender to obtain desired consistency.

Nutrient Analysis per Serving:

Regular	KCAL	PRO gm	CHO gm	FAT gm	Chol mg	SFA gm	PFA gm	VITA iu	VITC mg	THI mg	RIB mg	NIA mg	CA mg	NA mg	K+ mg	FE mg
	253	26.5	21.0	6.8	71.5	1.8	1.4	907	9.0	0.1	0.1	11.7	26.0	676	437	1.4

Sodium Restricted	NA mg	Diabetic	Kcal	Milk exg	Veg exg	Fruit exg	Bread exg	Meat exg	Fat exg	Low Fat & Low Chol	FAT gm	Chol mg	SFA gm	PFA gm
	70.8		206	0.0	1.0	0.5	0.0	3.0-L	0.0		2.2	48.1	0.5	0.4

Chicken Fricassee

Portion: 3 ounces cooked edible protein portion with 2 ounces gravy

Ingredients	50 portions		6 portions	
	weights	measures	weights	measures
Chicken fryers, ready-to-cook, 2 1/2 lb to 3 lb each, cut into desired pieces[1]	35 lb AP	13 each	4 1/2 lb AP	2 each
Pepper, black		1 Tbsp		3/4 tsp
Flour, all-purpose	8 oz	2 cups	1 oz	1/4 cup
Margarine, low sodium melted, #1	1 lb	2 cups	2 oz	1/4 cup
Onions, chopped	10 2/3 oz	2 cups	1 1/3 oz	1/4 cup
Celery, chopped	10 2/3 oz	2 cups	1 1/3 oz	1/4 cup
Carrots, chopped	10 2/3 oz	2 cups	1 1/3 oz	1/4 cup
Water, boiling		to cover		to cover
Gravy:				
Flour, all-purpose	6 oz	1 1/2 cups	3/4 oz	3 Tbsp
Chicken stock, saved from roasting pan		3 qt		1 1/2 cups
Margarine, low sodium, melted, #2	8 oz	1 cup	1 oz	2 Tbsp

Method

1. Cut chicken into desired pieces and season with pepper.
2. Dip each piece into flour and brown in hot margarine #1.
3. Place in roasting pan and cover with vegetables and boiling water. Cover and simmer in oven until tender (about 1 1/2 to 2 hours). Add more water if necessary. When tender remove from stock.
4. Prepare gravy:
   a. Puree vegetables and stock for gravy. Make gravy in pan in which chicken was browned.
   b. Add flour and margarine #2 to chicken stock/puree vegetables. Simmer until thickened.
5. Pour gravy over chicken.

Notes

[1]Chicken pieces vary, for a 3 oz cooked edible protein portion, purchase a 6 1/2 oz chicken leg with thigh, a 5 3/4 oz chicken breast half, or 2 chicken wings weighing 4 1/2 oz each.

Directions for Diet Preparations

Sodium Restricted (SR): Prepare as directed.
Low Fat/Low Cholesterol (LF): 2 oz cooked edible portion, 2 oz LF gravy and **Diabetic** (DB): 3 oz cooked edible portion, 2 oz LF gravy. Remove skin. Omit step #2. Omit margarine #1. Dip each piece into flour and brown in oven. Omit step #5 (omit flour and margarine in gravy). Puree vegetables and chicken stock to make low fat gravy.
Mechanical Soft (SFT): Prepare as directed. Remove chicken from bone. Chop.
Soft/Low Fiber (SLF): Omit onions, celery, and black pepper.
Puree (PUR): Prepare as directed. Remove chicken from bone. Add gravy to chicken; blender to obtain desired consistency.

Nutrient Analysis per Serving:

Regular	KCAL	PRO gm	CHO gm	FAT gm	Chol mg	SFA gm	PFA gm	VITA iu	VITC mg	THI mg	RIB mg	NIA mg	CA mg	NA mg	K+ mg	FE mg
	380	25	3.0	29	121	7.4	7.0	1748	4.4	0.11	0.24	8.0	23	117	331	1.6

Sodium Restricted	NA mg	Diabetic	Kcal	Milk exg	Veg exg	Fruit exg	Bread exg	Meat exg	Fat exg	Low Fat & Low Chol	FAT gm	Chol mg	SFA gm	PFA gm
	117		201	0.0	0.2	0.0	0.0	3.0-L	0.7		7.4	72	1.7	2.0

Portion: 1 leg with thigh or 1/2 breast (3 ounces cooked edible protein)

INGREDIENTS	50 portions		6 portions	
	weights	**measures**	**weights**	**measures**
Chicken[1], leg with thigh or	20 1/3 lb	50 each	2 1/2 lb	6 each
1/2 breast	18 lb	50 each	2 1/4 lb	6 each
Margarine, low sodium, melted	1 1/2 lb	3 cups	3 oz	1/3 cup
Bread crumbs, dry	3 lb	3 qt	6 oz	1 1/2 cups
Parsley, chopped, fresh or dried	1 1/3 oz	1 cup	1/8 oz	2 Tbsp
Garlic powder		1 Tbsp		1/4 tsp
Oregano leaves		2 Tbsp		3/4 tsp
Basil leaves		1 Tbsp		1/4 tsp
Pepper, black		1 Tbsp		1/4 tsp
Parmesan cheese, grated	11 1/2 oz	2 1/2 cups	1 1/2 oz	1/3 cup

Method

1. Combine bread crumbs, parsley, garlic, oregano, basil, pepper, and parmesan cheese.
2. Dip chicken in melted margarine, then roll in bread crumbs mixture.
3. Place chicken in shallow pans with skin side up.
4. Bake at 350°F for 1 hour or until chicken is tender.

Notes

[1]Chicken pieces vary, for a 3 oz cooked edible protein portion, purchase a 6 1/2 oz chicken leg with thigh, a 5 3/4 oz chicken breast half, or 2 chicken wings weighing 4 1/2 oz each.

Directions for Diet Preparations

Sodium Restricted (SR): Use low sodium bread crumbs. Use half the amount of parmesan cheese.

Low Fat/Low Cholesterol (LF): 2 oz cooked edible portion and **Diabetic** (DB): 3 oz cooked edible portion. Remove skin. Omit margarine. Use half the amount of parmesan cheese specified. Dip chicken in broth, then roll in bread crumbs, seasonings, and parmesan cheese. Bake at 350°F for 30 to 45 minutes or until chicken is tender.

Mechanical Soft (SFT): Prepare as directed. Remove chicken from bone. Chop.

Soft/Low Fiber (SLF): Omit black pepper and parmesan cheese.

Puree (PUR): Prepare as directed. Remove chicken from bone. Add liquid (i.e. broth or sauce) to chicken; blender to obtain desired consistency.

Nutrient Analysis per Serving:

Regular	KCAL	PRO gm	CHO gm	FAT gm	Chol mg	SFA gm	PFA gm	VITA iu	VITC mg	THI mg	RIB mg	NIA mg	CA mg	NA mg	K+ mg	FE mg
	378	28.8	14.4	22.0	83.7	5.6	5.4	569	1.1	0.12	0.23	8.6	95.6	285	251	2.1

Sodium Restricted	NA mg	Diabetic	Kcal	Milk exg	Veg exg	Fruit exg	Bread exg	Meat exg	Fat exg	Low Fat & Low Chol	FAT gm	Chol mg	SFA gm	PFA gm
	115		226	0.0	0.0	0.0	0.75	3.0-L	0.0		4.9	51.8	1.4	1.0

Portion: 1 leg with thigh or 1/2 breast (3 ounces cooked edible protein)

INGREDIENTS	50 portions		6 portions	
	weights	measures	weights	measures
Chicken[1], leg with thigh or	20 1/3 lb	50 each	2 1/2 lb	6 each
1/2 breast	18 lb	50 each	2 1/4 lb	6 each
Eggs	1 lb	2 cups	2 oz	1/4 cup
		(8 large)		(1 large)
Lemon juice		2 1/2 cups		1/3 cup
Bread crumbs, dry	2 lb	2 qt	4 oz	1 cup
Paprika		2 Tbsp		3/4 tsp
Lemon peel	1 oz	1/4 cup	1/8 oz	1/2 Tbsp
Margarine, low sodium, melted	12 oz	1 1/2 cups	1 1/2 oz	3 Tbsp

Method

1. Combine eggs and lemon juice.
2. Combine bread crumbs, paprika, and lemon peel.
3. Dip in egg/lemon juice mixture, then in bread crumbs.
4. Place chicken (skin side up) in single layer in greased baking sheets.
5. Brush chicken with melted margarine.
6. Bake at 350°F for 1 hour or until chicken is browned and tender.

Notes

[1]Chicken pieces vary, for a 3 oz cooked edible protein portion, purchase a 6 1/2 oz chicken leg with thigh, a 5 3/4 oz chicken breast half, or 2 chicken wings weighing 4 1/2 oz each.

Directions for Diet Preparations

Sodium Restricted (SR): Use low sodium bread crumbs.
Low Fat/Low Cholesterol (LF): 2 oz cooked edible portion and **Diabetic** (DB): 3 oz cooked edible portion. Remove skin. Omit eggs, substitute with an equal amount of egg whites. Dip chicken in egg whites/lemon juice, then in bread crumbs, paprika, and lemon peel. Omit margarine. Brush chicken with lemon juice. Bake at 350°F for 30 to 45 minutes or until chicken is tender.
Mechanical Soft (SFT): Prepare as directed. Remove chicken from bone. Chop.
Soft/Low Fiber (SLF): Omit paprika.
Puree (PUR): Prepare as directed. Remove chicken from bone. Add liquid (i.e. gravy or broth) to chicken; blender to obtain desired consistency.

Nutrient Analysis per Serving:

Regular	KCAL	PRO gm	CHO gm	FAT gm	Chol mg	SFA gm	PFA gm	VITA iu	VITC mg	THI mg	RIB mg	NIA mg	CA mg	NA mg	K+ mg	FE mg
	376	23.3	13.3	25.1	136	6.4	5.9	605	9.2	0.14	0.27	7.2	39	219	285	2.0

Sodium Restricted	NA mg	Diabetic	Kcal	Milk exg	Veg exg	Fruit exg	Bread exg	Meat exg	Fat exg	Low Fat & Low Chol	FAT gm	Chol mg	SFA gm	PFA gm
	102		192	0.0	0.0	0.1	0.3	3.0-L	0.0		3.5	65.7	0.9	0.8

Portion: 1 leg with thigh or 1/2 breast (3 ounces cooked edible protein)

INGREDIENTS	50 portions		6 portions	
	weights	measures	weights	measures
Chicken[1], leg with thigh or	20 1/3 lb	50 each	2 1/2 lb	6 each
1/2 breast	18 lb	50 each	2 1/4 lb	6 each
Milk, skim, or water		1 qt		1/2 cup
Cornflake crumbs	2 1/4 lb	2 1/2 qt	4 1/2 oz	1 1/4 cups
Paprika		2 Tbsp		1 tsp
Pepper, black		2 tsp		1/4 tsp
Parsley, dry		3 Tbsp		1 tsp

Method

1. Combine cornflakes, paprika, pepper, and parsley.
2. Dip each piece of chicken in milk (or water) and then dredge in seasoned cornflake crumbs.
3. Put chicken on well greased sheet pans. Do not crowd.
4. Bake at 350°F for 1 hour or until tender.

Notes

[1]Chicken pieces vary, for a 3 oz cooked edible protein portion, purchase a 6 1/2 oz chicken leg with thigh, a 5 3/4 oz chicken breast half, or 2 chicken wings weighing 4 1/2 oz each.

Directions for Diet Preparations

Sodium Restricted (SR): Use low sodium cornflake crumbs.

Low Fat/Low Cholesterol (LF): 2 oz cooked edible portion and **Diabetic** (DB): 3 oz cooked edible portion. Remove skin. Dip in chicken broth, then dredge in seasoned cornflake crumbs. Place on non-stick sheet pans. Bake at 350°F for 30 to 45 minutes or until chicken is tender.

Mechanical Soft (SFT): Prepare as directed. Remove chicken from bone. Chop.

Soft/Low Fiber (SLF): Omit paprika and black pepper.

Puree (PUR): Prepare as directed. Remove chicken from bone. Add liquid (i.e. gravy or broth) to chicken; blender to obtain desired consistency.

Nutrient Analysis per Serving:

Regular	KCAL	PRO gm	CHO gm	FAT gm	Chol mg	SFA gm	PFA gm	VITA iu	VITC mg	THI mg	RIB mg	NIA mg	CA mg	NA mg	K+ mg	FE mg
	222	23.6	4.1	11.6	74.8	3.2	2.5	359	2.6	0.11	0.22	8.0	14.5	117	201	1.5

Sodium Restricted	NA mg	Diabetic	Kcal	Milk exg	Veg exg	Fruit exg	Bread exg	Meat exg	Fat exg	Low Fat & Low Chol	FAT gm	Chol mg	SFA gm	PFA gm
	70.6		193	0.0	0.0	0.0	0.4	3.0-L	0.0		5.5	52.7	1.5	1.3

Oven Fried Chicken

Portion: 1 leg with thigh or 1/2 breast or 2 wings (3 ounces cooked edible protein)

Ingredients	50 portions		6 portions	
	weights	measures	weights	measures
Chicken fryers, ready-to-cook, 2 1/2 lb to 3 lb each, cut into desired pieces[1]	35 lb	13 each	4 1/2 lb	2 each
Chicken, leg with thigh or	20 1/3 lb	50 each	2 1/2 lb	6 each
1/2 breast or	18 lb	50 each	2 1/4 lb	6 each
wings	15 lb	100 each	1 3/4 lb	12 each
Eggs	1 lb	2 cups (8 large)	2 oz	1/4 cup (1 large)
Flour, all-purpose	1 lb	1 qt	2 oz	1/2 cup
Paprika		2 Tbsp		1 tsp
Pepper, black		2 tsp		1/4 tsp
Margarine, low sodium, melted	1 lb	2 cups	2 oz	1/4 cup

Method

1. Combine flour, paprika, and black pepper.
2. Dip chicken in eggs, then dredge in seasoned flour.
3. Place chicken (skin side up) in single layer on greased baking sheets.
4. Brush chicken with melted margarine.
5. Bake at 350°F for 1 hour or until chicken is browned and tender.

Notes

[1]Chicken pieces vary, for a 3 oz cooked edible protein portion, purchase a 6 1/2 oz chicken leg with thigh, a 5 3/4 oz chicken breast half, or 2 chicken wings weighing 4 1/2 oz each.

Directions for Diet Preparations

Sodium Restricted (SR): Prepare as directed.

Low Fat/Low Cholesterol (LF): 2 oz cooked edible portion and **Diabetic** (DB): 3 oz cooked edible portion. Remove skin before baking. Omit eggs, substitute with an equal amount of egg whites or a commercial egg substitute. Dredge chicken in seasoned flour. Omit margarine. Brush chicken with chicken broth. Bake at 350°F for 30 to 40 minutes or until chicken is tender.

Mechanical Soft (SFT): Prepare as directed. Remove chicken from bone. Chop.

Soft/Low Fiber (SLF): Omit black pepper and paprika.

Puree (PUR): Prepare as directed. Remove chicken from bone. Add liquid (i.e. gravy or broth) to chicken; blender to obtain desired consistency.

Nutrient Analysis per Serving:

Regular	KCAL	PRO gm	CHO gm	FAT gm	Chol mg	SFA gm	PFA gm	VITA iu	VITC mg	THI mg	RIB mg	NIA mg	CA mg	NA mg	K+ mg	FE mg
	266	26.8	7.4	13.4	123	3.7	2.8	272	0.09	0.12	0.21	8.2	20.0	88.7	225	1.8

Sodium Restricted	NA mg	Diabetic	Kcal	Milk exg	Veg exg	Fruit exg	Bread exg	Meat exg	Fat exg	Low Fat & Low Chol	FAT gm	Chol mg	SFA gm	PFA gm
	88.7		200	0.0	0.0	0.0	0.5	3.0-L	0.0		4.3	50.5	1.1	1.0

Roast Chicken

Portion: 1 leg with thigh or 1/2 breast or 2 wings (3 ounces cooked edible protein)

INGREDIENTS	50 portions		6 portions	
	weights	measures	weights	measures
Chicken fryers, ready-to-cook, 2 1/2 lb to 3 lb each, cut into desired pieces[1]	35 lb	13 each	4 1/2 lb	2 each
Chicken, leg with thigh or	20 1/3 lb	50 each	2 1/2 lb	6 each
1/2 breast or	18 lb	50 each	2 1/4 lb	6 each
wings	15 lb	100 each	1 3/4 lb	12 each
Paprika		2 Tbsp		1 tsp
Pepper, black		2 tsp		1/4 tsp
Chicken stock[2]		as needed		as needed

Method

1. Put pieces of chicken, skin side up on lightly greased sheet pans.
2. Sprinkle paprika and pepper onto chicken.
3. Bake at 350°F for 1 hour or until lightly browned.
4. Place chicken in roasting pans. Add about 1/2-inch of chicken stock to bottom of roaster. Cover and cook 30 minutes or until chicken is tender.

Notes

[1]Chicken pieces vary, for a 3 oz cooked edible protein portion, purchase a 6 1/2 oz chicken leg with thigh, a 5 3/4 oz chicken breast half, or 2 chicken wings weighing 4 1/2 oz each.

[2]May use a concentrated soup base as a quick stock. Prepare as directed by manufacturer.

Directions for Diet Preparations

Sodium Restricted (SR): Use low sodium chicken stock.

Low Fat/Low Cholesterol (LF): 2 oz cooked edible portion (without skin and bone) and **Diabetic** (DB): 3 oz cooked edible portion (without skin and bone). Remove skin and season about 10 minutes before cooking is finished.

Mechanical Soft (SFT): Prepare as directed. Remove chicken from bone. Chop.

Soft/Low Fiber (SLF): Omit black pepper and paprika.

Puree (PUR): Prepare as directed. Remove chicken from bone. Add liquid (i.e. gravy or broth) to chicken; blender to obtain desired consistency.

Nutrient Analysis per Serving:

Regular	KCAL	PRO gm	CHO gm	FAT gm	Chol mg	SFA gm	PFA gm	VITA iu	VITC mg	THI mg	RIB mg	NIA mg	CA mg	NA mg	K+ mg	FE mg
	209	23.8	0.4	11.8	74.8	3.3	2.5	306	0.2	0.06	0.16	7.6	15.1	168	224	1.2

Sodium Restricted	NA mg	Diabetic	Kcal	Milk exg	Veg exg	Fruit exg	Bread exg	Meat exg	Fat exg	Low Fat & Low Chol	FAT gm	Chol mg	SFA gm	PFA gm
	86.6		143	0.0	0.0	0.0	0.0	3.0-L	0.0		2.1	48.2	0.6	0.4

Tahitian Chicken

Portion: 1 leg with thigh or 1/2 breast (3 ounces cooked edible protein)

INGREDIENTS	50 portions		6 portions	
	weights	measures	weights	measures
Chicken[1], leg with thigh or	20 1/3 lb	50 each	2 1/2 lb	6 each
1/2 breast	18 lb	50 each	2 1/4 lb	6 each
Margarine, low sodium, melted #1	4 oz	4 oz	1 Tbsp	1 Tbsp
Pineapple tidbits, unsweetened	12 oz	1 1/2 cups	1 1/2 oz	3 Tbsp
Pineapple juice, unsweetened		2 qt		1 cup
Soy sauce	1 oz	2 Tbsp	1/8 oz	3/4 tsp
Margarine, low sodium, melted #2	8 oz	1 cup	1 oz	2 Tbsp
Ginger, ground		2 Tbsp		3/4 tsp

Method

1. Arrange chicken in lightly greased pans in single layer. Brush with margarine #1.
2. Brown chicken in 425°F oven for 20 to 30 minutes.
3. Combine pineapple tidbits, juice, soy sauce, margarine #2, and ginger. Pour oven chicken.
4. Brush chicken with pineapple mixture.
5. Bake at 325°F for 30 to 40 minutes, basting as needed.

Notes

[1]Chicken pieces vary, for a 3 oz cooked edible protein portion, purchase a 6 1/2 oz chicken leg with thigh, a 5 3/4 oz chicken breast half, or 2 chicken wings weighing 4 1/2 oz each.

Directions for Diet Preparations

Sodium Restricted (SR): Omit soy sauce, substitute with low sodium soy sauce.

Low Fat/Low Cholesterol (LF): 2 oz cooked edible protein portion; 1 1/2 oz sauce and **Diabetic** (DB): 3 oz cooked edible protein portion; 1 1/2 oz sauce. Remove skin before basting in pineapple mixture. Omit margarine #2 from pineapple mixture. Brush chicken with pineapple mixture. Bake at 325°F for 20 to 30 minutes or until chicken is tender. Baste as needed.

Mechanical Soft (SFT): Prepare as directed. Remove chicken from bone. Chop.

Soft/Low Fiber (SLF): Omit ginger.

Puree (PUR): Prepare as directed. Remove chicken from bone. Add additional sauce to chicken; blender to obtain desired consistency.

Nutrient Analysis per Serving:

Regular	KCAL	PRO gm	CHO gm	FAT gm	Chol mg	SFA gm	PFA gm	VITA iu	VITC mg	THI mg	RIB mg	NIA mg	CA mg	NA mg	K+ mg	FE mg
	280	23.4	6.9	17.0	74.8	4.1	4.9	366	4.9	0.08	0.16	7.3	22.7	118	259	1.2

Sodium Restricted	NA mg	Diabetic	Kcal	Milk exg	Veg exg	Fruit exg	Bread exg	Meat exg	Fat exg	Low Fat & Low Chol	FAT gm	Chol mg	SFA gm	PFA gm
	96.1		205	0.0	0.0	0.4	0.0	3.0-L	0.0		5.4	50.5	1.3	1.3

Baked Chicken Tarragon

Portion: 1 leg with thigh or 1/2 breast (3 ounces cooked edible protein)

INGREDIENTS	50 portions		6 portions	
	weights	measures	weights	measures
Chicken[1], leg with thigh or	20 1/3 lb	50 each	2 1/2 lb	6 each
1/2 breast	18 lb	50 each	2 1/4 lb	6 each
Eggs	1 lb	2 cups (8 large)	2 oz	1/4 cup (1 large)
Flour, all-purpose	1 lb	1 qt	2 oz	1/2 cup
Pepper, white		2 tsp		1/4 tsp
Tarragon, ground		3 Tbsp		1 tsp
Parsley, dry		3 Tbsp		1 tsp
Margarine, low sodium, melted	1 lb	2 cups	2 oz	1/4 cup

Method

1. Combine flour, pepper, tarragon, and parsley.
2. Dip chicken in eggs, then dredge in seasoned flour.
3. Place chicken (skin side up) in single layer greased baking sheets.
4. Brush chicken with melted margarine.
5. Bake at 350°F for 1 hour or until chicken is tender.

Notes

[1]Chicken pieces vary, for a 3 oz cooked edible protein portion, purchase a 6 1/2 oz chicken leg with thigh, a 5 3/4 oz chicken breast half, or 2 chicken wings weighing 4 1/2 oz each.

Directions for Diet Preparations

Sodium Restricted (SR): Prepare as directed.

Low Fat/Low Cholesterol (LF): 2 oz cooked edible portion and **Diabetic** (DB): 3 oz cooked edible portion. Remove skin. Omit eggs, substitute with an equal amount of egg whites or a commercial egg substitute. Dredge chicken in seasoned flour. Omit margarine. Brush chicken with chicken broth. Bake at 350°F for 30 to 45 minutes or until chicken is tender.

Mechanical Soft (SFT): Prepare as directed. Remove chicken from bone. Chop.

Soft/Low Fiber (SLF): Omit white pepper.

Puree (PUR): Prepare as directed. Remove chicken from bone. Add liquid (i.e. gravy or broth) to chicken; blend to obtain desired consistency.

Nutrient Analysis per Serving:

Regular	KCAL	PRO gm	CHO gm	FAT gm	Chol mg	SFA gm	PFA gm	VITA iu	VITC mg	THI mg	RIB mg	NIA mg	CA mg	NA mg	K+ mg	FE mg
	320	24.8	7.5	20.7	123	4.9	5.3	522	0.1	0.12	0.22	8.2	26.6	88.7	237	1.9

Sodium Restricted	NA mg	Diabetic	Kcal	Milk exg	Veg exg	Fruit exg	Bread exg	Meat exg	Fat exg	Low Fat & Low Chol	FAT gm	Chol mg	SFA gm	PFA gm
	88.7		201	0.0	0.0	0.0	0.5	3.0-L	0.0		4.2	50.5	1.1	1.0

Portion: 5 ounces stuffed chicken, 2 ounces gravy

INGREDIENTS	48 portions		6 portions	
	weights	measures	weights	measures
Chicken breasts, skinned, boned (4 oz each)	12 lb	48 breasts	1 1/2 lb	6 breasts
Spinach, frozen, chopped	5 1/2 lb	2 3/4 qt	12 oz	1 1/2 cups
Mushrooms, fresh, finely chopped	11 oz	1 qt	1 1/3 oz	1/2 cup
Parmesan cheese, grated	4 2/3 oz	1 cup	2/3 oz	2 Tbsp
Margarine, low sodium, #1	4 oz	1/2 cup	1/2 oz	1 Tbsp
Garlic powder		2 tsp		1/4 tsp
Flour, all-purpose	6 oz	1 1/2 cups	3/4 oz	3 Tbsp
Eggs, slightly beaten	12 oz	1 1/2 cups (6 large)	2 oz	1/4 cup (1 large)
Bread crumbs, fine, dry	1 1/8 lb	1 1/8 qt	2 1/4 oz	1/2 cup
Margarine, low sodium, melted, #2	12 oz	1 1/2 cups	1 1/2 oz	3 Tbsp
Chicken gravy		3 qt		1 1/2 cups

Method

1. Flatten chicken breasts by pounding with a mallet.
2. Steam or boil spinach and mushrooms. Drain well.
3. Add parmesan cheese, margarine, and garlic powder to spinach and mushrooms. Mix.
4. Spread 1/4 cup of spinach mixture over each chicken breast. Roll the chicken breast around the spinach mixture and skewer with a toothpick.
5. Dip chicken rolls in flour, then in beaten eggs, and roll in bread crumbs.
6. Sauté in margarine at moderate temperature until lightly browned.
7. Place chicken breasts in serving pans.
8. Prepare chicken gravy. Pour gravy over chicken breasts.
9. Bake at 350°F for about 1 hour or until chicken is tender.

Directions for Diet Preparations

Sodium Restricted (SR): Omit parmesan cheese. Use low sodium bread crumbs and low sodium chicken gravy.

Low Fat/Low Cholesterol (LF): 4 oz. Omit margarine #1 in Step #3. Omit eggs, substitute with a commercial egg substitute as per manufacturer's directions. Use 2 oz low fat chicken gravy. Low fat diets should consider individual tolerance to garlic.

Diabetic (DB): 5 oz. Omit margarine #1 in Step #3. Use 2 oz low fat chicken gravy.

Mechanical Soft (SFT): Prepare as directed. Chop meat. Consider individual tolerance.

Soft/Low Fiber (SLF): Omit parmesan cheese and garlic.

Puree (PUR): Prepare as directed. Add gravy to chicken; blend to obtain desired consistency.

Nutrient Analysis per Serving:

Regular	KCAL	PRO gm	CHO gm	FAT gm	Chol mg	SFA gm	PFA gm	VITA iu	VITC mg	THI mg	RIB mg	NIA mg	CA mg	NA mg	K+ mg	FE mg
	308	29.8	15.7	13.6	101	2.8	3.9	4536	14.9	0.22	0.33	14.2	125.2	428	572	3.5

Sodium Restricted	NA mg	Diabetic	Kcal	Milk exg	Veg exg	Fruit exg	Bread exg	Meat exg	Fat exg	Low Fat & Low Chol	FAT gm	Chol mg	SFA gm	PFA gm
	151		248	0.0	0.5	0.0	0.75	3.0(L)	0.25		6.7	50.1	1.6	1.7

Arroz con Pollo

Portion: 1 or 2 pieces[1] (3 ounces cooked edible protein), 1/2 cup rice-vegetables

INGREDIENTS	50 portions		6 portions	
	weights	measures	weights	measures
Chicken fryers, ready-to-cook, 2 1/2 lb to 3 lb each, cut into desired pieces[1]	35 lb	13 each	4 1/2 lb	2 each
Paprika		1 Tbsp		1/2 tsp
Olive oil	2 2/3 oz	1/3 cup	1/2 oz	1 Tbsp
Garlic, minced		2 tsp		1/4 tsp
Onions, chopped	10 3/4 oz	2 cups	1 1/3 oz	1/4 cup
Green peppers, chopped	1 lb	3 cups	2 oz	1/3 cup
Red peppers, chopped	10 3/4 oz	2 cups	1 1/3 oz	1/4 cup
Chicken stock, low sodium		2 1/2 qt		1 1/4 cups
Rice, long-grain, uncooked	2 3/4 lb	1 1/2 qt	5 1/4 oz	3/4 cup
Tomatoes, whole, canned, drained, cut up	3 lb	1 1/2 qt	6 oz	3/4 cup
Oregano, dried		1 Tbsp		1/2 tsp
Peas, frozen, thawed	1 lb	3 cups	2 oz	1/3 cup

Method

1. Place pieces of chicken skin side up on lightly greased sheet pans.
2. Sprinkle with paprika.
3. Bake at 350°F for about 40 minutes or until lightly browned. Place chicken in roasting pans.
4. Sauté garlic, onions, and bell peppers in oil until tender.
5. Bring stock to a boil. Add rice, tomatoes, and oregano to stock. Pour over chicken.
6. Cover and bake at 350°F for 30 to 35 minutes or until chicken and rice is cooked.
7. Right before serving time stir in the peas. Heat to serving temperature of 160°F.

Notes

[1]Chicken pieces vary, for a 3 oz cooked edible protein portion, purchase a 6 1/2 oz chicken leg with thigh, a 5 3/4 oz chicken breast half, or 2 chicken wings weighing 4 1/2 oz each.

Directions for Diet Preparations

Sodium Restricted (SR): Use low sodium tomatoes.

Low Fat/Low Cholesterol (LF): 2 oz, cooked, deboned and **Diabetic** (DB): 3 oz, cooked, deboned. In step #1 remove skin prior to baking. Sprinkle with paprika. Continue with recipe as written at step #3.

Mechanical Soft (SFT): Prepare as directed. Remove chicken from bone. Chop chicken. Cook vegetables until very soft.

Soft/Low Fiber (SLF): Omit onions, garlic, and peas. Cook vegetables until soft.

Puree (PUR): Remove chicken from bone. Add chicken stock to chicken; blender to obtain desired consistency. Add tomato juice to rice-vegetable mixture; blender to obtain desired consistency.

Nutrient Analysis per Serving:

Regular	KCAL	PRO gm	CHO gm	FAT gm	Chol mg	SFA gm	PFA gm	VITA iu	VITC mg	THI mg	RIB mg	NIA mg	CA mg	NA mg	K+ mg	FE mg
	321	26.2	18.3	15.1	75.6	3.9	3.1	417	20.1	0.16	0.19	8.6	34.6	130	446	2.6

Sodium Restricted	NA mg	Diabetic	Kcal	Milk exg	Veg exg	Fruit exg	Bread exg	Meat exg	Fat exg	Low Fat & Low Chol	FAT gm	Chol mg	SFA gm	PFA gm
	83.5		241	0.0	0.3	0.0	0.9	3.0-L	0.0		6.4	54.8	1.5	1.3

Portion: 1 split hen (3 ounces cooked edible protein)

INGREDIENTS	50 portions		6 portions	
	weights	measures	weights	measures
Rock cornish hens, split	22 lb		2 3/4 lb	
Lemon juice	6 oz	3/4 cup	3/4 oz	1 1/2 Tbsp
Apricot jam	1 lb	1 1/2 cups	2 oz	3 Tbsp
Apple juice concentrate	8 oz	1 cup	1 oz	2 Tbsp
Water		1 cup		2 Tbsp
Pepper, white, ground		1 1/2 Tbsp		1/8 tsp
Apricot halves, canned, unsweetened	3 1/2 lb	1 3/4 qt	8 oz	1 cup

Method

1. Rinse birds, rub with lemon juice.
2. Place 12 hens per pan and brown in oven at 400°F for 10 minutes.
3. Melt apricot jam. Add apple juice concentrate, water, and pepper to jam; simmer 10 minutes.
4. Pour glaze over hens; top each hen with an apricot half. Bake 15 to 20 minutes.

Directions for Diet Preparations

Sodium Restricted (SR): Prepare as directed.
Low Fat/Low Cholesterol (LF): 1 split hen. After step #2, remove skin, then follow directions as written.
Diabetic (DB): 1 split hen. After step #2, remove skin. Use an unsweetened apricot jam.
Mechanical Soft (SFT): Prepare as directed.
Soft/Low Fiber (SLF): Omit jam, substitute with an apricot jelly. Remove skin from apricots.
Puree (PUR): Prepare as directed. Remove chicken from bone. Add additional liquid (i.e. chicken broth or apple juice); blender to obtain desired consistency.

Nutrient Analysis per Serving:

Regular	KCAL	PRO gm	CHO gm	FAT gm	Chol mg	SFA gm	PFA gm	VITA iu	VITC mg	THI mg	RIB mg	NIA mg	CA mg	NA mg	K+ mg	FE mg
	267	25.5	11.7	12.6	81.1	3.5	2.7	596	4.4	0.07	0.17	7.9	20.5	79.2	310	1.5

Sodium Restricted	NA mg	Diabetic	Kcal	Milk exg	Veg exg	Fruit exg	Bread exg	Meat exg	Fat exg	Low Fat & Low Chol	FAT gm	Chol mg	SFA gm	PFA gm
	79.2		184	0.0	0.0	0.3	0.0	3.0	0.0		6.3	75.7	1.7	1.5

Portion: 3/4 cup, 6 ounces (3 ounces cooked edible protein)

INGREDIENTS	50 portions		6 portions	
	weights	**measures**	**weights**	**measures**
Turkey, cooked or chicken, cooked, diced	9 1/2 lb	1 3/4 gal	1 1/8 lb	3 1/2 cups
Green peppers, cut into strips	11 oz EP (13 3/4 lb AP)	2 cups	1 1/3 oz EP (1 3/4 oz AP)	1/4 cup
Onions, diced	12 1/3 oz	1 cup	1 1/2 oz	2 Tbsp
Margarine, low sodium, melted #1	3 oz	1/3 cup	1/3 oz	2 tsp
Chicken stock[1]		1 qt		1/2 cup
Milk, skim		3 qt		1 1/2 cups
Flour, all-purpose	8 oz	2 cups	1 oz	1/4 cup
Margarine, low sodium, melted #2	8 oz	1 cup	1 oz	2 Tbsp
Mushroom pieces or slices, canned	12 oz	1 1/2 cups	1 1/2 oz	3 Tbsp
Red sweet peppers, diced	5 1/2 oz	1 cup	3/4 oz	2 Tbsp

Method

1. Sauté green pepper and onions in margarine #1 until almost tender but crunch. Set aside.
2. Heat chicken stock and milk until simmering.
3. Prepare roux. Combine flour and margarine #2 over moderate heat. Stir until blended and smooth.
4. Add roux to milk/stock. Stir constantly until sauce boils. Hold at 160°F, serving temperature.
5. Add turkey or chicken, mushrooms, red peppers, green peppers, and onions to milk/stock. Mix.
6. Serving Suggestions: May be served on a bed of rice or noodles, over cornbread, biscuits, or toast point.

Notes

[1]May use a concentrated soup base as a quick stock. Prepare as directed by manufacturer.

Directions for Diet Preparations

Sodium Restricted (SR): Prepare as directed. May use a low sodium soup base as directed by manufacturer, instead of the stock.

Low Fat/Low Cholesterol (LF): 1/2 cup and **Diabetic** (DB): 3/4 cup. Omit margarine in step #1. Cook vegetables in broth until tender. Omit margarine #2, substitute with an equal amount of reduced calorie margarine.

Mechanical Soft (SFT): Prepare as directed. Consider individual tolerance.

Soft/Low Fiber (SLF): Omit peppers and onions, substitute with allowed cooked canned vegetables (i.e. green beans and carrots). May use if able to calculate milk into daily food plan.

Puree (PUR): Prepare as directed. Blender. Add additional liquid if necessary to obtain desired consistency.

Nutrient Analysis per Serving:

Regular	KCAL	PRO gm	CHO gm	FAT gm	Chol mg	SFA gm	PFA gm	VITA iu	VITC mg	THI mg	RIB mg	NIA mg	CA mg	NA mg	K+ mg	FE mg
	249	27.5	7.4	11.5	76.7	2.6	3.1	401	8.6	0.12	0.26	8.3	90.3	132	335	1.4

Sodium Restricted	NA mg	Diabetic	Kcal	Milk exg	Veg exg	Fruit exg	Bread exg	Meat exg	Fat exg	Low Fat & Low Chol	FAT gm	Chol mg	SFA gm	PFA gm
	132		222	0.25	0.1	0.0	0.25	3.0-L	0.0		5.6	51.1	1.4	1.4

Turkey (Chicken) Chow Mein

Portion: 1 cup, 8 ounces (3 ounces cooked edible protein)

INGREDIENTS	50 portions		6 portions	
	weights	measures	weights	measures
Turkey or chicken cooked, diced	9 1/2 lb	1 3/4 gal	1 1/8 lb	3 1/2 cup
Celery, diagonally sliced	2 lb	1 1/2 qt	4 oz	3/4 cup
Onions, sliced	2 lb	1 qt	4 oz	3/4 cup
Green pepper, diced	10 3/4 oz	2 cups	1 1/3 oz	1/4 cup
Chicken stock[1]		2 1/2 qt		1 1/4 cup
Mushrooms, sliced	1 1/2 lb	3 cups	3 oz	1/3 cup
Cornstarch	5 1/3 oz	1 cup	3/4 oz	2 Tbsp
Soy sauce	8 oz	1 cup	1 oz	2 Tbsp
Bean sprouts, canned, well drained	3 lb	3 qt	6 oz	1 1/2 cup
Water chestnuts, sliced, drained	1 lb	2 cups	2 oz	1/4 cup

Method

1. Add celery, onions, and green pepper to chicken stock. Cover. Simmer until vegetables are almost tender but crunchy.
2. Add mushrooms. Simmer 2 minutes.
3. Dissolve cornstarch in soy sauce. Add to vegetables. Stir constantly until sauce boils. Reduce heat.
4. Add cooked turkey or chicken to vegetables. Blend. Hold at 160°F, serving temperature.
5. Add bean sprouts and water chestnuts. Mix.

Notes

[1]May use a concentrated soup base as a quick stock. Prepare as directed by manufacturer.

Directions for Diet Preparations

Sodium Restricted (SR): May use a low sodium chicken soup base as directed by manufacturer, instead of the chicken stock.
50 portions: Omit soy sauce, substitute with a 1/2 cup low sodium soy sauce and 1/2 cup cold water.
6 portions: Omit soy sauce, substitute with 1 Tbsp low sodium soy sauce and 1 Tbsp cold water.
Low Fat/Low Cholesterol (LF): 3/4 cup and **Diabetic** (DB): 1 cup. Prepare as directed. Low fat diets should consider individual tolerance to onions.
Mechanical Soft (SFT): Cook vegetables until tender and soft. Consider individual tolerance.
Soft/Low Fiber (SLF): Omit onions. Cook vegetables until tender and soft. Consider individual tolerance.
Puree (PUR): Prepare as directed. Puree, add additional liquid (e.g. chicken stock) if necessary to obtain desired consistency.

Nutrient Analysis per Serving:

Regular	KCAL	PRO gm	CHO gm	FAT gm	Chol mg	SFA gm	PFA gm	VITA iu	VITC mg	THI mg	RIB mg	NIA mg	CA mg	NA mg	K+ mg	FE mg
	180	23.6	7.2	3.5	73.2	0.9	0.7	121.6	15.8	0.1	0.20	12.9	39.8	481	484	1.8

Sodium Restricted	NA mg	Diabetic	Kcal	Milk exg	Veg exg	Fruit exg	Bread exg	Meat exg	Fat exg	Low Fat & Low Chol	FAT gm	Chol mg	SFA gm	PFA gm
	225		180	0.0	1.0	0.0	0.0	3.0-L	0.0		2.6	54.9	0.6	0.6

Portion: 1 cup, 8 ounces (3 ounces cooked edible protein)

INGREDIENTS	50 portions		6 portions	
	weights	measures	weights	measures
Turkey or chicken, cooked, diced	8 1/2 lb	1 2/3 gal	1 lb	3 cups
Tomatoes, crushed	10 3/4 lb	1 1/2 gal	1 1/3 lb	3 cups
Rice, uncooked	1 3/4 lb	1 qt	3 1/2 oz	1/2 cup
Catsup	2 lb	1 qt	4 oz	1/2 cup
Worcestershire sauce	2 oz	1/4 cup	1/4 oz	1/2 Tbsp
Thyme, ground		1 Tbsp		1/2 tsp
Paprika		1 Tbsp		1/2 tsp
Pepper, black		1 Tbsp		1/2 tsp
Garlic powder		1 Tbsp		1/2 tsp
Onions, chopped	1 1/2 lb	1 qt	2 3/4 oz	1/2 cup
Celery, chopped	1 2/3 lb	1 1/4 qt	3 1/3 oz	2/3 cup
Green pepper, chopped	1 1/2 lb	1 qt	2 3/4 oz	1/2 cup
Margarine, melted	4 oz	1/2 cup	1/2 oz	1 Tbsp
Ham, cooked, diced	1 lb	3 cups	2 oz	1/3 cup

Method

1. Combine tomatoes, rice, catsup, worcestershire sauce, thyme, paprika, black pepper, and garlic. Cover. Simmer 45 minutes or until rice is tender.
2. Sauté onions, celery, and green pepper in margarine until tender. Add to sauce. Blend.
3. Add diced turkey or chicken and ham to vegetables and sauce. Blend.
4. Heat to 160°F.

Directions for Diet Preparations

Sodium Restricted (SR): Use low sodium tomatoes (or fresh tomatoes). Use low sodium catsup.
50 portions: Omit ham. Increase turkey or chicken to 9 1/2 lbs.
6 portions: Omit ham. Increase turkey or chicken to 1 1/8 lbs.
Low Fat/Low Cholesterol (LF): 3/4 cup. Low fat diets should consider individual tolerance to onions and garlic.
50 portions: Omit ham. Increase turkey or chicken to 9 1/2 lbs.
6 portions: Omit ham. Increase turkey or chicken to 1 1/8 lbs.
Diabetic (DB): 1 cup. Prepare as directed.
Mechanical Soft (SFT): Prepare as directed. Cook vegetables until tender and soft. Consider individual tolerance.
Soft/Low Fiber (SLF): Not recommended.
Puree (PUR): Prepare as directed. Blenderize. Add additional liquid (i.e. chicken stock) if necessary to obtain desired consistency.

Nutrient Analysis per Serving:

Regular	KCAL	PRO gm	CHO gm	FAT gm	Chol mg	SFA gm	PFA gm	VITA iu	VITC mg	THI mg	RIB mg	NIA mg	CA mg	NA mg	K+ mg	FE mg
	274	26.7	22.2	8.7	74.0	2.2	2.1	1310	38.6	0.26	0.23	9.2	62.5	732	709	2.4

Sodium Restricted	NA mg	Diabetic	Kcal	Milk exg	Veg exg	Fruit exg	Bread exg	Meat exg	Fat exg	Low Fat & Low Chol	FAT gm	Chol mg	SFA gm	PFA gm
	105		274	0.0	2.0	0.0	0.5	3.0-L	0.0		6.4	57.5	1.5	1.6

Roast Turkey

Portion: 3 ounces cooked edible protein

INGREDIENTS	50 portions		12 portions	
	weights	measures	weights	measures
Turkey[1], whole, ready to cook	22 lb		6 lb	
Oregano, ground		1 Tbsp		1 tsp
Vegetable oil	6 oz	3/4 cup	1 1/2 oz	3 Tbsp

Method

1. Wash thawed turkey inside and outside with running water; drain thoroughly; pat dry with paper towels.
2. Rub inside cavity of turkey with oregano. Brush skin of turkey with oil.
3. Place turkey breast side up in roasting pan. Do not cover pan.
4. Insert meat thermometer in center of inside muscle of thigh. Bake at 325°F. Cook to an internal temperature of 180°F or until the drumstick joint can be moved easily up and down.
5. Baste turkey every half hour with drippings. If turkey begins to get too brown, cover loosely with aluminum foil.

Size	Time
5 to 8 lb	3 to 3 1/2 hours
8 to 12 lb	3 1/2 to 4 1/2 hours
12 to 16 lb	4 1/2 to 5 1/2 hours
16 to 20 lb	5 1/2 to 6 1/2 hours
20 to 24 lb	6 1/2 to 7 hours

6. Cool cooked turkey 20 minutes; slice and serve hot.

Notes

[1]For a 3 oz cooked edible protein portion, purchase a 6 3/4 oz piece of turkey with bone and skin.

Directions for Diet Preparations

Sodium Restricted (SR): 3 oz. Prepare as directed.
Low Fat/Low Cholesterol (LF): 2 oz and **Diabetic** (DB): 3 oz. Prepare as directed. Remove skin.
Mechanical Soft (SFT): Prepare as directed. Chop meat.
Soft/Low Fiber (SLF): Prepare as directed.
Puree (PUR): Prepare as directed. Blenderize. Add additional liquid to obtain desired consistency.

Nutrient Analysis per Serving:

Regular	KCAL	PRO gm	CHO gm	FAT gm	Chol mg	SFA gm	PFA gm	VITA iu	VITC mg	THI mg	RIB mg	NIA mg	CA mg	NA mg	K+ mg	FE mg
	197	23.8	0.06	10.6	70	2.8	3.5	6.3	0.0	0.05	0.16	4.2	24.4	59.0	239	1.6

Sodium Restricted	NA mg	Diabetic	Kcal	Milk exg	Veg exg	Fruit exg	Bread exg	Meat exg	Fat exg	Low Fat & Low Chol	FAT gm	Chol mg	SFA gm	PFA gm
	59.0		165	0.0	0.0	0.0	0.0	2.7(L)	0.4		4.4	39.5	1.16	1.72

Fish

F1 — Fishburger on Bun

Portion: 3 1/2 ounces cooked fillet (3 ounces cooked edible protein), one bun

INGREDIENTS	50 portions		6 portions	
	weights	**measures**	**weights**	**measures**
Fish fillets, cut 4 per pound	12 1/2 lb	50 fillets	1 1/2 lb	6 fillets
Pepper, white		2 tsp		1/4 tsp
Milk, skim		2 qt		1 cup
Bread crumbs, dry	2 lb	2 qt	4 oz	1 cup
Margarine, low sodium, melted	1 lb	2 cups	2 oz	1/4 cup
Hamburger, bun		50 buns		6 buns
Tartar sauce	1 3/4 lb	3 1/4 cups	3 oz	6 Tbsp

Method

1. Combine milk and pepper.
2. Dip fillets in seasoned milk, then in bread crumbs. Coat well.
3. Place fillets on greased baking pans.
4. Brush margarine over fish.
5. Bake at 375°F for 25 to 35 minutes or until fish flakes easily.
6. Serve fillet on a bun with 1 Tbsp tartar sauce.

Directions for Diet Preparations

Sodium Restricted (SR): Use low sodium bread crumbs. Use low sodium tartar sauce.
Low Fat/Low Cholesterol (LF): 2 1/2 oz fillet, one bun and **Diabetic** (DB): 3 1/2 oz fillet, one bun. Brush lightly with margarine. May use 1 tsp tartar sauce, if able to calculate into daily food plan.
Mechanical Soft (SFT): Prepare as directed. Chop fish. Consider individual tolerance when using bun.
Soft/Low Fiber (SLF): Omit pepper and tartar sauce.
Puree (PUR): Prepare as directed. Omit bun. Add liquid (i.e. milk or cheese sauce) to fish; blenderize to obtain desired consistency.

Nutrient Analysis per Serving:

Regular	KCAL	PRO gm	CHO gm	FAT gm	Chol mg	SFA gm	PFA gm	VITA iu	VITC mg	THI mg	RIB mg	NIA mg	CA mg	NA mg	K+ mg	FE mg
without bun	262	29.3	13.8	9.1	63.9	1.6	2.9	437	1.5	0.17	0.2	3.6	87.1	230	370	1.2
with bun	381	32.6	35.0	11.4	66.3	2.1	3.1	437	1.5	0.32	0.3	4.9	116	432	408	2.3

Sodium Restricted	NA mg	Diabetic	Kcal	Milk exg	Veg exg	Fruit exg	Bread exg	Meat exg	Fat exg	Low Fat & Low Chol	FAT gm	Chol mg	SFA gm	PFA gm
without bun	113		230	0.0	0.0	0.0	1.0	3.0-L	0.0		4.0	45.6	0.7	1.2
with bun	316		349	0.0	0.0	0.0	2.6	3.0-L	0.0		6.2	48.0	1.2	1.4

Portion: 3 ounces cooked edible protein

INGREDIENTS	50 portions		6 portions	
	weights	measures	weights	measures
Fish fillets (cod, flounder, sole), cut 4 per pound	12 1/2 lb	50 fillets	1 1/2 lb	6 fillets
Vegetable oil	12 oz	1 1/2 cups	1 1/2 oz	3 Tbsp
Lemon juice	8 oz	1 cup	1 oz	2 Tbsp
Thyme, ground		2 tsp		1/4 tsp
Paprika		1 1/2 Tbsp		3/4 tsp
Lemon slices	10 lemons	50 slices	2 lemons	6 slices

Method

1. If frozen thaw in refrigerator. Cut into 4 oz fillets. Place in a single layer on well greased baking pans.
2. Combine oil, lemon juice, thyme, and paprika. Mix well. Brush fish generously with oil mixture.
3. Bake at 350°F for 25 to 30 minutes or until fish flakes easily when tested with a fork.
4. Serve hot. Garnish with a lemon slice.

Directions for Diet Preparations

Sodium Restricted (SR): 3 oz. Prepare as directed.
Low Fat/Low Cholesterol (LF): 3 oz and **Diabetic** (DB): 3 oz. Brush fish lightly with oil mixture.
Mechanical Soft (SFT): 3 oz. Prepare as directed.
Soft/Low Fiber (SLF): Omit paprika.
Puree (PUR): Prepare as directed. Puree, add liquid (i.e. broth or cheese sauce) to obtain desired consistency.

Nutrient Analysis per Serving:

Regular	KCAL	PRO gm	CHO gm	FAT gm	Chol mg	SFA gm	PFA gm	VITA iu	VITC mg	THI mg	RIB mg	NIA mg	CA mg	NA mg	K+ mg	FE mg
	160	21.0	2.9	7.5	49.9	1.0	4.2	178	19.9	0.09	0.08	2.4	27.7	71.5	264	0.7

Sodium Restricted	NA mg	Diabetic	Kcal	Milk exg	Veg exg	Fruit exg	Bread exg	Meat exg	Fat exg	Low Fat & Low Chol	FAT gm	Chol mg	SFA gm	PFA gm
	71.5		144	0.0	0.0	0.0	0.0	3.0-L	0.0		4.6	49.9	0.7	2.2

Portion: 3 ounces fish, 2 ounces sauce

INGREDIENTS	50 portions		6 portions	
	weights	measures	weights	measures
Fish fillets or steaks, cut 4 per pound	12 1/2 lb	50 fillets	1 1/2 lb	6 fillets
Creole sauce	6 1/4 lb	3 1/8 qt	12 oz	1 1/2 cups

Method

1. Place fish in greased baking pans.
2. Pour creole sauce over fish.
3. Bake at 350°F for about 30 to 35 minutes or until fish flakes easily.

Directions for Diet Preparations

Sodium Restricted (SR): Use low sodium creole sauce.

Low Fat/Low Cholesterol (LF): 3 oz fish, 2 oz low fat creole sauce. Prepare as directed. Use low fat creole sauce.

Diabetic (DB): 3 oz fish, 2 oz diabetic creole sauce. Prepare as directed. Use diabetic creole sauce.

Mechanical Soft (SFT): Prepare as directed. Chop fish. Consider individual tolerance when using sauce.

Soft/Low Fiber (SLF): Omit creole sauce, substitute with tomato sauce.

Puree (PUR): Prepare as directed. Blenderize and strain sauce. Add sauce to fish; blenderize to obtain desired consistency.

Nutrient Analysis per Serving:

Regular	KCAL	PRO gm	CHO gm	FAT gm	Chol mg	SFA gm	PFA gm	VITA iu	VITC mg	THI mg	RIB mg	NIA mg	CA mg	NA mg	K+ mg	FE mg
	125	20.0	4.1	2.8	46.8	0.4	0.9	416	11.2	0.11	0.08	2.5	28.9	143	334	0.8

Sodium Restricted	NA mg	Diabetic	Kcal	Milk exg	Veg exg	Fruit exg	Bread exg	Meat exg	Fat exg	Low Fat & Low Chol	FAT gm	Chol mg	SFA gm	PFA gm
	74.8		115	0.0	0.0	0.0	0.0	3.0-L	0.0		1.8	46.8	0.3	0.6

Oven Fried Fish

Portion: 3 ounces cooked edible protein

INGREDIENTS	50 portions		6 portions	
	weights	measures	weights	measures
Fish fillets (cod, flounder, sole), cut 4 per pound	12 1/2 lb	50 fillets	1 1/2 lb	6 fillets
Pepper, white		2 tsp		1/4 tsp
Milk, skim		2 qt		1 cup
Bread crumbs, dry	2 lb	2 qt	4 oz	1 cup
Margarine, low sodium, melted	1 lb	2 cups	2 oz	1/4 cup

Method

1. Combine milk and pepper.
2. Dip fillets in seasoned milk, then in bread crumbs. Coat well.
3. Place fillets on greased baking pans.
4. Brush margarine over fish.
5. Bake at 375°F for 25 to 35 minutes or until fish flakes easily.
6. Serve with lemon wedge or 1 Tbsp tartar sauce.

Directions for Diet Preparations

Sodium Restricted (SR): Use low sodium bread crumbs. Serve with lemon wedge.
Low Fat/Low Cholesterol (LF): 2 oz fillet and **Diabetic** (DB): 3 oz fillet. Brush fillets lightly with reduced calorie margarine. Serve with lemon wedge.
Mechanical Soft (SFT): Prepare as directed. Chop fish.
Soft/Low Fiber (SLF): Omit pepper.
Puree (PUR): Prepare as directed. Add liquid (i.e. cheese sauce or milk) to fish; blenderize to obtain desired consistency.

Nutrient Analysis per Serving:

Regular	KCAL	PRO gm	CHO gm	FAT gm	Chol mg	SFA gm	PFA gm	VITA iu	VITC mg	THI mg	RIB mg	NIA mg	CA mg	NA mg	K+ mg	FE mg
	204	21.9	11.2	7.7	70.8	1.4	2.3	352	0.3	0.1	0.15	2.5	79.8	203	474	1.4

Sodium Restricted	NA mg	Diabetic	Kcal	Milk exg	Veg exg	Fruit exg	Bread exg	Meat exg	Fat exg	Low Fat & Low Chol	FAT gm	Chol mg	SFA gm	PFA gm
	112		178	0.0	0.0	0.0	0.1	3.0-L	0.0		4.8	70.8	1.0	1.5

Portion: 3 ounces cooked edible protein

INGREDIENTS	50 portions		6 portions	
	weights	**measures**	**weights**	**measures**
Fish fillets or steaks, cut 4 per lb	12 1/2 lb	50 fillets	1 1/2 lb	6 fillets
Lemon juice	8 oz	1 cup	1 oz	2 Tbsp
Margarine, low sodium, melted	8 oz	1 cup	1 oz	2 Tbsp
Paprika		1 Tbsp		1/2 tsp
Parsley, chopped		1/4 cup		1/2 Tbsp

Method

1. Place fish in greased baking pans.
2. Combine lemon juice, margarine, paprika, and parsley. Mix. Pour over fish.
3. Bake at 350°F for about 30 to 35 minutes or until fish flakes easily.
4. Serve with lemon wedge or tartar sauce.

Directions for Diet Preparations

Sodium Restricted (SR): Prepare as directed. Serve with lemon wedge.

Low Fat/Low Cholesterol (LF): 2 oz cooked and **Diabetic** (DB): 3 oz cooked. Use half the amount of margarine specified. Serve with lemon wedge.

Mechanical Soft (SFT): Prepare as directed. Chop fish.

Soft/Low Fiber (SLF): Prepare as directed.

Puree (PUR): Prepare as directed. Add liquid (i.e. sauce or broth) to fish; blenderize to obtain desired consistency.

Nutrient Analysis per Serving:

Regular	KCAL	PRO gm	CHO gm	FAT gm	Chol mg	SFA gm	PFA gm	VITA iu	VITC mg	THI mg	RIB mg	NIA mg	CA mg	NA mg	K+ mg	FE mg
	184	26.3	0.6	6.8	43.6	1.1	2.3	464	2.6	0.08	0.11	7.9	66.1	75	625	1.2

Sodium Restricted	NA mg	Diabetic	Kcal	Milk exg	Veg exg	Fruit exg	Bread exg	Meat exg	Fat exg	Low Fat & Low Chol	FAT gm	Chol mg	SFA gm	PFA gm
	75		168	0.0	0.0	0.0	0.0	3.0-L	0.0		4.2	36.3	0.6	1.5

Portion: 4 ounces cooked (3 ounces edible protein)

INGREDIENTS	50 portions		6 portions	
	weights	measures	weights	measures
Salmon, canned	9 1/2 lb	4 3/4 qt	1 1/8 lb	2 1/3 cups
Cracker crumbs	2 lb	2 1/4 qt	4 oz	1 1/8 cups
Eggs, slightly beaten[1]	1 1/2 lb	3 cups (12 large)	4 oz	1/4 cup (2 large)
Onions, diced	5 1/3 oz EP	1 cup	2/3 oz	2 Tbsp
Milk, skim		3 cups		1/3 cup

Method

1. Remove skin and bones from salmon. Place salmon in mixing bowl.
2. Add cracker, eggs, onions, and milk to salmon. Mix at low speed to blend.
3. With a No. 8 dipper, place salmon mixture on greased sheet pans. Flatten salmon to form patties.
4. Bake at 400°F for 15 to 20 minutes or until golden brown on bottom of patties. Turn over and bake 10 minutes longer.

Note

[1]May use frozen pasteurized eggs. Prepare as directed by manufacturer.

Directions for Diet Preparations

Sodium Restricted (SR): Use low sodium salmon and low sodium cracker crumbs.

Low Fat/Low Cholesterol (LF): 3 oz cooked. Omit eggs, substitute with an equal measure of egg whites or a commercial egg substitute. Bake with non-stick cookware or spray.

Diabetic (DB): 4 oz cooked. Bake with non-stick cookware or spray.

Mechanical Soft (SFT) and **Soft/Low Fiber** (SLF): Omit onions.

Puree (PUR): Prepare as directed. Add liquid (i.e. milk or broth) to salmon patties; blenderize to obtain desired consistency.

Nutrient Analysis per Serving:

Regular	KCAL	PRO gm	CHO gm	FAT gm	Chol mg	SFA gm	PFA gm	VITA iu	VITC mg	THI mg	RIB mg	NIA mg	CA mg	NA mg	K+ mg	FE mg
	214	21.0	14.4	7.3	113	1.9	2.0	139	0.4	0.1	0.27	6.4	229	629	350	1.7

Sodium Restricted	NA mg	Diabetic	Kcal	Milk exg	Veg exg	Fruit exg	Bread exg	Meat exg	Fat exg	Low Fat & Low Chol	FAT gm	Chol mg	SFA gm	PFA gm
	71.0		214	0.0	0.0	0.0	0.7	3.0-L	0.0		4.8	36.0	1.2	1.5

Baked Vegetable Scrod

Portion: 3 ounces fish (3 ounces cooked edible protein), 1/2 cup vegetables

INGREDIENTS	50 portions		6 portions	
	weights	measures	weights	measures
Fish fillets, scrod, cut 4 per lb	12 1/2 lb	50 fillets	1 1/2 lb	6 fillets
Onions, finely chopped	5 1/3 oz	1 cup	2/3 oz	2 Tbsp
Green peppers, diced	1 lb	3 cups	2 oz	1/3 cup
Carrots, sliced, cooked	1 lb	3 cups	2 oz	1/3 cup
Margarine, low sodium	6 oz	3/4 cup	3/4 oz	1 1/2 Tbsp
Tomatoes, crushed, canned	9 lb	4 1/2 qt	1 1/8 lb	2 1/4 cups
Parsley, chopped	2/3 oz	1/2 cup		1 Tbsp

Method

1. If necessary, thaw fish. Place in a single layer in greased serving pan(s).
2. Sauté onions, green peppers, and carrots in margarine until onions are golden.
3. Add tomatoes and parsley to onion mixture. Cook, stirring occasionally.
4. Pour only enough tomato vegetable mixture over fillets to barely cover them.
5. Bake at 350°F for about 30 to 40 minutes or until fish flakes easily.

Directions for Diet Preparations

Sodium Restricted (SR): Use low sodium tomatoes.
Low Fat/Low Cholesterol (LF): 2 oz fish, 1/2 cup vegetables and **Diabetic** (DB): 3 oz fish, 1/2 cup vegetables. Omit margarine, substitute with an equal amount of reduced calorie margarine. Low fat diets should consider individual tolerance to onions.
Mechanical Soft (SFT): Prepare as directed. Chop fish. Cook vegetables until tender.
Soft/Low Fiber (SLF): Omit onions and green peppers.
Puree (PUR): 8 oz. Prepare as directed. Add sauce and vegetables to fish; blenderize to obtain desired consistency.

Nutrient Analysis per Serving:

Regular	KCAL	PRO gm	CHO gm	FAT gm	Chol mg	SFA gm	PFA gm	VITA iu	VITC mg	THI mg	RIB mg	NIA mg	CA mg	NA mg	K+ mg	FE mg
	164	25.2	7.0	3.9	58.6	0.7	1.3	3016	21.2	0.15	0.13	3.5	54.9	291	803	1.3

Sodium Restricted	NA mg	Diabetic	Kcal	Milk exg	Veg exg	Fruit exg	Bread exg	Meat exg	Fat exg	Low Fat & Low Chol	FAT gm	Chol mg	SFA gm	PFA gm
	94		140	0.0	1.0	0.0	0.0	3.0-L	0.0		1.0	51.2	0.18	0.3

Snapper Veracruz

Portion: 3 ounces cooked fish, 2 Tablespoons vegetables

INGREDIENTS	50 portions		6 portions	
	weights	measures	weights	measures
Fish fillets, red snapper 4 per lb	12 1/2 lb	50 fillets	1 1/2 lb	6 fillets
Lime juice		2 cups		1/4 cup
Paprika		1 Tbsp		1/2 tsp
Margarine, low sodium, melted	4 oz	1/2 cup	1/2 oz	1 Tbsp
Onions, diced	5 1/3 oz	1 cup	2/3 oz	2 Tbsp
Green peppers, chopped	10 2/3 oz	2 cups	1 1/3 oz	1/4 cup
Tomatoes, diced	1 1/3 lb	3 cups	2 2/3 oz	1/3 cup
Parsley, chopped	2/3 oz	1/2 cup		1 Tbsp

Method

1. Combine lime juice and paprika.
2. Dip each fillet into lime mixture; place in single layer in greased serving pans. Set aside for 1 hour.
3. Sauté onions and green peppers until tender. Add tomatoes. Cook an additional 2 minutes.
4. Add parsley.
5. Drain lime juice from the serving pans.
6. Top each portion with 2 Tbsp vegetable mixture.
7. Bake at 400°F for about 10 minutes or until fish flakes easily and flesh becomes opaque.

Directions for Diet Preparations

Sodium Restricted (SR): Prepare as directed.
Low Fat/Low Cholesterol (LF): 2 oz fish, 2 Tbsp vegetables and **Diabetic** (DB): 3 oz fish, 2 Tbsp vegetables. Omit margarine, substitute with an equal amount of reduced calorie margarine. Bake fish using a non-stick cooking spray. Low fat diets should consider individual tolerance to onions.
Mechanical Soft (SFT): Prepare as directed. Chop fish. Cook vegetables until tender.
Soft/Low Fiber (SLF): Omit onions and green peppers.
Puree (PUR): Prepare as directed. Add tomato sauce or juice to vegetables and fish; blenderize to obtain desired consistency.

Nutrient Analysis per Serving:

Regular	KCAL	PRO gm	CHO gm	FAT gm	Chol mg	SFA gm	PFA gm	VITA iu	VITC mg	THI mg	RIB mg	NIA mg	CA mg	NA mg	K+ mg	FE mg
	202	26.9	5.2	3.4	69.8	0.7	1.2	370	11.5	0.09	0.01	0.6	63.6	122	823	0.5

Sodium Restricted	NA mg	Diabetic	Kcal	Milk exg	Veg exg	Fruit exg	Bread exg	Meat exg	Fat exg	Low Fat & Low Chol	FAT gm	Chol mg	SFA gm	PFA gm
	122		194	0.0	1.0	0.0	0.0	3.0-L	0.0		1.9	52.4	0.4	0.6

Sole Almondine

Portion: 3 ounces cooked

INGREDIENTS	50 portions		6 portions	
	weights	**measures**	**weights**	**measures**
Fillet of sole, 4 per pound	12 1/2 lb	50 fillets	1 1/2 lb	6 fillets
Margarine, low sodium, melted	1 lb	2 cups	2 oz	1/4 cup
Pepper, white		2 tsp		1/4 tsp
Lemon juice	8 oz	1 cup	1 oz	2 Tbsp
Almonds, slivered	10 3/4 oz	2 cups	1 1/3 oz	1/4 cup

Method

1. Arrange fish fillets on greased baking pans.
2. Combine margarine, pepper, and lemon juice. Spread over fish.
3. Sprinkle almonds over fish.
4. Bake at 375°F for 15 to 20 minutes or until fish flakes easily.

Directions for Diet Preparations

Sodium Restricted (SR): Prepare as directed.
Low Fat/Low Cholesterol (LF): 2 oz cooked and **Diabetic** (DB): 3 oz cooked. Use half the amount of margarine specified in Step #2.
Mechanical Soft (SFT): Omit almonds.
Soft/Low Fiber (SLF): Omit pepper and almonds.
Puree (PUR): Omit almonds. Add liquid (i.e. sauce or broth) to fish; blenderize to obtain desired consistency.

Nutrient Analysis per Serving:

Regular	KCAL	PRO gm	CHO gm	FAT gm	Chol mg	SFA gm	PFA gm	VITA iu	VITC mg	THI mg	RIB mg	NIA mg	CA mg	NA mg	K+ mg	FE mg
	196	21.2	2.0	11.2	48.7	1.6	3.3	350	3.4	0.09	0.11	2.5	38.3	64.5	525	0.6

Sodium Restricted	NA mg	Diabetic	Kcal	Milk exg	Veg exg	Fruit exg	Bread exg	Meat exg	Fat exg	Low Fat & Low Chol	FAT gm	Chol mg	SFA gm	PFA gm
	64.5		164	0.0	0.0	0.0	0.0	3.0-L	0.0		5.1	32.5	0.7	1.4

Tuna Noodle Casserole

Portion: 8 ounces; 1 cup (3 ounces edible protein)

INGREDIENTS	50 portions		6 portions	
	weights	measures	weights	measures
Tuna fish, canned, packed in water, drained well	9 1/2 lb	4 3/4 qt	1 1/8 lb	2 1/3 cups
Noodles, dry	3 lb AP	1 gal	6 oz AP	2 cups
Water, boiling		5 gal		2 1/2 qt
Cream of mushroom soup, condensed	4 lb	2 qt	8 oz	1 cup
Milk, skim		2 qt		1 cup
Mushrooms canned, drained well	2 lb	1 qt	4 oz	1 cup
Mixed vegetables, frozen	2 3/4 lb	2 qt	5 1/2 oz	1 cup
Bread crumbs, dry	1 lb	1 qt	2 oz	1/2 cup
Margarine, low sodium, melted	8 oz	1 cup	1 oz	2 Tbsp
Cheddar cheese, shredded	1 lb	3 1/2 cups	2 1/3 oz	1/2 cup
Paprika		1 Tbsp		1/2 tsp

Method

1. Place noodles in boiling water. Stir lightly to mix. Cook, uncovered over medium heat about 12 minutes or until noodles are tender. Drain noodles.
2. Combine soup and milk. Mix together until smooth. Add to noodles. Mix.
3. Flake tuna. Add tuna, mushrooms, and mixed vegetables to noodles. Stir lightly to mix well.
4. Place tuna/noodle mixture in greased baking pans.
5. Combine bread crumbs, margarine, cheddar cheese, and paprika. Mix well. Sprinkle over tuna/noodle mixture.
6. Bake at 350°F for 30 to 35 minutes or until lightly browned and heated through.

Directions for Diet Preparations

Sodium Restricted (SR): Use low sodium soup, low sodium tuna fish, and low sodium bread crumbs. Omit cheddar cheese, substitute with a low sodium cheese.

Low Fat/Low Cholesterol (LF): 6 ounces (3/4 cup) and **Diabetic** (DB): 8 ounces (1 cup). Omit margarine in step #5, substitute with an equal amount of reduced calorie margarine. Omit cheddar cheese, substitute with a low fat cheese.

Mechanical Soft (SFT): Prepare as directed.

Soft/Low Fiber (SLF): Omit paprika.

Puree (PUR): Prepare as directed. Blenderize. Add additional cream of mushroom soup if necessary to obtain desired consistency.

Nutrient Analysis per Serving:

Regular	KCAL	PRO gm	CHO gm	FAT gm	Chol mg	SFA gm	PFA gm	VITA iu	VITC mg	THI mg	RIB mg	NIA mg	CA mg	NA mg	K+ mg	FE mg
	399	33.5	35.8	11.9	52.1	4.0	2.9	1772	1.7	0.36	0.39	13.5	164	841	493	4.5

Sodium Restricted	NA mg	Diabetic	Kcal	Milk exg	Veg exg	Fruit exg	Bread exg	Meat exg	Fat exg	Low Fat & Low Chol	FAT gm	Chol mg	SFA gm	PFA gm
	198		345	0.5	1.25	0.0	1.0	3.0-L	0.0		4.4	33.8	1.1	1.2

Cheese and Egg Entrees

G1 — Cheese Fettucini

Portion: 6 ounces, 3/4 cup (3 ounces edible protein)

INGREDIENTS	50 portions		6 portions	
	weights	measures	weights	measures
Fettucini, dry	3 lb AP	1 gal	6 oz AP	2 cups
Water, boiling		3 gal		1 1/2 qt
Margarine, low sodium, melted	8 oz	1 cup	1 oz	2 Tbsp
Flour, all-purpose	6 oz	1 1/2 cups	3/4 oz	3 Tbsp
Milk, skim		3 qt		1 1/2 cups
Mozzarella cheese, part skim, shredded	3 lb	2 2/3 qt	6 oz	1 1/3 cups
Cottage cheese, dry, drained, low fat	4 lb	2 qt	8 oz	1 cup
Basil, crumbled		1 Tbsp		1/2 tsp
Garlic powder		2 tsp		1/4 tsp

Method

1. Stir fettucini into boiling water, cook 10 to 12 minutes or until tender, stirring occasionally, drain well.
2. Mix margarine with flour. Stir. Cook 5 to 10 minutes.
3. Add milk gradually, stirring constantly. Cook until thickened.
4. Add mozzarella, cottage cheese, basil, and garlic to sauce. Stir until smooth.
5. Pour cheese sauce over fettucini, mix well.
6. Bake at 350°F for 20 to 30 minutes or until heated through.

Directions for Diet Preparations

Sodium Restricted (SR): Use low sodium cottage cheese and low sodium mozzarella. May use if able to calculate into daily food plan.

Low Fat/Low Cholesterol (LF): 6 oz and **Diabetic** (DB): 6 oz. Substitute reduced calorie margarine for regular margarine in equal amount.

Mechanical Soft (SFT): Prepare as directed.

Soft/Low Fiber (SLF): Omit garlic powder.

Puree (PUR): Prepare as directed. Blenderize. Add additional liquid (i.e. cheese sauce) if necessary to obtain desired consistency.

Nutrient Analysis per Serving:

Regular	KCAL	PRO gm	CHO gm	FAT gm	Chol mg	SFA gm	PFA gm	VITA iu	VITC mg	THI mg	RIB mg	NIA mg	CA mg	NA mg	K+ mg	FE mg
	262	16.9	28.2	8.8	18.3	3.7	1.3	451	0.6	0.3	0.36	2.1	278	307	159	1.1

Sodium Restricted	NA mg	Diabetic	Kcal	Milk exg	Veg exg	Fruit exg	Bread exg	Meat exg	Fat exg	Low Fat & Low Chol	FAT gm	Chol mg	SFA gm	PFA gm
	188		246	0.25	0.0	0.0	1.0	3.0-L	0.0		6.9	18.3	3.3	0.7

Cheese Lasagna

Portion: 2″ × 4″ portion; 6 ounces (3 ounces edible protein)

INGREDIENTS	48 portions		12 portions	
	weights	measures	weights	measures
Tomato sauce	6 lb	3 qt	1 1/2 lb	3 cups
Tomato paste	2 lb	1 qt	8 oz	1 cup
Basil, crumbled		1 Tbsp		1 tsp
Oregano, crumbled		2 Tbsp		2 tsp
Noodles, lasagna	2 1/2 lb		10 oz	
Water, boiling		2 gal		2 qt
Mozzarella cheese, part skim, grated	4 lb	3 1/2 qt	1 lb	3 1/2 cups
Parmesan cheese, grated	6 oz	1 1/3 cups	1 1/2 oz	5 Tbsp
Cottage cheese, dry, drained, low fat	5 lb	2 1/2 qt	1 1/4 lb	2 1/2 cups

Method

1. Combine tomato sauce, tomato paste, basil and oregano. Simmer 15 minutes, stirring occasionally.
2. Stir noodles into boiling water, cook 10 to 12 minutes or until tender, stirring occasionally; drain well.
3. Combine mozzarella, parmesan, and cottage cheese. Mix.
4. 48 portions: Arrange in (2) 12 x 20 x 2-inch counter pans in the following layers:
   Tomato sauce, 1 qt
   Lasagna noodles, overlapping, 1 3/4 lb
   Cheeses, 2 1/4 lb
   Repeat. Top with remainder of meat sauce.
   12 portions: Arrange in 13 x 9-inch baking dish in the following layers:
   Tomato sauce, 1 cup
   Lasagna noodles, overlapping, 7 oz
   Cheeses, 9 oz
   Repeat.
5. Top with remainder of tomato sauce.
6. Bake at 350°F for 40 to 45 minutes.
7. 48 portions: Cut 6 x 4 (2" x 4" pieces).
   12 portions: Cut 6 x 2 (2" x 4" pieces).

Directions for Diet Preparations

Sodium Restricted (SR): Use low sodium tomato sauce, low sodium tomato paste, and low sodium cottage cheese. Omit parmesan cheese.

Low Fat/Low Cholesterol (LF): 6 oz. Use low fat tomato sauce. Omit parmesan cheese.

Diabetic (DB): 6 oz. Use diabetic tomato sauce. Omit parmesan cheese.

Mechanical Soft (SFT): Prepare as directed.

Soft/Low Fiber (SLF): Use mild cheeses.

Puree (PUR): Prepare as directed. Blenderize. Add additional sauce if necessary to obtain desired consistency.

Nutrient Analysis per Serving:

Regular	KCAL	PRO gm	CHO gm	FAT gm	Chol mg	SFA gm	PFA gm	VITA iu	VITC mg	THI mg	RIB mg	NIA mg	CA mg	NA mg	K+ mg	FE mg
	318	21.1	30.2	12.5	26.4	5.4	1.7	1856	21.7	0.3	0.38	3.0	343	784	429	2.2

Sodium Restricted	NA mg	Diabetic	Kcal	Milk exg	Veg exg	Fruit exg	Bread exg	Meat exg	Fat exg	Low Fat & Low Chol	FAT gm	Chol mg	SFA gm	PFA gm
	232		254	0.0	1.0	0.0	1.0	3.0-L	0.0		6.5	16.7	2.7	0.9

Portion: 3″ × 3″ square; 6 ounces (3 ounces edible protein)

INGREDIENTS	50 portions		6 portions	
	weights	measures	weights	measures
Bread, white, trim off crust	4 1/2 lb	72 slices	9 oz	9 slices
Margarine, low sodium soft	12 oz	1 1/2 cup	1 1/2 oz	3 Tbsp
Cheddar cheese, mild, sliced	5 lb	105 slices	10 oz	14 slices
Milk, skim		5 qt		2 1/2 cups
Eggs, beaten	3 1/4 lb	6 1/2 cup (26 large)	14 oz	1 3/4 cups (7 large)
American cheese or mild cheddar, grated	1 1/4 lb	1 qt	2 1/2 oz	1/2 cup

Method

1. Spread margarine on bread.
2. Place single layer, fat side down in steam table or baking pan.
3. Layer cheese on top of bread, top with another layer of bread and repeat.
4. Combine milk and eggs. Pour over layered cheese and bread.
5. Top with grated cheese.
6. Bake at 325°F for 30 to 40 minutes.

Directions for Diet Preparations

Sodium Restricted (SR): Use low sodium bread and low sodium cheese. May use if able to calculate into daily food plan.
Low Fat/Low Cholesterol (LF): Not recommended.
Diabetic (DB): 6 oz. Omit margarine in step #1, use a non-stick spray or pan. Use reduced calorie margarine in half the amount specified for margarine. Use low fat cheese.
Mechanical Soft (SFT): Prepare as directed.
Soft/Low Fiber (SLF): Prepare as directed.
Puree (PUR): Prepare as directed. Blenderize. Add additional liquid (i.e. milk) if necessary to obtain desired consistency.

Nutrient Analysis per Serving:

Regular	KCAL	PRO gm	CHO gm	FAT gm	Chol mg	SFA gm	PFA gm	VITA iu	VITC mg	THI mg	RIB mg	NIA mg	CA mg	NA mg	K+ mg	FE mg
	462	24.2	26.4	28.6	204	14.2	2.7	1162	0.9	0.23	0.53	1.5	576	647	291	2.1

Sodium Restricted	NA mg	Diabetic	Kcal	Milk exg	Veg exg	Fruit exg	Bread exg	Meat exg	Fat exg	Low Fat & Low Chol	Not Recommended
	303		301	0.25	0.0	0.0	1.0	3.0-M	0.0		

Cheese Stuffed Potato

Portion: 1 medium potato, 1/2 cup filling (3 ounces edible protein)

INGREDIENTS	50 portions		6 portions	
	weights	measures	weights	measures
Potato, baking, uniform size	16 3/4 lb	50 medium	1 1/3 lb	4 medium
Margarine, low sodium, melted	4 oz	1/2 cup	1/3 oz	1 Tbsp
Pepper, white		2 tsp		1/4 tsp
Milk, skim		3 cups		1/4 cup
Cottage cheese, dry, low fat	9 1/2 lb	1 1/2 gal	12 oz	1 1/2 cups
Paprika		2 tsp		1/4 tsp

Method

1. Scrub potatoes and remove blemishes.
2. Brush lightly with margarine. Place on baking sheets.
3. Bake at 400°F for 1 to 1 1/2 hours or until tender.
4. Cut hot potatoes into halves lengthwise. Scoop out contents.
5. Mash contents. Add pepper, milk and cottage cheese to mashed potatoes. Mix well.
6. Top baked potato with potato/cheese mixture. Use No. 8 dipper.
7. Sprinkle with paprika.
8. Bake at 425°F until potatoes are hot, about 15 to 25 minutes.

Directions for Diet Preparations

Sodium Restricted (SR): Use low sodium cottage cheese.

Low Fat/Low Cholesterol (LF): one medium potato, 1/2 cup filling and **Diabetic** (DB): one small potato, 1/2 cup filling. Omit margarine in step #2.

Mechanical Soft (SFT): Remove skin. Consider individual tolerance.

Soft/Low Fiber (SLF): Remove skin from the potato.

Puree (PUR): Remove skin. Add liquid (i.e cottage cheese or milk) to potato/cheese mixture; blenderize to obtain desired consistency.

Nutrient Analysis per Serving:

Regular	KCAL	PRO gm	CHO gm	FAT gm	Chol mg	SFA gm	PFA gm	VITA iu	VITC mg	THI mg	RIB mg	NIA mg	CA mg	NA mg	K+ mg	FE mg
	304	15.7	54.0	2.9	4.0	0.9	0.7	192	26.2	0.23	0.23	3.4	90.5	373	943	2.9

Sodium Restricted	NA mg	Diabetic	Kcal	Milk exg	Veg exg	Fruit exg	Bread exg	Meat exg	Fat exg	Low Fat & Low Chol	FAT gm	Chol mg	SFA gm	PFA gm
	155		232	0.0	0.0	0.0	1.0	3.0-L	0.0		1.1	4.0	0.6	0.1

Portion: 4 ounces (2 ounces edible protein)

INGREDIENTS	48 portions		6 portions	
	weights	measures	weights	measures
Margarine, low sodium, melted	8 oz	1 cup	1 oz	2 Tbsp
Flour, all-purpose	4 oz	1 cup	1/2 oz	2 Tbsp
Pepper, white		2 tsp		1/4 tsp
Milk, skim		2 qt		1 cup
Eggs, beaten	12 lb	1 1/2 gal (96 large)	1 1/2 lb	3 cups (12 large)

Method

1. Combine margarine, flour, and pepper. Stir until smooth. Cook 5 minutes.
2. Add milk gradually, stirring constantly. Cook until thick.
3. Add eggs. Mix well.
4. Pour into greased counter pans or baking pan(s).
5. Set pans in hot water.
6. Bake at 325°F for 45 minutes or until set. Cut 4 × 6 (4 oz).

Directions for Diet Preparations

Sodium Restricted (SR), **Mechanical Soft** (SFT), and **Puree** (PUR): Prepare as directed.
Low Fat/Low Cholesterol (LF): Not recommended. Use egg whites or a commercial egg substitute as per manufacturer's directions.
Diabetic (DB): 4 oz. Omit margarine and flour in step #1.
Soft/Low Fiber (SLF): Omit pepper.

Nutrient Analysis per Serving:

Regular	KCAL	PRO gm	CHO gm	FAT gm	Chol mg	SFA gm	PFA gm	VITA iu	VITC mg	THI mg	RIB mg	NIA mg	CA mg	NA mg	K+ mg	FE mg
	215	13.8	5.1	15.0	547	4.0	2.7	762	0.4	0.11	0.36	0.2	109	160	202	2.2

Sodium Restricted	NA mg	Diabetic	Kcal	Milk exg	Veg exg	Fruit exg	Bread exg	Meat exg	Fat exg	Low Fat & Low Chol	FAT gm	Chol mg	SFA gm	PFA gm
	160		172	0.25	0.0	0.0	0.0	2.0-M	0.0		4.2	1.2	0.8	2.0

Portion: 4 1/2 ounces (2 1/2 ounces edible protein)

INGREDIENTS	48 portions		6 portions	
	weights	**measures**	**weights**	**measures**
Margarine, low sodium, melted	8 oz	1 cup	1 oz	2 Tbsp
Flour, all-purpose	4 oz	1 cup	1/2 oz	2 Tbsp
Pepper, white		2 tsp		1/4 tsp
Milk, skim		2 qt		1 cup
Eggs, beaten	12 lb	1 1/2 gal (96 large)	1 1/2 lb	3 cups (12 large)
Cheese, shredded	1 1/2 lb	1 1/2 qt	3 oz	3/4 cup

Method

1. Combine margarine, flour, and pepper. Stir until smooth. Cook 5 minutes.
2. Add milk gradually, stirring constantly. Cook until thick.
3. Add eggs. Mix well.
4. Add cheese. Mix well.
5. Pour into greased counter pans or baking pan(s).
6. Set pans in hot water.
7. Bake at 325°F for 45 minutes or until set. Cut 4 × 6 (4 1/2 oz).

Directions for Diet Preparations

Sodium Restricted (SR): Use low sodium cheese. May use if able to calculate into daily food plan.

Low Fat/Low Cholesterol (LF): Not recommended. Use egg whites or a commercial egg substitute as per manufacturer's directions. Add a low fat cheese to LF omelet.

Diabetic (DB): 4 oz. Omit margarine and flour in step #1. Use low fat cheese.

Mechanical Soft (SFT): Prepare as directed.

Soft/Low Fiber (SLF): Omit white pepper. Use a mild cheese.

Puree (PUR): Prepare as directed.

Nutrient Analysis per Serving:

Regular	KCAL	PRO gm	CHO gm	FAT gm	Chol mg	SFA gm	PFA gm	VITA iu	VITC mg	THI mg	RIB mg	NIA mg	CA mg	NA mg	K+ mg	FE mg
	272	17.3	5.3	19.7	562	7.0	2.8	912	0.4	0.12	0.42	0.2	211	248	216	2.3

Sodium Restricted	NA mg	Diabetic	Kcal	Milk exg	Veg exg	Fruit exg	Bread exg	Meat exg	Fat exg	Low Fat & Low Chol	FAT gm	Chol mg	SFA gm	PFA gm
	213		197	0.2	0.0	0.0	0.0	2.5-M	0.0		5.1	5.2	0.8	2.0

Ham Omelet

Portion: 5 ounces (3 ounces edible protein)

INGREDIENTS	48 portions		6 portions	
	weights	measures	weights	measures
Margarine, low sodium, melted	8 oz	1 cup	1 oz	2 Tbsp
Flour, all-purpose	4 oz	1 cup	1/2 oz	2 Tbsp
Pepper, white		2 tsp		1/4 tsp
Milk, skim		2 qt		1 cup
Eggs, beaten	12 lb	1 1/2 gal (96 large)	1 1/2 lb	3 cups (12 large)
Ham, cooked, diced	3 lb	2 1/4 qt	6 oz	1 1/8 cup

Method

1. Combine margarine, flour, and pepper. Stir until smooth. Cook 5 minutes.
2. Add milk gradually, stirring constantly. Cook until thick.
3. Add eggs. Mix well.
4. Add ham. Mix to blend.
5. Pour into greased counter pans or baking pan(s).
6. Set pans in hot water.
7. Bake at 325°F for 45 minutes or until set. Cut 4 × 6 (5 oz).

Directions for Diet Preparations

Sodium Restricted (SR): Omit ham.
Low Fat/Low Cholesterol (LF): Not recommended. Use egg whites or a commercial egg substitute as per manufacturer's directions. Omit ham.
Diabetic (DB): 5 oz. Omit margarine and flour in step #1.
Mechanical Soft (SFT): Prepare as directed.
Soft/Low Fiber (SLF): Omit pepper and ham.
Puree (PUR): Combine white pepper, milk, eggs, and ham. Blenderize to desired consistency. Follow step #7 until set.

Nutrient Analysis per Serving:

Regular	KCAL	PRO gm	CHO gm	FAT gm	Chol mg	SFA gm	PFA gm	VITA iu	VITC mg	THI mg	RIB mg	NIA mg	CA mg	NA mg	K+ mg	FE mg
	260	20.9	5.1	16.6	563	4.5	2.9	762	0.4	0.31	0.44	1.6	111	537	292	2.4

Sodium Restricted	NA mg	Diabetic	Kcal	Milk exg	Veg exg	Fruit exg	Bread exg	Meat exg	Fat exg	Low Fat & Low Chol	FAT gm	Chol mg	SFA gm	PFA gm
	160		217	0.1	0.0	0.0	0.0	3.0-M	0.0		4.2	1.2	0.8	2.0

Portion: 5 1/2 ounces (2 ounces edible protein)

INGREDIENTS	48 portions		6 portions	
	weights	**measures**	**weights**	**measures**
Margarine, low sodium, melted	8 oz	1 cup	1 oz	2 Tbsp
Flour, all-purpose	4 oz	1 cup	1/2 oz	2 Tbsp
Pepper, white		2 tsp		1/4 tsp
Milk, skim		2 qt		1 cup
Eggs, beaten	12 lb	1 1/2 gal (96 large)	1 1/2 lb	3 cups (12 large)
Potatoes, diced, cooked	3 lb EP (3 3/4 lb AP)	2 qt	6 oz EP (8 oz AP)	1 cup
Spinach, cooked, drained	1 lb	2 1/2 cups	2 oz	1/3 cup
Mushrooms, canned, sliced	12 oz	1 1/2 cups	1 1/2 oz	3 Tbsp

Method

1. Combine margarine, flour, and pepper. Stir until smooth. Cook 5 minutes.
2. Add milk gradually, stirring constantly. Cook until thick.
3. Add eggs. Mix well.
4. Add potatoes, spinach, and mushrooms to egg mixture. Mix well.
5. Pour into greased counter or baking pan(s).
6. Set pans in hot water.
7. Bake at 325°F for 45 minutes or until set. Cut 4 × 6 (5 1/2 oz).

Directions for Diet Preparations

Sodium Restricted (SR): Prepare as directed. Use fresh vegetables or sodium restricted canned vegetables.

Low Fat/Low Cholesterol (LF): Not recommended. Use egg whites or a commercial egg substitute as per manufacturer's directions. Add vegetables as directed.

Diabetic (DB): 5 1/2 oz. Omit margarine and flour in step #1.

Mechanical Soft (SFT): Cook vegetables until soft. Prepare as directed.

Soft/Low Fiber (SLF): Omit white pepper. Cook vegetables until soft.

Puree (PUR): Puree vegetables. Prepare as directed.

Nutrient Analysis per Serving:

Regular	KCAL	PRO gm	CHO gm	FAT gm	Chol mg	SFA gm	PFA gm	VITA iu	VITC mg	THI mg	RIB mg	NIA mg	CA mg	NA mg	K+ mg	FE mg
	243	14.7	11.4	15.1	547	4.0	2.7	1540	3.6	0.15	0.41	0.8	124	169	357	2.7

Sodium Restricted	NA mg	Diabetic	Kcal	Milk exg	Veg exg	Fruit exg	Bread exg	Meat exg	Fat exg	Low Fat & Low Chol	FAT gm	Chol mg	SFA gm	PFA gm
	169		200	0.1	1.0	0.0	0.2	2.0-M	0.0		4.2	1.2	0.8	2.0

Portion: 5 ounces (2 1/4 ounces edible protein)

INGREDIENTS	48 portions		6 portions	
	weights	**measures**	**weights**	**measures**
Margarine, low sodium, melted	8 oz	1 cup	1 oz	2 Tbsp
Flour, all-purpose	4 oz	1 cup	1/2 oz	2 Tbsp
Pepper, white		2 tsp		1/4 tsp
Milk, skim		2 qt		1 cup
Eggs, beaten	12 lb	1 1/2 gal	1 1/2 lb	3 cups
		(96 large)		(12 large)
Onions, diced	1 lb EP	3 cups	2 oz EP	1/3 cup
Green pepper, diced	1 lb EP	3 cups	2 oz EP	1/3 cup
Ham, cooked, diced	1 lb	3 cups	2 oz	1/3 cup

Method

1. Combine margarine, flour, and pepper. Stir until smooth. Cook 5 minutes.
2. Add milk gradually, stirring constantly. Cook until thick.
3. Add eggs. Mix well.
4. Sauté onions, green pepper and ham. Add to egg mixture. Mix well.
5. Pour into greased counter or baking pan(s).
6. Set pans in hot water.
7. Bake at 325°F for 45 minutes or until set. Cut 4 × 6 (5 oz).

Directions for Diet Preparations

Sodium Restricted (SR): Omit ham.
Low Fat/Low Cholesterol (LF): Not recommended. Use egg whites or a commercial egg substitute as per manufacturer's directions. Add onions and green peppers to LF omelet. Omit ham.
Diabetic (DB): 5 oz. Omit margarine and flour in step #1.
Mechanical Soft (SFT): Prepare as directed. Sauté vegetables until soft. Consider individual tolerance when using onions.
Soft/Low Fiber (SLF): Not recommended.
Puree (PUR): Puree ham, onions, and green pepper. Prepare as directed.

Nutrient Analysis per Serving:

Regular	KCAL	PRO gm	CHO gm	FAT gm	Chol mg	SFA gm	PFA gm	VITA iu	VITC mg	THI mg	RIB mg	NIA mg	CA mg	NA mg	K+ mg	FE mg
	235	16.3	6.2	15.6	552	4.2	2.8	796	9.3	0.19	0.39	0.7	112	286	260	2.4

Sodium Restricted	NA mg	Diabetic	Kcal	Milk exg	Veg exg	Fruit exg	Bread exg	Meat exg	Fat exg	Low Fat & Low Chol	FAT gm	Chol mg	SFA gm	PFA gm
	161		192	0.2	0.2	0.0	0.0	2.25-M	0.0		4.2	1.2	0.8	2.0

Portion: 2″ × 4″; 6 ounces (3 ounces edible protein)

INGREDIENTS	48 portions		6 portions	
	weights	measures	weights	measures
Eggplant	12 lb AP	162 slices	1 1/2 lb	25 slices
Breading:				
Flour, all-purpose	12 oz	3 cups	1 1/2 oz	1/3 cup
Oregano, ground		2 Tbsp		1/2 tsp
Eggs, beaten	1 1/2 lb	3 cups (12 large)	4 oz	1/2 cup (2 large)
Bread crumbs, dry	2 lb	2 qt	4 oz	1 cup
Parsley, chopped	1 1/3 oz	1 cup	1/8 oz	2 Tbsp
Oil for frying		as needed		as needed
Mozzarella cheese, part skim, sliced	8 1/2 lb	178 slices	1 lb	21 slices
Tomato sauce	6 lb	3 qt	12 oz	1 1/2 cups
Parmesan cheese, grated	9 oz	2 cups	1 1/8 oz	1/4 cup

Method

1. Wash and trim eggplants. Peel. Cut crosswise into 1/4-inch slices. Soak eggplant for 30 minutes in enough water to cover. Drain, pat dry.
2. Prepare breading.
   a. Combine flour and oregano.
   b. Combine bread crumbs and parsley.
   c. Dip eggplant in seasoned flour, then in eggs, then in seasoned bread crumbs.
3. Pan-fry breaded eggplant on both sides until browned. Remove and drain on absorbent paper.
4. Arrange in layers in counter or baking pan(s) in the following order:
   a. eggplant, sauce, mozzarella cheese, sauce.
   b. repeat.
5. Sprinkle with parmesan cheese.
6. Bake at 350°F for 30 to 40 minutes.
7. Cut 4″ × 2″ (6 oz portions).

Directions for Diet Preparations

Sodium Restricted (SR): 6 oz. Omit regular bread crumbs, substitute with low sodium bread crumbs. Omit mozzarella cheese, substitute with part skim ricotta cheese. Use low sodium tomato sauce. Omit parmesan cheese.

Low Fat/Low Cholesterol (LF): 6 oz. Omit eggs in step #4, dip eggplant in egg whites. Omit frying in step #5. Broil on both sides until browned. Bake at 350°F for 30–40 minutes. Omit mozzarella cheese, substitute with part skim ricotta cheese. Use low fat tomato sauce. Continue with step #6 with food items substituted. Omit parmesan cheese.

Diabetic (DB): 6 oz. Omit frying in step #5. Broil on both sides until browned. Bake at 350°F for 30–40 minutes. Omit mozzarella cheese, substitute with part skim ricotta cheese. Use diabetic tomato sauce. Continue with step #6 with food items substituted. Omit parmesan cheese.

Mechanical Soft (SFT): Use SFT tomato sauce.

Soft/Low Fiber (SLF): Not recommended.

Puree (PUR): Prepare as directed. Blenderize. Add additional sauce if necessary to obtain desired consistency.

Nutrient Analysis per Serving:

Regular	KCAL	PRO gm	CHO gm	FAT gm	Chol mg	SFA gm	PFA gm	VITA iu	VITC mg	THI mg	RIB mg	NIA mg	CA mg	NA mg	K+ mg	FE mg
	491	26.6	30.4	29.3	117	11.1	7.5	1736	15.3	0.25	0.41	2.3	639	727	510	2.5

Sodium Restricted	NA mg	Diabetic	Kcal	Milk exg	Veg exg	Fruit exg	Bread exg	Meat exg	Fat exg	Low Fat & Low Chol	FAT gm	Chol mg	SFA gm	PFA gm
	132		274	0.0	2.0	0.0	0.75	3.0-L	0.0		9.2	24.7	4.3	1.0

Portion: 8 ounces; 1 cup (3 ounces edible protein)

INGREDIENTS	50 portions		6 portions	
	weights	measures	weights	measures
Macaroni, dry	3 lb AP	3 qt	6 oz AP	1 1/2 cups
Water, boiling		3 gal		1 1/2 qt
Margarine, low sodium, melted #1	8 oz	1 cup	1 oz	2 Tbsp
Flour, all-purpose	6 oz	1 1/2 cups	3/4 oz	3 Tbsp
Milk, skim		3 qt		1 1/2 cups
Cheese, shredded	9 1/3 lb	2 gal	1 1/8 lb	1 qt
Bread crumbs, dry	12 oz	3 cups	1 1/2 oz	1/3 cup
Margarine, low sodium, melted #2	4 oz	1 1/2 cup	1/2 oz	1 Tbsp

Method

1. Stir macaroni into boiling water, cook 10 to 12 minutes or until tender, stirring occasionally; drain well.
2. Mix margarine #1 with flour. Stir. Cook 5 to 10 minutes.
3. Add milk gradually, stirring constantly. Cook until thickened.
4. Add cheese to sauce; stir until smooth.
5. Pour cheese sauce over macaroni; Mix well.
6. Combine bread crumbs and margarine #2. Sprinkle over macaroni and cheese.
7. Bake at 350°F for 30 to 40 minutes or until lightly browned.

Directions for Diet Preparations

Sodium Restricted (SR): 6 oz. Use low sodium cheese and low sodium bread crumbs. May use if able to calculate into daily food plan.

Low Fat/Low Cholesterol (LF): 6 oz and **Diabetic** (DB): 6 oz. Substitute reduced calorie margarine for regular margarine #1 in equal amounts. Use low fat cheese. Omit margarine #2.

Mechanical Soft (SFT): Prepare as directed.

Soft/Low Fiber (SLF): Use a mild cheese.

Puree (PUR): Prepare as directed. Blenderize. Add additional liquid (e.g. milk or cheese sauce) if necessary to obtain desired consistency.

Nutrient Analysis per Serving:

Regular	KCAL	PRO gm	CHO gm	FAT gm	Chol mg	SFA gm	PFA gm	VITA iu	VITC mg	THI mg	RIB mg	NIA mg	CA mg	NA mg	K+ mg	FE mg
	549	27.7	31.5	34.4	90.5	18.9	2.7	1248	0.5	0.3	0.5	2.2	704	604	251	1.7

Sodium Restricted	NA mg	Diabetic	Kcal	Milk exg	Veg exg	Fruit exg	Bread exg	Meat exg	Fat exg	Low Fat & Low Chol	FAT gm	Chol mg	SFA gm	PFA gm
	350		310	0.3	0.0	0.0	1.5	3.0-L	0.0		13.1	1.0	0.3	0.5

Portion: 1/6 quiche (3 ounces edible protein)

INGREDIENTS	48 portions; 8, 8-inch pies		6 portions; 1, 8-inch pie	
	weights	measures	weights	measures
Pie Shells:[1]				
Flour, all-purpose	2 lb	2 qt	4 oz	1 cup
Margarine, low sodium	1 lb	2 cups	2 oz	1/4 cup
Water, cold	10 oz	1 1/4 cups	1 1/4 oz	2 1/2 Tbsp
Filling:				
Eggs	2 2/3 lb	5 1/4 cups (21 large)	6 oz	3/4 cup (3 large)
Cream, half & half		5 1/3 cups		3/4 cup
Milk, skim		1 qt		3/4 cup
Pepper, white		2 tsp		1/4 tsp
Swiss cheese, grated	3 1/2 lb	3 qt	7 oz	1 1/2 cups
Bacon, chopped, cooked, drained	12 oz	1 1/2 cups	1 1/2 oz	3 Tbsp
Parmesan cheese, grated	8 oz	1 3/4 cups	1 oz	3 1/2 Tbsp

Method

1. Prepare pie shells.
   a. Mix flour and margarine (low speed) for 1 minute.
   b. Add water. Mix (low speed) until dough is formed, about 40 seconds.
   c. Portion into 5 oz balls. Let stand 10 minutes in refrigerator.
   d. Roll into circle 2 inches larger than pie pan. Trim, allowing 1/2 inch extra to build up edge.
   e. Bake in 375°F oven until partially baked.
2. Prepare filling.
   a. Beat eggs. Add cream, milk, and pepper.
   b. Add cheese to egg mixture.
3. Sprinkle bottom of shell(s) with bacon.
4. Pour egg mixture into pie shells, 3 cups per pie.
5. Sprinkle with parmesan cheese.
6. Bake at 375°F oven until custard is set and browned, 25 to 30 minutes.

Notes

[1]May purchase commercially prepared pie shell.

Directions for Diet Preparations

Sodium Restricted (SR): Omit bacon and parmesan cheese.

Low Fat/Low Cholesterol (LF): 1/6 quiche. Use reduced-calorie margarine in equal amounts to margarine in step #1.
48 portions: Omit eggs, replace with 20 egg whites and a commercial liquid egg substitute equal to 11 eggs. Beat egg whites. Fold in egg substitute. Omit cream, use 2 2/3 quart skim milk. Use low fat swiss cheese. Omit bacon and parmesan cheese. Increase cooking time to allow custard to set.
6 portions: Omit eggs, replace with 4 egg whites and a commercial liquid egg substitute equal to 1 egg. Beat egg whites. Fold in egg substitute. Omit cream, use 1 1/4 cups skim milk. Use low fat swiss cheese. Omit bacon and parmesan cheese. Increase cooking time to allow custard to set.

Diabetic (DB): 1/8 quiche. Use reduced-calorie margarine in equal amounts to margarine in step #1.
48 portions: Omit cream, use 2 2/3 quart skim milk. Use low fat swiss cheese. Omit bacon and parmesan cheese.
6 portions: Omit cream, use 1 1/4 cups skim milk. Use low fat swiss cheese. Omit bacon and parmesan cheese.

Mechanical Soft (SFT): Prepare as directed. Consider individual tolerance.

Soft/Low Fiber (SLF): Omit white pepper and swiss cheese, substitute with a mild cheese (i.e. American). Omit bacon and parmesan cheese.

Puree (PUR): Prepare as directed. Add liquid to quiche and blenderize to obtain desired consistency.

Nutrient Analysis per Serving:

Regular	KCAL	PRO gm	CHO gm	FAT gm	Chol mg	SFA gm	PFA gm	VITA iu	VITC mg	THI mg	RIB mg	NIA mg	CA mg	NA mg	K+ mg	FE mg
	363	18.0	12.2	26.7	168	11.6	3.8	889	2.8	0.16	0.33	1.1	426	304	185	1.1

Sodium Restricted	NA mg	Diabetic	Kcal	Milk exg	Veg exg	Fruit exg	Bread exg	Meat exg	Fat exg	Low Fat & Low Chol	FAT gm	Chol mg	SFA gm	PFA gm
	140		183	0.0	0.0	0.0	0.26	3.0-L	0.0		6.8	10.3	0.8	1.5

Portion: 1/6 quiche (3 ounces edible protein)

INGREDIENTS	48 portions; 8, 8-inch pies		6 portions; 1, 8-inch pie	
	weights	measures	weights	measures
Pie Shells[1]				
Flour, all-purpose	2 lb	2 qt	4 oz	1 cup
Margarine, low sodium	1 lb	2 cups	2 oz	1/4 cup
Water, cold	10 oz	1 1/4 cups	1 1/4 oz	2 1/2 Tbsp
Filling:				
Eggs	2 2/3 lb	5 1/4 cups (21 large)	6 oz	3/4 cup (3 large)
Cream, half & half		5 1/3 cups		3/4 cup
Milk, skim		1 qt		1/2 cup
Pepper, white		2 tsp		1/4 tsp
Swiss cheese, grated	3 1/2 lb	3 qt	7 oz	1 1/2 cups
Spinach, chopped, drained well or	3 1/4 lb	2 qt	6 1/2 oz	1 cup
broccoli, chopped, drained	2 lb	2 qt	4 oz	1 cup

Method

1. Prepare pie shells.
   a. Mix flour and margarine (low speed) for 1 minute.
   b. Add water. Mix (low speed) until dough is formed, about 40 seconds.
   c. Portion into 5 oz balls. Let stand 10 minutes in refrigerator.
   d. Roll into circle 2 inches larger than pie pan. Trim, allowing 1/2 inch extra to build up edge.
   e. Bake in 375°F oven until partially baked.
2. Prepare filling.
   a. Beat eggs. Add cream, milk, and pepper.
   b. Add cheese and spinach (or broccoli) to egg mixture.
3. Pour egg/cheese mixture into pie shells.
4. Bake at 375°F oven until custard is set and browned, 25 to 30 minutes.

Notes

[1]May purchase commercially prepared pie shell.

Directions for Diet Preparations

Sodium Restricted (SR): Use low sodium cheese. Use fresh spinach.

Low Fat/Low Cholesterol (LF): 1/6 quiche. Use reduced-calorie margarine in equal amounts to margarine in step #1. Consider individual tolerance to broccoli.

48 portions: Omit eggs, replace with 20 egg whites and a commercial liquid egg substitute equal to 11 eggs. Beat egg whites. Fold in egg substitute. Omit cream, use 2 2/3 quart skim milk. Use low fat swiss cheese. Increase cooking time to allow custard to set.

6 portions: Omit eggs, replace with 4 egg whites and a commercial liquid egg substitute equal to 1 egg. Beat egg whites. Fold in egg substitute. Omit cream, use 1 1/4 cups skim milk. Use low fat swiss cheese. Increase cooking time to allow custard to set.

Diabetic (DB): 1/6 quiche. Use reduced-calorie margarine in equal amounts to margarine in step #1.

48 portions: Omit cream, use 2 2/3 qt skim milk. Use low fat swiss cheese.

6 portions: Omit cream, use 1 1/4 cups skim milk. Use low fat swiss cheese.

Mechanical Soft (SFT): Prepare as directed. Consider individual tolerance.

Soft/Low Fiber (SLF): Omit white pepper and swiss cheese, substitute with a mild cheese (i.e. American). Broccoli is not recommended, substitute with an allowed vegetable.

Puree (PUR): Prepare as directed. Add liquid (i.e. milk) to quiche; blenderize to obtain desired consistency.

Nutrient Analysis per Serving:

Regular	KCAL	PRO gm	CHO gm	FAT gm	Chol mg	SFA gm	PFA gm	VITA iu	VITC mg	THI mg	RIB mg	NIA mg	CA mg	NA mg	K+ mg	FE mg
Spinach	329	16.7	13.3	23.3	162	10.3	3.4	3376	3.4	0.14	0.38	0.8	466	212	293	2.1
Broccoli	331	16.8	13.8	23.3	162	10.3	3.4	1476	12.8	0.13	0.33	0.8	441	271	207	1.2

Sodium Restricted	NA mg	Diabetic	Kcal	Milk exg	Veg exg	Fruit exg	Bread exg	Meat exg	Fat exg	Low Fat & Low Chol	FAT gm	Chol mg	SFA gm	PFA gm
Spinach	162		191	0.25	0.24	0.0	0.5	3.0-L	0.0		6.9	10.3	0.8	1.6
Broccoli	221		192	0.25	0.25	0.0	0.5	3.0-L	0.0		6.8	10.3	0.8	1.6

Vegetarian Entrees

H1	Bean Burger

Portion: 8 ounces (2 patties)

INGREDIENTS	50 portions		6 portions	
	weights	**measures**	**weights**	**measures**
Chickpeas, cooked or canned, drained and mashed	19 lb	2 gal	2 1/3 lb	1 qt
Celery, finely chopped	1 1/4 lb EP	1 1/4 qt	2 1/2 oz EP	2/3 cup
Onion, minced	14 oz EP	2 cups	1 3/4 oz EP	1/4 cup
Carrots, grated	3 1/4 lb EP	2 1/3 qt	6 1/2 oz EP	1 1/8 cups
Flour, whole wheat	1 1/8 lb	1 qt	2 1/4 oz	1/2 cup
Oregano, ground		1 Tbsp		1/2 tsp
Pepper, black		to taste		to taste
Vegetable oil		2/3 cup		1 1/4 Tbsp

Method

1. Mix all ingredients together, except vegetable oil.
2. Use a No. 8 dipper (1/2 cup) and shape into patties.
3. Fry in oiled pan over medium-high heat for 8 minutes, until burgers are golden brown.
4. Turn and fry for another 8 minutes on the other side. Drain.
5. Serve on a bun or with vegetarian gravy.

Directions for Diet Preparations

Sodium Restricted (SR): 6 oz. Rinse chickpeas before mashing.

Low Fat/Low Cholesterol (LF): 8 oz and **Diabetic** (DB): 8 oz. Omit frying. Broil for 8 minutes on each side until golden brown.

Mechanical Soft (SFT): Prepare as directed.

Soft/Low Fiber (SLF): Not recommended. Provide appropriate food substitute.

Puree (PUR): Prepare as directed. Add additional liquid (i.e. vegetable broth); blenderize to obtain desired consistency.

Nutrient Analysis per Serving:

Regular	KCAL	PRO gm	CHO gm	FAT gm	Chol mg	SFA gm	PFA gm	VITA iu	VITC mg	THI mg	RIB mg	NIA mg	CA mg	NA mg	K+ mg	FE mg
	229	7.5	40.1	4.5	0.0	0.5	2.5	5816	8.1	0.15	0.10	1.1	54.2	403	343	2.7

Sodium Restricted	NA mg	Diabetic	Kcal	Milk exg	Veg exg	Fruit exg	Bread exg	Meat exg	Fat exg	Low Fat & Low Chol	FAT gm	Chol mg	SFA gm	PFA gm
	102		203	0.0	0.5	0.0	2.75	0.0	0.0		1.6	0.0	0.2	0.7

H2 — Lentil Stew

Portion: 12 ounces (1 1/2 cups)

INGREDIENTS	50 portions		6 portions	
	weights	measures	weights	measures
Lentils, dry	5 lb	2 1/2 qt	10 oz	1 1/4 cups
Water, boiling		1 1/3 gal		2 2/3 cups
Macaroni, dry	2 1/2 lb	2 1/2 qt	5 oz	1 1/4 cups
Tomato paste	4 lb	2 qt	8 oz	1 cup
Onions, finely chopped	2 1/4 lb EP	5 1/2 cups (10 medium)	7 1/4 oz	1 cup (2 medium)
Oregano, ground		2 Tbsp		3/4 tsp
Garlic powder		3 Tbsp		1 1/4 tsp
Water		2 1/2 gal		2 1/2 qt

Method

1. Add lentils to boiling water. Boil 2 minutes.
2. Remove from heat. Cover and let soak 30 minutes.
3. Cook lentils in soaking water. Bring to a boil. Simmer 1 to 1 1/2 hours. Do not stir.
4. Combine all ingredients in a large pot.
5. Cook until tender, approximately 20 minutes.

Directions for Diet Preparations

Sodium Restricted (SR): Use low sodium tomato paste.
Low Fat/Low Cholesterol (LF): 12 oz, **Diabetic** (DB): 12 oz, and **Mechanical Soft** (SFT): Prepare as directed.
Soft/Low Fiber (SLF): Not recommended. Provide appropriate food substitute.
Puree (PUR): Prepare as directed. Blenderize. Add additional liquid (i.e. tomato sauce), if necessary to obtain desired consistency.

Nutrient Analysis per Serving:

Regular	KCAL	PRO gm	CHO gm	FAT gm	Chol mg	SFA gm	PFA gm	VITA iu	VITC mg	THI mg	RIB mg	NIA mg	CA mg	NA mg	K+ mg	FE mg
	281	17.5	52.6	1.2	0.0	0.18	0.5	1086	22.3	0.5	0.29	4.3	51.2	342	882	6.4

Sodium Restricted	NA mg	Diabetic	Kcal	Milk exg	Veg exg	Fruit exg	Bread exg	Meat exg	Fat exg	Low Fat & Low Chol	FAT gm	Chol mg	SFA gm	PFA gm
	30.2		281	0.0	1.5	0.0	3.2	0.0	0.0		1.2	0.0	0.2	0.5

Macaroni and Bean Casserole

Portion: 12 ounces (1 1/2 cup)

INGREDIENTS	50 portions		6 portions	
	weights	**measures**	**weights**	**measures**
Water, boiling		6 gal		3 qt
Macaroni shells or other pasta, dry	6 lb	1 1/2 gal	12 oz	3 cups
Onions, chopped	2 1/4 lb EP (2 1/2 lb AP)	6 2/3 cups (12 medium)	4 1/2 oz EP (5 oz AP)	3/4 cup (1 large)
Garlic, minced	2 oz	1/3 cup (16 cloves)	1/4 oz	2 tsp (2 cloves)
Green pepper, chopped	3 1/4 lb EP (4 lb AP)	2 1/3 qt (12 large)	6 2/3 oz EP (8 1/4 oz AP)	1 1/4 cups (2 medium)
Olive oil		1/2 cup		1 Tbsp
Tomato sauce	9 1/8 lb	4 1/2 qt	1 1/8 lb	2 1/4 cups
Kidney beans, dry, cooked	18 lb	3 gal	2 1/4 lb	1 1/2 qt
Soy sauce, low sodium		1/4 cup		1 1/2 tsp
Chili powder		3 Tbsp		1 1/4 tsp
Pepper, black		to taste		to taste

Method

1. Add pasta gradually to boiling water, while stirring. Bring water back to a boil. Cook uncovered. Stir occasionally. Cook until tender, about 10 minutes. Drain
2. Sauté onions, garlic, and green peppers in olive oil for 5 minutes or until vegetables are soft.
3. Stir in tomato sauce, kidney beans, soy sauce, and seasonings.
4. Simmer until heated through. Serve at 160°F.

Directions for Diet Preparations

Sodium Restricted (SR): Use low sodium tomato sauce.
Low Fat/Low Cholesterol (LF): 12 oz and **Diabetic** (DB): 10 oz. Prepare as directed. Low fat diets should consider individual tolerance to onions and garlic.
Mechanical Soft (SFT): Prepare as directed.
Soft/Low Fiber (SLF): Not recommended. Provide appropriate food substitute.
Puree (PUR): Prepare as directed. Blenderize. Add additional tomato sauce, if necessary to obtain desired consistency.

Nutrient Analysis per Serving:

Regular	KCAL	PRO gm	CHO gm	FAT gm	Chol mg	SFA gm	PFA gm	VITA iu	VITC mg	THI mg	RIB mg	NIA mg	CA mg	NA mg	K+ mg	FE mg
	537	27.2	101	4.2	0.0	0.5	0.9	981	41.1	0.93	0.44	6.1	89.6	629	1286	9.2

Sodium Restricted	NA mg	Diabetic	Kcal	Milk exg	Veg exg	Fruit exg	Bread exg	Meat exg	Fat exg	Low Fat & Low Chol	FAT gm	Chol mg	SFA gm	PFA gm
	108		415	0.0	1.0	0.0	3.3	2.3-L	0.3		4.2	0.0	0.5	0.9

Portion: 6 ounces (1 patty)

INGREDIENTS	50 portions		6 portions	
	weights	**measures**	**weights**	**measures**
Brown rice, pre-cooked	12 lb	1 1/2 gal	1 1/2 lb	3 cups
Bread crumbs, soft	12 oz	1 1/2 qt	1 1/2 oz	3/4 cup
Celery, finely chopped	1 1/3 lb EP (1 5/8 lb AP)	1 qt	2 2/3 oz EP (3 3/4 oz AP)	1/2 cup
Carrots, finely chopped	1 1/3 lb EP (1 1/2 lb AP)	1 qt	2 2/3 oz EP (3 1/8 oz AP)	1/2 cup
Onions, minced	1 1/3 lb EP (1 1/2 lb AP)	1 qt	2 2/3 oz EP (3 1/8 oz AP)	1/2 cup
Pepper, black		to taste		to taste
Tarragon, ground		1 Tbsp		1/2 tsp
Vegetable oil		1 cup		2 Tbsp

Method

1. Combine all ingredients together, except vegetable oil.
2. Use a No. 6 dipper (3/4 cup) and shape into patties about 3/4-inch thick.
3. Fry in oiled pan over medium-high heat for 8 minutes on each side, until patties are golden brown. Drain.

Directions for Diet Preparations

Sodium Restricted (SR): Use low sodium bread crumbs.

Low Fat/Low Cholesterol (LF): 6 oz and **Diabetic** (DB): 6 oz. Omit frying. Broil for 8 minutes on each side until golden brown.

Mechanical Soft (SFT): Prepare as directed. Consider individual tolerance.

Soft/Low Fiber (SLF): Not recommended. Provide appropriate food substitute.

Puree (PUR): Prepare as directed. Add additional liquid (i.e. vegetarian gravy); blenderize to obtain desired consistency.

Nutrient Analysis per Serving:

Regular	KCAL	PRO gm	CHO gm	FAT gm	Chol mg	SFA gm	PFA gm	VITA iu	VITC mg	THI mg	RIB mg	NIA mg	CA mg	NA mg	K+ mg	FE mg
	190	4.0	30.5	5.8	0.6	0.8	2.9	2520	2.5	0.14	0.07	2.0	32.4	105	132	1.0

Sodium Restricted	NA mg	Diabetic	Kcal	Milk exg	Veg exg	Fruit exg	Bread exg	Meat exg	Fat exg	Low Fat & Low Chol	FAT gm	Chol mg	SFA gm	PFA gm
	18.1		151	0.0	0.25	0.0	2.0	0.0	0.0		1.4	0.6	0.3	0.3

Portion: 10 ounces (2 cups) tofu and vegetables with 8 ounces (1 cup) brown rice

INGREDIENTS	50 portions		6 portions	
	weights	measures	weights	measures
Brown rice, raw	6 lb	3 3/4 qt	12 oz	1 5/8 cups
Water		7 1/2 qt		3 3/4 cups
Carrots, sliced thin	5 1/3 lb EP (7 2/3 lb AP)	1 gal (26 medium)	13 oz EP (1 1/4 lb AP)	2 1/2 cups (4 medium)
Broccoli, chopped	3 1/4 lb EP (4 lb AP)	3 qt	8 3/4 oz EP (10 2/3 oz AP)	2 cups
Zucchini, sliced thin	4 3/4 lb EP (5 1/2 lb AP)	1 gal (10 medium)	9 1/2 oz EP (11 oz AP)	2 cups (2 medium)
Red peppers, chopped	1 lb EP (1 1/4 lb AP)	3 cups	1 3/4 oz EP (2 1/4 oz AP)	1/3 cup
Vegetable oil		1 1/2 cups		3 Tbsp
Mushrooms, sliced	5 lb AP	2 gal	10 oz AP	1 qt
Tofu, cut into small pieces	10 lb	1 2/3 gal	1 1/4 lb	3 1/4 cups
Soy sauce, low sodium		3/4 cup		1 1/2 Tbsp

Method

1. Cook rice in boiling water for 50 minutes or until tender.
2. Sauté carrots, broccoli, zucchini, and red peppers in oil over medium-high heat for 5 minutes.
3. Add mushrooms, tofu, and soy sauce. Sauté for 5 minutes.
4. Serve hot over brown rice.

Directions for Diet Preparations

Sodium Restricted (SR), **Low Fat/Low Cholesterol** (LF): 2 cups tofu/vegetables and 1 cup rice, and **Diabetic** (DB): 2 cups tofu/vegetables and 1 cup rice. Prepare as directed.

Mechanical Soft (SFT): Prepare as directed. Cook vegetables until soft and tender.

Soft/Low Fiber (SLF):

50 portions: Use 7 qt canned carrots. Omit broccoli, zucchini, and red pepper, substitute with 4 3/4 qt canned green beans.

6 portions: Use 4 1/2 cups canned carrots. Omit broccoli, zucchini, and red pepper, substitute with 2 1/2 cups canned green beans.

Puree (PUR): Prepare as directed. Add additional liquid (i.e. vegetarian gravy); blenderize to obtain desired consistency.

Nutrient Analysis per Serving:

Regular	KCAL	PRO gm	CHO gm	FAT gm	Chol mg	SFA gm	PFA gm	VITA iu	VITC mg	THI mg	RIB mg	NIA mg	CA mg	NA mg	K+ mg	FE mg
	369	14.4	52.0	12.9	0.0	1.8	7.1	10576	27.7	0.36	0.37	5.6	145	159	712	6.8

Sodium Restricted	NA mg	Diabetic	Kcal	Milk exg	Veg exg	Fruit exg	Bread exg	Meat exg	Fat exg	Low Fat & Low Chol	FAT gm	Chol mg	SFA gm	PFA gm
	159		369	0.0	1.5	0.0	2.7	2.0-L	0.5		12.9	0.0	1.8	7.1

Portion: 6 ounces (1 patty)

INGREDIENTS	50 portions		6 portions	
	weights	**measures**	**weights**	**measures**
Tofu, mashed	16 lb	2 gal	2 lb	1 qt
Wheat germ	2 lb	2 qt	4 oz	1 cup
Green pepper, finely chopped	10 2/3 oz EP (13 1/4 oz AP)	2 cups	1 1/3 oz EP (1 2/3 oz AP)	1/4 cup
Red pepper, finely chopped	10 2/3 oz EP (13 1/4 oz AP)	2 cups	1 1/3 oz EP (1 2/3 oz AP)	1/4 cup
Garlic powder		6 Tbsp		2 tsp
Onion powder		6 Tbsp		2 tsp
Soy sauce, low sodium		2 cups		1/4 cup
Pepper, black		2 Tbsp		3/4 tsp
Parsley, finely chopped	8 oz	1 qt	1 oz	1/2 cup
Vegetable oil		1 cup		2 Tbsp

Method

1. Mix all ingredients together, except vegetable oil.
2. Form patties with approximately 1 cup of mixture and about 3/4-inch thick.
3. Fry in oiled pan over medium-high heat for 8 minutes on each side, until patties are golden brown. Drain.
4. Serve on a bun or bread.

Directions for Diet Preparations

Sodium Restricted (SR): 5 oz patty. Use half the amount of low sodium soy sauce.

Low Fat/Low Cholesterol (LF): 6 oz and **Diabetic** (DB): 6 oz. Omit frying. Broil for 8 minutes on each side until golden brown. Low fat diets should consider individual tolerance to garlic and onions.

Mechanical Soft (SFT): Prepare as directed. Consider individual tolerance.

Soft/Low Fiber (SLF): Not recommended. Provide appropriate food substitute.

Puree (PUR): Prepare as directed. Add liquid (i.e. vegetarian gravy); blenderize to obtain desired consistency.

Nutrient Analysis per Serving:

Regular	KCAL	PRO gm	CHO gm	FAT gm	Chol mg	SFA gm	PFA gm	VITA iu	VITC mg	THI mg	RIB mg	NIA mg	CA mg	NA mg	K+ mg	FE mg
	232	17.9	14.4	13.3	0.0	1.9	7.7	376	5.7	0.44	0.24	1.6	173	322	413	10.0

Sodium Restricted	NA mg	Diabetic	Kcal	Milk exg	Veg exg	Fruit exg	Bread exg	Meat exg	Fat exg	Low Fat & Low Chol	FAT gm	Chol mg	SFA gm	PFA gm
	133		193	0.0	0.0	0.0	0.5	2.8-L	0.0		8.9	0.0	1.3	5.1

Portion: 8 ounces (1 cup)

INGREDIENTS	50 portions		6 portions	
	weights	measures	weights	measures
Parsley, fresh, finely chopped	5 oz	1 1/4 qt	2/3 oz	2/3 cup
Oregano, ground		2 tsp		1/4 tsp
Garlic powder		2 tsp		1/4 tsp
Onions, chopped	1 2/3 lb EP (2 lb AP)	1 1/4 qt (9 medium)	3 oz EP (3 1/2 oz AP)	1/2 cup (1 medium)
Celery, chopped	2 lb EP (2 1/2 lb AP)	1 1/2 qt (20 stalks)	4 oz EP (4 3/4 oz AP)	3/4 cup (2 1/2 stalks)
Margarine, low sodium, melted	12 oz	1 1/2 cups	1 1/2 oz	3 Tbsp
Tomato sauce	9 lb	4 1/2 qt	1 1/8 lb	2 1/4 cups
Water		1 1/4 gal		2 1/2 cups
Bulgar (cracked wheat), dry	3 3/4 lb	2 1/2 qt	7 1/2 oz	1 1/4 cups

Method

1. Sauté parsley, seasonings, onions, and celery in margarine until vegetables are soft.
2. Add tomato sauce, water, and bulgar. Cook over medium heat until bulgar is done, about 25 minutes.
3. Serve with a baked potato or spaghetti.

Directions for Diet Preparations

Sodium Restricted (SR): Use low sodium tomato sauce.
Low Fat/Low Cholesterol (LF): 8 oz and **Diabetic** (DB): 8 oz. Sauté in half the amount of margarine specified. Low fat diets should consider individual tolerance to garlic and onions.
Mechanical Soft (SFT): Prepare as directed.
Soft/Low Fiber (SLF): Not recommended. Provide appropriate food substitute.
Puree (PUR): Prepare as directed. Add additional liquid (i.e. tomato sauce); blenderize to obtain desired consistency.

Nutrient Analysis per Serving:

Regular	KCAL	PRO gm	CHO gm	FAT gm	Chol mg	SFA gm	PFA gm	VITA iu	VITC mg	THI mg	RIB mg	NIA mg	CA mg	NA mg	K+ mg	FE mg
	205	5.9	35.0	6.2	0.0	1.0	2.1	1364	18.4	0.16	0.1	2.8	43.8	517	552	2.0

Sodium Restricted	NA mg	Diabetic	Kcal	Milk exg	Veg exg	Fruit exg	Bread exg	Meat exg	Fat exg	Low Fat & Low Chol	FAT gm	Chol mg	SFA gm	PFA gm
	41.5		180	0.0	1.0	0.0	1.8	0.0	0.5		3.4	0.0	0.6	1.2

Portion: 12 ounces (1 3/4 cups)

INGREDIENTS	50 portions		6 portions	
	weights	measures	weights	measures
Onions, chopped	2 1/3 lb EP (2 3/4 lb AP)	1 3/4 qt (10 large)	3 3/4 oz EP (4 1/2 oz AP)	3/4 cup (1 large)
Garlic, minced finely	3 oz	1/2 cup (24 cloves)	1/3 oz	1 Tbsp (3 cloves)
Green peppers, chopped	4 lb EP (5 lb AP)	3 qt (10 large)	12 3/4 oz EP (1 lb AP)	2 1/2 cups (2 large)
Celery, chopped	1 1/3 lb EP (1 2/3 lb AP)	1 qt (13 stalks)	3 1/4 oz EP (4 oz AP)	2/3 cup (2 stalks)
Vegetable oil		1 1/4 cups		2 1/2 Tbsp
Water		5 qt		2 1/2 cups
Red kidney beans, dry, cooked	10 1/4 lb	1 3/4 gal	1 1/4 lb	3 1/2 cups
Tomatoes, fresh, chopped or Tomatoes, canned, chopped	12 1/2 lb EP (13 3/4 lb AP)	1 3/4 gal (37 medium)	1 2/3 lb EP (1 3/4 lb AP)	3 3/4 cups (5 medium)
Corn kernels, frozen, fresh, or canned, drained	2 lb	1 1/2 qt	4 oz	3/4 cup
Chili powder		6 Tbsp		3/4 Tbsp
Pepper, black, ground		to taste		to taste

Method

1. Sauté onions, garlic, green peppers, and celery in vegetable oil over medium heat until the vegetables are soft, about 5 minutes.
2. Add water, kidney beans, tomatoes, corn, and seasonings. Cook over medium heat for 25 minutes, stirring occasionally.

Directions for Diet Preparations

Sodium Restricted (SR): Use fresh tomatoes.
Low Fat/Low Cholesterol (LF): 12 oz and **Diabetic** (DB): 12 oz. Sauté onions and green peppers in half the amount of oil specified. Low fat diets should consider individual tolerance to onions and garlic.
Mechanical Soft (SFT): Prepare as directed.
Soft/Low Fiber (SLF): Not recommended. Provide appropriate food substitute.
Puree (PUR): Prepare as directed. Blenderize. Add additional tomato sauce, if necessary to obtain desired consistency.

Nutrient Analysis per Serving:

Regular	KCAL	PRO gm	CHO gm	FAT gm	Chol mg	SFA gm	PFA gm	VITA iu	VITC mg	THI mg	RIB mg	NIA mg	CA mg	NA mg	K+ mg	FE mg
	270	13.4	42.5	6.8	0.0	0.8	3.8	1024	56.9	0.31	0.15	2.2	85.2	244	965	5.2

Sodium Restricted	NA mg	Diabetic	Kcal	Milk exg	Veg exg	Fruit exg	Bread exg	Meat exg	Fat exg	Low Fat & Low Chol	FAT gm	Chol mg	SFA gm	PFA gm
	34.0		246	0.0	1.5	0.0	2.1	0.2-L	0.5		4.0	0.0	0.5	2.2

Sandwiches and Cold Plates

I1 — Bean Taco

Portion: 2 taco shells with 2 ounces (1/4 cup) of beans in each shell

INGREDIENTS	50 portions		6 portions	
	weights	measures	weights	measures
Red kidney beans, cooked or canned, drained	7 1/4 lb	1 1/4 gal	14 1/2 oz	2 1/2 cups
Onions, minced	1 2/3 lb	1 qt (6 large)	3 1/4 oz	1/2 cup (1 medium)
Vegetable oil		3/4 cup		1 1/2 Tbsp
Tomato paste	3 lb	1 1/2 qt	6 oz	3/4 cup
Chili powder	2 oz	1/2 cup	1/4 oz	1 Tbsp
Pepper, black, ground		to taste		to taste
Lettuce, shredded	1 1/4 lb EP (1 3/4 lb AP)	2 1/2 qt (2 heads)	2 1/2 oz EP (3 1/2 oz AP)	1 1/4 cups (1/4 head)
Tomatoes, fresh, chopped	1 3/4 lb EP (2 lb AP)	1 qt	3 1/2 oz EP (4 oz AP)	1/2 cup
Taco shells		100 shells		12 shells

Method

1. Mash kidney beans and set aside.
2. Sauté onions in vegetable oil.
3. Add tomato paste, seasonings, and mashed beans to the onions. Cook over medium heat until beans are heated through.
4. To prepare taco, place 2 oz (1/4 cup) bean mixture in a taco shell with 1/4 cup shredded lettuce and chopped tomatoes.
5. Serving size: 2 tacos with salsa on the side.

Directions for Diet Preparations

Sodium Restricted (SR): Use raw, cooked kidney beans. Use low sodium tomato paste.

Low Fat/Low Cholesterol (LF): 1 taco shell with 4 oz bean filling and **Diabetic** (DB): 1 taco shell with 4 oz bean filling. Prepare as directed.

Mechanical Soft (SFT): Omit taco shell, substitute with a flour tortilla.

Soft/Low Fiber (SLF): Not recommended. Provide appropriate food substitute.

Puree (PUR): Omit taco shell. Prepare bean filling as directed. Blenderize. Add additional liquid (i.e. tomato sauce), if necessary to obtain desired consistency.

Nutrient Analysis per Serving:

Regular	KCAL	PRO gm	CHO gm	FAT gm	Chol mg	SFA gm	PFA gm	VITA iu	VITC mg	THI mg	RIB mg	NIA mg	CA mg	NA mg	K+ mg	FE mg
	300	11.3	42.9	10.3	0.0	0.5	2.3	1007	19.4	0.28	0.13	2.9	46.2	361	751	4.6

Sodium Restricted	NA mg	Diabetic	Kcal	Milk exg	Veg exg	Fruit exg	Bread exg	Meat exg	Fat exg	Low Fat & Low Chol	FAT gm	Chol mg	SFA gm	PFA gm
	36		241	0.0	1.0	0.0	1.4	1.1-L	1.1		7.3	0.0	0.5	2.3

12   Grilled Cheese Sandwich

Portion: 2 slices bread; 3 ounces cheese

Ingredients	50 portions		1 portion	
	weights	measures	weights	measures
Bread	6 1/3 lb	100 slices (4 1/4 loaves)	2 oz	2 slices
Cheese	9 1/3 lb	150 slices	3 oz	3 slices
Margarine, low sodium, melted	1 lb	2 cups		2 tsp

Method

1. Assemble sandwiches with 3 ounces of cheese.
2. Brush both sides of bread with margarine.
3. Grill on hot griddle until lightly browned on both sides.
4. Cut diagonally.

Open Faced Grilled Cheese

1. Place one ounce cheese on one slice bread.
2. Broil until cheese melts.

Directions for Diet Preparations

Sodium Restricted (SR): Use low sodium bread and low sodium cheese. May use if able to calculate into daily food plan.

Low Fat/Low Cholesterol (LF): 2 slices bread, 2 oz low fat cheese and **Diabetic** (DB): 2 slices bread, 3 oz low fat cheese. Omit margarine. Use low fat cheese.

Mechanical Soft (SFT): Consider individual tolerance to toasted bread.

Soft/Low Fiber (SLF): Use mild cheese and white bread.

Puree (PUR): Not recommended. Use appropriate food alternative.

Nutrient Analysis per Serving:

Regular	KCAL	PRO gm	CHO gm	FAT gm	Chol mg	SFA gm	PFA gm	VITA iu	VITC mg	THI mg	RIB mg	NIA mg	CA mg	NA mg	K+ mg	FE mg
2 slices	522	23.2	26.6	35.8	81.7	18.5	3.4	1344	0.01	0.22	0.4	1.7	561	1472	183	1.7
open faced	207	8.4	13.0	13.5	27.5	6.4	1.5	500	0.01	0.11	0.16	0.8	193	533	68.9	0.8

Sodium Restricted	NA mg	Diabetic	Kcal	Milk exg	Veg exg	Fruit exg	Bread exg	Meat exg	Fat exg	Low Fat & Low Chol	FAT gm	Chol mg	SFA gm	PFA gm
2 slices	227		284	0.0	0.0	0.0	2.0	3.0-L	0.0		5.5	17.5	0.5	0.7
open faced	77.7		117	0.0	0.0	0.0	1.0	1.0-L	0.0		2.7	8.7	0.2	0.3

Portion: 1/2 cup salad, 2 slices bread (3 ounces edible protein)

INGREDIENTS	50 portions		6 portions	
	weights	measures	weights	measures
Chicken, cooked, diced	9 1/2 lb	1 3/4 gal	1 1/4 lb	3 1/2 cups
Celery, chopped	1 lb EP (1 1/4 lb AP)	3 cup	2 oz EP (2 1/2 oz AP)	1/3 cup
Almonds, slivered, unsalted	9 oz	2 cups	1 oz	3 1/2 Tbsp
Pineapple chunks, drained, unsweetened	3 lb	1 1/2 qt	6 oz	3/4 cup
Grapes, seedless	1 1/2 lb	3 3/4 cups	3 1/4 oz	1/2 cup
Mayonnaise	2 lb	1 qt	4 oz	1/2 cup
Lettuce leaf	2 lb EP (3 lb AP)	50 leaves	4 oz EP (6 oz AP)	6 leaves
Bread	6 1/3 lb	100 slices (4 1/4 loaves)	12 oz	12 slices (1/2 loaf)

Method

1. Combine all ingredients.
2. Mix lightly.
3. Chill until serving time.
4. Assemble sandwich. Place lettuce leaf on each sandwich.
5. Portion chicken salad with No. 8 dipper.

Directions for Diet Preparations

Sodium Restricted (SR): Use unsalted almonds. Use low sodium mayonnaise and low sodium bread.

Low Fat/Low Cholesterol (LF): and **Diabetic** (DB): 1/2 cup salad; 2 slices bread. Omit almonds. Omit mayonnaise, substitute with half the amount of reduced-calorie low cholesterol mayonnaise.

Mechanical Soft (SFT) and **Soft/Low Fiber** (SLF): Omit celery, almonds, grapes, and lettuce. Combine chicken, pineapple, and mayonnaise. Use white bread.

Puree (PUR): Omit celery, almonds, grapes, lettuce, and bread. Combine chicken, pineapple, and mayonnaise. Add additional mayonnaise and pineapple juice. Blenderize to obtain desired consistency.

Nutrient Analysis per Serving:

Regular	KCAL	PRO gm	CHO gm	FAT gm	Chol mg	SFA gm	PFA gm	VITA iu	VITC mg	THI mg	RIB mg	NIA mg	CA mg	NA mg	K+ mg	FE mg
salad only	349	26.1	8.5	23.5	86.2	3.5	11.8	127	3.5	0.11	0.21	8.1	39.9	182	332	1.6
with bread	484	30.5	33.7	25.1	87.7	4.1	11.9	127	3.5	0.31	0.32	9.7	74.9	436	374	3.0

Sodium Restricted	NA mg	Diabetic	Kcal	Milk exg	Veg exg	Fruit exg	Bread exg	Meat exg	Fat exg	Low Fat & Low Chol	FAT gm	Chol mg	SFA gm	PFA gm
salad only	87.0		254	0.0	0.0	0.75	0.0	3.0-L	1.0		12.5	75.7	2.0	2.0
with bread	92.3		388	0.0	0.0	0.75	2.0	3.0-L	1.0		14.1	77.2	2.5	2.0

Cold Cut Sandwiches

Portion: 3 ounces meat, 2 slices bread

INGREDIENTS	50 portions		1 portions	
	weights	measures	weights	measures
Salami (1 oz slices) or	9 1/3 lb	150 slices	3 oz	3 slices
Roast Beef or	9 1/3 lb	150 slices	3 oz	3 slices
Turkey or	9 1/3 lb	150 slices	3 oz	3 slices
Bologna or	9 1/3 lb	150 slices	3 oz	3 slices
Ham or	9 1/3 lb	150 slices	3 oz	3 slices
Cheese	9 1/3 lb	150 slices	3 oz	3 slices
Lettuce leaf	2 lb EP (3 lb AP)	50 leaves	1 leaf	1 leaf
Bread	6 1/3 lb	100 slices (4 1/4 loaves)	2 oz	2 slices

Method

1. Assemble sandwiches with 3 oz of meat and/or cheese.
2. Place lettuce leaf on each sandwich.
3. Serve with catsup, mustard, or mayonnaise.

Directions for Diet Preparations

Sodium Restricted (SR): May use roast beef, low sodium turkey, and low sodium cheeses. Use low sodium bread, low sodium catsup, low sodium mustard, and low sodium mayonnaise.

Low Fat/Low Cholesterol (LF): 2 slices bread, 2 oz meat or cheese. May use roast beef, turkey, and low fat cheeses. Use reduced-calorie low cholesterol mayonnaise.

Diabetic (DB): 2 slices bread, 3 oz meat or cheese. May use all meats and low fat cheeses, if able to calculate into daily food plan. Use reduced-calorie mayonnaise, catsup, or mustard.

Mechanical Soft (SFT): Prepare as directed. Consider individual tolerance.

Soft/Low Fiber (SLF): Use roast beef, turkey, and/or mild cheeses. Use white bread.

Puree (PUR): Not recommended. Use appropriate food alternative.

Nutrient Analysis per Serving:

Regular	KCAL	PRO gm	CHO gm	FAT gm	Chol mg	SFA gm	PFA gm	VITA iu	VITC mg	THI mg	RIB mg	NIA mg	CA mg	NA mg	K+ mg	FE mg
	327	24.9	25.7	13.2	58.3	7.0	0.8	342	7.8	0.51	0.34	4.6	218	1000	271	2.3

Sodium Restricted	NA mg	Diabetic	Kcal	Milk exg	Veg exg	Fruit exg	Bread exg	Meat exg	Fat exg	Low Fat & Low Chol	FAT gm	Chol mg	SFA gm	PFA gm
	151		301	0.0	0.0	0.0	2.0	3.0-L	0.0		8.0	23.0	0.9	0.4

Portion: 1 chef salad, (3 ounces edible protein)

INGREDIENTS	50 portions		6 portions	
	weights	measures	weights	measures
Lettuce, iceberg	11 lb EP (14 1/2 lb AP)	4 1/8 gal	1 1/2 lb EP (1 3/4 lb AP)	2 qt
Carrot, shredded	3 1/8 lb EP (4 1/2 lb AP)	3 1/8 qt	6 1/4 oz EP (9 oz AP)	1 1/2 cups
Turkey, cooked, slice into thin strips	3 lb	2 1/4 qt	6 oz	1 1/8 cups
Ham, cooked, diced	3 lb	2 1/4 qt	6 oz	1 1/8 cups
Swiss cheese	3 lb	3 qt	6 oz	1 1/2 cups
Green pepper rings	1 1/4 lb EP (1 1/2 lb AP)	50 rings	2 1/2 oz EP (3 oz AP)	6 rings
Salad dressing	3 lb	1 1/2 qt	6 oz	3/4 cup

Method

1. Tear lettuce into bite-size pieces.
2. Add shredded carrots to lettuce. Toss lightly.
3. Portion lettuce, carrots into individual salad bowls; 4 1/2 oz (1 1/2 cup) per bowl.
4. Arrange 1 oz each of turkey, ham, and cheese on top of lettuce.
5. Place one green pepper ring and two tomato wedges on each salad.
6. Serve each salad with 1 oz salad dressing.

Directions for Diet Preparations

Sodium Restricted (SR): Omit ham. Serve an additional 1 oz turkey. Use low sodium cheese and low sodium salad dressing.

Low Fat/Low Cholesterol (LF): 1 chef salad with 2 oz meat. Omit ham. Serve 1 oz turkey and 1 oz low fat cheese. Use reduced-calorie low cholesterol or low calorie salad dressing.

Diabetic (DB): 1 chef salad with 3 oz meat. Use lean, low fat meats and cheeses. Use reduced calorie or low calorie salad dressing.

Mechanical Soft (SFT): Omit raw vegetables. Serve with appropriate cooked vegetables or juice. Chop meat and cheese.

Soft/Low Fiber (SLF): Not recommended. Use appropriate food substitute.

Puree (PUR): Not recommended. Serve appropriate puree vegetable or juice and puree meat and/or cheese.

Nutrient Analysis per Serving:

Regular	KCAL	PRO gm	CHO gm	FAT gm	Chol mg	SFA gm	PFA gm	VITA iu	VITC mg	THI mg	RIB mg	NIA mg	CA mg	NA mg	K+ mg	FE mg
	224	22.1	8.6	11.0	61.4	5.7	1.1	16160	26.8	0.31	0.31	3.9	240	910	570	1.7

Sodium Restricted	NA mg	Diabetic	Kcal	Milk exg	Veg exg	Fruit exg	Bread exg	Meat exg	Fat exg	Low Fat & Low Chol	FAT gm	Chol mg	SFA gm	PFA gm
	169		200	0.0	1.0	0.0	0.0	3.0-L	0.0		6.6	21.5	0.5	0.5

Portion: 1/2 cup, 4 ounces (3 ounces edible protein)

INGREDIENTS	50 portions		6 portions	
	weights	**measures**	**weights**	**measures**
Chicken, (or turkey) cooked, diced	9 1/2 lb	1 3/4 gal	1 1/4 lb	3 1/2 cups
Celery, diced	2 lb EP (2 1/2 lb AP)	2 qt	4 oz EP (5 oz AP)	1 cup
Onions, diced	5 1/3 oz EP	1 cup	3/4 oz EP	2 Tbsp
Red peppers, chopped	1 lb EP (1 1/4 lb AP)	3 cups	2 oz EP (2 1/2 oz AP)	1/3 cup
Mayonnaise	2 lb	1 qt	4 oz	1/2 cup

Method

1. Prepare close to serving time.
2. Combine all ingredients. Mix lightly. Chill.
3. Serve with No. 8 dipper.

Directions for Diet Preparations

Sodium Restricted (SR): Use low sodium mayonnaise.

Low Fat/Low Cholesterol (LF): 1/2 cup and **Diabetic** (DB): 1/2 cup. Use reduced-calorie low cholesterol mayonnaise in half the amount specified for regular mayonnaise.

Mechanical Soft (SFT) and **Soft/Low Fiber** (SLF): Omit celery, onions, and red peppers.

Puree (PUR): Omit celery, onions, and red peppers. Add additional mayonnaise to salad; blenderize to obtain desired consistency.

Nutrient Analysis per Serving:

Regular	KCAL	PRO gm	CHO gm	FAT gm	Chol mg	SFA gm	PFA gm	VITA iu	VITC mg	THI mg	RIB mg	NIA mg	CA mg	NA mg	K+ mg	FE mg
chicken	294	24.9	1.5	20.5	86.2	3.2	11.2	151	9.0	0.06	0.16	7.9	23.4	191	280	1.2
turkey	277	25.3	1.5	18.4	75.1	2.9	11.0	106	9.0	0.06	0.16	4.7	31.9	178	327	1.7

Sodium Restricted	NA mg	Diabetic	Kcal	Milk exg	Veg exg	Fruit exg	Bread exg	Meat exg	Fat exg	Low Fat & Low Chol	FAT gm	Chol mg	SFA gm	PFA gm
chicken	95.8		198	0.0	0.2	0.0	0.0	3.0-L	0.3		9.5	75.7	1.7	1.4
turkey	82.2		181	0.0	0.2	0.0	0.0	3.0-L	0.3		7.4	64.6	1.4	1.2

Chickpea Salad

Portion: 3/4 cup (6 ounces)

INGREDIENTS	50 portions		6 portions	
	weights	measures	weights	measures
Chickpeas, dry, cooked	16 2/3 lb	1 3/4 gal	2 lb	3 1/2 cups
Celery, finely chopped	1 2/3 lb EP (2 lb AP)	1 1/4 qt (16 stalks)	3 1/2 oz EP (4 1/8 oz AP)	2/3 cup (2 stalks)
Onions, minced	1 3/4 lb EP (2 1/8 lb AP)	1 qt (8 medium)	3 1/2 oz EP (4 1/4 oz AP)	1/2 cup (1 medium)
Red peppers, finely chopped	1 lb EP (1 1/4 lb AP)	3 cups (5 large)	2 oz EP (2 1/2 oz AP)	1/3 cup (1 small)
Mayonnaise	1 lb	2 cups	2 oz	1/4 cup
Pepper, black		to taste		to taste

Method

1. Prepare close to serving time.
2. Combine all ingredients. Mix lightly. Chill.
3. Serve with No. 6 dipper.

Directions for Diet Preparations

Sodium Restricted (SR): Use low sodium mayonnaise.

Low Fat/Low Cholesterol (LF): 3/4 cup and **Diabetic** (DB): 3/4 cup. Use reduced-calorie low cholesterol mayonnaise in half the amount specified for regular mayonnaise.

Mechanical Soft (SFT): Omit celery, onions, and red peppers.

Soft/Low Fiber (SLF): Not recommended. Provide appropriate food substitute.

Puree (PUR): Omit celery, onions, and red peppers. Add mayonnaise to salad; blenderize to obtain desired consistency.

Nutrient Analysis per Serving:

Regular	KCAL	PRO gm	CHO gm	FAT gm	Chol mg	SFA gm	PFA gm	VITA iu	VITC mg	THI mg	RIB mg	NIA mg	CA mg	NA mg	K+ mg	FE mg
	251	9.9	31.9	10.1	5.2	1.0	6.2	105	11.6	0.25	0.11	0.8	61.6	73.6	502	3.3

Sodium Restricted	NA mg	Diabetic	Kcal	Milk exg	Veg exg	Fruit exg	Bread exg	Meat exg	Fat exg	Low Fat & Low Chol	FAT gm	Chol mg	SFA gm	PFA gm
	25.8		203	0.0	0.27	0.0	2.1	0.0	0.9		4.6	0.0	0.3	1.3

Portion: 3 ounces cold cuts, lettuce leaf, 2 slices tomato, 1 green pepper ring, 1 black olive, and 1/2 cup side salad

INGREDIENTS	50 portions		6 portions	
	weights	measures	weights	measures
Roast beef, cooked	3 1/8 lb	2 1/3 qt	6 oz	1 cup
Ham, cooked	3 1/8 lb	2 1/3 qt	6 oz	1 cup
Turkey, cooked	3 1/8 lb	2 1/3 qt	6 oz	1 cup
Lettuce leaves	2 lb EP (3 lb AP)	50 leaves	4 oz EP (6 oz AP)	6 leaves
Tomatoes, sliced	7 lb EP (7 3/4 lb AP)	100 slices	13 1/2 oz EP (4 3/4 oz AP)	12 slices
Green pepper rings	1 1/4 lb EP (1 3/4 lb AP)	50 rings	2 1/2 oz EP (3 1/2 oz AP)	6 rings
Black olives	6 oz	50 each	3/4 oz	6 each
Side salad (see recipe list for menu ideas)	varies	6 1/4 qt	varies	3 cups

Method

1. Cut meats in thin slices.
2. Place lettuce leaf on each plate.
3. Roll meats. Place 1 oz of each meat on plate.
4. Arrange on each plate:
   a. 2 slices tomato.
   b. 1 green pepper ring.
   c. 1 black olive.
   d. 1/2 cup side salad.

Directions for Diet Preparations

Sodium Restricted (SR): Omit ham. Use 2 oz turkey and 1 oz roast beef. Omit black olive. Use low sodium mustard, low sodium catsup, and low sodium mayonnaise. Use low sodium side salad.

Low Fat/Low Cholesterol (LF): 2 oz meat, 1/2 cup low fat side salad. Omit ham. Use 2 oz lean meat. Omit black olives. Use LF side salad. Use reduced-calorie low cholesterol mayonnaise if able to calculate into daily food plan.

Diabetic (DB): 3 oz meat; 1/2 cup side salad. Use lean meat. Use low fat and/or diabetic side salad. Use reduced-calorie mayonnaise if able to calculate into daily food plan.

Mechanical Soft (SFT), **Soft/Low Fiber** (SLF), and **Puree** (PUR): Not recommended, use appropriate food alternatives.

Nutrient Analysis per Serving:

Regular	KCAL	PRO gm	CHO gm	FAT gm	Chol mg	SFA gm	PFA gm	VITA iu	VITC mg	THI mg	RIB mg	NIA mg	CA mg	NA mg	K+ mg	FE mg
	159	23.3	2.7	5.6	55.8	1.9	0.7	413	38.0	0.37	0.21	4.7	24.3	405	401	2.3

Sodium Restricted	NA mg	Diabetic	Kcal	Milk exg	Veg exg	Fruit exg	Bread exg	Meat exg	Fat exg	Low Fat & Low Chol	FAT gm	Chol mg	SFA gm	PFA gm
	64.9		159	0.0	0.5	0.0	0.0	3.0-L	0.0		3.6	47.3	1.4	0.5

Portion: 1/2 cup; 4 ounces (3 ounces edible protein)

INGREDIENTS	50 portions		6 portions	
	weights	measures	weights	measures
Eggs, hard-cooked, chopped	9 1/3 lb	1 1/2 gal (83 large)	1 1/4 lb	3 cups (10 large)
Celery, diced	2 lb	2 qt	4 oz	1 cup
Onions, diced	10 2/3 oz EP	2 cup	1 1/3 oz EP	1/4 cup
Red peppers, chopped	1 lb EP (1 1/4 lb AP)	3 cup	2 oz EP (2 1/2 oz AP)	1/3 cup
Mayonnaise	2 lb	1 qt	4 oz	1/2 cup

Method

1. Prepare close to serving time.
2. Combine all ingredients. Mix lightly.
3. Serve with No. 8 dipper.

Directions for Diet Preparations

Sodium Restricted (SR): Use low sodium mayonnaise.
Low Fat/Low Cholesterol (LF): Not recommended.
Diabetic (DB): 1/2 cup. Use reduced-calorie mayonnaise in half the amount specified for regular mayonnaise.
Mechanical Soft (SFT) and **Soft/Low Fiber** (SLF): Omit celery, onions, and red peppers.
Puree (PUR): Omit celery, onions, and red peppers. Add mayonnaise to egg salad; blenderize to obtain desired consistency.

Nutrient Analysis per Serving:

Regular	KCAL	PRO gm	CHO gm	FAT gm	Chol mg	SFA gm	PFA gm	VITA iu	VITC mg	THI mg	RIB mg	NIA mg	CA mg	NA mg	K+ mg	FE mg
	304	13.5	3.2	26.2	600	5.1	11.3	668	9.5	0.09	0.31	0.16	72.6	267	223	2.5

Sodium Restricted	NA mg	Diabetic	Kcal	Milk exg	Veg exg	Fruit exg	Bread exg	Meat exg	Fat exg	Low Fat & Low Chol		Not Recommended
	172		190	0.0	0.25	0.0	0.0	3.0-M	0.0			

Fruit Festival

Portion: 1/2 cup cottage cheese, 1/2 cup gelatin, 2/3 cup fruit

INGREDIENTS	48 portions		6 portions	
	weights	**measures**	**weights**	**measures**
Lettuce leaves	4 lb EP (6 1/8 lb AP)	96 leaves	8 oz EP (12 1/4 oz AP)	12 leaves
Cottage cheese, low fat	12 lb	1 1/2 gal	1 1/2 lb	3 cups
Strawberry gelatin, prepared, cut into cubes		1 1/2 gal		3 cups
Peach slices, drained	6 lb	3 qt	12 oz	1 1/2 cups
Banana, slices, cut diagonally	4 1/2 lb	3 1/2 qt	9 oz	1 3/4 cups
Lemon juice	2 oz	1/4 cup	1/4 oz	1/2 Tbsp
Pineapple chunks, drained	6 lb	3 qt	12 oz	1 1/2 cups

Method

1. For each salad, line plate with lettuce leaves.
2. Arrange the following on each plate:
   a. 1/2 cup cottage cheese.
   b. 1/2 cup gelatin cubes.
   c. 1/4 cup sliced peaches.
   d. 3 banana slices (1 1/2 oz). Sprinkle with lemon juice.
   e. 1/4 cup pineapple chunks.

Directions for Diet Preparations

Sodium Restricted (SR): Use low sodium cottage cheese and low sodium gelatin.

Low Fat/Low Cholesterol (LF): 1/2 cup cottage cheese, 1/2 cup gelatin cubes, 2/3 cup fruit. Prepare as directed.

Diabetic (DB): 1/2 cup cottage cheese, 1/2 cup unsweetened gelatin cubes, 2/3 cup unsweetened fruit. Use unsweetened gelatin and unsweetened or fresh fruit.

Mechanical Soft (SFT) and **Soft/Low Fiber** (SLF): Omit lettuce leaves. Use canned peaches and canned pineapple.

Puree (PUR): 1/2 cup cottage cheese, 1/2 cup gelatin, puree peaches and pineapple.

Nutrient Analysis per Serving:

Regular	KCAL	PRO gm	CHO gm	FAT gm	Chol mg	SFA gm	PFA gm	VITA iu	VITC mg	THI mg	RIB mg	NIA mg	CA mg	NA mg	K+ mg	FE mg
	246	17.1	43.7	1.5	4.9	0.8	0.1	509	12.9	0.11	0.28	1.0	85.5	524	518	0.8

Sodium Restricted	NA mg	**Diabetic**	Kcal	Milk exg	Veg exg	Fruit exg	Bread exg	Meat exg	Fat exg	**Low Fat & Low Chol**	FAT gm	Chol mg	SFA gm	PFA gm
	178		184	0.0	0.0	1.25	0.0	2.0-L	0.0		1.5	4.9	0.8	0.1

Portion: 3 ounces fish, lettuce leaf, 2 slices tomato, 1 green pepper ring, 1 black olive, 2 slices onion, and 1/2 cup side salad

Ingredients	50 portions		6 portions	
	weights	measures	weights	measures
Lettuce leaves	4 lb EP (6 1/8 lb AP)	100 leaves	8 oz EP (12 1/4 oz AP)	12 leaves
Gefilte fish, prepared	9 1/3 lb		1 1/8 lb	
Tomatoes, sliced	7 lb EP (7 3/4 lb AP)	100 slices	14 oz EP (15 1/2 oz AP)	12 slices
Green pepper rings	1 1/4 lb EP (1 3/4 lb AP)	50 rings	2 1/2 oz EP (3 1/2 oz AP)	6 rings
Black olives	6 oz	50 olives	3/4 oz	6 olives
Onion slices	1 lb EP (1 1/4 lb AP)	100 slices (2 cup)	2 oz EP (2 1/2 oz AP)	12 slices (1/4 cup)
Side salad (see recipe list for menu ideas)	varies	6 1/4 qt	varies	3 cups
Horseradish, prepared	10 oz	1 1/4 cups	1 oz	2 Tbsp

Method

1. For each salad, line plate with lettuce leaves.
2. Place 3 oz gefilte fish on each plate.
3. Arrange on each plate:
   a. 2 slices tomato.
   b. 1 green pepper ring.
   c. 1 black olive.
   d. 2 slices onion.
   e. 1/2 cup side salad.
4. Serve with 1 tsp horseradish.

Directions for Diet Preparations

Sodium Restricted (SR): Not recommended.

Low Fat/Low Cholesterol (LF): 3 oz gefilte fish. Use low fat side salad. Omit horseradish.

Diabetic (DB): 3 oz gefilte fish. Use low fat and/or diabetic side salad.

Mechanical Soft (SFT): Omit raw vegetables and side salad, substitute with allowed vegetables.

Soft/Low Fiber (SLF): Omit raw vegetables, side salad, and horseradish, substitute with allowed vegetables.

Puree (PUR): Omit raw vegetables and salad. Add liquid to fish; blenderize to obtain desired consistency.

Nutrient Analysis per Serving (does not include side salad):

Regular	KCAL	PRO gm	CHO gm	FAT gm	Chol mg	SFA gm	PFA gm	VITA iu	VITC mg	THI mg	RIB mg	NIA mg	CA mg	NA mg	K+ mg	FE mg
	123	21.0	5.4	1.7	28.0	0.3	0.4	572	32.9	0.08	0.11	2.3	38.3	916	548	1.1

Sodium Restricted	Diabetic	Kcal	Milk exg	Veg exg	Fruit exg	Bread exg	Meat exg	Fat exg		Low Fat & Low Chol	FAT gm	Chol mg	SFA gm	PFA gm
Not Recommended		123	0.0	1.0	0.0	0.0	3.0-L	0.0			1.0	28.0	0.2	0.3

Ham Salad

Portion: 1/2 cup, 4 ounces (3 ounces edible protein)

INGREDIENTS	50 portions		6 portions	
	weights	measures	weights	measures
Ham, cooked, diced	9 1/2 lb	1 3/4 gal	1 1/4 lb	3 1/2 cups
Celery, diced	2 lb	2 qt	4 oz	1 cup
Onions, diced	12 oz	2 cups	1 1/2 oz	1/4 cup
Red peppers, chopped	1 lb	3 cups	2 oz	1/3 cup
Mayonnaise	2 lb	1 qt	4 oz	1/2 cup

Method

1. Prepare close to serving time.
2. Combine all ingredients. Mix lightly.
3. Serve with No. 8 dipper.

Directions for Diet Preparations

Sodium Restricted (SR): Not recommended. Use appropriate food alternative.

Low Fat/Low Cholesterol (LF): 1/2 cup and **Diabetic** (DB): 1/2 cup. Use reduced-calorie low cholesterol mayonnaise in half the amount specified for regular mayonnaise. May use ham if able to calculate into daily food plan.

Mechanical Soft (SFT): Omit celery, onions, and red peppers.

Soft/Low Fiber (SLF): Not recommended. Use appropriate food alternative.

Puree (PUR): Omit celery, onions, and red peppers. Add mayonnaise to ham salad; blenderize to obtain desired consistency.

Nutrient Analysis per Serving:

Regular	KCAL	PRO gm	CHO gm	FAT gm	Chol mg	SFA gm	PFA gm	VITA iu	VITC mg	THI mg	RIB mg	NIA mg	CA mg	NA mg	K+ mg	FE mg
	250	18.4	2.4	18.3	36.0	2.9	10.2	106	32.9	0.89	0.21	4.2	17.2	1084	379	1.0

Sodium Restricted	Diabetic	Kcal	Milk exg	Veg exg	Fruit exg	Bread exg	Meat exg	Fat exg		Low Fat & Low Chol	FAT gm	Chol mg	SFA gm	PFA gm
Not Recommended		154	0.0	0.25	0.0	0.0	3.0-L	0.0			7.4	25.5	1.3	0.4

Portion: 3 ounces herring, lettuce leaf, 2 slices tomato, 1 green pepper ring, 2 slices onion, and 1/2 cup side salad

INGREDIENTS	50 portions		6 portions	
	weights	measures	weights	measures
Lettuce leaves	4 lb EP (6 1/8 lb AP)	100 leaves	8 oz EP (12 1/4 oz AP)	12 leaves
Herring, wine or creamed sauce	9 1/3 lb		1 1/8 lb	
Tomatoes, sliced	7 lb EP (7 3/4 lb AP)	100 slices	14 oz EP (15 1/2 oz AP)	12 slices
Green pepper rings	1 1/4 lb EP (1 3/4 lb AP)	50 rings	2 1/2 oz EP (3 1/2 oz AP)	6 rings
Onion slices	1 lb EP (1 1/4 lb AP)	100 slices (2 cups)	2 oz EP (2 1/2 oz AP)	12 slices (1/4 cup)
Side salad (see recipe list for menu ideas)	varies	6 1/4 qt	varies	3 cups

Method

1. For each salad, line plate with lettuce leaves.
2. Place 3 oz herring on each plate.
3. Arrange on each plate:
   a. 2 slices tomato.
   b. 1 green pepper ring.
   c. 2 slices onion.
   d. 1/2 cup side salad.

Directions for Diet Preparations

Sodium Restricted (SR): Use sodium restricted herring and sodium restricted side salad.

Low Fat/Low Cholesterol (LF): 2 oz herring, 1/2 cup low fat/low cholesterol side salad. Do not use cream sauce.

Diabetic (DB): 3 oz herring, 1/2 cup low fat/low cholesterol and/or diabetic side salad. Do not use cream sauce.

Mechanical Soft (SFT): Omit raw vegetables. Chop herring.

Soft/Low Fiber (SLF): Not recommended.

Puree (PUR): Omit raw vegetables. Add liquid (i.e. cream sauce) to herring; blenderize to obtain desired consistency.

Nutrient Analysis per Serving (does not include side salad):

Regular	KCAL	PRO gm	CHO gm	FAT gm	Chol mg	SFA gm	PFA gm	VITA iu	VITC mg	THI mg	RIB mg	NIA mg	CA mg	NA mg	K+ mg	FE mg
	246	13.0	13.0	15.5	11.0	2.0	1.5	1140	32.9	0.09	0.14	3.1	81.5	745	231	1.6

Sodium Restricted	NA mg	Diabetic	Kcal	Milk exg	Veg exg	Fruit exg	Bread exg	Meat exg	Fat exg	Low Fat & Low Chol	FAT gm	Chol mg	SFA gm	PFA gm
	68		246	0.0	2.0	0.0	0.0	3.0-L	0.75		10.4	7.3	1.3	1.1

Portion: 1/2 cup, 3 1/4 ounces (3 ounces edible protein)

INGREDIENTS	50 portions		6 portions	
	weights	**measures**	**weights**	**measures**
Liver, beef or calf	11 1/2 lb		1 1/2 lb	
Eggs, hard-cooked, chopped	1 1/2 lb	3 cups (12 large)	4 oz	1/2 cup (2 large)
Onions, finely diced	1 lb	2 cups	2 oz	1/4 cup
Margarine, low sodium melted	8 oz	1 cup	1 oz	2 Tbsp

Method

1. Slice liver one-inch thick.
2. Broil liver 5 to 10 minutes or till light brown on both sides. Remove veins and skin.
3. Combine liver and eggs. Put through a food grinder to form a smooth paste.
4. Sauté onions in margarine until browned. Add onions and margarine to liver paste. Mix until smooth.
5. Serve with No. 8 dipper.

Directions for Diet Preparations

Sodium Restricted (SR): Prepare as directed.
Low Fat/Low Cholesterol (LF): Not recommended.
Diabetic (DB): 1/2 cup. Omit margarine, use reduced-calorie margarine in half the amount specified for regular margarine.
Mechanical Soft (SFT) and **Soft/Low Fiber** (SLF): Omit onions. Consider individual tolerance.
Puree (PUR): Omit onions. Blenderize to obtain desired consistency.

Nutrient Analysis per Serving:

Regular	KCAL	PRO gm	CHO gm	FAT gm	Chol mg	SFA gm	PFA gm	VITA iu	VITC mg	THI mg	RIB mg	NIA mg	CA mg	NA mg	K+ mg	FE mg
	187	22.2	1.4	9.7	602	2.5	2.1	14144	13.9	0.14	1.5	3.7	21.4	61	146	7.5

Sodium Restricted	NA mg	Diabetic	Kcal	Milk exg	Veg exg	Fruit exg	Bread exg	Meat exg	Fat exg	Low Fat & Low Chol	Not Recommended
	61		163	0.0	0.1	0.0	0.0	3.0-L	0.0		

Portion: 3 ounces fish, lettuce leaf, 2 slices tomato, 1 green pepper ring, 1 black olive, 2 slices onion, and 1/2 cup side salad

INGREDIENTS	50 portions		6 portions	
	weights	measures	weights	measures
Lettuce leaves	4 lb EP (6 1/8 lb AP)	100 leaves	8 oz EP (12 1/4 oz AP)	12 leaves
Salmon, canned, drained	9 1/3 lb	1 1/4 gal	1 1/8 lb	2 1/2 cups
Tomatoes, sliced	7 lb EP (7 3/4 lb AP)	100 slices	14 oz EP (15 1/2 oz AP)	12 slices
Green pepper rings	1 1/4 lb EP (1 3/4 lb AP)	50 rings	2 1/2 oz EP (3 1/2 oz AP)	6 rings
Black olives	6 oz	50 olives	3/4 oz	6 olives
Onion slices	1 lb EP (1 1/4 lb AP)	100 slices (2 cup)	2 oz EP (2 1/2 oz AP)	12 slices (1/4 cup)
Side salad (see recipe list for menu ideas)	varies	6 1/4 qt	varies	3 cups
Oil and vinegar dressing	2 lb	1 qt	4 oz	1/2 cup

Method

1. For each salad, line plate with lettuce leaves.
2. Place 3 oz salmon on each plate.
3. Arrange on each plate:
   a. 2 slices tomato.
   b. 1 green pepper ring.
   c. 1 black olive.
   d. 2 slices onion.
   e. 1/2 cup side salad.
4. Serve with one oz oil and vinegar dressing.

Directions for Diet Preparations

Sodium Restricted (SR): Use low sodium salmon. Omit black olives. Use low sodium side salad.

Low Fat/Low Cholesterol (LF): 2 oz salmon. Use low fat/low cholesterol side salad. Use 2 tsp low-calorie salad dressing.

Diabetic (DB): 3 oz salmon. Use low fat and/or diabetic side salad. Use 2 tsp low-calorie salad dressing.

Mechanical Soft (SFT) and **Soft/Low Fiber** (SLF): May use salmon. All other foods listed in recipe should be omitted, substitute with appropriate food alternatives.

Puree (PUR): May use salmon. Add mayonnaise to salmon; blenderize to obtain desired consistency. All other foods listed in recipe should be omitted, substitute with appropriate food alternatives.

Nutrient Analysis per Serving (does not include side salad):

Regular	KCAL	PRO gm	CHO gm	FAT gm	Chol mg	SFA gm	PFA gm	VITA iu	VITC mg	THI mg	RIB mg	NIA mg	CA mg	NA mg	K+ mg	FE mg
123	21.0	5.4	1.7	28.0	0.3	0.4	572	32.9	0.08	0.11	2.3	38.3	916	548	1.1	

Sodium Restricted	NA mg	Diabetic	Kcal	Milk exg	Veg exg	Fruit exg	Bread exg	Meat exg	Fat exg	Low Fat & Low Chol	FAT gm	Chol mg	SFA gm	PFA gm
	56		189	0.0	1.0	0.0	0.0	3.0-L	0.0		8.2	31.2	1.4	3.9

Salmon Salad

Portion: 1/2 cup, 4 ounces (3 ounces edible protein)

INGREDIENTS	50 portions		6 portions	
	weights	**measures**	**weights**	**measures**
Salmon, canned, drained	9 1/3 lb	1 1/4 gal	1 1/8 lb	2 1/2 cups
Celery, diced	2 lb	2 qt	4 oz	1 cup
Onions, diced	12 oz	2 cups	1 1/2 oz	1/4 cup
Red peppers, chopped	1 lb	3 cups	2 oz	1/3 cup
Mayonnaise	2 lb	1 qt	4 oz	1/2 cup

Method

1. Prepare close to serving time.
2. Combine all ingredients. Mix lightly. Chill.
3. Serve with No. 8 dipper.

Directions for Diet Preparations

Sodium Restricted (SR): Use low sodium salmon. Use low sodium mayonnaise.

Low Fat/Low Cholesterol (LF): 1/2 cup and **Diabetic** (DB): 1/2 cup. Use reduced-calorie low cholesterol mayonnaise in half the amount specified for regular mayonnaise.

Mechanical Soft (SFT) and **Soft/Low Fiber** (SLF): Omit celery, onions, and red peppers.

Puree (PUR): Omit celery, onions, and red peppers. Add mayonnaise to salmon salad; blenderize to obtain desired consistency.

Nutrient Analysis per Serving:

Regular	KCAL	PRO gm	CHO gm	FAT gm	Chol mg	SFA gm	PFA gm	VITA iu	VITC mg	THI mg	RIB mg	NIA mg	CA mg	NA mg	K+ mg	FE mg
	313	17.0	1.9	26.1	39.3	5.1	9.8	302	9.5	0.04	0.12	6.2	143	428	394	1.0

Sodium Restricted	NA mg	Diabetic	Kcal	Milk exg	Veg exg	Fruit exg	Bread exg	Meat exg	Fat exg	Low Fat & Low Chol	FAT gm	Chol mg	SFA gm	PFA gm
	63		217	0.0	0.25	0.0	0.0	3.0-L	1.0		15.1	28.8	3.6	0.03

Portion: 1 bell pepper, 1/2 cup salmon salad, 1/2 cup pasta salad, 4 ounces perfection salad, lettuce leaf, 2 black olives, 1 carrot curl, and 1/2 cup side salad

INGREDIENTS	50 portions		6 portions	
	weights	measures	weights	measures
Salmon, canned, drained	9 1/3 lb	1 1/4 gal	1 1/8 lb	2 1/2 cups
Celery, diced	2 lb	2 qt	4 oz	1 cup
Onions, diced	12 oz	2 cups	1 1/2 oz	1/4 cup
Green peppers, chopped	1 lb	3 cups	2 oz	1/3 cup
Mayonnaise	2 lb	1 qt	4 oz	1/2 cup
Red peppers	12 lb AP	50 medium	1 1/2 lb	6 medium
Lettuce leaves	4 lb EP (6 1/8 lb AP)	100 leaves	8 oz EP (12 1/4 oz AP)	12 leaves
Perfection salad		6 1/4 qt		3 cups
Pasta salad		6 1/4 qt		3 cups
Carrot curls		50 curls		6 curls
Black olives	12 oz	100 olives	1 1/2 oz	12 olives

Method

1. Prepare close to serving time.
2. Combine salmon, celery, onions, green peppers, and mayonnaise. Mix lightly. Chill.
3. Wash red peppers and remove stem end. Remove seeds and tough white portion.
4. For each serving, line plate with lettuce leaves.
5. Arrange on each plate:
   a. one red pepper.
   b. portion salmon salad with a No. 8 dipper. Fill red bell pepper with salmon salad.
   c. 4 oz perfection salad.
   d. 1/2 cup pasta salad.
   e. 1 carrot curl.
   f. 2 black olives.

Directions for Diet Preparations

Sodium Restricted (SR): Use low sodium salmon, low sodium mayonnaise, low sodium perfection salad, low sodium pasta salad. Omit olives.

Low Fat/Low Cholesterol (LF): 1/2 cup LF salmon salad stuffed pepper, 1/2 cup LF pasta salad, 4 oz LF perfection salad. Use water-packed salmon. Use reduced-calorie low cholesterol mayonnaise in half the amount specified for regular mayonnaise. Omit olives.

Diabetic (DB): 1/2 cup LF salmon salad stuffed pepper, 1/2 cup LF pasta salad, 4 oz DB perfection salad. Use water-packed salmon. Use reduced-calorie mayonnaise in half the amount specified for regular mayonnaise. Serve one olive.

Mechanical Soft (SFT) and **Soft/Low Fiber** (SLF): Omit celery, green and red pepper, lettuce, olives, and carrots. Serve 1/2 cup salmon salad, 1/2 cup SFT pasta salad, and 4 oz SFT perfection salad. Consider individual tolerance.

Puree (PUR): Omit celery, green and red pepper, lettuce, olives, and carrots. Blenderize salmon salad. Serve 1/2 cup puree salmon salad, 1/2 cup PUR pasta salad, and 4 oz PUR perfection salad.

Nutrient Analysis per Serving:

Regular	KCAL	PRO gm	CHO gm	FAT gm	Chol mg	SFA gm	PFA gm	VITA iu	VITC mg	THI mg	RIB mg	NIA mg	CA mg	NA mg	K+ mg	FE mg
	543	23.2	58.6	24.9	109.7	5.4	6.5	5518	47.8	0.4	0.4	8.2	166	676	741	3.2

Sodium Restricted	NA mg	Diabetic	Kcal	Milk exg	Veg exg	Fruit exg	Bread exg	Meat exg	Fat exg	Low Fat & Low Chol	FAT gm	Chol mg	SFA gm	PFA gm
	115		338	0.0	2.0	0.0	1.0	3.0-L	1.0		16.3	24.6	3.1	0.1

118 Seafood Salad

Portion: 1/2 cup, 4 ounces (3 ounces edible protein)

INGREDIENTS	50 portions		6 portions	
	weights	measures	weights	measures
Shrimp, cooked, shelled, deveined	5 lb	1 gal	10 oz	2 cups
Crabmeat, flaked	4 1/3 lb	3 3/4 qt	8 oz	1 3/4 cups
Celery, diced	2 lb	2 qt	4 oz	1 cup
Onions, diced	12 oz	2 cups	1 1/2 oz	1/4 cup
Mayonnaise	2 lb	1 qt	4 oz	1/2 cup

Method

1. Prepare close to serving time.
2. Combine all ingredients. Mix lightly. Chill.
3. Serve with No. 8 dipper.

Directions for Diet Preparations

Sodium Restricted (SR): Use low sodium fish. Use low sodium mayonnaise.

Low Fat/Low Cholesterol (LF): 1/2 cup and **Diabetic** (DB): 1/2 cup. Use reduced-calorie low cholesterol mayonnaise in half the amount specified for regular mayonnaise. Low cholesterol diets should choose seafood that is low in cholesterol.

Mechanical Soft (SFT) and **Soft/Low Fiber** (SLF): Omit celery and onions.

Puree (PUR): Omit celery and onions. Add mayonnaise to seafood salad; blenderize to obtain desired consistency.

Nutrient Analysis per Serving:

Regular	KCAL	PRO gm	CHO gm	FAT gm	Chol mg	SFA gm	PFA gm	VITA iu	VITC mg	THI mg	RIB mg	NIA mg	CA mg	NA mg	K+ mg	FE mg
	219	14.6	5.9	15.2	106	1.7	10.2	231	10.5	0.04	0.03	1.3	34.9	547	200	1.8

Sodium Restricted	NA mg	Diabetic	Kcal	Milk exg	Veg exg	Fruit exg	Bread exg	Meat exg	Fat exg	Low Fat & Low Chol	FAT gm	Chol mg	SFA gm	PFA gm
	139		123	0.0	0.0	0.0	0.0	3.0-L	0.0		4.2	96.1	0.2	0.4

Portion: 3/4 cup, 6 ounces (2 ounces edible protein)

INGREDIENTS	50 portions		6 portions	
	weights	**measures**	**weights**	**measures**
Tofu, mashed	16 lb	2 gal	2 lb	1 qt
Celery, finely chopped	10 oz EP	2 1/2 cups	(1 1/4 oz EP)	1/3 cup
	(12 oz AP)	(8 stalks)	(1 1/2 oz AP)	(1 stalk)
Carrots, peeled, grated	2 lb EP	1 1/2 qt	4 oz EP	3/4 cup
	(2 3/4 lb AP)	(8 medium)	(5 3/4 oz AP)	(1 medium)
Red peppers, finely chopped	1 lb EP	3 cups	2 oz EP	1/3 cup
	(1 1/4 lb AP)	(5 large)	(2 1/2 oz AP)	(1 small)
Garlic powder		1/4 cup		1/2 Tbsp
Dill weed		1/4 cup		1/2 Tbsp
Pepper, black		to taste		to taste
Mustard, dijon-style		1 cup	1 oz	2 Tbsp
Mayonnaise	1 lb	2 cups	2 oz	1/4 cup

Method

1. Prepare close to serving time.
2. Combine all ingredients. Mix lightly. Chill.
3. Serve with No. 6 dipper.
4. Serve as a tomato stuffing or in a pita bread with lettuce and tomato.

Directions for Diet Preparations

Sodium Restricted (SR): Use low sodium mayonnaise and low sodium mustard.

Low Fat/Low Cholesterol (LF): 3/4 cup and **Diabetic** (DB): 3/4 cup. Use reduced-calorie low cholesterol mayonnaise in half the amount specified for regular mayonnaise. Low fat diets should consider individual tolerance to garlic.

Mechanical Soft (SFT) and **Soft/Low Fiber** (SLF): Omit celery, red peppers, mustard, garlic, and black pepper.

Puree (PUR): Prepare as directed. Add additional liquid (i.e. mayonnaise); blenderize to obtain desired consistency.

Nutrient Analysis per Serving:

Regular	KCAL	PRO gm	CHO gm	FAT gm	Chol mg	SFA gm	PFA gm	VITA iu	VITC mg	THI mg	RIB mg	NIA mg	CA mg	NA mg	K+ mg	FE mg
	201	13.7	6.0	15.1	5.2	1.9	9.2	3964	9.5	0.15	0.09	0.5	187	138	292	9.1

Sodium Restricted	NA mg	Diabetic	Kcal	Milk exg	Veg exg	Fruit exg	Bread exg	Meat exg	Fat exg	Low Fat & Low Chol	FAT gm	Chol mg	SFA gm	PFA gm
	26		153	0.0	0.5	0.0	0.1	2.0-L	0.5		9.6	0.0	1.1	4.3

Portion: 1/2 cup, 4 ounces (3 ounces edible protein)

INGREDIENTS	50 portions		6 portions	
	weights	measures	weights	measures
Tuna, flaked, water packed, drained	9 1/3 lb	1 1/3 gal	1 1/8 lb	2 1/2 cups
Celery, diced	2 lb	2 qt	4 oz	1 cup
Onions, diced	12 oz	2 cups	1 1/2 oz	1/4 cup
Red peppers, chopped	1 lb EP	3 cups	2 oz EP	1/3 cup
	(1 1/4 lb AP)	(5 large)	(2 1/2 oz AP)	(1 small)
Mayonnaise	2 lb	1 qt	4 oz	1/2 cup

Method

1. Prepare close to serving time.
2. Combine all ingredients. Mix lightly. Chill.
3. Serve with No. 8 dipper.

Directions for Diet Preparations

Sodium Restricted (SR): Use low sodium tuna and low sodium mayonnaise.

Low Fat/Low Cholesterol (LF): 1/2 cup and **Diabetic** (DB): 1/2 cup. Use reduced-calorie low cholesterol mayonnaise in half the amount specified for regular mayonnaise.

Mechanical Soft (SFT) and **Soft/Low Fiber** (SLF): Omit celery, onions, and red peppers.

Puree (PUR): Omit celery, onions, and red peppers. Add mayonnaise to tuna salad; blenderize to obtain desired consistency.

Nutrient Analysis per Serving:

Regular	KCAL	PRO gm	CHO gm	FAT gm	Chol mg	SFA gm	PFA gm	VITA iu	VITC mg	THI mg	RIB mg	NIA mg	CA mg	NA mg	K+ mg	FE mg
	246	25.5	1.9	14.6	25.8	1.6	9.9	173	9.5	0.04	0.11	10.6	22.4	421	350	3.0

Sodium Restricted	NA mg	Diabetic	Kcal	Milk exg	Veg exg	Fruit exg	Bread exg	Meat exg	Fat exg	Low Fat & Low Chol	FAT gm	Chol mg	SFA gm	PFA gm
	56		150	0.0	0.0	0.0	0.0	3.0-L	0.0		3.6	15.3	0.1	0.1

Curry Tuna Salad

Portion: 1/2 cup, 4 ounces (3 ounces edible protein)

INGREDIENTS	50 portions		6 portions	
	weights	measures	weights	measures
Tuna, flaked, water packed, drained	9 1/3 lb	1 1/3 gal	1 1/8 lb	2 1/2 cups
Mayonnaise	2 lb	1 qt	4 oz	1/2 cup
Curry powder		1 Tbsp		3/4 tsp
Celery, diced	2 lb	2 qt	4 oz	1 cup
Onions, diced	12 oz	2 cups	1 1/2 oz	1/4 cup

Method

1. Prepare close to serving time.
2. Add curry powder to mayonnaise. Mix well.
3. Combine all ingredients. Mix lightly. Chill.
4. Serve with No. 8 dipper.

Directions for Diet Preparations

Sodium Restricted (SR): Use low sodium tuna and low sodium mayonnaise.

Low Fat/Low Cholesterol (LF): 1/2 cup and **Diabetic** (DB): 1/2 cup. Use reduced-calorie low cholesterol mayonnaise in half the amount specified for regular mayonnaise.

Mechanical Soft (SFT): Omit celery and onions.

Soft/Low Fiber (SLF): Omit celery, onions, and curry powder.

Puree (PUR): Omit celery and onions. Add mayonnaise to tuna salad; blenderize to obtain desired consistency.

Nutrient Analysis per Serving:

Regular	KCAL	PRO gm	CHO gm	FAT gm	Chol mg	SFA gm	PFA gm	VITA iu	VITC mg	THI mg	RIB mg	NIA mg	CA mg	NA mg	K+ mg	FE mg
	244	25.5	1.7	14.6	25.8	1.6	9.9	142	1.8	0.04	0.1	10.6	22.6	421	340	2.9

Sodium Restricted	NA mg	Diabetic	Kcal	Milk exg	Veg exg	Fruit exg	Bread exg	Meat exg	Fat exg	Low Fat & Low Chol	FAT gm	Chol mg	SFA gm	PFA gm
	56		149	0.0	0.0	0.0	0.0	3.0-L	0.0		3.7	15.3	0.15	0.1

Portion: 1/2 cup salad, lettuce leaf, 2 slices tomato, 1 green pepper ring, 2 slices onion, and 1/2 cup side salad

INGREDIENTS	50 portions		6 portions	
	weights	measures	weights	measures
Choose two entree salads:				
Chicken salad		3 1/8 qt		1 1/2 cups
Turkey salad		3 1/8 qt		1 1/2 cups
Egg salad		3 1/8 qt		1 1/2 cups
Ham salad		3 1/8 qt		1 1/2 cups
Tuna salad		3 1/8 qt		1 1/2 cups
Seafood salad		3 1/8 qt		1 1/2 cups
Lettuce leaves	4 lb EP (6 1/8 lb AP)	100 leaves	8 oz EP (12 1/4 oz AP)	12 leaves
Tomatoes, sliced	7 lb EP (7 3/4 lb AP)	100 slices	14 oz EP (15 1/2 oz AP)	12 slices
Green pepper rings	1 1/4 lb EP (1 3/4 lb AP)	50 rings	2 1/2 oz EP (3 1/2 oz AP)	6 rings
Onion slices	1 lb EP (1 1/4 lb AP)	100 slices 2 cups	2 oz EP (2 1/2 oz AP)	12 slices 1/4 cup
Side salad (see recipe list for menu ideas)	varies	6 1/4 qt	varies	3 cups

Method

1. Prepare two of the salad entree recipes as directed.
2. For each serving, line plate with lettuce leaves.
3. Arrange on each plate:
   a. 2 salad entrees. Portion each with No. 16 dipper.
   b. 2 slices tomato.
   c. 1 green pepper ring.
   d. 2 onion slices.
   e. 1/2 cup side salad.

Directions for Diet Preparations

Sodium Restricted (SR): Use low sodium salad entrees and low sodium side salad.

Low Fat/Low Cholesterol (LF): 1/2 cup low fat/low cholesterol salad entree, 1/2 cup low fat/low cholesterol side salad. Arrange platter as directed.

Diabetic (DB): 1/2 cup low fat/low cholesterol salad entree, 1/2 cup low fat/low cholesterol and/or diabetic side salad. Arrange platter as directed.

Mechanical Soft (SFT) and **Soft/Low Fiber** (SLF): Use SFT/SLF salad entrees. Omit raw vegetables.

Puree (PUR): Use PUR salad entrees. Omit raw vegetables.

Nutrient Analysis: See individual recipes for analysis

Portion: 1 medium tomato, 1/2 cup salad entree, lettuce leaf, green pepper ring, 2 slices onion, and 1/2 cup side salad

Ingredients	50 portions		6 portions	
	weights	measures	weights	measures
Tomatoes	16 1/2 lb AP	50 medium	2 lb AP	6 medium
Choose one entree salad:				
Chicken salad		6 1/4 qt		3 cups
Turkey salad		6 1/4 qt		3 cups
Egg salad		6 1/4 qt		3 cups
Ham salad		6 1/4 qt		3 cups
Tuna salad		6 1/4 qt		3 cups
Seafood salad		6 1/4 qt		3 cups
Lettuce leaves	4 lb EP (6 1/8 lb AP)	100 leaves	8 oz EP (12 1/4 oz AP)	12 leaves
Green pepper rings	1 1/4 lb EP (1 3/4 lb AP)	50 rings	2 1/2 oz EP (3 1/2 oz AP)	6 rings
Onion slices	1 lb EP (1 1/4 lb AP)	100 slices 2 cups	2 oz EP (2 1/2 oz AP)	12 slices 1/4 cup
Side salad (see recipe list for menu ideas)	varies	6 1/4 qt	varies	3 cups

Method

1. Turn tomato stem-end down. Cut into fourths to within 1/4 inch of bottom.
2. Choose one of the salad entrees. Prepare as directed.
3. Portion salad entree with No. 8 dipper. Fill tomato with salad.
4. For each serving, line plate with lettuce leaves.
5. Arrange on each plate:
   a. stuffed tomato.
   b. 1 green pepper ring.
   d. 2 onion slices.
   e. 1/2 cup side salad.

Directions for Diet Preparations

Sodium Restricted (SR): Use low sodium salad entrees and low sodium side salad. Omit olives.

Low Fat/Low Cholesterol (LF): 1/2 cup low fat/low cholesterol salad entree, 1/2 cup low fat/low cholesterol side salad. Arrange plate as directed.

Diabetic (DB): 1/2 cup low fat/low cholesterol salad entree, 1/2 cup low fat/low cholesterol and/or diabetic side salad. Arrange plate as directed.

Mechanical Soft (SFT) and **Soft/Low Fiber** (SLF): Omit tomato and raw vegetables. Use SFT/SLF salad entrees.

Puree (PUR): Omit tomato and raw vegetables. Use PUR salad entrees.

Nutrient Analysis: See individual recipes for analysis

Vegetables and Starchy Vegetables

J1 — Asparagus

Portion: 1/2 cup (3 ounces)

INGREDIENTS	50 portions		6 portions	
	weights	measures	weights	measures
Fresh asparagus	18–20 lb AP (9 1/2–10 1/2 lb EP)	2 gal	2 1/4–2 1/2 lb AP (1 1/4–1 1/3 lb EP)	1 qt
Cuts or	9 lb EP	1 1/2 gal	1 1/8 lb EP	3 cups
Spears	11 1/4 lb EP	1 1/2 gal	1 1/2 lb EP	3 cups
Water, boiling		1 gal		2 cups
or				
Frozen cuts, tips, and spears	12 1/2 lb	1 1/2 gal	1 2/3 lb	3 cups
Water, boiling		1 1/2 qt		3/4 cup
or				
Canned cuts, drain half liquid	12 1/2 lb	2 #10 cans (1 3/4 gal)	1 2/3 lb	3 1/2 cups

Method

Fresh
1. Cut off tough part of stems. Wash and clean remaining portions. Spears may be tied in bundles of 1–2 lbs each for boiling. For cuts, cut into 1-inch pieces.
2. Boil cuts 5–15 minutes. Boil spears 10–25 minutes or
3. Steam cuts 5–10 minutes and spears 7–10 minutes. Omit water. (5–6 lb pressure).

Frozen
1. Boil 5–10 minutes or
2. Steam 5–10 minutes. Omit water. (5–6 lb pressure).

Canned
1. Heat long enough to bring to serving temperature or
2. Steam about 1 minute (5–6 lb pressure) or
3. Heat in 350°F oven until serving temperature is reached.

Directions for Diet Preparations

Sodium Restricted (SR), **Low Fat/Low Cholesterol** (LF), 1/2 cup, **Diabetic** (DB): 1/2 cup, **Mechanical Soft** (SFT), **Soft/Low Fiber** (SLF): Prepare as directed.
Puree (PUR): Prepare as directed. Add liquid (i.e. sauce or gravy); blenderize to obtain desired consistency.

Nutrient Analysis per Serving:

Regular	KCAL	PRO gm	CHO gm	FAT gm	Chol mg	SFA gm	PFA gm	VITA iu	VITC mg	THI mg	RIB mg	NIA mg	CA mg	NA mg	K+ mg	FE mg
	22.8	2.3	4.0	0.2	0.0	0.06	0.1	757	24.7	0.09	0.11	0.96	21.9	3.6	283	0.6

Sodium Restricted	NA mg	Diabetic	Kcal	Milk exg	Veg exg	Fruit exg	Bread exg	Meat exg	Fat exg	Low Fat & Low Chol	FAT gm	Chol mg	SFA gm	PFA gm
	3.6		22.8	0.0	1.0	0.0	0.0	0.0	0.0		0.2	0.0	0.06	0.1

Seasoned Asparagus

Portion: 1/2 cup (3 ounces)

INGREDIENTS	50 portions[1]		6 portions[2]	
	weights	measures	weights	measures
Asparagus, fresh	18–20 lb AP (10 lb EP)	2 gal	2 1/4–2 1/2 lb AP (1 1/4 EP)	1 qt
Thyme		2 tsp		1/4 tsp
Parsley, chopped		1 Tbsp		1/4 tsp

Method

1. Cut off tough part of stems. Wash and clean thoroughly.
2. Spears may be tied in bundles of 1–2 lbs each for boiling. For cuts, cut into 1-inch pieces.
3. Boil or Steam
   a. Boil cuts 5–15 minutes. Boil spears 10–25 minutes. or
   b. Steam cuts 5–10 minutes and spears 7–10 minutes. Omit water (5–6 lb pressure).
4. Drain.
5. Sprinkle with seasonings. Toss lightly.

Directions for Diet Preparations

Sodium Restricted (SR), **Low Fat/Low Cholesterol (LF)**, 1/2 cup, **Diabetic (DB)**: 1/2 cup, **Mechanical Soft (SFT)**, **Soft/Low Fiber (SLF)**: Prepare as directed.
Puree (PUR): Prepare as directed. Add liquid (i.e. sauce or gravy); blenderize to obtain desired consistency.

Notes

[1] 50 portions: May use frozen (12 1/2 lb) or canned (2 No. 10 cans).
[2] 6 portions: May use frozen (1 2/3 lb) or canned (1 2/3 lb).

Nutrient Analysis per Serving:

Regular	KCAL	PRO gm	CHO gm	FAT gm	Chol mg	SFA gm	PFA gm	VITA iu	VITC mg	THI mg	RIB mg	NIA mg	CA mg	NA mg	K+ mg	FE mg
	26.5	2.8	5.6	0.4	0.0	0.1	0.1	1120	26.4	0.1	0.1	1.1	68.7	10.4	344	3.7

Sodium Restricted	NA mg	Diabetic	Kcal	Milk exg	Veg exg	Fruit exg	Bread exg	Meat exg	Fat exg	Low Fat & Low Chol	FAT gm	Chol mg	SFA gm	PFA gm
	10.4		26.5	0.0	1.0	0.0	0.0	0.0	0.0		0.4	0.0	0.1	0.1

Portion: 1/2 cup (3 ounces)

INGREDIENTS	50 portions		6 portions	
	weights	measures	weights	measures
Fresh beans, green or wax (Ready-to-cook weight)	12 lb AP	2 gal	1 1/2 lb AP	1 qt
Beans, green or wax	10 1/2 lb	1 3/4 gal	1 1/3 lb	3 1/2 cups
Water, boiling		2 1/2 qt		1 1/4 cups
or				
Frozen beans, green or wax	12 lb	2 1/4 gal	1 1/2 lb	1 1/8 qt
Water, boiling		1 qt		1/2 cup
or				
Canned beans, green or wax	12 1/2 lb	2 #10 cans (1 3/4 gal)	1 2/3 lb	3 1/2 cups

Method

Fresh
1. Wash beans. Trim ends and remove strings. Cut or break into one-inch pieces.
2. Boil beans 10 to 30 minutes or
3. Steam 15–25 minutes. Omit water (5–6 lb pressure).

Frozen
1. Boil 10 to 20 minutes or
2. Steam 10 to 15 minutes. Omit water. (5–6 lb pressure).

Canned
1. Drain off half the liquid from can.
2. Heat long enough to bring to serving temperature or
3. Steam about 1 minute (5–6 lb pressure) or
4. Heat in 350°F oven until serving temperature is reached.

Directions for Diet Preparations

Sodium Restricted (SR), **Low Fat/Low Cholesterol** (LF), 1/2 cup, **Diabetic** (DB): 1/2 cup, **Mechanical Soft** (SFT), **Soft/Low Fiber** (SLF): Prepare as directed.
Puree (PUR): Prepare as directed. Add liquid (i.e. sauce or gravy); blenderize to obtain desired consistency.

Nutrient Analysis per Serving:

Regular	KCAL	PRO gm	CHO gm	FAT gm	Chol mg	SFA gm	PFA gm	VITA iu	VITC mg	THI mg	RIB mg	NIA mg	CA mg	NA mg	K+ mg	FE mg
	22.1	1.1	4.9	0.1	0.0	0.04	0.09	422	6.1	0.04	0.06	0.38	29.1	1.9	189	0.8

Sodium Restricted	NA mg	Diabetic	Kcal	Milk exg	Veg exg	Fruit exg	Bread exg	Meat exg	Fat exg	Low Fat & Low Chol	FAT gm	Chol mg	SFA gm	PFA gm
	1.9		22.1	0.0	1.0	0.0	0.0	0.0	0.0		0.1	0.0	0.04	0.09

Green Beans and Mushrooms

Portion: 1/2 cup

INGREDIENTS	50 portions[1]		6 portions[2]	
	weights	measures	weights	measures
Green beans, fresh	12 lb AP (10 1/2 lb EP)	2 gal 1 3/4 gal	1 1/2 lb AP (1 1/3 lb EP)	1 qt (3 1/2 cups)
Mushrooms, sliced	2 lb	3 1/2 qt	4 oz	1 3/4 cups
Water, boiling[3]		2 1/2 qt		1 1/4 cups
Thyme		1 Tbsp		1/2 tsp
Oregano, ground		1 Tbsp		1/2 tsp

Method

1. Wash beans. Trim ends and remove strings. Cut or break into one-inch pieces.
2. Add mushrooms and seasonings to green beans. Mix.
3. Boil beans 15 to 20 minutes. Drain water.
4. Serve with a No. 8 scoop.

Notes

[1]50 portions: May use 12 lb frozen green beans. Boil 10 to 12 minutes.
6 portions: May use 1 1/2 lb frozen green beans. Boil 10 to 12 minutes.
[2]50 portions: May use 2 No. 10 cans. Heat long enough to bring to serving temperature.
6 portions: May use 1 2/3 lb canned green beans. Heat long enough to bring to serving temperature.
[3]May steam fresh green beans 20 to 30 minutes at 5 to 6 lb pressure. Omit water.

Directions for Diet Preparations

Sodium Restricted (SR), **Low Fat/Low Cholesterol** (LF), 1/2 cup, **Diabetic** (DB): 1/2 cup, **Mechanical Soft** (SFT), **Soft/Low Fiber** (SLF): Prepare as directed.
Puree (PUR): Prepare as directed. Add liquid (i.e. sauce or gravy); blenderize to obtain desired consistency.

Nutrient Analysis per Serving:

Regular	KCAL	PRO gm	CHO gm	FAT gm	Chol mg	SFA gm	PFA gm	VITA iu	VITC mg	THI mg	RIB mg	NIA mg	CA mg	NA mg	K+ mg	FE mg
	33.1	2.0	7.4	0.2	0.0	0.04	0.09	617	15	0.09	0.17	1.41	39	5.5	257	1.3

Sodium Restricted	NA mg	Diabetic	Kcal	Milk exg	Veg exg	Fruit exg	Bread exg	Meat exg	Fat exg	Low Fat & Low Chol	FAT gm	Chol mg	SFA gm	PFA gm
	5.5		33.1	0.0	1.0	0.0	0.0	0.0	0.0		0.2	0.0	0.04	0.09

J5 Ejotes con Limón (Green beans with lemon)

Portion: 1/2 cup

INGREDIENTS	50 portions[1]		6 portions[2]	
	weights	measures	weights	measures
Green beans, fresh[3]	12 lb AP (10 1/2 lb EP)	3 gal 1 3/4 gal	1 1/2 lb AP (1 1/3 lb EP)	1 qt (3 1/2 cups)
Margarine, low sodium, melted	4 oz	1/2 cup	1/2 oz	1 Tbsp
Parsley, chopped	2/3 oz	1/2 cup		1 Tbsp
Lemon juice	2 2/3 oz	1/3 cup	1/3 oz	2 tsp

Method

1. Wash beans. Trim ends and remove strings. Break into one-inch pieces.
2. Boil 15 to 20 minutes. Drain water.
3. Combine margarine, parsley, and lemon juice. Pour over green beans. Mix.
4. Serve with a No. 8 scoop.

Notes

[1]50 portions: May use 12 lb frozen green beans. Boil 10 to 12 minutes.
6 portions: May use 1 1/2 lb frozen green beans. Boil 10 to 12 minutes.
[2]50 portions: May use 2 No. 10 cans. Heat long enough to bring to serving temperature.
6 portions: May use 1 2/3 lb canned green beans. Heat long enough to bring to serving temperature.
[3]May steam fresh green beans 20 to 30 minutes at 5 to 6 lb pressure. Omit water.

Directions for Diet Preparations

Sodium Restricted (SR): Prepare as directed.
Low Fat/Low Cholesterol (LF) and **Diabetic** (DB): 1/2 cup. Omit margarine.
Mechanical Soft (SFT) and **Soft/Low Fiber** (SLF): Prepare as directed. 1/2 cup. Prepare as directed.
Puree (PUR): 1/2 cup. Prepare as directed. Blenderize. Add additional liquid (i.e. gravy or sauce) if necessary to obtain desired consistency.

Nutrient Analysis per Serving:

Regular	KCAL	PRO gm	CHO gm	FAT gm	Chol mg	SFA gm	PFA gm	VITA iu	VITC mg	THI mg	RIB mg	NIA mg	CA mg	NA mg	K+ mg	FE mg
	34.0	1.0	4.1	1.8	0.0	0.3	0.6	479	10.3	0.05	0.06	0.4	22.1	4.2	122	0.6

Sodium Restricted	NA mg	Diabetic	Kcal	Milk exg	Veg exg	Fruit exg	Bread exg	Meat exg	Fat exg	Low Fat & Low Chol	FAT gm	Chol mg	SFA gm	PFA gm
	4.2		17.8	0.0	0.6	0.01	0.0	0.0	0.0		0.1	0.0	0.01	0.03

Portion: 1/2 cup (3 ounces)

INGREDIENTS	50 portions[1]		6 portions[2]	
	weights	measures	weights	measures
Beans, green or wax, frozen	12 lb AP	2 gal	1 1/2 lb	1 qt
Water, boiling		1 qt		1/2 cup
Basil		1 Tbsp		1/2 tsp
Garlic powder		2 tsp		1/4 tsp
Margarine, low sodium, melted	4 oz	1/2 cup	1/2 oz	1 Tbsp

Method

1. Place green or wax beans in boiling water.
2. Sprinkle with basil and garlic powder.
3. Boil beans 10 to 20 minutes. Drain.
4. Add melted margarine. Toss lightly.
5. Serve with No. 8 dipper.

Notes

[1]50 portions: May use fresh (12 lb AP) or canned beans (2 #10 cans).
[2]6 portions: May use fresh (1 1/2 lb AP) or canned beans (1 2/3 lb).

Directions for Diet Preparations

Sodium Restricted (SR) and **Mechanical Soft** (SFT): Prepare as directed.
Low Fat/Low Cholesterol (LF), 1/2 cup, **Diabetic** (DB): 1/2 cup. Omit margarine.
Soft/Low Fiber (SLF): Omit garlic powder.
Puree (PUR): Prepare as directed. Add liquid (i.e. gravy or sauce); blenderize to obtain desired consistency.

Nutrient Analysis per Serving:

Regular	KCAL	PRO gm	CHO gm	FAT gm	Chol mg	SFA gm	PFA gm	VITA iu	VITC mg	THI mg	RIB mg	NIA mg	CA mg	NA mg	K+ mg	FE mg
	34.5	1.0	4.3	1.9	0.0	0.3	0.6	444	5.7	0.03	0.05	0.29	32.9	9.6	80.7	0.6

Sodium Restricted	NA mg	Diabetic	Kcal	Milk exg	Veg exg	Fruit exg	Bread exg	Meat exg	Fat exg	Low Fat & Low Chol	FAT gm	Chol mg	SFA gm	PFA gm
	9.6		18.2	0.0	0.6	0.0	0.0	0.0	0.0		0.1	0.0	0.02	0.05

Portion: 1/2 cup

INGREDIENTS	50 portions		6 portions	
	weights	measures	weights	measures
Fresh Beets				
Beets, Whole AP	14 lb AP (10 3/4 lb EP)	2 1/8 gal 1 1/2 gal	1 3/4 lb AP (1 1/3 lb EP)	4 1/4 cups 3 cups
Water, boiling		to cover		to cover
or				
Canned Beets				
Diced (Harvard or plain) or	13 lb	2 #10 cans	1 2/3 lb	3 1/2 cups
Shoestring or sliced or	13 lb	2 #10 cans	1 2/3 lb	3 1/2 cups
Whole, baby beets (pickled or plain)	13 lb	2 #10 cans	1 2/3 lb	3 1/2 cups

Method

Fresh

1. Remove tops, leaving 2-inch stems on beets. Wash. Remove stems, roots, and skin after cooking to 20 minutes. Drain.
2. Boil 45–60 minutes or
3. Steam 60–75 minutes (5–6 lb pressure). Omit water.

Canned

1. Drain off half the liquid.
2. Heat long enough to bring to serving temperature or
3. Steam about 1 minute (5–6 lb pressure). Omit water.

Directions for Diet Preparations

Sodium Restricted (SR): Use low sodium canned beets or fresh beets.

Low Fat/Low Cholesterol (LF), 1/2 cup, **Diabetic** (DB): 1/2 cup, **Mechanical Soft** (SFT), **Soft/Low Fiber** (SLF): Prepare as directed.

Puree (PUR): Prepare as directed. Add liquid (i.e. gravy or sauce); blenderize to obtain desired consistency.

Nutrient Analysis per Serving (Analysis is based on fresh beets):

Regular	KCAL	PRO gm	CHO gm	FAT gm	Chol mg	SFA gm	PFA gm	VITA iu	VITC mg	THI mg	RIB mg	NIA mg	CA mg	NA mg	K+ mg	FE mg
	26.7	0.9	5.7	0.04	0.0	0.01	0.01	11.2	4.7	0.02	0.01	0.2	9.4	42.2	269	0.5

Sodium Restricted	NA mg	Diabetic	Kcal	Milk exg	Veg exg	Fruit exg	Bread exg	Meat exg	Fat exg	Low Fat & Low Chol	FAT gm	Chol mg	SFA gm	PFA gm
	42.2		332	26.7	0.0	1.0	0.0	0.0	0.0		0.04	0.0	0.01	0.01

Julienne Beets

Portion: 1/2 cup (3 ounces)

INGREDIENTS	50 portions[1]		6 portions[2]	
	weights	measures	weights	measures
Beets, canned, shoestring, drained	13 lb	2 #10 cans	1 2/3 lb	3 1/2 cups
Margarine, low sodium	4 oz	1/2 cup	1/2 oz	1 Tbsp
Lemon juice	8 oz	1 cup	1 oz	2 Tbsp

Method

1. Season beets with mixture of margarine and lemon juice.
2. Heat to serving temperature.
3. Serve with No. 8 dipper.

Notes

[1]50 portions: May prepare beets by steaming, boiling, or heating. May use 14 lb AP fresh beets.
[2]6 portions: May prepare beets by steaming, boiling, or heating. May use 1 3/4 lb AP fresh beets.

Directions for Diet Preparations

Sodium Restricted (SR): Use low sodium beets.
Low Fat/Low Cholesterol (LF), 1/2 cup, **Diabetic** (DB): 1/2 cup. Omit margarine.
Mechanical Soft (SFT) and **Soft/Low Fiber** (SLF): Prepare as directed.
Puree (PUR): Prepare as directed. Blenderize. Add additional liquid if necessary to obtain desired consistency.

Nutrient Analysis per Serving:

Regular	KCAL	PRO gm	CHO gm	FAT gm	Chol mg	SFA gm	PFA gm	VITA iu	VITC mg	THI mg	RIB mg	NIA mg	CA mg	NA mg	K+ mg	FE mg
	46.6	0.9	7.2	1.9	0.0	0.3	0.6	86.2	6.1	0.01	0.04	0.2	15.0	258	146	1.7

Sodium Restricted	NA mg	Diabetic	Kcal	Milk exg	Veg exg	Fruit exg	Bread exg	Meat exg	Fat exg	Low Fat & Low Chol	FAT gm	Chol mg	SFA gm	PFA gm
	42.8		30.4	0.0	1.0	0.1	0.0	0.0	0.0		0.1	0.0	0.02	0.04

Orange Julienne Beets

Portion: 1/2 cup (3 ounces)

INGREDIENTS	50 portions[1]		6 portions[2]	
	weights	measures	weights	measures
Beets, canned, shoestring, drained	13 lb	2 # 10 cans	1 2/3 lb	3 1/2 cups
Margarine, low sodium	4 oz	1/2 cup	1/2 oz	1 Tbsp
Orange juice, unsweetened		2 cups		1/4 cup
Lemon juice		1/4 cup		1/2 Tbsp
Mandarin oranges, unsweetened	1 1/3 lb	1 qt	2 2/3 oz	1/2 cup

Method

1. Combine beets, margarine, orange juice, and lemon juice. Bring to a boil.
2. Reduce heat and add mandarin oranges.
3. Heat to serving temperature, 170°F.
4. Serve with a No. 8 dipper.

Notes

[1]50 portions: May prepare beets by steaming, boiling, or heating. May use 14 lb AP fresh beets.
[2]6 portions: May prepare beets by steaming, boiling, or heating. May use 1 3/4 lb AP fresh beets.

Directions for Diet Preparations

Sodium Restricted (SR): Use low sodium beets.
Low Fat/Low Cholesterol (LF): 1/2 cup and **Diabetic** (DB): 1/2 cup. Omit margarine.
Mechanical Soft (SFT) and **Soft/Low Fiber** (SLF): Prepare as directed.
Puree (PUR): Prepare as directed. Add additional orange juice if necessary; blenderize to obtain desired consistency.

Nutrient Analysis per Serving:

Regular	KCAL	PRO gm	CHO gm	FAT gm	Chol mg	SFA gm	PFA gm	VITA iu	VITC mg	THI mg	RIB mg	NIA mg	CA mg	NA mg	K+ mg	FE mg
	50.7	1.0	7.9	1.9	0.0	0.3	0.6	268	15.6	0.05	0.02	0.3	11.8	258	274	0.5

Sodium Restricted	NA mg	Diabetic	Kcal	Milk exg	Veg exg	Fruit exg	Bread exg	Meat exg	Fat exg	Low Fat & Low Chol	FAT gm	Chol mg	SFA gm	PFA gm
	37.2		34.5	0.0	0.75	0.2	0.0	0.0	0.0		0.07	0.0	0.01	0.02

Portion: 1/2 cup

INGREDIENTS	50 portions[1]		6 portions[2]	
	weights	measures	weights	measures
Broccoli, fresh	16–20 lb AP (14 1/2 lb EP)	3 gal (1 3/4 gal)	2–2 1/2 lb AP (1 3/4 lb EP)	1 1/2 qt (3 1/2 cups)
Margarine, low sodium melted	4 oz	1/2 cup	1/2 oz	1 Tbsp

Method

1. Trim off large leaves. Remove tough ends of lower stems. Wash.
2. Boil or steam broccoli.
3. Pour margarine over cooked broccoli.

Steam

a. 5–6 lb per batch at 5–6 psi for 5 to 10 minutes.

Boil

a. Add broccoli to 1 qt boiling water.
b. Cover and bring water quickly back to a boil.
c. Continue boiling 10–15 minutes or until broccoli is tender.
d. Drain and place in serving pans.

Notes

[1]50 portions: May use frozen broccoli: Broccoli spears - 12 lb; Chopped broccoli - 10 lb.
[2]6 portions: May use frozen broccoli: Broccoli spears - 1 1/2 lb; Chopped broccoli - 1 1/4 lb.

Directions for Diet Preparations

Sodium Restricted (SR): Prepare as directed.
Low Fat/Low Cholesterol (LF): 1/2 cup. Omit margarine. Consider individual tolerance.
Diabetic (DB): 1/2 cup. Omit margarine.
Mechanical Soft (SFT): Prepare as directed. Consider individual tolerance.
Soft/Low Fiber (SLF): Not recommended. Provide appropriate food substitute.
Puree (PUR): Prepare as directed. Add liquid (i.e. sauce or gravy); blenderize to obtain desired consistency.

Nutrient Analysis per Serving:

Regular	KCAL	PRO gm	CHO gm	FAT gm	Chol mg	SFA gm	PFA gm	VITA iu	VITC mg	THI mg	RIB mg	NIA mg	CA mg	NA mg	K+ mg	FE mg
	41.6	2.7	4.7	2.1	0.0	0.3	0.6	1472	84.3	0.06	0.11	0.58	44.1	25.1	295	0.8

Sodium Restricted	NA mg	Diabetic	Kcal	Milk exg	Veg exg	Fruit exg	Bread exg	Meat exg	Fat exg	Low Fat & Low Chol	FAT gm	Chol mg	SFA gm	PFA gm
	25.1		26.1	0.0	1.0	0.0	0.0	0.0	0.0		0.11	0.0	0.02	0.05

Seasoned Broccoli

Portion: 1/2 cup

INGREDIENTS	50 portions[1]		6 portions[2]	
	weights	measures	weights	measures
Broccoli, frozen	12 lb	2 gal	1 1/2 lb	1 qt
Water, boiling		1 1/2 qt		3/4 cup
Parsley, chopped	1 oz	3/4 cup	1/8 oz	1 1/2 Tbsp
Pepper, black		2 tsp		1/4 tsp
Rosemary		1 Tbsp		3/4 tsp

Method

1. Boil 10 to 15 minutes or
2. Steam 5 to 10 minutes. Omit water. (5–6 lb pressure).
3. Add seasonings to broccoli. Toss lightly.
4. Serve with No. 8 dipper.

Notes

[1]50 portions: May use fresh broccoli (16 to 20 lb AP).
[2]6 portions: May use fresh broccoli (2 to 2 1/2 lb AP).

Directions for Diet Preparations

Sodium Restricted (SR) and **Diabetic** (DB): 1/2 cup. Prepare as directed.
Low Fat/Low Cholesterol (LF): 1/2 cup. Prepare as directed. Low fat diets should consider individual tolerance when using broccoli.
Mechanical Soft (SFT): Prepare as directed. Chop.
Soft/Low Fiber (SLF): Not recommended. Provide appropriate food substitute.
Puree (PUR): Prepare as directed. Add liquid (i.e. sauce or gravy); blenderize to obtain desired consistency.

Nutrient Analysis per Serving:

Regular	KCAL	PRO gm	CHO gm	FAT gm	Chol mg	SFA gm	PFA gm	VITA iu	VITC mg	THI mg	RIB mg	NIA mg	CA mg	NA mg	K+ mg	FE mg
	27.2	2.5	5.3	0.3	0.0	0.04	0.1	1226	50.2	0.07	0.17	0.6	53.6	11.1	157	1.6

Sodium Restricted	NA mg	Diabetic	Kcal	Milk exg	Veg exg	Fruit exg	Bread exg	Meat exg	Fat exg	Low Fat & Low Chol	FAT gm	Chol mg	SFA gm	PFA gm
	11.1		27.2	0.0	1.0	0.0	0.0	0.0	0.0		0.3	0.0	0.04	0.1

Portion: 1/2 cup

INGREDIENTS	50 portions		6 portions	
	weights	measures	weights	measures
Fresh Cabbage	14 lb AP	3 1/8 gal	1 3/4 lb AP	1 1/2 qt
Ready-to-cook shredded or	10 lb	2 1/2 gal	1 1/4 lb	1 1/4 qt
wedges	12 lb		1 1/2 lb	
Water, boiling		1 qt		1/2 cup

Method

1. Remove wilted outside leaves. Wash and core.
2. Cut cabbage into wedges or shred.
3. Boil in water.
   a. Boil shredded cabbage 5 to 10 minutes.
   b. Boil wedges 15 to 20 minutes.
4. Drain.

Directions for Diet Preparations

Sodium Restricted (SR), **Low Fat/Low Cholesterol** (LF): 1/2 cup, **Diabetic** (DB): 1/2 cup. Prepare as directed. Low fat diets should consider individual tolerance to cabbage.

Mechanical Soft (SFT): Shred finely. Cook until soft and tender. Consider individual tolerance.

Soft/Low Fiber (SLF): Not recommended, substitute with appropriate food alternative.

Puree (PUR): Prepare as directed. Cook cabbage until soft and tender. Add liquid (i.e. broth or gravy); blenderize to obtain desired consistency.

Nutrient Analysis per Serving:

Regular	KCAL	PRO gm	CHO gm	FAT gm	Chol mg	SFA gm	PFA gm	VITA iu	VITC mg	THI mg	RIB mg	NIA mg	CA mg	NA mg	K+ mg	FE mg
	15.4	0.7	3.5	0.18	0.0	0.02	0.08	63.1	17.8	0.04	0.04	0.16	24.2	13.9	150	0.2

Sodium Restricted	NA mg	Diabetic	Kcal exg	Milk exg	Veg exg	Fruit exg	Bread exg	Meat exg	Fat	Low Fat & Low Chol	FAT gm	Chol mg	SFA gm	PFA gm
	13.9		15.4	0.0	0.5	0.0	0.0	0.0	0.0		0.18	0.0	0.02	0.08

Portion: 1/2 cup

INGREDIENTS	50 portions		6 portions	
	weights	measures	weights	measures
Fresh collard greens	14 1/2 lb EP (18 lb AP)	3 gal	1 3/4 lb EP (2 1/4 lb AP)	1 1/2 qt
Water, boiling		1 qt		1/2 cup
Basil, ground		2 tsp		1/4 tsp
Oregano, ground		1 Tbsp		1/2 tsp
or				
Frozen collard greens, chopped	14 lb	1 3/4 gal	1 3/4 lb	3 1/2 cups
Water, boiling		2 qt		1 cup
Basil, ground		2 tsp		1/4 tsp
Oregano, ground		1 Tbsp		1/2 tsp
or				
Canned collard greens	14 lb	1 3/4 gal	1 3/4 lb	3 1/2 cups
Basil, ground		2 tsp		1/4 tsp
Oregano, ground		1 Tbsp		1/2 tsp

Method

Fresh: Boiling
1. Remove tough stems and discolored parts. Wash thoroughly. Shake sand out in several changes of water.
2. Boil covered 8 minutes, then uncovered 10 minutes.
3. Drain by lifting collards from cooking water so sand stays behind. Chop.
4. Add seasoning. Mix to blend.

Frozen: Boiling
1. Boil 8–12 minutes.
2. Add seasoning. Mix to blend.

Canned
1. Drain off half the liquid from can.
2. Heat long enough to bring to serving temperature or
3. Steam about 1 minute (5–6 lb pressure) or
4. Heat in 350°F oven until serving temperature is reached.

Directions for Diet Preparations

Sodium Restricted (SR): Prepare as directed.
Low Fat/Low Cholesterol (LF): 1/2 cup and **Diabetic** (DB): 1/2 cup. Prepare as directed.
Mechanical Soft (SFT) and **Soft/Low Fiber** (SLF): Prepare as directed. Chop.
Puree (PUR): Prepare as directed. Add liquid (i.e. broth or gravy); blenderize to obtain desired consistency.

Nutrient Analysis per Serving (Analysis is based on fresh collard greens):

Regular	KCAL	PRO gm	CHO gm	FAT gm	Chol mg	SFA gm	PFA gm	VITA iu	VITC mg	THI mg	RIB mg	NIA mg	CA mg	NA mg	K+ mg	FE mg
	13.7	1.1	2.6	0.2	0.0	0.0	0.0	2140	9.4	0.02	0.04	0.23	76.6	18.3	91.5	0.4

Sodium Restricted	NA mg	Diabetic	Kcal	Milk exg	Veg exg	Fruit exg	Bread exg	Meat exg	Fat exg	Low Fat & Low Chol	FAT gm	Chol mg	SFA gm	PFA gm
	18.3		13.7	0.0	0.5	0.0	0.0	0.0	0.0		0.2	0.0	0.0	0.0

Carrots

Portion: 1/2 cup

INGREDIENTS	50 portions		6 portions	
	weights	**measures**	**weights**	**measures**
Fresh carrots	14 lb AP	2 gal	1 3/4 lb AP	1 qt
	(10 lb EP)	1 1/2 gal	(1 1/4 lb EP)	3 cups
Ready-to-cook weight whole or sliced	9 3/4 lb	2 gal	1 1/4 lb	1 qt
Water, boiling		2 qt		1 cup
or				
Frozen carrots	12 lb	2 1/2 gal	1 1/2 lb	1 1/4 qt
Water, boiling		1 qt		1/2 cup
or				
Canned carrots, diced or sliced	13 lb	2 #10 cans	1 2/3 lb	1 qt

Method

Fresh
1. Wash. Remove tips, tops, and brown spots. Scrape or peel with vegetable peeler. Chop or cut into slices or sticks.
2. Boil whole 20 to 30 minutes or
3. Boil sliced 10 to 20 minutes or
4. Steam whole or sliced 15–30 minutes. Omit water. (5–6 lb pressure).

Frozen
1. Boil 8–10 minutes or
2. Steam 3–5 minutes. Omit water. (5–6 lb pressure).

Canned
1. Drain off half the liquid from can.
2. Heat long enough to bring to serving temperature or
3. Steam about 1 minute (5–6 lb pressure) or
4. Heat in 350°F oven until serving temperature is reached.

Directions for Diet Preparations

Sodium Restricted (SR), **Low Fat/Low Cholesterol** (LF): 1/2 cup, **Diabetic** (DB): 1/2 cup, **Mechanical Soft** (SFT), **Soft/Low Fiber** (SLF): Prepare as directed.

Puree (PUR): Prepare as directed. Add liquid (i.e. sauce or gravy); blenderize to obtain desired consistency.

Nutrient Analysis per Serving (Analysis is based on fresh carrots):

Regular	KCAL	PRO gm	CHO gm	FAT gm	Chol mg	SFA gm	PFA gm	VITA iu	VITC mg	THI mg	RIB mg	NIA mg	CA mg	NA mg	K+ mg	FE mg
	35.5	0.8	8.2	0.1	0.0	0.02	0.06	19392	1.8	0.02	0.04	0.39	24.5	52.1	179	0.4

Sodium Restricted	NA mg	Diabetic	Kcal	Milk exg	Veg exg	Fruit exg	Bread exg	Meat exg	Fat exg	Low Fat & Low Chol	FAT gm	Chol mg	SFA gm	PFA gm
	52.1		35.5	0.0	1.2	0.0	0.0	0.0	0.0		0.1	0.0	0.02	0.06

Glazed Carrots

Portion: 1/2 cup

INGREDIENTS	50 portions[1]		6 portions[2]	
	weights	measures	weights	measures
Carrots, fresh, sliced	14 lb AP (10 lb EP)	2 gal	1 3/4 lb AP (1 1/4 lb EP)	1 qt
Margarine, low sodium	8 oz	1 cup	1 oz	2 Tbsp
Sugar, brown, solid packed	8 oz	1 cup	1 oz	2 Tbsp
Orange juice, unsweetened	12 oz	1 1/2 cups	1 1/2 oz	3 Tbsp

Method

1. Steam or boil carrots until tender. Drain.
2. Melt margarine and sugar over low heat; stirring constantly.
3. Combine orange juice, margarine, sugar, and carrots. Simmer 5 to 10 minutes.

Notes

[1]50 portions: May use frozen or canned carrots: Frozen—12 lb; Canned—2 No. 10 cans.
[2]6 portions: May use frozen or canned carrots: Frozen—1 1/2 lb; Canned—1 2/3 lbs.

Directions for Diet Preparations

Sodium Restricted (SR), **Mechanical Soft** (SFT), and **Soft/Low Fiber** (SLF): Prepare as directed.
Low Fat/Low Cholesterol (LF): 1/2 cup. Omit margarine.
Diabetic (DB): 1/2 cup. Omit margarine and sugar.
Puree (PUR): Prepare as directed. Add additional orange juice if necessary; blenderize to obtain desired consistency.

Nutrient Analysis per Serving:

Regular	KCAL	PRO gm	CHO gm	FAT gm	Chol mg	SFA gm	PFA gm	VITA iu	VITC mg	THI mg	RIB mg	NIA mg	CA mg	NA mg	K+ mg	FE mg
	88.0	1.1	13.3	3.9	0.0	0.6	1.3	4240	7.1	0.04	0.04	0.6	34.8	56.2	195	0.7

Sodium Restricted	NA mg	Diabetic	Kcal	Milk exg	Veg exg	Fruit exg	Bread exg	Meat exg	Fat exg	Low Fat & Low Chol	FAT gm	Chol mg	SFA gm	PFA gm
	56.2		38.6	0.0	1.0	0.17	0.0	0.0	0.0		0.21	0.0	0.04	0.09

Hot Marinated Carrots

Portion: 1/2 cup

INGREDIENTS	50 portions		6 portions	
	weights	measures	weights	measures
Carrots, fresh, ready-to-cook or	9 3/4 lb	2 gal	1 1/4 lb	1 qt
Carrots, frozen	12 lb	2 1/2 gal	1 1/2 lb	1 1/4 qt
Vinegar, cider	4 oz	1/2 cup	1/2 oz	1 Tbsp
Sugar, granulated	1 1/2 lb	3 1/3 cups	3 oz	6 1/2 Tbsp
Margarine, low sodium	8 oz	1 cup	1 oz	2 Tbsp
Parsley, chopped	1 oz	3/4 cup	1/8 oz	1 1/2 Tbsp

Method

1. Trim, peel, and wash carrots.
2. Cut into 3-inch lengths and into strips 1/2-inch wide.
3. Place carrots in pans for steaming.
4. Cook until carrots are tender, about 10 minutes.
5. Combine vinegar, sugar, and margarine. Heat in a saucepan to boiling. Pour over carrots.
6. Bake carrots at 350°F for 15 to 20 minutes.
7. Just before serving, sprinkle with parsley.
8. Serve with a No. 8 dipper.

Directions for Diet Preparations

Sodium Restricted (SR), **Mechanical Soft** (SFT), and **Soft/Low Fiber** (SLF): Prepare as directed.
Low Fat/Low Cholesterol (LF): 1/2 cup. Use margarine in half the amount specified.
Diabetic (DB): 1/2 cup. Omit sugar. Use an artificial sweetener as per manufacturer's directions. Use margarine in half the amount specified.
Puree (PUR): Prepare as directed. Add liquid (i.e. juice); blenderize to obtain desired consistency.

Nutrient Analysis per Serving:

Regular	KCAL	PRO gm	CHO gm	FAT gm	Chol mg	SFA gm	PFA gm	VITA iu	VITC mg	THI mg	RIB mg	NIA mg	CA mg	NA mg	K+ mg	FE mg
	115	0.9	20.5	3.8	0.0	0.6	1.3	19584	2.6	0.02	0.04	0.4	27.0	53.9	188	0.5

Sodium Restricted	NA mg	Diabetic	Kcal	Milk exg	Veg exg	Fruit exg	Bread exg	Meat exg	Fat exg	Low Fat & Low Chol	FAT gm	Chol mg	SFA gm	PFA gm
	53.9		54.7	0.0	1.3	0.0	0.0	0.0	0.3		1.9	0.0	0.3	0.6

Portion: 1/2 cup

INGREDIENTS	50 portions		6 portions	
	weights	measures	weights	measures
Carrots, fresh, sliced,	14 lb AP		1 3/4 lb AP	
ready-to-cook or	9 3/4 lb	2 gal	1 1/4 lb	1 qt
Carrots, frozen, sliced or	12 lb	2 1/2 gal	1 1/2 lb	1 1/4 qt
Carrots, sliced, canned	13 lb	2 #10 cans	1 2/3 lb	1 qt
Margarine, low sodium	8 oz	1 cup	1 oz	2 Tbsp
Sugar, brown, packed	8 oz	1 cup	1 oz	2 Tbsp
Raisins, seedless	1 lb	3 cups	2 oz	1/3 cup

Method

1. Steam or boil carrots until tender. Place in serving or baking pan(s).
2. Combine margarine and sugar. Heat in a saucepan to boiling.
3. Add raisins to sauce.
4. Pour raisin sauce over carrots. Toss lightly.
5. Bake carrots at 350°F for 15 to 20 minutes or simmer until carrots and sauce are heated through.

Directions for Diet Preparations

Sodium Restricted (SR): Prepare as directed.
Low Fat/Low Cholesterol (LF): 1/2 cup. Omit margarine. Use reduced-calorie margarine in half the amount specified for regular margarine.
Diabetic (DB): 1/2 cup.
50 portions: Omit brown sugar, substitute with an artificial sweetener equivalent to 1 cup sugar (approximately 1 Tbsp artificial sweetener). Omit margarine. Use reduced-calorie margarine in half the amount specified for regular margarine.
6 portions: Omit brown sugar, substitute with an artificial sweetener equivalent to 2 Tbsp sugar (approximately 1/2 tsp artificial sweetener). Omit margarine. Use reduced-calorie margarine in half the amount specified for regular margarine.
Mechanical Soft (SFT) and **Soft/Low Fiber** (SLF): Omit raisins.
Puree (PUR): Prepare as directed. Blenderize. Add additional liquid if necessary to obtain desired consistency.

Nutrient Analysis per Serving:

Regular	KCAL	PRO gm	CHO gm	FAT gm	Chol mg	SFA gm	PFA gm	VITA iu	VITC mg	THI mg	RIB mg	NIA mg	CA mg	NA mg	K+ mg	FE mg
	100	1.1	17.1	3.7	0.0	0.6	1.2	11376	2.1	0.03	0.03	0.36	27.8	41.1	188	0.6

Sodium Restricted	NA mg	Diabetic	Kcal	Milk exg	Veg exg	Fruit exg	Bread exg	Meat exg	Fat exg	Low Fat & Low Chol	FAT gm	Chol mg	SFA gm	PFA gm
	41.1		60	0.0	0.75	0.6	0.0	0.0	0.0		1.0	0.0	0.2	0.3

Sunshine Carrots

Portion: 1/2 cup

INGREDIENTS	50 portions[1]		6 portions[2]	
	weights	measures	weights	measures
Carrots, sliced, ready-to-cook weight	9 3/4 lb	2 gal	1 1/4 lb	1 qt
Sugar, granulated	5 oz	3/4 cup	2/3 oz	1 1/2 Tbsp
Cornstarch	1 oz	3 Tbsp	1/8 oz	1 1/8 tsp
Ginger, ground		1 Tbsp		1/4 tsp
Orange juice, unsweetened		3 cups		1/3 cup
Margarine, low sodium	6 oz	3/4 cup	3/4 oz	1 1/2 Tbsp

Method

1. Boil carrots 10 to 20 minutes or until tender. Drain.
2. Combine sugar, cornstarch, ginger, and orange juice. Cook over low heat, stirring constantly until thickened. Cook 1 minute.
3. Add margarine to sauce. Stir until blended.
4. Pour sauce over carrots. Mix lightly to coat evenly.
5. Serve with No. 8 dipper.

Notes

[1]50 portions: May use 12 lb frozen carrots or 2 #10 cans.
[2]6 portions: May use 1 1/2 lb frozen carrots or 1 2/3 lb canned carrots.

Directions for Diet Preparations

Sodium Restricted (SR), **Mechanical Soft** (SFT), and **Soft/Low Fiber** (SLF): Prepare as directed.
Low Fat/Low Cholesterol (LF): 1/2 cup. Omit margarine and cornstarch.
Diabetic (DB): 1/2 cup.
50 portions: Omit sugar, substitute with an artificial sweetener equivalent to 3/4 cup of granulated sugar (approximately 3 tsp). Omit margarine and cornstarch.
6 portions: Omit sugar, substitute with an artificial sweetener equivalent to 1 1/2 Tbsp of granulated sugar (approximately 1/4 tsp). Omit margarine and cornstarch.
Puree (PUR): Prepare as directed. Add additional orange juice if necessary; blenderize to obtain desired consistency.

Nutrient Analysis per Serving:

Regular	KCAL	PRO gm	CHO gm	FAT gm	Chol mg	SFA gm	PFA gm	VITA iu	VITC mg	THI mg	RIB mg	NIA mg	CA mg	NA mg	K+ mg	FE mg
	81	1.0	13.3	2.9	0.0	0.5	1.0	19488	6.7	0.04	0.04	0.4	27.0	53.3	211	0.5

Sodium Restricted	NA mg	Diabetic	Kcal	Milk exg	Veg exg	Fruit exg	Bread exg	Meat exg	Fat exg	Low Fat & Low Chol	FAT gm	Chol mg	SFA gm	PFA gm
	53.3		43	0.0	1.5	0.0	0.0	0.0	0.01		0.2	0.0	0.03	0.08

Carrot Tzimmes

Portion: 1/2 cup

Ingredients	50 portions[1]		6 portions[2]	
	weights	measures	weights	measures
Carrots, fresh, diced	9 3/4 lb	2 gal	1 1/4 lb	1 qt
Water, boiling		2 qt		1 cup
Flour, all-purpose	8 oz	2 cups	1 oz	1/4 cup
Margarine, low sodium	8 oz	1 cup	1 oz	2 Tbsp
Sugar, brown	1 lb	2 cups	2 oz	1/4 cup
Prunes, dried, pitted, chopped	2 lb	1 qt	4 oz	1/2 cup

Method

1. Boil carrots 10 to 20 minutes or until tender. Drain and reserve cooking liquid and carrots.
2. Make a roux with the flour and margarine.
3. Add cooking liquid to roux; whip smooth.
4. Add brown sugar to roux. Simmer briefly.
5. Place carrots and prunes in greased baking pan(s) and pour sauce over them.
6. Bake at 350 °F about 1 1/2 hours.

Notes

[1]50 portions: May use 12 lb frozen carrots or 2 #10 cans.
[2]6 portions: May use 1 1/2 lb frozen carrots or 1 2/3 lb canned carrots.

Directions for Diet Preparations

Sodium Restricted (SR): Prepare as directed.
Low Fat/Low Cholesterol (LF): 1/2 cup. Omit margarine and flour.
Diabetic (DB): 1/2 cup. Omit margarine, flour, and sugar. Cook carrots, drain. Add prunes to carrots. Add artificial sweetener to taste. Heat until serving temperature is reached.
Mechanical Soft (SFT): Prepare as directed. Consider individual tolerance when using prunes.
Soft/Low Fiber (SLF): Omit prunes, substitute with canned sliced apples.
Puree (PUR): Prepare as directed. Add additional liquid (i.e. juice) if necessary; blenderize to obtain desired consistency.

Nutrient Analysis per Serving:

Regular	KCAL	PRO gm	CHO gm	FAT gm	Chol mg	SFA gm	PFA gm	VITA iu	VITC mg	THI mg	RIB mg	NIA mg	CA mg	NA mg	K+ mg	FE mg
	131	1.4	23.8	3.9	0.0	0.6	1.3	16480	2.0	0.05	0.07	0.7	34.0	48.1	244	1.1

Sodium Restricted	NA mg	Diabetic	Kcal	Milk exg	Veg exg	Fruit exg	Bread exg	Meat exg	Fat exg	Low Fat & Low Chol	FAT gm	Chol mg	SFA gm	PFA gm
	48.1		48.5	0.0	1.0	0.3	0.0	0.0	0.0		0.1	0.0	0.02	0.06

Portion: 1/2 cup

INGREDIENTS	50 portions		6 portions	
	weights	**measures**	**weights**	**measures**
Fresh cauliflower, medium heads	16 lb AP (10 lb EP)	16 heads (2 1/2 gal)	2 lb AP (1 1/4 lb EP)	2 heads 1 1/4 qt
Florets, ready-to-cook weight	7 3/4 lb	2 gal	1 lb	1 qt
Water, boiling		1 1/2 gal		3 cups
or				
Frozen cauliflower	12 lb	3 gal	1 1/2 lb	1 1/2 qt
Water, boiling		1 1/2 qt		3/4 cup

Method

Fresh

1. Remove outer leaves and stalks. Break into florets. Wash.
2. Boil florets 15 to 20 minutes, uncovered or
3. Steam florets 8 to 12 minutes. Omit water. (5–6 lb pressure).

Frozen

1. Boil 8 to 12 minutes or
2. Steam 10 to 15 minutes. Omit water. (5–6 lb pressure).

Directions for Diet Preparations

Sodium Restricted (SR), **Diabetic** (DB): 1/2 cup, and **Mechanical Soft** (SFT): Prepare as directed.

Low Fat/Low Cholesterol (LF): 1/2 cup. Prepare as directed. Consider individual tolerance.

Soft/Low Fiber (SLF): Not recommended, substitute with an appropriate food alternative.

Puree (PUR): Prepare as directed. Add liquid (i.e. sauce or gravy); blenderize to obtain desired consistency.

Nutrient Analysis per Serving:

Regular	KCAL	PRO gm	CHO gm	FAT gm	Chol mg	SFA gm	PFA gm	VITA iu	VITC mg	THI mg	RIB mg	NIA mg	CA mg	NA mg	K+ mg	FE mg
15.2	1.1	2.9	0.1	0.0	0.02	0.07	8.8	35.0	0.03	0.03	0.3	17.0	3.8	204	0.2	

Sodium Restricted	NA mg	Diabetic	Kcal	Milk exg	Veg exg	Fruit exg	Bread exg	Meat exg	Fat exg	Low Fat & Low Chol	FAT gm	Chol mg	SFA gm	PFA gm
	3.8		15.2	0.0	0.5	0.0	0.0	0.0	0.0		0.1	0.0	0.02	0.07

J21   Cauliflower Pollanese

Portion: 1/2 cup

INGREDIENTS	50 portions		6 portions	
	weights	measures	weights	measures
Cauliflower, chopped, frozen	12 lb	3 gal	1 1/2 lb	1 1/2 qt
Water, boiling		1 1/2 qt		3/4 cup
Bread crumbs, dry	4 oz	1 cup	1/2 oz	2 Tbsp
Margarine, low sodium, melted	4 oz	1/2 cup	1/2 oz	1 Tbsp

Method

1. Boil cauliflower in water 8 to 10 minutes or until tender. Drain.
2. Lightly brown bread crumbs in melted margarine. Sprinkle over cauliflower, Mix lightly.
3. Serve with No. 8 dipper.

Directions for Diet Preparations

Sodium Restricted (SR): Prepare as directed.
Low Fat/Low Cholesterol (LF): 1/2 cup and **Diabetic** (DB): 1/2 cup. Use half the amount of margarine specified. Low fat diets should consider individual tolerance to cauliflower.
Mechanical Soft (SFT): Prepare as directed. Consider individual tolerance.
Soft/Low Fiber (SLF): Not recommended, substitute with an appropriate food alternative.
Puree (PUR): Prepare as directed. Add liquid (i.e. sauce or gravy); blenderize to obtain desired consistency.

Nutrient Analysis per Serving:

Regular	KCAL	PRO gm	CHO gm	FAT gm	Chol mg	SFA gm	PFA gm	VITA iu	VITC mg	THI mg	RIB mg	NIA mg	CA mg	NA mg	K+ mg	FE mg
	39.5	1.4	4.4	2.0	0.1	0.3	0.7	84.8	35.0	0.04	0.04	0.4	20.1	19.2	208	0.3

Sodium Restricted	NA mg	Diabetic	Kcal	Milk exg	Veg exg	Fruit exg	Bread exg	Meat exg	Fat exg	Low Fat & Low Chol	FAT gm	Chol mg	SFA gm	PFA gm
	19.2		31.3	0.0	1.0	0.0	0.0	0.0	0.1		1.1	0.1	0.2	0.4

Portion: 1/2 cup

INGREDIENTS	50 portions		6 portions	
	weights	measures	weights	measures
Broccoli, cuts, frozen	2 lb	2 qt	4 oz	1 cup
Carrots, sliced, frozen	1 1/2 lb	1 1/2 qt	3 oz	3/4 cup
Pea pods, frozen	1 lb	3 cups	2 oz	1/3 cup
Water, boiling		1 qt		1/2 cup
Water chestnuts, sliced, drained, canned	1 lb	3 cups	2 oz	1/3 cup
Bamboo shoots, sliced, drained	14 oz	3 cups	1 3/4 oz	1/3 cup
Mushrooms, canned	1 1/2 lb	3 cups	3 oz	1/3 cup

Method

1. Add broccoli, carrots, and pea pods to boiling water. Boil 10 to 15 minutes from the time the water returns to boiling.
2. Add water chestnuts, bamboo shoots, and mushrooms to the above vegetables.
3. Heat just long enough to bring to serving temperature. Drain vegetables and place in serving or baking pan(s).
4. Serve with No. 8 dipper.

Notes

[1]May prepare vegetables by steaming. May use fresh vegetables.

Directions for Diet Preparations

Sodium Restricted (SR): Use fresh mushrooms or low sodium canned mushrooms

Low Fat/Low Cholesterol (LF): 1/2 cup, **Diabetic** (DB): 1/2 cup and **Mechanical Soft** (SFT): Prepare as directed. Low fat diets should consider individual tolerance to broccoli.

Soft/Low Fiber (SLF): Omit broccoli and peas.

Puree (PUR): Prepare as directed. Add liquid (i.e. sauce or gravy); blenderize to obtain desired consistency.

Nutrient Analysis per Serving:

Regular	KCAL	PRO gm	CHO gm	FAT gm	Chol mg	SFA gm	PFA gm	VITA iu	VITC mg	THI mg	RIB mg	NIA mg	CA mg	NA mg	K+ mg	FE mg
	26.4	1.5	5.5	0.1	0.0	0.02	0.07	4824	20.4	0.04	0.1	0.7	22.8	54.3	182	0.8

Sodium Restricted	NA mg	Diabetic	Kcal	Milk exg	Veg exg	Fruit exg	Bread exg	Meat exg	Fat exg	Low Fat & Low Chol	FAT gm	Chol mg	SFA gm	PFA gm
	14.2		26.4	0.0	1.0	0.0	0.0	0.0	0.0		0.1	0.0	0.02	0.07

Portion: 1/2 cup or one medium cob

INGREDIENTS	50 portions		6 portions	
	weights	measures	weights	measures
Fresh corn on cob	16 1/2 lb EP	50 medium	2 lb AP	6 medium
(Corn on cob with husk)	(21 lb AP)		(2 1/2 lb AP)	
Water, boiling		1 1/4 gal		2 1/2 cups
or				
Frozen corn, whole kernel	10 lb	1 3/4 gal	1 1/4 lb	3 1/2 cups
Water, boiling		1 1/2 qt		3/4 cup
or				
Canned corn, whole kernel	13 1/4 lb	2 #10 cans	1 2/3 lb	3 cups

Method

Fresh
1. Husk. Remove silks. Wash. Do not allow to stand in water.
2. Boil 15 to 20 minutes or
3. Steam 10 to 15 minutes. Omit water. (5–6 lb pressure).

Frozen
1. Boil 5–10 minutes or
2. Steam 8–13 minutes. Omit water (5–6 lb pressure).

Canned
1. Drain off half the liquid from can.
2. Heat long enough to bring to serving temperature or
3. Steam about 1 minute (5–6 lb pressure) or
4. Heat in 350 °F oven until serving temperature is reached.

Directions for Diet Preparations

Sodium Restricted (SR): Use fresh corn or sodium restricted canned corn.

Low Fat/Low Cholesterol (LF): 1/2 cup or 1 medium cob and **Diabetic** (DB): 1/2 cup or 1 medium cob. Prepare as directed. Low fat diets should consider individual tolerance to corn.

Mechanical Soft (SFT) and **Puree** (PUR): Corn on cob is not recommended. Whole kernel corn can be prepared as directed. Add liquid (i.e. gravy or sauce); blenderize to obtain desired consistency. Consider individual tolerance.

Soft/Low Fiber (SLF): Not recommended, substitute with appropriate food alternative.

Nutrient Analysis per Serving:

Regular	KCAL	PRO gm	CHO gm	FAT gm	Chol mg	SFA gm	PFA gm	VITA iu	VITC mg	THI mg	RIB mg	NIA mg	CA mg	NA mg	K+ mg	FE mg
On the Cob	58.5	1.9	14.0	0.4	0.0	0.07	0.22	132	3.0	0.1	0.04	0.9	1.8	2.5	158	0.3
whole kernel	89.6	2.7	20.8	1.0	0.0	0.1	0.5	180	5.1	0.17	0.05	1.3	1.6	210	206	0.5

Sodium Restricted	NA mg	Diabetic	Kcal	Milk exg	Veg exg	Fruit exg	Bread exg	Meat exg	Fat exg	Low Fat & Low Chol	FAT gm	Chol mg	SFA gm	PFA gm
On the Cob	2.5		58.5	0.0	0.0	0.0	0.8	0.0	0.0		0.4	0.0	0.07	0.2
whole kernel	4.2		89.6	0.0	0.0	0.0	1.2	0.0	0.0		1.0	0.0	0.1	0.5

Corn Confetti

Portion: 1/2 cup

INGREDIENTS	50 portions		6 portions	
	weights	measures	weights	measures
Green peppers, chopped	10 2/3 oz EP	2 cups	1 1/3 oz EP	1/4 cup
Red peppers, chopped	5 1/3 oz	1 cup	3/4 oz	2 Tbsp
Margarine, low sodium, melted	8 oz	1 cup	1 oz	2 Tbsp
Corn, whole kernel, canned	13 1/4 lb	2 #10 cans	1 2/3 lb	3 cups

Method

1. Sauté green and red peppers in margarine until tender.
2. Simmer corn in its own juice 10 to 20 minutes. Drain well.
3. Add corn to peppers. Mix well.
4. Serve with No. 8 dipper.

Directions for Diet Preparations

Sodium Restricted (SR): Use low sodium corn.

Low Fat/Low Cholesterol (LF): 1/2 cup and **Diabetic** (DB): 1/2 cup. Omit margarine. Cook green and red peppers in boiling water. Drain. Add to corn. Mix well. Low fat diets should consider individual tolerance to corn.

Mechanical Soft (SFT) and **Puree** (PUR): Prepare as directed. Add liquid (i.e. broth or gravy); blenderize to obtain desired consistency.

Soft/Low Fiber (SLF): Not recommended, substitute with an appropriate food alternative.

Nutrient Analysis per Serving:

Regular	KCAL	PRO gm	CHO gm	FAT gm	Chol mg	SFA gm	PFA gm	VITA iu	VITC mg	THI mg	RIB mg	NIA mg	CA mg	NA mg	K+ mg	FE mg
	93.6	2.0	13.9	4.4	0.0	0.7	1.5	298	14.0	0.02	0.06	0.9	5.2	237	156	0.7

Sodium Restricted	NA mg	Diabetic	Kcal	Milk exg	Veg exg	Fruit exg	Bread exg	Meat exg	Fat exg	Low Fat & Low Chol	FAT gm	Chol mg	SFA gm	PFA gm
	5.1		60.7	0.0	0.0	0.0	0.8	0.0	0.0		0.7	0.0	0.1	0.3

Portion: 1/2 cup

INGREDIENTS	50 portions		6 portions	
	weights	measures	weights	measures
Eggplant, cut into 1/2-inch slices, pared	9 3/4 lb EP (12 lb AP)	96 slices	1 1/4 lb EP (1 1/2 lb AP)	12 slices
Water, cold		as needed		as needed
Tomato sauce	5 lb	2 1/2 qt	10 oz	1 1/4 cups
Parmesan cheese, grated	3 1/2 oz	3/4 cup	1/2 oz	1 1/2 Tbsp
Oregano		1 Tbsp		1/2 tsp
Bread crumbs	12 oz	3 cups	1 1/2 oz	1/3 cup
Margarine, low sodium, melted	8 oz	1 cup	1 oz	2 Tbsp

Method

1. Soak eggplant in water (enough to cover) for 30 minutes. Drain.
2. Cook in frying pan on each side for 3 minutes with a little water. Place in baking pan(s).
3. Combine tomato sauce, parmesan cheese, and oregano. Pour sauce over eggplants.
4. Lightly brown bread crumbs in melted margarine. Sprinkle over eggplant.
5. Bake at 350°F for 30 minutes.

Directions for Diet Preparations

Sodium Restricted (SR): Use SR tomato sauce and low sodium bread crumbs. Omit parmesan cheese.

Low Fat/Low Cholesterol (LF): 1/2 cup. Use LF tomato sauce. Omit margarine.

Diabetic (DB): 1/2 cup. Use DB tomato sauce. Omit margarine.

Mechanical Soft (SFT): Prepare as directed. Consider individual tolerance.

Soft/Low Fiber (SLF): Not recommended, substitute with an appropriate food alternative.

Puree (PUR): Prepare as directed. Add additional tomato sauce; blenderize to obtain desired consistency.

Nutrient Analysis per Serving:

Regular	KCAL	PRO gm	CHO gm	FAT gm	Chol mg	SFA gm	PFA gm	VITA iu	VITC mg	THI mg	RIB mg	NIA mg	CA mg	NA mg	K+ mg	FE mg
	129	2.2	12.7	7.9	1.1	1.4	2.4	1021	10.5	0.08	0.05	1.0	37.3	212	247	0.9

Sodium Restricted	NA mg	Diabetic	Kcal	Milk exg	Veg exg	Fruit exg	Bread exg	Meat exg	Fat exg	Low Fat & Low Chol	FAT gm	Chol mg	SFA gm	PFA gm
	9.8		78	0.0	1.0	0.0	0.5	0.0	0.3		2.4	1.1	0.6	0.7

Portion: 1/2 cup

INGREDIENTS	50 portions		6 portions	
	weights	measures	weights	measures
Frozen italian vegetables	12 lb	2 1/4 gal	1 1/2 lb	4 1/2 cups
Water, boiling		1 qt		1/2 cup
or				
Canned italian vegetables	13 lb	2 #10 cans	1 2/3 lb	1 qt

Method

Frozen
1. Boil 12 to 20 minutes or
2. Steam 12 to 20 minutes. Omit water. (5–6 lb pressure).

Canned
1. Drain off half the liquid from can.
2. Heat long enough to bring to serving temperature or
3. Steam about 1 minute (5–6 lb pressure) or
4. Heat in 350°F oven until serving temperature is reached.

Directions for Diet Preparations

Sodium Restricted (SR): Use frozen or low sodium Italian mixed vegetables.

Low Fat/Low Cholesterol (LF): 1/2 cup and **Diabetic** (DB): 1/2 cup. Prepare as directed.

Mechanical Soft (SFT): Prepare as directed. Consider individual tolerance.

Soft/Low Fiber (SLF): Not recommended, substitute with an appropriate food alternative.

Puree (PUR): Prepare as directed. Add liquid (i.e. broth or gravy); blenderize to obtain desired consistency.

Nutrient Analysis per Serving (Analysis is based on frozen italian mixed vegetables):

Regular	KCAL	PRO gm	CHO gm	FAT gm	Chol mg	SFA gm	PFA gm	VITA iu	VITC mg	THI mg	RIB mg	NIA mg	CA mg	NA mg	K+ mg	FE mg
	36.7	1.9	8.0	0.1	0.0	0.02	0.06	2212	3.5	0.05	0.07	0.6	21.1	17.2	187	0.6

Sodium Restricted	NA mg	Diabetic	Kcal	Milk exg	Veg exg	Fruit exg	Bread exg	Meat exg	Fat exg	Low Fat & Low Chol	FAT gm	Chol mg	SFA gm	PFA gm
	17.2		36.7	0.0	0.6	0.0	0.25	0.0	0.0		0.1	0.0	0.02	0.06

Portion: 1/2 cup

INGREDIENTS	50 portions		6 portions	
	weights	measures	weights	measures
Frozen mixed vegetables	12 lb	2 1/4 gal	1 1/2 lb	4 1/2 cups
Water, boiling		1 qt		1/2 cup
or				
Canned mixed vegetables	13 lb	2 #10 cans	1 2/3 lb	1 qt

Method

Frozen
1. Boil 12 to 20 minutes or
2. Steam 12 to 20 minutes. Omit water. (5–6 lb pressure).

Canned
1. Drain off half the liquid from can.
2. Heat long enough to bring to serving temperature or
3. Steam about 1 minute (5–6 lb pressure) or
4. Heat in 350°F oven until serving temperature is reached.

Directions for Diet Preparations

Sodium Restricted (SR): Use frozen or low sodium mixed vegetables.

Low Fat/Low Cholesterol (LF): 1/2 cup and **Diabetic** (DB): 1/2 cup. Prepare as directed.

Mechanical Soft (SFT): Prepare as directed. Consider individual tolerance.

Soft/Low Fiber (SLF): Not recommended, substitute with an appropriate food alternative.

Puree (PUR): Prepare as directed. Add liquid (i.e. broth or gravy); blenderize to obtain desired consistency.

Nutrient Analysis per Serving (Analysis is based on frozen mixed vegetables):

Regular	KCAL	PRO gm	CHO gm	FAT gm	Chol mg	SFA gm	PFA gm	VITA iu	VITC mg	THI mg	RIB mg	NIA mg	CA mg	NA mg	K+ mg	FE mg
	54.3	2.6	12.0	0.1	0.0	0.02	0.06	3936	2.9	0.06	0.11	0.7	23.0	32.2	155	0.7

Sodium Restricted	NA mg	Diabetic	Kcal	Milk exg	Veg exg	Fruit exg	Bread exg	Meat exg	Fat exg	Low Fat & Low Chol	FAT gm	Chol mg	SFA gm	PFA gm
	32.2		54.3	0.0	0.6	0.0	0.5	0.0	0.0		0.1	0.0	0.02	0.06

Portion: 1/2 cup

INGREDIENTS	50 portions		6 portions	
	weights	measures	weights	measures
Celery, fresh, chopped	6 lb EP (7 1/4 lb AP)	1 1/8 gal	12 oz EP (14 1/2 oz AP)	2 1/4 cups
Water, boiling		2 qt		1 cup
Mushrooms, canned, drained	4 lb	2 qt	8 oz	1 cup
Margarine, low sodium, melted	8 oz	1 cup	1 oz	2 Tbsp

Method

1. Wash and trim celery. Cut in diagonal slices. Boil 10 minutes or steam 4 minutes (5–6 lb pressure). Drain well.
2. Sauté mushrooms in margarine for about 2 minutes.
3. Add mushrooms and margarine to celery. Serve hot.
4. Serve with No. 8 dipper.

Directions for Diet Preparations

Sodium Restricted (SR): Use low sodium mushrooms.
Low Fat/Low Cholesterol (LF): 1/2 cup and **Diabetic** (DB): 1/2 cup. Omit margarine.
Mechanical Soft (SFT): Prepare as directed. Cook until soft and tender. Consider individual tolerance.
Soft/Low Fiber (SLF): Omit celery.
Puree (PUR): Prepare as directed. Add liquid (i.e. broth or gravy); blenderize to obtain desired consistency.

Nutrient Analysis per Serving:

Regular	KCAL	PRO gm	CHO gm	FAT gm	Chol mg	SFA gm	PFA gm	VITA iu	VITC mg	THI mg	RIB mg	NIA mg	CA mg	NA mg	K+ mg	FE mg
	47.5	0.8	3.1	3.8	0.0	0.6	1.3	208	3.4	0.03	0.09	1.2	21.3	127.3	274	0.5

Sodium Restricted	NA mg	Diabetic	Kcal	Milk exg	Veg exg	Fruit exg	Bread exg	Meat exg	Fat exg	Low Fat & Low Chol	FAT gm	Chol mg	SFA gm	PFA gm
	34.8		14.5	0.0	0.5	0.0	0.0	0.0	0.0		0.1	0.0	0.02	0.07

Okra and Tomatoes

Portion: 1/2 cup

INGREDIENTS	50 portions		6 portions	
	weights	measures	weights	measures
Okra, fresh	10 lb AP		1 1/4 lb AP	
Onions, sliced	1 lb	3 cups	2 oz	1/3 cup
Margarine, low sodium	8 oz	1 cup	1 oz	2 Tbsp
Tomatoes, diced canned	7 lb	3 1/2 qt	14 oz	1 3/4 cups
or fresh	8 lb AP	3 1/2 qt	1 lb	1 3/4 cups
Sugar, granulated	2 1/2 oz	1/3 cup	1/3 oz	2 tsp

Method

1. Cut off stems. Wash in cold water and slice in 1/2-inch pieces.
2. Simmer onions in margarine for 10 minutes.
3. Add okra, tomatoes, and sugar to onions.
4. Simmer 30 minutes or until okra is tender.
5. Portion with a No 8 dipper.

Directions for Diet Preparations

Sodium Restricted (SR): Use low sodium diced tomatoes or dice fresh tomatoes.

Low Fat/Low Cholesterol (LF): 1/2 cup. Omit margarine. Simmer onions in small amount of water until tender. Drain. Continue recipe at step #3.

Diabetic (DB): 1/2 cup. Omit margarine. Simmer onions in small amount of water until tender. Drain. Omit sugar, substitute with artificial sweetener to taste. Add okra and tomatoes to onions. Continue recipe at step #4.

Mechanical Soft (SFT): Prepare as directed. Consider individual tolerance to onions.

Soft/Low Fiber (SLF): Not recommended, substitute with an appropriate food alternative.

Puree (PUR): Prepare as directed. Add additional liquid (i.e. tomato juice); blenderize to obtain desired consistency.

Nutrient Analysis per Serving:

Regular	KCAL	PRO gm	CHO gm	FAT gm	Chol mg	SFA gm	PFA gm	VITA iu	VITC mg	THI mg	RIB mg	NIA mg	CA mg	NA mg	K+ mg	FE mg
	63.4	1.0	7.0	3.8	0.0	0.6	1.3	590	13.1	0.09	0.03	0.6	37.1	100	210	0.5

Sodium Restricted	NA mg	Diabetic	Kcal	Milk exg	Veg exg	Fruit exg	Bread exg	Meat exg	Fat exg	Low Fat & Low Chol	FAT gm	Chol mg	SFA gm	PFA gm
	4.9		27.8	0.0	1.0	0.0	0.0	0.0	0.0		0.15	0.0	0.03	0.06

Smothered Onions

Portion: 1/2 cup

INGREDIENTS	50 portions		6 portions	
	weights	measures	weights	measures
Onions, large	10 lb AP (8 3/4 lb EP)	40 medium	1 1/4 lb AP (1 1/8 lb EP)	5 medium
Margarine, low sodium, melted	8 oz	1 cup	1 oz	2 Tbsp
Water	4 oz	1/2 cup	1/2 oz	1 Tbsp

Method

1. Peel onions and cut crosswise into 1/8-inch slices. Separate into rings.
2. Combine water, margarine, and onions. Cook covered over moderate direct heat for 10 minutes or until tender, stirring occasionally.

Directions for Diet Preparations

Sodium Restricted (SR): Prepare as directed.
Low Fat/Low Cholesterol (LF): 1/2 cup and **Diabetic** (DB): 1/2 cup. Omit margarine. Low fat diets should consider individual tolerance when using onions.
Mechanical Soft (SFT): Prepare as directed. Cook until soft and tender. Consider individual tolerance.
Soft/Low Fiber (SLF) and **Puree** (PUR): Not recommended, substitute with an appropriate food alternative.

Nutrient Analysis per Serving:

Regular	KCAL	PRO gm	CHO gm	FAT gm	Chol mg	SFA gm	PFA gm	VITA iu	VITC mg	THI mg	RIB mg	NIA mg	CA mg	NA mg	K+ mg	FE mg
	62.6	0.9	6.7	3.8	0.0	0.6	1.2	152	6.0	0.05	0.01	0.08	29.9	9.7	163	0.2

Sodium Restricted	NA mg	Diabetic	Kcal	Milk exg	Veg exg	Fruit exg	Bread exg	Meat exg	Fat exg	Low Fat & Low Chol	FAT gm	Chol mg	SFA gm	PFA gm
	9.7		29.7	0.0	1.0	0.0	0.0	0.0	0.0		0.1	0.0	0.02	0.06

Green Peas

Portion: 1/2 cup

INGREDIENTS	50 portions		6 portions	
	weights	measures	weights	measures
Fresh Green Peas	25 lb AP		3 1/8 lb AP	
Green peas, ready-to-cook weight	12 1/2 lb	1 3/4 gal	1 1/2 lb	3 1/2 cups
Water, boiling		2 qt		1 cup
or				
Frozen Green Peas	12 lb	2 gal	1 1/2 lb	1 qt
Water, boiling		1 qt		1/2 cup
or				
Canned Green Peas	10 lb	2 #10 cans (1 1/2 gal)	1 1/4 lb	3 cups

Method

Fresh
1. Shell and rinse.
2. Boil peas 10 to 20 minutes or
3. Steam peas 10 to 20 minutes. Omit water. (5–6 lb pressure).

Frozen
1. Boil 5–10 minutes or
2. Steam 3 to 5 minutes. Omit water. (5–6 lb pressure).

Canned
1. Drain off half the liquid from can.
2. Heat long enough to bring to serving temperature or
3. Steam about 1 minute (5–6 lb pressure) or
4. Heat in 350°F oven until serving temperature is reached.

Directions for Diet Preparations

Sodium Restricted (SR), **Low Fat/Low Cholesterol** (LF), 1/2 cup, **Diabetic** (DB): 1/2 cup, and **Mechanical Soft** (SFT): Prepare as directed.

Soft/Low Fiber (SLF): Not recommended, substitute with an appropriate food alternative.

Puree (PUR): Prepare as directed. Add liquid (i.e. broth or garvy); blenderize to obtain desired consistency.

Nutrient Analysis per Serving (Analysis based on fresh green peas):

Regular	KCAL	PRO gm	CHO gm	FAT gm	Chol mg	SFA gm	PFA gm	VITA iu	VITC mg	THI mg	RIB mg	NIA mg	CA mg	NA mg	K+ mg	FE mg
	68.0	4.3	12.6	0.1	0.0	0.03	0.08	484	11.5	0.2	0.12	1.6	21.8	2.4	219	1.2

Sodium Restricted	NA mg	Diabetic	Kcal	Milk exg	Veg exg	Fruit exg	Bread exg	Meat exg	Fat exg	Low Fat & Low Chol	FAT gm	Chol mg	SFA gm	PFA gm
	2.4		68.0	0.0	0.0	0.0	0.9	0.0	0.02		0.1	0.0	0.03	0.08

Seasoned Green Peas

Portion: 1/2 cup

INGREDIENTS	50 portions		6 portions	
	weights	measures	weights	measures
Green peas, frozen	12 lb	2 gal	1 1/2 lb	1 qt
Water, boiling		1 qt		1/2 cup
Thyme		2 Tbsp		3/4 tsp
Margarine, low sodium, melted	4 oz	1/2 cup	1/2 oz	1 Tbsp

Method

1. Boil peas in boiling water for 5 to 10 minutes.
2. Season with thyme.
3. Add melted margarine. Toss lightly.
4. Serve with No. 8 dipper.

Directions for Diet Preparations

Sodium Restricted (SR): Use low sodium peas.
Low Fat/Low Cholesterol (LF): 1/2 cup and **Diabetic** (DB): 1/2 cup. Omit margarine.
Mechanical Soft (SFT): Prepare as directed. Consider individual tolerance.
Soft/Low Fiber (SLF): Not recommended, substitute with an appropriate food alternative.
Puree (PUR): Prepare as directed. Add liquid (i.e. broth or gravy); blenderize to obtain desired consistency.

Nutrient Analysis per Serving:

Regular	KCAL	PRO gm	CHO gm	FAT gm	Chol mg	SFA gm	PFA gm	VITA iu	VITC mg	THI mg	RIB mg	NIA mg	CA mg	NA mg	K+ mg	FE mg
	80.1	4.2	11.7	2.1	0.0	0.3	0.7	623	8.0	0.23	0.08	1.2	23.3	71.1	138	1.4

Sodium Restricted	NA mg	Diabetic	Kcal	Milk exg	Veg exg	Fruit exg	Bread exg	Meat exg	Fat exg	Low Fat & Low Chol	FAT gm	Chol mg	SFA gm	PFA gm
	3.1		63.6	0.0	0.0	0.0	0.9	0.0	0.0		0.2	0.0	0.04	0.1

Potatoes

Portion: 1/2 cup (one small)

INGREDIENTS	50 portions		6 portions	
	weights	measures	weights	measures
Fresh Potatoes				
whole, ready-to-cook weight or	12 1/2 lb AP	50 small	1 2/3 lb	6 small
diced, ready-to-cook weight or	10 lb	1 3/4 gal	1 1/4 lb	3 1/2 cups
sliced, ready-to-cook weight or	10 lb	1 3/4 gal	1 1/4 lb	3 1/2 cups
for mashing	11 3/4 lb	1 1/2 gal	1 1/2 lb	3 cups
Water, boiling		1 1/4 gal		2 1/2 cups
or				
Canned, small, whole or sliced	10 lb	2 #10 cans	1 1/4 lb	3 cups

Method

Fresh
1. Wash, scrubbing with vegetable brush. Cook in skins or pare and remove eyes. Cut into serving size.
2. Boil 30 to 40 minutes or
3. Steam 30 to 45 minutes. Omit water, (5–6 lb pressure).

Canned
1. Heat long enough to bring to serving temperature or
2. Steam about 1 minute (5–6 lb pressure) or
3. Heat in 350°F oven until serving temperature is reached.

Directions for Diet Preparations

Sodium Restricted (SR), **Low Fat/Low Cholesterol** (LF): 1/2 cup or 1 small and **Diabetic** (DB): 1/2 cup or 1 small. Prepare as directed.

Mechanical Soft (SFT) and **Soft/Low Fiber** (SLF): Remove skin.

Puree (PUR): Remove skin. Add liquid (i.e. broth or gravy); blenderize to obtain desired consistency.

Nutrient Analysis per Serving (Analysis is based on fresh potatoes):

Regular	KCAL	PRO gm	CHO gm	FAT gm	Chol mg	SFA gm	PFA gm	VITA iu	VITC mg	THI mg	RIB mg	NIA mg	CA mg	NA mg	K+ mg	FE mg
	87.0	1.7	20.2	0.1	0.0	0.02	0.04	0.0	7.4	0.09	0.01	1.3	8.1	5.0	331	0.3

Sodium Restricted	NA mg	Diabetic	Kcal	Milk exg	Veg exg	Fruit exg	Bread exg	Meat exg	Fat exg	Low Fat & Low Chol	FAT gm	Chol mg	SFA gm	PFA gm
	5.0		87.0	0.0	0.0	0.0	1.1	0.0	0.0		0.1	0.0	0.02	0.04

J34   Red Bliss Potatoes

Portion: 4 ounces (2 to 3 small)

INGREDIENTS	50 portions		6 portions	
	weights	measures	weights	measures
Potatoes, red skinned	12 1/2 lb AP	100–150 small	1 1/2 lb AP	12–18 small
Margarine, low sodium, melted	8 oz	1 cup	1 oz	2 Tbsp
Rosemary		2 Tbsp		3/4 tsp

Method

1. Wash potatoes. Remove eyes.
2. Leave potatoes whole. If necessary cut potatoes to a uniform size.
3. Steam or boil until tender.
4. Distribute margarine uniformly over cooked potatoes.
5. Sprinkle rosemary over potatoes and toss lightly.

Steam

a. 5–6 lb per batch at 12–15 psi for 5 to 6 minutes.

Boil

a. Add potatoes to 3 qt boiling water. Cover and bring water quickly back to a boil.
b. Continue boiling 30 to 40 minutes or until potatoes are tender.
c. Drain and place in serving pans.

Directions for Diet Preparations

Sodium Restricted (SR): Prepare as directed.
Low Fat/Low Cholesterol (LF): 3 oz and **Diabetic** (DB): 3 oz. Omit margarine.
Mechanical Soft (SFT) and **Soft/Low Fiber** (SLF): Remove skin.
Puree (PUR): Remove skin. Add liquid (i.e. sauce or gravy); blenderize to obtain desired consistency.

Nutrient Analysis per Serving:

Regular	KCAL	PRO gm	CHO gm	FAT gm	Chol mg	SFA gm	PFA gm	VITA iu	VITC mg	THI mg	RIB mg	NIA mg	CA mg	NA mg	K+ mg	FE mg
	99.1	2.4	14.7	3.7	0.0	0.6	1.3	154.0	4.5	0.03	0.03	1.04	41.1	13.2	349	5.2

Sodium Restricted	NA mg	Diabetic	Kcal	Milk exg	Veg exg	Fruit exg	Bread exg	Meat exg	Fat exg	Low Fat & Low Chol	FAT gm	Chol mg	SFA gm	PFA gm
	13.2		66.6	0.0	0.0	0.0	0.9	0.0	0.0		0.0	0.02	0.03	0.0

Baked Potato

Portion: one medium

INGREDIENTS	50 portions		6 portions	
	weights	measures	weights	measures
Baking potatoes, uniform size	17 lb	50 medium	2 lb	6 medium

Method

1. Scrub potatoes and remove blemishes.
2. Place on baking pan(s). Bake at 400°F for 1 to 1 1/2 hours or until soft.

Directions for Diet Preparations

Sodium Restricted (SR), **Low Fat/Low Cholesterol** (LF): one medium, and **Diabetic** (DB): one small. Prepare as directed.

Mechanical Soft (SFT) and **Soft/Low Fiber** (SLF): Remove skin.

Puree (PUR): Remove skin. Add liquid (i.e. broth or gravy); blenderize to obtain desired consistency.

Nutrient Analysis per Serving:

Regular	KCAL	PRO gm	CHO gm	FAT gm	Chol mg	SFA gm	PFA gm	VITA iu	VITC mg	THI mg	RIB mg	NIA mg	CA mg	NA mg	K+ mg	FE mg
	147	3.1	34	0.1	0.0	0.03	0.06	trace	17	0.14	0.04	2.2	13	11	563	1.8

Sodium Restricted	NA mg	Diabetic	Kcal	Milk exg	Veg exg	Fruit exg	Bread exg	Meat exg	Fat exg	Low Fat & Low Chol	FAT gm	Chol mg	SFA gm	PFA gm
	11		87	0.0	0.0	0.0	1.0	0.0	0.0		0.1	0.0	0.03	0.06

Home Fried Potatoes

Portion: 1/2 cup

INGREDIENTS	50 portions		6 portions	
	weights	**measures**	**weights**	**measures**
Potatoes, white	17 lb AP	50 medium	2 lb AP	6 medium
Margarine, low sodium, melted	12 oz	1 1/2 cups	1 1/2 oz	3 Tbsp
Paprika		2 tsp		1/4 tsp

Method

1. Peel and cut potatoes, 1/8-inch slices.
2. Place potatoes in greased shallow pans in a thin layer.
3. Brush potatoes with melted margarine, turn to cover all sides.
4. Sprinkle with paprika.
5. Bake at 450°F for 20 to 30 minutes, or until golden brown, turn once or twice for even browning.

Directions for Diet Preparations

Sodium Restricted (SR): Prepare as directed.
Low Fat/Low Cholesterol (LF): 1/2 cup and **Diabetic** (DB): 1/2 cup. Use margarine in one-third the amount specified. May use if able to calculate into daily food plan.
Mechanical Soft (SFT) and **Soft/Low Fiber** (SLF): Prepare as directed.
Puree (PUR): Prepare as directed. Add liquid (i.e. broth or gravy); blenderize to obtain desired consistency.

Nutrient Analysis per Serving:

Regular	KCAL	PRO gm	CHO gm	FAT gm	Chol mg	SFA gm	PFA gm	VITA iu	VITC mg	THI mg	RIB mg	NIA mg	CA mg	NA mg	K+ mg	FE mg
	118	1.4	15.9	5.6	0.0	0.9	1.9	284	5.9	0.07	0.01	1.0	8.3	5.8	263	0.2

Sodium Restricted	NA mg	Diabetic	Kcal	Milk exg	Veg exg	Fruit exg	Bread exg	Meat exg	Fat exg	Low Fat & Low Chol	FAT gm	Chol mg	SFA gm	PFA gm
	5.8		84.6	0.0	0.0	0.0	1.0	0.0	0.2		1.9	0.0	0.3	0.6

Portion: 1/2 cup

Ingredients	50 portions		6 portions	
	weights	measures	weights	measures
Potatoes, pared, cut into uniform size pieces	12 lb EP (15 lb AP)	2 gal (36 medium)	1 1/2 lb EP (1 1/2 lb AP)	1 qt (4 1/2 medium)
Milk, skim, hot		2 qt		1 cup
Margarine, low sodium, melted	8 oz	1 cup	1 oz	2 Tbsp

Method

1. Steam or boil potatoes.
2. When done, drain and mash in mixer on low speed until smooth.
3. Whip at high speed about 2 minutes.
4. Add milk and margarine. Mix.
5. Portion with a No. 8 dipper.

Notes

[1]May use instant mashed potatoes. Read manufacturer's directions for preparation. Read label, not all modified diets will be allowed to use instant mashed potatoes.

Directions for Diet Preparations

Sodium Restricted (SR), **Mechanical Soft** (SFT), **Soft/Low Fiber** (SLF), and **Puree** (PUR): Prepare as directed.

Low Fat/Low Cholesterol (LF): 1/2 cup and **Diabetic** (DB): 1/2 cup. Omit margarine.

Nutrient Analysis per Serving:

Regular	KCAL	PRO gm	CHO gm	FAT gm	Chol mg	SFA gm	PFA gm	VITA iu	VITC mg	THI mg	RIB mg	NIA mg	CA mg	NA mg	K+ mg	FE mg
	114	2.7	17.8	3.8	0.6	0.7	1.3	230	6.3	0.09	0.07	1.1	55.8	25.3	326	0.3

Sodium Restricted	NA mg	Diabetic	Kcal	Milk exg	Veg exg	Fruit exg	Bread exg	Meat exg	Fat exg	Low Fat & Low Chol	FAT gm	Chol mg	SFA gm	PFA gm
	25.3		82	0.0	0.0	0.0	1.1	0.0	0.0		0.1	0.6	0.07	0.04

Portion: 1/2 cup (4 ounces)

INGREDIENTS	50 portions		6 portions	
	weights	measures	weights	measures
Potatoes, cut into 1 1/2 inch cubes	12 1/2 lb EP (15 1/2 lb AP)	2 gal	1 1/2 lb EP (1 3/4 lb AP)	1 qt
Water, boiling		to cover		to cover
Margarine, low sodium, #1	8 oz	1 cup	1 oz	2 Tbsp
Onions, chopped	10 2/3 oz	2 cups	1 1/3 oz	1/4 cup
Red pepper, chopped	5 1/3 oz	1 cup	3/4 oz	2 Tbsp
Margarine, low sodium, #2	4 oz	1/2 cup	1/2 oz	1 Tbsp

Method

1. Cover potatoes in boiling water, simmer 15 to 20 minutes or until tender, drain well.
2. Heat margarine #1 in roasting pan. Put potatoes in pan.
3. Bake at 450°F for 20 to 25 minutes stirring about every 5 minutes, until potatoes are browned.
4. Sauté onions and red pepper in margarine #2 until onions are golden.
5. Add onions and red peppers to potatoes about 5 minutes before they are finished cooking.

Directions for Diet Preparations

Sodium Restricted (SR): Prepare as directed.

Low Fat/Low Cholesterol (LF): 1/2 cup and **Diabetic** (DB): 1/2 cup. Omit margarine #1. Use margarine #2 in half the amount specified. Boil onions and red pepper in water until tender. Low fat diets should consider individual tolerance to onions.

Mechanical Soft (SFT) and **Soft/Low Fiber** (SLF): Omit onions. Sauté red pepper until soft and tender. Consider individual tolerance.

Puree (PUR): Prepare as directed. Add liquid (i.e. broth or gravy) to potatoes; blenderize to obtain desired consistency.

Nutrient Analysis per Serving:

Regular	KCAL	PRO gm	CHO gm	FAT gm	Chol mg	SFA gm	PFA gm	VITA iu	VITC mg	THI mg	RIB mg	NIA mg	CA mg	NA mg	K+ mg	FE mg
	121	1.6	16.5	5.6	0.0	0.9	1.8	237.7	13.4	0.09	0.02	1.1	7.5	5.2	316	0.3

Sodium Restricted	NA mg	Diabetic	Kcal	Milk exg	Veg exg	Fruit exg	Bread exg	Meat exg	Fat exg	Low Fat & Low Chol	FAT gm	Chol mg	SFA gm	PFA gm
	5.2		79.5	0.0	0.0	0.0	1.0	0.0	0.1		1.0	0.0	0.2	0.3

Oven Browned Potatoes

Portion: one medium potato or 4 quarters

Ingredients	50 portions[1]		6 portions[2]	
	weights	measures	weights	measures
Potatoes, peeled, cut into quarters	17 lb AP (13 1/2 lb EP)	50 medium	2 lb AP (1 3/4 lb EP)	6 medium
Margarine, low sodium, melted	8 oz	1 cup	1 oz	2 Tbsp
Paprika		1 Tbsp		1/4 tsp

Method

1. Place in greased or non-stick baking pan.[3]
2. Pour margarine over potatoes. Sprinkle with paprika.
3. Turn potatoes so that all sides are coated with margarine.
4. Bake at 425°F oven for about 1 hour or until tender and well browned.
5. Turn potatoes once during baking for even browning.

Directions for Diet Preparations

Sodium Restricted (SR), **Mechanical Soft** (SFT), and **Soft/Low Fiber** (SLF): Prepare as directed.

Low Fat/Low Cholesterol (LF): 1 small potato and **Diabetic** (DB): 1 small potato. Use margarine in half the amount specified.

Puree (PUR): Prepare as directed. Add liquid (i.e. broth or gravy); blenderize to obtain desired consistency.

Notes

[1]50 portions: May use canned new potatoes (2 #10 cans) instead of fresh potatoes.
[2]6 portions: May use 1 2/3 lb canned new potatoes instead of fresh potatoes.
[3]Potatoes can be boiled 10 minutes and drained before baking in order to shorten the baking time.

Nutrient Analysis per Serving:

Regular	KCAL	PRO gm	CHO gm	FAT gm	Chol mg	SFA gm	PFA gm	VITA iu	VITC mg	THI mg	RIB mg	NIA mg	CA mg	NA mg	K+ mg	FE mg
	120	1.7	20.3	3.7	0.0	0.6	1.2	234	7.5	0.1	0.02	1.3	9.5	6.3	336	0.3

Sodium Restricted	NA mg	Diabetic	Kcal	Milk exg	Veg exg	Fruit exg	Bread exg	Meat exg	Fat exg	Low Fat & Low Chol	FAT gm	Chol mg	SFA gm	PFA gm
	6.3		95.5	0.0	0.0	0.0	1.2	0.0	0.2		1.0	0.0	0.2	0.3

Potato Pancakes

Portion: 2, 2 ounce pancakes (3 inches each)

INGREDIENTS	60 portions		10 portions	
	weights	measures	weights	measures
Potatoes	10 lb AP	30 medium	1 3/4 lb AP	5 medium
Onions	2 3/4 lb AP	4 large	7 1/3 oz AP	1 medium
Eggs, beaten	1 1/2 lb	3 cups (12 large)	4 oz	1/2 cup (2 large)
Flour, all-purpose	3 oz	3/4 cup	1/2 oz	2 Tbsp
Vegetable oil		for frying		for frying

Method

1. Peel potatoes.
2. Shred or grate potatoes. Drain well.
3. Grate onions.
4. Mix onions and potatoes. Drain well.
5. Combine all ingredients. Mix lightly. Allow to set for 5 minutes.
6. Drop potato mixture with No. 20 dipper on hot greased griddle.
7. Fry until browned on both sides.
8. May be served with applesauce.

Notes

[1]60 portions: May use 1 cup matzo meal, instead of flour.
[2]10 portions: May use 2 2/3 Tbsp matzo meal, instead of flour.
[3]May be served with applesauce.

Directions for Diet Preparations

Sodium Restricted (SR): Prepare as directed.
Low Fat/Low Cholesterol (LF): 2 oz. Omit eggs, substitute with an equal measure of egg whites or a commercial egg substitute. Omit steps #6 and #7. Drop potato mixture with No. 20 dipper in non-stick baking pan. Bake in oven at 350°F for 30 to 45 minutes or until golden brown on both sides.
Diabetic (DB): 2 oz. Omit steps #6 and #7. Drop potato mixture with No. 20 dipper in non-stick baking pan. Bake in oven at 350°F for 30 to 45 minutes or until golden brown on both sides.
Mechanical Soft (SFT): Prepare as directed. Consider individual tolerance.
Soft/Low Fiber (SLF): Omit onions.
Puree (PUR): Prepare as directed. Add liquid (i.e. broth or gravy) to pancakes; blenderize to obtain desired consistency.

Nutrient Analysis per Serving:

Regular	KCAL	PRO gm	CHO gm	FAT gm	Chol mg	SFA gm	PFA gm	VITA iu	VITC mg	THI mg	RIB mg	NIA mg	CA mg	NA mg	K+ mg	FE mg
	171	2.8	17.3	10.4	54.6	1.5	5.5	51.9	6.7	0.1	0.05	1.0	15.2	17.8	282	0.5

Sodium Restricted	NA mg	Diabetic	Kcal	Milk exg	Veg exg	Fruit exg	Bread exg	Meat exg	Fat exg	Low Fat & Low Chol	FAT gm	Chol mg	SFA gm	PFA gm
	17.8		90.6	0.0	0.0	0.0	1.0	0.0	0.4		0.5	0.1	0.1	0.2

Parsley Potatoes

Portion: 3 ounces (one small or 1/2 cup cubed)

INGREDIENTS	50 portions		6 portions	
	weights	measures	weights	measures
Potatoes, small or	12 1/2 lbs AP	50 small	1 2/3 lb	6 small
cubed	10 lb EP	1 3/4 gal	1 1/4 lb	3 1/2 cups
Margarine, low sodium, melted	8 oz	1 cup	1 oz	2 Tbsp
Parsley, chopped	1 oz	3/4 cup	1/8 oz	1 1/2 Tbsp

Method

1. Wash and peel potatoes. Remove eyes.
2. Cut potatoes into 1 1/2-inch cubes or leave whole.
3. Steam or boil potatoes until tender.
4. Pour margarine over potatoes, distribute uniformly.
5. Sprinkle with parsley.

Directions for Diet Preparations

Sodium Restricted (SR), **Mechanical Soft** (SFT), and **Soft/Low Fiber** (SLF): Prepare as directed.
Low Fat/Low Cholesterol (LF): 3 oz (or 1/2 cup) and **Diabetic** (DB): 3 oz (or 1/2 cup). Omit margarine.
Puree (PUR): Prepare as directed. Add liquid (i.e. broth or gravy) to potatoes; blenderize to obtain desired consistency.

Nutrient Analysis per Serving:

Regular	KCAL	PRO gm	CHO gm	FAT gm	Chol mg	SFA gm	PFA gm	VITA iu	VITC mg	THI mg	RIB mg	NIA mg	CA mg	NA mg	K+ mg	FE mg
	111	1.6	18.2	3.7	0.0	0.6	1.2	199	7.5	0.09	0.02	1.2	9.6	6.1	303	0.3

Sodium Restricted	NA mg	Diabetic	Kcal	Milk exg	Veg exg	Fruit exg	Bread exg	Meat exg	Fat exg	Low Fat & Low Chol	FAT gm	Chol mg	SFA gm	PFA gm
	6.1		73.3	0.0	0.0	0.0	1.0	0.0	0.0		0.08	0.0	0.02	0.03

Portion: 4 ounces (2 rosettes)

INGREDIENTS	50 portions		6 portions	
	weights	measures	weights	measures
Potatoes, pared, cut into	12 lb EP	2 gal	1 1/2 lb EP	1 qt
uniform size pieces	(15 lb AP)	(36 medium)	(1 3/4 lb AP)	(4 1/2 medium)
Milk, skim, hot		1 3/4 qt		3/4 cup
Margarine, low sodium, melted	8 oz	1 cup	1 oz	2 Tbsp
Eggs, beaten	2 1/4 lb	1 1/8 qt	6 oz	3/4 cup
		(18 large)		(3 large)

Method

1. Steam or boil potatoes.[1]
2. When done, drain and mash in mixer on low speed until smooth.
3. Whip at high speed about 2 minutes.
4. Add milk, margarine, and eggs. Mix. Add additional milk if necessary to obtain desired consistency.
5. Put potato mixture into pastry tube and bag out into rosettes, about 1 1/2-inches in diameter and 1-inch high.
6. Bake at 350°F for about 15 minutes or until lightly browned.

Directions for Diet Preparations

Sodium Restricted (SR): Prepare as directed.

Low Fat/Low Cholesterol (LF): 3 oz. Use margarine in half the amount specified. Omit eggs, replace with commercial egg substitute as per manufacturer's directions.

Diabetic (DB): 3 oz. Use margarine in half the amount specified.

Mechanical Soft (SFT) and **Soft/Low Fiber** (SLF): Prepare as directed.

Puree (PUR): Prepare as directed. Mash potatoes when serving.

Notes

[1]May substitute instant mashed potatoes for potatoes, milk, and margarine. Follow manufacturer's directions for preparation. Read label, not all modified diets will be allowed.

Nutrient Analysis per Serving:

Regular	KCAL	PRO gm	CHO gm	FAT gm	Chol mg	SFA gm	PFA gm	VITA iu	VITC mg	THI mg	RIB mg	NIA mg	CA mg	NA mg	K+ mg	FE mg
	152	5.7	21.3	5.1	66.9	1.2	1.5	354	6.7	0.1	0.16	1.2	119	111	416	0.6

Sodium Restricted	NA mg	Diabetic	Kcal	Milk exg	Veg exg	Fruit exg	Bread exg	Meat exg	Fat exg	Low Fat & Low Chol	FAT gm	Chol mg	SFA gm	PFA gm
	111		96.0	0.3	0.0	0.0	0.75	0.4	0.4		1.3	1.1	0.3	0.5

Whipped Potatoes

Portion: 1/2 cup

INGREDIENTS	50 portions		6 portions	
	weights	**measures**	**weights**	**measures**
Potatoes[1]	15 lb AP (12 lb EP)	36 medium	1 3/4 lb AP (1 1/2 lb EP)	4 1/2 medium
Margarine, low sodium, melted	8 oz	1 cup	1 oz	2 Tbsp
Pepper, white		2 tsp		1/4 tsp

Method

1. Peel and eye potatoes. Cut in uniform size.
2. Steam or boil potatoes. Drain.
3. Mash in mixer on low speed until smooth. Whip at high speed about 2 minutes.
4. Add margarine and pepper. Whip on high for about 1 to 3 minutes or until light and fluffy.
5. Pour into greased pans. Cover and bake at 350°F for 20 minutes or until thoroughly heated.
6. Portion with a No. 8 dipper.

Notes

[1]May use instant mashed potatoes to make whipped potatoes. Read manufacturer's directions for preparation. Not all modified diets are allowed instant mashed potatoes. Read the label for ingredients listed.

Directions for Diet Preparations

Sodium Restricted (SR), **Mechanical Soft** (SFT), and **Puree** (PUR): Prepare as directed.
Low Fat/Low Cholesterol (LF): 1/2 cup and **Diabetic** (DB): 1/2 cup. Omit margarine, substitute with reduced-calorie margarine in half the amount specified for regular margarine. May need additional liquid (i.e chicken broth) to obtain desired consistency.
Soft/Low Fiber (SLF): Omit pepper.

Nutrient Analysis per Serving:

Regular	KCAL	PRO gm	CHO gm	FAT gm	Chol mg	SFA gm	PFA gm	VITA iu	VITC mg	THI mg	RIB mg	NIA mg	CA mg	NA mg	K+ mg	FE mg
	101	1.3	15.8	3.7	0.0	0.6	1.2	152	5.8	0.07	0.01	1.0	7.6	5.2	260	0.2

Sodium Restricted	NA mg	Diabetic	Kcal	Milk exg	Veg exg	Fruit exg	Bread exg	Meat exg	Fat exg	Low Fat & Low Chol	FAT gm	Chol mg	SFA gm	PFA gm
	5.2		84.5	0.0	0.0	0.0	1.0	0.0	0.1		1.9	0.0	0.3	0.6

Baked Sweet Potato

Portion: one small potato (4 ounces)

INGREDIENTS	50 portions		6 portions	
	weights	measures	weights	measures
Sweet potatoes, similar in size	13 lb AP	50 small	1 1/2 lb AP	6 small

Method

1. Scrub potatoes thoroughly. Remove blemishes. Pierce in two places.
2. Place on greased baking pans.
3. Bake at 425°F for 45 minutes or until tender.
4. Remove from oven and cut a short cross-shaped gash in each. Press potatoes to open slightly after cutting.

Directions for Diet Preparations

Sodium Restricted (SR), **Low Fat/Low Cholesterol** (LF): 1 small, and **Diabetic** (DB): 1/2 small. Prepare as directed.

Mechanical Soft (SFT) and **Soft/Low Fiber** (SLF): Remove skin.

Puree (PUR): Remove skin. Add liquid (i.e. apple juice or gravy); blenderize to obtain desired consistency.

Nutrient Analysis per Serving:

Regular	KCAL	PRO gm	CHO gm	FAT gm	Chol mg	SFA gm	PFA gm	VITA iu	VITC mg	THI mg	RIB mg	NIA mg	CA mg	NA mg	K+ mg	FE mg
	116	1.9	27.5	0.1	0.0	0.02	0.05	24722	27.8	0.08	0.14	0.68	31.7	11.3	394	0.5

Sodium Restricted	NA mg	Diabetic	Kcal	Milk exg	Veg exg	Fruit exg	Bread exg	Meat exg	Fat exg	Low Fat & Low Chol	FAT gm	Chol mg	SFA gm	PFA gm
	11.3		58.4	0.0	0.0	0.0	0.8	0.0	0.0		0.1	0.0	0.02	0.05

Sweet Potatoes with Apples

Portion: 1/2 cup

INGREDIENTS	50 portions[1]		6 portions[2]	
	weights	**measures**	**weights**	**measures**
Apples, tart, pared, sliced	3 lb EP (4 lb AP)	3 qt	6 oz EP (8 oz AP)	1 1/2 cup
Yams or sweet potatoes, canned in water	10 lb	2 #10 cans	1 1/4 lb	3 cups
Sugar, brown packed	1 lb	2 cups	2 oz	1/4 cup
Margarine, low sodium, melted	8 oz	1 cup	1 oz	2 Tbsp
Water		1/2 cup		1 Tbsp

Method

1. Place apples in greased baking pans.
2. Drain yams or sweet potatoes.
3. Cover apples with sweet potatoes.
4. Combine brown sugar, margarine, and water. Mix 1 minute at low speed.
5. Pour brown sugar syrup over sweet potatoes and apples.
6. Bake at 350°F for 1 hour or until lightly browned and hot.

Notes

[1]50 portions: May use fresh sweet potatoes (11 lb AP or 33 medium). Peel, slice, and cook.
[2]6 portions: May use fresh sweet potatoes (1 1/3 lb AP or 4 medium). Peel, slice, and cook.

Directions for Diet Preparations

Sodium Restricted (SR): Prepare as directed.
Low Fat/Low Cholesterol (LF): 1/2 cup.
50 portions: Omit margarine. Increase water to 1 1/2 cups.
6 portions: Omit margarine. Increase water to 3 Tbsp.
Diabetic (DB): 1/3 cup.
50 portions: Omit brown sugar. Use artificial sweetener equal to 2 cups granular sugar (follow manufacturer's directions). Omit margarine. Increase water to 1 1/2 cups.
6 portions: Omit brown sugar. Use artificial sweetener equal to 1/4 cup granular sugar (follow manufacturer's directions). Omit margarine. Increase water to 3 Tbsp.
Mechanical Soft (SFT) and **Soft/Low Fiber** (SLF): Prepare as directed. Consider individual tolerance.
Puree (PUR): Prepare as directed. Blenderize. Add additional liquid if necessary to obtain desired consistency.

Nutrient Analysis per Serving:

Regular	KCAL	PRO gm	CHO gm	FAT gm	Chol mg	SFA gm	PFA gm	VITA iu	VITC mg	THI mg	RIB mg	NIA mg	CA mg	NA mg	K+ mg	FE mg
	171	1.5	33.4	4.0	0.0	0.7	1.3	14864	15.8	0.05	0.12	0.59	27.9	15.1	221	0.8

Sodium Restricted	NA mg	Diabetic	Kcal	Milk exg	Veg exg	Fruit exg	Bread exg	Meat exg	Fat exg	Low Fat & Low Chol	FAT gm	Chol mg	SFA gm	PFA gm
	15.1		72	0.0	0.0	0.2	0.8	0.0	0.0		0.3	0.0	0.06	0.1

Portion: 1/2 cup

INGREDIENTS	50 portions		6 portions	
	weights	measures	weights	measures
Sweet potatoes, canned and drained or	14 lb	1 3/4 gal	1 3/4 lb	3 1/2 cups
Sweet potatoes, raw, peeled	15 lb AP (10 lb EP)	45 medium	2 lb AP (1 1/3 lb EP)	6 medium
Margarine, low sodium, melted	1 lb	2 cups	2 oz	1/4 cup
Nutmeg, ground		2 tsp		1/4 tsp

Method

1. Steam or boil potatoes. Drain.
2. Place in mixer and whip.
3. Add margarine and nutmeg and whip for 2 minutes or until fluffy.
4. Pour into greased pan(s). Cover and bake at 350°F for 20 minutes or until heated.

Directions for Diet Preparations

Sodium Restricted (SR), **Mechanical Soft** (SFT), **Soft/Low Fiber** (SLF), and **Puree** (PUR): Prepare as directed.

Low Fat/Low Cholesterol (LF): 1/2 cup and **Diabetic** (DB): 1/3 cup.

50 portions: Omit margarine, substitute 12 ounces reduced-calorie margarine.

6 portions: Omit margarine, substitute 1 1/2 ounces reduced-calorie margarine.

Nutrient Analysis per Serving:

Regular	KCAL	PRO gm	CHO gm	FAT gm	Chol mg	SFA gm	PFA gm	VITA iu	VITC mg	THI mg	RIB mg	NIA mg	CA mg	NA mg	K+ mg	FE mg
	177	1.8	26.1	7.6	0.0	1.3	2.2	596	18.3	0.06	0.15	0.7	25.1	16.5	201	0.6

Sodium Restricted	NA mg	Diabetic	Kcal	Milk exg	Veg exg	Fruit exg	Bread exg	Meat exg	Fat exg	Low Fat & Low Chol	FAT gm	Chol mg	SFA gm	PFA gm
	16.5		82	0.0	0.0	0.0	0.9	0.0	0.3		2.9	0.0	0.6	0.9

Spinach

Portion: 1/2 cup

INGREDIENTS	50 portions		6 portions	
	weights	**measures**	**weights**	**measures**
Fresh spinach	2 1/3 lb AP		4 2/3 oz AP	
Spinach, ready-to-cook weight	2 lb EP	1 2/3 gal	4 oz EP	3 cups
Water, boiling		clinging to leaves		clinging to leaves
or				
Frozen spinach	13 lb	1 3/4 gal	1 2/3 lb	3 1/2 cups
Water, boiling		1 qt		1/2 cup
or				
Canned spinach	12 1/2 lb	1 2/3 gal	1 2/3 lb	3 1/2 cups

Method

Fresh
1. Sort and trim. Cut off tough stems and roots. Wash thoroughly, at least 5 times. Discard damaged leaves.
2. Boil spinach 10 to 20 minutes or
3. Steam 4 to 8 minutes. Omit water. (5–6 lb pressure).

Frozen
1. Boil 5–10 minutes or
2. Steam 5–10 minutes. Omit water. (5–6 lb pressure).

Canned
1. Drain off half the liquid from can.
2. Heat long enough to bring to serving temperature or
3. Steam about 1 minute (5–6 lb pressure) or
4. Heat in 350°F oven until serving temperature is reached.

Directions for Diet Preparations

Sodium Restricted (SR), **Low Fat/Low Cholesterol** (LF), 1/2 cup, **Diabetic** (DB) 1/2 cup and **Soft/Low Fiber** (SLF): Prepare as directed.

Mechanical Soft (SFT): Prepare as directed. Chop.

Puree (PUR): Prepare as directed. Add liquid (i.e. broth or gravy); blenderize to obtain desired consistency.

Nutrient Analysis per Serving (Analysis is based on frozen spinach):

Regular	KCAL	PRO gm	CHO gm	FAT gm	Chol mg	SFA gm	PFA gm	VITA iu	VITC mg	THI mg	RIB mg	NIA mg	CA mg	NA mg	K+ mg	FE mg
	21	2.7	3.4	0.2	0.0	0.03	0.1	7464	8.9	0.09	0.21	0.4	124	63.8	425	3.2

Sodium Restricted	NA mg	Diabetic	Kcal	Milk exg	Veg exg	Fruit exg	Bread exg	Meat exg	Fat exg	Low Fat & Low Chol	FAT gm	Chol mg	SFA gm	PFA gm
	63.8		21	0.0	0.7	0.0	0.0	0.0	0.0		0.2	0.0	0.03	0.1

Herbed Seasoned Spinach

Portion: 1/2 cup

INGREDIENTS	50 portions		6 portions	
	weights	measures	weights	measures
Spinach, frozen, chopped	12 1/2 lb	1 2/3 gal	1 2/3 lb	3 1/2 cups
Water, boiling		1 qt		1/2 cup
Thyme		1 Tbsp		1/4 tsp
Oregano, ground		1 Tbsp		1/4 tsp

Method

1. Boil or steam spinach for 5 to 10 minutes. Drain water.
2. Add seasonings. Mix to blend.
3. Serve with a No. 8 scoop.

Directions for Diet Preparations

Sodium Restricted (SR); Use fresh spinach or sodium restricted canned or frozen spinach.

Low Fat/Low Cholesterol (LF): 1/2 cup, **Diabetic** (DB): 1/2 cup, and **Soft/Low Fiber** (SLF): Prepare as directed.

Mechanical Soft (SFT): Prepare as directed. Chop.

Puree (PUR): Prepare as directed. Add liquid (i.e. broth or gravy) to spinach; blenderize to obtain desired consistency.

Nutrient Analysis per Serving (Analysis is based on frozen spinach):

Regular	KCAL	PRO gm	CHO gm	FAT gm	Chol mg	SFA gm	PFA gm	VITA iu	VITC mg	THI mg	RIB mg	NIA mg	CA mg	NA mg	K+ mg	FE mg
	21.4	2.7	3.4	0.24	0.0	0.04	0.1	7344	8.8	0.09	0.21	0.45	125	62.8	419	3.34

Sodium Restricted	NA mg	Diabetic	Kcal	Milk exg	Veg exg	Fruit exg	Bread exg	Meat exg	Fat exg	Low Fat & Low Chol	FAT gm	Chol mg	SFA gm	PFA gm
	62.8		21.4	0.0	0.75	0.0	0.0	0.0	0.0		0.24	0.0	0.04	0.10

Portion: 1/2 cup

INGREDIENTS	50 portions		6 portions	
	weights	**measures**	**weights**	**measures**
Frozen succotash	12 lb	2 1/4 gal	1 1/2 lb	4 1/2 cups
Water, boiling		2 qt		1 cup
or				
Canned succotash	13 lb	2 #10 cans	1 2/3 lb	1 qt

Method

Frozen
1. Boil 6 to 15 minutes or
2. Steam 12 to 20 minutes. Omit water. (5–6 lb pressure).

Canned
1. Drain off half the liquid from can.
2. Heat long enough to bring to serving temperature or
3. Steam about 1 minute (5–6 lb pressure) or
4. Heat in 350°F oven until serving temperature is reached.

Directions for Diet Preparations

Sodium Restricted (SR): Use frozen or low sodium succotash.

Low Fat/Low Cholesterol (LF): 1/2 cup and **Mechanical Soft** (SFT): Prepare as directed. Consider individual tolerance.

Diabetic (DB): 1/2 cup. Prepare as directed.

Soft/Low Fiber (SLF): Not recommended, substitute with an appropriate food alternative.

Puree (PUR): Prepare as directed. Add liquid (i.e broth or gravy); blenderize to obtain desired consistency.

Nutrient Analysis per Serving (Analysis is based on frozen succotash):

Regular	KCAL	PRO gm	CHO gm	FAT gm	Chol mg	SFA gm	PFA gm	VITA iu	VITC mg	THI mg	RIB mg	NIA mg	CA mg	NA mg	K+ mg	FE mg
	111	4.9	23.7	0.7	0.0	0.1	0.3	286	7.9	0.16	0.09	1.2	16.5	16.5	399	1.4

Sodium Restricted	NA mg	Diabetic	Kcal	Milk exg	Veg exg	Fruit exg	Bread exg	Meat exg	Fat exg	Low Fat & Low Chol	FAT gm	Chol mg	SFA gm	PFA gm
	16.5		111	0.0	0.0	0.0	1.5	0.0	0.0		0.7	0.0	0.1	0.3

Stewed Tomatoes

Portion: 1/2 cup

INGREDIENTS	50 portions		6 portions	
	weights	**measures**	**weights**	**measures**
Onions, chopped	5 1/3 oz	1 cup	3/4 oz	2 Tbsp
Margarine, low sodium, melted	4 oz	1/2 cup	1/2 oz	1 Tbsp
Tomatoes, canned, crushed	12 3/4 lb	1 1/2 gal (2 #10 cans)	1 2/3 lb	3 cups
Sugar, granulated	2 1/3 oz	1/3 cup	1/3 oz	2 tsp
Celery powder		1 tsp		1/8 tsp

Method

1. Sauté onions in margarine until golden.
2. Add remaining ingredients to onions. Mix well. Bring to a boil, simmer, covered 10 to 20 minutes.
3. Portion with a 4 oz ladle.

Directions for Diet Preparations

Sodium Restricted (SR): Use low sodium canned tomatoes or crush fresh tomatoes.

Low Fat/Low Cholesterol (LF): 1/2 cup. Omit margarine, sauté onions in a small amount of water. Consider individual tolerance when using onions.

Diabetic (DB): 1/2 cup.
  50 portions: Omit margarine, sauté onions in a small amount of water. Omit sugar, substitute with artificial sweetener equivalent to 1/3 cup granulated sugar (approx. 1 tsp artificial sweetener).
  6 portions: Omit margarine, sauté onions in a small amount of water. Omit sugar, substitute with artificial sweetener to taste.

Mechanical Soft (SFT): Prepare as directed.

Soft/Low Fiber (SLF): Omit onions.

Puree (PUR): Prepare as directed. Blenderize and strain.

Nutrient Analysis per Serving:

Regular	KCAL	PRO gm	CHO gm	FAT gm	Chol mg	SFA gm	PFA gm	VITA iu	VITC mg	THI mg	RIB mg	NIA mg	CA mg	NA mg	K+ mg	FE mg
	49.3	1.3	7.3	2.1	0.0	0.4	0.7	878	20.3	0.06	0.04	0.9	36.7	217	300	0.8

Sodium Restricted	NA mg	**Diabetic**	Kcal	Milk exg	Veg exg	Fruit exg	Bread exg	Meat exg	Fat exg	**Low Fat & Low Chol**	FAT gm	Chol mg	SFA gm	PFA gm
	13.6		28.1	0.0	1.0	0.0	0.0	0.0	0.0		0.3	0.0	0.05	0.1

Vegetable Medley[1]

Portion: 1/2 cup

INGREDIENTS	50 portions		6 portions	
	weights	measures	weights	measures
Green beans, frozen	2 1/2 lb	2 qt	5 oz	1 cup
Carrots, sliced, frozen	3 lb	2 1/2 qt	6 oz	1 1/4 cups
Cauliflower florets, frozen	2 lb	2 qt	4 oz	1 cup
Green peas, frozen	2 1/2 lb	2 qt	5 oz	1 cup
Water, boiling		1 1/2 qt		3/4 cup
Oregano		1 Tbsp		1/4 tsp

Method

1. Combine all vegetables.
2. Boil 10 to 20 minutes or until tender. Drain water.
3. Sprinkle with oregano. Mix to blend.
4. Serve with a No. 8 dipper.

Notes

[1]May use fresh or canned vegetables.

Directions for Diet Preparations

Sodium Restricted (SR), **Low Fat/Low Cholesterol** (LF): 1/2 cup, and **Diabetic** (DB): 1/2 cup. Prepare as directed. Low fat diets should consider individual tolerance to cauliflower.

Mechanical Soft (SFT): Cook vegetables until soft and tender.

Soft/Low Fiber (SLF): Omit cauliflower and peas.

Puree (PUR): Prepare as directed. Add liquid (i.e. broth or gravy) to vegetables; blenderize to obtain desired consistency.

Nutrient Analysis per Serving:

Regular	KCAL	PRO gm	CHO gm	FAT gm	Chol mg	SFA gm	PFA gm	VITA iu	VITC mg	THI mg	RIB mg	NIA mg	CA mg	NA mg	K+ mg	FE mg
	33.6	1.7	6.9	0.1	0.0	0.02	0.07	6176	12.3	0.07	0.05	0.5	24.4	35.3	156	0.6

Sodium Restricted	NA mg	Diabetic	Kcal	Milk exg	Veg exg	Fruit exg	Bread exg	Meat exg	Fat exg	Low Fat & Low Chol	FAT gm	Chol mg	SFA gm	PFA gm
	35.3		33.6	0.0	1.2	0.0	0.0	0.0	0.0		0.1	0.0	0.02	0.07

Portion: 1/2 cup

INGREDIENTS	50 portions		6 portions	
	weights	measures	weights	measures
Fresh zucchini	12 lb AP		1 1/2 lb AP	
Zucchini, sliced	11 lb EP	2 1/4 gal	1 3/8 lb EP	4 1/2 cups
(ready-to-cook weight)				
Water, boiling		2 qt		1 cup
or				
Frozen zucchini, sliced	10 lb	2 gal	1 1/4 lb	1 qt
Water, boiling		1 qt		1/2 cup

Method

Fresh
1. Wash. Cut off ends. Do not peel. Slice or cut as desired.
2. Boil 10 to 20 minutes or
3. Steam 8 to 20 minutes. Omit water. (5–6 lb pressure).

Frozen
1. Boil 5 to 10 minutes or
2. Steam 5 to 10 minutes. Omit water. (5–6 lb pressure).

Directions for Diet Preparations

Sodium Restricted (SR), **Low Fat/Low Cholesterol** (LF): 1/2 cup, and **Diabetic** (DB): 1/2 cup. Prepare as directed.

Mechanical Soft (SFT) and **Soft/Low Fiber** (SLF): Remove skin.

Puree (PUR): Remove skin from zucchini. Add liquid (i.e. broth or gravy); blenderize to obtain desired consistency.

Nutrient Analysis per Serving:

Regular	KCAL	PRO gm	CHO gm	FAT gm	Chol mg	SFA gm	PFA gm	VITA iu	VITC mg	THI mg	RIB mg	NIA mg	CA mg	NA mg	K+ mg	FE mg
	14.6	0.6	3.6	0.05	0.0	0.01	0.02	219	4.2	0.04	0.04	0.4	11.9	2.7	231	0.3

Sodium Restricted	NA mg	Diabetic	Kcal	Milk exg	Veg exg	Fruit exg	Bread exg	Meat exg	Fat exg	Low Fat & Low Chol	FAT gm	Chol mg	SFA gm	PFA gm
	2.7		14.6	0.0	0.5	0.0	0.0	0.0	0.0		0.05	0.0	0.01	0.02

Portion: 1/2 cup

INGREDIENTS	50 portions[1]		6 portions[2]	
	weights	measures	weights	measures
Margarine, low sodium, melted	4 oz	1/2 cup	1/2 oz	1 Tbsp
Onions, chopped	5 1/3 oz EP (6 oz AP)	1 cup	3/4 oz EP (3/4 oz AP)	2 Tbsp
Red peppers, seeded, diced	5 1/3 oz EP (6 1/2 lb AP)	1 cup	3/4 oz EP (7/8 oz AP)	2 Tbsp
Corn kernels, frozen	1 1/3 lb	1 qt	2 2/3 oz	1/2 cup
Garlic cloves		2 each		1/2 clove
Zucchini, fresh, thinly sliced	8 lb EP (9 1/2 lb AP)	1 3/4 gal	1 lb EP (1 1/4 lb AP)	3 1/2 cups

Method

1. Sauté onions, bell peppers, corn, and garlic in margarine until tender.
2. Boil zucchini 10 to 20 minutes. Drain.
3. Add vegetables to zucchini. Toss lightly to mix.
4. Serve with No. 8 dipper.

Notes

[1]50 portions: May use frozen zucchini (8 lb). Boil 5 to 10 minutes in 1 qt water.
[2]6 portions: May use frozen zucchini (1 lb). Boil 5 to 10 minutes in 1/2 cup water.

Directions for Diet Preparations

Sodium Restricted (SR): Prepare as directed.
Low Fat/Low Cholesterol (LF): 1/2 cup and **Diabetic** (DB): 1/2 cup. Omit margarine. Low fat diets should consider individual tolerance when using onion and corn.
Mechanical Soft (SFT) and **Soft/Low Fiber** (SLF): Not recommended, substitute with appropriate food alternative.
Puree (PUR): Serve 1/2 cup puree zucchini. Remove skin from zucchini. Add liquid (i.e. sauce or gravy); blenderize to obtain desired consistency.

Nutrient Analysis per Serving:

Regular	KCAL	PRO gm	CHO gm	FAT gm	Chol mg	SFA gm	PFA gm	VITA iu	VITC mg	THI mg	RIB mg	NIA mg	CA mg	NA mg	K+ mg	FE mg
	33.9	1.3	5.7	1.1	0.0	0.2	0.3	417	7.6	0.05	0.04	0.6	15.0	2.3	196	0.5

Sodium Restricted	NA mg	Diabetic	Kcal	Milk exg	Veg exg	Fruit exg	Bread exg	Meat exg	Fat exg	Low Fat & Low Chol	FAT gm	Chol mg	SFA gm	PFA gm
	2.3		25.8	0.0	0.5	0.0	0.2	0.0	0.0		0.2	0.0	0.04	0.1

Tarragon Zucchini

Portion: 1/2 cup

INGREDIENTS	50 portions[1]		6 portions[2]	
	weights	measures	weights	measures
Zucchini, fresh, sliced	11 lb EP (12 lb AP)	2 1/4 gal	1 3/8 lb EP (1 1/2 lb AP)	4 1/2 cups
Water, boiling		2 qt		1 cup
Tarragon	1 oz	2 Tbsp	1/8 oz	3/4 tsp
Margarine, low sodium, melted	4 oz	1/2 cup	1/2 oz	2 Tbsp

Method

1. Boil zucchini 10 to 20 minutes. Drain.
2. Season with tarragon.
3. Add melted margarine. Toss lightly.

Notes

[1]50 portions: May use frozen zucchini (10 lb). Boil 5 to 10 minutes in 1 qt water.
[2]6 portions: May use frozen zucchini (1 1/4 lb). Boil 5 to 10 minutes in 1/2 cup water.

Directions for Diet Preparations

Sodium Restricted (SR): Prepare as directed.
Low Fat/Low Cholesterol (LF): 1/2 cup and **Diabetic** (DB): 1/2 cup. Omit margarine.
Mechanical Soft (SFT) and **Soft/Low Fiber** (SLF): Remove skin from zucchini.
Puree (PUR): Remove skin from zucchini. Add liquid (i.e. broth or gravy); blenderize to obtain desired consistency.

Nutrient Analysis per Serving:

Regular	KCAL	PRO gm	CHO gm	FAT gm	Chol mg	SFA gm	PFA gm	VITA iu	VITC mg	THI mg	RIB mg	NIA mg	CA mg	NA mg	K+ mg	FE mg
	36.0	1.3	4.1	1.9	0.0	0.3	0.6	571	4.1	0.04	0.04	0.4	22.0	3.0	225	0.6

Sodium Restricted	NA mg	Diabetic	Kcal	Milk exg	Veg exg	Fruit exg	Bread exg	Meat exg	Fat exg	Low Fat & Low Chol	FAT gm	Chol mg	SFA gm	PFA gm
	3.0		19.7	0.0	0.7	0.0	0.0	0.0	0.0		0.2	0.0	0.03	0.06

Sauté Zucchini and Onions

Portion: 1/2 cup

INGREDIENTS	50 portions		6 portions	
	weights	**measures**	**weights**	**measures**
Margarine, low sodium, melted	8 oz	1 cup	1 oz	2 Tbsp
Onions, chopped finely	3 lb	2 1/4 qt	6 oz	1 1/8 cups
Zucchini, fresh, sliced	8 lb EP	1 3/4 gal	1 lb EP	3 1/2 cups
	(9 1/2 lb AP)		(1 1/4 lb AP)	

Method

1. Add onions to margarine. Sauté until tender.
2. Add zucchini. Sauté over medium heat until zucchini is tender.

Directions for Diet Preparations

Sodium Restricted (SR): Prepare as directed.

Low Fat/Low Cholesterol (LF): 1/2 cup and **Diabetic** (DB): 1/2 cup. Omit margarine. Cook onions and zucchini in low fat broth until vegetables are tender.

Mechanical Soft (SFT) and **Soft/Low Fiber** (SLF): Omit onions. Remove skin from zucchini. Cook zucchini until soft and tender.

Puree (PUR): Remove skin from zucchini. Cook vegetables until soft and tender. Add liquid (i.e. broth or gravy); blenderize to obtain desired consistency.

Nutrient Analysis per Serving:

Regular	KCAL	PRO gm	CHO gm	FAT gm	Chol mg	SFA gm	PFA gm	VITA iu	VITC mg	THI mg	RIB mg	NIA mg	CA mg	NA mg	K+ mg	FE mg
	47.3	0.7	4.7	3.1	0.0	0.5	1.0	302	5.3	0.04	0.03	0.3	16.5	3.7	223	0.3

Sodium Restricted	NA mg	Diabetic	Kcal	Milk exg	Veg exg	Fruit exg	Bread exg	Meat exg	Fat exg	Low Fat & Low Chol	FAT gm	Chol mg	SFA gm	PFA gm
	3.7		19.9	0.0	0.7	0.0	0.0	0.0	0.0		0.1	0.0	0.02	0.04

Side Salads

K1 — Bean Sprout Salad

Portion: 1/2 cup

INGREDIENTS	50 portions[1]		6 portions[2]	
	weights	measures	weights	measures
Bean sprouts, rinsed, drained, fresh	2 lb	1 gal	4 oz	2 cups
Carrots, shredded	1 lb EP (1 1/2 lb AP)	1 qt	2 oz EP (3 oz AP)	1/2 cup
Green pepper, chopped	1 lb EP (1 1/4 lb AP)	3 cups	2 oz EP (2 1/2 oz AP)	1/3 cup
Cucumbers, peeled, diced	1 lb (1 1/4 lb AP)	3 1/2 cups	2 1/3 oz EP (2 3/4 oz AP)	1/2 cup
Soy sauce	2 oz	1/4 cup	1/4 oz	2 tsp
Vegetable oil	2 oz	1/4 cup	1/4 oz	2 tsp
Sesame oil	2 oz	1/4 cup	1/4 oz	2 tsp
Parsley, chopped		2 Tbsp		2 tsp

Method

1. Combine bean sprouts, carrots, green peppers, and cucumbers. Toss lightly.
2. Combine soy sauce, oils, and parsley. Pour over vegetables. Toss lightly.

Notes

[1] 50 portions: 4 lb canned bean sprouts may be substituted for 2 lb fresh bean sprouts.
[2] 6 portions: 8 oz canned bean sprouts may be substituted for 4 oz fresh bean sprouts.

Directions for Diet Preparations

Sodium Restricted (SR): Use low sodium soy sauce.
Low Fat/Low Cholesterol (LF): 1/2 cup and **Diabetic** (DB): 1/2 cup. Use half the amount of oil specified. May use if able to calculate into daily food plan.
Mechanical Soft (SFT), **Soft/Low Fiber** (SLF), and **Puree** (PUR): Not recommended, substitute with appropriate food alternative.

Nutrient Analysis per Serving:

Regular	KCAL	PRO gm	CHO gm	FAT gm	Chol mg	SFA gm	PFA gm	VITA iu	VITC mg	THI mg	RIB mg	NIA mg	CA mg	NA mg	K+ mg	FE mg
	29.7	0.6	1.9	2.3	0.0	0.3	1.1	2568	9.9	0.02	0.02	0.2	7.7	87.5	63.5	0.2

Sodium Restricted	NA mg	Diabetic	Kcal	Milk exg	Veg exg	Fruit exg	Bread exg	Meat exg	Fat exg	Low Fat & Low Chol	FAT gm	Chol mg	SFA gm	PFA gm
	42.7		19.9	0.0	0.5	0.0	0.0	0.0	0.1		1.2	0.0	0.1	0.6

Asparagus, spears or tips	Break off the tough ends of the stalk. Wash. If sandy under scales, scrape off scales. Brush gently with a soft brush. Leave as spears or cut into tips.
Beans, blackeye beans, peas, or limas	Shell. (Scald pods to make shelling easier.) Rinse.
Beans, green or wax	Wash. Trim ends and remove any strings. Break or cut into 1-inch pieces or slit lengthwise into thin strips.
Beets	Remove tops. Leave 2-inch stem. Wash. After cooking remove stems, roots, and skin.
Broccoli	Cut off tough stalk ends. Wash. Cut broccoli lengthwise, chop or leave as florets.
Brussel sprouts	Remove discolored outer leaves. Cut an X in the stem to shorten cooking time.
Cabbage	Remove discolored outer leaves. Wash thoroughly. Quarter and core. Crisp in cold water. Shred or cut into wedges.
Carrots	Wash. Scrape or peel with vegetable peeler. Cut off ends. Chop, shred, or cut into slices or sticks.
Cauliflower	Remove outer leaves and stalks. Break into florets. Wash.
Celery	Separate branches. Wash celery and scrub grooves. Trim off root and blemishes. Chop or cut into slices or sticks.
Corn on the cob	Husk; remove silks. Rinse, do not stand in water.
Cucumbers	Wash and pare, or score lengthwise. Crisp and let stand in ice water for 15 minutes. Cut into slices or wedges.
Eggplant	Wash. Pare and cut into desired pieces or slices.
Endive, chicory, escarole, and watercress	Wash and remove undesirable portions. Drain, place in plastic bag and refrigerate.
Lettuce, head	Remove ragged and undesirable leaves from heads. For a garnish, cut out stem and core. Hold heads under cold running water, heads should be core side up. Turn head right side up and drain. Separate leaves. Stack 6 leaves, invert and pack in covered container or plastic bag. Place in refrigerator for 2 hours or more to crisp.
Lettuce, romaine or leaf	Wash and drain. Place in covered container or plastic bag and refrigerate.
Okra	Wash, leaving small pods whole, and thickly slice the large ones.
Onions	Pour water over onions to cover. Under water, remove wilted leaves, outer layer, root end, and all bruised parts. Chop or cut as desired.
Peppers, green, red, or yellow	Wash. Cut out stem, remove seed and fibrous portion. Wash the inside and cut or chop as desired.
Potatoes	Wash and scrub. Pare. Remove eyes and blemishes. Cut as desired. Cook with skins on or off.
Spinach	Remove tough stems. Discard discolored, wilted, or slimy leave. Wash in warm water. Then wash in cold water as many times necessary to remove sand. Crisp.
Squash, summer	Wash, cut off stem. It is not necessary to peel. Slice or chop.
Tomatoes	Wash. Cut out core. Cut into quarters, wedges, or slices. Tomatoes may be peeled by scalding. Dip into boiling water for 1 minute. Plunge into cold water and slip off skin. After peeling, core and cut as desired.

Pickled Beets

Portion: 1/2 cup

INGREDIENTS	50 portions[1]		6 portions[2]	
	weights	measures	weights	measures
Beets, canned, sliced, drained	13 lb	1 3/4 gal (2 #10 cans)	1 2/3 lb	3 1/2 cups
Beet juice		1 1/2 qt		3/4 cup
Vinegar, cider		1 1/2 qt		3/4 cup
Sugar, granulated	14 oz	2 cups	1 3/4 oz	1/4 cup
Cloves, whole		2 tsp		1/4 tsp
Cinnamon sticks		4 sticks		1 stick

Method

1. Combine beet juice, vinegar, sugar, and spices. Bring to a boil.
2. Add beets and return to boil.
3. Chill 24 hours before serving.

Notes

[1]*50 portions:* May use fresh beets (14 lb AP). Boil or steam until tender. Omit beet juice, use 1 1/2 qt water. Chill 24 hours before serving.

[2]*6 portions:* May use fresh beets (1 3/4 lb AP). Boil or steam until tender. Omit beet juice, use 3/4 cup water. Chill 24 hours before serving.

Directions for Diet Preparations

Sodium Restricted (SR): Use low sodium beets.

Low Fat/Low Cholesterol (LF): 1/2 cup. Prepare as directed.

Diabetic (DB): 1/2 cup.

50 portions: Omit sugar, substitute with artificial sweetener equivalent to 2 cups of granulated sugar.

6 portions: Omit sugar, substitute with artificial sweetener equivalent to 1/4 cup of granulated sugar.

Mechanical Soft (SFT): Prepare as directed. Chop. Consider individual tolerance.

Soft/Low Fiber (SLF): Omit cloves. Consider individual tolerance.

Puree (PUR): Prepare as directed. Blenderize. Add additional liquid (i.e. beet juice) if necessary to obtain desired consistency.

Nutrient Analysis per Serving:

Regular	KCAL	PRO gm	CHO gm	FAT gm	Chol mg	SFA gm	PFA gm	VITA iu	VITC mg	THI mg	RIB mg	NIA mg	CA mg	NA mg	K+ mg	FE mg
	80	1.2	20.2	0.1	0.0	0.02	0.03	17.3	6.1	0.01	0.05	0.23	24.2	406	249	1.2

Sodium Restricted	NA mg	Diabetic	Kcal	Milk exg	Veg exg	Fruit exg	Bread exg	Meat exg	Fat exg	Low Fat & Low Chol	FAT gm	Chol mg	SFA gm	PFA gm
	52.8		50	0.0	1.0	0.3	0.0	0.0	0.0		0.1	0.0	0.02	0.03

Cabbage Apple Salad

Portion: 1/2 cup

INGREDIENTS	50 portions		6 portions	
	weights	measures	weights	measures
Apples, fresh, unpared, diced	2 lb EP (2 1/4 lb AP)	1 3/4 qt	4 1/2 oz EP (5 1/8 oz AP)	1 cup
Lemon juice		1/4 cup		1/2 Tbsp
Cabbage, fresh, shredded	3 1/2 lb EP (4 1/2 lb AP)	3 1/2 qt	12 oz EP (15 1/2 oz AP)	3 cups
Thousand island dressing		3 cups		1/3 cup

Method

1. Coat apples with lemon juice. Drain off excess juice.
2. Toss together apples and cabbage.
3. Add dressing to cabbage mixture. Mix thoroughly.
4. Chill. Portion 1/2 cup.

Directions for Diet Preparations

Sodium Restricted (SR): Use low sodium thousand island dressing.

Low Fat/Low Cholesterol (LF): 1/2 cup and **Diabetic** (DB): 1/2 cup. Use low fat thousand island dressing in half the amount specified. Low fat diets should consider individual tolerance to cabbage.

Mechanical Soft (SFT), **Soft/Low Fiber** (SLF), and **Puree** (PUR): Not recommended, substitute with appropriate food alternative.

Nutrient Analysis per Serving:

Regular	KCAL	PRO gm	CHO gm	FAT gm	Chol mg	SFA gm	PFA gm	VITA iu	VITC mg	THI mg	RIB mg	NIA mg	CA mg	NA mg	K+ mg	FE mg
	93.7	0.7	5.3	8.1	10.0	0.9	5.5	361	22.1	0.02	0.01	0.1	23.3	70.5	145	0.3

Sodium Restricted	NA mg	Diabetic	Kcal	Milk exg	Veg exg	Fruit exg	Bread exg	Meat exg	Fat exg	Low Fat & Low Chol	FAT gm	Chol mg	SFA gm	PFA gm
	12.4		38.5	0.0	0.5	0.25	0.0	0.0	0.2		1.8	0.0	0.01	0.05

Carrot Raisin Salad

Portion: 1/2 cup

INGREDIENTS	50 portions		6 portions	
	weights	measures	weights	measures
Raisins, seedless	13 oz	2 1/2 cups	1 2/3 oz	5 Tbsp
Carrots, peeled, shredded	6 lb EP (8 3/4 lb AP)	1 1/2 gal	12 oz EP (1 lb AP)	3 cups
Mayonnaise	2 lb	1 qt	4 oz	1/2 cup

Method

1. Combine carrots, raisins, and mayonnaise. Mix lightly.
2. Serve with No. 8 dipper.

Directions for Diet Preparations

Sodium Restricted (SR): Use low sodium mayonnaise.

Low Fat/Low Cholesterol (LF): 1/2 cup and **Diabetic** (DB): 1/3 cup. Use reduced-calorie low cholesterol mayonnaise in half the amount specified for regular mayonnaise.

Mechanical Soft (SFT), **Soft/Low Fiber** (SLF), and **Puree** (PUR): Not recommended, substitute with appropriate food alternative.

Nutrient Analysis per Serving:

Regular	KCAL	PRO gm	CHO gm	FAT gm	Chol mg	SFA gm	PFA gm	VITA iu	VITC mg	THI mg	RIB mg	NIA mg	CA mg	NA mg	K+ mg	FE mg
	117	0.9	15.4	6.5	4.9	0.9	3.4	14144	4.9	0.06	0.04	0.5	19.8	153	218	0.4

Sodium Restricted	NA mg	Diabetic	Kcal	Milk exg	Veg exg	Fruit exg	Bread exg	Meat exg	Fat exg	Low Fat & Low Chol	FAT gm	Chol mg	SFA gm	PFA gm
	23.8		37.1	0.0	0.7	0.2	0.0	0.0	0.2		1.3	4.5	0.2	0.05

Portion: 1/2 cup

INGREDIENTS	50 portions		6 portions	
	weights	measures	weights	measures
Cabbage, shredded	8 1/2 lb EP (11 lb AP)	2 1/8 gal	12 oz EP (1 lb AP)	3 cups
Vinegar, cider		3 1/2 cups		1/3 cup
Sugar, granulated	1 1/2 lb	3 1/3 cups	3 2/3 oz	1/2 cup
Celery seed		1 Tbsp		1/2 tsp

Method

1. Combine vinegar, sugar, and celery seed. Add to cabbage. Mix lightly.
2. Serve with No. 8 dipper.

Directions for Diet Preparations

Sodium Restricted (SR): Prepare as directed.

Low Fat/Low Cholesterol (LF): 1/2 cup. Prepare as directed. Consider individual tolerance to cabbage.

Diabetic (DB): 1/2 cup.

50 portions: Omit sugar, substitute with artificial sweetener in amount equal to 1 1/2 lb of granulated sugar (approx. 3 Tbsp artificial sweetener).

6 portions: Omit sugar, substitute with artificial sweetener in amount equal to 3 2/3 oz of granulated sugar (approx. 2 tsp artificial sweetener).

Mechanical Soft (SFT), **Soft/Low Fiber** (SLF), and **Puree** (PUR): Not recommended, substitute with appropriate food alternative.

Nutrient Analysis per Serving:

Regular	KCAL	PRO gm	CHO gm	FAT gm	Chol mg	SFA gm	PFA gm	VITA iu	VITC mg	THI mg	RIB mg	NIA mg	CA mg	NA mg	K+ mg	FE mg
	73.5	0.9	18.6	0.2	0.0	0.02	0.07	95.7	35.8	0.04	0.02	0.2	39.0	14.2	206	0.6

Sodium Restricted	NA mg	Diabetic	Kcal	Milk exg	Veg exg	Fruit exg	Bread exg	Meat exg	Fat exg	Low Fat & Low Chol	FAT gm	Chol mg	SFA gm	PFA gm
	14.2		24.3	0.0	0.9	0.0	0.0	0.0	0.0		0.2	0.0	0.02	0.07

Poppy Seed Cole Slaw

Portion: 1/2 cup

INGREDIENTS	50 portions		6 portions	
	weights	measures	weights	measures
Cabbage, shredded	8 1/2 lb EP (11 lb AP)	2 1/8 gal	12 oz EP (1 lb AP)	3 cups
Vinegar, cider		3 1/2 cups		1/3 cup
Sugar, granulated	1 3/4 lb	1 qt	3 2/3 oz	1/2 cup
Poppy seeds	2 oz	6 Tbsp	1/4 oz	2 1/4 tsp

Method

1. Combine vinegar, sugar, and poppy seed. Add to cabbage. Mix lightly.
2. Serve with No 8 dipper.

Directions for Diet Preparations

Sodium Restricted (SR): Prepare as directed.

Low Fat/Low Cholesterol (LF): 1/2 cup. Prepare as directed. Consider individual tolerance.

Diabetic (DB): 1/2 cup.

50 portions: Omit sugar, substitute with artificial sweetener in amount equal to 1 3/4 lb of granulated sugar (approx. 4 Tbsp artificial sweetener).

6 portions: Omit sugar, substitute with artificial sweetener in amount equal to 3 2/3 ounces of granulated sugar (approx. 2 tsp artificial sweetener).

Mechanical Soft (SFT), **Soft/Low Fiber** (SLF), and **Puree** (PUR): Not recommended, substitute with appropriate food alternative.

Nutrient Analysis per Serving:

Regular	KCAL	PRO gm	CHO gm	FAT gm	Chol mg	SFA gm	PFA gm	VITA iu	VITC mg	THI mg	RIB mg	NIA mg	CA mg	NA mg	K+ mg	FE mg
	87.6	1.1	21.1	0.6	0.0	0.07	0.4	97.1	36.3	0.05	0.02	0.24	52.7	14.4	214	0.6

Sodium Restricted	NA mg	Diabetic	Kcal	Milk exg	Veg exg	Fruit exg	Bread exg	Meat exg	Fat exg	Low Fat & Low Chol	FAT gm	Chol mg	SFA gm	PFA gm
	14.4		29.5	0.0	1.1	0.0	0.0	0.0	0.0		0.6	0.0	0.07	0.4

Portion: 1/2 cup

INGREDIENTS	50 portions		6 portions	
	weights	measures	weights	measures
Cabbage, green, fresh, shredded	8 lb EP (10 lb AP)	2 gal	1 lb EP (1 1/4 AP)	1 qt
Onions, diced	3 oz	1/2 cup	1/3 oz	1 Tbsp
Cilantro, fresh, minced		4 Tbsp		1/2 Tbsp
Pepper, black, ground		1 tsp		1/8 tsp
Dressing:				
Vegetable oil	14 oz	1 3/4 cups	1 3/4 oz	3 1/2 Tbsp
Lime juice	8 oz	1 cup	1 oz	2 Tbsp
Garlic cloves, minced		2 cloves		1/4 clove

Method

1. Combine cabbage, onions, cilantro, and black pepper. Toss lightly.
2. Prepare dressing.
   a. Combine vegetable oil, lime juice, and garlic. Whisk ingredients together.
3. Add dressing to vegetables. Mix lightly. Chill.

Directions for Diet Preparations

Sodium Restricted (SR): Prepare as directed.
Low Fat/Low Cholesterol (LF): 1/2 cup and **Diabetic** (DB): 1/2 cup. Use 2 tsp dressing. May use if able to calculate into daily food plan. Low fat diets should consider individual tolerance to cabbage.
Mechanical Soft (SFT), **Soft/Low Fiber** (SLF), and **Puree** (PUR): Not recommended, substitute with appropriate food alternative.

Nutrient Analysis per Serving:

Regular	KCAL	PRO gm	CHO gm	FAT gm	Chol mg	SFA gm	PFA gm	VITA iu	VITC mg	THI mg	RIB mg	NIA mg	CA mg	NA mg	K+ mg	FE mg
	88.5	0.9	4.6	7.8	0.0	0.9	4.6	98.5	37.4	0.04	0.02	0.2	36.8	13.7	195	0.4

Sodium Restricted	NA mg	Diabetic	Kcal	Milk exg	Veg exg	Fruit exg	Bread exg	Meat exg	Fat exg	Low Fat & Low Chol	FAT gm	Chol mg	SFA gm	PFA gm
	13.7		43.8	0.0	1.0	0.0	0.0	0.0	0.3		2.9	0.0	0.3	1.7

Corn Relish

Portion: 1/2 cup

INGREDIENTS	50 portions		6 portions	
	weights	measures	weights	measures
Green beans, cut, cooked	2 lb EP (2 1/3 lb AP)	1 1/2 qt	4 oz EP (4 2/3 oz AP)	3/4 cup
Corn, whole kernel, canned	5 lb	3 3/4 qt	8 oz	1 1/2 cups
Celery, chopped	1 1/2 lb EP (2 lb AP)	1 1/8 qt	2 2/3 oz EP (3 1/2 oz AP)	1/2 cup
Red peppers, chopped	1 lb EP (1 1/4 lb AP)	3 cups	1 3/4 oz EP (2 1/4 oz AP)	1/3 cup
Vinegar, cider		3 1/2 cups		1/3 cup
Sugar, granulated	1 3/4 lb	1 qt	3 2/3 oz	1/2 cup

Method

1. Combine all ingredients. Stir until sugar is dissolved.
2. Serve with No. 8 dipper.

Directions for Diet Preparations

Sodium Restricted (SR): Use low sodium vegetables.
Low Fat/Low Cholesterol (LF): 1/2 cup. Prepare as directed. Consider individual tolerance to corn.
Diabetic (DB): 1/2 cup.
50 portions: Omit sugar, substitute with artificial sweetener in amount equal to 1 3/4 lb of granulated sugar (approx. 3 Tbsp artificial sweetener).
6 portions: Omit sugar, substitute with artificial sweetener in amount equal to 3.6 oz of granulated sugar (approx. 2 tsp artificial sweetener).
Mechanical Soft (SFT), **Soft/Low Fiber** (SLF), and **Puree** (PUR): Not recommended, substitute with appropriate food alternative.

Nutrient Analysis per Serving:

Regular	KCAL	PRO gm	CHO gm	FAT gm	Chol mg	SFA gm	PFA gm	VITA iu	VITC mg	THI mg	RIB mg	NIA mg	CA mg	NA mg	K+ mg	FE mg
	83.1	1.8	20.1	0.6	0.0	0.1	0.3	224	11.4	0.1	0.04	0.84	11.2	119	194	0.6

Sodium Restricted	NA mg	Diabetic	Kcal	Milk exg	Veg exg	Fruit exg	Bread exg	Meat exg	Fat exg	Low Fat & Low Chol	FAT gm	Chol mg	SFA gm	PFA gm
	16.5		56.1	0.0	0.25	0.0	0.75	0.0	0.0		0.6	0.0	0.1	0.3

Portion: 1/2 cup

INGREDIENTS	50 portions		6 portions	
	weights	measures	weights	measures
Marinade:				
Lemon juice		2 1/2 Tbsp		1 tsp
Vinegar, white		1/3 cup		2 tsp
Salad oil	8 oz	1 cup	1 oz	2 Tbsp
Water		1/3 cup		2 tsp
Onion, finely chopped	2 oz	1/3 cup	1/4 oz	2 tsp
Red pepper, chopped		1/4 cup		1 1/2 tsp
Parsley, finely chopped		1/4 cup		1 1/2 tsp
Sugar, granulated		1 Tbsp		1 tsp
Tarragon		1 Tbsp		1 tsp
Cucumbers, peeled, sliced	9 lb EP (10 3/4 lb AP)	2 gal (18 large)	1 1/8 lb EP (1 1/3 lb AP)	3 1/2 cups (2–3 large)

Method

1. Combine all ingredients, except cucumbers. Mix well.
2. Pour marinade over cucumbers. Mix thoroughly.
3. Refrigerate for 2 to 3 hours.
4. Drain off most of the marinade before serving.
5. Serve with No. 8 dipper.

Directions for Diet Preparations

Sodium Restricted (SR): Prepare as directed.
Low Fat/Low Cholesterol (LF): 1/2 cup. Omit vegetable oil. Low fat diets should consider individual tolerance to onions.
Diabetic (DB): 1/2 cup. Omit vegetable oil and sugar. Use artificial sweetener to taste.
Mechanical Soft (SFT), **Soft/Low Fiber** (SLF), and **Puree** (PUR): Not recommended, substitute with appropriate food alternative.

Nutrient Analysis per Serving:

Regular	KCAL	PRO gm	CHO gm	FAT gm	Chol mg	SFA gm	PFA gm	VITA iu	VITC mg	THI mg	RIB mg	NIA mg	CA mg	NA mg	K+ mg	FE mg
	45.5	0.6	3.6	3.4	0.0	0.5	1.9	71.3	6.3	0.03	0.02	0.3	17.0	2.3	170	0.3

Sodium Restricted	NA mg	Diabetic	Kcal	Milk exg	Veg exg	Fruit exg	Bread exg	Meat exg	Fat exg	Low Fat & Low Chol	FAT gm	Chol mg	SFA gm	PFA gm
	2.3		15.5	0.0	0.5	0.0	0.0	0.0	0.0		0.1	0.0	0.03	0.05

Portion: 1/2 cup

INGREDIENTS	50 portions		6 portions	
	weights	**measures**	**weights**	**measures**
Marinade:				
Lemon juice		2 1/2 Tbsp		1 tsp
Vinegar, white		1/3 cup		2 tsp
Salad oil	8 oz	1 cup	1 oz	2 Tbsp
Water		1/3 cup		2 tsp
Onion, finely chopped	2 oz	1/3 cup	1/4 oz	2 tsp
Red pepper, chopped		1/4 cup		1 1/2 tsp
Parsley, finely chopped		1/4 cup		1 1/2 tsp
Sugar, granulated		1 Tbsp		1 tsp
Tarragon		1 Tbsp		1 tsp
Cucumbers, peeled, sliced	7 1/2 lb EP (9 lb AP)	1 1/2 gal (15 large)	15 oz EP (1 1/8 lb AP)	3 1/2 cups (2–3 large)
Onions, thinly sliced	1 1/2 lb EP (3/4 lb AP)	3 cups	3 oz EP (3 1/2 oz AP)	1/3 cup

Method

1. Combine all ingredients, except cucumbers and onions. Mix well.
2. Pour marinade over cucumbers and onions. Mix thoroughly.
3. Refrigerate for 2 to 3 hours.
4. Drain off most of the marinade before serving.
5. Serve with No. 8 dipper.

Directions for Diet Preparations

Sodium Restricted (SR): Prepare as directed.
Low Fat/Low Cholesterol (LF): 1/2 cup. Omit vegetable oil. Consider individual tolerance to onions.
Diabetic (DB): 1/2 cup. Omit vegetable oil and sugar. Use artificial sweetener to taste.
Mechanical Soft (SFT), **Soft/Low Fiber** (SLF), and **Puree** (PUR): Not recommended, substitute with appropriate food alternative.

Nutrient Analysis per Serving:

Regular	KCAL	PRO gm	CHO gm	FAT gm	Chol mg	SFA gm	PFA gm	VITA iu	VITC mg	THI mg	RIB mg	NIA mg	CA mg	NA mg	K+ mg	FE mg
	53.4	0.5	3.3	4.5	0.0	0.6	2.6	53.3	5.3	0.03	0.02	0.2	13.9	1.8	126	0.3

Sodium Restricted	NA mg	Diabetic	Kcal	Milk exg	Veg exg	Fruit exg	Bread exg	Meat exg	Fat exg	Low Fat & Low Chol	FAT gm	Chol mg	SFA gm	PFA gm
	1.8		13.4	0.0	0.5	0.0	0.0	0.0	0.0		0.1	0.0	0.02	0.04

K11 — Marinated Green Beans

Portion: 1/2 cup

INGREDIENTS	50 portions weights	50 portions measures	6 portions weights	6 portions measures
Marinade:				
Lemon juice		2 1/2 Tbsp		1 tsp
Vinegar, white		1/3 cup		2 tsp
Salad oil	8 oz	1 cup	1 oz	2 Tbsp
Water		1/3 cup		2 tsp
Onion, finely chopped	2 oz	1/3 cup	1/4 oz	2 tsp
Red pepper, chopped		1/4 cup		1 1/2 tsp
Parsley, finely chopped		1/4 cup		1 1/2 tsp
Sugar, granulated		1 Tbsp		1 tsp
Tarragon		1 Tbsp		1 tsp
Green beans, canned, drained	8 1/3 lb EP	1 1/2 gal	1 lb EP	3 cups

Method

1. Combine all ingredients, except green beans. Mix well.
2. Pour marinade over cucumbers. Mix thoroughly.
3. Refrigerate for 2 to 3 hours.
4. Drain off most of the marinade before serving.
5. Serve with No. 8 dipper.

Directions for Diet Preparations

Sodium Restricted (SR): Prepare as directed.

Low Fat/Low Cholesterol (LF): 1/2 cup. Omit vegetable oil. Low fat diets should consider individual tolerance to onions.

Diabetic (DB): 1/2 cup. Omit vegetable oil and sugar. Use artificial sweetener to taste.

Mechanical Soft (SFT), **Soft/Low Fiber** (SLF), and **Puree** (PUR): Not recommended, substitute with appropriate food alternative.

Nutrient Analysis per Serving:

Regular	KCAL	PRO gm	CHO gm	FAT gm	Chol mg	SFA gm	PFA gm	VITA iu	VITC mg	THI mg	RIB mg	NIA mg	CA mg	NA mg	K+ mg	FE mg
	55.6	1.3	6.0	3.5	0.0	0.4	2.0	484	8.0	0.05	0.06	0.44	33.8	2.3	216	0.9

Sodium Restricted	NA mg	Diabetic	Kcal	Milk exg	Veg exg	Fruit exg	Bread exg	Meat exg	Fat exg	Low Fat & Low Chol	FAT gm	Chol mg	SFA gm	PFA gm
	2.3		25.7	0.0	1.0	0.0	0.0	0.0	0.0		0.2	0.0	0.04	0.1

K12   Italian Vegetable Salad

Portion: 1/2 cup

Ingredients	50 portions		6 portions	
	weights	measures	weights	measures
Macaroni, dry	12 oz	3 cups	1 1/2 oz	1/3 cup
Water, boiling		3 qt		1 1/2 cups
Broccoli florets	2 lb EP (2 1/2 lb AP)	2 qt	4 oz EP (5 oz AP)	1 cup
Cauliflower florets	1 lb EP (1 3/4 lb AP)	1 qt	2 oz EP (3 1/2 oz AP)	1/2 cup
Carrots, sliced	2 lb EP (3 lb AP)	1 1/2 qt	4 oz EP (6 oz AP)	3/4 cup
Mushrooms, fresh	8 oz EP	3 cups	3/4 oz	1/3 cup
Onion, sliced	1 lb EP (1 1/8 lb AP)	2 cups	2 oz EP (2 1/3 oz AP)	1/4 cup
Italian dressing	3 lb	1 1/2 qt	6 oz	3/4 cup

Method

1. Cook macaroni in boiling water. Cook uncovered at a fast boil until tender, 5 to 10 minutes, stir occasionally. Drain. Rinse in cold water, drain well.
2. Combine all vegetables. Add to pasta.
3. Pour italian dressing over vegetables and pasta.
4. Marinate at least 2 hours.
5. Drain off most of the marinate before serving.
6. Serve with No. 8 dipper.

Directions for Diet Preparations

Sodium Restricted (SR): Prepare as directed.
Low Fat/Low Cholesterol (LF): 1/2 cup and **Diabetic** (DB): 1/2 cup. Use half the amount of italian dressing. Low fat diets should consider individual tolerance to broccoli, cauliflower, and onions.
Mechanical Soft (SFT), **Soft/Low Fiber** (SLF), and **Puree** (PUR): Not recommended, substitute with appropriate food alternative.

Nutrient Analysis per Serving:

Regular	KCAL	PRO gm	CHO gm	FAT gm	Chol mg	SFA gm	PFA gm	VITA iu	VITC mg	THI mg	RIB mg	NIA mg	CA mg	NA mg	K+ mg	FE mg
	127	1.9	9.6	9.4	0.0	1.1	5.4	4912	18.1	0.09	0.09	0.8	22.4	15.6	151	0.6

Sodium Restricted	NA mg	Diabetic	Kcal	Milk exg	Veg exg	Fruit exg	Bread exg	Meat exg	Fat exg	Low Fat & Low Chol	FAT gm	Chol mg	SFA gm	PFA gm
	15.6		58.3	0.0	1.0	0.0	0.25	0.0	0.25		1.7	0.0	0.2	0.9

Portion: 1/2 cup

INGREDIENTS	50 portions		6 portions	
	weights	measures	weights	measures
Macaroni, elbow	3 lb	3 qt	6 oz	1 1/2 cups
Water, boiling		3 gal		1 1/2 qt
Eggs, hard-cooked	1 lb	3 cups (8 large)	2 oz	1/4 cup (1 large)
Celery, finely chopped	1 lb EP (1 1/4 lb AP)	1 qt	2 oz EP (2 1/2 oz AP)	1/2 cup
Onion, finely chopped	3 oz	1/2 cup	1/3 oz	1 Tbsp
Mayonnaise	1 1/2 lb	3 cups	3 oz	1/3 cup

Method

1. Cook macaroni in boiling water. Cook uncovered at a fast boil until tender, 5 to 10 minutes, stir occasionally. Drain. Rinse in cold water, drain well.
2. Peel and chop eggs.
3. Add eggs and remaining ingredients to macaroni. Mix lightly. Chill.
4. Serve with No. 8 dipper.

Directions for Diet Preparations

Sodium Restricted (SR): Use low sodium mayonnaise.
Low Fat/Low Cholesterol (LF): 1/2 cup and **Diabetic** (DB): 1/2 cup. Omit eggs. Use reduced-calorie low cholesterol mayonnaise in half the amount specified for regular mayonnaise. Low fat diets should consider individual tolerance to onions.
Mechanical Soft (SFT) and **Soft/Low Fiber** (SLF): Omit celery and onions.
Puree (PUR): Omit celery and onions. Add additional liquid (i.e. mayonnaise); blenderize to obtain desired consistency.

Nutrient Analysis per Serving:

Regular	KCAL	PRO gm	CHO gm	FAT gm	Chol mg	SFA gm	PFA gm	VITA iu	VITC mg	THI mg	RIB mg	NIA mg	CA mg	NA mg	K+ mg	FE mg
	204	4.6	18.8	12.2	73.3	1.5	7.5	112	0.7	0.11	0.09	0.8	19.3	101	96.0	1.0

Sodium Restricted	NA mg	Diabetic	Kcal	Milk exg	Veg exg	Fruit exg	Bread exg	Meat exg	Fat exg	Low Fat & Low Chol	FAT gm	Chol mg	SFA gm	PFA gm
	30.0		114	0.0	0.1	0.0	1.0	0.0	0.8		2.7	0.0	0.0	0.01

Portion: 1/2 cup

INGREDIENTS	50 portions		6 portions	
	weights	**measures**	**weights**	**measures**
Pasta[1]	3 lb	varies	6 oz	varies
Water, boiling		3 gal		1 1/2 qt
Eggs, hard-cooked	1 3/4 lb	3 1/2 cups (14 large)	2 oz	1/4 cup (1 large)
Celery, finely chopped	8 oz EP (12 oz AP)	2 cups	1 oz EP (1 1/2 oz AP)	1/4 cup
Onion, finely chopped	3 oz	1/2 cup	1/3 oz	1 Tbsp
Zucchini, diced	1 lb EP	2 cups	2 oz EP	1/4 cup
Mayonnaise	1 1/2 lb	3 cups	3 oz	1/3 cup

Method

1. Cook macaroni in boiling water. Cook uncovered at a fast boil until tender, 5 to 10 minutes, stir occasionally. Drain. Rinse in cold water, drain well.
2. Peel and chop eggs.
3. Add eggs and remaining ingredients to macaroni. Mix lightly. Chill.
4. Serve with No 8 dipper.

Notes

[1]May use elbow macaroni, shell macaroni, rotini, or other pasta shape.

Directions for Diet Preparations

Sodium Restricted (SR): Use low sodium mayonnaise.
Low Fat/Low Cholesterol (LF): 1/2 cup and **Diabetic** (DB): 1/2 cup. Omit eggs. Use reduced-calorie low cholesterol mayonnaise in half the amount specified for regular mayonnaise. Low fat diets should consider individual tolerance when using onions.
Mechanical Soft (SFT) and **Soft/Low Fiber** (SLF): Omit celery, onions, and zucchini. Consider individual tolerance.
Puree (PUR): Omit celery, onions, and zucchini. Add liquid (i.e. mayonnaise); blenderize to obtain desired consistency.

Nutrient Analysis per Serving:

Regular	KCAL	PRO gm	CHO gm	FAT gm	Chol mg	SFA gm	PFA gm	VITA iu	VITC mg	THI mg	RIB mg	NIA mg	CA mg	NA mg	K+ mg	FE mg
	180	5.3	24.9	6.6	80.1	1.2	2.8	131	5.6	0.3	0.2	1.9	15.8	126	42.4	1.3

Sodium Restricted	NA mg	Diabetic	Kcal	Milk exg	Veg exg	Fruit exg	Bread exg	Meat exg	Fat exg	Low Fat & Low Chol	FAT gm	Chol mg	SFA gm	PFA gm
	28.7		111	0.0	0.3	0.0	1.0	0.0	0.7		2.7	0.0	0.0	0.01

Cheesy Macaroni Salad

Portion: 1/2 cup

INGREDIENTS	50 portions		6 portions	
	weights	measures	weights	measures
Macaroni, elbow	3 lb	3 qt	6 oz	1 1/2 cups
Water, boiling		3 gal		1 1/2 qt
Eggs, hard-cooked	1 lb	3 cups (8 large)	2 oz	1/4 cup (1 large)
Cheddar, mild, shredded	1 1/2 lb	1 1/3 qt	3 oz	2/3 cup
Celery, finely chopped	1 lb EP (1 1/4 lb AP)	1 qt	2 oz EP (2 1/2 oz AP)	1/2 cup
Onion, finely chopped	3 oz	1/2 cup	1/3 oz	1 Tbsp
Red pepper, finely chopped	3 oz	1/2 cup	1/3 oz	1 Tbsp
Mayonnaise	1 1/2 lb	3 cups	3 oz	1/3 cup

Method

1. Cook macaroni in boiling water. Cook uncovered at a fast boil until tender, 5 to 10 minutes, stir occasionally. Drain. Rinse in cold water, drain well.
2. Peel and chop eggs.
3. Add eggs and remaining ingredients to macaroni. Mix lightly. Chill.
4. Serve with No. 8 dipper.

Directions for Diet Preparations

Sodium Restricted (SR): Use low sodium cheese in half the amount specified for cheddar cheese. Use low sodium mayonnaise.

Low Fat/Low Cholesterol (LF): 1/3 cup and **Diabetic** (DB): 1/3 cup. Omit eggs. Use low fat cheese. Use reduced-calorie low cholesterol mayonnaise in half the amount specified for regular mayonnaise.

Mechanical Soft (SFT) and **Soft/Low Fiber** (SLF): Omit celery, onions, and red peppers. Consider individual tolerance.

Puree (PUR): Omit celery, onions, and red peppers. Add additional liquid (i.e. mayonnaise or cheese sauce); blenderize to obtain desired consistency.

Nutrient Analysis per Serving:

Regular	KCAL	PRO gm	CHO gm	FAT gm	Chol mg	SFA gm	PFA gm	VITA iu	VITC mg	THI mg	RIB mg	NIA mg	CA mg	NA mg	K+ mg	FE mg
	259	8.0	19.0	16.7	87.7	4.4	7.6	261	1.9	0.12	0.14	0.8	117	186	111	1.1

Sodium Restricted	NA mg	Diabetic	Kcal	Milk exg	Veg exg	Fruit exg	Bread exg	Meat exg	Fat exg	Low Fat & Low Chol	FAT gm	Chol mg	SFA gm	PFA gm
	55.2		101	0.0	0.0	0.0	0.75	0.5-L	0.5		3.4	0.0	0.0	0.01

Portion: 1/2 cup

INGREDIENTS	50 portions		6 portions	
	weights	measures	weights	measures
Marinade:				
Lemon juice		2 1/2 Tbsp		1 tsp
Vinegar, white		1/3 cup		2 tsp
Salad oil	8 oz	1 cup	1 oz	2 Tbsp
Water		1/3 cup		2 tsp
Onion, finely chopped	2 oz	1/3 cup	1/4 oz	2 tsp
Red pepper, chopped		1/4 cup		1 1/2 tsp
Parsley, finely chopped		1/4 cup		1 1/2 tsp
Sugar, granulated		1 Tbsp		1 tsp
Tarragon		1 Tbsp		1 tsp
Mixed vegetables, frozen, cooked	12 lb	2 1/4 gal	1 1/2 lb	1 qt

Method

1. Combine all ingredients, except green beans. Mix well.
2. Pour marinade over cucumbers. Mix thoroughly.
3. Refrigerate for 2 to 3 hours.
4. Drain off most of the marinade before serving.
5. Serve with No. 8 dipper.

Directions for Diet Preparations

Sodium Restricted (SR): Prepare as directed.

Low Fat/Low Cholesterol (LF): 1/2 cup. Omit vegetable oil. Consider individual tolerance to onions and corn.

Diabetic (DB): 1/2 cup. Omit vegetable oil and granulated sugar. Add artificial sweetener to taste.

Mechanical Soft (SFT), **Soft/Low Fiber** (SLF), and **Puree** (PUR): Not recommended, substitute appropriate food alternative.

Nutrient Analysis per Serving:

Regular	KCAL	PRO gm	CHO gm	FAT gm	Chol mg	SFA gm	PFA gm	VITA iu	VITC mg	THI mg	RIB mg	NIA mg	CA mg	NA mg	K+ mg	FE mg
	85.7	2.6	12.5	3.4	0.0	0.4	2.0	3956	4.2	0.07	0.11	0.7	24.9	32.4	164	0.8

Sodium Restricted	NA mg	Diabetic	Kcal	Milk exg	Veg exg	Fruit exg	Bread exg	Meat exg	Fat exg	Low Fat & Low Chol	FAT gm	Chol mg	SFA gm	PFA gm
	32.4		55.8	0.0	1.0	0.0	0.3	0.0	0.0		0.15	0.0	0.02	0.06

Portion: 1 cup

INGREDIENTS	50 portions		6 portions	
	weights	measures	weights	measures
Bean sprouts, rinsed, drained, fresh	2 1/2 lb AP	1 1/4 gal	5 oz	2 1/2 cups
Lettuce, chopped	1 1/2 lb EP (2 3/4 lb AP)	3 qt (2–4 heads)	3 oz EP (5 1/2 oz AP)	1 1/2 cups (1/2 head)
Onion, thinly sliced	1 lb EP (1 1/4 lb AP)	3 cups	2 oz EP (2 1/2 oz AP)	1/3 cup
Celery, finely chopped	1 1/4 lb EP (1 1/2 lb AP)	1 1/4 qt	2 1/2 oz EP (3 oz AP)	2/3 cup
Water chestnuts, sliced	2 1/3 lb	1 1/2 qt	4 2/3 oz	3/4 cup
Green peas, cooked	1 3/4 lb	1 qt	3 1/2 oz	1/2 cup
Dressing:				
Soy sauce	2 oz	1/4 cup	1/4 oz	1/2 Tbsp
Vegetable oil	8 oz	1 cup	1 oz	2 Tbsp
Parsley, chopped		2 Tbsp		3/4 tsp

Method

1. Combine vegetables. Toss lightly.
2. Prepare dressing.
   a. Combine soy sauce, oil, and parsley. Pour over vegetables. Toss lightly.
3. Portion 1 cup per serving.

Directions for Diet Preparations

Sodium Restricted (SR): Use low sodium soy sauce.
Low Fat/Low Cholesterol (LF): 1 cup and **Diabetic** (DB): 1 cup. Use half the amount of oil specified. Low fat diets should consider individual tolerance to onions.
Mechanical Soft (SFT), **Soft/Low Fiber** (SLF), and **Puree** (PUR): Not recommended, substitute appropriate food alternative.

Nutrient Analysis per Serving:

Regular	KCAL	PRO gm	CHO gm	FAT gm	Chol mg	SFA gm	PFA gm	VITA iu	VITC mg	THI mg	RIB mg	NIA mg	CA mg	NA mg	K+ mg	FE mg
	70.0	1.8	6.2	4.6	0.0	0.5	2.6	167	5.3	0.06	0.05	0.5	18.2	98.0	140	0.7

Sodium Restricted	NA mg	Diabetic	Kcal	Milk exg	Veg exg	Fruit exg	Bread exg	Meat exg	Fat exg	Low Fat & Low Chol	FAT gm	Chol mg	SFA gm	PFA gm
	53.3		50.5	0.0	1.0	0.0	0.0	0.0	0.5		2.4	0.0	0.3	1.3

Mustard Rice Salad

Portion: 1/2 cup

INGREDIENTS	50 portions		6 portions	
	weights	measures	weights	measures
Rice, converted, cooked	10 lb EP (2 1/2 lb AP)	1 1/4 gal	1 1/4 lb EP (5 oz AP)	2 1/2 cups
Mayonnaise	1 lb	2 cups	2 oz	1/4 cup
Mustard, dijon	4 oz	1/2 cup	1/2 oz	1 Tbsp
Onions, chopped	1 1/2 lb EP (2 lb AP)	1 qt	3 oz EP (4 oz AP)	1/2 cup
Tomatoes, chopped	1 1/2 lb EP (1 3/4 lb AP)	3 1/2 cups	3 1/2 oz EP (4 oz AP)	1/2 cup

Method

1. Cook rice.
2. Add onions and tomatoes to rice.
3. In a bowl, combine mayonnaise and mustard. Add to hot rice. Mix well.
4. Cover and refrigerate. Serve chilled.

Directions for Diet Preparations

Sodium Restricted (SR): Use low sodium mayonnaise and mustard.

Low Fat/Low Cholesterol (LF): 1/2 cup and **Diabetic** (DB): 1/3 cup.

50 portions: Replace 2 cups mayonnaise with 1 cup reduced-calorie low cholesterol mayonnaise. May use if able to calculate into daily food plan.

6 portions: Replace 1/4 cup mayonnaise with 2 Tbsp reduced-calorie low cholesterol mayonnaise. May use if able to calculate into daily food plan.

Mechanical Soft (SFT): Omit onions and tomatoes. Consider individual tolerance.

Soft/Low Fiber (SLF) and **Puree** (PUR): Not recommended, substitute with appropriate food alternative.

Nutrient Analysis per Serving:

Regular	KCAL	PRO gm	CHO gm	FAT gm	Chol mg	SFA gm	PFA gm	VITA iu	VITC mg	THI mg	RIB mg	NIA mg	CA mg	NA mg	K+ mg	FE mg
	161	2.0	21.4	7.3	5.2	0.7	4.9	86.8	1.7	0.02	0.01	0.3	15.8	84.2	56.0	0.3

Sodium Restricted	NA mg	Diabetic	Kcal	Milk exg	Veg exg	Fruit exg	Bread exg	Meat exg	Fat exg	Low Fat & Low Chol	FAT gm	Chol mg	SFA gm	PFA gm
	3.8		75.4	0.0	0.08	0.0	0.8	0.0	0.3		1.8	0.0	0.03	0.01

Portion: 3/4 cup

INGREDIENTS	48 portions		8 portions	
	weights	**measures**	**weights**	**measures**
Brown rice, cooked	7 1/2 lb	3 3/4 qt	1 1/4 lb	2 1/2 cups
Green onions, chopped	1 lb EP (1 1/4 lb AP)	3 cups	2 2/3 oz EP (3 1/4 oz AP)	1/2 cup
Cucumbers, diced	13 3/4 oz EP (1 lb AP)	3 cups	2 1/3 oz EP (2 3/4 oz AP)	1/2 cup
Carrot, grated	1 lb EP (1 1/8 lb AP)	3 cups (4 medium)	2 2/3 oz EP (3 oz AP)	1/2 cup (1 medium)
Parsley, fresh, chopped	2 2/3 oz	2 cups	2/3 oz	1/2 cup
Walnuts, coarsely chopped	1 1/4 lb	4 1/2 cups	3 1/2 oz	3/4 cup
Apple, grated	2 lb	1 1/2 qt (6 medium)	5 1/3 oz	1 cup (1 medium)
Dressing:				
Salad oil	12 oz	1 1/2 cups	2 oz	1/4 cup
Lemon juice	12 oz	1 1/2 cups	2 oz	1/4 cup
Mayonnaise	10 oz	1 1/4 cups	1 2/3 oz	3 Tbsp
Curry powder		2 Tbsp		1 tsp
Garlic powder		3/4 tsp		1/8 tsp
Apple juice concentrate	1 oz	2 Tbsp	1/8 oz	1/2 tsp

Method

1. Combine the rice, onion, cucumber, carrot, parsley, and walnuts; chill well.
2. Prepare dressing.
   a. Whisk all the dressing ingredients together until smooth.
   b. Grate the apple into the dressing.
3. Toss dressing with the salad.
4. Arrange salad on a plate of lettuce leaves and garnish with tomato wedges.

Directions for Diet Preparations

Sodium Restricted (SR): Use low sodium mayonnaise.
Low Fat/Low Cholesterol (LF) 3/4 cup and **Diabetic** (DB): 3/4 cup. Use reduced-calorie low cholesterol mayonnaise. Use half the amount of dressing. Omit walnuts. Low fat diets should consider individual tolerance to garlic.
Mechanical Soft (SFT) and **Soft/Low Fiber** (SLF): Not recommended. Provide appropriate food substitute.
Puree (PUR): Prepare as directed. Add additional liquid (i.e. dressing); blenderize to obtain desired consistency.

Nutrient Analysis per Serving:

Regular	KCAL	PRO gm	CHO gm	FAT gm	Chol mg	SFA gm	PFA gm	VITA iu	VITC mg	THI mg	RIB mg	NIA mg	CA mg	NA mg	K+ mg	FE mg
	247	3.3	19.1	18.4	3.2	2.0	11.4	2048	8.2	0.11	0.04	1.0	27.3	39.3	170	0.8

Sodium Restricted	NA mg	Diabetic	Kcal	Milk exg	Veg exg	Fruit exg	Bread exg	Meat exg	Fat exg	Low Fat & Low Chol	FAT gm	Chol mg	SFA gm	PFA gm
	9.5		115	0.0	0.25	0.15	0.8	0.0	0.8		4.9	0.0	0.5	2.1

Portion: 1/2 cup

INGREDIENTS	50 portions		6 portions	
	weights	measures	weights	measures
Green peas, canned, drained, or frozen cooked	10 lb	2 #10 cans (1 1/2 gal)	1 1/4 lb	3 cups
Eggs, hard-cooked	1 3/4 lb	3 1/2 cups (14 large)	2 oz	1/4 cup (1 large)
Cheddar, mild diced or shredded	1 1/2 lb	1 1/2 qt	3 oz	3/4 cup
Onion, finely chopped	3 oz	1/2 cup	1/3 oz	1 Tbsp
Celery, finely chopped	12 oz	3 cups	1 1/2 oz	1/3 cup
Red peppers, finely chopped	5 1/3 oz	1 cup	2/3 oz	2 Tbsp
Mayonnaise	1 1/2 lb	3 cups	3 oz	1/3 cup

Method

1. Peel and chop eggs.
2. Combine all ingredients. Mix lightly.
3. Serve with No. 8 dipper.

Directions for Diet Preparations

Sodium Restricted (SR): Use low sodium peas, low sodium cheese, and low sodium mayonnaise.

Low Fat/Low Cholesterol (LF) 1/2 cup and **Diabetic** (DB): 1/2 cup. Use low fat cheese. Omit eggs. Use reduced-calorie low cholesterol mayonnaise in half the amount specified for regular mayonnaise. Low fat diets should consider individual tolerance to onions.

Mechanical Soft (SFT): Cook peas until mushy. Omit celery, onions, and peppers. Consider individual tolerance.

Soft/Low Fiber (SLF): Not recommended, substitute appropriate food alternative.

Puree (PUR): Omit celery, onions, and peppers. Blenderize. Add additional liquid (i.e mayonnaise or cheese sauce) if necessary to obtain desired consistency.

Nutrient Analysis per Serving:

Regular	KCAL	PRO gm	CHO gm	FAT gm	Chol mg	SFA gm	PFA gm	VITA iu	VITC mg	THI mg	RIB mg	NIA mg	CA mg	NA mg	K+ mg	FE mg
	153	7.7	11.9	8.5	94.7	3.1	2.2	688	13.9	0.18	0.14	1.1	96.2	230	145	1.4

Sodium Restricted	NA mg	Diabetic	Kcal	Milk exg	Veg exg	Fruit exg	Bread exg	Meat exg	Fat exg	Low Fat & Low Chol	FAT gm	Chol mg	SFA gm	PFA gm
	67.3		87.7	0.0	0.2	0.0	1.0	0.0	0.2		2.6	2.4	0.2	0.1

Portion: 1/2 cup

INGREDIENTS	50 portions		6 portions	
	weights	**measures**	**weights**	**measures**
Potatoes, white or red, pared	12 lb AP (9 3/4 lb EP)	36 medium	1 1/2 lb AP (1 1/4 lb EP)	5 medium
Salad oil	4 oz	1/2 cup	1/2 oz	1 Tbsp
Vinegar, cider	4 oz	1/2 cup	1/2 oz	1 Tbsp
Lemon juice		1 Tbsp		1/2 tsp
Mustard, prepared		1 Tbsp		1/2 tsp
Eggs, hard-cooked, diced	1 lb	2 3/4 cups (10 large)	1 2/3 oz	1/4 cup (1 large)
Onions, finely chopped	5 1/3 oz	1 cup	3/4 oz	2 Tbsp
Celery, diced	12 oz	3 cups	1 1/2 oz	1/3 cup
Mayonnaise	8 oz	1 cup	1 oz	2 Tbsp
Yogurt, plain, nonfat	12 oz	1 1/2 cups	1 1/2 oz	3 Tbsp

Method

1. Cook potatoes in steamer or stock pot until tender. Drain well.
2. Dice potatoes.
3. Combine oil, vinegar, lemon juice, and mustard to make marinade.
4. Add marinade to potatoes. Mix gently. Marinate until cold. Drain.
5. Add eggs, celery, and onions to potatoes. Mix lightly.
6. Add mayonnaise and yogurt. Mix carefully to blend.
7. Chill 1 to 2 hours before serving.
8. Serve with No. 8 dipper.

Directions for Diet Preparations

Sodium Restricted (SR): Use low sodium mayonnaise.

Low Fat/Low Cholesterol (LF): 1/2 cup and **Diabetic** (DB): 1/2 cup. Omit salad oil and eggs. Use reduced-calorie low cholesterol mayonnaise in half the amount specified for regular mayonnaise. Low fat diets should consider individual tolerance to onions.

Mechanical Soft (SFT) and **Soft/Low Fiber** (SLF): Cook potatoes until soft. Omit vinegar, mustard, celery, and onions. Consider individual tolerance.

Puree (PUR): Cook potatoes until soft. Omit celery and onions. Blenderize. Add additional liquid (i.e. mayonnaise) if necessary to obtain desired consistency.

Nutrient Analysis per Serving:

Regular	KCAL	PRO gm	CHO gm	FAT gm	Chol mg	SFA gm	PFA gm	VITA iu	VITC mg	THI mg	RIB mg	NIA mg	CA mg	NA mg	K+ mg	FE mg
	135	3.5	18.2	5.5	83.1	1.0	2.4	97.7	6.7	0.09	0.07	1.1	28.4	72.6	307	0.6

Sodium Restricted	NA mg	Diabetic	Kcal	Milk exg	Veg exg	Fruit exg	Bread exg	Meat exg	Fat exg	Low Fat & Low Chol	FAT gm	Chol mg	SFA gm	PFA gm
	19.6		77.0	0.0	0.2	0.0	1.0	0.0	0.0		0.4	1.2	0.1	0.04

Three Bean Salad

Portion: 1/2 cup

INGREDIENTS	50 portions		6 portions	
	weights	measures	weights	measures
Kidney beans, canned	2 lb	1 1/2 qt	4 oz	3/4 cup
Green beans, cut or french style, canned	3 lb	2 1/4 qt	6 oz	1 1/8 cups
Wax beans, cut, canned	2 lb	1 1/2 qt	4 oz	3/4 cup
Marinade:				
Onions, sliced thin	1 lb	2 cups	2 oz	1/4 cup
Green pepper, diced	10 oz	2 cups	1 1/4 oz	1/4 cup
Vinegar, cider		2 cups		1/4 cup
Sugar, granulated	1 lb	2 1/4 cups	2 oz	4 1/2 Tbsp
Soy sauce		1/4 cup		1/2 Tbsp
Salad oil	8 oz	1 cup	1 oz	2 Tbsp

Method

1. Rinse beans thoroughly. Drain. Combine.
2. Combine onions, green pepper, vinegar, sugar, and soy sauce to make marinade.
3. Pour marinade over beans. Refrigerate overnight.
4. Just before serving, drain off marinade.
5. Add oil. Toss lightly.
6. Serve with No. 8 dipper.

Directions for Diet Preparations

Sodium Restricted (SR): Use low sodium beans. Omit soy sauce, substitute with low sodium soy sauce.

Low Fat/Low Cholesterol (LF): 1/2 cup. Omit salad oil. Low fat diets should consider individual tolerance to onions.

Diabetic (DB): 1/2 cup.

50 portions: Omit sugar, substitute with artificial sweetener equivalent to 1 lb granulated sugar (approx. 2 Tbsp artificial sweetener). Omit salad oil.

6 portions: Omit sugar, substitute with artificial sweetener equivalent to 2 oz granulated sugar (approx. 3/4 tsp artificial sweetener). Omit salad oil.

Mechanical Soft (SFT), **Soft/Low Fiber** (SLF), **Puree** (PUR): Not recommended, substitute with appropriate food alternative.

Nutrient Analysis per Serving:

Regular	KCAL	PRO gm	CHO gm	FAT gm	Chol mg	SFA gm	PFA gm	VITA iu	VITC mg	THI mg	RIB mg	NIA mg	CA mg	NA mg	K+ mg	FE mg
	63.1	1.6	9.8	2.3	0.0	0.3	1.3	179	8.1	0.03	0.04	0.2	18.9	218	120	0.7

Sodium Restricted	NA mg	Diabetic	Kcal	Milk exg	Veg exg	Fruit exg	Bread exg	Meat exg	Fat exg	Low Fat & Low Chol	FAT gm	Chol mg	SFA gm	PFA gm
	21.6		29.0	0.0	1.0	0.0	0.0	0.0	0.0		0.1	0.0	0.02	0.07

Portion: 1/2 cup

INGREDIENTS	50 portions		6 portions	
	weights	measures	weights	measures
Marinade:				
Lemon juice		2 1/2 Tbsp		1 tsp
Vinegar, white		1/3 cup		2 tsp
Salad oil	8 oz	1 cup	1 oz	2 Tbsp
Water		1/3 cup		2 tsp
Onion, finely chopped	2 oz	1/3 cup	1/4 oz	2 tsp
Red pepper, chopped		1/4 cup		1 1/2 tsp
Parsley, finely chopped		1/4 cup		1 1/2 tsp
Sugar, granulated		1 Tbsp		1 tsp
Tarragon		1 Tbsp		1 tsp
Zucchini, fresh, sliced	12 lb AP	50 small	1 1/2 lb AP	6–7 small
	(10 lb EP)	1 3/4 gal	(1 1/4 lb EP)	3 1/2 cups

Method

1. Combine all ingredients, except zucchini. Mix well.
2. Pour marinade over zucchini. Mix thoroughly.
3. Refrigerate for 2 to 3 hours.
4. Drain off most of the marinade before serving.
5. Serve with No. 8 dipper.

Directions for Diet Preparations

Sodium Restricted (SR): Prepare as directed.
Low Fat/Low Cholesterol (LF): 1/2 cup. Omit vegetable oil. Low fat diets should consider individual tolerance to onions.
Diabetic (DB): 1/2 cup. Omit vegetable oil and sugar. Use artificial sweetener to taste.
Mechanical Soft (SFT), **Soft/Low Fiber** (SLF), and **Puree** (PUR): Not recommended, substitute with appropriate food alternative.

Nutrient Analysis per Serving:

Regular	KCAL	PRO gm	CHO gm	FAT gm	Chol mg	SFA gm	PFA gm	VITA iu	VITC mg	THI mg	RIB mg	NIA mg	CA mg	NA mg	K+ mg	FE mg
	46.0	0.6	4.1	3.3	0.0	0.4	1.9	241	5.4	0.03	0.03	0.4	13.7	2.9	239	0.3

Sodium Restricted	NA mg	Diabetic	Kcal	Milk exg	Veg exg	Fruit exg	Bread exg	Meat exg	Fat exg	Low Fat & Low Chol	FAT gm	Chol mg	SFA gm	PFA gm
	2.9		16.0	0.0	0.5	0.0	0.0	0.0	0.0		0.06	0.0	0.01	0.02

Portion: 1 cup

INGREDIENTS	50 portions		6 portions	
	weights	**measures**	**weights**	**measures**
Lettuce, iceberg	5 lb EP (6 3/4 lb AP)	2 1/4 gal (3–4 heads)	10 oz EP (13 1/2 oz AP)	1 qt (1/2 head)
Carrots, shredded	8 oz EP (11 1/2 oz AP)	2 cups	1 oz EP (1 1/2 oz AP)	1/4 cup
Tomatoes, diced	1 1/3 lb EP (1 1/2 lb AP)	3 cups	2 2/3 oz EP (3 oz AP)	1/3 cup
Green peppers, diced	1 lb EP (1 1/4 lb AP)	3 cups	2 oz EP (2 1/2 oz AP)	1/3 cup
Onion, chopped	5 1/3 oz EP	1 cup	3/4 oz	2 Tbsp
Zucchini, sliced	8 oz EP	2 cups	1 oz EP	1/4 cup
Green peas, cooked, chilled	14 oz	2 cups	1 3/4 oz	1/4 cup
Mushrooms, sliced	5 oz	2 cups	2/3 oz	1/4 cup

Method

1. Wash and drain lettuce thoroughly. Cut or tear into bite size pieces. Place in mixing bowl.
2. Add remaining ingredients to lettuce. Toss lightly.
3. Portion into individual salad bowls. Portion 1 cup per serving.
4. Serve with appropriate salad dressing according to diet.

Directions for Diet Preparations

Sodium Restricted (SR): Prepare as directed. Use SR salad dressing.

Low Fat/Low Cholesterol (LF): 1 cup and **Diabetic** (DB): 1 cup. Use low-calorie low cholesterol salad dressing. Low fat diets should consider individual tolerance to onions and peas.

Mechanical Soft (SFT): Use shredded lettuce if tolerated. If unable to tolerate, substitute with an appropriate food alternative. Use a SFT salad dressing.

Soft/Low Fiber (SLF) and **Puree** (PUR): Not recommended, substitute with appropriate food alternative.

Nutrient Analysis per Serving:

Regular	KCAL	PRO gm	CHO gm	FAT gm	Chol mg	SFA gm	PFA gm	VITA iu	VITC mg	THI mg	RIB mg	NIA mg	CA mg	NA mg	K+ mg	FE mg
	21.1	1.3	4.0	0.2	trace	0.03	0.1	1614	13.2	0.07	0.05	0.5	17.6	8.5	189	0.6

Sodium Restricted	NA mg	Diabetic	Kcal	Milk exg	Veg exg	Fruit exg	Bread exg	Meat exg	Fat exg	Low Fat & Low Chol	FAT gm	Chol mg	SFA gm	PFA gm
	8.5		21.1	0.0	0.8	0.0	0.0	0.0	0.0		0.2	trace	0.03	0.1

Portion: 1 cup

INGREDIENTS	50 portions		6 portions	
	weights	measures	weights	measures
Lettuce, iceberg	4 1/2 lb AP (3 lb EP)	2–3 heads (1 1/2 gal)	9 oz AP (6 oz EP)	1/3 head 3 cups
Spinach	11 oz AP	3 qt	1 1/2 oz AP	1 1/2 cups
Cucumbers, sliced	2 2/3 lb EP (3 lb AP)	2 qt (8 large)	5 1/4 oz EP (6 oz AP)	1 cup (1 large)
Broccoli florets	1 1/2 lb EP (2 lb AP)	1 1/2 qt	3 oz EP (4 oz AP)	3/4 cup

Method

1. Wash and drain lettuce and spinach thoroughly. Cut or tear into bite size pieces. Place in mixing bowl.
2. Add remaining ingredients to lettuce and spinach. Toss lightly.
3. Portion into individual salad bowls. Portion 1 cup per serving.
4. Serve with appropriate salad dressing according to diet.

Directions for Diet Preparations

Sodium Restricted (SR): Prepare as directed. Use SR salad dressing.

Low Fat/Low Cholesterol (LF): 1 cup and **Diabetic** (DB): 1 cup. Use low-calorie low cholesterol salad dressing. Low fat diets should consider individual tolerance to broccoli.

Mechanical Soft (SFT): Use shredded lettuce if tolerated. If unable to tolerate, substitute with an appropriate food alternative. Use a SFT salad dressing.

Soft/Low Fiber (SLF) and **Puree** (PUR): Not recommended, substitute with appropriate food alternative.

Nutrient Analysis per Serving:

Regular	KCAL	PRO gm	CHO gm	FAT gm	Chol mg	SFA gm	PFA gm	VITA iu	VITC mg	THI mg	RIB mg	NIA mg	CA mg	NA mg	K+ mg	FE mg
	11.6	1.0	2.0	0.1	0.0	0.02	0.07	1174	15.5	0.03	0.04	0.2	26.0	16.3	178	0.6

Sodium Restricted	NA mg	Diabetic	Kcal	Milk exg	Veg exg	Fruit exg	Bread exg	Meat exg	Fat exg	Low Fat & Low Chol	FAT gm	Chol mg	SFA gm	PFA gm
	16.3		11.6	0.0	0.4	0.0	0.0	0.0	0.0		0.1	0.0	0.02	0.07

Portion: 1 cup

INGREDIENTS	50 portions		6 portions	
	weights	**measures**	**weights**	**measures**
Spinach, fresh	4 lb AP (3 1/4 lb EP)	2 1/2 gal	8 oz AP (6 1/2 oz EP)	1 1/4 qt
Cucumbers, sliced	1 lb EP (1 1/4 lb AP)	3 cups (3–4 large)	2 oz EP (2 1/3 oz AP)	1/3 cup (1/2 large)
Broccoli florets	12 oz EP	3 cups	1 1/2 oz EP	1/3 cup
Green peppers, chopped	1 lb EP (1 1/4 lb AP)	3 cups	2 oz EP (2 1/2 oz AP)	1/3 cup
Scallions, diced	8 oz EP (10 oz AP)	1 cup	1 oz EP (1 1/4 oz AP)	2 Tbsp

Method

1. Wash and drain spinach thoroughly. Cut or tear into bite size pieces. Place in mixing bowl.
2. Add remaining ingredients to spinach. Toss lightly.
3. Portion into individual salad bowls. Portion 1 cup per serving.
4. Serve with appropriate salad dressing according to diet.

Directions for Diet Preparations

Sodium Restricted (SR): Prepare as directed. Use SR salad dressing.

Low Fat/Low Cholesterol (LF): 1 cup and **Diabetic** (DB): 1 cup. Use low-calorie low cholesterol salad dressing. Low fat diets should consider individual tolerance to broccoli.

Mechanical Soft (SFT): Use shredded lettuce if tolerated. If unable to tolerate, substitute with an appropriate food alternative. Use a SFT salad dressing.

Soft/Low Fiber (SLF) and **Puree** (PUR): Not recommended, substitute with appropriate food alternative.

Nutrient Analysis per Serving:

Regular	KCAL	PRO gm	CHO gm	FAT gm	Chol mg	SFA gm	PFA gm	VITA iu	VITC mg	THI mg	RIB mg	NIA mg	CA mg	NA mg	K+ mg	FE mg
	14.9	1.5	2.6	0.2	0.0	0.03	0.09	3160	26.0	0.04	0.09	0.4	49.5	37.6	296	1.3

Sodium Restricted	NA mg	**Diabetic**	Kcal	Milk exg	Veg exg	Fruit exg	Bread exg	Meat exg	Fat exg	**Low Fat & Low Chol**	FAT gm	Chol mg	SFA gm	PFA gm
	37.6		14.9	0.0	0.5	0.0	0.0	0.0	0.0		0.2	0.0	0.03	0.09

Israeli Salad

Portion: 1 cup

INGREDIENTS	50 portions		6 portions	
	weights	measures	weights	measures
Lettuce, iceberg	7 lb AP (5 lb EP)	3–4 heads (2 1/2 gal)	14 oz AP (10 oz EP)	1/2 head (1 1/4 qt)
Tomatoes, diced	1 1/3 lb EP (1 1/2 lb AP)	3 cups	2 2/3 oz EP (3 oz AP)	1/3 cup
Green peppers, diced	1 lb EP (1 1/4 lb AP)	3 cups	2 oz EP (2 1/2 oz AP)	1/3 cup
Onion, chopped	5 1/3 oz EP	1 cup	3/4 oz EP	2 Tbsp
Cucumbers, diced	1 lb EP (1 1/4 lb AP)	3 cups	2 oz EP (2 1/2 oz AP)	1/3 cup
Italian parsley, chopped	1 1/3 oz	1 cup	1/8 oz	2 Tbsp
Lemon juice	8 oz	1 cup	1 oz	2 Tbsp
Olive oil	8 oz	1 cup	1 oz	2 Tbsp

Method

1. Wash and drain lettuce thoroughly. Cut or tear into bite size pieces. Place in mixing bowl.
2. Add tomatoes, green pepper, onions, cucumbers, and parsley to lettuce. Toss lightly.
3. Add lemon juice and oil to salad. Toss lightly.
4. Portion into individual salad bowls. Portion 1 cup per serving.

Directions for Diet Preparations

Sodium Restricted (SR), **Low Fat/Low Cholesterol** (LF): 1 cup and **Diabetic** (DB): 1 cup. Prepare as directed.

Mechanical Soft (SFT): Use shredded lettuce if tolerated. If unable to tolerate, substitute with appropriate food alternative.

Soft/Low Fiber (SLF) and **Puree** (PUR): Not recommended, substitute with appropriate food alternative.

Nutrient Analysis per Serving:

Regular	KCAL	PRO gm	CHO gm	FAT gm	Chol mg	SFA gm	PFA gm	VITA iu	VITC mg	THI mg	RIB mg	NIA mg	CA mg	NA mg	K+ mg	FE mg
	52.9	0.9	2.8	4.5	0.0	0.6	0.5	371	15.1	0.04	0.03	0.2	16.4	7.1	151	0.5

Sodium Restricted	NA mg	Diabetic	Kcal	Milk exg	Veg exg	Fruit exg	Bread exg	Meat exg	Fat exg	Low Fat & Low Chol	FAT gm	Chol mg	SFA gm	PFA gm
	7.1		52.9	0.0	1.1	0.0	0.0	0.0	0.5		4.5	0.0	0.6	0.5

Mixed Field Greens

Portion: 1 cup

INGREDIENTS	50 portions		6 portions	
	weights	**measures**	**weights**	**measures**
Lettuce, iceberg	3 lb EP (4 1/2 lb AP)	1 1/2 gal (3 heads)	6 oz EP (9 oz AP)	3 cups (1/3 head)
Lettuce, romaine	3 lb EP (4 1/2 lb AP)	1 1/2 gal (3 heads)	6 oz EP (9 oz AP)	3 cups (1/3 head)
Green peppers, chopped	10 2/3 oz EP (13 1/4 oz AP)	2 cups	1 1/3 oz EP (1 2/3 oz AP)	1/4 cup
Green onions, chopped	1 lb EP (1 1/4 lb AP)	3 cups	2 oz EP (2 1/2 oz AP)	1/3 cup

Method

1. Wash and drain lettuce thoroughly. Cut or tear into bite size pieces. Place in mixing bowl.
2. Add green peppers and onions to lettuce. Toss gently until the greens are uniformly mixed.
3. Refrigerate until ready to serve.
4. Portion 1 cup per salad bowl.
5. Serve with appropriate salad dressing according to diet. The salad dressing may be served in a separate container or added just before serving.

Directions for Diet Preparations

Sodium Restricted (SR): Prepare as directed. Use SR salad dressing.

Low Fat/Low Cholesterol (LF): 1 cup and **Diabetic** (DB): 1 cup. Use low-calorie low cholesterol salad dressing. Low fat diets should consider individual tolerance to onions.

Mechanical Soft (SFT): Use shredded lettuce if tolerated. If unable to tolerate, substitute with appropriate food alternative. Use a SFT salad dressing.

Soft/Low Fiber (SLF) and **Puree** (PUR): Not recommended, substitute with appropriate food alternative.

Nutrient Analysis per Serving:

Regular	KCAL	PRO gm	CHO gm	FAT gm	Chol mg	SFA gm	PFA gm	VITA iu	VITC mg	THI mg	RIB mg	NIA mg	CA mg	NA mg	K+ mg	FE mg
	13.7	1.2	2.2	0.2	0.0	0.02	0.09	1316	17.4	0.06	0.06	0.3	24.3	7.3	195	0.8

Sodium Restricted	NA mg	Diabetic	Kcal	Milk exg	Veg exg	Fruit exg	Bread exg	Meat exg	Fat exg	Low Fat & Low Chol	FAT gm	Chol mg	SFA gm	PFA gm
	7.3		13.7	0.0	0.5	0.0	0.0	0.0	0.0		0.2	0.0	0.02	0.09

Tossed Salad

Portion: 1 cup

INGREDIENTS	50 portions		6 portions	
	weights	measures	weights	measures
Lettuce, iceberg	5 lb EP (7 lb AP)	2 1/2 gal (3–4 heads)	10 oz EP (14 oz AP)	1 1/4 qt (1/2 head)
Tomatoes, diced	4 1/2 lb EP (5 lb AP)	2 1/2 qt	9 oz EP (10 oz AP)	1 1/4 cups

Method

1. Wash and drain lettuce thoroughly. Cut or tear into bite size pieces. Place in mixing bowl.
2. Add tomato to lettuce. Toss lightly.
3. Portion into individual salad bowls. Portion 1 cup per serving.
4. Serve with appropriate salad dressing according to diet. The salad dressing may be served in a separate container or added just before serving.

Directions for Diet Preparations

Sodium Restricted (SR): Prepare as directed. Use SR salad dressing.

Low Fat/Low Cholesterol (LF): 1 cup and **diabetic** (DB): 1 cup. Use low-calorie low cholesterol salad dressing.

Mechanical Soft (SFT): Use shredded lettuce if tolerated. If unable to tolerate, substitute with appropriate food alternative. Use a SFT salad dressing.

Soft/Low Fiber (SLF) and **Puree** (PUR): Not recommended, substitute with appropriate food alternative.

Nutrient Analysis per Serving:

Regular	KCAL	PRO gm	CHO gm	FAT gm	Chol mg	SFA gm	PFA gm	VITA iu	VITC mg	THI mg	RIB mg	NIA mg	CA mg	NA mg	K+ mg	FE mg
	9.9	0.6	1.9	0.1	0.0	0.02	0.06	398	5.7	0.03	0.02	0.2	9.7	5.7	114	0.3

Sodium Restricted	NA mg	Diabetic	Kcal	Milk exg	Veg exg	Fruit exg	Bread exg	Meat exg	Fat exg	Low Fat & Low Chol	FAT gm	Chol mg	SFA gm	PFA gm
	5.7		9.9	0.0	0.4	0.0	0.0	0.0	0.0		0.1	0.0	0.02	0.06

Portion: 1 cup

INGREDIENTS	50 portions		6 portions	
	weights	**measures**	**weights**	**measures**
Lettuce, iceberg	5 lb EP (7 lb AP)	2 1/2 gal (3–4 heads)	10 oz EP (14 oz AP)	1 1/4 qt (1/2 head)
Green peas, cooked, chilled	1 1/3 lb	3 cups	2 2/3 oz	1/3 cup
Green peppers, chopped	1 1/3 lb EP (1 3/4 lb AP)	1 qt	2 2/3 oz EP (3 1/2 oz AP)	1/2 cup
Zucchini, sliced	12 oz EP (13 oz AP)	3 cups	1 1/2 oz EP (1 2/3 oz AP)	1/3 cup

Method

1. Wash and drain lettuce thoroughly. Cut or tear into bite size pieces. Place in mixing bowl.
2. Add remaining ingredients to lettuce. Toss lightly.
3. Portion into individual salad bowls. Portion 1 cup per serving.
4. Serve with appropriate salad dressing according to diet. The salad dressing may be served in a separate container or added just before serving.

Directions for Diet Preparations

Sodium Restricted (SR): Prepare as directed. Use SR salad dressing.

Low Fat/Low Cholesterol (LF): 1 cup and **Diabetic** (DB): 1 cup. Use low-calorie low cholesterol salad dressing. Low fat diets should consider individual tolerance to peas.

Mechanical Soft (SFT): Use shredded lettuce if tolerated. If unable to tolerate, substitute with appropriate food alternative. Use a SFT salad dressing.

Soft/Low Fiber (SLF) and **Puree** (PUR): Not recommended, substitute with appropriate food alternative.

Nutrient Analysis per Serving:

Regular	KCAL	PRO gm	CHO gm	FAT gm	Chol mg	SFA gm	PFA gm	VITA iu	VITC mg	THI mg	RIB mg	NIA mg	CA mg	NA mg	K+ mg	FE mg
	17.5	1.1	3.2	0.1	0.0	0.02	0.07	270	11.4	0.06	0.03	0.4	13.2	4.9	139	0.5

Sodium Restricted	NA mg	**Diabetic**	Kcal	Milk exg	Veg exg	Fruit exg	Bread exg	Meat exg	Fat exg	**Low Fat & Low Chol**	FAT gm	Chol mg	SFA gm	PFA gm
	4.9		17.4	0.0	0.6	0.0	0.0	0.0	0.0		0.1	0.0	0.02	0.07

Portion: 1 cup

INGREDIENTS	50 portions		6 portions	
	weights	**measures**	**weights**	**measures**
Lettuce, iceberg	4 lb EP (5 1/4 lb AP)	2 gal (2–3 heads)	8 oz EP (10 1/2 oz AP)	1 qt (1/3 head)
Pineapple tidbits, unsweetened, drained	3 lb	1 1/2 qt	6 oz	3/4 cup
Carrots, shredded	1 1/2 lb EP (2 1/4 lb AP)	1 1/2 qt	3 oz EP (4 1/2 oz AP)	3/4 cup
Green peppers, diced	1 1/2 lb EP (2 lb AP)	1 1/8 qt	3 oz EP (4 oz AP)	1/2 cup
Dressing:				
Honey	4 oz	1/2 cup	1/2 oz	1 Tbsp
Vinegar, cider	4 oz	1/2 cup	1/2 oz	1 Tbsp
Lemon juice		2 1/2 tsp		1/2 tsp
Onion, grated		2 tsp		1/4 tsp
Salad oil	12 oz	1 1/2 cups	1 1/2 oz	3 Tbsp
Mustard, dry		1 1/2 tsp		1/8 tsp
Celery seed		1 1/2 tsp		1/8 tsp

Method

1. Wash and drain lettuce thoroughly. Cut or tear into bite size pieces. Place in mixing bowl.
2. Add remaining ingredients to lettuce. Toss lightly.
3. Prepare dressing.
   a. Combine salad dressing ingredients. Mix well. Pour over salad. Toss lightly.
4. Portion into individual salad bowls. Portion 1 cup per serving.

Directions for Diet Preparations

Sodium Restricted (SR): Prepare as directed.

Low Fat/Low Cholesterol (LF): 1 cup. Use half the amount of salad oil specified. Serve 2 tsp salad dressing per 1 cup.

Diabetic (DB): 1 cup. Use half the amount of salad oil specified. Omit honey, substitute with an artificial sweetener to taste. Serve 2 tsp salad dressing per 1 cup.

Mechanical Soft (SFT) and **Soft/Low Fiber** (SLF): Not recommended. Serve canned pineapple tidbits with cooked canned carrots. Omit onions, mustard, and celery seeds from dressing. Add to pineapple and carrots.

Puree (PUR): Not recommended. Serve canned pineapple tidbits with cooked canned carrots. Strain dressing. Add dressing to pineapple and carrots; blenderize to obtain desired consistency.

Nutrient Analysis per Serving:

Regular	KCAL	PRO gm	CHO gm	FAT gm	Chol mg	SFA gm	PFA gm	VITA iu	VITC mg	THI mg	RIB mg	NIA mg	CA mg	NA mg	K+ mg	FE mg
	92.2	0.7	8.0	6.8	0.0	0.8	3.9	3936	16.7	0.06	0.03	0.3	17.7	8.8	162	0.5

Sodium Restricted	NA mg	Diabetic	Kcal	Milk exg	Veg exg	Fruit exg	Bread exg	Meat exg	Fat exg	Low Fat & Low Chol	FAT gm	Chol mg	SFA gm	PFA gm
	8.8		53.0	0.0	0.5	0.25	0.0	0.0	0.5		3.5	0.0	0.4	2.0

Portion: 1 cup

INGREDIENTS	50 portions		6 portions	
	weights	measures	weights	measures
Lettuce, iceberg	5 lb EP (7 lb AP)	2 1/2 gal (3–4 heads)	10 oz EP (14 oz AP)	1 1/4 qt (1/2 head)
Tomatoes, diced	1 3/4 lb EP (2 lb AP)	1 qt	3 1/2 oz EP (4 oz AP)	1/2 cup
Green peas, cooked, chilled	1 1/3 lb	3 cups	2 2/3 oz	1/3 cup
Mushrooms, sliced, fresh	7 oz	3 cups	3/4 oz	1/3 cup

Method

1. Wash and drain lettuce thoroughly. Cut or tear into bite size pieces. Place in mixing bowl.
2. Add remaining ingredients to lettuce. Toss lightly.
3. Portion into individual salad bowls. Portion 1 cup per serving.
4. Serve with appropriate salad dressing according to diet. The salad dressing may be served in a separate container or added just before serving.

Directions for Diet Preparations

Sodium Restricted (SR): Prepare as directed. Use SR salad dressing.

Low Fat/Low Cholesterol (LF): 1 cup and **Diabetic** (DB): 1 cup. Use low-calorie low cholesterol salad dressing. Low fat diets should consider individual tolerance to peas.

Mechanical Soft (SFT): Use shredded lettuce if tolerated. If unable to tolerate, substitute with appropriate food alternative. Use a SFT salad dressing.

Soft/Low Fiber (SLF) and **Puree** (PUR): Not recommended, substitute with appropriate food alternative.

Nutrient Analysis per Serving:

Regular	KCAL	PRO gm	CHO gm	FAT gm	Chol mg	SFA gm	PFA gm	VITA iu	VITC mg	THI mg	RIB mg	NIA mg	CA mg	NA mg	K+ mg	FE mg
	15.9	1.1	2.8	0.1	0.0	0.02	0.07	297	4.1	0.05	0.04	0.4	11.7	13.2	118	0.4

Sodium Restricted	NA mg	Diabetic	Kcal	Milk exg	Veg exg	Fruit exg	Bread exg	Meat exg	Fat exg	Low Fat & Low Chol	FAT gm	Chol mg	SFA gm	PFA gm
	13.2		15.9	0.0	0.3	0.0	0.1	0.0	0.0		0.1	0.0	0.02	0.07

Portion: 3/4 cup

INGREDIENTS	50 portions		6 portions	
	weights	measures	weights	measures
Spinach, fresh	2 1/2 lb EP (3 lb AP)	2 gal	5 oz EP (6 oz AP)	1 qt
Mushrooms, white, fresh, sliced thin	2 lb	3 1/2 qt	4 oz	1 3/4 cups
Eggs, hard-cooked, chopped	14 oz	2 1/3 cups (8 large)	1 3/4 oz	1/4 cup (1 large)
Bacon, cooked, crisp, crumbled	1 3/4 lb AP	1 qt	3 1/2 oz	1/2 cup

Method

1. Wash spinach in cold water several times, until there is no trace of sand. Drain well. Cut or tear into bite size pieces.
2. Combine spinach, mushrooms, and eggs. Toss lightly.
3. At serving time, sprinkle with crumbled bacon.
4. Serve with appropriate salad dressing according to diet. The salad dressing may be served in a separate container or added just before serving.

Directions for Diet Preparations

Sodium Restricted (SR): Omit bacon. Use SR salad dressing.

Low Fat/Low Cholesterol (LF): 3/4 cup and **Diabetic** (DB): 3/4 cup. Omit eggs and bacon. Use low-calorie low cholesterol salad dressing.

Mechanical Soft (SFT), **Soft/Low Fiber** (SLF), and **Puree** (PUR): Not recommended, substitute with appropriate food alternative.

Nutrient Analysis per Serving:

Regular	KCAL	PRO gm	CHO gm	FAT gm	Chol mg	SFA gm	PFA gm	VITA iu	VITC mg	THI mg	RIB mg	NIA mg	CA mg	NA mg	K+ mg	FE mg
	96.5	6.0	1.7	7.3	75.6	2.4	0.9	1280	9.7	0.12	0.19	1.8	27.0	221	248	1.2

Sodium Restricted	NA mg	Diabetic	Kcal	Milk exg	Veg exg	Fruit exg	Bread exg	Meat exg	Fat exg	Low Fat & Low Chol	FAT gm	Chol mg	SFA gm	PFA gm
	35.2		10.4	0.0	0.4	0.0	0.0	0.0	0.0		0.1	0.0	0.02	0.07

Portion: 4 ounces or 1/2 cup

INGREDIENTS	50 portions		6 portions	
	weights	measures	weights	measures
Gelatin, orange	1 1/2 lb	3 1/2 cups	3 oz	3/8 cup
Water, boiling		2 qt		1 cup
Orange juice, unsweetened, cold		2 qt		1 cup
Mandarin oranges, unsweetened, drained	3 lb	1 1/2 qt	6 oz	3/4 cup
Carrots, grated	8 oz EP (11 1/2 oz AP)	1 1/2 cups	1 oz EP (1 3/8 oz AP)	3 Tbsp

Method

1. Pour boiling water over gelatin. Stir until dissolved.
2. Add orange juice to gelatin. Chill.
3. Place mandarin oranges and carrots into counter pan(s) or gelatin mold.
4. When gelatin begins to congeal, pour over oranges and carrots.
5. Place in refrigerator to congeal completely.

Directions for Diet Preparations

Sodium Restricted (SR): Prepare as directed.
Low Fat/Low Cholesterol (LF): 4 oz or 1/2 cup. Prepare as directed.
Diabetic (DB): 4 oz or 1/2 cup. Use unsweetened orange gelatin as per manufacturer's directions.
Mechanical Soft (SFT) and **Soft/Low Fiber** (SLF): Substitute raw carrots with canned diced carrots.
Puree (PUR): Substitute raw carrots with canned carrots. Puree oranges and carrots. Pour gelatin over puree oranges and carrots. Place in refrigerator to congeal.

Nutrient Analysis per Serving:

Regular	KCAL	PRO gm	CHO gm	FAT gm	Chol mg	SFA gm	PFA gm	VITA iu	VITC mg	THI mg	RIB mg	NIA mg	CA mg	NA mg	K+ mg	FE mg
	84.0	1.9	19.8	0.2	0.0	0.02	0.04	1038	27.7	0.07	0.02	0.2	16.5	44.8	168	0.1

Sodium Restricted	NA mg	Diabetic	Kcal	Milk exg	Veg exg	Fruit exg	Bread exg	Meat exg	Fat exg	Low Fat & Low Chol	FAT gm	Chol mg	SFA gm	PFA gm
	44.8		41.1	0.0	0.3	0.5	0.0	0.0	0.0		0.2	0.0	0.02	0.04

Portion: 4 ounces or 1/2 cup

INGREDIENTS	50 portions		6 portions	
	weights	**measures**	**weights**	**measures**
Gelatin, lemon	1 1/2 lb	3 1/2 cups	3 oz	3/8 cup
Water, boiling		1 3/4 qt		3/4 cup
Water, cold		2 qt		1 cup
Carrots, grated	1 1/3 lb EP (1 3/4 lb AP)	1 qt	2 2/3 oz EP (3 2/3 oz AP)	1/2 cup
Celery, chopped, fine	10 2/3 oz EP (12 3/4 lb AP)	2 cups	1 1/3 oz EP (1 2/3 oz AP)	1/4 cup
Green peas, cooked	1 3/4 lb	1 qt	3 3/8 oz	1/2 cup
Onions, diced	10 2/3 oz EP (12 1/8 oz AP)	2 cups	1 1/3 oz EP (1 1/2 oz AP)	1/4 cup
Vinegar	8 oz	1 cup	1 oz	2 Tbsp

Method

1. Pour boiling water over gelatin. Stir until dissolved.
2. Add cold water to gelatin. Chill until gelatin begins to congeal.
3. Combine vegetables. Pour vinegar over vegetables. Allow to marinate 30 minutes.
4. Place marinated vegetables into counter pan(s) or gelatin mold.
5. Pour partially congealed gelatin over vegetables.
6. Place in refrigerator to congeal completely.

Directions for Diet Preparations

Sodium Restricted (SR): Prepare as directed.
Low Fat/Low Cholesterol (LF): 4 oz or 1/2 cup. Prepare as directed. Low fat diets should consider individual tolerance to onions.
Diabetic (DB): 4 oz or 1/2 cup. Use unsweetened gelatin as per manufacturer's directions.
Mechanical Soft (SFT) and **Soft/Low Fiber** (SLF): 4 oz or 1/2 cup.

50 portions: Omit raw vegetables at Step #3, substitute with 1 1/2 qt canned carrots and 1 1/2 qt canned chopped spinach. Pour gelatin over marinated vegetables. Place in refrigerator to congeal.

6 portions: Omit raw vegetables at Step #3, substitute with 3/4 cup canned carrots and 3/4 cup canned chopped spinach. Pour gelatin over marinated vegetables. Place in refrigerator to congeal.

Puree (PUR): 4 oz or 1/2 cup.
50 portions: Omit raw vegetables at Step #3, substitute with 1 1/2 qt canned carrots and 1 1/2 qt canned chopped spinach. Puree marinated carrots and spinach. Pour gelatin over puree marinated vegetables. Place in refrigerator to congeal.

6 portions: Omit raw vegetables at Step #3, substitute with 3/4 cup canned carrots and 3/4 cup canned chopped spinach. Puree marinated carrots and spinach. Pour gelatin over puree marinated vegetables. Place in refrigerator to congeal.

Nutrient Analysis per Serving:

Regular	KCAL	PRO gm	CHO gm	FAT gm	Chol mg	SFA gm	PFA gm	VITA iu	VITC mg	THI mg	RIB mg	NIA mg	CA mg	NA mg	K+ mg	FE mg
	68.1	2.1	15.7	0.07	0.0	0.01	0.03	2600	2.9	0.05	0.02	0.3	9.1	62.1	107	0.3

Sodium Restricted	NA mg	Diabetic	Kcal	Milk exg	Veg exg	Fruit exg	Bread exg	Meat exg	Fat exg	Low Fat & Low Chol	FAT gm	Chol mg	SFA gm	PFA gm
	62.1		25.2	0.0	0.9	0.0	0.0	0.0	0.0		0.07	0.0	0.01	0.03

Blushing Pear Salad

Portion: 1 pear half with lettuce leaf

INGREDIENTS	50 portions		6 portions	
	weights	**measures**	**weights**	**measures**
Pear halves, canned, drained, unsweetened	7 lb	1 gal (50 halves)	14 oz	2 cups (6 halves)
Gelatin, raspberry	14 oz	2 cups	1 3/4 oz	1/4 cup
Lettuce leaves	3 lb EP (4 1/2 lb AP)	100 leaves (2–3 heads)	6 oz EP (9 oz AP)	12 leaves (1/2 head)

Method

1. Place pears in counter pan cut side down.
2. Sprinkle gelatin over pears through mesh strainer. Allow to stand a few minutes until pears take on red color.
3. Arrange lettuce leaf on each salad plate. Place pear half cut side down on each lettuce leaf.

Directions for Diet Preparations

Sodium Restricted (SR): Prepare as directed.
Low Fat/Low Cholesterol (LF): 1 pear half with lettuce leaf. Prepare as directed.
Diabetic (DB): 1 pear half with lettuce leaf. Use unsweetened gelatin as per manufacturer's directions.
Mechanical Soft (SFT) and **Soft/Low Fiber** (SLF): Omit lettuce.
Puree (PUR): 1/2 cup. Omit lettuce. Blenderize pears. Add additional pear juice to pears, if necessary to obtain desired consistency.

Nutrient Analysis per Serving:

Regular	KCAL	PRO gm	CHO gm	FAT gm	Chol mg	SFA gm	PFA gm	VITA iu	VITC mg	THI mg	RIB mg	NIA mg	CA mg	NA mg	K+ mg	FE mg
	78.3	1.0	19.5	0.3	0.0	0.01	0.07	18.4	3.3	0.02	0.03	0.08	9.2	25.3	121	0.2

Sodium Restricted	NA mg	Diabetic	Kcal	Milk exg	Veg exg	Fruit exg	Bread exg	Meat exg	Fat exg	Low Fat & Low Chol	FAT gm	Chol mg	SFA gm	PFA gm
	25.3		52.8	0.0	0.0	0.9	0.0	0.0	0.0		0.3	0.0	0.01	0.07

Portion: 4 ounces or 1/2 cup

INGREDIENTS	50 portions		6 portions	
	weights	**measures**	**weights**	**measures**
Gelatin, lemon	1 1/2 lb	3 1/3 cup	3 oz	3/8 cup
Water, boiling		1 3/4 qt		3/4 cup
Water, cold		2 qt		1 cup
Vinegar, cider	8 oz	1 cup	1 oz	2 Tbsp
Cabbage, chopped	1 1/2 lb EP (2 lb AP)	1 1/2 qt	3 oz EP (4 oz AP)	3/4 cup
Celery, chopped	11 oz EP (14 oz AP)	2 cup	1 1/3 oz EP (1 3/4 oz AP)	1/4 cup
Green pepper, diced	4 oz	3/4 cup	1/2 oz	1 1/2 Tbsp
Red pepper, diced	4 oz	3/4 cup	1/2 oz	1 1/2 Tbsp

Method

1. Pour boiling water over gelatin. Stir until dissolved.
2. Add cold water and vinegar to gelatin. Chill until gelatin begins to congeal.
3. Add vegetables to partially congealed gelatin. Pour into counter pan(s) or gelatin mold.
4. Place in refrigerator to congeal completely.

Directions for Diet Preparations

Sodium Restricted (SR): Prepare as directed.

Low Fat/Low Cholesterol (LF): 4 oz or 1/2 cup. Prepare as directed. Low fat diets should consider individual tolerance to cabbage.

Diabetic (DB): 4 oz or 1/2 cup. Use unsweetened gelatin as per manufacturer's directions.

Mechanical Soft (SFT) and **Soft/Low Fiber** (SLF): 4 oz or 1/2 cup.

50 portions: Omit raw vegetables (cabbage, celery, green peppers, and red peppers), substitute with 1 3/4 qt of cooked tolerated vegetables. (Example: green beans, carrots, spinach).

6 portions: Omit raw vegetables (cabbage, celery, green peppers, and red peppers), substitute with 1 cup of cooked tolerated vegetables. (Example: green beans, carrots, spinach).

Puree (PUR): 4 oz or 1/2 cup.

50 portions: Omit raw vegetables (cabbage, celery, green peppers, and red peppers), substitute with 1 3/4 qt of cooked puree vegetables. (Example: green beans, carrots, spinach).

6 portions: Omit raw vegetables (cabbage, celery, green peppers, and red peppers), substitute with 1 cup of puree tolerated vegetables. (Example: green beans, carrots, spinach).

Nutrient Analysis per Serving:

Regular	KCAL	PRO gm	CHO gm	FAT gm	Chol mg	SFA gm	PFA gm	VITA iu	VITC mg	THI mg	RIB mg	NIA mg	CA mg	NA mg	K+ mg	FE mg
	57.1	1.5	13.5	0.05	0.0	0.01	0.02	45.2	12.7	0.01	0.01	0.08	10.8	51.0	98.0	0.2

Sodium Restricted	NA mg	Diabetic	Kcal	Milk exg	Veg exg	Fruit exg	Bread exg	Meat exg	Fat exg	Low Fat & Low Chol	FAT gm	Chol mg	SFA gm	PFA gm
	51.0		14.2	0.0	0.5	0.0	0.0	0.0	0.0		0.05	0.0	0.01	0.02

Portion: 4 ounces or 1/2 cup

INGREDIENTS	50 portions		6 portions	
	weights	**measures**	**weights**	**measures**
Gelatin, lemon	1 1/2 lb	3 1/3 cup	3 oz	3/8 cup
Water, boiling		1 3/4 qt		3/4 cup
Water, cold		2 qt		1 cup
Vinegar, cider	8 oz	1 cup	1 oz	2 Tbsp
Cabbage, chopped	1 1/2 lb EP (2 lb AP)	1 1/2 qt	3 oz EP (4 oz AP)	3/4 cup
Mixed vegetables, canned, cooked, chilled	1 1/4 lb	3 1/2 cups	2 3/4 oz	1/2 cup

Method

1. Pour boiling water over gelatin. Stir until dissolved.
2. Add cold water and vinegar to gelatin. Chill until gelatin begins to congeal.
3. Add vegetables to partially congealed gelatin. Pour into counter pan(s) or gelatin mold.
4. Place in refrigerator to congeal completely.

Directions for Diet Preparations

Sodium Restricted (SR): Prepare as directed.
Low Fat/Low Cholesterol (LF): 4 oz or 1/2 cup.
50 portions: Omit cabbage and mixed vegetables, substitute with 1 qt cooked, chilled green beans and 3 cups diced cooked, chilled carrots.
6 portions: Omit cabbage and mixed vegetables, substitute with 1/2 cup cooked, chilled green beans and 1/3 cup diced cooked, chilled carrots.
Diabetic (DB): 4 oz or 1/2 cup. Use unsweetened gelatin as per manufacturer's directions.
Mechanical Soft (SFT) and **Soft/Low Fiber** (SLF): 4 oz or 1/2 cup.
50 portions: Omit cabbage and mixed vegetables, substitute with 1 qt cooked, chilled green beans and 3 cups diced cooked, chilled carrots.
6 portions: Omit cabbage and mixed vegetables, substitute with 1/2 cup cooked, chilled green beans and 1/3 cup diced cooked, chilled carrots.
Puree (PUR): 4 oz or 1/2 cup.
50 portions: Omit cabbage and mixed vegetables, substitute with 1 qt cooked, puree green beans and 3 cups cooked, puree carrots.
6 portions: Omit cabbage and mixed vegetables, substitute with 1/2 cup cooked, puree green beans and 1/3 cup cooked, puree carrots.

Nutrient Analysis per Serving:

Regular	KCAL	PRO gm	CHO gm	FAT gm	Chol mg	SFA gm	PFA gm	VITA iu	VITC mg	THI mg	RIB mg	NIA mg	CA mg	NA mg	K+ mg	FE mg
	91.6	2.1	21.4	0.2	0.0	0.01	0.04	590	10.7	0.02	0.01	0.17	9.6	43.4	73.7	0.2

Sodium Restricted	NA mg	Diabetic	Kcal	Milk exg	Veg exg	Fruit exg	Bread exg	Meat exg	Fat exg	Low Fat & Low Chol	FAT gm	Chol mg	SFA gm	PFA gm
	43.4		23.2	0.0	0.8	0.0	0.0	0.0	0.0		0.2	0.0	0.01	0.02

Portion: 1/2 cup

INGREDIENTS	50 portions		6 portions	
	weights	measures	weights	measures
Dressing:				
Mayonnaise	2 2/3 oz	1/3 cup	1/3 oz	2 tsp
Yogurt, plain, low fat	1 lb	2 cup	2 oz	1/4 cup
Honey		2 Tbsp		3/4 tsp
Pineapple juice, unsweetened		2 Tbsp		3/4 tsp
Lemon juice		2 tsp		1/4 tsp
Orange peel, grated		1 tsp		1/8 tsp
Salad:				
Apples, tart, red skinned, unpeeled	4 1/2 lb EP (5 lb AP)	1 gal	9 oz EP (10 oz AP)	2 cups
Pineapple, crushed, unsweetened	1 lb	2 cups	2 oz	1/4 cup
Celery, chopped	1 lb EP (1 1/4 lb AP)	3 cups	2 oz EP (2 1/2 oz AP)	1/3 cup
Kiwifruit, peeled, diced	2 lb AP	1 qt (16 kiwifruit)	4 oz AP	1/2 cup (2 kiwifruit)
Lettuce leaves	3 lb EP (4 1/2 lb AP)	100 leaves (2–3 heads)	6 oz EP (9 oz AP)	12 leaves (1/2 head)

Method

1. Prepare dressing.
   a. Combine mayonnaise, yogurt, honey, pineapple juice, lemon juice, and orange peel. Beat well. Refrigerate.
2. Combine apples, pineapple, celery, and kiwifruit. Mix lightly.
3. Add dressing to fruit salad. Toss lightly until all ingredients are coated with dressing.
4. Arrange lettuce leaves on individual salad plates. Using a No. 8 dipper serve 1/2 cup fruit salad on lettuce.

Directions for Diet Preparations

Sodium Restricted (SR): Prepare as directed.
Low Fat/Low Cholesterol (LF): 1/2 cup. Use reduced-calorie low cholesterol mayonnaise.
Diabetic (DB): 1/2 cup. Use reduced-calorie mayonnaise. Omit honey, substitute with artificial sweetener to taste.
Mechanical Soft (SFT), **Soft/Low Fiber** (SLF), and **Puree** (PUR): Not recommended, substitute with appropriate food alternative.

Nutrient Analysis per Serving:

Regular	KCAL	PRO gm	CHO gm	FAT gm	Chol mg	SFA gm	PFA gm	VITA iu	VITC mg	THI mg	RIB mg	NIA mg	CA mg	NA mg	K+ mg	FE mg
	55.6	1.0	12.3	0.8	0.4	0.1	0.4	157	22.7	0.04	0.04	0.2	28.9	25.9	179	0.3

Sodium Restricted	NA mg	Diabetic	Kcal	Milk exg	Veg exg	Fruit exg	Bread exg	Meat exg	Fat exg	Low Fat & Low Chol	FAT gm	Chol mg	SFA gm	PFA gm
	25.9		48.9	0.0	0.0	0.8	0.0	0.0	0.0		0.5	0.7	0.06	0.07

Waldorf Salad

Portion: 1/2 cup

INGREDIENTS	50 portions		6 portions	
	weights	**measures**	**weights**	**measures**
Apples, tart, red skinned, unpeeled	7 lb AP	1 3/4 qt (21 medium)	1 lb AP	1 cup (3 medium)
Pineapple, crushed, unsweetened	1 lb	2 cups	2 oz	1/4 cup
Mayonnaise	1 lb	2 cups	2 oz	1/4 cup
Celery, chopped	2 lb EP (2 1/2 lb AP)	1 1/2 qt	4 oz EP (5 oz AP)	3/4 cup
Walnuts, coarsely chopped	4 oz	1 cup	1/2 oz	2 Tbsp

Method

1. Cut apples in quarters, remove cores, slice into thin slices.
2. Add pineapple to apple slices.
3. Combine mayonnaise with apples and pineapple. Add celery. Mix lightly until all ingredients are coated with mayonnaise.
4. Add walnuts to salad right before serving time. Mix lightly.

Directions for Diet Preparations

Sodium Restricted (SR): Use sodium restricted mayonnaise.

Low Fat/Low Cholesterol (LF): 1/2 cup and **Diabetic** (DB): 1/2 cup. Use reduced-calorie low cholesterol mayonnaise. Omit walnuts.

Mechanical Soft (SFT), **Soft/Low Fiber** (SLF), and **Puree** (PUR): Not recommended, substitute with appropriate food alternative.

Nutrient Analysis per Serving:

Regular	KCAL	PRO gm	CHO gm	FAT gm	Chol mg	SFA gm	PFA gm	VITA iu	VITC mg	THI mg	RIB mg	NIA mg	CA mg	NA mg	K+ mg	FE mg
	124	0.7	12.6	8.6	5.2	0.9	5.8	88.0	5.8	0.03	0.02	0.15	16.1	66.5	151	0.3

Sodium Restricted	NA mg	Diabetic	Kcal	Milk exg	Veg exg	Fruit exg	Bread exg	Meat exg	Fat exg	Low Fat & Low Chol	FAT gm	Chol mg	SFA gm	PFA gm
	32.3		64.8	0.0	0.0	0.7	0.0	0.0	0.4		2.1	0.0	0.04	0.08

Portion: 1/2 cup or 3 1/2 ounces

INGREDIENTS	50 portions		6 portions	
	weights	measures	weights	measures
Gelatin, raspberry	1 1/2 lb	3 1/3 cups	3 oz	3/8 cup
Water, boiling		2 qt		1 cup
Water, cold		2 qt		1 cup
Apples, unpeeled, diced	2 lb EP (2 1/4 lb AP)	1 3/4 qt	4 2/3 oz EP (5 1/8 oz AP)	1 cup
Celery, diced finely	12 oz EP (1 lb AP)	3 cups	1 1/2 oz EP (2 oz AP)	1/3 cup
Walnuts, chopped	4 oz	1 cup	1/2 oz	2 Tbsp

Method

1. Pour boiling water over gelatin. Stir until dissolved.
2. Add cold water to gelatin. Chill.
3. When gelatin begins to congeal, add apples, celery, and walnuts.
4. Place in refrigerator to congeal.

Directions for Diet Preparations

Sodium Restricted (SR): Prepare as directed.

Low Fat/Low Cholesterol (LF): 1/2 cup or 3 1/2 oz. Omit walnuts.

Diabetic (DB): 1/2 cup or 3 1/2 oz. Use unsweetened gelatin as per manufacturer's directions. Omit walnuts.

Mechanical Soft (SFT), **Soft/Low Fiber** (SLF), and **Puree** (PUR): Not recommended, substitute with appropriate food alternative.

Nutrient Analysis per Serving:

Regular	KCAL	PRO gm	CHO gm	FAT gm	Chol mg	SFA gm	PFA gm	VITA iu	VITC mg	THI mg	RIB mg	NIA mg	CA mg	NA mg	K+ mg	FE mg
	76.2	1.9	14.9	1.4	0.0	0.1	0.9	25.0	1.4	0.01	0.01	0.05	5.1	49.7	80.5	0.1

Sodium Restricted	NA mg	Diabetic	Kcal	Milk exg	Veg exg	Fruit exg	Bread exg	Meat exg	Fat exg	Low Fat & Low Chol	FAT gm	Chol mg	SFA gm	PFA gm
	49.7		18.3	0.0	0.0	0.3	0.0	0.0	0.0		0.06	0.0	0.01	0.02

Portion: 1/2 cup or 4 ounces

INGREDIENTS	48 portions		6 portions	
	weights	measures	weights	measures
Gelatin, raspberry	1 1/2 lb	3 1/3 cups	3 oz	3/8 cup
Water, boiling		2 qt		1 cup
Cranberry sauce, whole	6 1/2 lb	3 1/4 qt	13 oz	1 2/3 cups
Oranges, ground	1 lb	2 cups	2 oz	1/4 cup

Method

1. Dissolve gelatin in hot water.
2. Add cranberry sauce and oranges.
3. Pour into counter pan(s) or gelatin mold. Place in refrigerator to congeal.

Directions for Diet Preparations

Sodium Restricted (SR): Prepare as directed.

Low Fat/Low Cholesterol (LF): 1/2 cup or 4 oz. Prepare as directed.

Diabetic (DB): 1/2 cup or 4 oz. Use unsweetened gelatin as per manufacturer's directions. Omit cranberry sauce. Mix oranges with gelatin; garnish with orange slice.

Mechanical Soft (SFT): and **Puree** (PUR): Puree cranberry sauce and oranges. Mix with gelatin. Place in refrigerator to congeal.

Soft/Low Fiber (SLF): Omit cranberry sauce. Mix oranges with gelatin; garnish with orange slice.

Nutrient Analysis per Serving:

Regular	KCAL	PRO gm	CHO gm	FAT gm	Chol mg	SFA gm	PFA gm	VITA iu	VITC mg	THI mg	RIB mg	NIA mg	CA mg	NA mg	K+ mg	FE mg
	207	1.8	52.3	0.3	0.0	0.0	0.0	47.2	12.3	0.03	0.02	0.14	9.9	64.1	47.1	0.19

Sodium Restricted	NA mg	Diabetic	Kcal	Milk exg	Veg exg	Fruit exg	Bread exg	Meat exg	Fat exg	Low Fat & Low Chol	FAT gm	Chol mg	SFA gm	PFA gm
	64.1		15.2	0.0	0.0	0.25	0.0	0.0	0.0		0.27	0.0	0.0	0.0

Portion: 2 Tablespoons

INGREDIENTS	50 portions		6 portions	
	weights	measures	weights	measures
Yogurt, plain, low fat	12 oz	1 1/2 cups	1 1/2 oz	3 Tbsp
Avocado pulp	1 1/2 lb	3 cups	3 oz	1/3 cup
Lime juice		1 Tbsp		1/2 tsp
Garlic powder		1 tsp		1/8 tsp
Cilantro, finely chopped, fresh		2 Tbsp		3/4 tsp
Onions, chopped	2 2/3 oz EP	1/2 cup	1/3 oz EP	1 Tbsp
Tomatoes, fresh, diced	1 lb	2 1/4 cups	1 3/4 oz	1/4 cup

Method

1. Pour yogurt into a fine sieve or cheesecloth. Let drain about 10 minutes.
2. Add avocado. Mix until smooth.
3. Add remaining ingredients. Mix until evenly distributed.
4. Chill.

Directions for Diet Preparations

Sodium Restricted (SR): Prepare as directed.
Low Fat/Low Cholesterol (LF) and **Diabetic** (DB): 2 Tbsp. May use if able to calculate into daily food plan.
Mechanical Soft (SFT), **Soft/Low Fiber** (SLF), and **Puree** (PUR): Omit onions. Blenderize to obtain desired consistency.

Nutrient Analysis per Serving:

Regular	KCAL	PRO gm	CHO gm	FAT gm	Chol mg	SFA gm	PFA gm	VITA iu	VITC mg	THI mg	RIB mg	NIA mg	CA mg	NA mg	K+ mg	FE mg
	36.3	0.7	2.2	3.0	0.0	0.5	0.4	165.2	2.4	0.02	0.03	0.4	11.9	5.9	130	0.2

Sodium Restricted	NA mg	Diabetic	Kcal	Milk exg	Veg exg	Fruit exg	Bread exg	Meat exg	Fat exg	Low Fat & Low Chol	FAT gm	Chol mg	SFA gm	PFA gm
	5.9		36.3	0.0	0.5	0.0	0.0	0.0	0.5		3.0	0.0	0.5	0.4

Portion: 1 serving (3 ounces)

INGREDIENTS	50 portions		6 portions	
	weights	measures	weights	measures
Carrots, peel and cut each into 6 sticks	3 1/2 lb AP	100 sticks	7 oz AP	12 sticks
Celery, cut each into 4 sticks	2 lb AP	100 sticks	4 oz AP	12 sticks
Broccoli florets	3 lb AP	100 florets (3 heads)	6 oz AP	12 florets (1/3 head)
Tomatoes, cut each into 6 slices	5 1/2 lb AP	100 slices (12 medium)	11 oz AP	12 slices (1 1/2 medium)
Onions, cut each into 10 slices	3 1/2 lb AP	100 slices (14 medium)	7 oz AP	12 slices (1 3/4 medium)

Method

1. Arrange on small individual side plates:
   a. 2 carrot sticks.
   b. 2 celery sticks.
   c. 2 broccoli florets.
   d. 2 tomato slices.
   e. 2 onion slices.

Directions for Diet Preparations

Sodium Restricted (SR): Prepare as directed.
Low Fat/Low Cholesterol (LF): 3 oz. Prepare as directed. Consider individual tolerance to broccoli and onions.
Diabetic (DB): 3 oz. Prepare as directed.
Mechanical Soft (SFT), **Soft/Low Fiber** (SLF), **Puree** (PUR): Not recommended, substitute with appropriate food alternative.

Nutrient Analysis per Serving:

Regular	KCAL	PRO gm	CHO gm	FAT gm	Chol mg	SFA gm	PFA gm	VITA iu	VITC mg	THI mg	RIB mg	NIA mg	CA mg	NA mg	K+ mg	FE mg
	27.3	1.2	6.0	0.2	0.0	0.03	0.09	6776	24.5	0.06	0.05	0.5	28.5	35.6	261	0.5

Sodium Restricted	NA mg	Diabetic	Kcal	Milk exg	Veg exg	Fruit exg	Bread exg	Meat exg	Fat exg	Low Fat & Low Chol	FAT gm	Chol mg	SFA gm	PFA gm
	35.6		27.3	0.0	1.0	0.0	0.0	0.0	0.0		0.2	0.0	0.03	0.09

Portion: 1 serving (3 ounces)

INGREDIENTS	50 portions		6 portions	
	weights	measures	weights	measures
Carrots, peel and cut each into 6 sticks	3 1/2 lb AP	100 sticks	7 oz AP	12 sticks
Celery, cut each into 4 sticks	2 lb AP	100 sticks	4 oz AP	12 sticks
Radishes, cut into roses	1 1/4 lb AP	50 roses	2 1/2 oz AP	6 roses
Olives, black, medium	1 lb AP	100 olives	2 oz AP	12 olives
Onions, cut each into 10 slices	3 1/2 lb AP	100 slices (14 medium)	7 oz AP	12 slices (1 3/4 medium)

Method

1. Arrange on small individual side plates:
   a. 2 carrot sticks.
   b. 2 celery sticks.
   c. 1 radish rose.
   d. 2 black olives.
   e. 2 onion slices.

Directions for Diet Preparations

Sodium Restricted (SR), **Low Fat/Low Cholesterol** (LF): 3 oz, and **Diabetic** (DB): 3 oz. Omit olives.

Mechanical Soft (SFT), **Soft/Low Fiber** (SLF), **Puree** (PUR): Not recommended, substitute with appropriate food alternative.

Nutrient Analysis per Serving:

Regular	KCAL	PRO gm	CHO gm	FAT gm	Chol mg	SFA gm	PFA gm	VITA iu	VITC mg	THI mg	RIB mg	NIA mg	CA mg	NA mg	K+ mg	FE mg
	41.4	0.9	6.8	1.5	0.0	0.1	0.2	8960	9.3	0.05	0.03	0.4	33.3	107	232	0.5

Sodium Restricted	NA mg	Diabetic	Kcal	Milk exg	Veg exg	Fruit exg	Bread exg	Meat exg	Fat exg	Low Fat & Low Chol	FAT gm	Chol mg	SFA gm	PFA gm
	30.4		29.2	0.0	1.0	0.0	0.0	0.0	0.0		0.2	0.0	0.03	0.07

Grains and Legumes

L1 — Rice Cookery

Portion: 1/2 cup

INGREDIENTS	50 portions		6 portions	
	weights	measures	weights	measures
Rice, converted[1]	3 1/2 lb	2 1/4 qt	6 oz	1 cup
Water, hot		4 1/4 qt		1 3/4 cups

Method

Steamer:

50 portions: Place rice in a 12 × 20 × 2-inch counter pan. Pour hot water over rice. Stir. Steam uncovered for 30 to 40 minutes. Fluff with fork.

6 portions: Place rice in sauce pan. Pour hot water over rice. Stir. Steam uncovered for 30 to 40 minutes. Fluff with fork.

Boiled:

Bring water to boil. Add rice. Stir. cover tightly. Cook on low heat until rice is tender and all water is absorbed, about 15 minutes. Remove from heat and let stand covered about 5 minutes. Fluff with fork.

Oven:

50 portions: Place rice in a 12 × 20 × 2-inch counter pan. Pour hot water over rice. Stir. Cover pan tightly. Bake at 350°F for 1 hour. Remove from oven and let stand covered for 5 minutes. Fluff with fork.

6 portions: Place rice in greased 1 1/2 qt casserole. Pour hot water over rice. Cover and bake at 350°F for 30 minutes or until rice is tender and water is absorbed.

Directions for Diet Preparations

Sodium Restricted (SR), Low Fat/Low Cholesterol (LF): 1/2 cup, **Diabetic (DB):** 1/3 cup, **Mechanical Soft (SFT),** and **Soft/Low Fiber (SLF):** Prepare as directed.

Puree (PUR): Prepare as directed. Add liquid (i.e. broth or gravy) to rice; blenderize to obtain desired consistency.

Notes

[1]One lb uncooked rice yields 2 qt cooked rice.

Nutrient Analysis per Serving:

Regular	KCAL	PRO gm	CHO gm	FAT gm	Chol mg	SFA gm	PFA gm	VITA iu	VITC mg	THI mg	RIB mg	NIA mg	CA mg	NA mg	K+ mg	FE mg
	94.0	1.8	20.6	0.1	0.0	0.0	0.0	0.0	0.0	0.09	0.01	1.1	16.8	0.0	38.1	0.7

Sodium Restricted	NA mg	Diabetic	Kcal	Milk exg	Veg exg	Fruit exg	Bread exg	Meat exg	Fat exg	Low Fat & Low Chol	FAT gm	Chol mg	SFA gm	PFA gm
	0.0		62.6	0.0	0.0	0.0	0.8	0.0	0.0		0.1	0.0	0.0	0.0

Rice Chantilly

Portion: 1/2 cup

INGREDIENTS	50 portions		6 portions	
	weights	measures	weights	measures
Rice, converted, uncooked	3 lb AP	7 1/2 cups	6 oz	1 cup
Water, hot		3 3/4 qt		1 3/4 cups
Cheddar cheese, mild, shredded	1 1/2 lb	1 1/2 qt	3 oz	3/4 cup
Sour cream	1 lb	2 cups	2 oz	1/4 cup

Method

1. Place rice in a 12 × 20 × 2-inch counter pan (50 portions) or 1 1/2 qt greased casserole (6 portions).
2. Pour hot water over rice. Stir.
3. Cover pan tightly.
4. 50 portions: Bake at 350°F for 1 hour.
   6 portions: Bake at 350°F for 30 minutes.
5. Remove from oven and let stand covered for 5 minutes.
6. Add sour cream and cheese to rice. Mix.
7. Bake at 350°F for 20 minutes or until thoroughly heated.

Directions for Diet Preparations

Sodium Restricted (SR): Use low sodium cheese.
Low Fat/Low Cholesterol (LF): 1/2 cup and **Diabetic** (DB): 1/3 cup.
50 portions: Use low fat cheese. Omit sour cream, substitute with 1 cup low fat plain yogurt.
6 portions: Use low fat cheese. Omit sour cream, substitute with 1/4 cup low fat plain yogurt.
Mechanical Soft (SFT) and **Soft/Low Fiber** (SLF): Prepare as directed.
Puree (PUR): Prepare as directed. Add liquid (i.e. cheese sauce); blenderize to obtain desired consistency.

Nutrient Analysis per Serving:

Regular	KCAL	PRO gm	CHO gm	FAT gm	Chol mg	SFA gm	PFA gm	VITA iu	VITC mg	THI mg	RIB mg	NIA mg	CA mg	NA mg	K+ mg	FE mg
	188	5.7	25.8	6.5	18.4	4.1	0.27	217	0.08	0.12	0.07	1.1	119	89.2	56.0	1.0

Sodium Restricted	NA mg	Diabetic	Kcal	Milk exg	Veg exg	Fruit exg	Bread exg	Meat exg	Fat exg	Low Fat & Low Chol	FAT gm	Chol mg	SFA gm	PFA gm
	55.3		104	0.0	0.0	0.0	1.2	0.3	0.0		2.5	0.16	0.01	0.07

Rice Florentine

Portion: 1/2 cup

INGREDIENTS	50 portions		6 portions	
	weights	**measures**	**weights**	**measures**
Rice, converted, uncooked	2 1/2 lb	1 1/2 qt	5 oz	3/4 cup
Water, hot		3 qt		1 1/2 cups
Margarine, low sodium, melted	4 oz	1/2 cup	1/2 oz	1 Tbsp
Onion, chopped	5 1/3 oz	1 cup	3/4 oz	2 Tbsp
Spinach, frozen, chopped, thawed	3 lb	1 1/2 qt	6 oz	3/4 cup
Lemon juice	4 oz	1/2 cup	1/2 oz	1 Tbsp
Cheddar cheese, mild, shredded	6 oz	1 1/2 cups	3/4 oz	3 Tbsp

Method

1. Add rice to boiling water. Return to a boil; stir and cover. Reduce heat and simmer about 15 minutes or until rice is tender and liquid is absorbed. Remove from heat; let stand covered 5 additional minutes.
2. Sauté onions in margarine until soft but not brown.
3. Remove excess water from spinach; mix in with onions.
4. Stir in lemon juice. Remove from heat.
5. Combine vegetable and rice mixture; mix gently.
6. Portion rice and vegetable mixture into baking pan(s).
7. Sprinkle with cheese.
8. Bake at 325°F for 25 minutes or until hot.
9. Portion with No. 8 scoop.

Directions for Diet Preparations

Sodium Restricted (SR): Use low sodium cheese.
Low Fat/Low Cholesterol (LF): 1/2 cup and **Diabetic** (DB): 1/3 cup. Use low fat cheese. Omit margarine. Low fat diets should consider individual tolerance when using onions.
Mechanical Soft (SFT) and **Soft/Low Fiber** (SLF): Omit onions.
Puree (PUR): Prepare as directed. Add liquid (i.e. cheese sauce); blenderize to obtain desired consistency.

Nutrient Analysis per Serving:

Regular	KCAL	PRO gm	CHO gm	FAT gm	Chol mg	SFA gm	PFA gm	VITA iu	VITC mg	THI mg	RIB mg	NIA mg	CA mg	NA mg	K+ mg	FE mg
	137	4.2	19.8	4.5	7.9	1.9	0.7	2264	8.01	0.04	0.08	0.5	91.6	68.7	125	0.8

Sodium Restricted	NA mg	Diabetic	Kcal	Milk exg	Veg exg	Fruit exg	Bread exg	Meat exg	Fat exg	Low Fat & Low Chol	FAT gm	Chol mg	SFA gm	PFA gm
	36.3		67.6	0.0	0.3	0.0	0.75	0.1-L	0.0		0.8	0.0	0.01	0.03

Hawaiian Rice

Portion: 1/2 cup

INGREDIENTS	50 portions		6 portions	
	weights	**measures**	**weights**	**measures**
Rice, converted, uncooked	2 1/2 lb	1 1/2 qt	5 oz	3/4 cup
Water, hot		3 qt		1 1/2 cups
Green peppers, diced	10 3/4 oz EP (13 1/2 lb AP)	2 cups	1 1/3 oz EP (1 3/4 oz AP)	1/4 cup
Margarine, low sodium, melted	4 oz	1/2 cup	1/2 oz	1 Tbsp
Pineapple tidbits, unsweetened	3 lb	1 1/2 qt	6 oz	3/4 cup

Method

1. Add rice to boiling water. Return to a boil; stir and cover. Reduce heat and simmer about 15 minutes or until rice is tender and liquid is absorbed.
2. Sauté green peppers in margarine until tender.
3. Combine green peppers and pineapple. Add to rice the last 5 minutes of cooking.
4. Remove from heat and let stand covered about 5 minutes. Stir.

Directions for Diet Preparations

Sodium Restricted (SR): Prepare as directed.
Low Fat/Low Cholesterol (LF): 1/2 cup and **Diabetic** (DB): 1/3 cup. Omit margarine.
Mechanical Soft (SFT) and **Soft/Low Fiber** (SLF): Omit green peppers.
Puree (PUR): Prepare as directed. Add liquid (i.e. pineapple juice); blenderize to obtain desired consistency.

Nutrient Analysis per Serving:

Regular	KCAL	PRO gm	CHO gm	FAT gm	Chol mg	SFA gm	PFA gm	VITA iu	VITC mg	THI mg	RIB mg	NIA mg	CA mg	NA mg	K+ mg	FE mg
	117	1.7	23.1	1.9	0.0	0.3	0.6	108	8.0	0.13	0.01	0.9	10.4	2.1	66.1	0.8

Sodium Restricted	NA mg	Diabetic	Kcal	Milk exg	Veg exg	Fruit exg	Bread exg	Meat exg	Fat exg	Low Fat & Low Chol	FAT gm	Chol mg	SFA gm	PFA gm
	2.1		67.4	0.0	0.0	0.2	0.75	0.0	0.0		0.1	0.0	0.0	0.02

Portion: 1/2 cup

INGREDIENTS	50 portions		6 portions	
	weights	**measures**	**weights**	**measures**
Margarine, low sodium	6 oz	3/4 cup	3/4 oz	1 1/2 Tbsp
Rice, converted, uncooked	3 lb	7 1/2 cups	6 oz	1 cup
Onions, chopped	4 oz EP (4 1/2 oz AP)	3/4 cup	1/2 oz EP (2/3 oz AP)	1 1/2 Tbsp
Green peppers, chopped	5 1/3 oz EP (6 2/3 oz AP)	1 cup	3/4 oz (5/8 oz AP)	2 Tbsp
Mushrooms, canned, sliced	8 oz	1 cup	1 oz	2 Tbsp
Chicken or vegetable stock[1]		3 qt		1 1/2 cups

Method

1. Place margarine in baking pans. Melt in oven at 350°F. Remove pans from oven.
2. Mix rice, onions, green peppers, and mushrooms. Place in baking pan(s).
3. Prepare chicken or vegetable stock.
4. Pour stock over rice. Cover pan(s) tightly and bake at 350°F for 30 to 45 minutes.
5. Remove from oven and let stand covered for 5 minutes. Serve with a No. 8 scoop.

Directions for Diet Preparations

Sodium Restricted (SR): Use low sodium stock.

Low Fat/Low Cholesterol (LF): 1/2 cup and **Diabetic** (DB): 1/3 cup. Prepare as directed. Low fat diets should consider individual tolerance to onions.

Mechanical Soft (SFT) and **Soft/Low Fiber** (SLF): Omit onions and green peppers.

Puree (PUR): Prepare as directed. Add additional liquid (i.e. broth); blenderize to obtain desired consistency.

Notes

[1]May use a concentrated soup base as a quick stock. Prepare as directed by manufacturer.

Nutrient Analysis per Serving:

Regular	KCAL	PRO gm	CHO gm	FAT gm	Chol mg	SFA gm	PFA gm	VITA iu	VITC mg	THI mg	RIB mg	NIA mg	CA mg	NA mg	K+ mg	FE mg
	107	1.6	18.3	3.2	0.0	0.4	0.8	110	3.2	0.09	0.02	1.1	3.5	202	21	0.7

Sodium Restricted	NA mg	Diabetic	Kcal	Milk exg	Veg exg	Fruit exg	Bread exg	Meat exg	Fat exg	Low Fat & Low Chol	FAT gm	Chol mg	SFA gm	PFA gm
	26.1		71.4	0.0	0.03	0.0	0.7	0.0	0.4		3.2	0.0	0.4	0.8

Portion: 1/2 cup

INGREDIENTS	50 portions		6 portions	
	weights	**measures**	**weights**	**measures**
Onions, finely chopped	10 3/4 oz EP (12 1/4 oz AP)	2 cups	1 1/3 oz EP (1 1/2 oz AP)	1/4 cup
Green peppers, chopped	10 3/4 oz (13 1/2 oz AP)	2 cups	1 1/3 oz EP (1 3/4 oz AP)	1/4 cup
Celery, chopped	2 2/3 oz	1/2 cup	1/3 oz	1 Tbsp
Margarine, low sodium, melted	3 oz	1/3 cup	1/2 oz	2 tsp
Rice, converted	3 lb	7 1/2 cups	6 oz	1 cup
Tomato juice		2 1/2 qt		1 1/4 cups
Chicken or vegetable stock, low sodium		1 3/4 qt		3/4 cup
Garlic powder		2 tsp		1/4 tsp
Parsley, chopped		1/4 cup		1/2 Tbsp

Method

1. Sauté onions, green peppers, and celery in margarine.
2. Add raw rice. Stir about 2 minutes until grains are coated with margarine.
3. 50 portions: Place in counter pan (12 × 20 × 4-inch). 6 portions: Place in 1 1/2 quart casserole.
4. Combine tomato juice, chicken or vegetable stock, and seasonings. Pour over rice. Stir to combine.
5. Cover pan tightly.
6. 50 portions: Bake at 350°F for 45 minutes. Stir before serving.
   6 portions: Bake at 350°F for 20–30 minutes. Stir before serving.
7. Serve with No. 8 dipper.

Directions for Diet Preparations

Sodium Restricted (SR): Use low sodium tomato juice.
Low Fat/Low Cholesterol (LF): 1/2 cup and **Diabetic** (DB): 1/3 cup. Omit steps #1 and 2. Combine vegetables with raw rice. Place in pan. Combine tomato juice, low fat chicken or vegetable stock, and seasonings. Pour over rice. Continue with recipe at step #5 as written.

Low fat diets should consider individual tolerance when using onions.
Mechanical Soft (SFT) and **Soft/Low Fiber** (SLF): 1/2 cup.
50 portions: Omit onions, peppers, and celery, substitute with 2 1/2 cups canned cooked carrots and 2 cups canned cooked green beans. Omit garlic powder.
6 portions: Omit onions, peppers, and celery, substitute with 1/4 cup canned cooked carrots and 1/4 cup canned cooked green beans. Omit garlic powder.
Puree (PUR): 1/2 cup.
50 portions: Omit onions, peppers, and celery, substitute with 2 1/2 cups canned cooked carrots and 2 cups canned cooked green beans. Continue with recipe at step #2 as written. Add additional liquid if necessary (i.e. tomato juice); blenderize to obtain desired consistency.
6 portions: Omit onions, peppers, and celery, substitute with 1/4 cup canned cooked carrots and 1/4 cup canned cooked green beans. Continue with recipe at step #2 as written. Add additional liquid if necessary (i.e. tomato juice); blenderize to obtain desired consistency.

Nutrient Analysis per Serving:

Regular	KCAL	PRO gm	CHO gm	FAT gm	Chol mg	SFA gm	PFA gm	VITA iu	VITC mg	THI mg	RIB mg	NIA mg	CA mg	NA mg	K+ mg	FE mg
	142	2.8	28.5	1.6	0.0	0.2	0.5	663	19.6	0.1	0.03	1.6	19.0	191	148	1.3

Sodium Restricted	NA mg	Diabetic	Kcal	Milk exg	Veg exg	Fruit exg	Bread exg	Meat exg	Fat exg	Low Fat & Low Chol	FAT gm	Chol mg	SFA gm	PFA gm
	17.5		87.2	0.0	0.0	0.0	1.2	0.0	0.0		0.4	0.0	0.01	0.1

Portion: 1/2 cup

INGREDIENTS	50 portions		6 portions	
	weights	measures	weights	measures
Brown rice	3 1/2 lb	2 1/4 qt	7 oz	1 1/8 cups
Water, hot		4 1/4 qt		1 3/4 cups

Method

Steamer
1. Place rice in a 12 × 20 × 2-inch counter pan (50 portions) or sauce pan (6 portions).
2. Pour hot water over rice. Stir.
3. Steam uncovered for 50 to 60 minutes.

Boiled
1. Bring water to boil.
2. Add rice. Stir. Cover tightly.
3. Cook on low heat until rice is tender and all water is absorbed, about 40 to 45 minutes.
4. Remove from heat and let stand covered about 5 to 10 minutes.

Oven
1. Place rice in a 12 × 20 × 2-inch counter pan (50 portions) or 1 1/2 qt casserole (6 portions).
2. Pour hot water over rice. Stir.
3. Cover pan tightly.
4. Bake at 350°F for 1 1/2 hours. Remove from oven and let stand covered for 5 minutes.

Directions for Diet Preparations

Sodium Restricted (SR), **Low Fat/Low Cholesterol** (LF): 1/2 cup, **Diabetic** (DB): 1/3 cup, and **Mechanical Soft** (SFT): Prepare as directed.

Soft/Low Fiber (SLF): Not recommended, substitute with an appropriate food alternative.

Puree (PUR): Prepare as directed. Add liquid (i.e. broth or gravy) to rice; blenderize to obtain desired consistency.

Nutrient Analysis per Serving:

Regular	KCAL	PRO gm	CHO gm	FAT gm	Chol mg	SFA gm	PFA gm	VITA iu	VITC mg	THI mg	RIB mg	NIA mg	CA mg	NA mg	K+ mg	FE mg
	105	2.2	22.5	0.5	0.0	0.0	0.2	0.0	0.0	0.07	0.02	1.2	10.6	0.0	62.1	0.4

Sodium Restricted	NA mg	Diabetic	Kcal	Milk exg	Veg exg	Fruit exg	Bread exg	Meat exg	Fat exg	Low Fat & Low Chol	FAT gm	Chol mg	SFA gm	PFA gm
	0.0		70.2	0.0	0.0	0.0	1.0	0.0	0.1		0.5	0.0	0.0	0.2

Brown Rice and Raisins

Portion: 1/2 cup

INGREDIENTS	50 portions		6 portions	
	weights	**measures**	**weights**	**measures**
Brown rice	3 lb	2 qt	6 oz	1 cup
Water, hot		3 3/4 qt		2 cups
Raisins, seedless	10 3/4 oz	2 cups	1 1/3 oz	1/4 cup

Method

1. Bring water to a boil.
2. Add rice. Stir. Cover tightly.
3. Cook on low heat until rice is tender and all water is absorbed, about 40 to 45 minutes.
4. Add raisins the last 5 minutes of cooking.
5. Remove from heat and let stand covered 5 to 10 minutes.

Directions for Diet Preparations

Sodium Restricted (SR), **Low Fat/Low Cholesterol** (LF): 1/2 cup, and **Diabetic** (DB): 1/3 cup. Prepare as directed.
Mechanical Soft (SFT): Omit raisins.
Soft/Low Fiber (SLF): Not recommended, substitute with an appropriate food alternative.
Puree (PUR): Prepare as directed. Add liquid (i.e. broth or gravy) to rice; blenderize to obtain desired consistency.

Nutrient Analysis per Serving:

Regular	KCAL	PRO gm	CHO gm	FAT gm	Chol mg	SFA gm	PFA gm	VITA iu	VITC mg	THI mg	RIB mg	NIA mg	CA mg	NA mg	K+ mg	FE mg
	114	2.2	25.4	0.5	0.0	0.0	0.2	0.5	0.2	0.08	0.02	1.2	12.7	0.7	101	0.5

Sodium Restricted	NA mg	Diabetic	Kcal	Milk exg	Veg exg	Fruit exg	Bread exg	Meat exg	Fat exg	Low Fat & Low Chol	FAT gm	Chol mg	SFA gm	PFA gm
	0.7		68.8	0.0	0.0	0.2	0.8	0.0	0.0		0.5	0.0	0.0	0.2

Portion: 1/2 cup

Ingredients	50 portions		6 portions	
	weights	**measures**	**weights**	**measures**
Wild rice, raw[1]	2 3/4 lb	2 qt	5 1/2 oz	1 cup
Water, boiling		1 gal		2 cups

Method

1. Rinse wild rice. Drain.
2. Add rice slowly to boiling water. Cover and simmer for 1 hour or until the rice is tender and fluffy and all liquid has been absorbed. Do not stir.

Notes

[1]1 lb (2 3/4 cups) raw wild rice, raw yields 2 1/2 lb (2 1/3 qt) cooked wild rice.

Directions for Diet Preparations

Sodium Restricted (SR), **Low Fat/Low Cholesterol** (LF): 1/2 cup, **Diabetic** (DB): 1/2 cup, and **Mechanical Soft** (SFT): Prepare as directed.
Soft/Low Fiber (SLF): Not recommended. Use white rice or other appropriate food alternative.
Puree (PUR): Prepare as directed. Add liquid (i.e. broth) to rice; blenderize to obtain desired consistency.

Nutrient Analysis per Serving:

Regular	KCAL	PRO gm	CHO gm	FAT gm	Chol mg	SFA gm	PFA gm	VITA iu	VITC mg	THI mg	RIB mg	NIA mg	CA mg	NA mg	K+ mg	FE mg
	82.7	3.3	17.6	0.2	0.0	0.0	0.0	0.0	0.0	0.1	0.14	1.5	4.5	1.6	51.5	0.9

Sodium Restricted	NA mg	Diabetic	Kcal	Milk exg	Veg exg	Fruit exg	Bread exg	Meat exg	Fat exg	Low Fat & Low Chol	FAT gm	Chol mg	SFA gm	PFA gm
	1.6		82.7	0.0	0.0	0.0	1.1	0.0	0.0		0.2	0.0	0.0	0.0

Dry Bean Cookery

Portion: 1/2 cup

INGREDIENTS	50 portions		6 portions		
	weights	**measures**	**weights**	**measures**	**Cooking Time**
Black-eyed beans or peas or	4 1/4 lb	2 7/8 qt	8 3/8 oz	1 1/2 cups	2 hr
Red beans:					
kidney or pinto or	4 1/4 lb	2 2/3 qt	8 1/2 oz	1 1/3 cups	2 hr
White beans:					
great northern or	4 1/2 lb	2 5/8 qt	9 oz	1 3/8 cups	1–1 1/2 hr
Lima beans:					
small or	4 1/4 lb	2 2/3 qt	8 3/8 oz	1 1/3 cups	1 1/2–2 hr
large or	4 1/2 lb	2 5/8 qt	9 oz	1 3/8 cups	1–2 hr
Pea beans:					
navy or small white	4 1/4 lb	2 3/8 qt	8 3/8 oz	1 1/4 cup	2–2 1/2 hr
Water, boiling		2 gal		1 qt	

Method

1. Sort and wash beans.
2. Add beans to boiling water. Boil 2 minutes.
3. Remove from heat. Cover and let soak overnight in refrigerator.
4. Cook beans in soaking water for the time indicated or until tender. Begin counting cooking time when water returns to boiling. Add boiling water if beans become dry.

Directions for Diet Preparations

Sodium Restricted (SR), **Low Fat/Low Cholesterol** (LF): 1/2 cup, and **Diabetic** (DB): 1/3 cup. Prepare as directed.

Mechanical Soft (SFT): Prepare as directed. Consider individual tolerance.

Soft/Low Fiber (SLF): Not recommended, substitute with appropriate food alternative.

Puree (PUR): Prepare as directed. Add liquid (i.e. broth or gravy); blenderize to obtain desired consistency.

Nutrient Analysis per Serving:

Regular	KCAL	PRO gm	CHO gm	FAT gm	Chol mg	SFA gm	PFA gm	VITA iu	VITC mg	THI mg	RIB mg	NIA mg	CA mg	NA mg	K+ mg	FE mg
Blackeye	124	7.8	22.8	0.5	0.0	0.1	0.2	6.3	0.2	0.32	0.07	0.7	45.3	1.8	541	1.8
Kidney	142	9.7	25.5	0.5	0.0	0.0	0.3	0.0	1.3	0.17	0.06	0.6	31.4	2.2	452	3.3
Pinto	136	8.1	25.4	0.5	0.0	0.1	0.2	1.9	2.0	0.18	0.09	0.3	47.6	1.9	464	2.5
Great North	107	7.5	19.1	0.4	0.0	0.1	0.2	0.9	1.1	0.14	0.05	0.6	61.9	1.8	356	1.9
Lima	106	5.8	20.3	0.2	0.0	0.1	0.1	319	8.7	0.12	0.08	0.8	27.5	14.6	491	2.1
Navy	141	8.6	26.1	0.5	0.0	0.1	0.2	1.9	0.9	0.20	0.06	0.5	69.5	0.9	365	2.4

Sodium Restricted	NA mg	Diabetic	Kcal	Milk exg	Veg exg	Fruit exg	Bread exg	Meat exg	Fat exg	Low Fat & Low Chol	FAT gm	Chol mg	SFA gm	PFA gm
Blackeye	1.8		83.0	0.0	0.0	0.0	1.1	0.0	0.0		0.5	0.0	0.1	0.2
Kidney	2.2		94.9	0.0	0.0	0.0	1.1	0.0	0.0		0.5	0.0	0.0	0.3
Pinto	1.9		97.1	0.0	0.0	0.0	1.3	0.0	0.0		0.5	0.0	0.1	0.2
Great North	1.8		71.5	0.0	0.0	0.0	0.9	0.0	0.0		0.4	0.0	0.1	0.2
Lima	14.6		70.6	0.0	0.0	0.0	0.9	0.0	0.0		0.2	0.0	0.1	0.1
Navy	0.9		100	0.0	0.0	0.0	1.3	0.0	0.0		0.5	0.0	0.1	0.2

Portion: 1/2 cup

INGREDIENTS	50 portions		6 portions	
	weights	measures	weights	measures
Split peas, dry	5 lb	2 5/8 qt	10 1/2 oz	1 1/2 cups
Water, boiling		1 1/3 gal		2 2/3 cups

Method

Boiling
1. Sort and wash peas.
2. Add peas to boiling water. Boil 2 minutes.
3. Remove from heat. Cover and let soak 30 minutes.
4. Cook peas in soaking water. Bring to a boil. Simmer 1 to 1 1/2 hours. Do not stir.

Oven
1. Place peas and soaking liquid in baking pan(s). Cover pan tightly.
2. Bake at 350°F for 35 minutes.

Directions for Diet Preparations

Sodium Restricted (SR), **Low Fat/Low Cholesterol** (LF): 1/2 cup, and **Diabetic** (DB): 1/3 cup. Prepare as directed.

Mechanical Soft (SFT): Prepare as directed. Consider individual tolerance.

Soft/Low Fiber (SLF): Not recommended, substitute with appropriate food alternative.

Puree (PUR): Prepare as directed. Add liquid (i.e. broth or gravy); blenderize to obtain desired consistency.

Nutrient Analysis per Serving:

Regular	KCAL	PRO gm	CHO gm	FAT gm	Chol mg	SFA gm	PFA gm	VITA iu	VITC mg	THI mg	RIB mg	NIA mg	CA mg	NA mg	K+ mg	FE mg
	119	8.4	21.4	0.3	0.0	0.05	0.17	7.1	0.4	0.19	0.05	0.9	14.2	2.0	367	1.3

Sodium Restricted	NA mg	Diabetic	Kcal	Milk exg	Veg exg	Fruit exg	Bread exg	Meat exg	Fat exg	Low Fat & Low Chol	FAT gm	Chol mg	SFA gm	PFA gm
	2.0		79.8	0.0	0.0	0.0	1.0	0.0	0.0		0.3	0.0	0.05	0.17

L12 — Black-Eyed Peas

Portion: 1/2 cup

INGREDIENTS	50 portions		6 portions	
	weights	measures	weights	measures
Black-eyed peas	4 lb	2 3/4 qt	8 3/4 oz	1 1/2 cups
Water, cold		2 gal		1 qt
Cayenne pepper		1/4 tsp		dash
Onions, chopped	5 1/3 oz EP (6 oz AP)	1 cup	3/4 oz EP (3/4 oz AP)	2 Tbsp

Method

1. Sort beans and wash.
2. Soak overnight in cold water. Do not drain.
3. Bring to a boil. Skim foam off.
4. Add cayenne pepper and onions.
5. Simmer 2 hours or until beans are tender.

Directions for Diet Preparations

Sodium Restricted (SR), Low Fat/Low Cholesterol (LF): 1/2 cup, **Diabetic** (DB): 1/3 cup, and **Mechanical Soft** (SFT): Prepare as directed. Low fat diets should consider individual tolerance to onions.

Soft/Low Fiber (SLF): Not recommended, substitute with appropriate food alternative.

Puree (PUR): Prepare as directed. Add liquid (i.e. broth or gravy) to rice; blenderize to obtain desired consistency.

Nutrient Analysis per Serving:

Regular	KCAL	PRO gm	CHO gm	FAT gm	Chol mg	SFA gm	PFA gm	VITA iu	VITC mg	THI mg	RIB mg	NIA mg	CA mg	NA mg	K+ mg	FE mg
	125	7.9	22.8	0.5	0.0	0.1	0.2	6.3	0.2	0.3	0.07	0.7	45.3	1.9	541	1.8

Sodium Restricted	NA mg	Diabetic	Kcal	Milk exg	Veg exg	Fruit exg	Bread exg	Meat exg	Fat exg	Low Fat & Low Chol	FAT gm	Chol mg	SFA gm	PFA gm
	1.9		83	0.0	0.0	0.0	1.2	0.0	0.0		0.5	0.0	0.1	0.2

Portion: 1/2 cup

INGREDIENTS	50 portions		6 portions	
	weights	measures	weights	measures
Black beans or black turtle beans	4 lb	2 1/4 qt	8 oz	1 1/8 cups
Water, boiling		2 gal		1 qt
Garlic powder		2 tsp		1/4 tsp
Onions, chopped	5 1/3 oz EP	1 cup	3/4 oz EP	2 Tbsp

Method

1. Sort beans and wash.
2. Add beans to boiling water. Boil 3 minutes.
3. Remove from heat. Cover and let soak overnight in refrigerator.
4. Add garlic powder and onions.
5. Cook beans in soaking water. Bring to a boil. Reduce heat to low, cover and simmer 2 to 3 hours or until beans are tender. Stir occasionally. Add additional boiling water if beans become dry.

Directions for Diet Preparations

Sodium Restricted (SR), **Low Fat/Low Cholesterol** (LF): 1/2 cup, **Diabetic** (DB): 1/3 cup, **Mechanical Soft** (SFT): Prepare as directed. Low fat diets should consider individual tolerance to onions and garlic.

Soft/Low Fiber (SLF): Not recommended. Use appropriate food alternative.

Puree (PUR): Prepare as directed. Add liquid and blenderize to obtain desired consistency.

Nutrient Analysis per Serving:

Regular	KCAL	PRO gm	CHO gm	FAT gm	Chol mg	SFA gm	PFA gm	VITA iu	VITC mg	THI mg	RIB mg	NIA mg	CA mg	NA mg	K+ mg	FE mg
	113	7.5	20.3	0.4	0.0	0.1	0.1	5.1	0.1	0.2	0.05	0.4	23.4	0.9	305	1.8

Sodium Restricted	NA mg	Diabetic	Kcal	Milk exg	Veg exg	Fruit exg	Bread exg	Meat exg	Fat exg	Low Fat & Low Chol	FAT gm	Chol mg	SFA gm	PFA gm
	0.9		75.4	0.0	0.0	0.0	1.0	0.0	0.0		0.4	0.0	0.1	0.2

Pastas

M1   Pasta Cookery: Macaroni, Noodles, and Spaghetti

Portion: 1/2 cup

INGREDIENTS	50 portions		6 portions	
	weights	measures	weights	measures
Water, boiling		3 1/4 gal		6 1/2 cups
Macaroni or	3 1/4 lb	3 1/4 qt	6 1/2 oz	1 3/4 cups
Noodles or	3 1/4 lb	4 1/3 qt	6 1/2 oz	2 1/8 cups
Spaghetti	3 1/4 lb	3 1/4 qt	6 1/2 oz	1 3/4 cups

Method

1. Add pasta gradually to boiling water, while stirring.
2. Return to a boil. Continue cooking uncovered at a fast boil until pasta is tender, but firm; about 10 minutes for noodles and about 12 minutes for macaroni and spaghetti. Stir occasionally to prevent sticking.
3. Drain.

Directions for Diet Preparations

Sodium Restricted (SR), **Low Fat/Low Cholesterol** (LF): 1/2 cup, **Diabetic** (DB): 1/2 cup, **Mechanical Soft** (SFT), and **Soft/Low Fiber** (SLF): Prepare as directed.

Puree (PUR): Prepare as directed. Add liquid (i.e. broth or sauce); blenderize to obtain desired consistency.

Nutrient Analysis per Serving:

Regular	KCAL	PRO gm	CHO gm	FAT gm	Chol mg	SFA gm	PFA gm	VITA iu	VITC mg	THI mg	RIB mg	NIA mg	CA mg	NA mg	K+ mg	FE mg
spaghetti	79	2.4	16.3	0.2	0.0	0.0	0.0	0.0	0.0	0.09	0.05	0.7	5.7	0.7	43.3	0.6
macaroni	105	3.5	21.3	0.3	0.0	0.0	0.0	0.0	0.0	0.12	0.07	0.9	7.8	0.7	56.0	0.7
noodles	101	3.3	18.9	1.2	25.2	0.0	0.0	0.0	0.0	0.1	0.06	0.9	8.1	1.6	35.8	0.7

Sodium Restricted	NA mg	Diabetic	Kcal	Milk exg	Veg exg	Fruit exg	Bread exg	Meat exg	Fat exg	Low Fat & Low Chol	FAT gm	Chol mg	SFA gm	PFA gm
spaghetti	0.7		79	0.0	0.0	0.0	1.0	0.0	0.1		0.2	0.0	0.0	0.0
macaroni	0.7		105	0.0	0.0	0.0	1.1	0.0	0.0		0.3	0.0	0.0	0.0
noodles	1.6		101	0.0	0.0	0.0	1.2	0.0	0.2		1.2	25.2	0.0	0.0

Lyonnaise Noodles

Portion: 1/2 cup

Ingredients	50 portions		6 portions	
	weights	**measures**	**weights**	**measures**
Noodles, dry	3 1/4 lb	1 gal	6 1/2 oz	2 cups
Water, boiling		3 1/4 gal		1 2/3 qt
Margarine, low sodium, melted	4 oz	1/2 cup	1/2 oz	1 Tbsp
Onions, chopped	8 oz	1 1/2 cups	1 oz	3 Tbsp
Parmesan cheese, grated	2 1/4 oz	1/2 cup	1/4 oz	1 Tbsp
Parsley, fresh, chopped		1/4 cup		1/2 Tbsp

Method

1. Cook noodles in boiling water. Drain and rinse under cold water. Set aside.
2. Sauté onions in margarine until tender.
3. Combine noodles, onions, parmesan cheese, and parsley. Mix to blend.
4. Heat at 350°F for 5 minutes or until heated through.

Directions for Diet Preparations

Sodium Restricted (SR): Omit parmesan cheese.

Low Fat/Low Cholesterol (LF): 1/2 cup and **Diabetic** (DB): 1/3 cup. Use half the amount of margarine specified. Low fat diets should consider individual tolerance to onions. Low cholesterol diets should not use egg noodles.

Mechanical Soft (SFT): Prepare as directed. Consider individual tolerance.

Soft/Low Fiber (SLF): Omit onions and parmesan cheese.

Puree (PUR): Prepare as directed. Add liquid (i.e. broth or gravy); blenderize to obtain desired consistency.

Nutrient Analysis per Serving:

Regular	KCAL	PRO gm	CHO gm	FAT gm	Chol mg	SFA gm	PFA gm	VITA iu	VITC mg	THI mg	RIB mg	NIA mg	CA mg	NA mg	K+ mg	FE mg
	126	3.9	21.7	2.4	0.5	0.4	0.6	97.0	0.6	0.13	0.07	1.0	20.1	15.2	66.8	0.8

Sodium Restricted	NA mg	Diabetic	Kcal	Milk exg	Veg exg	Fruit exg	Bread exg	Meat exg	Fat exg	Low Fat & Low Chol	FAT gm	Chol mg	SFA gm	PFA gm
	1.5		78.7	0.0	0.0	0.0	0.9	0.0	0.2		1.5	0.5	0.2	0.3

Parsley Noodles

Portion: 1/2 cup

INGREDIENTS	50 portions		6 portions	
	weights	measures	weights	measures
Noodles, dry	4 lb	1 1/4 gal	8 oz	2 1/2 cups
Water		4 gal		2 qt
Margarine, low sodium, melted	8 oz	1 cup	1 oz	2 Tbsp
Parsley, fresh, chopped	1 1/3 oz	1 cup	1/8 oz	2 Tbsp

Method

1. Bring water to a boil.
2. Add noodles gradually, while stirring. Return to boil. Do not cover noodles.
3. Continue to boil until noodles are tender, about 5 to 10 minutes. Stir occasionally to prevent sticking.
4. Test for doneness. Noodles should be firm to the bite.
5. Drain.
6. Distribute margarine uniformly over cooked noodles. Sprinkle with parsley. Toss lightly.

Directions for Diet Preparations

Sodium Restricted (SR), **Mechanical Soft** (SFT), and **Soft/Low Fiber** (SLF): Prepare as directed.
Low Fat/Low Cholesterol (LF): 1/2 cup and **Diabetic** (DB): 1/2 cup. Omit margarine. Low cholesterol diet should not use egg noodles.
Puree (PUR): Prepare as directed. Add liquid (i.e. broth or gravy); blenderize to obtain desired consistency.

Nutrient Analysis per Serving:

Regular	KCAL	PRO gm	CHO gm	FAT gm	Chol mg	SFA gm	PFA gm	VITA iu	VITC mg	THI mg	RIB mg	NIA mg	CA mg	NA mg	K+ mg	FE mg
	111	2.4	16.4	3.9	0.0	0.6	1.2	213.0	1.1	0.01	0.01	0.2	8.4	2.4	51.5	0.4

Sodium Restricted	NA mg	Diabetic	Kcal	Milk exg	Veg exg	Fruit exg	Bread exg	Meat exg	Fat exg	Low Fat & Low Chol	FAT gm	Chol mg	SFA gm	PFA gm
	2.4		79.1	0.0	0.0	0.0	1.1	0.0	0.0		0.29	0.0	0.0	0.0

Noodle Pudding (Kugel)

Portion: 4 ounces

INGREDIENTS	48 portions		6 portions	
	weights	measures	weights	measures
Noodles, dry, medium	4 lb	1 1/4 gal	8 oz	2 1/2 cups
Water, boiling		4 gal		2 qt
Eggs, large	3 lb	1 1/2 qt	6 oz	3/4 cup
		(24 large)		(3 large)
Sugar, granulated	1 3/4 lb	1 qt	3 1/2 oz	1/2 cup
Margarine, low sodium, melted	6 oz	3/4 cup	3/4 oz	1 1/2 Tbsp
Orange juice, unsweetened	10 oz	1 1/4 cups	1 1/4 oz	2 1/2 Tbsp
Cinnamon, ground		2 tsp		1/4 tsp
Nutmeg		1 tsp		1/8 tsp
Raisins, seedless	2 lb	1 1/2 qt	4 oz	3/4 cup

Method

1. Cook noodles in boiling water. Drain and rinse under cold water. Place in mixing bowl.
2. Beat eggs with sugar until well mixed. Add margarine, orange juice, cinnamon, and nutmeg. Mix.
3. Add raisins. Stir until all ingredients are distributed evenly.
4. Place noodle mixture in lightly greased or non-stick spray coated baking pan(s). Cover.
5. Bake at 350°F for 40 minutes.
6. Remove cover and bake 10 to 20 minutes longer, or until kugel is firm.
7. Let cool slightly before cutting.

Directions for Diet Preparations

Sodium Restricted (SR) and **Mechanical Soft** (SFT): Prepare as directed.

Low Fat/Low Cholesterol (LF): 4 oz.

48 portions: Omit eggs, substitute with 24 large egg whites and an egg substitute equal to 12 large eggs (3 cups). Omit margarine, substitute with equal amount of reduced-calorie margarine.

6 portions: Omit eggs, substitute with 3 large egg whites and an egg substitute equal to 3 large eggs (3 oz). Omit margarine, substitute with equal amount of reduced-calorie margarine.

Diabetic (DB): 3 oz.

48 portions: Omit sugar, substitute with artificial sweetener in amount equivalent to 1 3/4 lb granulated sugar (approximately 4 Tbsp artificial sweetener). Omit margarine, substitute with equal amount of reduced-calorie margarine.

6 portions: Omit sugar, substitute with artificial sweetener in amount equivalent to 3 1/2 oz granulated sugar (approximately 2 tsp artificial sweetener). Omit margarine, substitute with equal amount of reduced-calorie margarine.

Soft/Low Fiber (SLF): Omit nutmeg and raisins.

Puree (PUR): Prepare as directed. Add additional orange juice; blenderize to obtain desired consistency.

Nutrient Analysis per Serving:

Regular	KCAL	PRO gm	CHO gm	FAT gm	Chol mg	SFA gm	PFA gm	VITA iu	VITC mg	THI mg	RIB mg	NIA mg	CA mg	NA mg	K+ mg	FE mg
	293	7.2	53.6	6.1	136	1.3	1.3	255	2.7	0.18	0.16	1.2	33.0	38.6	240	1.7

Sodium Restricted	NA mg	Diabetic	Kcal	Milk exg	Veg exg	Fruit exg	Bread exg	Meat exg	Fat exg	Low Fat & Low Chol	FAT gm	Chol mg	SFA gm	PFA gm
	38.6		163	0.0	0.0	0.75	1.1	0.3	0.5		2.4	0.1	0.4	0.7

Pasta Primavera

Portion: 3/4 cup

INGREDIENTS	50 portions		6 portions	
	weights	**measures**	**weights**	**measures**
Pasta, dry	3 1/4 lb	1 gal	6 1/2 oz	2 cups
Water, boiling		3 1/4 gal		6 1/2 cups
Broccoli florets	12 oz	3 cups	1 1/2 oz	1/3 cup
Carrots, sliced	1 lb EP (1 3/8 lb AP)	3 cups	2 oz EP (2 7/8 oz AP)	1/3 cup
Margarine, low sodium, melted #1	8 oz	1 cup	1 oz	2 Tbsp
Green peppers, diced	1 lb EP (1 1/4 lb AP)	3 cups	2 oz EP (2 1/2 oz AP)	1/3 cup
Onions, chopped	5 1/3 oz EP (6 oz AP)	1 cup	2/3 oz EP (3/4 oz AP)	2 Tbsp
Tomatoes, diced	1 lb EP (18 oz AP)	2 1/2 cups	2 oz EP (2 1/4 oz AP)	1/3 cup
Basil leaves, dried		1/4 cup		1/2 Tbsp
Parsley, finely chopped	1 1/3 oz	1 cup	1/8 oz	2 Tbsp
Margarine, low sodium, melted, #2	6 oz	3/4 cup	3/4 oz	1 1/2 Tbsp
Parmesan cheese, grated	7 oz	1 1/2 cups	7/8 oz	3 Tbsp

Method

1. Cook pasta in boiling water. Drain.
2. Steam broccoli and carrots until tender crisp.
3. Sauté green peppers and onions in margarine #1 until tender.
4. Add broccoli, carrots, tomatoes, basil, and parsley to green peppers/onions. Cook until vegetables are tender and heated through. Stir to combine.
5. Add vegetables, margarine #2, and parmesan cheese to pasta. Toss to coat.

Directions for Diet Preparations

Sodium Restricted (SR): Use fresh tomatoes. Omit parmesan cheese.

Low Fat/Low Cholesterol (LF): 3/4 cup and **Diabetic** (DB): 3/4 cup. Omit margarine #1. Steam all vegetables until tender. Omit margarine #2, substitute with reduced-calorie margarine in equal amounts to regular margarine. Omit parmesan cheese. Low fat diets should consider individual tolerance when using broccoli and onions.

Mechanical Soft (SFT) and **Soft/Low Fiber** (SLF): 3/4 cup.

50 portions: Omit broccoli, green peppers, onions, and parmesan cheese. Use 1 qt canned carrots, 3 cups canned, peeled, diced tomatoes, and 3 cups canned green beans. Add vegetables and margarine to pasta.

6 portions: Omit broccoli, green peppers, onions, and parmesan cheese. Use 1/2 cup canned carrots, 1/3 cup canned, peeled, diced tomatoes, and 1/3 cup canned green beans. Add vegetables and margarine to pasta.

Puree (PUR): Prepare as directed. Add liquid (i.e. tomato sauce); blenderize to obtain desired consistency.

Nutrient Analysis per Serving:

Regular	KCAL	PRO gm	CHO gm	FAT gm	Chol mg	SFA gm	PFA gm	VITA iu	VITC mg	THI mg	RIB mg	NIA mg	CA mg	NA mg	K+ mg	FE mg
	183	5.1	23.9	7.4	1.7	1.5	2.1	2896	16.1	0.15	0.1	1.2	53.9	52.5	136	1.2

Sodium Restricted	NA mg	Diabetic	Kcal	Milk exg	Veg exg	Fruit exg	Bread exg	Meat exg	Fat exg	Low Fat & Low Chol	FAT gm	Chol mg	SFA gm	PFA gm
	11.3		128	0.0	0.5	0.0	1.0	0.0	1.0		1.8	0.0	0.2	0.4

Breads and Muffins

N1	Biscuits

Portion: 2-inch biscuit

INGREDIENTS	50 portions		6 portions	
	weights	measures	weights	measures
Flour, all-purpose	2 lb	2 qt	4 oz	1 cup
Baking powder	2 oz	4 2/3 Tbsp	1/4 oz	1 3/4 tsp
Salt		2 1/4 tsp		1/4 tsp
Milk, nonfat dry	2 3/4 oz	1 cup	3/4 oz	2 Tbsp
Margarine, low sodium	8 oz	1 cup	1 oz	2 Tbsp
Water		2 3/4 cups		1/3 cup

Method

1. Combine flour, baking powder, salt, and nonfat dry milk in mixing bowl. Mix on low speed until blended.
2. Add margarine to flour mixture. Mix on medium speed for 1 to 2 minutes. The mixture will be crumbly.
3. Add water. Mix on low speed to form a soft dough, about 30 seconds.
4. Turn out on lightly floured board, divide into halves. Knead lightly 15 to 20 times.
5. Roll out to 1/2-inch thickness. Cut with 2-inch biscuit cutter and place on baking sheets or place dough on baking sheets and cut into 2-inch squares.
6. Bake at 425°F for 12 to 15 minutes.

Directions for Diet Preparations

Sodium Restricted (SR): Use low sodium baking powder. Omit salt.

Low Fat/Low Cholesterol (LF): 1 biscuit and **Diabetic** (DB): 1 biscuit. Prepare as directed. May use if able to calculate into daily food plan.

Mechanical Soft (SFT) and **Soft/Low Fiber** (SLF): Prepare as directed.

Puree (PUR): Not recommended.

Nutrient Analysis per Serving:

Regular	KCAL	PRO gm	CHO gm	FAT gm	Chol mg	SFA gm	PFA gm	VITA iu	VITC mg	THI mg	RIB mg	NIA mg	CA mg	NA mg	K+ mg	FE mg
	107	2.4	15.3	3.9	0.2	0.6	1.3	185	0.08	0.12	0.10	1.0	32.8	300	43.2	0.8

Sodium Restricted	NA mg	Diabetic	Kcal	Milk exg	Veg exg	Fruit exg	Bread exg	Meat exg	Fat exg	Low Fat & Low Chol	FAT gm	Chol mg	SFA gm	PFA gm
	9.3		107	0.0	0.0	0.0	1.0	0.0	0.75		3.9	0.2	0.6	1.3

Portion: 2-inch biscuit

INGREDIENTS	50 portions		6 portions	
	weights	measures	weights	measures
Flour, all-purpose	2 lb	2 qt	4 oz	1 cup
Baking powder	2 oz	4 2/3 Tbsp	1/4 oz	1 3/4 tsp
Salt		2 1/4 tsp		1/4 tsp
Milk, nonfat dry	2 3/4 oz	1 cup	3/4 oz	2 Tbsp
Cheese, mild, shredded	6 oz	1 1/2 cups	3/4 oz	3 Tbsp
Margarine, low sodium	6 oz	3/4 cup	3/4 oz	1 1/2 Tbsp
Water		2 3/4 cups		1/3 cup

Method

1. Combine flour, baking powder, salt, nonfat dry milk, and grated cheese in mixing bowl. Mix on low speed until blended.
2. Add margarine to flour mixture. Mix on medium speed for 1 to 2 minutes. The mixture will be crumbly.
3. Add water. Mix on low speed to form a soft dough, about 30 seconds.
4. Turn out on lightly floured board, divide into halves. Knead lightly 15 to 20 times.
5. Roll out to 1/2-inch thickness. Cut with 2-inch biscuit cutter and place on baking sheets or place dough on baking sheets and cut into 2-inch squares.
6. Bake at 425°F for 12 to 15 minutes.

Directions for Diet Preparations

Sodium Restricted (SR): Use low sodium baking powder and low sodium cheese. Omit salt.

Low Fat/Low Cholesterol (LF): 1 biscuit and **Diabetic** (DB): 1 biscuit. Use low fat cheese. May use if able to calculate into daily food plan.

Mechanical Soft (SFT) and **Soft/Low Fiber** (SLF): Prepare as directed.

Puree (PUR): Not recommended.

Nutrient Analysis per Serving:

Regular	KCAL	PRO gm	CHO gm	FAT gm	Chol mg	SFA gm	PFA gm	VITA iu	VITC mg	THI mg	RIB mg	NIA mg	CA mg	NA mg	K+ mg	FE mg
	112	3.3	15.3	4.1	3.8	1.1	1.0	182	0.08	0.12	0.11	1.0	57.0	214	46.1	0.8

Sodium Restricted	NA mg	Diabetic	Kcal	Milk exg	Veg exg	Fruit exg	Bread exg	Meat exg	Fat exg	Low Fat & Low Chol	FAT gm	Chol mg	SFA gm	PFA gm
	21.6		108	0.0	0.0	0.0	1.0	0.0	0.8		3.5	0.25	0.5	1.0

Portion: 2-inch biscuit

INGREDIENTS	50 portions		6 portions	
	weights	measures	weights	measures
Flour, all-purpose	1 1/4 lb	1 1/4 qt	2 1/2 oz	2/3 cup
Cornmeal	6 oz	1 1/8 cups	3/4 oz	2 1/4 Tbsp
Baking powder	2 oz	4 2/3 Tbsp	1/4 oz	1 3/4 tsp
Salt		2 1/4 tsp		1/4 tsp
Milk, nonfat dry	2 3/4 oz	1 cup	3/4 oz	2 Tbsp
Margarine, low sodium	8 oz	1 cup	1 oz	2 Tbsp
Water		2 3/4 cups		1/3 cup

Method

1. Combine flour, cornmeal, baking powder, salt, and nonfat dry milk in mixing bowl. Mix on low speed until blended.
2. Add margarine to flour mixture. Mix on medium speed for 1 to 2 minutes. The mixture will be crumbly.
3. Add water. Mix on low speed to form a soft dough, about 30 seconds.
4. Turn out on lightly floured board, divide into halves. Knead lightly 15 to 20 times.
5. Roll out to 1/2-inch thickness. Cut with 2-inch biscuit cutter and place on baking sheets or place dough on baking sheets and cut into 2-inch squares.
6. Bake at 425°F for 12 to 15 minutes.

Directions for Diet Preparations

Sodium Restricted (SR): Use low sodium baking powder. Omit salt.
Low Fat/Low Cholesterol (LF): 1 biscuit and **Diabetic** (DB): 1 biscuit. Prepare as directed. May use if able to calculate into daily food plan.
Mechanical Soft (SFT): Prepare as directed.
Soft/Low Fiber (SLF) and **Puree** (PUR): Not recommended.

Nutrient Analysis per Serving:

Regular	KCAL	PRO gm	CHO gm	FAT gm	Chol mg	SFA gm	PFA gm	VITA iu	VITC mg	THI mg	RIB mg	NIA mg	CA mg	NA mg	K+ mg	FE mg
	93.5	2.0	12.5	3.8	0.2	0.6	1.3	185	0.08	0.08	0.07	0.6	32.0	300	40.4	0.5

Sodium Restricted	NA mg	Diabetic	Kcal	Milk exg	Veg exg	Fruit exg	Bread exg	Meat exg	Fat exg	Low Fat & Low Chol	FAT gm	Chol mg	SFA gm	PFA gm
	9.2		93.5	0.0	0.0	0.0	1.0	0.0	0.5		3.8	0.2	0.6	1.3

Drop Biscuits

Portion: 2-inch biscuit

INGREDIENTS	50 portions		6 portions	
	weights	measures	weights	measures
Flour, all-purpose	2 lb	2 qt	4 oz	1 cup
Baking powder	2 oz	4 2/3 Tbsp	1/4 oz	1 3/4 tsp
Salt		2 1/4 tsp		1/4 tsp
Milk, nonfat dry	2 3/4 oz	1 cup	1/3 oz	2 Tbsp
Margarine, low sodium	8 oz	1 cup	1 oz	2 Tbsp
Water		3 1/2 cups		7 Tbsp

Method

1. Combine flour, baking powder, salt, and nonfat dry milk in mixing bowl. Mix on low speed until blended.
2. Add margarine to flour mixture. Mix on medium speed for 1 to 2 minutes. The mixture will be crumbly.
3. Add water. Mix on low speed to form a soft dough, about 30 seconds.
4. Turn out on lightly floured board, divide into halves. Knead lightly 15 to 20 times.
5. Portion with spoon or No. 30 dipper. Place on baking sheets.
6. Bake at 425°F for 12 to 15 minutes.

Directions for Diet Preparations

Sodium Restricted (SR): Use low sodium baking powder. Omit salt.

Low Fat/Low Cholesterol (LF): 1 biscuit and **Diabetic** (DB): 1 biscuit. Prepare as directed. May use if able to calculate into daily food plan.

Mechanical Soft (SFT) and **Soft/Low Fiber** (SLF): Prepare as directed.

Puree (PUR): Not recommended.

Nutrient Analysis per Serving:

Regular	KCAL	PRO gm	CHO gm	FAT gm	Chol mg	SFA gm	PFA gm	VITA iu	VITC mg	THI mg	RIB mg	NIA mg	CA mg	NA mg	K+ mg	FE mg
	107	2.4	15.3	3.9	0.2	0.6	1.3	185	0.08	0.12	0.10	1.0	32.8	300	43.2	0.8

Sodium Restricted	NA mg	Diabetic	Kcal	Milk exg	Veg exg	Fruit exg	Bread exg	Meat exg	Fat exg	Low Fat & Low Chol	FAT gm	Chol mg	SFA gm	PFA gm
	9.3		107	0.0	0.0	0.0	1.0	0.0	0.75		3.9	0.2	0.6	1.3

Portion: 2-inch biscuit

INGREDIENTS	50 portions		6 portions	
	weights	**measures**	**weights**	**measures**
Flour, all-purpose	1 1/4 lb	1 1/4 qt	2 1/2 oz	2/3 cup
Flour, whole wheat	6 oz	1 3/8 cups	3/4 oz	2 7/8 Tbsp
Baking powder	2 oz	4 2/3 Tbsp	1/4 oz	1 3/4 tsp
Salt		2 1/4 tsp		1/4 tsp
Milk, nonfat dry	2 3/4 oz	1 cup	1/3 oz	2 Tbsp
Margarine, low sodium	8 oz	1 cup	1 oz	2 Tbsp
Water		2 3/4 cups		1/3 cup

Method

1. Combine flours, baking powder, salt, and nonfat dry milk in mixing bowl. Mix on low speed until blended.
2. Add margarine to flour mixture. Mix on medium speed for 1 to 2 minutes. The mixture will be crumbly.
3. Add water. Mix on low speed to form a soft dough, about 30 seconds.
4. Turn out on lightly floured board, divide into halves. Knead lightly 15 to 20 times.
5. Roll out to 1/2-inch thickness. Cut with 2-inch biscuit cutter and place on baking sheets or place dough on baking sheets and cut into 2-inch squares.
6. Bake at 425°F for 12 to 15 minutes.

Directions for Diet Preparations

Sodium Restricted (SR): Use low sodium baking powder. Omit salt.

Low Fat/Low Cholesterol (LF): 1 biscuit and **Diabetic** (DB): 1 biscuit. Prepare as directed. May use if able to calculate into daily food plan.

Mechanical Soft (SFT): Prepare as directed.

Soft/Low Fiber (SLF) and **Puree** (PUR): Not recommended.

Nutrient Analysis per Serving:

Regular	KCAL	PRO	CHO	FAT	Chol	SFA	PFA	VITA	VITC	THI	RIB	NIA	CA	NA	K+	FE
		gm	gm	gm	mg	gm	gm	iu	mg	mg	mg	mg	mg	mg	mg	mg
	93.0	2.2	12.3	3.8	0.25	0.6	1.3	184	0.08	0.09	0.07	0.7	33.1	300	49.0	0.6

Sodium	NA	Diabetic	Kcal	Milk	Veg	Fruit	Bread	Meat	Fat	Low Fat &	FAT	Chol	SFA	PFA
Restricted	mg			exg	exg	exg	exg	exg	exg	Low Chol	gm	mg	gm	gm
	9.2		93.0	0.0	0.0	0.0	1.0	0.0	0.5		3.8	0.25	0.6	1.3

Portion: 1 slice

INGREDIENTS	60 portions		15 portions	
	1 pan (12 × 20 × 2″) **cut 6 × 10**		**1 pan (9 × 9″)** **cut 5 × 3**	
	weights	measures	weights	measures
Flour, all-purpose	2 1/8 lb	2 1/8 qt	8 oz	2 1/8 cups
Cornmeal, yellow	2 lb	1 1/2 qt	8 oz	1 1/2 cups
Baking powder	3 1/8 oz	7 Tbsp	3/4 oz	1 3/4 Tbsp
Milk, skim		1 1/2 qt		1 1/2 cups
Sugar, granulated	9 oz	1 1/4 cups	2 1/4 oz	1/3 cup
Salt		2 tsp		1/2 tsp
Eggs, beaten	1 lb	2 cup (8 large)	4 oz	1/2 cup (2 large)
Margarine, low sodium, melted	9 oz	1 1/8 cups	2 1/4 oz	4 1/2 Tbsp

Method

1. Combine flour, cornmeal, baking powder, sugar, and salt in mixing bowl. Blend on low speed for 4 minutes.
2. Combine milk, eggs, margarine, and water. Add to dry ingredients. Mix on low speed until dry ingredients are moistened.
3. Pour batter into greased or non-stick baking pan(s).
4. Bake at 375°F for 25 minutes or until browned.
5. Cut into slices.

Directions for Diet Preparations

Sodium Restricted (SR): Use low sodium baking powder as per manufacturer's directions. Omit salt.

Low Fat/Low Cholesterol (LF): 1 slice. Omit eggs, substitute with an equal amount of egg whites or a commercial egg substitute. Omit margarine, substitute with equal amount of reduced-calorie margarine. May use if able to calculate into daily food plan.

Diabetic (DB): 1 slice.

60 portions: Replace 1 1/4 cup granulated sugar with 2 Tbsp granulated sugar and an artificial sweetener equivalent to 1 cup granulated sugar (approximately 4 tsp artificial sweetener). Omit margarine, substitute with equal amount of reduced-calorie margarine. May use if able to calculate into daily food plan.

15 portions: Replace 1/3 cup granulated sugar with 1/2 Tbsp granulated sugar and an artificial sweetener equivalent to 1/4 cup granulated sugar (approximately 1 tsp artificial sweetener). Omit margarine, substitute with equal amount of reduced-calorie margarine. May use if able to calculate into daily food plan.

Mechanical Soft (SFT): Prepare as directed. Consider individual tolerance.

Soft/Low Fiber (SLF) and **Puree** (PUR): Not recommended.

Nutrient Analysis per Serving:

Regular	KCAL	PRO gm	CHO gm	FAT gm	Chol mg	SFA gm	PFA gm	VITA iu	VITC mg	THI mg	RIB mg	NIA mg	CA mg	NA mg	K+ mg	FE mg
	101	2.2	14.7	3.6	18.4	0.6	1.1	169	0.1	0.06	0.06	0.5	28.2	185	42.4	0.5

Sodium Restricted	NA mg	Diabetic	Kcal	Milk exg	Veg exg	Fruit exg	Bread exg	Meat exg	Fat exg	Low Fat & Low Chol	FAT gm	Chol mg	SFA gm	PFA gm
	12.3		80.7	0.0	0.0	0.0	1.0	0.0	0.2		1.8	0.2	0.3	0.6

Portion: 1 slice (1/2 inch, 16 slices per loaf)

INGREDIENTS	48 portions, 3 loaves		16 portions, 1 loaf	
	weights	measures	weights	measures
Dates, chopped	1 1/8 lb	3 1/3 cups	6 oz	1 1/8 cups
Baking soda		1 Tbsp		1 tsp
Water, boiling		2 1/2 cups		3/4 cup
Margarine, low sodium	2 1/4 oz	4 1/2 Tbsp	3/4 oz	1 1/2 Tbsp
Sugar, granulated	1 1/3 lb	3 cups	7 oz	1 cup
Eggs	6 oz	3/4 cup (3 large)	2 oz	1/4 cup (1 large)
Vanilla		1 Tbsp		1 tsp
Flour, all-purpose	1 1/2 lb	1 1/2 qt	8 oz	2 cups
Pecans, chopped	6 oz	1 1/2 cups	2 oz	1/2 cup

Method

1. Combine dates, baking soda, and water. Let stand 15 minutes.
2. Cream margarine and sugar on medium speed for 5 minutes using flat beater.
3. Add eggs and vanilla to creamed mixture. Mix on medium speed for 2 minutes.
4. Combine flour and nuts. Add to creamed mixture.
5. Add dates to creamed mixture. Mix to blend.
6. Scale batter into 3 greased or non-stick loaf pans.
7. Bake at 350°F for about 40 to 50 minutes.

Directions for Diet Preparations

Sodium Restricted (SR): Prepare as directed. May use if able to calculate into daily food plan.

Low Fat/Low Cholesterol (LF): 1/2-inch slice. Omit margarine, substitute with equal amount of reduced-calorie margarine. Omit pecans. May use if able to calculate into daily food plan.

Diabetic (DB): 1/2-inch slice.

48 portions: Replace 1 1/3 lb granulated sugar with 3 Tbsp granulated sugar and an artificial sweetener equivalent to 2 1/2 cups granulated sugar (approximately 2 1/2 Tbsp artificial sweetener). Omit margarine, substitute with equal amount of reduced-calorie margarine. Omit pecans. Bake at 350°F for about 35 minutes. Consider individual tolerance when using granulated sugar. May use if able to calculate into daily food plan.

16 portions: Replace 7 oz granulated sugar with 1 Tbsp granulated sugar and an artificial sweetener equivalent to 3/4 cup granulated sugar (approximately 1 Tbsp artificial sweetener). Omit margarine, substitute with equal amount of reduced-calorie margarine. Omit pecans. Bake at 350°F for about 35 minutes. Consider individual tolerance when using granulated sugar. May use if able to calculate into daily food plan.

Mechanical Soft (SFT): Omit pecans. Consider individual tolerance.

Soft/Low Fiber (SLF) and **Puree** (PUR): Not recommended.

Nutrient Analysis per Serving:

Regular	KCAL	PRO gm	CHO gm	FAT gm	Chol mg	SFA gm	PFA gm	VITA iu	VITC mg	THI mg	RIB mg	NIA mg	CA mg	NA mg	K+ mg	FE mg
	165	2.2	31.8	3.8	11.4	0.4	1.0	64.8	0.1	0.1	0.08	1.0	8.4	55.3	99.4	0.9

Sodium Restricted	NA mg	Diabetic	Kcal	Milk exg	Veg exg	Fruit exg	Bread exg	Meat exg	Fat exg	Low Fat & Low Chol	FAT gm	Chol mg	SFA gm	PFA gm
	55.3		94.6	0.0	0.0	0.4	1.0	0.0	0.0		1.0	11.4	0.2	0.3

Portion: 1 slice (2 inches)

INGREDIENTS	48 portions		6 portions	
	weights	measures	weights	measures
Bread, french (12 × 4 inch loaf)		2 loaves		1/4 loaf
Margarine, low sodium	1 lb	2 cups	2 oz	1/4 cup
Garlic powder	1 1/3 oz	4 Tbsp	1/8 oz	1/2 Tbsp

Method

1. Cut french bread in half lengthwise.
2. Place on sheet pan.
3. Brush with margarine.
4. Sprinkle lightly with garlic powder.
5. Bake at 400°F for 5 to 10 minutes.
6. Cut crosswise every 2 inches.

Directions for Diet Preparations

Sodium Restricted (SR): Use sodium-restricted bread.

Low Fat/Low Cholesterol (LF): 1 slice and **Diabetic** (DB): 1 oz. May use 1 tsp reduced-calorie margarine if able to calculate into daily meal plan. Low fat diets should consider individual tolerance to garlic.

Mechanical Soft (SFT): Use white bread. Brush with margarine. Sprinkle with garlic powder.

Soft/Low Fiber (SLF) and **Puree** (PUR): Not recommended.

Nutrient Analysis per Serving:

Regular	KCAL	PRO gm	CHO gm	FAT gm	Chol mg	SFA gm	PFA gm	VITA iu	VITC mg	THI mg	RIB mg	NIA mg	CA mg	NA mg	K+ mg	FE mg
	152	2.7	16.2	8.4	0.8	1.4	2.5	312	0.01	0.11	0.07	0.9	15.2	167	36.8	0.8

Sodium Restricted	NA mg	Diabetic	Kcal	Milk exg	Veg exg	Fruit exg	Bread exg	Meat exg	Fat exg	Low Fat & Low Chol	FAT gm	Chol mg	SFA gm	PFA gm
	5.7		84.6	0.0	0.0	0.0	1.1	0.0	0.0		0.8	0.8	0.18	0.0

Portion: 1 slice (17 slices per loaf)

INGREDIENTS	51 portions, 3 loaves		17 portions, 1 loaf	
	weights	measures	weights	measures
Margarine, low sodium, melted	8 oz	1 cup	2 2/3 oz	1/3 cup
Sugar, brown	2 lb	1 1/2 qt	10 2/3 oz	2 cups
Eggs, well beaten	2 oz	1 1/2 cups (6 large)	4 oz	1/2 cup (2 large)
Pumpkin, canned	1 1/2 lb	3 cups	8 oz	1 cup
Flour, all-purpose	1 1/4 lb	1 1/4 qt	6 2/3 oz	1 2/3 cup
Baking powder		3/4 tsp		1/4 tsp
Baking soda		1 Tbsp		1 tsp
Salt		2 1/4 tsp		3/4 tsp
Nutmeg		1 1/2 tsp		1/2 tsp
Cinnamon, ground		2 tsp		1/2 tsp
Water		1 cup		1/3 cup
Walnuts, chopped	6 oz	1 1/2 cups	2 oz	1/2 cup

Method

1. Cream margarine and sugar on medium speed for 3 minutes.
2. Add eggs. Mix.
3. Add pumpkin gradually. Mix at medium speed for 5 minutes.
4. Combine flour, baking powder, baking soda, salt, and spices. Gradually add to creamed mixture alternately with water. (Preheat oven to 350°F.)
5. Mix on low speed for 3 minutes. Do not over beat.
6. Fold in nuts.
7. Pour into greased loaf pans (9" × 5" × 3"). Divide batter in equal amounts.
8. Bake at 350°F for 45–50 minutes or until browned on top and toothpick inserted in center of loaf comes out clean.
9. Remove from oven, cool in pans 15 minutes. Remove from pans. Place on wire rack. When cooled, wrap. Refrigerate before slicing.

Directions for Diet Preparations

Sodium Restricted (SR): 1 slice. Omit baking powder, substitute with low sodium baking powder as per manufacturer's directions. Omit salt.

Low Fat/Low Cholesterol (LF): 1 slice.
51 portions: Omit margarine, substitute with reduced-calorie margarine in equal amounts. Omit eggs, substitute with 1 1/2 cups commercial egg substitute. Omit walnuts. May use if able to calculate into daily food plan.
17 portions: Omit margarine, substitute with reduced-calorie margarine in equal amounts. Omit eggs, substitute with 1/2 cup commercial egg substitute. Omit walnuts. May use if able to calculate into daily food plan.

Diabetic (DB): 1 slice.
51 portions: Omit margarine, substitute with reduced-calorie margarine in equal amounts. Use 1/2 lb granulated sugar and artificial sweetener equivalent to 1 1/2 lb of granulated sugar (approx. 4 Tbsp). Omit walnuts. May use if able to calculate into daily food plan.
17 portions: Omit margarine, substitute with reduced-calorie margarine in equal amounts. Use 1/2 cup granulated sugar and artificial sweetener equivalent to 1 1/2 cups of granulated sugar (approx. 1 1/2 Tbsp). Omit walnuts. May use if able to calculate into daily food plan.

Mechanical Soft (SFT): Omit walnuts.
Soft/Low Fiber (SLF) and **Puree** (PUR): Not recommended.

Nutrient Analysis per Serving:

Regular	KCAL	PRO gm	CHO gm	FAT gm	Chol mg	SFA gm	PFA gm	VITA iu	VITC mg	THI mg	RIB mg	NIA mg	CA mg	NA mg	K+ mg	FE mg
	180	2.7	28	6.7	32	1.0	3.0	940	0.8	0.1	0.08	0.7	17	163	72	1.0

Sodium Restricted	NA mg	Diabetic	Kcal	Milk exg	Veg exg	Fruit exg	Bread exg	Meat exg	Fat exg	Low Fat & Low Chol	FAT gm	Chol mg	SFA gm	PFA gm
	59		89	0.0	0.0	0.3	1.0	0.0	0.0		2.5	0.2	0.3	0.6

Portion: 1 muffin

INGREDIENTS	78 portions		10 portions	
	weights	measures	weights	measures
Flour, all-purpose	2 1/2 lb	2 1/2 qt	5 oz	1 1/4 cups
Baking powder	2 oz	4 2/3 Tbsp	1/4 oz	1 3/4 tsp
Salt		2 tsp		1/4 tsp
Sugar, granulated	7 oz	1 cup	5/8 oz	2 Tbsp
Eggs, beaten	8 oz	1 cup (4 large)	1 1/2 oz	3 Tbsp (1 small)
Milk, skim		1 1/2 qt		3/4 cup
Margarine, low sodium, melted, cooled	8 oz	1 cup	1 oz	2 Tbsp

Method

1. Combine flour, baking powder, salt, and sugar. Blend on low speed for 10 seconds.
2. Combine eggs, milk, and margarine. Add to dry ingredients. Mix at low speed only to blend, about 25 seconds.
3. Measure with No. 24 dipper into greased or non-stick muffin pans.
4. Dip batter all at oz. Handle as little as possible.
5. Bake at 400°F for about 25 minutes or until golden brown.
6. Remove from pans as soon as baked.

Directions for Diet Preparations

Sodium Restricted (SR): Use low sodium baking powder as per manufacturer's directions. Omit salt.

Low Fat/Low Cholesterol (LF): 1 muffin.

78 portions: Omit eggs, substitute with 1 cup commercial egg substitute. Omit margarine, substitute with reduced-calorie margarine in equal amount to regular margarine. May use if able to calculate into daily food plan.

10 portions: Omit eggs, substitute with 3 Tbsp commercial egg substitute. Omit margarine, substitute with reduced-calorie margarine in equal amount to regular margarine. May use if able to calculate into daily food plan.

Diabetic (DB): 1 muffin.

78 portions: Omit sugar, substitute with artificial sweetener equal to 1 cup granulated sugar (approximately 4 tsp artificial sweetener). Omit margarine, substitute with reduced-calorie margarine in equal amount to regular margarine. May use if able to calculate into daily food plan.

10 portions: Omit sugar, substitute with artificial sweetener equal to 2 Tbsp granulated sugar (approximately 1/2 tsp artificial sweetener). Omit margarine, substitute with reduced-calorie margarine in equal amount to regular margarine. May use if able to calculate into daily food plan.

Mechanical Soft (SFT) and **Soft/Low Fiber** (SLF): Prepare as directed.

Puree (PUR): Not recommended. Use white bread if tolerated.

Nutrient Analysis per Serving:

Regular	KCAL	PRO gm	CHO gm	FAT gm	Chol mg	SFA gm	PFA gm	VITA iu	VITC mg	THI mg	RIB mg	NIA mg	CA mg	NA mg	K+ mg	FE mg
	97.1	2.5	15.1	2.8	14.3	0.5	0.9	149	0.2	0.10	0.09	0.8	35.6	193	50.4	0.7

Sodium Restricted	NA mg	Diabetic	Kcal	Milk exg	Veg exg	Fruit exg	Bread exg	Meat exg	Fat exg	Low Fat & Low Chol	FAT gm	Chol mg	SFA gm	PFA gm
	14.5		77.3	0.0	0.0	0.0	1.0	0.0	0.0		1.4	0.3	0.2	0.5

Apple Muffin

Portion: 1 muffin

INGREDIENTS	78 portions		10 portions	
	weights	measures	weights	measures
Flour, all-purpose	2 1/2 lb	2 1/2 qt	5 oz	1 1/4 cups
Baking powder	2 oz	4 2/3 Tbsp	1/4 oz	1 3/4 tsp
Salt		2 tsp		1/4 tsp
Sugar, granulated	7 oz	1 cup	5/8 oz	2 Tbsp
Eggs, beaten	8 oz	1 cup	1 1/2 oz	3 Tbsp
		(4 large)		(1 small)
Milk, skim		1 1/2 qt		3/4 cup
Margarine, low sodium, melted, cooled	8 oz	1 cup	1 oz	2 Tbsp
Apples, peeled, chopped	1 lb EP	3 1/2 cups	2 1/3 oz EP	1/2 cup
	(1 1/2 lb AP)		(3 1/2 oz AP)	

Method

1. Combine flour, baking powder, salt, and sugar. Blend on low speed for 10 seconds.
2. Combine eggs, milk, and margarine. Add to dry ingredients. Mix at low speed only to blend, about 25 seconds.
3. Fold apples into batter.
4. Measure with No. 24 dipper into greased or non-stick muffin pans.
5. Dip batter all at once. Handle as little as possible.
6. Bake at 400°F for about 25 minutes or until golden brown.
7. Remove from pans as soon as baked.

Directions for Diet Preparations

Sodium Restricted (SR): Use low sodium baking powder as per manufacturer's directions. Omit salt.

Low Fat/Low Cholesterol (LF): 1 muffin.

78 portions: Omit eggs, substitute with 1 cup commercial egg substitute. Omit margarine, substitute with reduced-calorie margarine in equal amount to regular margarine. May use if able to calculate into daily food plan.

10 portions: Omit eggs, substitute with 3 Tbsp commercial egg substitute. Omit margarine, substitute with reduced-calorie margarine in equal amount to regular margarine. May use if able to calculate into daily food plan.

Diabetic (DB): 1 muffin.

78 portions: Omit sugar, substitute with artificial sweetener equal to 1 cup granulated sugar (approximately 4 tsp artificial sweetener). Omit margarine, substitute with reduced-calorie margarine in equal amount to regular margarine. May use if able to calculate into daily food plan.

10 portions: Omit sugar, substitute with artificial sweetener equal to 2 Tbsp granulated sugar (approximately 1/2 tsp artificial sweetener). Omit margarine, substitute with reduced-calorie margarine in equal amount to regular margarine. May use if able to calculate into daily food plan.

Mechanical Soft (SFT) and **Soft/Low Fiber** (SLF): 1 muffin.

78 portions: Omit apples, substitute with 1 cup applesauce.

10 portions: Omit apples, substitute with 1/4 cup applesauce.

Puree (PUR): Not recommended. Use white bread if tolerated.

Nutrient Analysis per Serving:

Regular	KCAL	PRO gm	CHO gm	FAT gm	Chol mg	SFA gm	PFA gm	VITA iu	VITC mg	THI mg	RIB mg	NIA mg	CA mg	NA mg	K+ mg	FE mg
	100	2.5	15.8	2.8	14.3	0.5	0.9	152	0.4	0.11	0.09	0.8	35.8	193	56.0	0.7

Sodium Restricted	NA mg	Diabetic	Kcal	Milk exg	Veg exg	Fruit exg	Bread exg	Meat exg	Fat exg	Low Fat & Low Chol	FAT gm	Chol mg	SFA gm	PFA gm
	14.5		80.2	0.0	0.0	0.13	1.0	0.0	0.0		1.5	0.3	0.2	0.5

Portion: 1 muffin

INGREDIENTS	78 portions		10 portions	
	weights	measures	weights	measures
Flour, all-purpose	2 1/2 lb	2 1/2 qt	5 oz	1 1/4 cups
Baking powder	2 oz	4 2/3 Tbsp	1/4 oz	1 3/4 tsp
Salt		2 tsp		1/4 tsp
Sugar, granulated	11 oz	1 1/2 cups	1 3/8 oz	3 Tbsp
Eggs, beaten	8 oz	1 cup (4 large)	1 1/2 oz	3 Tbsp (1 small)
Milk, skim		1 1/2 qt		3/4 cup
Margarine, low sodium, melted, cooled	8 oz	1 cup	1 oz	2 Tbsp
Blueberries, well-drained, unsweetened	1 lb	3 cups	2 oz	1/3 cup

Method

1. Combine flour, baking powder, salt, and sugar. Blend on low speed for 10 seconds.
2. Combine eggs, milk, and margarine. Add to dry ingredients. Mix at low speed only to blend, about 25 seconds.
3. Fold blueberries into batter.
4. Measure with No. 24 dipper into greased or non-stick muffin pans.
5. Dip batter all at once. Handle as little as possible.
6. Bake at 400°F for about 25 minutes or until golden brown.
7. Remove from pans as soon as baked.

Directions for Diet Preparations

Sodium Restricted (SR): Use low sodium baking powder as per manufacturer's directions. Omit salt.

Low Fat/Low Cholesterol (LF): 1 muffin.

78 portions: Omit eggs, substitute with 1 cup commercial egg substitute. Omit margarine, substitute with reduced-calorie margarine in equal amount to regular margarine. May use if able to calculate into daily food plan.

10 portions: Omit eggs, substitute with 3 Tbsp commercial egg substitute. Omit margarine, substitute with reduced-calorie margarine in equal amount to regular margarine. May use if able to calculate into daily food plan.

Diabetic (DB): 1 muffin.

78 portions: Omit sugar, substitute with artificial sweetener equal to 1 1/2 cups granulated sugar (approximately 1 3/4 Tbsp artificial sweetener). Omit margarine, substitute with reduced-calorie margarine in equal amount to regular margarine. May use if able to calculate into daily food plan.

10 portions: Omit sugar, substitute with artificial sweetener equal to 3 Tbsp granulated sugar (approximately 3/4 tsp artificial sweetener). Omit margarine, substitute with reduced-calorie margarine in equal amount to regular margarine. May use if able to calculate into daily food plan.

Mechanical Soft (SFT): Prepare as directed.

Soft/Low Fiber (SLF) and **Puree** (PUR): Not recommended, substitute with appropriate food alternative.

Nutrient Analysis per Serving:

Regular	KCAL	PRO gm	CHO gm	FAT gm	Chol mg	SFA gm	PFA gm	VITA iu	VITC mg	THI mg	RIB mg	NIA mg	CA mg	NA mg	K+ mg	FE mg
	104	2.5	16.9	2.8	14.3	0.5	0.9	154	0.3	0.10	0.09	0.8	36.1	193	53.7	0.7

Sodium Restricted	NA mg	Diabetic	Kcal	Milk exg	Veg exg	Fruit exg	Bread exg	Meat exg	Fat exg	Low Fat & Low Chol	FAT gm	Chol mg	SFA gm	PFA gm
	14.6		80.6	0.0	0.0	0.0	1.0	0.0	0.0		1.5	0.3	0.2	0.5

Blueberry Muffin (variation)

Portion: 1 muffin

INGREDIENTS	48 portions		12 portions	
	weights	**measures**	**weights**	**measures**
Banana, ripe, peeled	1 1/4 lb	2 1/2 cups (6 medium)	5 oz	2/3 cup (1 1/2 medium)
Maple syrup	3 oz	6 Tbsp	3/4 oz	1 1/2 Tbsp
Margarine, low sodium	12 oz	1 1/2 cups	3 oz	6 Tbsp
Cornstarch	2 oz	6 Tbsp	1/3 oz	1 1/2 Tbsp
Flour, whole wheat pastry	1 2/3 lb	1 1/2 qt	6 1/2 oz	1 1/2 cups
Nutmeg		4 tsp		1 tsp
Cinnamon, ground		2 tsp		1/2 tsp
Applesauce, unsweetened	1 1/2 lb	3 cups	6 oz	3/4 cup
Water		1 1/2 cups		6 Tbsp
Blueberries, fresh or frozen, thawed, unsweetened	1 lb	3 cups	4 oz	3/4 cup

Method

1. Cream together bananas, maple syrup, and margarine.
2. Add cornstarch, flour, nutmeg, cinnamon, applesauce, and water. Mix well.
3. Fold blueberries into batter.
4. Measure with No. 16 dipper into greased or non-stick muffin pans.
5. Pre-heat oven to 350°F.
6. Bake at 350°F for about 40 minutes or until golden brown.
7. Cool on rack.

Directions for Diet Preparations

Sodium Restricted (SR): Prepare as directed.
Low Fat/Low Cholesterol (LF): 1 muffin. Prepare as directed. May use if able to calculate into daily food plan.
Diabetic (DB): 1 muffin. Prepare as directed. Consider individual tolerance to maple syrup.
Mechanical Soft (SFT): Prepare as directed.
Soft/Low Fiber (SLF) and **Puree** (PUR): Not recommended, substitute with appropriate food alternative.

Nutrient Analysis per Serving:

Regular	KCAL	PRO gm	CHO gm	FAT gm	Chol mg	SFA gm	PFA gm	VITA iu	VITC mg	THI mg	RIB mg	NIA mg	CA mg	NA mg	K+ mg	FE mg
	138	2.3	19.9	6.2	0.0	1.1	2.0	263	5.7	0.08	0.05	1.1	11.8	4.1	144	0.7

Sodium Restricted	NA mg	Diabetic	Kcal	Milk exg	Veg exg	Fruit exg	Bread exg	Meat exg	Fat exg	Low Fat & Low Chol	FAT gm	Chol mg	SFA gm	PFA gm
	4.1		138	0.0	0.0	0.5	0.75	0.0	1.1		6.2	0.0	1.1	2.0

Portion: 1 muffin

INGREDIENTS	48 portions		12 portions	
	weights	**measures**	**weights**	**measures**
Flour, all-purpose	1 1/3 lb	5 1/4 cups	5 1/4 oz	1 1/3 cups
Baking powder	2 oz	4 2/3 Tbsp	1/2 oz	3 1/2 tsp
Salt		1 tsp		1/4 tsp
Sugar, granulated	3 1/2 oz	1/2 cup	5/8 oz	2 Tbsp
Bran cereal	8 oz	1 qt	2 oz	1 cup
Milk, skim		1 qt		1 cup
Margarine, low sodium, melted	6 oz	3/4 cup	1 1/2 oz	3 Tbsp
Eggs, beaten	8 oz	1 cup	2 oz	1/4 cup
		(4 large)		(1 large)

Method

1. Combine flour, baking powder, salt, and sugar. Blend on low speed for 10 seconds.
2. Combine bran cereal and milk. Mix on medium speed until blended. Let stand 5 minutes or until cereal has softened.
3. Add margarine, eggs, and flour mixture. Mix on low speed until thoroughly combined.
4. Measure with No. 24 dipper into greased or non-stick muffin pans.
5. Bake at 400°F for about 25 minutes or until golden brown.

Directions for Diet Preparations

Sodium Restricted (SR): Use low sodium baking powder as per manufacturer's directions. Omit salt. Use a low sodium bran cereal.

Low Fat/Low Cholesterol (LF): 1 muffin.

48 portions: Omit eggs, substitute with 1 cup commercial egg substitute. Omit margarine, substitute with reduced-calorie margarine in equal amount to regular margarine. May use if able to calculate into daily food plan.

12 portions: Omit eggs, substitute with 1/4 cup commercial egg substitute. Omit margarine, substitute with reduced-calorie margarine in equal amount to regular margarine. May use if able to calculate into daily food plan.

Diabetic (DB): 1 muffin.

48 portions: Omit sugar, substitute with artificial sweetener equal to 1/2 cup granulated sugar (approximately 2 tsp artificial sweetener). Omit margarine, substitute with reduced-calorie margarine in equal amount to regular margarine. May use if able to calculate into daily food plan.

12 portions: Omit sugar, substitute with artificial sweetener equal to 2 Tbsp granulated sugar (approximately 1/2 tsp artificial sweetener). Omit margarine, substitute with reduced-calorie margarine in equal amount to regular margarine. May use if able to calculate into daily food plan.

Mechanical Soft (SFT): Prepare as directed. Consider individual tolerance.

Soft/Low Fiber (SLF) and **Puree** (PUR): Not recommended, substitute with appropriate food alternative.

Nutrient Analysis per Serving:

Regular	KCAL	PRO gm	CHO gm	FAT gm	Chol mg	SFA gm	PFA gm	VITA iu	VITC mg	THI mg	RIB mg	NIA mg	CA mg	NA mg	K+ mg	FE mg
	113	3.6	18.5	3.6	23.1	0.6	1.1	499	4.0	0.18	0.20	1.9	48.7	340	142	1.8

Sodium Restricted	NA mg	Diabetic	Kcal	Milk exg	Veg exg	Fruit exg	Bread exg	Meat exg	Fat exg	Low Fat & Low Chol	FAT gm	Chol mg	SFA gm	PFA gm
	61.2		93.0	0.0	0.0	0.0	1.0	0.0	0.46		1.9	0.4	0.3	0.6

Portion: 1 muffin

INGREDIENTS	78 portions		10 portions	
	weights	measures	weights	measures
Flour, all-purpose	1 1/2 lb	1 1/2 qt	3 oz	3/4 cup
Cornmeal, white	1 lb	3 cups	2 oz	1/3 cup
Baking powder	2 oz	4 2/3 Tbsp	1/4 oz	1 3/4 tsp
Salt		2 tsp		1/4 tsp
Sugar, granulated	7 oz	1 cup	5/8 oz	2 Tbsp
Eggs, beaten	8 oz	1 cup (4 large)	1 1/2 oz	3 Tbsp (1 small)
Milk, skim		1 1/2 qt		3/4 cup
Margarine, low sodium, melted, cooled	8 oz	1 cup	1 oz	2 Tbsp

Method

1. Combine flour, cornmeal, baking powder, salt, and sugar. Blend on low speed for 10 seconds.
2. Combine eggs, milk, and margarine. Add to dry ingredients. Mix at low speed only to blend, about 25 seconds.
3. Measure with No. 24 dipper into greased or non-stick muffin pans.
4. Dip batter all at once. Handle as little as possible.
5. Bake at 400°F for about 25 minutes or until golden brown.
6. Remove from pans as soon as baked.

Directions for Diet Preparations

Sodium Restricted (SR): Use low sodium baking powder as per manufacturer's directions. Omit salt.

Low Fat/Low Cholesterol (LF): 1 muffin.

78 portions: Omit eggs, substitute with 1 cup commercial egg substitute. Omit margarine, substitute with reduced-calorie margarine in equal amount to regular margarine. May use if able to calculate into daily food plan.

10 portions: Omit eggs, substitute with 3 Tbsp commercial egg substitute. Omit margarine, substitute with reduced-calorie margarine in equal amount to regular margarine. May use if able to calculate into daily food plan.

Diabetic (DB): 1 muffin.

78 portions: Omit sugar, substitute with artificial sweetener equal to 1 cup granulated sugar (approximately 4 tsp artificial sweetener). Omit margarine, substitute with reduced-calorie margarine in equal amount to regular margarine. May use if able to calculate into daily food plan.

10 portions: Omit sugar, substitute with artificial sweetener equal to 2 Tbsp granulated sugar (approximately 1/2 tsp artificial sweetener). Omit margarine, substitute with reduced-calorie margarine in equal amount to regular margarine. May use if able to calculate into daily food plan.

Mechanical Soft (SFT): Prepare as directed. Consider individual tolerance.

Puree (PUR) and **Soft/Low Fiber (SLF):** Not recommended, substitute with appropriate food alternative.

Nutrient Analysis per Serving:

Regular	KCAL	PRO gm	CHO gm	FAT gm	Chol mg	SFA gm	PFA gm	VITA iu	VITC mg	THI mg	RIB mg	NIA mg	CA mg	NA mg	K+ mg	FE mg
	93.6	2.3	14.4	2.9	14.3	0.5	0.9	167	0.2	0.08	0.07	0.56	41.8	179	58.3	0.5

Sodium Restricted	NA mg	Diabetic	Kcal	Milk exg	Veg exg	Fruit exg	Bread exg	Meat exg	Fat exg	Low Fat & Low Chol	FAT gm	Chol mg	SFA gm	PFA gm
	14.3		75.4	0.0	0.0	0.0	1.0	0.0	0.0		1.4	0.3	0.24	0.5

Portion: 1 muffin

INGREDIENTS	78 portions		10 portions	
	weights	measures	weights	measures
Flour, all-purpose	1 1/2 lb	1 1/2 qt	3 oz	3/4 cup
Cornmeal, white	1 lb	3 cups	2 oz	1/3 cup
Baking powder	2 oz	4 2/3 Tbsp	1/4 oz	1 3/4 tsp
Salt		2 tsp		1/4 tsp
Sugar, granulated	7 oz	1 cup	5/8 oz	2 Tbsp
Eggs, beaten	8 oz	1 cup (4 large)	1 1/2 oz	3 Tbsp (1 small)
Milk, skim		1 1/2 qt		3/4 cup
Margarine, low sodium, melted, cooled	8 oz	1 cup	1 oz	2 Tbsp
Green pepper, diced	10 2/3 oz EP	2 cups	1 1/3 oz EP	1/4 cup
Red pepper, diced	10 2/3 oz EP	2 cups	1 1/3 oz EP	1/4 cup

Method

1. Combine flour, cornmeal, baking powder, salt, and sugar. Blend on low speed for 10 seconds.
2. Combine eggs, milk, and margarine. Add to dry ingredients. Mix at low speed only to blend, about 25 seconds.
3. Add diced green and red peppers. Fold into batter.
4. Measure with No. 24 dipper into greased or non-stick muffin pans.
5. Dip batter all at once. Handle as little as possible.
6. Bake at 400°F for about 25 minutes or until golden brown.
7. Remove from pans as soon as baked.

Directions for Diet Preparations

Sodium Restricted (SR): Use low sodium baking powder as per manufacturer's directions. Omit salt.
Low Fat/Low Cholesterol (LF): 1 muffin.
78 portions: Omit eggs, substitute with 1 cup commercial egg substitute. Omit margarine, substitute with reduced-calorie margarine in equal amount to regular margarine. May use if able to calculate into daily food plan.

10 portions: Omit eggs, substitute with 3 Tbsp commercial egg substitute. Omit margarine, substitute with reduced-calorie margarine in equal amount to regular margarine. May use if able to calculate into daily food plan.
Diabetic (DB): 1 muffin.
78 portions: Omit sugar, substitute with artificial sweetener equal to 1 cup granulated sugar (approximately 4 tsp artificial sweetener). Omit margarine, substitute with reduced-calorie margarine in equal amount to regular margarine. May use if able to calculate into daily food plan.
10 portions: Omit sugar, substitute with artificial sweetener equal to 2 Tbsp granulated sugar (approximately 1/2 tsp artificial sweetener). Omit margarine, substitute with reduced-calorie margarine in equal amount to regular margarine. May use if able to calculate into daily food plan.
Mechanical Soft (SFT): Prepare as directed. Consider individual tolerance.
Puree (PUR) and **Soft/Low Fiber** (SLF): Not recommended, substitute with appropriate food alternative.

Nutrient Analysis per Serving:

Regular	KCAL	PRO gm	CHO gm	FAT gm	Chol mg	SFA gm	PFA gm	VITA iu	VITC mg	THI mg	RIB mg	NIA mg	CA mg	NA mg	K+ mg	FE mg
	94.8	2.3	14.6	2.9	14.3	0.5	0.9	172.2	6.0	0.08	0.07	0.6	34.8	130	66.5	0.6

Sodium Restricted	NA mg	Diabetic	Kcal	Milk exg	Veg exg	Fruit exg	Bread exg	Meat exg	Fat exg	Low Fat & Low Chol	FAT gm	Chol mg	SFA gm	PFA gm
	14.5		76.2	0.0	0.04	0.0	1.0	0.0	0.1		1.7	14.3	0.3	0.5

Portion: 1 muffin

INGREDIENTS	78 portions		10 portions	
	weights	measures	weights	measures
Flour, all-purpose	2 1/2 lb	2 1/2 qt	5 oz	1 1/4 cup
Baking powder	2 oz	4 2/3 Tbsp	1/4 oz	1 3/4 tsp
Salt		2 tsp		1/4 tsp
Sugar, granulated	11 oz	1 1/2 cups	1 3/8 oz	3 Tbsp
Eggs, beaten	8 oz	1 cup (4 large)	1 1/2 oz	3 Tbsp (1 small)
Milk, skim		1 1/2 qt		3/4 cup
Margarine, low sodium, melted, cooled	8 oz	1 cup	1 oz	2 Tbsp
Date, chopped	1 lb	3 cups	2 oz	1/3 cup

Method

1. Combine flour, baking powder, salt, and sugar. Blend on low speed for 10 seconds.
2. Combine eggs, milk, and margarine. Add to dry ingredients. Mix at low speed only to blend, about 25 seconds.
3. Fold dates into batter.
4. Measure with No. 24 dipper into greased or non-stick muffin pans.
5. Dip batter all at once. Handle as little as possible.
6. Bake at 400°F for about 25 minutes or until golden brown.
7. Remove from pans as soon as baked.

Directions for Diet Preparations

Sodium Restricted (SR): Use low sodium baking powder as per manufacturer's directions. Omit salt.

Low Fat/Low Cholesterol (LF): 1 muffin.

78 portions: Omit eggs, substitute with 1 cup commercial egg substitute. Omit margarine, substitute with reduced-calorie margarine in equal amount to regular margarine. May use if able to calculate into daily food plan.

10 portions: Omit eggs, substitute with 3 Tbsp commercial egg substitute. Omit margarine, substitute with reduced-calorie margarine in equal amount to regular margarine. May use if able to calculate into daily food plan.

Diabetic (DB): 1 muffin.

78 portions: Omit sugar, substitute with artificial sweetener equal to 1 1/2 cup granulated sugar (approximately 1 3/4 Tbsp artificial sweetener). Omit margarine, substitute with reduced-calorie margarine in equal amount to regular margarine. May use if able to calculate into daily food plan.

10 portions: Omit sugar, substitute with artificial sweetener equal to 3 Tbsp granulated sugar (approximately 3/4 tsp artificial sweetener). Omit margarine, substitute with reduced-calorie margarine in equal amount to regular margarine. May use if able to calculate into daily food plan.

Mechanical Soft (SFT): Prepare as directed.

Soft/Low Fiber (SLF) and **Puree** (PUR): Not recommended, substitute with appropriate food alternative.

Nutrient Analysis per Serving:

Regular	KCAL	PRO gm	CHO gm	FAT gm	Chol mg	SFA gm	PFA gm	VITA iu	VITC mg	THI mg	RIB mg	NIA mg	CA mg	NA mg	K+ mg	FE mg
	116	2.6	20.2	2.8	14.3	0.5	0.9	153	0.19	0.11	0.10	0.9	37.8	193	95.5	0.8

Sodium Restricted	NA mg	Diabetic	Kcal	Milk exg	Veg exg	Fruit exg	Bread exg	Meat exg	Fat exg	Low Fat & Low Chol	FAT gm	Chol mg	SFA gm	PFA gm
	14.7		96.3	0.0	0.0	0.4	1.0	0.0	0.0		1.5	0.3	0.2	0.5

Portion: 1 muffin

INGREDIENTS	48 portions		12 portions	
	weights	**measures**	**weights**	**measures**
Flour, all-purpose	1 lb	1 qt	4 oz	1 cup
Flour, whole wheat	17 oz	1 qt	4 1/4 oz	1 cup
Baking powder		1 1/2 Tbsp		1 1/8 tsp
Baking soda		2 tsp		1/2 tsp
Sugar, brown, packed	1 lb	2 cups	4 oz	1/2 cup
Cinnamon, ground		2 tsp		1/2 tsp
Nutmeg		1 tsp		1/4 tsp
Pumpkin, canned	2 lb	1 qt	8 oz	1 cup
Milk, skim		2 cups		1/2 cup
Margarine, low sodium, melted	8 oz	1 cup	2 oz	1/4 cup
Maple syrup, reduced-calorie	4 oz	1/2 cup	1 oz	2 Tbsp
Eggs, beaten	8 oz	1 cup (4 large)	1 1/2 oz	3 Tbsp (1 small)
Maple flavoring		2 tsp		1/2 tsp

Method

1. Combine dry ingredients. Mix well. Make a well in the center of mixture.
2. Combine pumpkin, milk, margarine, maple syrup, eggs, and flavoring. Mix well.
3. Add liquid ingredients to dry ingredients. Mix only until dry ingredients are moistened.
4. Measure with No. 24 dipper into greased or non-stick muffin pans.
5. Bake at 400°F for about 20 minutes, or until lightly browned.
6. Remove from pans as soon as baked.

Directions for Diet Preparations

Sodium Restricted (SR): Use low sodium baking powder as per manufacturer's directions. May use if able to calculate into daily food plan.

Low Fat/Low Cholesterol (LF): 1 muffin.

48 portions: Omit margarine, substitute with reduced-calorie margarine in equal amount to regular margarine. Omit eggs, substitute with a commercial egg substitute equivalent to 4 eggs. May use if able to calculate into daily food plan.

12 portions: Omit margarine, substitute with reduced-calorie margarine in equal amount to regular margarine. Omit eggs, substitute with a commercial egg substitute equivalent to 1 egg. May use if able to calculate into daily food plan.

Diabetic (DB): 1 muffin.

48 portions: Replace 2 cups of brown sugar with 2 Tbsp of brown sugar and artificial sweetener equal to 1 3/4 cups brown sugar (approximately 7 tsp artificial sweetener). Omit margarine, substitute with reduced-calorie margarine in equal amount to regular margarine. May use if able to calculate into daily food plan.

12 portions: Replace 1/2 cup of brown sugar with 1/2 Tbsp of brown sugar and artificial sweetener equal to 1/2 cup brown sugar (approximately 2 tsp artificial sweetener). Omit margarine, substitute with reduced-calorie margarine in equal amount to regular margarine. May use if able to calculate into daily food plan.

Mechanical Soft (SFT): Prepare as directed. Consider individual tolerance.

Puree (PUR) and **Soft/Low Fiber** (SLF): Not recommended. Use white bread if tolerated.

Nutrient Analysis per Serving:

Regular	KCAL	PRO gm	CHO gm	FAT gm	Chol mg	SFA gm	PFA gm	VITA iu	VITC mg	THI mg	RIB mg	NIA mg	CA mg	NA mg	K+ mg	FE mg
	155	3.4	25.7	4.7	22.9	0.8	1.4	4760	1.0	0.14	0.09	1.1	44.1	112	140	1.4

Sodium Restricted	NA mg	Diabetic	Kcal	Milk exg	Veg exg	Fruit exg	Bread exg	Meat exg	Fat exg	Low Fat & Low Chol	FAT gm	Chol mg	SFA gm	PFA gm
	50.0		110	0.0	0.0	0.26	1.0	0.0	0.5		2.4	0.2	0.4	0.8

Portion: 1 muffin

Ingredients	78 portions		10 portions	
	weights	**measures**	**weights**	**measures**
Flour, all-purpose	2 1/2 lb	2 1/2 qt	5 oz	1 1/4 cups
Baking powder	2 oz	4 2/3 Tbsp	1/4 oz	1 3/4 tsp
Salt		2 tsp		1/4 tsp
Sugar, granulated	7 oz	1 cup	5/8 oz	2 Tbsp
Eggs, beaten	8 oz	1 cup (4 large)	1 1/2 oz	3 Tbsp (1 small)
Milk, skim		1 1/2 qt		3/4 cup
Margarine, low sodium, melted, cooled	8 oz	1 cup	1 oz	2 Tbsp
Raisins, seedless	1 lb	3 cups	2 oz	1/3 cup
Pecans, chopped	6 oz	1 1/8 cups	3/4 oz	2 1/4 Tbsp
	6 oz	1 1/2 cups	3/4 oz	3 Tbsp

Method

1. Combine flour, baking powder, salt, and sugar. Blend on low speed for 10 seconds.
2. Combine eggs, milk, and margarine. Add to dry ingredients. Mix at low speed only to blend, about 25 seconds.
3. Fold raisins and pecans into batter.
4. Measure with No. 24 dipper into greased or non-stick muffin pans.
5. Dip batter all at once. Handle as little as possible.
6. Bake at 400°F for about 25 minutes or until golden brown.
7. Remove from pans as soon as baked.

Directions for Diet Preparations

Sodium Restricted (SR): Use low sodium baking powder as per manufacturer's directions. Omit salt.

Low Fat/Low Cholesterol (LF): 1 muffin.

78 portions: Omit eggs, substitute with 1 cup commercial egg substitute. Omit margarine, substitute with reduced-calorie margarine in equal amount to regular margarine. May use if able to calculate into daily food plan.

10 portions: Omit eggs, substitute with 3 Tbsp commercial egg substitute. Omit margarine, substitute with reduced-calorie margarine in equal amount to regular margarine. May use if able to calculate into daily food plan.

Diabetic (DB): 1 muffin.

78 portions: Omit sugar, substitute with artificial sweetener equal to 1 cup granulated sugar (approximately 4 teaspoons artificial sweetener). Omit margarine, substitute with reduced-calorie margarine in equal amount to regular margarine. May use if able to calculate into daily food plan.

10 portions: Omit sugar, substitute with artificial sweetener equal to 2 Tbsp granulated sugar (approximately 1/2 tsp artificial sweetener). Omit margarine, substitute with reduced-calorie margarine in equal amount to regular margarine. May use if able to calculate into daily food plan.

Mechanical Soft (SFT), **Soft/Low Fiber** (SLF), and **Puree** (PUR): Not recommended, substitute with appropriate food alternative.

Nutrient Analysis per Serving:

Regular	KCAL	PRO gm	CHO gm	FAT gm	Chol mg	SFA gm	PFA gm	VITA iu	VITC mg	THI mg	RIB mg	NIA mg	CA mg	NA mg	K+ mg	FE mg
	117	2.8	17.2	4.2	14.3	0.6	1.2	152	0.3	0.11	0.09	0.8	37.4	193	74.2	0.8

Sodium Restricted	NA mg	Diabetic	Kcal	Milk exg	Veg exg	Fruit exg	Bread exg	Meat exg	Fat exg	Low Fat & Low Chol	FAT gm	Chol mg	SFA gm	PFA gm
	14.8		98.0	0.0	0.0	0.25	1.0	0.0	0.25		1.4	0.3	0.2	0.5

Portion: 1 muffin

INGREDIENTS	78 portions		10 portions	
	weights	**measures**	**weights**	**measures**
Flour, all-purpose	2 1/2 lb	2 1/2 qt	5 oz	1 1/4 cups
Baking powder	2 oz	4 2/3 Tbsp	1/4 oz	1 3/4 tsp
Sugar, granulated	7 oz	1 cup	5/8 oz	2 Tbsp
Cinnamon, ground		1 1/2 tsp		1/8 tsp
Ginger, ground		1 tsp		1/8 tsp
Allspice		1/2 tsp		pinch
Eggs, beaten	8 oz	1 cup (4 large)	1 1/2 oz	3 Tbsp (1 small)
Milk, skim		1 1/2 qt		3/4 cup
Margarine, low sodium, melted, cooled	8 oz	1 cup	1 oz	2 Tbsp

Method

1. Combine dry ingredients, blend on low speed for 10 seconds.
2. Combine eggs, milk, and margarine. Add to dry ingredients. Mix at low speed only to blend, about 25 seconds.
3. Measure with No. 24 dipper into greased or non-stick muffin pans.
4. Dip batter all at once. Handle as little as possible.
5. Bake at 400°F for about 25 minutes or until golden brown.
6. Remove from pans as soon as baked.

Directions for Diet Preparations

Sodium Restricted (SR): Use low sodium baking powder as per manufacturer's directions. Omit salt.

Low Fat/Low Cholesterol (LF): 1 muffin.

78 portions: Omit eggs, substitute with 1 cup commercial egg substitute. Omit margarine, substitute with reduced-calorie margarine in equal amount to regular margarine. May use if able to calculate into daily food plan.

10 portions: Omit eggs, substitute with 3 Tbsp commercial egg substitute. Omit margarine, substitute with reduced-calorie margarine in equal amount to regular margarine. May use if able to calculate into daily food plan.

Diabetic (DB): 1 muffin.

78 portions: Omit sugar, substitute with artificial sweetener equal to 1 cup granulated sugar (approximately 4 teaspoons artificial sweetener). Omit margarine, substitute with reduced-calorie margarine in equal amount to regular margarine. May use if able to calculate into daily food plan.

10 portions: Omit sugar, substitute with artificial sweetener equal to 2 Tbsp granulated sugar (approximately 1/2 tsp artificial sweetener). Omit margarine, substitute with reduced-calorie margarine in equal amount to regular margarine. May use if able to calculate into daily food plan.

Mechanical Soft (SFT): Prepare as directed. Consider individual tolerance.

Puree (PUR) and **Soft/Low Fiber** (SLF): Not recommended, substitute with appropriate food alternative.

Nutrient Analysis per Serving:

Regular	KCAL	PRO gm	CHO gm	FAT gm	Chol mg	SFA gm	PFA gm	VITA iu	VITC mg	THI mg	RIB mg	NIA mg	CA mg	NA mg	K+ mg	FE mg
	93.7	2.5	14.4	2.8	14.3	0.5	0.8	148.5	0.2	0.1	0.09	0.8	35.9	130	50.6	0.7

Sodium Restricted	NA mg	Diabetic	Kcal	Milk exg	Veg exg	Fruit exg	Bread exg	Meat exg	Fat exg	Low Fat & Low Chol	FAT gm	Chol mg	SFA gm	PFA gm
	14.5		75.1	0.0	0.0	0.0	1.0	0.0	0.0		1.4	0.3	0.2	0.5

Portion: 1 slice (2 halves)

INGREDIENTS	50 portions		6 portions	
	weights	measures	weights	measures
Toast, white	3 1/8 lb	50 slices	6 oz	6 slices
Margarine, low sodium, melted	2 oz	1/4 cup	1/4 oz	1/2 Tbsp
Sugar, brown, packed	5 1/3 oz	1 cup	2/3 oz	2 Tbsp
Cinnamon, ground	1 1/2 oz	6 Tbsp	1/8 oz	2 1/4 tsp

Method

1. Brush melted margarine over warm toast.
2. Combine brown sugar and cinnamon. Sprinkle over toast.
3. Cut toast diagonally. Serve 2 halves.

Directions for Diet Preparations

Sodium Restricted (SR): Use low sodium bread.

Low Fat/Low Cholesterol (LF): 1 slice. Omit margarine. Use 1 tsp reduced-calorie margarine on each slice of toast. May use if able to calculate into food plan.

Diabetic (DB): 1 slice. Omit margarine. Use 1 tsp reduced-calorie margarine on each slice of toast. Omit brown sugar, substitute with artificial sweetener as per manufacturer's directions. May use if able to calculate into food plan.

Mechanical Soft (SFT) and **Soft/Low Fiber** (SLF): Do not toast bread. Consider individual tolerance.

Puree (PUR): Not recommended.

Nutrient Analysis per Serving:

Regular	KCAL	PRO gm	CHO gm	FAT gm	Chol mg	SFA gm	PFA gm	VITA iu	VITC mg	THI mg	RIB mg	NIA mg	CA mg	NA mg	K+ mg	FE mg
	119	2.2	17.3	4.6	0.7	0.9	1.2	160	0.2	0.1	0.06	0.8	28.9	128	27.2	1.0

Sodium Restricted	NA mg	Diabetic	Kcal	Milk exg	Veg exg	Fruit exg	Bread exg	Meat exg	Fat exg	Low Fat & Low Chol	FAT gm	Chol mg	SFA gm	PFA gm
	4.3		87.5	0.0	0.0	0.0	1.0	0.0	0.3		2.7	0.75	0.5	0.6

Portion: 1 muffin

INGREDIENTS	50 portions		10 portions	
	weights	**measures**	**weights**	**measures**
Matzo meal	3 3/4 lb	3 3/4 qt	12 oz	3 cups
Water, boiling		2 1/2 qt		2 cups
Margarine, low sodium	10 oz	1 1/4 cups	2 oz	1/4 cup
Eggs, beaten	2 1/2 lb	5 cups (20 large)	8 oz	1 cup (4 large)
Cinnamon, ground		1 Tbsp		1/2 tsp
Raisins, seedless	6 2/3 oz	1 1/4 cups	1 1/3 oz	1/4 cup
Apples, grated	2 lb	2 qt (5 large)	6 3/8 oz	1 2/3 cups (1 large)
Sugar, granulated	2 1/3 oz	1/3 cup	3/8 oz	1 Tbsp

Method

1. Combine matzo meal, water, and margarine. Mix well.
2. Combine remaining ingredients. Add to matzo meal mixture. Mix thoroughly.
3. Measure with No. 20 dipper into greased or non-stick muffin pans.
4. Bake at 350°F for about 30 minutes or until golden brown.
5. Remove from pans as soon as baked.

Directions for Diet Preparations

Sodium Restricted (SR): Prepare as directed.
Low Fat/Low Cholesterol (LF): 1 muffin.
50 portions: Omit margarine, substitute with an equal amount of reduced-calorie margarine. Omit eggs, substitute with 40 eggs whites (5 cups). May use if able to calculate into daily food plan.
10 portions: Omit margarine, substitute with an equal amount of reduced-calorie margarine. Omit eggs, substitute with 8 egg whites (1 cup). May use if able to calculate into daily food plan.
Diabetic (DB): 1 muffin.
50 portions: Omit margarine, substitute with an equal amount of reduced-calorie margarine. Omit sugar, substitute with artificial sweetener equal to 1/3 cup granulated sugar (approximately 1 tsp artificial sweetener). May use if able to calculate into daily food plan.
10 portions: Omit margarine, substitute with an equal amount of reduced-calorie margarine. Omit sugar, substitute with artificial sweetener equal to 1 Tbsp granulated sugar (approximately 1/4 tsp artificial sweetener). May use if able to calculate into daily food plan.
Mechanical Soft (SFT), **Soft/Low Fiber** (SLF), and **Puree** (PUR): Not recommended.

Nutrient Analysis per Serving:

Regular	KCAL	PRO gm	CHO gm	FAT gm	Chol mg	SFA gm	PFA gm	VITA iu	VITC mg	THI mg	RIB mg	NIA mg	CA mg	NA mg	K+ mg	FE mg
	241	6.2	38.5	6.6	99.4	1.3	1.7	275	0.9	0.02	0.06	0.06	16.5	28.8	115	0.5

Sodium Restricted	NA mg	Diabetic	Kcal	Milk exg	Veg exg	Fruit exg	Bread exg	Meat exg	Fat exg	Low Fat & Low Chol	FAT gm	Chol mg	SFA gm	PFA gm
	28.8		218	0.0	0.0	0.5	2.0	0.0	1.0		2.7	0.0	0.3	0.7

Portion: 2 latkas

INGREDIENTS	50 portions		6 portions	
	weights	measures	weights	measures
Matzo meal	1 1/8 lb	4 1/2 cups	2 oz	1/2 cup
Sugar, granulated		3 Tbsp		1 1/8 tsp
Water, cold		6 3/4 cups		3/4 cup
Eggs	3 1/3 lb	6 3/4 cups (27 large)	8 oz	1 cup (4 large)
Honey	1 1/3 lb	1 3/4 cups	2 2/3 oz	3 1/2 Tbsp

Method

1. Combine matzo meal with sugar.
2. Separate eggs. Beat yolks slightly and combine with water. Add yolk mixture to the dry ingredients. Let stand 15 to 20 minutes.
3. Beat egg whites until stiff. Fold into matzo meal mixture.
4. Use a No. 24 dipper to drop batter into a well greased griddle or frying pan. Brown both sides to make latkas.
5. Layer latkas into baking pans.
6. Drizzle 1/2 tsp honey over each pancake.
7. Heat in 250°F oven to keep warm before serving.

Directions for Diet Preparations

Sodium Restricted (SR): Prepare as directed.

Low Fat/Low Cholesterol (LF): 2 latkas. Omit eggs, substitute with commercial egg substitute as per manufacturer's directions. Use a non-stick surface to cook latkas.

Diabetic (DB): 2 latkas. Omit sugar and honey, substitute with artificial sweetener to taste. Use a non-stick surface to cook latkas.

Mechanical Soft (SFT) and **Soft/Low Fiber** (SLF): Prepare as directed. Consider individual tolerance.

Puree (PUR): 1/2 cup. Prepare as directed. Add liquid (i.e. milk with dairy meal; apple juice with meat or dairy meal) to latkas; blenderize to obtain desired consistency.

Nutrient Analysis per Serving:

Regular	KCAL	PRO gm	CHO gm	FAT gm	Chol mg	SFA gm	PFA gm	VITA iu	VITC mg	THI mg	RIB mg	NIA mg	CA mg	NA mg	K+ mg	FE mg
	120	4.2	19.3	2.9	137	0.8	0.4	130	0.1	0.02	0.08	0.05	14.5	35.6	51.1	0.6

Sodium Restricted	NA mg	Diabetic	Kcal	Milk exg	Veg exg	Fruit exg	Bread exg	Meat exg	Fat exg	Low Fat & Low Chol	FAT gm	Chol mg	SFA gm	PFA gm
	35.6		85.8	0.0	0.0	0.0	1.2	0.0	0.0		0.1	0.0	0.0	0.0

Portion: 1 roll

INGREDIENTS	60 portions		15 portions	
	weights	**measures**	**weights**	**measures**
Matzo meal	2 1/2 lb	2 1/2 qt	10 oz	2 1/2 cups
Sugar, granulated	2 1/3 oz	1/3 cup	1/2 oz	4 tsp
Water		1 1/2 qt		1 1/2 cups
Peanut oil	10 oz	1 1/4 cups	2 1/2 oz	5 Tbsp
Eggs	8 oz	1 cup (4 large)	2 oz	1/4 cup (1 large)

Method

1. Combine matzo meal with sugar.
2. Bring oil and water to a boil. Add to matzo meal mixture and mix well.
3. Beat in eggs thoroughly. Let stand 15 minutes.
4. Measure dough using a No. 20 dipper. Shape dough into rolls.
5. Place on a well greased pan.
6. Bake at 375°F for 50 minutes or until golden brown.

Directions for Diet Preparations

Sodium Restricted (SR): Prepare as directed.
Low Fat/Low Cholesterol (LF): 1 roll.
60 rolls: Omit eggs, substitute with 8 egg whites or 1 cup of egg whites. Use a non-stick surface to cook rolls. May use if able to calculate into daily food plan.
15 rolls: Omit eggs, substitute with 2 egg whites or 1/4 cup of egg whites. Use a non-stick surface to cook rolls. May use if able to calculate into daily food plan.
Diabetic (DB): 1 roll.
60 rolls: Omit sugar, substitute with artificial sweetener equivalent to 1/3 cup granulated sugar (approximately 1 tsp artificial sweetener). Use a non-stick surface to cook rolls. May use if able to calculate into daily food plan.
15 rolls: Omit sugar, substitute with artificial sweetener equivalent to 4 tsp granulated sugar (approximately 1/4 tsp artificial sweetener). Use a non-stick surface to cook rolls. May use if able to calculate into daily food plan.
Mechanical Soft (SFT), **Soft/Low Fiber** (SLF), and **Puree** (PUR): Not recommended.

Nutrient Analysis per Serving:

Regular	KCAL	PRO gm	CHO gm	FAT gm	Chol mg	SFA gm	PFA gm	VITA iu	VITC mg	THI mg	RIB mg	NIA mg	CA mg	NA mg	K+ mg	FE mg
	162	4.4	20.6	6.6	91.1	1.3	1.7	86.6	0.0	0.01	0.05	0.01	9.3	24.1	48.3	0.4

Sodium Restricted	NA mg	Diabetic	Kcal	Milk exg	Veg exg	Fruit exg	Bread exg	Meat exg	Fat exg	Low Fat & Low Chol	FAT gm	Chol mg	SFA gm	PFA gm
	24.1		158	0.0	0.0	0.0	1.5	0.0	1.0		4.7	0.0	0.7	1.4

Portion: 1 scone

INGREDIENTS	48 portions		12 portions	
	weights	**measures**	**weights**	**measures**
Flour, all-purpose	3 lb	3 qt	12 oz	3 cups
Vegetable shortening	5 oz	2/3 cup	1 1/4 oz	2 1/2 Tbsp
Baking soda	1/2 oz	1 Tbsp	1/8 oz	3/4 tsp
Baking powder	3 oz	6 3/4 Tbsp	3/4 oz	1 3/4 Tbsp
Sugar, granulated	1 oz	2 1/4 Tbsp	1/3 oz	2 tsp
Buttermilk	2 lb	1 qt	8 oz	1 cup

Method

1. Mix together flour, shortening, baking soda, baking powder, and sugar to form a coarse crumb.
2. Add buttermilk to make a soft dough. Do not knead.
3. Roll out dough one-inch thick on floured surface. Cut into 3" × 2" squares. Then cut diagonally to make triangles.
4. Wash with buttermilk.
5. Place 24 scones on a sheet pan.
6. Bake at 400°F for about 15 minutes.

Directions for Diet Preparations

Sodium Restricted (SR): Use low sodium baking powder as per manufacture's directions.
Low Fat/Low Cholesterol (LF): 1 scone. Prepare as directed. May use if able to calculate into daily food plan.
Diabetic (DB): 1 scone. Prepare as directed.
Mechanical Soft (SFT): Prepare as directed.
Soft/Low Fiber (SLF): Prepare as directed.
Puree (PUR): Not recommended. Provide appropriate food substitute.

Nutrient Analysis per Serving:

Regular	KCAL	PRO gm	CHO gm	FAT gm	Chol mg	SFA gm	PFA gm	VITA iu	VITC mg	THI mg	RIB mg	NIA mg	CA mg	NA mg	K+ mg	FE mg
	141	3.6	23.6	3.3	0.7	0.6	0.7	6.8	0.20	0.22	0.17	1.6	45.8	355	61.6	1.3

Sodium Restricted	NA mg	Diabetic	Kcal	Milk exg	Veg exg	Fruit exg	Bread exg	Meat exg	Fat exg	Low Fat & Low Chol	FAT gm	Chol mg	SFA gm	PFA gm
	73.6		141	0.1	0.0	0.0	1.5	0.0	0.5		3.3	0.7	0.6	0.7

Sauces and Gravies

O1   Basic White Sauce

Portion: 2 ounces (1/4 cup)

INGREDIENTS	64 portions (1 gallon)		8 portions (2 cups)	
	weights	measures	weights	measures
Thin Consistency				
Milk, skim		1 gal		2 cups
Flour, all-purpose	6 oz	1 1/2 cups	3/4 oz	3 Tbsp
Margarine, low sodium	6 oz	3/4 cup	3/4 oz	1 1/2 Tbsp
Medium Consistency				
Milk, skim		1 gal		2 cups
Flour, all-purpose	8 oz	2 cups	1 oz	3/4 cup
Margarine, low sodium	8 oz	1 cup	1 oz	2 Tbsp
Thick Consistency				
Milk, skim		1 gal		2 cups
Flour, all-purpose	12 oz	3 cups	1 1/2 oz	1/3 cup
Margarine, low sodium	12 oz	1 1/2 cups	1 1/2 oz	3 Tbsp

Method

1. Melt margarine, remove from heat.
2. Add flour, stir until smooth. Cook 5 to 10 minutes.
3. Add milk gradually, stirring constantly with wire whip. Cook and stir until smooth and thick, about 15 minutes.

Directions for Diet Preparations

Sodium Restricted (SR): Prepare as directed. May use if able to calculate into daily food plan.

Low Fat/Low Cholesterol (LF): 2 oz and **Diabetic** (DB): 2 oz. Use reduced-calorie margarine. May use if able to calculate into daily food plan.

Mechanical Soft (SFT) and **Puree** (PUR): Prepare as directed.

Soft/Low Fiber (SLF): Prepare as directed. May use if able to calculate into daily food plan.

Nutrient Analysis per Serving:

Regular	KCAL	PRO gm	CHO gm	FAT gm	Chol mg	SFA gm	PFA gm	VITA iu	VITC mg	THI mg	RIB mg	NIA mg	CA mg	NA mg	K+ mg	FE mg
Thin	50.9	2.4	5.1	2.3	1.1	0.4	0.7	215	0.6	0.04	0.09	0.2	77.7	32.7	106	0.1
Medium	60.6	2.5	5.8	3.0	1.1	0.5	0.9	245	0.6	0.04	0.10	0.2	78.1	33.0	107	0.1
Thick	80.2	2.7	7.2	4.4	1.1	0.8	1.4	304	0.6	0.05	0.11	0.3	78.8	33.5	110	0.2

Sodium Restricted	NA mg	Diabetic	Kcal	Milk exg	Veg exg	Fruit exg	Bread exg	Meat exg	Fat exg	Low Fat & Low Chol	FAT gm	Chol mg	SFA gm	PFA gm
Thin	32.7		41.1	0.0	0.0	0.0	0.0	0.0	0.9		1.2	1.1	0.2	0.4
Medium	33.0		47.6	0.0	0.0	0.0	0.0	0.0	1.0		1.5	1.1	0.3	0.5
Thick	33.5		60.6	0.0	0.0	0.0	0.0	0.0	1.3		2.3	1.1	0.4	0.7

Barbecue Sauce

Portion: 2 ounces (1/4 cup)

INGREDIENTS	64 portions (1 gallon)		8 portions (2 cups)	
	weights	measures	weights	measures
Catsup	7 lb	3 1/2 qt (1 #10 can)	14 oz	1 3/4 cups
Vinegar, cider		3 cup		1/3 cup
Sugar, granulated	12 oz	1 3/4 cup	1 1/2 oz	1/4 cup
Onion, grated	4 oz	5 Tbsp	1/2 oz	2 tsp

Method

1. Mix all ingredients.

Directions for Diet Preparations

Sodium Restricted (SR): Use low sodium catsup.

Low Fat/Low Cholesterol (LF): 2 oz. Prepare as directed. Low fat diets should consider individual tolerance when using onions.

Diabetic (DB): 2 oz.

1 gallon: Replace granulated sugar with artificial sweetener equivalent to 1 1/2 cups granulated sugar (approximately 2 Tbsp artificial sweetener).

2 cups: Replace granulated sugar with artificial sweetener equivalent to 1/4 cup granulated sugar (approximately 1 tsp artificial sweetener).

Mechanical Soft (SFT): 2 oz.

1 gallon: Omit grated onions, substitute with 1/2 tsp onion powder.

2 cups: Omit grated onions, substitute with a pinch onion powder.

Soft/Low Fiber (SLF): Not recommended.

Puree (PUR): Prepare as directed. Blenderize and strain.

Nutrient Analysis per Serving:

Regular	KCAL	PRO gm	CHO gm	FAT gm	Chol mg	SFA gm	PFA gm	VITA iu	VITC mg	THI mg	RIB mg	NIA mg	CA mg	NA mg	K+ mg	FE mg
	85.4	1.2	21.1	0.2	0.0	0.0	0.0	828	9.0	0.05	0.04	0.95	14.1	616	229	0.5

Sodium Restricted	NA mg	Diabetic	Kcal	Milk exg	Veg exg	Fruit exg	Bread exg	Meat exg	Fat exg	Low Fat & Low Chol	FAT gm	Chol mg	SFA gm	PFA gm
	10.5		66	0.0	1.0	0.63	0.0	0.0	0.0		0.2	0.0	0.0	0.0

Brown Gravy

Portion: 2 ounces (1/4 cup)

Ingredients	64 portions (1 gallon)		8 portions (2 cups)	
	weights	measures	weights	measures
Beef stock[1]		1 gal		2 cups
Margarine, low sodium, melted	10 oz	1 1/4 cups	1 1/4 oz	2 1/2 Tbsp
Flour, all-purpose	8 oz	2 cups	1 oz	1/4 cup

Method

1. Prepare stock.
2. Combine flour and margarine. Blend.
3. Add stock to roux gradually, stirring constantly with wire whip.
4. Cook until thickened and smooth.

Notes

[1]May use a concentrated soup base as a quick beef stock. Prepare as directed by manufacturer.

Directions for Diet Preparations

Sodium Restricted (SR): Prepare as directed. May use a low sodium soup base as directed by manufacturer, instead of the stock.

Low Fat/Low Cholesterol (LF): 2 oz and **Diabetic** (DB): 2 oz. Omit margarine, substitute reduced-calorie margarine in equal amount specified for regular margarine.

Mechanical Soft (SF), **Soft/Low Fiber** (SLF), and **Puree** (PUR): Prepare as directed.

Nutrient Analysis per Serving:

Regular	KCAL	PRO gm	CHO gm	FAT gm	Chol mg	SFA gm	PFA gm	VITA iu	VITC mg	THI mg	RIB mg	NIA mg	CA mg	NA mg	K+ mg	FE mg
	53.1	0.9	3.3	4.0	0.0	0.6	1.2	148	0.01	0.02	0.03	0.5	1.7	20.3	5.1	0.4

Sodium Restricted	NA mg	Diabetic	Kcal	Milk exg	Veg exg	Fruit exg	Bread exg	Meat exg	Fat exg	Low Fat & Low Chol	FAT gm	Chol mg	SFA gm	PFA gm
	20.3		36.8	0.0	0.0	0.0	0.0	0.0	0.8		2.1	0.0	0.3	0.6

O4 Cheese Sauce

Portion: 2 ounces (1/4 cup)

INGREDIENTS	64 portions (1 gallon)		8 portions (2 cups)	
	weights	measures	weights	measures
Margarine, low sodium, melted	8 oz	1 cup	1 oz	2 Tbsp
Flour, all-purpose	8 oz	2 cups	1 oz	1/4 cup
Milk, skim		1 gal		2 cups
Cheese, cheddar, shredded	2 lb	2 qt	4 oz	1 cup

Method

1. Melt margarine, remove from heat.
2. Add flour, stir until smooth. Cook 5 to 10 minutes.
3. Add milk, gradually stirring constantly with wire whip.
4. Add cheese. Stir to melt cheese.
5. Cook and stir as necessary until smooth and thick, about 15 minutes.

Directions for Diet Preparations

Sodium Restricted (SR): Use low sodium cheese. May use if able to calculate into daily food plan.

Low Fat/Low Cholesterol (LF): 2 oz and **Diabetic** (DB): 2 oz. Replace reduced-calorie margarine for regular margarine in equal amounts. Use low fat cheese. May use if able to calculate into daily food plan.

Mechanical Soft (SFT) and **Puree** (PUR): Prepare as directed.

Soft/Low Fiber (SLF): Use mild cheddar. Consider individual tolerance.

Nutrient Analysis per Serving:

Regular	KCAL	PRO gm	CHO gm	FAT gm	Chol mg	SFA gm	PFA gm	VITA iu	VITC mg	THI mg	RIB mg	NIA mg	CA mg	NA mg	K+ mg	FE mg
	117	6.0	6.0	7.7	15.9	3.5	1.1	395	0.6	0.04	0.15	0.2	180	120	121	0.2

Sodium Restricted	NA mg	Diabetic	Kcal	Milk exg	Veg exg	Fruit exg	Bread exg	Meat exg	Fat exg	Low Fat & Low Chol	FAT gm	Chol mg	SFA gm	PFA gm
	85.5		87.8	0.0	0.0	0.0	0.0	0.7	1.0		4.0	1.1	0.3	0.5

Portion: 2 ounces (1/4 cup)

Ingredients	64 portions (1 gallon)		8 portions (2 cups)	
	weights	measures	weights	measures
Chicken stock[1]		1 gal		2 cups
Margarine, low sodium	8 oz	1 cup	1 oz	2 Tbsp
Flour, all-purpose	8 oz	2 cups	1 oz	1/4 cup
Parsley, minced	1 oz	3/4 cup	1/8 oz	1 1/2 Tbsp

Method

1. Prepare chicken stock. Heat until simmering.
2. Melt margarine. Add flour and parsley. Cook over low heat 3 to 5 minutes. Stir while cooking.
3. Add roux to chick stock. Stir constantly until gravy boils.
4. Reduce heat to hold at 160°F serving temperature.

Notes

[1]May use a concentrated chicken soup base as a quick chicken stock. Prepare as directed by manufacturer.

Directions for Diet Preparations

Sodium Restricted (SR): Prepare as directed. May use a low sodium soup base as directed by manufacturer, instead of the stock.

Low Fat/Low Cholesterol (LF): 2 oz and **Diabetic** (DB): 2 oz. Replace reduced-calorie margarine for regular margarine in equal amounts. May use if able to calculate into daily food plan.

Mechanical Soft (SFT) and **Soft/Low Fiber** (SLF): Prepare as directed.

Puree (PUR): Prepare as directed. Strain.

Nutrient Analysis per Serving:

Regular	KCAL	PRO gm	CHO gm	FAT gm	Chol mg	SFA gm	PFA gm	VITA iu	VITC mg	THI mg	RIB mg	NIA mg	CA mg	NA mg	K+ mg	FE mg
	50.1	1.7	3.2	3.3	0.0	0.58	1.03	147.8	0.55	0.06	0.03	0.92	10.5	22.1	74.7	0.6

Sodium Restricted	NA mg	Diabetic	Kcal	Milk exg	Veg exg	Fruit exg	Bread exg	Meat exg	Fat exg	Low Fat & Low Chol	FAT gm	Chol mg	SFA gm	PFA gm
	22.1		25.0	0.0	0.0	0.0	0.0	0.0	0.6		1.6	0.0	0.24	0.5

Portion: 2 ounces (1/4 cup)

INGREDIENTS	48 portions (3 quarts)		6 portions (1 1/2 cups)	
	weights	measures	weights	measures
Cranberries	2 1/2 lb AP	2 1/2 qt	5 oz AP	1 1/4 cups
Sugar, granulated	2 1/2 lb	1 3/8 qt	5 oz	3/4 cup
Water		2 1/2 cups		1/3 cup

Method

1. Wash cranberries. Remove stems and spoiled berries.
2. Combine all ingredients. Bring to a boil.
3. Boil gently until skin bursts.
4. Puree.
5. Chill.
6. Serve with No. 16 dipper.

Directions for Diet Preparations

Sodium Restricted (SR) and **Low Fat/Low Cholesterol** (LF): 1/4 cup. Prepare as directed.

Diabetic (DB): 1/4 cup. Omit sugar, substitute with artificial sweetener as per manufacturer's directions.

Mechanical Soft (SFT): Prepare as directed. Consider individual tolerance.

Soft/Low Fiber (SLF): Not recommended.

Puree (PUR): Prepare as directed. Blenderize and strain.

Nutrient Analysis per Serving:

Regular	KCAL	PRO gm	CHO gm	FAT gm	Chol mg	SFA gm	PFA gm	VITA iu	VITC mg	THI mg	RIB mg	NIA mg	CA mg	NA mg	K+ mg	FE mg
	102	0.08	26.3	0.04	0.0	0.0	0.0	10.3	3.0	0.01	0.0	0.02	1.5	0.4	16.6	0.1

Sodium Restricted	NA mg	Diabetic	Kcal	Milk exg	Veg exg	Fruit exg	Bread exg	Meat exg	Fat exg	Low Fat & Low Chol	FAT gm	Chol mg	SFA gm	PFA gm
	0.4		17.0	0.0	0.0	0.3	0.0	0.0	0.0		0.04	0.0	0.0	0.0

Portion: 2 ounces (1/4 cup)

INGREDIENTS	48 portions (3 quarts)		6 portions (1 1/2 cups)	
	weights	measures	weights	measures
Onions, chopped	1 lb	3 cups	2 oz	1/3 cup
Celery, chopped	5 oz	1 cup	2/3 oz	2 Tbsp
Green pepper, diced	5 oz	1 cup	2/3 oz	2 Tbsp
Margarine, low sodium, melted	4 oz	1/2 cup	1/2 oz	1 Tbsp
Flour, all-purpose	2 oz	1/2 cup	1/4 oz	1 Tbsp
Sugar, granulated		2 Tbsp		3/4 tsp
Bay leaf		4 leaves		1 leaf
Basil		2 tsp		1/4 tsp
Tomatoes, canned	4 1/2 lb	2 1/4 qt	9 oz	1 1/8 cups

Method

1. Sauté onions, celery, and green pepper in margarine until tender.
2. Add flour and stir.
3. Add sugar, bay leaf, basil, and tomatoes. Simmer, covered, stirring occasionally for 15 minutes.
4. Remove bay leaf before serving.

Directions for Diet Preparations

Sodium Restricted (SR): Use low sodium tomatoes for fresh tomatoes.

Low Fat/Low Cholesterol (LF): 2 oz. Use half the amount of margarine specified. Low fat diets should consider individual tolerance to onions.

Diabetic (DB): 2 oz. Use half the amount of margarine specified. Omit sugar, substitute with artificial sweetener to taste.

Mechanical Soft (SFT): Prepare as directed. Consider individual tolerance.

Soft/Low Fiber (SLF): Not recommended.

Puree (PUR): Prepare as directed. Blenderize and strain.

Nutrient Analysis per Serving:

Regular	KCAL	PRO gm	CHO gm	FAT gm	Chol mg	SFA gm	PFA gm	VITA iu	VITC mg	THI mg	RIB mg	NIA mg	CA mg	NA mg	K+ mg	FE mg
	36.2	0.6	4.1	2.0	0.0	0.3	0.7	377	10.3	0.03	0.02	0.4	17.0	77.3	126	0.4

Sodium Restricted	NA mg	Diabetic	Kcal	Milk exg	Veg exg	Fruit exg	Bread exg	Meat exg	Fat exg	Low Fat & Low Chol	FAT gm	Chol mg	SFA gm	PFA gm
	8.5		25.6	0.0	0.5	0.0	0.0	0.0	0.25		1.1	0.0	0.2	0.3

Portion: 2 ounces (1/4 cup)

INGREDIENTS	48 portions (3 quarts)		6 portions (1 1/2 cups)	
	weights	measures	weights	measures
Margarine, low sodium	8 oz	1 cup	1 oz	2 Tbsp
Bread crumbs, soft	1 1/4 lb	2 1/2 qt	2 1/2 oz	1 1/4 cups
Lemon juice	8 oz	1 cup	1 oz	2 Tbsp
Parsley, chopped	1 1/4 oz	1 cup	1/8 oz	2 Tbsp

Method

1. Melt margarine.
2. Add bread crumbs. Cook until golden; tossing lightly.
3. Stir in lemon juice and parsley.
4. Portion 1/4 cup per serving.

Directions for Diet Preparations

Sodium Restricted (SR): Use low sodium bread crumbs.

Low Fat/Low Cholesterol (LF): 1/4 cup and **Diabetic** (DB): 1/4 cup. Use margarine in half the amount specified. May use if able to calculate into daily food plan.

Mechanical Soft (SFT) and **Soft/Low Fiber** (SLF): Prepare as directed.

Puree (PUR): Prepare as directed. Add additional liquid (i.e. lemon juice or broth); blenderize to obtain desired consistency.

Nutrient Analysis per Serving:

Regular	KCAL	PRO gm	CHO gm	FAT gm	Chol mg	SFA gm	PFA gm	VITA iu	VITC mg	THI mg	RIB mg	NIA mg	CA mg	NA mg	K+ mg	FE mg
	117	2.7	15.8	4.8	1.0	0.8	1.2	225	3.5	0.07	0.07	1.0	28.6	155	46.6	0.9

Sodium Restricted	NA mg	Diabetic	Kcal	Milk exg	Veg exg	Fruit exg	Bread exg	Meat exg	Fat exg	Low Fat & Low Chol	FAT gm	Chol mg	SFA gm	PFA gm
	5.2		100	0.0	0.0	0.0	1.0	0.0	0.5		2.8	1.0	0.5	0.6

O9   Almond Butter Sauce

Portion: 1 1/2 ounces (3 Tablespoons)

INGREDIENTS	50 portions (2 1/2 quarts)		8 portions (1 1/2 cups)	
	weights	measures	weights	measures
Margarine, low sodium, melted, hot	2 1/2 oz	5 Tbsp	3/8 oz	2 1/2 tsp
Flour, all-purpose	5 oz	1 1/4 cups	5/8 oz	1/4 cup
Water, hot		2 1/2 qt		1 2/3 cups
Margarine, low sodium, cut into pieces	8 oz	1 cup	1 1/3 oz	2 2/3 Tbsp
Lemon juice	2 2/3 oz	1/3 cup	3/8 oz	1 Tbsp
Almonds, sliced, toasted, low sodium	6 oz	1 1/4 cups	1 oz	1/4 cup

Method

1. Add flour to melted margarine. Blend.
2. Gradually add hot water while stirring. Cook 5 minutes.
3. When ready to serve, add margarine pieces. Beat until blended.
4. Add lemon juice and almonds. Mix.

Directions for Diet Preparations

Sodium Restricted (SR): Prepare as directed.
Low Fat/Low Cholesterol (LF): 1 1/2 oz and **Diabetic** (DB): 1 1/2 oz. Omit margarine, substitute with reduced-calorie margarine equal to the amount specified for regular margarine. Use half the amount of almonds specified. May use if able to calculate into daily food plan.
Mechanical Soft (SFT), **Soft/Low Fiber** (SLF), and **Puree** (PUR): Omit almonds.

Nutrient Analysis per Serving:

Regular	KCAL	PRO gm	CHO gm	FAT gm	Chol mg	SFA gm	PFA gm	VITA iu	VITC mg	THI mg	RIB mg	NIA mg	CA mg	NA mg	K+ mg	FE mg
	73.3	1.0	3.1	6.5	0.0	0.9	1.9	200	0.7	0.02	0.03	0.2	11.3	2.1	32.0	0.3

Sodium Restricted	NA mg	Diabetic	Kcal	Milk exg	Veg exg	Fruit exg	Bread exg	Meat exg	Fat exg	Low Fat & Low Chol	FAT gm	Chol mg	SFA gm	PFA gm
	2.1		42.1	0.0	0.0	0.0	0.0	0.0	0.9		3.2	0.0	0.4	0.9

Portion: 1 1/2 ounces (3 Tablespoons)

INGREDIENTS	50 portions (2 1/2 quarts)		8 portions (1 1/2 cups)	
	weights	measures	weights	measures
Margarine, low sodium, melted, hot	2 1/2 oz	5 Tbsp	3/8 oz	2 1/2 tsp
Flour, all-purpose	5 oz	1 1/4 cups	5/8 oz	1/4 cup
Water, hot		2 1/2 qt		1 2/3 cups
Margarine, low sodium, cut into pieces	8 oz	1 cup	1 1/3 oz	2 2/3 Tbsp

Method

1. Add flour to melted margarine. Blend.
2. Gradually add hot water while stirring. Cook 5 minutes.
3. When ready to serve, add margarine pieces. Beat until blended.

Directions for Diet Preparations

Sodium Restricted (SR): Prepare as directed.
Low Fat/Low Cholesterol (LF): 1 1/2 oz and **Diabetic** (DB): 1 1/2 oz. Omit margarine, substitute with reduced-calorie margarine equal to the amount specified for regular margarine. May use if able to calculate into daily food plan.
Mechanical Soft (SFT), **Soft/Low Fiber** (SLF), and **Puree** (PUR): Prepare as directed.

Nutrient Analysis per Serving:

Regular	KCAL	PRO gm	CHO gm	FAT gm	Chol mg	SFA gm	PFA gm	VITA iu	VITC mg	THI mg	RIB mg	NIA mg	CA mg	NA mg	K+ mg	FE mg
	53.8	0.3	2.2	4.8	0.0	0.8	1.6	199	0.01	0.02	0.01	0.1	2.1	1.7	5.1	0.1

Sodium Restricted	NA mg	Diabetic	Kcal	Milk exg	Veg exg	Fruit exg	Bread exg	Meat exg	Fat exg	Low Fat & Low Chol	FAT gm	Chol mg	SFA gm	PFA gm
	1.7		32.5	0.0	0.0	0.0	0.0	0.0	0.7		2.4	0.0	0.4	0.8

O11   Lemon Butter Sauce

Portion: 1 1/2 ounces (3 Tablespoons)

INGREDIENTS	50 portions (2 1/2 quarts)		8 portions (1 1/2 cups)	
	weights	measures	weights	measures
Margarine, low sodium, melted, hot	2 1/2 oz	5 Tbsp	3/8 oz	2 1/2 tsp
Flour, all-purpose	5 oz	1 1/4 cups	5/8 oz	1/4 cup
Water, hot		2 1/2 qt		1 2/3 cups
Margarine, low sodium, cut into pieces	8 oz	1 cup	1 1/3 oz	2 2/3 Tbsp
Lemon peel, grated		1 1/4 Tbsp		3/4 tsp
Lemon juice	2 2/3 oz	1/3 cup	3/8 oz	1 Tbsp

Method

1. Add flour to melted margarine. Blend.
2. Gradually add hot water while stirring. Cook 5 minutes.
3. When ready to serve, add margarine pieces. Beat until blended.
4. Add grated lemon peel and lemon juice. Mix.

Directions for Diet Preparations

Sodium Restricted (SR): Prepare as directed.
Low Fat/Low Cholesterol (LF): 1 1/2 oz and **Diabetic** (DB): 1 1/2 oz. Omit margarine, substitute with reduced-calorie margarine equal to the amount specified for regular margarine. May use if able to calculate into daily food plan.
Mechanical Soft (SFT), **Soft/Low Fiber** (SLF), and **Puree** (PUR): Prepare as directed.

Nutrient Analysis per Serving:

Regular	KCAL	PRO gm	CHO gm	FAT gm	Chol mg	SFA gm	PFA gm	VITA iu	VITC mg	THI mg	RIB mg	NIA mg	CA mg	NA mg	K+ mg	FE mg
	54.3	0.3	2.4	4.8	0.0	0.8	1.6	200	0.9	0.01	0.01	0.1	2.3	1.7	7.3	0.1

Sodium Restricted	NA mg	Diabetic	Kcal	Milk exg	Veg exg	Fruit exg	Bread exg	Meat exg	Fat exg	Low Fat & Low Chol	FAT gm	Chol mg	SFA gm	PFA gm
	1.7		32.7	0.0	0.0	0.0	0.0	0.0	0.7		2.4	0.0	0.40	0.8

O12   Parsley Butter Sauce

Portion: 1 1/2 ounces (3 Tablespoons)

INGREDIENTS	50 portions (2 1/2 quarts)		8 portions (1 1/2 cups)	
	weights	measures	weights	measures
Margarine, low sodium, melted, hot	2 1/2 oz	5 Tbsp	3/8 oz	2 1/2 tsp
Flour, all-purpose	5 oz	1 1/4 cups	5/8 oz	1/4 cup
Water, hot		2 1/2 qt		1 2/3 cups
Margarine, low sodium, cut into pieces	8 oz	1 cup	1 1/3 oz	2 2/3 Tbsp
Parsley, chopped	2 oz	1 1/2 cups	1/3 oz	1/4 cup

Method

1. Add flour to melted margarine. Blend.
2. Gradually add hot water while stirring. Cook 5 minutes.
3. When ready to serve, add margarine pieces. Beat until blended.
4. Add parsley. Mix.

Directions for Diet Preparations

Sodium Restricted (SR): Prepare as directed.
Low Fat/Low Cholesterol (LF): 1 1/2 oz and **Diabetic** (DB): 1 1/2 oz. Omit margarine, substitute with reduced-calorie margarine equal to the amount specified for regular margarine. May use if able to calculate into daily food plan.
Mechanical Soft (SFT), **Soft/Low Fiber** (SLF), and **Puree** (PUR): Prepare as directed.

Nutrient Analysis per Serving:

Regular	KCAL	PRO gm	CHO gm	FAT gm	Chol mg	SFA gm	PFA gm	VITA iu	VITC mg	THI mg	RIB mg	NIA mg	CA mg	NA mg	K+ mg	FE mg
	54.5	0.3	2.4	4.8	0.0	0.81	1.6	294	1.6	0.02	0.01	0.1	4.4	2.4	14.8	0.2

Sodium Restricted	NA mg	Diabetic	Kcal	Milk exg	Veg exg	Fruit exg	Bread exg	Meat exg	Fat exg	Low Fat & Low Chol	FAT gm	Chol mg	SFA gm	PFA gm
	2.4		32.8	0.0	0.0	0.0	0.0	0.0	0.7		2.4	0.0	0.4	0.8

Brown Mushroom Gravy

Portion: 2 ounces (1/4 cup)

INGREDIENTS	64 portions (1 gallon)		8 portions (2 cups)	
	weights	measures	weights	measures
Beef stock[1]		1 gal		2 cups
Flour, all-purpose	8 oz	2 cups	1 oz	1/4 cup
Margarine, low sodium, melted	8 oz	1 cup	1 oz	2 Tbsp
Mushroom, pieces, cooked	2 lb	1 1/2 qt	4 oz	3/4 cup
Onions, diced	2 3/4 oz	1/2 cup	1/3 oz	1 Tbsp

Method

1. Heat beef stock. Simmer.
2. Combine flour and margarine to form roux.
3. Add beef stock to roux gradually, stirring constantly with wire whip.
4. Add mushrooms and onions to gravy. Stir to blend.
5. Cook until thickened.

Notes

[1]May use a concentrated soup base as a quick beef stock. Prepare as directed by manufacturer.

Directions for Diet Preparations

Sodium Restricted (SR): Prepare as directed. May use a low sodium soup base as directed by manufacturer, instead of the stock.

Low Fat/Low Cholesterol (LF): 2 oz and **Diabetic** (DB): 2 oz. Substitute reduced-calorie margarine for regular margarine in equal amount specified for regular margarine. Low fat diet should consider individual tolerance to onions.

Mechanical Soft (SF): 2 oz.

1 gallon: Omit onions, substitute with 1 tsp onion powder.
2 cups: Omit onions, substitute with 1/8 tsp onion powder.

Soft/Low Fiber (SLF): Omit onions.

Puree (PUR): Prepare as directed. Blenderize and strain.

Nutrient Analysis per Serving:

Regular	KCAL	PRO gm	CHO gm	FAT gm	Chol mg	SFA gm	PFA gm	VITA iu	VITC mg	THI mg	RIB mg	NIA mg	CA mg	NA mg	K+ mg	FE mg
	51.1	1.3	4.2	3.3	0.0	0.4	1.0	118	0.7	0.04	0.07	1.2	2.7	20.4	59.5	0.7

Sodium Restricted	NA mg	Diabetic	Kcal	Milk exg	Veg exg	Fruit exg	Bread exg	Meat exg	Fat exg	Low Fat & Low Chol	FAT gm	Chol mg	SFA gm	PFA gm
	20.4		38.2	0.0	0.0	0.0	0.0	0.0	0.8		1.9	0.0	0.2	0.5

O14 — Creamed Mushroom Gravy

Portion: 2 ounces (1/4 cup)

INGREDIENTS	64 portions (1 gallon)		8 portions (2 cups)	
	weights	measures	weights	measures
Margarine, low sodium, #1	8 oz	1 cup	1 oz	2 Tbsp
Flour, all-purpose	8 oz	2 cups	1 oz	1/4 cup
Milk, skim		1 gal		2 cups
Mushroom, sliced	2 lb	1 1/2 qt	4 oz	3/4 cup
Onions, diced	2 3/4 oz	1/2 cup	1/3 oz	1 Tbsp
Margarine, low sodium, melted, #2	4 oz	1/2 cup	1/2 oz	1 Tbsp

Method

1. Melt margarine #1, remove from heat. Add flour, stir until smooth. Cook 5 to 10 minutes.
2. Add milk gradually, stirring constantly with wire whip.
3. Sauté mushrooms and onions in margarine #2. Add to white sauce.
4. Continue to cook and stir until smooth and thick, about 15 minutes.

Directions for Diet Preparations

Sodium Restricted (SR): Prepare as directed.

Low Fat/Low Cholesterol (LF): 2 oz and **Diabetic** (DB): 2 oz. Omit margarine #1, substitute with reduced-calorie margarine in equal amount specified for regular margarine. Omit margarine #2, sauté mushrooms and onions in water until soft. Add to white sauce. Low fat diet should consider individual tolerance to onions.

Mechanical Soft (SF): 2 oz.

1 gallon: Omit onions, substitute with 1 tsp onion powder.

2 cups: Omit onions, substitute with 1/8 tsp onion powder.

Soft/Low Fiber (SLF): Omit onions. Consider individual tolerance. May use if able to calculate into daily food plan.

Puree (PUR): Prepare as directed. Blenderize and strain.

Nutrient Analysis per Serving:

Regular	KCAL	PRO gm	CHO gm	FAT gm	Chol mg	SFA gm	PFA gm	VITA iu	VITC mg	THI mg	RIB mg	NIA mg	CA mg	NA mg	K+ mg	FE mg
	78.0	2.8	6.6	4.5	1.1	0.8	1.5	304	1.3	0.05	0.14	0.9	79.7	33.8	163	0.4

Sodium Restricted	NA mg	Diabetic	Kcal	Milk exg	Veg exg	Fruit exg	Bread exg	Meat exg	Fat exg	Low Fat & Low Chol	FAT gm	Chol mg	SFA gm	PFA gm
	33.8		58.6	0.25	0.0	0.0	0.0	0.0	0.8		2.3	1.1	0.4	0.7

O15 — Cream Gravy

Portion: 2 ounces (1/4 cup)

INGREDIENTS	64 portions (1 gallon)		8 portions (2 cups)	
	weights	measures	weights	measures
Chicken stock[1]		1 qt		1/2 cup
Margarine, low sodium, melted	1 lb	2 cups	2 oz	1/4 cup
Flour, all-purpose	8 oz	2 cups	1 oz	1/4 cup
Milk, skim, hot		3 qt		1 1/2 cups

Method

1. Prepare stock.
2. Combine margarine and flour. Blend. Simmer on low heat for 5 minutes.
3. Add stock and milk to flour mixture gradually, stirring constantly with wire whip.
4. Cook until thickened and smooth.

Notes

[1]May use a concentrated soup base as a quick stock. Prepare as directed by manufacturer.

Directions for Diet Preparations

Sodium Restricted (SR): Prepare as directed. May use a low sodium soup base as directed by manufacturer, instead of the stock.

Low Fat/Low Cholesterol (LF): 2 oz and **Diabetic** (DB): 2 oz. Omit margarine, substitute reduced-calorie margarine in equal amount specified for regular margarine.

Mechanical Soft (SF) and **Puree** (PUR): Prepare as directed.

Soft/Low Fiber (SLF): Prepare as directed. May use if able to calculate into daily food plan.

Nutrient Analysis per Serving:

Regular	KCAL	PRO gm	CHO gm	FAT gm	Chol mg	SFA gm	PFA gm	VITA iu	VITC mg	THI mg	RIB mg	NIA mg	CA mg	NA mg	K+ mg	FE mg
	82.8	2.1	5.2	5.9	0.8	1.0	1.9	332	0.4	0.04	0.08	0.3	59.9	30.7	83.2	0.2

Sodium Restricted	NA mg	Diabetic	Kcal	Milk exg	Veg exg	Fruit exg	Bread exg	Meat exg	Fat exg	Low Fat & Low Chol	FAT gm	Chol mg	SFA gm	PFA gm
	30.7		57.1	0.25	0.0	0.0	0.0	0.0	0.8		3.1	0.8	0.5	0.9

O16 Onion Gravy

Portion: 2 ounces (1/4 cup)

INGREDIENTS	64 portions (1 gallon)		8 portions (2 cups)	
	weights	measures	weights	measures
Margarine, low sodium, melted, hot	8 oz	1 cup	1 oz	2 Tbsp
Onions, thinly sliced	3 lb EP (3 1/2 lb AP)	1 1/2 qt	6 oz EP (7 oz AP)	3/4 cup
Flour, all-purpose	8 oz	2 cups	1 oz	1/4 cup
Beef or chicken stock[1]		1 gal		2 cups

Method

1. Lightly brown onions in margarine.
2. Add flour to onions. Blend. Simmer on low heat for 5 minutes.
3. Gradually add stock to flour/onion mixture, stir constantly with wire whip.
4. Cook until smooth and thickened.

Notes

[1]May use a concentrated soup base as a quick stock. Prepare as directed by manufacturer.

Directions for Diet Preparations

Sodium Restricted (SR): Prepare as directed. May use a low sodium soup base as directed by manufacturer, instead of the stock.

Low Fat/Low Cholesterol (LF): 2 oz and **Diabetic** (DB): 2 oz. Omit margarine, substitute with reduced-calorie margarine in equal amount specified for regular margarine. May use if able to calculate into daily food plan. Low fat diets should consider individual tolerance to onions.

Mechanical Soft (SF): 2 oz.
1 gallon: Omit onions, substitute with 1 tsp onion powder.
2 cups: Omit onions, substitute with 1/8 tsp onion powder.

Soft/Low Fiber (SLF): Not recommended.

Puree (PUR): Prepare as directed. Blenderize and strain.

Nutrient Analysis per Serving:

Regular	KCAL	PRO gm	CHO gm	FAT gm	Chol mg	SFA gm	PFA gm	VITA iu	VITC mg	THI mg	RIB mg	NIA mg	CA mg	NA mg	K+ mg	FE mg
	51.8	1.1	4.5	3.3	0.0	0.5	1.0	118	1.2	0.03	0.03	0.59	5.3	20.4	28.3	0.5

Sodium Restricted	NA mg	Diabetic	Kcal	Milk exg	Veg exg	Fruit exg	Bread exg	Meat exg	Fat exg	Low Fat & Low Chol	FAT gm	Chol mg	SFA gm	PFA gm
	20.4		39.0	0.0	0.0	0.0	0.0	0.0	0.9		1.9	0.0	0.2	0.5

O17 — Pan Gravy

Portion: 2 ounces (1/4 cup)

INGREDIENTS	64 portions (1 gallon)		8 portions (2 cups)	
	weights	measures	weights	measures
Beef or chicken stock[1]		1 gal		2 cups
Fat, hot, meat drippings	8 oz	1 cup	1 oz	2 Tbsp
Flour, all-purpose	8 oz	2 cups	1 oz	1/4 cup

Method

1. Prepare stock.
2. Combine flour to fat. Blend.
3. Add stock to roux gradually, stirring constantly with wire whip.
4. Cook until thickened and smooth.

Notes

[1]May use concentrated soup base as a quick stock. Prepare as directed by manufacturer.

Directions for Diet Preparations

Sodium Restricted (SR): Prepare as directed. May use a low sodium soup base as directed by manufacturer, instead of the stock.

Low Fat/Low Cholesterol (LF): 2 oz and **Diabetic** (DB): 2 oz. Delete meat drippings, substitute with reduced-calorie margarine in equal amount specified for fat.

Mechanical Soft (SFT) and **Puree** (PUR): Prepare as directed.

Soft/Low Fiber (SLF): Not recommended.

Nutrient Analysis per Serving:

Regular	KCAL	PRO gm	CHO gm	FAT gm	Chol mg	SFA gm	PFA gm	VITA iu	VITC mg	THI mg	RIB mg	NIA mg	CA mg	NA mg	K+ mg	FE mg
	50.1	0.9	3.3	3.6	2.7	0.9	0.7	0.0	0.0	0.03	0.03	0.5	0.5	19.1	3.4	0.4

Sodium Restricted	NA mg	Diabetic	Kcal	Milk exg	Veg exg	Fruit exg	Bread exg	Meat exg	Fat exg	Low Fat & Low Chol	FAT gm	Chol mg	SFA gm	PFA gm
	19.1		33.6	0.0	0.0	0.0	0.0	0.0	0.75		1.8	0.0	0.2	0.5

O18   Pan Giblet Gravy

Portion: 2 ounces (1/4 cup)

INGREDIENTS	64 portions (1 gallon)		8 portions (2 cups)	
	weights	measures	weights	measures
Turkey or chicken fat, hot	8 oz	1 cup	1 oz	2 Tbsp
Flour, all-purpose	8 oz	2 cups	1 oz	1/4 cup
Chicken stock[1]		1 gal		2 cups
Giblets, cooked	2 lb	1 qt	4 oz	1/2 cup

Method

1. Add flour to fat and blend.
2. Prepare chicken stock.
3. Add stock gradually, stirring constantly until mixture starts to thicken.
4. Add precooked, chopped giblets; blend.
5. Heat to serving temperature.

Notes

[1]May use concentrated soup base as a quick stock. Prepare as directed by manufacturer.

Directions for Diet Preparations

Sodium Restricted (SR): Prepare as directed. May use a low sodium soup base as directed by manufacturer, instead of the stock.

Low Fat/Low Cholesterol (LF) and **Soft/Low Fiber** (SLF): Not recommended.

Diabetic (DB): 2 oz. Prepare as directed. Strain. May use if able to calculate into daily food plan.

Mechanical Soft (SF): Prepare as directed.

Puree (PUR): Prepare as directed. Blenderize and strain.

Nutrient Analysis per Serving:

Regular	KCAL	PRO gm	CHO gm	FAT gm	Chol mg	SFA gm	PFA gm	VITA iu	VITC mg	THI mg	RIB mg	NIA mg	CA mg	NA mg	K+ mg	FE mg
	65.4	3.0	3.6	4.2	40.8	1.1	0.8	550	0.15	0.02	0.1	0.9	1.7	24.5	21.5	0.7

Sodium Restricted	NA mg	Diabetic	Kcal	Milk exg	Veg exg	Fruit exg	Bread exg	Meat exg	Fat exg	Low Fat & Low Chol	Not Recommended
	24.5		51.1	0.0	0.0	0.0	0.25	0.0	0.75		

O19   Italian Sauce

Portion: 2 ounces (1/4 cup)

INGREDIENTS	64 portions (1 gallon)		8 portions (2 cups)	
	weights	measures	weights	measures
Onions, chopped	10 1/2 oz	2 cups	1 1/3 oz	1/4 cup
Olive oil	4 oz	1/2 cup	1/2 oz	1 Tbsp
Oregano, crushed		2 tsp		1/4 tsp
Basil, diced		1/4 cup		1/2 Tbsp
Garlic powder		2 tsp		1/4 tsp
Bay leaves		4 leaves		1 leaf
Tomato juice		3 1/2 qt		1 3/4 cups
Tomato paste	14 oz	1 3/4 cups	1 3/4 oz	1/4 cup

Method

1. Sauté onions in olive oil until tender.
2. Add oregano, basil, garlic powder, and bay leaves to onions. Mix well. Adjust spices to taste.
3. Add tomato juice and paste to onions. Heat to boiling.
4. Reduce heat and simmer uncovered 20 minutes.
5. Remove bay leaves.

Directions for Diet Preparations

Sodium Restricted (SR): Use low sodium tomato juice and low sodium tomato paste.

Low Fat/Low Cholesterol (LF): 2 oz and **Diabetic** (DB): 2 oz. Prepare as directed. Low fat diets should consider individual tolerance to onions and garlic.

Mechanical Soft (SF): 2 oz.

1 gallon: Omit onions, substitute with 1 tsp onion powder.
2 cups: Omit onions, substitute with 1/8 tsp onion powder.

Soft/Low Fiber (SLF): Omit onions and garlic powder. Consider individual tolerance.

Puree (PUR): Prepare as directed. Blenderize and strain.

Nutrient Analysis per Serving:

Regular	KCAL	PRO gm	CHO gm	FAT gm	Chol mg	SFA gm	PFA gm	VITA iu	VITC mg	THI mg	RIB mg	NIA mg	CA mg	NA mg	K+ mg	FE mg
	34.3	0.7	4.4	1.8	0.0	0.2	0.2	839	18.5	0.03	0.03	0.6	16.8	253	190	0.6

Sodium Restricted	NA mg	Diabetic	Kcal	Milk exg	Veg exg	Fruit exg	Bread exg	Meat exg	Fat exg	Low Fat & Low Chol	FAT gm	Chol mg	SFA gm	PFA gm
	10.2		34.3	0.0	0.5	0.0	0.0	0.0	0.5		1.8	0.0	0.2	0.2

Marinara Sauce

Portion: 2 ounces (1/4 cup)

INGREDIENTS	64 portions (1 gallon)		8 portions (2 cups)	
	weights	measures	weights	measures
Tomato puree	6 1/2 lb	3 1/4 qt (1 #10 can)	13 oz	1 2/3 cups
Onions, chopped	5 1/3 oz	1 cup	2/3 oz	2 Tbsp
Green pepper, chopped	5 1/3 oz	1 cup	2/3 oz	2 Tbsp
Worcestershire sauce		1 Tbsp		1/2 tsp
Oregano, ground		1 Tbsp		1/2 tsp
Garlic powder		1 Tbsp		1/2 tsp
Parsley, flakes		1/4 cup		1/2 Tbsp

Method

1. Combine all ingredients.
2. Heat to a boil. Simmer uncovered for 30 minutes.

Directions for Diet Preparations

Sodium Restricted (SR): Use low sodium tomato puree or fresh tomatoes.

Low Fat/Low Cholesterol (LF): 2 oz. Prepare as directed. Consider individual tolerance when using onions and garlic powder.

Diabetic (DB): 2 oz. Prepare as directed.

Mechanical Soft (SF) and **Puree** (PUR): Prepare as directed. Blenderize and strain.

Soft/Low Fiber (SLF): Not recommended.

Nutrient Analysis per Serving:

Regular	KCAL	PRO gm	CHO gm	FAT gm	Chol mg	SFA gm	PFA gm	VITA iu	VITC mg	THI mg	RIB mg	NIA mg	CA mg	NA mg	K+ mg	FE mg
	47.5	2.1	10.6	0.5	0.0	0.07	0.2	1360	25.6	0.08	0.10	1.7	21.4	429	516	1.7

Sodium Restricted	NA mg	Diabetic	Kcal	Milk exg	Veg exg	Fruit exg	Bread exg	Meat exg	Fat exg	Low Fat & Low Chol	FAT gm	Chol mg	SFA gm	PFA gm
	37.1		47.5	0.0	1.0	0.0	0.0	0.0	0.4		0.5	0.0	0.07	0.2

Spaghetti Sauce with Meat

Portion: 6 ounces (3/4 cup)

INGREDIENTS	50 portions (2 1/2 gallons)		8 portions (1 1/2 quarts)	
	weights	measures	weights	measures
Ground beef, lean	13 lb	1 2/3 gal	1 2/3 lb	3 1/4 cups
Tomato puree	9 lb	4 1/2 qt	1 1/8 lb	2 1/4 cups
Water		3 1/2 cups		6 1/2 Tbsp
Catsup	3 lb	1 1/2 qt	6 oz	3/4 cup
Onions, chopped	9 oz	1 3/4 cups	1 oz	3 Tbsp
Bay leaves		4 leaves		1 leaf
Thyme, crushed		2 tsp		1/4 tsp
Garlic powder		2 tsp		1/4 tsp
Oregano, ground		1 Tbsp		1/2 tsp
Basil		2 tsp		1/4 tsp
Sugar, granulated		1 1/2 Tbsp		1/2 tsp
Worcestershire sauce		2 Tbsp		3/4 tsp

Method

1. Brown meat. Drain fat.
2. Add remaining ingredients to beef.
3. Simmer about 30 minutes or until thickened.

Directions for Diet Preparations

Sodium Restricted (SR): Use low sodium tomato puree or puree fresh tomatoes. Use low sodium catsup.

Low Fat/Low Cholesterol (LF): 4 oz (1/2 cup). Prepare as directed. Low fat diets should consider individual tolerance to onions and garlic.

Diabetic (DB): 6 oz (3/4 cup). Omit sugar, substitute with artificial sweetener as per manufacturer's directions.

Mechanical Soft (SF): Prepare as directed.

Soft/Low Fiber (SLF): Omit onions, garlic powder, and worcestershire sauce.

Puree (PUR): Prepare as directed. Blenderize to obtain desired consistency.

Nutrient Analysis per Serving:

Regular	KCAL	PRO	CHO	FAT	Chol	SFA	PFA	VITA	VITC	THI	RIB	NIA	CA	NA	K+	FE
		gm	gm	gm	mg	gm	gm	iu	mg	mg	mg	mg	mg	mg	mg	mg
	316	26.4	17.9	15.5	85.7	5.9	0.7	1586	25.4	0.15	0.31	7.1	39.4	780	853	3.9

Sodium Restricted	NA	Diabetic	Kcal	Milk	Veg	Fruit	Bread	Meat	Fat	Low Fat & Low Chol	FAT	Chol	SFA	PFA
	mg			exg	exg	exg	exg	exg	exg		gm	mg	gm	gm
	116		314	0.0	2.0	0.0	0.0	3.0-L	2.0		10.3	57.1	3.9	0.5

Tomato Sauce

Portion: 2 ounces (1/4 cup)

INGREDIENTS	64 portions (1 gallon)		8 portions (2 cups)	
	weights	measures	weights	measures
Margarine, low sodium	12 oz	1 1/2 cups	1 1/2 oz	3 Tbsp
Flour, all-purpose	8 oz	2 cups	1 oz	1/4 cup
Tomato juice		1 gal		2 cups
Onions, chopped	5 1/3 oz	1 cup	2/3 oz	2 Tbsp
Sugar, granulated		2 Tbsp		3/4 tsp
Worcestershire sauce		1 tsp		1/8 tsp

Method

1. Melt margarine. Blend in flour.
2. Add tomato juice to flour. Stir.
3. Add onions, sugar, and worcestershire sauce.
4. Simmer 15 to 20 minutes, uncovered.

Directions for Diet Preparations

Sodium Restricted (SR): Use low sodium tomato juice. Omit worcestershire sauce.

Low Fat/Low Cholesterol (LF): 1 oz. Omit margarine, substitute with reduced-calorie margarine in equal amount specified for regular margarine. Low fat diets should consider individual tolerance when using onions.

Diabetic (DB): 1 oz. Omit margarine, substitute with reduced-calorie margarine in equal amount specified for regular margarine. Omit sugar, substitute with artificial sweetener to taste.

Mechanical Soft (SF): 2 oz.
1 gallon: Omit onions, substitute with 1 tsp onion powder.
2 cups: Omit onions, substitute with 1/8 tsp onion powder.

Soft/Low Fiber (SLF): Omit onions and worcestershire sauce.

Puree (PUR): Prepare as directed. Blenderize and strain.

Nutrient Analysis per Serving:

Regular	KCAL	PRO gm	CHO gm	FAT gm	Chol mg	SFA gm	PFA gm	VITA iu	VITC mg	THI mg	RIB mg	NIA mg	CA mg	NA mg	K+ mg	FE mg
	67.0	0.8	6.1	4.3	0.0	0.7	1.4	1030	12.3	0.04	0.03	0.6	11.4	181	141.7	0.5

Sodium Restricted	NA mg	Diabetic	Kcal	Milk exg	Veg exg	Fruit exg	Bread exg	Meat exg	Fat exg	Low Fat & Low Chol	FAT gm	Chol mg	SFA gm	PFA gm
	7.7		22.1	0.0	0.5	0.0	0.0	0.0	0.2		1.1	0.0	0.2	0.4

Salsa

Portion: 1 ounce (2 Tbsp)

INGREDIENTS	64 portions (2 quarts)		8 portions (1 cup)	
	weights	measures	weights	measures
Tomatoes, canned, diced or crushed	2 1/2 lb	1 1/4 qt	5 oz	2/3 cup
Green peppers, chopped	8 oz	1 1/2 cups	1 oz	3 Tbsp
Onions, chopped	8 oz	1 1/2 cups	1 oz	3 Tbsp
Garlic, minced		1 clove		1/4 clove
Vinegar, cider	4 oz	1/2 cup	1/2 oz	1 Tbsp
Tomato juice	1 1/2 lb	3 cups	3 oz	1/3 cup
Oregano		1 Tbsp		1/2 tsp
Cumin, ground		1/4 tsp		pinch

Method

1. Drain tomatoes. Reserve juice.
2. Chop tomato until pureed.
3. Place tomatoes and reserved juice in large pot.
4. Add remaining ingredients to tomatoes.
5. Simmer 15 minutes or until desired consistency.

Directions for Diet Preparations

Sodium Restricted (SR): Use low sodium canned tomatoes and low sodium tomato juice.
Low Fat/Low Cholesterol (LF) 1 oz and **Diabetic** (DB) 1 oz. Prepare as directed.
Mechanical Soft (SFT) and **Puree** (PUR): Strain.
Soft/Low Fiber (SLF): Not recommended.

Nutrient Analysis per Serving:

Regular	KCAL	PRO gm	CHO gm	FAT gm	Chol mg	SFA gm	PFA gm	VITA iu	VITC mg	THI mg	RIB mg	NIA mg	CA mg	NA mg	K+ mg	FE mg
	8.2	0.3	1.8	0.1	0.0	0.0	0.03	262	9.4	0.02	0.01	0.2	7.6	73.0	76.8	0.2

Sodium Restricted	NA mg	Diabetic	Kcal	Milk exg	Veg exg	Fruit exg	Bread exg	Meat exg	Fat exg	Low Fat & Low Chol	FAT gm	Chol mg	SFA gm	PFA gm
	3.6		8.2	0.0	0.3	0.0	0.0	0.0	0.0		0.1	0.0	0.01	0.03

Portion: 1 ounce (2 Tbsp)

INGREDIENTS	64 portions (2 quarts)		8 portions (1 cup)	
	weights	measures	weights	measures
Margarine, low sodium, melted	8 oz	1 cup	1 oz	2 Tbsp
Flour, all-purpose	4 oz	1 cup	1/2 oz	2 Tbsp
Chicken stock[1]		1 qt		1/2 cup
Milk, skim, hot		1 qt		1/2 cup
Nutmeg		1/4 tsp		pinch
Parmesan cheese, grated	4 1/2 oz	3/4 cup	2/3 oz	1 1/2 Tbsp
Swiss cheese, shredded	4 oz	1 cup	1/2 oz	2 Tbsp

Method

1. Add flour to melted margarine. Stir until smooth. Cook 5 to 10 minutes.
2. Add stock and milk gradually, stirring constantly with wire whip.
3. Add nutmeg and cheeses. Stir until cheeses melt.
4. Cook and stir as necessary until smooth and thick.

Notes

[1]May use a concentrated soup base as a quick stock. Prepare as directed by manufacturer.

Directions for Diet Preparations

Sodium Restricted (SR): 1 Tbsp, **Low Fat/Low Cholesterol** (LF): 1 Tbsp, and **Diabetic** (DB): 1 Tbsp.

2 quarts: Use low sodium reduced-calorie margarine in equal amount specified for low sodium margarine. Use a low sodium chicken stock. Omit parmesan cheese and swiss cheese, substitute with 1 3/4 cups of low sodium reduced-calorie cheese. May use if able to calculate into daily food plan.

1 cup: Use low sodium reduced-calorie margarine in equal amount specified for low sodium margarine. Use a low sodium chicken stock. Omit parmesan cheese and swiss cheese, substitute with 3 1/2 Tbsp of low sodium reduced-calorie cheese. May use if able to calculate into daily food plan.

Mechanical Soft (SFT) and **Puree** (PUR): Prepare as directed.

Soft/Low Fiber (SLF): Not recommended.

Nutrient Analysis per Serving:

Regular	KCAL	PRO gm	CHO gm	FAT gm	Chol mg	SFA gm	PFA gm	VITA iu	VITC mg	THI mg	RIB mg	NIA mg	CA mg	NA mg	K+ mg	FE mg
	56.3	2.1	2.5	4.2	4.3	1.3	0.9	189	0.16	0.02	0.05	0.2	61.8	93.2	41.2	0.2

Sodium Restricted	NA mg	Diabetic	Kcal	Milk exg	Veg exg	Fruit exg	Bread exg	Meat exg	Fat exg	Low Fat & Low Chol	FAT gm	Chol mg	SFA gm	PFA gm
	13.4		24.6	0.0	0.0	0.0	0.0	0.0	0.5		1.8	0.1	0.2	0.5

Tartar Sauce

Portion: 1 ounce (2 Tbsp)

INGREDIENTS	64 portions (2 quarts)		8 portions (1 cup)	
	weights	measures	weights	measures
Mayonnaise	3 1/4 lb	6 1/2 cups	6 oz	3/4 cup
Sweet relish	10 oz	1 1/4 cups	1 1/2 oz	3 Tbsp
Onions, minced	6 oz	1/2 cup	3/4 oz	1 Tbsp
Lemon juice	1 oz	2 Tbsp	1/8 oz	3/4 tsp
Parsley, chopped		2 Tbsp		3/4 tsp

Method

1. Combine all ingredients. Blend well.
2. Chill.

Directions for Diet Preparations

Sodium Restricted (SR): Use low sodium mayonnaise. Omit sweet relish, substitute with diced green and red peppers.

Low Fat/Low Cholesterol (LF): 2 tsp and **Diabetic** (DB): 2 tsp. Omit mayonnaise, substitute with reduced-calorie low cholesterol mayonnaise in equal amounts specified for regular mayonnaise. May use if able to calculate into daily food plan.

Mechanical Soft (SF): Prepare as directed. Consider individual tolerance.

Soft/Low Fiber (SLF) and **Puree** (PUR): Omit relish and onions.

Nutrient Analysis per Serving:

Regular	KCAL	PRO gm	CHO gm	FAT gm	Chol mg	SFA gm	PFA gm	VITA iu	VITC mg	THI mg	RIB mg	NIA mg	CA mg	NA mg	K+ mg	FE mg
	83.8	0.1	1.01	9.0	6.6	0.9	6.2	39.7	0.4	0.0	0.0	0.0	2.7	77.6	9.5	0.1

Sodium Restricted	NA mg	Diabetic	Kcal	Milk exg	Veg exg	Fruit exg	Bread exg	Meat exg	Fat exg	Low Fat & Low Chol	FAT gm	Chol mg	SFA gm	PFA gm
	3.7		13.5	0.0	0.0	0.0	0.0	0.0	0.3		1.1	4.25	0.19	0.0

Portion: 1 ounce (2 Tbsp)

INGREDIENTS	64 portions (2 quarts)		8 portions (1 cup)	
	weights	measures	weights	measures
Tahini (sesame butter)	2 lb	1 qt	4 oz	1/2 cup
Lemon juice		2 cups		1/4 cup
Garlic powder		1 tsp		1/8 tsp
Sea salt		2 tsp		1/4 tsp
Water, cold		2 cups		1/4 cup

Method

1. In a bowl, combine the tahini, lemon juice, garlic, and salt.
2. Slowly beat in the water until the mixture is a thick sauce.
3. Serve over vegetables or rice.

Directions for Diet Preparations

Sodium Restricted (SR): Omit salt.
Low Fat/Low Cholesterol (LF): 2 tsp and **Diabetic** (DB): 2 tsp. Prepare as directed.
Mechanical Soft (SFT): Prepare as directed.
Soft/Low Fiber (SLF): Not recommended. Provide appropriate food substitute.
Puree (PUR): Prepare as directed.

Nutrient Analysis per Serving:

Regular	KCAL	PRO gm	CHO gm	FAT gm	Chol mg	SFA gm	PFA gm	VITA iu	VITC mg	THI mg	RIB mg	NIA mg	CA mg	NA mg	K+ mg	FE mg
	98.3	2.9	4.8	8.2	0.0	1.1	3.6	9.6	3.5	0.04	0.03	1.1	156	76.0	104	3.1

Sodium Restricted	NA mg	Diabetic	Kcal	Milk exg	Veg exg	Fruit exg	Bread exg	Meat exg	Fat exg	Low Fat & Low Chol	FAT gm	Chol mg	SFA gm	PFA gm
	2.0		32.7	0.0	0.0	0.0	0.0	0.0	0.7		2.7	0.0	0.4	1.2

O27   Vegetarian Gravy

Portion: 2 ounce (1/4 cup)

INGREDIENTS	64 portions (1 gallon)		8 portions (2 cups)	
	weights	measures	weights	measures
Margarine, low sodium	2 1/4 oz	4 1/2 Tbsp	1/4 oz	1 3/4 tsp
Flour, all-purpose	9 oz	2 1/4 cups	1 1/8 oz	4 1/2 Tbsp
Water		3 1/2 qt		1 3/4 cups
Soy sauce, low sodium		2 1/4 cups		4 1/2 Tbsp
Lemon juice		1/2 cup		3 1/2 tsp

Method

1. Melt margarine. Add flour to form a paste.
2. Add water and soy sauce. Whisk for 5 minutes or until smooth.
3. Add lemon juice. Heat to serving temperature.

Directions for Diet Preparations

Sodium Restricted (SR): Use half the amount of low sodium soy sauce specified.

Low Fat/Low Cholesterol (LF): 2 oz and **Diabetic** (DB): 2 oz. Prepare as directed.

Mechanical Soft (SFT): Prepare as directed.

Soft/Low Fiber (SLF): Not recommended. Provide appropriate food substitute.

Puree (PUR): Prepare as directed.

Nutrient Analysis per Serving:

Regular	KCAL	PRO gm	CHO gm	FAT gm	Chol mg	SFA gm	PFA gm	VITA iu	VITC mg	THI mg	RIB mg	NIA mg	CA mg	NA mg	K+ mg	FE mg
	26.9	0.8	4.0	0.8	0.0	0.1	0.3	33.8	0.8	0.03	0.03	0.5	2.4	282	21.8	0.3

Sodium Restricted	NA mg	Diabetic	Kcal	Milk exg	Veg exg	Fruit exg	Bread exg	Meat exg	Fat exg	Low Fat & Low Chol	FAT gm	Chol mg	SFA gm	PFA gm
	146		26.9	0.0	0.0	0.0	0.0	0.0	0.0		0.6	0.0	0.1	0.3

Salad Dressing, Spreads, and Stuffing

P1	French Dressing[1]

Portion: 1 ounce (2 Tbsp)

INGREDIENTS	48 portions (1 1/2 quarts)		8 portions (1 cup)	
	weights	measures	weights	measures
Paprika		1 Tbsp		1/2 tsp
Mustard, dry		1 Tbsp		1/2 tsp
Garlic powder		1 tsp		1/8 tsp
Basil, sweet		1 Tbsp		1/2 tsp
Tomato juice	6 oz	3/4 cup	1 oz	2 Tbsp
Vinegar, cider	1 lb	2 cups	2 2/3 oz	1/3 cup
Salad oil	1 2/3 lb	3 1/4 cups	4 oz	1/2 cup

Method

1. Combine all ingredients.
2. Mix on high speed until blended.
3. Chill.
4. Shake vigorously just before serving.

Notes

1. May use individual prepared packets of salad dressing.
   a. Low calorie: 2 Tbsp for low fat and diabetic are free.
   b. Reduced calorie: 2 Tbsp equals one fat exchange (5 grams fat).
   c. May purchase low sodium salad dressing.

Directions for Diet Preparations

Sodium Restricted (SR): Use low sodium tomato juice.
Low Fat/Low Cholesterol (LF): 2 tsp and **Diabetic** (DB): 2 tsp. Prepare as directed. May use if able to calculate into daily food plan.
Mechanical Soft (SFT): Prepare as directed.
Soft/Low Fiber (SLF): Omit mustard and garlic. Consider individual tolerance.
Puree (PUR): Prepare as directed. Strain.

Nutrient Analysis per Serving:

Regular	KCAL	PRO gm	CHO gm	FAT gm	Chol mg	SFA gm	PFA gm	VITA iu	VITC mg	THI mg	RIB mg	NIA mg	CA mg	NA mg	K+ mg	FE mg
	136	0.1	1.0	15.0	0.0	1.9	8.8	141	1.2	0.0	0.0	0.07	4.5	14.1	26.4	0.2

Sodium Restricted	NA mg	Diabetic	Kcal	Milk exg	Veg exg	Fruit exg	Bread exg	Meat exg	Fat exg	Low Fat & Low Chol	FAT gm	Chol mg	SFA gm	PFA gm
	0.5		45.3	0.0	0.0	0.0	0.0	0.0	1.0		5.0	0.0	0.6	2.9

French Lemon Dressing

Portion: 1 ounce (2 Tbsp)

INGREDIENTS	48 portions (1 1/2 quarts)		8 portions (1 cup)	
	weights	measures	weights	measures
Salad oil	16 oz	2 cups	3 oz	1/3 cup
Lemon juice	24 oz	3 cups	4 oz	1/2 cup
Lemon peel, grated		2 Tbsp		1 tsp
Vinegar, cider		3/4 cup		2 Tbsp
Mustard, dry		3 Tbsp		2 tsp
Apple juice concentrate	3 oz	6 Tbsp	1/2 oz	1 Tbsp
Miso (soy paste)		2 Tbsp		1 tsp
Pepper, white, ground		1 1/2 tsp		1/4 tsp

Method

1. Combine all ingredients. Shake well and chill.
2. Shake vigorously just before serving.

Directions for Diet Preparations

Sodium Restricted (SR), **Low Fat/Low Cholesterol** (LF): 2 tsp, **Diabetic** (DB): 2 tsp, **Mechanical Soft** (SFT), **Soft/Low Fiber** (SLF), and **Puree** (PUR): Prepare as directed.

Nutrient Analysis per Serving:

Regular	KCAL	PRO gm	CHO gm	FAT gm	Chol mg	SFA gm	PFA gm	VITA iu	VITC mg	THI mg	RIB mg	NIA mg	CA mg	NA mg	K+ mg	FE mg
	94.2	0.3	2.9	9.4	0.0	1.1	5.4	3.6	7.4	0.01	0.1	0.07	5.9	21.7	38.3	0.1

Sodium Restricted	NA mg	Diabetic	Kcal	Milk exg	Veg exg	Fruit exg	Bread exg	Meat exg	Fat exg	Low Fat & Low Chol	FAT gm	Chol mg	SFA gm	PFA gm
	21.7		31.4	0.0	0.0	0.0	0.0	0.0	0.7		3.1	0.0	0.3	1.8

Portion: 1 ounce (2 Tbsp)

INGREDIENTS	48 portions (1 1/2 quarts)		8 portions (1 cup)	
	weights	measures	weights	measures
Avocado	1 lb	2 medium	3 oz	1/3 medium
Lemon juice	2 2/3 oz	1/3 cup	3/8 oz	2 3/4 tsp
Mayonnaise	1 1/4 lb	1 1/4 qt	3 oz	3/4 cup
Vinegar, tarragon	2 2/3 oz	1/3 cup	3/8 oz	2 3/4 tsp
Chives, chopped		1/2 cup		4 tsp
Parsley, chopped		1/4 cup		2 tsp
Onions, finely, chopped	1 3/4 oz	1/3 cup	1/3 oz	2 3/4 tsp

Method

1. Peel avocado and remove seed. Cut into small pieces. Add lemon juice.
2. Combine remaining ingredients. Add to avocado mixture.
3. Mix on low speed until well blended.
4. Chill.

Directions for Diet Preparations

Sodium Restricted (SR): Use low sodium mayonnaise.
Low Fat/Low Cholesterol (LF): 2 tsp and **Diabetic** (DB): 2 tsp. Omit mayonnaise, substitute with reduced-calorie low cholesterol mayonnaise in equal amount to regular mayonnaise. May use if able to calculate into daily food plan. Low fat diets should consider individual tolerance to onions.
Mechanical Soft (SFT), **Soft/Low Fiber** (SLF), and **Puree** (PUR): Omit onions.

Nutrient Analysis per Serving:

Regular	KCAL	PRO gm	CHO gm	FAT gm	Chol mg	SFA gm	PFA gm	VITA iu	VITC mg	THI mg	RIB mg	NIA mg	CA mg	NA mg	K+ mg	FE mg
	108	0.4	6.7	9.2	6.4	1.4	4.6	142	2.1	0.01	0.02	0.13	5.5	177	48.3	0.2

Sodium Restricted	NA mg	Diabetic	Kcal	Milk exg	Veg exg	Fruit exg	Bread exg	Meat exg	Fat exg	Low Fat & Low Chol	FAT gm	Chol mg	SFA gm	PFA gm
	7.8		14.3	0.0	0.0	0.0	0.0	0.0	0.3		3.1	0.0	0.05	0.04

Italian Dressing[1]

Portion: 1 ounce (2 Tbsp)

INGREDIENTS	48 portions (1 1/2 quarts)		8 portions (1 cup)	
	weights	measures	weights	measures
Mustard, dry		1 Tbsp		1/2 tsp
Oregano, ground		1 Tbsp		1/2 tsp
Garlic powder		1 tsp		1/8 tsp
Basil, sweet		2 tsp		1/2 tsp
Vinegar, cider	1 lb	2 cups	2 2/3 oz	1/3 cup
Salad oil	2 lb	1 qt	5 1/3 oz	2/3 cup

Method

1. Combine all ingredients.
2. Mix on high speed until blended.
3. Chill.
4. Shake vigorously just before serving.

Notes

1. May use individual prepared packets of salad dressing.
   a. Low calorie: 2 Tbsp for low fat and diabetic are free.
   b. Reduced calorie: 2 Tbsp equals one fat exchange (5 grams fat).
   c. May purchase low sodium salad dressing.

Directions for Diet Preparations

Sodium Restricted (SR) and **Mechanical Soft** (SFT): Prepare as directed.

Low Fat/Low Cholesterol (LF): 2 tsp and **Diabetic** (DB): 2 tsp. Prepare as directed. May use if able to calculate into daily food plan.

Soft/Low Fiber (SLF): Omit mustard and garlic. Consider individual tolerance.

Puree (PUR): Prepare as directed. Strain.

Nutrient Analysis per Serving:

Regular	KCAL	PRO gm	CHO gm	FAT gm	Chol mg	SFA gm	PFA gm	VITA iu	VITC mg	THI mg	RIB mg	NIA mg	CA mg	NA mg	K+ mg	FE mg
	165	0.1	0.7	18.4	0.0	2.3	10.7	5.2	0.02	0.001	0.001	0.02	3.0	0.1	13.5	0.1

Sodium Restricted	NA mg	Diabetic	Kcal	Milk exg	Veg exg	Fruit exg	Bread exg	Meat exg	Fat exg	Low Fat & Low Chol	FAT gm	Chol mg	SFA gm	PFA gm
	0.1		55.0	0.0	0.0	0.0	0.0	0.0	1.2		6.1	0.0	0.7	3.6

Lemon Miso Dressing

Portion: 1 ounce (2 Tbsp)

INGREDIENTS	48 portions (1 1/2 quarts)		8 portions (1 cup)	
	weights	measures	weights	measures
Yogurt, plain, low fat	2 lb	1 qt	5 3/8 oz	2/3 cup
White miso		1 cup		2 1/2 Tbsp
Olive oil		1 cup		2 1/2 Tbsp
Mustard, prepared		2 1/2 Tbsp		1 1/4 tsp
Horseradish, prepared		1 Tbsp		1/2 tsp
Lemon juice		1/2 cup		4 tsp
Lemon peel, grated		1 Tbsp		1/2 tsp
Pepper, white, ground		3/4 tsp		1/8 tsp

Method

1. Combine all ingredients. Whisk until smooth.
2. Chill.

Directions for Diet Preparations

Sodium Restricted (SR): 2 tsp. Use half the amount of white miso specified.

Low Fat/Low Cholesterol (LF): 2 tsp and **Diabetic** (DB): 2 tsp. Prepare as directed.

Mechanical Soft (SFT) and **Puree** (PUR): Prepare as directed.

Soft/Low Fiber (SLF): Not recommended. Provide appropriate food substitute.

Nutrient Analysis per Serving:

Regular	KCAL	PRO gm	CHO gm	FAT gm	Chol mg	SFA gm	PFA gm	VITA iu	VITC mg	THI mg	RIB mg	NIA mg	CA mg	NA mg	K+ mg	FE mg
	61.8	1.6	3.1	4.9	0.3	0.6	0.3	1.9	1.5	0.01	0.04	0.02	39.2	193	53.5	0.06

Sodium Restricted	NA mg	Diabetic	Kcal	Milk exg	Veg exg	Fruit exg	Bread exg	Meat exg	Fat exg	Low Fat & Low Chol	FAT gm	Chol mg	SFA gm	PFA gm
	36.4		20.6	0.0	0.0	0.0	0.0	0.0	0.5		1.6	0.1	0.2	0.1

Portion: 1 ounce (2 Tbsp)

INGREDIENTS	48 portions (1 1/2 quarts)		8 portions (1 cup)	
	weights	measures	weights	measures
Salad oil	1 1/2 lb	3 cups	4 oz	1/2 cup
Vinegar, cider	1 1/2 lb	3 cups	4 oz	1/2 cup
Parsley, fresh, chopped		1/4 cup		2 tsp

Method

1. Combine all ingredients.
2. Mix well.
3. Chill.
4. Shake vigorously just before serving.

Notes

1. May use individual prepared packets of salad dressing.
   a. Low calorie: 2 Tbsp for low fat and diabetic are free.
   b. Reduced calorie: 2 Tbsp equals one fat exchange (5 grams fat).
   c. May purchase low sodium salad dressing.

Directions for Diet Preparations

Sodium Restricted (SR): Prepare as directed.
Low Fat/Low Cholesterol (LF): 2 tsp and **Diabetic** (DB): 2 tsp. Prepare as directed. May use if able to calculate into daily food plan.
Mechanical Soft (SFT), **Soft/Low Fiber** (SLF), and **Puree** (PUR): Prepare as directed.

Nutrient Analysis per Serving:

Regular	KCAL	PRO gm	CHO gm	FAT gm	Chol mg	SFA gm	PFA gm	VITA iu	VITC mg	THI mg	RIB mg	NIA mg	CA mg	NA mg	K+ mg	FE mg
	124	0.01	0.9	13.8	0.0	1.7	8.1	16.4	0.3	0.0	0.00	0.0	1.3	0.3	16.9	0.1

Sodium Restricted	NA mg	Diabetic	Kcal	Milk exg	Veg exg	Fruit exg	Bread exg	Meat exg	Fat exg	Low Fat & Low Chol	FAT gm	Chol mg	SFA gm	PFA gm
	0.3		41.3	0.0	0.0	0.0	0.0	0.0	0.9		4.6	0.0	0.6	2.7

Russian Dressing

Portion: 1 ounce (2 Tbsp)

INGREDIENTS	48 portions (1 1/2 quarts		8 portions (1 cup)	
	weights	measures	weights	measures
Mayonnaise	2 1/4 lb	4 1/2 cup	6 oz	3/4 cup
Catsup	9 oz	1 1/8 cup	2 oz	1/4 cup

Method

1. Combine all ingredients.
2. Mix well until blended.
3. Chill.

Notes

1. May use individual prepared packets of salad dressing.
   a. Low calorie: 2 Tbsp for low fat and diabetic are free.
   b. Reduced calorie: 2 Tbsp equals one fat exchange (5 grams fat).
   c. May purchase low sodium salad dressing.

Directions for Diet Preparations

Sodium Restricted (SR): Use low sodium mayonnaise and low sodium catsup.

Low Fat/Low Cholesterol (LF): 2 tsp and **Diabetic** (DB): 2 tsp. Omit mayonnaise, substitute low calorie low cholesterol mayonnaise in equal amount to regular mayonnaise. May use if able to calculate into daily food plan.

Mechanical Soft (SFT), **Soft/Low Fiber** (SLF), and **Puree** (PUR): Prepare as directed.

Nutrient Analysis per Serving:

Regular	KCAL	PRO gm	CHO gm	FAT gm	Chol mg	SFA gm	PFA gm	VITA iu	VITC mg	THI mg	RIB mg	NIA mg	CA mg	NA mg	K+ mg	FE mg
	156	0.3	2.2	16.5	12.3	1.8	11.4	149	0.9	0.005	0.004	0.1	5.1	186	30.6	0.2

Sodium Restricted	NA mg	Diabetic	Kcal	Milk exg	Veg exg	Fruit exg	Bread exg	Meat exg	Fat exg	Low Fat & Low Chol	FAT gm	Chol mg	SFA gm	PFA gm
	7.8		27.2	0.0	0.0	0.0	0.0	0.0	0.6		2.5	0.0	0.0	0.0

Portion: 1 ounce (2 Tbsp)

INGREDIENTS	48 portions (1 1/2 quarts)		8 portions (1 cup)	
	weights	measures	weights	measures
Eggs, hard-cooked, chopped fine	1/2 oz	1/2 cup (2 large)	1 1/2 oz	3 Tbsp (1 small)
Onion, minced	1 oz	1 1/3 Tbsp	1/8 oz	3/4 tsp
Chili sauce	9 oz	1 1/8 cups	1 1/2 oz	3 Tbsp
Pickle relish	2 oz	1/4 cup	1/3 oz	2 tsp
Mayonnaise	2 1/4 lb	4 1/2 cups	6 oz	3/4 cup

Method

1. Combine all ingredients.
2. Mix well until blended.
3. Chill.

Notes

1. May use individual prepared packets of salad dressing.
   a. Low calorie: 2 Tbsp for low fat and diabetic are free.
   b. Reduced calorie: 2 Tbsp equals one fat exchange (5 grams fat).
   c. May purchase low sodium salad dressing.

Directions for Diet Preparations

Sodium Restricted (SR): Omit chili sauce, substitute with low sodium catsup. Omit pickle relish, substitute with diced red and green peppers. Use low sodium mayonnaise.

Low Fat/Low Cholesterol (LF): 2 tsp and **Diabetic** (DB): 2 tsp. Omit eggs. Omit pickle relish, substitute with diced red and green peppers. Omit mayonnaise, substitute low calorie low cholesterol mayonnaise in equal amount to regular mayonnaise. May use if able to calculate into daily food plan. Low fat diets should consider individual tolerance to onions.

Mechanical Soft (SFT): Prepare as directed.
Soft/Low Fiber (SLF): Not recommended.
Puree (PUR): Prepare as directed. Strain.

Nutrient Analysis per Serving:

Regular	KCAL	PRO gm	CHO gm	FAT gm	Chol mg	SFA gm	PFA gm	VITA iu	VITC mg	THI mg	RIB mg	NIA mg	CA mg	NA mg	K+ mg	FE mg
	155	0.4	1.2	16.7	20.8	1.8	11.5	627	1.8	0.0	0.01	0.03	5.4	131	45.0	0.2

Sodium Restricted	NA mg	Diabetic	Kcal	Milk exg	Veg exg	Fruit exg	Bread exg	Meat exg	Fat exg	Low Fat & Low Chol	FAT gm	Chol mg	SFA gm	PFA gm
	9.9		26.5	0.0	0.0	0.0	0.0	0.0	0.5		2.4	0.0	0.0	0.0

Portion: 1 ounce (2 Tbsp)

INGREDIENTS	50 portions (1 3/4 quarts)		8 portions (1 cup)	
	weights	**measures**	**weights**	**measures**
Cream cheese, softened	2 lb	1 qt	5 1/8 oz	2/3 cup
Yogurt, plain, non-fat	8 oz	1 cup	1 1/4 oz	2 1/2 Tbsp
Mayonnaise	8 oz	1 cup	1 1/4 oz	2 1/2 Tbsp
Milk, skim	8 oz	1 cup	1 1/4 oz	2 1/2 Tbsp
Vinegar, tarragon	2 1/2 oz	5 Tbsp	3/8 oz	2 1/2 tsp
Tarragon		1 Tbsp		1/2 tsp

Method

1. Combine all ingredients. Blenderize until smooth.
2. Cover and refrigerate until ready to use.

Directions for Diet Preparations

Sodium Restricted (SR): 2 Tbsp, **Low Fat/Low Cholesterol** (LF): 2 Tbsp, and **Diabetic** (DB): 2 Tbsp. Substitute imitation reduced-calorie cream cheese for regular cream cheese in equal amounts. Substitute reduced-calorie low cholesterol low sodium mayonnaise for regular mayonnaise in equal amounts. May use if able to calculate into daily food plan.

Mechanical Soft (SFT), **Soft/Low Fiber** (SLF), and **Puree** (PUR): Prepare as directed.

Nutrient Analysis per Serving:

Regular	KCAL	PRO gm	CHO gm	FAT gm	Chol mg	SFA gm	PFA gm	VITA iu	VITC mg	THI mg	RIB mg	NIA mg	CA mg	NA mg	K+ mg	FE mg
	67.1	1.4	1.8	6.2	16.6	3.3	0.8	221	0.04	0.0	0.04	0.02	22.2	72.1	27.2	0.2

Sodium Restricted	NA mg	Diabetic	Kcal	Milk exg	Veg exg	Fruit exg	Bread exg	Meat exg	Fat exg	Low Fat & Low Chol	FAT gm	Chol mg	SFA gm	PFA gm
	23.0		49.9	0.0	0.0	0.0	0.0	0.0	1.1		4.6	1.5	1.9	0.09

Portion: 1 ounce (2 Tbsp)

INGREDIENTS	50 portions (1 3/4 quarts)		8 portions (1 cup)	
	weights	measures	weights	measures
Cucumbers, peeled, seeded, finely chopped	2 1/4 lb AP	6 1/2 cups	5 1/2 oz AP	1 cup
Yogurt, plain, nonfat	8 oz	1 cup	1 1/3 oz	2 1/2 Tbsp
Mayonnaise	10 oz	1 1/4 cups	1 2/3 oz	3 1/4 Tbsp
Cottage cheese, 1% low fat	1 lb	2 cups	2 1/2 oz	1/3 cup
Parsley, fresh, minced		1/2 cup		1 1/4 Tbsp
Chives, fresh, minced		1 Tbsp		1/2 tsp
Garlic powder		1 tsp		1/8 tsp
Pepper, black		1 tsp		1/8 tsp

Method

1. Combine all ingredients.
2. Mix well until blended.
3. Cover and refrigerate until ready to use.

Directions for Diet Preparations

Sodium Restricted (SR): 1 Tbsp, **Low Fat/Low Cholesterol** (LF): 1 Tbsp, and **Diabetic** (DB): 1 Tbsp. Substitute reduced-calorie low cholesterol low sodium mayonnaise for regular mayonnaise in equal amounts. May use if able to calculate into daily food plan.

Mechanical Soft (SFT) and **Puree** (PUR): Prepare as directed.

Soft/Low Fiber (SLF): Omit garlic powder and black pepper.

Nutrient Analysis per Serving:

Regular	KCAL	PRO gm	CHO gm	FAT gm	Chol mg	SFA gm	PFA gm	VITA iu	VITC mg	THI mg	RIB mg	NIA mg	CA mg	NA mg	K+ mg	FE mg
	25.0	1.1	1.0	1.7	0.3	0.05	0.01	35.9	0.9	0.01	0.02	0.03	11.5	59.5	22.8	0.1

Sodium Restricted	NA mg	Diabetic	Kcal	Milk exg	Veg exg	Fruit exg	Bread exg	Meat exg	Fat exg	Low Fat & Low Chol	FAT gm	Chol mg	SFA gm	PFA gm
	29.7		12.5	0.0	0.0	0.0	0.0	0.0	0.3		0.8	0.1	0.02	0.0

Portion: 1/2 cup

INGREDIENTS	50 portions		6 portions	
	weights	measures	weights	measures
Margarine, low sodium, melted	4 oz	1/2 cup	1/2 oz	1 Tbsp
Onions, chopped	1 lb	3 cups	2 oz	1/3 cup
Celery, chopped	1 1/2 lb	1 1/8 qt	2 3/4 oz	1/2 cup
Cornbread, stale, dry, crumble	3 1/2 lb	1 1/3 gal	7 oz	2 2/3 cups
Bread, stale, dry, cubed	1 3/4 lb	3 1/2 qt	3 1/2 oz	1 3/4 cups
Chicken stock[1]		3 qt		1 1/2 cups
Sage		1 Tbsp		1/4 tsp

Method

1. Sauté onions and celery in margarine until tender.
2. Add cornbread and bread to sauté vegetables.
3. Combine chicken stock and sage. Pour over bread mixture. Stir to moisten.
4. Place dressing in greased baking pan(s).
5. Bake at 375°F for 20 to 30 minutes or until hot and lightly browned.
6. Serve with No. 8 dipper.

Notes

[1]May use concentrated soup base as a quick chicken stock. Prepare as directed by manufacturer.

Directions for Diet Preparations

Sodium Restricted (SR): Use low sodium bread. May use a low sodium soup base as directed by manufacturer, instead of the stock.

Low Fat/Low Cholesterol (LF): 1/4 cup. Omit margarine, sauté vegetables in small amount of water. Use low fat cornbread and low fat chicken stock. Low fat diets should consider individual tolerance to onions.

Diabetic (DB): 1/4 cup. Omit margarine, sauté vegetables in small amount of water. Use diabetic cornbread and low fat chicken stock.

Mechanical Soft (SFT): 1/2 cup.
50 portions: Omit onions, substitute with 1 tsp onion powder. Consider individual tolerance.
6 portions: Omit onions, substitute with 1/8 tsp onion powder. Consider individual tolerance.

Soft/Low Fiber (SLF): Omit onions and celery.

Puree (PUR): Prepare as directed. Add additional chicken stock; blenderize to obtain desired consistency.

Nutrient Analysis per Serving:

Regular	KCAL	PRO gm	CHO gm	FAT gm	Chol mg	SFA gm	PFA gm	VITA iu	VITC mg	THI mg	RIB mg	NIA mg	CA mg	NA mg	K+ mg	FE mg
	139	3.8	21.2	4.2	10.0	0.7	1.1	150	1.1	0.10	0.11	1.3	40.6	240	81.2	1.2

Sodium Restricted	NA mg	Diabetic	Kcal	Milk exg	Veg exg	Fruit exg	Bread exg	Meat exg	Fat exg	Low Fat & Low Chol	FAT gm	Chol mg	SFA gm	PFA gm
	29.2		64.1	0.0	0.0	0.0	0.75	0.0	0.2		1.0	0.5	0.1	0.2

Portion: 1/2 cup

Ingredients	50 portions		6 portions	
	weights	**measures**	**weights**	**measures**
Dry bread, cubed	5 lb	2 1/2 gal	10 oz	1 1/4 qt
Sage		1 Tbsp		1/4 tsp
Onions, chopped finely	1 lb EP	3 cups	2 oz EP	1/3 cup
Celery, chopped finely	2 lb EP	1 1/2 qt	4 oz EP	3/4 cup
Margarine, low sodium, melted	1 lb	2 cups	2 oz	1/4 cup
Chicken stock[1]		3 qt		1 1/2 cups
Eggs, beaten	1 lb	2 cups (8 large)	2 oz	1/4 cup (1 large)
Raisins, seedless	5 1/3 oz	1 cup	2/3 oz	2 Tbsp

Method

1. Add sage to bread. Mix.
2. Sauté onions and celery in margarine until tender. Add to bread mixture. Mix.
3. Add chicken stock, eggs, and raisins to bread mixture; mix lightly.
4. Place in greased counter pan (12 × 20 × 2-inches) or baking pan(s). Bake at 350°F for 1/2 hours or until top is browned.
5. Serve with a No. 8 dipper.

Notes

[1]May use concentrated soup base as a quick chicken stock. Prepare as directed by manufacturer.

Directions for Diet Preparations

Sodium Restricted (SR): Use low sodium bread. May use a low sodium soup base as directed by manufacturer, instead of the stock.

Low Fat/Low Cholesterol (LF): 1/4 cup. Omit eggs, substitute with a commercial egg substitute as per manufacturer's directions.

Diabetic (DB): 1/4 cup. Prepare as directed.

Mechanical Soft (SFT): Omit raisins.

Soft/Low Fiber (SLF): Not recommended.

Puree (PUR): Omit raisins. Add additional chicken stock; blenderize to obtain desired consistency.

Nutrient Analysis per Serving:

Regular	KCAL	PRO gm	CHO gm	FAT gm	Chol mg	SFA gm	PFA gm	VITA iu	VITC mg	THI mg	RIB mg	NIA mg	CA mg	NA mg	K+ mg	FE mg
	244	7.1	30.6	10.2	45.4	2.2	2.4	363	1.8	0.19	0.18	2.6	55.2	481	187	1.9

Sodium Restricted	NA mg	Diabetic	Kcal	Milk exg	Veg exg	Fruit exg	Bread exg	Meat exg	Fat exg	Low Fat & Low Chol	FAT gm	Chol mg	SFA gm	PFA gm
	47.4		122	0.0	0.1	0.0	1.0	0.1	0.8		5.1	1.1	0.9	1.4

Portion: 1/2 cup

INGREDIENTS	48 portions (1 1/2 quarts)		8 portions (1 cup)	
	weights	measures	weights	measures
Vegetable oil	6 oz	3/4 cup	3/4 oz	1 1/2 Tbsp
Onions, finely chopped	1 1/2 lb EP	4 1/2 cups	2 2/3 oz EP	1/2 cup
Celery, diced	1 lb EP	3 cups	2 oz EP	1/3 cup
Mushrooms, diced, canned	1 1/2 lb	3 cups	3 oz	1/3 cup
Chicken stock[1]		1 3/4 qt		3/4 cup
Matzo farfel	3 3/8 lb	1 1/2 gal	6 5/8 oz	3 cups
Paprika		1 Tbsp		1/2 tsp
Dill weed		1 Tbsp		1/2 tsp
Parsley flakes		2 Tbsp		3/4 tsp
Eggs, beaten	12 oz	1 1/2 cups (6 large)	2 oz	1/4 cup (1 large)

Method

1. Sauté onions, celery, and mushrooms in oil.
2. Add chicken stock to matzo farfel. Mix. Let stand 15 minutes. Add to vegetables.
3. Combine paprika, dill, parsley, and eggs. Add to matzo mixture. Mix well.
4. Cover pot and keep hot until ready to serve.
5. Serve with a No. 8 dipper.

Notes

[1]May use concentrated soup base as a quick chicken stock. Prepare as directed by manufacturer.

Directions for Diet Preparations

Sodium Restricted (SR): Prepare as directed. May use a low sodium soup base as directed by manufacturer, instead of the chicken stock.

Low Fat/Low Cholesterol (LF): 1/2 cup.

50 portions: Omit vegetable oil. Sauté vegetables in water until tender. Omit whole eggs, substitute with nine egg whites. Low fat diets should consider individual tolerance to onions.

6 portions: Omit vegetable oil. Sauté vegetables in water until tender. Omit whole eggs, substitute with two egg whites. Low fat diets should consider individual tolerance to onions.

Diabetic (DB): 1/3 cup. Omit vegetable oil. Sauté vegetables in water until tender.

Mechanical Soft (SFT): Prepare as directed.

Soft/Low Fiber (SLF): Omit onions and celery.

Puree (PUR): Prepare as directed. Add additional chicken stock and blenderize to obtain desired consistency.

Nutrient Analysis per Serving:

Regular	KCAL	PRO gm	CHO gm	FAT gm	Chol mg	SFA gm	PFA gm	VITA iu	VITC mg	THI mg	RIB mg	NIA mg	CA mg	NA mg	K+ mg	FE mg
	126	4.3	20.1	4.3	30.5	0.8	1.8	72.1	1.9	0.02	0.05	0.4	12.3	22.1	177	0.6

Sodium Restricted	NA mg	Diabetic	Kcal	Milk exg	Veg exg	Fruit exg	Bread exg	Meat exg	Fat exg	Low Fat & Low Chol	FAT gm	Chol mg	SFA gm	PFA gm
	22.1		66.7	0.0	0.2	0.0	0.9	0.0	0.0		0.6	0.1	0.1	0.7

Cakes and Cookies

Q1   Angel Food Cake

Portion: 1 slice (14 slices per cake)

INGREDIENTS	56 portions; 4, 10" cakes		14 portions; 1, 10" cake	
	weights	measures	weights	measures
Egg whites, fresh or frozen	2 2/3 lb	5 1/4 cups (39 large)	11 oz	1 1/3 cups (10 large)
Cream of tartar		1 3/4 Tbsp		1 1/3 tsp
Salt		1 tsp		1/4 tsp
Sugar, granulated #1	1 lb	2 1/4 cups	4 oz	5/8 cup
Vanilla	1/2 oz	1 Tbsp	1/8 oz	3/4 tsp
Sugar, granulated #2	1 3/4 lb	1 qt	7 oz	1 cup
Flour, cake	1 lb	3 3/4 cups	4 oz	7/8 cup

Method

1. Beat egg whites on medium speed until frothy, about 1 minute.
2. Add cream of tartar and salt. Continue beating until egg whites are stiff enough to hold their shape.
3. Gradually add sugar #1 while beating on medium speed.
4. Add vanilla. Continue beating on high speed for 2 minutes.
5. Mix sugar #2 and flour. Sift. Gradually add to egg whites on low speed. Mix only to combine.
6. 56 portions: Scale into 4, 10-inch tube pans.
   14 portions: Scale into 1, 10-inch tube pan.
7. Bake at 350°F for 50 minutes or until brown and done.
8. Remove from oven, turn upside down to cool.

Directions for Diet Preparations

Sodium Restricted (SR), **Low Fat/Low Cholesterol** (LF): 1 slice, **Mechanical Soft** (SFT), and **Soft/Low Fiber** (SLF): Prepare as directed.

Diabetic (DB): 1 slice. Prepare as directed. Consider individual tolerance when using granulated sugar.

Puree (PUR): Not recommended. Use appropriate food alternative.

Nutrient Analysis per Serving:

Regular	KCAL	PRO gm	CHO gm	FAT gm	Chol mg	SFA gm	PFA gm	VITA iu	VITC mg	THI mg	RIB mg	NIA mg	CA mg	NA mg	K+ mg	FE mg
	142	3.3	32.4	0.1	0.0	0.0	0.0	0.0	0.0	0.0	0.08	0.1	4.4	110	56.9	0.1

Sodium Restricted	NA mg	Diabetic	Kcal	Milk exg	Veg exg	Fruit exg	Bread exg	Meat exg	Fat exg	Low Fat & Low Chol	FAT gm	Chol mg	SFA gm	PFA gm
	110		142	0.0	0.0	1.2	1.0	0.0	0.0		0.1	0.0	0.0	0.0

Portion: 1 slice (3″ × 2″)

INGREDIENTS	78 portions, 1 sheet cake (18 × 26 × 2″), cut 6 × 13		18 portions, 1 cake (13 × 9 × 2″), cut 6 × 3	
	weights	measures	weights	measures
Sugar, granulated	2 1/2 lb	5 2/3 cups	10 oz	1 1/3 cups
Margarine, low sodium	1 lb	2 cups	4 oz	1/2 cup
Vanilla		1 Tbsp		3/4 tsp
Eggs	1 lb	2 cups (8 large)	4 oz	1/2 cup (2 large)
Bananas, mashed	2 lb	1 qt	8 oz	1 cup
Flour, cake	2 lb	1 3/4 qt	8 oz	1 3/4 cups
Baking powder		2 tsp		1/2 tsp
Baking soda		1 Tbsp		3/4 tsp
Buttermilk, skim	12 oz	1 1/2 cups	3 oz	1/3 cup

Method

1. Cream margarine, sugar, and vanilla on high speed until light, about 5 minutes.
2. Add eggs to creamed mixture and mix on medium speed for 3 minutes.
3. Add bananas to creamed mixture and mix for 2 minutes.
4. Combine flour, baking powder, and soda.
5. Add dry ingredients alternately with buttermilk. Mix on low speed to combine.
6. Mix on medium speed for 2 minutes.
7. Pour batter into greased floured pan.
8. Bake at 350°F for 25 to 30 minutes or until done.
9. Cool. Remove from pans and frost.
10. Cut into slices.
11. Suggested Frosting: Cream cheese frosting.

Directions for Diet Preparations

Sodium Restricted (SR): 2″ × 2″. Use low sodium baking powder as per manufacturer's directions. Omit frosting. May use if able to calculate into food plan.

Low Fat/Low Cholesterol (LF): 2″ × 2″.

78 portions: Omit margarine, substitute with reduced-calorie margarine in equal amount specified for regular margarine. Omit eggs, substitute with a commercial egg substitute equal to 2 cups eggs. Omit frosting. May use if able to calculate into daily food plan.

18 portions: Omit margarine, substitute with reduced-calorie margarine in equal amount specified for regular margarine. Omit eggs, substitute with a commercial egg substitute equal to 1/2 cup eggs. Omit frosting. May use if able to calculate into daily food plan.

Diabetic (DB): 2″ × 2″.

78 portions: Replace 2 1/2 lb granulated sugar with 1 1/8 cups granulated sugar and artificial sweetener equivalent to 4 1/2 cups granulated sugar (approximately 5 Tbsp artificial sweetener). Omit margarine, substitute with reduced-calorie margarine in equal amount specified for regular margarine. Increase baking powder to 1 Tbsp. Omit frosting. May use if able to calculate into daily food plan. Consider individual tolerance when using granulated sugar.

18 portions: Replace 10 oz granulated sugar with 1/3 cup granulated sugar and artificial sweetener equivalent to 1 cup granulated sugar (approximately 1 Tbsp artificial sweetener). Omit margarine, substitute with reduced-calorie margarine in equal amount specified for regular margarine. Increase baking powder to 3/4 tsp. Omit frosting. May use if able to calculate into daily food plan. Consider individual tolerance when using granulated sugar.

Mechanical Soft (SFT) and **Soft/Low Fiber** (SLF): Prepare as directed.

Puree (PUR): Not recommended. Use appropriate food alternative.

Nutrient Analysis per Serving:

Regular	KCAL	PRO gm	CHO gm	FAT gm	Chol mg	SFA gm	PFA gm	VITA iu	VITC mg	THI mg	RIB mg	NIA mg	CA mg	NA mg	K+ mg	FE mg
	161	1.8	26.8	5.4	28.1	1.0	1.6	229	1.1	0.01	0.03	0.15	13.7	62.8	73.6	0.2

Sodium Restricted	NA mg	Diabetic	Kcal	Milk exg	Veg exg	Fruit exg	Bread exg	Meat exg	Fat exg	Low Fat & Low Chol	FAT gm	Chol mg	SFA gm	PFA gm
	45.7		98.1	0.0	0.0	0.5	0.75	0.0	0.3		2.7	0.2	0.4	0.8

Portion: 1 slice (3″ × 2″)

INGREDIENTS	72 portions, 2 cakes (18 × 26 × 2″), cut 4 × 9		18 portions, 1 cake (13 × 9 × 2″), cut 6 × 3	
	weights	measures	weights	measures
Flour, cake	2 1/3 lb	2 1/8 qt	9 1/4 oz	2 1/8 cups
Baking powder		3 3/4 Tbsp		1 Tbsp
Margarine, low sodium	1 lb	2 cups	4 oz	1/2 cup
Sugar, granulated	2 3/4 lb	1 1/2 qt	11 oz	1 1/2 cups
Salt		2 tsp		1/2 tsp
Milk, skim		4 1/2 cups		1 1/8 cups
Eggs	1 lb	2 cups (8 large)	4 oz	1/2 cup (2 large)
Vanilla		4 tsp		1 tsp
Filling:				
Cornstarch	2 oz	1/3 cup	1/2 oz	1 1/2 Tbsp
Sugar, granulated	5 1/3 oz	3/4 cup	1 1/3 oz	3 Tbsp
Milk, skim, cold	5 oz	2/3 cup	1 1/4 oz	2 1/2 Tbsp
Milk, skim, hot	1 2/3 lb	3 1/3 cups	6 2/3 oz	5/8 cup
Eggs, beaten	6 oz	3/4 cup (3 large)	1 1/2 oz	3 Tbsp (1 small)
Vanilla		3/4 tsp		1/4 tsp
Glaze:				
Chocolate, unsweetened	4 oz	4 squares	1 oz	1 square
Margarine, low sodium	3 oz	1/3 cup	3/4 oz	1 1/2 Tbsp
Sugar, powdered, sifted	1 1/4 lb	1 1/8 qt	5 oz	1 1/8 cup
Vanilla	1/2 oz	1 Tbsp	1/8 oz	3/4 tsp
Water, boiling	8 oz	1 cup	2 oz	1/4 cup

Method

1. Combine flour, baking powder, and margarine in mixing bowl. Mix on low speed for 5 minutes.
2. Combine sugar, salt, and milk. Add to flour mixture. Mix on low speed for 5 minutes.
3. Combine eggs and vanilla. Add to flour mixture. Mix for 3 to 5 minutes.
4. 72 portions: Scale batter into 4 pans (12 × 18 × 2 inch). 18 portions: Scale batter into 2 pans (13 × 9 × 2 inch).
5. Bake at 350°F for 35 to 40 minutes.
6. **Filling:**
   a. Combine cornstarch and sugar. Add cold milk, stir until smooth.
   b. Add cold mixture to hot milk. Stir constantly with wire whip. Cook over hot water until thick.
   c. Add eggs. Stir constantly, about 5 to 7 minutes.
   d. Remove from heat. Add vanilla, mix. Cool.
7. Divide filling in half, spread half on two cakes. Place other 2 cakes on top of each of the cakes.
8. **Glaze:**
   a. Melt chocolate and margarine over low heat.
   b. Add sugar, vanilla, and water. Beat until smooth.
9. Cover with glaze.
10. Cut into slices.

Directions for Diet Preparations

Sodium Restricted (SR): Use low sodium baking powder. Omit salt.

Low Fat/Low Cholesterol (LF), **Diabetic** (DB), **Soft/Low Fiber** (SLF), and **Puree** (PUR): Not recommended, substitute with appropriate food alternative.

Mechanical Soft (SFT): Prepare as directed. Consider individual tolerance.

Nutrient Analysis per Serving:

Regular	KCAL	PRO gm	CHO gm	FAT gm	Chol mg	SFA gm	PFA gm	VITA iu	VITC mg	THI mg	RIB mg	NIA mg	CA mg	NA mg	K+ mg	FE mg
	245	3.2	41.8	7.6	42.2	1.6	2.1	347	0.3	0.02	0.07	0.1	52.3	198	85.6	0.4

| Sodium Restricted | NA mg 28.3 | | **Diabetic** Not recommended | | | | | **Low Fat & Low Chol** | Not recommended | | | | | | | |

Carrot Raisin Cake

Portion: 1 slice (3″ × 2″)

INGREDIENTS	78 portions, 1 cake (18 × 26 × 2″), cut 6 × 13		18 portions, 1 cake (13 × 9 × 2″), cut 6 × 3	
	weights	measures	weights	measures
Sugar, granulated	2 3/8 lb	1 1/3 qt	9 1/2 oz	1 1/3 cups
Cooking oil	1 1/4 lb	2 1/2 cups	5 oz	2/3 cup
Eggs	1 lb	2 cups (8 large)	4 oz	1/2 cup (2 large)
Flour, all-purpose	1 3/4 lb	1 3/4 qt	7 oz	1 3/4 cups
Salt		2 tsp		1/2 tsp
Baking soda		1 1/2 Tbsp		1 1/8 tsp
Cinnamon, ground		2 Tbsp		1 1/2 tsp
Carrots, raw, grated	2 1/2 lb	2 qt	10 oz	2 cups
Raisins, seedless	13 1/3 oz	2 1/2 cups	3 1/3 oz	2/3 cup

Method

1. Combine sugar, oil, and eggs. Beat 2 minutes on medium speed.
2. Combine flour, salt, baking soda, and cinnamon. Add to sugar/oil mixture, beat 1 minute on medium speed.
3. Add carrots and raisins. Mix until blended.
4. Pour batter into pan.
5. Bake at 325°F for 40 to 45 minutes.
6. Frost with cream cheese frosting.
7. Cut into slices.

Directions for Diet Preparations

Sodium Restricted (SR): Omit salt and frosting.
Low Fat/Low Cholesterol (LF): 3″ × 2″.
78 portions: Omit cooking oil, substitute with an equal amount of reduced-calorie margarine. Omit eggs, substitute with 16 large egg whites or a commercial egg substitute as per manufacturer's directions. Omit frosting. May use if able to calculate into daily food plan.
18 portions: Omit cooking oil, substitute with an equal amount of reduced-calorie margarine. Omit eggs, substitute with 4 large egg whites or a commercial egg substitute as per manufacturer's directions. Omit frosting. May use if able to calculate into daily food plan.
Diabetic (DB): 3″ × 2″.
78 portions: Replace 2 3/8 lb granulated sugar with 1 cup granulated sugar and artificial sweetener equivalent to 4 1/4 cups granulated sugar (approximately 3 Tbsps artificial sweetener). Increase baking soda to 2 Tbsp. Omit cooking oil, substitute with an equal amount of reduced-calorie margarine. Omit frosting. May use if able to calculate into daily food plan. Consider individual tolerance when using granulated sugar.
18 portions: Replace 9 1/2 oz granulated sugar with 1/3 cup granulated sugar and artificial sweetener equivalent to 1 cup granulated sugar (approximately 4 tsp artificial sweetener). Increase baking soda to 1 1/2 tsp. Omit cooking oil, substitute with an equal amount of reduced-calorie margarine. Omit frosting. May use if able to calculate into daily food plan. Consider individual tolerance when using granulated sugar.
Mechanical Soft (SFT): Omit raisins. Consider individual tolerance.
Soft/Low Fiber (SLF) and **Puree** (PUR): Not recommended. Use appropriate food alternative.

Nutrient Analysis per Serving:

Regular	KCAL	PRO gm	CHO gm	FAT gm	Chol mg	SFA gm	PFA gm	VITA iu	VITC mg	THI mg	RIB mg	NIA mg	CA mg	NA mg	K+ mg	FE mg
	182	2.0	26.9	7.7	28.0	1.0	4.2	4112	1.5	0.09	0.06	0.7	13.0	121	100	0.8

Sodium Restricted	NA mg	Diabetic	Kcal	Milk exg	Veg exg	Fruit exg	Bread exg	Meat exg	Fat exg	Low Fat & Low Chol	FAT gm	Chol mg	SFA gm	PFA gm
	60.5		98.5	0.0	0.0	0.5	1.0	0.0	0.0		2.5	0.0	0.3	1.0

Q5   Cherry Pecan Coffeecake

Portion: 1 slice (3" × 3 1/3")

INGREDIENTS	78 portions, 1 cake (18 × 26 × 2"), cut 6 × 13		18 portions, 1 cake (13 × 9 × 2"), cut 6 × 3	
	weights	**measures**	**weights**	**measures**
Margarine, low sodium	10 oz	1 1/4 cups	2 1/2 oz	5 Tbsp
Sugar, granulated	1 1/2 lb	3 1/3 cups	6 oz	5/8 cup
Eggs	10 oz	1 1/4 cups (5 large)	3 oz	1/3 cup (2 small)
Flour, all-purpose	2 lb	2 qt	8 oz	2 cups
Baking powder	2 oz	4 2/3 Tbsp	1/2 oz	3 1/2 tsp
Salt		1 Tbsp		3/4 tsp
Cinnamon, ground		1 tsp		1/4 tsp
Milk, skim		3 1/2 cups		5/8 cup
Vanilla		1 Tbsp		3/4 tsp
Cherries, drained, unsweetened, fresh or canned	2 lb	1 1/2 qt	8 oz	1 1/2 cups
Topping:				
Sugar, granulated	12 oz	1 2/3 cups	3 oz	1/3 cup
Flour, all-purpose	4 oz	1 cup	1 oz	1/4 cup
Cinnamon, ground		1 Tbsp		3/4 tsp
Margarine, low sodium, softened	4 oz	1/2 cup	1 oz	2 Tbsp
Pecans, chopped	8 oz	2 cups	2 oz	1/2 cup

Method

1. Cream margarine and sugar on medium speed until light and fluffy.
2. Add eggs. Beat on medium speed for 5 minutes.
3. Mix dry ingredients (flour, baking powder, salt, and cinnamon).
4. Add dry ingredients alternately with milk and vanilla to creamed mixture. Mix on low speed.
5. Mix cherries carefully into batter.
6. Divide batter equally and spread into greased pans.
7. Topping: Combine sugar, flour, cinnamon, margarine, and pecans. Mix until blended. Sprinkle over batter.
8. Bake at 350°F for 40 minutes or until browned on top and toothpick inserted into center comes out clean. Let cool.
9. Cut into slices.

Directions for Diet Preparations

Sodium Restricted (SR): Use low sodium baking powder. Omit salt.

Low Fat/Low Cholesterol (LF): (3" × 3 1/3"). In Steps #1 and #7 substitute reduced-calorie margarine for margarine in equal amounts. Omit eggs, substitute with a commercial egg substitute as per manufacturer's directions. In Step #7 omit pecans.

Diabetic (DB): (3" × 3 1/3").

78 portions: In Step #1 substitute reduced-calorie margarine for margarine in equal amounts. In Step #1 omit sugar and substitute with an artificial sweetener equivalent to 1 1/2 lb granulated sugar. (Approx. 4 1/2 Tbsp artificial sweetener). Increase baking powder to 5 Tbsp. Omit topping.

18 portions: In Step #1 substitute reduced-calorie margarine for margarine in equal amounts. In Step #1 omit sugar and substitute with an artificial sweetener equivalent to 6 oz granulated sugar. (Approx. 1 Tbsp artificial sweetener). Increase baking powder to 4 tsp. Omit topping.

Mechanical Soft (SFT): Omit pecans and cherries. Consider individual tolerance.

Puree (PUR) and **Soft/Low Fiber** (SLF): Not recommended. Provide appropriate food substitute.

Nutrient Analysis per Serving:

Regular	KCAL	PRO gm	CHO gm	FAT gm	Chol mg	SFA gm	PFA gm	VITA iu	VITC mg	THI mg	RIB mg	NIA mg	CA mg	NA mg	K+ mg	FE mg
	273	4.0	42.1	10.3	28.7	1.5	3.1	373	0.7	0.16	0.14	1.3	60.2	286	104	1.3

Sodium Restricted	NA mg	Diabetic	Kcal	Milk exg	Veg exg	Fruit exg	Bread exg	Meat exg	Fat exg	Low Fat & Low Chol	FAT gm	Chol mg	SFA gm	PFA gm
	19.7		118	0.0	0.0	0.5	1.0	0.0	0.4		3.8	0.4	0.6	1.3

Portion: 1 slice (3" × 2")

INGREDIENTS	78 portions, 1 cake (18 × 26 × 2"), cut 6 × 13		18 portions, 1 cake (13 × 9 × 2"), cut 6 × 3	
	weights	measures	weights	measures
Flour, cake	2 1/4 lb	2 1/8 qt	9 oz	2 1/8 cups
Baking powder		3 1/2 Tbsp		2 1/2 tsp
Margarine, low sodium	1 1/8 lb	2 1/4 cups	4 1/2 oz	1/2 cup
Sugar, granulated	2 1/4 lb	1 1/4 qt	9 oz	1 1/4 cups
Milk, skim		3 1/3 cups		3/4 cup
Egg white	13 oz	1 2/3 cups (12 large)	3 1/4 oz	3/8 cup (3 large)
Vanilla		1 Tbsp		3/4 tsp
Chocolate chip	12 oz	2 cups	3 oz	1/2 cup

Method

1. Combine flour, baking powder, and margarine. Mix on low speed for 5 minutes.
2. Combine sugar and milk. Add to flour mixture. Mix on low speed for 5 minutes.
3. Combine egg whites and vanilla. Mix on low for 4 minutes.
4. Add chocolate chips to batter. Mix to blend.
5. Pour batter into pan.
6. Bake at 350°F for 35 to 40 minutes.
7. Cool.
8. Cut into slices.

Directions for Diet Preparations

Sodium Restricted (SR): Use low sodium baking powder as per manufacturer's directions.

Low Fat/Low Cholesterol (LF): 2" × 2". Omit margarine, substitute with reduced-calorie margarine in equal amount specified for regular margarine. May use if able to calculate into daily food plan.

Diabetic (DB): 2" × 2" slice.

78 portions: Increase baking powder to 4 Tbsp. Omit margarine, substitute with reduced-calorie margarine in equal amount specified for regular margarine. Replace 2 1/4 lb granulated sugar with 1 cup granulated sugar and artificial sweetener equivalent to 4 cups granulated sugar (approximately 5 Tbsp artificial sweetener). May use if able to calculate into daily food plan. Consider individual tolerance when using granulated sugar.

18 portions: Increase baking powder to 1 Tbsp. Omit margarine, substitute with reduced-calorie margarine in equal amount specified for regular margarine. Replace 9 oz granulated sugar with 1/4 cup granulated sugar and artificial sweetener equivalent to 1 cup granulated sugar (approximately 4 tsp artificial sweetener). May use if able to calculate into daily food plan. Consider individual tolerance when using granulated sugar.

Mechanical Soft (SFT): Prepare as directed. Consider individual tolerance.

Soft/Low Fiber (SLF) and **Puree** (PUR): Not recommended. Use appropriate food alternative.

Nutrient Analysis per Serving:

Regular	KCAL	PRO gm	CHO gm	FAT gm	Chol mg	SFA gm	PFA gm	VITA iu	VITC mg	THI mg	RIB mg	NIA mg	CA mg	NA mg	K+ mg	FE mg
	174	2.1	26.7	7.0	0.2	1.8	1.7	241	0.1	0.01	0.04	0.1	24.1	102	53.7	0.2

Sodium Restricted	NA mg	Diabetic	Kcal	Milk exg	Veg exg	Fruit exg	Bread exg	Meat exg	Fat exg	Low Fat & Low Chol	FAT gm	Chol mg	SFA gm	PFA gm
	15.4		75.0	0.0	0.0	0.0	1.0	0.0	0.0		2.9	0.1	0.9	0.6

Portion: 1 slice (3" × 2")

INGREDIENTS	78 portions, 1 cake (18 × 26 × 2"), cut 6 × 13		18 portions, 1 cake (13 × 9 × 2"), cut 6 × 3	
	weights	measures	weights	measures
Water, boiling		2 1/4 cups		1/2 cup
Chocolate, unsweetened, melted	8 oz	1 cup	2 oz	1/4 cup
Margarine, low sodium	12 oz	1 1/4 cups	3 oz	1/3 cup
Sugar, granulated	2 lb	4 1/2 cups	8 oz	1 1/8 cups
Vanilla		1 Tbsp		3/4 tsp
Eggs	18 oz	2 1/4 cups (9 large)	4 oz	1/2 cup (2 large)
Flour, cake	1 3/4 lb	6 1/2 cups	7 oz	1 2/3 cups
Baking soda		2 tsp		1/2 tsp
Baking powder		1 Tbsp		3/4 tsp
Buttermilk, skim		2 cups		1/2 cup
Chocolate frosting		1 1/4 qt		1 1/4 cups

Method

1. Add boiling water to melted chocolate. Mix well. Bring to a boil, while stirring. Cool.
2. Cream margarine and sugar on high speed until light and fluffy.
3. Add chocolate to creamed mixture. Mix.
4. Add eggs and vanilla to creamed mixture. Mix well on high speed.
5. Sift together flour, soda, and baking powder.
6. Add dry ingredients alternately with buttermilk into creamed mixture. Mix on low speed to combine.
7. Pour batter into greased or non-stick pan.
8. Bake at 325°F for 40 to 45 minutes or until done. Cool.
9. Cut into slices.
10. When cake is cooled, frost with chocolate frosting.

Directions for Diet Preparations

Sodium Restricted (SR): Use low sodium baking powder as per manufacturer's directions. May use if able to calculate into daily food plan.

Low Fat/Low Cholesterol (LF): 3" × 2". Omit margarine, substitute with reduced-calorie margarine in equal amount specified for regular margarine. Omit eggs, substitute with commercial egg substitute as per manufacturer's directions. Omit frosting. May use if able to calculate into daily food plan.

Diabetic (DB): 3" × 2".

78 portions: Omit margarine, substitute with reduced-calorie margarine in equal amount specified for regular margarine. Replace 4 1/2 cups granulated sugar with 1 cup granulated sugar and artificial sweetener equivalent to 3 1/2 cups granulated sugar (approximately 4 Tbsp artificial sweetener). Increase baking powder to 1 1/2 Tbsp. Omit frosting. May use if able to calculate into daily food plan. Consider individual tolerance when using granulated sugar.

18 portions: Omit margarine, substitute with reduced-calorie margarine in equal amount specified for regular margarine. Replace 8 oz granulated sugar with 1/4 cup granulated sugar and artificial sweetener equivalent to 3/4 cup granulated sugar (approximately 1 Tbsp artificial sweetener). Increase baking powder to 1 1/4 tsp. Omit frosting. May use if able to calculate into daily food plan. Consider individual tolerance when using granulated sugar.

Mechanical Soft (SFT): Prepare as directed. Consider individual tolerance.

Puree (PUR) and **Soft/Low Fiber** (SLF): Not recommended. Use appropriate food alternative.

Nutrient Analysis per Serving:

Regular	KCAL	PRO gm	CHO gm	FAT gm	Chol mg	SFA gm	PFA gm	VITA iu	VITC mg	THI mg	RIB mg	NIA mg	CA mg	NA mg	K+ mg	FE mg
	206	2.2	35.6	6.8	31.7	1.3	1.9	274	0.1	0.01	0.04	0.14	21.3	66.1	69.6	0.6

Sodium Restricted	NA mg	Diabetic	Kcal	Milk exg	Veg exg	Fruit exg	Bread exg	Meat exg	Fat exg	Low Fat & Low Chol		FAT gm	Chol mg	SFA gm	PFA gm
	40.4		77.5	0.0	0.0	0.0	1.1	0.0	0.0			3.5	0.3	0.7	1.1

Portion: 1 slice (3" × 2")

INGREDIENTS	78 portions, 1 cake (18 × 26 × 2"), cut 6 × 13		18 portions, 1 cake (13 × 9 × 2"), cut 6 × 3	
	weights	measures	weights	measures
Flour, cake	2 1/3 lb	2 1/8 qt	9 1/4 oz	2 1/8 cups
Baking powder		3 3/4 Tbsp		2 3/4 tsp
Margarine, low sodium	1 lb	2 cups	4 oz	1/2 cup
Sugar, granulated	2 3/4 lb	1 1/2 qt	11 oz	1 1/2 cups
Salt		2 tsp		1/2 tsp
Milk, skim or water		4 1/2 cups		1 1/8 cups
Eggs	1 lb	2 cups (8 large)	4 oz	1/2 cup (2 large)
Vanilla		4 tsp		1 tsp
Cocoa		3 Tbsp		2 1/4 tsp
Cinnamon, ground		1 Tbsp		3/4 tsp
Nutmeg		1 tsp		1/4 tsp

Method

1. Cream flour, baking powder, and margarine. Mix on low high speed for 5 minutes.
2. Combine sugar, salt, and milk (or water). Add to flour mixture. Mix on low speed for 5 minutes.
3. Combine eggs and vanilla. Add to flour mixture. Mix for 3 minutes.
4. Divide batter into 2 portions. To batter #1 add cocoa, cinnamon, and nutmeg.
5. Pour batter #2 into pan. Pour batter #1 over batter #2. Swirl with a knife.
6. Bake at 350°F for 35 to 40 minutes. Cool.
7. Cut into slices.

Directions for Diet Preparations

Sodium Restricted (SR): Omit salt. Use low sodium baking powder as per manufacturer's directions. May use if able to calculate into daily food plan.

Low Fat/Low Cholesterol (LF): 3" × 2". Omit margarine, substitute with reduced-calorie margarine in equal amount specified for regular margarine. Omit eggs, substitute with a commercial egg substitute as per manufacturer's directions. May use if able to calculate into daily food plan.

Diabetic (DB): 3" × 2".

78 portions: Increase baking powder to 4 Tbsp. Omit margarine, substitute with reduced-calorie margarine in equal amount specified for regular margarine. Replace 2 3/4 lb granulated sugar with 1 1/2 cups granulated sugar and artificial sweetener equivalent to 4 1/2 cups granulated sugar (approximately 5 Tbsp artificial sweetener). May use if able to calculate into daily food plan. Consider individual tolerance when using granulated sugar.

18 portions: Increase baking powder to 1 Tbsp. Omit margarine, substitute with reduced-calorie margarine in equal amount specified for regular margarine. Replace 11 oz granulated sugar with 1/3 cup granulated sugar and artificial sweetener equivalent to 1 cup granulated sugar (approximately 1 Tbsp artificial sweetener). May use if able to calculate into daily food plan. Consider individual tolerance when using granulated sugar.

Mechanical Soft (SFT): Prepare as directed. Consider individual tolerance.

Soft/Low Fiber (SLF) and **Puree** (PUR): Not recommended. Use appropriate food alternative.

Nutrient Analysis per Serving:

Regular	KCAL	PRO gm	CHO gm	FAT gm	Chol mg	SFA gm	PFA gm	VITA iu	VITC mg	THI mg	RIB mg	NIA mg	CA mg	NA mg	K+ mg	FE mg
	158	2.2	25.4	5.5	28.2	1.0	1.6	251	0.2	0.01	0.04	0.12	32.8	180	54.6	0.3

Sodium Restricted	NA mg	Diabetic	Kcal	Milk exg	Veg exg	Fruit exg	Bread exg	Meat exg	Fat exg	Low Fat & Low Chol		FAT gm	Chol mg	SFA gm	PFA gm
	16.5		102	0.0	0.0	0.5	1.0	0.0	0.0			2.7	0.3	0.4	1.0

Portion: 1 slice; 3/4-inch (12 slices per loaf)

INGREDIENTS	48 portions, 4 loaves (9 × 5″)		12 portions, 1 loaf (9 × 5″)	
	weights	measures	weights	measures
Flour, cake, sifted	1 2/3 lb	1 1/2 qt	6 1/2 oz	1 1/2 cups
Sugar, granulated	2 lb	1 1/8 qt	8 oz	1 1/8 cups
Salt		2 tsp		1/2 tsp
Baking powder		1/2 tsp		1/8 tsp
Eggs	1 1/4 lb	2 1/2 cups (10 large)	5 3/8 oz	2/3 cup (3 medium)
Margarine, low sodium	1 1/8 lb	2 1/8 cups	4 1/2 oz	9 Tbsp
Milk, skim		1 3/4 cups		7 Tbsp
Vanilla		2 tsp		1/2 tsp

Method

1. Combine dry ingredients in mixer bowl. Blend on low speed for 1 minute, using flat beater.
2. Add eggs to dry ingredients. Blend until ingredients are evenly mixed.
3. Add margarine and 1/2 the milk to mixture. Cream on medium speed for about 5 minutes, until light.
4. Add remaining milk and vanilla slowly. Mix on low speed for 2 to 3 minutes or just until blended.
5. Scale batter into greased loaf pan(s).
6. Bake at 325°F for 1 1/4 hours or until done.
7. Cool.
8. Slice each loaf into 12 slices (3/4-inch slice).

Directions for Diet Preparations

Sodium Restricted (SR): Omit salt. Use low sodium baking powder as per manufacturer's directions.

Low Fat/Low Cholesterol (LF): 1/2-inch slice. Omit eggs, substitute with a commercial egg substitute as per manufacturer's directions. Omit margarine, substitute with reduced-calorie margarine in equal amount specified for regular margarine. May use if able to calculate into daily food plan.

Diabetic (DB): 1/2-inch slice.

48 portions: Replace 2 lb granulated sugar with 1 cup granulated sugar and artificial sweetener equivalent to 3 1/2 cups granulated sugar (approximately 4 1/2 Tbsp artificial sweetener). Omit margarine, substitute with reduced-calorie margarine in equal amount specified for regular margarine. May use if able to calculate into daily food plan. Consider individual tolerance when using granulated sugar.

12 portions: Replace 8 oz granulated sugar with 1/4 cup granulated sugar and artificial sweetener equivalent to 3/4 cup granulated sugar (approximately 1 Tbsp artificial sweetener). Omit margarine, substitute with reduced-calorie margarine in equal amount specified for regular margarine. May use if able to calculate into daily food plan. Consider individual tolerance when using granulated sugar.

Mechanical Soft (SFT) and **Soft/Low Fiber** (SLF): Prepare as directed.

Puree (PUR): Not recommended. Use appropriate food alternative.

Nutrient Analysis per Serving:

Regular	KCAL	PRO gm	CHO gm	FAT gm	Chol mg	SFA gm	PFA gm	VITA iu	VITC mg	THI mg	RIB mg	NIA mg	CA mg	NA mg	K+ mg	FE mg
	224	2.7	31.6	9.8	57.1	1.7	3.0	422	0.09	0.02	0.05	0.1	22.0	127	46.3	0.3

Sodium Restricted	NA mg	Diabetic	Kcal	Milk exg	Veg exg	Fruit exg	Bread exg	Meat exg	Fat exg	Low Fat & Low Chol	FAT gm	Chol mg	SFA gm	PFA gm
	22.0		88.0	0.0	0.0	0.2	1.0	0.0	0.0		3.0	0.1	0.5	1.2

Portion: 1 slice (2-inch shortcake, 1/4 cup strawberries)

INGREDIENTS	50 portions		12 portions	
	weights	measures	weights	measures
Flour, all-purpose	2 1/2 lb	2 1/2 qt	10 oz	2 1/2 cups
Baking powder	2 oz	4 2/3 Tbsp	1/2 oz	3 1/2 tsp
Sugar, granulated	7 oz	1 cup	1 3/4 oz	1/4 cup
Margarine, low sodium	1 lb	2 cups	4 oz	1/2 cup
Milk, skim		2 1/2 cups		2/3 cup
Eggs, beaten	4 oz	1/2 cup (2 large)	1 1/2 oz	3 Tbsp (1 small)
Strawberries, fresh, sliced or mashed	5 2/3 lb EP (6 1/2 lb AP)	4 1/4 qt	1 3/8 lb EP (1 2/3 lb AP)	4 1/4 cups
Sugar, granulated		to taste		to taste
Whipped topping		1 qt		1 cup

Method

1. Mix flour, baking powder, and sugar.
2. Cut margarine into dry ingredients.
3. Combine milk and eggs. Stir into dry ingredients to form soft dough.
4. Knead dough 10 times on lightly floured board.
5. Roll 3/4-inch thick. Cut with 2-inch cutter. Place on ungreased baking sheet.
6. Bake at 425°F for 15 minutes.
7. Split cakes and serve 1/4 cup strawberries between layers and on top. Sprinkle with sugar.
8. Serve with 1 Tbsp whipped topping.

Directions for Diet Preparations

Sodium Restricted (SR): Use low sodium baking powder as per manufacturer's directions.
Low Fat/Low Cholesterol (LF): 2-inch shortcake, 1/4 cup strawberries. Omit margarine, substitute with reduced-calorie margarine in equal amount specified for regular margarine. Omit eggs, substitute with a commercial egg substitute as per manufacturer's directions. May use if able to calculate into daily food plan.
Diabetic (DB): 2-inch shortcake.

50 portions: Increase baking powder to 5 Tbsp. Replace 1 cup granulated sugar with 2 Tbsp granulated sugar and artificial sweetener equivalent to 3/4 cup granulated sugar (approximately 1 Tbsp artificial sweetener). Omit margarine, substitute with reduced-calorie margarine in equal amount specified for regular margarine. In step #7 do not sprinkle with granulated sugar, substitute with artificial sweetener to taste. Serve with 1 Tbsp whipped topping. May use if able to calculate into daily food plan. Consider individual tolerance when using granulated sugar.

12 portions: Increase baking powder to 4 tsp. Replace 1/4 cup granulated sugar with 1 1/2 tsp granulated sugar and artificial sweetener equivalent to 3 Tbsp granulated sugar (approximately 3/4 tsp artificial sweetener). Omit margarine, substitute with reduced-calorie margarine in equal amount specified for regular margarine. In step #7 do not sprinkle with granulated sugar, substitute with artificial sweetener to taste. Serve with 1 Tbsp whipped topping. May use if able to calculate into daily food plan. Consider individual tolerance when using granulated sugar.

Mechanical Soft (SFT): Prepare as directed. Consider individual tolerance when using strawberries.
Soft/Low Fiber (SLF) and **Puree** (PUR): Not recommended. Use appropriate food alternative.

Nutrient Analysis per Serving:

Regular	KCAL	PRO gm	CHO gm	FAT gm	Chol mg	SFA gm	PFA gm	VITA iu	VITC mg	THI mg	RIB mg	NIA mg	CA mg	NA mg	K+ mg	FE mg
	200	3.4	26.7	9.0	7.5	2.3	2.7	385	27.5	0.2	0.1	1.3	40.3	194	128	1.2

Sodium Restricted	NA mg	Diabetic	Kcal	Milk exg	Veg exg	Fruit exg	Bread exg	Meat exg	Fat exg	Low Fat & Low Chol	FAT gm	Chol mg	SFA gm	PFA gm
	12.9		154	0.0	0.0	0.6	1.0	0.0	1.0		5.4	7.5	1.7	1.5

Portion: 1 slice

INGREDIENTS	50 portions, 1 cake (18 × 26 × 2″), cut 5 × 10		12 portions, 1 cake (13 × 9 × 2″), cut 4 × 3	
	weights	measures	weights	measures
Eggs, separated	1 1/2 lb	3 cups (12 large)	6 oz	3/4 cup (3 large)
Sugar, granulated	14 oz	2 cups	3 1/2 oz	1/2 cup
Lemon rind, grated		1 lemon		1/4 lemon
Lemon juice		1 Tbsp		3/4 tsp
Water, cold		1/4 cup		1 Tbsp
Matzo cake flour		1 cup		1/4 cup
Potato starch		1 cup		1/4 cup

Method

1. Beat yolks with sugar until thick and creamy.
2. Add lemon rind, lemon juice, and water to yolks.
3. Add matzo cake flour and potato flour to mixture. Stir.
4. Beat egg whites until stiff. Fold lightly into batter.
5. Pour batter into greased or non-stick pans. (Bake cake on double pans to prevent excessive bottom heat from scorching the bottom.)
6. Bake at 325°F for 50 minutes to 1 hour or until edges are crisp and a toothpick inserted in the center comes out dry.
7. Turn out on rack to cool.
8. 50 portions: Cut 5 × 10 (3 1/2″ × 2 1/2″).
   12 portions: Cut 4 × 3 (3 1/4″ × 3″).

Directions for Diet Preparations

Sodium Restricted (SR), **Mechanical Soft** (SFT), and **Soft/Low Fiber** (SLF): Prepare as directed.

Low Fat/Low Cholesterol (LF): 3 1/2″ × 2 1/2″.

50 portions: Omit eggs, substitute with 24 egg whites.

12 portions: Omit eggs, substitute with 6 egg whites.

Diabetic (DB): 3 1/2″ × 2 1/2″.

50 portions: Omit sugar, substitute with artificial sweetener equivalent to 1 cup granulated sugar (approximately 4 tsp) and 1 cup unsweetened applesauce.

12 portions: Omit sugar, substitute with artificial sweetener equivalent to 1/4 cup granulated sugar (approximately 1 tsp) and 1/4 cup unsweetened applesauce.

Puree (PUR): Not recommended. Use appropriate food alternative.

Nutrient Analysis per Serving:

Regular	KCAL	PRO gm	CHO gm	FAT gm	Chol mg	SFA gm	PFA gm	VITA iu	VITC mg	THI mg	RIB mg	NIA mg	CA mg	NA mg	K+ mg	FE mg
	73.9	2.0	13.4	1.4	65.6	0.4	0.2	62.4	0.1	0.01	0.04	0.01	6.8	18.1	76.5	0.3

Sodium Restricted	NA mg	Diabetic	Kcal	Milk exg	Veg exg	Fruit exg	Bread exg	Meat exg	Fat exg	Low Fat & Low Chol	FAT gm	Chol mg	SFA gm	PFA gm
	18.1		45.7	0.0	0.0	0.0	0.6	0.0	0.0		0.05	0.0	0.0	0.0

Portion: 2 cookies

INGREDIENTS	60 portions		15 portions	
	weights	**measures**	**weights**	**measures**
Flour, whole wheat	2 1/8 lb	2 qt	8 1/2 oz	2 cups
Baking powder, low sodium	1 1/8 oz	2 1/2 Tbsp	1/3 oz	2 tsp
Sea salt		1 tsp		1/4 tsp
Margarine, low sodium	1 lb	2 cups	4 oz	1/2 cup
Almonds, blanched, chopped, unsalted	9 1/8 oz	2 cups	2 1/3 oz	1/2 cup
Maple syrup	1 lb	2 cups	4 oz	1/2 cup
Egg	8 oz	1 cup (4 large)	2 oz	1/4 cup (1 large)
Almond extract		4 tsp		1 tsp
Vanilla extract		4 tsp		1 tsp
Almonds, blanched, unsalted	6 oz	1 cup (120 medium)	1 1/2 oz	1/4 cup (30 medium)

Method

1. Sift the flour, baking powder, and salt together.
2. In a saucepan, melt the margarine; stir in the chopped almonds, maple syrup, egg, almond extract, vanilla extract. Add to the dry ingredients, a little at a time, and mix well.
3. Roll into 1-inch balls and place on oiled cookie sheets.
4. Gently press a blanched almond into the center of each ball.
5. Bake at 350°F for about 20 minutes or until light golden brown; cool and serve.

Directions for Diet Preparations

Sodium Restricted (SR): Omit salt.
Low Fat/Low Cholesterol (LF), **Diabetic** (DB), **Mechanical Soft** (SFT), **Soft/Low Fiber** (SLF), and **Puree** (PUR): Not recommended. Provide appropriate food substitute.

Nutrient Analysis per Serving:

Regular	KCAL	PRO gm	CHO gm	FAT gm	Chol mg	SFA gm	PFA gm	VITA iu	VITC mg	THI mg	RIB mg	NIA mg	CA mg	NA mg	K+ mg	FE mg
	186	4.1	20.3	10.6	14.1	1.5	3.0	274	0.05	0.10	0.11	1.2	60.0	48.3	163	1.1

Sodium Restricted	NA mg 8.9	**Diabetic:** Not recommended		Low Fat & Low Chol	Not recommended

Apricot Strips

Portion: 1 slice (3 × 2")

Ingredients	78 portions, 1 pan (18 × 26 × 2"), cut 6 × 13		18 portions, 1 pan (13 × 9 × 2"), cut 6 × 3	
	weights	measures	weights	measures
Apricots, dried, chopped, 1/4-inch pieces	2 lb	1 1/2 qt	8 oz	1 1/2 cups
Sugar, granulated	1 1/4 lb	2 3/4 cups	5 oz	2/3 cup
Water	2 lb	1 qt	8 oz	1 cup
Lemon juice	2 oz	1/4 cup	1/2 oz	1 Tbsp
Quick oats	1 3/4 lb	2 2/3 qt	7 oz	2 2/3 cups
Flour, all-purpose	1 lb	1 qt	4 oz	1 cup
Sugar, brown	2 1/2 lb	1 1/4 qt	10 oz	1 1/4 cups
Margarine, low sodium	1 3/4 lb	3 1/2 cups	7 oz	5/8 cup

Method

1. Combine apricots, sugar, and water. Bring to a boil. Cook over low heat, stirring constantly until thick, about 10 minutes. Stir in lemon juice. Cool.
2. Combine oats, flour, and brown sugar. Mix well.
3. Cut margarine into oats mixture. Mixture should be crumbly in appearance.
4. Sprinkle half of oats/margarine mixture on greased sheet pan. Pat down with rolling pin.
5. Spread apricot mixture over crumbs.
6. Top apricot mixture with remaining crumb mixture. (Do not pat down).
7. Bake at 375°F for 30 minutes or until browned.
8. Cut into slices.

Directions for Diet Preparations

Sodium Restricted (SR): Prepare as directed.
Low Fat/Low Cholesterol (LF): 2" × 2". Omit margarine, substitute with reduced-calorie margarine in equal amount specified for regular margarine. Omit step numbers 4 to 6. Fold apricot mixture into batter. Continue with step number 7. May use if able to calculate into daily food plan.

Diabetic(DB): 2" × 2".
78 portions: Omit granulated sugar, substitute with artificial sweetener equivalent to 2 cups granulated sugar (approximately 2 Tbsp artificial sweetener). Omit brown sugar, substitute with 3 1/2 cups unsweetened applesauce and artificial sweetener equivalent to 1 1/2 cups granulated sugar (approximately 1 1/2 Tbsp artificial sweetener). Omit margarine, substitute with reduced-calorie margarine in equal amount specified for regular margarine. Omit step numbers 4 to 6. Fold apricot mixture into batter. Continue with step 7. May use if able to calculate into daily food plan.
18 portions: Omit granulated sugar, substitute with artificial sweetener equivalent to 1/2 cup granulated sugar (approximately 1 1/2 tsp artificial sweetener). Omit brown sugar, substitute with 3/4 cup unsweetened applesauce and artificial sweetener equivalent to 1/3 cup granulated sugar (approximately 1 1/8 tsp artificial sweetener). Omit margarine, substitute with reduced-calorie margarine in equal amount specified for regular margarine. Omit step numbers 4 to 6. Fold apricot mixture into batter. Continue with step 7. May use if able to calculate into daily food plan.
Mechanical Soft (SFT), **Soft/Low Fiber** (SLF), and **Puree** (PUR): Not recommended. Use appropriate food alternative.

Nutrient Analysis per Serving:

Regular	KCAL	PRO gm	CHO gm	FAT gm	Chol mg	SFA gm	PFA gm	VITA iu	VITC mg	THI mg	RIB mg	NIA mg	CA mg	NA mg	K+ mg	FE mg
	231	2.3	37.8	8.8	0.0	1.5	2.9	1818	1.4	0.08	0.04	0.5	27.5	9.1	305	1.6

Sodium Restricted	NA mg	Diabetic	Kcal	Milk exg	Veg exg	Fruit exg	Bread exg	Meat exg	Fat exg	Low Fat & Low Chol	FAT gm	Chol mg	SFA gm	PFA gm
	9.1		78.6	0.0	0.0	0.5	0.7	0.0	0.0		3.1	0.0	0.5	1.1

Portion: 1 cookie (2 1/2-inch cookie)

INGREDIENTS	60 portions		15 portions	
	weights	**measures**	**weights**	**measures**
Margarine, low sodium	1 lb	2 cups	4 oz	1/2 cup
Sugar, granulated	7 oz	1 cup	1 3/4 oz	1/4 cup
Sugar, brown, packed firm	8 oz	1 cup	2 oz	1/4 cup
Eggs	8 oz	1 cup (4 large)	2 oz	1/4 cup (1 large)
Vanilla		1 Tbsp		3/4 tsp
Flour, all-purpose	17 oz	4 1/4 cups	4 1/4 oz	1 1/8 cups
Baking soda		2 tsp		1/2 tsp
Salt		1/2 tsp		1/8 tsp
Chocolate chips, semisweet	12 oz	2 cups	3 oz	1/3 cup

Method

1. Combine margarine and sugars in mixer bowl. Mix at medium speed until light and fluffy.
2. Add eggs and vanilla to creamed mixture. Blend on medium speed for 2 minutes.
3. Combine flour, baking soda, and salt. Add to creamed mixture. Mix until blended.
4. Add chocolate chips to dough. Mix only until chips are mixed into dough.
5. Using a No. 40 dipper, drop dough onto lightly greased or non-stick sheet pans.
6. Bake at 350°F for about 12 to 15 minutes or until cookies are lightly browned.
7. Remove cookies to wire racks to cool.

Directions for Diet Preparations

Sodium Restricted (SR): Omit salt.
Low Fat/Low Cholesterol (LF): 1 cookie.
60 cookies: Substitute reduced-calorie margarine for margarine in equal amounts. Omit eggs, replace with 1 cup liquid egg substitute. Omit chocolate chips, substitute with 2 cups raisins. Drop by spoonful onto a non-stick baking sheet.
15 cookies: Substitute reduced-calorie margarine for margarine in equal amounts. Omit eggs, replace with 1/4 cup liquid egg substitute. Omit chocolate chips, substitute with 1/2 cup raisins. Drop by spoonful onto a non-stick baking sheet.

Diabetic (DB): 1 cookie.
60 cookies: Substitute reduced-calorie margarine for margarine in equal amounts. Replace 1 cup granulated sugar and 1 cup brown sugar with 1/4 cup granulated sugar and artificial sweetener equivalent to 3/4 cup granulated sugar (approx. 1 Tbsp). Omit chocolate chips, substitute with 2 cups raisins. Drop by spoonful onto a non-stick baking sheet. Consider individual tolerance when using granulated sugar.
15 cookies: Substitute reduced-calorie margarine for margarine in equal amounts. Replace 1/4 cup granulated sugar and 1/4 cup brown sugar with 1 Tbsp granulated sugar and artificial sweetener equivalent to 3 Tbsp granulated sugar (approx. 3/4 tsp). Omit chocolate chips, substitute with 1/2 cup raisins. Drop by spoonful onto a non-stick baking sheet. Consider individual tolerance when using granulated sugar.

Mechanical Soft (SFT): Prepare as directed. Consider individual tolerance.
Soft/Low Fiber (SLF) and **Puree** (PUR): Not recommended, substitute with appropriate food alternative.

Nutrient Analysis per Serving:

Regular	KCAL	PRO gm	CHO gm	FAT gm	Chol mg	SFA gm	PFA gm	VITA iu	VITC mg	THI mg	RIB mg	NIA mg	CA mg	NA mg	K+ mg	FE mg
	145	1.5	16.6	8.5	15.1	2.2	2.0	269	0.01	0.05	0.04	0.4	9.7	54.4	45.5	0.7

Sodium Restricted	NA mg	Diabetic	Kcal	Milk exg	Veg exg	Fruit exg	Bread exg	Meat exg	Fat exg	Low Fat & Low Chol	FAT gm	Chol mg	SFA gm	PFA gm
	34.6		83.1	0.0	0.0	0.5	0.5	0.0	0.5		3.2	0.04	0.6	1.2

Portion: 1 serving (3 × 2")

INGREDIENTS	78 portions, 1 pan (18 × 26 × 2"), cut 6 × 13		18 portions, 1 cake (13 × 9 × 2") cut 6 × 3	
	weights	measures	weights	measures
Quick oats	2 1/4 lb	3 1/3 qt	9 oz	3 1/3 cups
Flour, all-purpose	1 1/4 lb	1 1/4 qt	5 oz	1 1/4 cups
Sugar #1, brown, solid packed	3 1/4 lb	6 1/2 cups	13 oz	1 2/3 cups
Margarine, low sodium	2 lb	1 qt	8 oz	1 cup
Dates, chopped	1 3/4 lb	4 1/3 cups	7 oz	1 1/8 cups
Water		1 qt		1 cup
Sugar #2, brown, solid packed	1 1/4 lb	2 1/2 cups	5 oz	2/3 cup

Method

1. Combine oats, flour, and brown sugar #1. Mix thoroughly.
2. Cut margarine into oats mixture. Mixture should be crumbly.
3. Spread oats/margarine mixture into greased or nonstick pan.
4. Combine dates, water, and brown sugar #2. Bring to a boil. Simmer 25 minutes or until soft and thick. Spread evenly over crumb mixture.
5. Bake at 375°F until browned, about 45 minutes.
6. Let cool.
7. Cut into individual servings.

Directions for Diet Preparations

Sodium Restricted (SR): Prepare as directed.
Low Fat/Low Cholesterol (LF): 2" × 2". Replace margarine with reduced-calorie margarine in equal amount specified for regular margarine. May use if able to calculate into daily food plan.
Diabetic (DB), **Mechanical Soft** (SFT), **Soft/Low Fiber** (SLF), and **Puree** (PUR): Not recommended. Use appropriate food alternative.

Nutrient Analysis per Serving:

Regular	KCAL	PRO gm	CHO gm	FAT gm	Chol mg	SFA gm	PFA gm	VITA iu	VITC mg	THI mg	RIB mg	NIA mg	CA mg	NA mg	K+ mg	FE mg
	289	3.3	47.3	10.4	0.0	1.7	3.5	409	0.01	0.16	0.07	0.7	36.5	11.8	215	1.9

Sodium Restricted	NA mg 11.8	Diabetic	Not Recommended							Low Fat & Low Chol			FAT gm 3.7	Chol mg 0.0	SFA gm 0.6	PFA gm 1.5

Portion: 1 cookie

INGREDIENTS	72 portions		18 portions	
	weights	**measures**	**weights**	**measures**
Margarine, low sodium, melted	8 oz	1 cup	2 oz	1/4 cup
Sugar, brown, light, packed firm	8 oz	1 cup	2 oz	1/4 cup
Egg	4 oz	1/2 cup (2 large)	1 1/2 oz	3 Tbsp (1 small)
Flour, whole wheat	10 2/3 oz	2 1/2 cups	2 2/3 oz	2/3 cup
Baking powder		1 tsp		1/4 tsp
Cinnamon, ground		2 tsp		1/2 tsp
Cloves, ground		1/2 tsp		1/8 tsp
Nutmeg, ground		1/2 tsp		1/8 tsp
Milk, skim	4 oz	1/2 cup	1 oz	2 Tbsp
Pecans, chopped	4 oz	1 cup	1 oz	1/4 cup
Raisins, seedless	6 oz	1 cup	1 1/2 oz	1/4 cup
Apricots, dried, chopped	5 1/3 oz	1 cup	1 1/3 oz	1/4 cup
Dates, chopped	5 1/3 oz	1 cup	1 1/3 oz	1/4 cup

Method

1. Cream margarine and sugar. Add eggs.
2. Combine dry ingredients (flour, baking powder, cinnamon, cloves, and nutmeg). Add dry ingredients alternately with milk to creamed mixture. Mix on low speed.
3. Mix pecans, raisins, apricots, and dates carefully into batter.
4. Drop by spoonful onto a lightly greased baking sheet.
5. Bake at 350°F for about 10 minutes.
6. Cool on wire rack and store in closed containers.

Directions for Diet Preparations

Sodium Restricted (SR): Prepare as directed.
Low Fat/Low Cholesterol (LF): 1 cookie.
72 cookies: Substitute reduced-calorie margarine for margarine in equal amounts. Omit eggs, substitute with 4 large egg whites. Omit pecans. Use a non-stick spray to coat baking sheet.

18 cookies: Substitute reduced-calorie margarine for margarine in equal amounts. Omit eggs, substitute with 2 small egg whites. Omit pecans. Use a non-stick spray to coat baking sheet.
Diabetic (DB): 1 cookie.
72 cookies: Substitute reduced-calorie margarine for margarine in equal amounts. Use 1/4 cup brown sugar. Use an artificial sweetener equivalent to 3/4 cup granulated sugar (approx. 3 tsp). Omit pecans. Use a non-stick spray to coat baking sheet. Consider individual tolerance when using brown sugar.
18 cookies: Substitute reduced-calorie margarine for margarine in equal amounts. Use 1 Tbsp brown sugar. Use an artificial sweetener equivalent to 3 Tbsp granulated sugar (approx. 3/4 tsp). Omit pecans. Use a non-stick spray to coat baking sheet. Consider individual tolerance when using brown sugar.
Mechanical Soft (SFT), **Soft/Low Fiber** (SLF), **Puree** (PUR): Not recommended. Use appropriate food alternative.

Nutrient Analysis per Serving:

Regular	KCAL	PRO gm	CHO gm	FAT gm	Chol mg	SFA gm	PFA gm	VITA iu	VITC mg	THI mg	RIB mg	NIA mg	CA mg	NA mg	K+ mg	FE mg
	80.7	1.0	11.4	3.8	7.6	0.6	1.1	329	0.31	0.02	0.02	0.19	12.3	11.6	88.7	0.4

Sodium Restricted	NA mg	Diabetic	Kcal	Milk exg	Veg exg	Fruit exg	Bread exg	Meat exg	Fat exg	Low Fat & Low Chol	FAT gm	Chol mg	SFA gm	PFA gm
	11.6		50.9	0.0	0.0	0.25	0.5	0.0	0.0		1.4	0.04	0.2	0.5

Oatmeal Cookies

Portion: 2 cookies

INGREDIENTS	60 portions		12 portions	
	weights	**measures**	**weights**	**measures**
Maple syrup		1 1/2 cups		5 Tbsp
Vegetable oil		2 1/2 cups		1/2 cup
Bananas, ripe, peeled and mashed	1 1/2 lb	2 cups (5 medium)	6 oz	1/2 cup (2 small)
Water		1 1/2 cups		1/3 cup
Flour, whole wheat pastry	1 1/8 lb	4 1/4 cups	3 2/3 oz	5/8 cup
Baking soda		2 1/2 tsp		1/2 tsp
Baking powder		2 1/2 tsp		1/2 tsp
Cinnamon, ground		2 1/2 tsp		1/2 tsp
Nutmeg		2 tsp		1/4 tsp
Oats, rolled	1 1/4 lb	7 1/2 cups	4 oz	1 1/2 cups
Raisins, seedless	1 lb	3 cups	3 2/3 oz	2/3 cup

Method

1. Cream together maple syrup, oil, and bananas.
2. Add remaining ingredients. Mix well.
3. Preheat oven to 400°F.
4. Dip with #40 dipper or drop large tablespoons onto lightly oiled cookie sheets. Flatten cookies.
5. Bake at 400°F for 8 to 10 minutes or until cookies begin to brown on bottom.
6. Cool on rack.

Directions for Diet Preparations

Sodium Restricted (SR): Use low sodium baking powder as per manufacturer's directions.
Mechanical Soft (SFT): Prepare as directed.
Low Fat/Low Cholesterol (LF), **Diabetic** (DB), **Soft/Low Fiber** (SLF), and **Puree** (PUR): **Not recommended, provide appropriate food substitute.**

Nutrient Analysis per Serving:

Regular	KCAL	PRO gm	CHO gm	FAT gm	Chol mg	SFA gm	PFA gm	VITA iu	VITC mg	THI mg	RIB mg	NIA mg	CA mg	NA mg	K+ mg	FE mg
	198	3.0	25.8	10.0	0.0	1.3	5.6	18.1	1.1	0.1	0.05	0.7	23.3	64.6	175	1.0

Sodium Restricted	NA mg 36.8	Diabetic	Not recommended						Low Fat & Low Chol	Not recommended

Portion: 1 cookie (2-inch cookie)

INGREDIENTS	60 portions		15 portions	
	weights	**measures**	**weights**	**measures**
Margarine, low sodium	8 oz	1 cup	2 oz	1/4 cup
Sugar, granulated	8 oz	1 1/8 cups	2 oz	4 1/2 Tbsp
Eggs	4 oz	1/2 cup (2 large)	1 1/2 oz	3 Tbsp (1 small)
Vanilla		1 1/2 tsp		1/2 tsp
Flour, all-purpose	12 oz	3 cups	3 oz	3/4 cup
Salt		1 tsp		1/4 tsp
Baking powder		1 tsp		1/4 tsp

Method

1. Cream margarine and sugar.
2. Add eggs and vanilla to creamed mixture. Blend on medium speed for 2 minutes.
3. Combine flour, salt, and baking powder. Add to creamed mixture. Mix until blended.
4. Roll out dough 1/8-inch thick on a surface that has been lightly dusted with flour.
5. Cut dough into desired shapes.
6. Place on lightly greased baking sheets.
7. Bake at 375°F for about 10 minutes or until lightly browned.
8. Remove cookies to wire racks to cool.

Variation

Sprinkled Cookies: After Step #6, brush cookies lightly with water and decorate with colored sprinkles.

Directions for Diet Preparations

Sodium Restricted (SR): Omit salt. Use low sodium baking powder as per manufacturer's directions.
Low Fat/Low Cholesterol (LF): 1 cookie.
60 cookies: Substitute reduced-calorie margarine for regular margarine in equal amounts. Omit eggs, substitute with 4 large egg whites. Omit steps #4 and #5. Drop by spoonful onto a non stick baking sheet. May decorate with colored sprinkles.
15 cookies: Substitute reduced calorie margarine for regular margarine in equal amounts. Omit eggs, substitute with 2 small egg whites. Omit steps #4 and #5. Drop by spoonful onto a non-stick baking sheet. May decorate with colored sprinkles.
Diabetic (DB): 1 cookie.
60 cookies: Substitute reduced-calorie margarine for margarine in equal amounts. Use 4 oz granulated sugar. Use an artificial sweetener equivalent to 4 oz granulated sugar (approx. 2 tsp). Omit steps #4 and #5. Drop by spoonful onto a non-stick baking sheet. Omit sprinkles. Consider individual tolerance when using granulated sugar.
15 cookies: Substitute reduced-calorie margarine for margarine in equal amounts. Use 1 oz granulated sugar. Use an artificial sweetener equivalent to 1 oz granulated sugar (approx. 1/4 tsp). Omit steps #4 and #5. Drop by spoonful onto a non-stick baking sheet. Omit sprinkles. Consider individual tolerance when using granulated sugar.
Mechanical Soft (SFT) and **Soft/Low Fiber** (SFL): Prepare as directed. Consider individual tolerance.
Puree (PUR): Not recommended. Use appropriate food alternative.

Nutrient Analysis per Serving:

Regular	KCAL	PRO gm	CHO gm	FAT gm	Chol mg	SFA gm	PFA gm	VITA iu	VITC mg	THI mg	RIB mg	NIA mg	CA mg	NA mg	K+ mg	FE mg
	72.5	0.9	9.9	3.2	9.0	0.5	1.0	134	0.08	0.04	0.03	0.3	7.5	48.0	10.7	0.4

Sodium Restricted	NA mg	Diabetic	Kcal	Milk exg	Veg exg	Fruit exg	Bread exg	Meat exg	Fat exg	Low Fat & Low Chol	FAT gm	Chol mg	SFA gm	PFA gm
	3.6		45.1	0.0	0.0	0.2	0.5	0.0	0.0		2.0	0.0	0.3	0.6

Pies, Cobblers, Crisps, and Pastries

R1 — Pastry Shell, 1-Crust Pie

Portion: 1/8 pie

INGREDIENTS	64 portions; 8, 8-inch pies (3 1/2 lb)		8 portions; 1, 8-inch pie (7 oz)	
	weights	measures	weights	measures
Flour, all-purpose	2 lb	2 qt	4 oz	1 cup
Margarine, low sodium	1 lb	2 cups	2 oz	1/4 cup
Water, cold	10 oz	1 3/4 cups	1 1/4 oz	2 1/2 Tbsp
Salt		2 tsp		1/4 tsp

Method

1. Mix flour and shortening on low speed for 2 to 3 minutes.
2. Dissolve salt in small amount of water. Add to flour mixture.
3. Mix on low speed until a dough is formed, about 40 seconds.
4. Portion into 5 oz balls, for 8-inch pies.
5. Roll dough into a circle at least 2 inches larger than pie pan.
6. Fit pastry loosely into pan so there are no air spaces between the crust and pan. Trim, allow 1/2-inch edge.
7. Bake at 425°F for 10 minutes or until light brown. Cool.
8. Fill baked crust with desired filling.

Directions for Diet Preparations

Sodium Restricted (SR): Omit salt.
Low Fat/Low Cholesterol (LF): 1/8 pie and **Diabetic** (DB): 1/8 pie. Substitute reduced-calorie margarine for regular margarine in equal amounts. May use if able to calculate into daily food plan.
Mechanical Soft (SFT) and **Soft/Low Fiber** (SLF): Prepare as directed. Consider individual tolerance to filling.
Puree (PUR): Not recommended.

Nutrient Analysis per Serving:

Regular	KCAL	PRO gm	CHO gm	FAT gm	Chol mg	SFA gm	PFA gm	VITA iu	VITC mg	THI mg	RIB mg	NIA mg	CA mg	NA mg	K+ mg	FE mg
	102	1.5	10.8	5.8	0.0	0.9	1.9	234	0.01	0.09	0.05	0.7	4.2	76.1	16.1	0.6

Sodium Restricted	NA mg	Diabetic	Kcal	Milk exg	Veg exg	Fruit exg	Bread exg	Meat exg	Fat exg	Low Fat & Low Chol	FAT gm	Chol mg	SFA gm	PFA gm
	2.2		76.0	0.0	0.0	0.0	0.75	0.0	0.5		2.8	0.0	0.4	1.2

Table R-1   Using Frozen Fruits in Pies and Cobblers

Ingredients	64 portions; 8, 8-inch pies		8 portions; 1, 8-inch pie	
	weights	measures	weights	measures
Fruit, frozen	10 lb	5 qt	1 1/4 lb	2 1/2 cups
Sugar, granulated		see below		see below
Cornstarch or		see below		see below
Waxy maize		see below		see below
Seasonings		see below		see below

Method

1. Thaw fruit.
2. 64 portions: Measure juice. If necessary add water to juice to bring total liquid to 1 1/2 qt.
   8 portions: Measure juice. If necessary add water to juice to bring total liquid to 3/4 cup.
3. Combine sugar and starch (cornstarch or waxy maize).
4. Add to hot liquid, stirring with wire whip.
5. Add seasonings to liquid. Pour over fruit.
6. Mix carefully, do not mash fruit.

Measures for Sugar and Starch

Fruit	Sugar		Cornstarch		Waxy Maize		Seasoning
	64 portions	8 portions	64 portions	8 portions	64 portions	8 portions	
Apples	1 1/2 lb	3 oz	3 oz	3/8 oz	2 1/2 oz	1/3 oz	nutmeg, cinnamon
Apricots	2 lb	4 oz	5 oz	2/3 oz	4 oz	1/2 oz	cinnamon
Berries	3 lb	6 oz	6 oz	3/4 oz	5 oz	2/3 oz	lemon juice
Cherries	1 3/4 lb	7 oz	7 oz	5/8 oz	5 oz	2/3 oz	
Peaches	1 1/2 lb	3 oz	5 oz	2/3 oz	4 oz	1/2 oz	nutmeg, cinnamon
Pineapples	2 lb	4 oz	5 oz	2/3 oz	4 oz	1/2 oz	
Strawberries	2 lb	4 oz	12 oz	1 1/2 oz	8 oz	1 oz	lemon juice

Directions for Diet Preparations

Sodium Restricted (SR): Prepare as directed.
Low Fat/Low Cholesterol (LF): 1/8 pie. Prepare as directed.
Diabetic (DB): 1/8 pie. Use unsweetened or no sugar added fruit. Omit granulated sugar and starch. Use as artificial sweetener to taste.
Mechanical Soft (SFT): Prepare as directed. Consider individual tolerance when using strawberries.
Soft/Low Fiber (SLF): The following fruits are not recommended: berries, pineapple, and strawberries.
Puree (PUR): Prepare as directed. Add additional liquid if necessary; blenderize to obtain desired consistency.

Pastry Shell, 2-Crust Pie

Portion: 1/8 pie

INGREDIENTS	64 portions; 8, 8-inch pies (7 lb)		8 portions; 1, 8-inch pie (14 oz)	
	weights	measures	weights	measures
Flour, all-purpose	4 lb	1 gal	8 oz	2 cups
Margarine, low sodium	2 lb	1 qt	4 oz	1/2 cup
Water, cold	1 1/4 lb	2 1/2 cups	2 1/2 oz	5 Tbsp
Salt		1 Tbsp		1/2 tsp

Method

1. Mix flour and shortening on low speed for 1 minute, using flat beater or pastry knife.
2. Scrape down sides of bowl and continue mixing until margarine is evenly distributed, 1 to 2 minutes.
3. Dissolve salt in small amount of cold water. Add to flour mixture. Mix on low speed until dough is formed, about 35 to 45 seconds.
4. Portion into 5 oz balls for bottom crust and 4 oz balls for top crust. Roll each ball of dough into a circle.
5. Place pastry for bottom crust in pie pan. Ease into pans. Trim off overhanging dough. Add desired filling.
6. Moisten edge of bottom crust with water.
7. Cover with top crust. Cut slits near center of top crust.
8. Trim top crust to extend 1/2 inch beyond edge of pan.
9. Fold edge of top crust under lower crust, seal by pressing the 2 crusts together and fluting with fingertips.

Directions for Diet Preparations

Sodium Restricted (SR): Omit salt.

Low Fat/Low Cholesterol (LF): 1/8 pie and **Diabetic** (DB): 1/8 pie. Substitute reduced-calorie margarine for regular margarine in equal amounts. May use if able to calculate into daily food plan.

Mechanical Soft (SFT) and **Soft/Low Fiber** (SLF): Prepare as directed. Consider individual tolerance to filling.

Puree (PUR): Not recommended.

Nutrient Analysis per Serving:

Regular	KCAL	PRO gm	CHO gm	FAT gm	Chol mg	SFA gm	PFA gm	VITA iu	VITC mg	THI mg	RIB mg	NIA mg	CA mg	NA mg	K+ mg	FE mg
	204	3.0	21.6	11.6	0.0	1.9	3.9	468	0.02	0.18	0.11	1.5	8.4	115	32.2	1.2

Sodium Restricted	NA mg	Diabetic	Kcal	Milk exg	Veg exg	Fruit exg	Bread exg	Meat exg	Fat exg	Low Fat & Low Chol	FAT gm	Chol mg	SFA gm	PFA gm
	4.4		152	0.0	0.0	0.0	1.5	0.0	1.0		5.7	0.0	0.9	2.4

Portion: 1/8 pie

INGREDIENTS	64 portions; 8, 8-inch pies		8 portions; 1, 8-inch pie	
	weights	measures	weights	measures
Pastry shells, 2 crust pies	7 lb		14 oz	
Apples, tart	15 lb AP (12 lb EP)	52 medium (3 gal)	1 5/8 lb AP (1 1/2 lb EP)	7 medium (1 1/2 qt)
Sugar, granulated	3 lb	1 2/3 qt	6 oz	5/8 cup
Flour, all-purpose	4 oz	1 cup	1/2 oz	2 Tbsp
Cinnamon, ground		2 tsp		1/4 tsp
Nutmeg		1 tsp		1/8 tsp
Margarine, low sodium, melted	8 oz	1 cup	1 oz	2 Tbsp

Method

1. Make two crust pastry shell.
2. Peel, core, and slice apples. Combine sugar, flour, and spices. Add to apples and mix carefully.
3. Portion two pounds filling into each unbaked crust. Add one ounce margarine to each pie. Moisten edge of bottom crust. Cover with perforated top crust. Seal edge, trim excess dough, and flute edges.
4. Bake at 400°F for 45 minutes or until apples are tender.

Directions for Diet Preparations

Sodium Restricted (SR): 1/8 pie. Use sodium restricted pastry shell.

Low Fat/Low Cholesterol (LF): 1/8 pie. Use low fat pie shell. Substitute reduced calorie margarine in equal amounts specified for regular margarine. May use if able to calculate into daily food plan.

Diabetic (DB): 1/8 pie.

64 portions: Use low fat pie shell. Replace 3 lbs granulated sugar with 1 cup granulated sugar and artificial sweetener equivalent to 5 3/4 cups granulated sugar (approximately 7 1/3 Tbsp artificial sweetener. Substitute reduced calorie margarine in equal amounts specified for regular margarine. May use if able to calculate into daily food plan. Consider individual tolerance when using granulated sugar.

8 portions: Use low fat pie shell. Replace 6 oz granulated sugar with 2 Tbsp granulated sugar and artificial sweetener equivalent to 3/4 cup granulated sugar (approximately 1 Tbsp artificial sweetener. Substitute reduced calorie margarine in equal amounts specified for regular margarine. May use if able to calculate into daily food plan. Consider individual tolerance when using granulated sugar.

Mechanical Soft (SFT) and **Soft/Low Fiber** (SLF): Prepare as directed. Consider individual tolerance to filling.

Puree (PUR): Not recommended. Use appropriate food alternative.

Nutrient Analysis per Serving:

Regular	KCAL	PRO gm	CHO gm	FAT gm	Chol mg	SFA gm	PFA gm	VITA iu	VITC mg	THI mg	RIB mg	NIA mg	CA mg	NA mg	K+ mg	FE mg
	366	3.4	56.6	14.8	0.0	2.4	5.0	623	3.3	0.2	0.1	1.6	13.9	116	130	1.4

Sodium Restricted	NA mg	Diabetic	Kcal	Milk exg	Veg exg	Fruit exg	Bread exg	Meat exg	Fat exg	Low Fat & Low Chol	FAT gm	Chol mg	SFA gm	PFA gm
	5.7		235	0.0	0.0	1.0	1.8	0.0	1.0		7.4	0.0	1.1	3.1

Portion: 1/8 pie

INGREDIENTS	64 portions; 8, 8-inch pies		8 portions; 1, 8-inch pie	
	weights	measures	weights	measures
Pastry shell, one crust pie[1]	3 1/2 lb		7 oz	
Water		2 1/4 qt		1 1/8 cups
Salt		2 tsp		1/4 tsp
Lemon rinds, grated	1 1/2 oz	6 Tbsp	1/8 oz	2 1/4 tsp
Cornstarch	12 oz	2 1/4 cups	1 1/2 oz	4 1/2 Tbsp
Sugar, granulated	3 1/2 lb	7 3/4 cups	7 1/4 oz	1 cup
Water, cold		3 cups		1/3 cup
Egg yolks, beaten	1 lb	2 cups (16 large)	2 oz	1/4 cup (2 large)
Margarine, low sodium	3 oz	1/3 cup	1/3 oz	2 tsp
Lemon juice	12 oz	1 1/2 cup	1 1/2 oz	3 Tbsp
Meringue	2 lb	1 qt	4 oz	1/2 cup

Method

1. Make crust for pies. Line pies with pastry shell. Flute edges and prick with fork.
2. Bake at 425°F for 10 minutes or until light brown.
3. Heat water, salt, and lemon peel to boiling point.
4. Mix cornstarch and sugar. Add cold water and stir until mixed. Add slowly to boiling water stirring constantly with wire whip. Cook until clear and thickened. Remove from heat.
5. While stirring add hot mixture to egg yolks.
6. Return to heat and cook about 5 minutes.
7. Remove from heat.
8. Add margarine and lemon juice. Blend.
9. Scale into pie shells, 3 cups per pie.
10. Top with meringue.
11. Bake at 375°F for 10 to 12 minutes or until meringue is golden brown.

Notes

[1]May use prepared pie shells.

Directions for Diet Preparations

Sodium Restricted (SR): Use sodium restricted pastry shell. Omit salt in step #3.

Low Fat/Low Cholesterol (LF): 1/8 pie. Omit filling, substitute with a low fat, unsweetened lemon pudding. Prepare pudding as per manufacturer's directions. Fill pie shell with pudding. Chill. Top each serving with meringue. May use if able to calculate into daily food plan.

Diabetic (DB): 1/8 pie. Use low fat pie shell. Omit filling, substitute with a low fat, unsweetened lemon pudding. Prepare pudding as per manufacturer's directions. Fill pie shell with pudding. Chill. Omit meringue. Top each serving with 1 Tbsp of whipped topping. May use if able to calculate into daily food plan.

Mechanical Soft (SFT) and **Soft/Low Fiber** (SLF): Prepare as directed.

Puree (PUR): Not recommended, substitute with appropriate food alternative.

Nutrient Analysis per Serving:

Regular	KCAL	PRO gm	CHO gm	FAT gm	Chol mg	SFA gm	PFA gm	VITA iu	VITC mg	THI mg	RIB mg	NIA mg	CA mg	NA mg	K+ mg	FE mg
	273	3.0	47.8	8.0	68.0	1.5	2.4	349	3.4	0.10	0.09	0.7	12.9	165	40.0	0.9

Sodium Restricted	NA mg	Diabetic	Kcal	Milk exg	Veg exg	Fruit exg	Bread exg	Meat exg	Fat exg	Low Fat & Low Chol	FAT gm	Chol mg	SFA gm	PFA gm
	17.5		145	0.5	0.0	0.0	1.0	0.0	0.75		2.8	0.0	0.4	1.2

Portion: 1/8 pie

INGREDIENTS	64 portions; 8, 8-inch pies		8 portions; 1, 8-inch pie	
	weights	measures	weights	measures
Pastry shell, one crust pie[1]	3 1/2 lb		7 oz	
Sugar, granulated	5 lb	2 3/4 qt	10 oz	1 1/3 cups
Margarine, low sodium	5 oz	2/3 cup	2/3 oz	4 tsp
Eggs, beaten	3 3/4 lb	7 1/2 cups (30 large)	8 oz	1 cup (4 large)
Corn syrup	2 2/3 lb	1 qt	5 1/4 oz	1/2 cup
Vanilla	1 1/2 oz	3 Tbsp	1/8 oz	1 1/8 tsp
Pecan halves, unsalted	2 lb	2 qt	4 oz	1 cup

Method

1. Make crust for pies. Line pies with pastry shell. Flute edges and prick with fork.
2. Cream sugar and margarine on medium speed until fluffy.
3. Add eggs to creamed mixture. Mix well.
4. Add corn syrup and vanilla. Mix to blend.
5. Place 4 oz pecans in each unbaked pie shell.
6. Pour 2 1/2 cups egg/creamed mixture over pecans.
7. Bake at 350°F for 40 minutes, or until filling is set.

Notes

[1]May use prepared pie shells.

Directions for Diet Preparations

Sodium Restricted (SR): Use sodium restricted pie shell.

Diabetic (DB): 1/10 pie.

64 portions: Use low fat pie shell. Omit granulated sugar, substitute with 1 cup granulated sugar and artificial sweetener equivalent to 4 1/2 lb granulated sugar (approximately 3/4 cup artificial sweetener). Substitute reduced-calorie margarine for regular margarine in equal amounts. Omit corn syrup, replace with 1 3/4 quarts unsweetened applesauce. Use one oz pecan pieces per pie; sprinkle on top of creamed mixture. May use if able to calculate into daily food plan. Consider individual tolerance when using granulated sugar.

8 portions: Use low fat pie shell. Omit granulated sugar, substitute with 2 Tbsp granulated sugar and artificial sweetener equivalent to 9 oz granulated sugar (approximately 1 1/2 Tbsp artificial sweetener). Substitute reduced-calorie margarine for regular margarine in equal amounts. Omit corn syrup, replace with 3/4 cup unsweetened applesauce. Use one oz pecan pieces per pie; sprinkle on top of creamed mixture. May use if able to calculate into daily food plan. Consider individual tolerance when using granulated sugar.

Low Fat/Low Cholesterol (LF), **Mechanical Soft** (SFT), **Soft/Low Fiber** (SLF), and **Puree** (PUR): Not recommended. Prepare appropriate food alternative.

Nutrient Analysis per Serving:

Regular	KCAL	PRO gm	CHO gm	FAT gm	Chol mg	SFA gm	PFA gm	VITA iu	VITC mg	THI mg	RIB mg	NIA mg	CA mg	NA mg	K+ mg	FE mg
	415	4.9	60.3	18.2	127	2.59	4.79	404	0.3	0.12	0.12	0.6	31.0	118	95.8	2.0

Sodium Restricted	NA mg	Diabetic	Kcal	Milk exg	Veg exg	Fruit exg	Bread exg	Meat exg	Fat exg	Low Fat & Low Chol	Not Recommended
	49.2		122	0.0	0.0	0.7	0.5	0.0	1.0		

Apple Cobbler

Portion: 1/8 pie

INGREDIENTS	64 portions; 8, 8-inch pies		8 portions; 1, 8-inch pie	
	weights	measures	weights	measures
Apples, fresh, sliced, peeled[1]	3 1/8 lb EP (4 lb AP)	3 qt (16 medium)	6 oz EP (8 oz AP)	1 1/2 cups (2 medium)
Oatmeal, dry	1 1/3 lb	2 qt	2 2/3 oz	1 cup
Walnuts, ground	8 3/4 oz	2 1/2 cups	1 oz	1/3 cup
Brown rice flour	8 oz	2 cups	1 oz	1/4 cup
Cinnamon, ground		2 Tbsp		1 tsp
Raisins	10 2/3 oz	2 cups	1 1/3 oz	1/4 cup
Apple juice concentrate	1 lb	2 cups	4 oz	1/4 cup
Lemon juice		4 tsp		1/2 tsp

Method

1. Grease 9-inch pie pan. Cover the bottom with apples.
2. Combine oatmeal, walnuts, flour, cinnamon, raisins, apple juice concentrate, and lemon juice. Mix well. Sprinkle over apples.
3. Bake at 375°F for 20 to 25 minutes or until the apples are soft.

Notes

[1]Variations: cherry, peach, pears, apricots, and berries.

Directions for Diet Preparations

Sodium Restricted (SR): Prepare as directed.
Low Fat/Low Cholesterol (LF): 1/10 pie and **Diabetic** (DB): 1/10 pie. Omit walnuts.
Mechanical Soft (SFT): Prepare as directed. Consider individual tolerance.
Soft/Low Fiber (SLF) and **Puree** (PUR): Not recommended. Provide appropriate food substitute.

Nutrient Analysis per Serving:

Regular	KCAL	PRO gm	CHO gm	FAT gm	Chol mg	SFA gm	PFA gm	VITA iu	VITC mg	THI mg	RIB mg	NIA mg	CA mg	NA mg	K+ mg	FE mg
	124	3.2	21.3	3.5	0.0	0.3	2.0	34.1	1.5	0.09	0.03	0.3	15.7	3.3	161	0.8

Sodium Restricted	NA mg	Diabetic	Kcal	Milk exg	Veg exg	Fruit exg	Bread exg	Meat exg	Fat exg	Low Fat & Low Chol	FAT gm	Chol mg	SFA gm	PFA gm
	3.3		99.8	0.0	0.0	0.8	0.5	0.0	0.4		2.8	0.0	0.2	1.7

Portion: 1 serving (3 × 2″)

INGREDIENTS	40 portions; 1 pan (12 × 20 × 2″), cut 4 × 10		12 portions; 1 pan (8 × 8″), cut 4 × 3	
	weights	measures	weights	measures
Fruit, fresh[1]	7 1/2 lb EP	1 1/2 gal	2 1/2 lb EP	2 qt
Sugar, granulated	7 oz	1 cup	2 1/3 oz	1/3 cup
Lemon juice	1 1/2 oz	3 Tbsp	1/2 oz	1 Tbsp
Margarine, low sodium, soft	10 oz	1 1/4 cups	3 1/3 oz	1/3 cup
Flour, all-purpose	6 oz	1 1/2 cups	2 oz	1/2 cup
Rolled oats, quick cooking, uncooked	6 oz	2 1/4 cups	2 oz	3/4 cup
Sugar, brown, lightly packed	1 lb	3 cups	5 1/3 oz	1 cup
Cinnamon, ground		1 tsp		1/4 tsp

Method

1. Mix sugar and lemon juice with apples.
2. Arrange in greased baking pan.
3. Combine margarine, flour, oats, brown sugar, and cinnamon. Mix until crumbly.
4. Spread evenly over fruit.
5. Bake at 350°F for 45 minutes.
6. Cut into individual servings.
7. Serve with whipped topping, ice cream or cheese.

Notes

[1]Variations: apple, cherry, peach, pears, apricots, and berries. May use fresh, frozen, or canned (drained) fruit.

Directions for Diet Preparations

Sodium Restricted (SR): Prepare as directed.
Low Fat/Low Cholesterol (LF): 2″ × 2″.
40 portions: Replace 10 oz regular margarine with 7 oz reduced-calorie margarine. May use if able to calculate into daily food plan.
12 portions: Replace 3 1/3 oz regular margarine with 4 1/2 Tbsp reduced-calorie margarine. May use if able to calculate into daily food plan.
Diabetic (DB): 2″ × 2″.
40 portions: Omit sugar in step #1, sprinkle with artificial sweetener. Replace 10 oz regular margarine with 7 oz reduced-calorie margarine. Omit brown sugar, substitute with artificial sweetener equivalent to 2 cups brown sugar (approximately 2 Tbsp artificial sweetener). May use if able to calculate into daily food plan.
12 portions: Omit sugar in step #1, sprinkle with artificial sweetener. Replace 3 1/3 oz regular margarine with 4 1/2 Tbsp reduced-calorie margarine. Omit brown sugar, substitute with artificial sweetener equivalent to 2/3 cup brown sugar (approximately 2 tsp artificial sweetener). May use if able to calculate into daily food plan.
Mechanical Soft (SFT): Prepare as directed. Consider individual tolerance.
Soft/Low Fiber (SLF): Not recommended, substitute with appropriate food alternative.
Puree (PUR): Prepare as directed. Add juice and blenderize to obtain desired consistency.

Nutrient Analysis per Serving:

Regular	KCAL	PRO gm	CHO gm	FAT gm	Chol mg	SFA gm	PFA gm	VITA iu	VITC mg	THI mg	RIB mg	NIA mg	CA mg	NA mg	K+ mg	FE mg
	202	1.8	37.0	6.1	0.0	1.0	2.0	694	6.1	0.07	0.06	1.1	24.0	7.2	249	1.0

Sodium Restricted	NA mg	Diabetic	Kcal	Milk exg	Veg exg	Fruit exg	Bread exg	Meat exg	Fat exg	Low Fat & Low Chol	FAT gm	Chol mg	SFA gm	PFA gm
	7.2		58.9	0.0	0.0	0.5	0.4	0.0	0.0		1.5	0.0	0.2	0.6

Portion: 1 tart

INGREDIENTS	48 portions		12 portions	
	weights	**measures**	**weights**	**measures**
Pastry tart:				
Flour, all-purpose	1 5/8 lb	7 1/2 cups	7 1/2 oz	1 5/8 cups
Sugar, granulated	7 oz	1 cup	1 3/4 oz	1/4 cup
Cocoa powder, unsweetened	3 1/3 oz	1 cup	5/8 oz	1/4 cup
Margarine, low sodium	1 1/2 lb	3 1/8 cups	6 1/4 oz	3/4 cup
Water, cold	7 1/2 oz	1 cup	1 5/8 oz	3 3/4 Tbsp
Filling:				
Sugar, granulated	7 oz	1 cup	1 3/4 oz	1/4 cup
Strawberries, frozen, unsweetened, defrosted	4 lb	3 qt	1 lb	3 cups
Cream cheese	1 3/4 lb	3 1/2 cups	7 oz	5/8 cup
Sugar, powdered	6 oz	1 1/4 cups	1 1/2 oz	5 Tbsp
Yogurt, nonfat, vanilla	2 1/2 lb	5 cups	10 oz	1 1/4 cups
Vanilla		1 1/2 Tbsp		1 1/4 tsp
Whipped topping, prepared		3 3/4 cups		1 cup

Method

1. Combine flour, sugar, and cocoa.
2. Cut in margarine until pieces are the size of small peas.
3. Add water. Mix until all of dough is moistened.
4. Flour board and roll dough to 1/8-inch thickness. Cut pastry into 5-inch circles.
5. Ease pastry circles into 2 3/4-inch muffin cups. Be careful not to stretch pastry. Pierce in several places with toothpick. Crimp edges.
6. Bake at 400°F for 12 to 15 minutes or until done. Carefully remove from pans. Cool.
7. Sprinkle sugar over strawberries. Toss lightly to mix.
8. Combine cream cheese, powdered sugar, yogurt, and vanilla. Mix well. Fold in whipped topping.
9. Spoon 3 Tbsp filling into each tart. Fill remaining tart with strawberries. Chill.

Directions for Diet Preparations

Sodium Restricted (SR): Prepare as directed.
Low Fat/Low Cholesterol (LF): 1 tart, 2 Tbsp filling, 1/4 cup strawberries. Replace regular margarine with reduced-calorie margarine in equal amount. Omit water in step #3. Replace imitation cream cheese for regular cream cheese in equal amounts. May use if able to calculate into daily food plan.
Diabetic (DB): 1 tart, 2 Tbsp filling, 1/4 cup strawberries.

48 portions: Replace 7 oz granulated sugar in step #1 with 2 Tbsp granulated sugar and artificial sweetener equivalent to 1 cup granulated sugar (approximately 4 tsp artificial sweetener). Replace regular margarine with reduced-calorie margarine in equal amount. Omit water in step #3. Omit granulated sugar in step #7, substitute with artificial sweetener to taste. Replace imitation cream cheese for regular cream cheese in equal amounts. May use if able to calculate into daily food plan. Consider individual tolerance when using granulated sugar.

12 portions: Replace 1 3/4 oz granulated sugar in step #1 with 1 1/2 tsp granulated sugar and artificial sweetener equivalent to 1/4 cup granulated sugar (approximately 1 tsp artificial sweetener). Replace regular margarine with reduced-calorie margarine in equal amount. Omit water in step #3. Omit granulated sugar in step #7, substitute with artificial sweetener to taste. Replace imitation cream cheese for regular cream cheese in equal amounts. May use if able to calculate into daily food plan. Consider individual tolerance when using granulated sugar.

Mechanical Soft (SFT): Prepare as directed. Consider individual tolerance. If unable to tolerate tart serve 1/2 cup strawberries with filling.
Soft/Low Fiber (SLF): Not recommended. Provide appropriate food substitute.
Puree (PUR): Omit tart. Puree strawberries; strain. Serve 1/2 cup strawberries with filling.

Nutrient Analysis per Serving:

Regular	KCAL	PRO gm	CHO gm	FAT gm	Chol mg	SFA gm	PFA gm	VITA iu	VITC mg	THI mg	RIB mg	NIA mg	CA mg	NA mg	K+ mg	FE mg
	310	4.6	32.2	18.9	16.4	6.6	4.4	771	14.1	0.13	0.16	1.2	55.9	62.1	122	1.5

Sodium Restricted	NA mg	Diabetic	Kcal	Milk exg	Veg exg	Fruit exg	Bread exg	Meat exg	Fat exg	Low Fat & Low Chol	FAT gm	Chol mg	SFA gm	PFA gm
	62.1		170	0.2	0.0	0.3	1.0	0.0	1.5		9.0	5.5	2.9	2.2

Fruits, Gelatins, Whips, Puddings, and Frozen Desserts

S1 — Baked Apple

Portion: 1 medium apple

INGREDIENTS	50 portions		6 portions	
	weights	**measures**	**weights**	**measures**
Apples, baking	14 lb	50 medium	1 3/4 lb	6 medium
Sugar, granulated	3 lb	1 3/4 qt	5 1/8 oz	3/4 cup
Water, hot		3 cups		1/3 cup
Cinnamon, ground		2 tsp		1/4 tsp

Method

1. Wash and core apples. Pare down about 1/4 of the way from top.
2. Place in baking pan, pared side up.
3. Mix sugar, water, and cinnamon. Pour over apples.
4. Baste occasionally while cooking to glaze.
5. Bake at 375°F for about 45 minutes or until tender.

Directions for Diet Preparations

Sodium Restricted (SR) and **Low Fat/Low Cholesterol** (LF): 1 medium. Prepare as directed.

Diabetic (DB): 1 small.

50 portions: Omit sugar and water, substitute with 3 cups diet black cherry soda or other flavor. Follow baking directions.

6 portions: Omit sugar and water, substitute with 1/3 cup diet black cherry soda or other flavor. Follow baking directions.

Mechanical Soft (SFT) and **Soft/Low Fiber** (SLF): Remove skin. Consider individual tolerance.

Puree (PUR): Remove skin. Add additional liquid (i.e. apple juice); blenderize to obtain desired consistency.

Nutrient Analysis per Serving:

Regular	KCAL	PRO gm	CHO gm	FAT gm	Chol mg	SFA gm	PFA gm	VITA iu	VITC mg	THI mg	RIB mg	NIA mg	CA mg	NA mg	K+ mg	FE mg
	134	0.3	34.6	0.5	0.0	0.1	0.1	73.2	7.8	0.02	0.02	0.1	10.8	0.2	159	0.3

Sodium Restricted	NA mg	Diabetic	Kcal	Milk exg	Veg exg	Fruit exg	Bread exg	Meat exg	Fat exg	Low Fat & Low Chol	FAT gm	Chol mg	SFA gm	PFA gm
	0.2		61.2	0.0	0.0	1.0	0.0	0.0	0.0		0.5	0.0	0.1	0.1

S2 | Spiced Applesauce

Portion: 1/2 cup

Ingredients	48 portions		6 portions	
	weights	measures	weights	measures
Applesauce, canned	12 lb	1 1/2 gal	1 1/2 lb	3 cups
Cinnamon, ground		2 Tbsp		3/4 tsp
Sugar, granulated	10 2/3 oz	1 1/2 cups	1 1/3 oz	6 Tbsp

Method

1. Combine cinnamon and sugar.
2. Add cinnamon/sugar into applesauce. Mix well.
3. Heat applesauce, if desired.
4. Serve with No. 8 dipper.

Directions for Diet Preparations

Sodium Restricted (SR), **Low Fat/Low Cholesterol** (LF): 1/2 cup, **Mechanical Soft** (SFT), **Soft/Low Fiber** (SLF), and **Puree** (PUR): Prepare as directed.
Diabetic (DB): 1/2 cup. Use unsweetened applesauce. Replace granulated sugar with artificial sweetener to taste.

Nutrient Analysis per Serving:

Regular	KCAL	PRO gm	CHO gm	FAT gm	Chol mg	SFA gm	PFA gm	VITA iu	VITC mg	THI mg	RIB mg	NIA mg	CA mg	NA mg	K+ mg	FE mg
	98.5	0.2	25.8	0.2	0.0	0.05	0.07	14.4	2.2	0.02	0.04	0.2	5.8	3.9	79.4	0.5

Sodium Restricted	NA mg	Diabetic	Kcal	Milk exg	Veg exg	Fruit exg	Bread exg	Meat exg	Fat exg	Low Fat & Low Chol	FAT gm	Chol mg	SFA gm	PFA gm
	3.9		53.3	0.0	0.0	0.9	0.0	0.0	0.0		0.2	0.0	0.05	0.07

Portion: 1/2 cup

INGREDIENTS	50 portions		6 portions	
	weights	measures	weights	measures
Grapefruit sections, canned, unsweetened	6 lb	3 qt	12 oz	1 1/2 cups
Orange sections, canned, unsweetened	7 lb	3 1/2 qt	14 oz	1 3/4 cups
Orange juice, unsweetened		1 qt		1/2 cup

Method

1. Combine all ingredients.
2. Chill.
3. Serve with No. 8 dipper.

Directions for Diet Preparations

Sodium Restricted (SR), **Low Fat/Low Cholesterol** (LF): 1/2 cup, and **Diabetic** (DB): 1/2 cup. Prepare as directed.

Mechanical Soft (SFT) and **Soft/Low Fiber** (SLF): Use canned citrus fruits. Consider individual tolerance.

Puree (PUR): Prepare as directed. Add additional liquid if necessary (i.e. orange juice), blenderize to obtain desired consistency.

Nutrient Analysis per Serving:

Regular	KCAL	PRO gm	CHO gm	FAT gm	Chol mg	SFA gm	PFA gm	VITA iu	VITC mg	THI mg	RIB mg	NIA mg	CA mg	NA mg	K+ mg	FE mg
	46.5	0.8	11.4	0.2	0.0	0.0	0.0	128	39.9	0.07	0.03	0.3	25.3	1.2	177	0.3

Sodium Restricted	NA mg	Diabetic	Kcal	Milk exg	Veg exg	Fruit exg	Bread exg	Meat exg	Fat exg	Low Fat & Low Chol	FAT gm	Chol mg	SFA gm	PFA gm
	1.2		46.5	0.0	0.0	0.7	0.0	0.0	0.0		0.2	0.0	0.0	0.0

S4 — Fruit Compote

Portion: 1/2 cup

INGREDIENTS	50 portions		6 portions	
	weights	measures	weights	measures
Prunes, pitted	3 lb	2 1/4 qt	6 oz	1 1/8 cups
Apricots, dried	3 lb	2 1/4 qt	6 oz	1 1/8 cups
Pear halves, canned, unsweetened	3 3/4 lb	2 qt	7 1/2 oz	1 cup
Water		to cover		to cover

Method

1. Combine prunes and apricots. Cover with water just barely covering the fruit.
2. Simmer 30 minutes or until prunes are plump.
3. Add pear halves.
4. Chill.

Directions for Diet Preparations

Sodium Restricted (SR), **Low Fat/Low Cholesterol** (LF): 1/2 cup, **Diabetic** (DB): 1/3 cup, and **Mechanical Soft** (SFT): Prepare as directed.

Soft/Low Fiber (SLF): Not recommended, substitute with appropriate food alternative.

Puree (PUR): Prepare as directed. Add additional liquid if necessary, blenderize to obtain desired consistency.

Nutrient Analysis per Serving:

Regular	KCAL	PRO gm	CHO gm	FAT gm	Chol mg	SFA gm	PFA gm	VITA iu	VITC mg	THI mg	RIB mg	NIA mg	CA mg	NA mg	K+ mg	FE mg
	98.6	1.0	25.8	0.2	0.0	0.01	0.03	984	2.1	0.01	0.05	0.6	16.5	2.8	330	1.1

Sodium Restricted	NA mg	Diabetic	Kcal	Milk exg	Veg exg	Fruit exg	Bread exg	Meat exg	Fat exg	Low Fat & Low Chol	FAT gm	Chol mg	SFA gm	PFA gm
	2.8		65.7	0.0	0.0	1.1	0.0	0.0	0.0		0.16	0.0	0.01	0.03

Portion: 1/2 cup

INGREDIENTS	50 portions		6 portions	
	weights	measures	weights	measures
Fruit cocktail, canned, drained, unsweetened	4 1/3 lb	1 1/8 gal	8 2/3 oz	2 1/4 cups
Orange sections, unsweetened	1 1/2 lb	3 cups	3 oz	1/3 cup
Melon, cut in balls	1 lb	2 cups	2 oz	1/4 cup
Strawberries, fresh	10 2/3 oz	2 cups	1 1/3 oz	1/4 cup

Method

1. Combine all fruit. Mix lightly.
2. Chill.

Directions for Diet Preparations

Sodium Restricted (SR), **Low Fat/Low Cholesterol** (LF): 1/2 cup, and **Diabetic** (DB): 1/2 cup. Prepare as directed.

Mechanical Soft (SFT): Prepare as directed. Consider individual tolerance.

Soft/Low Fiber (SLF): Omit strawberries.

Puree (PUR): Prepare as directed. Add liquid (i.e. orange juice); blenderize to obtain desired consistency.

Nutrient Analysis per Serving:

Regular	KCAL	PRO gm	CHO gm	FAT gm	Chol mg	SFA gm	PFA gm	VITA iu	VITC mg	THI mg	RIB mg	NIA mg	CA mg	NA mg	K+ mg	FE mg
	37.8	0.5	9.8	0.09	0.0	0.0	0.03	455	13.8	0.02	0.01	0.4	10.4	4.2	134	0.2

Sodium Restricted	NA mg	Diabetic	Kcal	Milk exg	Veg exg	Fruit exg	Bread exg	Meat exg	Fat exg	Low Fat & Low Chol	FAT gm	Chol mg	SFA gm	PFA gm
	4.2		37.8	0.0	0.0	0.6	0.0	0.0	0.0		0.09	0.0	0.0	0.03

Portion: 1/2 cup

INGREDIENTS	50 portions		6 portions	
	weights	measures	weights	measures
Pineapple tidbits, unsweetened	4 lb	2 qt	8 oz	1 cup
Peaches, diced, unsweetened	4 lb	2 qt	8 oz	1 cup
Banana, slices	1 1/3 lb EP (2 lb AP)	1 qt (6 medium)	3 1/2 oz EP (5 1/3 oz AP)	2/3 cup (1 medium)
Apples, unpared, diced	1 1/2 lb EP (2 lb AP)	1 1/4 qt	3 oz EP (4 oz AP)	2/3 cup
Pineapple juice, unsweetened		1 qt		1/2 cup

Method

1. Combine all fruits and juice.
2. Chill.
3. Serve with 1/2 cup slotted spoon.

Note

[1]May use fresh or canned fruit.

Directions for Diet Preparations

Sodium Restricted (SR), **Low Fat/Low Cholesterol** (LF): 1/2 cup, and **Diabetic** (DB): 1/2 cup. Prepare as directed.

Mechanical Soft (SFT) and **Soft/Low Fiber** (SLF): Omit apples. Use only canned fruit.

Puree (PUR): Peel apples. Add additional pineapple juice if necessary; blenderize to obtain desired consistency.

Nutrient Analysis per Serving:

Regular	KCAL	PRO gm	CHO gm	FAT gm	Chol mg	SFA gm	PFA gm	VITA iu	VITC mg	THI mg	RIB mg	NIA mg	CA mg	NA mg	K+ mg	FE mg
	56.6	0.6	14.4	0.1	0.0	0.04	0.05	236	8.4	0.06	0.04	0.4	11.7	1.9	201	0.4

Sodium Restricted	NA mg	Diabetic	Kcal	Milk exg	Veg exg	Fruit exg	Bread exg	Meat exg	Fat exg	Low Fat & Low Chol	FAT gm	Chol mg	SFA gm	PFA gm
	1.9		56.6	0.0	0.0	0.9	0.0	0.0	0.0		0.1	0.0	0.04	0.05

Fruit Parfait

Portion: 1/2 cup

INGREDIENTS	50 portions		6 portions	
	weights	measures	weights	measures
Bananas, peeled and sliced	4 lb EP (6 1/4 lb AP)	3 qt (18 medium)	10 2/3 oz EP (1 lb AP)	2 cups (3 medium)
Pineapple, diced	1 1/2 lb	3 cups	3 oz	1/3 cup
Oranges, diced	3 lb	1 1/2 qt	6 oz	3/4 cup
Apples, peeled and diced	2 lb	1 3/4 qt	4 oz	3/4 cup
Non-dairy whipped topping		3 1/4 cups		6 Tbsp

Method

1. Combine fruit. Mix.
2. Serve with 1/2 cup slotted spoon in parfait glasses.
3. Top each serving with one Tbsp of non-dairy whipped topping.

Directions for Diet Preparations

Sodium Restricted (SR), **Low Fat/Low Cholesterol** (LF): 1/2 cup, and **Diabetic** (DB): 1/3 cup. Prepare as directed.

Mechanical Soft (SFT) and **Soft/Low Fiber** (SLF): Use canned fruit cocktail and bananas.

Puree (PUR): Use canned fruit cocktail and bananas. Add apple juice; blenderize to obtain desired consistency.

Nutrient Analysis per Serving:

Regular	KCAL	PRO gm	CHO gm	FAT gm	Chol mg	SFA gm	PFA gm	VITA iu	VITC mg	THI mg	RIB mg	NIA mg	CA mg	NA mg	K+ mg	FE mg
	99.4	1.0	22.7	1.2	0.0	1.2	0.1	159	23	0.07	0.08	0.5	17	2.0	325	0.3

Sodium Restricted	NA mg	Diabetic	Kcal	Milk exg	Veg exg	Fruit exg	Bread exg	Meat exg	Fat exg	Low Fat & Low Chol	FAT gm	Chol mg	SFA gm	PFA gm
	2.0		66.2	0.0	0.0	1.0	0.0	0.0	0.14		1.2	0.0	1.19	0.12

Portion: 1/2 cup

Ingredients	48 portions		6 portions	
	weights	measures	weights	measures
Peaches, sliced, canned, unsweetened	13 3/4 lb	1 1/2 gal (2 #10 cans)	1 3/4 lb	3 cups
Almond extract		2 tsp		1/4 tsp
Whipped cream		2 3/4 cups		6 Tbsp
Almonds, slivered, toasted	4 1/2 oz	1 cup	1/2 oz	2 Tbsp

Method

1. Drain peaches.
2. Combine whip cream and almond extract. Whip until soft peaks form.
3. Serve 1/2 cup sliced peaches. Top with 1 Tbsp whipped cream and 1 tsp almonds.

Directions for Diet Preparations

Sodium Restricted (SR) and **Diabetic** (DB): 1/2 cup. Prepare as directed.
Low Fat/Low Cholesterol (LF): 1/2 cup, **Mechanical Soft** (SFT), and **Soft/Low Fiber** (SLF): Omit almonds.
Puree (PUR): Omit almonds. Blenderize; add apple juice if necessary to obtain desired consistency.

Nutrient Analysis per Serving:

Regular	KCAL	PRO gm	CHO gm	FAT gm	Chol mg	SFA gm	PFA gm	VITA iu	VITC mg	THI mg	RIB mg	NIA mg	CA mg	NA mg	K+ mg	FE mg
	73.2	1.1	8.5	4.3	10.3	1.8	0.4	767	3.6	0.01	0.04	0.7	15.5	6.8	150	0.5

Sodium Restricted	NA mg	Diabetic	Kcal	Milk exg	Veg exg	Fruit exg	Bread exg	Meat exg	Fat exg	Low Fat & Low Chol	FAT gm	Chol mg	SFA gm	PFA gm
	6.8		73.2	0.0	0.0	1.0	0.0	0.0	0.2		1.2	0.0	1.05	0.05

Spiced Peaches

Portion: 1/2 cup

INGREDIENTS	48 portions		6 portions	
	weights	**measures**	**weights**	**measures**
Peaches, sliced, canned, drained, unsweetened	13 3/4 lb	1 1/2 gal (2 #10 cans)	1 3/4 lb	3 cups
Cinnamon, ground		1 tsp		1/8 tsp
Ginger		3/4 tsp		pinch
Nutmeg		3/4 tsp		pinch

Method

1. Combine all ingredients. Mix.
2. Chill.
3. Serve with No. 8 dipper.

Directions for Diet Preparations

Sodium Restricted (SR), **Low Fat/Low Cholesterol** (LF): 1/2 cup, **Diabetic** (DB): 1/2 cup, **Mechanical Soft** (SFT), and **Soft/Low Fiber** (SLF): Prepare as directed.
Puree (PUR): Prepare as directed. Blenderize; add apple juice if necessary to obtain desired consistency.

Nutrient Analysis per Serving:

Regular	KCAL	PRO gm	CHO gm	FAT gm	Chol mg	SFA gm	PFA gm	VITA iu	VITC mg	THI mg	RIB mg	NIA mg	CA mg	NA mg	K+ mg	FE mg
	29.8	0.5	7.7	0.08	0.0	0.01	0.04	657	3.6	0.01	0.02	0.6	2.8	3.7	123	0.4

Sodium Restricted	NA mg	Diabetic	Kcal	Milk exg	Veg exg	Fruit exg	Bread exg	Meat exg	Fat exg	Low Fat & Low Chol	FAT gm	Chol mg	SFA gm	PFA gm
	3.7		29.8	0.0	0.0	0.5	0.0	0.0	0.0		0.08	0.0	0.01	0.04

S10   Baked Pears with Raspberry Sauce

Portion: 1/2 pear with 3 Tablespoons sauce

INGREDIENTS	50 portions		6 portions	
	weights	measures	weights	measures
Red raspberries, frozen, unsweetened	4 1/2 lb	3 1/3 qt	9 oz	1 2/3 cups
Sugar, granulated	7 oz	1 cup	5/8 oz	2 Tbsp
Water		2 cups		1/4 cup
Pears, mature[1]	7 lb	25 medium	14 oz	3 medium

Method

1. Defrost raspberries. Do not drain. Mash raspberries and strain to remove seeds.
2. Add sugar and water to raspberry juice. Heat to boiling. Simmer for 5 minutes.
3. Wash pears. Cut in half and remove core. Place in baking pan cut side down.
4. Pour sauce over pears.
5. Bake at 350°F for 45 minutes or until tender.
6. Serve warm or chilled.

Note

[1]May substitute canned pear halves for raw pears. If canned pears are used, pour sauce over individual servings. Do not bake.

Directions for Diet Preparations

Sodium Restricted (SR) and **Low Fat/Low Cholesterol** (LF): 1/2 pear and 3 Tbsp sauce. Prepare as directed.

Diabetic (DB): 1/2 pear and 3 DB Tbsp sauce.

50 portions: Omit sugar, substitute with artificial sweetener equal to 1 1/2 cups granulated sugar (approximately 2 Tbsp artificial sweetener). If using canned pears purchase unsweetened.

6 portions: Omit sugar, substitute with artificial sweetener equal to 3 Tbsp granulated sugar (approximately 3/4 tsp artificial sweetener). If using canned pears purchase unsweetened.

Mechanical Soft (SFT): 1/2 pear and 3 Tbsp sauce. Use canned pear halves.

Soft/Low Fiber (SLF): Use canned pear halves. Omit sauce.

Puree (PUR): Use canned pear halves. Strain sauce. Add sauce to pears; blenderize to obtain desired consistency.

Nutrient Analysis per Serving:

Regular	KCAL	PRO gm	CHO gm	FAT gm	Chol mg	SFA gm	PFA gm	VITA iu	VITC mg	THI mg	RIB mg	NIA mg	CA mg	NA mg	K+ mg	FE mg
	94.3	0.6	24.1	0.4	0.0	0.02	0.08	52.6	6.9	0.02	0.05	0.3	15.1	0.4	149	0.4

Sodium Restricted	NA mg	Diabetic	Kcal	Milk exg	Veg exg	Fruit exg	Bread exg	Meat exg	Fat exg	Low Fat & Low Chol	FAT gm	Chol mg	SFA gm	PFA gm
	0.4		63.1	0.0	0.0	1.0	0.0	0.0	0.0		0.4	0.0	0.02	0.08

Stewed Prunes

Portion: 3 prunes

INGREDIENTS	50 portions		6 portions	
	weights	measures	weights	measures
Prunes, whole, pitted, unsweetened	5 lb	3 3/4 qt	10 2/3 oz	2 cups
Water		to cover		to cover
Lemon, fresh, cut in quarters	4 oz	4 slices	1 oz	1 slice

Method

1. Cover prunes with cold water, about 1/2 inch over prunes.
2. Add lemon.
3. Simmer 30 minutes until prunes are plump.
4. Cool.

Directions for Diet Preparations

Sodium Restricted (SR), Low Fat/Low Cholesterol (LF): 3 prunes, **Diabetic (DB):** 3 prunes, and **Mechanical Soft (SFT):** Prepare as directed.

Soft/Low Fiber (SLF): Not recommended, substitute with appropriate food alternative.

Puree (PUR): Prepare as directed. Add additional liquid if necessary (i.e. prune juice); blenderize to obtain desired consistency.

Nutrient Analysis per Serving:

Regular	KCAL	PRO gm	CHO gm	FAT gm	Chol mg	SFA gm	PFA gm	VITA iu	VITC mg	THI mg	RIB mg	NIA mg	CA mg	NA mg	K+ mg	FE mg
	60.1	0.7	15.8	0.1	0.0	0.01	0.03	500	0.8	0.02	0.04	0.5	12.8	1.0	187	0.6

Sodium Restricted	NA mg	Diabetic	Kcal	Milk exg	Veg exg	Fruit exg	Bread exg	Meat exg	Fat exg	Low Fat & Low Chol	FAT gm	Chol mg	SFA gm	PFA gm
	1.0		60.1	0.0	0.0	1.0	0.0	0.0	0.0		0.1	0.0	0.01	0.03

Gelatin

Portion: 1/2 cup or 3 ounces

INGREDIENTS	50 portions		12 portions	
	weights	**measures**	**weights**	**measures**
Gelatin, flavored	1 1/2 lb	3 1/3 cups	6 oz	5/8 cup
Water, boiling		2 qt		2 cups
Fruit juice or cold water		2 qt		2 cups

Method

1. Pour boiling water over gelatin. Stir until dissolved.
2. Add juice or cold water to gelatin.
3. 50 portions: Place in counter pan (12 × 20 × 2"). 12 portions: Place in pan (8 × 8").
4. Place in refrigerator to congeal.
5. 50 portions: Portion with No. 8 dipper or cut 5 × 10. 12 portions: Portion with No. 8 dipper or cut 4 × 3.

Directions for Diet Preparations

Sodium Restricted (SR), **Low Fat/Low Cholesterol** (LF): 1/2 cup, **Mechanical Soft** (SFT), **Soft/Low Fiber** (SLF), and **Puree** (PUR): Prepare as directed.

Diabetic (DB): 1/2 cup. Use unsweetened gelatin as per manufacturer's directions.

Variations

Suggested gelatin flavors: orange, raspberry, strawberry, lemon and lime.

Nutrient Analysis per Serving (with Fruit Cocktail):

Regular	KCAL	PRO gm	CHO gm	FAT gm	Chol mg	SFA gm	PFA gm	VITA iu	VITC mg	THI mg	RIB mg	NIA mg	CA mg	NA mg	K+ mg	FE mg
	81.4	1.5	19.9	0.1	0.0	0.0	0.0	0.0	3.6	0.0	0.0	0.0	0.0	41.3	0.0	0.0

Sodium Restricted	NA mg	**Diabetic**	Kcal	Milk exg	Veg exg	Fruit exg	Bread exg	Meat exg	Fat exg	**Low Fat & Low Chol**	FAT gm	Chol mg	SFA gm	PFA gm
	41.3		8.0	0.0	0.0	0.0	0.0	0.1	0.0		0.1	0.0	0.0	0.0

Portion: 1/2 cup or 3 ounces

INGREDIENTS	50 portions		12 portions	
	weights	measures	weights	measures
Gelatin, flavored	1 1/2 lb	3 1/3 cups	6 oz	5/8 cup
Water, boiling		2 qt		2 cups
Fruit juice or cold water		2 qt		2 cups
Fruit, canned, drained, unsweetened	4 lb	varies	1 lb	varies

Method

1. Pour boiling water over gelatin. Stir until dissolved.
2. Add juice or cold water to gelatin. Chill until gelatin begins to congeal.
3. 50 portions: Arrange fruit in counter pan (12 × 20 × 2").
   12 portions: Arrange fruit in pan (8 × 8").
4. Pour partially congealed gelatin over fruit.
5. Refrigerate to congeal completely.
6. 50 portions: Portion with No. 8 dipper or cut 5 × 10.
   12 portions: Portion with No. 8 dipper or cut 4 × 3.

Variations

Suggested gelatin flavors: orange, raspberry, strawberry, lemon and lime.
Suggested fruits (canned): fruit cocktail, apricots, peaches, and pears.

Directions for Diet Preparations

Sodium Restricted (SR), **Low Fat/Low Cholesterol (LF)**: 1/2 cup, and **Mechanical Soft (SFT)**: Prepare as directed.
Diabetic (DB): 1/2 cup. Use unsweetened gelatin as per manufacturer's directions.
Soft/Low Fiber (SLF): Use allowed canned fruit. Prepare as directed.
Puree (PUR): Puree fruit. Prepare as directed.

Nutrient Analysis per Serving:

Regular	KCAL	PRO gm	CHO gm	FAT gm	Chol mg	SFA gm	PFA gm	VITA iu	VITC mg	THI mg	RIB mg	NIA mg	CA mg	NA mg	K+ mg	FE mg
	70.6	0.7	17.4	0.06	0.0	0.0	0.0	250	3.6	0.0	0.0	0.2	0.0	20.6	0.0	0.1

Sodium Restricted	NA mg	Diabetic	Kcal	Milk exg	Veg exg	Fruit exg	Bread exg	Meat exg	Fat exg	Low Fat & Low Chol	FAT gm	Chol mg	SFA gm	PFA gm
	20.6		34.0	0.0	0.0	0.5	0.0	0.0	0.0		0.06	0.0	0.0	0.0

Portion: 1/2 cup or 3 ounces

INGREDIENTS	50 portions		12 portions	
	weights	measures	weights	measures
Gelatin, flavored	1 1/2 lb	3 1/3 cups	6 oz	5/8 cup
Water, boiling		2 qt		2 cups
Water, cold		2 qt		2 cups
Blueberries, unsweetened, fresh or canned, drained	4 lb	3 qt 2 1/4 qt	1 lb	3 cups 2 1/4 cups

Method

1. Pour boiling water over gelatin. Stir until dissolved.
2. Add juice or cold water to gelatin. Chill until gelatin begins to congeal.
3. 50 portions: Arrange blueberries in counter pan (12 × 20 × 2").
   12 portions: Arrange blueberries in pan (8 × 8").
4. Pour partially congealed gelatin over fruit.
5. Refrigerate to congeal completely.
6. 50 portions: Portion with No. 8 dipper or cut 5 × 10.
   12 portions: Portion with No. 8 dipper or cut 4 × 3.

Directions for Diet Preparations

Sodium Restricted (SR), **Low Fat/Low Cholesterol** (LF): 1/2 cup, and **Mechanical Soft** (SFT): Prepare as directed.

Diabetic (DB): 1/2 cup. Use unsweetened gelatin as per manufacturer's directions.

Soft/Low Fiber (SLF): Omit blueberries.

Puree (PUR): Puree and strain fruit. Prepare as directed.

Nutrient Analysis per Serving:

Regular	KCAL	PRO gm	CHO gm	FAT gm	Chol mg	SFA gm	PFA gm	VITA iu	VITC mg	THI mg	RIB mg	NIA mg	CA mg	NA mg	K+ mg	FE mg
	67.5	1.2	16.5	0.2	0.0	0.0	0.0	38.6	7.4	0.01	0.01	0.09	7.4	28.1	45.8	0.1

Sodium Restricted	NA mg	Diabetic	Kcal	Milk exg	Veg exg	Fruit exg	Bread exg	Meat exg	Fat exg	Low Fat & Low Chol	FAT gm	Chol mg	SFA gm	PFA gm
	28.1		17.5	0.0	0.0	0.3	0.0	0.0	0.0		0.2	0.0	0.0	0.0

Portion: 1/2 cup

INGREDIENTS	50 portions		12 portions	
	weights	**measures**	**weights**	**measures**
Gelatin, flavored	1 1/2 lb	3 1/3 cups	6 oz	5/8 cup
Water, boiling		2 qt		2 cups
Fruit juice or cold water		2 qt		2 cups
Fruit, puree, unsweetened		2 1/2 qt		2 1/2 cups
Lemon juice	2 oz	1/4 cup	1/2 oz	1 Tbsp

Method

1. Pour boiling water over gelatin. Stir until dissolved.
2. Add juice or cold water to gelatin. Chill until thick, but not set. Whip until light and fluffy.
3. Combine fruit puree and lemon juice. Fold into gelatin.
4. Refrigerate.
5. Serve with No 8 dipper. Top each serving with 1 Tbsp whipped topping.

Variations

Suggested gelatin flavors: orange, raspberry, strawberry, lemon and lime.
Suggested fruit puree: Prune, apricots, peach, pear, and fruit cocktail.

Directions for Diet Preparations

Sodium Restricted (SR): Use low sodium gelatin.
Low Fat/Low Cholesterol (LF): 1/2 cup, **Mechanical Soft** (SFT), and **Puree** (PUR): Prepare as directed.
Diabetic (DB): 1/2 cup. Use unsweetened gelatin and unsweetened fruit. Prepare gelatin as directed by manufacturer.
Soft/Low Fiber (SLF): Use allowed canned fruit (Prunes are not recommended). Prepare as directed.

Nutrient Analysis per Serving:

Regular	KCAL	PRO gm	CHO gm	FAT gm	Chol mg	SFA gm	PFA gm	VITA iu	VITC mg	THI mg	RIB mg	NIA mg	CA mg	NA mg	K+ mg	FE mg
	91.9	1.9	22.5	0.1	0.0	0.0	0.0	833	5.0	0.01	0.01	0.2	3.8	46.4	72.4	0.2

Sodium Restricted	NA mg	Diabetic	Kcal	Milk exg	Veg exg	Fruit exg	Bread exg	Meat exg	Fat exg	Low Fat & Low Chol	FAT gm	Chol mg	SFA gm	PFA gm
	14.1		18.4	0.0	0.0	0.3	0.0	0.0	0.0		0.01	0.0	0.0	0.0

S16   Chocolate Pudding[1]

Portion: 1/2 cup

INGREDIENTS	50 portions		6 portions	
	weights	**measures**	**weights**	**measures**
Sugar, granulated	2 1/4 lb	1 1/4 qt	4 1/2 oz	2/3 cup
Flour, all-purpose	6 oz	1 1/2 cups	3/4 oz	3 Tbsp
Cornstarch	3 oz	9 Tbsp	1/3 oz	3 1/4 Tbsp
Cocoa	8 oz	2 1/4 cups	1 oz	4 1/2 Tbsp
Milk, skim		1 gal		2 cups
Margarine, low sodium	8 oz	1 cup	1 oz	2 Tbsp
Vanilla	1 oz	2 Tbsp	1/8 oz	3/4 tsp

Method

1. Combine sugar, flour, cornstarch, and cocoa.
2. Pour milk into stock pot.
3. Gradually add dry ingredient to milk, while stirring briskly with a wire whip.
4. Heat to boiling point. Cook until thickened, about 20 minutes. Stir occasionally.
5. Remove from heat.
6. Add margarine and vanilla. Blend.
7. Cover with plastic wrap while cooling or cooking.
8. Serve with No. 8 dipper.

Note

[1]May purchase commercially packaged puddings for regular and modified diets.

Directions for Diet Preparations

Sodium Restricted (SR): Prepare as directed. May use if able to calculate into daily food plan.

Low Fat/Low Cholesterol (LF) and **Diabetic** (DB): Not recommended. Use a commercially packaged pudding for low fat and/or diabetic diets.

Mechanical Soft (SFT): Prepare as directed.

Soft/Low Fiber (SLF): Not recommended, substitute with appropriate food alternative.

Puree (PUR): Prepare as directed.

Nutrient Analysis per Serving:

RegularKCAL		PRO	CHO	FAT	Chol	SFA	PFA	VITA	VITC	THI	RIB	NIA	CA	NA	K+	FE
		gm	gm	gm	mg	gm	gm	iu	mg	mg	mg	mg	mg	mg	mg	mg
	167	4.0	30.9	4.2	1.4	0.8	1.2	314	0.7	0.05	0.14	0.3	106	42.6	206	0.6

Sodium	NA	**Diabetic**	Not Recommended				**Low Fat &**	Not Recommended
Restricted	mg						**Low Chol**	
	42.6							

Portion: 1/2 cup

INGREDIENTS	50 portions		6 portions	
	weights	measures	weights	measures
Milk, skim		4 1/2 qt		2 1/4 cups
Sugar, granulated	1 3/4 lb	1 qt	3 1/2 oz	1/2 cup
Cornstarch	8 oz	1 1/2 cups	1 oz	3 Tbsp
Flour, all-purpose	3 oz	3/4 cup	1/3 oz	1 1/2 Tbsp
Egg yolks, beaten	1 1/4 lb	2 1/2 cups (20 large)	2 3/8 oz	4 1/2 Tbsp (3 medium)
Margarine, low sodium	6 oz	3/4 cup	3/4 oz	1 1/2 Tbsp
Vanilla	1 1/2 oz	3 Tbsp	1/4 oz	1 1/8 tsp

Method

1. Heat milk to boiling point.
2. Sift sugar, cornstarch, and flour together.
3. Combine egg yolks into dry ingredients.
4. Add egg yolks and dry ingredients slowly into hot milk, stir constantly.
5. Continue to cook on low heat until thickened, stirring frequently.
6. Remove from heat.
7. Stir in margarine and vanilla.
8. Cover with plastic wrap while cooling.
9. Serve with No. 8 dipper.

Note

[1]May purchase commercially packaged puddings for regular and modified diets.

Directions for Diet Preparations

Sodium Restricted (SR) and **Soft/Low Fiber** (SLF): Prepare as directed. May use if able to calculate into daily food plan.

Low Fat/Low Cholesterol (LF) and **Diabetic** (DB): Not recommended. Use a commercially packaged pudding for low fat and/or diabetic diets.

Mechanical Soft (SFT) and **Puree** (PUR): Prepare as directed.

Nutrient Analysis per Serving:

Regular	KCAL	PRO gm	CHO gm	FAT gm	Chol mg	SFA gm	PFA gm	VITA iu	VITC mg	THI mg	RIB mg	NIA mg	CA mg	NA mg	K+ mg	FE mg
	168	4.3	26.0	5.1	110	1.2	1.2	419	0.8	0.06	0.16	0.1	121	50.4	157	0.5

Sodium Restricted	NA mg 50.4	Diabetic	Not Recommended					Low Fat & Low Chol	Not Recommended

Jericalla (Spiced Custard)

Portion: 1/2 cup (4 ounces)

INGREDIENTS	50 portions[1]		12 portions[2]	
	weights	measures	weights	measures
Eggs	2 1/2 lb	5 cups (20 large)	10 oz	1 1/4 cups (5 large)
Sugar, granulated	1 1/4 lb	2 3/4 cups	4 5/8 oz	2/3 cup
Milk, skim, cold		1 qt		1 cup
Cinnamon, ground		1 tsp		1/4 cup
Vanilla	1 oz	2 Tbsp	1/4 oz	1 1/2 tsp
Milk, skim		1 gal		1 qt

Method[1]

1. Beat eggs slightly, using wire whip.
2. Add sugar, cold milk, cinnamon, and sugar. Mix on low speed until blended.
3. Scald milk by heating to point just before boiling. Add to egg mixture and blend.
4. Pour mixture into custard cups that have been arranged in baking pan(s). Pour hot water around cups.
5. Bake at 325°F for 40 to 45 minutes or until a knife inserted in custard comes out clean.

Note

[1]50 portions: May bake in a 12 × 20 × 2-inch pan set in hot water. Cut 5 × 10.
[2]12 portions: May bake in a 8 × 8-inch pan set in hot water. Cut 4 × 3.

Directions for Diet Preparations

Sodium Restricted (SR): Prepare as directed. May use if able to calculate into daily food plan.

Low Fat/Low Cholesterol (LF): 4 oz (1/2 cup). Omit eggs, substitute with an egg substitute as directed by manufacturer.

Diabetic (DB): 4 oz (1/2 cup).
50 portions: Omit sugar, substitute with 2 tsp artificial sweetener and 2 cups unsweetened applesauce.
12 portions: Omit sugar, substitute with 1/2 tsp artificial sweetener and 1/2 cup unsweetened applesauce.

Mechanical Soft (SFT), **Soft/Low Fiber** (SLF), and **Puree** (PUR): Prepare as directed.

Nutrient Analysis per Serving:

Regular	KCAL	PRO gm	CHO gm	FAT gm	Chol mg	SFA gm	PFA gm	VITA iu	VITC mg	THI mg	RIB mg	NIA mg	CA mg	NA mg	K+ mg	FE mg
	129	8.2	13.4	4.6	220	1.4	0.6	409	0.9	0.07	0.2	0.1	144	106	215	0.9

Sodium Restricted	NA mg	Diabetic	Kcal	Milk exg	Veg exg	Fruit exg	Bread exg	Meat exg	Fat exg	Low Fat & Low Chol	FAT gm	Chol mg	SFA gm	PFA gm
	106		76.5	0.3	0.0	0.0	0.0	0.5	0.3		1.8	2.3	0.4	0.8

Portion: 1 slice (5 ounces)

INGREDIENTS	48 portions		6 portions	
	weights	measures	weights	measures
Lime sherbet	6 1/4 lb	1 1/4 gal	12 1/2 oz	2 1/2 cups
Strawberry ice milk	6 1/4 lb	1 1/4 gal	12 1/2 oz	2 1/2 cups

Method

1. Soften sherbet.
2. 48 portions: Line 6 loaf pans with wax paper.
   6 portions: Line 1 loaf pan with wax paper.
3. Spread lime sherbet on bottom of loaf pans. Freeze 30 minutes to 1 hour.
4. Soften strawberry ice milk.
5. Spread strawberry ice milk evenly over lime sherbet.
6. Cover and freeze several hours or until firm.
7. Invert frozen loaf onto a serving platter. Remove wax paper.
8. Slice 1" (5 ounces) slice per serving.

Directions for Diet Preparations

Sodium Restricted (SR): Prepare as directed.
Low Fat/Low Cholesterol (LF) and **Diabetic** (DB): 1/2 slice; 2 1/2 oz. Prepare as directed. Consider individual tolerance when using concentrated sweets.
Mechanical Soft (SFT) and **Puree** (PUR): Prepare as directed.
Soft/Low Fiber (SLF): Use strawberry ice milk without seeds.

Nutrient Analysis per Serving:

Regular	KCAL	PRO gm	CHO gm	FAT gm	Chol mg	SFA gm	PFA gm	VITA iu	VITC mg	THI mg	RIB mg	NIA mg	CA mg	NA mg	K+ mg	FE mg
	175	3.3	36.0	2.3	7.6	1.5	0.09	89.5	0.3	0.05	0.2	0.05	114	43.7	111	0.1

Sodium Restricted	NA mg	Diabetic	Kcal	Milk exg	Veg exg	Fruit exg	Bread exg	Meat exg	Fat exg	Low Fat & Low Chol	FAT gm	Chol mg	SFA gm	PFA gm
	43.7		87.5	0.25	0.0	1.0	0.0	0.0	0.2		1.1	3.8	0.7	0.04

Star-Spangled Sundae

Portion: 1/2 cup ice milk, 1/2 cup berries

INGREDIENTS	48 portions		6 portions	
	weights	measures	weights	measures
Strawberries, fresh, sliced	4 lb	3 qt	8 oz	1 1/2 cups
Blueberries, fresh	4 lb	3 qt	8 oz	1 1/2 cups
Ice milk, vanilla, low fat		1 1/2 gal		3 cups

Method

1. Combine strawberries and blueberries.
2. Per Serving:
   a. Scoop 1/2 cup ice milk into sundae dish.
   b. Scoop 1/2 cup berries over ice milk.

Directions for Diet Preparations

Sodium Restricted (SR): Prepare as directed.
Low Fat/Low Cholesterol (LF) and **Diabetic** (DB): 1/3 cup ice milk and 1/2 cup berries. **Mechanical Soft** (SFT), **Soft/Low Fiber** (SLF), and **Puree** (PUR): 1/2 cup ice milk with 2 oz strained strawberry syrup.

Nutrient Analysis per Serving:

Regular	KCAL	PRO gm	CHO gm	FAT gm	Chol mg	SFA gm	PFA gm	VITA iu	VITC mg	THI mg	RIB mg	NIA mg	CA mg	NA mg	K+ mg	FE mg
	123	3.0	22.3	3.1	9.1	1.7	0.2	153	26.4	0.06	0.21	0.3	95.8	55.0	228	0.3

Sodium Restricted	NA mg	Diabetic	Kcal	Milk exg	Veg exg	Fruit exg	Bread exg	Meat exg	Fat exg	Low Fat & Low Chol	FAT gm	Chol mg	SFA gm	PFA gm
	55.0		86.9	0.2	0.0	0.9	0.0	0.0	0.3		1.9	5.4	1.1	0.1

Dessert Sauces, Frostings, and Toppings

T1 — Chocolate Frosting

INGREDIENTS	Yield: 1 1/4 quart[1]		Yield: 1 cup[2]	
	weights	measures	weights	measures
Margarine, low sodium, softened	8 oz	1 cup	1 2/3 oz	3 1/4 Tbsp
Sugar, powdered	2 lb	7 1/2 cups	6 3/8 oz	1 1/2 cups
Cocoa	3 1/2 oz	1 cup	3/4 oz	3 1/4 Tbsp
Vanilla		1 Tbsp		3/4 tsp
Corn syrup, light	8 oz	3/4 cup	1 2/3 oz	2 1/2 Tbsp
Water, hot		1/2 cup		1 3/4 Tbsp

Method

1. Combine margarine, sugar, cocoa, and vanilla in mixing bowl.
2. Combine syrup and water; heat to simmering. Do not boil. Add to sugar/margarine mixture.
3. Beat at low speed until frosting is smooth.
4. Spread frosting on cool cake.

Note

[1]Yields enough frosting for 1 sheet cake, 6 dozen cupcakes, or (3) 2-layer cakes.
[2]Yields enough frosting for 1 dozen cupcakes, or 1-layer or 2-layers cake.

Directions for Diet Preparations

Sodium Restricted (SR), **Mechanical Soft** (SFT), and **Puree** (PUR): Prepare as directed.
Low Fat/Low Cholesterol (LF):
1 1/4 quart: Omit margarine, substitute with reduced-calorie margarine in equal amount to regular margarine. Decrease corn syrup to 1/2 cup and decrease hot water to 1/4 cup. May use if able to calculate into daily food plan.
1 cup: Omit margarine, substitute with reduced-calorie margarine in equal amount to regular margarine. Decrease corn syrup to 1 3/4 Tbsp and decrease hot water to 2 1/2 tsp. May use if able to calculate into daily food plan.
Diabetic (DB) and **Soft/Low Fiber** (SLF): Not recommended.

Nutrient Analysis per One Tablespoon:

Regular	KCAL	PRO gm	CHO gm	FAT gm	Chol mg	SFA gm	PFA gm	VITA iu	VITC mg	THI mg	RIB mg	NIA mg	CA mg	NA mg	K+ mg	FE mg
	76.0	0.3	14.4	2.4	0.0	0.4	0.7	95.1	0.0	0.0	0.01	0.03	4.1	3.1	20.7	0.2

Sodium Restricted	NA mg 3.1	**Diabetic:** Not Recommended					Low Fat & Low Chol		FAT gm 1.2	Chol mg 0.0	SFA gm 0.2	PFA gm 0.4

T2 | Cream Cheese Frosting

INGREDIENTS	Yield: 1 3/4 quart[1]		Yield: 1 cup[2]	
	weights	measures	weights	measures
Cream cheese, softened	12 oz	1 1/2 cups	1 3/4 oz	3 1/2 Tbsp
Margarine, low sodium, softened	4 oz	1/2 cup	2/3 oz	1 1/8 Tbsp
Sugar, powdered, sifted	2 3/4 lb	2 2/3 qt	6 1/3 oz	1 1/2 cups
Vanilla		1 Tbsp		1/2 tsp

Method

1. Combine cream cheese and margarine. Beat until smooth.
2. Add sugar gradually to cheese/margarine mixture.
3. Add vanilla and beat until smooth and spreading consistently.
4. Spread frosting on cool cake.

Note

[1]Yields enough frosting for 1 sheet cake, 6 dozen cupcakes, or (3) 2-layer cakes.
[2]Yields enough frosting for 1 dozen cupcakes, or (1) layer cake.

Directions for Diet Preparations

Sodium Restricted (SR), **Mechanical Soft** (SFT), **Soft/ Low Fiber** (SLF), and **Puree** (PUR): Prepare as directed.
Low Fat/Low Cholesterol (LF) and **Diabetic** (DB): Not recommended.

Nutrient Analysis per One Tablespoon:

Regular	KCAL	PRO gm	CHO gm	FAT gm	Chol mg	SFA gm	PFA gm	VITA iu	VITC mg	THI mg	RIB mg	NIA mg	CA mg	NA mg	K+ mg	FE mg
	61.0	0.2	11.2	1.8	3.3	0.8	0.3	76.7	0.0	0.0	0.0	0.0	2.6	9.3	4.3	0.04

| Sodium Restricted | NA mg 9.8 | **Diabetic:** Not Recommended | | | | | Low Fat & Low Chol | | Not Recommended | | | | | | | |

Vanilla Frosting

INGREDIENTS	Yield: 1 1/4 quart[1]		Yield: 1 cup[2]	
	weights	measures	weights	measures
Margarine, low sodium, softened	6 oz	3/4 cup	1 1/4 oz	2 1/2 Tbsp
Sugar, powdered	2 lb	1 3/4 qt	6 3/8 oz	1 1/2 cups
Water, boiling		1/2 cup		1 3/4 Tbsp
Vanilla		4 tsp		3/4 tsp

Method

1. Cream margarine until light and fluffy.
2. Add powdered sugar and water alternately to creamed mixture. Beat well after each addition.
3. Blend in vanilla. Beat until light and fluffy.

Note

[1]Yields enough frosting for 1 sheet cake, 6 dozen cupcakes, or (3) 2-layer cakes.
[2]Yields enough frosting for 1 dozen cupcakes, or (1) layer cake.

Directions for Diet Preparations

Sodium Restricted (SR), **Mechanical Soft** (SFT), **Soft/ Low Fiber** (SLF), and **Puree** (PUR): Prepare as directed.

Low Fat/Low Cholesterol (LF): Omit margarine, substitute with reduced-calorie margarine in equal amount to regular margarine. May use if able to calculate into daily food plan.

Diabetic (DB): Not recommended.

Nutrient Analysis per One Tablespoon:

Regular	KCAL	PRO gm	CHO gm	FAT gm	Chol mg	SFA gm	PFA gm	VITA iu	VITC mg	THI mg	RIB mg	NIA mg	CA mg	NA mg	K+ mg	FE mg
	42.5	0.0	8.1	1.2	0.0	0.2	0.4	50.1	0.0	0.0	0.0	0.0	0.4	0.4	0.8	0.0

Sodium Restricted	NA mg 0.4	**Diabetic:** Not Recommended								Low Fat & Low Chol			FAT gm 0.5	Chol mg 0.0	SFA gm 0.09	PFA gm 0.2

INGREDIENTS	64 portions; 8, 8-inch pies		8 portions; 1, 8-inch pie	
	weights	measures	weights	measures
Egg whites, at room temperature	1 1/8 lb	2 1/4 cups (16 large)	2 1/4 oz	4 3/8 Tbsp (2 large)
Cream of tartar		1/2 tsp		1/8 tsp
Sugar, granulated	1 lb	2 1/4 cups	2 oz	1/4 cup

Method

1. Beat egg whites and cream of tartar on high speed for about 1 1/2 minutes with wire whip.
2. Gradually add sugar, beating until whites are stiff enough to hold peaks.
3. Spread about 4 oz of meringue on filled pies.
4. Brown in 375°F oven for 10 minutes or until golden brown.

Directions for Diet Preparations

Sodium Restricted (SR), **Low Fat/Low Cholesterol** (LF), **Mechanical Soft** (SFT), **Soft/Low Fiber** (SLF), and **Puree** (PUR): Prepare as directed.
Diabetic (DB): Not recommended.

Nutrient Analysis per One Tablespoon:

Regular	KCAL	PRO gm	CHO gm	FAT gm	Chol mg	SFA gm	PFA gm	VITA iu	VITC mg	THI mg	RIB mg	NIA mg	CA mg	NA mg	K+ mg	FE mg
	30.7	0.7	7.1	0.0	0.0	0.0	0.0	0.0	0.0	0.0	0.02	0.0	0.7	12.5	10.8	0.0

Sodium Restricted	NA mg 12.5	Diabetic	Not Recommended								Low Fat & Low Chol	FAT gm 0.0	Chol mg 0.0	SFA gm 0.0	PFA gm 0.0

Chocolate Sauce

Portion: 2 Tablespoons (1 ounce)

INGREDIENTS	48 portions; 1 1/2 quarts		8 portions; 1 cup	
	weights	measures	weights	measures
Sugar, granulated	12 oz	1 2/3 cups	2 oz	4 1/2 Tbsp
Cornstarch	2 oz	6 Tbsp	1/3 oz	1 Tbsp
Cocoa	3 oz	5/8 cup	1/2 oz	2 1/4 Tbsp
Water		4 1/2 cups		3/4 cup
Margarine, low sodium	6 oz	3/4 cup	1 oz	2 Tbsp
Vanilla		1 tsp		1/8 tsp

Method

1. Combine sugar, cornstarch, and cocoa.
2. Gradually add water stirring constantly until smooth.
3. Boil slowly for about 5 minutes, continue stirring until thickened.
4. Remove from heat.
5. Add margarine and vanilla. Stir to blend.
6. Serve over cake, fruit, ice cream, bread or rice pudding.

Directions for Diet Preparations

Sodium Restricted (SR), **Mechanical Soft** (SFT), and **Puree** (PUR): Prepare as directed.

Low Fat/Low Cholesterol (LF): 2 Tbsp. Substitute regular margarine with reduced-calorie margarine in equal amount. May use if able to calculate into daily food plan.

Diabetic (DB) and **Soft/Low Fiber** (SLF): Not recommended.

Nutrient Analysis per Two Tablespoons:

Regular	KCAL	PRO gm	CHO gm	FAT gm	Chol mg	SFA gm	PFA gm	VITA iu	VITC mg	THI mg	RIB mg	NIA mg	CA mg	NA mg	K+ mg	FE mg
	60.5	0.3	9.1	2.9	0.0	0.5	0.9	117	0.0	0.0	0.0	0.0	3.6	1.1	28.5	0.2

Sodium Restricted	NA mg 1.1	**Diabetic:** Not Recommended									Low Fat & Low Chol		FAT gm 1.5	Chol mg 0.0	SFA gm 0.2	PFA gm 0.5

Strawberry Sauce

Portion: 2 Tablespoons (1 ounce)

INGREDIENTS	48 portions; 1 1/2 quarts		8 portions; 1 cup	
	weights	measures	weights	measures
Strawberry juice, frozen, thawed	2 1/4 lb	4 1/2 cups	6 oz	3/4 cup
Cornstarch	2 1/2 oz	1/2 cup	3/8 oz	1 1/3 Tbsp
Lemon juice		2 tsp		1/4 tsp
Strawberries, frozen, drained, thawed, strained	8 oz	1 1/2 cups	1 1/3 oz	1/4 cup

Method

1. 48 portions: Bring 2 cups strawberry juice to boil.
   8 portions: Bring 1/3 cup strawberry juice to boil.
2. Combine cornstarch and remaining strawberry juice. Mix to form a paste. Add to boiling juice.
3. Add lemon juice and strawberries.
4. Serve at room temperature.

Directions for Diet Preparations

Sodium Restricted (SR), **Low Fat/Low Cholesterol** (LF), **Mechanical Soft** (SFT), and **Puree** (PUR): Prepare as directed.

Diabetic (DB) and **Soft/Low Fiber** (SLF): Not recommended.

Nutrient Analysis per Two Tablespoons:

Regular	KCAL	PRO	CHO	FAT	Chol	SFA	PFA	VITA	VITC	THI	RIB	NIA	CA	NA	K+	FE
		gm	gm	gm	mg	gm	gm	iu	mg	mg	mg	mg	mg	mg	mg	mg
	25.6	0.1	6.7	0.0	0.0	0.0	0.0	7.0	10.3	0.0	0.02	0.07	2.8	0.2	25.7	0.1

Sodium Restricted	NA mg 0.2	**Diabetic:** Not Recommended					Low Fat & Low Chol	FAT gm 0.0	Chol mg 0.0	SFA gm 0.0	PFA gm 0.0

Vanilla Sauce

Portion: 2 Tablespoons (1 ounce)

INGREDIENTS	48 portions; 1 1/2 quarts		8 portions; 1 cup	
	weights	measures	weights	measures
Sugar, granulated	1 1/3 lb	3 cups	3 1/2 oz	1/2 cup
Cornstarch	2 1/2 oz	1/2 cup	3/8 oz	1 1/3 Tbsp
Water, boiling		1 qt		2/3 cup
Margarine, low sodium	2 oz	1/4 cup	1/3 oz	2 tsp
Vanilla		2 tsp		1/2 tsp

Method

1. Combine sugar and cornstarch.
2. Gradually add water, stirring constantly until slightly thickened.
3. Remove from heat. Add margarine and vanilla. Stir to blend.
4. Serve over cake, fruit, ice cream, bread or rice pudding.

Directions for Diet Preparations

Sodium Restricted (SR), **Mechanical Soft** (SFT), **Soft/Low Fiber** (SLF), and **Puree** (PUR): Prepare as directed.

Low Fat/Low Cholesterol (LF): 2 Tbsp. Substitute regular margarine with reduced-calorie margarine in equal amount. May use if able to calculate into daily food plan.

Diabetic (DB): Not recommended.

Nutrient Analysis per Two Tablespoons:

Regular	KCAL	PRO gm	CHO gm	FAT gm	Chol mg	SFA gm	PFA gm	VITA iu	VITC mg	THI mg	RIB mg	NIA mg	CA mg	NA mg	K+ mg	FE mg
	63.1	0.0	13.9	0.9	0.0	0.1	0.3	39.0	0.0	0.0	0.0	0.0	0.3	0.4	0.8	0.0

Sodium Restricted	NA mg 0.4	**Diabetic:** Not Recommended								Low Fat & Low Chol		FAT gm 0.9	Chol mg 0.0	SFA gm 0.1	PFA gm 0.3

PART IV

Menu Planning

Menu planning is the key to a successful diet. When planning a menu consider nutritional needs, variety of foods, eye appeal, food texture, flavor, and food preferences.

The menus contained in this book have been designed to meet the needs of individuals with special nutritional considerations. Each menu contains recipe codes and serving sizes. Most of the menus are in a four-week cycle format.

A cycle menu is a menu that has been designed for a specific period of time and then is repeated. Most of the menus found in this book cover a four-week period.

The recipe codes found on the menus correspond to recipes in this book. When you locate the recipe, choose the directions that coincide with your dietary needs.

You will notice serving sizes next to each food item. The serving sizes indicated on the following diets are recommended minimum amounts: regular, liberal bland, no added salt, puree, mechanical soft, low fiber, no concentrated sweets, and vegetarian. The serving sizes on the 1 to 2 gram sodium, low fat, low cholesterol, and calorie-controlled diabetic diets are required amounts necessary to adhere to the diet restrictions.

Nutrition analysis of the menus can be found in the appendix.

Menus for individuals with special needs. These menus are recommended for people with specific nutri-

tional or medical needs. Each diet contains four weeks of menus.

Vegetarian Menu. This is a one-week menu meeting the nutritional needs of the individual on a vegetarian diet.

Menus for Health Care Facilities. This is a four-week cycle, nonselective menu which describes the foods needed for 16 different diets. The nonselective menu does not offer food choices. However, many facilities have established standard food substitutions. The menu is prepared in a spreadsheet format. Each page represents one day of menus with all the modified diets listed on the same page. This style of menu is recommended for health care facilities, such as: long-term care facilities, retirement homes, and hospitals using a nonselective format.

Federal and state regulations governing the development of menus were followed in preparing the health care facility menus. The regular and modified menus were designed using the Recommended Dietary Allowances (RDA) of the Food and Nutrition Board of the National Research Council. A diet manual was used as the standard reference in planning the regular and modified diets.

Senior Citizen Nutrition Program. This is a four-week cycle menu. It meets one-third of the Recommended Daily Allowances for individuals 51 years or older. The menu was prepared using the guidelines set forth by the Older Americans Act.

Special Holidays and Themes. This section uses the same format as the menus for health care facilities. For individuals wanting to stay on their diet, these menus provide traditional holiday favorites without guilt of cheating. For health care facilities it offers a diversity of foods to celebrate special occasions. In addition, most health care facilities are required by state regulations to provide menus for special holidays.

11

Menus for Individuals with Special Needs

Recipe	Monday	Recipe	Tuesday	Recipe	Wednesday	Recipe	Thursday
	Breakfast						
	1/2c Orange Juice		1/2c Apple Juice		1/2c Grapefruit Juice or		1/2c Pineapple Juice
B1	1/2c Farina or	B1	1/2c Wheatena or		1 small Banana	B1	1/2c Oatmeal or
	3/4c Dry Cereal		3/4c Dry Cereal	B1	1/2c Cream of Rice or		3/4c Dry Cereal
B4	1 Soft-Cooked Egg	G6	2 oz Cheese Omelet		3/4c Dry Cereal	I2	1 oz Grilled Cheese
	1 sl Toast		1 English Muffin	B5	1 Scrambled Egg		on 1 sl Toast
	1 tsp Margarine		1 tsp Margarine		1 sl Toast		1 tsp Margarine
	1 tsp Jam or Jelly		1 tsp Jam or Jelly		1 tsp Margarine		1c Milk
	1c Milk		1c Milk		1 tsp Jam or Jelly		Coffee or Tea
	Coffee or Tea		Coffee or Tea		1c Milk		
					Coffee or Tea		
	Lunch						
K29	1c Tossed Salad with	K35	1/2c Molded Vegetable Salad	K25	1c Green Salad with	K22	1/2c Three Bean Salad
P1	1 oz French Dressing	E4	3 oz Lemon Chicken	P4	1 oz Italian Dressing	E14	1c Turkey Chow Mein
D6	8 oz Pepper Steak	J39	4 oz Oven Browned Potatoes	D26	5 oz Veal Parmesan	L1	1/2c White Rice
L3	1/2c Rice Florentine	J10	1/2c Broccoli	M1	1/2c Spaghetti with		1/4c Chinese Noodles
	1 Dinner Roll		1 Dinner Roll	O22	2 oz Tomato Sauce		1 Dinner Roll
	1 tsp Margarine		1 tsp Margarine	J55	1/2c Saute Zucchini-Onions		1 tsp Margarine
	1/2c Milk		1/2c Milk		1 Dinner Roll		1/2c Milk
	Coffee or Tea		Coffee or Tea		1 tsp Margarine		Coffee or Tea
	1/2c Sliced Peaches	S3	1/2c Citrus Cup		1/2c Milk		2 Plums
					Coffee or Tea		
				S10	1/2 Baked Pear		
	Dinner						
C23	2/3c Split Pea Soup	C12	2/3c Cream Mushroom Soup	C27	2/3c Chunky Vegetable Soup	C18	2/3c Onion Soup
I12	1/2c Ham Salad[2] on	D17	4 oz Sloppy Joe on	I18	1/2c Seafood Salad on	G13	1/6 pie Spinach Quiche
	Lettuce Leaves		1 Bun		1 Croissant	K32	1c Tossed Vegetable Salad
	3 sl Tomatoes and	J24	1/2c Corn Confetti	K40	1/2c Waldorf Salad	P1–8	with 1 oz Salad Dressing
	3 sl Cucumbers		1/2c Milk		1/2c Milk		1 Dinner Roll
K5	1/2c Cole Slaw		Coffee or Tea		Coffee or Tea		1 tsp Margarine
	1 Dinner Roll		1/2c Ice Cream	S12	1/2c Orange Gelatin		1/2c Milk
	1 tsp Margarine						Coffee or Tea
	1/2c Milk						2 Cookies
	Coffee or Tea						
Q7	3×2" sl Devil's Food Cake						
	Snacks—Choice of:						
	1/2c Juice or Milk		1/2c Juice or Milk		1/2c Juice or Milk		1/2c Juice or Milk
	2 Cookies or Crackers		2 Cookies or Crackers		2 Cookies or Crackers		2 Cookies or Crackers
S12	1/2c Gelatin or Ice Cream	S12	1/2c Gelatin or Ice Cream	S12	1/2c Gelatin or Ice Cream	S12	1/2c Gelatin or Ice Cream
	Fresh Fruit		Fresh Fruit		Fresh Fruit		Fresh Fruit

1. *Liberal Bland:* Follow a regular diet. Use decaffeinated products. Omit pepper and chili powder.

2. *No Added Salt (3–4 gm sodium):* Follow a regular diet. Use sodium restricted soups and sodium restricted canned meats. Omit salt packets (and shakers), bacon, sausage, smoked, and cured meats, substitute with sodium restricted food choices (see recipes).

Amounts specified for food items that contain bone is equivalent to cooked, edible deboned portion.

Recipe	Friday	Recipe	Saturday	Recipe	Sunday
S11	1/2c Cranberry Juice or	B1	1/2c Apple Juice	B1	1/2c Orange Juice
B1	3 Stewed Prunes		1/2c Wheatena or		1/2c Farina or
	1/2c Cream of Wheat or		3/4c Dry Cereal		3/4c Dry Cereal
	3/4c Dry Cereal	B4	1 Hard-Boiled Egg	B4,5	1 Egg of Choice
B4	1 Poached Egg		1 sl Toast	B9	2 Pancakes with
	1 Sweet Roll		1 tsp Margarine		2 oz Maple Syrup
	1 tsp Margarine		1 tsp Jam or Jelly		1 tsp Margarine
	1 tsp Jam or Jelly		1c Milk		1 tsp Jam or Jelly
	1c Milk		Coffee or Tea		1c Milk
	Coffee or Tea				Coffee or Tea
K20	1/2c Cheesy Pea Salad	K9	1/2c Marinated Cucumbers	K24	1c Garden Salad with
F4	3 1/2 oz Oven Fried Fish	D15	4 oz Meatloaf with	P1–8	1 oz Salad Dressing
O25	with 2 Tbsp Tartar Sauce[2]	O16	2 oz Onion Gravy	D31	3 oz Roast Pork with
M2	1/2c Lyonnaise Noodles	J37	1/2c Mashed Potatoes	O3	2 oz Brown Gravy
J15	1/2c Glazed Carrots	J51	1/2c Vegetable Medley	P11	1/2c Cornbread Stuffing
	1 Dinner Roll		1 Dinner Roll	J47	1/2c Spinach
	1 tsp Margarine		1 tsp Margarine		1 Dinner Roll
	1/2c Milk		1/2c Milk		1 tsp Margarine
	Coffee or Tea		Coffee or Tea		1/2c Milk
	1/2c Fruit Cocktail		1/2c Apricot Halves		Coffee or Tea
					1/2c Applesauce
C8	2/3c Chicken Rice Soup	C4	2/3c Bean Soup	C15	2/3c Creole Soup
E2	3 oz Chicken Fricassee	I5	Chef Salad: 3 oz Ham[2],	F10	8 oz Tuna Noodle Casserole[2]
	with 2 oz Gravy		Turkey and Cheese	J8	1/2c Julienne Beets
J41	3 oz Parsley Potatoes		1c Lettuce, Tomatoes,		1 Dinner Roll
J1	1/2c Asparagus Tips		Onions, and Cucumbers		1 tsp Margarine
	1 Dinner Roll	P1–8	1 oz Salad Dressing		1/2c Milk
	1 tsp Margarine		1 Dinner Roll or		Coffee or Tea
	1/2c Milk		4 Crackers		1/2c Sherbet
	Coffee or Tea		1 tsp Margarine		
Q10	2" Strawberry Shortcake		1/2c Milk		
			Coffee or Tea		
		S16	1/2c Chocolate Pudding		
	1/2c Juice or Milk		1/2c Juice or Milk		1/2c Juice or Milk
	2 Cookies or Crackers		2 Cookies or Crackers		2 Cookies or Crackers
S12	1/2c Gelatin or Ice Cream	S12	1/2c Gelatin or Ice Cream	S12	1/2c Gelatin or Ice Cream
	Fresh Fruit		Fresh Fruit		Fresh Fruit

Recipe	Monday	Recipe	Tuesday	Recipe	Wednesday	Recipe	Thursday
	Breakfast						
	1/2c Pineapple Juice or		1/2c Grapefruit Juice		1/2c Cranberry Juice		1/2c Orange Juice or
	1 small Banana	B1	1/2c Farina or	B1	1/2c Wheatena or		1/2c Melon Cubes
B1	1/2c Cream of Wheat or		3/4c Dry Cereal		3/4c Dry Cereal	B1	1/2c Cream of Rice or
	3/4c Dry Cereal	B4	1 Soft-Cooked Egg		1 Tbsp Peanut Butter and		3/4c Dry Cereal
B5	1 Scrambled Egg		1 sl Toast		1 Tbsp Jelly on	B4	1 Poached Egg
D33	1 Sausage Link[2]		1 tsp Margarine		1 sl Raisin Bread	N12	1 Blueberry Muffin
	1 sl Toast		1 tsp Jam or Jelly		1 tsp Margarine		1 tsp Margarine
	1 tsp Margarine		1c Milk		1c Milk		1 tsp Jam or Jelly
	1 tsp Jam or Jelly		Coffee or Tea		Coffee or Tea		1c Milk
	1c Milk						Coffee or Tea
	Coffee or Tea						
	Lunch						
K28	1c Mixed Field Greens	K2	1/2c Pickled Beets	K31	1c Hawaiian Tossed Salad	K22	1/2c Three Bean Salad
P1–8	with 1 oz Salad Dressing	D2	8 oz Beef Stew	D27	3 1/2 oz Veal Patty with	D37	3 oz Braised Liver with
E8	3 oz Tahitian Chicken	M1	1/2c Noodles	O13	2 oz Mushroom Gravy		1/4c Sauté Onions
	with 1 1/2 oz Sauce	N1	1 Biscuit	J24	1/2c Corn Confetti	M2	1/2c Lyonnaise Noodles
L5	1/2c Rice Pilaf		1 tsp Margarine	J50	1/2c Stewed Tomatoes	J18	1/2c Sunshine Carrots
J10	1/2c Steamed Broccoli		1/2c Milk		1 Dinner Roll		1 Dinner Roll
	1 Dinner Roll		Coffee or Tea		1 tsp Margarine		1 tsp Margarine
	1 tsp Margarine		2 Pear Halves		1/2c Milk		1/2c Milk
	1/2c Milk				Coffee or Tea		Coffee or Tea
	Coffee or Tea				1/2c Ice Cream		
S8	1/2c Almond Peaches					S2	1/2c Spiced Applesauce
	Dinner						
C28	2/3c French Vegetable Soup	C8	2/3c Chicken Rice Soup	C13	2/3c Cream of Spinach Soup	C21	2/3c Minestrone Soup
I2	3 oz Grilled Cheese	E16	3 oz Turkey on	I9	1/2c Egg Salad Platter	M1	1/2c Spaghetti and
	Sandwich, 2 sl Bread		1 sl Bread with		Lettuce Leaves,	D13	3 oz Meatballs with
	1/2c Lettuce Leaves with	O5	2 oz Chicken Gravy		1 Radish Rose,	O20	2 oz Marinara Sauce
	4 sl Tomatoes	J37	1/2c Mashed Potatoes		3 sl Cucumbers	J26	1/2c Italian Mix Vegetables
P1–8	1 oz Salad Dressing	J27	1/2c Mixed Vegetables	K13	1/2c Macaroni Salad		1 sl Italian Bread
	1/2c Milk		1 tsp Margarine		1 Dinner Roll		1 tsp Margarine
	Coffee or Tea		1/2c Milk		1 tsp Margarine		1/2c Milk
Q4	3×2" sl Carrot Raisin Cake		Coffee or Tea		1/2c Milk		Coffee or Tea
		Q18	2 Sugar Cookies		Coffee or Tea	R4	1/8 Lemon Pie
					1/2c Fruit Cocktail		
	Snacks—Choice of:						
	1/2c Juice or Milk		1/2c Juice or Milk		1/2c Juice or Milk		1/2c Juice or Milk
	2 Cookies or Crackers		2 Cookies or Crackers		2 Cookies or Crackers		2 Cookies or Crackers
S12	1/2c Gelatin or Ice Cream	S12	1/2c Gelatin or Ice Cream	S12	1/2c Gelatin or Ice Cream	S12	1/2c Gelatin or Ice Cream
	Fresh Fruit		Fresh Fruit		Fresh Fruit		Fresh Fruit

1. *Liberal Bland:* Follow a regular diet. Use decaffeinated products. Omit pepper and chili powder.
2. *No Added Salt (3–4 gm sodium):* Follow a regular diet. Use sodium restricted soups and sodium restricted canned meats. Omit salt packets (and shakers), bacon, sausage, smoked, and cured meats, substitute with sodium restricted food choices (see recipes).
Amounts specified for food items that contain bone is equivalent to cooked, edible deboned portion.

Recipe	Friday	Recipe	Saturday	Recipe	Sunday
B1	1/2c Apple Juice 1/2c Oatmeal or 3/4c Dry Cereal	B1	1/2c Grapefruit Juice 1/2c Cream of Wheat or 3/4c Dry Cereal	B1	1/2c Pineapple Juice 1/2c Wheatena or 3/4c Dry Cereal
B4	1 Hard-Boiled Egg 1 sl Toast 1 tsp Margarine 1 tsp Jam or Jelly 1c Milk Coffee or Tea	B5 N7	1 Scrambled Egg 1/2" sl Date Nut Bread 1 oz Cream Cheese or 1 tsp Margarine 1 tsp Jam or Jelly 1c Milk Coffee or Tea	B8	1 sl French Toast with 2 oz Maple Syrup 1 tsp Margarine 1 tsp Jam or Jelly 1c Milk Coffee or Tea
K24 P1–8 F3 O7 L1 J47	1c Garden Salad with 1 oz Salad Dressing 3 oz Fish Creole with 2 oz Creole Sauce 1/2c White Rice 1/2c Spinach 1 Dinner Roll 1 tsp Margarine 1/2c Milk Coffee or Tea 1/2c Chilled Apricots	K3 D29 J46 J6	1/2c Cabbage Apple Salad 3 oz Breaded Pork Chops 1/2c Whipped Sweet Potatoes 1/2c Seasoned Green Beans 1 Dinner Roll 1 tsp Margarine 1/2c Milk Coffee or Tea 1/2c Sherbet	K26 P6 D19 J41 J54 S7	1c Green Vegetable Salad with 1 oz Oil & Vinegar 3 oz Swiss Steak with 1 1/2 oz Gravy 3 oz Parsley Potatoes 1/2c Tarragon Zucchini 1 Dinner Roll 1 tsp Margarine 1/2c Milk Coffee or Tea 1/2c Fruit Parfait with Whipped Topping
C7 E5 J35 J8 Q9	2/3c Beef Noodle Soup 3 oz Oven Crisp Chicken 1 sm Baked Potato with 1 oz Sour Cream 1/2c Julienne Beets 1 Dinner Roll 1 tsp Margarine 1/2c Milk Coffee or Tea 3/4" sl Pound Cake	C29 G11 J49	2/3c Old Fashion Vegtble Soup 8 oz Macaroni and Cheese 1/2c Succotash 1 Dinner Roll 1 tsp Margarine 1/2c Milk Coffee or Tea 2 Plums	C12 F1 O25 K5 S12	2/3c Cream Mushroom Soup 3 1/2 oz Fish Burger on 1 Bun 2 Tbsp Tartar Sauce[2] 2 Lettuce Leaves 2 sl Tomatoes 1/2c Cole Slaw 1/2c Milk Coffee or Tea 1/2c Cherry Gelatin
S12	1/2c Juice or Milk 2 Cookies or Crackers 1/2c Gelatin or Ice Cream Fresh Fruit	S12	1/2c Juice or Milk 2 Cookies or Crackers 1/2c Gelatin or Ice Cream Fresh Fruit	S12	1/2c Juice or Milk 2 Cookies or Crackers 1/2c Gelatin or Ice Cream Fresh Fruit

Recipe	Monday	Recipe	Tuesday	Recipe	Wednesday	Recipe	Thursday
	Breakfast						
B1	1/2c Cranberry Juice		1/2c Orange Juice or		1/2c Apple Juice		1/2c Grapefruit Juice
	1/2c Oatmeal or		1/2c Fresh Berries	B1	1/2c Farina or	B1	1/2c Wheatena or
	3/4c Dry Cereal	B1	1/2c Cream of Wheat or		3/4c Dry Cereal		3/4c Dry Cereal
B4	1 Hard-Boiled Egg		3/4c Dry Cereal	B4	1 Poached Egg		1/4c Cottage Cheese with
	1 sl Toast	G7	2 oz Ham[2] Omelet		1 English Muffin		Brown Sugar & Cinnamon
	1 tsp Margarine		1 sl Toast		1 tsp Margarine		on 1 sl Raisin Toast
	1 tsp Jam or Jelly		1 tsp Margarine		1 tsp Jam or Jelly		1 tsp Margarine
	1c Milk		1 tsp Jam or Jelly		1c Milk		1 tsp Jam or Jelly
	Coffee or Tea		1c Milk		Coffee or Tea		1c Milk
			Coffee or Tea				Coffee or Tea
	Lunch						
K10	1/2c Cucumber Onion Salad	K4	1/2c Carrot-Raisin Salad	K25	1c Green Salad with	K24	1c Garden Salad with
E3	3 oz Chicken Italiano	D25	4 oz Veal Loaf with	P1	1 oz French Dressing	P1–8	1 oz Salad Dressing
M1	1/2c Spaghetti with	O3	2 oz Brown Gravy	E15	1c Turkey Jambalaya	D14	3 oz Sweet-n-Sour Meatballs
O22	2 oz Tomato Sauce	J37	1/2c Mashed Potatoes	J3	1/2c Green Beans		with 2 oz Sauce
J26	1/2c Italian Mix Vegetables	J1	1/2c Asparagus Tips		1 Dinner Roll	M1	1/2c Noodles
	1 sl Italian Bread		1 Dinner Roll		1 tsp Margarine	J48	1/2c Seasoned Spinach
	1 tsp Margarine		1 tsp Margarine		1/2c Milk		1 Dinner Roll
	1/2c Milk		1/2c Milk		Coffee or Tea		1 tsp Margarine
	Coffee or Tea		Coffee or Tea	S17	1/2c Vanilla Pudding		1/2c Milk
	1/2c Sliced Peaches	R7	3×2" srv Apple Crisp				Coffee or Tea
							1/2c Apricots
	Dinner						
C20	2/3c Julienne Soup	C3	2/3c Clear Vegetable Soup	C14	2/3c Cream Tomato Soup	C19	2/3c French Onion Soup
I10	Fruit Festival with	G3	6 oz Cheese Strata	I22	Salad Sampler Platter with	G12	1/6 pie Quiche Lorraine[2]
	1/2c Cottage Cheese	J51	1/2c Vegetable Medley	I12	1/4c Ham Salad[2]	J28	1/2c Sauté Mushrooms
	2/3c Seasonal Fruit		1 Dinner Roll	I6	1/4c Chicken Salad		and Celery
S12	1/2c Gelatin Cubes		1 tsp Margarine		Lettuce Leaves, 2 sl Onions,		1 Dinner Roll
N10–20	1 Muffin		1/2c Milk		and 2 Green Pepper Rings		1 tsp Margarine
	1 tsp Margarine		Coffee or Tea	K21	1/2c Potato Salad		1/2c Milk
	1 tsp Jam or Jelly		1/2c Pineapple Chunks		1 Dinner Roll		Coffee or Tea
	1/2c Milk				1 tsp Margarine		1/2c Ice Cream
	Coffee or Tea				1/2c Milk		
Q6	3×2" sl Chocolate Chip Cake				Coffee or Tea		
				S5	1/2c Fruit Cup		
	Snacks—Choice of:						
	1/2c Juice or Milk		1/2c Juice or Milk		1/2c Juice or Milk		1/2c Juice or Milk
	2 Cookies or Crackers		2 Cookies or Crackers		2 Cookies or Crackers		2 Cookies or Crackers
S12	1/2c Gelatin or Ice Cream	S12	1/2c Gelatin or Ice Cream	S12	1/2c Gelatin or Ice Cream	S12	1/2c Gelatin or Ice Cream
	Fresh Fruit		Fresh Fruit		Fresh Fruit		Fresh Fruit

1. *Liberal Bland:* Follow a regular diet. Use decaffeinated products. Omit pepper and chili powder.
2. *No Added Salt (3–4 gm sodium):* Follow a regular diet. Use sodium restricted soups and sodium restricted canned meats. Omit salt packets (and shakers), bacon, sausage, smoked, and cured meats, substitute with sodium restricted food choices (see recipes).
Amounts specified for food items that contain bone is equivalent to cooked, edible deboned portion.

Recipe	Friday	Recipe	Saturday	Recipe	Sunday
B1 B5	1/2c Orange Juice or 1 small Banana 1/2c Cream of Rice or 3/4c Dry Cereal 1 Scrambled Egg 1 sl Toast 1 tsp Margarine 1 tsp Jam or Jelly 1c Milk Coffee or Tea	B1 B4	1/2c Apple Juice 1/2c Oatmeal or 3/4c Dry Cereal 1 Hard-Boiled Egg 1 sl Toast 1 tsp Margarine 1 tsp Jam or Jelly 1c Milk Coffee or Tea	B1 B4,5 B12	1/2c Cranberry Juice 1/2c Farina or 3/4c Dry Cereal 1 Egg of Choice 1 Waffle with 2 oz Maple Syrup 1 tsp Margarine 1 tsp Jam or Jelly 1c Milk Coffee or Tea
K2 F5 O25 L5 J27	1/2c Pickled Beets 3 oz Catch of the Day with 2 Tbsp Tartar Sauce[2] Lemon Wedge 1/2c Rice Pilaf 1/2c Mixed Vegetables 1 Dinner Roll 1 tsp Margarine 1/2c Milk Coffee or Tea 2 Pear Halves	K29 P1–8 D28 J45 J3 S13	1c Tossed Salad with 1 oz Salad Dressing 3 oz Baked Glazed Ham[2] 1/2c Sweet Potatoes/Apples 1/2c String Beans 1 Dinner Roll 1 tsp Margarine 1/2c Milk Coffee or Tea 1/2c Fruited Lime Gelatin	K16 D3 J40 J10	1/2c Mixed Vegetable Salad 3 oz Brisket of Beef with 2 oz Gravy 4 oz Potato Pancakes 1/2c Broccoli Cuts 1 Dinner Roll 1 tsp Margarine 1/2c Milk Coffee or Tea 1/2c Applesauce
C23 E7 J35 J19 Q8	2/3c Split Pea Soup 3 oz Roast Chicken 1 medium Baked Potato with 1 oz Sour Cream 1/2c Carrot Tzimmes 1 Dinner Roll 1 tsp Margarine 1/2c Milk Coffee or Tea 3×2" sl Marble Cake	C21 G1 J55	2/3c Minestrone Soup 6 oz Cheese Fettucine 1/2c Sauté Zucchini-Onions 1 sl Italian Bread 1 tsp Margarine 1/2c Milk Coffee or Tea 2 Plums	C27 I18 I23 K15	2/3c Chunky Vegetable Soup 1/2c Seafood Salad Stuffed Tomato 1/2c Cheesy Macaroni Salad 1 Dinner Roll 1 tsp Margarine 1/2c Milk Coffee or Tea 1/2c Sherbet
S12	1/2c Juice or Milk 2 Cookies or Crackers 1/2c Gelatin or Ice Cream Fresh Fruit	S12	1/2c Juice or Milk 2 Cookies or Crackers 1/2c Gelatin or Ice Cream Fresh Fruit	S12	1/2c Juice or Milk 2 Cookies or Crackers 1/2c Gelatin or Ice Cream Fresh Fruit

Recipe	Monday	Recipe	Tuesday	Recipe	Wednesday	Recipe	Thursday
	Breakfast						
	1/2c Apple Juice or		1/2c Orange Juice		1/2c Pineapple Juice		1/2c Apple Juice or
	1/2c Fresh Fruit	B1	1/2c Oatmeal or	B1	1/2c Cream of Wheat or	S11	3 Stewed Prunes
B1	1/2c Cream of Rice or		3/4c Dry Cereal		3/4c Dry Cereal	B1	1/2c Farina or
	3/4c Dry Cereal	B4	1 Poached Egg	B4	1 Soft-Cooked Egg		3/4c Dry Cereal
I2	1 oz Grilled Cheese on		1 English Muffin		1 sl Toast	B4,5	1 Egg to Order
	1 sl Toast		1 tsp Margarine		1 tsp Margarine		1 sl Raisin Toast
	1 tsp Margarine		1 tsp Jam or Jelly		1 tsp Jam or Jelly		1 tsp Margarine
	1 tsp Jam or Jelly		1c Milk		1c Milk		1 tsp Jam or Jelly
	1c Milk		Coffee or Tea		Coffee or Tea		1c Milk
	Coffee or Tea						Coffee or Tea
	Lunch						
K29	1c Tossed Salad with	K23	1/2c Marinated Zucchini	K32	1c Tossed Vegetable Salad	K25	1c Green Salad with
P8	1 oz Thousand Island Dressing	D22	3 1/2 oz Breaded Veal with	P1–8	with 1 oz Salad Dressing	P6	1 oz Oil & Vinegar
E1	3 oz Barbecue Chicken	O20	2 oz Marinara Sauce	D1	3 1/2 oz Beef Teriyaki	D30	3 oz Pork Chops with
O2	with 2 oz Barbecue Sauce	M5	3/4c Pasta Primavera	J22	1/2c Chinese Vegetables		1/4c Apple Stuffing
J31	1/2c Green Peas		1 sl Italian Bread	L1	1/2c White Rice	J1	1/2c Asparagus Tips
J14	1/2c Carrots		1 tsp Margarine		1 Dinner Roll		1 Dinner Roll
	1 Dinner Roll		1/2c Milk		1 tsp Margarine		1 tsp Margarine
	1 tsp Margarine		Coffee or Tea		1/2c Milk		1/2c Milk
	1/2c Milk	S5	1/2c Fresh Fruit Cup		Coffee or Tea		Coffee or Tea
	Coffee or Tea				1/2c Ice Cream	S16	1/2c Chocolate Pudding
	1/2c Sliced Peaches						
	Dinner						
C11	2/3c Cream Celery Soup	C4	2/3c Bean Soup	C26	2/3c Vegetable Beef Soup	C21	2/3c Minestrone Soup
G8	5 1/2 oz Vegetable Omelet	I4	Asst Cold Cut Sandwiches	E13	3/4c Turkey ala King with	D12	8 oz Beef Macaroni Casserole
J36	1/2c Home Fried Potatoes		2 sl Bread (cut in quarters)		2 Toast Points	J6	1/2c Seasoned Green Beans
	1 Dinner Roll		with 3 oz Roast Beef, Ham[2],	J47	1/2c Spinach		1 Dinner Roll
	1 tsp Margarine		Turkey, Bologna[2], & Salami[2]		1/2c Milk		1 tsp Margarine
	1/2c Milk		Lettuce Leaves		Coffee or Tea		1/2c Milk
	Coffee or Tea		2 sl Tomatoes		2 Plums		Coffee or Tea
Q2	3×2" sl Banana Cake	K5	1/2c Cole Slaw				1/2c Chilled Apricots
			1 tsp Catsup, 1 tsp Mustard				
			1 Tbsp Mayonnaise				
			1/2c Milk				
			Coffee or Tea				
		S12	1/2c Strawberry Gelatin				
	Snacks—Choice of:						
	1/2c Juice or Milk		1/2c Juice or Milk		1/2c Juice or Milk		1/2c Juice or Milk
	2 Cookies or Crackers		2 Cookies or Crackers		2 Cookies or Crackers		2 Cookies or Crackers
S12	1/2c Gelatin or Ice Cream	S12	1/2c Gelatin or Ice Cream	S12	1/2c Gelatin or Ice Cream	S12	1/2c Gelatin or Ice Cream
	Fresh Fruit		Fresh Fruit		Fresh Fruit		Fresh Fruit

1. *Liberal Bland:* Follow a regular diet. Use decaffeinated products. Omit pepper and chili powder.

2. *No Added Salt (3–4 gm sodium):* Follow a regular diet. Use sodium restricted soups and sodium restricted canned meats. Omit salt packets (and shakers), bacon, sausage, smoked, and cured meats, substitute with sodium restricted food choices (see recipes).

Amounts specified for food items that contain bone is equivalent to cooked, edible deboned portion.

Recipe	Friday	Recipe	Saturday	Recipe	Sunday
B1	1/2c Grapefruit Juice 1/2c Wheatena or 3/4c Dry Cereal		1/2c Cranberry Juice or 1 small Banana 1/2c Cream of Rice or 3/4c Dry Cereal	B1	1/2c Pineapple Juice 1/2c Oatmeal or 3/4c Dry Cereal
B5	1 Scrambled Egg	B1		B8	1 sl French Toast with 2 oz Maple Syrup
N14	1 Bran Muffin 1 tsp Margarine 1 tsp Jam or Jelly 1c Milk Coffee or Tea	G9	2 1/2 oz Western Omelet[2] 1 sl Toast 1 tsp Margarine 1 tsp Jam or Jelly 1c Milk Coffee or Tea		1 tsp Margarine 1 tsp Jam or Jelly 1c Milk Coffee or Tea
K9	1/2c Marinated Cucumbers	K37	4 oz Perfection Salad	K42	1/2c Cranberry Mold
F9	3 oz Sole Almondine	D18	6 oz Stuffed Cabbage	E16	3 oz Roast Turkey with
O25	2 Tbsp Tartar Sauce[2] Lemon Wedge	J43	1/2c Whipped Potatoes	O18	2 oz Giblet Gravy
L2	1/2c Rice Chantilly	J15	1/2c Glazed Carrots	P12	1/2c Raisin Bread Stuffing
J51	1/2c Vegetable Medley 1 Dinner Roll 1 tsp Margarine 1/2c Milk Coffee or Tea		1 Dinner Roll 1 tsp Margarine 1/2c Milk Coffee or Tea 1/2c Pineapple Tidbits	J52	1/2c Zucchini 1 Dinner Roll 1 tsp Margarine 1/2c Milk Coffee or Tea
Q3	3×2" sl Boston Cream Cake			R3	1 sl Apple Pie
C9	2/3c Chicken Matzo Ball Soup	C24	2/3c Tomato Soup	C3	2/3c Clear Vegetable Soup
E9	3 oz Baked Chicken Tarragon	I21	1/2c Curry Tuna[2] Salad Platter Lettuce Leaves, 2 sl	G2	6 oz Lasagna
M4	4 oz Noodle Pudding		Onions, 3 sl Cucumbers,	J27	1/2c Mixed Vegetables
J10	1/2c Steamed Broccoli 1 Dinner Roll		1 Radish Rose	N8	1 sl Garlic Bread 1 tsp Margarine
	1 tsp Margarine 1/2c Milk Coffee or Tea	K13	1/2c Macaroni Salad 1 Dinner Roll or 4 Crackers 1 tsp Margarine 1/2c Milk Coffee or Tea 1/2c Sherbet		1/2c Milk Coffee or Tea
S1	1 medium Baked Apple			S4	1/2c Fruit Compote
S12	1/2c Juice or Milk 2 Cookies or Crackers 1/2c Gelatin or Ice Cream Fresh Fruit	S12	1/2c Juice or Milk 2 Cookies or Crackers 1/2c Gelatin or Ice Cream Fresh Fruit	S12	1/2c Juice or Milk 2 Cookies or Crackers 1/2c Gelatin or Ice Cream Fresh Fruit

Recipe	Monday	Recipe	Tuesday	Recipe	Wednesday	Recipe	Thursday
	Breakfast						
	1/2c Orange Juice		1/2c Apple Juice		1/2c Grapefruit Juice or		1/2c Pineapple Juice
B1	1/2c Farina or	B1	1/2c Wheatena or		1 small Banana	B1	1/2c Oatmeal or
	3/4c SR Dry Cereal		3/4c SR Dry Cereal	B1	1/2c Cream of Rice or		3/4c SR Dry Cereal
B4	1 Soft-Cooked Egg	G6	2 oz SR Cheese Omelet		3/4c SR Dry Cereal	I2	1 oz SR Grilled Cheese
	1 sl Toast		1 English Muffin	B5	1 Scrambled Egg		on 1 sl Toast
	1 tsp SR Margarine		1 tsp SR Margarine		1 sl Toast		1 tsp SR Margarine
	1 tsp Jam or Jelly		1 tsp Jam or Jelly		1 tsp SR Margarine		1c Milk
	1c Milk		1c Milk		1 tsp Jam or Jelly		Coffee or Tea
	Coffee or Tea		Coffee or Tea		1c Milk		
					Coffee or Tea		
	Lunch						
K29	1c Tossed Salad with	K35	1/2c Molded Vegetable Salad	K25	1c Green Salad with	K22	1/2c SR Three Bean Salad
P1	1 oz SR French Dressing	E4	3 oz SR Lemon Chicken	P4	1 oz Italian Dressing	E14	1c SR Turkey Chow Mein
D6	8 oz SR Pepper Steak	J39	4 oz Oven Browned Potatoes	D26	5 oz SR Veal Parmesan	11	1/2c White Rice
13	1/2c SR Rice Florentine	J10	1/2c Broccoli	M1	1/2c Spaghetti with		1 Dinner Roll
	1 Dinner Roll		1 Dinner Roll	O22	2 oz SR Tomato Sauce		1 tsp SR Margarine
	1 tsp SR Margarine		1 tsp SR Margarine	J55	1/2c Sauté Zucchini-Onions		1/2c Milk
	1/2c Milk		1/4c Milk		1 Dinner Roll		Coffee or Tea
	Coffee or Tea		Coffee or Tea		1 tsp SR Margarine		2 Plums
	1/2c Sliced Peaches	S3	1/2c Citrus Cup		1/2c Milk		
					Coffee or Tea		
				S10	1/2 Baked Pear		
	Dinner						
C23	2/3c SR Split Pea Soup	C12	2/3c Cream Mushroom Soup	C27	2/3c SR Chunky Vegetable Soup	C18	2/3c Onion Soup
I6	1/2c Turkey Salad on	D17	4 oz SR Sloppy Joe on	I18	1/2c SR Seafood Salad on	G13	1/6 pie SR Spinach Quiche
	Lettuce Leaves		1 Bun		1 Croissant	K32	1c Tossed Vegetable Salad
	3 sl Tomatoes and	J24	1/2c SR Corn Confetti	K40	1/2c Waldorf Salad	P1–8	with 1 oz SR Salad Dressing
	3 sl Cucumbers		1/4c Milk		1/2c Milk		1 Dinner Roll
K5	1/2c Cole Slaw		Coffee or Tea		Coffee or Tea		1 tsp SR Margarine
	1 Dinner Roll		1/2c Ice Cream	S12	1/2c Orange Gelatin		1/2c Milk
	1 tsp SR Margarine						Coffee or Tea
	1/2c Milk						2 Cookies
	Coffee or Tea						
Q7	3×2" sl Devil's Food Cake						
	Snacks—Choice of:						
	1/2c Juice		1/2c Juice		1/2c Juice		1/2c Juice
	2 SR Cookies or SR Crackers		2 SR Cookies or SR Crackers		2 SR Cookies or SR Crackers		2 SR Cookies or SR Crackers
S12	1/2c Gelatin	S12	1/2c Gelatin	S12	1/2c Gelatin	S12	1/2c Gelatin
	Fresh Fruit		Fresh Fruit		Fresh Fruit		Fresh Fruit

TERMS: SR = Sodium or Salt Restricted
Amounts specified for food items that contain bone is equivalent to cooked, edible deboned portion.

Recipe	Friday	Recipe	Saturday	Recipe	Sunday
S11 B1 B4	1/2c Cranberry Juice or 3 Stewed Prunes 1/2c Cream of Wheat or 3/4c SR Dry Cereal 1 Poached Egg 1 Sweet Roll 1 tsp SR Margarine 1 tsp Jam or Jelly 1c Milk Coffee or Tea	B1 B4	1/2c Apple Juice 1/2c Wheatena or 3/4c SR Dry Cereal 1 Hard-Boiled Egg 1 sl Toast 1 tsp SR Margarine 1 tsp Jam or Jelly 1c Milk Coffee or Tea	B1 B4,5 B9	1/2c Orange Juice 1/2c Farina or 3/4c SR Dry Cereal 1 Egg of Choice 2 SR Pancakes with 2 oz Maple Syrup 1 tsp SR Margarine 1 tsp Jam or Jelly 1c Milk Coffee or Tea
K20 F4 M2 J15	1/2c SR Cheesy Pea Salad 3 1/2 oz SR Oven Fried Fish with 1 Tbsp SR Mayonnaise 1/2c Lyonnaise Noodles 1/2c Glazed Carrots 1 Dinner Roll 1 tsp SR Margarine 1/2c Milk Coffee or Tea 1/2c Fruit Cocktail	K9 D15 O16 J37 J51	1/2c Marinated Cucumbers 4 oz Meatloaf with 2 oz SR Onion Gravy 1/2c Mashed Potatoes 1/2c Vegetable Medley 1 Dinner Roll 1 tsp SR Margarine 1/2c Milk Coffee or Tea 1/2c Apricot Halves	K24 P1–8 D31 O3 P11 J47	1c Garden Salad with 1 oz SR Salad Dressing 3 oz Roast Pork with 2 oz SR Brown Gravy 1/2c SR Cornbread Stuffing 1/2c Spinach 1 Dinner Roll 1 tsp SR Margarine 1/2c Milk Coffee or Tea 1/2c Applesauce
C8 E2 J41 J1 Q10	2/3c Chicken Rice Soup 3 oz Chicken Fricassee with 2 oz Gravy 3 oz Parsley Potatoes 1/2c Asparagus Tips 1 Dinner Roll 1 tsp SR Margarine 1/2c Milk Coffee or Tea 2" SR Strawberry Shortcake	C4 I5 P1–8 S16	2/3c SR/LF Bean Soup Chef Salad: 2 oz Turkey and 1 oz SR Cheese 1c Lettuce, Tomatoes, Onions, and Cucumbers 1 oz SR Salad Dressing 1 Dinner Roll or 4 SR Crackers 1 tsp SR Margarine 1/4c Milk Coffee or Tea 1/2c Chocolate Pudding	C15 F10 J8	2/3c SR Creole Soup 8 oz SR Tuna Noodle Casserole 1/2c SR Julienne Beets 1 Dinner Roll 1 tsp SR Margarine 1/4c Milk Coffee or Tea 1/2c Sherbet
S12	1/2c Juice 2 SR Cookies or SR Crackers 1/2c Gelatin Fresh Fruit	S12	1/2c Juice 2 SR Cookies or SR Crackers 1/2c Gelatin Fresh Fruit	S12	1/2c Juice 2 SR Cookies or SR Crackers 1/2c Gelatin Fresh Fruit

Recipe	Monday	Recipe	Tuesday	Recipe	Wednesday	Recipe	Thursday
	Breakfast						
	1/2c Pineapple Juice or		1/2c Grapefruit Juice		1/2c Cranberry Juice		1/2c Orange Juice or
	1 small Banana	B1	1/2c Farina or	B1	1/2c Wheatena or		1/2c Melon Cubes
B1	1/2c Cream of Wheat or		3/4c SR Dry Cereal		3/4c SR Dry Cereal	B1	1/2c Cream of Rice or
	3/4c SR Dry Cereal	B4	1 Soft-Cooked Egg		1 Tbsp SR Peanut Butter		3/4c SR Dry Cereal
B5	1 Scrambled Egg		1 sl Toast		and 1 Tbsp Jelly on	B4	1 Poached Egg
	1 sl Toast		1 tsp SR Margarine		1 sl Raisin Bread	N12	1 SR Blueberry Muffin
	1 tsp SR Margarine		1 tsp Jam or Jelly		1 tsp SR Margarine		1 tsp SR Margarine
	1 tsp Jam or Jelly		1c Milk		1c Milk		1 tsp Jam or Jelly
	1c Milk		Coffee or Tea		Coffee or Tea		1c Milk
	Coffee or Tea						Coffee or Tea
	Lunch						
K28	1c Mixed Field Greens	K2	1/2c SR Beets	K31	1c Hawaiian Tossed Salad	K22	1/2c SR Three Bean Salad
P1–8	with 1 oz SR Salad Dressing	D2	8 oz Beef Stew	D27	3 1/2 oz Veal Patty with	D37	3 oz Braised Liver with
E8	3 oz SR Tahitian Chicken	M1	1/2c Noodles	O13	2 oz SR Mushroom Gravy		1/4c Sauté Onions
	with 1 1/2 oz SR Sauce	N1	1 SR Biscuit	J24	1/2c SR Corn Confetti	M2	1/2c SR Lyonnaise Noodles
L5	1/2c SR Rice Pilaf		1 tsp SR Margarine	J50	1/2c SR Stewed Tomatoes	J18	1/2c Sunshine Carrots
J10	1/2c Steamed Broccoli		1/2c Milk		1 Dinner Roll		1 Dinner Roll
	1 Dinner Roll		Coffee or Tea		1 tsp SR Margarine		1 tsp SR Margarine
	1 tsp SR Margarine		2 Pear Halves		1/4c Milk		1/2c Milk
	1/2c Milk				Coffee or Tea		Coffee or Tea
	Coffee or Tea				1/2c Ice Cream	S2	1/2c Spiced Applesauce
S8	1/2c Almond Peaches						
	Dinner						
C28	2/3c SR French Vegetable Soup	C8	2/3c SR Chicken Rice Soup	C13	2/3c Cream of Spinach Soup	C21	2/3c SR Minestrone Soup
I2	3 oz SR Grilled Cheese		3 oz Turkey on	I9	1/2c SR Egg Salad Platter	M1	1/2c Spaghetti and
	Sandwich, 2 sl Bread	E16	1 sl Bread with		Lettuce Leaves,	D13	3 oz Meatballs with
	1/2c Lettuce Leaves with	O5	2 oz SR Chicken Gravy		1 Radish Rose,	O20	2 oz SR Marinara Sauce
	4 sl Tomatoes	J37	1/2c Mashed Potatoes		3 sl Cucumbers	J26	1/2c Italian Mix Vegetables
P1–8	1 oz SR Salad Dressing	J27	1/2c Mixed Vegetables	K13	1/2c Macaroni Salad		1 sl Italian Bread
	1/2c Milk		1 tsp SR Margarine		1 Dinner Roll		1 tsp SR Margarine
	Coffee or Tea		1/2c Milk		1 tsp SR Margarine		1/2c Milk
Q4	3×2" sl Carrot Raisin Cake		Coffee or Tea		1/4c Milk		Coffee or Tea
		Q18	2 Sugar Cookies		Coffee or Tea	R4	1/8 Lemon Pie
					1/2c Fruit Cocktail		
	Snacks—Choice of:						
	1/2c Juice		1/2c Juice		1/2c Juice		1/2c Juice
	2 SR Cookies or SR Crackers		2 SR Cookies or SR Crackers		2 SR Cookies or SR Crackers		2 SR Cookies or SR Crackers
S12	1/2c Gelatin	S12	1/2c Gelatin	S12	1/2c Gelatin	S12	1/2c Gelatin
	Fresh Fruit		Fresh Fruit		Fresh Fruit		Fresh Fruit

TERMS: SR = Sodium or Salt Restricted

Amounts specified for food items that contain bone is equivalent to cooked, edible deboned portion.

Recipe	Friday	Recipe	Saturday	Recipe	Sunday
B1	1/2c Apple Juice 1/2c Oatmeal or 3/4c SR Dry Cereal	B1	1/2c Grapefruit Juice 1/2c Cream of Wheat or 3/4c SR Dry Cereal	B1	1/2c Pineapple Juice 1/2c Wheatena or 3/4c SR Dry Cereal
B4	1 Hard-Boiled Egg 1 sl Toast 1 tsp SR Margarine 1 tsp Jam or Jelly 1c Milk Coffee or Tea	B5 N7	1 Scrambled Egg 1/2" sl Date Nut Bread 1 oz Cream Cheese or 1 tsp SR Margarine 1 tsp Jam or Jelly 1c Milk Coffee or Tea	B8	1 sl SR French Toast with 2 oz Maple Syrup 1 tsp SR Margarine 1 tsp Jam or Jelly 1c Milk Coffee or Tea
K24 P1–8 F3 O7 L1 J47	1c Garden Salad with 1 oz SR Salad Dressing 3 oz SR Fish Creole with 2 oz SR Creole Sauce 1/2c White Rice 1/2c Spinach 1 Dinner Roll 1 tsp SR Margarine 1/2c Milk Coffee or Tea 1/2c Chilled Apricots	K3 D29 J46 J6	1/2c SR Cabbage Apple Salad 3 oz Breaded Pork Chops 1/2c Whipped Sweet Potatoes 1/2c Seasoned Green Beans 1 Dinner Roll 1 tsp SR Margarine 1/2c Milk Coffee or Tea 1/2c Sherbet	K26 P6 D19 J41 J54 S7	1c Green Vegetable Salad with 1 oz Oil & Vinegar 3 oz Swiss Steak with 1 1/2 oz Gravy 3 oz Parsley Potatoes 1/2c Tarragon Zucchini 1 Dinner Roll 1 tsp SR Margarine 1/2c Milk Coffee or Tea 1/2c Fruit Parfait with Whipped Topping
C7 E5 J35 J8 Q9	2/3c SR Beef Noodle Soup 3 oz Oven Crisp Chicken 1 sm Baked Potato with 1 oz Sour Cream 1/2c SR Julienne Beets 1 Dinner Roll 1 tsp SR Margarine 1/2c Milk Coffee or Tea 3/4" sl Pound Cake	C29 G11 J49	2/3c SR Old Fashion Veg Soup 6 oz SR Macaroni & Cheese 1/2c SR Succotash 1 Dinner Roll 1 tsp SR Margarine 1/2c Milk Coffee or Tea 2 Plums	C12 F1 K5 S12	2/3c Cream Mushroom Soup 3 1/2 oz SR Fish Burger on 1 Bun 1 Tbsp SR Mayonnaise 2 Lettuce Leaves 2 sl Tomatoes 1/2c Cole Slaw 1/4c Milk Coffee or Tea 1/2c Cherry Gelatin
S12	1/2c Juice 2 SR Cookies or SR Crackers 1/2c Gelatin Fresh Fruit	S12	1/2c Juice 2 SR Cookies or SR Crackers 1/2c Gelatin Fresh Fruit	S12	1/2c Juice 2 SR Cookies or SR Crackers 1/2c Gelatin Fresh Fruit

Recipe	Monday	Recipe	Tuesday	Recipe	Wednesday	Recipe	Thursday
	Breakfast						
B1	1/2c Cranberry Juice		1/2c Orange Juice or		1/2c Apple Juice		1/2c Grapefruit Juice
	1/2c Oatmeal or		1/2c Fresh Berries	B1	1/2c Farina or	B1	1/2c Wheatena or
	3/4c SR Dry Cereal	B1	1/2c Cream of Wheat or		3/4c SR Dry Cereal		3/4c SR Dry Cereal
B4	1 Hard-Boiled Egg		3/4c SR Dry Cereal	B4	1 Poached Egg		1/4c Cottage Cheese with
	1 sl Toast	G5	2 oz Plain Omelet		1 English Muffin		Brown Sugar & Cinnamon
	1 tsp SR Margarine		1 sl Toast		1 tsp SR Margarine		on 1 sl Raisin Toast
	1 tsp Jam or Jelly		1 tsp SR Margarine		1 tsp Jam or Jelly		1 tsp SR Margarine
	1c Milk		1 tsp Jam or Jelly		1c Milk		1 tsp Jam or Jelly
	Coffee or Tea		1c Milk		Coffee or Tea		1c Milk
			Coffee or Tea				Coffee or Tea
	Lunch						
K10	1/2c Cucumber Onion Salad	K4	1/2c Carrot-Raisin Salad	K25	1c Green Salad with	K24	1c Garden Salad with
E3	3 oz SR Chicken Italiano	D25	4 oz Veal Loaf with	P1	1 oz SR French Dressing	P1–8	1 oz SR Salad Dressing
M1	1/2c Spaghetti with	O3	2 oz SR Brown Gravy	E15	1c SR Turkey Jambalaya	D14	3 oz SR Sweet-n-Sour Meatballs
O22	2 oz SR Tomato Sauce	J37	1/2c Mashed Potatoes	J3	1/2c Green Beans		with 2 oz SR Sauce
J26	1/2c Italian Mix Vegetables	J1	1/2c Asparagus Tips		1 Dinner Roll	M1	1/2c Noodles
	1 sl Italian Bread		1 Dinner Roll		1 tsp SR Margarine	J48	1/2c SR Seasoned Spinach
	1 tsp SR Margarine		1 tsp SR Margarine		1/4c Milk		1 Dinner Roll
	1/2c Milk		1/2c Milk		Coffee or Tea		1 tsp SR Margarine
	Coffee or Tea		Coffee or Tea	S17	1/2c Vanilla Pudding		1/2c Milk
	1/2c Sliced Peaches	R7	3×2" srv Apple Crisp				Coffee or Tea
							1/2c Apricots
	Dinner						
C20	2/3c SR Julienne Soup	C3	2/3c Clear Vegetable Soup	C14	2/3c SR Cream Tomato Soup	C19	2/3c SR French Onion Soup
I10	Fruit Festival with	G3	6 oz SR Cheese Strata	I22	Salad Sampler Platter with	G12	1/8 pie SR Quiche Lorraine
	1/2c Cottage Cheese	J51	1/2c Vegetable Medley	I9	1/4c Egg Salad	J28	1/2c Saute Mushrooms and
	2/3c Seasonal Fruit		1 Dinner Roll	I6	1/4c Chicken Salad		Celery
S12	1/2c Gelatin Cubes		1 tsp SR Margarine		Lettuce Leaves, 2 sl Onions,		1 Dinner Roll
N10–20	1 SR Muffin		1/4c Milk		and 2 Green Pepper Rings		1 tsp SR Margarine
	1 tsp SR Margarine		Coffee or Tea	K21	1/2c SR Potato Salad		1/4c Milk
	1 tsp Jam or Jelly		1/2c Pineapple Chunks		1 Dinner Roll		Coffee or Tea
	1/2c Milk				1 tsp SR Margarine		1/2c Ice Cream
	Coffee or Tea				1/4c Milk		
Q6	3×2" sl Chocolate Chip Cake				Coffee or Tea		
				S5	1/2c Fruit Cup		
	Snacks—Choice of:						
	1/2c Juice		1/2c Juice		1/2c Juice		1/2c Juice
	2 SR Cookies or SR Crackers		2 SR Cookies or SR Crackers		2 SR Cookies or SR Crackers		2 SR Cookies or SR Crackers
S12	1/2c Gelatin	S12	1/2c Gelatin	S12	1/2c Gelatin	S12	1/2c Gelatin
	Fresh Fruit		Fresh Fruit		Fresh Fruit		Fresh Fruit

TERMS: SR = Sodium or Salt Restricted
Amounts specified for food items that contain bone is equivalent to cooked, edible deboned portion.

Recipe	Friday	Recipe	Saturday	Recipe	Sunday
B1 B5	1/2c Orange Juice or 1 small Banana 1/2c Cream of Rice or 3/4c SR Dry Cereal 1 Scrambled Egg 1 sl Toast 1 tsp SR Margarine 1 tsp Jam or Jelly 1c Milk Coffee or Tea	B1 B4	1/2c Apple Juice 1/2c Oatmeal or 3/4c SR Dry Cereal 1 Hard-Boiled Egg 1 sl Toast 1 tsp SR Margarine 1 tsp Jam or Jelly 1c Milk Coffee or Tea	B1 B4,5 B12	1/2c Cranberry Juice 1/2c Farina or 3/4c SR Dry Cereal 1 Egg of Choice 1 Waffle with 2 oz Maple Syrup 1 tsp SR Margarine 1 tsp Jam or Jelly 1c Milk Coffee or Tea
K2 F5 L5 J27	1/2c SR Beets 3 oz Catch of the Day with 1 Tbsp SR Mayonnaise Lemon Wedge 1/2c SR Rice Pilaf 1/2c Mixed Vegetables 1 Dinner Roll 1 tsp SR Margarine 1/2c Milk Coffee or Tea 2 Pear Halves	K29 P1–8 D31 J45 J3 S13	1c Tossed Salad with 1 oz SR Salad Dressing 3 oz Roast Pork 1/2c Sweet Potatoes/Apples 1/2c String Beans 1 Dinner Roll 1 tsp SR Margarine 1/2c Milk Coffee or Tea 1/2c Fruited Lime Gelatin	K16 D3 J40 J10	1/2c Mixed Vegetable Salad 3 oz Brisket of Beef with 2 oz Gravy 4 oz Potato Pancakes 1/2c Broccoli Cuts 1 Dinner Roll 1 tsp SR Margarine 1/2c Milk Coffee or Tea 1/2c Applesauce
C23 E7 J35 J19 Q8	2/3c SR Split Pea Soup 3 oz Roast Chicken 1 medium Baked Potato with 1 oz Sour Cream 1/2c Carrot Tzimmes 1 Dinner Roll 1 tsp SR Margarine 1/2c Milk Coffee or Tea 3×2" sl Marble Cake	C21 G1 J55	2/3c SR Minestrone Soup 6 oz SR Cheese Fettucine 1/2c Sauté Zucchini-Onions 1 sl Italian Bread 1 tsp SR Margarine 1/2c Milk Coffee or Tea 2 Plums	C27 I18 I23 K15	2/3c SR Chunky Vegetable Soup 1/2c SR Seafood Salad Stuffed Tomato 1/2c SR Cheesy Macaroni Salad 1 Dinner Roll 1 tsp SR Margarine 1/2c Milk Coffee or Tea 1/2c Sherbet
S12	1/2c Juice 2 SR Cookies or SR Crackers 1/2c Gelatin Fresh Fruit	S12	1/2c Juice 2 SR Cookies or SR Crackers 1/2c Gelatin Fresh Fruit	S12	1/2c Juice 2 SR Cookies or SR Crackers 1/2c Gelatin Fresh Fruit

Recipe	Monday	Recipe	Tuesday	Recipe	Wednesday	Recipe	Thursday
	Breakfast						
B1	1/2c Apple Juice or	B1	1/2c Orange Juice	B1	1/2c Pineapple Juice	S11	1/2c Apple Juice or
	1/2c Fresh Fruit		1/2c Oatmeal or		1/2c Cream of Wheat or		3 Stewed Prunes
	1/2c Cream of Rice or		3/4c SR Dry Cereal		3/4c SR Dry Cereal	B1	1/2c Farina or
	3/4c SR Dry Cereal	B4	1 Poached Egg	B4	1 Soft-Cooked Egg		3/4c SR Dry Cereal
I2	1 oz SR Grilled Cheese on		1 English Muffin		1 sl Toast	B4,5	1 Egg to Order
	1 sl Toast		1 tsp SR Margarine		1 tsp SR Margarine		1 sl Raisin Toast
	1 tsp SR Margarine		1 tsp Jam or Jelly		1 tsp Jam or Jelly		1 tsp SR Margarine
	1 tsp Jam or Jelly		1c Milk		1c Milk		1 tsp Jam or Jelly
	1c Milk		Coffee or Tea		Coffee or Tea		1c Milk
	Coffee or Tea						Coffee or Tea
	Lunch						
K29	1c Tossed Salad with	K23	1/2c Marinated Zucchini	K32	1c Tossed Vegetable Salad	K25	1c Green Salad with
P8	1 oz SR Thousand Island Dressing	D22	3 1/2 oz SR Breaded Veal	P1–8	with 1 oz SR Salad Dressing	P6	1 oz Oil & Vinegar
E1	3 oz SR Barbecue Chicken	O20	with 2 oz SR Marinara Sauce	D1	3 1/2 oz SR Beef Teriyaki	D30	3 oz Pork Chops with
O2	with 2 oz SR Barbecue Sauce	M5	3/4c Pasta Primavera	J22	1/2c SR Chinese Vegetables		1/4c Apple Stuffing
J31	1/2c Green Peas		1 sl Italian Bread	L1	1/2c White Rice	J1	1/2c Asparagus Tips
J14	1/2c Carrots		1 tsp SR Margarine		1 Dinner Roll		1 Dinner Roll
	1 Dinner Roll		1/2c Milk		1 tsp SR Margarine		1 tsp SR Margarine
	1 tsp SR Margarine		Coffee or Tea		1/4c Milk		1/4c Milk
	1/2c Milk	S5	1/2c Fresh Fruit Cup		Coffee or Tea		Coffee or Tea
	Coffee or Tea				1/2c Ice Cream	S16	1/2c Chocolate Pudding
	1/2c Sliced Peaches						
	Dinner						
C11	2/3c Cream Celery Soup	C4	2/3c SR/LF Bean Soup	C26	2/3c SR Vegetable Beef Soup	C21	2/3c SR Minestrone Soup
G8	5 1/2 oz Vegetable Omelet	I4	Asst Cold Cut Sandwiches	E13	3/4c SR Turkey à la King	D12	6 oz SR Beef Macaroni Casserole
J36	1/2c Home Fried Potatoes		2 sl Bread (cut in quarters)		with 2 Toast Points	J6	1/2c Seasoned Green Beans
	1 Dinner Roll		with 3 oz Roast Beef and	J47	1/2c Spinach		1 Dinner Roll
	1 tsp SR Margarine		Turkey		1/2c Milk		1 tsp SR Margarine
	1/4c Milk		Lettuce Leaves		Coffee or Tea		1/2c Milk
	Coffee or Tea		2 sl Tomatoes		2 Plums		Coffee or Tea
Q2	3×2" sl Banana Cake	K5	1/2c Cole Slaw				1/2c Chilled Apricots
			1 tsp SR Catsup				
			1 Tbsp SR Mayonnaise				
			1/2c Milk				
			Coffee or Tea				
		S12	1/2c Strawberry Gelatin				
	Snacks—Choice of:						
	1/2c Juice		1/2c Juice		1/2c Juice		1/2c Juice
	2 SR Cookies or SR Crackers		2 SR Cookies or SR Crackers		2 SR Cookies or SR Crackers		2 SR Cookies or SR Crackers
S12	1/2c Gelatin	S12	1/2c Gelatin	S12	1/2c Gelatin	S12	1/2c Gelatin
	Fresh Fruit		Fresh Fruit		Fresh Fruit		Fresh Fruit

TERMS: SR = Sodium or Salt Restricted

Amounts specified for food items that contain bone is equivalent to cooked, edible deboned portion.

Recipe	Friday	Recipe	Saturday	Recipe	Sunday
B1	1/2c Grapefruit Juice 1/2c Wheatena or 3/4c SR Dry Cereal	B1	1/2c Cranberry Juice or 1 small Banana 1/2c Cream of Rice or 3/4c SR Dry Cereal	B1	1/2c Pineapple Juice 1/2c Oatmeal or 3/4c SR Dry Cereal
B5 N14	1 Scrambled Egg 1 SR Bran Muffin 1 tsp SR Margarine 1 tsp Jam or Jelly 1c Milk Coffee or Tea	G9	2 1/2 oz SR Western Omelet 1 sl Toast 1 tsp SR Margarine 1 tsp Jam or Jelly 1c Milk Coffee or Tea	B8	1 sl SR French Toast with 2 oz Maple Syrup 1 tsp SR Margarine 1 tsp Jam or Jelly 1c Milk Coffee or Tea
K9 F9	1/2c Marinated Cucumbers 3 oz Sole Almondine 1 Tbsp SR Mayonnaise Lemon Wedge	K37 D18 J43 J15	4 oz Perfection Salad 6 oz SR Stuffed Cabbage 1/2c Whipped Potatoes 1/2c Glazed Carrots	K42 E16 O18 P12	1/2c Cranberry Mold 3 oz Roast Turkey with 2 oz SR Giblet Gravy 1/2c SR Raisin Bread Stuffing
L2 J51	1/2c SR Rice Chantilly 1/2c Vegetable Medley 1 Dinner Roll 1 tsp SR Margarine 1/2c Milk Coffee or Tea		1 Dinner Roll 1 tsp SR Margarine 1/2c Milk Coffee or Tea 1/2c Pineapple Tidbits	J52	1/2c Zucchini 1 Dinner Roll 1 tsp SR Margarine 1/2c Milk Coffee or Tea
Q3	3×2" sl SR Boston Cream Cake			R3	1 sl SR Apple Pie
C9 E9 M4 J10	2/3c Chicken Matzo Ball Soup 3 oz Baked Chicken Tarragon 4 oz Noodle Pudding 1/2c Steamed Broccoli 1 Dinner Roll 1 tsp SR Margarine 1/2c Milk Coffee or Tea	C24 I21	2/3c SR Tomato Soup 1/2c SR Curry Tuna Salad Platter Lettuce Leaves, 2 sl Onions, 3 sl Cucumbers, 1 Radish Rose	C3 G2 J27 N8	2/3c Clear Vegetable Soup 6 oz SR Lasagna 1/2c Mixed Vegetables 1 sl SR Garlic Bread 1 tsp SR Margarine 1/2c Milk Coffee or Tea
		K13	1/2c Macaroni Salad 1 Dinner Roll or 4 SR Crackers 1 tsp SR Margarine 1/2c Milk Coffee or Tea 1/2c Sherbet	S4	1/2c Fruit Compote
S1	1 medium Baked Apple				
S12	1/2c Juice 2 SR Cookies or SR Crackers 1/2c Gelatin Fresh Fruit	S12	1/2c Juice 2 SR Cookies or SR Crackers 1/2c Gelatin Fresh Fruit	S12	1/2c Juice 2 SR Cookies or SR Crackers 1/2c Gelatin Fresh Fruit

Recipe	Monday	Recipe	Tuesday	Recipe	Wednesday	Recipe	Thursday
	Breakfast						
	1/2c Orange Juice		1/2c Apple Juice		1/2c Grapefruit Juice or		1/2c Pineapple Juice
B1	1/2c LF Farina or	B1	1/2c LF Wheatena or		1 small Banana	B1	1/2c LF Oatmeal or
	3/4c Dry Cereal		3/4c Dry Cereal	B1	1/2c LF Cream of Rice or		3/4c Dry Cereal
B4	1 Egg Substitute	G6	2 oz Egg Substitute		3/4c Dry Cereal	I2	1 oz LF Grilled Cheese
	1 sl Toast		with LF Cheese	B4	1 Egg Substitute		on 1 sl Toast
	1 tsp Margarine		1 English Muffin		1 sl Toast		1 tsp Margarine
	1 tsp Jam or Jelly		1 tsp Margarine		1 tsp Margarine		1c Skim Milk
	1c Skim Milk		1 tsp Jam or Jelly		1 tsp Jam or Jelly		Coffee or Tea
	Coffee or Tea		1c Skim Milk		1c Skim Milk		
			Coffee or Tea		Coffee or Tea		
	Lunch						
K29	1c Tossed Salad with	K35	1/2c Molded Vegetable Salad	K25	1c Green Salad with	K22	1/2c LF Three Bean Salad
P1	1 Tbsp LC French Dressing	E4	2 oz LF Lemon Chicken	P4	2 tsp Italian Dressing	E14	3/4c Turkey Chow Mein
D6	6 oz LF Pepper Steak	J39	4 oz LF Oven Browned Potatoes	D26	4 oz LF Veal Parmesan	L1	1/2c White Rice
L3	1/2c LF Rice Florentine	J10	1/2c LF Broccoli+	M1	1/2c Spaghetti with		1 Dinner Roll
	1 Dinner Roll		1 Dinner Roll	O22	1 oz LF Tomato Sauce		1/2c Skim Milk
	1/2c Skim Milk		1/2c Skim Milk	J55	1/2c LF Zucchini-Onions		Coffee or Tea
	Coffee or Tea		Coffee or Tea		1 Dinner Roll		2 Plums
	1/2c Sliced Peaches	S3	1/2c Citrus Cup		1/2c Skim Milk		
					Coffee or Tea		
				S10	1/2 LF Baked Pear		
	Dinner						
C23	2/3c LF Split Pea Soup	C12	2/3c LF Cream Mushroom Soup	C27	2/3c Chunky Vegetable Soup	C18	2/3c LF Onion Soup+
I12	1/2c LF Ham Salad on	D17	3 oz LF Sloppy Joe on	I18	1/2c LF Seafood Salad on	G13	1/8 pie LF Spinach Quiche
	Lettuce Leaves		1 Bun		2 sl Bread	K32	1c Tossed Vegetable Salad
	3 sl Tomatoes and	J24	1/2c LF Corn Confetti	K40	1/2c LF Waldorf Salad	P1–8	with 1 Tbsp LC Salad Dressing
	3 sl Cucumbers		1/2c Skim Milk		1/2c Skim Milk		1 Dinner Roll
K5	1/2c Cole Slaw+		Coffee or Tea		Coffee or Tea		1/2c Skim Milk
	1 Dinner Roll		1/2c LF Ice Milk	S12	1/2c Orange Gelatin		Coffee or Tea
	1/2c Skim Milk						2 LF Cookies
	Coffee or Tea						
S17	1/2c LF Vanilla Pudding						
	Snacks—Choice of:						
	1/2c Juice or Skim Milk		1/2c Juice or Skim Milk		1/2c Juice or Skim Milk		1/2c Juice or Skim Milk
	2 LF Cookies or LF Crackers		2 LF Cookies or LF Crackers		2 LF Cookies or LF Crackers		2 LF Cookies or LF Crackers
S12	1/2c Gelatin or Fresh Fruit	S12	1/2c Gelatin or Fresh Fruit	S12	1/2c Gelatin or Fresh Fruit	S12	1/2c Gelatin or Fresh Fruit

TERMS: LF = Low Fat; FF = Fat Free; LCH = Low Cholesterol; RC = Reduced Calorie; LC = Low Calorie; SR = Sodium or Salt Restricted. +Consider individual tolerance.
Amounts specified for food items that contain bone is equivalent to cooked, edible deboned portion.

Recipe	Friday	Recipe	Saturday	Recipe	Sunday
S11 B1 B4	1/2c Cranberry Juice or 3 Stewed Prunes 1/2c LF Cream of Wheat or 3/4c Dry Cereal 1 Egg Substitute 1 sl Toast 1 tsp Margarine 1 tsp Jam or Jelly 1c Skim Milk Coffee or Tea	B1 B4	1/2c Apple Juice 1/2c LF Wheatena or 3/4c Dry Cereal 1 Egg Substitute 1 sl Toast 1 tsp Margarine 1 tsp Jam or Jelly 1c Skim Milk Coffee or Tea	B1 B4 B9	1/2c Orange Juice 1/2c LF Farina or 3/4c Dry Cereal 1 Egg Substitute 2 LF Pancakes with 2 oz Maple Syrup 1 tsp Jam or Jelly 1c Skim Milk Coffee or Tea
K20 F4 O25 M2 J15	1/2c LF Cheesy Pea Salad 3 oz LF Oven Fried Fish with 1 tsp LF Tartar Sauce 1/2c LF Lyonnaise Noodles 1/2c LF Glazed Carrots 1 Dinner Roll 1/2c Skim Milk Coffee or Tea 1/2c Fruit Cocktail	K9 D15 O16 J37 J51	1/2c LF Marinated Cucumbers 3 oz LF Meatloaf with 2 oz LF Onion Gravy+ 1/2c LF Mashed Potatoes 1/2c Vegetable Medley+ 1 Dinner Roll 1/2c Skim Milk Coffee or Tea 1/2c Apricot Halves	K24 P1–8 D31 O3 P11 J47	1c Garden Salad with 1 Tbsp LC Salad Dressing 2 oz Roast Pork with 2 oz LF Brown Gravy 1/2c LF Cornbread Stuffing 1/2c Spinach 1 Dinner Roll 1/2c Skim Milk Coffee or Tea 1/2c Applesauce
C8 E2 J41 J1 Q10	2/3c Chicken Rice Soup 2 oz LF Chicken Fricassee with 2 oz LF Gravy 3 oz LF Parsley Potatoes 1/2c Asparagus Tips 1 Dinner Roll 1/2c Skim Milk Coffee or Tea 2" LF Strawberry Shortcake	C4 I5 P1–8 S16	2/3c SR/LF Bean Soup Chef Salad: 1 oz Turkey and 1 oz LF Cheese 1c Lettuce, Tomatoes, Onions, and Cucumbers 1 Tbsp LC Salad Dressing 1 Dinner Roll or 4 LF Crackers 1/2c Skim Milk Coffee or Tea 1/2c LF Chocolate Pudding	C15 F10 J8	2/3c Creole Soup 6 oz LF Tuna Noodle Casserole 1/2c LF Julienne Beets 1 Dinner Roll 1 tsp Margarine 1/2c Skim Milk Coffee or Tea 1/2c LF Sherbet
  S12	1/2c Juice or Skim Milk 2 LF Cookies or LF Crackers 1/2c Gelatin or Fresh Fruit	 S12	1/2c Juice or Skim Milk 2 LF Cookies or LF Crackers 1/2c Gelatin or Fresh Fruit	 S12	1/2c Juice or Skim Milk 2 LF Cookies or LF Crackers 1/2c Gelatin or Fresh Fruit

Recipe	Monday	Recipe	Tuesday	Recipe	Wednesday	Recipe	Thursday
	Breakfast						
	1/2c Pineapple Juice or		1/2c Grapefruit Juice		1/2c Cranberry Juice		1/2c Orange Juice or
	1 small Banana	B1	1/2c LF Farina or	B1	1/2c LF Wheatena or		1/2c Melon Cubes
B1	1/2c LF Cream of Wheat		3/4c Dry Cereal		3/4c Dry Cereal	B1	1/2c LF Cream of Rice or
	or 3/4c Dry Cereal	B4	1 Egg Substitute		1/4c LF Cottage Cheese		3/4c Dry Cereal
B4	1 Egg Substitute		1 sl Toast		1 Tbsp Jelly on	B4	1 Egg Substitute
	1 sl Toast		1 tsp Margarine		1 sl Raisin Bread	N12	1 LF sm Blueberry Muffin
	1 tsp Margarine		1 tsp Jam or Jelly		1c Skim Milk		1 tsp Margarine
	1 tsp Jam or Jelly		1c Skim Milk		Coffee or Tea		1 tsp Jam or Jelly
	1c Skim Milk		Coffee or Tea				1c Skim Milk
	Coffee or Tea						Coffee or Tea
	Lunch						
K28	1c Mixed Field Greens	K2	1/2c Pickled Beets	K31	1c LF Hawaiian Tossed Salad	K22	1/2c LF Three Bean Salad
P1–8	with 1 Tbsp LC Salad Dressing	D2	6 oz Beef Stew	D27	2 1/2 oz LF Veal Patty with	E16	2 oz Sliced Turkey with
E8	2 oz LF Tahitian Chicken	M1	1/2c Noodles	O13	2 oz LF Mushroom Gravy	O30	1/4c LF Sauté Onions+
	with 1 1/2 oz LF Sauce	N1	1 Biscuit	J24	1/2c LF Corn Confetti	M2	1/2c LF Lyonnaise Noodles
L5	1/2c Rice Pilaf+		1/2c Skim Milk	J50	1/2c LF Stewed Tomatoes	J18	1/2c LF Sunshine Carrots
J10	1/2c LF Steamed Broccoli		Coffee or Tea		1 Dinner Roll		1 Dinner Roll
	1 Dinner Roll		2 Pear Halves		1 tsp Margarine		1/2c Skim Milk
	1/2c Skim Milk				1/2c Skim Milk		Coffee or Tea
	Coffee or Tea				Coffee or Tea	S2	1/2c Spiced Applesauce
S8	1/2c Almond Peaches				1/2c LF Ice Milk		
	Dinner						
C28	2/3c French Vegetable Soup+	C8	2/3c Chicken Rice Soup+	C13	2/3c Cream of Spinach Soup	C21	2/3c Minestrone Soup+
I2	2 oz LF Grilled Cheese	E16	2 oz Turkey on	I6	1/2c LF Chicken Salad	M1	1/2c Spaghetti and
	Sandwich, 2 sl Bread		1 sl Bread with		Lettuce Leaves,	D13	2 oz LF Meatballs with
	1/2c Lettuce Leaves with	O5	2 oz LF Chicken Gravy		1 Radish Rose,	O20	2 oz Marinara Sauce
	4 sl Tomatoes	J37	1/2c LF Mashed Potatoes		3 sl Cucumbers	J26	1/2c Italian Mix Vegetables
P1–8	1 Tbsp LC Salad Dressing	J27	1/2c Mixed Vegetables+	K13	1/2c LF Macaroni Salad		1 sl Italian Bread
	1/2c Skim Milk		1/2c Skim Milk		1 Dinner Roll		1/2c Skim Milk
	Coffee or Tea		Coffee or Tea		1/2c Skim Milk		Coffee or Tea
Q4	3×2" sl LF Carrot Raisin Cake		4 Vanilla Wafers		Coffee or Tea	R4	1/8 LF Lemon Pie
					1/2c Fruit Cocktail		
	Snacks—Choice of:						
	1/2c Juice or Skim Milk		1/2c Juice or Skim Milk		1/2c Juice or Skim Milk		1/2c Juice or Skim Milk
	2 LF Cookies or LF Crackers		2 LF Cookies or LF Crackers		2 LF Cookies or LF Crackers		2 LF Cookies or LF Crackers
S12	1/2c Gelatin or Fresh Fruit	S12	1/2c Gelatin or Fresh Fruit	S12	1/2c Gelatin or Fresh Fruit	S12	1/2c Gelatin or Fresh Fruit

TERMS: LF = Low Fat; FF = Fat Free; LCH = Low Cholesterol; RC = Reduced Calorie; LC = Low Calorie; SR = Sodium or Salt Restricted. +Consider individual tolerance.
Amounts specified for food items that contain bone is equivalent to cooked, edible deboned portion.

Recipe	Friday	Recipe	Saturday	Recipe	Sunday
B1	1/2c Apple Juice 1/2c LF Oatmeal or 3/4c Dry Cereal	B1	1/2c Grapefruit Juice 1/2c LF Cream of Wheat or 3/4c Dry Cereal	B1	1/2c Pineapple Juice 1/2c LF Wheatena or 3/4c Dry Cereal
B4	1 Egg Substitute 1 sl Toast 1 tsp Margarine 1 tsp Jam or Jelly 1c Skim Milk Coffee or Tea	B4 N7	1 Egg Substitute 1/2"sl LF Date Nut Bread 1 Tbsp Cream Cheese or 1 tsp Margarine 1 tsp Jam or Jelly 1c Skim Milk Coffee or Tea	B8	1 sl LF French Toast with 2 oz Maple Syrup 1 tsp Jam or Jelly 1c Skim Milk Coffee or Tea
K24 P1–8 F3 O7 L1 J47	1c Garden Salad with 1 Tbsp LC Salad Dressing 3 oz LF Fish Creole with 2 oz LF Creole Sauce 1/2c White Rice 1/2c Spinach 1 Dinner Roll 1/2c Skim Milk Coffee or Tea 1/2c Chilled Apricots	K3 D29 J46 J6	1/2c LF Cabbage Apple Salad+ 2 oz LF Breaded Pork Chops 1/2c LF Whipped Sweet Potatoes 1/2c LF Seasoned Green Beans 1 Dinner Roll 1/2c Skim Milk Coffee or Tea 1/2c LF Sherbet	K26 P1–8 D19 J41 J54 S7	1c Green Vegetable Salad with 1 Tbsp LC Salad Dressing 1 oz LF Swiss Steak with 1 1/2 oz LF Gravy 3 oz LF Parsley Potatoes 1/2c LF Tarragon Zucchini 1 Dinner Roll 1/2c Skim Milk Coffee or Tea 1/2c Fruit Parfait
C7 E5 J35 J8 Q9	2/3c Beef Noodle Soup 2 oz LF Oven Crisp Chicken 1 sm Baked Potato 1/2c LF Julienne Beets 1 Dinner Roll 1 tsp Margarine 1/2c Skim Milk Coffee or Tea 1/2" sl LF Pound Cake	C29 G11 J49	2/3c Old Fashion Vegetable Soup 6 oz LF Macaroni & Cheese 1/2c Succotash 1 Dinner Roll 1/2c Skim Milk Coffee or Tea 2 Plums	C12 F1 O25 K5 S12	2/3c LF Cream Mushroom Soup 3 1/2 oz LF Fish Burger on 1 Bun 1 tsp LF Tartar Sauce 2 Lettuce Leaves 2 sl Tomatoes 1/2c Cole Slaw+ 1/2c Skim Milk Coffee or Tea 1/2c Cherry Gelatin
S12	1/2c Juice or Skim Milk 2 LF Cookies or LF Crackers 1/2c Gelatin or Fresh Fruit	S12	1/2c Juice or Skim Milk 2 LF Cookies or LF Crackers 1/2c Gelatin or Fresh Fruit	S12	1/2c Juice or Skim Milk 2 LF Cookies or LF Crackers 1/2c Gelatin or Fresh Fruit

Recipe	Monday	Recipe	Tuesday	Recipe	Wednesday	Recipe	Thursday
	Breakfast						
B1	1/2c Cranberry Juice 1/2c LF Oatmeal or 3/4c Dry Cereal		1/2c Orange Juice or 1/2c Fresh Berries	B1	1/2c Apple Juice 1/2c LF Farina or 3/4c Dry Cereal	B1	1/2c Grapefruit Juice 1/2c LF Wheatena or 3/4c Dry Cereal
B4	1 Egg Substitute 1 sl Toast 1 tsp Margarine 1 tsp Jam or Jelly 1c Skim Milk Coffee or Tea	B1 B4	1/2c LF Cream of Wheat or 3/4c Dry Cereal 1 Egg Substitute 1 sl Toast 1 tsp Margarine 1 tsp Jam or Jelly 1c Skim Milk Coffee or Tea	B4	1 Egg Substitute 1 English Muffin 1 tsp Margarine 1 tsp Jam or Jelly 1c Skim Milk Coffee or Tea		1/4c LF Cottage Cheese, Brown Sugar & Cinnamon on 1 sl Raisin Toast 1 tsp Jam or Jelly 1c Skim Milk Coffee or Tea
	Lunch						
K10	1/2c LF Cucumber Onion Salad	K4	1/2c LF Carrot-Raisin Salad	K25	1c Green Salad with	K24	1c Garden Salad with
E3	2 oz LF Chicken Italiano	D25	3 oz LF Veal Loaf with	P1	1 Tbsp LC French Dressing	P1–8	1 Tbsp LC Salad Dressing
M1	1/2c Spaghetti with	O3	2 oz LF Brown Gravy	E15	3/4c LF Turkey Jambalaya	D14	2 oz LF Sweet-n-Sour Meatballs
O22	2 oz LF Tomato Sauce	J37	1/2c LF Mashed Potatoes	J3	1/2c Green Beans		with 2 oz LF Sauce
J26	1/2c Italian Mix Vegetables+	J1	1/2c Asparagus Tips		1 Dinner Roll	M1	1/2c Noodles
	1 sl Italian Bread		1 Dinner Roll		1/2c Skim Milk	J48	1/2c Seasoned Spinach
	1/2c Skim Milk		1/2c Skim Milk		Coffee or Tea		1 Dinner Roll
	Coffee or Tea		Coffee or Tea	S17	1/2c LF Vanilla Pudding		1/2c Skim Milk
	1/2c Sliced Peaches	R7	2×2" srv LF Apple Crisp				Coffee or Tea
							1/2c Apricots
	Dinner						
C20	2/3c Julienne Soup	C3	2/3c Clear Vegetable Soup	C14	2/3c LF Cream Tomato Soup	C19	2/3c LF Onion Soup
I10	Fruit Festival with	G2	6 oz LF Cheese Lasagna	I22	Salad Sampler Platter with	G13	1/8 pie LF Broccoli Quiche
	1/2c LF Cottage Cheese	J51	1/2c Vegetable Medley+	I12	1/4c LF Ham Salad	J28	1/2c LF Mushrooms & Celery
	2/3c Seasonal Fruit		1 Dinner Roll	I6	1/4c LF Chicken Salad		1 Dinner Roll
S12	1/2c Gelatin Cubes		1/2c Skim Milk		Lettuce Leaves, 2 sl Onions,		1 tsp Margarine
N10–20	1 LF Muffin		Coffee or Tea		and 2 Green Pepper Rings		1/2c Skim Milk
	1 tsp Jam or Jelly		1/2c Pineapple Chunks	K21	1/2c LF Potato Salad		Coffee or Tea
	1/2c Skim Milk				1 Dinner Roll		1/2c LF Ice Milk
	Coffee or Tea				1/2c Skim Milk		
Q6	2×2" sl LF Chocolate Chip Cake				Coffee or Tea		
				S5	1/2c Fruit Cup		
	Snacks—Choice of:						
	1/2c Juice or Skim Milk 2 LF Cookies or LF Crackers		1/2c Juice or Skim Milk 2 LF Cookies or LF Crackers		1/2c Juice or Skim Milk 2 LF Cookies or LF Crackers		1/2c Juice or Skim Milk 2 LF Cookies or LF Crackers
S12	1/2c Gelatin or Fresh Fruit	S12	1/2c Gelatin or Fresh Fruit	S12	1/2c Gelatin or Fresh Fruit	S12	1/2c Gelatin or Fresh Fruit

TERMS: LF = Low Fat; FF = Fat Free; LCH = Low Cholesterol; RC = Reduced Calorie; LC = Low Calorie; SR = Sodium or Salt Restricted. +Consider individual tolerance.
Amounts specified for food items that contain bone is equivalent to cooked, edible deboned portion.

Recipe	Friday	Recipe	Saturday	Recipe	Sunday
B1	1/2c Orange Juice or 1 small Banana 1/2c LF Cream of Rice or 3/4c Dry Cereal	B1	1/2c Apple Juice 1/2c LF Oatmeal or 3/4c Dry Cereal	B1	1/2c Cranberry Juice 1/2c LF Farina or 3/4c Dry Cereal
B4	1 Egg Substitute 1 sl Toast 1 tsp Margarine 1 tsp Jam or Jelly 1c Skim Milk Coffee or Tea	B4	1 Egg Substitute 1 sl Toast 1 tsp Margarine 1 tsp Jam or Jelly 1c Skim Milk Coffee or Tea	B4 B12	1 Egg Substitute 1 Waffle with 2 oz Maple Syrup 1 tsp Jam or Jelly 1c Skim Milk Coffee or Tea
K2 F5 O25 L5 J27	1/2c Pickled Beets 3 oz LF Catch of the Day with 1 tsp LF Tartar Sauce Lemon Wedge 1/2c Rice Pilaf+ 1/2c Mixed Vegetables+ 1 Dinner Roll 1/2c Skim Milk Coffee or Tea 2 Pear Halves	K29 P1–8 D28 J45 J3 S13	1c Tossed Salad with 1 Tbsp LC Salad Dressing 2 oz Baked Glazed Ham 1/2c LF Sweet Potatoes/Apples 1/2c String Beans 1 Dinner Roll 1/2c Skim Milk Coffee or Tea 1/2c Fruited Lime Gelatin	K16 D3 C1 J40 J10	1/2c LF Mixed Vegetable Salad 2 oz Brisket of Beef with 2 oz LF Broth 4 oz LF Potato Pancakes 1/2c LF Broccoli Cuts+ 1 Dinner Roll 1 tsp Margarine 1/2c Skim Milk Coffee or Tea 1/2c Applesauce
C23 E7 J35 J19 Q8	2/3c LF Split Pea Soup 2 oz LF Roast Chicken 1 medium Baked Potato with 1 Tbsp Sour Cream 1/2c LF Carrot Tzimmes 1 Dinner Roll 1/2c Skim Milk Coffee or Tea 3×2" sl LF Marble Cake	C21 G1 J55	2/3c Minestrone Soup+ 5 oz Cheese Fettucine 1/2c LF Zucchini-Onions 1 sl Italian Bread 1/2c Skim Milk Coffee or Tea 2 Plums	C27 I18 I23 K15	2/3c Chunky Vegetable Soup 1/2c LF Seafood Salad Stuffed Tomato 1/2c LF Cheesy Macaroni Salad 1 Dinner Roll 1/2c Skim Milk Coffee or Tea 1/2c LF Sherbet
S12	1/2c Juice or Skim Milk 2 LF Cookies or LF Crackers 1/2c Gelatin or Fresh Fruit	S12	1/2c Juice or Skim Milk 2 LF Cookies or LF Crackers 1/2c Gelatin or Fresh Fruit	S12	1/2c Juice or Skim Milk 2 LF Cookies or LF Crackers 1/2c Gelatin or Fresh Fruit

Recipe	Monday	Recipe	Tuesday	Recipe	Wednesday	Recipe	Thursday
	Breakfast						
	1/2c Apple Juice or		1/2c Orange Juice		1/2c Pineapple Juice		1/2c Apple Juice or
	1/2c Fresh Fruit	B1	1/2c LF Oatmeal or	B1	1/2c LF Cream of Wheat or	S11	3 Stewed Prunes
B1	1/2c LF Cream of Rice or		3/4c Dry Cereal		3/4c Dry Cereal	B1	1/2c LF Farina or
	3/4c Dry Cereal	B4	1 Egg Substitute	B4	1 Egg Substitute		3/4c Dry Cereal
I2	1 oz LF Grilled Cheese on		1 English Muffin		1 sl Toast	B4	1 Egg Substitute
	1 sl Toast		1 tsp Margarine		1 tsp Margarine		1 sl Raisin Toast
	1 tsp Margarine		1 tsp Jam or Jelly		1 tsp Jam or Jelly		1 tsp Margarine
	1 tsp Jam or Jelly		1c Skim Milk		1c Skim Milk		1 tsp Jam or Jelly
	1c Skim Milk		Coffee or Tea		Coffee or Tea		1c Skim Milk
	Coffee or Tea						Coffee or Tea
	Lunch						
K29	1c Tossed Salad with	K23	1/2c LF Marinated Zucchini	K32	1c Tossed Vegetable Salad	K25	1c Green Salad with
P8	1 Tbsp LC Thousand	D22	2 1/2 oz LF Breaded Veal		with 1 Tbsp LC Salad Dressing	P1–8	1 Tbsp LC Salad Dressing
	Island Dressing	O20	with 2 oz Marinara Sauce+	D1	3 oz LF Beef Teriyaki	D30	2 oz Pork Chops with
E1	2 oz LF Barbecue Chicken	M5	3/4c LF Pasta Primavera	J22	1/2c Chinese Vegetables		1/4c LC Apple Stuffing
O2	with 2 oz Barbecue Sauce+		1 sl Italian Bread	L1	1/2c White Rice	J1	1/2c Asparagus Tips
J31	1/2c Green Peas		1/2c Skim Milk		1 Dinner Roll		1 Dinner Roll
J14	1/2c Carrots		Coffee or Tea		1/2c Skim Milk		1/2c Skim Milk
	1 Dinner Roll	S5	1/2c Fresh Fruit Cup		Coffee or Tea		Coffee or Tea
	1/2c Skim Milk				1/2c LF Ice Milk	S16	1/2c LF Chocolate Pudding
	Coffee or Tea						
	1/2c Sliced Peaches						
	Dinner						
C11	2/3c LF Cream Celery Soup	C4	2/3c SR/LF Bean Soup	C26	2/3c Vegetable Beef Soup	C21	2/3c Minestrone Soup+
G8	5 1/2 oz Egg Substitute with	I4	Asst Cold Cut Sandwiches	E13	2/3c LF Turkey à la King	D12	6 oz LF Beef Macaroni Casserole
	Vegetables		2 sl Bread (cut in quarters)		with 2 Toast Points	J6	1/2c LF Seasoned Green Beans
J36	1/2c Home Fried Potatoes		with 3 oz Roast Beef and	J47	1/2c Spinach		1 Dinner Roll
	1 Dinner Roll		Turkey		1/2c Skim Milk		1/2c Skim Milk
	1/2c Skim Milk		Lettuce Leaves		Coffee or Tea		Coffee or Tea
	Coffee or Tea		2 sl Tomatoes		2 Plums		1/2c Chilled Apricots
Q2	2 ×2" sl LF Banana Cake	K5	1/2c Cole Slaw+				
			1 tsp Catsup, 1 tsp Mustard				
			1 Tbsp LF Mayonnaise				
			1/2c Skim Milk				
			Coffee or Tea				
		S12	1/2c Strawberry Gelatin				
	Snacks—Choice of:						
	1/2c Juice or Skim Milk		1/2c Juice or Skim Milk		1/2c Juice or Skim Milk		1/2c Juice or Skim Milk
	2 LF Cookies or LF Crackers		2 LF Cookies or LF Crackers		2 LF Cookies or LF Crackers		2 LF Cookies or LF Crackers
S12	1/2c Gelatin or Fresh Fruit	S12	1/2c Gelatin or Fresh Fruit	S12	1/2c Gelatin or Fresh Fruit	S12	1/2c Gelatin or Fresh Fruit

TERMS: LF = Low Fat; FF = Fat Free; LCH = Low Cholesterol; RC = Reduced Calorie; LC = Low Calorie; SR = Sodium or Salt Restricted. +Consider individual tolerance.
Amounts specified for food items that contain bone is equivalent to cooked, edible deboned portion.

Recipe	Friday	Recipe	Saturday	Recipe	Sunday
B1	1/2c Grapefruit Juice		1/2c Cranberry Juice or	B1	1/2c Pineapple Juice
	1/2c LF Wheatena or		1 small Banana		1/2c LF Oatmeal or
	3/4c Dry Cereal	B1	1/2c LF Cream of Rice or		3/4c Dry Cereal
B4	1 Egg Substitute		3/4c Dry Cereal	B8	1 sl LF French Toast with
N14	1 LF Bran Muffin	G9	2 1/2 oz Western Egg		2 oz Maple Syrup
	1 tsp Margarine		Substitute		1 tsp Margarine
	1 tsp Jam or Jelly		1 sl Toast		1 tsp Jam or Jelly
	1c Skim Milk		1 tsp Margarine		1c Skim Milk
	Coffee or Tea		1 tsp Jam or Jelly		Coffee or Tea
			1c Skim Milk		
			Coffee or Tea		
K9	1/2c LF Marinated Cucumbers	K37	4 oz Perfection Salad	K42	1/2c Cranberry Mold
F9	2 oz LF Sole Almondine	D18	4 oz LF Stuffed Cabbage+	E16	2 oz LF Roast Turkey with
O25	1 tsp LF Tartar Sauce	J43	1/2c LF Whipped Potatoes	O5	2 oz LF Chicken Gravy
	Lemon Wedge	J15	1/2c LF Glazed Carrots	P12	1/4c LF Raisin Bread Stuffing
L2	1/2c LF Rice Chantilly		1 Dinner Roll	J52	1/2c Zucchini
J51	1/2c Vegetable Medley+		1/2c Skim Milk		1 Dinner Roll
	1 Dinner Roll		Coffee or Tea		1 tsp Margarine
	1/2c Skim Milk		1/2c Pineapple Tidbits		1/2c Skim Milk
	Coffee or Tea				Coffee or Tea
	3 Vanilla Wafers			R3	1/8 LF Apple Pie
C9	2/3c LF Chicken Matzo Ball Soup	C24	2/3c LF Tomato Soup	C3	2/3c Clear Vegetable Soup
E9	2 oz LF Baked Chicken Tarragon	I21	1/2c LF Curry Tuna Salad	G2	5 oz LF Lasagna
M4	4 oz LF Noodle Pudding		Lettuce Leaves,	J27	1/2c Mixed Vegetables+
J10	1/2c LF Steamed Broccoli+		2 sl Onions, 3 sl Cucumbers,	N8	1 sl LF Garlic Bread
	1 Dinner Roll		1 Radish Rose		1/2c Skim Milk
	1/2c Skim Milk	K13	1/2c LF Macaroni Salad		Coffee or Tea
	Coffee or Tea		1 Dinner Roll or	S4	1/2c Fruit Compote
S1	1 medium Baked Apple		4 LF Crackers		
			1/2c Skim Milk		
			Coffee or Tea		
			1/2c LF Sherbet		
	1/2c Juice or Skim Milk		1/2c Juice or Skim Milk		1/2c Juice or Skim Milk
	2 LF Cookies or LF Crackers		2 LF Cookies or LF Crackers		2 LF Cookies or LF Crackers
S12	1/2c Gelatin or Fresh Fruit	S12	1/2c Gelatin or Fresh Fruit	S12	1/2c Gelatin or Fresh Fruit

Recipe	Monday	Recipe	Tuesday	Recipe	Wednesday	Recipe	Thursday
	Breakfast						
	1/2c UNSW Orange Juice		1/2c UNSW Apple Juice		1/2c UNSW Grapefruit Juice		1/2c UNSW Pineapple Juice
B1	1/2c DB Farina or	B1	1/2c DB Wheatena or		or 1 small Banana	B1	1/2c DB Oatmeal or
	3/4c UNSW Dry Cereal		3/4c UNSW Dry Cereal	B1	1/2c DB Cream of Rice or		3/4c UNSW Dry Cereal
B4	1 Soft-Cooked Egg	G6	2 oz DB Cheese Omelet		3/4c UNSW Dry Cereal	I2	1 oz LF Grilled Cheese
	1 sl Toast		1 English Muffin	B5	1 Scrambled Egg		on 1 sl Toast
	1 tsp Margarine		1 tsp Margarine		1 sl Toast		1 tsp Margarine
	1 tsp DB Jam/Jelly		1 tsp DB Jam/Jelly		1 tsp Margarine		1c Skim Milk
	1c Skim Milk		1c Skim Milk		1 tsp DB Jam/Jelly		Coffee or Tea
	Coffee or Tea		Coffee or Tea		1c Skim Milk		
					Coffee or Tea		
	Lunch						
K29	1c Tossed Salad with	K35	1/2c DB Molded Veg Salad	K25	1c Green Salad with	K22	1/2c DB Three Bean Salad
P1	1 Tbsp LC French Dressing	E4	3 oz LF Lemon Chicken	P4	1 Tbsp Italian Dressing	E14	1c Turkey Chow Mein
D6	8 oz LF Pepper Steak	J39	4 oz LF Oven Browned Potatoes	D26	5 oz DB Veal Parmesan	L1	1/2c White Rice
L3	1/2c LF Rice Florentine	J10	1/2c LF Broccoli	M1	1/2c Spaghetti with		1/4c Chinese Noodles
	1 Dinner Roll		1 Dinner Roll	O22	2 oz DB Tomato Sauce		1 Dinner Roll
	1 tsp Margarine		1 tsp Margarine	J55	1/2c LF Zucchini-Onions		1 tsp Margarine
	1/2c Skim Milk		1/2c Skim Milk		1 Dinner Roll		1/2c Skim Milk
	Coffee or Tea		Coffee or Tea		1 tsp Margarine		Coffee or Tea
	1/2c UNSW Sliced Peaches	S3	1/2c Citrus Cup		1/2c Skim Milk		2 UNSW Plums
					Coffee or Tea		
				S10	1/2 DB Baked Pear		
	Dinner						
C23	2/3c LF Split Pea Soup	C12	2/3c LF Cream Mushroom Soup	C27	2/3c Chunky Vegetable Soup	C18	2/3c LF Onion Soup
I12	1/2c LF Ham Salad on	D17	4 oz LF Sloppy Joe on	I18	1/2c LF Seafood Salad on	G13	1/6 pie DB Spinach Quiche
	Lettuce Leaves		1 Bun		1 Croissant	K32	1c Tossed Vegetable Salad
	3 sl Tomatoes and	J24	1/2c LF Corn Confetti	K40	1/2c LF Waldorf Salad	P1–8	1 Tbsp LC Salad Dressing
	3 sl Cucumbers		1/2c Skim Milk		1/2c Skim Milk		1 Dinner Roll
K5	1/2c DB Cole Slaw		Coffee or Tea		Coffee or Tea		1 tsp Margarine
	1 Dinner Roll		1/2c LF Ice Milk	S12	1/2c DB Orange Gelatin		1/2c Skim Milk
	1 tsp Margarine						Coffee or Tea
	1/2c Skim Milk						3 Graham Crackers
	Coffee or Tea						
S17	1/2c DB Vanilla Pudding						
	Snacks:						
	1/2 Milk Exchange		1/2 Milk Exchange		1/2 Milk Exchange		1/2 Milk Exchange
	1 Starch/Bread Exchange		1 Starch/Bread Exchange		1 Starch/Bread Exchange		1 Starch/Bread Exchange
	1 Meat Exchange		1 Meat Exchange		1 Meat Exchange		1 Meat Exchange
	1 Fat Exchange		1 Fat Exchange		1 Fat Exchange		1 Fat Exchange

TERMS: LF = Low Fat; FF = Fat Free; SR = Sodium or Salt Restricted; STR = Strained; DB = Diabetic; UNSW = Unsweetened; RC = Reduced Calorie; LC = Low Calorie; EXCH = Diabetic Exchange.
Amounts specified for food items that contain bone is equivalent to cooked, edible deboned portion.

Recipe	Friday	Recipe	Saturday	Recipe	Sunday
S11	1/2c UNSW Cranberry Juice or 3 medium Stewed Prunes	B1	1/2c UNSW Apple Juice 1/2c DB Wheatena or	B1	1/2c UNSW Orange Juice 1/2c DB Farina or
B1	1/2c DB Cream of Wheat or 3/4c UNSW Dry Cereal	B4	3/4c UNSW Dry Cereal 1 Hard-Boiled Egg	B4,5	3/4c UNSW Dry Cereal 1 Egg of Choice
B4	1 Poached Egg		1 sl Toast	B9	2 DB Pancakes (4" across)
	1 sl Toast		1 tsp Margarine		with 1 oz DB Maple Syrup
	1 tsp Margarine		1 tsp DB Jam/Jelly		1 tsp Margarine
	1 tsp DB Jam/Jelly		1c Skim Milk		1 tsp DB Jam/Jelly
	1c Skim Milk		Coffee or Tea		1c Skim Milk
	Coffee or Tea				Coffee or Tea
K20	1/2c LF Cheesy Pea Salad	K9	1/2c DB Marinated	K24	1c Garden Salad with
F4	3 1/2 oz LF Oven Fried Fish	D15	Cucumbers	P1–8	1 Tbsp LC Salad Dressing
O25	2 Tbsp LF Tartar Sauce	O16	4 oz Meatloaf with	D31	3 oz Roast Pork with
M2	1/2c LF Lyonnaise Noodles	J37	2 oz LF Onion Gravy	O3	2 oz LF Brown Gravy
J15	1/2c DB Glazed Carrots	J51	1/2c LF Mashed Potatoes	P11	1/2c DB Cornbread Stuffing
	1 Dinner Roll		1/2c Vegetable Medley	J47	1/2c Spinach
	1 tsp Margarine		1 Dinner Roll		1 Dinner Roll
	1/2c Skim Milk		1 tsp Margarine		1 tsp Margarine
	Coffee or Tea		1/2c Skim Milk		1/2c Skim Milk
	1/2c UNSW Fruit Cocktail		Coffee or Tea		Coffee or Tea
			1/2c UNSW Apricot Halves		1/2c UNSW Applesauce
C8	2/3c Chicken Rice Soup	C4	2/3c SR/LF Bean Soup	C15	2/3c Creole Soup
E2	3 oz LF Chicken Fricassee	I5	Chef Salad: 1 oz LF Ham,	F10	8 oz LF Tuna Noodle Casserole
	with 2 oz LF Gravy		1 oz Turkey and	J8	1/2c DB Julienne Beets
J41	3 oz LF Parsley Potatoes		1 oz LF Cheese		1 Dinner Roll
J1	1/2c Asparagus Tips		1c Lettuce, Tomatoes,		1 tsp Margarine
	1 Dinner Roll		Onions, and Cucumbers		1/2c Skim Milk
	1 tsp Margarine	P1–8	1 Tbsp LC Salad Dressing		Coffee or Tea
	1/2c Skim Milk		1 Dinner Roll or		1/2c LF Sherbet
	Coffee or Tea		4 LF Crackers		
Q10	2" DB Strawberry Shortcake		1 tsp Margarine		
			1/2c Skim Milk		
			Coffee or Tea		
		S16	1/2c DB Chocolate Pudding		
	1/2 Milk Exchange		1/2 Milk Exchange		1/2 Milk Exchange
	1 Starch/Bread Exchange		1 Starch/Bread Exchange		1 Starch/Bread Exchange
	1 Meat Exchange		1 Meat Exchange		1 Meat Exchange
	1 Fat Exchange		1 Fat Exchange		1 Fat Exchange

Recipe	Monday	Recipe	Tuesday	Recipe	Wednesday	Recipe	Thursday
	Breakfast						
	1/2c UNSW Pineapple Juice		1/2c UNSW Grapefruit Juice		1/2c UNSW Cranberry Juice		1/2c UNSW Orange Juice
	or 1 small Banana	B1	1/2c DB Farina or	B1	1/2c DB Wheatena or		or 1/2c Melon Cubes
B1	1/2c DB Cream of Wheat		3/4c UNSW Dry Cereal		3/4c UNSW Dry Cereal	B1	1/2c DB Cream of Rice or
	or 3/4c UNSW Dry Cereal	B4	1 Soft-Cooked Egg		1 Tbsp Peanut Butter and		3/4c UNSW Dry Cereal
B5	1 Scrambled Egg		1 sl Toast		1Tbsp DB Jelly on	B4	1 Poached Egg
D33	1 Sausage Link		1 tsp Margarine		1sl Raisin Bread	N12	1 sm DB Blueberry Muffin
	1 sl Toast		1 tsp DB Jam/Jelly		1 tsp Margarine		1 tsp Margarine
	1 tsp Margarine		1c Skim Milk		1c Skim Milk		1 tsp DB Jam/Jelly
	1 tsp DB Jam/Jelly		Coffee or Tea		Coffee or Tea		1c Skim Milk
	1c Skim Milk						Coffee or Tea
	Coffee or Tea						
	Lunch						
K28	1c Mixed Field Greens	K2	1/2c DB Pickled Beets	K31	1c DB Hawaiian Tossed Salad	K22	1/2c DB Three Bean Salad
P1–8	1 Tbsp LC Salad Dressing	D2	8 oz Beef Stew	D27	3 1/2 oz Veal Patty with	D37	3 oz DB Braised Liver with
E8	3 oz LF Tahitian Chicken	M1	1/2c Noodles	O13	2 oz LF Mushroom Gravy		1/4c LF Sauté Onions
	with 1 1/2 oz LF Sauce	n1	1 Biscuit	J24	1/2c LF Corn Confetti	M2	1/2c LF Lyonnaise Noodles
L5	1/2c Rice Pilaf		1 tsp Margarine	J50	1/2c DB Stewed Tomatoes	J18	1/2c DB Sunshine Carrots
J10	1/2c LF Steamed Broccoli		1/2c Skim Milk		1 Dinner Roll		1 Dinner Roll
	1 Dinner Roll		Coffee or Tea		1 tsp Margarine		1 tsp Margarine
	1 tsp Margarine		2 UNSW Pear Halves		1/2c Skim Milk		1/2c Skim Milk
	1/2c Skim Milk				Coffee or Tea		Coffee or Tea
	Coffee or Tea				1/2c LF Ice Milk	S2	1/2c DB Spiced Applesauce
S8	1/2c Almond Peaches						
	Dinner						
C28	2/3c French Vegetable Soup	C8	2/3c Chicken Rice Soup	C13	2/3c LF Cream of Spinach Soup	C21	2/3c Minestrone Soup
I2	3 oz LF Grilled Cheese	E16	3 oz Turkey on	I9	1/2c DB Egg Salad Platter	M1	1/2c Spaghetti and
	Sandwich, 2 sl Bread		1 sl Bread with		Lettuce Leaves,	D13	3 oz Meatballs with
	1/2c Lettuce Leaves with	O5	2 oz LF Chicken Gravy		1 Radish Rose,	O20	2 oz Marinara Sauce
	4 sl Tomatoes	J37	1/2c LF Mashed Potatoes		3 sl Cucumbers	J26	1/2c Italian Mix Vegetables
P1–8	1 Tbsp LC Salad Dressing	J27	1/2c Mixed Vegetables	K13	1/2c LF Macaroni Salad		1 sl Italian Bread
	1/2c Skim Milk		1 tsp Margarine		1 Dinner Roll		1 tsp Margarine
	Coffee or Tea		1/2c Skim Milk		1 tsp Margarine		1/2c Skim Milk
Q4	3×2" sl DB Carrot Raisin Cake		Coffee or Tea		1/2c Skim Milk		Coffee or Tea
			4 Vanilla Wafers		Coffee or Tea	R4	1/8 DB Lemon Pie
					1/2c UNSW Fruit Cocktail		
	Snacks:						
	1/2 Milk Exchange		1/2 Milk Exchange		1/2 Milk Exchange		1/2 Milk Exchange
	1 Starch/Bread Exchange		1 Starch/Bread Exchange		1 Starch/Bread Exchange		1 Starch/Bread Exchange
	1 Meat Exchange		1 Meat Exchange		1 Meat Exchange		1 Meat Exchange
	1 Fat Exchange		1 Fat Exchange		1 Fat Exchange		1 Fat Exchange

TERMS: LF = Low Fat; FF = Fat Free; SR = Sodium or Salt Restricted; STR = Strained; DB = Diabetic; UNSW = Unsweetened; RC = Reduced Calorie; LC = Low Calorie; EXCH = Diabetic Exchange.
Amounts specified for food items that contain bone is equivalent to cooked, edible deboned portion.

Recipe	Friday	Recipe	Saturday	Recipe	Sunday
B1	1/2c UNSW Apple Juice 1/2c DB Oatmeal or 3/4c UNSW Dry Cereal	B1	1/2c UNSW Grapefruit Juice 1/2c DB Cream of Wheat or 3/4c UNSW Dry Cereal	B1	1/2c UNSW Pineapple Juice 1/2c DB Wheatena or 3/4c UNSW Dry Cereal
B4	1 Hard-Boiled Egg 1 sl Toast 1 tsp Margarine 1 tsp DB Jam/Jelly 1c Skim Milk Coffee or Tea	B5 N7	1 Scrambled Egg 1/2" sl DB Date Nut Bread 1 Tbsp Cream Cheese or 1 tsp Margarine 1 tsp DB Jam/Jelly 1c Skim Milk Coffee or Tea	B8	1 sl French Toast with 1 oz DB Maple Syrup 1 tsp Margarine 1 tsp DB Jam/Jelly 1c Skim Milk Coffee or Tea
K24 P1–8 F3 O7 L1 J47	1c Garden Salad with 1 Tbsp LC Salad Dressing 3 oz DB Fish Creole with 2 oz DB Creole Sauce 1/2c White Rice 1/2c Spinach 1 Dinner Roll 1 tsp Margarine 1/2c Skim Milk Coffee or Tea 1/2c UNSW Chilled Apricots	K3 D29 J46 J6	1/2c DB Cabbage Apple Salad 3 oz DB Breaded Pork Chops 1/2c LF Whipped Sweet Potatoes 1/2c LF Seasoned Green Beans 1 Dinner Roll 1 tsp Margarine 1/2c Skim Milk Coffee or Tea 1/2c LF Sherbet	K26 P1–8 D19 J41 J54 S7	1c Green Vegetable Salad 1 Tbsp LC Salad Dressing 3 oz LF Swiss Steak with 1 1/2 oz LF Gravy 3 oz LF Parsley Potatoes 1/2c LF Tarragon Zucchini 1 Dinner Roll 1 tsp Margarine 1/2c Skim Milk Coffee or Tea 1/2c Fruit Parfait with 1 Tbsp Whipped Topping
C7 E5 J35 J8 Q9	2/3c Beef Noodle Soup 3 oz LF Oven Crisp Chicken 1 sm Baked Potato with 1 oz Sour Cream 1/2c LF Julienne Beets 1 Dinner Roll 1 tsp Margarine 1/2c Skim Milk Coffee or Tea 3/4" sl DB Pound Cake	C29 G11 J49	2/3c Old Fashion Vegtble Soup 8 oz LF Macaroni & Cheese 1/2c Succotash 1 Dinner Roll 1 tsp Margarine 1/2c Skim Milk Coffee or Tea 2 UNSW Plums	C12 F1 O25 K5 S12	2/3c LF Cream Mushroom Soup 3 1/2 oz LF Fish Burger on 1 Bun 2 Tbsp LF Tartar Sauce 2 Lettuce Leaves 2 sl Tomatoes 1/2c DB Cole Slaw 1/2c Skim Milk Coffee or Tea 1/2c DB Cherry Gelatin
	1/2 Milk Exchange 1 Starch/Bread Exchange 1 Meat Exchange 1 Fat Exchange		1/2 Milk Exchange 1 Starch/Bread Exchange 1 Meat Exchange 1 Fat Exchange		1/2 Milk Exchange 1 Starch/Bread Exchange 1 Meat Exchange 1 Fat Exchange

Recipe	Monday	Recipe	Tuesday	Recipe	Wednesday	Recipe	Thursday
	Breakfast						
B1	1/2c UNSW Cranberry Juice 1/2c DB Oatmeal or 3/4c UNSW Dry Cereal		1/2c UNSW Orange Juice or 1/2c Fresh Berries	B1	1/2c UNSW Apple Juice 1/2c DB Farina or 3/4c UNSW Dry Cereal	B1	1/2c UNSW Grapefruit Juice 1/2c DB Wheatena or 3/4c UNSW Dry Cereal
B4	1 Hard-Boiled Egg	B1	1/2c DB Cream of Wheat or 3/4c UNSW Dry Cereal	B4	1 Poached Egg		1/4c LF Cottage Cheese with Artificial Sweetener
	1 sl Toast	G7	2 oz DB Ham Omelet		1 English Muffin		and Cinnamon
	1 tsp Margarine		1 sl Toast		1 tsp Margarine		on 1 sl Raisin Toast
	1 tsp DB Jam/Jelly		1 tsp Margarine		1 tsp DB Jam/Jelly		1 tsp Margarine
	1c Skim Milk		1 tsp DB Jam/Jelly		1c Skim Milk		1 tsp DB Jam/Jelly
	Coffee or Tea		1c Skim Milk		Coffee or Tea		1c Skim Milk
			Coffee or Tea				Coffee or Tea
	Lunch						
K10	1/2c DB Cucumber Onion Salad	K4	1/2c LF Carrot-Raisin Salad	K25	1c Green Salad with	K24	1c Garden Salad with
E3	3 oz LF Chicken Italiano	D25	4 oz Veal Loaf with	P1	1 Tbsp LC French Dressing	P1–8	1 Tbsp LC Salad Dressing
M1	1/2c Spaghetti with	O3	2 oz LF Brown Gravy	E15	1c Turkey Jambalaya	D14	3 oz DB Sweet-n-Sour Meatballs
O22	2 oz DB Tomato Sauce	J37	1/2c LF Mashed Potatoes	J3	1/2c Green Beans		with 2 oz DB Sauce
J26	1/2c Italian Mix Vegetables	J1	1/2c Asparagus Tips		1 Dinner Roll	M1	1/2c Noodles
	1 sl Italian Bread		1 Dinner Roll		1 tsp Margarine	J48	1/2c Seasoned Spinach
	1 tsp Margarine		1 tsp Margarine		1/2c Skim Milk		1 Dinner Roll
	1/2c Skim Milk		1/2c Skim Milk		Coffee or Tea		1 tsp Margarine
	Coffee or Tea		Coffee or Tea	S17	1/2c DB Vanilla Pudding		1/2c Skim Milk
	1/2c UNSW Sliced Peaches	R7	2×2" srv DB Apple Crisp				Coffee or Tea
							1/2c UNSW Apricots
	Dinner						
C20	2/3c Julienne Soup	C3	2/3c Clear Vegetable Soup	C14	2/3c LF Cream Tomato Soup	C19	2/3c LF Onion Soup
I10	Fruit Festival with	G3	6 oz DB Cheese Strata	I22	Salad Sampler Platter with	G12	1/6 pie DB Quiche Lorraine
	1/2c Cottage Cheese	J51	1/2c Vegetable Medley	I12	1/4c LF Ham Salad	J28	1/2c LF Mushrooms & Celery
	2/3c Seasonal Fruit		1 Dinner Roll	I6	1/4c LF Chicken Salad		1 Dinner Roll
S12	1/2c DB Gelatin Cubes		1 tsp Margarine		Lettuce Leaves, 2 sl Onions,		1 tsp Margarine
N10–20	1 DB Muffin		1/2c Skim Milk		and 2 Green Pepper Rings		1/2c Skim Milk
	1 tsp Margarine		Coffee or Tea	K21	1/2c LF Potato Salad		Coffee or Tea
	1 tsp DB Jam/Jelly		1/2c UNSW Pineapple		1 Dinner Roll		1/2c LF Ice Milk
	1/2c Skim Milk		Chunks		1 tsp Margarine		
	Coffee or Tea				1/2c Skim Milk		
Q6	2×2" sl DB Chocolate Chip Cake				Coffee or Tea		
				S5	1/2c Fruit Cup		
	Snacks:						
	1/2 Milk Exchange		1/2 Milk Exchange		1/2 Milk Exchange		1/2 Milk Exchange
	1 Starch/Bread Exchange		1 Starch/Bread Exchange		1 Starch/Bread Exchange		1 Starch/Bread Exchange
	1 Meat Exchange		1 Meat Exchange		1 Meat Exchange		1 Meat Exchange
	1 Fat Exchange		1 Fat Exchange		1 Fat Exchange		1 Fat Exchange

TERMS: LF = Low Fat; FF = Fat Free; SR = Sodium or Salt Restricted; STR = Strained; DB = Diabetic; UNSW = Unsweetened; RC = Reduced Calorie; LC = Low Calorie; EXCH = Diabetic Exchange.
Amounts specified for food items that contain bone is equivalent to cooked, edible deboned portion.

Recipe	Friday	Recipe	Saturday	Recipe	Sunday
B1	1/2c UNSW Orange Juice or 1 small Banana 1/2c DB Cream of Rice or 3/4c UNSW Dry Cereal	B1	1/2c UNSW Apple Juice 1/2c DB Oatmeal or 3/4c UNSW Dry Cereal	B1	1/2c UNSW Cranberry Juice 1/2c DB Farina or 3/4c UNSW Dry Cereal
B5	1 Scrambled Egg 1 sl Toast 1 tsp Margarine 1 tsp DB Jam/Jelly 1c Skim Milk Coffee or Tea	B4	1 Hard-Boiled Egg 1 sl Toast 1 tsp Margarine 1 tsp DB Jam/Jelly 1c Skim Milk Coffee or Tea	B4,5 B12	1 Egg of Choice 1 DB Waffle (4 1/2" sq) with 1 oz DB Maple Syrup 1 tsp Margarine 1 tsp DB Jam/Jelly 1c Skim Milk Coffee or Tea
K2 F5 O25 L5 J27	1/2c DB Pickled Beets 3 oz LF Catch of the Day 2 Tbsp LF Tartar Sauce Lemon Wedge 1/2c Rice Pilaf 1/2c Mixed Vegetables 1 Dinner Roll 1 tsp Margarine 1/2c Skim Milk Coffee or Tea 2 UNSW Pear Halves	K29 P1–8 D28 J45 J3 S13	1c Tossed Salad with 1 Tbsp LC Salad Dressing 3 oz DB Baked Ham 1/2c DB Sweet Potatoes/Apples 1/2c String Beans 1 Dinner Roll 1 tsp Margarine 1/2c Skim Milk Coffee or Tea 1/2c DB Fruited Lime Gelatin	K16 D3 C1 J40 J10	1/2c DB Mixed Vegetable Salad 3 oz Brisket of Beef with 2 oz LF Broth 4 oz DB Potato Pancakes 1/2c LF Broccoli Cuts 1 Dinner Roll 1 tsp Margarine 1/2c Skim Milk Coffee or Tea 1/2c UNSW Applesauce
C23 E7 J35 J19 Q8	2/3c LF Split Pea Soup 3 oz LF Roast Chicken 1 medium Baked Potato with 1 oz Sour Cream 1/2c DB Carrot Tzimmes 1 Dinner Roll 1 tsp Margarine 1/2c Skim Milk Coffee or Tea 3×2" sl DB Marble Cake	C21 G1 J55	2/3c Minestrone Soup 6 oz LF Cheese Fettucine 1/2c LF Zucchini-Onions 1 sl Italian Bread 1 tsp Margarine 1/2c Skim Milk Coffee or Tea 2 UNSW Plums	C27 I18 I23 K15	2/3c Chunky Vegetable Soup 1/2c LF Seafood Salad Stuffed Tomato 1/2c LF Cheesy Macaroni Salad 1 Dinner Roll 1 tsp Margarine 1/2c Skim Milk Coffee or Tea 1/2c LF Sherbet
	1/2 Milk Exchange 1 Starch/Bread Exchange 1 Meat Exchange 1 Fat Exchange		1/2 Milk Exchange 1 Starch/Bread Exchange 1 Meat Exchange 1 Fat Exchange		1/2 Milk Exchange 1 Starch/Bread Exchange 1 Meat Exchange 1 Fat Exchange

Recipe	Monday	Recipe	Tuesday	Recipe	Wednesday	Recipe	Thursday
	Breakfast						
	1/2c UNSW Apple Juice or		1/2c UNSW Orange Juice		1/2c UNSW Pineapple Juice		1/2c UNSW Apple Juice or
	1/2c Fresh Fruit	B1	1/2c DB Oatmeal or	B1	1/2c DB Cream of Wheat	S11	3 medium Stewed Prunes
B1	1/2c DB Cream of Rice or		3/4c UNSW Dry Cereal		or 3/4c UNSW Dry Cereal	B1	1/2c DB Farina or
	3/4c UNSW Dry Cereal	B4	1 Poached Egg	B4	1 Soft-Cooked Egg		3/4c UNSW Dry Cereal
I2	1 oz Grilled Cheese on		1 English Muffin		1 sl Toast	B4,5	1 Egg to Order
	1 sl Toast		1 tsp Margarine		1 tsp Margarine		1 sl Raisin Toast
	1 tsp Margarine		1 tsp DB Jam/Jelly		1 tsp DB Jam/Jelly		1 tsp Margarine
	1 tsp DB Jam/Jelly		1c Skim Milk		1c Skim Milk		1 tsp DB Jam/Jelly
	1c Skim Milk		Coffee or Tea		Coffee or Tea		1c Skim Milk
	Coffee or Tea						Coffee or Tea
	Lunch						
K29	1c Tossed Salad with	K23	1/2c DB Marinated Zucchini	K32	1c Tossed Vegetable Salad	K25	1c Green Salad with
P8	1 Tbsp LC Salad Dressing	D22	3 1/2 oz DB Breaded Veal	P1–8	1 Tbsp LC Salad Dressing	P1–8	1 Tbsp LC Salad Dressing
E1	3 oz LF Barbecue Chicken	O20	with 2 oz Marinara Sauce	D1	3 1/2 oz LF Beef Teriyaki	D30	3 oz Pork Chops with
O2	with 2 oz DB Barbecue Sauce	M5	3/4c LF Pasta Primavera	J22	1/2c Chinese Vegetables		1/4c LF Apple Stuffing
J31	1/2c Green Peas		1 sl Italian Bread	L1	1/2c White Rice	J1	1/2c Asparagus Tips
J14	1/2c Carrots		1 tsp Margarine		1 Dinner Roll		1 Dinner Roll
	1 Dinner Roll		1/2c Skim Milk		1 tsp Margarine		1 tsp Margarine
	1 tsp Margarine		Coffee or Tea		1/2c Skim Milk		1/2c Skim Milk
	1/2c Skim Milk	S5	1/2c Fresh Fruit Cup		Coffee or Tea		Coffee or Tea
	Coffee or Tea				1/2c LF Ice Milk	S16	1/2c DB Chocolate Pudding
	1/2c UNSW Sliced Peaches						
	Dinner						
C11	2/3c LF Cream Celery Soup	C4	2/3c SR/LF Bean Soup	C26	2/3c Vegetable Beef Soup	C21	2/3c Minestrone Soup
G8	5 1/2 oz DB Vegetable Omelet	I4	Asst Cold Cut Sandwiches	E13	3/4c LF Turkey à la King	D12	8 oz LF Beef Macaroni Casserole
J36	1/2c LF Home Fried Potatoes		2 sl Bread (cut in quarters)		with 2 Toast Points	J6	1/2c LF Seasoned Green Beans
	1 Dinner Roll		with 3 oz Roast Beef, Ham,	J47	1/2c Spinach		1 Dinner Roll
	1 tsp Margarine		Turkey, Bologna, & Salami		1/2c Skim Milk		1 tsp Margarine
	1/2c Skim Milk		Lettuce Leaves		Coffee or Tea		1/2c Skim Milk
	Coffee or Tea		2 sl Tomatoes		2 UNSW Plums		Coffee or Tea
Q2	2×2" sl DB Banana Cake	K5	1/2c DB Cole Slaw				1/2c UNSW Chilled Apricots
			1 tsp Catsup, 1 tsp Mustard				
			1 Tbsp LF Mayonnaise				
			1/2c Skim Milk				
			Coffee or Tea				
		S12	1/2c DB Strawberry Gelatin				
	Snacks:						
	1/2 Milk Exchange		1/2 Milk Exchange		1/2 Milk Exchange		1/2 Milk Exchange
	1 Starch/Bread Exchange		1 Starch/Bread Exchange		1 Starch/Bread Exchange		1 Starch/Bread Exchange
	1 Meat Exchange		1 Meat Exchange		1 Meat Exchange		1 Meat Exchange
	1 Fat Exchange		1 Fat Exchange		1 Fat Exchange		1 Fat Exchange

TERMS: LF = Low Fat; FF = Fat Free; SR = Sodium or Salt Restricted; STR = Strained; DB = Diabetic; UNSW = Unsweetened; RC = Reduced Calorie; LC = Low Calorie; EXCH = Diabetic Exchange.

Amounts specified for food items that contain bone is equivalent to cooked, edible deboned portion.

Recipe	Friday	Recipe	Saturday	Recipe	Sunday
B1	1/2c UNSW Grapefruit Juice 1/2c DB Wheatena or 3/4c UNSW Dry Cereal		1/2c UNSW Cranberry Juice or 1 small Banana 1/2c DB Cream of Rice or	B1	1/2c UNSW Pineapple Juice 1/2c DB Oatmeal or 3/4c UNSW Dry Cereal
B5	1 Scrambled Egg	B1	3/4c UNSW Dry Cereal	B8	1 sl French Toast with
N14	1 DB Bran Muffin 1 tsp Margarine 1 tsp DB Jam/Jelly 1c Skim Milk Coffee or Tea	G9	2 1/2 oz DB Western Omelet 1 sl Toast 1 tsp Margarine 1 tsp DB Jam/Jelly 1c Skim Milk Coffee or Tea		1 oz DB Maple Syrup 1 tsp Margarine 1 tsp DB Jam/Jelly 1c Skim Milk Coffee or Tea
K9	1/2c DB Marinated Cucumbers	K37	4 oz DB Perfection Salad	K42	1/2c DB Cranberry Mold
F9	3 oz LF Sole Almondine	D18	6 oz Stuffed Cabbage	E16	3 oz LF Roast Turkey with
O25	2 Tbsp LF Tartar Sauce	J43	1/2c LF Whipped Potatoes	O18	2 oz STR Giblet Gravy
	Lemon Wedge	J15	1/2c DB Glazed Carrots	P12	1/4c Raisin Bread Stuffing
L2	1/2c Rice Chantilly		1 Dinner Roll	J52	1/2c Zucchini
J51	1/2c Vegetable Medley 1 Dinner Roll 1 tsp Margarine 1/2c Skim Milk Coffee or Tea 3 Vanilla Wafers		1 tsp Margarine 1/2c Skim Milk Coffee or Tea 1/2c UNSW Pineapple Tidbits	R3	1 Dinner Roll 1 tsp Margarine 1/2c Skim Milk Coffee or Tea 1/8 DB Apple Pie
C9	2/3c Chicken Matzo Ball Soup	C24	2/3c LF Tomato Soup	C3	2/3c Clear Vegetable Soup
E9	3 oz LF Chicken Tarragon	I21	1/2c LF Curry Tuna Salad	G2	6 oz DB Lasagna
M4	4 oz DB Noodle Pudding		Platter Lettuce Leaves,	J27	1/2c Mixed Vegetables
J10	1/2c LF Steamed Broccoli		2 sl Onions, 3 sl	N8	1 sl LF Garlic Bread
	1 Dinner Roll		Cucumbers, 1 Radish Rose		1/2c Skim Milk
	1 tsp Margarine	K13	1/2c LF Macaroni Salad		Coffee or Tea
	1/2c Skim Milk		1 Dinner Roll or	S4	1/3c Fruit Compote
	Coffee or Tea		4 LF Crackers		
S1	1 small DB Baked Apple		1 tsp Margarine 1/2c Skim Milk Coffee or Tea 1/2c LF Sherbet		
	1/2 Milk Exchange 1 Starch/Bread Exchange 1 Meat Exchange 1 Fat Exchange		1/2 Milk Exchange 1 Starch/Bread Exchange 1 Meat Exchange 1 Fat Exchange		1/2 Milk Exchange 1 Starch/Bread Exchange 1 Meat Exchange 1 Fat Exchange

Recipe	Monday	Recipe	Tuesday	Recipe	Wednesday	Recipe	Thursday
	Breakfast						
B1	1/2c UNSW Orange Juice 1/2c DB Farina or 3/4c UNSW Dry Cereal	B1	1/2c UNSW Apple Juice 1/2c DB Wheatena or 3/4c UNSW Dry Cereal	B1	1/2c UNSW Grapefruit Juice or 1/2 small Banana 1/2c DB Cream of Rice or 3/4c UNSW Dry Cereal	B1	1/2c UNSW Pineapple Juice 1/2c DB Oatmeal or 3/4c UNSW Dry Cereal
B4	1 Soft-Cooked Egg 1 sl Toast 1 tsp Margarine 1 tsp DB Jam/Jelly 1/2c Skim Milk Coffee or Tea	G6	2 oz DB Cheese Omelet 1/2 English Muffin 1 tsp DB Jam/Jelly 1/2c Skim Milk Coffee or Tea	B5	1 Scrambled Egg 1 sl Toast 1 tsp DB Jam/Jelly 1/2c Skim Milk Coffee or Tea	I2	1 oz LF Grilled Cheese on 1 sl Toast 1/2c Skim Milk Coffee or Tea
	Lunch						
K29 P1 D6 L3	1c Tossed Salad with 1 Tbsp LC French Dressing 6 oz LF Pepper Steak 1/3c LF Rice Florentine 1/2c Skim Milk Coffee or Tea 1/2c UNSW Sliced Peaches	K35 E4 J39 J10 S3	1/2c DB Molded Veg Salad 2 oz LF Lemon Chicken 2 oz LF Oven Browned Potatoes 1/2c LF Broccoli 1/2c Skim Milk Coffee or Tea 1/2c Citrus Cup	K25 P4 D26 M1 O22 J55 S10	1c Green Salad with 1 tsp Italian Dressing 4 oz DB Veal Parmesan 1/2c Spaghetti with 1 oz DB Tomato Sauce 1/2c LF Zucchini-Onions 1/2c Skim Milk Coffee or Tea 1/2 DB Baked Pear	K22 E14 L1	1/2c DB Three Bean Salad 3/4 Turkey Chow Mein 1/3c White Rice 1/2c Skim Milk Coffee or Tea 2 UNSW Plums
	Dinner						
C23 I12 K5 S17	2/3c LF Split Pea Soup 1/2c LF Ham Salad on Lettuce Leaves 3 sl Tomatoes and 3 sl Cucumbers 1/2c DB Cole Slaw 1/4c Skim Milk Coffee or Tea 1/2c DB Vanilla Pudding	C12 D17 J24	2/3c LF Cream Mushroom Soup 3 oz LF Sloppy Joe on 1/2 Bun 1/4c LF Corn Confetti 1/4c Skim Milk Coffee or Tea 1/2c LF Ice Milk	C27 I18 K40 S12	2/3c Chunky Vegetable Soup 1/2c LF Seafood Salad 1/2c LF Waldorf Salad 1/2c Skim Milk Coffee or Tea 1/2c DB Orange Gelatin	C18 G13 K32 P1–8	2/3c LF Onion Soup 1/8 pie DB Spinach Quiche 1c Tossed Vegetable Salad 1 Tbsp LC Salad Dressing 1/2c Skim Milk Coffee or Tea 2 Graham Crackers
	Snacks: 1/2 Milk Exchange 1 Starch/Bread Exchange		1/2 Milk Exchange 1 Starch/Bread Exchange		1/2 Milk Exchange 1 Starch/Bread Exchange		1/2 Milk Exchange 1 Starch/Bread Exchange

TERMS: LF = Low Fat; FF = Fat Free; SR = Sodium or Salt Restricted; STR = Strained; DB = Diabetic; UNSW = Unsweetened; RC = Reduced Calorie; LC = Low Calorie; EXCH = Diabetic Exchange.

Amounts specified for food items that contain bone is equivalent to cooked, edible deboned portion.

Recipe	Friday	Recipe	Saturday	Recipe	Sunday
S11	1/3c UNSW Cranberry Juice	B1	1/2c UNSW Apple Juice	B1	1/2c UNSW Orange Juice
B1	or 3 medium Stewed Prunes		1/2c DB Wheatena or		1/2c DB Farina or
	1/2c DB Cream of Wheat		3/4c UNSW Dry Cereal		3/4c UNSW Dry Cereal
	or 3/4c UNSW Dry Cereal	B4	1 Hard-Boiled Egg	B4,5	1 Egg of Choice
B4	1 Poached Egg		1 sl Toast	B9	2 DB Pancakes (4" across)
	1 sl Toast		1 tsp DB Jam/Jelly		with 1 oz DB Maple Syrup
	1 tsp DB Jam/Jelly		1/2c Skim Milk		1 tsp DB Jam/Jelly
	1/2c Skim Milk		Coffee or Tea		1/2c Skim Milk
	Coffee or Tea				Coffee or Tea
	1c Shredded Lettuce	K9	1/2c DB Marinated Cucumbers	K24	1c Garden Salad with
P1–8	1 Tbsp LC Salad Dressing	D15	3 oz Meatloaf with	P1–8	1 Tbsp LC Salad Dressing
F4	2 1/2 oz LF Oven Fried Fish	O16	1 oz LF Onion Gravy	D31	2 oz Roast Pork with
	Lemon Wedge	J37	1/2c LF Mashed Potatoes	C1	2 oz LF Broth
M2	1/3c LF Lyonnaise Noodles	J51	1/2c Vegetable Medley	P11	1/4c DB Cornbread Stuffing
J15	1/2c DB Glazed Carrots		1/2c Skim Milk	J47	1/2c Spinach
	1/2c Skim Milk		Coffee or Tea		1/2c Skim Milk
	Coffee or Tea		1/2c UNSW Apricot Halves		Coffee or Tea
	1/2c UNSW Fruit Cocktail				1/2c UNSW Applesauce
C8	2/3c STR Chicken Rice Soup	C4	2/3c SR/LF Bean Soup	C15	2/3c Creole Soup
E2	2 oz LF Chicken Fricassee	I5	Chef Salad:	F10	6 oz LF Tuna Noodle Casserole
	with 2 oz LF Gravy		1 oz Turkey and	J8	1/2c DB Julienne Beets
J41	2 oz LF Parsley Potatoes		1 oz LF Cheese		1/2c Skim Milk
J1	1/2c Asparagus Tips		1c Lettuce, Tomatoes,		Coffee or Tea
	1/2c Skim Milk		Onions, and Cucumbers		1/2c LF Sherbet
	Coffee or Tea	P1–8	1 Tbsp LC Salad Dressing		
Q10	1" DB Strawberry Shortcake		2 LF Crackers		
			1/4c Skim Milk		
			Coffee or Tea		
		S16	1/2c DB Chocolate Pudding		
	1/2 Milk Exchange		1/2 Milk Exchange		1/2 Milk Exchange
	1 Starch/Bread Exchange		1 Starch/Bread Exchange		1 Starch/Bread Exchange

Recipe	Monday	Recipe	Tuesday	Recipe	Wednesday	Recipe	Thursday
	Breakfast						
	1/2c UNSW Pineapple Juice		1/2c UNSW Grapefruit Juice		1/3c UNSW Cranberry Juice		1/2c UNSW Orange Juice
	or 1/2 small Banana	B1	1/2c DB Farina or	B1	1/2c DB Wheatena or		or 1c Melon Cubes
B1	1/2c DB Cream of Wheat		3/4c UNSW Dry Cereal		3/4c UNSW Dry Cereal	B1	1/2c DB Cream of Rice or
	or 3/4c UNSW Dry Cereal	B4	1 Soft-Cooked Egg		1 Tbsp Peanut Butter and		3/4c UNSW Dry Cereal
B5	1 Scrambled Egg		1 sl Toast		2 tsp DB Jelly on	B4	1 Poached Egg
	1 sl Toast		1 tsp DB Jam/Jelly		1 sl Raisin Bread	N12	1 sm DB Blueberry Muffin
	1 tsp DB Jam/Jelly		1/2c Skim Milk		1/2c Skim Milk		1 tsp DB Jam/Jelly
	1/2c Skim Milk		Coffee or Tea		Coffee or Tea		1/2c Skim Milk
	Coffee or Tea						Coffee or Tea
	Lunch						
K28	1c Mixed Field Greens	K2	1/2c DB Pickled Beets	K31	1c DB Hawaiian Tossed Salad	K22	1/2c DB Three Bean Salad
P1–8	1 Tbsp LC Salad Dressing	D2	6 oz Beef Stew	D27	2 1/2 oz Veal Patty	D37	2 oz DB Braised Liver with
E8	2 oz LF Tahitian Chicken	M1	1/4c Noodles	J24	1/3c LF Corn Confetti		1/4c LF Sauté Onions
	with 1 1/2 oz LF Sauce		1/2c Skim Milk	J50	1/2c DB Stewed Tomatoes	M2	1/2c LF Lyonnaise Noodles
L5	1/3c Rice Pilaf		Coffee or Tea		1/2c Skim Milk	J18	1/2c DB Sunshine Carrots
J10	1/2c LF Steamed Broccoli		2 UNSW Pear Halves		Coffee or Tea		1/2c Skim Milk
	1/2c Skim Milk				1/2c LF Ice Milk		Coffee or Tea
	Coffee or Tea					S2	1/2c DB Spiced Applesauce
S8	1/2c Almond Peaches						
	Dinner						
C28	2/3c French Vegetable Soup	C8	2/3c Chicken Rice Soup	C1	2/3c Broth	C21	2/3c STR Minestrone Soup
I2	2 oz LF Grilled Cheese	E16	2 oz Turkey on	I9	1/2c DB Egg Salad Platter	M1	1/2c Spaghetti and
	Sandwich, 2 sl Diet Bread		1 sl Bread with		Lettuce Leaves,	D13	2 oz Meatballs with
	1/2c Lettuce Leaves with	O5	1 oz LF Chicken Gravy		1 Radish Rose,	O20	1 oz Marinara Sauce
	4 sl Tomatoes	J37	1/2c LF Mashed Potatoes		3 sl Cucumbers	J26	1/2c Italian Mix Vegetables
P1–8	1 Tbsp LC Salad Dressing	J27	1/4c Mixed Vegetables	K13	1/3c LF Macaroni Salad		1/2c Skim Milk
	1/2c Skim Milk		1/2c Skim Milk		1/2c Skim Milk		Coffee or Tea
	Coffee or Tea		Coffee or Tea		Coffee or Tea	R4	1/8 DB Lemon Pie
Q4	2×2" sl DB Carrot Raisin Cake		3 Vanilla Wafers		1/2c UNSW Fruit Cocktail		
	Snacks:						
	1/2 Milk Exchange		1/2 Milk Exchange		1/2 Milk Exchange		1/2 Milk Exchange
	1 Starch/Bread Exchange		1 Starch/Bread Exchange		1 Starch/Bread Exchange		1 Starch/Bread Exchange

TERMS: LF = Low Fat; FF = Fat Free; SR = Sodium or Salt Restricted; STR = Strained; DB = Diabetic; UNSW = Unsweetened; RC = Reduced Calorie; LC = Low Calorie; EXCH = Diabetic Exchange.
Amounts specified for food items that contain bone is equivalent to cooked, edible deboned portion.

Recipe	Friday	Recipe	Saturday	Recipe	Sunday
B1	1/2c UNSW Apple Juice 1/2c DB Oatmeal or 3/4c UNSW Dry Cereal	B1	1/2c UNSW Grapefruit Juice 1/2c DB Cream of Wheat or 3/4c UNSW Dry Cereal	B1	1/2c UNSW Pineapple Juice 1/2c DB Wheatena or 3/4c UNSW Dry Cereal
B4	1 Hard-Boiled Egg 1 sl Toast 1 tsp DB Jam/Jelly 1/2c Skim Milk Coffee or Tea	B5 N7	1 Scrambled Egg 1/2" sl DB Date Nut Bread 1 Tbsp Cream Cheese or 1 tsp Margarine 1 tsp DB Jam/Jelly 1/2c Skim Milk Coffee or Tea	B8	1 sl French Toast with 1 oz DB Maple Syrup 1 tsp DB Jam/Jelly 1/2c Skim Milk Coffee or Tea
K24 P1–8 F3 O7 L1 J47	1c Garden Salad with 1 Tbsp LC Salad Dressing 2 oz DB Fish Creole with 1 1/2 oz DB Creole Sauce 1/3c White Rice 1/2c Spinach 1/2c Skim Milk Coffee or Tea 1/2c UNSW Chilled Apricots	P1–8 D29 J46 J6	1c Shredded Lettuce 1 Tbsp LC Salad Dressing 2 oz DB Breaded Pork Chops 1/3c LF Whipped Sweet Potatoes 1/2c LF Seasoned Green Beans 1/4c Skim Milk Coffee or Tea 1/3c LF Sherbet	K26 P1–8 D19 J41 J54 S7	1c Green Vegetable Salad 1 Tbsp LC Salad Dressing 2 oz LF Swiss Steak with 1 oz LF Gravy 3 oz LF Parsley Potatoes 1/2c LF Tarragon Zucchini 1/2c Skim Milk Coffee or Tea 1/3c Fruit Parfait
C7 E5 J35 J8 Q9	2/3c Beef Noodle Soup 2 oz LF Oven Crisp Chicken 1/2 sm Baked Potato with 1/2c LF Julienne Beets 1/2c Skim Milk Coffee or Tea 1/2" sl DB Pound Cake	C29 G11 J49	2/3c Old Fashion Vegtble Soup 6 oz LF Macaroni & Cheese 1/2c Succotash 1/2c Skim Milk Coffee or Tea 2 UNSW Plums	C12 F1 K5 S12	2/3c LF Cream Mushroom Soup 3 oz LF Fish Burger on 1/2 Bun Lemon Wedge 2 Lettuce Leaves 2 sl Tomatoes 1/2c DB Cole Slaw 1/2c Skim Milk Coffee or Tea 1/2c DB Cherry Gelatin
	1/2 Milk Exchange 1 Starch/Bread Exchange		1/2 Milk Exchange 1 Starch/Bread Exchange		1/2 Milk Exchange 1 Starch/Bread Exchange

Recipe	Monday	Recipe	Tuesday	Recipe	Wednesday	Recipe	Thursday
	Breakfast						
B1	1/3c UNSW Cranberry Juice 1/2c DB Oatmeal or		1/2c UNSW Orange Juice or 3/4c Fresh Berries	B1	1/2c UNSW Apple Juice 1/2c DB Farina or	B1	1/2c UNSW Grapefruit Juice 1/2c DB Wheatena or
	3/4c UNSW Dry Cereal	B1	1/2c DB Cream of Wheat		3/4c UNSW Dry Cereal		3/4c UNSW Dry Cereal
B4	1 Hard-Boiled Egg		or 3/4c UNSW Dry Cereal	B4	1 Poached Egg		1/4c LF Cottage Cheese
	1 sl Toast	G7	2 oz DB Ham Omelet		1/2 English Muffin		with Artificial Sweetener
	1 tsp DB Jam/Jelly		1 sl Toast		1 tsp Margarine		and Cinnamon
	1/2c Skim Milk		1 tsp DB Jam/Jelly		1 tsp DB Jam/Jelly		on 1 sl Raisin Toast
	Coffee or Tea		1/2c Skim Milk		1/2c Skim Milk		1 tsp DB Jam/Jelly
			Coffee or Tea		Coffee or Tea		1/2c Skim Milk
							Coffee or Tea
	Lunch						
K10	1/2c DB Cucumber Onion Salad	K4	1/3c LF Carrot-Raisin Salad	K25	1c Green Salad with	K24	1c Garden Salad with
E3	2 oz LF Chicken Italiano	D25	3 oz Veal Loaf with	P1	1 Tbsp LC French Dressing	P1–8	1 Tbsp LC Salad Dressing
M1	1/2c Spaghetti with	O3	2 oz LF Brown Gravy	E15	3/4c Turkey Jambalaya	D14	2 oz DB Sweet-n-Sour Meatballs
O22	1 oz DB Tomato Sauce	J37	1/4c LF Mashed Potatoes	J3	1/2c Green Beans		with 1 oz DB Sauce
J26	1/2c Italian Mix Vegetables	J1	1/2c Asparagus Tips		1/4c Skim Milk	M1	1/2c Noodles
	1/2c Skim Milk		1/2c Skim Milk		Coffee or Tea	J48	1/2c Seasoned Spinach
	Coffee or Tea		Coffee or Tea	S17	1/2c DB Vanilla Pudding		1/2c Skim Milk
	1/2c UNSW Sliced Peaches	R7	2×2" srv DB Apple Crisp				Coffee or Tea
							1/2c UNSW Apricots
	Dinner						
C20	2/3c Julienne Soup	C3	2/3c Clear Vegetable Soup	C14	2/3c LF Cream Tomato Soup	C19	2/3c LF Onion Soup
I10	Fruit Festival with	G3	4 oz DB Cheese Strata	I22	Salad Sampler Platter with	G12	1/8 pie DB Quiche Lorraine
	1/2c Cottage Cheese	J51	1/2c Vegetable Medley	I12	1/4c LF Ham Salad	J28	1/2c LF Mushrooms & Celery
	1/2c Seasonal Fruit		1/2c Skim Milk	I6	1/2c LF Chicken Salad		1/4c Skim Milk
S12	1/2c DB Gelatin Cubes		Coffee or Tea		Lettuce Leaves, 2 sl Onions,		Coffee or Tea
N10–20	1 small DB Muffin		1/3c UNSW Pineapple		and 2 Green Pepper Rings		1/3c LF Ice Milk
	1 tsp DB Jam/Jelly		Chunks	K21	1/4c LF Potato Salad		
	1/2c Skim Milk				1/2c Skim Milk		
	Coffee or Tea				Coffee or Tea		
Q6	2×2" sl DB Chocolate Chip Cake			S5	1/2c Fruit Cup		
	Snacks:						
	1/2 Milk Exchange		1/2 Milk Exchange		1/2 Milk Exchange		1/2 Milk Exchange
	1 Starch/Bread Exchange		1 Starch/Bread Exchange		1 Starch/Bread Exchange		1 Starch/Bread Exchange

TERMS: LF = Low Fat; FF = Fat Free; SR = Sodium or Salt Restricted; STR = Strained; DB = Diabetic; UNSW = Unsweetened; RC = Reduced Calorie; LC = Low Calorie; EXCH = Diabetic Exchange.

[1]*2000 Calorie Diet:* Follow 1800 calorie diet with the following additions: Breakfast—add 1/2 milk exchange and 1 bread exchange; Snack—add 1 medium-fat meat exchange. Amounts specified for food items that contain bone is equivalent to cooked, edible deboned portion.

Recipe	Friday	Recipe	Saturday	Recipe	Sunday
B1 B5	1/2c UNSW Orange Juice or 1/2 small Banana 1/2c DB Cream of Rice or 3/4c UNSW Dry Cereal 1 Scrambled Egg 1 sl Toast 1 tsp DB Jam/Jelly 1/2c Skim Milk Coffee or Tea	B1 B4	1/2c UNSW Apple Juice 1/2c DB Oatmeal or 3/4c UNSW Dry Cereal 1 Hard-Boiled Egg 1 sl Toast 1 tsp DB Jam/Jelly 1/2c Skim Milk Coffee or Tea	B1 B4,5 B12	1/3c UNSW Cranberry Juice 1/2c DB Farina or 3/4c UNSW Dry Cereal 1 Egg of Choice 1 DB Waffle (4 1/2" sq) with 1 oz DB Maple Syrup 1 tsp DB Jam/Jelly 1/2c Skim Milk Coffee or Tea
K2 F5 L5 J27	1/2c DB Pickled Beets 2 oz LF Catch of the Day Lemon Wedge 1/3c Rice Pilaf 1/4c Mixed Vegetables 1/2c Skim Milk Coffee or Tea 2 UNSW Pear Halves	K29 P1–8 D28 J45 J3 S13	1c Tossed Salad with 1 Tbsp LC Salad Dressing 2 oz DB Baked Ham 1/4c DB Sweet Potatoes/Apples 1/2c String Beans 1/2c Skim Milk Coffee or Tea 1/2c DB Fruited Lime Gelatin	P1–8 D3 C1 J40 J10	1c Shredded Lettuce 1 Tbsp LC Salad Dressing 2 oz Brisket of Beef with 2 oz LF Broth 2 oz DB Potato Pancakes 1/2c LF Broccoli Cuts 1/2c Skim Milk Coffee or Tea 1/2c UNSW Applesauce
C23 E7 J35 J19 Q8	2/3c LF Split Pea Soup 2 oz LF Roast Chicken 1/2 small Baked Potato 1/2c DB Carrot Tzimmes 1/2c Skim Milk Coffee or Tea 2×2" sl DB Marble Cake	C21 G1 J55	2/3c STR Minestrone Soup 5 oz LF Cheese Fettucine 1/2c LF Zucchini-Onions 1/2c Skim Milk Coffee or Tea 2 UNSW Plums	C27 I18 I23 K15	2/3c Chunky Vegetable Soup 1/2c LF Seafood Salad Stuffed Tomato 1/4c LF Cheesy Macaroni Salad 1/2c Skim Milk Coffee or Tea 1/2c LF Sherbet
	1/2 Milk Exchange 1 Starch/Bread Exchange		1/2 Milk Exchange 1 Starch/Bread Exchange		1/2 Milk Exchange 1 Starch/Bread Exchange

Recipe	Monday	Recipe	Tuesday	Recipe	Wednesday	Recipe	Thursday
	Breakfast						
	1/2c UNSW Apple Juice or		1/2c UNSW Orange Juice		1/2c UNSW Pineapple Juice		1/2c UNSW Apple Juice or
	1/2c Fresh Fruit	B1	1/2c DB Oatmeal or	B1	1/2c DB Cream of Wheat	S11	3 medium Stewed Prunes
B1	1/2c DB Cream of Rice or		3/4c UNSW Dry Cereal		or 3/4c UNSW Dry Cereal	B1	1/2c DB Farina or
	3/4c UNSW Dry Cereal	B4	1 Poached Egg	B4	1 Soft Cooked Egg		3/4c UNSW Dry Cereal
I2	1 oz Grilled Cheese on		1/2 English Muffin		1 sl Toast	B4,5	1 Egg to Order
	1 sl Toast		1 tsp DB Jam/Jelly		1 tsp DB Jam/Jelly		1 sl Raisin Toast
	1 tsp DB Jam/Jelly		1/2c Skim Milk		1/2c Skim Milk		1 tsp DB Jam/Jelly
	1/2c Skim Milk		Coffee or Tea		Coffee or Tea		1/2c Skim Milk
	Coffee or Tea						Coffee or Tea
	Lunch						
K29	1c Tossed Salad with	K23	1/2c DB Marinated Zucchini	K32	1c Tossed Vegetable Salad	K25	1c Green Salad with
P8	1 Tbsp LC Salad Dressing	D22	2 1/2 oz DB Breaded Veal	P1–8	2 Tbsp LC Salad Dressing	P1–8	1 Tbsp LC Salad Dressing
E1	2 oz LF Barbecue Chicken	O20	with 1 oz Marinara Sauce	D1	2 1/2 oz LF Beef Teriyaki	D30	2 oz Pork Chops with
O2	with 1 oz DB Barbecue Sauce	M5	1/2c LF Pasta Primavera	J22	1/2c Chinese Vegetables		1/4c LF Apple Stuffing
J31	1/4c Green Peas		1/2c Skim Milk	L1	1/3c White Rice	J1	1/2c Asparagus Tips
J14	1/2c Carrots		Coffee or Tea		1/4c Skim Milk		1/4c Skim Milk
	1/2c Skim Milk	S5	1/2c Fresh Fruit Cup		Coffee or Tea		Coffee or Tea
	Coffee or Tea				1/2c LF Ice Milk	S16	1/2c DB Chocolate Pudding
	1/2c UNSW Sliced Peaches						
	Dinner						
C11	2/3c LF Cream Celery Soup	C4	2/3c SR/LF Bean Soup	C26	2/3c Vegetable Beef Soup	C21	2/3c Minestrone Soup
G8	5 oz DB Vegetable Omelet	I4	Asst Cold Cut Sandwiches	E13	2/3c LF Turkey à la King	D12	6 oz LF Beef Macaroni Casserole
J36	1/2c LF Home Fried Potatoes		2 sl Bread (cut in quarters)		with 2 Toast Points	J6	1/2c LF Seasoned Green Beans
	1 small Dinner Roll		with 3 oz Roast Beef, Ham,	J47	1/2c Spinach		1 small Dinner Roll
	1 tsp Margarine		Turkey, Bologna, & Salami		1/2c Skim Milk		1 tsp Margarine
	1/2c Skim Milk		Lettuce Leaves		Coffee or Tea		1/2c Skim Milk
	Coffee or Tea		2 sl Tomatoes		2 UNSW Plums		Coffee or Tea
Q2	2 × 1" sl DB Banana Cake	K5	1/2c DB Cole Slaw				1/2c UNSW Chilled Apricots
			1 tsp Catsup, 1 tsp Mustard				
			1/2c Skim Milk				
			Coffee or Tea				
		S12	1/2c DB Strawberry Gelatin				
	Snacks:						
	1/2 Milk Exchange		1/2 Milk Exchange		1/2 Milk Exchange		1/2 Milk Exchange
	1 Starch/Bread Exchange		1 Starch/Bread Exchange		1 Starch/Bread Exchange		1 Starch/Bread Exchange

TERMS: LF=Low Fat; FF=Fat Free; SR=Sodium or Salt Restricted; STR=Strained; DB=Diabetic; UNSW=Unsweetened; RC=Reduced Calorie; LC=Low Calorie; EXCH=Diabetic Exchange.

[1]*2000 Calorie Diet:* Follow 1800 calorie diet with the following additions: Breakfast—add 1/2 milk exchange and 1 bread exchange; Snack—add 1 medium-fat meat exchange. Amounts specified for food items that contain bone is equivalent to cooked, edible deboned portion.

Recipe	Friday	Recipe	Saturday	Recipe	Sunday
B1	1/2c UNSW Grapefruit Juice 1/2c DB Wheatena or 3/4c UNSW Dry Cereal	B1	1/3c UNSW Cranberry Juice or 1/2 small Banana 1/2c DB Cream of Rice or 3/4c UNSW Dry Cereal	B1	1/2c UNSW Pineapple Juice 1/2c DB Oatmeal or 3/4c UNSW Dry Cereal
B5	1 Scrambled Egg	G9	2 1/2 oz DB Western Omelet	B8	1 sl French Toast with
N14	1 small DB Bran Muffin 1 tsp DB Jam/Jelly 1/2c Skim Milk Coffee or Tea		1 sl Toast 1 tsp DB Jam/Jelly 1/2c Skim Milk Coffee or Tea		1 oz DB Maple Syrup 1 tsp DB Jam/Jelly 1/2c Skim Milk Coffee or Tea
K9	1/2c DB Marinated Cucumbers	K37	4 oz DB Perfection Salad	K42	1/2c DB Cranberry Mold
F9	2 oz LF Sole Almondine Lemon Wedge	D18	5 oz Stuffed Cabbage	E16	2 oz LF Roast Turkey with
		J43	1/2c LF Whipped Potatoes	O18	1 oz STR Giblet Gravy
L2	1/4c Rice Chantilly	J15	1/2c DB Glazed Carrots	P12	1/4c Raisin Bread Stuffing
J51	1/2c Vegetable Medley 1/2c Skim Milk Coffee or Tea 3 Vanilla Wafers		1/2c Skim Milk Coffee or Tea 1/3c UNSW Pineapple Tidbits	J52	1/2c Zucchini 1/2c Skim Milk Coffee or Tea
				R3	1/12 DB Apple Pie
C9	2/3c Chicken Matzo Ball Soup	C24	2/3c LF Tomato Soup	C3	2/3c Clear Vegetable Soup
E9	2 oz LF Chicken Tarragon	I21	1/2c LF Curry Tuna Salad	G2	5 oz DB Lasagna
M4	4 oz DB Noodle Pudding		Platter Lettuce Leaves,	J27	1/2c Mixed Vegetables
J10	1/2c LF Steamed Broccoli		2 sl Onions, 3 sl	N8	1 sl LF Garlic Bread
	1 small Dinner Roll		Cucumbers, 1 Radish Rose		1/2c Skim Milk
	1 tsp Margarine	K13	1/2c LF Macaroni Salad		Coffee or Tea
	1/2c Skim Milk		1 small Dinner Roll or	S4	1/3c Fruit Compote
	Coffee or Tea		5 LF Crackers		
S1	1 small DB Baked Apple		1 tsp Margarine 1/2c Skim Milk Coffee or Tea 1/2c LF Sherbet		
	1/2 Milk Exchange 1 Starch/Bread Exchange		1/2 Milk Exchange 1 Starch/Bread Exchange		1/2 Milk Exchange 1 Starch/Bread Exchange

Recipe	Monday	Recipe	Tuesday	Recipe	Wednesday	Recipe	Thursday
	Breakfast						
B1	1/2c UNSW Orange Juice	B1	1/2c UNSW Apple Juice		1/2c UNSW Grapefruit Juice	B1	1/2c UNSW Pineapple Juice
	1/2c DB Farina or		1/2c DB Wheatena or		or 1/2 small Banana		1/2c DB Oatmeal or
	3/4c UNSW Dry Cereal		3/4c UNSW Dry Cereal	B1	1/2c DB Cream of Rice or		3/4c UNSW Dry Cereal
B4	1 Soft Cooked Egg	G6	2 oz DB Cheese Omelet		3/4c UNSW Dry Cereal	I2	1 oz LF Grilled Cheese
	1 sl Toast		1/2 English Muffin	B5	1 Scrambled Egg		on 1 sl Toast
	1 tsp Margarine		1 tsp Margarine		1 sl Toast		1 tsp Margarine
	1 tsp DB Jam/Jelly		1 tsp DB Jam/Jelly		1 tsp DB Jam/Jelly		1/2c Skim Milk
	1/2c Skim Milk		1/2c Skim Milk		1/2c Skim Milk		Coffee or Tea
	Coffee or Tea		Coffee or Tea		Coffee or Tea		
	Lunch						
K29	1c Tossed Salad with	K35	1/2c DB Molded Veg Salad	K25	1c Green Salad with	K22	1/2c DB Three Bean Salad
P1	1 Tbsp LC French Dressing	E4	3 oz LF Lemon Chicken	P4	1 tsp Italian Dressing	E14	1c Turkey Chow Mein
D6	8 oz LF Pepper Steak	J39	4 oz LF Oven Browned Potatoes	D26	5 oz DB Veal Parmesan	L1	1/3c White Rice
I3	1/3c LF Rice Florentine	J10	1/2c LF Broccoli	M1	1/2c Spaghetti with		1/2c Skim Milk
	1 small Dinner Roll		1/2c Skim Milk	O22	1 oz DB Tomato Sauce		Coffee or Tea
	1/2c Skim Milk		Coffee or Tea	J55	1/2c LF Zucchini-Onions		2 UNSW Plums
	Coffee or Tea	S3	1/2c Citrus Cup		1 small Dinner Roll		
	1/2c UNSW Sliced Peaches				1 tsp Margarine		
					1/2c Skim Milk		
					Coffee or Tea		
				S10	1/2 DB Baked Pear		
	Dinner						
C23	2/3c LF Split Pea Soup	C12	2/3c LF Cream Mushroom Soup	C27	2/3c Chunky Vegetable Soup	C18	2/3c LF Onion Soup
I12	3/4c LF Ham Salad on	D17	4 oz LF Sloppy Joe on	I18	3/4c LF Seafood Salad on	G13	1/6 pie DB Spinach Quiche
	Lettuce Leaves		1 Bun		1/2 Croissant	K32	1c Tossed Vegetable Salad
	3 sl Tomatoes and	J24	1/2c LF Corn Confetti	K40	1/2c LF Waldorf Salad	P1–8	1 Tbsp LC Salad Dressing
	3 sl Cucumbers		1/4c Skim Milk		1/2c Skim Milk		1/2c Skim Milk
K5	1/2c DB Cole Slaw		Coffee or Tea		Coffee or Tea		Coffee or Tea
	1 small Dinner Roll		1/2c LF Ice Milk	S12	1/2c DB Orange Gelatin		2 Graham Crackers
	1 tsp Margarine						
	1/4c Skim Milk						
	Coffee or Tea						
S17	1/2c DB Vanilla Pudding						
	Snacks:						
	1/2 Milk Exchange		1/2 Milk Exchange		1/2 Milk Exchange		1/2 Milk Exchange
	1 Starch/Bread Exchange		1 Starch/Bread Exchange		1 Starch/Bread Exchange		1 Starch/Bread Exchange

TERMS: LF = Low Fat; FF = Fat Free; SR = Sodium or Salt Restricted; STR = Strained; DB = Diabetic; UNSW = Unsweetened; RC = Reduced Calorie; LC = Low Calorie; EXCH = Diabetic Exchange.

Amounts specified for food items that contain bone is equivalent to cooked, edible deboned portion.

Recipe	Friday	Recipe	Saturday	Recipe	Sunday
S11 B1 B4	1/3c UNSW Cranberry Juice or 3 medium Stewed Prunes 1/2c DB Cream of Wheat or 3/4c UNSW Dry Cereal 1 Poached Egg 1 sl Toast 1 tsp Margarine 1 tsp DB Jam/Jelly 1/2c Skim Milk Coffee or Tea	B1 B4	1/2c UNSW Apple Juice 1/2c DB Wheatena or 3/4c UNSW Dry Cereal 1 Hard-Boiled Egg 1 sl Toast 1 tsp DB Jam/Jelly 1/2c Skim Milk Coffee or Tea	B1 B4,5 B9	1/2c UNSW Orange Juice 1/2c DB Farina or 3/4c UNSW Dry Cereal 1 Egg of Choice 2 DB Pancakes (4" across) with 1 oz DB Maple Syrup 1 tsp Margarine 1 tsp DB Jam/Jelly 1/2c Skim Milk Coffee or Tea
K20 F4 M2 J15	1/2c LF Cheesy Pea Salad 3 1/2 oz LF Oven Fried Fish Lemon Wedge 1/2c LF Lyonnaise Noodles 1/2c DB Glazed Carrots 1/2c Skim Milk Coffee or Tea 1/2c UNSW Fruit Cocktail	K9 D15 O16 J37 J51	1/2c DB Marinated Cucumbers 4 oz Meatloaf with 1 oz LF Onion Gravy 1/2c LF Mashed Potatoes 1/2c Vegetable Medley 1 small Dinner Roll 1 tsp Margarine 1/2c Skim Milk Coffee or Tea 1/2c UNSW Apricot Halves	K24 P1–8 D31 O3 P11 J47	1c Garden Salad with 1 Tbsp LC Salad Dressing 3 oz Roast Pork with 1 oz LF Brown Gravy 1/4c DB Cornbread Stuffing 1/2c Spinach 1/2c Skim Milk Coffee or Tea 1/2c UNSW Applesauce
C8 E2 J41 J1 Q10	2/3c STR Chicken Rice Soup 3 oz LF Chicken Fricassee with 2 oz LF Gravy 3 oz LF Parsley Potatoes 1/2c Asparagus Tips 1/2c Skim Milk Coffee or Tea 2" DB Strawberry Shortcake	C4 I5 P1–8 S16	2/3c SR/LF Bean Soup Chef Salad: 1 oz LF Ham, 1 oz Turkey and 1 oz LF Cheese 1c Lettuce, Tomatoes, Onions, and Cucumbers 1 Tbsp LC Salad Dressing 1 small Dinner Roll or 5 LF Crackers 1/4c Skim Milk Coffee or Tea 1/2c DB Chocolate Pudding	C15 F10 J8	2/3c Creole Soup 8 oz LF Tuna Noodle Casserole 1/2c DB Julienne Beets 1 small Dinner Roll 1 tsp Margarine 1/2c Skim Milk Coffee or Tea 1/2c LF Sherbet
	1/2 Milk Exchange 1 Starch/Bread Exchange		1/2 Milk Exchange 1 Starch/Bread Exchange		1/2 Milk Exchange 1 Starch/Bread Exchange

Recipe	Monday	Recipe	Tuesday	Recipe	Wednesday	Recipe	Thursday
	Breakfast						
	1/2c UNSW Pineapple Juice		1/2c UNSW Grapefruit Juice		1/3c UNSW Cranberry Juice		1/2c UNSW Orange Juice
	or 1/2 small Banana	B1	1/2c DB Farina or	B1	1/2c DB Wheatena or		or 1c Melon Cubes
B1	1/2c DB Cream of Wheat		3/4c UNSW Dry Cereal		3/4c UNSW Dry Cereal	B1	1/2c DB Cream of Rice or
	or 3/4c UNSW Dry Cereal	B4	1 Soft Cooked Egg		1 Tbsp Peanut Butter and		3/4c UNSW Dry Cereal
B5	1 Scrambled Egg		1 sl Toast		2 tsp DB Jelly on	B4	1 Poached Egg
	1 sl Toast		1 tsp DB Jam/Jelly		1 sl Raisin Bread	N12	1 sm DB Blueberry Muffin
	1 tsp DB Jam/Jelly		1/2c Skim Milk		1/2c Skim Milk		1 tsp Margarine
	1/2c Skim Milk		Coffee or Tea		Coffee or Tea		1 tsp DB Jam/Jelly
	Coffee or Tea						1/2c Skim Milk
							Coffee or Tea
	Lunch						
K28	1c Mixed Field Greens	K2	1/2c DB Pickled Beets	K31	1c DB Hawaiian Tossed Salad	K22	1/2c DB Three Bean Salad
P1–8	1 Tbsp LC Salad Dressing	D2	8 oz Beef Stew	D27	3 1/2 oz Veal Patty	D37	3 oz DB Braised Liver with
E8	3 oz LF Tahitian Chicken	M1	1/2c Noodles	J24	1/2c LF Corn Confetti		1/4c LF Sauté Onions
	with 1 1/2 oz LF Sauce		1/2c Skim Milk	J50	1/2c DB Stewed Tomatoes	M2	1/2c LF Lyonnaise Noodles
L5	1/3c Rice Pilaf		Coffee or Tea		1 small Dinner Roll	J18	1/2c DB Sunshine Carrots
J10	1/2c LF Steamed Broccoli		2 UNSW Pear Halves		1/2c Skim Milk		1 small Dinner Roll
	1/2c Skim Milk				Coffee or Tea		1/2c Skim Milk
	Coffee or Tea				1/2c LF Ice Milk		Coffee or Tea
S8	1/2c Almond Peaches					S2	1/2c DB Spiced Applesauce
	Dinner						
C28	2/3c French Vegetable Soup	C8	2/3c Chicken Rice Soup	C13	2/3c LF Cream of Spinach Soup	C21	2/3c Minestrone Soup
I2	3 oz LF Grilled Cheese	E16	3 oz Turkey on	I9	3/4c DB Egg Salad Platter	M1	1/2c Spaghetti and
	Sandwich, 2 sl Bread		1 sl Bread with		Lettuce Leaves,	D13	3 oz Meatballs with
	1/2c Lettuce Leaves with	O5	1 oz LF Chicken Gravy		1 Radish Rose,	O20	1 oz Marinara Sauce
	4 sl Tomatoes	J37	1/2c LF Mashed Potatoes		3 sl Cucumbers	J26	1/2c Italian Mix Vegetables
P1–8	1 Tbsp LC Salad Dressing	J27	1/4c Mixed Vegetables	K13	1/3c LF Macaroni Salad		1/2c Skim Milk
	1/2c Skim Milk		1/2c Skim Milk		1 small Dinner Roll		Coffee or Tea
	Coffee or Tea		Coffee or Tea		1/2c Skim Milk	R4	1/8 DB Lemon Pie
Q4	3×2" sl DB Carrot Raisin Cake		3 Vanilla Wafers		Coffee or Tea		
					1/2c UNSW Fruit Cocktail		
	Snacks:						
	1/2 Milk Exchange		1/2 Milk Exchange		1/2 Milk Exchange		1/2 Milk Exchange
	1 Starch/Bread Exchange		1 Starch/Bread Exchange		1 Starch/Bread Exchange		1 Starch/Bread Exchange

TERMS: LF = Low Fat; FF = Fat Free; SR = Sodium or Salt Restricted; STR = Strained; DB = Diabetic; UNSW = Unsweetened; RC = Reduced Calorie; LC = Low Calorie; EXCH = Diabetic Exchange.
Amounts specified for food items that contain bone is equivalent to cooked, edible deboned portion.

Recipe	Friday	Recipe	Saturday	Recipe	Sunday
B1	1/2c UNSW Apple Juice 1/2c DB Oatmeal or 3/4c UNSW Dry Cereal	B1	1/2c UNSW Grapefruit Juice 1/2c DB Cream of Wheat or 3/4c UNSW Dry Cereal	B1	1/2c UNSW Pineapple Juice 1/2c DB Wheatena or 3/4c UNSW Dry Cereal
B4	1 Hard Boiled Egg 1 sl Toast 1 tsp Margarine 1 tsp DB Jam/Jelly 1/2c Skim Milk Coffee or Tea	B5 N7	1 Scrambled Egg 1/2" sl DB Date Nut Bread 1 Tbsp Cream Cheese or 1 tsp Margarine 1 tsp DB Jam/Jelly 1/2c Skim Milk Coffee or Tea	B8	1 sl French Toast with 1 oz DB Maple Syrup 1 tsp Margarine 1 tsp DB Jam/Jelly 1/2c Skim Milk Coffee or Tea
K24 P1–8 F3 O7 L1 J47	1c Garden Salad with 1 Tbsp LC Salad Dressing 3 oz DB Fish Creole with 2 oz DB Creole Sauce 1/3c White Rice 1/2c Spinach 1/2c Skim Milk Coffee or Tea 1/2c UNSW Chilled Apricots	K3 D29 J46 J6	1/2c DB Cabbage Apple Salad 3 oz DB Breaded Pork Chops 1/3c LF Whipped Sweet Potatoes 1/2c LF Seasoned Green Beans 1 small Dinner Roll 1 tsp Margarine 1/4c Skim Milk Coffee or Tea 1/3c LF Sherbet	K26 P1–8 D19 J41 J54 S7	1c Green Vegetable Salad 1 Tbsp LC Salad Dressing 3 oz LF Swiss Steak with 1 1/2 oz LF Gravy 3 oz LF Parsley Potatoes 1/2c LF Tarragon Zucchini 1/2c Skim Milk Coffee or Tea 1/2c Fruit Parfait with 1 Tbsp Whipped Topping
C7 E5 J35 J8 Q9	2/3c Beef Noodle Soup 3 oz LF Oven Crisp Chicken 1 sm Baked Potato with 1 Tbsp Sour Cream 1/2c LF Julienne Beets 1/2c Skim Milk Coffee or Tea 1/2" sl DB Pound Cake	C29 G11 J49	2/3c Old Fashion Vegtble Soup 8 oz LF Macaroni & Cheese 1/2c Succotash 1/2c Skim Milk Coffee or Tea 2 UNSW Plums	C12 F1 O25 K5 S12	2/3c LF Cream Mushroom Soup 3 1/2 oz LF Fish Burger on 1 Bun 2 tsp LF Tartar Sauce 2 Lettuce Leaves 2 sl Tomatoes 1/2c DB Cole Slaw 1/2c Skim Milk Coffee or Tea 1/2c DB Cherry Gelatin
	1/2 Milk Exchange 1 Starch/Bread Exchange		1/2 Milk Exchange 1 Starch/Bread Exchange		1/2 Milk Exchange 1 Starch/Bread Exchange

Recipe	Monday	Recipe	Tuesday	Recipe	Wednesday	Recipe	Thursday
	Breakfast						
B1	1/3c UNSW Cranberry Juice		1/2c UNSW Orange Juice		1/2c UNSW Apple Juice		1/2c UNSW Grapefruit Juice
	1/2c DB Oatmeal or		or 3/4c Fresh Berries	B1	1/2c DB Farina or	B1	1/2c DB Wheatena or
	3/4c UNSW Dry Cereal	B1	1/2c DB Cream of Wheat		3/4c UNSW Dry Cereal		3/4c UNSW Dry Cereal
B4	1 Hard Boiled Egg		or 3/4c UNSW Dry Cereal	B4	1 Poached Egg		1/4c LF Cottage Cheese
	1 sl Toast	G7	2 oz DB Ham Omelet		1/2 English Muffin		with Artificial Sweetener
	1 tsp Margarine		1 sl Toast		1 tsp Margarine		and Cinnamon
	1 tsp DB Jam/Jelly		1 tsp Margarine		1 tsp DB Jam/Jelly		on 1 sl Raisin Toast
	1/2c Skim Milk		1 tsp DB Jam/Jelly		1/2c Skim Milk		1 tsp DB Jam/Jelly
	Coffee or Tea		1/2c Skim Milk		Coffee or Tea		1/2c Skim Milk
			Coffee or Tea				Coffee or Tea
	Lunch						
K10	1/2c DB Cucumber Onion Salad	K4	1/3c LF Carrot-Raisin Salad	K25	1c Green Salad with	K24	1c Garden Salad with
E3	3 oz LF Chicken Italiano	D25	4 oz Veal Loaf with	P1	1 Tbsp LC French Dressing	P1–8	1 Tbsp LC Salad Dressing
M1	1/2c Spaghetti with	O3	2 oz LF Brown Gravy	E15	1c Turkey Jambalaya	D14	3 oz DB Sweet-n-Sour Meatballs
O22	2 oz DB Tomato Sauce	J37	1/2c LF Mashed Potatoes	J3	1/2c Green Beans		with 1 oz DB Sauce
J26	1/2c Italian Mix Vegetables	J1	1/2c Asparagus Tips		1/2c Skim Milk	M1	1/2c Noodles
	1/2c Skim Milk		1/2c Skim Milk		Coffee or Tea	J48	1/2c Seasoned Spinach
	Coffee or Tea		Coffee or Tea	S17	1/2c DB Vanilla Pudding		1/2c Skim Milk
	1/2c UNSW Sliced Peaches	R7	2×2" srv DB Apple Crisp				Coffee or Tea
							1/2c UNSW Apricots
	Dinner						
C20	2/3c Julienne Soup	C3	2/3c Clear Vegetable Soup	C14	2/3c LF Cream Tomato Soup	C19	2/3c LF Onion Soup
I10	Fruit Festival with	G3	6 oz DB Cheese Strata	I22	Salad Sampler Platter with	G12	1/6 pie DB Quiche Lorraine
	3/4c Cottage Cheese	J51	1/2c Vegetable Medley	I12	1/4c LF Ham Salad	J28	1/2c LF Mushrooms & Celery
	1/2c Seasonal Fruit		1/2c Skim Milk	I6	1/2c LF Chicken Salad		1 small Dinner Roll
S12	1/2c DB Gelatin Cubes		Coffee or Tea		Lettuce Leaves, 2 sl Onions,		1/4c Skim Milk
N10-20	1 small DB Muffin		1/3c UNSW Pineapple		and 2 Green Pepper Rings		Coffee or Tea
	1 tsp DB Jam/Jelly		Chunks	K21	1/2c LF Potato Salad		1/2c LF Ice Milk
	1/2c Skim Milk				1 medium Dinner Roll		
	Coffee or Tea				1/2c Skim Milk		
Q6	2×2" sl DB Chocolate Chip Cake				Coffee and Tea		
				S5	1/2c Fruit Cup		
	Snacks:						
	1/2 Milk Exchange		1/2 Milk Exchange		1/2 Milk Exchange		1/2 Milk Exchange
	1 Starch/Bread Exchange		1 Starch/Bread Exchange		1 Starch/Bread Exchange		1 Starch/Bread Exchange

TERMS: LF = Low Fat; FF = Fat Free; SR = Sodium or Salt Restricted; STR = Strained; DB = Diabetic; UNSW = Unsweetened; RC = Reduced Calorie; LC = Low Calorie; EXCH = Diabetic Exchange.

Amounts specified for food items that contain bone is equivalent to cooked, edible deboned portion.

Recipe	Friday	Recipe	Saturday	Recipe	Sunday
B1 B5	1/2c UNSW Orange Juice or 1/2 small Banana 1/2c DB Cream of Rice or 3/4c UNSW Dry Cereal 1 Scrambled Egg 1 sl Toast 1 tsp Margarine 1 tsp DB Jam/Jelly 1/2c Skim Milk Coffee or Tea	B1 B4	1/2c UNSW Apple Juice 1/2c DB Oatmeal or 3/4c UNSW Dry Cereal 1 Hard-Boiled Egg 1 sl Toast 1 tsp Margarine 1 tsp DB Jam/Jelly 1/2c Skim Milk Coffee or Tea	B1 B4,5 B12	1/3c UNSW Cranberry Juice 1/2c DB Farina or 3/4c UNSW Dry Cereal 1 Egg of Choice 1 DB Waffle (4 1/2"sq) with 1 oz DB Maple Syrup 1 tsp DB Jam/Jelly 1/2c Skim Milk Coffee or Tea
K2 F5 L5 J27	1/2c DB Pickled Beets 3 oz LF Catch of the Day Lemon Wedge 1/3c Rice Pilaf 1/2c Mixed Vegetables 1/2c Skim Milk Coffee or Tea 2 UNSW Pear Halves	K29 P1–8 D28 J45 J3 S13	1c Tossed Salad with 1 Tbsp LC Salad Dressing 3 oz DB Baked Ham 1/2c DB Sweet Potatoes/Apples 1/2c String Beans 1 small Dinner Roll 1 tsp Margarine 1/2c Skim Milk Coffee or Tea 1/2c DB Fruited Lime Gelatin	K16 D3 C1 J40 J10	1/2c DB Mixed Vegetable Salad 3 oz Brisket of Beef with 2 oz LF Broth 4 oz DB Potato Pancakes 1/2c LF Broccoli Cuts 1/2c Skim Milk Coffee or Tea 1/2c UNSW Applesauce
C23 E7 J35 J19 Q8	2/3c LF Split Pea Soup 3 oz LF Roast Chicken 1 small Baked Potato with 1 Tbsp Sour Cream 1/2c DB Carrot Tzimmes 1/2c Skim Milk Coffee or Tea 3×2" sl DB Marble Cake	C21 G1 J55	2/3c Minestrone Soup 6 oz LF Cheese Fettucine 1/2c LF Zucchini-Onions 1/2c Skim Milk Coffee or Tea 2 UNSW Plums	C27 I18 I23 K15	2/3c Chunky Vegetable Soup 3/4c LF Seafood Salad Stuffed Tomato 1/3c LF Cheesy Macaroni Salad 1 small Dinner Roll 1/2c Skim Milk Coffee or Tea 1/2c LF Sherbet
	1/2 Milk Exchange 1 Starch/Bread Exchange		1/2 Milk Exchange 1 Search/Bread Exchange		1/2 Milk Exchange 1 Starch/Bread Exchange

Recipe	Monday	Recipe	Tuesday	Recipe	Wednesday	Recipe	Thursday
	Breakfast						
	1/2c UNSW Apple Juice or		1/2c UNSW Orange Juice		1/2c UNSW Pineapple Juice		1/2c UNSW Apple Juice or
	1/2c Fresh Fruit	B1	1/2c DB Oatmeal or	B1	1/2c DB Cream of Wheat	S11	3 medium Stewed Prunes
B1	1/2c DB Cream of Rice or		3/4c UNSW Dry Cereal		or 3/4c UNSW Dry Cereal	B1	1/2c DB Farina or
	3/4c UNSW Dry Cereal	B4	1 Poached Egg	B4	1 Soft Cooked Egg		3/4c UNSW Dry Cereal
I2	1 oz Grilled Cheese on		1 English Muffin		1 sl Toast	B4,5	1 Egg to Order
	1 sl Toast		1 tsp Margarine		1 tsp Margarine		1 sl Raisin Toast
	1 tsp DB Jam/Jelly		1 tsp DB Jam/Jelly		1 tsp DB Jam/Jelly		1 tsp Margarine
	1/2c Skim Milk		1/2c Skim Milk		1/2c Skim Milk		1 tsp DB Jam/Jelly
	Coffee or Tea		Coffee or Tea		Coffee or Tea		1/2c Skim Milk
							Coffee or Tea
	Lunch						
K29	1c Tossed Salad with	K23	1/2c DB Marinated Zucchini	K32	1c Tossed Vegetable Salad	K25	1c Green Salad with
P8	1 Tbsp LC Salad Dressing	D22	3 1/2 oz DB Breaded Veal	P1–8	2 Tbsp LC Salad Dressing	P1–8	1 Tbsp LC Salad Dressing
E1	3 oz LF Barbecue Chicken	O20	with 1 oz Marinara Sauce	D1	3 1/2 oz LF Beef Teriyaki	D30	3 oz Pork Chops with
O2	with 2 oz DB Barbecue Sauce	M5	3/4c LF Pasta Primavera	J22	1/2c Chinese Vegetables		1/4c LF Apple Stuffing
J31	1/2c Green Peas		1/2c Skim Milk	L1	1/3c White Rice	J1	1/2c Asparagus Tips
J14	1/2c Carrots		Coffee or Tea		1 small Dinner Roll		1 small Dinner Roll
	1/2c Skim Milk	S5	1/2c Fresh Fruit Cup		1/4c Skim Milk		1/4c Skim Milk
	Coffee or Tea				Coffee or Tea		Coffee or Tea
	1/2c UNSW Sliced Peaches				1/2c LF Ice Milk	S16	1/2c DB Chocolate Pudding
	Dinner						
C11	2/3c LF Cream Celery Soup	C4	2/3c SR/LF Bean Soup	C26	2/3c Vegetable Beef Soup	C21	2/3c Minestrone Soup
G8	5 1/2 oz DB Vegetable Omelet	I4	Asst Cold Cut Sandwiches	E13	3/4c LF Turkey à la King	D12	8 oz LF Beef Macaroni Casserole
J36	1/2c LF Home Fried Potatoes		2 sl Bread (cut in quarters)		with 2 Toast Points	J6	1/2c LF Seasoned Green Beans
	1 small Dinner Roll		with 3 oz Roast Beef, Ham,	J47	1/2c Spinach		1/2c Skim Milk
	1/2c Skim Milk		Turkey, Bologna, & Salami		1/2c Skim Milk		Coffee or Tea
	Coffee or Tea		Lettuce Leaves		Coffee or Tea		1/2c UNSW Chilled Apricots
Q2	2×1" sl DB Banana Cake		2 sl Tomatoes		2 UNSW Plums		
		K5	1/2c DB Cole Slaw				
			1 tsp Catsup, 1 tsp Mustard				
			1/2c Skim Milk				
			Coffee or Tea				
		S12	1/2c DB Strawberry Gelatin				
	Snacks:						
	1/2 Milk Exchange		1/2 Milk Exchange		1/2 Milk Exchange		1/2 Milk Exchange
	1 Starch/Bread Exchange		1 Starch/Bread Exchange		1 Starch/Bread Exchange		1 Starch/Bread Exchange

TERMS: LF = Low Fat; FF = Fat Free; SR = Sodium or Salt Restricted; STR = Strained; DB = Diabetic; UNSW = Unsweetened; RC = Reduced Calorie; LC = Low Calorie; EXCH = Diabetic Exchange.
Amounts specified for food items that contain bone is equivalent to cooked, edible deboned portion.

Recipe	Friday	Recipe	Saturday	Recipe	Sunday
B1	1/2c UNSW Grapefruit Juice		1/3c UNSW Cranberry Juice	B1	1/2c UNSW Pineapple Juice
	1/2c DB Wheatena or		or 1/2 small Banana		1/2c DB Oatmeal or
	3/4c UNSW Dry Cereal	B1	1/2c DB Cream of Rice or		3/4c UNSW Dry Cereal
B5	1 Scrambled Egg		3/4c UNSW Dry Cereal	B8	1 sl French Toast with
N14	1 small DB Bran Muffin	G9	2 1/2 oz DB Western Omelet		1 oz DB Maple Syrup
	1 tsp Margarine		1 sl Toast		1 tsp DB Jam/Jelly
	1 tsp DB Jam/Jelly		1 tsp DB Jam/Jelly		1/2c Skim Milk
	1/2c Skim Milk		1/2c Skim Milk		Coffee or Tea
	Coffee or Tea		Coffee or Tea		
K9	1/2c DB Marinated Cucumbers	K37	4 oz DB Perfection Salad	K42	1/2c DB Cranberry Mold
F9	3 oz LF Sole Almondine	D18	6 oz Stuffed Cabbage	E16	3 oz LF Roast Turkey with
O25	2 tsp LF Tartar Sauce	J43	1/2c LF Whipped Potatoes	O18	2 oz STR Giblet Gravy
	Lemon Wedge	J15	1/2c DB Glazed Carrots	P12	1/4c Raisin Bread Stuffing
L2	1/2c Rice Chantilly		1/2c Skim Milk	J52	1/2c Zucchini
J51	1/2c Vegetable Medley		Coffee or Tea		1/2c Skim Milk
	1/2c Skim Milk		1/3c UNSW Pineapple Tidbits		Coffee or Tea
	Coffee or Tea			R3	1/12 DB Apple Pie
	3 Vanilla Wafers				
C9	2/3c Chicken Matzo Ball Soup	C24	2/3c LF Tomato Soup	C3	2/3c Clear Vegetable Soup
E9	3 oz LF Chicken Tarragon	I21	3/4c LF Curry Tuna Salad	G2	6 oz DB Lasagna
M4	4 oz DB Noodle Pudding		Platter Lettuce Leaves,	J27	1/3c Mixed Vegetables
J10	1/2c LF Steamed Broccoli		2 sl Onions, 3 sl	N8	1 sl LF Garlic Bread
	1/2c Skim Milk		Cucumbers, 1 Radish Rose		1/2c Skim Milk
	Coffee or Tea	K13	1/2c LF Macaroni Salad		Coffee or Tea
S1	1 small DB Baked Apple		1 small Dinner Roll or	S4	1/3c Fruit Compote
			5 LF Crackers		
			1/2c Skim Milk		
			Coffee or Tea		
			1/2c LF Sherbet		
	1/2 Milk Exchange		1/2 Milk Exchange		1/2 Milk Exchange
	1 Starch/Bread Exchange		1 Starch/Bread Exchange		1 Starch/Bread Exchange

Recipe	Monday	Recipe	Tuesday	Recipe	Wednesday	Recipe	Thursday
	Breakfast						
B1	1/2c UNSW Orange Juice 1/2c DB Farina or 3/4c UNSW Dry Cereal	B1	1/2c UNSW Apple Juice 1/2c DB Wheatena or 3/4c UNSW Dry Cereal	B1	1/2c UNSW Grapefruit Juice or 1/2 small Banana 1/2c DB Cream of Rice or	B1	1/2c UNSW Pineapple Juice 1/2c DB Oatmeal or 3/4c UNSW Dry Cereal
B4	1 Soft Cooked Egg 1 sl Toast 1 tsp Margarine 1 tsp DB Jam/Jelly 1/2c Skim Milk Coffee or Tea	G6	2 oz DB Cheese Omelet 1 English Muffin 1 tsp Margarine 1 tsp DB Jam/Jelly 1/2c Skim Milk Coffee or Tea	B5	3/4c UNSW Dry Cereal 1 Scrambled Egg 1 sl Toast 1 tsp Margarine 1 tsp DB Jam/Jelly 1/2c Skim Milk Coffee or Tea	I2	1 oz LF Grilled Cheese on 1 sl Toast 1 tsp Margarine 1/2c Skim Milk Coffee or Tea
	Lunch						
K29 P1 D6 L3	1c Tossed Salad with 1 Tbsp LC French Dressing 8 oz LF Pepper Steak 1/3c LF Rice Florentine 1 small Dinner Roll 1 tsp Margarine 1/2c Skim Milk Coffee or Tea 1/2c UNSW Sliced Peaches	K35 E4 J39 J10 S3	1/2c DB Molded Veg Salad 3 oz LF Lemon Chicken 4 oz LF Oven Browned Potatoes 1/2c LF Broccoli 1 sm Dinner Roll 1 tsp Margarine 1/2c Skim Milk Coffee or Tea 1/2c Citrus Cup	K25 P4 D26 M1 O22 J55 S10	1c Green Salad with 1 tsp Italian Dressing 5 oz DB Veal Parmesan 1/2c Spaghetti with 2 oz DB Tomato Sauce 1/2c LF Zucchini-Onions 1 small Dinner Roll 1 tsp Margarine 1/2c Skim Milk Coffee or Tea 1/2 DB Baked Pear	K22 E14 L1	1/2c DB Three Bean Salad 1c Turkey Chow Mein 1/2c White Rice 1/4c Chinese Noodles 1 small Dinner Roll 1/2c Skim Milk Coffee or Tea 2 UNSW Plums
	Dinner						
C23 I12 K5 S17	2/3c LF Split Pea Soup 3/4c LF Ham Salad on Lettuce Leaves 3 sl Tomatoes and 3 sl Cucumbers 1/2c DB Cole Slaw 1 medium Dinner Roll 1 tsp Margarine 1/4c Skim Milk Coffee or Tea 1/2c DB Vanilla Pudding	C12 D17 J24	2/3c LF Cream Mushroom Soup 4 oz LF Sloppy Joe on 1 Bun 1/2c LF Corn Confetti 1/2c Skim Milk Coffee or Tea 1/2c LF Ice Milk	C27 I18 K40 S12	2/3c Chunky Vegetable Soup 3/4c LF Seafood Salad on 1 Croissant 1/2c LF Waldorf Salad 1/2c Skim Milk Coffee or Tea 1/2c DB Orange Gelatin	C18 G13 K32 P1–8	2/3c LF Onion Soup 1/6 pie DB Spinach Quiche 1c Tossed Vegetable Salad 1 Tbsp LC Salad Dressing 1/2c Skim Milk Coffee or Tea 3 Graham Crackers
	Snacks: 1/2 Milk Exchange 1 Starch/Bread Exchange 1 Fat Exchange		1/2 Milk Exchange 1 Starch/Bread Exchange 1 Fat Exchange		1/2 Milk Exchange 1 Starch/Bread Exchange 1 Fat Exchange		1/2 Milk Exchange 1 Starch/Bread Exchange 1 Fat Exchange

TERMS: LF = Low Fat; FF = Fat Free; SR = Sodium or Salt Restricted; STR = Strained; DB = Diabetic; UNSW = Unsweetened; RC = Reduced Calorie; LC = Low Calorie; EXCH = Diabetic Exchange.

[1] *2000 Calorie Diet:* Follow 1800 calorie diet with the following additions: Breakfast—add 1/2 milk exchange and 1 bread exchange; Snack—add 1 medium-fat meat exchange. Amounts specified for food items that contain bone is equivalent to cooked, edible deboned portion.

Recipe	Friday	Recipe	Saturday	Recipe	Sunday
S11	1/3c UNSW Cranberry Juice or 3 medium Stewed Prunes	B1	1/2c UNSW Apple Juice 1/2c DB Wheatena or	B1	1/2c UNSW Orange Juice 1/2c DB Farina or
B1	1/2c DB Cream of Wheat or 3/4c UNSW Dry Cereal	B4	3/4c UNSW Dry Cereal 1 Hard-Boiled Egg	B4,5	3/4c UNSW Dry Cereal 1 Egg of Choice
B4	1 Poached Egg 1 sl Toast 1 tsp Margarine 1 tsp DB Jam/Jelly 1/2c Skim Milk Coffee or Tea		2 sl Toast 1 tsp Margarine 1 tsp DB Jam/Jelly 1/2c Skim Milk Coffee or Tea	B9	2 DB Pancakes (4"across) with 1 oz DB Maple Syrup 1 tsp Margarine 1 tsp DB Jam/Jelly 1/2c Skim Milk Coffee or Tea
K20	1/2c LF Cheesy Pea Salad	K9	1/2c DB Marinated Cucumbers	K24	1c Garden Salad with
F4	3 1/2 oz LF Oven Fried Fish	D15	4 oz Meatloaf with	P1–8	1 Tbsp LC Salad Dressing
O25	2 tsp LF Tartar Sauce	O16	2 oz LF Onion Gravy	D31	3 oz Roast Pork with
M2	1/2c LF Lyonnaise Noodles	J37	1/2c LF Mashed Potatoes	O3	2 oz LF Brown Gravy
J15	1/2c DB Glazed Carrots	J51	1/2c Vegetable Medley	P11	1/4c DB Cornbread Stuffing
	1 small Dinner Roll		1 small Dinner Roll	J47	1/2c Spinach
	1/2c Skim Milk		1 tsp Margarine		1 small Dinner Roll
	Coffee or Tea		1/2c Skim Milk		1 tsp Margarine
	1/2c UNSW Fruit Cocktail		Coffee or Tea		1/2c Skim Milk
			1/2c UNSW Apricot Halves		Coffee or Tea
					1/2c UNSW Applesauce
C8	2/3c STR Chicken Rice Soup	C4	2/3c SR/LF Bean Soup	C15	2/3c Creole Soup
E2	3 oz LF Chicken Fricassee with 2 oz LF Gravy	I5	Chef Salad: 1 oz LF Ham, 1 oz Turkey and	F10	8 oz LF Tuna Noodle Casserole
J41	3 oz LF Parsley Potatoes		1 oz LF Cheese	J8	1/2c DB Julienne Beets
J1	1/2c Asparagus Tips		1c Lettuce, Tomatoes,		1 small Dinner Roll
	1 small Dinner Roll		Onions, and Cucumbers		1 tsp Margarine
	1 tsp Margarine	P1–8	1 Tbsp LC Salad Dressing		1/2c Skim Milk
	1/2c Skim Milk		1 medium Dinner Roll or		Coffee or Tea
	Coffee or Tea		10 LF Crackers		1/2c LF Sherbet
Q10	2" DB Strawberry Shortcake		1/2c Skim Milk		
			Coffee or Tea		
		S16	1/2c DB Chocolate Pudding		
	1/2 Milk Exchange 1 Starch/Bread Exchange 1 Fat Exchange		1/2 Milk Exchange 1 Starch/Bread Exchange 1 Fat Exchange		1/2 Milk Exchange 1 Starch/Bread Exchange 1 Fat Exchange

Recipe	Monday	Recipe	Tuesday	Recipe	Wednesday	Recipe	Thursday
	Breakfast						
	1/2c UNSW Pineapple Juice		1/2c UNSW Grapefruit Juice		1/3c UNSW Cranberry Juice		1/2c UNSW Orange Juice
	or 1/2 small Banana	B1	1/2c DB Farina or	B1	1/2c DB Wheatena or		or 1c Melon Cubes
B1	1/2c DB Cream of Wheat		3/4c UNSW Dry Cereal		3/4c UNSW Dry Cereal	B1	1/2c DB Cream of Rice or
	or 3/4c UNSW Dry Cereal	B4	1 Soft Cooked Egg		1 Tbsp Peanut Butter and		3/4c UNSW Dry Cereal
B5	1 Scrambled Egg		1 sl Toast		2 tsp DB Jelly on	B4	1 Poached Egg
	2 sl Toast		1 tsp Margarine		1 sl Raisin Bread	N12	1 sm DB Blueberry Muffin
	1 tsp Margarine		1 tsp DB Jam/Jelly		1/2c Skim Milk		1 tsp Margarine
	1 tsp DB Jam/Jelly		1/2c Skim Milk		Coffee or Tea		1 tsp DB Jam/Jelly
	1/2c Skim Milk		Coffee or Tea				1/2c Skim Milk
	Coffee or Tea						Coffee or Tea
	Lunch						
K28	1c Mixed Field Greens	K2	1/2c DB Pickled Beets	K31	1c DB Hawaiian Tossed Salad	K22	1/2c DB Three Bean Salad
P1–8	1 Tbsp LC Salad Dressing	D2	8 oz Beef Stew	D27	3 1/2 oz Veal Patty	d37	3 oz DB Braised Liver with
E8	3 oz LF Tahitian Chicken	M1	1/2c Noodles	J24	1/2c LF Corn Confetti		1/4c LF Sauté Onions
	with 1 1/2 oz LF Sauce		1 Biscuit	J50	1/2c DB Stewed Tomatoes	M2	1/2c LF Lyonnaise Noodles
L5	1/3c Rice Pilaf		1 tsp Margarine		1 small Dinner Roll	J18	1/2c DB Sunshine Carrots
J10	1/2c LF Steamed Broccoli		1/2c Skim Milk		1 tsp Margarine		1 small Dinner Roll
	1 small Dinner Roll		Coffee or Tea		1/2c Skim Milk		1 tsp Margarine
	1 tsp Margarine		2 UNSW Pear Halves		Coffee or Tea		1/2c Skim Milk
	1/2c Skim Milk				1/2c LF Ice Milk		Coffee or Tea
	Coffee or Tea					S2	1/2c DB Spiced Applesauce
S8	1/2c Almond Peaches						
	Dinner						
C28	2/3c French Vegetable Soup	C8	2/3c Chicken Rice Soup	C13	2/3c LF Cream of Spinach Soup	C21	2/3c Minestrone Soup
I2	3 oz LF Grilled Cheese	E16	3 oz Turkey on	I9	3/4c DB Egg Salad Platter	M1	1/2c Spaghetti and
	Sandwich, 2 sl Bread		1 sl Bread with		Lettuce Leaves,	D13	3 oz Meatballs with
	1/2c Lettuce Leaves with	O5	2 oz LF Chicken Gravy		1 Radish Rose,	O20	2 oz Marinara Sauce
	4 sl Tomatoes	J37	1/2c LF Mashed Potatoes		3 sl Cucumbers	J26	1/2c Italian Mix Vegetables
P1–8	1 Tbsp LC Salad Dressing	J27	1/2c Mixed Vegetables	K13	1/2c LF Macaroni Salad		1 sl Italian Bread
	1/2c Skim Milk		1/2c Skim Milk		1 small Dinner Roll		1 tsp Margarine
	Coffee or Tea		Coffee or Tea		1 tsp Margarine		1/2c Skim Milk
Q4	3×2" sl DB Carrot Raisin Cake		3 Vanilla Wafers		1/2c Skim Milk		Coffee or Tea
					Coffee or Tea	R4	1/8 DB Lemon Pie
					1/2c UNSW Fruit Cocktail		
	Snacks:						
	1/2 Milk Exchange		1/2 Milk Exchange		1/2 Milk Exchange		1/2 Milk Exchange
	1 Starch/Bread Exchange		1 Starch/Bread Exchange		1 Starch/Bread Exchange		1 Starch/Bread Exchange
	1 Fat Exchange		1 Fat Exchange		1 Fat Exchange		1 Fat Exchange

TERMS: LF = Low Fat; FF = Fat Free; SR = Sodium or Salt Restricted; STR = Strained; DB = Diabetic; UNSW = Unsweetened; RC = Reduced Calorie; LC = Low Calorie; EXCH = Diabetic Exchange.

[1] *2000 Calorie Diet:* Follow 1800 calorie diet with the following additions: Breakfast—add 1/2 milk exchange and 1 bread exchange; Snack—add 1 medium-fat meat exchange. Amounts specified for food items that contain bone is equivalent to cooked, edible deboned portion.

Recipe	Friday	Recipe	Saturday	Recipe	Sunday
B1	1/2c UNSW Apple Juice 1/2c DB Oatmeal or 3/4c UNSW Dry Cereal	B1	1/2c UNSW Grapefruit Juice 1/2c DB Cream of Wheat or 3/4c UNSW Dry Cereal	B1	1/2c UNSW Pineapple Juice 1/2c DB Wheatena or 3/4c UNSW Dry Cereal
B4	1 Hard-Boiled Egg 1 sl Toast 1 tsp Margarine 1 tsp DB Jam/Jelly 1/2c Skim Milk Coffee or Tea	B5 N7	1 Scrambled Egg 1/2" sl DB Date Nut Bread 1 Tbsp Cream Cheese or 1 tsp Margarine 1 tsp DB Jam/Jelly 1/2c Skim Milk Coffee or Tea	B8	1 sl French Toast with 1 oz DB Maple Syrup 1 tsp Margarine 1 tsp DB Jam/Jelly 1/2c Skim Milk Coffee or Tea
K24 P1–8 F3 O7 L1 J47	1c Garden Salad with 1 Tbsp LC Salad Dressing 3 oz DB Fish Creole with 2 oz DB Creole Sauce 1/3c White Rice 1/2c Spinach 1 small Dinner Roll 1 tsp Margarine 1/2c Skim Milk Coffee or Tea 1/2c UNSW Chilled Apricots	K3 D29 J46 J6	1/2c DB Cabbage Apple Salad 3 oz DB Breaded Pork Chops 1/4c LF Whipped Sweet Potatoes 1/2c LF Seasoned Green Beans 1 small Dinner Roll 1 tsp Margarine 1/4c Skim Milk Coffee or Tea 1/2c LF Sherbet	K26 P1–8 D19 J41 J54 S7	1c Green Vegetable Salad 1 Tbsp LC Salad Dressing 3 oz LF Swiss Steak with 1 1/2 oz LF Gravy 3 oz LF Parsley Potatoes 1/2c LF Tarragon Zucchini 1 small Dinner Roll 1 tsp Margarine 1/2c Skim Milk Coffee or Tea 1/2c Fruit Parfait with 1 Tbsp Whipped Topping
C7 E5 J35 J8 Q9	2/3c Beef Noodle Soup 3 oz LF Oven Crisp Chicken 1 sm Baked Potato with 1 oz Sour Cream 1/2c LF Julienne Beets 1 small Dinner Roll 1 tsp Margarine 1/2c Skim Milk Coffee or Tea 1/2" sl DB Pound Cake	C29 G11 J49	2/3c Old Fashion Vegtble Soup 8 oz LF Macaroni & Cheese 1/2c Succotash 1 small Dinner Roll 1 tsp Margarine 1/2c Skim Milk Coffee or Tea 2 UNSW Plums	C12 F1 O25 K5 S12	2/3c LF Cream Mushroom Soup 3 1/2 oz LF Fish Burger on 1 Bun 2 tsp LF Tartar Sauce 2 Lettuce Leaves 2 sl Tomatoes 1/2c DB Cole Slaw 1/2c Skim Milk Coffee or Tea 1/2c DB Cherry Gelatin
	1/2 Milk Exchange 1 Starch/Bread Exchange 1 Fat Exchange		1/2 Milk Exchange 1 Starch/Bread Exchange 1 Fat Exchange		1/2 Milk Exchange 1 Starch/Bread Exchange 1 Fat Exchange

Recipe	Monday	Recipe	Tuesday	Recipe	Wednesday	Recipe	Thursday
	Breakfast						
	1/3c UNSW Cranberry Juice		1/2c UNSW Orange Juice		1/2c UNSW Apple Juice		1/2c UNSW Grapefruit Juice
B1	1/2c DB Oatmeal or		or 3/4c Fresh Berries	B1	1/2c DB Farina or	B1	1/2c DB Wheatena or
	3/4c UNSW Dry Cereal	B1	1/2c DB Cream of Wheat		3/4c UNSW Dry Cereal		3/4c UNSW Dry Cereal
B4	1 Hard-Boiled Egg		or 3/4c UNSW Dry Cereal	B4	1 Poached Egg		1/4c LF Cottage Cheese
	1 sl Toast	G7	2 oz DB Ham Omelet		1 English Muffin		with Artificial Sweetener
	1 tsp Margarine		1 sl Toast		2 tsp Margarine		and Cinnamon
	1 tsp DB Jam/Jelly		1 tsp Margarine		1 tsp DB Jam/Jelly		on 1 sl Raisin Toast
	1/2c Skim Milk		1 tsp DB Jam/Jelly		1/2c Skim Milk		1 tsp DB Jam/Jelly
	Coffee or Tea		1/2c Skim Milk		Coffee or Tea		1/2c Skim Milk
			Coffee or Tea				Coffee or Tea
	Lunch						
K10	1/2c DB Cucumber Onion Salad	K4	1/3c LF Carrot-Raisin Salad	K25	1c Green Salad with	K24	1c Garden Salad with
E3	3 oz LF Chicken Italiano	D25	4 oz Veal Loaf with	P1	1 Tbsp LC French Dressing	P1-8	1 Tbsp LC Salad Dressing
M1	1/2c Spaghetti with	O3	2 oz LF Brown Gravy	E15	1c Turkey Jambalaya	D14	3 oz DB Sweet-n-Sour Meatballs
O22	2 oz DB Tomato Sauce	J37	1/2c LF Mashed Potatoes	J3	1/2c Green Beans		with 2 oz DB Sauce
J26	1/2c Italian Mix Vegetables	J1	1/2c Asparagus Tips		1 small Dinner Roll	M1	3/4c Noodles
	1 sl Italian Bread		1 small Dinner Roll		1 tsp Margarine	J48	1/2c Seasoned Spinach
	1 tsp Margarine		1 tsp Margarine		1/2c Skim Milk		1 small Dinner Roll
	1/2c Skim Milk		1/2c Skim Milk		Coffee or Tea		1 tsp Margarine
	Coffee or Tea		Coffee or Tea	s17	1/2c DB Vanilla Pudding		1/2c Skim Milk
	1/2c UNSW Sliced Peaches	R7	2× 2" srv DB Apple Crisp				Coffee or Tea
							1/2c UNSW Apricots
	Dinner						
C20	2/3c Julienne Soup	C3	2/3c Clear Vegetable Soup	C14	2/3c LF Cream Tomato Soup	C19	2/3c LF Onion Soup
I10	Fruit Festival with	G3	6 oz DB Cheese Strata	I22	Salad Sampler Platter with	G12	1/6 pie DB Quiche Lorraine
	3/4c Cottage Cheese	J51	1/2c Vegetable Medley	I12	1/4c LF Ham Salad	J28	1/2c LF Mushrooms & Celery
	1/2c Seasonal Fruit		1 small Dinner Roll	I6	1/2c LF Chicken Salad		1 small Dinner Roll
S12	1/2c DB Gelatin Cubes		1 tsp Margarine		Lettuce Leaves, 2 sl Onions,		1 tsp Margarine
N10–20	1 small DB Muffin		1/2c Skim Milk		and 2 Green Pepper Rings		1/4c Skim Milk
	1 tsp Margarine		Coffee or Tea	K21	1/2c LF Potato Salad		Coffee or Tea
	1 tsp DB Jam/Jelly		1/3c UNSW Pineapple Chunks		1 medium Dinner Roll		1/2c LF Ice Milk
	1/2c Skim Milk				1/2c Skim Milk		
	Coffee or Tea				Coffee or Tea		
Q6	2 × 2" sl DB Chocolate Chip Cake			S5	1/2c Fruit Cup		
	Snacks:						
	1/2 Milk Exchange		1/2 Milk Exchange		1/2 Milk Exchange		1/2 Milk Exchange
	1 Starch/Bread Exchange		1 Starch/Bread Exchange		1 Starch/Bread Exchange		1 Starch/Bread Exchange
	1 Fat Exchange		1 Fat Exchange		1 Fat Exchange		1 Fat Exchange

TERMS: LF = Low Fat; FF = Fat Free; SR = Sodium or Salt Restricted; STR = Strained; DB = Diabetic; UNSW = Unsweetened; RC = Reduced Calorie; LC = Low Calorie; EXCH = Diabetic Exchange.

[1]*2000 Calorie Diet:* Follow 1800 calorie diet with the following additions: Breakfast—add 1/2 milk exchange and 1 bread exchange; Snack—add 1 medium-fat meat exchange.
Amounts specified for food items that contain bone is equivalent to cooked, edible deboned portion.

Recipe	Friday	Recipe	Saturday	Recipe	Sunday
B1	1/2c UNSW Orange Juice or 1/2 small Banana 1/2c DB Cream of Rice or 3/4c UNSW Dry Cereal	B1	1/2c UNSW Apple Juice 1/2c DB Oatmeal or 3/4c UNSW Dry Cereal	B1	1/3c UNSW Cranberry Juice 1/2c DB Farina or 3/4c UNSW Dry Cereal
B5	1 Scrambled Egg 1 sl Toast 1 tsp Margarine 1 tsp DB Jam/Jelly 1/2c Skim Milk Coffee or Tea	B4	1 Hard-Boiled Egg 1 sl Toast 1 tsp Margarine 1 tsp DB Jam/Jelly 1/2c Skim Milk Coffee or Tea	B4,5 B12	1 Egg of Choice 1 DB Waffle (4 1/2" sq) with 1 oz DB Maple Syrup 1 tsp Margarine 1 tsp DB Jam/Jelly 1/2c Skim Milk Coffee or Tea
K2 F5 O25 L5 J27	1/2c DB Pickled Beets 3 oz LF Catch of the Day 2 tsp LF Tartar Sauce Lemon Wedge 1/3c Rice Pilaf 1/2c Mixed Vegetables 1 small Dinner Roll 1 tsp Margarine 1/2c Skim Milk Coffee or Tea 2 UNSW Pear Halves	K29 P1-8 D28 J45 J3 S13	1c Tossed Salad with 1 Tbsp LC Salad Dressing 3 oz DB Baked Ham 1/2c DB Sweet Potatoes/Apples 1/2c String Beans 1 small Dinner Roll 1 tsp Margarine 1/2c Skim Milk Coffee or Tea 1/2c DB Fruited Lime Gelatin	K16 D3 C1 J40 J10	1/2c DB Mixed Vegetable Salad 3 oz Brisket of Beef with 2 oz LF Broth 4 oz DB Potato Pancakes 1/2c LF Broccoli Cuts 1 small Dinner Roll 1 tsp Margarine 1/2c Skim Milk Coffee or Tea 1/2c UNSW Applesauce
C23 E7 J35 J19 Q8	2/3c LF Split Pea Soup 3 oz LF Roast Chicken 1 small Baked Potato with 1 oz Sour Cream 1/2c DB Carrot Tzimmes 1 small Dinner Roll 1 tsp Margarine 1/2c Skim Milk Coffee or Tea 3 × 2" sl DB Marble Cake	C21 G1 J55	2/3c Minestrone Soup 6 oz LF Cheese Fettucine 1/2c LF Zucchini-Onions 1 sl Italian Bread 1 tsp Margarine 1/2c Skim Milk Coffee or Tea 2 UNSW Plums	C27 I18 I23 K15	2/3c Chunky Vegetable Soup 3/4c LF Seafood Salad Stuffed Tomato 1/2c LF Cheesy Macaroni Salad 1 small Dinner Roll 1/2c Skim Milk Coffee or Tea 1/2c LF Sherbet
	1/2 Milk Exchange 1 Starch/Bread Exchange 1 Fat Exchange		1/2 Milk Exchange 1 Starch/Bread Exchange 1 Fat Exchange		1/2 Milk Exchange 1 Starch/Bread Exchange 1 Fat Exchange

Recipe	Monday	Recipe	Tuesday	Recipe	Wednesday	Recipe	Thursday
	Breakfast						
	1/2c UNSW Apple Juice or		1/2c UNSW Orange Juice		1/2c UNSW Pineapple Juice		1/2c UNSW Apple Juice or
	1/2c Fresh Fruit	B1	1/2c DB Oatmeal or	B1	1/2c DB Cream of Wheat	S11	3 medium Stewed Prunes
B1	1/2c DB Cream of Rice or		or 3/4c UNSW Dry Cereal		or 3/4c UNSW Dry Cereal	B1	1/2c DB Farina or
	3/4c UNSW Dry Cereal	B4	1 Poached Egg	B4	1 Soft-Cooked Egg		3/4c UNSW Dry Cereal
I2	1 oz Grilled Cheese on		1 English Muffin		1 sl Toast	B4,5	1 Egg to Order
	1 sl Toast		1 tsp Margarine		1 tsp Margarine		1 sl Raisin Toast
	1 tsp Margarine		1 tsp DB Jam/Jelly		1 tsp DB Jam/Jelly		1 tsp Margarine
	1 tsp DB Jam/Jelly		1/2c Skim Milk		1/2c Skim Milk		1 tsp DB Jam/Jelly
	1/2c Skim Milk		Coffee or Tea		Coffee or Tea		1/2c Skim Milk
	Coffee or Tea						Coffee or Tea
	Lunch						
K29	1c Tossed Salad with	K23	1/2c DB Marinated Zucchini	K32	1c Tossed Vegetable Salad	K25	1c Green Salad with
P8	1 Tbsp LC Salad Dressing	D22	3 1/2 oz DB Breaded Veal	P1-8	2 Tbsp LC Salad Dressing	P1-8	1 Tbsp LC Salad Dressing
E1	3 oz LF Barbecue Chicken	O20	with 2 oz Marinara Sauce	D1	3 1/2 oz LF Beef Teriyaki	D30	3 oz Pork Chops with
O2	with 2 oz DB Barbecue Sauce	M5	1c LF Pasta Primavera	J22	1/2c Chinese Vegetables		1/2c LF Apple Stuffing
J31	1/2c Green Peas		1 sl Italian Bread	L1	2/3c White Rice	J1	1/2c Asparagus Tips
J14	1/2c Carrots		1 tsp Margarine		1 small Dinner Roll		1 small Dinner Roll
	1 small Dinner Roll		1/2c Skim Milk		1 tsp Margarine		1 tsp Margarine
	1 tsp Margarine		Coffee or Tea		1/2c Skim Milk		1/2c Skim Milk
	1/2c Skim Milk	S5	1/2c Fresh Fruit Cup		Coffee or Tea		Coffee or Tea
	Coffee or Tea				1/2c LF Ice Milk	S16	1/2c DB Chocolate Pudding
	1/2c UNSW Sliced Peaches						
	Dinner						
C11	2/3c LF Cream Celery Soup	C4	2/3c SR/LF Bean Soup	C26	2/3c Vegetable Beef Soup	C21	2/3c Minestrone Soup
G8	5 1/2 oz DB Vegetable Omelet	I4	Asst Cold Cut Sandwiches	E13	3/4c LF Turkey à la King	D12	8 oz LF Beef Macaroni Casserole
J36	1/2c LF Home Fried Potatoes		2 sl Bread (cut in quarters)		with 2 Toast Points	J6	1/2c LF Seasoned Green Beans
	1 small Dinner Roll		with 3 oz Roast Beef, Ham,	J47	1/2c Spinach		1 small Dinner Roll
	1 tsp Margarine		Turkey, Bologna, & Salami		1/2c Skim Milk		1 tsp Margarine
	1/2c Skim Milk		Lettuce Leaves		Coffee or Tea		1/2c Skim Milk
	Coffee or Tea		2 sl Tomatoes		2 UNSW Plums		Coffee or Tea
Q2	2 × 1" sl DB Banana Cake	K5	1/2c DB Cole Slaw				1/2c UNSW Chilled Apricots
			1 tsp Catsup, 1 tsp Mustard				
			1/2c Skim Milk				
			Coffee or Tea				
		S12	1/2c DB Strawberry Gelatin				
	Snacks:						
	1/2 Milk Exchange		1/2 Milk Exchange		1/2 Milk Exchange		1/2 Milk Exchange
	1 Starch/Bread Exchange		1 Starch/Bread Exchange		1 Starch/Bread Exchange		1 Starch/Bread Exchange
	1 Fat Exchange		1 Fat Exchange		1 Fat Exchange		1 Fat Exchange

TERMS: LF = Low Fat; FF = Fat Free; SR = Sodium or Salt Restricted; STR = Strained; DB = Diabetic; UNSW = Unsweetened; RC = Reduced Calorie; LC = Low Calorie; EXCH = Diabetic Exchange.

[1]*2000 Calorie Diet:* Follow 1800 calorie diet with the following additions: Breakfast—add 1/2 milk exchange and 1 bread exchange; Snack—add 1 medium-fat meat exchange. Amounts specified for food items that contain bone is equivalent to cooked, edible deboned portion.

Recipe	Friday	Recipe	Saturday	Recipe	Sunday
B1	1/2c UNSW Grapefruit Juice		1/3c UNSW Cranberry Juice	B1	1/2c UNSW Pineapple Juice
	1/2c DB Wheatena or		or 1/2 small Banana		1/2c DB Oatmeal or
	3/4c UNSW Dry Cereal	B1	1/2c DB Cream of Rice or		3/4 UNSW Dry Cereal
B5	1 Scrambled Egg		3/4c UNSW Dry Cereal	B8	1 sl French Toast with
N14	1 small DB Bran Muffin	G9	2 1/2 oz DB Western Omelet		1 oz DB Maple Syrup
	1 tsp Margarine		1 sl Toast		1 tsp Margarine
	1 tsp DB Jam/Jelly		1 tsp Margarine		1 tsp DB Jam/Jelly
	1/2c Skim Milk		1 tsp DB Jam/Jelly		1/2c Skim Milk
	Coffee or Tea		1/2c Skim Milk		Coffee or Tea
			Coffee or Tea		
K9	1/2c DB Marinated Cucumbers	K37	4 oz DB Perfection Salad	K42	1/2c DB Cranberry Mold
F9	3 oz LF Sole Almondine	D18	6 oz Stuffed Cabbage	E16	3 oz LF Roast Turkey with
O25	2 tsp LF Tartar Sauce	J43	1/2c LF Whipped Potatoes	O18	2 oz STR Giblet Gravy
	Lemon Wedge	J15	1/2c DB Glazed Carrots	P12	1/3c Raisin Bread Stuffing
L2	1/2c Rice Chantilly		1 small Dinner Roll	J52	1/2c Zucchini
J51	1/2c Vegetable Medley		1 tsp Margarine		1 small Dinner Roll
	1 small Dinner Roll		1/2c Skim Milk		1 tsp Margarine
	1 tsp Margarine		Coffee or Tea		1/2c Skim Milk
	1/2c Skim Milk		1/3c UNSW Pineapple Tidbits		Coffee or Tea
	Coffee or Tea			R3	1/12 DB Apple Pie
	3 Vanilla Wafers				
C9	2/3c Chicken Matzo Ball Soup	C24	2/3c LF Tomato Soup	C3	2/3c Clear Vegetable Soup
E9	3 oz LF Chicken Tarragon	I21	3/4c LF Curry Tuna Salad	G2	6 oz DB Lasagna
M4	4 oz DB Noodle Pudding		Platter Lettuce Leaves,	J27	1/2c Mixed Vegetables
J10	1/2c LF Steamed Broccoli		2 sl Onions, 3 sl	N8	1 sl LF Garlic Bread
	1 small Dinner Roll		Cucumbers, 1 Radish Rose		1/2c Skim Milk
	1 tsp Margarine	K13	1/2c LF Macaroni Salad		Coffee or Tea
	1/2c Skim Milk		1 small Dinner Roll or	S4	1/3c Fruit Compote
	Coffee or Tea		5 LF Crackers		
S1	1 small DB Baked Apple		1 tsp Margarine		
			1/2c Skim Milk		
			Coffee or Tea		
			1/2c LF Sherbet		
	1/2 Milk Exchange		1/2 Milk Exchange		1/2 Milk Exchange
	1 Starch/Bread Exchange		1 Starch/Bread Exchange		1 Starch/Bread Exchange
	1 Fat Exchange		1 Fat Exchange		1 Fat Exchange

Recipe	Monday	Recipe	Tuesday	Recipe	Wednesday	Recipe	Thursday
	Breakfast						
B1	1/2c Orange Juice 1/2c Farina or 3/4c Dry Cereal with 2 Tbsp Wheat Germ	B1	1/2c oz Apple Juice 1/2c Wheatena or 3/4c Dry Cereal with 1 Tbsp Wheat Germ	B1	1/2c Pineapple Juice 3/4c Oatmeal or 1c Dry Cereal with 2 Tbsp Wheat Germ	B1	1/2c Grapefruit Juice 3/4c Cream of Rice or 1 cup Dry Cereal with 2 Tbsp Wheat Germ
B15	1c Scrambled Tofu 1 sl Toast 1 tsp Margarine 1 tsp Jam or Jelly 1 cup Fortified Soy Milk Coffee or Tea	B13	1 Blueberry Oatmeal Waffle with 2 oz Maple Syrup 1 tsp Margarine 1 cup Fortified Soy Milk Coffee or Tea		1 sliced Banana 1 sl Toast 1 tsp Margarine 1 tsp Jam or Jelly 1 cup Fortified Soy Milk Coffee or Tea	N13	3/4c Diced Seasonal Fruit 1 Blueberry Muffin (v) 1 tsp Margarine 1 tsp Jam or Jelly 1 cup Fortified Soy Milk Coffee or Tea
	Lunch						
K29 P2 H3	1c Tossed Salad with 1 oz French Lemon Miso Dressing 12 oz Macaroni & Bean Casserole 1 Dinner Roll 1 tsp Margarine 1/2c Fortified Soy Milk Coffee or Tea 1/2c Sliced Peaches	K22 H5 L7	1/2c Three Bean Salad 2c Stir Fry Tofu and Vegetables 1 cup Brown Rice 1 Dinner Roll 1 tsp Margarine 1/2c Fortified Soy Milk Coffee or Tea 1/2c Ice Cream	K23 H2 S3	1/2c Marinated Zucchini 1 1/2 cup Lentil Stew 1 Dinner Roll 1 tsp Margarine 1/2c Fortified Soy Milk Coffee or Tea 1/2c Citrus Cup	C11 G13 K24 P5	2/3c Cream Celery Soup 1/6 Spinach Quiche 1c Garden Salad with 1 oz Lemon Miso Dressing 1 Dinner Roll 1 tsp Margarine 1/2c Fortified Soy Milk Coffee or Tea 1/2c Sherbet
	Dinner						
C15 I7 K40 Q17	2/3c Creole Soup 3/4 cup Chickpea Salad on 2 sl Bread with 2 Lettuce Leaves 3 sl Tomatoes 1/2c Waldorf Salad 1/2c Fortified Soy Milk Coffee or Tea 2 Oatmeal Cookies	C27 H1 O27 J41 J51	2/3c Chunky Veg Soup 8 oz Bean Burger with 2 oz Vegetarian Gravy 3 oz Parsley Potatoes 1/2c Vegetable Medley 1 Dinner Roll 1 tsp Margarine 1/2c Fortified Soy Milk Coffee or Tea 1 Seasonal Fruit	C24 I19 K19 R6	2/3c Tomato Soup 3/4c Tofu Salad on Lettuce with 3 sl Cucumbers 3/4c Rice Walnut Salad 1 Dinner Roll 1 tsp Margarine 1/2c Fortified Soy Milk Coffee or Tea 1/8 Apple Cobbler	I1 O23	2 Bean Tacos, contains 2 Taco Shells with 2 oz Bean Mixture in each shell 1c Shredded Lettuce and Diced Tomatoes 1 oz Salsa 1/2c Fortified Soy Milk Coffee or Tea 1/2c Pineapple Chunks
	Snacks—Choice of: 1/2c Fruit Juice or 1/2c Fortified Soy Milk 2 Cookies, 2 Crackers, or 1 Fresh Fruit		1/2c Fruit Juice or 1/2c Fortified Soy Milk 2 Cookies, 2 Crackers, or 1 Fresh Fruit		1/2c Fruit Juice or 1/2c Fortified Soy Milk 2 Cookies, 2 Crackers, or 1 Fresh Fruit		1/2c Fruit Juice or 1/2c Fortified Soy Milk 2 Cookies, 2 Crackers, or 1 Fresh Fruit

Recipe	Friday	Recipe	Saturday	Recipe	Sunday
B1	1/2c Cranberry Juice 1/2c Farina or 3/4c Dry Cereal with 1 Tbsp Wheat Germ and 2 Tbsp Raisins	B1	1/2c Peach Nectar 1/2c Oatmeal or 3/4c Dry Cereal with 1 Tbsp Wheat germ	B1	1/2c Pineapple Juice 3/4c Wheatena or 1c Dry Cereal with 2 Tbsp Wheat Germ 3/4c Diced Seasonal Fruit
B15	1c Scrambled Tofu 1 sl Toast 1 tsp Margarine 1 tsp Jam or Jelly 1 cup Fortified Soy Milk Coffee or Tea	B11	3 Banana Pancakes with 2 oz Maple Syrup 1 tsp Margarine 1 cup Fortified Soy Milk Coffee or Tea		1 sl Toast 1 tsp Margarine 1 tsp Jam or Jelly 1 cup Fortified Soy Milk Coffee or Tea
K28 P2 G2 J26	1c Mixed Field Greens with 1 oz French Lemon Dressing 6 oz Cheese Lasagna 1/2c Italian Mix Vegetables 1 Dinner Roll 1 tsp Margarine 1/2c Fortified Soy Milk Coffee or Tea 1/2c Fruit Cocktail	K32 P5 H8 L1	1c Toss Vegetable Salad with 1 oz Lemon Miso Dressing 12 oz Vegetarian Chili 1/2c White Rice 1 Dinner Roll 1 tsp Margarine 1/2c Fortified Soy Milk Coffee or Tea 1/2c Apricot Halves	K9 H7 J35 J14 S17	1/2c Marinated Cucumbers 8 oz Tomato Bulgar 1 medium Baked Potato 1/2c Sliced Carrots 1 Dinner Roll 1 tsp Margarine 1/2c Fortified Soy Milk Coffee or Tea 1/2c Vanilla Pudding
C18 H4 K44	2/3c Onion Soup 6 oz Rice Patty on 1 Whole Wheat Bun 2 Lettuce Leaves 3 sl Tomatoes 3 oz Raw Vegetable Condiments 1/2c Fortified Soy Milk Coffee or Tea 2 Plums	C28 G11 J50 G12	2/3c French Vegetable Soup 8 oz Macaroni and Cheese 1/2c Stewed Tomatoes 1 Dinner Roll 1 tsp Margarine 1/2c Fortified Soy Milk Coffee or Tea 2 Almond Cookies	c4 H6	2/3c Bean Soup 6 oz Tofu Burger on 1 Bun 2 Lettuce Leaves 2 sl Tomatoes 2 sl Onions 1 tsp Catsup 1/2c Fortified Soy Milk Coffee or Tea 1 Pear Halves
	1/2c Fruit Juice or 1/2c Fortified Soy Milk 2 Cookies, 2 Crackers, or 1 Fresh Fruit		1/2c Fruit Juice or 1/2c Fortified Soy Milk 2 Cookies, 2 Crackers, or 1 Fresh Fruit		1/2c Fruit Juice or 1/2c Fortified Soy Milk 2 Cookies, 2 Crackers, or 1 Fresh Fruit

12

Menus for Health Care Facilities

Recipe	Regular, Liberal Bland[1], No Added Salt[2]	1–2 gm Na (Low Sodium)	Mechanical Soft	Puree
	Breakfast			
	1/2c Orange Juice	1/2c Orange Juice	1/2c Orange Juice	1/2c STR Orange Juice
B1	1/2c Farina or	1/2c Farina or	1/2c Farina or	1c Farina
	3/4c Asst Dry Cereals	3/4c SR Asst Dry Cereals	3/4c Asst Dry Cereals+	NO
B4	1 Soft-Cooked Egg	1 Soft-Cooked Egg	1 Soft-Cooked Egg	1 Soft-Cooked Egg
	1 sl Toast	1 sl Toast	1 sl Bread	1 sl Bread+
	1 tsp Margarine	1 tsp SR Margarine	1 tsp Margarine	1 tsp Margarine
	1 tsp Jam/Jelly	1 tsp Jam/Jelly	1 tsp Jelly	1 tsp Jelly
	1c Milk	1c Milk	1c Milk	1c Milk
	Coffee/Tea/Decaf	Coffee/Tea/Decaf	Coffee/Tea/Decaf	Coffee/Tea/Decaf
	Lunch			
K29	1c Tossed Salad	1c Tossed Salad	1/2c Juice	1/2c STR Juice
P1	1 oz French Dressing	1 oz SR French Dressing	NO	NO
D6	8 oz Pepper Steak	8 oz SR Pepper Steak	8 oz CHP Pepper Steak	8 oz PUR Pepper Steak
I3	1/2c Rice Florentine	1/2c SR Rice Florentine	1/2c SFT Rice Florentine	1/2c PUR Rice Florentine
	1 Dinner Roll	1 Dinner Roll	1 SFT Dinner Roll+	1 sl Bread+
	1 tsp Margarine	1 tsp SR Margarine	1 tsp Margarine	1 tsp Margarine
	1/2c Milk	1/2c Milk	1/2c Milk	1/2c Milk
	Coffee/Tea/Decaf	Coffee/Tea/Decaf	Coffee/Tea/Decaf	Coffee/Tea/Decaf
	1/2c Sliced Peaches	1/2c Sliced Peaches	1/2c Sliced Peaches	1/2c PUR Peaches
	Dinner			
C23,1	2/3c Split Pea Soup	2/3c SR Split Pea Soup	2/3c Split Pea Soup+	2/3c PUR/STR Pea Soup
I12,6	1/2c Ham[2] Salad	1/2c SR Turkey Salad	1/2c SFT Ham Salad+	1/2c PUR Ham Salad
	Lettuce Leaves	Lettuce Leaves	CHP Lettuce Leaves+	NO
J50	3 Tomato Slices	3 Tomato Slices	1/2c Stewed Tomatoes	1/2c PUR/STR Tomatoes
	3 Cucumber Slices	3 Cucumber Slices	1/2c Juice	1/2c STR Juice
K5,J47	1/2c Cole Slaw	1/2c Cole Slaw	1/2c Cooked Spinach	1/2c PUR Spinach
	1 Dinner Roll	1 Dinner Roll	1 SFT Dinner Roll+	1 sl Bread+
	1 tsp Margarine	1 tsp SR Margarine	1 tsp Margarine	1 tsp Margarine
	1/2c Milk	1/2c Milk	1/2c Milk	1/2c Milk
	Coffee/Tea/Decaf	Coffee/Tea/Decaf	Coffee/Tea/Decaf	Coffee/Tea/Decaf
Q7,S17	3×2" sl Devil's Food Cake	3×2" sl Devil's Food Cake	3×2" sl Devil's Food Cake+	1/2c Vanilla Pudding
	Snacks			
	Milk or Juice	Juice	Milk or Juice	Milk or STR Juice
	Cookies, Crackers,	SR Cookies, SR Crackers,	Plain Cookies, Gelatin,	Applesauce, SFT Banana,
	Gelatin, Ice Cream,	Gelatin, Fresh Fruit	Plain Crackers+, Ice Cream,	Gelatin, Ice Cream
	Fresh Fruit		Banana	

TERMS: SFT = Soft; SLF = Soft/Low Fiber; GRD = Ground; CHP = Chopped Finely; PUR = Puree; STR = Strained; SR = Sodium or Salt Restricted; LF = Low Fat; FF = Fat Free; LCH = Low Cholesterol; DB = Diabetic; UNSW = Unsweetened; RC = Reduced Calorie; LC = Low Calorie; EXCH = Diabetic Exchange

SERVING UTENSILS: #6 Scoop = 2/3 cup-6 oz; #8 Scoop = 1/2 cup-4 oz; #10 Scoop = 3/8 cup-3 to 4 oz; #12 Scoop = 1/3 cup-2.5 to 3 oz; #16 Scoop = 1/4 cup-2 oz; #30 Scoop = 2 tbsp-1 oz; #60 Scoop = 1 tbsp-1/2 oz. Ounces will vary, based on food used.

1. *Liberal Bland:* Follow a regular diet. Use decaffeinated products. Omit pepper and chili powder.

2. *No Added Salt (3–4 gm Na):* Follow a regular diet. Use SR soups and SR canned meats. Omit salt packets (and shakers), bacon, sausage, smoked, and cured meats, substitute with SR food choices.

3. *Low Fiber:* Follow a soft diet. Do not exceed 2 cups of milk per day. Soft/Low Fiber—Omit pepper, garlic, and onions from recipes.

4. *2200 Calorie Diet:* Follow 2000 calorie diet with the following additions: Lunch—add 1 bread exchange and 1 fat exchange; Dinner—add 1 bread exchange.

+Consider individual tolerance. Daily alternatives: Lunch and Dinner—Chicken, Hamburger, Cottage Cheese Fruit Plate, or Assorted Sandwiches. Individual preferences are provided upon request.

Amounts specified for food items that contain bone is equivalent to cooked, edible deboned portion.

Soft, Low Fiber[3]	Low Cholesterol, Low Fat (40–50 gm)	No Concentrated Sweets (Diabetic)	1200	1500	1800	2000[4]
			\multicolumn 4 Diabetic/Calorie-Controlled			
1/2c STR Orange Juice	1/2c Orange Juice	1/2 UNSW Orange Juice	1/2c	1/2c	1/2c	1/2c
1/2c Farina or	1/2c LF Farina or	1/2c DB Farina or	1/2c	1/2c	1/2c	1/2c
3/4c Asst Refined Cereals	3/4c Dry Cereals	3/4c UNSW Dry Cereals	3/4c	3/4c	3/4c	3/4c
1 Soft-Cooked Egg	1 Egg Substitute	1 Soft-Cooked Egg	1	1	1	1
1 sl White Toast	1 sl Toast	1 sl Toast	1 sl	1 sl	1 sl	2 sl
1 tsp Margarine	1 tsp Margarine	1 tsp Margarine	1 tsp	1 tsp	1 tsp	1 tsp
1 tsp Jelly	1 tsp Jam/Jelly	1 tsp DB Jam/Jelly	1 tsp	1 tsp	1 tsp	1 tsp
1c Milk	1c Skim Milk	1c Skim Milk	1/2c	1/2c	1/2c	1c
Coffee/Tea/Decaf	Coffee/Tea/Decaf	Coffee/Tea/Decaf	free	free	free	free
1/2c STR Juice	1c Tossed Salad	1c Tossed Salad	1c	1c	1c	1c
NO	1 Tbsp LC French Dressing	1 Tbsp LC Frch Sld Drsg	1 Tbsp	1 Tbsp	1 Tbsp	1 Tbsp
8 oz SLF Pepper Steak	6 oz LF Pepper Steak	8 oz LF Pepper Steak	6 oz	8 oz	8 oz	8 oz
1/2c SFT Rice Florentine	1/2c LF Rice Florentine	1c LF Rice Florentine	1/3c	1/3c	2/3c	2/3c
1 SFT Refined Dinner Roll	1 Dinner Roll	1 Dinner Roll	0	1 sm	1 sm	1 sm
1 tsp Margarine	NO	1 tsp Margarine	0	0	1 tsp	1 tsp
1/2c Milk	1/2c Skim Milk	1/2c Skim Milk	1/2c	1/2c	1/2c	1/2c
Coffee/Tea/Decaf	Coffee/Tea/Decaf	Coffee/Tea/Decaf	free	free	free	free
1/2c Sliced Peaches	1/2c Sliced Peaches	1/2c UNSW Sliced Peaches	1/2c	1/2c	1/2c	1/2c
2/3c SLF Broth	2/3c LF Split Pea Soup	2/3c LF Split Pea Soup	2/3c	2/3c	2/3c	2/3c
1/2c SFT Ham Salad	1/2c LF Ham Salad	1/2c LF Ham Salad	1/2c	3/4c	3/4c	3/4c
NO	Lettuce Leaves	Lettuce Leaves	free	free	free	free
1/2c SLF Stewed Tomatoes	3 Tomato Slices	3 Tomato Slices	3 sl	3 sl	3 sl	3 sl
1/2c STR Juice	3 Cucumber Slices	3 Cucumber Slices	3 sl	3 sl	3 sl	3 sl
1/2c Cooked Spinach	1/2c Cole Slaw+	1/2c DB Cole Slaw	1/2c	1/2c	1/2c	1/2c
1 SFT Refined Dinner Roll	1 Dinner Roll	1 Dinner Roll	0	1 sm	1 med	1 med
1 tsp Margarine	NO	1 tsp Margarine	0	0	1 tsp	1 tsp
1/2c Milk (1/4c)[3]	1/2c Skim Milk	1/2c Skim Milk	1/4c	1/4c	1/4c	1/4c
Coffee/Tea/Decaf	Coffee/Tea/Decaf	Coffee/Tea/Decaf	free	free	free	free
1/2c Vanilla Pudding	1/2c LF Vanilla Pudding	1/2c DB Vanilla Pudding	1/2c	1/2c	1/2c	1/2c
Milk[3] or STR Juice	Skim Milk or Juice	1/2c Skim Milk	1/2c	1/2c	1/2c	1/2c
Plain Cookies, Gelatin,	LF Cookies, LF Crackers,	1 Starch/Bread Exch	1	1	1	1
Plain Crackers, Banana,	Gelatin, Fresh Fruit	1 Meat Exch	0	0	0	1
Vanilla Ice Cream[3]		1 Fat Exch	0	0	1	1

Recipe	Regular, Liberal Bland[1], No Added Salt[2]	1–2 gm Na (Low Sodium)	Mechanical Soft	Puree
	Breakfast			
	1/2c Apple Juice	1/2c Apple Juice	1/2c Apple Juice	1/2c STR Apple Juice
B1	1/2c Wheatena or	1/2c Wheatena or	1/2c Wheatena or	1c Wheatena
	3/4c Asst Dry Cereals	3/4c SR Asst Dry Cereals	3/4c Asst Dry Cereals+	NO
G6	2 oz Cheese Omelette	2 oz SR Cheese Omelette	2 oz Cheese Omelette	2 oz Cheese Omelette
	1 English Muffin	1 English Muffin	1 sl Bread	1 sl Bread+
	1 tsp Margarine	1 tsp SR Margarine	1 tsp Margarine	1 tsp Margarine
	1 tsp Jam/Jelly	1 tsp Jam/Jelly	1 tsp Jelly	1 tsp Jelly
	1c Milk	1c Milk	1c Milk	1c Milk
	Coffee/Tea/Decaf	Coffee/Tea/Decaf	Coffee/Tea/Decaf	Coffee/Tea/Decaf
	Lunch			
K35	1/2c Molded Veg Salad	1/2c Molded Veg Salad	1/2c SFT Molded Veg Salad	1/2c PUR Molded Veg Salad
E4	3 oz Lemon Chicken	3 oz SR Lemon Chicken	3 oz CHP Lemon Chicken	4 oz PUR Lemon Chicken
J39	4 oz Oven Browned Potatoes	4 oz Oven Browned Potatoes	4 oz Oven Br Potatoes	1/2c PUR Oven Br Potatoes
J10,7	1/2c Broccoli	1/2c Broccoli	1/2c CHP Broccoli	1/2c PUR Broccoli
	1 Dinner Roll	1 Dinner Roll	1 SFT Dinner Roll+	1 sl Bread+
	1 tsp Margarine	1 tsp SR Margarine	1 tsp Margarine	1 tsp Margarine
	1/2c Milk	1/4c Milk	1/2c Milk	1/2c Milk
	Coffee/Tea/Decaf	Coffee/Tea/Decaf	Coffee/Tea/Decaf	Coffee/Tea/Decaf
S3	1/2c Citrus Cup	1/2c Citrus Cup	1/2c Canned Citrus Cup	1/2c PUR Citrus Cup
	Dinner			
C12	2/3c Cr of Mushroom Soup	2/3c Cr Mushroom Soup	2/3c Cr of Mushroom Soup	2/3c PUR/STR Cr Mshrm Soup
D17	4 oz Sloppy Joe	4 oz SR Sloppy Joe	4 oz Sloppy Joe	4 oz PUR Sloppy Joe
	1 Bun	1 Bun	1 Bun+	1 sl Bread+
J24,14	1/2c Corn Confetti	1/2c SR Corn Confetti	1/2c PUR Corn Confetti	1/2c PUR Corn Confetti
	1/2c Milk	1/4c Milk	1/2c Milk	1/2c Milk
	Coffee/Tea/Decaf	Coffee/Tea/Decaf	Coffee/Tea/Decaf	Coffee/Tea/Decaf
	1/2c Ice Cream	1/2c Ice Cream	1/2c Ice Cream	1/2c Ice Cream
	Snacks			
	Milk or Juice	Juice	Milk or Juice	Milk or STR Juice
	Cookies, Crackers,	SR Cookies, SR Crackers,	Plain Cookies, Gelatin,	Applesauce, SFT Banana,
	Gelatin, Ice Cream,	Gelatin, Fresh Fruit	Plain Crackers+, Ice Cream,	Gelatin, Ice Cream
	Fresh Fruit	Banana		Vanilla Ice Cream[3]

TERMS: SFT = Soft; SLF = Soft/Low Fiber; GRD = Ground; CHP = Chopped Finely; PUR = Puree; STR = Strained; SR = Sodium or Salt Restricted; LF = Low Fat; FF = Fat Free; LCH = Low Cholesterol; DB = Diabetic; UNSW = Unsweetened; RC = Reduced Calorie; LC = Low Calorie; EXCH = Diabetic Exchange

SERVING UTENSILS: #6 Scoop = 2/3 cup-6 oz; #8 Scoop = 1/2 cup-4 oz; #10 Scoop = 3/8 cup-3 to 4 oz; #12 Scoop = 1/3 cup-2.5 to 3 oz; #16 Scoop = 1/4 cup-2 oz; #30 Scoop = 2 tbsp-1 oz; #60 Scoop = 1 tbsp-1/2 oz. Ounces will vary, based on food used.

1. *Liberal Bland:* Follow a regular diet. Use decaffeinated products. Omit pepper and chili powder.

2. *No Added Salt (3–4 gm NA):* Follow a regular diet. Use SR soups and SR canned meats. Omit salt packets (and shakers), bacon, sausage, smoked, and cured meats, substitute with SR food choices.

3. *Low Fiber:* Follow a soft diet. Do not exceed 2 cups of milk per day. Soft/Low Fiber—Omit pepper, garlic, and onions from recipes.

4. *2200 Calorie Diet:* Follow 2000 calorie diet with the following additions: Lunch—add 1 bread exchange and 1 fat exchange; Dinner—add 1 bread exchange.

+Consider individual tolerance. Daily Alternatives: Lunch and Dinner—Chicken, Hamburger, Cottage Cheese Fruit Plate, or Assorted Sandwiches. Individual preferences are provided upon request.

Amounts specified for food items that contain bone is equivalent to cooked, edible deboned portion.

Soft, Low Fiber[3]	Low Cholesterol, Low Fat (40–50 gm)	No Concentrated Sweets (Diabetic)	1200	1500	1800	2000[4]
			Diabetic/Calorie-Controlled			
1/2c STR Apple Juice	1/2c Apple Juice	1/2c UNSW Apple Juice	1/2c	1/2c	1/2c	1/2c
1/2c Wheatena or	1/2c LF Wheatena or	1/2c DB Wheatena or	1/2c	1/2c	1/2c	1/2c
3/4c Asst Refined Cereals	3/4c Dry Cereals	3/4c UNSW Dry Cereals	3/4c	3/4c	3/4c	3/4c
2 oz SLF Cheese Omelette	2 oz Egg Sub w/LF Cheese	2 oz DB Cheese Omelette	2 oz	2 oz	2 oz	2 oz
1 sl White Toast	1 English Muffin	1 English Muffin	1/2	1/2	1	1
1 tsp Margarine	1 tsp Margarine	1 tsp Margarine	0	1 tsp	1 tsp	1 tsp
1 tsp Jelly	1 tsp Jam/Jelly	1 tsp DB Jam/Jelly	1 tsp	1 tsp	1 tsp	1 tsp
1c Milk	1c Skim Milk	1c Skim Milk	1/2c	1/2c	1/2c	1c
Coffee/Tea/Decaf	Coffee/Tea/Decaf	Coffee/Tea/Decaf	free	free	free	free
1/2c SFT Molded Veg Salad	1/2c Molded Veg Salad	1/2c DB Molded Veg Salad	1/2c	1/2c	1/2c	1/2c
3 oz SLF Lemon Chicken	2 oz LF Lemon Chicken	3 oz LF Lemon Chicken	2 oz	3 oz	3 oz	3 oz
4 oz Oven Browned Potatoes	4 oz LF Oven Br Potatoes	4 oz LF Oven Br Potatoes	2 oz	4 oz	4 oz	6 oz
1/2c Beets	1/2c LF Broccoli+	1/2c LF Broccoli	1/2c	1/2c	1/2c	1/2c
1 SFT Refined Dinner Roll	1 Dinner Roll	1 Dinner Roll	0	0	1 sm	1 sm
1 tsp Margarine	NO	1 tsp Margarine	0	0	1 tsp	1 tsp
1/2c Milk (1/4c)[3]	1/2c Skim Milk	1/2c Skim Milk	1/2c	1/2c	1/2c	1/2c
Coffee/Tea/Decaf	Coffee/Tea/Decaf	Coffee/Tea/Decaf	free	free	free	free
1/2c Canned Citrus Cup	1/2c Citrus Cup	1/2c	1/2c	1/2c	1/2c	
2/3c SLF Cr Mushroom Soup	2/3c LF Cr Mushroom Soup	2/3c LF Cr Mushroom Soup	2/3c	2/3c	2/3c	2/3c
4 oz SLF Sloppy Joe	3 oz LF Sloppy Joe	4 oz LF Sloppy Joe	3 oz	4 oz	4 oz	4 oz
1 SFT Refined Bun	1 Bun	1 Bun	1/2	1	1	1
1/2c Carrots	1/2c LF Corn Confetti	1/2c LF Corn Confetti	1/4c	1/2c	1/2c	1/2c
1/2c Milk (1/4c)[3]	1/2c Skim Milk	1/2c Skim Milk	1/4c	1/4c	1/2c	1/2c
Coffee/Tea/Decaf	Coffee/Tea/Decaf	Coffee/Tea/Decaf	free	free	free	free
1/2c Vanilla Ice Cream	1/2c LF Ice Milk	1/2c LF Ice Milk	1/2c	1/2c	1/2c	1/2c
Milk[3] or STR Juice	Skim Milk or Juice	1/2c Skim Milk	1/2c	1/2c	1/2c	1/2c
Plain Cookies, Gelatin,	LF Cookies, LF Crackers,	1 Starch/Bread Exch	1	1	1	1
Plain Crackers, Banana,	Gelatin, Fresh Fruit	1 Meat Exch	0	0	0	1
	1 Fat Exch	0	0	1	1	

Recipe	Regular, Liberal Bland[1], No Added Salt[2]	1–2 gm Na (Low Sodium)	Mechanical Soft	Puree
	Breakfast			
	1/2c Grapefruit Juice or	1/2c Grapefruit Juice or	1/2c Grapefruit Juice or	1/2c STR Grapefruit Jce or
	1 small Banana	1 small Banana	1 small Banana	1 small Banana-Mashed
B1	1/2c Cream of Rice or	1/2c Cream of Rice or	1/2c Cream of Rice or	1c Cream of Rice
	3/4c Asst Dry Cereals	3/4c SR Asst Dry Cereals	3/4c Asst Dry Cereals+	NO
B5	1 Scrambled Egg	1 Scrambled Egg	1 Scrambled Egg	1 Scrambled Egg
	1 sl Toast	1 sl Toast	1 sl Bread	1 sl Bread+
	1 tsp Margarine	1 tsp SR Margarine	1 tsp Margarine	1 tsp Margarine
	1 tsp Jam/Jelly	1 tsp Jam/Jelly	1 tsp Jelly	1 tsp Jelly
	1c Milk	1c Milk	1c Milk	1c Milk
	Coffee/Tea/Decaf	Coffee/Tea/Decaf	Coffee/Tea/Decaf	Coffee/Tea/Decaf
	Lunch			
K25	1c Green Salad	1c Green Salad	1/2c Juice	1/2c STR Juice
P4	1 oz Italian Dressing	1 oz Italian Dressing	NO	NO
D26	5 oz Veal Parmesan	5 oz SR Veal Parmesan	5 oz CHP Veal Parmesan	5 oz PUR Veal Parmesan
M1	1/2c Spaghetti	1/2c Spaghetti	1/2c Spaghetti	1/2c PUR Spaghetti
O22	2 oz Tomato Sauce	2 oz SR Tomato Sauce	2 oz SFT Tomato Sauce	2 oz STR Tomato Sauce
J55,52	1/2c Sauté Zucchini-Onions	1/2c Sauté Zucchini-Onions	1/2c SFT Zucchini-Onions	1/2c PUR Zucchini-Onions
	1 Dinner Roll	1 Dinner Roll	1 SFT Dinner Roll+	1 sl Bread+
	1 tsp Margarine	1 tsp SR Margarine	1 tsp Margarine	1 tsp Margarine
	1/2c Milk	1/2c Milk	1/2c Milk	1/2c Milk
	Coffee/Tea/Decaf	Coffee/Tea/Decaf	Coffee/Tea/Decaf	Coffee/Tea/Decaf
S10	1/2 Baked Pear	1/2 Baked Pear	1/2 Canned Baked Pear	1/2c PUR/STR Baked Pear
	Dinner			
C27,1	2/3c Chunky Vegetable Soup	2/3c SR Chunky Veg Soup	2/3c Chunky Vegetable Soup	2/3c PUR/STR Chunky Veg Soup
I18	1/2c Seafood Salad	1/2c SR Seafood Salad	1/2c SFT Seafood Salad	1/2c PUR Seafood Salad
	1 Croissant	1 Croissant	1 Croissant+	1 sl Bread+
K40,21	1/2c Waldorf Salad	1/2c Waldorf Salad	1/2c SFT Potato Salad	1/2c PUR Potato Salad
	1/2c Milk	1/2c Milk	1/2c Milk	1/2c Milk
	Coffee/Tea/Decaf	Coffee/Tea/Decaf	Coffee/Tea/Decaf	Coffee/Tea/Decaf
S12	1/2c Orange Gelatin	1/2c Orange Gelatin	1/2c Orange Gelatin	1/2c Orange Gelatin
	Snacks			
	Milk or Juice	Juice	Milk or Juice	Milk or STR Juice
	Cookies, Crackers,	SR Cookies, SR Crackers,	Plain Cookies, Gelatin,	Applesauce, SFT Banana,
	Gelatin, Ice Cream,	Gelatin, Fresh Fruit	Plain Crackers+, Ice Cream,	Gelatin, Ice Cream
	Fresh Fruit		Banana	

TERMS: SFT = Soft; SLF = Soft/Low Fiber; GRD = Ground; CHP = Chopped Finely; PUR = Puree; STR = Strained; SR = Sodium or Salt Restricted; LF = Low Fat; FF = Fat Free; LCH = Low Cholesterol; DB = Diabetic; UNSW = Unsweetened; RC = Reduced Calorie; LC = Low Calorie; EXCH = Diabetic Exchange

SERVING UTENSILS: #6 Scoop = 2/3 cup-6 oz; #8 Scoop = 1/2 cup-4 oz; #10 Scoop = 3/8 cup-3 to 4 oz; #12 Scoop = 1/3 cup-2.5 to 3 oz; #16 Scoop = 1/4 cup-2 oz; #30 Scoop = 2 tbsp-1 oz; #60 Scoop = 1 tbsp-1/2 oz. Ounces will vary, based on food used.

1. *Liberal Bland:* Follow a regular diet. Use decaffeinated products. Omit pepper and chili powder.

2. *No Added Salt (3–4 gm NA):* Follow a regular diet. Use SR soups and SR canned meats. Omit salt packets (and shakers), bacon, sausage, smoked, and cured meats, substitute with SR food choices.

3. *Low Fiber:* Follow a soft diet. Do not exceed 2 cups of milk per day. Soft/Low Fiber—Omit pepper, garlic, and onions from recipes.

4. *2200 Calorie Diet:* Follow 2000 calorie diet with the following additions: Lunch—add 1 bread exchange and 1 fat exchange; Dinner—add 1 bread exchange. +Consider individual tolerance. Daily Alternatives: Lunch and Dinner—Chicken, Hamburger, Cottage Cheese Fruit Plate, or Assorted Sandwiches. Individual preferences are provided upon request.

Amounts specified for food items that contain bone is equivalent to cooked, edible deboned portion.

Soft, Low Fiber[3]	Low Cholesterol, Low Fat (40–50 gm)	No Concentrated Sweets (Diabetic)	1200	1500	1800	2000[4]
			Diabetic/Calorie-Controlled			
1/2c STR Grapefruit Juice or	1/2c Grapefruit Jce or	1/2c UNSW Grpefruit Jce or	1/2c	1/2c	1/2c	1/2c
1 small Banana	1 small Banana	1 small Banana	1/2	1/2	1/2	1/2
1/2c Cream of Rice or	1/2c LF Cream of Rice or	1/2c DB Cream of Rice or	1/2c	1/2c	1/2c	1/2c
3/4c Asst Refined Cereals	3/4c Dry Cereals	3/4c UNSW Dry Cereals	3/4c	3/4c	3/4c	3/4c
1 Scrambled Egg	1 Egg Substitute	1 Scrambled Egg	1	1	1	1
1 sl White Toast	1 sl Toast	1 sl Toast	1 sl	1 sl	1 sl	2 sl
1 tsp Margarine	1 tsp Margarine	1 tsp Margarine	0	0	1 tsp	1 tsp
1 tsp Jelly	1 tsp Jam/Jelly	1 tsp DB Jam/Jelly	1 tsp	1 tsp	1 tsp	1 tsp
1c Milk	1c Skim Milk	1c Skim Milk	1/2c	1/2c	1/2c	1c
Coffee/Tea/Decaf	Coffee/Tea/Decaf	Coffee/Tea/Decaf	free	free	free	free
1/2c STR Juice	1c Green Salad	1c Green Salad	1c	1c	1c	1c
NO	2 tsp Italian Dressing	1 Tbsp Italian Drsg	1 tsp	1 tsp	2 tsp	1 Tbsp
5 oz SLF Veal Parmesan	4 oz LF Veal Parmesan	5 oz DB Veal Parmesan	4 oz	5 oz	5 oz	5 oz
1/2c Spaghetti	1/2c Spaghetti	1/2c Spaghetti	1/2c	1/2c	1/2c	1/2c
2 oz SLF Tomato Sauce	1 oz LF Tomato Sauce	2 oz DB Tomato Sauce	1 oz	1 oz	2 oz	2 oz
1/2c Zucchini	1/2c LF Zucchini-Onions	1/2c LF Zucchini-Onions	1/2c	1/2c	1/2c	1/2c
1 SFT Refined Dinner Roll	1 Dinner Roll	1 Dinner Roll	0	1 sm	1 sm	1 sm
1 tsp Margarine	NO	1 tsp Margarine	0	1 tsp	1 tsp	1 tsp
1/2c Milk	1/2c Skim Milk	1/2c Skim Milk	1/2c	1/2c	1/2c	1/2c
Coffee/Tea/Decaf	Coffee/Tea/Decaf	Coffee/Tea/Decaf	free	free	free	free
1/2 SLF Canned Baked Pear	1/2 LF Baked Pear	1/2 DB Baked Pear	1/2	1/2	1/2	1/2
2/3c SLF Broth	2/3c Chunky Veg Soup	2/3c Chunky Veg Soup	2/3c	2/3c	2/3c	2/3c
1/2c SFT Seafood Salad	1/2c LF Seafood Salad	1/2c LF Seafood Salad	1/2c	3/4c	3/4c	3/4c
2 sl White Bread	2 sl Bread	1 Croissant	0	1/2	1	1
1/2c SFT Potato Salad	1/2c LF Waldorf Salad	1/2c LF Waldorf Salad	1/2c	1/2c	1/2c	1/2c
1/2c Milk	1/2c Skim Milk	1/2c Skim Milk	1/2c	1/2c	1/2c	1/2c
Coffee/Tea/Decaf	Coffee/Tea/Decaf	Coffee/Tea/Decaf	free	free	free	free
1/2c Orange Gelatin	1/2c Orange Gelatin	1/2c DB Orange Gelatin	1/2c	1/2c	1/2c	1/2c
Milk[3] or STR Juice	Skim Milk or Juice	1/2c Skim Milk	1/2c	1/2c	1/2c	1/2c
Plain Cookies, Gelatin,	LF Cookies, LF Crackers,	1 Starch/Bread Exch	1	1	1	1
Plain Crackers, Banana,	Gelatin, Fresh Fruit	1 Meat Exch	0	0	0	1
Vanilla Ice Cream[3]		1 Fat Exch	0	0	1	1

Recipe	Regular, Liberal Bland[1], No Added Salt[2]	1–2 gm Na (Low Sodium)	Mechanical Soft	Puree
	Breakfast			
B1	1/2c Pineapple Juice	1/2c Pineapple Juice	1/2c Pineapple Juice	1/2c STR Pineapple Juice
	1/2c Oatmeal or	1/2c Oatmeal or	1/2c Oatmeal or	1c Oatmeal
I2	3/4c Asst Dry Cereals	3/4c SR Asst Dry Cereals	3/4c Asst Dry Cereals+	NO
	1 oz Cheese-Grilled on	1 oz SR Cheese-Grilled on	1 oz Cheese on	1/2c PUR Cottage Cheese
	1 sl Toast	1 sl Toast	1 sl Bread	1 sl Bread+
	1 tsp Margarine	1 tsp SR Margarine	1 tsp Margarine	1 tsp Margarine
	1c Milk	1c Milk	1c Milk	1c Milk
	Coffee/Tea/Decaf	Coffee/Tea/Decaf	Coffee/Tea/Decaf	Coffee/Tea/Decaf
	Lunch			
K22	1/2c Three Bean Salad	1/2c SR Three Bean Salad	1/2c Juice	1/2c STR Juice
E14	1c Turkey Chow Mein	1c SR Turkey Chow Mein	1c SFT Turkey Chow Mein	1c PUR Turkey Chow Mein
	1/4c Chinese Noodles	NO	NO	NO
L1	1/2c White Rice	1/2c White Rice	1/2c White Rice	1/2c PUR White Rice
	1 Dinner Roll	1 Dinner Roll	1 SFT Dinner Roll+	1 sl Bread+
	1 tsp Margarine	1 tsp SR Margarine	1 tsp Margarine	1 tsp Margarine
	1/2c Milk	1/2c Milk	1/2c Milk	1/2c Milk
	Coffee/Tea/Decaf	Coffee/Tea/Decaf	Coffee/Tea/Decaf	Coffee/Tea/Decaf
	2 Plums	2 Plums	2 Plums—No Skin	1/2c PUR Plums
	Dinner			
C18,1	2/3c Onion Soup	2/3c Onion Soup	2/3c Onion Soup	2/3c PUR/STR Onion Soup
G13	1/6 pie Spinach Quiche	1/6 pie SR Spinach Quiche	1/6 pie Spinach Quiche	6 oz PUR Spinach Quiche
K32	1c Tossed Veg Salad	1c Tossed Veg Salad	1/2c Juice	1/2c STR Juice
P1-8	1 oz Salad Dressing	1 oz SR Salad Dressing	NO	NO
	1 Dinner Roll	1 Dinner Roll	1 SFT Dinner Roll+	1 sl Bread+
	1 tsp Margarine	1 tsp SR Margarine	1 tsp Margarine	1 tsp Margarine
	1/2c Milk	1/2c Milk	1/2c Milk	1/2c Milk
	Coffee/Tea/Decaf	Coffee/Tea/Decaf	Coffee/Tea/Decaf	Coffee/Tea/Decaf
	2 Cookies	2 Cookies	2 Plain Cookies	1/2c PUR Peaches
	Snacks			
	Milk or Juice	Juice	Milk or Juice	Milk or STR Juice
	Cookies, Crackers,	SR Cookies, SR Crackers,	Plain Cookies, Gelatin,	Applesauce, SFT Banana,
	Gelatin, Ice Cream,	Gelatin, Fresh Fruit	Plain Crackers+, Ice Cream,	Gelatin, Ice Cream
	Fresh Fruit		Banana	

TERMS: SFT = Soft; SLF = Soft/Low Fiber; GRD = Ground; CHP = Chopped Finely; PUR = Puree; STR = Strained; SR = Sodium or Salt Restricted; LF = Low Fat; FF = Fat Free; LCH = Low Cholesterol; DB = Diabetic; UNSW = Unsweetened; RC = Reduced Calorie; LC = Low Calorie; EXCH = Diabetic Exchange

SERVING UTENSILS: #6 Scoop = 2/3 cup-6 oz; #8 Scoop = 1/2 cup-4 oz; #10 Scoop = 3/8 cup-3 to 4 oz; #12 Scoop = 1/3 cup-2.5 to 3 oz; #16 Scoop = 1/4 cup-2 oz; #30 Scoop = 2 tbsp-1 oz; #60 Scoop = 1 tbsp-1/2 oz. Ounces will vary, based on food used.

1. *Liberal Bland:* Follow a regular diet. Use decaffeinated products. Omit pepper and chili powder.

2. *No Added Salt (3–4 gm NA):* Follow a regular diet. Use SR soups and SR canned meats. Omit salt packets (and shakers), bacon, sausage, smoked, and cured meats, substitute with SR food choices.

3. *Low Fiber:* Follow a soft diet. Do not exceed 2 cups of milk per day. Soft/Low Fiber—Omit pepper, garlic, and onions from recipes.

4. *2200 Calorie Diet:* Follow 2000 calorie diet with the following additions: Lunch—add 1 bread exchange and 1 fat exchange; Dinner—add 1 bread exchange.

+Consider individual tolerance. Daily Alternatives: Lunch and Dinner—Chicken, Hamburger, Cottage Cheese Fruit Plate, or Assorted Sandwiches. Individual preferences are provided upon request.

Amounts specified for food items that contain bone is equivalent to cooked, edible deboned portion.

Soft, Low Fiber[3]	Low Cholesterol, Low Fat (40–50 gm)	No Concentrated Sweets (Diabetic)	1200	1500	1800	2000[4]
			Diabetic/Calorie-Controlled			
1/2c STR Apple Juice	1/2c Pineapple Juice	1/2c UNSW Pineapple Juice	1/2c	1/2c	1/2c	1/2c
1/2c Oatmeal or	1/2c LF Oatmeal or	1/2c DB Oatmeal or	1/2c	1/2c	1/2c	1/2c
3/4c Asst Refined Cereals	3/4c Dry Cereals	3/4c UNSW Dry Cereals	3/4c	3/4c	3/4c	3/4c
1 oz Mild Chse-Grilled on	1 oz LF Cheese-Grilled on	1 oz LF Cheese-Grilled on	1 oz	1 oz	1 oz	1 oz
1 sl White Toast	1 sl Toast	1 sl Toast	1 sl	1 sl	1 sl	2 sl
1 tsp Margarine	1 tsp Margarine	1 tsp Margarine	0	1 tsp	1 tsp	1 tsp
1c Milk	1c Skim Milk	1c Skim Milk	1/2c	1/2c	1/2c	1c
Coffee/Tea/Decaf	Coffee/Tea/Decaf	Coffee/Tea/Decaf	free	free	free	free
1/2c STR Juice	1/2c LF Three Bean Salad	1/2c DB Three Bean Salad	1/2c	1/2c	1/2c	1/2c
1c SLF Turkey Chow Mein	3/4c Turkey Chow Mein	1c Turkey Chow Mein	3/4c	1c	1c	1c
NO	NO	1/4c Chinese Noodles	0	0	1/4c	1/4c
1/2c White Rice	1/2c White Rice	1/2c White Rice	1/3c	1/3c	1/3c	1/3c
1 SFT Refined Dinner Roll	1 Dinner Roll	1 Dinner Roll	0	0	1 sm	1 sm
1 tsp Margarine	NO	1 tsp Margarine	0	0	0	1 tsp
1/2c Milk	1/2c Skim Milk	1/2c Skim Milk	1/2c	1/2c	1/2c	1/2c
Coffee/Tea/Decaf	Coffee/Tea/Decaf	Coffee/Tea/Decaf	free	free	free	free
2 Plums—No Skin	2 Plums	2 UNSW Plums	2	2	2	2
2/3c SLF Broth	2/3c LF Onion Soup+	2/3c LF Onion Soup	2/3c	2/3c	2/3c	2/3c
1/6 pie SLF Spinach Quiche	1/8 pie LF Spinach Quiche	1/6 pie DB Spinach Quiche	1/8	1/6	1/6	1/6
1/2c STR Juice	1c Tossed Veg Salad	1c Tossed Veg Salad	1c	1c	1c	1c
NO	1 Tbsp LC Salad Dressing	1 Tbsp LC Sld Dressing	1 Tbsp	1 Tbsp	1 Tbsp	1 Tbsp
1 SFT Refined Dinner Roll	1 Dinner Roll	1 Dinner Roll	0	0	1 sm	1 sm
1 tsp Margarine	NO	1 tsp Margarine	0	0	1 tsp	1 tsp
1/2c Milk	1/2c Skim Milk	1/2c Skim Milk	1/2c	1/2c	1/2c	1/2c
Coffee/Tea/Decaf	Coffee/Tea/Decaf	Coffee/Tea/Decaf	free	free	free	free
2 Plain Cookies	2 LF Cookies	3 Graham Crackers	2	2	3	3
Milk[3] or STR Juice	Skim Milk or Juice	1/2c Skim Milk	1/2c	1/2c	1/2c	1/2c
Plain Cookies, Gelatin,	LF Cookies, LF Crackers,	1 Starch/Bread Exch	1	1	1	1
Plain Crackers, Banana,	Gelatin, Fresh Fruit	1 Meat Exch	0	0	0	1
Vanilla Ice Cream[3]		1 Fat Exch	0	0	1	1

Recipe	Regular, Liberal Bland[1], No Added Salt[2]	1–2 gm Na (Low Sodium)	Mechanical Soft	Puree
	Breakfast			
	1/2c Cranberry Juice or	1/2c Cranberry Juice or	1/2c Cranberry Juice or	1/2c STR Cranberry Juice or
S11	1/2c Stewed Prunes	1/2c Stewed Prunes	1/2c Stewed Prunes+	1/4c PUR Prunes
B1	1/2c Cream of Wheat or	1/2c Cream of Wheat or	1/2 Cream of Wheat or	1c Cream of Wheat
	3/4c Asst Dry Cereals	3/4c SR Asst Dry Cereals	3/4c Asst Dry Cereals+	NO
B4	1 Poached Egg	1 Poached Egg	1 Poached Egg	1 Poached Egg
	1 Sweet Roll	1 Sweet Roll	1 sl Bread	1 sl Bread+
	1 tsp Margarine	1 tsp SR Margarine	1 tsp Margarine	1 tsp Margarine
	1 tsp Jam/Jelly	1 tsp Jam/Jelly	1 tsp Jelly	1 tsp Jelly
	1c Milk	1c Milk	1c Milk	1c Milk
	Coffee/Tea/Decaf	Coffee/Tea/Decaf	Coffee/Tea/Decaf	Coffee/Tea/Decaf
	Lunch			
K20	1/2c Cheesy Pea Salad	1/2c SR Cheesy Pea Salad	1/2c SFT Cheesy Pea Salad	1/2c PUR Cheesy Pea Salad
F4	3.5 oz Oven Fried Fish	3.5 oz SR Oven Fried Fish	3.5 oz CHP Oven Fried Fish	3.5 oz PUR Oven Fried Fish
O25	2 Tbsp Tartar Sauce[2]	1 Tbsp SR Mayonnaise	2 Tbsp Tartar Sauce	2 Tbsp Mayonnaise
	Lemon Wedge	Lemon Wedge	Lemon Wedge	Lemon Wedge
M2	1/2c Lyonnaise Noodles	1/2c Lyonnaise Noodles	1/2c Lyonnaise Noodles	1/2c PUR Lyonnaise Noodles
J15	1/2c Glazed Carrots	1/2c Glazed Carrots	1/2c Glazed Carrots	1/2c PUR Glazed Carrots
	1 Dinner Roll	1 Dinner Roll	1 SFT Dinner Roll+	1 sl Bread+
	1 tsp Margarine	1 tsp SR Margarine	1 tsp Margarine	1 tsp Margarine
	1/2c Milk	1/2c Milk	1/2c Milk	1/2c Milk
	Coffee/Tea/Decaf	Coffee/Tea/Decaf	Coffee/Tea/Decaf	Coffee/Tea/Decaf
	1/2c Fruit Cocktail	1/2c Fruit Cocktail	1/2c Fruit Cocktail	1/2c PUR Fruit Cocktail
	Dinner			
C8	2/3c Chicken Rice Soup	2/3c Chicken Rice Soup	2/3c Chicken Rice Soup	2/3c PUR/STR Chicken Rice Soup
E2	3 oz Chicken Fricassee	3 oz Chicken Fricassee	3 oz CHP Chicken Fricassee	4 oz PUR Chicken Fricassee
	with 2 oz Gravy	with 2 oz Gravy	with 2 oz Gravy	with 2 oz STR Gravy
J41	3 oz Parsley Potatoes	3 oz Parsley Potatoes	3 oz Parsley Potatoes	1/2c PUR Parsley Potatoes
J1	1/2c Asparagus Tips	1/2c Asparagus Tips	1/2c Asparagus Tips	1/2 PUR Asparagus Tips
	1 Dinner Roll	1 Dinner Roll	1 SFT Dinner Roll+	1 sl Bread+
	1 tsp Margarine	1 tsp SR Margarine	1 tsp Margarine	1 tsp Margarine
	1/2c Milk	1/2c Milk	1/2c Milk	1/2c Milk
	Coffee/Tea/Decaf	Coffee/Tea/Decaf	Coffee/Tea/Decaf	Coffee/Tea/Decaf
Q10,1	2" Strawberry Shortcake	2" Strawberry Shortcake	2" Strawberry Shortcake+	1/2c Applesauce
	Snacks			
	Milk or Juice	Juice	Milk or Juice	Milk or STR Juice
	Cookies, Crackers,	SR Cookies, SR Crackers,	Plain Cookies, Gelatin,	Applesauce, SFT Banana,
	Gelatin, Ice Cream,	Gelatin, Fresh Fruit	Plain Crackers+, Ice Cream,	Gelatin, Ice Cream
	Fresh Fruit		Banana	

TERMS: SFT = Soft; SLF = Soft/Low Fiber; GRD = Ground; CHP = Chopped Finely; PUR = Puree; STR = Strained; SR = Sodium or Salt Restricted; LF = Low Fat; FF = Fat Free; LCH = Low Cholesterol; DB = Diabetic; UNSW = Unsweetened; RC = Reduced Calorie; LC = Low Calorie; EXCH = Diabetic Exchange

SERVING UTENSILS: #6 Scoop = 2/3 cup-6 oz; #8 Scoop = 1/2 cup-4 oz; #10 Scoop = 3/8 cup-3 to 4 oz; #12 Scoop = 1/3 cup-2.5 to 3 oz; #16 Scoop = 1/4 cup-2 oz; #30 Scoop = 2 tbsp-1 oz; #60 Scoop = 1 tbsp-1/2 oz. Ounces will vary, based on food used.

1. *Liberal Bland:* Follow a regular diet. Use decaffeinated products. Omit pepper and chili powder.

2. *No Added Salt (3–4 gm NA):* Follow a regular diet. Use SR soups and SR canned meats. Omit salt packets (and shakers), bacon, sausage, smoked, and cured meats, substitute with SR food choices.

3. *Low Fiber:* Follow a soft diet. Do not exceed 2 cups of milk per day. Soft/Low Fiber—Omit pepper, garlic, and onions from recipes.

4. *2200 Calorie Diet:* Follow 2000 calorie diet with the following additions: Lunch—add 1 bread exchange and 1 fat exchange; Dinner—add 1 bread exchange.

+Consider individual tolerance. Daily Alternatives: Lunch and Dinner—Chicken, Hamburger, Cottage Cheese Fruit Plate, or Assorted Sandwiches. Individual preferences are provided upon request.

Amounts specified for food items that contain bone is equivalent to cooked, edible deboned portion.

Soft, Low Fiber[3]	Low Cholesterol, Low Fat (40–50 gm)	No Concentrated Sweets (Diabetic)	1200	1500	1800	2000[4]
			Diabetic/Calorie-Controlled			
1/2c STR Cranberry Juice	1/2c Cranberry Juice or	1/2c UNSW Cranberry Jce or	1/3c	1/3c	1/3c	1/3c
NO	1/2c Stewed Prunes	3 med Stewed Prunes	3 med	3 med	3 med	3 med
1/2c Cream of Wheat or	1/2c LF Cream of Wheat or	1/2c DB Cream of Wheat or	1/2c	1/2c	1/2c	1/2c
3/4c Asst Refined Cereals	3/4c Dry Cereals	3/4c UNSW Dry Cereals	3/4c	3/4c	3/4c	3/4c
1 Poached Egg	1 Egg Substitute	1 Poached Egg	1	1	1	1
1 sl White Toast	1 sl Toast	1 sl Toast	1 sl	1 sl	1 sl	2 sl
1 tsp Margarine	1 tsp Margarine	1 tsp Margarine	0	1 tsp	1 tsp	1 tsp
1 tsp Jelly	1 tsp Jam/Jelly	1 tsp DB Jam/Jelly	1 tsp	1 tsp	1 tsp	1 tsp
1c Milk	1c Skim Milk	1c Skim Milk	1/2c	1/2c	1/2c	1c
Coffee/Tea/Decaf	Coffee/Tea/Decaf	Coffee/Tea/Decaf	free	free	free	free
1/2c STR Juice	1/2c LF Cheesy Pea Salad	1/2c LF Cheesy Pea Salad	Lett	1/2c	1/2c	1/2c
3.5 oz SLF Oven Fried Fish	3 oz LF Oven Fried Fish	3.5 oz LF Oven Fried Fish	2.5 oz	3.5 oz	3.5 oz	3.5 oz
2 Tbsp Mayonnaise	1 tsp LF Tartar Sauce	2 Tbsp LF Tartar Sauce	0	0	2 tsp	2 tsp
Lemon Wedge	Lemon Wedge	Lemon Wedge	Lemon	Lemon	Lemon	Lemon
1/2c SLF Lyonnaise Noodles	1/2c LF Lyonnaise Noodles	1/2c LF Lyonnaise Noodles	1/3c	1/2c	1/2c	1/2c
1/2c Glazed Carrots	1/2c LF Glazed Carrots	1/2c DB Glazed Carrots	1/2c	1/2c	1/2c	1/2c
1 SFT Refined Dinner Roll	1 Dinner Roll	1 Dinner Roll	0	0	1 sm	1 sm
1 tsp Margarine	NO	1 tsp Margarine	0	0	0	0
1/2c Milk	1/2c Skim Milk	1/2c Skim Milk	1/2c	1/2c	1/2c	1/2c
Coffee/Tea/Decaf	Coffee/Tea/Decaf	Coffee/Tea/Decaf	free	free	free	free
1/2c Fruit Cocktail	1/2c Fruit Cocktail	1/2c UNSW Fruit Cocktail	1/2c	1/2c	1/2c	1/2c
2/3c SLF Chicken Rice Soup	2/3c Chicken Rice Soup	2/3c Chicken Rice Soup	STR	STR	2/3c	2/3c
3 oz SLF Chicken Fricassee	2 oz LF Chicken Fricassee	3 oz LF Chicken Fricassee	2 oz	3 oz	3 oz	3 oz
with 2 oz Gravy	with 2 oz LF Gravy	with 2 oz LF Gravy	2 oz	2 oz	2 oz	2 oz
3 oz Parsley Potatoes	3 oz LF Parsley Potatoes	3 oz LF Parsley Potatoes	2 oz	3 oz	3 oz	3 oz
1/2c Asparagus Tips	1/2c Asparagus Tips	1/2c Asparagus Tips	1/2c	1/2c	1/2c	1/2c
1 SFT Refined Dinner Roll	1 Dinner Roll	1 Dinner Roll	0	0	1 sm	1 sm
1 tsp Margarine	NO	1 tsp Margarine	0	0	0	0
1/2c Milk	1/2c Skim Milk	1/2c Skim Milk	1/2c	1/2c	1/2c	1/2c
Coffee/Tea/Decaf	Coffee/Tea/Decaf	Coffee/Tea/Decaf	free	free	free	free
1 sl Angelfood Cake	2" LF Strawberry Shortcake	2" DB Strawberry Shortcake	1"	2"	2"	2"
Milk[3] or STR Juice	Skim Milk or Juice	1/2c Skim Milk	1/2c	1/2c	1/2c	1/2c
Plain Cookies, Gelatin,	LF Cookies, LF Crackers,	1 Starch/Bread Exch	1	1	1	1
Plain Crackers, Banana,	Gelatin, Fresh Fruit	1 Meat Exch	0	0	0	1
Vanilla Ice Cream[3]		1 Fat Exch	0	0	1	1

Recipe	Regular, Liberal Bland[1], No Added Salt[2]	1–2 gm Na (Low Sodium)	Mechanical Soft	Puree
	Breakfast			
B1	1/2c Apple Juice	1/2c Apple Juice	1/2c Apple Juice	1/2c STR Apple Juice
	1/2c Wheatena or	1/2c Wheatena or	1/2c Wheatena or	1c Wheatena
	3/4c Asst Dry Cereals	3/4c SR Asst Dry Cereals	3/4c Asst Dry Cereals+	NO
B4	1 Hard-Boiled Egg	1 Hard-Boiled Egg	1 Hard-Boiled Egg	1 Soft-Cooked Egg
	1 sl Toast	1 sl Toast	1 sl Bread	1 sl Bread+
	1 tsp Margarine	1 tsp SR Margarine	1 tsp Margarine	1 tsp Margarine
	1 tsp Jam/Jelly	1 tsp Jam/Jelly	1 tsp Jelly	1 tsp Jelly
	1c Milk	1c Milk	1c Milk	1c Milk
	Coffee/Tea/Decaf	Coffee/Tea/Decaf	Coffee/Tea/Decaf	Coffee/Tea/Decaf
	Lunch			
K9	1/2c Marinated Cucumbers	1/2c Marinated Cucumbers	1/2c Juice	1/2c STR Juice
D15	4 oz Meatloaf	4 oz Meatloaf	4 oz Meatloaf	4 oz PUR Meatloaf
O16,15	2 oz Onion Gravy	2 oz SR Onion Gravy	2 oz SFT Onion Gravy	2 oz SFT Onion Gravy
J37	1/2c Mashed Potatoes	1/2c Mashed Potatoes	1/2c Mashed Potatoes	1/2c PUR Mashed Potatoes
J51	1/2c Vegetable Medley	1/2c Vegetable Medley	1/2c SFT Vegetable Medley	1/2c PUR Vegetable Medley
	1 Dinner Roll	1 Dinner Roll	1 SFT Dinner Roll+	1 sl Bread+
	1 tsp Margarine	1 tsp SR Margarine	1 tsp Margarine	1 tsp Margarine
	1/2c Milk	1/2c Milk	1/2c Milk	1/2c Milk
	Coffee/Tea/Decaf	Coffee/Tea/Decaf	Coffee/Tea/Decaf	Coffee/Tea/Decaf
	1/2c Apricot Halves	1/2c Apricot Halves	1/2c Apricot Halves	1/2c PUR Apricot
	Dinner			
C4,1	2/3c Bean Soup	2/3c SR/LF Bean Soup	2/3c Bean Soup	2/3c PUR Bean Soup
I5	Chef Salad with	Chef Salad with	Chef Salad with	NO
	2 oz Ham[2]-Turkey	2 oz Turkey	2 oz CHP Ham-Turkey	4 oz PUR Ham-Turkey
	1 oz Cheese	1 oz SR Cheese	1 oz Cheese	NO
	Lettuce Leaves	Lettuce Leaves	CHP Lettuce Leaves+	NO
J50	4 Tomato Slices	4 Tomato Slices	1/2c Stewed Tomatoes	1/2c PUR/STR Tomatoes
K13	4 Onion Slices	4 Onion Slices	1/2c SFT Macaroni Salad	1/2c PUR Macaroni Salad
	4 Cucumber Slices	4 Cucumber Slices	1/2c Juice	1/2c STR Juice
P1-8	1 oz Salad Dressing	1 oz SR Salad Dressing	1 Tbsp Salad Dressing	NO
	1 Dinner Roll or	1 Dinner Roll or	1 SFT Dinner Roll+	1 sl Bread+
	4 Crackers	4 SR Crackers	NO	NO
	1 tsp Margarine	1 tsp SR Margarine	1 tsp Margarine	1 tsp Margarine
	1/2c Milk	1/4c Milk	1/2c Milk	1/2c Milk
	Coffee/Tea/Decaf	Coffee/Tea/Decaf	Coffee/Tea/Decaf	Coffee/Tea/Decaf
S16,17	1/2c Chocolate Pudding	1/2c Chocolate Pudding	1/2c Chocolate Pudding	1/2c Chocolate Pudding
	Snacks			
	Milk or Juice	Juice	Milk or Juice	Milk or STR Juice
	Cookies, Crackers,	SR Cookies, SR Crackers,	Plain Cookies, Gelatin,	Applesauce, SFT Banana,
	Gelatin, Ice Cream,	Gelatin, Fresh Fruit	Plain Crackers+, Ice Cream,	Gelatin, Ice Cream
	Fresh Fruit	Banana		Vanilla Ice Cream[3]

TERMS: SFT = Soft; SLF = Soft/Low Fiber; GRD = Ground; CHP = Chopped Finely; PUR = Puree; STR = Strained; SR = Sodium or Salt Restricted; LF = Low Fat; FF = Fat Free; LCH = Low Cholesterol; DB = Diabetic; UNSW = Unsweetened; RC = Reduced Calorie; LC = Low Calorie; EXCH = Diabetic Exchange

SERVING UTENSILS: #6 Scoop = 2/3 cup-6 oz; #8 Scoop = 1/2 cup-4 oz; #10 Scoop = 3/8 cup-3 to 4 oz; #12 Scoop = 1/3 cup-2.5 to 3 oz; #16 Scoop = 1/4 cup-2 oz; #30 Scoop = 2 tbsp-1 oz; #60 Scoop = 1 tbsp-1/2 oz. Ounces will vary, based on food used.

1. *Liberal Bland:* Follow a regular diet. Use decaffeinated products. Omit pepper and chili powder.

2. *No Added Salt (3–4 gm NA):* Follow a regular diet. Use SR soups and SR canned meats. Omit salt packets (and shakers), bacon, sausage, smoked, and cured meats, substitute with SR food choices.

3. *Low Fiber:* Follow a soft diet. Do not exceed 2 cups of milk per day. Soft/Low Fiber—Omit pepper, garlic, and onions from recipes.

4. *2200 Calorie Diet:* Follow 2000 calorie diet with the following additions: Lunch—add 1 bread exchange and 1 fat exchange; Dinner—add 1 bread exchange.

+Consider individual tolerance. Daily Alternatives: Lunch and Dinner—Chicken, Hamburger, Cottage Cheese Fruit Plate, or Assorted Sandwiches. Individual preferences are provided upon request.

Amounts specified for food items that contain bone is equivalent to cooked, edible deboned portion.

Soft, Low Fiber[3]	Low Cholesterol, Low Fat (40–50 gm)	No Concentrated Sweets (Diabetic)	1200	1500	1800	2000[4]
			Diabetic/Calorie-Controlled			

Soft, Low Fiber[3]	Low Cholesterol, Low Fat (40–50 gm)	No Concentrated Sweets (Diabetic)	1200	1500	1800	2000[4]
1/2c STR Apple Juice	1/2c Apple Juice	1/2c UNSW Apple Juice	1/2c	1/2c	1/2c	1/2c
1/2c Wheatena or	1/2c LF Wheatena or	1/2c DB Wheatena or	1/2c	1/2c	1/2c	1/2c
3/4c Asst Refined Cereals	3/4c Dry Cereals	3/4c UNSW Dry Cereals	3/4c	3/4c	3/4c	3/4c
1 Hard-Boiled Egg	1 Egg Substitute	1 Hard-Boiled Egg	1	1	1	1
1 sl White Toast	1 sl Toast	1 sl Toast	1 sl	1 sl	2 sl	2 sl
1 tsp Margarine	1 tsp Margarine	1 tsp Margarine	0	0	1 tsp	2 tsp
1 tsp Jelly	1 tsp Jam/Jelly	1 tsp DB Jam/Jelly	1 tsp	1 tsp	1 tsp	1 tsp
1c Milk	1c Skim Milk	1c Skim Milk	1/2c	1/2c	1/2c	1c
Coffee/Tea/Decaf	Coffee/Tea/Decaf	Coffee/Tea/Decaf	free	free	free	free
1/2c STR Juice	1/2c LF Marinated Cucumbers	1/2c DB Marinated Cucumbers	1/2c	1/2c	1/2c	1/2c
4 oz SLF MeatLoaf	3 oz LF Meatloaf+	4 oz Meatloaf	3 oz	4 oz	4 oz	4 oz
2 oz Cream Gravy	2 oz LF Onion Gravy+	2 oz LF Onion Gravy	1 oz	1 oz	2 oz	2 oz
1/2c Mashed Potatoes	1/2c LF Mashed Potatoes	1/2c LF Mashed Potatoes	1/2c	1/2c	1/2c	1/2c
1/2c Green Beans-Carrots	1/2c Vegetable Medley+	1/2c Vegetable Medley	1/2c	1/2c	1/2c	1/2c
1 SFT Refined Dinner Roll	1 Dinner Roll	1 Dinner Roll	0	1 sm	1 sm	1 med
1 tsp Margarine	NO	1 tsp Margarine	0	1 tsp	1 tsp	1 tsp
1/2c Milk	1/2c Skim Milk	1/2c Skim Milk	1/2c	1/2c	1/2c	1/2c
Coffee/Tea/Decaf	Coffee/Tea/Decaf	Coffee/Tea/Decaf	free	free	free	free
1/2c Apricot Halves	1/2c Apricot Halves	1/2c UNSW Apricot Halves	1/2c	1/2c	1/2c	1/2c
2/3c SLF Broth	2/3c SR/LF Bean Soup	2/3c SR/LF Bean Soup	2/3c	2/3c	2/3c	2/3c
Chef Salad with	Chef Salad with	Chef Salad with				
2 oz Turkey	1 oz Turkey	2 oz LF Ham-Turkey	1 oz	2 oz	2 oz	2 oz
1 oz Mild Cheese	1 oz LF Cheese	1 oz LF Cheese	1 oz	1 oz	1 oz	1 oz
NO	Lettuce Leaves	Lettuce Leaves	free	free	free	free
1/2c SLF Stewed Tomatoes	4 Tomato Slices	4 Tomato Slices	4 sl	4 sl	4 sl	4 sl
1/2c SFT Macaroni Salad	4 Onion Slices+	4 Onion Slices	4 sl	4 sl	4 sl	4 sl
1/2c STR Juice	4 Cucumber Slices	4 Cucumber Slices	4 sl	4 sl	4 sl	4 sl
NO	1 Tbsp LC Salad Dressing	1 Tbsp LC Salad Dressing	1 Tbsp	1 Tbsp	1 Tbsp	1 Tbsp
1 SFT Refined Dinner Roll or	1 Dinner Roll or	1 Dinner Roll or	0	1 sm	1 med	1 med
4 Plain Crackers	4 LF Crackers	4 LF Crackers	2	5	10	10
1 tsp Margarine	NO	1 tsp Margarine	0	0	1 tsp	1 tsp
1/2c Milk (1/4c)[3]	1/2c Skim Milk	1/2c Skim Milk	1/4c	1/4c	1/2c	1/2c
Coffee/Tea/Decaf	Coffee/Tea/Decaf	Coffee/Tea/Decaf	free	free	free	free
1/2c Vanilla Pudding	1/2c LF Chocolate Pudding	1/2c DB Chocolate Pudding	1/2c	1/2c	1/2c	1/2c
Milk[3] or STR Juice	Skim Milk or Juice	1/2c Skim Milk	1/2c	1/2c	1/2c	1/2c
Plain Cookies, Gelatin,	LF Cookies, LF Crackers,	1 Starch/Bread Exch	1	1	1	1
Plain Crackers, Banana,	Gelatin, Fresh Fruit	1 Meat Exch	0	0	0	1
	1 Fat Exch	0	0	1	1	

Recipe	Regular, Liberal Bland[1], No Added Salt[2]	1–2 gm Na (Low Sodium)	Mechanical Soft	Puree
	Breakfast			
	1/2c Orange Juice	1/2c Orange Juice	1/2c Orange Juice	1/2c STR Orange Juice
B1	1/2c Farina or	1/2c Farina or	1/2c Farina or	1c Farina
	3/4c Asst Dry Cereals	3/4c SR Asst Dry Cereals	3/4c Asst Dry Cereals+	NO
B4,5	1 Egg to Order	1 Egg to Order	1 Egg to Order	1 PUR Egg to Order
B9	2 Pancakes	2 SR Pancakes	2 Pancakes	1 sl Bread+
	2 oz Maple Syrup	2 oz Maple Syrup	2 oz Maple Syrup	NO
	1 tsp Margarine	1 tsp SR Margarine	1 tsp Margarine	1 tsp Margarine
	1 tsp Jam/Jelly	1 tsp Jam/Jelly	1 tsp Jelly	1 tsp Jelly
	1c Milk	1c Milk	1c Milk	1c Milk
	Coffee/Tea/Decaf	Coffee/Tea/Decaf	Coffee/Tea/Decaf	Coffee/Tea/Decaf
	Lunch			
K24	1c Garden Salad	1c Garden Salad	1/2c Juice	1/2c STR Juice
P1–8	1 oz Salad Dressing	1 oz SR Salad Dressing	NO	NO
D31	3 oz Roast Pork with	3 oz Roast Pork with	3 oz CHP Roast Pork with	4 oz PUR Roast Pork with
O3	2 oz Brown Gravy	2 oz SR Brown Gravy	2 oz Brown Gravy	2 oz Brown Gravy
P11	1/2c Cornbread Stuffing	1/2c SR Cornbread Stuffing	1/2c SFT Cornbread Stuffing	1/2c PUR Stuffing
J47	1/2c Spinach	1/2c Spinach	1/2c Spinach	1/2c PUR Spinach
	1 Dinner Roll	1 Dinner Roll	1 SFT Dinner Roll+	1 sl Bread+
	1 tsp Margarine	1 tsp SR Margarine	1 tsp Margarine	1 tsp Margarine
	1/2c Milk	1/2c Milk	1/2c Milk	1/2c Milk
	Coffee/Tea/Decaf	Coffee/Tea/Decaf	Coffee/Tea/Decaf	Coffee/Tea/Decaf
	1/2c Applesauce	1/2c Applesauce	1/2c Applesauce	1/2c Applesauce
	Dinner			
C15,1	2/3c Creole Soup	2/3c SR Creole Soup	2/3c Creole Soup	2/3c PUR Creole Soup
F10	8 oz Tuna Noodle Casserole[2]	8 oz SR Tuna Ndle Casserole	8 oz Tuna Noodle Casserole	8 oz PUR Tuna Ndle Csserle
J8	1/2c Julienne Beets	1/2c SR Julienne Beets	1/2c Julienne Beets	1/2c PUR Julienne Beets
	1 Dinner Roll	1 Dinner Roll	1 SFT Dinner Roll+	1 sl Bread+
	1 tsp Margarine	1 tsp SR Margarine	1 tsp Margarine	1 tsp Margarine
	1/2c Milk	1/4c Milk	1/2c Milk	1/2c Milk
	Coffee/Tea/Decaf	Coffee/Tea/Decaf	Coffee/Tea/Decaf	Coffee/Tea/Decaf
	1/2c Sherbet	1/2c Sherbet	1/2c Sherbet	1/2c Sherbet
	Snacks			
	Milk or Juice	Juice	Milk or Juice	Milk or STR Juice
	Cookies, Crackers,	SR Cookies, SR Crackers,	Plain Cookies, Gelatin,	Applesauce, SFT Banana,
	Gelatin, Ice Cream,	Gelatin, Fresh Fruit	Plain Crackers+, Ice Cream,	Gelatin, Ice Cream
	Fresh Fruit		Banana	

TERMS: SFT = Soft; SLF = Soft/Low Fiber; GRD = Ground; CHP = Chopped Finely; PUR = Puree; STR = Strained; SR = Sodium or Salt Restricted; LF = Low Fat; FF = Fat Free; LCH = Low Cholesterol; DB = Diabetic; UNSW = Unsweetened; RC = Reduced Calorie; LC = Low Calorie; EXCH = Diabetic Exchange

SERVING UTENSILS: #6 Scoop = 2/3 cup-6 oz; #8 Scoop = 1/2 cup-4 oz; #10 Scoop = 3/8 cup-3 to 4 oz; #12 Scoop = 1/3 cup-2.5 to 3 oz; #16 Scoop = 1/4 cup-2 oz; #30 Scoop = 2 tbsp-1 oz; #60 Scoop = 1 tbsp-1/2 oz. Ounces will vary, based on food used.

1. *Liberal Bland:* Follow a regular diet. Use decaffeinated products. Omit pepper and chili powder.

2. *No Added Salt (3–4 gm NA):* Follow a regular diet. Use SR soups and SR canned meats. Omit salt packets (and shakers), bacon, sausage, smoked, and cured meats, substitute with SR food choices.

3. *Low Fiber:* Follow a soft diet. Do not exceed 2 cups of milk per day. Soft/Low Fiber—Omit pepper, garlic, and onions from recipes.

4. *2200 Calorie Diet:* Follow 2000 calorie diet with the following additions: Lunch—add 1 bread exchange and 1 fat exchange; Dinner—add 1 bread exchange.

+Consider individual tolerance. Daily Alternatives: Lunch and Dinner—Chicken, Hamburger, Cottage Cheese Fruit Plate, or Assorted Sandwiches. Individual preferences are provided upon request.

Amounts specified for food items that contain bone is equivalent to cooked, edible deboned portion.

Soft, Low Fiber[3]	Low Cholesterol, Low Fat (40–50 gm)	No Concentrated Sweets (Diabetic)	1200	1500	1800	2000[4]
			Diabetic/Calorie-Controlled			
1/2c STR Orange Juice	1/2c Orange Juice	1/2c UNSW Orange Juice	1/2c	1/2c	1/2c	1/2c
1/2c Farina or	1/2c LF Farina or	1/2c DB Farina or	1/2c	1/2c	1/2c	1/2c
3/4c Asst Refined Cereals	3/4c Dry Cereals	3/4c UNSW Dry Cereals	3/4c	3/4c	3/4c	3/4c
1 Egg to Order	1 Egg Substitute	1 Egg to Order	1	1	1	1
2 Pancakes	2 LF Pancakes	2 DB Pancakes – 4" across	2	2	2	3
2 oz Maple Syrup	2 oz Maple Syrup	1 oz DB Maple Syrup	1 oz	1 oz	1 oz	1 oz
1 tsp Margarine	NO	1 tsp Margarine	0	1 tsp	2 tsp	2 tsp
1 tsp Jelly	1 tsp Jam/Jelly	1 tsp DB Jam/Jelly	1 tsp	1 tsp	1 tsp	1 tsp
1c Milk	1c Skim Milk	1c Skim Milk	1/2c	1/2c	1/2c	1c
Coffee/Tea/Decaf	Coffee/Tea/Decaf	Coffee/Tea/Decaf	free	free	free	free
1/2c STR Juice	1c Garden Salad	1c Garden Salad	1c	1c	1c	1c
NO	1 Tbsp LC Salad Dressing	1 Tbsp LC Sld Dressing	1 Tbsp	1 Tbsp	1 Tbsp	1 Tbsp
3 oz SLF Roast Pork with	2 oz Roast Pork with	3 oz Roast Pork with	2 oz	3 oz	3 oz	3 oz
2 oz Brown Gravy	2 oz LF Brown Gravy	2 oz LF Brown Gravy	Broth	1 oz	2 oz	2 oz
1/2c SLF Cornbread Stuffing	1/2c LF Cornbread Stuffing	1/2c DB Cornbread Stuffing	1/4c	1/4c	1/2c	1/2c
1/2c Spinach	1/2c Spinach	1/2c Spinach	1/2c	1/2c	1/2c	1/2c
1 SFT Refined Dinner Roll	1 Dinner Roll	1 Dinner Roll	0	0	1 sm	1 sm
1 tsp Margarine	NO	1 tsp Margarine	0	0	1 tsp	1 tsp
1/2c Milk	1/2c Skim Milk	1/2c Skim Milk	1/2c	1/2c	1/2c	1/2c
Coffee/Tea/Decaf	Coffee/Tea/Decaf	Coffee/Tea/Decaf	free	free	free	free
1/2c Applesauce	1/2c Applesauce	1/2c UNSW Applesauce	1/2c	1/2c	1/2c	1/2c
2/3c SLF Broth	2/3c Creole Soup	2/3c Creole Soup	2/3c	2/3c	2/3c	2/3c
8 oz SLF Tuna Ndle Casserole	6 oz LF Tuna Ndle Casserole	8 oz LF Tuna Ndle Casserole	6 oz	8 oz	8 oz	8 oz
1/2c Julienne Beets	1/2c LF Julienne Beets	1/2c DB Julienne Beets	1/2c	1/2c	1/2c	1/2c
1 SFT Refined Dinner Roll	1 Dinner Roll	1 Dinner Roll	0	1 sm	1 sm	1 sm
1 tsp Margarine	1 tsp Margarine	1 tsp Margarine	0	1 tsp	1 tsp	1 tsp
1/2c Milk (1/4c)[3]	1/2c Skim Milk	1/2c Skim Milk	1/2c	1/2c	1/2c	1/2c
Coffee/Tea/Decaf	Coffee/Tea/Decaf	Coffee/Tea/Decaf	free	free	free	free
1/2c Orange Sherbet	1/2c LF Sherbet	1/2c LF Sherbet	1/2c	1/2c	1/2c	1/2c
Milk[3] or STR Juice	Skim Milk or Juice	1/2c Skim Milk	1/2c	1/2c	1/2c	1/2c
Plain Cookies, Gelatin,	LF Cookies, LF Crackers,	1 Starch/Bread Exch	1	1	1	1
Plain Crackers, Banana,	Gelatin, Fresh Fruit	1 Meat Exch	0	0	0	1
Vanilla Ice Cream[3]		1 Fat Exch	0	0	1	1

Recipe	Regular, Liberal Bland[1], No Added Salt[2]	1–2 gm Na (Low Sodium)	Mechanical Soft	Puree
	Breakfast			
	1/2c Pineapple Juice or	1/2c Pineapple Juice or	1/2c Pineapple Juice or	1/2c STR Pineapple Jce or
	1 small Banana	1 small Banana	1 small Banana	1 small Banana-Mashed
B1	1/2c Cream of Wheat or	1/2c Cream of Wheat or	1/2c Cream of Wheat or	1c Cream of Wheat
	3/4c Asst Dry Cereals	3/4c SR Asst Dry Cereals	3/4c Asst Dry Cereals+	NO
B5	1 Scrambled Egg	1 Scrambled Egg	1 Scrambled Egg	1 Scrambled Egg
D33	1 Sausage Link[2]	NO	1 CHP Sausage Link	NO
	1 sl Toast	1 sl Toast	1 sl Bread	1 sl Bread+
	1 tsp Margarine	1 tsp SR Margarine	1 tsp Margarine	1 tsp Margarine
	1 tsp Jam/Jelly	1 tsp Jam/Jelly	1 tsp Jelly	1 tsp Jelly
	1c Milk	1c Milk	1c Milk	1c Milk
	Coffee/Tea/Decaf	Coffee/Tea/Decaf	Coffee/Tea/Decaf	Coffee/Tea/Decaf
	Lunch			
K28	1c Mixed Field Greens	1c Mixed Field Greens	1/2c Juice	1/2c STR Juice
P1–8	1 oz Salad Dressing	1 oz SR Salad Dressing	NO	NO
E8	3 oz Tahitian Chicken	3 oz SR Tahitian Chicken	3 oz CHP Tahitian Chicken	4 oz PUR Tahitian Chicken
	with 1 1/2 oz Sauce	with 1 1/2 oz SR Sauce	with 1 1/2 oz Sauce	with 1 1/2 oz STR Sauce
L5	1/2c Rice Pilaf	1/2c SR Rice Pilaf	1/2c SFT Rice Pilaf	1/2c PUR Rice Pilaf
J10,14	1/2c Steamed Broccoli	1/2c Steamed Broccoli	1/2c CHP Steamed Broccoli	1/2c PUR Steamed Broccoli
	1 Dinner Roll	1 Dinner Roll	1 SFT Dinner Roll+	1 sl Bread+
	1 tsp Margarine	1 tsp SR Margarine	1 tsp Margarine	1 tsp Margarine
	1/2c Milk	1/2c Milk	1/2c Milk	1/2c Milk
	Coffee/Tea/Decaf	Coffee/Tea/Decaf	Coffee/Tea/Decaf	Coffee/Tea/Decaf
S8	1/2c Almond Peaches	1/2c Almond Peaches	1/2c Sliced Peaches	1/2c PUR Peaches
	Dinner			
C28,1	2/3c French Vegetable Soup	2/3c SR French Veg Soup	2/3c French Vegetable Soup	2/3c PUR French Veg Soup
I2	3 oz Grilled Cheese	3 oz SR Grilled Cheese	3 oz Grilled Cheese	1/2c PUR Cottage Cheese
	Sandwich, 2 sl Bread	Sandwich, 2 sl Bread	Sandwich, 2 sl Bread+	1 sl Bread+
J3	Lettuce Leaves	Lettuce Leaves	1/2c Green Beans	1/2c PUR Green Beans
J46	4 Tomato Slices	4 Tomato Slices	NO	1/2c Whipped Sweet Potatoes
P1–8	1 oz Salad Dressing	1 oz SR Salad Dressing	NO	1 tsp Margarine
	1/2c Milk	1/2c Milk	1/2c Milk	1/2c Milk
	Coffee/Tea/Decaf	Coffee/Tea/Decaf	Coffee/Tea/Decaf	Coffee/Tea/Decaf
Q4,S12	3×2" sl Carrot-Raisin Cake	3×2" sl Carrot-Raisin Cake	3×2" sl SFT Carrot Cake+	1/2c Gelatin
	Snacks			
	Milk or Juice	Juice	Milk or Juice	Milk or STR Juice
	Cookies, Crackers,	SR Cookies, SR Crackers,	Plain Cookies, Gelatin,	Applesauce, SFT Banana,
	Gelatin, Ice Cream,	Gelatin, Fresh Fruit	Plain Crackers+, Ice Cream,	Gelatin, Ice Cream
	Fresh Fruit		Banana	

TERMS: SFT = Soft; SLF = Soft/Low Fiber; GRD = Ground; CHP = Chopped Finely; PUR = Puree; STR = Strained; SR = Sodium or Salt Restricted; LF = Low Fat; FF = Fat Free; LCH = Low Cholesterol; DB = Diabetic; UNSW = Unsweetened; RC = Reduced Calorie; LC = Low Calorie; EXCH = Diabetic Exchange

SERVING UTENSILS: #6 Scoop = 2/3 cup-6 oz; #8 Scoop = 1/2 cup-4 oz; #10 Scoop = 3/8 cup-3 to 4 oz; #12 Scoop = 1/3 cup-2.5 to 3 oz; #16 Scoop = 1/4 cup-2 oz; #30 Scoop = 2 tbsp-1 oz; #60 Scoop = 1 tbsp-1/2 oz. Ounces will vary, based on food used.

1. *Liberal Bland:* Follow a regular diet. Use decaffeinated products. Omit pepper and chili powder.

2. *No Added Salt (3–4 gm NA):* Follow a regular diet. Use SR soups and SR canned meats. Omit salt packets (and shakers), bacon, sausage, smoked, and cured meats, substitute with SR food choices.

3. *Low Fiber:* Follow a soft diet. Do not exceed 2 cups of milk per day. Soft/Low Fiber—Omit pepper, garlic, and onions from recipes.

4. *2200 Calorie Diet:* Follow 2000 calorie diet with the following additions: Lunch—add 1 bread exchange and 1 fat exchange; Dinner—add 1 bread exchange.

+Consider individual tolerance. Daily Alternatives: Lunch and Dinner—Chicken, Hamburger, Cottage Cheese Fruit Plate, or Assorted Sandwiches. Individual preferences are provided upon request.

Amounts specified for food items that contain bone is equivalent to cooked, edible deboned portion.

Soft, Low Fiber[3]	Low Cholesterol, Low Fat (40–50 gm)	No Concentrated Sweets (Diabetic)	1200	1500	1800	2000[4]
				Diabetic/Calorie-Controlled		
1/2c STR Cranberry Juice or	1/2c Pineapple Juice or	1/2c UNSW Pineapple Jce or	1/2c	1/2c	1/2c	1/2c
1 small Banana	1 small Banana	1 small Banana	1/2	1/2	1/2	1/2
1/2c Cream of Wheat or	1/2c LF Cream of Wheat or	1/2c DB Cream of Wheat or	1/2c	1/2c	1/2c	1/2c
3/4c Asst Refined Cereals	3/4c Dry Cereals	3/4c UNSW Dry Cereals	3/4c	3/4c	3/4c	3/4c
1 Scrambled Egg	1 Egg Substitute	1 Scrambled Egg	1	1	1	1
NO	NO	1 Sausage Link	0	0	0	0
1 sl White Toast	1 sl Toast	1 sl Toast	1 sl	1 sl	2 sl	2 sl
1 tsp Margarine	1 tsp Margarine	1 tsp Margarine	0	1 tsp	1 tsp	1 tsp
1 tsp Jelly	1 tsp Jam/Jelly	1 tsp DB Jam/Jelly	1 tsp	1 tsp	1 tsp	1 tsp
1c Milk	1c Skim Milk	1c Skim Milk	1/2c	1/2c	1/2c	1c
Coffee/Tea/Decaf	Coffee/Tea/Decaf	Coffee/Tea/Decaf	free	free	free	free
1/2c STR Juice	1c Mixed Field Greens	1c Mixed Field Greens	1c	1c	1c	1c
NO	1 Tbsp LC Salad Dressing	1 Tbsp LC Sld Dressing	1 Tbsp	1 Tbsp	2 Tbsp	2 Tbsp
3 oz SLF Tahitian Chicken	2 oz LF Tahitian Chicken	3 oz LF Tahitian Chicken	2 oz	3 oz	3 oz	3 oz
NO	with 1 1/2 oz LF Sauce	with 1 1/2 oz LF Sauce	1 1/2 oz	1 1/2 oz	1 1/2 oz	1 1/2 oz
1/2c SFT Rice Pilaf	1/2c Rice Pilaf+	1/2c Rice Pilaf	1/3c	1/3c	1/3c	2/3c
1/2c Carrots	1/2c LF Steamed Broccoli+	1/2c LF Steamed Broccoli	1/2c	1/2c	1/2c	1/2c
1 SFT Refined Dinner Roll	1 Dinner Roll	1 Dinner Roll	0	0	1 sm	1 sm
1 tsp Margarine	NO	1 tsp Margarine	0	0	1 tsp	1 tsp
1/2c Milk	1/2c Skim Milk	1/2c Skim Milk	1/2c	1/2c	1/2c	1/2c
Coffee/Tea/Decaf	Coffee/Tea/Decaf	Coffee/Tea/Decaf	free	free	free	free
1/2c Sliced Peaches	1/2c Sliced Peaches	1/2c Almond Peaches	1/2c	1/2c	1/2c	1/2c
2/3c SLF Broth	2/3c French Veg Soup+	2/3c French Veg Soup	2/3c	2/3c	2/3c	2/3c
3 oz Mild Grilled Cheese	2 oz LF Grilled Cheese	3 oz LF Grilled Cheese	2 oz	3 oz	3 oz	3 oz
Sandwich, 2 sl White Bread	Sandwich, 2 sl Bread	Sandwich, 2 sl Bread	2sl diet	2 sl	2 sl	2 sl
1/2c Green Beans	Lettuce Leaves	Lettuce Leaves	Lett	Lett	Lett	Lett
NO	4 Tomato Slices	4 Tomato Slices	4 sl	4 sl	4 sl	4 sl
NO	1 Tbsp LC Salad Dressing	1 Tbsp LC Sld Dressing	1 Tbsp	1 Tbsp	1 Tbsp	1 Tbsp
1/2c Milk	1/2c Skim Milk	1/2c Skim Milk	1/2c	1/2c	1/2c	1/2c
Coffee/Tea/Decaf	Coffee/Tea/Decaf	Coffee/Tea/Decaf	free	free	free	free
1/2c Gelatin	3×2" sl LF Carrot-Raisin Cake	3×2" sl DB Carrot-Raisin Cake	2×2"	3×2"	3×2"	3×2"
Milk[3] or STR Juice	Skim Milk or Juice	1/2c Skim Milk	1/2c	1/2c	1/2c	1/2c
Plain Cookies, Gelatin,	LF Cookies, LF Crackers,	1 Starch/Bread Exch	1	1	1	1
Plain Crackers, Banana,	Gelatin, Fresh Fruit	1 Meat Exch	0	0	0	1
Vanilla Ice Cream[3]		1 Fat Exch	0	0	1	1

Recipe	Regular, Liberal Bland[1], No Added Salt[2]	1–2 gm Na (Low Sodium)	Mechanical Soft	Puree
	Breakfast			
B1	1/2c Grapefruit Juice	1/2c Grapefruit Juice	1/2c Grapefruit Juice	1/2c STR Grapefruit Juice
	1/2c Farina or	1/2c Farina or	1/2c Farina or	1c Farina
	3/4c Asst Dry Cereals	3/4c SR Asst Dry Cereals	3/4c Asst Dry Cereals+	NO
B4	1 Soft-Cooked Egg	1 Soft-Cooked Egg	1 Soft-Cooked Egg	1 Soft-Cooked Egg
	1 sl Toast	1 sl Toast	1 sl Bread	1 sl Bread+
	1 tsp Margarine	1 tsp SR Margarine	1 tsp Margarine	1 tsp Margarine
	1 tsp Jam/Jelly	1 tsp Jam/Jelly	1 tsp Jelly	1 tsp Jelly
	1c Milk	1c Milk	1c Milk	1c Milk
	Coffee/Tea/Decaf	Coffee/Tea/Decaf	Coffee/Tea/Decaf	Coffee/Tea/Decaf
	Lunch			
K2	1/2c Pickled Beets	1/2c SR Beets	1/2c Pickled Beets+	1/2c PUR Pickled Beets
D2	8 oz Beef Stew	8 oz Beef Stew	8 oz Beef Stew	8 oz PUR Beef Stew
M1	1/2c Noodles	1/2c Noodles	1/2c Noodles	1/2c PUR Noodles
N1	1 Biscuit	1 SR Biscuit	1 Biscuit	1 sl Bread+
	1 tsp Margarine	1 tsp SR Margarine	1 tsp Margarine	1 tsp Margarine
	1/2c Milk	1/2c Milk	1/2c Milk	1/2c Milk
	Coffee/Tea/Decaf	Coffee/Tea/Decaf	Coffee/Tea/Decaf	Coffee/Tea/Decaf
	2 Pear Halves	2 Pear Halves	2 Pear Halves	1/2c PUR Pears
	Dinner			
C8	2/3c Chicken-Rice Soup	2/3c SR Chicken-Rice Soup	2/3c Chicken-Rice Soup	2/3c PUR/STR Soup
E16	3 oz Hot Turkey with	3 oz Hot Turkey with	3 oz Hot Turkey with	4 oz PUR Hot Turkey with
O5	2 oz Chicken Gravy on	2 oz SR Chicken Gravy on	2 oz Chicken Gravy	2 oz STR Chicken Gravy
	1 sl Bread	1 sl Bread	1 sl Bread	1 sl Bread+
J37	1/2c Mashed Potatoes	1/2c Mashed Potatoes	1/2c Mashed Potatoes	1/2c Mashed Potatoes
J27,47	1/2c Mixed Vegetables	1/2c Mixed Vegetables	1/2c Mixed Vegetables+	1/2c PUR Mixed Vegetables
	1 tsp Margarine	1 tsp SR Margarine	1 tsp Margarine	1 tsp Margarine
	1/2c Milk	1/2c Milk	1/2c Milk	1/2c Milk
	Coffee/Tea/Decaf	Coffee/Tea/Decaf	Coffee/Tea/Decaf	Coffee/Tea/Decaf
Q18	2 Sugar Cookies	2 Sugar Cookies	2 Sugar Cookies+	1/2c PUR Pineapple
	Snacks			
	Milk or Juice	Juice	Milk or Juice	Milk or STR Juice
	Cookies, Crackers,	SR Cookies, SR Crackers,	Plain Cookies, Gelatin,	Applesauce, SFT Banana,
	Gelatin, Ice Cream,	Gelatin, Fresh Fruit	Plain Crackers+, Ice Cream,	Gelatin, Ice Cream
	Fresh Fruit		Banana	

TERMS: SFT = Soft; SLF = Soft/Low Fiber; GRD = Ground; CHP = Chopped Finely; PUR = Puree; STR = Strained; SR = Sodium or Salt Restricted; LF = Low Fat; FF = Fat Free; LCH = Low Cholesterol; DB = Diabetic; UNSW = Unsweetened; RC = Reduced Calorie; LC = Low Calorie; EXCH = Diabetic Exchange

SERVING UTENSILS: #6 Scoop = 2/3 cup-6 oz; #8 Scoop = 1/2 cup-4 oz; #10 Scoop = 3/8 cup-3 to 4 oz; #12 Scoop = 1/3 cup-2.5 to 3 oz; #16 Scoop = 1/4 cup-2 oz; #30 Scoop = 2 tbsp-1 oz; #60 Scoop = 1 tbsp-1/2 oz. Ounces will vary, based on food used.

1. *Liberal Bland:* Follow a regular diet. Use decaffeinated products. Omit pepper and chili powder.

2. *No Added Salt (3–4 gm NA):* Follow a regular diet. Use SR soups and SR canned meats. Omit salt packets (and shakers), bacon, sausage, smoked, and cured meats, substitute with SR food choices.

3. *Low Fiber:* Follow a soft diet. Do not exceed 2 cups of milk per day. Soft/Low Fiber—Omit pepper, garlic, and onions from recipes.

4. *2200 Calorie Diet:* Follow 2000 calorie diet with the following additions: Lunch—add 1 bread exchange and 1 fat exchange; Dinner—add 1 bread exchange.

+Consider individual tolerance. Daily Alternatives: Lunch and Dinner—Chicken, Hamburger, Cottage Cheese Fruit Plate, or Assorted Sandwiches, Individual preferences are provided upon request.

Amounts specified for food items that contain bone is equivalent to cooked, edible deboned portion.

Soft, Low Fiber[3]	Low Cholesterol, Low Fat (40–50 gm)	No Concentrated Sweets (Diabetic)	1200	1500	1800	2000[4]
			Diabetic/Calorie-Controlled			
1/2c STR Grapefruit Juice	1/2c Grapefruit Juice	1/2c UNSW Grapefruit Juice	1/2c	1/2c	1/2c	1/2c
1/2c Farina or	1/2c LF Farina or	1/2c DB Farina or	1/2c	1/2c	1/2c	1/2c
3/4c Asst Refined Cereals	3/4c Dry Cereals	3/4c UNSW Dry Cereals	3/4c	3/4c	3/4c	3/4c
1 Soft-Cooked Egg	1 Egg Substitute	1 Soft-Cooked Egg	1	1	1	1
1 sl White Toast	1 sl Toast	1 sl Toast	1 sl	1 sl	1 sl	2 sl
1 tsp Margarine	1 tsp Margarine	1 tsp Margarine	0	0	1 tsp	1 tsp
1 tsp Jelly	1 tsp Jam/Jelly	1 tsp DB Jam/Jelly	1 tsp	1 tsp	1 tsp	1 tsp
1c Milk	1c Skim Milk	1c Skim Milk	1/2c	1/2c	1/2c	1c
Coffee/Tea/Decaf	Coffee/Tea/Decaf	Coffee/Tea/Decaf	free	free	free	free
1/2c SLF Pickled Beets	1/2c Pickled Beets	1/2c DB Pickled Beets	1/2c	1/2c	1/2c	1/2c
8 oz SLF Beef Stew	6 oz Beef Stew	8 oz Beef Stew	6 oz	8 oz	8 oz	8 oz
1/2c Noodles	1/2c Noodles	1/2c Noodles	1/4c	1/2c	1/2c	1/2c
1 Biscuit	1 Biscuit	1 Biscuit	0	0	1	1
1 tsp Margarine	NO	1 tsp Margarine	0	0	1 tsp	1 tsp
1/2c Milk	1/2c Skim Milk	1/2c Skim Milk	1/2c	1/2c	1/2c	1/2c
Coffee/Tea/Decaf	Coffee/Tea/Decaf	Coffee/Tea/Decaf	free	free	free	free
2 Pear Halves	2 Pear Halves	2 UNSW Pear Halves	2	2	2	2
2/3c SLF Chicken-Rice Soup	2/3c Chicken-Rice Soup+	2/3c Chicken-Rice Soup	2/3c	2/3c	2/3c	2/3c
3 oz Hot Turkey with	2 oz Hot Turkey with	3 oz Hot Turkey with	2 oz	3 oz	3 oz	3 oz
2 oz Chicken Gravy on	2 oz LF Chicken Gravy on	2 oz LF Chicken Gravy on	2 Tbsp	2 Tbsp	2 oz	2 oz
1 sl White Bread	1 sl Bread	1 sl Bread	0	1 sl	1 sl	1 sl
1/2c Mashed Potatoes	1/2c LF Mashed Potatoes	1/2c LF Mashed Potatoes	1/4c	1/2c	1/2c	1/2c
1/2c Spinach	1/2c Mixed Vegetables+	1/2c Mixed Vegetables	1/4c	1/4c	1/2c	1/2c
1 tsp Margarine	NO	1 tsp Margarine	0	0	0	0
1/2c Milk	1/2c Skim Milk	1/2c Skim Milk	1/2c	1/2c	1/2c	1/2c
Coffee/Tea/Decaf	Coffee/Tea/Decaf	Coffee/Tea/Decaf	free	free	free	free
2 Sugar Cookies	4 Vanilla Wafers	4 Vanilla Wafers	3	3	3	5
Milk[3] or STR Juice	Skim Milk or Juice	1/2c Skim Milk	1/2c	1/2c	1/2c	1/2c
Plain Cookies, Gelatin,	LF Cookies, LF Crackers,	1 Starch/Bread Exch	1	1	1	1
Plain Crackers, Banana,	Gelatin, Fresh Fruit	1 Meat Exch	0	0	0	1
Vanilla Ice Cream[3]		1 Fat Exch	0	0	1	1

Recipe	Regular, Liberal Bland[1], No Added Salt[2]	1–2 gm Na (Low Sodium)	Mechanical Soft	Puree
	Breakfast			
B1	1/2c Cranberry Juice	1/2c Cranberry Juice	1/2c Cranberry Juice	1/2c STR Cranberry Juice
	1/2c Wheatena or	1/2c Wheatena or	1/2c Wheatena or	1c Wheatena
	3/4 Asst Dry Cereals	3/4c SR Asst Dry Cereals	3/4c Asst Dry Cereals+	NO
	1 Tbsp Peanut Butter &	1 Tbsp SR Peanut Butter &	1 Tbsp Smth Peanut Btter &	1/4c PUR Cottage Cheese
	1 Tbsp Jelly on	1 Tbsp Jelly on	1 Tbsp Jelly on	1 Tbsp Jelly
	1 sl Raisin Bread	1 sl Raisin Bread	1 sl White Bread	1 sl Bread+
	1 tsp Margarine	1 tsp SR Margarine	1 tsp Margarine	1 tsp Margarine
	1c Milk	1c Milk	1c Milk	1c Milk
	Coffee/Tea/Decaf	Coffee/Tea/Decaf	Coffee/Tea/Decaf	Coffee/Tea/Decaf
	Lunch			
K31	1c Hawaiian Tossed Salad	1c Hawaiian Tossed Salad	1/2c Juice	1/2c STR Juice
D27	3 1/2 oz Veal Patty with	3 1/2 oz Veal Patty with	3 1/2 oz Veal Patty with	4 oz PUR Veal Patty with
O13	2 oz Mushroom Gravy	2 oz SR Mushroom Gravy	2 oz SFT Mushroom Gravy	2 oz STR Mushroom Gravy
J24,3	1/2c Corn Confetti	1/2c SR Corn Confetti	1/2c PUR Corn Confetti+	1/2c PUR Corn Confetti
J50	1/2c Stewed Tomatoes	1/2c SR Stewed Tomatoes	1/2c Stewed Tomatoes	1/2c PUR Stewed Tomatoes
	1 Dinner Roll	1 Dinner Roll	1 SFT Dinner Roll+	1 sl Bread+
	1 tsp Margarine	1 tsp SR Margarine	1 tsp Margarine	1 tsp Margarine
	1/2c Milk	1/4c Milk	1/2c Milk	1/2c Milk
	Coffee/Tea/Decaf	Coffee/Tea/Decaf	Coffee/Tea/Decaf	Coffee/Tea/Decaf
	1/2c Ice Cream	1/2c Ice Cream	1/2c Ice Cream	1/2c Ice Cream
	Dinner			
C13	2/3c Cream Spinach Soup	2/3c Crm Spinach Soup	2/3c Cream Spinach Soup	2/3c PUR/STR Crm Spnch Soup
I9,6	1/2c Egg Salad	1/2c SR Egg Salad	1/2c SFT Egg Salad	1/2c PUR Egg Salad
	Lettuce Leaves	Lettuce Leaves	CHP Lettuce Leaves	NO
	1 Radish Rose	1 Radish Rose	1/2c Juice	1/2c STR Juice
	3 Cucumber Slices	3 Cucumber Slices	NO	NO
K13	1/2c Macaroni Salad	1/2c Macaroni Salad	1/2c SFT Macaroni Salad	1/2c PUR Macaroni Salad
	1 Dinner Roll	1 Dinner Roll	1 SFT Dinner Roll+	1 sl Bread+
	1 tsp Margarine	1 tsp SR Margarine	1 tsp Margarine	1 tsp Margarine
	1/2c Milk	1/4c Milk	1/2c Milk	1/2c Milk
	Coffee/Tea/Decaf	Coffee/Tea/Decaf	Coffee/Tea/Decaf	Coffee/Tea/Decaf
	1/2c Fruit Cocktail	1/2c Fruit Cocktail	1/2c Fruit Cocktail	1/2c PUR Fruit Cocktail
	Snacks			
	Milk or Juice	Juice	Milk or Juice	Milk or STR Juice
	Cookies, Crackers,	SR Cookies, SR Crackers,	Plain Cookies, Gelatin,	Applesauce, SFT Banana,
	Gelatin, Ice Cream,	Gelatin, Fresh Fruit	Plain Crackers+, Ice Cream,	Gelatin, Ice Cream
	Fresh Fruit		Banana	

TERMS: SFT = Soft; SLF = Soft/Low Fiber; GRD = Ground; CHP = Chopped Finely; PUR = Puree; STR = Strained; SR = Sodium or Salt Restricted; LF = Low Fat; FF = Fat Free; LCH = Low Cholesterol; DB = Diabetic; UNSW = Unsweetened; RC = Reduced Calorie; LC = Low Calorie; EXCH = Diabetic Exchange

SERVING UTENSILS: #6 Scoop = 2/3 cup-6 oz; #8 Scoop = 1/2 cup-4 oz; #10 Scoop = 3/8 cup-3 to 4 oz; #12 Scoop = 1/3 cup-2.5 to 3 oz; #16 Scoop = 1/4 cup-2 oz; #30 Scoop = 2 tbsp-1 oz; #60 Scoop = 1 tbsp-1/2 oz. Ounces will vary, based on food used.

1. *Liberal Bland:* Follow a regular diet. Use decaffeinated products. Omit pepper and chili powder.

2. *No Added Salt (3–4 gm NA):* Follow a regular diet. Use SR soups and SR canned meats. Omit salt packets (and shakers), bacon, sausage, smoked, and cured meats, substitute with SR food choices.

3. *Low Fiber:* Follow a soft diet. Do not exceed 2 cups of milk per day. Soft/Low Fiber—Omit pepper, garlic, and onions from recipes.

4. *2200 Calorie Diet:* Follow 2000 calorie diet with the following additions: Lunch—add 1 bread exchange and 1 fat exchange; Dinner—add 1 bread exchange.

+Consider individual tolerance. Daily Alternatives: Lunch and Dinner—Chicken, Hamburger, Cottage Cheese Fruit Plate, or Assorted Sandwiches, Individual preferences are provided upon request.

Amounts specified for food items that contain bone is equivalent to cooked, edible deboned portion.

Soft, Low Fiber[3]	Low Cholesterol, Low Fat (40–50 gm)	No Concentrated Sweets (Diabetic)	1200	1500	1800	2000[4]
			Diabetic/Calorie-Controlled			
1/2c STR Cranberry Juice	1/2c Cranberry Juice	1/2c UNSW Cranberry Juice	1/3c	1/3c	1/3c	1/3c
1/2c Wheatena or	1/2c LF Wheatena or	1/2c DB Wheatena or	1/2c	1/2c	1/2c	1/2c
3/4c Asst Refined Cereals	3/4c Dry Cereals	3/4c UNSW Dry Cereals	3/4c	3/4c	3/4c	3/4c
1 Tbsp Smth Peanut Btter &	1/4c LF Cottage Cheese	1 Tbsp Peanut Butter &	1 Tbsp	1 Tbsp	1 Tbsp	1 Tbsp
1 Tbsp Jelly on	1 Tbsp Jelly	1 Tbsp DB Jelly	2 tsp	2 tsp	2 tsp	2 tsp
1 sl White Toast	1 sl Raisin Bread	1 sl Raisin Bread	1 sl	1 sl	1 sl	2 sl
1 tsp Margarine	NO	1 tsp Margarine	0	0	0	0
1c Milk	1c Skim Milk	1c Skim Milk	1/2c	1/2c	1/2c	1c
Coffee/Tea/Decaf	Coffee/Tea/Decaf	Coffee/Tea/Decaf	free	free	free	free
1/2c STR Juice	1c LF Hawaiian Tossed Sld	1c DB Hawaiian Tossed Sld	1c	1c	1c	1c
3 1/2 oz SLF Veal Patty with	2 1/2 oz LF Veal Patty with	3 1/2 oz Veal Patty with	2 1/2 oz	3 1/2 oz	3 1/2 oz	3 1/2 oz
2 oz SLF Mushroom Gravy	2 oz LF Mushroom Gravy	2 oz LF Mushroom Gravy	0	0	2 oz	2 oz
1/2c Green Beans	1/2c LF Corn Confetti	1/2c LF Corn Confetti	1/3c	1/3c	1/2c	1/2c
1/2c SLF Stewed Tomatoes	1/2c LF Stewed Tomatoes	1/2c DB Stewed Tomatoes	1/2c	1/2c	1/2c	1/2c
1 SFT Refined Dinner Roll	1 Dinner Roll	1 Dinner Roll	0	1 sm	1 sm	1 sm
1 tsp Margarine	1 tsp Margarine	1 tsp Margarine	0	0	1 tsp	1 tsp
1/2c Milk (1/4c)[3]	1/2c Skim Milk	1/2c Skim Milk	1/2c	1/2c	1/2c	1/2c
Coffee/Tea/Decaf	Coffee/Tea/Decaf	Coffee/Tea/Decaf	free	free	free	free
1/2c Vanilla Ice Cream	1/2c LF Ice Milk	1/2c LF Ice Milk	1/2c	1/2c	1/2c	1/2c
2/3c SLF Cream Spinach Soup	2/3c LF Crm Spinach Soup	2/3c LF Crm Spinach Soup	Broth	2/3c	2/3c	2/3c
1/2c SFT Egg Salad	1/2c LF Chicken Salad	1/2c DB Egg Salad	1/2c	3/4c	3/4c	3/4c
NO	Lettuce Leaves	Lettuce Leaves	Lett	Lett	Lett	Lett
1/2c STR Juice	1 Radish Rose	1 Radish Rose	1	1	1	1
NO	3 Cucumber Slices	3 Cucumber Slices	3 sl	3 sl	3 sl	3 sl
1/2c SFT Macaroni Salad	1/2c LF Macaroni Salad	1/2c LF Macaroni Salad	1/3c	1/3c	1/2c	1/2c
1 SFT Refined Dinner Roll	1 Dinner Roll	1 Dinner Roll	0	1 sm	1 sm	1 sm
1 tsp Margarine	NO	1 tsp Margarine	0	0	1 tsp	1 tsp
1/2c Milk (1/4c)[3]	1/2c Skim Milk	1/2c Skim Milk	1/2c	1/2c	1/2c	1/2c
Coffee/Tea/Decaf	Coffee/Tea/Decaf	Coffee/Tea/Decaf	free	free	free	free
1/2c Fruit Cocktail	1/2c Fruit Cocktail	1/2c UNSW Fruit Cocktail	1/2c	1/2c	1/2c	1/2c
Milk[3] or STR Juice	Skim Milk or Juice	1/2c Skim Milk	1/2c	1/2c	1/2c	1/2c
Plain Cookies, Gelatin,	LF Cookies, LF Crackers,	1 Starch/Bread Exch	1	1	1	1
Plain Crackers, Banana,	Gelatin, Fresh Fruit	1 Meat Exch	0	0	0	1
Vanilla Ice Cream[3]		1 Fat Exch	0	0	1	1

Recipe	Regular, Liberal Bland[1], No Added Salt[2]	1–2 gm Na (Low Sodium)	Mechanical Soft	Puree
	Breakfast			
	1/2c Orange Juice or	1/2c Orange Juice or	1/2c Orange Juice or	1/2c STR Orange Juice
	1/2c Melon Cubes	1/2c Melon Cubes	1/2c Diced Melon+	NO
B1	1/2c Cream of Rice or	1/2c Cream of Rice or	1/2c Cream of Rice or	1c Cream of Rice
	3/4c Asst Dry Cereals	3/4c SR Asst Dry Cereals	3/4c Asst Dry Cereals+	NO
B4	1 Poached Egg	1 Poached Egg	1 Poached Egg	1 Poached Egg
N12	1 Blueberry Muffin	1 SR Blueberry Muffin	1 Blueberry Muffin	1 sl Bread+
	1 tsp Margarine	1 tsp SR Margarine	1 tsp Margarine	1 tsp Margarine
	1 tsp Jam/Jelly	1 tsp Jam/Jelly	1 tsp Jelly	1 tsp Jelly
	1c Milk	1c Milk	1c Milk	1c Milk
	Coffee/Tea/Decaf	Coffee/Tea/Decaf	Coffee/Tea/Decaf	Coffee/Tea/Decaf
	Lunch			
K22	1/2c Three Bean Salad	1/2c SR Three Bean Salad	1/2c Juice	1/2c STR Juice
D37,E16	3 oz Braised Liver with	3 oz Braised Liver with	3 oz Braised Liver with	4 oz PUR Braised Liver
	1/4c Sautéed Onions	1/4c Sautéed Onions	1/4c CHP Sautéed Onions	NO
M2	1/2c Lyonnaise Noodles	1/2c SR Lyonnaise Noodles	1/2c Lyonnaise Noodles	1/2c PUR Lyonnaise Noodles
J18	1/2c Sunshine Carrots	1/2c Sunshine Carrots	1/2c Sunshine Carrots	1/2c PUR Sunshine Carrots
	1 Dinner Roll	1 Dinner Roll	1 SFT Dinner Roll+	1 sl Bread+
	1 tsp Margarine	1 tsp SR Margarine	1 tsp Margarine	1 tsp Margarine
	1/2c Milk	1/2c Milk	1/2c Milk	1/2c Milk
	Coffee/Tea/Decaf	Coffee/Tea/Decaf	Coffee/Tea/Decaf	Coffee/Tea/Decaf
S2	1/2c Spiced Applesauce	1/2c Spiced Applesauce	1/2c Spiced Applesauce	1/2c Spiced Applesauce
	Dinner			
C21,1	2/3c Minestrone Soup	2/3c SR Minestrone Soup	2/3c Minestrone Soup	2/3c PUR/STR Minstrne Soup
M1	1/2c Spaghetti	1/2c Spaghetti	1/2c Spaghetti	1/2c PUR Spaghetti
D13	3 oz Meatballs	3 oz Meatballs	3 oz Meatballs	3 oz PUR Meatballs
O20,19	2 oz Marinara Sauce	2 oz SR Marinara Sauce	2 oz PUR/STR Marinara Sauce	2 oz PUR/STR Marinara Sauce
J26,52	1/2c Italian Mix Vegtbles	1/2c Italian Mix Vegtbles	1/2c Italian Mix Vegtbles	1/2c PUR Italian Mix Veg
	1 sl Italian Bread	1 sl Italian Bread	1 SFT Dinner Roll	1 sl Bread+
	1 tsp Margarine	1 tsp SR Margarine	1 tsp Margarine	1 tsp Margarine
	1/2c Milk	1/4c Milk	1/2c Milk	1/2c Milk
	Coffee/Tea/Decaf	Coffee/Tea/Decaf	Coffee/Tea/Decaf	Coffee/Tea/Decaf
R4	1/8 Lemon Pie	1/8 Lemon Pie	1/8 Lemon Pie	1/2c Lemon Pudding
	Snacks			
	Milk or Juice	Juice	Milk or Juice	Milk or STR Juice
	Cookies, Crackers,	SR Cookies, SR Crackers,	Plain Cookies, Gelatin,	Applesauce, SFT Banana,
	Gelatin, Ice Cream,	Gelatin, Fresh Fruit	Plain Crackers+, Ice Cream,	Gelatin, Ice Cream
	Fresh Fruit		Banana	

TERMS: SFT = Soft; SLF = Soft/Low Fiber; GRD = Ground; CHP = Chopped Finely; PUR = Puree; STR = Strained; SR = Sodium or Salt Restricted; LF = Low Fat; FF = Fat Free; LCH = Low Cholesterol; DB = Diabetic; UNSW = Unsweetened; RC = Reduced Calorie; LC = Low Calorie; EXCH = Diabetic Exchange
SERVING UTENSILS: #6 Scoop = 2/3 cup-6 oz; #8 Scoop = 1/2 cup-4 oz; #10 Scoop = 3/8 cup-3 to 4 oz; #12 Scoop = 1/3 cup-2.5 to 3 oz; #16 Scoop = 1/4 cup-2 oz; #30 Scoop = 2 tbsp-1 oz; #60 Scoop = 1 tbsp-1/2 oz. Ounces will vary, based on food used.
1. *Liberal Bland:* Follow a regular diet. Use decaffeinated products. Omit pepper and chili powder.
2. *No Added Salt (3–4 gm NA):* Follow a regular diet. Use SR soups and SR canned meats. Omit salt packets (and shakers), bacon, sausage, smoked, and cured meats, substitute with SR food choices.
3. *Low Fiber:* Follow a soft diet. Do not exceed 2 cups of milk per day. Soft/Low Fiber—Omit pepper, garlic, and onions from recipes.
4. *2200 Calorie Diet:* Follow 2000 calorie diet with the following additions: Lunch—add 1 bread exchange and 1 fat exchange; Dinner—add 1 bread exchange.
+Consider individual tolerance. Daily Alternatives: Lunch and Dinner—Chicken, Hamburger, Cottage Cheese Fruit Plate, or Assorted Sandwiches. Individual preferences are provided upon request.
Amounts specified for food items that contain bone is equivalent to cooked, edible deboned portion.

Soft, Low Fiber[3]	Low Cholesterol, Low Fat (40–50 gm)	No Concentrated Sweets (Diabetic)	1200	1500	1800	2000[4]
			Diabetic/Calorie-Controlled			
1/2c STR Orange Juice	1/2c Orange Juice or	1/2c UNSW Orange Juice or	1/2c	1/2c	1/2c	1/2c
NO	1/2c Melon Cubes	1/2c Melon Cubes	1c	1c	1c	1c
1/2c Cream of Rice or	1/2c LF Cream of Rice or	1/2c DB Cream of Rice or	1/2c	1/2c	1/2c	1/2c
3/4c Asst Refined Cereals	3/4c Dry Cereals	3/4c UNSW Dry Cereals	3/4c	3/4c	3/4c	3/4c
1 Poached Egg	1 Egg Substitute	1 Poached Egg	1	1	1	1
1 sl White Toast	1 sm LF Blueberry Muffin	1 sm DB Blueberry Muffin	1 sm	1 sm	1 sm	2 sm
1 tsp Margarine	1 tsp Margarine	1 tsp Margarine	0	1 tsp	1 tsp	1 tsp
1 tsp Jelly	1 tsp Jam/Jelly	1 tsp DB Jam/Jelly	1 tsp	1 tsp	1 tsp	1 tsp
1c Milk	1c Skim Milk	1c Skim Milk	1/2c	1/2c	1/2c	1c
Coffee/Tea/Decaf	Coffee/Tea/Decaf	Coffee/Tea/Decaf	free	free	free	free
1/2c STR Juice	1/2c LF Three Bean Salad	1/2c DB Three Bean Salad	1/2c	1/2c	1/2c	1/2c
3 oz Braised Liver	2 oz Sliced Turkey with	3 oz DB Braised Liver with	2 oz	3 oz	3 oz	3 oz
NO	1/4c LF Sautéed Onions+	1/4c LF Sautéed Onions	0	1/4c	1/4c	1/4c
1/2c SLF Lyonnaise Noodles	1/2c LF Lyonnaise Noodles	1/2c LF Lyonnaise Noodles	1/2c	1/2c	1/2c	1/2c
1/2c Sunshine Carrots	1/2c LF Sunshine Carrots	1/2c DB Sunshine Carrots	1/2c	1/2c	1/2c	1/2c
1 SFT Refined Dinner Roll	1 Dinner Roll	1 Dinner Roll	0	1 sm	1 sm	1 sm
1 tsp Margarine	NO	1 tsp Margarine	0	0	1 tsp	1 tsp
1/2c Milk	1/2c Skim Milk	1/2c Skim Milk	1/2c	1/2c	1/2c	1/2c
Coffee/Tea/Decaf	Coffee/Tea/Decaf	Coffee/Tea/Decaf	free	free	free	free
1/2c Spiced Applesauce	1/2c Spiced Applesauce	1/2c DB Spiced Applesauce	1/2c	1/2c	1/2c	1/2c
2/3c SLF Broth	2/3c Minestrone Soup+	2/3c Minestrone Soup	STR	2/3c	2/3c	2/3c
1/2c Spaghetti	1/2c Spaghetti	1/2c Spaghetti	1/2c	1/2c	1/2c	1/2c
3 oz SLF Meatballs	2 oz LF Meatballs	3 oz Meatballs	2 oz	3 oz	3 oz	3 oz
2 oz SLF Italian Sauce	2 oz Marinara Sauce+	2 oz Marinara Sauce	1 oz	1 oz	2 oz	2 oz
1/2c Zucchini	1/2c Italian Mix Vegtbles	1/2c Italian Mix Vegtbles	1/2c	1/2c	1/2c	1/2c
1 SFT Refined Dinner Roll	1 sl Italian Bread	1 sl Italian Bread	0	0	1 sl	1 sl
1 tsp Margarine	NO	1 tsp Margarine	0	0	1 tsp	1 tsp
1/2c Milk (1/4c)[3]	1/2c Skim Milk	1/2c Skim Milk	1/2c	1/2c	1/2c	1/2c
Coffee/Tea/Decaf	Coffee/Tea/Decaf	Coffee/Tea/Decaf	free	free	free	free
1/8 Lemon Pie	1/8 LF Lemon Pie	1/8 DB Lemon Pie	1/8	1/8	1/8	1/8
Milk[3] or STR Juice	Skim Milk or Juice	1/2c Skim Milk	1/2c	1/2c	1/2c	1/2c
Plain Cookies, Gelatin,	LF Cookies, LF Crackers,	1 Starch/Bread Exch	1	1	1	1
Plain Crackers, Banana,	Gelatin, Fresh Fruit	1 Meat Exch	0	0	0	1
Vanilla Ice Cream[3]		1 Fat Exch	0	0	1	1

Recipe	Regular, Liberal Bland[1], No Added Salt[2]	1–2 gm Na (Low Sodium)	Mechanical Soft	Puree
	Breakfast			
	1/2c Apple Juice	1/2c Apple Juice	1/2c Apple Juice	1/2c STR Apple Juice
B1	1/2c Oatmeal or	1/2c Oatmeal or	1/2c Oatmeal or	1c Oatmeal
	3/4c Asst Dry Cereals	3/4c SR Asst Dry Cereals	3/4c Asst Dry Cereals+	NO
B4	1 Hard-Boiled Egg	1 Hard-Boiled Egg	1 Hard-Boiled Egg	1 Soft-Cooked Egg
	1 sl Toast	1 sl Toast	1 sl Bread	1 sl Bread+
	1 tsp Margarine	1 tsp SR Margarine	1 tsp Margarine	1 tsp Margarine
	1 tsp Jam/Jelly	1 tsp Jam/Jelly	1 tsp Jelly	1 tsp Jelly
	1c Milk	1c Milk	1c Milk	1c Milk
	Coffee/Tea/Decaf	Coffee/Tea/Decaf	Coffee/Tea/Decaf	Coffee/Tea/Decaf
	Lunch			
K24	1c Garden Salad	1c Garden Salad	1/2c Juice	1/2c STR Juice
P1–8	1 oz Salad Dressing	1 oz SR Salad Dressing	NO	NO
F3	3 oz Fish Creole with	3 oz SR Fish Creole with	3 oz Fish Creole with	3 oz PUR Fish Creole with
O7,22	2 oz Creole Sauce	2 oz SR Creole Sauce	2 oz Creole Sauce	2 oz PUR/STR Creole Sauce
L1	1/2c White Rice	1/2c White Rice	1/2c White Rice	1/2c PUR White Rice
J47	1/2c Spinach	1/2c Spinach	1/2c CHP Spinach	1/2c PUR Spinach
	1 Dinner Roll	1 Dinner Roll	1 SFT Dinner Roll+	1 sl Bread+
	1 tsp Margarine	1 tsp SR Margarine	1 tsp Margarine	1 tsp Margarine
	1/2c Milk	1/2c Milk	1/2c Milk	1/2c Milk
	Coffee/Tea/Decaf	Coffee/Tea/Decaf	Coffee/Tea/Decaf	Coffee/Tea/Decaf
	1/2c Chilled Apricots	1/2c Chilled Apricots	1/2c Chilled Apricots	1/2c PUR Chilled Apricots
	Dinner			
C7	2/3c Beef Noodle Soup	2/3c SR Beef Noodle Soup	2/3c Beef Noodle Soup	2/3c PUR/STR Soup
E5	3 oz Oven Crisp Chicken	3 oz Oven Crisp Chicken	4 oz CHP Oven Crisp Chix	4 oz PUR Oven Crisp Chix
J35	1 Baked Potato with	1 Baked Potato with	1 Baked Potato (no skin)	1/2c PUR Baked Potato
	1 oz Sour Cream	1 oz Sour Cream	1 oz Sour Cream	1 oz Sour Cream
J8	1/2c Julienne Beets	1/2c SR Julienne Beets	1/2c Julienne Beets	1/2c PUR Beets
	1 Dinner Roll	1 Dinner Roll	1 SFT Dinner Roll+	1 sl Bread+
	1 tsp Margarine	1 tsp SR Margarine	1 tsp Margarine	1 tsp Margarine
	1/2c Milk	1/2c Milk	1/2c Milk	1/2c Milk
	Coffee/Tea/Decaf	Coffee/Tea/Decaf	Coffee/Tea/Decaf	Coffee/Tea/Decaf
Q9	3/4" sl Pound Cake	3/4" sl Pound Cake	3/4" sl Pound Cake+	1/2c Applesauce
	Snacks			
	Milk or Juice	Juice	Milk or Juice	Milk or STR Juice
	Cookies, Crackers,	SR Cookies, SR Crackers,	Plain Cookies, Gelatin,	Applesauce, SFT Banana,
	Gelatin, Ice Cream,	Gelatin, Fresh Fruit	Plain Crackers+, Ice Cream,	Gelatin, Ice Cream
	Fresh Fruit		Banana	

TERMS: SFT = Soft; SLF = Soft/Low Fiber; GRD = Ground; CHP = Chopped Finely; PUR = Puree; STR = Strained; SR = Sodium or Salt Restricted; LF = Low Fat; FF = Fat Free; LCH = Low Cholesterol; DB = Diabetic; UNSW = Unsweetened; RC = Reduced Calorie; LC = Low Calorie; EXCH = Diabetic Exchange

SERVING UTENSILS: #6 Scoop = 2/3 cup-6 oz; #8 Scoop = 1/2 cup-4 oz; #10 Scoop = 3/8 cup-3 to 4 oz; #12 Scoop = 1/3 cup-2.5 to 3 oz; #16 Scoop = 1/4 cup-2 oz; #30 Scoop = 2 tbsp-1 oz; #60 Scoop = 1 tbsp-1/2 oz. Ounces will vary, based on food used.

1. *Liberal Bland:* Follow a regular diet. Use decaffeinated products. Omit pepper and chili powder.

2. *No Added Salt (3–4 gm NA):* Follow a regular diet. Use SR soups and SR canned meats. Omit salt packets (and shakers), bacon, sausage, smoked, and cured meats, substitute with SR food choices.

3. *Low Fiber:* Follow a soft diet. Do not exceed 2 cups of milk per day. Soft/Low Fiber—Omit pepper, garlic, and onions from recipes.

4. *2200 Calorie Diet:* Follow 2000 calorie diet with the following additions: Lunch—add 1 bread exchange and 1 fat exchange; Dinner—add 1 bread exchange.

+Consider individual tolerance. Daily Alternatives: Lunch and Dinner—Chicken, Hamburger, Cottage Cheese Fruit Plate, or Assorted Sandwiches, Individual preferences are provided upon request.

Amounts specified for food items that contain bone is equivalent to cooked, edible deboned portion.

Soft, Low Fiber[3]	Low Cholesterol, Low Fat (40–50 gm)	No Concentrated Sweets (Diabetic)	1200	1500	1800	2000[4]
			Diabetic/Calorie-Controlled			

Soft, Low Fiber[3]	Low Cholesterol, Low Fat (40–50 gm)	No Concentrated Sweets (Diabetic)	1200	1500	1800	2000[4]
1/2c STR Apple Juice	1/2c Apple Juice	1/2c UNSW Apple Juice	1/2c	1/2c	1/2c	1/2c
1/2c Oatmeal or	1/2c LF Oatmeal or	1/2c DB Oatmeal or	1/2c	1/2c	1/2c	1/2c
3/4c Asst Refined Cereals	3/4c Dry Cereals	3/4c UNSW Dry Cereals	3/4c	3/4c	3/4c	3/4c
1 Hard-Boiled Egg	1 Egg Substitute	1 Hard-Boiled Egg	1	1	1	1
1 sl White Toast	1 sl Toast	1 sl Toast	1 sl	1 sl	1 sl	2 sl
1 tsp Margarine	1 tsp Margarine	1 tsp Margarine	0	1 tsp	1 tsp	1 tsp
1 tsp Jelly	1 tsp Jam/Jelly	1 tsp DB Jam/Jelly	1 tsp	1 tsp	1 tsp	1 tsp
1c Milk	1c Skim Milk	1c Skim Milk	1/2c	1/2c	1/2c	1c
Coffee/Tea/Decaf	Coffee/Tea/Decaf	Coffee/Tea/Decaf	free	free	free	free
1/2c STR Juice	1c Garden Salad	1c Garden Salad	1c	1c	1c	1c
NO	1 Tbsp LC Salad Dressing	1 Tbsp LC Sld Dressing	1 Tbsp	1 Tbsp	1 Tbsp	1 Tbsp
3 oz Baked Fish Fillet with	3 oz LF Fish Creole with	3 oz DB Fish Creole with	2 oz	3 oz	3 oz	3 oz
2 oz SLF Tomato Sauce	2 oz LF Creole Sauce	2 oz DB Creole Sauce	1 1/2 oz	2 oz	2 oz	2 oz
1/2c White Rice	1/2c White Rice	1/2c White Rice	1/3c	1/3c	1/3c	1/3c
1/2c Spinach	1/2c Spinach	1/2c Spinach	1/2c	1/2c	1/2c	1/2c
1 SFT Refined Dinner Roll	1 Dinner Roll	1 Dinner Roll	0	0	1 sm	1 sm
1 tsp Margarine	NO	1 tsp Margarine	0	0	1 tsp	1 tsp
1/2c Milk	1/2c Skim Milk	1/2c Skim Milk	1/2c	1/2c	1/2c	1/2c
Coffee/Tea/Decaf	Coffee/Tea/Decaf	Coffee/Tea/Decaf	free	free	free	free
1/2c Chilled Apricots	1/2c Chilled Apricots	1/2c UNSW Chilled Apricots	1/2c	1/2c	1/2c	1/2c
2/3c SLF Beef Noodle Soup	2/3c Beef Noodle Soup	2/3c Beef Noodle Soup	2/3c	2/3c	2/3c	2/3c
3 oz SLF Oven Crisp Chicken	2 oz LF Oven Crisp Chicken	3 oz LF Oven Crisp Chicken	2 oz	3 oz	3 oz	3 oz
1 Baked Potato (no skin)	1 Baked Potato	1 Baked Potato with	1/2 sm	1 sm	1 sm	1 sm
1 Tbsp Sour Cream	NO	1 oz Sour Cream	0	1 Tbsp	1 oz	1 oz
1/2c Julienne Beets	1/2c LF Julienne Beets	1/2c LF Julienne Beets	1/2c	1/2c	1/2c	1/2c
1 SFT Refined Dinner Roll	1 Dinner Roll	1 Dinner Roll	0	0	1 sm	1 sm
1 tsp Margarine	1 tsp Margarine	1 tsp Margarine	0	0	1 tsp	1 tsp
1/2c Milk	1/2c Skim Milk	1/2c Skim Milk	1/2c	1/2c	1/2c	1/2c
Coffee/Tea/Decaf	Coffee/Tea/Decaf	Coffee/Tea/Decaf	free	free	free	free
3/4" sl Pound Cake	1/2" sl LF Pound Cake	3/4" sl DB Pound Cake	1/2" sl	1/2" sl	1/2" sl	1/2" sl
Milk[3] or STR Juice	Skim Milk or Juice	1/2c Skim Milk	1/2c	1/2c	1/2c	1/2c
Plain Cookies, Gelatin,	LF Cookies, LF Crackers,	1 Starch/Bread Exch	1	1	1	1
Plain Crackers, Banana,	Gelatin, Fresh Fruit	1 Meat Exch	0	0	0	1
Vanilla Ice Cream[3]		1 Fat Exch	0	0	1	1

Recipe	Regular, Liberal Bland[1], No Added Salt[2]	1–2 gm Na (Low Sodium)	Mechanical Soft	Puree
	Breakfast			
	1/2c Grapefruit Juice	1/2c Grapefruit Juice	1/2c Grapefruit Juice	1/2c STR Grapefruit Juice
B1	1/2c Cream of Wheat or	1/2c Cream of Wheat or	1c Cream of Wheat	1/2c Cream of Wheat or
	3/4c Asst Dry Cereals	3/4c SR Asst Dry Cereals	3/4c Asst Dry Cereals+	NO
B5	1 Scrambled Egg	1 Scrambled Egg	1 Scrambled Egg	1 Scrambled Egg
N7	1/2" sl Date Nut Bread	1/2" sl Date Nut Bread	1 sl Bread	1 sl Bread+
	1 oz Cream Cheese or	1 oz Cream Cheese or	1 oz Cream Cheese or	1 oz Cream Cheese or
	1 tsp Margarine	1 tsp SR Margarine	1 tsp Margarine	1 tsp Margarine
	1 tsp Jam/Jelly	1 tsp Jam/Jelly	1 tsp Jelly	1 tsp Jelly
	1c Milk	1c Milk	1c Milk	1c Milk
	Coffee/Tea/Decaf	Coffee/Tea/Decaf	Coffee/Tea/Decaf	Coffee/Tea/Decaf
	Lunch			
K3	1/2c Cabbage Apple Salad	1/2c SR Cabbage Apple Salad	1/2c Juice	1/2c STR Juice
D29	3 oz Breaded Pork Chops	3 oz Breaded Pork Chops	3 oz CHP Breaded Pork	4 oz PUR Breaded Pork
J46	1/2c Whip Sweet Potatoes	1/2c Whip Sweet Potato	1/2c Whip Sweet Potatoes	1/2c Whip Sweet Potatoes
J6	1/2c Seasoned Green Beans	1/2c Seasoned Green Beans	1/2c Seasoned Green Beans	1/2c PUR Seasoned Gr Beans
	1 Dinner Roll	1 Dinner Roll	1 SFT Dinner Roll+	1 sl Bread+
	1 tsp Margarine	1 tsp SR Margarine	1 tsp Margarine	1 tsp Margarine
	1/2c Milk	1/2c Milk	1/2c Milk	1/2c Milk
	Coffee/Tea/Decaf	Coffee/Tea/Decaf	Coffee/Tea/Decaf	Coffee/Tea/Decaf
	1/2c Sherbet	1/2c Sherbet	1/2c Sherbet	1/2c Sherbet
	Dinner			
C29	2/3c Old Fash Veg Soup	2/3c SR Old Fash Veg Soup	2/3c Old Fash Veg Soup	2/3c PUR/STR Veg Soup
G11	8 oz Macaroni & Cheese	6 oz SR Macaroni & Cheese	8 oz Macaroni & Cheese	8 oz PUR Macaroni & Cheese
J49,14	1/2c Succotash	1/2c SR Succotash	1/2c Succotash	1/2c PUR Succotash
	1 Dinner Roll	1 Dinner Roll	1 SFT Dinner Roll+	1 sl Bread+
	1 tsp Margarine	1 tsp SR Margarine	1 tsp Margarine	1 tsp Margarine
	1/2c Milk	1/2c Milk	1/2c Milk	1/2c Milk
	Coffee/Tea/Decaf	Coffee/Tea/Decaf	Coffee/Tea/Decaf	Coffee/Tea/Decaf
	2 Plums	2 Plums	2 Plums—No Skin	1/2c PUR Plums
	Snacks			
	Milk or Juice	Juice	Milk or Juice	Milk or STR Juice
	Cookies, Crackers,	SR Cookies, SR Crackers,	Plain Cookies, Gelatin,	Applesauce, SFT Banana,
	Gelatin, Ice Cream,	Gelatin, Fresh Fruit	Plain Crackers+, Ice Cream,	Gelatin, Ice Cream
	Fresh Fruit		Banana	

TERMS: SFT = Soft; SLF = Soft/Low Fiber; GRD = Ground; CHP = Chopped Finely; PUR = Puree; STR = Strained; SR = Sodium or Salt Restricted; LF = Low Fat; FF = Fat Free; LCH = Low Cholesterol; DB = Diabetic; UNSW = Unsweetened; RC = Reduced Calorie; LC = Low Calorie; EXCH = Diabetic Exchange

SERVING UTENSILS: #6 Scoop = 2/3 cup-6 oz; #8 Scoop = 1/2 cup-4 oz; #10 Scoop = 3/8 cup-3 to 4 oz; #12 Scoop = 1/3 cup-2.5 to 3 oz; #16 Scoop = 1/4 cup-2 oz; #30 Scoop = 2 tbsp-1 oz; #60 Scoop = 1 tbsp-1/2 oz. Ounces will vary, based on food used.

1. *Liberal Bland:* Follow a regular diet. Use decaffeinated products. Omit pepper and chili powder.

2. *No Added Salt (3–4 gm NA):* Follow a regular diet. Use SR soups and SR canned meats. Omit salt packets (and shakers), bacon, sausage, smoked, and cured meats, substitute with SR food choices.

3. *Low Fiber:* Follow a soft diet. Do not exceed 2 cups of milk per day. Soft/Low Fiber—Omit pepper, garlic, and onions from recipes.

4. *2200 Calorie Diet:* Follow 2000 calorie diet with the following additions: Lunch—add 1 bread exchange and 1 fat exchange; Dinner—add 1 bread exchange.

+Consider individual tolerance. Daily Alternatives: Lunch and Dinner—Chicken, Hamburger, Cottage Cheese Fruit Plate, or Assorted Sandwiches. Individual preferences are provided upon request.

Amounts specified for food items that contain bone is equivalent to cooked, edible deboned portion.

Soft, Low Fiber[3]	Low Cholesterol, Low Fat (40–50 gm)	No Concentrated Sweets (Diabetic)	1200	1500	1800	2000[4] Diabetic/Calorie-Controlled
1/2c STR Grapefruit Juice	1/2c Grapefruit Juice	1/2c UNSW Grapefruit Juice	1/2c	1/2c	1/2c	1/2c
1/2c LF Cream of Wheat or	1/2c DB Cream of Wheat or	1/2c	1/2c	1/2c	1/2c	
3/4c Asst Refined Cereals	3/4c Dry Cereals	3/4c UNSW Dry Cereals	3/4c	3/4c	3/4c	3/4c
1 Scrambled Egg	1 Egg Substitute	1 Scrambled Egg	1	1	1	1
1 sl White Toast	1/2" sl LF Date Bread	1/2" sl DB Date Nut Bread	1/2"	1/2"	1/2"	3/4"
1 oz Cream Cheese or	1 Tbsp Cream Cheese or	1 Tbsp Cream Cheese or	1 Tbsp	1 Tbsp	1 Tbsp	1 Tbsp
1 tsp Margarine	1 tsp Margarine	1 tsp Margarine	1 tsp	1 tsp	1 tsp	1 tsp
1 tsp Jelly	1 tsp Jam/Jelly	1 tsp DB Jam/Jelly	1 tsp	1 tsp	1 tsp	1 tsp
1c Milk	1c Skim Milk	1c Skim Milk	1/2c	1/2c	1/2c	1c
Coffee/Tea/Decaf	Coffee/Tea/Decaf	Coffee/Tea/Decaf	free	free	free	free
1/2c STR Juice	1/2c LF Cabbage Apple Salad+	1/2c DB Cabbage Apple Salad	lett	1/2c	1/2c	1/2c
3 oz SLF Breaded Pork Chops	2 oz LF Breaded Pork Chops	3 oz DB Breaded Pork Chops	2 oz	3 oz	3 oz	3 oz
1/2c Whip Sweet Potatoes	1/2c LF Whip Sweet Potato	1/2c LF Whip Sweet Potato	1/3c	1/3c	1/2c	1/2c
1/2c SLF Season Green Beans	1/2c LF Seasoned Gr Beans	1/2c LF Season Green Beans	1/2c	1/2c	1/2c	1/2c
1 SFT Refined Dinner Roll	1 Dinner Roll	1 Dinner Roll	0	1 sm	1 sm	1 sm
1 tsp Margarine	NO	1 tsp Margarine	0	1 tsp	1 tsp	1 tsp
1/2c Milk (1/4c)[3]	1/2c Skim Milk	1/2c Skim Milk	1/4c	1/4c	1/2c	1/2c
Coffee/Tea/Decaf	Coffee/Tea/Decaf	Coffee/Tea/Decaf	free	free	free	free
1/2c Orange Sherbet	1/2c LF Sherbet	1/2c LF Sherbet	1/3c	1/3c	1/2c	1/2c
2/3c SLF Old Fash Veg Soup	2/3c Old Fash Veg Soup+	2/3c Old Fash Veg Soup	2/3c	2/3c	2/3c	2/3c
8 oz SLF Macaroni-Cheese	6 oz LF Macaroni & Cheese	8 oz LF Macaroni & Cheese	6 oz	8 oz	8 oz	8 oz
1/2c Carrots	1/2c Succotash+	1/2c Succotash	1/2c	1/2c	1/2c	1/2c
1 SFT Refined Dinner Roll	1 Dinner Roll	1 Dinner Roll	0	0	1 sm	1 sm
1 tsp Margarine	NO	1 tsp Margarine	0	0	0	1 tsp
1/2c Milk	1/2c Skim Milk	1/2c Skim Milk	1/2c	1/2c	1/2c	1/2c
Coffee/Tea/Decaf	Coffee/Tea/Decaf	Coffee/Tea/Decaf	free	free	free	free
2 Plums—No Skin	2 Plums	2 UNSW Plums	2	2	2	2
Milk[3] or STR Juice	Skim Milk or Juice	1/2c Skim Milk	1/2c	1/2c	1/2c	1/2c
Plain Cookies, Gelatin,	LF Cookies, LF Crackers,	1 Starch/Bread Exch	1	1	1	1
Plain Crackers, Banana,	Gelatin, Fresh Fruit	1 Meat Exch	0	0	0	1
Vanilla Ice Cream[3]		1 Fat Exch	0	0	1	1

Recipe	Regular, Liberal Bland[1], No Added Salt[2]	1–2 gm Na (Low Sodium)	Mechanical Soft	Puree
	Breakfast			
B1	1/2c Pineapple Juice	1/2c Pineapple Juice	1/2c Pineapple Juice	1/2c STR Pineapple Juice
	1/2c Wheatena or	1/2c Wheatena or	1/2c Wheatena or	1c Wheatena
	3/4c Asst Dry Cereals	3/4c SR Asst Dry Cereals	3/4c Asst Dry Cereals+	NO
B8,4	1 sl French Toast	1 sl SR French Toast	1 sl French Toast+	1 Soft-Boiled Egg
	2 oz Maple Syrup	2 oz Maple Syrup	2 oz Maple Syrup	1 sl Bread+
	1 tsp Margarine	1 tsp SR Margarine	1 tsp Margarine	1 tsp Margarine
	1 tsp Jam/Jelly	1 tsp Jam/Jelly	1 tsp Jelly	1 tsp Jelly
	1c Milk	1c Milk	1c Milk	1c Milk
	Coffee/Tea/Decaf	Coffee/Tea/Decaf	Coffee/Tea/Decaf	Coffee/Tea/Decaf
	Lunch			
K26	1c Green Vegetable Salad	1c Green Vegetable Salad	1/2c Juice	1/2c STR Juice
P6	1 oz Oil & Vinegar	1 oz Oil & Vinegar	NO	NO
D19	3 oz Swiss Steak with	3 oz Swiss Steak with	3 oz Swiss Steak with	3 oz PUR Swiss Steak with
	1 1/2 oz Gravy	1 1/2 oz Gravy	1 1/2 oz Gravy	1 1/2 oz STR Gravy
J41	3 oz Parsley Potatoes	3 oz Parsley Potatoes	1/2c CHP Parsley Potatoes	1/2c PUR Parsley Potatoes
J54	1/2c Tarragon Zucchini	1/2c Tarragon Zucchini	1/2c SFT Tarragon Zucchini	1/2c PUR Tarragon Zucchini
	1 Dinner Roll	1 Dinner Roll	1 SFT Dinner Roll+	1 sl Bread+
	1 tsp Margarine	1 tsp SR Margarine	1 tsp Margarine	1 tsp Margarine
	1/2c Milk	1/2c Milk	1/2c Milk	1/2c Milk
	Coffee/Tea/Decaf	Coffee/Tea/Decaf	Coffee/Tea/Decaf	Coffee/Tea/Decaf
S7	1/2c Fruit Parfait with	1/2c Fruit Parfait with	1/2c Canned Fruit Cocktail	1/2c PUR Fruit Cocktail
	1 Tbsp Whipped Topping	1 Tbsp Whipped Topping	w/1 Tbsp Whipped Topping	w/1 Tbsp Whipped Topping
	Dinner			
C12	2/3c Cr of Mushroom Soup	2/3c Cr Mushroom Soup	2/3c Cr of Mushroom Soup	2/3c PUR/STR Cr Mshrm Soup
F1	3 1/2 oz Fishburger on	3 1/2 oz SR Fishburger on	3 1/2 oz Fishburger	3 1/2 oz PUR Fishburger
	1 Bun	1 Bun	1 Bun+	1 sl Bread+
O25	2 Tbsp Tartar Sauce[2]	1 Tbsp SR Mayonnaise	2 Tbsp Tartar Sauce	2 Tbsp Mayonnaise
	Lettuce Leaves	Lettuce Leaves	CHP Lettuce Leaves+	NO
J50	2 Tomato Slices	2 Tomato Slices	1/2c Stewed Tomatoes	1/2c PUR Stewed Tomatoes
K5J47	1/2c Cole Slaw	1/2c Cole Slaw	1/2c Cooked Spinach	1/2c PUR Spinach
	1/2c Milk	1/4c Milk	1/2c Milk	1/2c Milk
	Coffee/Tea/Decaf	Coffee/Tea/Decaf	Coffee/Tea/Decaf	Coffee/Tea/Decaf
S12	1/2c Cherry Gelatin	1/2c Cherry Gelatin	1/2c Cherry Gelatin	1/2c Cherry Gelatin
	Snacks			
	Milk or Juice	Juice	Milk or Juice	Milk or STR Juice
	Cookies, Crackers,	SR Cookies, SR Crackers,	Plain Cookies, Gelatin,	Applesauce, SFT Banana,
	Gelatin, Ice Cream,	Gelatin, Fresh Fruit	Plain Crackers +, Ice Cream,	Gelatin, Ice Cream
	Fresh Fruit		Banana	

TERMS: SFT = Soft; SLF = Soft/Low Fiber; GRD = Ground; CHP = Chopped Finely; PUR = Puree; STR = Strained; SR = Sodium or Salt Restricted; LF = Low Fat; FF = Fat Free; LCH = Low Cholesterol; DB = Diabetic; UNSW = Unsweetened; RC = Reduced Calorie; LC = Low Calorie; EXCH = Diabetic Exchange

SERVING UTENSILS: #6 Scoop = 2/3 cup-6 oz; #8 Scoop = 1/2 cup-4 oz; #10 Scoop = 3/8 cup-3 to 4 oz; #12 Scoop = 1/3 cup-2.5 to 3 oz; #16 Scoop = 1/4 cup-2 oz; #30 Scoop = 2 tbsp-1 oz; #60 Scoop = 1 tbsp-1/2 oz. Ounces will vary, based on food used.

1. *Liberal Bland:* Follow a regular diet. Use decaffeinated products. Omit pepper and chili powder.

2. *No Added Salt (3–4 gm NA):* Follow a regular diet. Use SR soups and SR canned meats. Omit salt packets (and shakers), bacon, sausage, smoked, and cured meats, substitute with SR food choices.

3. *Low Fiber:* Follow a soft diet. Do not exceed 2 cups of milk per day. Soft/Low Fiber—Omit pepper, garlic, and onions from recipes.

4. *2200 Calorie Diet:* Follow 2000 calorie diet with the following additions: Lunch—add 1 bread exchange and 1 fat exchange; Dinner—add 1 bread exchange.

+ Consider individual tolerance. Daily Alternatives: Lunch and Dinner—Chicken, Hamburger, Cottage Cheese Fruit Plate, or Assorted Sandwiches. Individual preferences are provided upon request.

Amounts specified for food items that contain bone is equivalent to cooked, edible deboned portion.

Soft, Low Fiber[3]	Low Cholesterol, Low Fat (40–50 gm)	No Concentrated Sweets (Diabetic)	1200	1500	1800	2000[4]
			Diabetic/Calorie-Controlled			

Soft, Low Fiber[3]	Low Cholesterol, Low Fat (40–50 gm)	No Concentrated Sweets (Diabetic)	1200	1500	1800	2000[4]
1/2c STR Apple Juice	1/2c Pineapple Juice	1/2c UNSW Pineapple Juice	1/2c	1/2c	1/2c	1/2c
1/2c Wheatena or	1/2c LF Wheatena or	1/2c DB Wheatena or	1/2c	1/2c	1/2c	1/2c
3/4c Asst Refined Cereals	3/4c Dry Cereals	3/4c UNSW Dry Cereals	3/4c	3/4c	3/4c	3/4c
1 sl French Toast	1 sl LF French Toast	1 sl French Toast	1	1	1	2
2 oz Maple Syrup	2 oz Maple Syrup	1 oz DB Maple Syrup	1 oz	1 oz	1 oz	1 oz
1 tsp Margarine	NO	1 tsp Margarine	0	1 tsp	1 tsp	2 tsp
1 tsp Jelly	1 tsp Jam/Jelly	1 tsp DB Jam/Jelly	1 tsp	1 tsp	1 tsp	1 tsp
1c Milk	1c Skim Milk	1c Skim Milk	1/2c	1/2c	1/2c	1c
Coffee/Tea/Decaf	Coffee/Tea/Decaf	Coffee/Tea/Decaf	free	free	free	free
1/2c STR Juice	1c Green Vegetable Salad	1c Green Vegetable Salad	1c	1c	1c	1c
NO	1 Tbsp LC Salad Dressing	1 Tbsp LC Salad Dressing	1 Tbsp	1 Tbsp	1 Tbsp	1 Tbsp
3 oz SLF Swiss Steak with	2 oz LF Swiss Steak with	3 oz LF Swiss Steak with	2 oz	3 oz	3 oz	3 oz
1 1/2 oz SLF Gravy	1 1/2 oz LF Gravy	1 1/2 oz LF Gravy	1 oz	1 1/2 oz	1 1/2 oz	1 1/2 oz
3 oz Parsley Potatoes	3 oz LF Parsley Potatoes	3 oz LF Parsley Potatoes	3 oz	3 oz	3 oz	3 oz
1/2c SFT Tarragon Zucchini	1/2c LF Tarragon Zucchini	1/2c LF Tarragon Zucchini	1/2c	1/2c	1/2c	1/2c
1 SFT Refined Dinner Roll	1 Dinner Roll	1 Dinner Roll	0	0	1 sm	1 sm
1 tsp Margarine	NO	1 tsp Margarine	0	0	1 tsp	1 tsp
1/2c Milk	1/2c Skim Milk	1/2c Skim Milk	1/2c	1/2c	1/2c	1/2c
Coffee/Tea/Decaf	Coffee/Tea/Decaf	Coffee/Tea/Decaf	free	free	free	free
1/2c Canned Fruit Cocktail	1/2c Fruit Parfait	1/2c Fruit Parfait with	1/3c	1/3c	1/2c	1/2c
w/1 Tbsp Whipped Topping	NO	1 Tbsp Whipped Topping	No	1 Tbsp	1 Tbsp	1 Tbsp
2/3c SLF Cr Mushroom Soup	2/3c LF Cr Mushroom Soup	2/3c LF Cr Mushroom Soup	2/3c	2/3c	2/3c	2/3c
3 1/2 oz SLF Fishburger	3 oz LF Fishburger	3 1/2 oz LF Fishburger on	3 oz	3 1/2 oz	3 1/2 oz	3 1/2 oz
1 SFT Refined Bun	1 Bun	1 Bun	1/2	1	1	1
2 Tbsp Mayonnaise	1 tsp LF Tartar Sauce	2 Tbsp LF Tartar Sauce	lemon	2 tsp	2 tsp	2 tsp
NO	Lettuce Leaves	Lettuce Leaves	free	free	free	free
1/2c SLF Stewed Tomatoes	2 Tomato Slices	2 Tomato Slices	2 sl	2 sl	2 sl	2 sl
1/2c Cooked Spinach	1/2c Cole Slaw+	1/2c DB Cole Slaw	1/2c	1/2c	1/2c	1/2c
1/2c Milk (1/4c)[3]	1/2c Skim Milk	1/2c Skim Milk	1/2c	1/2c	1/2c	1/2c
Coffee/Tea/Decaf	Coffee/Tea/Decaf	Coffee/Tea/Decaf	free	free	free	free
1/2c Cherry Gelatin	1/2c Cherry Gelatin	1/2c DB Cherry Gelatin	1/2c	1/2c	1/2c	1/2c
Milk[3] or STR Juice	Skim Milk or Juice	1/2c Skim Milk	1/2c	1/2c	1/2c	1/2c
Plain Cookies, Gelatin,	LF Cookies, LF Crackers,	1 Starch/Bread Exch	1	1	1	1
Plain Crackers, Banana,	Gelatin, Fresh Fruit	1 Meat Exch	0	0	0	1
Vanilla Ice Cream[3]		1 Fat Exch	0	0	1	1

Recipe	Regular, Liberal Bland[1], No Added Salt[2]	1–2 gm Na (Low Sodium)	Mechanical Soft	Puree
	Breakfast			
	1/2c Cranberry Juice	1/2c Cranberry Juice	1/2c Cranberry Juice	1/2c STR Cranberry Juice
B1	1/2c Oatmeal or	1/2c Oatmeal or	1/2c Oatmeal or	1c Oatmeal
	3/4c Asst Dry Cereals	3/4c SR Asst Dry Cereals	3/4 Asst Dry Cereals+	NO
B4	1 Hard-Boiled Egg	1 Hard-Boiled Egg	1 Hard-Boiled Egg	1 Soft-Cooked Egg
	1 sl Toast	1 sl Toast	1 sl Bread	1 sl Bread+
	1 tsp Margarine	1 tsp SR Margarine	1 tsp Margarine	1 tsp Margarine
	1 tsp Jam/Jelly	1 tsp Jam/Jelly	1 tsp Jelly	1 tsp Jelly
	1c Milk	1c Milk	1c Milk	1c Milk
	Coffee/Tea/Decaf	Coffee/Tea/Decaf	Coffee/Tea/Decaf	Coffee/Tea/Decaf
	Lunch			
K10	1/2c Cucumber Onion Salad	1/2c Cucumber Onion Salad	1/2c Juice	1/2c STR Juice
E3	3 oz Chicken Italiano	3 oz SR Chicken Italiano	4 oz CHP Chicken Italiano	4 oz PUR Chicken Italiano
M1	1/2c Spaghetti	1/2c Spaghetti	1/2c CHP Spaghetti	1/2c PUR Spaghetti
O22	2 oz Tomato Sauce	2 oz SR Tomato Sauce	2 oz SFT Tomato Sauce	2 oz SFT Tomato Sauce
J26,3	1/2c Italian Mix Vegetables	1/2c Italian Mix Vegetables	1/2c Italian Mix Vegetables	1/2c PUR Italian Mix Vegetable
	1 sl Italian Bread	1 sl Italian Bread	1 SFT Dinner Roll	1 sl Bread+
	1 tsp Margarine	1 tsp SR Margarine	1 tsp Margarine	1 tsp Margarine
	1/2c Milk	1/2c Milk	1/2c Milk	1/2c Milk
	Coffee/Tea/Decaf	Coffee/Tea/Decaf	Coffee/Tea/Decaf	Coffee/Tea/Decaf
	1/2c Sliced Peaches	1/2c Sliced Peaches	1/2c Sliced Peaches	1/2c PUR Peaches
	Dinner			
C20	2/3c Julienne Soup	2/3c SR Julienne Soup	2/3c Julienne Soup	2/3c PUR/STR Julienne Soup
I10	Fruit Festival:	Fruit Festival:	Fruit Festival:	Fruit Festival:
	1/2c Cottage Cheese	1/2c Cottage Cheese	1/2c Cottage Cheese	1/2c Cottage Cheese
	2/3c Fresh Fruit in Season	2/3c Fresh Fruit in Season	2/3c Canned Fruit	2/3c PUR Fruit
S12	1/2c Gelatin Cubes	1/2c Gelatin Cubes	1/2c Gelatin Cubes	1/2c Gelatin Cubes
N10–20	1 Muffin	1 SR Muffin	1 SFT Muffin	1 sl Bread+
	1 tsp Margarine	1 tsp SR Margarine	1 tsp Margarine	1 tsp Margarine
	1 tsp Jam/Jelly	1 tsp Jam/Jelly	1 tsp Jelly	1 tsp Jelly
	1/2c Milk	1/4c Milk	1/2c Milk	1/2c Milk
	Coffee/Tea/Decaf	Coffee/Tea/Decaf	Coffee/Tea/Decaf	Coffee/Tea/Decaf
Q6	3×2" sl Chocolate Chip Cake	3×2" sl Chocolate Chip Cake	3×2" sl Chocolate Chip Cake +	1/2c Ice Cream
	Snacks			
	Milk or Juice	Juice	Milk or Juice	Milk or STR Juice
	Cookies, Crackers,	SR Cookies, SR Crackers,	Plain Cookies, Gelatin,	Applesauce, SFT Banana,
	Gelatin, Ice Cream,	Gelatin, Fresh Fruit	Plain Crackers+, Ice Cream,	Gelatin, Ice Cream
	Fresh Fruit		Banana	

TERMS: SFT = Soft; SLF = Soft/Low Fiber; GRD = Ground; CHP = Chopped Finely; PUR = Puree; STR = Strained; SR = Sodium or Salt Restricted; LF = Low Fat; FF = Fat Free; LCH = Low Cholesterol; DB = Diabetic; UNSW = Unsweetened; RC = Reduced Calorie; LC = Low Calorie; EXCH = Diabetic Exchange

SERVING UTENSILS: #6 Scoop = 2/3 cup-6 oz; #8 Scoop = 1/2 cup-4 oz; #10 Scoop = 3/8 cup-3 to 4 oz; #12 Scoop = 1/3 cup-2.5 to 3 oz; #16 Scoop = 1/4 cup-2 oz; #30 Scoop = 2 tbsp-1 oz; #60 Scoop =1 tbsp-1/2 oz. Ounces will vary, based on food used.

1. *Liberal Bland:* Follow a regular diet. Use decaffeinated products. Omit pepper and chili powder.

2. *No Added Salt (3–4 gm NA):* Follow a regular diet. Use SR soups and SR canned meats. Omit salt packets (and shakers), bacon, sausage, smoked, and cured meats, substitute with SR food choices.

3. *Low Fiber:* Follow a soft diet. Do not exceed 2 cups of milk per day. Soft/Low Fiber—Omit pepper, garlic, and onions from recipes.

4. *2200 Calorie Diet:* Follow 2000 calorie diet with the following additions: Lunch—add 1 bread exchange and 1 fat exchange; Dinner—add 1 bread exchange.

+ Consider individual tolerance. Daily Alternatives: Lunch and Dinner—Chicken, Hamburger, Cottage Cheese Fruit Plate, or Assorted Sandwiches. Individual preferences are provided upon request.

Amounts specified for food items that contain bone is equivalent to cooked, edible deboned portion.

Soft, Low Fiber[3]	Low Cholesterol, Low Fat (40–50 gm)	No Concentrated Sweets (Diabetic)	1200	1500	1800	2000[4] Diabetic/Calorie-Controlled
1/2c STR Cranberry Juice	1/2c Cranberry Juice	1/2c UNSW Cranberry Juice	1/3c	1/3c	1/3c	1/3c
1/2c Oatmeal or	1/2c LF Oatmeal or	1/2c DB Oatmeal or	1/2c	1/2c	1/2c	1/2c
3/4c Asst Refined Cereals	3/4c Dry Cereals	3/4c UNSW Dry Cereals	3/4c	3/4c	3/4c	3/4c
1 Hard-Boiled Egg	1 Egg Substitute	1 Hard-Boiled Egg	1	1	1	1
1 sl White Toast	1 sl Toast	1 sl Toast	1 sl	1 sl	1 sl	2 sl
1 tsp Margarine	1 tsp Margarine	1 tsp Margarine	0	1 tsp	1 tsp	1 tsp
1 tsp Jelly	1 tsp Jam/Jelly	1 tsp DB Jam/Jelly	1 tsp	1 tsp	1 tsp	1 tsp
1c Milk	1c Skim Milk	1c Skim Milk	1/2c	1/2c	1/2c	1c
Coffee/Tea/Decaf	Coffee/Tea/Decaf	Coffee/Tea/Decaf	free	free	free	free
1/2c STR Juice	1/2c LF Cucumber Onion Sld +	1/2c DB Cucumber Onion Sld	1/2c	1/2c	1/2c	1/2c
3 oz SLF Chicken Italiano	2 oz LF Chicken Italiano	3 oz LF Chicken Italiano	2 oz	3 oz	3 oz	3 oz
1/2c Spaghetti	1/2c Spaghetti	1/2c Spaghetti	1/2c	1/2c	3/4c	3/4c
2 oz SLF Tomato Sauce	2 oz LF Tomato Sauce	2 oz DB Tomato Sauce	1 oz	2 oz	2 oz	2 oz
1/2c Green Beans	1/2c Italian Mix Vegetables+	1/2c Italian Mix Vegetables	1/2c	1/2c	1/2c	1/2c
1 SFT Refined Dinner Roll	1 sl Italian Bread	1 sl Italian Bread	0	0	1 sl	1 sl
1 tsp Margarine	NO	1 tsp Margarine	0	0	1 tsp	1 tsp
1/2c Milk	1/2c Skim Milk	1/2c Skim Milk	1/2c	1/2c	1/2c	1/2c
Coffee/Tea/Decaf	Coffee/Tea/Decaf	Coffee/Tea/Decaf	free	free	free	free
1/2c Sliced Peaches	1/2c Sliced Peaches	1/2c UNSW Sliced Peaches	1/2c	1/2c	1/2c	1/2c
2/3c SLF Julienne Soup	2/3c Julienne Soup+	2/3c Julienne Soup	STR	2/3c	2/3c	2/3c
1/2c Cottage Cheese	1/2c LF Cottage Cheese	3/4c LF Cottage Cheese	1/2c	3/4c	3/4c	3/4c
2/3c Canned Fruit	2/3c Fresh Fruit in Season	2/3c Fresh Fruit in Season	1/2c	1/2c	2/3c	2/3c
1/2c Gelatin Cubes	1/2c Gelatin Cubes	1/2c DB Gelatin Cubes	1/2c	1/2c	1/2c	1/2c
1 SLF Muffin	1 LF Muffin	1 sm DB Muffin	1	1	1	1
1 tsp Margarine	NO	1 tsp Margarine	0	0	1 tsp	1 tsp
1 tsp Jelly	1 tsp Jam/Jelly	1 tsp DB Jam/Jelly	1 tsp	1 tsp	1 tsp	1 tsp
1/2c Milk (1/4c)[3]	1/2c Skim Milk	1/2c Skim Milk	1/2c	1/2c	1/2c	1/2c
Coffee/Tea/Decaf	Coffee/Tea/Decaf	Coffee/Tea/Decaf	free	free	free	free
1/2c Vanilla Ice Cream	2×2" sl LF Chocolate Chip Cake	2×2" sl DB Chocolate Chip Cake	2×2	2×2	2×2	2×2
Milk[3] or STR Juice	Skim Milk or Juice	1/2c Skim Milk	1/2c	1/2c	1/2c	1/2c
Plain Cookies, Gelatin,	LF Cookies, LF Crackers,	1 Starch/Bread Exch	1	1	1	1
Plain Crackers, Banana,	Gelatin, Fresh Fruit	1 Meat Exch	0	0	0	1
Vanilla Ice Cream[3]		1 Fat Exch	0	0	1	1

Recipe	Regular, Liberal Bland[1], No Added Salt[2]	1–2 gm Na (Low Sodium)	Mechanical Soft	Puree
	Breakfast			
	1/2c Orange Juice or	1/2c Orange Juice or	1/2c Orange Juice	1/2c STR Orange Juice
	1/2c Fresh Berries	1/2c Fresh Berries	NO	NO
B1	1/2c Cream of Wheat or	1/2c Cream of Wheat or	1/2c Cream of Wheat or	1c Cream of Wheat
	3/4c Asst Dry Cereals	3/4c SR Asst Dry Cereals	3/4c Asst Dry Cereals+	NO
G7,5	2 oz Ham[2] Omelette	2 oz Plain Omelette	2 oz Ham Omelette	2 oz PUR Ham Omelette
	1 sl Toast	1 sl Toast	1 sl Bread	1 sl Bread+
	1 tsp Margarine	1 tsp SR Margarine	1 tsp Margarine	1 tsp Margarine
	1 tsp Jam/Jelly	1 tsp Jam/Jelly	1 tsp Jelly	1 tsp Jelly
	1c Milk	1c Milk	1c Milk	1c Milk
	Coffee/Tea/Decaf	Coffee/Tea/Decaf	Coffee/Tea/Decaf	Coffee/Tea/Decaf
	Lunch			
K4	1/2c Carrot-Raisin Salad	1/2c Carrot-Raisin Salad	1/2c Juice	1/2c STR Juice
D25	4 oz Veal Loaf with	4 oz Veal Loaf with	4 oz Veal Loaf with	4 oz PUR Veal Loaf with
O3	2 oz Brown Gravy	2 oz SR Brown Gravy	2 oz Brown Gravy	2 oz Brown Gravy
J37	1/2c Mashed Potatoes	1/2c Mashed Potatoes	1/2c Mashed Potatoes	1/2c Mashed Potatoes
J1	1/2c Asparagus Tips	1/2c Asparagus Tips	1/2c Asparagus Tips	1/2c PUR Asparagus Tips
	1 Dinner Roll	1 Dinner Roll	1 SFT Dinner Roll+	1 sl Bread+
	1 tsp Margarine	1 tsp SR Margarine	1 tsp Margarine	1 tsp Margarine
	1/2c Milk	1/2c Milk	1/2c Milk	1/2c Milk
	Coffee/Tea/Decaf	Coffee/Tea/Decaf	Coffee/Tea/Decaf	Coffee/Tea/Decaf
R7	3×2" Apple Crisp	3×2" Apple Crisp	3×2" Apple Crisp+	1/2c Applesauce
	Dinner			
C3	2/3c Clear Vegetable Soup	2/3c Clear Vegtble Soup	2/3c Clear Vegetable Soup	2/3c PUR/STR Clr Veg Soup
G3,2	6 oz Cheese Strata	6 oz SR Cheese Strata	6 oz Cheese Strata	6 oz PUR Cheese Strata
J51	1/2c Vegetable Medley	1/2c Vegetable Medley	1/2c Vegetable Medley	1/2c PUR Vegetable Medley
	1 Dinner Roll	1 Dinner Roll	1 SFT Dinner Roll+	1 sl Bread+
	1 tsp Margarine	1 tsp SR Margarine	1 tsp Margarine	1 tsp Margarine
	1/2c Milk	1/4c Milk	1/2c Milk	1/2c Milk
	Coffee/Tea/Decaf	Coffee/Tea/Decaf	Coffee/Tea/Decaf	Coffee/Tea/Decaf
	1/2c Pineapple Chunks	1/2c Pineapple Chunks	1/2c Pineapple Chunks	1/2c PUR Pineapple
	Snacks			
	Milk or Juice	Juice	Milk or Juice	Milk or STR Juice
	Cookies, Crackers,	SR Cookies, SR Crackers,	Plain Cookies, Gelatin,	Applesauce, SFT Banana,
	Gelatin, Ice Cream,	Gelatin, Fresh Fruit	Plain Crackers+, Ice Cream,	Gelatin, Ice Cream
	Fresh Fruit		Banana	

TERMS: SFT = Soft; SLF = Soft/Low Fiber; GRD = Ground; CHP = Chopped Finely; PUR = Puree; STR = Strained; SR = Sodium or Salt Restricted; LF = Low Fat; FF = Fat Free; LCH = Low Cholesterol; DB = Diabetic; UNSW = Unsweetened; RC = Reduced Calorie; LC = Low Calorie; EXCH = Diabetic Exchange

SERVING UTENSILS: #6 Scoop = 2/3 cup-6 oz; #8 Scoop = 1/2 cup-4 oz; #10 Scoop = 3/8 cup-3 to 4 oz; #12 Scoop = 1/3 cup-2.5 to 3 oz; #16 Scoop = 1/4 cup-2 oz; #30 Scoop = 2 tbsp-1 oz; #60 Scoop =1 tbsp-1/2 oz. Ounces will vary, based on food used.

1. *Liberal Bland:* Follow a regular diet. Use decaffeinated products. Omit pepper and chili powder.

2. *No Added Salt (3–4 gm NA):* Follow a regular diet. Use SR soups and SR canned meats. Omit salt packets (and shakers), bacon, sausage, smoked, and cured meats, substitute with SR food choices.

3. *Low Fiber:* Follow a soft diet. Do not exceed 2 cups of milk per day. Soft/Low Fiber—Omit pepper, garlic, and onions from recipes.

4. *2200 Calorie Diet:* Follow 2000 calorie diet with the following additions: Lunch—add 1 bread exchange and 1 fat exchange; Dinner—add 1 bread exchange.

+ Consider individual tolerance. Daily Alternatives: Lunch and Dinner—Chicken, Hamburger, Cottage Cheese Fruit Plate, or Assorted Sandwiches. Individual preferences are provided upon request.

Amounts specified for food items that contain bone is equivalent to cooked, edible deboned portion.

Soft, Low Fiber[3]	Low Cholesterol, Low Fat (40–50 gm)	No Concentrated Sweets (Diabetic)	1200	1500	1800	2000[4]
			Diabetic/Calorie-Controlled			
1/2c STR Orange Juice	1/2c Orange Juice	1/2c UNSW Orange Juice or	1/2c	1/2c	1/2c	1/2c
NO	1/2c Fresh Berries	1/2c Fresh Berries	3/4c	3/4c	3/4c	3/4c
1/2c Cream of Wheat or	1/2c LF Cream of Wheat or	1/2c DB Cream of Wheat or	1/2c	1/2c	1/2c	1/2c
3/4c Asst Refined Cereals	3/4c Dry Cereals	3/4c UNSW Dry Cereals	3/4c	3/4c	3/4c	3/4c
2 oz Plain Omelette	1 Egg Substitute	2 oz DB Ham Omelette	2 oz	2 oz	2 oz	2 oz
1 sl White Toast	1 sl Toast	1 sl Toast	1 sl	1 sl	1 sl	2 sl
1 tsp Margarine	1 tsp Margarine	1 tsp Margarine	0	1 tsp	1 tsp	2 tsp
1 tsp Jelly	1 tsp Jam/Jelly	1 tsp DB Jam/Jelly	1 tsp	1 tsp	1 tsp	1 tsp
1c Milk	1c Skim Milk	1c Skim Milk	1/2c	1/2c	1/2c	1c
Coffee/Tea/Decaf	Coffee/Tea/Decaf	Coffee/Tea/Decaf	free	free	free	free
1/2c STR Juice	1/2c LF Carrot-Raisin Sld	1/2c LF Carrot-Raisin Sld	1/3c	1/3c	1/2c	1/2c
4 oz SLF Veal Loaf with	3 oz LF Veal Loaf+ with	4 oz Veal Loaf with	3 oz	4 oz	4 oz	4 oz
2 oz Brown Gravy	2 oz LF Brown Gravy	2 oz LF Brown Gravy	2 oz	2 oz	2 oz	2 oz
1/2c Mashed Potatoes	1/2c LF Mashed Potatoes	1/2c LF Mashed Potatoes	1/4c	1/2c	1/2c	1/2c
1/2c Asparagus Tips	1/2c Asparagus Tips	1/2c Asparagus Tips	1/2c	1/2c	1/2c	1/2c
1 SFT Refined Dinner Roll	1 Dinner Roll	1 Dinner Roll	0	0	1 sm	1 sm
1 tsp Margarine	NO	1 tsp Margarine	0	0	1 tsp	1 tsp
1/2c Milk	1/2c Skim Milk	1/2c Skim Milk	1/2c	1/2c	1/2c	1/2c
Coffee/Tea/Decaf	Coffee/Tea/Decaf	Coffee/Tea/Decaf	free	free	free	free
1/2c Applesauce	2×2" LF Apple Crisp	2×2" DB Apple Crisp	2×2"	2×2"	2×2"	2×2"
2/3c SLF Clear Vegetable Soup	2/3c Clear Vegtble Soup	2/3c Clear Vegtble Soup	2/3c	2/3c	2/3c	2/3c
6 oz Mild Cheese Strata	6 oz LF Cheese Lasagna	6 oz DB Cheese Strata	4 oz	6 oz	6 oz	6 oz
1/2c Carrots & Green Beans	1/2c Vegetable Medley+	1/2c Vegetable Medley	1/2c	1/2c	1/2c	1/2c
1 SFT Refined Dinner Roll	1 Dinner Roll	1 Dinner Roll	0	0	1 sm	1 sm
1 tsp Margarine	NO	1 tsp Margarine	0	0	1 tsp	1 tsp
1/2c Milk	1/2c Skim Milk	1/2c Skim Milk	1/2c	1/2c	1/2c	1/2c
Coffee/Tea/Decaf	Coffee/Tea/Decaf	Coffee/Tea/Decaf	free	free	free	free
2 Canned Pear Halves	1/2c Pineapple Chunks	1/2c UNSW Pineapple Chunks	1/3c	1/3c	1/3c	1/3c
Milk[3] or STR Juice	Skim Milk or Juice	1/2c Skim Milk	1/2c	1/2c	1/2c	1/2c
Plain Cookies, Gelatin,	LF Cookies, LF Crackers,	1 Starch/Bread Exch	1	1	1	1
Plain Crackers, Banana,	Gelatin, Fresh Fruit	1 Meat Exch	0	0	0	1
Vanilla Ice Cream[3]		1 Fat Exch	0	0	1	1

Recipe	Regular, Liberal Bland[1], No Added Salt[2]	1–2 gm Na (Low Sodium)	Mechanical Soft	Puree
	Breakfast			
	1/2c Apple Juice	1/2c Apple Juice	1/2c Apple Juice	1/2c STR Apple Juice
B1	1/2c Farina or	1/2c Farina or	1/2c Farina or	1c Farina
	3/4c Asst Dry Cereals	3/4c SR Asst Dry Cereals	3/4c Asst Dry Cereals+	NO
B4	1 Poached Egg	1 Poached Egg	1 Poached Egg	1 Poached Egg
	1 English Muffin	1 English Muffin	1 sl Bread	1 sl Bread +
	1 tsp Margarine	1 tsp SR Margarine	1 tsp Margarine	1 tsp Margarine
	1 tsp Jam/Jelly	1 tsp Jam/Jelly	1 tsp Jelly	1 tsp Jelly
	1c Milk	1c Milk	1c Milk	1c Milk
	Coffee/Tea/Decaf	Coffee/Tea/Decaf	Coffee/Tea/Decaf	Cofee/Tea/Decaf
	Lunch			
K25	1c Green Salad	1c Green Salad	1/2c Juice	1/2c STR Juice
P1	1 oz French Dressing	1 oz SR French Dressing	NO	NO
EL5,16	1c Turkey Jambalaya	1c SR Turkey Jambalaya	1c SFT Turkey Jambalaya	1c PUR Turkey Jambalaya
L1				
J3	1/2c Green Beans	1/2c Green Beans	1/2c Green Beans	1/2c PUR Green Beans
	1 Dinner Roll	1 Dinner Roll	1 SFT Dinner Roll+	1 sl Bread+
	1 tsp Margarine	1 tsp SR Margarine	1 tsp Margarine	1 tsp Margarine
	1/2c Milk	1/4c Milk	1/2c Milk	1/2c Milk
	Coffee/Tea/Decaf	Coffee/Tea/Decaf	Coffee/Tea/Decaf	Coffee/Tea/Decaf
S17	1/2c Vanilla Pudding	1/2c Vanilla Pudding	1/2c Vanilla Pudding	1/2c Vanilla Pudding
	Dinner			
C14	2/3c Cream Tomato Soup	2/3c SR Crm Tomato Soup	2/3c Crm Tomato Soup+	2/3c PUR/STR Crm Tomato Sp
I22	Salad Sampler Platter:	Salad Sampler Platter:	Salad Sampler Platter:	Salad Sampler Platter:
I12,9	1/4c Ham[2] Salad	1/4c SR Egg Salad	1/4c SFT Ham Salad	1/4c PUR Ham Salad
I6	1/4c Chicken Salad	1/4c Chicken Salad	1/4c SFT Chicken Salad	1/4c PUR Chicken Salad
	Lettuce Leaves	Lettuce Leaves	CHP Lettuce Leaves	NO
	2 Green Pepper Slices	2 Green Pepper Slices	NO	NO
	2 Onion Slices	2 Onion Slices	1/2c Juice	1/2c STR Juice
K21	1/2c Potato Salad	1/2c SR Potato Salad	1/2c SFT Potato Salad	1/2c PUR Potato Salad
	1 Dinner Roll	1 Dinner Roll	1 SFT Dinner Roll+	1 sl Bread+
	1 tsp Margarine	1 tsp SR Margarine	1 tsp Margarine	1 tsp Margarine
	1/2c Milk	1/4c Milk	1/2c Milk	1/2c Milk
	Coffee/Tea/Decaf	Coffee/Tea/Decaf	Coffee/Tea/Decaf	Coffee/Tea/Decaf
S5	1/2c Fruit Cup	1/2c Fruit Cup	1/2c Fruit Cup+	1/2c PUR Fruit Cocktail
	Snacks			
	Milk or Juice	Juice	Milk or Juice	Milk or STR Juice
	Cookies, Crackers,	SR Cookies, SR Crackers,	Plain Cookies, Gelatin,	Applesauce, SFT Banana,
	Gelatin, Ice Cream,	Gelatin, Fresh Fruit	Plain Crackers+, Ice Cream,	Gelatin, Ice Cream
	Fresh Fruit		Banana	

TERMS: SFT = Soft; SLF = Soft/Low Fiber; GRD = Ground; CHP = Chopped Finely; PUR = Puree; STR = Strained; SR = Sodium or Salt Restricted; LF = Low Fat; FF = Fat Free; LCH = Low Cholesterol; DB = Diabetic; UNSW = Unsweetened; RC = Reduced Calorie; LC = Low Calorie; EXCH = Diabetic Exchange

SERVING UTENSILS: #6 Scoop = 2/3 cup-6 oz; #8 Scoop = 1/2 cup-4 oz; #10 Scoop = 3/8 cup-3 to 4 oz; #12 Scoop = 1/3 cup-2.5 to 3 oz; #16 Scoop = 1/4 cup-2 oz; #30 Scoop = 2 tbsp-1 oz; #60 Scoop =1 tbsp-1/2 oz. Ounces will vary, based on food used.

1. *Liberal Bland:* Follow a regular diet. Use decaffeinated products. Omit pepper and chili powder.

2. *No Added Salt (3–4 gm NA):* Follow a regular diet. Use SR soups and SR canned meats. Omit salt packets (and shakers), bacon, sausage, smoked, and cured meats, substitute with SR food choices.

3. *Low Fiber:* Follow a soft diet. Do not exceed 2 cups of milk per day. Soft/Low Fiber—Omit pepper, garlic, and onions from recipes.

4. *2200 Calorie Diet:* Follow 2000 calorie diet with the following additions: Lunch—add 1 bread exchange and 1 fat exchange; Dinner—add 1 bread exchange.

+ Consider individual tolerance. Daily Alternatives: Lunch and Dinner—Chicken, Hamburger, Cottage Cheese Fruit Plate, or Assorted Sandwiches. Individual preferences are provided upon request.

Amounts specified for food items that contain bone is equivalent to cooked, edible deboned portion.

Soft, Low Fiber[3]	Low Cholesterol, Low Fat (40–50 gm)	No Concentrated Sweets (Diabetic)	1200	1500	1800	2000[4]
			Diabetic/Calorie-Controlled			
1/2c STR Apple Juice	1/2c Apple Juice	1/2c UNSW Apple Juice	1/2c	1/2c	1/2c	1/2c
1/2c Farina or	1/2c LF Farina or	1/2c DB Farina or	1/2c	1/2c	1/2c	1/2c
3/4c Asst Refined Cereals	3/4c Dry Cereals	3/4c UNSW Dry Cereals	3/4c	3/4c	3/4c	3/4c
1 Poached Egg	1 Egg Substitute	1 Poached Egg	1	1	1	1
1 sl White Toast	1 English Muffin	1 English Muffin	1/2	1/2	1	1
1 tsp Margarine	1 tsp Margarine	1 tsp Margarine	1 tsp	1 tsp	2 tsp	2 tsp
1 tsp Jelly	1 tsp Jam/Jelly	1 tsp DB Jam/Jelly	1 tsp	1 tsp	1 tsp	1 tsp
1c Milk	1c Skim Milk	1c Skim Milk	1/2c	1/2c	1/2c	1c
Coffee/Tea/Decaf	Coffee/Tea/Decaf	Coffee/Tea/Decaf	free	free	free	free
1/2c STR Juice	1c Green Salad	1c Green Salad	1c	1c	1c	1c
NO	1 Tbsp LC French Dressing	1 Tbsp LC French Dressing	1 Tbsp	1 Tbsp	1 Tbsp	1 Tbsp
3 oz Sliced Turkey	3/4c LF Turkey Jambalaya+	1c Turkey Jambalaya	3/4c	1c	1c	1c
1/2c White Rice						
1/2c Green Beans	1/2c Green Beans	1/2c Green Beans	1/2c	1/2c	1/2c	1/2c
1 SFT Refined Dinner Roll	1 Dinner Roll	1 Dinner Roll	0	0	1 sm	1 sm
1 tsp Margarine	NO	1 tsp Margarine	0	0	1 tsp	1 tsp
1/2c Milk (1/4c)[3]	1/2c Skim Milk	1/2c Skim Milk	1/4c	1/2c	1/2c	1/2c
Coffee/Tea/Decaf	Coffee/Tea/Decaf	Coffee/Tea/Decaf	free	free	free	free
1/2c Vanilla Pudding	1/2c LF Vanilla Pudding	1/2c DB Vanilla Pudding	1/2c	1/2c	1/2c	1/2c
2/3c SLF Crm Tomato Soup	2/3c LF Crm Tomato Soup+	2/3c LF Crm Tomato Soup	2/3c	2/3c	2/3c	2/3c
Salad Sampler Platter:	Salad Sampler Platter:	Salad Sampler Platter:				
1/4c SFT Egg Salad	1/4c LF Ham Salad	1/4c LF Ham Salad	1/4c	1/4c	1/4c	1/4c
1/4c SFT Chicken Salad	1/4c LF Chicken Salad	1/4c LF Chicken Salad	1/4c	1/2c	1/2c	1/2c
NO	Lettuce Leaves	Lettuce Leaves	Lett	Lett	Lett	Lett
NO	2 Green Pepper Slices	2 Green Pepper Slices	2 sl	2 sl	2 sl	2 sl
1/2c STR Juice	2 Onion Slices+	2 Onion Slices	2 sl	2 sl	2 sl	2 sl
1/2c SFT Potato Salad	1/2c LF Potato Salad	1/2c LF Potato Salad	1/4c	1/2c	1/2c	1/2c
1 SFT Refined Dinner Roll	1 Dinner Roll	1 Dinner Roll	0	1 med	1 med	1 med
1 tsp Margarine	NO	1 tsp Margarine	0	0	0	1 tsp
1/2c Milk (1/4c)[3]	1/2c Skim Milk	1/2c Skim Milk	1/2c	1/2c	1/2c	1/2c
Coffee/Tea/Decaf	Coffee/Tea/Decaf	Coffee/Tea/Decaf	free	free	free	free
1/2c SLF Fruit Cup	1/2c Fruit Cup	1/2c Fruit Cup	1/2c	1/2c	1/2c	1/2c
Milk[3] or STR Juice	Skim Milk or Juice	1/2c Skim Milk	1/2c	1/2c	1/2c	1/2c
Plain Cookies, Gelatin,	LF Cookies, LF Crackers,	1 Starch/Bread Exch	1	1	1	1
Plain Crackers, Banana,	Gelatin, Fresh Fruit	1 Meat Exch	0	0	0	1
Vanilla Ice Cream[3]		1 Fat Exch	0	0	1	1

Recipe	Regular, Liberal Bland[1], No Added Salt[2]	1–2 gm Na (Low Sodium)	Mechanical Soft	Puree
	Breakfast			
B1	1/2c Grapefruit Juice	1/2c Grapefruit Juice	1/2c Grapefruit Juice	1/2c STR Grapefruit Juice
	1/2c Wheatena or	1/2c Wheatena or	1/2c Wheatena or	1c Wheatena
	3/4c Asst Dry Cereals	3/4c SR Asst Dry Cereals	3/4c Asst Dry Cereals+	NO
	1/4c Cottage Cheese with	1/4c Cottage Cheese with	1/4c Cottage Cheese with	1/4c PUR Cottage Cheese with
	Brown Sugar-Cinnamon on	Brown Sugar-Cinnamon on	Brown Sugar-Cinnamon on	Brown Sugar-Cinnamon on
	1 sl Raisin Toast	1 sl Raisin Toast	1 sl Whole Wheat Bread	1 sl Bread+
	1 tsp Margarine	1 tsp SR Margarine	1 tsp Margarine	1 tsp Margarine
	1 tsp Jam/Jelly	1 tsp Jam/Jelly	1 tsp Jelly	1 tsp Jelly
	1c Milk	1c Milk	1c Milk	1c Milk
	Coffee/Tea/Decaf	Coffee/Tea/Decaf	Coffee/Tea/Decaf	Coffee/Tea/Decaf
	Lunch			
K24	1c Garden Salad	1c Garden Salad	1/2c Juice	1/2c STR Juice
P1–8	1 oz Salad Dressing	1 oz SR Salad Dressing	NO	NO
D14	3 oz Sweet-n-Sour Meatballs	3 oz SR Sweet-n-Sour Meatballs	3 oz Sweet-n-Sour Meatballs	4 oz PUR Swt-n-Sour Meatballs
	with 2 oz Sauce	with 2 oz SR Sauce	with 2 oz Sauce	with 2 oz PUR/STR Sauce
M1	1/2c Noodles	1/2c Noodles	1/2c Noodles	1/2c PUR Noodles
J48	1/2c Seasoned Spinach	1/2c SR Seasoned Spinach	1/2c Seasoned Spinach	1/2c PUR Seasoned Spinach
	1 Dinner Roll	1 Dinner Roll	1 SFT Dinner Roll+	1 sl Bread+
	1 tsp Margarine	1 tsp SR Margarine	1 tsp Margarine	1 tsp Margarine
	1/2c Milk	1/2c Milk	1/2c Milk	1/2c Milk
	Coffee/Tea/Decaf	Coffee/Tea/Decaf	Coffee/Tea/Decaf	Coffee/Tea/Decaf
	1/2c Apricot Halves	1/2c Apricot Halves	1/2c Apricot Halves	1/2c PUR Apricots
	Dinner			
C19,1	2/3c French Onion Soup	2/3c SR French Onion Soup	2/3c French Onion Soup	2/3c PUR/STR Onion Soup
G12,13	1/6 pie Quiche Lorraine[2]	1/8 pie SR Quiche Lorraine	1/6 pie Quiche Lorraine+	6 oz PUR Quiche Lorraine
J28	1/2c Mushrooms and Celery	1/2c Mushrooms and Celery	1/2c SFT Mushrooms & Celery+	1/2c PUR Mushrooms & Celery
	1 Dinner Roll	1 Dinner Roll	1 SFT Dinner Roll+	1 sl Bread+
	1 tsp Margarine	1 tsp SR Margarine	1 tsp Margarine	1 tsp Margarine
	1/2c Milk	1/4c Milk	1/2c Milk	1/2c Milk
	Coffee/Tea/Decaf	Coffee/Tea/Decaf	Coffee/Tea/Decaf	Coffee/Tea/Decaf
	1/2c Ice Cream	1/2c Ice Cream	1/2c Ice Cream	1/2c Ice Cream
	Snacks			
	Milk or Juice	Juice	Milk or Juice	Milk or STR Juice
	Cookies, Crackers,	SR Cookies, SR Crackers,	Plain Cookies, Gelatin,	Applesauce, SFT Banana,
	Gelatin, Ice Cream,	Gelatin, Fresh Fruit	Plain Crackers+, Ice Cream,	Gelatin, Ice Cream
	Fresh Fruit		Banana	

TERMS: SFT = Soft; SLF = Soft/Low Fiber; GRD = Ground; CHP = Chopped Finely; PUR = Puree; STR = Strained; SR = Sodium or Salt Restricted; LF = Low Fat; FF = Fat Free; LCH = Low Cholesterol; DB = Diabetic; UNSW = Unsweetened; RC = Reduced Calorie; LC = Low Calorie; EXCH = Diabetic Exchange

SERVING UTENSILS: #6 Scoop = 2/3 cup-6 oz; #8 Scoop = 1/2 cup-4 oz; #10 Scoop = 3/8 cup-3 to 4 oz; #12 Scoop = 1/3 cup-2.5 to 3 oz; #16 Scoop = 1/4 cup-2 oz; #30 Scoop = 2 tbsp-1 oz; #60 Scoop = 1 tbsp-1/2 oz. Ounces will vary, based on food used.

1. *Liberal Bland:* Follow a regular diet. Use decaffeinated products. Omit pepper and chili powder.

2. *No Added Salt (3–4 gm NA):* Follow a regular diet. Use SR soups and SR canned meats. Omit salt packets (and shakers), bacon, sausage, smoked, and cured meats, substitute with SR food choices.

3. *Low Fiber:* Follow a soft diet. Do not exceed 2 cups of milk per day. Soft/Low Fiber—Omit pepper, garlic, and onions from recipes.

4. *2200 Calorie Diet:* Follow 2000 calorie diet with the following additions: Lunch—add 1 bread exchange and 1 fat exchange; Dinner—add 1 bread exchange.

+ Consider individual tolerance. Daily Alternatives: Lunch and Dinner—Chicken, Hamburger, Cottage Cheese Fruit Plate, or Assorted Sandwiches. Individual preferences are provided upon request.

Amounts specified for food items that contain bone is equivalent to cooked, edible deboned portion.

Soft, Low Fiber[3]	Low Cholesterol, Low Fat (40–50 gm)	No Concentrated Sweets (Diabetic)	1200	1500	1800	2000[4] Diabetic/Calorie-Controlled
1/2c STR Grapefruit Juice	1/2c Grapefruit Juice	1/2c UNSW Grapefruit Juice	1/2c	1/2c	1/2c	1/2c
1/2c Wheatena or	1/2c LF Wheatena or	1/2c DB Wheatena or	1/2c	1/2c	1/2c	1/2c
3/4c Asst Refined Cereals	3/4c Dry Cereals	3/4c UNSW Dry Cereals	3/4c	3/4c	3/4c	3/4c
1/4c Cottage Cheese with	1/4c LF Cottage Cheese with	1/4c LF Cottage Cheese with	1/4c	1/4c	1/4c	1/4c
Brown Sugar-Cinnamon on	Brown Sugar-Cinnamon on	Artificial Sweetener/Cinnamon	yes	yes	yes	yes
1 sl White Toast	1 sl Raisin Toast	on 1 sl Raisin Toast	1 sl	1 sl	1 sl	2 sl
1 tsp Margarine	NO	1 tsp Margarine	0	0	0	0
1 tsp Jelly	1 tsp Jam/Jelly	1 tsp DB Jam/Jelly	1 tsp	1 tsp	1 tsp	1 tsp
1c Milk	1c Skim Milk	1c Skim Milk	1/2c	1/2c	1/2c	1c
Coffee/Tea/Decaf	Coffee/Tea/Decaf	Coffee/Tea/Decaf	free	free	free	free
1/2c STR Juice	1c Garden Salad	1c Garden Salad	1c	1c	1c	1c
NO	1 Tbsp LC Salad Dressing	1 Tbsp LC Sld Dressing	1 Tbsp	1 Tbsp	1 Tbsp	1 Tbsp
3 oz SLF Meatballs	2 oz LF Sweet-n-Sour Meatball	3 oz DB Swt-n-Sour Meatballs	2 oz	3 oz	3 oz	3 oz
NO	with 2 oz LF Sauce	with 2 oz DB Sauce	1 oz	1 oz	2 oz	2 oz
1/2c Noodles	1/2c Noodles	1/2c Noodles	1/2c	1/2c	3/4c	3/4c
1/2c Seasoned Spinach	1/2c Seasoned Spinach	1/2c Seasoned Spinach	1/2c	1/2c	1/2c	1/2c
1 SFT Refined Dinner Roll	1 Dinner Roll	1 Dinner Roll	0	0	1 sm	1 sm
1 tsp Margarine	NO	1 tsp Margarine	0	0	1 tsp	1 tsp
1/2c Milk	1/2c Skim Milk	1/2c Skim Milk	1/2c	1/2c	1/2c	1/2c
Coffee/Tea/Decaf	Coffee/Tea/Decaf	Coffee/Tea/Decaf	free	free	free	free
1/2c Apricot Halves	1/2c Apricot Halves	1/2c UNSW Apricot Halves	1/2c	1/2c	1/2c	1/2c
2/3c SLF Broth	2/3c LF Onion Soup+	2/3c LF Onion Soup	2/3c	2/3c	2/3c	2/3c
1/6 pie SLF Quiche	1/8 pie LF Broccoli Quiche	1/6 pie DB Quiche Lorraine	1/8	1/6	1/6	1/6
1/2c Sauté Mushrooms	1/2c LF Mushrooms & Celery	1/2c LF Mushrooms & Celery	1/2c	1/2c	1/2c	1/2c
1 SFT Refined Dinner Roll	1 Dinner Roll	1 Dinner Roll	0	1 sm	1 sm	1 sm
1 tsp Margarine	1 tsp Margarine	1 tsp Margarine	0	0	1 tsp	1 tsp
1/2c Milk (1/4c)[3]	1/2c Skim Milk	1/2c Skim Milk	1/4c	1/4c	1/4c	1/2c
Coffee/Tea/Decaf	Coffee/Tea Decaf	Coffee/Tea/Decaf	free	free	free	free
1/2c Vanilla Ice Cream	1/2c LF Ice Milk	1/2c LF Ice Milk	1/3c	1/2c	1/2c	1/2c
Milk[3] or STR Juice	Skim Milk or Juice	1/2c Skim Milk	1/2c	1/2c	1/2c	1/2c
Plain Cookies, Gelatin,	LF Cookies, LF Crackers,	1 Starch/Bread Exch	1	1	1	1
Plain Crackers, Banana,	Gelatin, Fresh Fruit	1 Meat Exch	0	0	0	1
Vanilla Ice Cream[3]		1 Fat Exch	0	0	1	1

Recipe	Regular, Liberal Bland[1], No Added Salt[2]	1–2 gm Na (Low Sodium)	Mechanical Soft	Puree
	Breakfast			
	1/2c Orange Juice or	1/2c Orange Juice or	1/2c Orange Juice or	1/2c STR Orange Juice
	1 small Banana	1 small Banana	1 small Banana	1 small Banana-Mashed
B1	1/2c Cream of Rice or	1/2c Cream of Rice or	1/2c Cream of Rice or	1c Cream of Rice
	3/4c Asst Dry Cereals	3/4c SR Asst Dry Cereals	3/4c Asst Dry Cereals+	NO
B5	1 Scrambled Egg	1 Scrambled Egg	1 Scrambled Egg	1 Scrambled Egg
	1 sl Toast	1 sl Toast	1 sl Bread	1 sl Bread+
	1 tsp Margarine	1 tsp SR Margarine	1 tsp Margarine	1 tsp Margarine
	1 tsp Jam/Jelly	1 tsp Jam/Jelly	1 tsp Jelly	1 tsp Jelly
	1c Milk	1c Milk	1c Milk	1c Milk
	Coffee/Tea/Decaf	Coffee/Tea/Decaf	Coffee/Tea/Decaf	Coffee/Tea/Decaf
	Lunch			
K2	1/2c Pickled Beets	1/2c SR Beets	1/2c Pickled Beets+	1/2c PUR Pickled Beets
F5	3 oz Catch of the Day	3 oz Catch of the Day	3 oz CHP Catch of the Day	4 oz PUR Catch of the Day
O25	2 Tbsp Tartar Sauce[2]	1 Tbsp SR Mayonnaise	2 Tbsp Tartar Sauce	2 Tbsp Mayonnaise
	Lemon Wedge	Lemon Wedge	Lemon Wedge	Lemon Wedge
L5	1/2c Rice Pilaf	1/2c SR Rice Pilaf	1/2c Rice Pilaf	1/2c PUR Rice Pilaf
J27,50	1/2c Mixed Vegetables	1/2c Mixed Vegetables	1/2c Mixed Vegetables	1/2c PUR Mixed Vegetables
	1 Dinner Roll	1 Dinner Roll	1 SFT Dinner Roll+	1 sl Bread+
	1 tsp Margarine	1 tsp SR Margarine	1 tsp Margarine	1 tsp Margarine
	1/2c Milk	1/2c Milk	1/2c Milk	1/2c Milk
	Coffee/Tea/Decaf	Coffee/Tea/Decaf	Coffee/Tea/Decaf	Coffee/Tea/Decaf
	2 Pear Halves	2 Pear Halves	2 Pear Halves	1/2c PUR Pears
	Dinner			
C23,1	2/3c Split Pea Soup	2/3c SR Split Pea Soup	2/3c Split Pea Soup+	2/3c PUR/STR Pea Soup
E7	3 oz Roast Chicken	3 oz Roast Chicken	3 oz CHP Roast Chicken	4 oz PUR Roast Chicken
J35	1 med Baked Potato with	1 med Baked Potato with	1 med Baked Potato (No Skin)	1/2c PUR Baked Potato
	1 oz Sour Cream	1 oz Sour Cream	1 oz Sour Cream	1 oz Sour Cream
J19	1/2c Carrot Tzimmes	1/2c Carrot Tzimmes	1/2c Carrot Tzimmes+	1/2c PUR Carrot Tzimmes
	1 Dinner Roll	1 Dinner Roll	1 SFT Dinner Roll+	1 sl Bread+
	1 tsp Margarine	1 tsp SR Margarine	1 tsp Margarine	1 tsp Margarine
	1/2c Milk	1/2c Milk	1/2c Milk	1/2c Milk
	Coffee/Tea/Decaf	Coffee/Tea/Decaf	Coffee/Tea/Decaf	Coffee/Tea/Decaf
Q8,1	3×2" sl Marble Cake	3×2" sl Marble Cake	3×2" sl Marble Cake+	1/2c Applesauce
	Snacks			
	Milk or Juice	Juice	Milk or Juice	Milk or STR Juice
	Cookies, Crackers,	SR Cookies, SR Crackers,	Plain Cookies, Gelatin,	Applesauce, SFT Banana,
	Gelatin, Ice Cream,	Gelatin, Fresh Fruit	Plain Crackers+, Ice Cream,	Gelatin, Ice Cream
	Fresh Fruit		Banana	

TERMS: SFT = Soft; SLF = Soft/Low Fiber; GRD = Ground; CHP = Chopped Finely; PUR = Puree; STR = Strained; SR = Sodium or Salt Restricted; LF = Low Fat; FF = Fat Free; LCH = Low Cholesterol; DB = Diabetic; UNSW = Unsweetened; RC = Reduced Calorie; LC = Low Calorie; EXCH = Diabetic Exchange

SERVING UTENSILS: #6 Scoop = 2/3 cup-6 oz; #8 Scoop = 1/2 cup-4 oz; #10 Scoop = 3/8 cup-3 to 4 oz; #12 Scoop = 1/3 cup-2.5 to 3 oz; #16 Scoop = 1/4 cup-2 oz; #30 Scoop = 2 tbsp-1 oz; #60 Scoop =1 tbsp-1/2 oz. Ounces will vary, based on food used.

1. *Liberal Bland:* Follow a regular diet. Use decaffeinated products. Omit pepper and chili powder.

2. *No Added Salt (3–4 gm NA):* Follow a regular diet. Use SR soups and SR canned meats. Omit salt packets (and shakers), bacon, sausage, smoked, and cured meats, substitute with SR food choices.

3. *Low Fiber:* Follow a soft diet. Do not exceed 2 cups of milk per day. Soft/Low Fiber—Omit pepper, garlic, and onions from recipes.

4. *2200 Calorie Diet:* Follow 2000 calorie diet with the following additions: Lunch—add 1 bread exchange and 1 fat exchange; Dinner—add 1 bread exchange.

+ Consider individual tolerance. Daily Alternatives: Lunch and Dinner—Chicken, Hamburger, Cottage Cheese Fruit Plate, or Assorted Sandwiches. Individual preferences are provided upon request.

Amounts specified for food items that contain bone is equivalent to cooked, edible deboned portion.

Soft, Low Fiber[3]	Low Cholesterol, Low Fat (40–50 gm)	No Concentrated Sweets (Diabetic)	1200	1500	1800	2000[4]
			Diabetic/Calorie-Controlled			
1/2c STR Orange Juice	1/2c Orange Juice or	1/2c UNSW Orange Juice or	1/2c	1/2c	1/2c	1/2c
1 small Banana	1 small Banana	1 small Banana	1/2	1/2	1/2	1/2
1/2c Cream of Rice or	1/2c LF Cream of Rice or	1/2c DB Cream of Rice or	1/2c	1/2c	1/2c	1/2c
3/4c Asst Refined Cereals	3/4c Dry Cereals	3/4c UNSW Dry Cereals	3/4c	3/4c	3/4c	3/4c
1 Scrambled Egg	1 Egg Substitute	1 Scrambled Egg	1	1	1	1
1 sl White Toast	1 sl Toast	1 sl Toast	1 sl	1 sl	1 sl	2 sl
1 tsp Margarine	1 tsp Margarine	1 tsp Margarine	0	1 tsp	1 tsp	1 tsp
1 tsp Jelly	1 tsp Jam/Jelly	1 tsp DB Jam/Jelly	1 tsp	1 tsp	1 tsp	1 tsp
1c Milk	1c Skim Milk	1c Skim Milk	1/2c	1/2c	1/2c	1c
Coffee/Tea/Decaf	Coffee/Tea/Decaf	Coffee/Tea/Decaf	free	free	free	free
1/2c SLF Pickled Beets	1/2c Pickled Beets	1/2c DB Pickled Beets	1/2c	1/2c	1/2c	1/2c
3 oz Catch of the Day	3 oz LF Catch of the Day	3 oz LF Catch of the Day	2 oz	3 oz	3 oz	3 oz
2 Tbsp Mayonnaise	1 tsp LF Tartar Sauce	2 Tbsp LF Tartar Sauce	0	0	2 tsp	2 tsp
Lemon Wedge	Lemon Wedge	Lemon Wedge	Lemon	Lemon	Lemon	Lemon
1/2c SFT Rice Pilaf	1/2c Rice Pilaf+	1/2c Rice Pilaf	1/3c	1/3c	1/3c	1/2c
1/2c SLF Stewed Tomatoes	1/2c Mixed Vegetables+	1/2c Mixed Vegetables	1/4c	1/2c	1/2c	1/2c
1 SFT Refined Dinner Roll	1 Dinner Roll	1 Dinner Roll	0	0	1 sm	1 sm
1 tsp Margarine	NO	1 tsp Margarine	0	0	1 tsp	1 tsp
1/2c Milk	1/2c Skim Milk	1/2c Skim Milk	1/2c	1/2c	1/2c	1/2c
Coffee/Tea/Decaf	Coffee/Tea/Decaf	Coffee/Tea/Decaf	free	free	free	free
2 Pear Halves	2 Pear Halves	2 UNSW Pear Halves	2	2	2	2
2/3c SLF Broth	2/3c LF Split Pea Soup	2/3c LF Split Pea Soup	2/3c	2/3c	2/3c	2/3c
3 oz SLF Roast Chicken	2 oz LF Roast Chicken	3 oz LF Roast Chicken	2 oz	3 oz	3 oz	3 oz
1 med Baked Potato (No Skin)	1 Baked Potato	1 Baked Potato with	1/2 sm	1 sm	1 sm	1 sm
1 oz Sour Cream	1 Tbsp Sour Cream	1 oz Sour Cream	0	1 Tbsp	1 oz	1 oz
1/2c SLF Carrot Tzimmes	1/2c LF Carrot Tzimmes	1/2c DB Carrot Tzimmes	1/2c	1/2c	1/2c	1/2c
1 SFT Refined Dinner Roll	1 Dinner Roll	1 Dinner Roll	0	0	1 sm	1 sm
1 tsp Margarine	NO	1 tsp Margarine	0	0	1 tsp	1 tsp
1/2c Milk	1/2c Skim Milk	1/2c Skim Milk	1/2c	1/2c	1/2c	1/2c
Coffee/Tea/Decaf	Coffee/Tea/Decaf	Coffee/Tea/Decaf	free	free	free	free
1 sl Angelfood Cake	3×2" sl LF Marble Cake	3×2" sl DB Marble Cake	2×2" sl	3×2" sl	3×2" sl	3×2" sl
Milk[3] or STR Juice	Skim Milk or Juice	1/2c Skim Milk	1/2c	1/2c	1/2c	1/2c
Plain Cookies, Gelatin,	LF Cookies, LF Crackers,	1 Starch/Bread Exch	1	1	1	1
Plain Crackers, Banana,	Gelatin, Fresh Fruit	1 Meat Exch	0	0	0	1
Vanilla Ice Cream[3]		1 Fat Exch	0	0	1	1

Recipe	Regular, Liberal Bland[1], No Added Salt[2]	1–2 gm Na (Low Sodium)	Mechanical Soft	Puree
	Breakfast			
	1/2c Apple Juice	1/2c Apple Juice	1/2c Apple Juice	1/2c STR Apple Juice
B1	1/2c Oatmeal or	1/2c Oatmeal or	1/2c Oatmeal or	1c Oatmeal
	3/4c Asst Dry Cereals	3/4c SR Asst Dry Cereals	3/4c Asst Dry Cereals+	NO
B4	1 Hard-Boiled Egg	1 Hard-Boiled Egg	1 Hard-Boiled Egg	1 Soft-Cooked Egg
	1 sl Toast	1 sl Toast	1 sl Bread	1 sl Bread+
	1 tsp Margarine	1 tsp SR Margarine	1 tsp Margarine	1 tsp Margarine
	1 tsp Jam/Jelly	1 tsp Jam/Jelly	1 tsp Jelly	1 tsp Jelly
	1c Milk	1c Milk	1c Milk	1c Milk
	Coffee/Tea/Decaf	Coffee/Tea/Decaf	Coffee/Tea/Decaf	Coffee/Tea/Decaf
	Lunch			
K29	1c Tossed Salad	1c Tossed Salad	1/2c Juice	1/2c STR Juice
P1–8	1 oz Salad Dressing	1 oz SR Salad Dressing	NO	NO
D28,31	3 oz Baked Glazed Ham[2]	3 oz Roast Pork	3 oz CHP Glazed Ham	4 oz PUR Glazed Ham
J45	1/2c Sweet Potatoes/Apples	1/2c Sweet Potatoes/Apples	1/2c Sweet Potatoes/Apples+	1/2c PUR Swt Potato/Apples
J3	1/2c String Beans	1/2c String Beans	1/2c String Beans	1/2c PUR String Beans
	1 Dinner Roll	1 Dinner Roll	1 SFT Dinner Roll+	1 sl Bread+
	1 tsp Margarine	1 tsp SR Margarine	1 tsp Margarine	1 tsp Margarine
	1/2c Milk	1/2c Milk	1/2c Milk	1/2c Milk
	Coffee/Tea/Decaf	Coffee/Tea/Decaf	Coffee/Tea/Decaf	Coffee/Tea/Decaf
S13	1/2c Fruited Lime Gelatin	1/2c Fruited Lime Gelatin	1/2c Fruited Lime Gelatin	1/2c PUR Fruit Gelatin
	Dinner			
C21,1	2/3c Minestrone Soup	2/3c SR Minestrone Soup	2/3c Minestrone Soup	2/3c PUR/STR Veg Soup
G1	6 oz Cheese Fettucine	6 oz SR Cheese Fettucine	6 oz Cheese Fettucine	6 oz PUR Cheese Fettucine
J55,52	1/2c Sauté Zucchini/Onions	1/2c Sauté Zucchini Onions	1/2c Sauté Zucchini	1/2c Sauté Zucchini/Onions
	1 sl Italian Bread	1 sl Italian Bread	1 SFT Dinner Roll	1 sl Bread+
	1 tsp Margarine	1 tsp SR Margarine	1 tsp Margarine	1 tsp Margarine
	1/2c Milk	1/2c Milk	1/2c Milk	1/2c Milk
	Coffee/Tea/Decaf	Coffee/Tea/Decaf	Coffee/Tea/Decaf	Coffee/Tea/Decaf
	2 Plums	2 Plums	2 Plums—No Skin	1/2c PUR Plums
	Snacks			
	Milk or Juice	Juice	Milk or Juice	Milk or STR Juice
	Cookies, Crackers,	SR Cookies, SR Crackers,	Plain Cookies, Gelatin,	Applesauce, SFT Banana
	Gelatin, Ice Cream,	Gelatin, Fresh Fruit	Plain Crackers +, Ice Cream,	Gelatin, Ice Cream
	Fresh Fruit		Banana	

TERMS: SFT = Soft; SLF = Soft/Low Fiber; GRD = Ground; CHP = Chopped Finely; PUR = Puree; STR = Strained; SR = Sodium or Salt Restricted; LF = Low Fat; FF = Fat Free; LCH = Low Cholesterol; DB = Diabetic; UNSW = Unsweetened; RC = Reduced Calorie; LC = Low Calorie; EXCH = Diabetic Exchange

SERVING UTENSILS: #6 Scoop = 2/3 cup-6 oz; #8 Scoop = 1/2 cup-4 oz; #10 Scoop = 3/8 cup-3 to 4 oz; #12 Scoop = 1/3 cup-2.5 to 3 oz; #16 Scoop = 1/4 cup-2 oz; #30 Scoop = 2 tbsp-1 oz; #60 Scoop = 1 tbsp-1/2 oz. Ounces will vary, based on food used.

1. *Liberal Bland:* Follow a regular diet. Use decaffeinated products. Omit pepper and chili powder.

2. *No Added Salt (3–4 gm NA):* Follow a regular diet. Use SR soups and SR canned meats. Omit salt packets (and shakers), bacon, sausage, smoked, and cured meats, substitute with SR food choices.

3. *Low Fiber:* Follow a soft diet. Do not exceed 2 cups of milk per day. Soft/Low Fiber—Omit pepper, garlic, and onions from recipes.

4. *2200 Calorie Diet:* Follow 2000 calorie diet with the following additions: Lunch—add 1 bread exchange and 1 fat exchange; Dinner—add 1 bread exchange.

+ Consider individual tolerance. Daily Alternatives: Lunch and Dinner—Chicken, Hamburger, Cottage Cheese Fruit Plate, or Assorted Sandwiches. Individual preferences are provided upon request.

Amounts specified for food items that contain bone is equivalent to cooked, edible deboned portion.

Soft, Low Fiber[3]	Low Cholesterol, Low Fat (40–50 gm)	No Concentrated Sweets (Diabetic)	1200	1500	1800	2000[4]
			Diabetic/Calorie-Controlled			
1/2c STR Apple Juice	1/2c Apple juice	1/2c UNSW Apple Juice	1/2c	1/2c	1/2c	1/2c
1/2c Oatmeal or	1/2c LF Oatmeal or	1/2c DB Oatmeal or	1/2c	1/2c	1/2c	1/2c
3/4c Asst Refined Cereals	3/4c Dry Cereals	3/4c UNSW Dry Cereals	3/4c	3/4c	3/4c	3/4c
1 Hard-Boiled Egg	1 Egg Substitute	1 Hard-Boiled Egg	1	1	1	1
1 sl White Toast	1 sl Toast	1 sl Toast	1 sl	1 sl	1 sl	2 sl
1 tsp Margarine	1 tsp Margarine	1 tsp Margarine	0	1 tsp	1 tsp	2 tsp
1 tsp Jelly	1 tsp Jam/Jelly	1 tsp DB Jam/Jelly	1 tsp	1 tsp	1 tsp	1 tsp
1c Milk	1c Skim Milk	1c Skim Milk	1/2c	1/2c	1/2c	1c
Coffee/Tea/Decaf	Coffee/Tea/Decaf	Coffee/Tea/Decaf	free	free	free	free
1/2c STR Juice	1c Tossed Salad	1c Tossed Salad	1c	1c	1c	1c
NO	1 Tbsp LC Salad Dressing	1 Tbsp LC Sld Dressing	1 Tbsp	1 Tbsp	1 Tbsp	1 Tbsp
3 oz SLF Roast Pork	2 oz Baked Glazed Ham	3 oz DB Baked Ham	2 oz	3 oz	3 oz	3 oz
1/2c Swt Potato/Apples+	1/2c LF Swt Potato/Apples	1/2c DB Swt Potato/Apples	1/4c	1/2c	1/2c	1/2c
1/2c String Beans	1/2c String Beans	1/2c String Beans	1/2c	1/2c	1/2c	1/2c
1 SFT Refined Dinner Roll	1 Dinner Roll	1 Dinner Roll	0	1 sm	1 sm	1 sm
1 tsp Margarine	NO	1 tsp Margarine	0	1 tsp	1 tsp	1 tsp
1/2c Milk	1/2c Skim Milk	1/2c Skim Milk	1/2c	1/2c	1/2c	1/2c
Coffee/Tea/Decaf	Coffee/Tea/Decaf	Coffee/Tea/Decaf	free	free	free	free
1/2c SLF Fruited Lime Gelatin	1/2c Fruited Lime Gelatin	1/2c DB Fruit Gelatin	1/2c	1/2c	1/2c	1/2c
2/3c SLF Broth	2/3c Minestrone Soup+	2/3c Minestrone Soup	STR	2/3c	2/3c	2/3c
6 oz SLF Cheese Fettucine	5 oz LF Cheese Fettucine	6 oz LF Cheese Fettucine	5 oz	6 oz	6 oz	6 oz
1/2c Sauté Zucchini	1/2c LF Sauté Zucchini/Onions	1/2c LF Sauté Zucchini/Onions	1/2c	1/2c	1/2c	1/2c
1 SFT Refined Dinner Roll	1 sl Italian Bread	1 sl Italian Bread	0	0	1 sl	1 sl
1 tsp Margarine	NO	1 tsp Margarine	0	0	1 tsp	1 tsp
1/2c Milk	1/2c Skim Milk	1/2c Skim Milk	1/2c	1/2c	1/2c	1/2c
Coffee/Tea/Decaf	Coffee/Tea/Decaf	Coffee/Tea/Decaf	free	free	free	free
2 Plums—No Skin	2 Plums	2 UNSW Plums	2	2	2	2
Milk[3] or STR Juice	Skim Milk or Juice	1/2c Skim Milk	1/2c	1/2c	1/2c	1/2c
Plain Cookies, Gelatin,	LF Cookies, LF Crackers,	1 Starch/Bread Exch	1	1	1	1
Plain Crackers, Banana,	Gelatin, Fresh Fruit	1 Meat Exch	0	0	0	1
Vanilla Ice Cream[3]		1 Fat Exch	0	0	1	1

Recipe	Regular, Liberal Bland[1], No Added Salt[2]	1–2 gm Na (Low Sodium)	Mechanical Soft	Puree
	Breakfast			
	1/2c Cranberry Juice	1/2c Cranberry Juice	1/2c Cranberry Juice	1/2c STR Cranberry Juice
B1	1/2c Farina or	1/2c Farina or	1/2c Farina or	1c Farina
	3/4c Asst Dry Cereals	3/4c SR Asst Dry Cereals	3/4c Asst Dry Cereals+	NO
B4,5	1 Egg to Order	1 Egg to Order	1 Egg to Order	1 PUR Egg to Order
B12	1 Waffle	1 Waffle	1 Waffle+	1 sl Bread+
	2 oz Maple Syrup	2 oz Maple Syrup	2 oz Maple Syrup	NO
	1 tsp Margarine	1 tsp SR Margarine	1 tsp Margarine	1 tsp Margarine
	1 tsp Jam/Jelly	1 tsp Jam/Jelly	1 tsp Jelly	1 tsp Jelly
	1c Milk	1c Milk	1c Milk	1c Milk
	Coffee/Tea/Decaf	Coffee/Tea/Decaf	Coffee/Tea/Decaf	Coffee/Tea/Decaf
	Lunch			
K16	1/2c Mixed Vegetable Salad	1/2c Mixed Vegetable Salad	1/2c Juice	1/2c STR Juice
D3	3 oz Brisket with	3 oz Brisket with	3 oz CHP Brisket with	4 oz PUR Brisket with
	2 oz Gravy	2 oz Gravy	2 oz Gravy	2 oz Gravy
J40	4 oz Potato Pancakes	4 oz Potato Pancakes	4 oz Potato Pancakes+	1/2c PUR Potato Pancakes
J10,47	1/2c Broccoli Cuts	1/2c Broccoli Cuts	1/2c Broccoli Cuts	1/2c PUR Broccoli
	1 Dinner Roll	1 Dinner Roll	1 SFT Dinner Roll+	1 sl Bread+
	1 tsp Margarine	1 tsp SR Margarine	1 tsp Margarine	1 tsp Margarine
	1/2c Milk	1/2c Milk	1/2c Milk	1/2c Milk
	Coffee/Tea/Decaf	Coffee/Tea/Decaf	Coffee/Tea/Decaf	Coffee/Tea/Decaf
	1/2c Applesauce	1/2c Applesauce	1/2c Applesauce	1/2c Applesauce
	Dinner			
C27,1	2/3c Chunky Veg Soup	2/3c SR Chunky Veg Soup	2/3c Chunky Veg Soup	2/3c PUR/STR Chunky Veg Soup
I18	1/2c Seafood Salad in	1/2c SR Seafood Salad in	1/2c SFT Seafood Salad	1/2c PUR Seafood Salad
I23	1 Whole Tomato	1 Whole Tomato	1/2c Stewed Tomatoes	1/2c PUR Stewed Tomatoes
	Lettuce Leaves	Lettuce Leaves	NO	NO
K15	1/2c Cheesy Macaroni Sld	1/2c SR Cheesy Macaroni Sld	1/2c SFT Cheesy Mcrni Sld	1/2 PUR Cheesy Mcrni Sld
	1 Dinner Roll	1 Dinner Roll	1 SFT Dinner Roll+	1 sl Bread+
	1 tsp Margarine	1 tsp SR Margarine	1 tsp Margarine	1 tsp Margarine
	1/2c Milk	1/2c Milk	1/2c Milk	1/2c Milk
	Coffee/Tea/Decaf	Coffee/Tea/Decaf	Coffee/Tea/Decaf	Coffee/Tea/Decaf
	1/2c Sherbet	1/2c Sherbet	1/2c Sherbet	1/2c Sherbet
	Snacks			
	Milk or Juice	Juice	Milk or Juice	Milk or STR Juice
	Cookies, Crackers,	SR Cookies, SR Crackers,	Plain Cookies, Gelatin,	Applesauce, SFT Banana,
	Gelatin, Ice Cream,	Gelatin, Fresh Fruit	Plain Crackers+, Ice Cream,	Gelatin, Ice Cream
	Fresh Fruit		Banana	

TERMS: SFT = Soft; SLF = Soft/Low Fiber; GRD = Ground; CHP = Chopped Finely; PUR = Puree; STR = Strained; SR = Sodium or Salt Restricted; LF = Low Fat; FF = Fat Free; LCH = Low Cholesterol; DB = Diabetic; UNSW = Unsweetened; RC = Reduced Calorie; LC = Low Calorie; EXCH = Diabetic Exchange

SERVING UTENSILS: #6 Scoop = 2/3 cup-6 oz; #8 Scoop = 1/2 cup-4 oz; #10 Scoop = 3/8 cup-3 to 4 oz; #12 Scoop = 1/3 cup-2.5 to 3 oz; #16 Scoop = 1/4 cup-2 oz; #30 Scoop = 2 tbsp-1 oz; #60 Scoop = 1 tbsp-1/2 oz. Ounces will vary, based on food used.

1. *Liberal Bland:* Follow a regular diet. Use decaffeinated products. Omit pepper and chili powder.

2. *No Added Salt (3–4 gm NA):* Follow a regular diet. Use SR soups and SR canned meats. Omit salt packets (and shakers), bacon, sausage, smoked, and cured meats, substitute with SR food choices.

3. *Low Fiber:* Follow a soft diet. Do not exceed 2 cups of milk per day. Soft/Low Fiber—Omit pepper, garlic, and onions from recipes.

4. *2200 Calorie Diet:* Follow 2000 calorie diet with the following additions: Lunch—add 1 bread exchange and 1 fat exchange; Dinner—add 1 bread exchange.

+Consider individual tolerance. Daily Alternatives: Lunch and Dinner—Chicken, Hamburger, Cottage Cheese Fruit Plate, or Assorted Sandwiches. Individual preferences are provided upon request.

Amounts specified for food items that contain bone is equivalent to cooked, edible deboned portion.

Soft, Low Fiber[3]	Low Cholesterol, Low Fat (40–50 gm)	No Concentrated Sweets (Diabetic)	1200	1500	1800	2000[4]
			Diabetic/Calorie-Controlled			
1/2c STR Cranberry Juice	1/2c Cranberry Juice	1/2c UNSW Cranberry Juice	1/3c	1/3c	1/2c	1/2c
1/2c Farina or	1/2c LF Farina or	1/2c DB Farina or	1/2c	1/2c	1/2c	1/2c
3/4c Asst Refined Cereals	3/4c Dry Cereals	3/4c UNSW Dry Cereals	3/4c	3/4c	3/4c	3/4c
1 Egg to Order	1 Egg Substitute	1 Egg to Order	1	1	1	1
1 Waffle+	1 LF Waffle	1 DB Waffle, 4,5"sq	1	1	1	1
2 oz Maple Syrup	2 oz Maple Syrup	1 oz DB Maple Syrup	1 oz	1 oz	1 oz	1 oz
1 tsp Margarine	NO	1 tsp Margarine	0	0	1 tsp	1 tsp
1 tsp Jelly	1 tsp Jam/Jelly	1 tsp DB Jam/Jelly	1 tsp	1 tsp	1 tsp	1 tsp
1c Milk	1c Skim Milk	1c Skim Milk	1/2c	1/2c	1/2c	1c
Coffee/Tea/Decaf	Coffee/Tea/Decaf	Coffee/Tea/Decaf	free	free	free	free
1/2c STR Juice	1/2c LF Mixed Vegtable Sld	1/2c DB Mixed Vegtable Sld	Lett	1/2c	1/2c	1/2c
3 oz SLF Brisket with	2 oz Brisket+ with	3 oz Brisket with	2 oz	3 oz	3 oz	3 oz
2 oz SLF Gravy	2 oz LF Broth	2 oz LF Broth	2 oz	2 oz	2 oz	2 oz
4 oz SLF Potato Pancakes	4 oz LF Potato Pancakes	4 oz DB Potato Pancakes	2 oz	4 oz	4 oz	4 oz
1/2c Spinach	1/2c LF Broccoli Cuts+	1/2c LF Broccoli Cuts	1/2c	1/2c	1/2c	1/2c
1 SFT Refined Dinner Roll	1 Dinner Roll	1 Dinner Roll	0	0	1 sm	1 sm
1 tsp Margarine	1 tsp Margarine	1 tsp Margarine	0	0	1 tsp	1 tsp
1/2c Milk	1/2c Skim Milk	1/2c Skim Milk	1/2c	1/2c	1/2c	1/2c
Coffee/Tea/Decaf	Coffee/Tea/Decaf	Coffee/Tea/Decaf	free	free	free	free
1/2c Applesauce	1/2c Applesauce	1/2c UNSW Applesauce	1/2c	1/2c	1/2c	1/2c
2/3c SLF Broth	2/3c Chunky Veg Soup+	2/3c Chunky Veg Soup	2/3c	2/3c	2/3c	2/3c
1/2c SFT Seafood Salad	1/2c LF Seafood Salad in	1/2c LF Seafood Salad in	1/2c	3/4c	3/4c	3/4c
1/2c SLF Stewed Tomatoes	1 Whole Tomato	1 Whole Tomato	1	1	1	1
NO	Lettuce Leaves	Lettuce Leaves	Lett	Lett	Lett	Lett
1/2c SFT Cheesy Macaroni Sld	1/2c LF Cheesy Macaroni Sld	1/2c LF Cheesy Macaroni Sld	1/4c	1/3c	1/2c	1/2c
1 SFT Refined Dinner Roll	1 Dinner Roll	1 Dinner Roll	0	1 sm	1 sm	1 sm
1 tsp Margarine	NO	1 tsp Margarine	0	0	0	1 tsp
1/2c Milk (1/4c)[3]	1/2c Skim Milk	1/2c Skim Milk	1/2c	1/2c	1/2c	1/2c
Coffee/Tea/Decaf	Coffee/Tea/Decaf	Coffee/Tea/Decaf	free	free	free	free
1/2c Orange Sherbet	1/2c LF Sherbet	1/2c LF Sherbet	1/2c	1/2c	1/2c	1/2c
Milk[3] or STR Juice	Skim Milk or Juice	1/2c Skim Milk	1/2c	1/2c	1/2c	1/2c
Plain Cookies, Gelatin,	LF Cookies, LF Crackers,	1 Starch/Bread Exch	1	1	1	1
Plain Crackers, Banana,	Gelatin, Fresh Fruit	1 Meat Exch	0	0	0	1
Vanilla Ice Cream[3]		1 Fat Exch	0	0	1	1

Recipe	Regular, Liberal Bland[1], No Added Salt[2]	1–2 gm Na (Low Sodium)	Mechanical Soft	Puree
	Breakfast			
	1/2c Apple Juice or	1/2c Apple Juice or	1/2c Apple Juice	1/2c STR Apple Juice
	1/2c Fresh Fruit	1/2c Fresh Fruit	NO	NO
B1	1/2c Cream of Rice or	1/2c Cream of Rice or	1/2c Cream of Rice or	1c Cream of Rice
	3/4c Asst Dry Cereals	3/4c SR Asst Dry Cereals	3/4c Asst Dry Cereals+	NO
I2	1 oz Cheese-Grilled on	1 oz SR Cheese-Grilled on	1 oz Cheese on	1/2c PUR Cottage Cheese
	1 sl Toast	1 sl Toast	1 sl Bread	1 sl Bread+
	1 tsp Margarine	1 tsp SR Margarine	1 tsp Margarine	1 tsp Margarine
	1 tsp Jam/Jelly	1 tsp Jam/Jelly	1 tsp Jelly	1 tsp Jelly
	1c Milk	1c Milk	1c Milk	1c Milk
	Coffee/Tea/Decaf	Coffee/Tea/Decaf	Coffee/Tea/Decaf	Coffee/Tea/Decaf
	Lunch			
K29	1c Tossed Salad	1c Tossed Salad	1/2c Juice	1/2c STR Juice
P8	1 oz 1000 Island Drsg	1 oz SR 1000 Isd Drsg	NO	NO
E1,7	3 oz BBQ Chicken with	3 oz SR BBQ Chicken with	3 oz CHP BBQ Chicken with	4 oz PUR BBQ Chicken with
O2	2 oz Barbecue Sauce	2 oz SR Barbecue Sauce	2 oz SFT Barbecue Sauce	2 oz SFT Barbecue Sauce
J31,3	1/2c Green Peas	1/2c Green Peas	1/2c Green Peas	1/2c PUR Green Peas
J14	1/2c Carrots	1/2c Carrots	1/2c Carrots	1/2c PUR Carrots
	1 Dinner Roll	1 Dinner Roll	1 SFT Dinner Roll+	1 sl Bread+
	1 tsp Margarine	1 tsp SR Margarine	1 tsp Margarine	1 tsp Margarine
	1/2c Milk	1/2c Milk	1/2c Milk	1/2c Milk
	Coffee/Tea/Decaf	Coffee/Tea/Decaf	Coffee/Tea/Decaf	Coffee/Tea/Decaf
	1/2c Sliced Peaches	1/2c Sliced Peaches	1/2c Sliced Peaches	1/2c PUR Peaches
	Dinner			
C11	2/3c Cream Celery Soup	2/3c Cream Celery Soup	2/3c Cream Celery Soup	2/3c PUR/STR Crm Celery Soup
G8	5 1/2 oz Vegetable Omelette	5 1/2 oz Vegetable Omelette	5 1/2 oz SFT Vegetable Omelette	5 1/2 oz PUR Vegetable Omelette
J36	1/2c Home Fried Potatoes	1/2c Home Fried Potatoes	1/2c Home Fried Potatoes	1/2c PUR Home Fries
	1 Dinner Roll	1 Dinner Roll	1 SFT Dinner Roll+	1 sl Bread+
	1 tsp Margarine	1 tsp SR Margarine	1 tsp Margarine	1 tsp Margarine
	1/2c Milk	1/4c Milk	1/2c Milk	1/2c Milk
	Coffee/Tea/Decaf	Coffee/Tea/Decaf	Coffee/Tea/Decaf	Coffee/Tea/Decaf
Q2	3 × 2" sl Banana Cake	3 × 2" sl Banana Cake	3 × 2" sl Banana Cake+	1/2c Banana Pudding
	Snacks			
	Milk or Juice	Juice	Milk or Juice	Milk or STR Juice
	Cookies, Crackers,	SR Cookies, SR Crackers,	Plain Cookies, Gelatin,	Applesauce, SFT Banana,
	Gelatin, Ice Cream,	Gelatin, Fresh Fruit	Plain Crackers+, Ice Cream,	Gelatin, Ice Cream
	Fresh Fruit		Banana	

TERMS: SFT = Soft; SLF = Soft/Low Fiber; GRD = Ground; CHP = Chopped Finely; PUR = Puree; STR = Strained; SR = Sodium or Salt Restricted; LF = Low Fat; FF = Fat Free; LCH = Low Cholesterol; DB = Diabetic; UNSW = Unsweetened; RC = Reduced Calorie; LC = Low Calorie; EXCH = Diabetic Exchange

SERVING UTENSILS: #6 Scoop = 2/3 cup-6 oz; #8 Scoop = 1/2 cup-4 oz; #10 Scoop = 3/8 cup-3 to 4 oz; #12 Scoop = 1/3 cup-2 1/2 to 3 oz; #16 Scoop = 1/4 cup-2 oz; #30 Scoop = 2 tbsp-1 oz; #60 Scoop = 1 tbsp-1/2 oz. Ounces will vary, based on food used.

1. *Liberal Bland:* Follow a regular diet. Use decaffeinated products. Omit pepper and chili powder.

2. *No Added Salt (3–4 gm NA):* Follow a regular diet. Use SR soups and SR canned meats. Omit salt packets (and shakers), bacon, sausage, smoked, and cured meats, substitute with SR food choices.

3. *Low Fiber:* Follow a soft diet. Do not exceed 2 cups of milk per day. Soft/Low Fiber—Omit pepper, garlic, and onions from recipes.

4. *2200 Calorie Diet:* Follow 2000 calorie diet with the following additions: Lunch—add 1 bread exchange and 1 fat exchange; Dinner—add 1 bread exchange.

+Consider individual tolerance. Daily Alternatives: Lunch and Dinner—Chicken, Hamburger, Cottage Cheese Fruit Plate, or Assorted Sandwiches. Individual preferences are provided upon request.

Amounts specified for food items that contain bone is equivalent to cooked, edible deboned portion.

Soft, Low Fiber[3]	Low Cholesterol, Low Fat (40–50 gm)	No Concentrated Sweets (Diabetic)	1200	1500	1800	2000[4]
			Diabetic/Calorie-Controlled			
1/2c STR Apple Juice	1/2c Apple Juice or	1/2c UNSW Apple Juice or	1/2c	1/2c	1/2c	1/2c
NO	1/2c Fresh Fruit	1/2c Fresh Fruit	1/2c	1/2c	1/2c	1/2c
1/2c Cream of Rice or	1/2c LF Cream of Rice or	1/2c DB Cream of Rice or	1/2c	1/2c	1/2c	1/2c
3/4c Asst Refined Cereals	3/4c Dry Cereals	3/4c UNSW Dry Cereals	3/4c	3/4c	3/4c	3/4c
1 oz Mild Chse-Grilled on	1 oz LF Cheese-Grilled on	1 oz LF Cheese-Grilled on	1 oz	1 oz	1 oz	1 oz
1 sl White Toast	1 sl Toast	1 sl Toast	1 sl	1 sl	1 sl	1 sl
1 tsp Margarine	1 tsp Margarine	1 tsp Margarine	0	0	1 tsp	1 tsp
1 tsp Jelly	1 tsp Jam/Jelly	1 tsp DB Jam/Jelly	1 tsp	1 tsp	1 tsp	1 tsp
1c Milk	1c Skim Milk	1c Skim Milk	1/2c	1/2c	1/2c	1c
Coffee/Tea/Decaf	Coffee/Tea/Decaf	Coffee/Tea/Decaf	free	free	free	free
1/2c STR Juice	1c Tossed Salad	1c Tossed Salad	1c	1c	1c	1c
NO	1 Tbsp LC 1000 Isd Drsg	1 Tbsp LC 1000 Isd Drsg	1 Tbsp	1 Tbsp	1 Tbsp	1 Tbsp
3 oz Roast Chicken	2 oz LF BBQ Chicken with	3 oz LF BBQ Chicken with	2 oz	3 oz	3 oz	3 oz
No	2 oz Barbecue Sauce+	2 oz DB Barbecue Sauce	1 oz	2 oz	2 oz	2 oz
1/2c Wax Beans	1/2c Green Peas	1/2c Green Peas	1/4c	1/2c	1/2c	1/2c
1/2c Carrots	1/2c Carrots	1/2c Carrots	1/2c	1/2c	1/2c	1/2c
1 SFT Refined Dinner Roll	1 Dinner Roll	1 Dinner Roll	0	0	1 sm	1 sm
1 tsp Margarine	NO	1 tsp Margarine	0	0	1 tsp	1 tsp
1/2c Milk	1/2c Skim Milk	1/2c Skim Milk	1/2c	1/2c	1/2c	1/2c
Coffee/Tea/Decaf	Coffee/Tea/Decaf	Coffee/Tea/Decaf	free	free	free	free
1/2c Sliced Peaches	1/2c Sliced Peaches	1/2c UNSW Sliced Peaches	1/2c	1/2c	1/2c	1/2c
2/3c PUR/STR Crm Celery Soup	2/3c LF Cream Celery Soup	2/3c LF Cream Celery Soup	2/3c	2/3c	2/3c	2/3c
5 1/2 oz SLF Vegetable Omelette	5 1/2 oz Egg Sub w/Vegetables	5 1/2 oz DB Vegetable Omelette	5 oz	5 1/2 oz	5 1/2 oz	5 1/2 oz
1/2c Home Fried Potatoes	1/2c LF Home Frd Potatoes	1/2c LF Home Frd Potatoes	1/2c	1/2c	1/2c	1/2c
1 SFT Refined Dinner Roll	1 Dinner Roll	1 Dinner Roll	0	1 sm	1 sm	1 med
1 tsp Margarine	NO	1 tsp Margarine	0	0	1 tsp	2 tsp
1/2c Milk (1/4c)[3]	1/2c Skim Milk	1/2c Skim Milk	1/2c	1/2c	1/2c	1/2c
Coffee/Tea/Decaf	Coffee/Tea/Decaf	Coffee/Tea/Decaf	free	free	free	free
3 × 2" sl Banana Cake	2 × 2" sl LF Banana Cake	2 × 2" sl DB Banana Cake	2 × 1"	2 × 1"	2 × 2"	2 × 2"
Milk[3] or STR Juice	Skim Milk or Juice	1/2c Skim Milk	1/2c	1/2c	1/2c	1/2c
Plain Cookies, Gelatin,	LF Cookies, LF Crackers,	1 Starch/Bread Exch	1	1	1	1
Plain Crackers, Banana,	Gelatin, Fresh Fruit	1 Meat Exch	0	0	0	1
Vanilla Ice Cream[3]		1 Fat Exch	0	0	1	1

Recipe	Regular, Liberal Bland[1], No Added Salt[2]	1–2 gm Na (Low Sodium)	Mechanical Soft	Puree
	Breakfast			
	1/2c Orange Juice	1/2c Orange Juice	1/2c Orange Juice	1/2c STR Orange Juice
B1	1/2c Oatmeal or	1/2c Oatmeal or	1/2c Oatmeal or	1c Oatmeal
	3/4c Asst Dry Cereals	3/4c SR Asst Dry Cereals	3/4c Asst Dry Cereals+	NO
B4	1 Poached Egg	1 Poached Egg	1 Poached Egg	1 Poached Egg
	1 English Muffin	1 English Muffin	1 sl Bread	1 sl Bread+
	1 tsp Margarine	1 tsp SR Margarine	1 tsp Margarine	1 tsp Margarine
	1 tsp Jam/Jelly	1 tsp Jam/Jelly	1 tsp Jelly	1 tsp Jelly
	1c Milk	1c Milk	1c Milk	1c Milk
	Coffee/Tea/Decaf	Coffee/Tea/Decaf	Coffee/Tea/Decaf	Coffee/Tea/Decaf
	Lunch			
K23	1/2c Marinated Zucchini	1/2c Marinated Zucchini	1/2c Juice	1/2c STR Juice
D22	3 1/2 oz Breaded Veal	3 1/2 oz SR Breaded Veal	3 1/2 oz CHP Breaded Veal	4 oz PUR Breaded Veal
O20,22	2 oz Marinara Sauce	2 oz SR Marinara Sauce	2 oz SFT Marinara Sauce	2 oz SFT Marinara Sauce
M5	3/4c Pasta Primavera	3/4c Pasta Primavera	3/4c SFT Pasta Primavera	3/4c PUR Pasta Primavera
	1 sl Italian Bread	1 sl Italian Bread	1 SFT Dinner Roll	1 sl Bread+
	1 tsp Margarine	1 tsp SR Margarine	1 tsp Margarine	1 tsp Margarine
	1/2c Milk	1/2c Milk	1/2c Milk	1/2c Milk
	Coffee/Tea/Decaf	Coffee/Tea/Decaf	Coffee/Tea/Decaf	Coffee/Tea/Decaf
S5	1/2c Fresh Fruit Cup	1/2c Fresh Fruit Cup	1/2c Fruit Cup+	1/2c PUR Fruit Cup
	Dinner			
C4,1	2/3c Bean Soup	2/3c SR/LF Bean Soup	2/3c Bean Soup	2/3c PUR Bean Soup
I4	Assorted Cold Cut Sandwiches:	Assorted Cold Cut Sandwiches:	Assorted Cold Cut Sandwiches:	Assorted Cold Cut Sandwiches:
	2 sl Bread with	2 sl Bread with	2 sl Bread+ with	1 sl Bread+
	3 oz Roast Beef, Ham[2], Turkey, Bologna[2], and Salami[2]	3 oz Roast Beef and Turkey	3 oz Roast Beef, Ham, Turkey, Bologna, and Salami	3 oz PUR Roast Beef, PUR Turkey, PUR Bologna PUR Ham and PUR Salami
	Lettuce Leaves	Lettuce Leaves	CHP Lettuce Leaves+	NO
J50	4 Tomato Slices	4 Tomato Slices	1/2c Stewed Tomatoes	1/2c PUR Stewed Tomatoes
K5,21	1/2c Cole Slaw	1/2c Cole Slaw	1/2c SFT Potato Salad	1/2c PUR Potato Salad
	1 tsp Catsup & Mustard	1 tsp SR Catsup	1 tsp Catsup & Mustard	1 tsp Catsup & Mustard
	1 Tbsp Mayonnaise	1 Tbsp SR Mayonnaise	1 Tbsp Mayonnaise	1 Tbsp Mayonnaise
	1/2c Milk	1/2c Milk	1/2c Milk	1/2c Milk
	Coffee/Tea/Decaf	Coffee/Tea/Decaf	Coffee/Tea/Decaf	Coffee/Tea/Decaf
S12	1/2c Strawberry Gelatin	1/2c Strawberry Gelatin	1/2c Strawberry Gelatin	1/2c Strawberry Gelatin
	Snacks			
	Milk or Juice	Juice	Milk or Juice	Milk or STR Juice
	Cookies, Crackers, Gelatin, Ice Cream, Fresh Fruit	SR Cookies, SR Crackers, Gelatin, Fresh Fruit	Plain Cookies, Gelatin, Plain Crackers+, Ice Cream, Banana	Applesauce, SFT Banana, Gelatin, Ice Cream

TERMS: SFT = Soft; SLF = Soft/Low Fiber; GRD = Ground; CHP = Chopped Finely; PUR = Puree; STR = Strained; SR = Sodium or Salt Restricted; LF = Low Fat; FF = Fat Free; LCH = Low Cholesterol; DB = Diabetic; UNSW = Unsweetened; RC = Reduced Calorie; LC = Low Calorie; EXCH = Diabetic Exchange

SERVING UTENSILS: #6 Scoop = 2/3 cup-6 oz; #8 Scoop = 1/2 cup-4 oz; #10 Scoop = 3/8 cup-3 to 4 oz; #12 Scoop = 1/3 cup-2 1/2 to 3 oz; #16 Scoop = 1/4 cup-2 oz; #30 Scoop = 2 tbsp-1 oz; #60 Scoop = 1 tbsp-1/2 oz. Ounces will vary, based on food used.

1. *Liberal Bland:* Follow a regular diet. Use decaffeinated products. Omit pepper and chili powder.

2. *No Added Salt (3–4 gm NA):* Follow a regular diet. Use SR soups and SR canned meats. Omit salt packets (and shakers), bacon, sausage, smoked, and cured meats, substitute with SR food choices.

3. *Low Fiber:* Follow a soft diet. Do not exceed 2 cups of milk per day. Soft/Low Fiber—Omit pepper, garlic, and onions from recipes.

4. *2200 Calorie Diet:* Follow 2000 calorie diet with the following additions: Lunch—add 1 bread exchange and 1 fat exchange; Dinner—add 1 bread exchange.

+Consider individual tolerance. Daily Alternatives: Lunch and Dinner—Chicken, Hamburger, Cottage Cheese Fruit Plate, or Assorted Sandwiches. Individual preferences are provided upon request.

Amounts specified for food items that contain bone is equivalent to cooked, edible deboned portion.

Soft, Low Fiber[3]	Low Cholesterol, Low Fat (40–50 gm)	No Concentrated Sweets (Diabetic)	1200	1500	1800	2000[4]
			Diabetic/Calorie-Controlled			
1/2c STR Orange Juice	1/2c Orange Juice	1/2c UNSW Orange Juice	1/2c	1/2c	1/2c	1/2c
1/2c Oatmeal or	1/2c LF Oatmeal or	1/2c DB Oatmeal or	1/2c	1/2c	1/2c	1/2c
3/4c Asst Refined Cereals	3/4c Dry Cereals	3/4c UNSW Dry Cereals	3/4c	3/4c	3/4c	3/4c
1 Poached Egg	1 Egg Substitute	1 Poached Egg	1	1	1	1
1 sl White Toast	1 English Muffin	1 English Muffin	1/2	1	1	1
1 tsp Margarine	1 tsp Margarine	1 tsp Margarine	0	1 tsp	1 tsp	2 tsp
1 tsp Jelly	1 tsp Jam/Jelly	1 tsp DB Jam/Jelly	1 tsp	1 tsp	1 tsp	1 tsp
1c Milk	1c Skim Milk	1c Skim Milk	1/2c	1/2c	1/2c	1c
Coffee/Tea/Decaf	Coffee/Tea/Decaf	Coffee/Tea/Decaf	free	free	free	free
1/2c STR Juice	1/2c LF Marinated Zucchini	1/2c DB Marinated Zucchini	1/2c	1/2c	1/2c	1/2c
3 1/2 oz SLF Breaded Veal	2 1/2 oz LF Breaded Veal	3 1/2 oz DB Breaded Veal	2 1/2 oz	3 1/2 oz	3 1/2 oz	3 1/2 oz
2 oz SLF Tomato Sauce	2 oz Marinara Sauce+	2 oz Marinara Sauce	1 oz	1 oz	2 oz	2 oz
3/4c SFT Pasta Primavera	3/4c LF Pasta Primavera	3/4c LF Pasta Primavera	1/2c	3/4c	1c	1c
1 SFT Refined Dinner Roll	1 sl Italian Bread	1 sl Italian Bread	0	0	1 sl	1 sl
1 tsp Margarine	NO	1 tsp Margarine	0	0	1 tsp	1 tsp
1/2c Milk	1/2c Skim Milk	1/2c Skim Milk	1/2c	1/2c	1/2c	1/2c
Coffee/Tea/Decaf	Coffee/Tea/Decaf	Coffee/Tea/Decaf	free	free	free	free
1/2c SLF Fruit Cup	1/2c Fresh Fruit Cup	1/2c Fresh Fruit Cup	1/2c	1/2c	1/2c	1/2c
2/3c SLF Broth	2/3c SR/LF Bean Soup	2/3c SR/LF Bean Soup	2/3c	2/3c	2/3c	2/3c
Assorted Cold Cut Sandwiches:	Assorted Cold Cut Sandwiches:	Assorted Cold Cut Sandwiches:				
2 sl White Bread with	2 sl Bread with	2 sl Bread with	2 sl	2 sl	2 sl	2 sl
3 oz Roast Beef and Turkey	2 oz Roast Beef and Turkey	3 oz Roast Beef, Ham, Turkey, Bologna, and Salami	2 oz	3 oz	3 oz	3 oz
NO	Lettuce Leaves	Lettuce Leaves	free	free	free	free
1/2c SLF Stewed Tomatoes	4 Tomato Slices	4 Tomato Slices	4 sl	4 sl	4 sl	4 sl
1/2c SFT Potato Salad	1/2c Cole Slaw+	1/2c DB Cole Slaw	1/2c	1/2c	1/2c	1/2c
1 tsp Catsup	1 tsp Catsup & Mustard	1 tsp Catsup & Mustard	1 tsp	1 tsp	1 tsp	1 tsp
1 Tbsp Mayonnaise	1 Tbsp LF Mayonnaise	1 Tbsp LF Mayonnaise	0	0	0	0
1/2c Milk	1/2c Skim Milk	1/2c Skim Milk	1/2c	1/2c	1/2c	1/2c
Coffee/Tea/Decaf	Coffee/Tea/Decaf	Coffee/Tea/Decaf	free	free	free	free
1/2c Strawberry Gelatin	1/2c Strawberry Gelatin	1/2c DB Strawberry Gelatin	1/2c	1/2c	1/2c	1/2c
Milk[3] or STR Juice	Skim Milk or Juice	1/2c Skim Milk	1/2c	1/2c	1/2c	1/2c
Plain Cookies, Gelatin,	LF Cookies, LF Crackers,	1 Starch/Bread Exch	1	1	1	1
Plain Crackers, Banana,	Gelatin, Fresh Fruit	1 Meat Exch	0	0	0	1
Vanilla Ice Cream[3]		1 Fat Exch	0	0	1	1

Recipe	Regular, Liberal Bland[1], No Added Salt[2]	1–2 gm Na (Low Sodium)	Mechanical Soft	Puree
	Breakfast			
	1/2c Pineapple Juice	1/2c Pineapple Juice	1/2c Pineapple Juice	1/2c STR Pineapple Juice
B1	1/2c Cream of Wheat or	1/2c Cream of Wheat or	1/2c Cream of Wheat or	1c Cream of Wheat
	3/4c Asst Dry Cereals	3/4c SR Asst Dry Cereals	3/4c Asst Dry Cereals+	NO
B4	1 Soft-Cooked Egg	1 Soft-Cooked Egg	1 Soft-Cooked Egg	1 Soft-Cooked Egg
	1 sl Toast	1 sl Toast	1 sl Bread	1 sl Bread+
	1 tsp Margarine	1 tsp SR Margarine	1 tsp Margarine	1 tsp Margarine
	1 tsp Jam/Jelly	1 tsp Jam/Jelly	1 tsp Jelly	1 tsp Jelly
	1c Milk	1c Milk	1c Milk	1c Milk
	Coffee/Tea/Decaf	Coffee/Tea/Decaf	Coffee/Tea/Decaf	Coffee/Tea/Decaf
	Lunch			
K32	1c Tossed Vegetable Salad	1c Tossed Vegetable Salad	1/2c Juice	1/2c STR Juice
P1-8	1 oz Salad Dressing	1 oz SR Salad Dressing	NO	NO
D1	3 1/2 oz Beef Teriyaki	3 1/2 oz SR Beef Teriyaki	3 1/2 oz Beef Teriyaki+	4 oz PUR Beef Teriyaki
J22	1/2c Chinese Vegetables	1/2c SR Chinese Vegetables	1/2c Chinese Vegetables+	1/2c PUR Chinese Vegetables
11	1/2c White Rice	1/2c White Rice	1/2c White Rice	1/2c PUR White Rice
	1 Dinner Roll	1 Dinner Roll	1 SFT Dinner Roll+	1 sl Bread+
	1 tsp Margarine	1 tsp SR Margarine	1 tsp Margarine	1 tsp Margarine
	1/2c Milk	1/4c Milk	1/2c Milk	1/2c Milk
	Coffee/Tea/Decaf	Coffee/Tea/Decaf	Coffee/Tea/Decaf	Coffee/Tea/Decaf
	1/2c Ice Cream	1/2c Ice Cream	1/2c Ice Cream	1/2c Ice Cream
	Dinner			
C26	2/3c Vegetable Beef Soup	2/3c SR Vegetable Beef Soup	2/3c Vegetable Beef Soup	2/3c PUR/STR Veg Beef Soup
E13	3/4c Turkey à la King	3/4c SR Turkey à la King	3/4c Turkey à la King	3/4c PUR Turkey à la King
	2 Toast Points	2 Toast Points	2 Toast Points	2 Bread Points+
J47	1/2c Spinach	1/2c Spinach	1/2c Spinach	1/2c PUR Spinach
	1/2c Milk	1/2c Milk	1/2c Milk	1/2c Milk
	Coffee/Tea/Decaf	Coffee/Tea/Decaf	Coffee/Tea/Decaf	Coffee/Tea/Decaf
	2 Plums	2 Plums	2 Plums—No Skin	1/2c PUR Plums
	Snacks			
	Milk or Juice	Juice	Milk or Juice	Milk or STR Juice
	Cookies, Crackers,	SR Cookies, SR Crackers,	Plain Cookies, Gelatin,	Applesauce, SFT Banana,
	Gelatin, Ice Cream,	Gelatin, Fresh Fruit	Plain Crackers+, Ice Cream,	Gelatin, Ice Cream
	Fresh Fruit		Banana	

TERMS: SFT = Soft; SLF = Soft/Low Fiber; GRD = Ground; CHP = Chopped Finely; PUR = Puree; STR = Strained; SR = Sodium or Salt Restricted; LF = Low Fat; FF = Fat Free; LCH = Low Cholesterol; DB = Diabetic; UNSW = Unsweetened; RC = Reduced Calorie; LC = Low Calorie; EXCH = Diabetic Exchange

SERVING UTENSILS: #6 Scoop = 2/3 cup-6 oz; #8 Scoop = 1/2 cup-4 oz; #10 Scoop = 3/8 cup-3 to 4 oz; #12 Scoop = 1/3 cup-2 1/2 to 3 oz; #16 Scoop = 1/4 cup-2 oz; #30 Scoop = 2 tbsp-1 oz; #60 Scoop = 1 tbsp-1/2 oz. Ounces will vary, based on food used.

1. *Liberal Bland:* Follow a regular diet. Use decaffeinated products. Omit pepper and chili powder.

2. *No Added Salt (3–4 gm NA):* Follow a regular diet. Use SR soups and SR canned meats. Omit salt packets (and shakers), bacon, sausage, smoked, and cured meats, substitute with SR food choices.

3. *Low Fiber:* Follow a soft diet. Do not exceed 2 cups of milk per day. Soft/Low Fiber—Omit pepper, garlic, and onions from recipes.

4. *2200 Calorie Diet:* Follow 2000 calorie diet with the following additions: Lunch—add 1 bread exchange and 1 fat exchange; Dinner—add 1 bread exchange.

+Consider individual tolerance. Daily Alternatives: Lunch and Dinner—Chicken, Hamburger, Cottage Cheese Fruit Plate, or Assorted Sandwiches. Individual preferences are provided upon request.

Amounts specified for food items that contain bone is equivalent to cooked, edible deboned portion.

Soft, Low Fiber[3]	Low Cholesterol, Low Fat (40–50 gm)	No Concentrated Sweets (Diabetic)	1200	1500	1800	2000[4]
			Diabetic/Calorie-Controlled			
1/2c STR Cranberry Juice	1/2c Pineapple Juice	1/2c UNSW Pineapple Juice	1/2c	1/2c	1/2c	1/2c
1/2c Cream of Wheat or	1/2c LF Cream of Wheat or	1/2c DB Cream of Wheat or	1/2c	1/2c	1/2c	1/2c
3/4c Asst Refined Cereals	3/4c Dry Cereals	3/4c UNSW Cereals	3/4c	3/4c	3/4c	3/4c
1 Soft-Cooked Egg	1 Egg Substitute	1 Soft-Cooked Egg	1	1	1	1
1 sl White Toast	1 sl Toast	1 sl Toast	1 sl	1 sl	1 sl	2 sl
1 tsp Margarine	1 tsp Margarine	1 tsp Margarine	0	1 tsp	1 tsp	2 tsp
1 tsp Jelly	1 tsp Jam/Jelly	1 tsp DB Jam/Jelly	1 tsp	1 tsp	1 tsp	1 tsp
1c Milk	1c Skim Milk	1c Skim Milk	1/2c	1/2c	1/2c	1c
Coffee/Tea/Decaf	Coffee/Tea/Decaf	Coffee/Tea/Decaf	free	free	free	free
1/2c STR Juice	1c Tossed Vegetable Salad	1c Tossed Vegetable Salad	1c	1c	1c	1c
NO	1 Tbsp LC Salad Dressing	1 Tbsp LC Salad Dressing	1 Tbsp	1 Tbsp	2 Tbsp	2 Tbsp
3 1/2 oz SLF Beef Patty	3 oz LF Beef Teriyaki	3 1/2 oz LF Beef Teriyaki	2 1/2 oz	3 1/2 oz	3 1/2 oz	3 1/2 oz
1/2c SLF Chinese Vegetables	1/2c Chinese Vegetables+	1/2c Chinese Vegetables	1/2c	1/2c	1/2c	1/2c
1/2c White Rice	1/2c White Rice	1/2c White Rice	1/3c	1/3c	2/3c	2/3c
1 SFT Refined Dinner Roll	1 Dinner Roll	1 Dinner Roll	0	1 sm	1 sm	1 sm
1 tsp Margarine	NO	1 tsp Margarine	0	0	1 tsp	1 tsp
1/2c Milk (1/4c)[3]	1/2c Skim Milk	1/2c Skim Milk	1/4c	1/4c	1/2c	1/2c
Coffee/Tea/Decaf	Coffee/Tea/Decaf	Coffee/Tea/Decaf	free	free	free	free
1/2c Vanilla Ice Cream	1/2c LF Ice Milk	1/2c LF Ice Milk	1/2c	1/2c	1/2c	1/2c
2/3c SLF Vegetable Beef Soup	2/3c Vegetable Beef Soup	2/3c Vegetable Beef Soup	2/3c	2/3c	2/3c	2/3c
3/4c SLF Turkey à la King	2/3c LF Turkey à la King	3/4c LF Turkey à la King	2/3c	3/4c	3/4c	3/4c
2 White Toast Points	2 Toast Points	2 Toast Points	2 pts	2 pts	3 pts	3 pts
1/2c Spinach	1/2c Spinach	1/2c Spinach	1/2c	1/2c	1/2c	1/2c
1/2c Milk (1/4c)[3]	1/2c Skim Milk	1/2c Skim Milk	1/4c	1/2c	1/2c	1/2c
Coffee/Tea/Decaf	Coffee/Tea/Decaf	Coffee/Tea/Decaf	free	free	free	free
2 Plums—No Skin	2 Plums	2 UNSW Plums	2	2	2	2
Milk[3] or STR Juice	Skim Milk or Juice	1/2c Skim Milk	1/2c	1/2c	1/2c	1/2c
Plain Cookies, Gelatin,	LF Cookies, LF Crackers,	1 Starch/Bread Exch	1	1	1	1
Plain Crackers, Banana,	Gelatin, Fresh Fruit	1 Meat Exch	0	0	0	1
Vanilla Ice Cream[3]		1 Fat Exch	0	0	1	1

Recipe	Regular, Liberal Bland[1], No Added Salt[2]	1–2 gm Na (Low Sodium)	Mechanical Soft	Puree
	Breakfast			
	1/2c Apple Juice or	1/2c Apple Juice or	1/2c Apple Juice or	1/2c STR Apple Juice
S11	1/2c Stewed Prunes	1/2c Stewed Prunes	1/2c Stewed Prunes+	1/4c PUR Prunes
B1	1/2c Farina or	1/2c Farina or	1/2c Farina or	1c Farina
	3/4c Asst Dry Cereals	3/4c SR Asst Dry Cereals	3/4c Asst Dry Cereals+	NO
B4,5	1 Egg to Order	1 Egg to Order	1 Egg to Order	1 PUR Egg to Order
	1 sl Raisin Toast	1 sl Raisin Toast	1 sl Bread	1 sl Bread+
	1 tsp Margarine	1 tsp SR Margarine	1 tsp Margarine	1 tsp Margarine
	1 tsp Jam/Jelly	1 tsp Jam/Jelly	1 tsp Jelly	1 tsp Jelly
	1c Milk	1c Milk	1c Milk	1c Milk
	Coffee/Tea/Decaf	Coffee/Tea/Decaf	Coffee/Tea/Decaf	Coffee/Tea/Decaf
	Lunch			
K25	1c Green Salad	1c Green Salad	1/2c Juice	1/2c STR Juice
P6	1 oz Oil & Vinegar	1 oz Oil & Vinegar	NO	NO
D30	3 oz Pork Chops with	3 oz Pork Chops with	3 oz CHP Pork with	4 oz PUR Pork with
J37	1/4c Apple Stuffing	1/4c Apple Stuffing	1/4c Apple Stuffing+	1/4c PUR Apple Stuffing
J1	1/2c Asparagus Tips	1/2c Asparagus Tips	1/2c Asparagus Tips	1/2c PUR Asparagus Tips
	1 Dinner Roll	1 Dinner Roll	1 SFT Dinner Roll+	1 sl Bread+
	1 tsp Margarine	1 tsp SR Margarine	1 tsp Margarine	1 tsp Margarine
	1/2c Milk	1/4c Milk	1/2c Milk	1/2c Milk
	Coffee/Tea/Decaf	Coffee/Tea/Decaf	Coffee/Tea/Decaf	Coffee/Tea/Decaf
S16,17	1/2c Chocolate Pudding	1/2c Chocolate Pudding	1/2c Chocolate Pudding	1/2c Chocolate Pudding
	Dinner			
C21,1	2/3c Minestrone Soup	2/3c SR Minestrone Soup	2/3c Minestrone Soup	2/3c PUR/STR Minestrone Soup
D12	8 oz Beef Macaroni Cassrle	6 oz SR Beef Macaroni Cassrle	8 oz Beef Macaroni Cassrle	8 oz PUR Beef Macaroni Cassrle
J6	1/2c Seasoned Green Beans	1/2c Seasoned Green Beans	1/2c Seasoned Green Beans	1/2c PUR Seasoned Green Beans
	1 Dinner Roll	1 Dinner Roll	1 SFT Dinner Roll+	1 sl Bread+
	1 tsp Margarine	1 tsp SR Margarine	1 tsp Margarine	1 tsp Margarine
	1/2c Milk	1/2c Milk	1/2c Milk	1/2c Milk
	Coffee/Tea/Decaf	Coffee/Tea/Decaf	Coffee/Tea/Decaf	Coffee/Tea/Decaf
	1/2c Chilled Apricots	1/2c Chilled Apricots	1/2c Chilled Apricots	1/2c PUR Chilled Apricots
	Snacks			
	Milk or Juice	Juice	Milk or Juice	Milk or STR Juice
	Cookies, Crackers,	SR Cookies, SR Crackers,	Plain Cookies, Gelatin,	Applesauce, SFT Banana,
	Gelatin, Ice Cream,	Gelatin, Fresh Fruit	Plain Crackers+, Ice Cream,	Gelatin, Ice Cream
	Fresh Fruit		Banana	

TERMS: SFT = Soft; SLF = Soft/Low Fiber; GRD = Ground; CHP = Chopped Finely; PUR = Puree; STR = Strained; SR = Sodium or Salt Restricted; LF = Low Fat; FF = Fat Free; LCH = Low Cholesterol; DB = Diabetic; UNSW = Unsweetened; RC = Reduced Calorie; LC = Low Calorie; EXCH = Diabetic Exchange

SERVING UTENSILS: #6 Scoop = 2/3 cup-6 oz; #8 Scoop = 1/2 cup-4 oz; #10 Scoop = 3/8 cup-3 to 4 oz; #12 Scoop = 1/3 cup-2 1/2 to 3 oz; #16 Scoop = 1/4 cup-2 oz; #30 Scoop = 2 tbsp-1 oz; #60 Scoop = 1 tbsp-1/2 oz. Ounces will vary, based on food used.

1. *Liberal Bland:* Follow a regular diet. Use decaffeinated products. Omit pepper and chili powder.

2. *No Added Salt (3–4 gm NA):* Follow a regular diet. Use SR soups and SR canned meats. Omit salt packets (and shakers), bacon, sausage, smoked, and cured meats, substitute with SR food choices.

3. *Low Fiber:* Follow a soft diet. Do not exceed 2 cups of milk per day. Soft/Low Fiber—Omit pepper, garlic, and onions from recipes.

4. *2200 Calorie Diet:* Follow 2000 calorie diet with the following additions: Lunch—add 1 bread exchange and 1 fat exchange; Dinner—add 1 bread exchange.

+Consider individual tolerance. Daily Alternatives: Lunch and Dinner—Chicken, Hamburger, Cottage Cheese Fruit Plate, or Assorted Sandwiches. Individual preferences are provided upon request.

Amounts specified for food items that contain bone is equivalent to cooked, edible deboned portion.

Soft, Low Fiber[3]	Low Cholesterol, Low Fat (40–50 gm)	No Concentrated Sweets (Diabetic)	1200	1500	1800	2000[4] Diabetic/Calorie-Controlled		
1/2c STR Apple Juice	1/2c Apple Juice or	1/2c UNSW Apple Juice or	1/2c	1/2c	1/2c	1/2c
NO	1/2c Stewed Prunes	3 med Stewed Prunes	3 med	3 med	3 med	3 med
1/2c Farina or	1/2c LF Farina or	1/2c DB Farina or	1/2c	1/2c	1/2c	1/2c
3/4c Asst Refined Cereals	3/4c Dry Cereals	3/4c UNSW Dry Cereals	3/4c	3/4c	3/4c	3/4c
1 Egg to Order	1 Egg Substitute	1 Egg to Order	1	1	1	1
1 sl White Toast	1 sl Raisin Toast	1 sl Raisin Toast	1 sl	1 sl	1 sl	2 sl
1 tsp Margarine	1 tsp Margarine	1 tsp Margarine	0	1 tsp	1 tsp	1 tsp
1 tsp Jelly	1 tsp Jam/Jelly	1 tsp DB Jam/Jelly	1 tsp	1 tsp	1 tsp	1 tsp
1c Milk	1c Skim Milk	1c Skim Milk	1/2c	1/2c	1/2c	1c
Coffee/Tea/Decaf	Coffee/Tea/Decaf	Coffee/Tea/Decaf	free	free	free	free
1/2c STR Juice	1c Green Salad	1c Green Salad	1c	1c	1c	1c
NO	1 Tbsp LC Salad Dressing	1 Tbsp LC Salad Dressing	1 Tbsp	1 Tbsp	1 Tbsp	1 Tbsp
3 oz Pork Chops	2 oz Pork Chops with	3 oz Pork Chops with	2 oz	3 oz	3 oz	3 oz
1/2c Mashed Potatoes	1/4c LF Apple Stuffing	1/4c LF Apple Stuffing	1/4c	1/4c	1/2c	1/2c
1/2c Asparagus Tips	1/2c Asparagus Tips	1/2c Asparagus Tips	1/2c	1/2c	1/2c	1/2c
1 SFT Refined Dinner Roll	1 Dinner Roll	1 Dinner Roll	0	1 sm	1 sm	1 sm
1 tsp Margarine	NO	1 tsp Margarine	0	0	1 tsp	1 tsp
1/2c Milk (1/4c)[3]	1/2c Skim Milk	1/2c Skim Milk	1/4c	1/4c	1/2c	1/2c
Coffee/Tea/Decaf	Coffee/Tea/Decaf	Coffee/Tea/Decaf	free	free	free	free
1/2c Vanilla Pudding	1/2c LF Chocolate Pudding	1/2c DB Chocolate Pudding	1/2c	1/2c	1/2c	1/2c
2/3c SLF Broth	2/3c Minestrone Soup+	2/3c Minestrone Soup	2/3c	2/3c	2/3c	2/3c
8 oz SLF Beef Macaroni Cassrle	6 oz LF Beef Macaroni Cassrle+	8 oz LF Beef Macaroni Cassrle	6 oz	8 oz	8 oz	8 oz
1/2c SLF Seasoned Green Beans	1/2c LF Seasoned Green Beans	1/2c LF Seasoned Green Beans	1/2c	1/2c	1/2c	1/2c
1 SFT Refined Dinner Roll	1 Dinner Roll	1 Dinner Roll	0	0	1 sm	1 sm
1 tsp Margarine	NO	1 tsp Margarine	0	0	1 tsp	1 tsp
1/2c Milk	1/2c Skim Milk	1/2c Skim Milk	1/2c	1/2c	1/2c	1/2c
Coffee/Tea/Decaf	Coffee/Tea/Decaf	Coffee/Tea/Decaf	free	free	free	free
1/2c Chilled Apricots	1/2c Chilled Apricots	1/2c UNSW Chilled Apricots	1/2c	1/2c	1/2c	1/2c
Milk[3] or STR Juice	Skim Milk or Juice	1/2c Skim Milk	1/2c	1/2c	1/2c	1/2c
Plain Cookies, Gelatin,	LF Cookies, LF Crackers,	1 Starch/Bread Exch	1	1	1	1
Plain Crackers, Banana,	Gelatin, Fresh Fruit	1 Meat Exch	0	0	0	1
Vanilla Ice Cream[3]		1 Fat Exch	0	0	1	1

Recipe	Regular, Liberal Bland[1], No Added Salt[2]	1–2 gm Na (Low Sodium)	Mechanical Soft	Puree
	Breakfast			
	1/2c Grapefruit Juice	1/2c Grapefruit Juice	1/2c Grapefruit Juice	1/2c STR Grapefruit Juice
B1	1/2c Wheatena or	1/2c Wheatena or	1/2c Wheatena or	1c Wheatena
	3/4c Asst Dry Cereals	3/4c SR Asst Dry Cereals	3/4c Asst Dry Cereals+	NO
B5	1 Scrambled Egg	1 Scrambled Egg	1 Scrambled Egg	1 Scrambled Egg
N14	1 Bran Muffin	1 SR Bran Muffin	1 Bran Muffin+	1 sl Bread+
	1 tsp Margarine	1 tsp SR Margarine	1 tsp Margarine	1 tsp Margarine
	1 tsp Jam/Jelly	1 tsp Jam/Jelly	1 tsp Jelly	1 tsp Jelly
	1c Milk	1c Milk	1c Milk	1c Milk
	Coffee/Tea/Decaf	Coffee/Tea/Decaf	Coffee/Tea/Decaf	Coffee/Tea/Decaf
	Lunch			
K9	1/2c Marinated Cucumbers	1/2c Marinated Cucumbers	1/2c Juice	1/2c STR Juice
F9	3 oz Sole Almondine	3 oz Sole Almondine	3 oz Baked Sole	4 oz PUR Baked Sole
O25	2 Tbsp Tartar Sauce[2]	1 Tbsp SR Mayonnaise	2 Tbsp Tartar Sauce	2 Tbsp Mayonnaise
	Lemon Wedge	Lemon Wedge	Lemon Wedge	Lemon Wedge
L2	1/2c Rice Chantilly	1/2c SR Rice Chantilly	1/2c Rice Chantilly	1/2c PUR Rice Chantilly
J51	1/2c Vegetable Medley	1/2c Vegetable Medley	1/2c SFT Vegetable Medley	1/2c PUR Vegetable Medley
	1 Dinner Roll	1 Dinner Roll	1 SFT Dinner Roll+	1 sl Bread+
	1 tsp Margarine	1 tsp SR Margarine	1 tsp Margarine	1 tsp Margarine
	1/2c Milk	1/2c Milk	1/2c Milk	1/2c Milk
	Coffee/Tea/Decaf	Coffee/Tea/Decaf	Coffee/Tea/Decaf	Coffee/Tea/Decaf
Q3	3×2" sl Boston Cream Cake	3×2" sl SR Boston Cream Cake	3×2" sl Boston Cream Cake+	1/2c PUR Pears
	Dinner			
C9	2/3c Chicken Matzo Ball Soup	2/3c Chicken Matzo Ball Soup	2/3c Chicken Matzo Ball Soup	2/3c PUR/STR Soup
E9	3 oz Chicken Tarragon	3 oz Chicken Tarragon	3 oz CHP Chicken Tarragon	4 oz PUR Chicken Tarragon
M4	4 oz Noodle Pudding	4 oz Noodle Pudding	4 oz Noddle Pudding	1/2c PUR Noodle Pudding
J10,7	1/2c Steamed Broccoli	1/2c Steamed Broccoli	1/2c Steamed Broccoli	1/2c PUR Steamed Broccoli
	1 Dinner Roll	1 Dinner Roll	1 SFT Dinner Roll+	1 sl Bread+
	1 tsp Margarine	1 tsp SR Margarine	1 tsp Margarine	1 tsp Margarine
	1/2c Milk	1/2c Milk	1/2c Milk	1/2c Milk
	Coffee/Tea/Decaf	Coffee/Tea/Decaf	Coffee/Tea/Decaf	Coffee/Tea/Decaf
S1	1 med Baked Apple	1 med Baked Apple	1 med Baked Apple-No Skin	1/2c PUR Baked Apple
	Snacks			
	Milk or Juice	Juice	Milk or Juice	Milk or STR Juice
	Cookies, Crackers,	SR Cookies, SR Crackers,	Plain Cookies, Gelatin,	Applesauce, SFT Banana,
	Gelatin, Ice Cream,	Gelatin, Fresh Fruit	Plain Crackers+, Ice Cream,	Gelatin, Ice Cream
	Fresh Fruit		Banana	

TERMS: SFT = Soft; SLF = Soft/Low Fiber; GRD = Ground; CHP = Chopped Finely; PUR = Puree; STR = Strained; SR = Sodium or Salt Restricted; LF = Low Fat; FF = Fat Free; LCH = Low Cholesterol; DB = Diabetic; UNSW = Unsweetened; RC = Reduced Calorie; LC = Low Calorie; EXCH = Diabetic Exchange

SERVING UTENSILS: #6 Scoop = 2/3 cup-6 oz; #8 Scoop = 1/2 cup-4 oz; #10 Scoop = 3/8 cup-3 to 4 oz; #12 Scoop = 1/3 cup-2 1/2 to 3 oz; #16 Scoop = 1/4 cup-2 oz; #30 Scoop = 2 tbsp-1 oz; #60 Scoop = 1 tbsp-1/2 oz. Ounces will vary, based on food used.

1. *Liberal Bland:* Follow a regular diet. Use decaffeinated products. Omit pepper and chili powder.

2. *No Added Salt (3–4 gm NA):* Follow a regular diet. Use SR soups and SR canned meats. Omit salt packets (and shakers), bacon, sausage, smoked, and cured meats, substitute with SR food choices.

3. *Low Fiber:* Follow a soft diet. Do not exceed 2 cups of milk per day. Soft/Low Fiber—Omit pepper, garlic, and onions from recipes.

4. *2200 Calorie Diet:* Follow 2000 calorie diet with the following additions: Lunch—add 1 bread exchange and 1 fat exchange; Dinner—add 1 bread exchange.

+Consider individual tolerance. Daily Alternatives: Lunch and Dinner—Chicken, Hamburger, Cottage Cheese Fruit Plate, or Assorted Sandwiches. Individual preferences are provided upon request.

Amounts specified for food items that contain bone is equivalent to cooked, edible deboned portion.

Soft, Low Fiber[3]	Low Cholesterol, Low Fat (40–50 gm)	No Concentrated Sweets (Diabetic)	1200	1500	1800	2000[4]
			Diabetic/Calorie-Controlled			
1/2c STR Grapefruit Juice	1/2c Grapefruit Juice	1/2c UNSW Grapefruit Juice	1/2c	1/2c	1/2c	1/2c
1/2c Wheatena or	1/2c LF Wheatena or	1/2c DB Wheatena or	1/2c	1/2c	1/2c	1/2c
3/4c Asst Refined Cereals	3/4c Dry Cereals	3/4c UNSW Dry Cereals	3/4c	3/4c	3/4c	3/4c
1 Scrambled Egg	1 Egg Substitute	1 Scrambled Egg	1	1	1	1
1 sl White Toast	1 small LF Bran Muffin	1 small DB Bran Muffin	1 sm	1 sm	1 sm	2 sm
1 tsp Margarine	1 tsp Margarine	1 tsp Margarine	0	1 tsp	1 tsp	1 tsp
1 tsp Jelly	1 tsp Jam/Jelly	1 tsp DB Jam/Jelly	1 tsp	1 tsp	1 tsp	1 tsp
1c Milk	1c Skim Milk	1c Skim Milk	1/2c	1/2c	1/2c	1c
Coffee/Tea/Decaf	Coffee/Tea/Decaf	Coffee/Tea/Decaf	free	free	free	free
1/2c STR Juice	1/2c LF Marinated Cucumbers	1/2c DB Marinated Cucumbers	1/2c	1/2c	1/2c	1/2c
3 oz Baked Sole	2 oz LF Sole Almondine	3 oz LF Sole Almondine	2 oz	3 oz	3 oz	3 oz
2 Tbsp Mayonnaise	1 tsp LF Tartar Sauce	2 Tbsp LF Tartar Sauce	0	2 tsp	2 tsp	2 tsp
Lemon Wedge	Lemon Wedge	Lemon Wedge	Lemon	Lemon	Lemon	Lemon
1/2c Rice Chantilly	1/2c LF Rice Chantilly	1/2c LF Rice Chantilly	1/4c	1/2c	1/2c	1/2c
1/2c SLF Vegetable Medley	1/2c Vegetable Medley+	1/2c Vegetable Medley	1/2c	1/2c	1/2c	1/2c
1 SFT Refined Dinner Roll	1 Dinner Roll	1 Dinner Roll	0	0	1 sm	1 sm
1 tsp Margarine	NO	1 tsp Margarine	0	0	1 tsp	1 tsp
1/2c Milk	1/2c Skim Milk	1/2c Skim Milk	1/2c	1/2c	1/2c	1/2c
Coffee/Tea/Decaf	Coffee/Tea/Decaf	Coffee/Tea/Decaf	free	free	free	free
4 Vanilla Wafers	3 Vanilla Wafers	3 Vanilla Wafers	3	3	3	3
2/3c Chicken Matzo Ball Soup	2/3c LF Chicken Matzo Ball Soup	2/3c Chicken Matzo Ball Soup	2/3c	2/3c	2/3c	2/3c
3 oz SLF Chicken Tarragon	2 oz LF Chicken Tarragon	3 oz LF Chicken Tarragon	2 oz	3 oz	3 oz	3 oz
4 oz SLF Noodle Pudding	4 oz LF Noodle Pudding	4 oz DB Noodle Pudding	2 oz	4 oz	4 oz	4 oz
1/2c Beets	1/2c LF Steamed Broccoli+	1/2c LF Steamed Broccoli	1/2c	1/2c	1/2c	1/2c
1 SFT Refined Dinner Roll	1 Dinner Roll	1 Dinner Roll	0	0	1 sm	1 sm
1 tsp Margarine	NO	1 tsp Margarine	0	0	1 tsp	1 tsp
1/2c Milk	1/2c Skim Milk	1/2c Skim Milk	1/2c	1/2c	1/2c	1/2c
Coffee/Tea/Decaf	Coffee/Tea/Decaf	Coffee/Tea/Decaf	free	free	free	free
1 med Baked Apple-No Skin	1 med Baked Apple	1 sm DB Baked Apple	1 sm	1 sm	1 sm	1 sm
Milk[3] or STR Juice	Skim Milk or Juice	1/2c Skim Milk	1/2c	1/2c	1/2c	1/2c
Plain Cookies, Gelatin,	LF Cookies, LF Crackers,	1 Starch/Bread Exch	1	1	1	1
Plain Crackers, Banana,	Gelatin, Fresh Fruit	1 Meat Exch	0	0	0	1
Vanilla Ice Cream[3]		1 Fat Exch	0	0	1	1

Recipe	Regular, Liberal Bland[1], No Added Salt[2]	1–2 gm Na (Low Sodium)	Mechanical Soft	Puree
	Breakfast			
	1/2c Cranberry Juice or	1/2c Cranberry Juice or	1/2c Cranberry Juice or	1/2c STR Cranberry Jce or
	1 small Banana	1 small Banana	1 small Banana	1 small Banana-Mashed
B1	1/2c Cream of Rice or	1/2c Cream of Rice or	1/2c Cream of Rice or	1c Cream of Rice
	3/4c Asst Dry Cereals	3/4c SR Asst Dry Cereals	3/4c Asst Dry Cereals+	NO
G9,5	2 1/2 oz Western Omelette[2]	2 1/2 oz SR Western Omelette	2 1/2 oz SFT Western Omelette	2 1/2 oz PUR Western Omelette
	1 sl Toast	1 sl Toast	1 sl Bread	1 sl Bread+
	1 tsp Margarine	1 tsp SR Margarine	1 tsp Margarine	1 tsp Margarine
	1 tsp Jam/Jelly	1 tsp Jam/Jelly	1 tsp Jelly	1 tsp Jelly
	1c Milk	1c Milk	1c Milk	1c Milk
	Coffee/Tea/Decaf	Coffee/Tea/Decaf	Coffee/Tea/Decaf	Coffee/Tea/Decaf
	Lunch			
K37	4 oz Perfection Salad	4 oz Perfection Salad	4 oz SFT Perfection Salad	4 oz PUR Perfection Salad
D18,19	6 oz Stuffed Cabbage	6 oz SR Stuffed Cabbage	4 oz Grd Beef Stuff/No Cabbage	4 oz PUR Beef Stuff/No Cabbage
J43	1/2c Whipped Potatoes	1/2c Whipped Potatoes	1/2c Whipped Potatoes	1/2c Whipped Potatoes
J15	1/2c Glazed Carrots	1/2c Glazed Carrots	1/2c Glazed Carrots	1/2c PUR Glazed Carrots
	1 Dinner Roll	1 Dinner Roll	1 SFT Dinner Roll+	1 sl Bread+
	1 tsp Margarine	1 tsp SR Margarine	1 tsp Margarine	1 tsp Margarine
	1/2c Milk	1/2c Milk	1/2c Milk	1/2c Milk
	Coffee/Tea/Decaf	Coffee/Tea/Decaf	Coffee/Tea/Decaf	Coffee/Tea/Decaf
	1/2c Pineapple Tidbits	1/2c Pineapple Tidbits	1/2c Pineapple Tidbits	1/2c PUR Pineapple
	Dinner			
C24	2/3c Tomato Soup	2/3c SR Tomato Soup	2/3c Tomato Soup	2/3c PUR/STR Tomato Soup
I21,20	1/2c Curry Tuna[2] Salad	1/2c SR Curry Tuna Salad	1/2c SFT Curry Tuna Salad	1/2c PUR Curry Tuna Salad
	Lettuce Leaves	Lettuce Leaves	CHP Lettuce Leaves+	NO
J47	2 Onion Slices	2 Onion Slices	1/2c Cooked Spinach	1/2c PUR Cooked Spinach
	3 Cucumber Slices	3 Cucumber Slices	NO	NO
	1 Radish Rose	1 Radish Rose	NO	NO
K13	1/2c Macaroni Salad	1/2c Macaroni Salad	1/2c SFT Macaroni Salad	1/2c PUR Macaroni Salad
	1 Dinner Roll or	1 Dinner Roll or	1 SFT Dinner Roll or+	1 sl Bread+
	4 Crackers	4 SR Crackers	4 Plain Crackers	NO
	1 tsp Margarine	1 tsp SR Margarine	1 tsp Margarine	1 tsp Margarine
	1/2c Milk	1/2c Milk	1/2c Milk	1/2c Milk
	Coffee/Tea/Decaf	Coffee/Tea/Decaf	Coffee/Tea/Decaf	Coffee/Tea/Decaf
	1/2c Sherbet	1/2c Sherbet	1/2c Sherbet	1/2c Sherbet
	Snacks			
	Milk or Juice	Juice	Milk or Juice	Milk or STR Juice
	Cookies, Crackers,	SR Cookies, SR Crackers,	Plain Cookies, Gelatin,	Applesauce, SFT Banana,
	Gelatin, Ice Cream,	Gelatin, Fresh Fruit	Plain Crackers+, Ice Cream,	Gelatin, Ice Cream
	Fresh Fruit		Banana	

TERMS: SFT = Soft; SLF = Soft/Low Fiber; GRD = Ground; CHP = Chopped Finely; PUR = Puree; STR = Strained; SR = Sodium or Salt Restricted; LF = Low Fat; FF = Fat Free; LCH = Low Cholesterol; DB = Diabetic; UNSW = Unsweetened; RC = Reduced Calorie; LC =Low Calorie; EXCH = Diabetic Exchange

SERVING UTENSILS: #6 = 2/3 cup-6 oz; #8 Scoop = 1/2 cup-4 oz; #10 Scoop = 3/8 cup-3 to 4 oz; #12 Scoop = 1/3 cup-2 1/2 to 3 oz; #16 Scoop = 1/4 cup-2 oz; #30 Scoop = 2 tbsp-1 oz; #60 Scoop = 1 tbsp-1/2 oz. Ounces will vary, based on food used.

1. *Liberal Bland:* Follow a regular diet. Use decaffeinated products. Omit pepper and chili powder.

2. *No Added Salt (3–4 gm NA):* Follow a regular diet. Use SR soups and SR canned meats. Omit salt packets (and shakers), bacon, sausage, smoked, and cured meats, substitute with SR food choices.

3. *Low Fiber:* Follow a soft diet. Do not exceed 2 cups of milk per day. Soft/Low Fiber—Omit pepper, garlic, and onions from recipes.

4. *2200 Calorie Diet:* Follow 2000 calorie diet with the following additions: Lunch—add 1 bread exchange and 1 fat exchange; Dinner—add 1 bread exchange.

+Consider individual tolerance. Daily Alternatives: Lunch and Dinner—Chicken, Hamburger, Cottage Cheese Fruit Plate, or Assorted Sandwiches. Individual preferences are provided upon request.

Amounts specified for food items that contain bone is equivalent to cooked, edible deboned portion.

Soft, Low Fiber[3]	Low Cholesterol, Low Fat (40–50 gm)	No Concentrated Sweets (Diabetic)	1200	1500	1800	2000[4]
			Diabetic/Calorie-Controlled			
1/2c STR Cranberry Juice or	1/2c Cranberry Juice or	1/2c UNSW Cranberry Jce or	1/3c	1/2c	1/2c	1/2c
1 small Banana	1 small Banana	1 Small Banana	1/2	1/2	1/2	1/2
1/2c Cream of Rice or	1/2c LF Cream of Rice or	1/2c DB Cream of Rice or	1/2c	1/2c	1/2c	1/2c
3/4c Asst Refined Cereals	3/4c Dry Cereals	3/4c UNSW Dry Cereals	3/4c	3/4c	3/4c	3/4c
2 oz Plain Omelette	1 LF Western Egg Sub Omelet	2 1/2 oz DB Western Omelette	2 1/2 oz	2 1/2 oz	2 1/2 oz	2 1/2 oz
1 sl White Toast	1 sl Toast	1 sl Toast	1 sl	1 sl	1 sl	1 sl
1 tsp Margarine	1 tsp Margarine	1 tsp Margarine	0	0	1 tsp	2 tsp
1 tsp Jelly	1 tsp Jam/Jelly	1 tsp DB Jam/Jelly	1 tsp	1 tsp	1 tsp	1 tsp
1c Milk	1c Skim Milk	1c Skim Milk	1/2c	1/2c	1/2c	1c
Coffee/Tea/Decaf	Coffee/Tea/Decaf	Coffee/Tea/Decaf	free	free	free	free
4 oz SFT Perfection Salad	4 oz Perfection Salad+	4 oz DB Perfection Salad	4 oz	4 oz	4 oz	4 oz
3 1/2 oz SLF Hamburger	4 oz LF Stuffed Cabbage+	6 oz Stuffed Cabbage	5 oz	6 oz	6 oz	6 oz
1/2c SLF Whipped Potatoes	1/2c LF Whipped Potatoes	1/2c LF Whipped Potatoes	1/2c	1/2c	1/2c	1/2c
1/2c Glazed Carrots	1/2c LF Glazed Carrots	1/2c DB Glazed Carrots	1/2c	1/2c	1/2c	1/2c
1 SFT Refined Dinner Roll	1 Dinner Roll	1 Dinner Roll	0	0	1 sm	1 sm
1 tsp Margarine	NO	1 tsp Margarine	0	0	1 tsp	1 tsp
1/2c Milk	1/2c Skim Milk	1/2c Skim Milk	1/2c	1/2c	1/2c	1/2c
Coffee/Tea/Decaf	Coffee/Tea/Decaf	Coffee/Tea/Decaf	free	free	free	free
2 Canned Pear Halves	1/2c Pineapple Tidbits	1/2c UNSW Pineapple Tidbits	1/3c	1/3c	1/3c	1/3c
2/3c SLF Tomato Soup	2/3c LF Tomato Soup+	2/3c LF Tomato Soup	2/3c	2/3c	2/3c	2/3c
1/2c SLF Tuna Salad	1/2c LF Curry Tuna Salad	1/2c LF Curry Tuna Salad	1/2c	3/4c	3/4c	3/4c
NO	Lettuce Leaves	Lettuce Leaves	free	free	free	free
1/2c Cooked Spinach	2 Onion Slices	2 Onion Slices	2 sl	2 sl	2 sl	2 sl
NO	3 Cucumber Slices	3 Cucumber Slices	3 sl	3 sl	3 sl	3 sl
NO	1 Radish Rose	1 Radish Rose	1	1	1	1
1/2c SFT Macaroni Salad	1/2c LF Macaroni Salad	1/2c LF Macaroni Salad	1/4c	1/2c	1/2c	1/2c
1 SFT Refined Dinner Roll or	1 Dinner Roll or	1 Dinner Roll or	0	1 sm	1 sm	1 sm
4 Plain Crackers	4 LF Crackers	4 LF Crackers	2	5	5	5
1 tsp Margarine	NO	1 tsp Margarine	0	0	1 tsp	1 tsp
1/2c Milk (1/4c)[3]	1/2c Skim Milk	1/2c Skim Milk	1/2c	1/2c	1/2c	1/2c
Coffee/Tea/Decaf	Coffee/Tea/Decaf	Coffee/Tea/Decaf	free	free	free	free
1/2c Orange Sherbet	1/2c LF Sherbet	1/2c LF Sherbet	1/2c	1/2c	1/2c	1/2c
Milk[3] or STR Juice	Skim Milk or Juice	1/2c Skim Milk	1/2c	1/2c	1/2c	1/2c
Plain Cookies, Gelatin,	LF Cookies, LF Crackers,	1 Starch/Bread Exch	1	1	1	1
Plain Crackers, Banana,	Gelatin, Fresh Fruit	1 Meat Exch	0	0	0	1
Vanilla Ice Cream[3]		1 Fat Exch	0	0	1	1

Recipe	Regular, Liberal Bland[1], No Added Salt[2]	1–2 gm Na (Low Sodium)	Mechanical Soft	Puree
	Breakfast			
B1	1/2c Pineapple Juice	1/2c Pineapple Juice	1/2c Pineapple Juice	1/2c STR Pineapple Juice
	1/2c Oatmeal or	1/2c Oatmeal or	1/2c Oatmeal or	1c Oatmeal
	3/4c Asst Dry Cereals	3/4c SR Asst Dry Cereals	3/4c Asst Dry Cereals+	NO
B8,4	1 sl French Toast	1 sl SR French Toast	1 sl French Toast+	1 Soft-Boiled Egg
	2 oz Maple Syrup	2 oz Maple Syrup	2 oz Maple Syrup	1 sl Bread+
	1 tsp Margarine	1 tsp SR Margarine	1 tsp Margarine	1 tsp Margarine
	1 tsp Jam/Jelly	1 tsp Jam/Jelly	1 tsp Jelly	1 tsp Jelly
	1c Milk	1c Milk	1c Milk	1c Milk
	Coffee/Tea/Decaf	Coffee/Tea/Decaf	Coffee/Tea/Decaf	Coffee/Tea/Decaf
	Lunch			
K42	1/2c Cranberry Mold	1/2c Cranberry Mold	1/2c PUR Cranberry Mold	1/2c PUR Cranberry Mold
E16	3 oz Roast Turkey	3 oz Roast Turkey	3 oz CHP Roast Turkey	4 oz PUR Roast Turkey
O18,5	2 oz Giblet Gravy	2 oz SR Giblet Gravy	2 oz Giblet Gravy	2 oz STR Giblet Gravy
P12,J46	1/2c Raisin Bread Stuffing	1/2c SR Raisin Bread Stuffing	1/2c SFT Bread Stuffing	1/2c PUR Bread Stuffing
J52	1/2c Zucchini	1/2c Zucchini	1/2c SFT Zucchini	1/2c PUR Zucchini
	1 Dinner Roll	1 Dinner Roll	1 SFT Dinner Roll+	1 sl Bread+
	1 tsp Margarine	1 tsp SR Margarine	1 tsp Margarine	1 tsp Margarine
	1/2c Milk	1/2c Milk	1/2c Milk	1/2c Milk
	Coffee/Tea/Decaf	Coffee/Tea/Decaf	Coffee/Tea/Decaf	Coffee/Tea/Decaf
R3	1/8 Apple Pie	1/8 SR Apple Pie	1/8 Apple Pie+	1/2c PUR Apple Pie Filling
	Dinner			
C3	2/3c Clear Vegetable Soup	2/3c Clear Vegetable Soup	2/3c Clear Vegetable Soup	2/3c Clear Veg Soup
G2	6 oz Lasagna	6 oz SR Lasagna	6 oz Lasagna	6 oz PUR Lasagna
J27,3	1/2c Mixed Vegetables	1/2c Mixed Vegetables	1/2c Mixed Vegetables+	1/2c PUR Mixed Vegetables
N8	1 sl Garlic Bread	1 sl SR Garlic Bread	1 SFT Dinner Roll	1 sl SFT Garlic Bread+
	1 tsp Margarine	1 tsp SR Margarine	1 tsp Margarine	1 tsp Margarine
	1/2c Milk	1/2c Milk	1/2c Milk	1/2c Milk
	Coffee/Tea/Decaf	Coffee/Tea/Decaf	Coffee/Tea/Decaf	Coffee/Tea/Decaf
S4	1/2c Fruit Compote	1/2c Fruit Compote	1/2c Fruit Compote	1/2c PUR Fruit Compote
	Snacks			
	Milk or Juice	Juice	Milk or Juice	Milk or STR Juice
	Cookies, Crackers,	SR Cookies, SR Crackers,	Plain Cookies, Gelatin,	Applesauce, SFT Banana,
	Gelatin, Ice Cream,	Gelatin, Fresh Fruit	Plain Crackers+, Ice Cream,	Gelatin, Ice Cream
	Fresh Fruit		Banana	

TERMS: SFT = Soft; SLF = Soft/Low Fiber; GRD = Ground; CHP = Chopped Finely; PUR = Puree; STR = Strained; SR = Sodium or Salt Restricted; LF = Low Fat; FF = Fat Free; LCH = Low Cholesterol; DB = Diabetic; UNSW = Unsweetened; RC = Reduced Calorie; LC = Low Calorie; EXCH = Diabetic Exchange

SERVING UTENSILS: #6 Scoop = 2/3 cup-6 oz; #8 Scoop = 1/2 cup-4 oz; #10 Scoop = 3/8 cup-3 to 4 oz; #12 Scoop = 1/3 cup-2 1/2 to 3 oz; #16 Scoop = 1/4 cup-2 oz; #30 Scoop = 2 tbsp-1 oz; #60 Scoop = 1 tbsp-1/2 oz.

1. *Liberal Bland:* Follow a regular diet. Use decaffeinated products. Omit pepper and chili powder.

2. *No Added Salt (3–4 gm NA):* Follow a regular diet. Use SR soups and SR canned meats. Omit salt packets (and shakers), bacon, sausage, smoked, and cured meats, substitute with SR food choices.

3. *Low Fiber:* Follow a soft diet. Do not exceed 2 cups of milk per day. Soft/Low Fiber—Omit pepper, garlic, and onion from recipes.

4. *2200 Calorie Diet:* Follow 2000 calorie diet with the following additions: Lunch—add 1 bread exchange and 1 fat exchange; Dinner—add 1 bread exchange.

+Consider individual tolerance. Daily Alternatives: Lunch and Dinner—Chicken, Hamburger, Cottage Cheese Fruit Plate, or Assorted Sandwiches. Individual preferences are provided upon request.

Amounts specified for food items that contain bone is equivalent to cooked, edible deboned portion.

Soft, Low Fiber[3]	Low Cholesterol, Low Fat (40–50 gm)	No Concentrated Sweets (Diabetic)	1200	1500	1800	2000[4]
			Diabetic/Calorie-Controlled			
1/2c STR Grape Juice	1/2c Pineapple Juice	1/2c UNSW Pineapple Juice	1/3c	1/3c	1/2c	1/2c
1/2c Oatmeal or	1/2c LF Oatmeal or	1/2c DB Oatmeal or	1/2c	1/2c	1/2c	1/2c
3/4c Asst Refined Cereals	3/4c Dry Cereals	3/4c UNSW Dry Cereals	3/4c	3/4c	3/4c	3/4c
1 sl French Toast	1 sl LF French Toast	1 sl French Toast	1	1	1	2
2 oz Maple Syrup	2 oz Maple Syrup	1 oz DB Maple Syrup	1 oz	1 oz	1 oz	1 oz
1 tsp Margarine	NO	1 tsp Margarine	0	0	1 tsp	1 tsp
1 tsp Jelly	1 tsp Jam/Jelly	1 tsp DB Jam/Jelly	1 tsp	1 tsp	1 tsp	1 tsp
1c Milk	1c Skim Milk	1c Skim Milk	1/2c	1/2c	1/2c	1c
Coffee/Tea/Decaf	Coffee/Tea/Decaf	Coffee/Tea/Decaf	free	free	free	free
1/2c STR Cranberry Juice	1/2c Cranberry Mold	1/2c DB Cranberry Mold	1/2c	1/2c	1/2c	1/2c
3 oz Roast Turkey	2 oz LF Roast Turkey	3 oz LF Roast Turkey	2 oz	3 oz	3 oz	3 oz
2 oz Chicken Gravy	2 oz LF Chicken Gravy	2 oz STR Giblet Gravy	1 oz	2 oz	2 oz	2 oz
1/2c Whip Sweet Potatoes	1/4c LF Raisin Bread Stuffing	1/4c Raisin Bread Stuffing	1/4c	1/4c	1/3c	1/3c
1/2c SFT Zucchini	1/2c Zucchini	1/2c Zucchini	1/2c	1/2c	1/2c	1/2c
1 SFT Refined Dinner Roll	1 Dinner Roll	1 Dinner Roll	0	0	1 sm	1 sm
1 tsp Margarine	NO	1 tsp Margarine	0	0	1 tsp	1 tsp
1/2c Milk	1/2c Skim Milk	1/2c Skim Milk	1/2c	1/2c	1/2c	1/2c
Coffee/Tea/Decaf	Coffee/Tea/Decaf	Coffee/Tea/Decaf	free	free	free	free
1/8 Apple Pie+	1/8 LF Apple Pie	1/8 DB Apple Pie	1/12	1/12	1/12	1/12
2/3c SLF Clear Vegetable Soup	2/3c Clear Vegetable Soup	2/3c Clear Vegetable Soup	2/3c	2/3c	2/3c	2/3c
6 oz SLF Lasagna	5 oz LF Lasagna	6 oz DB Lasagna	5 oz	6 oz	6 oz	6 oz
1/2c Wax Beans	1/2c Mixed Vegetables+	1/2c Mixed Vegetables	1/3c	1/3c	1/2c	1/2c
1 SFT Refined Dinner Roll	1 sl LF Garlic Bread+	1 sl LF Garlic Bread	0	1 sl	1 sl	1 sl
1 tsp Margarine	NO	NO	0	0	0	0
1/2c Milk	1/2c Skim Milk	1/2c Skim Milk	1/2c	1/2c	1/2c	1/2c
Coffee/Tea/Decaf	Coffee/Tea/Decaf	Coffee/Tea/Decaf	free	free	free	free
1/2c Canned Fruit Cocktail	1/2c Fruit Compote	1/3c Fruit Compote	1/3c	1/3c	1/3c	1/3c
Milk[3] or STR Juice	Skim Milk or Juice	1/2c Skim Milk	1/2c	1/2c	1/2c	1/2c
Plain Cookies, Gelatin,	LF Cookies, LF Crackers,	1 Starch/Bread Exch	1	1	1	1
Plain Crackers, Banana,	Gelatin, Fresh Fruit	1 Meat Exch	0	0	0	1
Vanilla Ice Cream[3]		1 Fat Exch	0	0	1	1

13

Senior Citizen Nutrition Program

Recipe	Monday	Recipe	Tuesday	Recipe	Wednesday
	Week One				
E4	3 oz Lemon Chicken	D26	5 oz Veal Parmesan	D15	4 oz Meatloaf with
J39	4 oz Oven Browned Potatoes	M1	1/2c Spaghetti with	O16	2 oz Onion Gravy
J10	1/2c Broccoli	O22	2 oz Tomato Sauce	J37	1/2c Mashed Potatoes
	1 Dinner Roll, 1 tsp Margarine	K30	1c Tossed Salad with	J51	1/2c Vegetable Medley
S16	1/2c Chocolate Pudding	P4	1 oz Italian Dressing		1 sl Wheat Bread, 1 tsp Margarine
	Diet: 1/2c DB Chocolate Pudding	J55	1/2c Sauté Zucchini & Onions		1 Banana
	1 cup Milk	S13	1/2c Fruited Gelatin		1 cup Milk
			Diet: 1/2c DB Fruited Gelatin		
			1 cup Milk		
	Week Two				
D2	8 oz Beef Stew, contains,	D29	3 oz Breaded Pork Chops	E5	3 oz Oven Crisp Chicken
	1/2c Stew Vegetables	J46	1/2c Whipped Sweet Potatoes	J35	1 sm Baked Potato with
K28	1c Green Vegetable Salad	J10	1/2c Steamed Broccoli		1 oz Sour Cream
P1–8	1 oz Salad Dressing		1 Dinner Roll, 1 tsp Margarine	J18	1/2c Sunshine Carrots
N1	1 Biscuit, 1 tsp Margarine	S5	1/2c Fruit Cup		1 sl Wheat Bread, 1 tsp Margarine
	2 Cookies		1 cup Milk		1 Orange
	Diet: 4 Vanilla Wafers				1 Cup Milk
	1 cup Milk				
	Week Three				
D11	6 oz Lasagna	I20	4 oz Tuna Salad Sandwich,	D22	3 1/2 oz Breaded Veal with
J26	1/2c Italian Vegetables		2 sl Whole Wheat Bread	O3	2 oz Brown Gravy
K29	1c Tossed Salad with		Lettuce Leaves, 2 sl Tomatoes	M3	1/2c Parsley Noodles
P4	1 oz Italian Dressing	C29	6 oz Old Fashioned Vegetable Soup	J11	1/2c Seasoned Broccoli
	1 sl Italian Bread, 1 tsp Margarine	K40	1/2c Waldorf Salad	K37	1/2c Perfection Salad
S12	1/2c Gelatin	Q6	3×2" sl Chocolate Chip Cake		1 Dinner Roll, 1 tsp Margarine
	Diet: 1/2c DB Gelatin		Diet: 3 Graham Crackers	S10	1 Baked Pear
	1 cup Milk		1 cup Milk		Diet: 1 DB Baked Pear
					1 cup Milk
	Week Four				
D14	3 oz Sweet-n-Sour Meatballs	E1	3 oz Barbecue Chicken	D28	3 oz Baked Glazed Ham
M1	1/2c Buttered Noodles	J23	1 sm Corn-on-the-Cob	J45	1/2c Sweet Potatoes with Apples
K23	1/2c Marinated Zucchini	K6	1/2c Poppy Seed Cole Slaw	J4	1/2c Green Beans & Mushrooms
J47	1/2c Spinach	N1	1 Biscuit, 1 tsp Margarine		1 Dinner Roll, 1 tsp Margarine
	1 Dinner Roll, 1 tsp Margarine		1 Seasonal Fruit	R4	1/8 Lemon Pie
	1 Banana		1 cup Milk		Diet: 1/2c DB Lemon Pudding
	1 cup Milk				1 cup Milk

TERMS: DB = Diabetic; UNSW = Unsweetened; EXCH = Diabetic Exchange.

Meals meet 1/3 RDA for individuals 51+. Meal Pattern Requirements are as follows: Meat or Alternative: 3 oz Cooked Edible Portion; Vegetables and/or Fruit: 2, 1/2c serving; Bread or Alternate: 1 serving; Butter or Fortified Margarine: 1 teaspoon; Dessert: 1/2 cup; Milk: 1 cup; Beverage (optional).

Notes:

(1) Amounts specified for food items that contain bone is equivalent to cooked, edible deboned portion.

(2) Recommend the use of Vitamin C enriched mashed potatoes, water or juice-packed canned fruit, and low-fat milk.

Recipe	Thursday	Recipe	Friday
F4	3 1/2 oz Oven Fried Fish	I12	4 oz Ham Salad Sandwich,
	1 Bun		2 sl Whole Wheat Bread
O25	1 Tbsp Tartar Sauce		Lettuce Leaf, 2 sl Tomatoes
K9	1/2c Marinated Cucumbers	C27	6 oz Chunky Vegetable Soup
J15	1/2c Glazed Carrots	K5	1/2c Cole Slaw
S3	1/2c Citrus Cup	Q7	3×2" sl Devil's Food Cake
	1 cup Milk		Diet: 3 Graham Crackers
			1 cup Milk
M1	1/2c Spaghetti and	E16	3 oz Sliced Turkey on
D13	4 oz Meatballs with		1 sl Bread with
O20	2 oz Marinara Sauce	O5	2 oz Chicken Gravy
J26	1/2c Italian Vegetables	J37	1/2c Mashed Potatoes
K32	1/2c Tossed Vegetable Salad	J6	1/2c Seasoned Green Beans
P1-8	with 1 oz Salad Dressing		1/2c Sliced Peaches
N8	1 sl Garlic Bread		1 cup Milk
	1/2c Sherbet		
	1 cup Milk		
E9	3 oz Tarragon Chicken	G11	8 oz Macaroni and Cheese
J43	1/2c Whipped Potatoes	J49	1/2c Succotash
J9	1/2c Orange Julienne Beets	K24	1c Garden Salad with
	1 Dinner Roll, 1 tsp Margarine	P1-8	1 oz Salad Dressing
S17	1/2c Vanilla Pudding		1 sl Wheat Bread, 1 tsp Margarine
	Diet: 1/2c DB Vanilla Pudding		1 Apple
	1 cup Milk		1 cup Milk
E14	1 cup Turkey Chow Mein,	D9	3 1/2 oz Hamburger on
	1/2c Chinese Vegetables		1 Bun
L1	1/2c White Rice		10 French Fries
J10	1/2c Broccoli		2 Lettuce Leaves, 2 sl Tomatoes,
	1 Dinner Roll, 1 tsp Margarine		2 sl Onions
	1/4c Chinese Noodles		1 Tbsp Catsup
	1/2c Pineapple Chunks		1 Orange
	1 cup Milk		1 cup Milk

14

Special Holidays & Themes

New Year's Eve

Breakfast
Chilled Apple Juice
Assorted Homemade Danish and Muffins
Farm Fresh Egg to Order
Cream of Wheat or
Assorted Cold Cereal
Assorted Condiments
Your Choice of Beverage

Lunch
Julienne Soup
Sole Almondine
Steamed White Rice
Spiced Peaches
Your Choice of Beverage

Dinner
Molded Vegetable Salad
Broiled Veal Chop
Oven Browned Potatoes
Seasoned Green Beans
Warm Dinner Rolls
Marble Cake
Your Choice of Beverage

Recipe	Regular, Liberal Bland[1], No Added Salt[2]	1–2 Gm Na (Low Sodium)	Mechanical Soft	Puree
	Breakfast			
	1/2c Apple Juice	1/2c Apple Juice	1/2c Apple Juice	1/2c STR Apple Juice
B1	1/2c Cream of Wheat or	1/2c Cream of Wheat or	1/2c Cream of Wheat or	1c Cream of Wheat
	3/4c Asst Dry Cereals	3/4c SR Asst Dry Cereals	3/4c Asst Dry Cereals+	NO
B4,5	1 Egg to Order	1 Egg to Order	1 Egg to Order	1 PUR Egg to Order
N10–20	2 Asst Danish/Muffin or	2 SR Asst Danish/SR Muffin or	2 SFT Asst Danish/SFT Muffin or	NO
	1 sl Toast	1 sl SR Toast	1 sl Bread	1 sl Bread+
	1 oz Cream Cheese or	1 oz Cream Cheese or	1 oz Cream Cheese or	1 oz Cream Cheese or
	1 tsp Margarine	1 tsp SR Margarine	1 tsp Margarine	1 tsp Margarine
	1 tsp Jelly/Jam	1 tsp Jelly/Jam	1 tsp Jelly	1 tsp Jelly
	1c Milk	1c Milk	1c Milk	1c Milk
	Coffee/Tea/Decaf	Coffee/Tea/Decaf	Coffee/Tea/Decaf	Coffee/Tea/Decaf
	Lunch			
C20	2/3c Julienne Soup	2/3c Julienne Soup	2/3c Julienne Soup	2/3c PUR/STR Julienne Soup
F9	3 oz Sole Almondine	3 oz Sole Almondine	3 oz Baked Sole	4 oz PUR Baked Sole
O25	2 Tbsp Tartar Sauce[2]	1 Tbsp SR Mayonnaise	2 Tbsp Tartar Sauce	2 Tbsp Mayonnaise
	Lemon Wedge	Lemon Wedge	Lemon Wedge	Lemon Wedge
L1	1/2c White Rice	1/2c White Rice	1/2c White Rice	1/2c PUR White Rice
J47	1/2c Spinach	1/2c Spinach	1/2c Spinach	1/2c PUR Spinach
	1 Dinner Roll	1 Dinner Roll	1 SFT Dinner Roll+	1 sl Bread+
	1 tsp Margarine	1 tsp SR Margarine	1 tsp Margarine	1 tsp Margarine
	1/2c Milk	1/2c Milk	1/2c Milk	1/2c Milk
	Coffee/Tea/Decaf	Coffee/Tea/Decaf	Coffee/Tea/Decaf	Coffee/Tea/Decaf
S9	1/2c Spiced Peaches	1/2c Spiced Peaches	1/2c Spiced Peaches	1/2c PUR Spiced Peaches
	Dinner			
K35	1/2c Molded Vegetable Sld	1/2c Molded Vegetable Sld	1/2c SFT Molded Vegetable Sld	1/2c PUR Molded Vegetable Sld
D23	3 oz Veal Chop	3 oz Veal Chop	3 oz CHP Veal Chop	4 oz PUR Veal Chop
J39	4 oz Oven Brown Potatoes	4 oz Oven Brown Potatoes	4 oz Oven Brown Potatoes	4 oz PUR Oven Brown Potatoes
J6	1/2c Seasoned Green Beans	1/2c Seasoned Green Beans	1/2c Seasoned Green Beans	1/2c PUR Seasoned Green Beans
	1 Dinner Roll	1 Dinner Roll	1 SFT Dinner Roll+	1 sl Bread+
	1 tsp Margarine	1 tsp SR Margarine	1 tsp Margarine	1 tsp Margarine
	1/2c Milk	1/2c Milk	1/2c Milk	1/2c Milk
	Coffee/Tea/Decaf	Coffee/Tea/Decaf	Coffee/Tea/Decaf	Coffee/Tea/Decaf
Q8	3×2" sl Marble Cake	3×2" sl Marble Cake	3×2" sl Marble Cake	1/2c Ice Cream
	Snacks			
	Milk or Juice	Juice	Milk or Juice	Milk or STR Juice
	Cookies, Crackers,	SR Cookies, SR Crackers,	Plain Cookies, Gelatin,	Applesauce, SFT Banana,
	Gelatin, Ice Cream,	Gelatin, Fresh Fruit	Plain Crackers+, Ice Cream,	Gelatin, Ice Cream,
	Fresh Fruit		Banana	

TERMS: SFT = Soft; SLF = Soft/Low Fiber; GRD = Ground; CHP = Chopped Finely; PUR = Puree; STR = Strained; SR = Sodium or Salt Restricted; LF = Low Fat; FF = Fat Free; LCH = Low Cholesterol; DB = Diabetic; UNSW = Unsweetened; RC = Reduced Calorie; LC = Low Calorie; EXCH = Diabetic Exchange

SERVING UTENSILS: #6 Scoop = 2/3 cup-6 oz; #8 Scoop = 1/2 cup-4 oz; #10 Scoop = 3/8 cup-3 to 4 oz; #12 Scoop = 1/3 cup-2.5 to 3 oz; #16 Scoop = 1/4 cup-2 oz; #30 Scoop = 2 tbsp-1 oz; #60 Scoop = 1 tbsp-1/2 oz. Ounces will vary, based on food used.

1. *Liberal Bland:* Follow a regular diet. Use decaffeinated products. Omit pepper and chill powder.

2. *No Added Salt (3–4 gm NA):* Follow a regular diet. Use SR soups and SR canned meats. Omit salt packets (and shakers), bacon, sausage, smoked, and cured meats, substitute with SR food choices.

3. *Low Fiber:* Follow a soft diet. Do not exceed 2 cups of milk per day. Soft/Low Fiber—Omit pepper, garlic, and onions from recipes.

4. *2200 Calorie Diet:* Follow 2000 calorie diet with the following additions: Lunch—add 1 bread exchange and 1 fat exchange; Dinner—add 1 bread exchange. +Consider individual tolerance. Daily Alternatives: Lunch and Dinner—Chicken, Hamburger, Cottage Cheese Fruit Plate, or Assorted Sandwiches. Individual preferences are provided upon request.

Amounts specified for food items that contain bone is equivalent to cooked, edible deboned portion.

Soft, Low Fiber[3]	Low Cholesterol, Low Fat (40–50 GM)	No Concentrated Sweets (Diabetic)	1200	1500	1800	2000[4]
			Diabetic/Calorie-Controlled			
1/2c STR Apple Juice	1/2c Apple Juice	1/2c UNSW Apple Juice	1/2c	1/2c	1/2c	1/2c
1/2c Cream of Wheat or	1/2c LF Cream of Wheat or	1/2c DB Cream of Wheat or	1/2c	1/2c	1/2c	1/2c
3/4c Asst Refined Cereals	3/4c Dry Cereals	3/4c UNSW Dry Cereals	3/4c	3/4c	3/4c	3/4c
1 Egg to Order	1 Egg Substitute	1 Egg to Order	1	1	1	1
2 SLF Muffin or	1 LF Muffin or	1 sm DB Muffin or	1	1	1	1
1 sl White Toast	1 sl Toast	1 sl Toast	1 sl	1 sl	1 sl	1 sl
1 oz LF Cream Cheese or	1 Tbsp Cream Cheese or	2 Tbsp Cream Cheese or	1 Tbsp	1 Tbsp	1 Tbsp	2 Tbsp
1 tsp Margarine	1 tsp Margarine	2 tsp Margarine	1 tsp	1 tsp	1 tsp	2 tsp
1 tsp Jelly	1 tsp Jelly/Jam	1 tsp UNSW Jelly/Jam	1 tsp	1 tsp	1 tsp	1 tsp
1c Milk	1c Skim Milk	1c Skim Milk	1/2c	1/2c	1/2c	1c
Coffee/Tea/Decaf	Coffee/Tea/Decaf	Coffee/Tea/Decaf	free	free	free	free
2/3c SLF Julienne Soup	2/3c Julienne Soup+	2/3c Julienne Soup	2/3c	2/3c	2/3c	2/3c
3 oz Baked Sole	2 oz LF Sole Almondine	3 oz LF Sole Almondine	2 oz	3 oz	3 oz	3 oz
2 Tbsp Mayonnaise	1 tsp LF Tartar Sauce	2 Tbsp LF Tartar Sauce	1 Tbsp	1 Tbsp	2 Tbsp	2 Tbsp
Lemon Wedge	Lemon Wedge	Lemon Wedge	Lemon	Lemon	Lemon	Lemon
1/2c White Rice	1/2c White Rice	1/2c White Rice	1/3c	1/3c	2/3c	2/3c
1/2c Spinach	1/2c Spinach	1/2c Spinach	1/2c	1/2c	1/2c	1/2c
1 SFT Refined Dinner Roll	1 Dinner Roll	1 Dinner Roll	0	1 sm	1 sm	1 sm
1 tsp Margarine	1 tsp Margarine	1 tsp Margarine	0	1 tsp	1 tsp	1 tsp
1/2c Milk (1/4c)[3]	1/2c Skim Milk	1/2c Skim Milk	1/4c	1/2c	1/2c	1/2c
Coffee/Tea/Decaf	Coffee/Tea/Decaf	Coffee/Tea/Decaf	free	free	free	free
1/2c Spiced Peaches	1/2c Spiced Peaches	1/2c Spiced Peaches	1/2c	1/2c	1/2c	1/2c
1/2c SFT Molded Vegetable Sld	1/2c Molded Vegetable Sld	1/2c DB Molded Vegetable Sld	1/2c	1/2c	1/2c	1/2c
3 oz SLF Veal Chop	2 oz LF Veal Chop	3 oz LF Veal Chop	2 oz	3 oz	3 oz	3 oz
4 oz Oven Brown Potatoes	4 oz LF Oven Brown Potatoes	4 oz LF Oven Brown Potatoes	2 oz	4 oz	4 oz	4 oz
1/2c SLF Seasoned Green Beans	1/2c LF Seasoned Green Beans	1/2c LF Season Green Beans	1/2c	1/2c	1/2c	1/2c
1 SFT Refined Dinner Roll	1 Dinner Roll	1 Dinner Roll	0	0	1	1
1 tsp Margarine	1 tsp Margarine	1 tsp Margarine	0	0	1 tsp	2 tsp
1/2c Milk (1/4c)[3]	1/2c Skim Milk	1/2c Skim Milk	1/4c	1/4c	1/2c	1/2c
Coffee/Tea/Decaf	Coffee/Tea/Decaf	Coffee/Tea/Decaf	free	free	free	free
1/2c Vanilla Ice Cream	3×2" sl LF Marble Cake	3×2" sl DB Marble Cake	2×2	2×2	3×2	3×2
Milk[3] or STR Juice	Skim Milk or Juice	1/2c Skim Milk	1/2c	1/2c	1/2c	1/2c
Plain Cookies, Gelatin,	LF Cookies, LF Crackers,	1 Starch/Bread Exch	1	1	1	1
Plain Crackers, Banana,	Gelatin, Fresh Fruit	1 Meat Exch	0	0	0	1
Vanilla Ice Cream[3]		1 Fat Exch	0	0	1	1

St. Valentine's Day

Breakfast

Chilled Passion Punch
Apple Delight Pancakes
with Maple Syrup
Farm Fresh Egg to Order
Hot Oatmeal or
Assorted Cold Cereals
Assorted Condiments
Your Choice of Beverage

Lunch

Garden Salad with
Green Goddess Dressing
Roast Brisket of Beef with
Tomato Sauce
Rosette Potatoes
Seasoned Asparagus
Crescent Rolls
Baked Pear
with Raspberry Sauce
Your Choice of Beverage

Dinner

Pureed Cauliflower Soup
Salmon Stuffed Red Bell Pepper
Molded-to-Perfection Salad
Cupid's Pasta Salad
Warm Dinner Rolls
Chocolate-Strawberry Tart
Your Choice of Beverage

Recipe	Regular, Liberal Bland[1], No Added Salt[2]	1–2 Gm Na (Low Sodium)	Mechanical Soft	Puree
	Breakfast			
A5	1/2c Passion Punch	1/2c Passion Punch	1/2c Passion Punch	1/2c STR Passion Punch
B1	1/2c Oatmeal or	1/2c Oatmeal or	1/2c Oatmeal or	1c Oatmeal
	3/4c Asst Dry Cereals	3/4c SR Asst Dry Cereals	3/4c Asst Dry Cereals+	NO
B10	2 Apple Pancakes with	2 SR Apple Pancakes with	2 SFT Apple Pancakes with	NO
	2 oz Maple Syrup	2 oz Maple Syrup	2 oz Maple Syrup	NO
B4,5	1 Egg to Order	1 Egg to Order	1 Egg to Order	1 PUR Egg to Order
	1 sl Toast	1 sl SR Toast	1 sl Bread	1 sl White Bread+
	1 tsp Margarine	1 tsp SR Margarine	1 tsp Margarine	1 tsp Margarine
	1 tsp Jam/Jelly	1 tsp Jam/Jelly	1 tsp Jelly	1 tsp Jelly
	1c Milk	1c Milk	1c Milk	1c Milk
	Coffee/Tea/Decaf	Coffee/Tea/Decaf	Coffee/Tea/Decaf	Coffee/Tea/Decaf
	Lunch			
K24	1c Garden Salad with	1c Garden Salad with	4 oz Juice	4 oz STR Juice
P3	1 oz Green Goddess Dressing	1 oz SR Green Goddess Dressing	NO	NO
D4	3 oz Roast Brisket of Beef	3 oz Roast Brisket of Beef	3 oz SFT Roast Brisket of Beef	4 oz PUR Roast Brisket of Beef
O22	with 2 oz Tomato Sauce	2 oz SR Tomato Sauce	2 oz SFT Tomato Sauce	2 oz SFT Tomato Sauce
J42	4 oz Rosette Potatoes	4 oz Rosette Potatoes	4 oz Rosette Potatoes	4 oz PUR Rosette Potatoes
J2	1/2c Seasoned Asparagus	1/2c Seasoned Asparagus	1/2c CHP Asparagus	1/2c PUR Asparagus
	1 Crescent Roll	1 Crescent Roll	1 Crescent Roll+	1 sl Bread+
	1 tsp Margarine	1 tsp SR Margarine	1 tsp Margarine	1 tsp Margarine
	1/2c Milk	1/2c Milk	1/2c Milk	1/2c Milk
	Coffee/Tea/Decaf	Coffee/Tea/Decaf	Coffee/Tea/Decaf	Coffee/Tea/Decaf
S10	1/2 Baked Pear with	1/2 Baked Pear with	1/2 SFT Baked Pear with	1/2 PUR Baked Pear with
	3 Tbsp Raspberry sauce	3 Tbsp Raspberry sauce	3 Tbsp Raspberry sauce	3 Tbsp Raspberry sauce
	Dinner			
C10,1	2/3c Pureed Cauliflower Soup	2/3c Cauliflower Soup	2/3c Pureed Cauliflower Soup+	2/3c PUR/STR Cauliflower Soup
I17	1/2c Salmon Salad in	1/2c SR Salmon Salad in	1/2c SFT Salmon Salad	4 oz PUR Salmon Salad
	1 Red Pepper	1 Red Pepper	NO	NO
K38	4 oz Perfection Salad	4 oz Perfection Salad	4 oz SFT Perfection Salad	4 oz PUR Perfection Salad
K14	1/2c Pasta Salad	1/2c SR Pasta Salad	1/2c SFT Pasta Salad	1/2c PUR Pasta Salad
	1 Carrot Curl	1 Carrot Curl	NO	NO
	2 Black Olives	NO	NO	NO
	1 Dinner Roll	1 Dinner Roll	1 SFT Dinner Roll+	1 sl Bread+
	1 tsp Margarine	1 tsp SR Margarine	1 tsp Margarine	1 tsp Margarine
	1/2c Milk	1/4c Milk	1/2c Milk	1/2c Milk
	Coffee/Tea/Decaf	Coffee/Tea/Decaf	Coffee/Tea/Decaf	Coffee/Tea/Decaf
R8,S17	1 Chocolate/Strawberry Tart	1 Chocolate/Strawberry Tart	1/2c Strawberries/Filling	1/2c PUR/STR Strawberries/Fill
	Snacks			
	Milk or Juice	Juice	Milk or Juice	Milk or STR Juice
	Cookies, Crackers,	SR Cookies, SR Crackers,	Plain Cookies, Gelatin,	Applesauce, SFT Banana,
	Gelatin, Ice Cream,	Gelatin, Fresh Fruit	Plain Crackers+, Ice Cream,	Gelatin, Ice Cream
	Fresh Fruit		Banana	

TERMS: SFT = Soft; SLF = Soft/Low Fiber; GRD = Ground; CHP = Chopped Finely; PUR = Puree; STR = Strained; SR = Sodium or Salt Restricted; LF = Low Fat; FF = Fat Free; LCH = Low Cholesterol; DB = Diabetic; UNSW = Unsweetened; RC = Reduced Calorie; LC = Low Calorie; EXCH = Diabetic Exchange

SERVING UTENSILS: #6 Scoop = 2/3 cup-6 oz; #8 Scoop = 1/2 cup-4 oz; #10 Scoop = 3/8 cup-3 to 4 oz; #12 Scoop = 1/3 cup-2.5 to 3 oz; #16 Scoop = 1/4 cup-2 oz; #30 Scoop = 2 tbsp-1 oz; #60 Scoop = 1 tbsp-1/2 oz. Ounces will vary, based on food used.

1. *Liberal Bland:* Follow a regular diet. Use decaffeinated products. Omit pepper and chili powder.

2. *No Added Salt (3–4 gm NA):* Follow a regular diet. Use SR soups and SR canned meats. Omit salt packets (and shakers), bacon, sausage, smoked, and cured meats, substitute with SR food choices.

3. *Low Fiber:* Follow a soft diet. Do not exceed 2 cups of milk per day. Soft/Low Fiber—Omit pepper, garlic, and onions from recipes.

4. *2200 Calorie Diet:* Follow 2000 calorie diet with the following additions: Lunch—add 1 bread exchange and 1 fat exchange; Dinner—add 1 bread exchange.

+Consider individual tolerance. Daily Alternatives: Lunch and Dinner—Chicken, Hamburger, Cottage Cheese Fruit Plate, or Assorted Sandwiches. Individual preferences are provided upon request.

Amounts specified for food items that contain bone is equivalent to cooked, edible deboned portion.

Soft, Low Fiber[3]	Low Cholesterol, Low Fat (40–50 GM)	No Concentrated Sweets (Diabetic)	1200	1500	1800	2000[4] Diabetic/Calorie-Controlled
1/2c STR Passion Punch	1/2c Passion Punch	1/2c Passion Punch	1/2c	1/2c	1/2c	1/2c
1/2c Oatmeal or	1/2c LF Oatmeal or	1/2c DB Oatmeal or	1/2c	1/2c	1/2c	1/2c
3/4c Asst Refined Cereals	3/4c Dry Cereals	3/4c UNSW Dry Cereals	3/4c	3/4c	3/4c	3/4c
2 SLF Apple Pancakes with	2 LF Apple Pancakes with	2 DB Apple Pancakes with	1	1	2	2
2 oz Maple Syrup	2 oz Maple Syrup	2 oz UNSW Maple Syrup	1 oz	1 oz	2 oz	2 oz
1 Egg to Order	1 Egg Substitute	1 Egg to Order	1	1	1	1
1 sl White Toast	1 sl Toast	1 sl Toast	0	0	0	1 sl
1 tsp Margarine	1 tsp Margarine	1 tsp Margarine	0	0	0	1 tsp
1 tsp Jelly	1 tsp Jam/Jelly	1 tsp DB Jam/Jelly	1 tsp	1 tsp	1 tsp	1 tsp
1c Milk	1c Skim Milk	1c Skim Milk	1/2c	1/2c	1/2c	1c
Coffee/Tea/Decaf	Coffee/Tea/Decaf	Coffee/Tea/Decaf	free	free	free	free
4 oz STR Juice	1c Garden Salad with	1c Garden Salad with	1c	1c	1c	1c
NO	2 tsp LF Green Goddess Dressing	2 tsp LF Green Goddess Dressing	2 tsp	2 tsp	2 tsp	2 tsp
3 oz SLF Roast Brisket of Beef	2 oz LF Roast Brisket of Beef	3 oz Roast Brisket of Beef	2 oz	3 oz	3 oz	3 oz
2 oz SLF Tomato Sauce	1 oz LF Tomato Sauce+	2 oz DB Tomato Sauce	1 oz	1 oz	1 oz	1 oz
4 oz Rosette Potatoes	3 oz LF Rosette Potatoes	3 oz DB Rosette Potatoes	2 oz	3 oz	3 oz	3 oz
1/2c Seasoned Asparagus	1/2c Seasoned Asparagus	1/2c Seasoned Asparagus	1/2c	1/2c	1/2c	1/2c
1 SFT Refined Dinner Roll	1 Crescent Roll	1 Crescent Roll	0	0	1	1
1 tsp Margarine	NO	1 tsp Margarine	0	0	0	0
1/2c Milk	1/2c Skim Milk	1/2c Skim Milk	1/2c	1/2c	1/2c	1/2c
Coffee/Tea/Decaf	Coffee/Tea/Decaf	Coffee/Tea/Decaf	free	free	free	free
1/2 SFT Baked Pear	1/2 Baked Pear with	1/2 DB Baked Pear with	1/2	1/2	1/2	1/2
NO	3 Tbsp Raspberry sauce	2 Tbsp DB Raspberry sauce	2 Tbsp	2 Tbsp	2 Tbsp	2 Tbsp
2/3c SLF Broth	2/3c LF Cauliflower Soup+	2/3c LF Cauliflower Soup	2/3c	2/3c	2/3c	2/3c
1/2c SFT Salmon Salad	1/2c LF Salmon Salad in	1/2c LF Salmon Salad in	1/3c	1/2c	1/2c	1/2c
NO	1 Red Pepper	1 Red Pepper	1	1	1	1
4 oz SFT Perfection Salad	4 oz LF Perfection Salad	4 oz DB Perfection Salad	4 oz	4 oz	4 oz	4 oz
1/2c SFT Pasta Salad	1/2c LF Pasta Salad	1/2c LF Pasta Salad	1/3c	1/3c	1/2c	1/2c
NO	1 Carrot Curl	1 Carrot Curl	1	1	1	1
NO	NO	2 Black Olives	0	0	1	1
1 SFT Refined Dinner Roll	1 Dinner Roll	1 Dinner Roll	0	0	1 sm	1 sm
1 tsp Margarine	NO	1 tsp Margarine	0	0	0	0
1/2c Milk (1/4c)[3]	1/2c Skim Milk	1/2c Skim Milk	1/4c	1/4c	1/4c	1/2c
Coffee/Tea/Decaf	Coffee/Tea/Decaf	Coffee/Tea/Decaf	free	free	free	free
1/2c Vanilla Pudding	1 LF Chocolate/Strawberry Tart	1 DB Chocolate/Strawberry Tart	0	1	1	1
		UNSW Strawberries	1/2c	0	0	0
Milk[3] or STR Juice	Skim Milk or Juice	1/2c Skim Milk	1/2c	1/2c	1/2c	1/2c
Plain Cookies, Gelatin,	LF Cookies, LF Crackers,	1 Starch/Bread Exch	1	1	1	1
Plain Crackers, Banana,	Gelatin, Fresh Fruit	1 Meat Exch	0	0	0	1
Vanilla Ice Cream[3]		1 Fat Exch	0	0	1	1

St. Patrick's Day

Breakfast
Chilled Cranberry Juice
Farm Fresh Egg to Order
Buttermilk Scone
Porridge of Oatmeal or
Assorted Cold Cereals
Assorted Condiments
Your Choice of Beverage

Lunch
Green Vegetable Salad with
Green Goddess Dressing
Irish Stew
Irish Soda Bread
Warm Dinner Roll
Lime Gelatin
Your Choice of Beverage

Dinner
Cream of Spinach Soup
Corned Beef Sandwich on
Rye Bread
Lettuce and Tomato Slices
Cole Slaw
Baked Green Apple
Your Choice of Beverage

Recipe	Regular, Liberal Bland[1], No Added Salt[2]	1–2 Gm Na (Low Sodium)	Mechanical Soft	Puree
	Breakfast			
	1/2c Cranberry Juice	1/2c Cranberry Juice	1/2c Cranberry Juice	1/2c STR Cranberry Juice
B1	1/2c Oatmeal or	1/2c Oatmeal or	1/2c Oatmeal or	1c Oatmeal
	3/4c Asst Dry Cereals	3/4c SR Asst Dry Cereals	3/4c Asst Dry Cereals+	NO
B4,5	1 Egg to Order	1 Egg to Order	1 Egg to Order	1 PUR Egg to Order
N25	1 Buttermilk Scone	1 SR Buttermilk Scone	1 Buttermilk Scone	1 sl Bread+
	1 tsp Margarine	1 tsp SR Margarine	1 tsp Margarine	1 tsp Margarine
	1 tsp Jam/Jelly	1 tsp Jam/Jelly	1 tsp Jelly	1 tsp Jelly
	1c Milk	1c Milk	1c Milk	1c Milk
	Coffee/Tea/Decaf	Coffee/Tea/Decaf	Coffee/Tea/Decaf	Coffee/Tea/Decaf
	Lunch			
K26	1c Green Veg Salad	1c Green Veg Salad	1/2c Juice	1/2c STR Juice
P3	1 oz Green Goddess Dressing	1 oz SR Green Goddess Dressing	NO	NO
D36	8 oz Irish Stew	8 oz Irish Stew	8 oz Irish Stew	8 oz PUR Irish Stew
	1 sl Irish Soda Bread	1 sl Irish Soda Bread	1 sl Bread	1 sl Bread+
	1 tsp Margarine	1 tsp SR Margarine	1 tsp Margarine	1 tsp Margarine
	1/2c Milk	1/2c Milk	1/2c Milk	1/2c Milk
	Coffee/Tea/Decaf	Coffee/Tea/Decaf	Coffee/Tea/Decaf	Coffee/Tea/Decaf
S12	1/2c Lime Gelatin	1/2c Lime Gelatin	1/2c Lime Gelatin	1/2c Lime Gelatin
	Dinner			
C13	2/3c Cream Spinach Soup	2/3c Cream Spinach Soup	2/3c Cream Spinach Soup	2/3c PUR/STR Soup
D5,E16	3 oz Corned Beef	3 oz Turkey	3 oz CHP Corned Beef Sandwich,	4 oz PUR Corned Beef
M1	Sandwich, 2 sl Rye Bread	Sandwich, 2 sl Rye Bread	2 sl Seedless Rye Bread	1/2c PUR Noodles
	Lettuce Leaves	Lettuce Leaves	NO	NO
	4 Tomato Slices	4 Tomato Slices	NO	NO
K5,J14	1/2c Cole Slaw	1/2c Cole Slaw	1/2c Cooked Carrots	1/2c PUR Carrots
	1 tsp Mustard	1 tsp SR Catsup	1 tsp Mustard	1 tsp Mustard
	1/2c Milk	1/4c Milk	1/2c Milk	1/2c Milk
	Coffee/Tea/Decaf	Coffee/Tea/Decaf	Coffee/Tea/Decaf	Coffee/Tea/Decaf
S1	1 med Baked Green Apple	1 med Baked Green Apple	1 med Bkd Green Apple-No Skin	1/2c PUR Baked Green Apple
	Snacks			
	Milk or Juice	Juice	Milk or Juice	Milk or STR Juice
	Cookies, Crackers,	SR Cookies, SR Crackers,	Plain Cookies, Gelatin,	Applesauce, SFT Banana,
	Gelatin, Ice Cream,	Gelatin, Fresh Fruit	Plain Crackers+, Ice Cream,	Gelatin, Ice Cream
	Fresh Fruit		Banana	

TERMS: SFT = Soft; SLF = Soft/Low Fiber; GRD = Ground; CHP = Chopped Finely; PUR = Puree; STR = Strained; SR = Sodium or Salt Restricted; LF = Low Fat; FF = Fat Free; LCH = Low Cholesterol; DB = Diabetic; UNSW = Unsweetened; RC = Reduced Calorie; LC = Low Calorie; EXCH = Diabetic Exchange

SERVING UTENSILS: #6 Scoop = 2/3 cup-6 oz; #8 Scoop = 1/2 cup-4 oz; #10 Scoop = 3/8 cup-3 to 4 oz; #12 Scoop = 1/3 cup-2.5 to 3 oz; #16 Scoop = 1/4 cup-2 oz; #30 Scoop = 2 tbsp-1 oz; #60 Scoop = 1 tbsp-1/2 oz. Ounces will vary, based on food used.

1. *Liberal Bland:* Follow a regular diet. Use decaffeinated products. Omit pepper and chili powder.

2. *No Added Salt (3–4 gm NA):* Follow a regular diet. Use SR soups and SR canned meats. Omit salt packets (and shakers), bacon, sausage, smoked, and cured meats, substitute with SR food choices.

3. *Low Fiber:* Follow a soft diet. Do not exceed 2 cups of milk per day. Soft/Low Fiber—Omit pepper, garlic, and onions from recipes.

4. *2200 Calorie Diet:* Follow 2000 calorie diet with the following additions: Lunch—add 1 bread exchange and 1 fat exchange; Dinner—add 1 bread exchange.

+Consider individual tolerance. Daily Alternatives: Lunch and Dinner—Chicken, Hamburger, Cottage Cheese Fruit Plate, or Assorted Sandwiches. Individual preferences are provided upon request.

Amounts specified for food items that contain bone is equivalent to cooked, edible deboned portion.

Soft, Low Fiber[3]	Low Cholesterol, Low Fat (40–50 GM)	No Concentrated Sweets (Diabetic)	1200	1500	1800	2000[4]
			Diabetic/Calorie-Controlled			
1/2c STR Cranberry Juice	1/2c Cranberry Juice	1/2c UNSW Cranberry Juice	1/3c	1/3c	1/2c	1/2c
1/2c Oatmeal or	1/2c LF Oàtmeal or	1/2c DB Oatmeal or	1/2c	1/2c	1/2c	1/2c
3/4c Asst Refined Cereals	3/4c Dry Cereals	3/4c UNSW Dry Cereals	3/4c	3/4c	3/4c	3/4c
1 Egg to Order	1 Egg Substitute	1 Egg to Order	1	1	1	1
1 Buttermilk Scone	1 Buttermilk Scone	1 Buttermilk Scone	1/2	1	1	1
1 tsp Margarine	NO	1 tsp Margarine	0	0	1 tsp	2 tsp
1 tsp Jelly	2 tsp Jam/Jelly	1 tsp DB Jam/Jelly	1 tsp	1 tsp	1 tsp	1 tsp
1c Milk	1c Skim Milk	1c Skim Milk	1/2c	1/2c	1/2c	1c
Coffee/Tea/Decaf	Coffee/Tea/Decaf	Coffee/Tea/Decaf	free	free	free	free
1/2c STR Juice	1c Green Veg Salad	1c Green Veg Salad	1c	1c	1c	1c
NO	2 tsp LF Green Goddess Dressing	2 Tbsp LF Green Goddess Dressing	2 tsp	2 tsp	1 Tbsp	2 Tbsp
8 oz SLF Irish Stew	6 oz Irish Stew	8 oz Irish Stew	6 oz	8 oz	8 oz	8 oz
1 SFT Refined Dinner Roll	1 sl Irish Soda Bread	1 sl Irish Soda Bread	0	0	1 sl	1 sl
1 tsp Margarine	NO	1 tsp Margarine	0	0	1 tsp	1 tsp
1/2c Milk	1/2c Skim Milk	1/2c Skim Milk	1/2c	1/2c	1/2c	1/2c
Coffee/Tea/Decaf	Coffee/Tea/Decaf	Coffee/Tea/Decaf	free	free	free	free
1/2c Lime Gelatin	1/2c Lime Gelatin	1/2c DB Lime Gelatin	1/2c	1/2c	1/2c	1/2c
2/3c SLF Cream Spinach Soup	2/3c LF Cream Spinach Soup	2/3c LF Cream Spinach Soup	2/3c	2/3c	2/3c	2/3c
3 oz Turkey Sandwich,	2 oz lean Corned Beef	3 oz lean Corned Beef	2 oz	3 oz	3 oz	3 oz
2 sl White Bread	Sandwich, 2 sl Rye Bread	Sandwich, 2 sl Rye Bread	2sl diet	2 sl	2 sl	2 sl
NO	Lettuce Leaves	Lettuce Leaves	Lett	Lett	Lett	Lett
NO	4 Tomato Slices	4 Tomato Slices	4 sl	4 sl	4 sl	4 sl
1/2c Cooked Carrots	1/2c Cole Slaw+	1/2c DB Cole Slaw	1/2c	1/2c	1/2c	1/2c
1 tsp Catsup	1 tsp Mustard	1 tsp Mustard	1 tsp	1 tsp	1 tsp	1 tsp
1/2c Milk (1/4c)[3]	1/2c Skim Milk	1/2c Skim Milk	1/4c	1/4c	1/2c	1/2c
Coffee/Tea/Decaf	Coffee/Tea/Decaf	Coffee/Tea/Decaf	free	free	free	free
1 med Bkd Green Apple-No Skin	1 med Baked Green Apple	1 sm DB Baked Green Apple	1 sm	1 sm	1 med	1 med
Milk[3] or STR Juice	Skim Milk or Juice	1/2c Skim Milk	1/2c	1/2c	1/2c	1/2c
Plain Cookies, Gelatin,	LF Cookies, LF Crackers,	1 Starch/Bread Exch	1	1	1	1
Plain Crackers, Banana,	Gelatin, Fresh Fruit	1 Meat Exch	0	0	0	1
Vanilla Ice Cream[3]		1 Fat Exch	0	0	1	1

Passover Sedar

Breakfast
Chilled Orange Juice or
Stewed Prunes
Matzo Meal Muffin
Farm Fresh Egg to Order
Hot Matzo Cereal
Assorted Matzos
Assorted Condiments
Your Choice of Beverage

Lunch
Israeli Salad with
Lemon Dressing
Cold Borscht with Sour Cream
Baked Vegetable Scrod
Honey Matzo Meal Latkas
Passover Rolls
Spiced Applesauce
Your Choice of Beverage

Dinner
Chicken Matzo Ball Soup
Roast Chicken
Farfel Stuffing
Steamed Zucchini
Assorted Matzos
Passover Sponge Cake
Your Choice of Beverage

Recipe	Regular, Liberal Bland[1], No Added Salt[2]	1–2 Gm Na (Low Sodium)	Mechanical Soft	Puree
	Breakfast			
S11	1/2c Orange Juice or 3 Stewed Prunes	1/2c Orange Juice or 3 Stewed Prunes	1/2c Orange Juice or 3 Stewed Prunes	1/2c STR Orange Juice or 1/4c PUR Prunes
N22	1 Matzo Meal Muffin or 1 sl Matzo	1 Matzo Meal Muffin or 1 sl Matzo	NO NO	NO NO
B4,5	1 Egg to Order	1 Egg to Order	1 Egg to Order	1 PUR Egg to Order
B3	3/4c Hot Matzo Cereal	3/4c Hot Matzo Cereal	1c Hot Matzo Cereal	1c PUR Hot Matzo Cereal
	1 tsp Margarine	1 tsp SR Margarine	1 tsp Margarine	1 tsp Margarine
	1 tsp Jam/Jelly	1 tsp Jam/Jelly	1 tsp Jelly	1 tsp Jelly
	1c Milk	1c Milk	1c Milk	1c Milk
	Coffee/Tea/Decaf	Coffee/Tea/Decaf	Coffee/Tea/Decaf	Coffeee/Tea/Decaf
	Lunch			
K27	1c Israeli Salad	1c Israeli Salad	4 oz Juice	4 oz STR Juice
C5	2/3c Cold Borscht with 1 oz Sour Cream	2/3c SR Cold Borscht with 1 oz Sour Cream	2/3c SFT Cold Borscht with 1 oz Sour Cream	2/3c PUR/STR Borscht with 1 oz Sour Cream
F7	3 oz Baked Scrod with 1/2c Vegetables & Tomato	3 oz Baked Scrod with 1/2c SR Vegetables & Tomato	3 oz Baked Scrod with 1/2c Vegetables & Tomato	8 oz PUR Scrod with PUR Vegetables & Tomato
N23	2 Honey Matzo Meal Latkas	2 Honey Matzo Meal Latkas	2 Honey Matzo Meal Latkas	1/2c PUR Matzo Meal Latkas
N24	1 Passover Roll	1 Passover Roll	NO	NO
	1 tsp Margarine	1 tsp SR Margarine	1 tsp Margarine	1 tsp Margarine
	1c Milk	1c Milk	1c Milk	1c Milk
	Coffee/Tea/Decaf	Coffee/Tea/Decaf	Coffee/Tea/Decaf	Coffee/Tea/Decaf
S2	1/2c Spiced Applesauce	1/2c Spiced Applesauce	1/2c Spiced Applesauce	1/2c Spiced Applesauce
	Dinner			
C9	2/3c Chix Matzo Ball Soup	2/3c Chix Matzo Ball Soup	2/3c Chix Matzo Ball Soup	2/3c PUR/STR Soup
E7	3 oz Roast Chicken	3 oz Roast Chicken	3 oz CHP Roast Chicken	4 oz PUR Roast Chicken
P13	1/2c Farfel Stuffing	1/2c Farfel Stuffing	3/4c Farfel Stuffing	3/4c PUR Farfel Stuffing
J52	1/2c Steamed Zucchini	1/2c Steamed Zucchini	1/2c SFT Steamed Zucchini	1/2c PUR Steamed Zucchini
	1 sl Matzo	1 sl Matzo	NO	NO
	1 tsp Margarine	1 tsp SR Margarine	1 tsp Margarine	1 tsp Margarine
	Coffee/Tea/Decaf	Coffee/Tea/Decaf	Coffee/Tea/Decaf	Coffee/Tea/Decaf
Q11	1 sl Passover Sponge Cake	1 sl Passover Sponge Cake	1 sl Passover Sponge Cake	1/2c PUR Peaches
	Snacks			
	Milk or Juice	Juice	Milk or Juice	Milk or STR Juice
	Cookies, Crackers,	SR Cookies, SR Crackers,	Plain Cookies, Gelatin,	Applesauce, SFT Banana,
	Gelatin, Ice Cream,	Gelatin, Fresh Fruit	Plain Crackers+, Ice Cream,	Gelatin, Ice Cream,
	Fresh Fruit		Banana	

TERMS: SFT = Soft; SLF = Soft/Low Fiber; GRD = Ground; CHP = Chopped Finely; PUR = Puree; STR = Strained; SR = Sodium or Salt Restricted; LF = Low Fat; FF = Fat Free; LCH = Low Cholesterol; DB = Diabetic; UNSW = Unsweetened; RC = Reduced Calorie; LC = Low Calorie; EXCH = Diabetic Exchange

SERVING UTENSILS: #6 Scoop = 2/3 cup-6 oz; #8 Scoop = 1/2 cup-4 oz; #10 Scoop = 3/8 cup-3 to 4 oz; #12 Scoop = 1/3 cup-2.5 to 3 oz; #16 Scoop = 1/4 cup-2 oz; #30 Scoop = 2 tbsp-1 oz; #60 Scoop = 1 tbsp-1/2 oz. Ounces will vary, based on food used.

1. *Liberal Bland:* Follow a regular diet. Use decaffeinated products. Omit pepper and chili powder.

2. *No Added Salt (3–4 gm NA):* Follow a regular diet. Use SR soups and SR canned meats. Omit salt packets (and shakers), bacon, sausage, smoked, and cured meats, substitute with SR food choices.

3. *Low Fiber:* Follow a soft diet. Do not exceed 2 cups of milk per day. Soft/Low Fiber—Omit pepper, garlic, and onions from recipes.

4. *2200 Calorie Diet:* Follow 2000 calorie diet with the following additions: Lunch—add 1 bread exchange and 1 fat exchange; Dinner—add 1 bread exchange.

+Consider individual tolerance. Daily Alternatives: Lunch and Dinner—Chicken, Hamburger, Cottage Cheese Fruit Plate, or Assorted Sandwiches. Individual preferences are provided upon request.

Amounts specified for food items that contain bone is equivalent to cooked, edible deboned portion.

Soft, Low Fiber[3]	Low Cholesterol, Low Fat (40–50 GM)	No Concentrated Sweets (Diabetic)	1200	1500	1800	2000[4]
			Diabetic/Calorie-Controlled			
1/2c STR Orange Juice	1/2c Orange Juice or	1/2c UNSW Orange Juice or	1/2c	1/2c	1/2c	1/2c
NO	3 med Stewed Prunes	3 Stewed Prunes	3	3	3	3
NO	1 LF Matzo Meal Muffin or	1 DB Matzo Meal Muffin (omit 1 fat)	0	1	1	1
1 sl Plain Matzo	1 sl Matzo	or 3/4 oz Matzo	3/4 oz	3/4 oz	3/4 oz	3/4 oz
1 Egg to Order	1 Egg Substitute	1 Egg to Order	1	1	1	1
3/4c Hot Matzo Cereal	3/4c Hot Matzo Cereal	3/4c Hot Matzo Cereal	1/2c	1/2c	1/2c	1/2c
1 tsp Margarine	1 tsp Margarine	1 tsp Margarine	1 tsp	1 tsp	1 tsp	1 tsp
1 tsp Jelly	1 tsp Jam/Jelly	1 tsp DB Jam/Jelly	1 tsp	1 tsp	1 tsp	1 tsp
1c Milk	1c Skim Milk	1c Skim Milk	1/2c	1/2c	1/2c	1c
Coffee/Tea/Decaf	Coffee/Tea/Decaf	Coffee/Tea/Decaf	free	free	free	free
4 oz STR Juice	1c Israeli Salad	1c Israeli Salad	1c	1c	1c	1c
2/3c SFT Cold Borscht with	2/3c Cold Borscht	2/3c DB Cold Borscht with	2/3c	2/3c	2/3c	2/3c
1 oz Sour Cream	NO	1 oz Sour Cream	0	0	1Tbsp	2Tbsp
3 oz Baked Scrod with	3 oz Baked Scrod with	3 oz Baked Scrod with	2 oz	3 oz	3 oz	3 oz
1/2c SLF Vegetables & Tomato	1/2c LF Vegetables & Tomato	1/2c LF Vegetables & Tomato	1/2c	1/2c	1/2c	1/2c
2 Honey Matzo Meal Latkas	1 LF Honey Matzo Meal Latkas	2 DB Matzo Meal Latkas	1	2	2	2
1 sl Plain Matzo	1 sl Matzo	1 DB Passover Roll	0	0	1	1
1 tsp Margarine	NO	1 tsp Margarine	0	0	0	0
1c Milk	1c Skim Milk	1c Skim Milk	1/4c	1/4c	1/4c	1c
Coffee/Tea/Decaf	Coffee/Tea/Decaf	Coffee/Tea/Decaf	free	free	free	free
1/2c Spiced Applesauce	1/2c Spiced Applesauce	1/2c DB Spiced Applesauce	1/2c	1/2c	1/2c	1/2c
2/3c Chix Matzo Ball Soup	2/3c LF Chix Matzo Ball Soup	2/3c Chix Matzo Ball Soup	Broth	2/3c	2/3c	2/3c
3 oz SLF Roast Chicken	2 oz LF Roast Chicken	3 oz LF Roast Chicken	2 oz	3 oz	3 oz	3 oz
1/2c SLF Farfel Stuffing+	3/4c LF Farfel Stuffing	1/2c DB Farfel Stuffing	1/3c	1/3c	1/3c	1/2c
1/2c SFT Steamed Zucchini	1/2c Steamed Zucchini	1/2c Steamed Zucchini	1/2c	1/2c	1/2c	1/2c
1 sl Plain Matzo	1 sl Matzo	3/4 oz Matzo	0	0	3/4 oz	3/4 oz
1 tsp Margarine	NO	1 tsp Margarine	0	0	0	1 tsp
Coffee/Tea/Decaf	Coffee/Tea/Decaf	Coffee/Tea/Decaf	free	free	free	free
1 sl Passover Sponge Cake	1 sl LF Passover Sponge Cake	1 sl DB Passover Sponge Cake	1 sl	1 sl	1 sl	1 sl
Milk[3] or STR Juice	Skim Milk or Juice	1/2c Skim Milk	1/2c	1/2c	1/2c	1/2c
Plain Cookies, Gelatin,	LF Cookies, LF Crackers,	1 Starch/Bread Exch	1	1	1	1
Plain Crackers, Banana,	Gelatin, Fresh Fruit	1 Meat Exch	0	0	0	1
Vanilla Ice Cream[3]		1 Fat Exch	0	0	1	1

Easter

Breakfast
Citrus Cup
Vegetable Omelette
Farm Fresh Egg to Order
Bran or Corn Muffin
Cream of Rice or
Assorted Cold Cereals
Assorted Condiments
Your Choice of Beverage

Lunch
Julienne Soup
Baked Glazed Ham
Baked Sweet Potato
Asparagus Spears
Warm Dinner Rolls
Lemon Meringue Pie
Your Choice of Beverage

Dinner
Tossed Vegetable Salad
with Assorted Salad Dressings
Tarragon Chicken
Lyonnaise Noodles
Sunshine Carrots
Warm Fresh Dinner Rolls
Angelfood Cake with
Fresh Berries
Your Choice of Beverage

Recipe	Regular, Liberal Bland[1], No Added Salt[2]	1–2 Gm Na (Low Sodium)	Mechanical Soft	Puree
	Breakfast			
S3	1/2c Citrus Cup	1/2c Citrus Cup	1/2c Canned Citrus Cup	1/2c PUR Citrus Cup
B1	1/2c Cream of Rice or	1/2c Cream of Rice or	1/2c Cream of Rice or	1c Cream of Rice
	3/4c Asst Dry Cereals	3/4c SR Asst Dry Cereals	3/4c Asst Dry Cereals+	NO
G8	3.5 oz Vegetable Omelette	3.5 oz Vegetable Omelette	3.5 oz SFT Vegetable Omelette	3.5 oz PUR Vegetable Omelette
N14,15	1 Bran or Corn Muffin	1 SR Bran or SR Corn Muffin	1 Bran+ or Corn Muffin	1 sl Bread+
	1 tsp Margarine	1 tsp SR Margarine	1 tsp Margarine	1 tsp Margarine
	1 tsp Jam/Jelly	1 tsp Jam/Jelly	1 tsp Jelly	1 tsp Jelly
	1c Milk	1c Milk	1c Milk	1c Milk
	Coffee/Tea/Decaf	Coffee/Tea/Decaf	Coffee/Tea/Decaf	Coffee/Tea/Decaf
	Lunch			
C20	2/3c Julienne Soup	2/3c SR Julienne Soup	2/3c Julienne Soup	2/3c PUR/STR Julienne Soup
D28,31	3 oz Baked Glazed Ham[2]	3 oz Roast Pork	3 oz CHP Glazed Ham	4 oz PUR Glazed Ham
J44	1 sm Baked Sweet Potato	1 sm Baked Sweet Potato	1 sm Bkd Sweet Potato-no skin	1/2c PUR Sweet Potatoes
J1	1/2c Asparagus Spears	1/2c Asparagus Spears	1/2c Asparagus Spears	1/2c PUR Asparagus Spears
	1 Dinner Roll	1 Dinner Roll	1 SFT Dinner Roll+	1 sl Bread+
	1 tsp Margarine	1 tsp SR Margarine	1 tsp Margarine	1 tsp Margarine
	1/2c Milk	1/2c Milk	1/2c Milk	1/2c Milk
	Coffee/Tea/Decaf	Coffee/Tea/Decaf	Coffee/Tea/Decaf	Coffee/Tea/Decaf
R4,T4	1/8 Lemon Meringue Pie	1/8 SR Lemon Meringue Pie	1/8 Lemon Meringue Pie	1/2c Lemon Pudding
	Dinner			
K32	1c Tossed Vegetable Salad	1c Tossed Vegetable Salad	1/2c Juice	1/2c STR Juice
P1–8	1 oz Salad Dressing	1 oz SR Salad Dressing	NO	NO
E9	3 oz Tarragon Chicken	3 oz Tarragon Chicken	3 oz CHP Tarragon Chicken	4 oz PUR Tarragon Chicken
M2	1/2c Lyonnaise Noodles	1/2c Lyonnaise Noodles	1/2c Lyonnaise Noodles	1/2c PUR Lyonnaise Noodles
J18	1/2c Sunshine Carrots	1/2c Sunshine Carrots	1/2c Sunshine Carrots	1/2c PUR Sunshine Carrots
	Coffee/Tea/Decaf	Coffee/Tea/Decaf	Coffee/Tea/Decaf	Coffee/Tea/Decaf
	1 Dinner Roll	1 Dinner Roll	1 SFT Dinner Roll+	1 sl Bread+
	1 tsp Margarine	1 tsp SR Margarine	1 tsp Margarine	1 tsp Margarine
	1/2c Milk	1/2c Milk	1/2c Milk	1/2c Milk
	Coffee/Tea/Decaf	Coffee/Tea/Decaf	Coffee/Tea/Decaf	Coffee/Tea/Decaf
Q1	1 sl Angelfood Cake with	1 sl Angelfood Cake with	1 sl Angelfood Cake with	NO
	1/4c Fresh Berries and	1/4c Fresh Berries and	1/4c Canned Sliced Peaches	1/2c PUR Peaches with
	1 Tbsp Whipped Cream	1 Tbsp Whipped Cream	1 Tbsp Whipped Cream	1 Tbsp Whipped Cream
	Snacks			
	Milk or Juice	Juice	Milk or Juice	Milk or STR Juice
	Cookies, Crackers,	SR Cookies, SR Crackers,	Plain Cookies, Gelatin,	Applesauce, SFT Banana,
	Gelatin, Ice Cream,	Gelatin, Fresh Fruit	Plain Crackers+, Ice Cream,	Gelatin, Ice Cream
	Fresh Fruit		Banana	

TERMS: SFT = Soft; SLF = Soft/Low Fiber; GRD = Ground; CHP = Chopped Finely; PUR = Puree; STR = Strained; SR = Sodium or Salt Restricted; LF = Low Fat; FF = Fat Free; LCH = Low Cholesterol; DB = Diabetic; UNSW = Unsweetened; RC = Reduced Calorie; LC = Low Calorie; EXCH = Diabetic Exchange

SERVING UTENSILS: #6 Scoop = 2/3 cup-6 oz; #8 Scoop = 1/2 cup-4 oz; #10 Scoop = 3/8 cup-3 to 4 oz; #12 Scoop = 1/3 cup-2.5 to 3 oz; #16 Scoop = 1/4 cup-2 oz; #30 Scoop = 2 tbsp-1 oz; #60 Scoop = 1 tbsp-1/2 oz. Ounces will vary, based on food used.

1. *Liberal Bland:* Follow a regular diet. Use decaffeinated products. Omit pepper and chili powder.

2. *No Added Salt (3–4 gm NA):* Follow a regular diet. Use SR soups and SR canned meats. Omit salt packets (and shakers), bacon, sausage, smoked, and cured meats, substitute with SR food choices.

3. *Low Fiber:* Follow a soft diet. Do not exceed 2 cups of milk per day. Soft/Low Fiber—Omit pepper, garlic, and onions from recipes.

4. *2200 Calorie Diet:* Follow 2000 calorie diet with the following additions: Lunch—add 1 bread exchange and 1 fat exchange; Dinner—add 1 bread exchange.

+Consider individual tolerance. Daily Alternatives: Lunch and Dinner—Chicken, Hamburger, Cottage Cheese Fruit Plate, or Assorted Sandwiches. Individual preferences are provided upon request.

Amounts specified for food items that contain bone is equivalent to cooked, edible deboned portion.

Soft, Low Fiber[3]	Low Cholesterol, Low Fat (40–50 GM)	No Concentrated Sweets (Diabetic)	1200	1500	1800	2000[4] Diabetic/Calorie-Controlled		
1/2c Canned Citrus Cup	1/2c Citrus Cup	1/2c Citrus Cup	1/2c	1/2c	1/2c	1/2c		
1/2c Cream of Rice or	1/2c LF Cream of Rice or	1/2c DB Cream of Rice or	1/2c	1/2c	1/2c	1/2c		
3/4c Asst Refined Cereals	3/4c Dry Cereals	3/4c UNSW Dry Cereals	3/4c	3/4c	3/4c	3/4c		
3.5 oz SLF Vegetable Omelette	3.5 oz LF Egg Sub w/Vegetables	3.5 oz DB Vegetable Omelette	3 oz	3 oz	3 oz	3.5 oz		
1 sl White Toast	1 LF Bran or LF Corn Muffin	1 DB Bran or DB Corn Muffin	1 sm	1 sm	1 sm	1 sm		
1 tsp Margarine	1 tsp Margarine	1 tsp Margarine	0	0	1 tsp	1 tsp		
1 tsp Jelly	1 tsp Jam/Jelly	1 tsp DB Jam/Jelly	1 tsp	1 tsp	1 tsp	1 tsp		
1c Milk	1c Skim Milk	1c Skim Milk	1/2c	1/2c	1/2c	1c		
Coffee/Tea/Decaf	Coffee/Tea/Decaf	Coffee/Tea/Decaf	free	free	free	free		
2/3c SLF Julienne Soup	2/3c Julienne Soup+	2/3c Julienne Soup	2/3c	2/3c	2/3c	2/3c		
3 oz SLF Roast Pork	2 oz Baked Glazed Ham	3 oz DB Baked Ham	2 oz	3 oz	3 oz	3 oz		
1 sm Bkd Sweet Potato-no skin	1 sm Baked Sweet Potato	1 sm Baked Sweet Potato	1/3 sm	1/3 sm	1/2 sm	1/2 sm		
1/2c Asparagus Spears	1/2c Asparagus Spears	1/2c Asparagus Spears	1/2c	1/2c	1/2c	1/2c		
1 SFT Refined Dinner Roll	1 Dinner Roll	1 Dinner Roll	0	0	1 sm	1 sm		
1 tsp Margarine	1 tsp Margarine	1 tsp Margarine	0	0	1 tsp	1 tsp		
1/2c Milk	1/2c Skim Milk	1/2c Skim Milk	1/2c	1/2c	1/2c	1/2c		
Coffee/Tea/Decaf	Coffee/Tea/Decaf	Coffee/Tea/Decaf	free	free	free	free		
1/8 Lemon Meringue Pie	1/8 LF Lemon Meringue Pie	1/8 DB Lemon Pie (no meringue)	1/12	1/12	1/8	1/8		
1/2c STR Juice	1c Tossed Vegetable Salad	1c Tossed Vegetable Salad	1c	1c	1c	1c		
NO	1 Tbsp LC Salad Dressing	1 Tbsp LC Sld Dressing	1 Tbsp	1 Tbsp	1 Tbsp	1 Tbsp		
3 oz SLF Tarragon Chicken	3 oz LF Tarragon Chicken	3 oz LF Tarragon Chicken	2 oz	3 oz	3 oz	3 oz		
1/2c SLF Lyonnaise Noodles	1/2c LF Lyonnaise Noodles	1/2c LF Lyonnaise Noodles	1/3c	1/3c	1/2c	1/2c		
1/2c Sunshine Carrots	1/2c LF Sunshine Carrots	1/2c DB Sunshine Carrots	1/2c	1/2c	1/2c	1/2c		
Coffee/Tea/Decaf	Coffee/Tea/Decaf	Coffee/Tea/Decaf	free	free	free	free		
1 SFT Refined Dinner Roll	1 Dinner Roll	1 Dinner Roll	0	0	0	1 sm		
1 tsp Margarine	NO	1 tsp Margarine	0	0	0	1 tsp		
1/2c Milk	1/2c Skim Milk	1/2c Skim Milk	1/2c	1/2c	1/2c	1/2c		
Coffee/Tea/Decaf	Coffee/Tea/Decaf	Coffee/Tea/Decaf	free	free	free	free		
1 sl Angelfood Cake with	1 sl Angelfood Cake with	1 sl Angelfood Cake with	0	3/4 sl	1 sl	1 sl		
1/4c Canned Sliced Peaches	1/4c Fresh Berries	1/4c Fresh Berries and	1/2c	1/4c	1/2c	1/2c		
1 Tbsp Whipped Cream	NO	1 Tbsp Whipped Cream	1 Tbsp	1 Tbsp	1 Tbsp	1 Tbsp		
Milk[3] or STR Juice	Skim Milk or Juice	1/2c Skim Milk	1/2c	1/2c	1/2c	1/2c		
Plain Cookies, Gelatin,	LF Cookies, LF Crackers,	1 Starch/Bread Exch	1	1	1	1		
Plain Crackers, Banana,	Gelatin, Fresh Fruit	1 Meat Exch	0	0	0	1		
Vanilla Ice Cream[3]		1 Fat Exch	0	0	1	1		

Mother's Day

Breakfast
Chilled White Grape Juice
Fresh Fruit Cup
Quiche Lorraine
Hot Homemade Muffins
Cream of Wheat or
Assorted Cold Cereals
Assorted Condiments
Your Choice of Beverage

Lunch
Marinated Cucumbers
Rock Cornish Game Hen with
Apricot Glaze
Rice Pilaf
Vegetable Medley
Warm Dinner Rolls
Mom's Apple Pie
Your Choice of Beverage

Dinner
Cream of Celery Soup
Seafood Salad in
Avocado Half
Lettuce, Tomato Slices, and
Green Pepper Rings
Assorted Salad Dressings
Warm Dinner Rolls
Rainbow Sherbet
Your Choice of Beverage

Recipe	Regular, Liberal Bland[1], No Added Salt[2]	1–2 Gm Na (Low Sodium)	Mechanical Soft	Puree
	Breakfast			
	1/2c White Grape Juice	1/2c White Grape Juice	1/2c White Grape Juice	1/2c STR White Grape Juice
S5	1/2c Fruit Cup	1/2c Fruit Cup	1/2c Fruit Cup	1/2c PUR Fruit Cup
B1	1/2c Cream of Wheat or	1/2c Cream of Wheat or	1/2c Cream of Wheat or	1c Cream of Wheat
	3/4c Asst Dry Cereals	3/4c SR Asst Dry Cereals	3/4c Asst Dry Cereals+	NO
G12,13	1/12 pie Quiche Lorraine[2]	1/12 pie SR Spinach Quiche	1/12 pie Quiche Lorraine+	1/2c PUR Quiche Lorraine
N10–20	1 Homemade Muffin	1 SR Homemade Muffin	1 Plain Muffin+	1 sl White Bread+
	1 tsp Margarine	1 tsp SR Margarine	1 tsp Margarine	1 tsp Margarine
	1 tsp Jelly/Jam	1 tsp Jelly/Jam	1 tsp Jelly	1 tsp Jelly
	1c Milk	1c Milk	1c Milk	1c Milk
	Coffee/Tea/Decaf	Coffee/Tea/Decaf	Coffee/Tea/Decaf	Coffee/Tea/Decaf
	Lunch			
K9	1/2c Marinated Cucumbers	1/2c Marinated Cucumbers	1/2c Juice	1/2c STR Juice
E12	3 oz Rock Cornish Game Hen	3 oz Rock Cornish Game Hen	3 oz Rock Cornish Game Hen	4 oz PUR Cornish Game Hen
	with Apricot Glaze	with Apricot Glaze	with Apricot Glaze	with STR Apricot Glaze
L5	1/2c Rice Pilaf	1/2c SR Rice Pilaf	1/2c SFT Rice Pilaf	1/2c PUR Rice Pilaf
J51	1/2c Vegetable Medley	1/2c Vegetable Medley	1/2c SFT Vegetable Medley	1/2c PUR Vegetable Medley
	1 Dinner Roll	1 Dinner Roll	1 SFT Dinner Roll+	1 sl Bread+
	1 tsp Margarine	1 tsp SR Margarine	1 tsp Margarine	1 tsp Margarine
	1/2c Milk	1/2c Milk	1/2c Milk	1/2c Milk
	Coffee/Tea/Decaf	Coffee/Tea/Decaf	Coffee/Tea/Decaf	Coffee/Tea/Decaf
R3	1/8 Apple Pie	1/8 SR Apple Pie	1/8 Apple Pie+	1/2c PUR Apple Pie Filling
	Dinner			
C11	2/3c Cream Celery Soup	2/3c Cream Celery Soup	2/3c Cream Celery Soup	2/3c PUR/STR Crm Celery Soup
I18	1/2c Seafood Salad in	1/2c SR Seafood Salad in	1/2c SFT Seafood Salad in	1/2c PUR Seafood Salad
K21	1 sm Avocado Half on	1 sm Avocado Half on	1 sm Avocado Half	1/4c PUR Avocado
	Lettuce Leaves	Lettuce Leaves	NO	NO
J50	3 Tomato Slices	3 Tomato Slices	1/2c Stewed Tomatoes	1/2c PUR Stewed Tomatoes
	3 Green Pepper Ring	3 Green Pepper Ring	NO	NO
P1–8	1 oz Salad Dressing	1 oz SR Salad Dressing	NO	NO
	1 Dinner Roll	1 Dinner Roll	1 SFT Dinner Roll+	1 sl Bread+
	1 tsp Margarine	1 tsp SR Margarine	1 tsp Margarine	1 tsp Margarine
	1/2c Milk	1/4c Milk	1/2c Milk	1/2c Milk
	Coffee/Tea/Decaf	Coffee/Tea/Decaf	Coffee/Tea/Decaf	Coffee/Tea/Decaf
	1/2c Rainbow Sherbet	1/2c Rainbow Sherbet	1/2c Rainbow Sherbet	1/2c Rainbow Sherbet
	Snacks			
	Milk or Juice	Juice	Milk or Juice	Milk or STR Juice
	Cookies, Crackers,	SR Cookies, SR Crackers,	Plain Cookies, Gelatin,	Applesauce, SFT Banana,
	Gelatin, Ice Cream,	Gelatin, Fresh Fruit	Plain Crackers+, Ice Cream,	Gelatin, Ice Cream,
	Fresh Fruit		Banana	

TERMS: SFT = Soft; SLF = Soft/Low Fiber; GRD = Ground; CHP = Chopped Finely; PUR = Puree; STR = Strained; SR = Sodium or Salt Restricted; LF = Low Fat; FF = Fat Free; LCH = Low Cholesterol; DB = Diabetic; UNSW = Unsweetened; RC = Reduced Calorie; LC = Low Calorie; EXCH = Diabetic Exchange

SERVING UTENSILS: #6 Scoop = 2/3 cup-6 oz; #8 Scoop = 1/2 cup-4 oz; #10 Scoop = 3/8 cup-3 to 4 oz; #12 Scoop = 1/3 cup-2.5 to 3 oz; #16 Scoop = 1/4 cup-2 oz; #30 Scoop = 2 tbsp-1 oz; #60 Scoop = 1 tbsp-1/2 oz. Ounces will vary, based on food used.

1. *Liberal Bland:* Follow a regular diet. Use decaffeinated products. Omit pepper and chili powder.

2. *No Added Salt (3–4 gm NA):* Follow a regular diet. Use SR soups and SR canned meats. Omit salt packets (and shakers), bacon, sausage, smoked, and cured meats, substitute with SR food choices.

3. *Low Fiber:* Follow a soft diet. Do not exceed 2 cups of milk per day. Soft/Low Fiber—Omit pepper, garlic, and onions from recipes.

4. *2200 Calorie Diet:* Follow 2000 calorie diet with the following additions: Lunch—add 1 bread exchange and 1 fat exchange; Dinner—add 1 bread exchange.

+Consider individual tolerance. Daily Alternatives: Lunch and Dinner—Chicken, Hamburger, Cottage Cheese Fruit Plate, or Assorted Sandwiches. Individual preferences are provided upon request.

Amounts specified for food items that contain bone is equivalent to cooked, edible deboned portion.

Soft, Low Fiber[3]	Low Cholesterol, Low Fat (40–50 GM)	No Concentrated Sweets (Diabetic)	1200	1500	1800	2000[4]
			Diabetic/Calorie-Controlled			

Soft, Low Fiber[3]	Low Cholesterol, Low Fat (40–50 GM)	No Concentrated Sweets (Diabetic)	1200	1500	1800	2000[4]
1/2c STR White Grape Juice	1/2c White Grape Juice	1/2c UNSW White Grape Juice	1/3c	1/3c	1/3c	1/3c
1/2c SLF Fruit Cup	1/2c Fruit Cup	or 1/2c Fruit Cup	1/2c	1/2c	1/2c	1/2c
1/2c Cream of Wheat or	1/2c LF Cream of Wheat or	1/2c DB Cream of Wheat or	1/2c	1/2c	1/2c	1/2c
3/4c Asst Refined Cereals	3/4c Dry Cereals	3/4c UNSW Dry Cereals	3/4c	3/4c	3/4c	3/4c
1/12 pie SLF Spinach Quiche	1/12 pie LF Spinach Quiche	1/12 pie DB Quiche Lorraine	1/12	1/12	1/12	1/12
1 SLF Muffin	1 LF Muffin	1 DB Muffin	1 sm	1 sm	1 sm	1 sm
1 tsp Margarine	1 tsp Margarine	1 tsp Margarine	0	0	1 tsp	1 tsp
1 tsp Jelly	1 tsp Jelly/Jam	1 tsp UNSW Jelly/Jam	1 tsp	1 tsp	1 tsp	1 tsp
1c Milk	1c Skim Milk	1c Skim Milk	1/2c	1/2c	1/2c	1c
Coffee/Tea/Decaf	Coffee/Tea/Decaf	Coffee/Tea/Decaf	free	free	free	free
1/2c STR Juice	1/2c LF Marinated Cucumbers	1/2c DB Marinated Cucumbers	1/2c	1/2c	1/2c	1/2c
3 oz SLF Cornish Game Hen	2 oz LF Rock Cornish Game Hen	3 oz DB Cornish Game Hen	2 oz	3 oz	3 oz	3 oz
with SLF Apricot Glaze	with Apricot Glaze	with DB Apricot Glaze				
1/2c SFT Rice Pilaf	1/2c Rice Pilaf+	1/2c Rice Pilaf	1/3c	1/3c	1/2c	1/2c
1/2c SLF Vegetable Medley	1/2c Vegetable Medley+	1/2c Vegetable Medley	1/2c	1/2c	1/2c	1/2c
1 SFT Refined Dinner Roll	1 Dinner Roll	1 Dinner Roll	0	0	1 sm	1 sm
1 tsp Margarine	NO	1 tsp Margarine	0	0	0	1 tsp
1/2c Milk (1/4c)[3]	1/2c Skim Milk	1/2c Skim Milk	1/4c	1/2c	1/2c	1/2c
Coffee/Tea/Decaf	Coffee/Tea/Decaf	Coffee/Tea/Decaf	free	free	free	free
1/8 Apple Pie+	1/8 LF Apple Pie	1/8 DB Apple Pie	1/12	1/12	1/12	1/12
2/3c PUR/STR Crm Celery Soup	2/3c LF Cream Celery Soup	2/3c LF Cream Celery Soup	Broth	2/3c	2/3c	2/3c
1/2c SFT Seafood Salad	1/2c LF Seafood Salad	1/2c LF Seafood Salad in	1/2c	3/4c	3/4c	3/4c
1/2c SFT Potato Salad	1/2c LF Potato Salad	1 sm Avocado Half on	0	1/4	1/4	1/2
NO	Lettuce Leaves	Lettuce Leaves	free	free	free	free
1/2c SLF Stewed Tomatoes	3 Tomato Slices	3 Tomato Slices	3 sl	3 sl	3 sl	3 sl
NO	3 Green Pepper Ring	3 Green Pepper Ring	3	3	3	3
NO	1 Tbsp LC Salad Dressing	1 Tbsp LC Sld Dressing	1 Tbsp	1 Tbsp	1 Tbsp	1 Tbsp
1 SFT Refined Dinner Roll	1 Dinner Roll	1 Dinner Roll	0	0	1	1
1 tsp Margarine	NO	1 tsp Margarine	0	0	1 tsp	1 tsp
1/2c Milk (1/4c)[3]	1/2c Skim Milk	1/2c Skim Milk	1/4c	1/4c	1/2c	1/2c
Coffee/Tea/Decaf	Coffee/Tea/Decaf	Coffee/Tea/Decaf	free	free	free	free
1/2c Orange Sherbet	1/2c LF Rainbow Sherbet	1/2c LF Rainbow Sherbet+	1/3c	1/2c	1/2c	1/2c
Milk[3] or STR Juice	Skim Milk or Juice	1/2c Skim Milk	1/2c	1/2c	1/2c	1/2c
Plain Cookies, Gelatin,	LF Cookies, LF Crackers	1 Starch/Bread Exch	1	1	1	1
Plain Crackers, Banana,	Gelatin, Fresh Fruit	1 Meat Exch	0	0	0	1
Vanilla Ice Cream[3]		1 Fat Exch	0	0	1	1

Father's Day

Breakfast
Fresh Squeezed Orange Juice
French Toast with
Maple Syrup or
Farm Fresh Egg to Order
Bacon Strips
Cream of Rice or
Assorted Cold Cereals
Assorted Condiments
Your Choice of Beverage

Lunch
Cucumber-Onion Salad
Savory Meatloaf
O'Brien Potatoes
Steamed Spinach
Warm Dinner Rolls
Baked Apple
Your Choice of Beverage

Dinner
Bean Soup
Deli Platter
Cheesy Pea Salad
Carrot-Raisin Salad
Warm Fresh Dinner Rolls
Chocolate Chip Cake
Your Choice of Beverage

Recipe	Regular, Liberal Bland[1], No Added Salt[2]	1–2 Gm Na (Low Sodium)	Mechanical Soft	Puree
	Breakfast			
B1	1/2c Orange Juice	1/2c Orange Juice	1/2c Orange Juice	1/2c STR Orange Juice
	1/2c Cream of Rice or	1/2c Cream of Rice or	1/2c Cream of Rice or	1c Cream of Rice
B8	3/4c Asst Dry Cereals	3/4c SR Asst Dry Cereals	3/4c Asst Dry Cereals+	NO
	1 sl French Toast with	1 sl SR French Toast with	1 sl French Toast with	NO
	2 oz Maple Syrup or	2 oz Maple Syrup or	2 oz Maple Syrup or	NO
B4,5	1 Egg to Order with	1 Egg to Order with	1 Egg to Order with	1 PUR Egg to Order with
	1 sl Toast	1 sl Toast	1 sl Toast+	1 sl White Bread+
D32	2 sl Bacon[2]	NO	2 sl Crisp Bacon	NO
	1 tsp Margarine	1 tsp SR Margarine	1 tsp Margarine	1 tsp Margarine
	1 tsp Jam/Jelly	1 tsp Jam/Jelly	1 tsp Jelly	1 tsp Jelly
	1c Milk	1c Milk	1c Milk	1c Milk
	Coffee/Tea/Decaf	Coffee/Tea/Decaf	Coffee/Tea/Decaf	Coffee/Tea/Decaf
	Lunch			
K10	1/2c Cucumber-Onion Salad	1/2c Cucumber-Onion Salad	1/2c Cranberry Juice	1/2c STR Cranberry Juice
D16	4 oz Savory Meatloaf	4 oz SR Savory Meatloaf	4 oz Savory Meatloaf	4 oz PUR Savory Meatloaf
J38	1/2c O'Brien Potatoes	1/2c O'Brien Potatoes	1/2c SFT O'Brien Potatoes	1/2c PUR O'Brien Potatoes
J47	1/2c Steamed Spinach	1/2c Steamed Spinach	1/2c Steamed Spinach	1/2c PUR Steamed Spinach
	1 Dinner Roll	1 Dinner Roll	1 SFT Dinner Roll+	1 sl Bread+
	1 tsp Margarine	1 tsp SR Margarine	1 tsp Margarine	1 tsp Margarine
	1/2c Milk	1/2c Milk	1/2c Milk	1/2c Milk
	Coffee/Tea/Decaf	Coffee/Tea/Decaf	Coffee/Tea/Decaf	Coffee/Tea/Decaf
S1	1 med Baked Apple	1 med Baked Apple	1 med SFT Bkd Apple-No skin	1/2c Applesauce
	Dinner			
C4,1	2/3c Bean Soup	2/3c SR/LF Bean Soup	2/3c Bean Soup	2/3c PUR/STR Bean Soup
I8	Deli Platter:	Deli Platter:	Deli Platter:	Deli Platter:
	1 oz Roast Beef	1 oz Roast Beef	1 oz CHP Roast Beef	1 oz PUR Roast Beef
	1 oz Turkey, 1 oz Ham[2]	2 oz Turkey	1 oz CHP Turkey, 1 oz CHP Ham	1 oz PUR Turkey, 1 oz PUR Ham
	Lettuce Leaves	Lettuce Leaves	NO	NO
	2 sl Tomatoes	2 sl Tomatoes	NO	NO
	1 Green Pepper Ring	1 Green Pepper Ring	NO	NO
	1 Black Olive	NO	NO	NO
K20,15	1/2c Cheesy Pea Salad	1/2c SR Cheesy Pea Salad	1/2c SFT Cheesy Pea Salad	1/2c PUR Cheesy Pea Salad
K4,J14	1/2c Carrot-Raisin Salad	1/2c SR Carrot-Raisin Salad	1/2c Cooked Carrots	1/2c PUR Cooked Carrots
	1 Dinner Roll	1 Dinner Roll	1 SFT Dinner Roll+	1 sl Bread+
	1 tsp Catsup, Mustard,	1 tsp SR Catsup, SR Mustard,	1 tsp Catsup, Mustard,	1 tsp Catsup, Mustard,
	and 1 Tbsp Mayonnaise	and 1 Tbsp SR Mayonnaise	and 1 Tbsp Mayonnaise	and 1 Tbsp Mayonnaise
	1/2c Milk	1/2c Milk	1/2c Milk	1/2c Milk
	Coffee/Tea/Decaf	Coffee/Tea/Decaf	Coffee/Tea/Decaf	Coffee/Tea/Decaf
Q6,1	3×2" sl Chocolate Chip Cake	3×2" sl Chocolate Chip Cake	3×2" sl Chocolate Chip Cake+	1/2c Ice Cream
	Snacks			
	Milk or Juice	Juice	Milk or Juice	Milk or STR Juice
	Cookies, Crackers,	SR Cookies, SR Crackers,	Plain Cookies, Gelatin,	Applesauce, SFT Banana,
	Gelatin, Ice Cream,	Gelatin, Fresh Fruit	Plain Crackers+, Ice Cream,	Gelatin, Ice Cream
	Fresh Fruit		Banana	

TERMS: SFT = Soft; SLF = Soft/Low Fiber; GRD = Ground; CHP = Chopped Finely; PUR = Puree; STR = Strained; SR = Sodium or Salt Restricted; LF = Low Fat; FF = Fat Free; LCH = Low Cholesterol; DB = Diabetic; UNSW = Unsweetened; RC = Reduced Calorie; LC = Low Calorie; EXCH = Diabetic Exchange

SERVING UTENSILS: #6 Scoop = 2/3 cup-6 oz; #8 Scoop = 1/2 cup-4 oz; #10 Scoop = 3/8 cup-3 to 4 oz; #12 Scoop = 1/3 cup-2.5 to 3 oz; #16 Scoop = 1/4 cup-2 oz; #30 Scoop = 2 tbsp-1 oz; #60 Scoop = 1 tbsp-1/2 oz. Ounces will vary, based on food used.

1. *Liberal Bland:* Follow a regular diet. Use decaffeinated products. Omit pepper and chili powder.

2. *No Added Salt (3–4 gm NA):* Follow a regular diet. Use SR soups and SR canned meats. Omit salt packets (and shakers), bacon, sausage, smoked, and cured meats, substitute with SR food choices.

3. *Low Fiber:* Follow a soft diet. Do not exceed 2 cups of milk per day. Soft/Low Fiber—Omit pepper, garlic, and onions from recipes.

4. *2200 Calorie Diet:* Follow 2000 calorie diet with the following additions: Lunch—add 1 bread exchange and 1 fat exchange; Dinner—add 1 bread exchange.

+Consider individual tolerance. Daily Alternatives: Lunch and Dinner—Chicken, Hamburger, Cottage Cheese Fruit Plate, or Assorted Sandwiches. Individual preferences are provided upon request.

Amounts specified for food items that contain bone is equivalent to cooked, edible deboned portion.

Soft, Low Fiber[3]	Low Cholesterol, Low Fat (40–50 GM)	No Concentrated Sweets (Diabetic)	1200	1500	1800	2000[4]
			Diabetic/Calorie-Controlled			
1/2c STR Orange Juice	1/2c Orange Juice	1/2c UNSW Orange Juice	1/2c	1/2c	1/2c	1/2c
1/2c Cream of Rice or	1/2c LF Cream of Rice or	1/2c DB Cream of Rice or	1/2c	1/2c	1/2c	1/2c
3/4c Asst Refined Cereals	3/4c Dry Cereals	3/4c UNSW Dry Cereals	3/4c	3/4c	3/4c	3/4c
1 sl French Toast with	1 sl LF French Toast with	1 sl DB French Toast with	1 sl	1 sl	1 sl	2 sl
2 oz Maple Syrup or	2 oz Maple Syrup or	2 oz DB Maple Syrup or	1 Tbsp	1 Tbsp	1 Tbsp	1 Tbsp
1 Egg to Order with	1 Egg Substitute	1 Egg to Order with	1	1	1	1
1 sl White Toast	1 sl Toast	1 sl Toast	1 sl	1 sl	1 sl	2 sl
NO	NO	2 sl Bacon	0	0	1 sl	1 sl
1 tsp Margarine	NO	1 tsp Margarine	0	1 tsp	2 tsp	2 tsp
1 tsp Jelly	1 tsp Jam/Jelly	1 tsp DB Jam/Jelly	1 tsp	1 tsp	1 tsp	1 tsp
1c Milk	1c Skim Milk	1c Skim Milk	1/2c	1/2c	1/2c	1c
Coffee/Tea/Decaf	Coffee/Tea/Decaf	Coffee/Tea/Decaf	free	free	free	free
1/2c STR Cranberry Juice	1/2c LF Cucumber-Onion Salad	1/2c DB Cucumber-Onion Salad	1/2c	1/2c	1/2c	1/2c
4 oz SLF Savory Meatloaf	3 oz LF Savory Meatloaf	4 oz DB Savory Meatloaf	3 oz	4 oz	4 oz	4 oz
1/2c SFT O'Brien Potatoes	1/2c LF O'Brien Potatoes	1/2c LF O'Brien Potatoes	1/2c	1/2c	1/2c	1/2c
1/2c Steamed Spinach	1/2c Steamed Spinach	1/2c Steamed Spinach	1/2c	1/2c	1/2c	1/2c
1 SFT Refined Dinner Roll	1 Dinner Roll	1 Dinner Roll	0	0	1 sm	1 sm
1 tsp Margarine	NO	1 tsp Margarine	0	0	1 tsp	1 tsp
1/2c Milk	1/2c Skim Milk	1/2c Skim Milk	1/2c	1/2c	1/2c	1/2c
Coffee/Tea/Decaf	Coffee/Tea/Decaf	Coffee/Tea/Decaf	free	free	free	free
1 med SFT Bkd Apple-No skin	1 med Baked Apple	1 sm DB Baked Apple	1 sm	1 sm	1 sm	1 sm
2/3c SLF Broth	2/3c SR/LF Bean Soup	2/3c SR/LF Bean Soup	Broth	2/3c	2/3c	2/3c
Deli Platter:	Deli Platter:	Deli Platter:				
1 oz Roast Beef	1 oz Roast Beef	1 oz Roast Beef	1 oz	1 oz	1 oz	1 oz
2 oz Turkey	1 oz Turkey	1 oz Turkey, 1 oz Ham	1 oz	1,1 oz	1,1 oz	1,1 oz
NO	Lettuce Leaves	Lettuce Leaves	lett	lett	lett	lett
NO	2 sl Tomatoes	2 sl Tomatoes	2 sl	2 sl	2 sl	2 sl
NO	1 Green Pepper Ring	1 Green Pepper Ring	1	1	1	1
NO	NO	1 Black Olive	1	1	1	1
1/2c SLF Cheesy Macaroni Sld	1/2c LF Cheesy Pea Salad	1/2c LF Cheesy Pea Salad	1/3c	1/3c	1/2c	1/2c
1/2c Cooked Carrots	1/2c LF Carrot-Raisin Salad	1/2c LF Carrot-Raisin Salad	1/3c	1/3c	1/3c	1/3c
1 SFT Refined Dinner Roll	1 Dinner Roll	1 Dinner Roll	0	1 sm	1 sm	1 sm
1 tsp Catsup	1 tsp Catsup, Mustard,	1 tsp Catsup, Mustard,	1,1 tsp	1,1 tsp	1,1 tsp	1,1 tsp
and 1 Tbsp Mayonnaise	and 1 tsp LF Mayonnaise	and 1 tsp LF Mayonnaise	0	1 tsp	1 tsp	1 tsp
1/2c Milk	1/2c Skim Milk	1/2c Skim Milk	1/2c	1/2c	1/2c	1/2c
Coffee/Tea/Decaf	Coffee/Tea/Decaf	Coffee/Tea/Decaf	free	free	free	free
1 sl Angel Food Cake	2×2" sl LF Chocolate Chip Cake	2×2" sl DB Chocolate Chip Cake	1×1" sl	1×1" sl	2×2" sl	2×2" sl
Milk[3] or STR Juice	Skim Milk or Juice	1/2c Skim Milk	1/2c	1/2c	1/2c	1/2c
Plain Cookies, Gelatin,	LF Cookies, LF Crackers,	1 Starch/Bread Exch	1	1	1	1
Plain Crackers, Banana,	Gelatin, Fresh Fruit	1 Meat Exch	0	0	0	1
Vanilla Ice Cream[3]		1 Fat Exch	0	0	1	1

Independence Day

Breakfast
Fresh Squeezed Orange Juice
Spice Muffin
Farm Fresh Egg to Order
Bacon Strips
Oatmeal with
Sliced Banana or
Assorted Cold Cereals
Assorted Condiments
Your Choice of Beverage

Lunch
Raw Vegetable Platter with
Creamy Tarragon Dip
Hamburger or
Frankfurter
Potato Salad
Cole Slaw
Bun
Apricot Strip
Assorted Condiments
Lemonade

Dinner
Chunky Vegetable Soup
Catch of the Day
Rice Florentine
Julienne Beets
Warm Fresh Dinner Rolls
Star-Spangled Sundae
Your Choice of Beverage

Recipe	Regular, Liberal Bland[1], No Added Salt[2]	1–2 Gm Na (Low Sodium)	Mechanical Soft	Puree
	Breakfast			
	1/2c Orange Juice	1/2c Orange Juice	1/2c Orange Juice	1/2c STR Orange Juice
B1	1/2c Oatmeal or	1/2c SR Oatmeal or	1/2c Oatmeal or	1c STR Oatmeal
	3/4c Asst Cold Cereals	3/4c SR Asst Cold Cereals	3/4c Asst Cold Cereals+	NO
B4,5	1 Egg to Order	1 Egg to Order	1 Egg to Order	1 PUR Egg to Order
N20	1 Spice Muffin or	1 SR Spice Muffin or	1 Spice Muffin+ or	NO
	1 sl Toast	1 sl Toast	1 sl Toast+	1 sl White Bread+
	1/3c Sliced Banana	1/3c Sliced Banana	1/3c Sliced Banana	1/3c PUR Banana
D32	2 sl Bacon[2]	NO	2 sl Crisp Bacon	NO
	1 tsp Margarine	1 tsp SR Margarine	1 tsp Margarine	1 tsp Margarine
	1 tsp Jam/Jelly	1 tsp Jam/Jelly	1 tsp Jelly	1 tsp Jelly
	1c Milk	1c Milk	1c Milk	1c Milk
	Coffee/Tea/Decaf	Coffee/Tea/Decaf	Coffee/Tea/Decaf	Coffee/Tea/Decaf
	Lunch			
K44	3 oz Raw Vegetables with	3 oz Raw Vegetables with	1/2c Apple Juice	1/2c STR Apple Juice
P9	1 oz Creamy Tarragon Dip	1 oz SR/LF Creamy Tarragon Dip	NO	NO
D9	3.5 oz Hamburger or	3.5 oz Hamburger	3.5 oz Hamburger or	4 oz PUR Hamburger or
D38	3 oz Frankfurter	NO	3 oz SFT Frankfurter+	4 oz PUR Frankfurter
K21	1/2c Potato Salad	1/2c SR Potato Salad	1/2c SFT Potato Salad	1/2c PUR Potato Salad
K5,J14	1/2c Cole Slaw	1/2c Cole Slaw	1/2c Carrots	1/2c PUR Carrots
	1 Hamburger/Hot Dog Bun	1 Hamburger Bun	1 Hamburger/Hot Dog Bun+	1 sl White Bread+
	1 tsp Catsup, Mustard,	1 tsp SR Catsup, SR Mustard	1 tsp Catsup, Mustard	1 tsp Catsup, Mustard
	and 1 tsp Relish	NO	NO	NO
	1/2c Milk	1/2c Milk	1/2c Milk	1/2c Milk
	Coffee/Tea/Decaf	Coffee/Tea/Decaf	Coffee/Tea/Decaf	Coffee/Tea/Decaf
A2	6 oz Lemonade	6 oz Lemonade	6 oz Lemonade	6 oz STR Lemonade
Q13	3"×2" Apricot Strips	3"×2" Apricot Strips	1/2c Apricots	1/2c PUR Apricots
	Dinner			
C27,1	2/3c Chunky Vegetable Soup	2/3c SR Chunky Vegetable Soup	2/3c Chunky Vegetable Soup	2/3c PUR/STR Soup
F5	3 oz Catch of the Day	3 oz Catch of the Day	3 oz CHP Catch of the Day	4 oz PUR Catch of the Day
O25	2 Tbsp Tartar Sauce[2]	1 Tbsp SR Mayonnaise	2 Tbsp Tartar Sauce	2 Tbsp Mayonnaise
	Lemon Wedge	Lemon Wedge	Lemon Wedge	Lemon Wedge
L3	1/2c Rice Florentine	1/2c SR Rice Florentine	1/2c SFT Rice Florentine	1/2c PUR Rice Florentine
J9	1/2c Julienne Beets	1/2c SR Julienne Beets	1/2c Julienne Beets	1/2c PUR Beets
	1 Dinner Roll	1 Dinner Roll	1 SFT Dinner Roll+	1 sl Bread+
	1 tsp Margarine	1 tsp SR Margarine	1 tsp Margarine	1 tsp Margarine
	1/2c Milk	1/4c Milk	1/2c Milk	1/2c Milk
	Coffee/Tea/Decaf	Coffee/Tea/Decaf	Coffee/Tea/Decaf	Coffee/Tea/Decaf
S20	Star-Spangled Sundae:			
	1/2c Ice Milk with	1/2c Ice Milk with	1/2c Ice Milk with	1/2c Ice Milk with
	1/2c Berries	1/2c Berries	2 oz STR Strawberry Sauce	2 oz STR Strawberry Sauce
	Snacks			
	Milk or Juice	Juice	Milk or Juice	Milk or STR Juice
	Cookies, Crackers,	SR Cookies, SR Crackers,	Plain Cookies, Gelatin,	Applesauce, SFT Bananas,
	Gelatin, Ice Cream,	Gelatin, Fresh Fruit	Plain Crackers+, Ice Cream,	Gelatin, Ice Cream
	Fresh Fruit		Banana	

TERMS: SFT = Soft; SLF = Soft/Low Fiber; GRD = Ground; CHP = Chopped Finely; PUR = Puree; STR = Strained; SR = Sodium or Salt Restricted; LF = Low Fat; FF = Fat Free; LCH = Low Cholesterol; DB = Diabetic; UNSW = Unsweetened; RC = Reduced Calorie; LC = Low Calorie; EXCH = Diabetic Exchange

SERVING UTENSILS: #6 Scoop = 2/3 cup-6 oz; #8 Scoop = 1/2 cup-4 oz; #10 Scoop = 3/8 cup-3 to 4 oz; #12 Scoop = 1/3 cup-2.5 to 3 oz; #16 Scoop = 1/4 cup-2 oz; #30 Scoop = 2 tbsp-1 oz; #60 Scoop = 1 tbsp-1/2 oz. Ounces will vary, based on food used.

1. *Liberal Bland:* Follow a regular diet. Use decaffeinated products. Omit pepper and chili powder.

2. *No Added Salt (3–4 gm NA):* Follow a regular diet. Use SR soups and SR canned meats. Omit salt packets (and shakers), bacon, sausage, smoked, and cured meats, substitute with SR food choices.

3. *Low Fiber:* Follow a soft diet. Do not exceed 2 cups of milk per day. Soft/Low Fiber—Omit pepper, garlic, and onions from recipes.

4. *2200 Calorie Diet:* Follow 2000 calorie diet with the following additions: Lunch—add 1 bread exchange and 1 fat exchange; Dinner—add 1 bread exchange.

+Consider individual tolerance. Daily Alternatives: Lunch and Dinner—Chicken, Hamburger, Cottage Cheese Fruit Plate, or Assorted Sandwiches. Individual preferences are provided upon request.

Amounts specified for food items that contain bone is equivalent to cooked, edible deboned portion.

Soft, Low Fiber[3]	Low Cholesterol, Low Fat (40–50 GM)	No Concentrated Sweets (Diabetic)	1200	1500	1800	2000[4]
			Diabetic/Calorie-Controlled			
1/2c STR Orange Juice	1/2c Orange Juice	1/2c UNSW Orange Juice	1/2c	1/2c	1/2c	1/2c
1/2c Oatmeal or	1/2c LF Oatmeal or	1/2c DB Oatmeal or	1/2c	1/2c	1/2c	1/2c
3/4c Asst Refined Cereals	3/4c Cold Cereals	3/4c UNSW Cold Cereals	3/4c	3/4c	3/4c	3/4c
1 Egg to Order	1 Egg Substitute	1 Egg to Order	1	1	1	1
NO	1 LF Spice Muffin or	1 DB Spice Muffin or	1	1	1	1
1 sl White Toast	1 sl Toast	1 sl Toast	1 sl	1 sl	1 sl	1 sl
1/3c Sliced Banana	1/3c Sliced Banana	1/3c Sliced Banana	0	0	0	1/3c
NO	NO	1 sl Bacon	0	0	1 sl	1 sl
1 tsp Margarine	1 tsp Margarine	1 tsp Margarine	0	0	1 tsp	1 tsp
1 tsp Jelly	1 tsp Jam/Jelly	1 tsp DB Jam/Jelly	1 tsp	1 tsp	1 tsp	1 tsp
1c Milk	1c Skim Milk	1c Skim Milk	1/2c	1/2c	1/2c	1c
Coffee/Tea/Decaf	Coffee/Tea/Decaf	Coffee/Tea/Decaf	free	free	free	free
1/2c STR Apple Juice	3 oz Raw Vegetables with	3 oz Raw Vegetables with	3 oz	3 oz	3 oz	3 oz
NO	1 Tbsp SR/LF Creamy Tarragon Dip	1 Tbsp SR/LF Creamy Tarragon Dip	1 Tbsp	1 Tbsp	1 Tbsp	1 Tbsp
3.5 oz SLF Hamburger	2.5 oz LF Hamburger or	3.5 oz Hamburger or	2.5 oz	3.5 oz	3.5 oz	3.5 oz
NO	2 oz LF Frankfurter	3 oz Frankfurter	2 oz	3 oz	3 oz	3 oz
1/2c SFT Potato Salad	1/2c LF Potato Salad	1/2c LF Potato Salad	0	0	1/2c	1/2c
1/2c Carrots	1/2c Cole Slaw+	1/2c DB Cole Slaw	1/2c	1/2c	1/2c	1/2c
1 Hamburger Bun	1 Hamburger/Hot Dog Bun	1 Hamburger/Hot Dog Bun	1/2	1	1	1
1 tsp Catsup	1 tsp Catsup, Mustard,	1 tsp Catsup, Mustard,	1,1 tsp	1,1 tsp	1,1 tsp	1,1 tsp
NO	and 1 tsp Relish	NO	No	No	No	No
1/2c Milk	1/2c Skim Milk	1/2c Skim Milk	1/4c	1/2c	1/2c	1/2c
Coffee/Tea/Decaf	Coffee/Tea/Decaf	Coffee/Tea/Decaf	free	free	free	free
6 oz STR Lemonade	6 oz Lemonade	6 oz DB Lemonade	6 oz	6 oz	6 oz	6 oz
1/2c Apricot	2"×2" LF Apricot Strips	2"×2" DB Apricot Strips	2×2	2×2	2×2	2×2
2/3c SLF Broth	2/3c Chunky Vegetable Soup	2/3c Chunky Vegetable Soup	2/3c	2/3c	2/3c	2/3c
3 oz CHP Catch of the Day	3 oz LF Catch of the Day	3 oz LF Catch of the Day	2 oz	3 oz	3 oz	3 oz
2 Tbsp Mayonnaise	1 tsp LF Tartar Sauce	2 Tbsp LF Tartar Sauce	0	0	1 Tbsp	1 Tbsp
Lemon Wedge	Lemon Wedge	Lemon Wedge	Lemon	Lemon	Lemon	Lemon
1/2c SFT Rice Florentine	1/2c LF Rice Florentine	1/2c LF Rice Florentine	1/3c	1/3c	1/2c	1/2c
1/2c Julienne Beets	1/2c LF Julienne Beets	1/2c LF Julienne Beets	1/2c	1/2c	1/3c	1/3c
1 SFT Refined Dinner Roll	1 Dinner Roll	1 Dinner Roll	0	0	1 sm	1 sm
1 tsp Margarine	NO	1 tsp Margarine	0	0	1 tsp	1 tsp
1/2c Milk (1/4c)[3]	1/2c Skim Milk	1/2c Skim Milk	1/4c	1/4c	1/4c	1/2c
Coffee/Tea/Decaf	Coffee/Tea/Decaf	Coffee/Tea/Decaf	free	free	free	free
1/2c Ice Milk with	1/3c Ice Milk with	1/3c Ice Milk with	1/3c	1/3c	1/3c	1/3c
2 oz STR Strawberry Sauce	1/2c Berries	1/2c Berries	1/2c	1/2c	1/2c	1/2c
Milk[3] or STR Juice	Skim Milk or Juice	1/2c Skim Milk	1/2c	1/2c	1/2c	1/2c
Plain Cookies, Gelatin,	LF Cookies, LF Crackers,	1 Starch/Bread Exch	1	1	1	1
Plain Crackers, Banana,	Gelatin, Fresh Fruit	1 Meat Exch	0	0	0	1
Vanilla Ice Cream[3]		1 Fat Exch	0	0	1	1

Labor Day

Breakfast
Grapefruit Half
Cheese Biscuit
Farm Fresh Egg to Order
Bacon Strips
Oatmeal or
Assorted Cold Cereals with
Sliced Peaches
Assorted Condiments
Your Choice of Beverage

Lunch
Relish Tray with
Cucumber-Yogurt Dip
Barbecue Chicken
Mustard Rice Salad
Three Bean Salad
Warm Dinner Rolls
Watermelon
Your Choice of Beverage

Dinner
Cream of Mushroom Soup
Oven Fried Fish
Sweet Potatoes and Apples
Tarragon Zucchini
Warm Fresh Cornbread
Chocolate Chip Cake
Your Choice of Beverage

Recipe	Regular, Liberal Bland[1], No Added Salt[2]	1–2 Gm Na (Low Sodium)	Mechanical Soft	Puree
	Breakfast			
	1/2 Grapefruit	1/2 Grapefruit	1/2c Grapefruit Sections	1/2c STR Grapefruit Juice
B1	1/2c Oatmeal or	1/2c Oatmeal or	1/2c Oatmeal or	1c Oatmeal
	3/4c Asst Dry Cereals	3/4c SR Asst Dry Cereals	3/4c Asst Dry Cereals+	NO
	1/2c Sliced Peaches	1/2c Sliced Peaches	1/2c Sliced Peaches	1/2c PUR Peaches
B4,5	1 Egg to Order	1 Egg to Order	1 Egg to Order	1 PUR Egg to Order
N2	1 Cheese Biscuit or	1 SR Cheese Biscuit or	1 Cheese Biscuit+ or	NO
	1 sl Toast	1 sl Toast	1 sl Toast+	1 sl Bread+
D32	2 sl Bacon[2]	NO	2 sl Crisp Bacon	NO
	1 tsp Margarine	1 tsp SR Margarine	1 tsp Margarine	1 tsp Margarine
	1 tsp Jam/Jelly	1 tsp Jam/Jelly	1 tsp Jelly	1 tsp Jelly
	1c Milk	1c Milk	1c Milk	1c Milk
	Coffee/Tea/Decaf	Coffee/Tea/Decaf	Coffee/Tea/Decaf	Coffee/Tea/Decaf
	Lunch			
K45	3 oz Relish Tray with	3 oz SR/LF Relish Tray with	1/2c Apple Juice	1/2c STR Apple Juice
P10	1 oz Cucumber-Yogurt Dip	1 oz Cucumber-Yogurt Dip	NO	NO
E1,7	3 oz BBQ Chicken with	3 oz SR BBQ Chicken with	3 oz CHP BBQ Chicken with	4 oz PUR BBQ Chicken with
O2	2 oz Barbecue Sauce	2 oz SR Barbecue Sauce	2 oz SFT Barbecue Sauce	2 oz SFT Barbecue Sauce
K18,11	1/2c Mustard-Rice Salad	1/2c Mustard-Rice Salad	1/2c SFT Mustard-Rice Salad	1/2c PUR White Rice
K22J3	1/2c Three Bean Salad	1/2c SR Three Bean Salad	1/2c Green Beans	1/2c PUR Green Beans
	1 Dinner Roll	1 Dinner Roll	1 SFT Dinner Roll+	1 sl Bread+
	1 tsp Margarine	1 tsp SR Margarine	1 tsp Margarine	1 tsp Margarine
	1/2c Milk	1/2c Milk	1/2c Milk	1/2c Milk
	Coffee/Tea/Decaf	Coffee/Tea/Decaf	Coffee/Tea/Decaf	Coffee/Tea/Decaf
	1/2c Watermelon Cubes	1/2c Watermelon Cubes	1/2c Watermelon Cubes	1/2c PUR Watermelon
	Dinner			
C12	2/3c Cream Mushroom Soup	2/3c Cream Mushroom Soup	2/3c Cream Mushroom Soup	2/3c PUR/STR Soup
F4	3.5 oz Oven Fried Fish	3.5 oz SR Oven Fried Fish	3.5 oz CHP Oven Fried Fish	4 oz PUR Oven Fried Fish
O25	2 Tbsp Tartar Sauce[2]	1 Tbsp SR Mayonnaise	2 Tbsp Tartar Sauce	2 Tbsp Mayonnaise
	Lemon Wedge	Lemon Wedge	Lemon Wedge	Lemon Wedge
J45	1/2c Sweet Potatoes-Apples	1/2c Sweet Potatoes-Apples	1/2c Sweet Potatoes-Apples	1/2c PUR Sweet Potatoes-Apples
J54	1/2c Tarragon Zucchini	1/2c Tarragon Zucchini	1/2c SFT Tarragon Zucchini	1/2c PUR Zucchini
N6	1 sl Cornbread	1 sl SR Cornbread	1 sl Cornbread+	1 sl Bread+
	1 tsp Margarine	1 tsp SR Margarine	1 tsp Margarine	1 tsp Margarine
	1/2c Milk	1/4c Milk	1/2c Milk	1/2c Milk
	Coffee/Tea/Decaf	Coffee/Tea/Decaf	Coffee/Tea/Decaf	Coffee/Tea/Decaf
Q6	3×2" sl Chocolate Chip Cake	3×2" sl Chocolate Chip Cake	3×2" sl Chocolate Chip Cake+	1/2c Ice Cream
	Snacks			
	Milk or Juice	Juice	Milk or Juice	Milk or STR Juice
	Cookies, Crackers,	SR Cookies, SR Crackers,	Plain Cookies, Gelatin,	Applesauce, SFT Banana,
	Gelatin, Ice Cream,	Gelatin, Fresh Fruit	Plain Crackers+, Ice Cream,	Gelatin, Ice Cream,
	Fresh Fruit		Banana	

TERMS: SFT = Soft; SLF = Soft/Low Fiber; GRD = Ground; CHP = Chopped Finely; PUR = Puree; STR = Strained; SR = Sodium or Salt Restricted; LF = Low Fat; FF = Fat Free; LCH = Low Cholesterol; DB = Diabetic; UNSW = Unsweetened; RC = Reduced Calorie; LC = Low Calorie; EXCH = Diabetic Exchange
SERVING UTENSILS: #6 Scoop = 2/3 cup-6 oz; #8 Scoop = 1/2 cup-4 oz; #10 Scoop = 3/8 cup-3 to 4 oz; #12 Scoop = 1/3 cup-2.5 to 3 oz; #16 Scoop = 1/4 cup-2 oz; #30 Scoop = 2 tbsp-1 oz; #60 Scoop = 1 tbsp-1/2 oz. Ounces will vary, based on food used.
1. *Liberal Bland:* Follow a regular diet. Use decaffeinated products. Omit pepper and chili powder.
2. *No Added Salt (3–4 gm NA):* Follow a regular diet. Use SR soups and SR canned meats. Omit salt packets (and shakers), bacon, sausage, smoked, and cured meats, substitute with SR food choices.
3. *Low Fiber:* Follow a soft diet. Do not exceed 2 cups of milk per day. Soft/Low Fiber—Omit pepper, garlic, and onions from recipes.
4. *2200 Calorie Diet:* Follow 2000 calorie diet with the following additions: Lunch—add 1 bread exchange and 1 fat exchange; Dinner—add 1 bread exchange.
+Consider individual tolerance. Daily Alternatives: Lunch and Dinner—Chicken, Hamburger, Cottage Cheese Fruit Plate, or Assorted Sandwiches. Individual preferences are provided upon request.
Amounts specified for food items that contain bone is equivalent to cooked, edible deboned portion.

Soft, Low Fiber[3]	Low Cholesterol, Low Fat (40–50 GM)	No Concentrated Sweets (Diabetic)	1200	1500	1800	2000[4] Diabetic/Calorie-Controlled		
1/2c STR Grapefruit Juice	1/2 Grapefruit	1/2 Grapefruit	1/2	1/2	1/2	1/2
1/2c Oatmeal or	1/2c LF Oatmeal or	1/2c DB Oatmeal or	1/2c	1/2c	1/2c	1/2c
3/4c Asst Refined Cereals	3/4c Dry Cereals	3/4c UNSW Dry Cereals	3/4c	3/4c	3/4c	3/4c
1/2c Sliced Peaches	1/2c Sliced Peaches	1/2c UNSW Sliced Peaches	0	0	0	1/2c
1 Egg to Order	1 Egg Substitute	1 Egg to Order	1	1	1	1
1 SLF Cheese Biscuit+ or	1 LF Cheese Biscuit or	1 LF Cheese Biscuit	1	1	1	1
1 sl White Toast	1 sl Toast	(omit 1 fat) or 1 sl Toast	1 sl	1 sl	1 sl	1 sl
NO	NO	1 sl Bacon	0	0	1 sl	1 sl
1 tsp Margarine	1 tsp Margarine	1 tsp Margarine	1 tsp	1 tsp	1 tsp	1 tsp
1 tsp Jelly	1 tsp Jam/Jelly	1 tsp DB Jam/Jelly	1 tsp	1 tsp	1 tsp	1 tsp
1c Milk	1c Skim Milk	1c Skim Milk	1/2c	1/2c	1/2c	1c
Coffee/Tea/Decaf	Coffee/Tea/Decaf	Coffee/Tea/Decaf	free	free	free	free
1/2c STR Apple Juice	3 oz SR/LF Relish Tray with	3 oz SR/LF Relish Tray with	3 oz	3 oz	3 oz	3 oz
NO	1 Tbsp SR/LF Cucumber-Yogurt Dip	1 Tbsp SR/LF Cucumber-Yogurt Dip	1 Tbsp	1 Tbsp	1 Tbsp	1 Tbsp
3 oz Roast Chicken	2 oz LF BBQ Chicken with	3 oz LF BBQ Chicken with	2 oz	3 oz	3 oz	3 oz
No	2 oz Barbecue Sauce+	2 oz DB Barbecue Sauce	1 oz	2 oz	2 oz	2 oz
1/2c White Rice	1/2c LF Mustard-Rice Salad	1/2c LF Mustard-Rice Salad	1/3c	1/3c	1/2c	1/2c
1/2c Green Beans	1/2c LF Three Bean Salad+	1/2c DB Three Bean Salad	1/2c	1/2c	1/2c	1/2c
1 SFT Refined Dinner Roll	1 Dinner Roll	1 Dinner Roll	0	0	1 sm	1 sm
1 tsp Margarine	NO	1 tsp Margarine	0	0	1 tsp	1 tsp
1/2c Milk	1/2c Skim Milk	1/2c Skim Milk	1/2c	1/2c	1/2c	1/2c
Coffee/Tea/Decaf	Coffee/Tea/Decaf	Coffee/Tea/Decaf	free	free	free	free
1/2c Sliced Banana	1/2c Watermelon Cubes	1/2c Watermelon Cubes	1c	1c	1c	1c
2/3c SLF Cream Mushroom Soup	2/3c LF Cream Mushroom Soup	2/3c LF Cream Mushroom Soup	2/3c	2/3c	2/3c	2/3c
3 oz SLF Oven Fried Fish	3 oz LF Oven Fried Fish	3.5 oz LF Oven Fried Fish	2.5 oz	3.5 oz	3.5 oz	3.5 oz
2 Tbsp Mayonnaise	1 tsp LF Tartar Sauce	2 Tbsp LF Tartar Sauce	0	1 Tbsp	1 Tbsp	1 Tbsp
Lemon Wedge	Lemon Wedge	Lemon Wedge	Lemon	Lemon	Lemon	Lemon
1/2c Sweet Potatoes-Apples	1/2c LF Sweet Potatoes-Apples	1/2c DB Sweet Potatoes-Apples	1/4c	1/3c	1/2c	1/2c
1/2c SFT Tarragon Zucchini	1/2c LF Tarragon Zucchini	1/2c LF Tarragon Zucchini	1/2c	1/2c	1/2c	1/2c
1 SFT Refined Dinner Roll	1 sl Cornbread	1 sl DB Cornbread	0	1 sl	1 sl	1 sl
1 tsp Margarine	1 tsp Margarine	1 tsp Margarine	0	0	1 tsp	1 tsp
1/2c Milk (1/4)[3]	1/2c Skim Milk	1/2c Skim Milk	1/4c	1/4c	1/2c	1/2c
Coffee/Tea/Decaf	Coffee/Tea/Decaf	Coffee/Tea/Decaf	free	free	free	free
1/2c Vanilla Ice Cream	2×2" sl LF Chocolate Chip Cake	2×2" sl DB Chocolate Chip Cake	2×2"	2×2"	2×2"	2×2"
Milk[3] or STR Juice	Skim Milk or Juice	1/2c Skim Milk	1/2c	1/2c	1/2c	1/2c
Plain Cookies, Gelatin,	LF Cookies, LF Crackers,	1 Starch/Bread Exch	1	1	1	1
Plain Crackers, Banana,	Gelatin, Fresh Fruit	1 Meat Exch	0	0	0	1
Vanilla Ice Cream[3]		1 Fat Exch	0	0	1	1

Halloween

Breakfast
Chilled Apple Cider
Pumpkin Muffin
Farm Fresh Egg to Order
Sausage Links
Farina or
Assorted Cold Cereals
Assorted Condiments
Your Choice of Beverage

Lunch
Virgin Bloody Mary
Pork Chops with
Apple Stuffing
Wild Rice
Seasoned Green Beans
Warm Dinner Rolls
Boo Berry Gelatin
Your Choice of Beverage

Dinner
Cream of Spinach Soup
Salmon Patty
Oven Browned Potatoes
Carrots with Raisins
Warm Dinner Rolls
Devil's Food Cake
Your Choice of Beverage

Recipe	Regular, Liberal Bland[1], No Added Salt[2]	1–2 Gm Na (Low Sodium)	Mechanical Soft	Puree
	Breakfast			
	1/2c Apple Cider	1/2c Apple Cider	1/2c Apple Cider	1/2c STR Apple Cider
B1	1/2c Farina or	1/2c SR Farina or	1/2c Farina or	1c STR Farina
	3/4c Asst Cold Cereals	3/4c SR Asst Cold Cereals	3/4c Asst Cold Cereals+	NO
B4,5	1 Egg to Order	1 Egg to Order	1 Egg to Order	1 PUR Egg to Order
N18	1 Pumpkin Muffin or	1 Pumpkin Muffin or	1 Pumpkin Muffin+ or	NO
	1 sl Toast	1 sl Toast	1 sl Toast+	1 sl White Bread+
D33	1 Sausage Link[2]	NO	1 Sausage Link	NO
	1 tsp Margarine	1 tsp SR Margarine	1 tsp Margarine	1 tsp Margarine
	1 tsp Jam/Jelly	1 tsp Jam/Jelly	1 tsp Jelly	1 tsp Jelly
	1c Milk	1c Milk	1c Milk	1c Milk
	Coffee/Tea/Decaf	Coffee/Tea/Decaf	Coffee/Tea/Decaf	Coffee/Tea/Decaf
	Lunch			
A7	4 oz Virgin Bloody Mary	4 oz SR Virgin Bloody Mary	4 oz Virgin Blood Mary	4 oz STR Virgin Bloody Mary
D30	3 oz Pork Chop with	3 oz Pork Chop with	3 oz CHP Pork Chop	4 oz PUR Pork Chop with
	1/4c Apple Stuffing	1/4c Apple Stuffing	1/4c Apple Stuffing+	1/4c PUR Apple Stuffing
L9,1	1/2c Wild Rice	1/2c Wild Rice	1/2c Wild Rice+	1/2c PUR White Rice
J6	1/2c Seasoned Green Beans	1/2c Seasoned Green Beans	1/2c Seasoned Green Beans	1/2c PUR Green Beans
	1 Dinner Roll	1 Dinner Roll	1 SFT Dinner Roll+	1 sl Bread+
	1 tsp Margarine	1 tsp SR Margarine	1 tsp Margarine	1 tsp Margarine
	1/2c Milk	1/2c Milk	1/2c Milk	1/2c Milk
	Coffee/Tea/Decaf	Coffee/Tea/Decaf	Coffee/Tea/Decaf	Coffee/Tea/Decaf
S14,12	1/2c Boo Berry Gelatin	1/2c Boo Berry Gelatin	1/2c Boo Berry Gelatin	1/2c Orange Gelatin
	Dinner			
C13	2/3c Cream Spinach Soup	2/3c Cream Spinach Soup	2/3c Cream Spinach Soup	2/3c PUR/STR Soup
F6	4 oz Salmon Patty	4 oz SR Salmon Patty	4 oz SFT Salmon Patty	4 oz PUR Salmon Patty
O25	2 Tbsp Tartar Sauce[2]	1 Tbsp SR Mayonnaise	2 Tbsp Tartar Sauce	2 Tbsp Mayonnaise
	Lemon Wedge	Lemon Wedge	Lemon Wedge	Lemon Wedge
J39	4 oz Oven Browned Potatoes	4 oz Oven Browned Potatoes	4 oz Oven Browned Potatoes	1/2c PUR Oven Brwn Potatoes
J17,14	1/2c Carrots/Raisins	1/2c Carrots/Raisins	1/2c Carrots	1/2c PUR Carrots/Raisins
	1 Dinner Roll	1 Dinner Roll	1 SFT Dinner Roll+	1 sl Bread+
	1 tsp Margarine	1 tsp SR Margarine	1 tsp Margarine	1 tsp Margarine
	1/2c Milk	1/4c Milk	1/2c Milk	1/2c Milk
	Coffee/Tea/Decaf	Coffee/Tea/Decaf	Coffee/Tea/Decaf	Coffee/Tea/Decaf
Q7	3×2 sl Devil's Food Cake	3×2 sl Devil's Food Cake	3×2 sl Devil's Food Cake+	1/2c PUR Peaches
	Snacks			
	Milk or Juice	Juice	Milk or Juice	Milk or STR Juice
	Cookies, Crackers,	SR Cookies, SR Crackers,	Plain Cookies, Gelatin,	Applesauce, SFT Banana,
	Gelatin, Ice Cream,	Gelatin, Fresh Fruit	Plain Crackers+, Ice Cream,	Gelatin, Ice Cream
	Fresh Fruit		Banana	

TERMS: SFT = Soft; SLF = Soft/Low Fiber; GRD = Ground; CHP = Chopped Finely; PUR = Puree; STR = Strained; SR = Sodium or Salt Restricted; LF = Low Fat; FF = Fat Free; LCH = Low Cholesterol; DB = Diabetic; UNSW = Unsweetened; RC = Reduced Calorie; LC = Low Calorie; EXCH = Diabetic Exchange

SERVING UTENSILS: #6 Scoop = 2/3 cup-6 oz; #8 Scoop = 1/2 cup-4 oz; #10 Scoop = 3/8 cup-3 to 4 oz; #12 Scoop = 1/3 cup-2.5 to 3 oz; #16 Scoop = 1/4 cup-2 oz; #30 Scoop = 2 tbsp-1 oz; #60 Scoop = 1 tbsp-1/2 oz. Ounces will vary, based on food used.

1. *Liberal Bland:* Follow a regular diet. Use decaffeinated products. Omit pepper and chili powder.

2. *No Added Salt (3–4 gm NA):* Follow a regular diet. Use SR soups and SR canned meats. Omit salt packets (and shakers), bacon, sausage, smoked, and cured meats, substitute with SR food choices.

3. *Low Fiber:* Follow a soft diet. Do not exceed 2 cups of milk per day. Soft/Low Fiber—Omit pepper, garlic, and onions from recipes.

4. *2200 Calorie Diet:* Follow 2000 calorie diet with the following additions: Lunch—add 1 bread exchange and 1 fat exchange; Dinner—add 1 bread exchange.

+Consider individual tolerance. Daily Alternatives: Lunch and Dinner—Chicken, Hamburger, Cottage Cheese Fruit Plate, or Assorted Sandwiches. Individual preferences are provided upon request.

Amounts specified for food items that contain bone is equivalent to cooked, edible deboned portion.

Soft, Low Fiber[3]	Low Cholesterol, Low Fat (40–50 GM)	No Concentrated Sweets (Diabetic)	1200	1500	1800	2000[4] Diabetic/Calorie-Controlled
1/2c STR Apple Cider	1/2c Apple Cider	1/2c Apple Cider	1/2c	1/2c	1/2c	1/2c
1/2c Farina or	1/2c LF Farina or	1/2c DB Farina or	1/2c	1/2c	1/2c	1/2c
3/4c Asst Refined Cereals	3/4c Cold Cereals	3/4c UNSW Cold Cereals	3/4c	3/4c	3/4c	3/4c
1 Egg to Order	1 Egg Substitute	1 Egg to Order	1	1	1	1
NO	1 LF Pumpkin Muffin or	1 DB Pumpkin Muffin (omit 1 fat)	1	1	1	1
1 sl White Toast	1 sl Toast	or 1 sl Toast	1 sl	1 sl	1 sl	1 sl
NO	NO	1 oz Sausage Link	0	0	0	0
1 tsp Margarine	1 tsp Margarine	1 tsp Margarine	1 tsp	1 tsp	1 tsp	1 tsp
1 tsp Jelly	1 tsp Jam/Jelly	1 tsp DB Jam/Jelly	1 tsp	1 tsp	1 tsp	1 tsp
1c Milk	1c Skim Milk	1c Skim Milk	1/2c	1/2c	1/2c	1c
Coffee/Tea/Decaf	Coffee/Tea/Decaf	Coffee/Tea/Decaf	free	free	free	free
4 oz STR Tomato Juice	4 oz Tomato Juice	4 oz Virgin Bloody Mary	4 oz	4 oz	4 oz	4 oz
3 oz Pork Chop	2 oz Pork Chop with	3 oz Pork Chop with	2 oz	3 oz	3 oz	3 oz
NO	1/4c LF Apple Stuffing	1/4c LF Apple Stuffing	1/4c	1/4c	1/4c	1/4c
1/2c White Rice	1/2c Wild Rice	1/2c Wild Rice	0	1/3c	1/2c	1/2c
1/2c SLF Seasoned Green Beans	1/2c LF Season Green Beans	1/2c LF Season Green Beans	1/2c	1/2c	1/2c	1/2c
1 SFT Refined Dinner Roll	1 Dinner Roll	1 Dinner Roll	0	0	1 sm	1 sm
1 tsp Margarine	NO	1 tsp Margarine	0	0	1 tsp	1 tsp
1/2c Milk	1/2c Skim Milk	1/2c Skim Milk	1/2c	1/2c	1/2c	1/2c
Coffee/Tea/Decaf	Coffee/Tea/Decaf	Coffee/Tea/Decaf	free	free	free	free
1/2c Orange Gelatin	1/2c Boo Berry Gelatin	1/2c DB Boo Berry Gelatin	1/2c	1/2c	1/2c	1/2c
2/3c SLF Cream Spinach Soup	2/3c LF Cream Spinach Soup	2/3c LF Cream Spinach Soup	2/3c	2/3c	2/3c	2/3c
4 oz SFT Salmon Patty	4 oz LF Salmon Patty	4 oz Salmon Patty	3 oz	4 oz	4 oz	4 oz
2 Tbsp Mayonnaise	1 tsp LF Tartar Sauce	2 Tbsp LF Tartar Sauce	0	0	1 Tbsp	1 Tbsp
Lemon Wedge	Lemon Wedge	Lemon Wedge	Lemon	Lemon	Lemon	Lemon
4 oz Oven Browned Potatoes	4 oz LF Oven Browned Potatoes	3 oz LF Oven Browned Potatoes	2 oz	3 oz	3 oz	3 oz
1/2c Carrots	1/2c LF Carrots/Raisins	1/2c DB Carrots/Raisins	1/3c	1/2c	1/2c	1/2c
1 SFT Refined Dinner Roll	1 Dinner Roll	1 Dinner Roll	0	0	1 sm	1 sm
1 tsp Margarine	NO	1 tsp Margarine	0	0	1 tsp	1 tsp
1/2c Milk (1/4c)[3]	1/2c Skim Milk	1/2c Skim Milk	1/4c	1/4c	1/2c	1/2c
Coffee/Tea/Decaf	Coffee/Tea/Decaf	Coffee/Tea/Decaf	free	free	free	free
1/2c Sliced Canned Peaches	3×2" sl LF Devil's Food Cake	3×2" sl DB Devil's Food Cake	2×1"	3×2"	3×2"	3×2"
Milk[3] or STR Juice	Skim Milk or Juice	1/2c Skim Milk	1/2c	1/2c	1/2c	1/2c
Plain Cookies, Gelatin,	LF Cookies, LF Crackers,	1 Starch/Bread Exch	1	1	1	1
Plain Crackers, Banana,	Gelatin, Fresh Fruit	1 Meat Exch	0	0	0	1
Vanilla Ice Cream[3]		1 Fat Exch	0	0	1	1

Thanksgiving Day

Breakfast
Chilled Apple Juice
Hot Homemade Muffins
Grilled Bacon Strips
Farm Fresh Egg to Order
Hot Cinnamon Oatmeal or
Assorted Cold Cereals
Assorted Condiments
Your Choice of Beverage

Lunch
Clear Chicken Consomme
Mixed Field Greens with
Assorted Salad Dressings
Roast Tom Turkey with
Pan Giblet Gravy
Raisin Bread Stuffing
Whipped Sweet Potatoes
Green Beans and Mushrooms
Cranberry Mold
Warm Dinner Rolls
Pilgrims Apple Pie
Your Choice of Beverage

Dinner
Old Fashioned Vegetable Soup
Baked Halibut Steak
Rice Pilaf
Herbed Seasoned Spinach
Pumpkin Bread
Fresh Fruit Parfait
Your Choice of Beverage

Recipe	Regular, Liberal Bland[1], No Added Salt[2]	1–2 Gm Na (Low Sodium)	Mechanical Soft	Puree
	Breakfast			
	1/2c Apple Juice	1/2c Apple Juice	1/2c Apple Juice	1/2c STR Apple Juice
N10–20	1 Homemade Muffin	1 SR Homemade Muffin	1 Plain Muffin+	1 sl White Bread+
B1	1/2c Cinnamon Oatmeal or	1/2c SR Cinnamon Oatmeal or	1/2c Cinnamon Oatmeal or	1c Cinnamon Oatmeal
	3/4c Asst Cold Cereals	3/4c SR Asst Cold Cereals	3/4c Asst Cold Cereals+	NO
B4,5	1 Egg to Order	1 Egg to Order	1 Egg to Order	1 PUR Egg to Order
D32	2 slices Bacon[2]	NO	2 slices Crisp Bacon+	NO
	1 tsp Margarine	1 tsp SR Margarine	1 tsp Margarine	1 tsp Margarine
	1 tsp Jam/Jelly	1 tsp Jam/Jelly	1 tsp Jelly	1 tsp Jelly
	1c Milk	1c Milk	1c Milk	1c Milk
	Coffee/Tea/Decaf	Coffee/Tea/Decaf	Coffee/Tea/Decaf	Coffee/Tea/Decaf
	Lunch			
C2	2/3c Chicken Consomme	2/3c SR Chicken Consomme	2/3c Chicken Consomme	2/3c Chicken Consomme
K28	1c Mixed Field Greens	1c Mixed Field Greens	4 oz Juice	4 oz STR Juice
P1–8	1 oz Salad Dressing	1 oz SR Salad Dressing	NO	NO
E16	3 oz Roast Turkey	3 oz Roast Turkey	3 oz CHP Roast Turkey	4 oz PUR Roast Turkey
O18,5	2 oz Giblet Gravy	2 oz SR Giblet Gravy	2 oz Giblet Gravy	2 oz STR Giblet Gravy
P12	1/2c Raisin Bread Stuffing	1/2c SR Raisin Bread Stuffing	1/2c SFT Bread Stuffing	1/2c PUR Bread Stuffing
J46	1/2c Whipped Sweet Potato	1/2c Whipped Sweet Potato	1/2c Whipped Sweet Potato	1/2c Whipped Sweet Potato
J4	1/2c Green Beans-Mushrms	1/2c Green Beans-Mushrms	1/2c Green Beans-Mushrms	1/2c PUR Green Beans-Mushrms
K42	1/2c Cranberry Mold	1/2c Cranberry Mold	1/2c PUR Cranberry Mold	1/2c SFT Cranberry Mold
	1 Dinner Roll	1 Dinner Roll	1 SFT Dinner Roll+	1 sl Bread+
	1 tsp Margarine	1 tsp SR Margarine	1 tsp Margarine	1 tsp Margarine
	1/2c Milk	1/2c Milk	1/2c Milk	1/2c Milk
	Coffee/Tea/Decaf	Coffee/Tea/Decaf	Coffee/Tea/Decaf	Coffee/Tea/Decaf
R3	1/8 Apple Pie	1/8 Apple Pie	1/8 Apple Pie+	1/2c PUR Apple Pie Filling
	Dinner			
C29	2/3c Old Fash Veg Soup	2/3c SR Old Fash Veg Soup	2/3c Old Fash Veg Soup	2/3c PUR/STR Veg Soup
F2	3 oz Baked Halibut Steak	3 oz Baked Halibut Steak	3 oz Baked Halibut Steak	4 oz PUR Bkd Halibut Steak
O25	2 Tbsp Tartar Sauce[2]	1 Tbsp SR Mayonnaise	2 Tbsp Tartar Sauce	2 Tbsp Mayonnaise
	Lemon Wedge	Lemon Wedge	Lemon Wedge	Lemon Wedge
L5	1/2c Rice Pilaf	1/2c SR Rice Pilaf	1/2c SFT Rice Pilaf	1/2c PUR Rice Pilaf
J48	1/2c Seasoned Spinach	1/2c Seasoned Spinach	1/2c CHP Seasoned Spinach	1/2c PUR Seasoned Spinach
N9	1 sl Pumpkin Bread	1 sl SR Pumpkin Bread	1 sl SFT Pumpkin Bread	1 sl Bread+
	1 tsp Margarine	1 tsp SR Margarine	1 tsp Margarine	1 tsp Margarine
	1/2c Milk	1/2c Milk	1/2c Milk	1/2c Milk
	Coffee/Tea/Decaf	Coffee/Tea/Decaf	Coffee/Tea/Decaf	Coffee/Tea/Decaf
S7	1/2c Fruit Parfait with	1/2c Fruit Parfait with	1/2c Canned Fruit Parfait	1/2c PUR Fruit Parfait
	1 Tbsp Whipped Topping	1 Tbsp Whipped Topping	1 Tbsp Whipped Topping	1 Tbsp Whipped Topping
	Snacks			
	Milk or Juice	Juice	Milk or Juice	Milk or STR Juice
	Cookies, Crackers,	SR Cookies, SR Crackers,	Plain Cookies, Gelatin,	Applesauce, SFT Banana,
	Gelatin, Ice Cream,	Gelatin, Fresh Fruit	Plain Crackers+, Ice Cream,	Gelatin, Ice Cream
	Fresh Fruit		Banana	

TERMS: SFT = Soft; SLF = Soft/Low Fiber; GRD = Ground; CHP = Chopped Finely; PUR = Puree; STR = Strained; SR = Sodium or Salt Restricted; LF = Low Fat; FF = Fat Free; LCH = Low Cholesterol; DB = Diabetic; UNSW = Unsweetened; RC = Reduced Calorie; LC = Low Calorie; EXCH = Diabetic Exchange

SERVING UTENSILS: #6 Scoop = 2/3 cup-6 oz; #8 Scoop = 1/2 cup-4 oz; #10 Scoop = 3/8 cup-3 to 4 oz; #12 Scoop = 1/3 cup-2.5 to 3 oz; #16 Scoop = 1/4 cup-2 oz; #30 Scoop = 2 tbsp-1 oz; #60 Scoop = 1 tbsp-1/2 oz. Ounces will vary, based on food used.

1. *Liberal Bland:* Follow a regular diet. Use decaffeinated products. Omit pepper and chili powder.

2. *No Added Salt (3–4 gm NA):* Follow a regular diet. Use SR soups and SR canned meats. Omit salt packets (and shakers), bacon, sausage, smoked, and cured meats, substitute with SR food choices.

3. *Low Fiber:* Follow a soft diet. Do not exceed 2 cups of milk per day. Soft/Low Fiber—Omit pepper, garlic, and onions from recipes.

4. *2200 Calorie Diet:* Follow 2000 calorie diet with the following additions: Lunch—add 1 bread exchange and 1 fat exchange; Dinner—add 1 bread exchange.

+Consider individual tolerance. Daily Alternatives: Lunch and Dinner—Chicken, Hamburger, Cottage Cheese Fruit Plate, or Assorted Sandwiches. Individual preferences are provided upon request.

Amounts specified for food items that contain bone is equivalent to cooked, edible deboned portion.

Soft, Low Fiber[3]	Low Cholesterol, Low Fat (40–50 GM)	No Concentrated Sweets (Diabetic)	1200	1500	1800	2000[4]
			Diabetic/Calorie-Controlled			
1/2c STR Apple Juice	1/2c Apple Juice	1/2c UNSW Apple Juice	1/2c	1/2c	1/2c	1/2c
1 SLF Muffin	1 LF Muffin	1 DB Muffin	1 sm	1 sm	1 sm	1 sm
1/2c Cinnamon Oatmeal or	1/2c LF Cinnamon Oatmeal or	1/2c DB Cinnamon Oatmeal or	1/2c	1/2c	1/2c	1/2c
3/4c Asst Refined Cereals	3/4c Cold Cereals	3/4c UNSW Cold Cereals	3/4c	3/4c	3/4c	3/4c
1 Egg to Order	1 Egg Substitute	1 Egg to Order	1	1	1	1
NO	NO	1 slice Bacon or	0	0	1 sl	1 sl
1 tsp Margarine	1 tsp Margarine	1 tsp Margarine	0	0	1 tsp	1 tsp
1 tsp Jelly	1 tsp Jam/Jelly	1 tsp DB Jam/Jelly	1 tsp	1 tsp	1 tsp	1 tsp
1c Milk	1c Skim Milk	1c Skim Milk	1/2c	1/2c	1/2c	1c
Coffee/Tea/Decaf	Coffee/Tea/Decaf	Coffee/Tea/Decaf	free	free	free	free
2/3c SLF Chicken Consomme	2/3c Chicken Consomme	2/3c Chicken Consomme	2/3c	2/3c	2/3c	2/3c
4 oz STR Juice	1c Mixed Field Greens	1c Mixed Field Greens	1c	1c	1c	1c
NO	1 Tbsp LC Salad Dressing	1 Tbsp LC Salad Dressing	1 Tbsp	1 Tbsp	1 Tbsp	1 Tbsp
3 oz Roast Turkey	2 oz LF Roast Turkey	3 oz LF Roast Turkey	2 oz	3 oz	3 oz	3 oz
2 oz Chicken Gravy	2 oz LF Chicken Gravy	2 oz STR Giblet Gravy	1 oz	1 oz	2 oz	2 oz
NO	1/4c LF Raisin Bread Stuffing	1/4c Raisin Bread Stuffing		1/4c	1/4c	1/4c
1/2c Whipped Sweet Potato	1/2c LF Whipped Sweet Potato	1/2c LF Whipped Sweet Potato	1/3c	1/4c	1/3c	1/3c
1/2c Green Beans-Mushrms	1/2c Green Beans-Mushrms	1/2c Green Beans-Mushrms	1/2c	1/2c	1/2c	1/2c
1/2c SLF Gelatin Mold	1/2c Cranberry Mold	1/2c DB Cranberry Mold	1/2c	1/2c	1/2c	1/2c
1 SFT Refined Dinner Roll	1 Dinner Roll	1 Dinner Roll	0	0	0	1 sm
1 tsp Margarine	NO	1 tsp Margarine	0	0	0	0
1/2c Milk	1/2c Skim Milk	1/2c Skim Milk	1/2c	1/2c	1/2c	1/2c
Coffee/Tea/Decaf	Coffee/Tea/Decaf	Coffee/Tea/Decaf	free	free	free	free
1/8 Apple Pie+	1/10 LF Apple Pie	1/8 DB Apple Pie	1/12	1/12	1/10	1/10
2/3c SLF Old Fash Veg Soup	2/3c Old Fash Veg Soup	2/3c Old Fash Veg Soup	STR	2/3c	2/3c	2/3c
3 oz SLF Baked Halibut Steak	3 oz LF Bkd Halibut Steak	3 oz LF Bkd Halibut Steak	2 oz	3 oz	3 oz	3 oz
2 Tbsp Mayonnaise	1 tsp LF Tartar Sauce	2 Tbsp LF Tartar Sauce	0	2 tsp	2 tsp	2 tsp
Lemon Wedge	Lemon Wedge	Lemon Wedge	Lemon	Lemon	Lemon	Lemon
1/2c SFT Rice Pilaf	1/2c Rice Pilaf	1/2c Rice Pilaf	1/3c	1/3c	1/2c	2/3c
1/2c Seasoned Spinach	1/2c Seasoned Spinach	1/2c Seasoned Spinach	1/2c	1/2c	1/2c	1/2c
1 SFT Refined Dinner Roll	1 sl LF Pumpkin Bread	1 sl DB Pumpkin Bread	0	0	1 sl	1 sl
1 tsp Margarine	NO	1 tsp Margarine	0	0	0	0
1/2c Milk	1/2c Skim Milk	1/2c Skim Milk	1/2c	1/2c	1/2c	1/2c
Coffee/Tea/Decaf	Coffee/Tea/Decaf	Coffee/Tea/Decaf	free	free	free	free
1/2c SFT Fruit Parfait	1/2c Fruit Parfait	1/2c Fruit Parfait with	1/3c	1/3c	1/2c	1/2c
1 Tbsp Whipped Topping	NO	1 Tbsp Whipped Topping	1 Tbsp	1 Tbsp	1 Tbsp	1 Tbsp
Milk[3] or STR Juice	Skim Milk or Juice	1/2c Skim Milk	1/2c	1/2c	1/2c	1/2c
Plain Cookies, Gelatin,	LF Cookies, LF Crackers,	1 Starch/Bread Exch	1	1	1	1
Plain Crackers, Banana,	Gelatin, Fresh Fruit	1 Meat Exch	0	0	0	1
Vanilla Ice Cream[3]		1 Fat Exch	0	0	1	1

Merry Christmas

Breakfast
Chilled Cranberry Juice
Cherry Pecan Coffee Cake
Farm Fresh Egg to Order
Hot Cream of Wheat
with Raisins or
Assorted Cold Cereals
Assorted Condiments
Your Choice of Beverage

Lunch
Cream of Tomato Soup
Waldorf Salad
Roast Lamb with
Mint Jelly
Red Bliss Potatoes
Steamed Broccoli
Warm Parker House Rolls
Frozen Christmas Loaf
Your Choice of Beverage

Dinner
Split Pea Soup
Stuffed Breast of Chicken
Parsley Noodles
Glazed Carrots
Warm Dinner Rolls
Homemade Christmas Cookies
Your Choice of Beverage

Recipe	Regular, Liberal Bland[1], No Added Salt[2]	1–2 Gm Na (Low Sodium)	Mechanical Soft	Puree
	Breakfast			
	1/2c Cranberry Juice	1/2c Cranberry Juice	1/2 Cranberry Juice	1/2c STR Cranberry Juice
Q5	1 sl Cherry Pecan Coffeecake	1 sl SR Cherry Pecan Coffeecake	1 sl SFT Coffeecake+	1 sl White Bread+
B1	1/2c Cream of Wheat with	1/2c Cream of Wheat with	1/2c Cream of Wheat	1c Cream of Wheat
	2 Tbsp Raisins or	2 Tbsp Raisins or	NO or	NO
	3/4c Asst Cold Cereals	3/4c SR Asst Cold Cereals	3/4c Asst Cold Cereals+	NO
B4,5	1 Egg to Order	1 Egg to Order	1 Egg to Order	1 PUR Egg to Order
	1 tsp Margarine	1 tsp SR Margarine	1 tsp Margarine	1 tsp Margarine
	1 tsp Jam/Jelly	1 tsp Jam/Jelly	1 tsp Jelly	1 tsp Jelly
	1c Milk	1c Milk	1c Milk	1c Milk
	Coffee/Tea/Decaf	Coffee/Tea/Decaf	Coffee/Tea/Decaf	Coffee/Tea/Decaf
	Lunch			
C14	2/3c Cream of Tomato Soup	2/3c SR Cream of Tomato Soup	2/3c Cream of Tomato Soup	2/3c Cream of Tomato Soup
	with 1 sl Lime	with 1 sl Lime	with 1 sl Lime	NO
K40	1/2c Waldorf Salad	1/2c SR Waldorf Salad	1/2c Juice	1/2c STR Juice
D35	3 oz Roast Lamb with	3 oz Roast Lamb with	3 oz CHP Roast Lamb with	4 oz PUR Roast Lamb with
	2 tsp Mint Jelly	2 tsp Mint Jelly	2 tsp Mint Jelly	2 tsp Mint Jelly
J34	4 oz Red Bliss Potatoes	4 oz Red Bliss Potatoes	4 oz SFT Red Bliss Potatoes	1/2c PUR Red Bliss Potatoes
J10,3	1/2c Steamed Broccoli	1/2c Steamed Broccoli	1/2c Steamed Broccoli	1/2c PUR Broccoli
	1 Parker House Roll	1 Parker House Roll	1 Parker House Roll+	1 sl White Bread+
	1 tsp Margarine	1 tsp SR Margarine	1 tsp Margarine	1 tsp Margarine
	1/2c Milk	1/4c Milk	1/2c Milk	1/2c Milk
	Coffee/Tea/Decaf	Coffee/Tea/Decaf	Coffee/Tea/Decaf	Coffee/Tea/Decaf
S19	1 sl Frozen Christmas Loaf	1 sl Frozen Christmas Loaf	1 sl Frozen Christmas Loaf	1 sl Frozen Christmas Loaf
	Dinner			
C23,1	2/3c Split Pea Soup	2/3c SR Split Pea Soup	2/3c Split Pea Soup	2/3c PUR/STR Pea Soup
E10	5 oz Stuffed Chicken	5 oz SR Stuffed Chicken	5 oz CHP Stuffed Chicken	6 oz PUR Stuffed Chicken
O5	2 oz Chicken Gravy	2 oz SR Chicken Gravy	2 oz Chicken Gravy	2 oz Chicken Gravy
M3	1/2c Parsley Noodles	1/2c Parsley Noodles	1/2c Parsley Noodles	1/2c PUR Parsley Noodles
J15	1/2c Glazed Carrots	1/2c Glazed Carrots	1/2c Glazed Carrots	1/2c PUR Glazed Carrots
	1 Dinner Roll	1 Dinner Roll	1 SFT Dinner Roll+	1 sl Bread+
	1 tsp Margarine	1 tsp SR Margarine	1 tsp Margarine	1 tsp Margarine
	1/2c Milk	1/2c Milk	1/2c Milk	1/2c Milk
	Coffee/Tea/Decaf	Coffee/Tea/Decaf	Coffee/Tea/Decaf	Coffee/Tea/Decaf
Q18	1 Sprinkled Sugar Cookie	1 Sprinkled Sugar Cookie	2 Sprinkled Sugar Cookie	1/2c PUR Fruit Cocktail
Q16	1 Fruitcake Cookie	1 Fruitcake Cookie		
	Snacks			
	Milk or Juice	Juice	Milk or Juice	Milk or STR Juice
	Cookies, Crackers,	SR Cookies, SR Crackers,	Plain Cookies, Gelatin,	Applesauce, SFT Banana,
	Gelatin, Ice Cream,	Gelatin, Fresh Fruit	Plain Crackers+, Ice Cream,	Gelatin, Ice Cream
	Fresh Fruit		Banana	

TERMS: SFT = Soft; SLF = Soft/Low Fiber; GRD = Ground; CHP = Chopped Finely; PUR = Puree; STR = Strained; SR = Sodium or Salt Restricted; LF = Low Fat; FF = Fat Free; LCH = Low Cholesterol; DB = Diabetic; UNSW = Unsweetened; RC = Reduced Calorie; LC = Low Calorie; EXCH = Diabetic Exchange

SERVING UTENSILS: #6 Scoop = 2/3 cup-6 oz; #8 Scoop = 1/2 cup-4 oz; #10 Scoop = 3/8 cup-3 to 4 oz; #12 Scoop = 1/3 cup-2.5 to 3 oz; #16 Scoop = 1/4 cup-2 oz; #30 Scoop = 2 tbsp-1 oz; #60 Scoop = 1 tbsp-1/2 oz. Ounces will vary, based on food used.

1. *Liberal Bland:* Follow a regular diet. Use decaffeinated products. Omit pepper and chili powder.

2. *No Added Salt (3-4 gm NA):* Follow a regular diet. Use SR soups and SR canned meats. Omit salt packets (and shakers), bacon, sausage, smoked, and cured meats, substitute with SR food choices.

3. *Low Fiber:* Follow a soft diet. Do not exceed 2 cups of milk per day. Soft/Low Fiber—Omit pepper, garlic, and onions from recipes.

4. *2200 Calorie Diet:* Follow 2000 calorie diet with the following additions: Lunch—add 1 bread exchange and 1 fat exchange; Dinner—add 1 bread exchange.

+Consider individual tolerance. Daily Alternatives: Lunch and Dinner—Chicken, Hamburger, Cottage Cheese Fruit Plate, or Assorted Sandwiches. Individual preferences are provided upon request.

Amounts specified for food items that contain bone is equivalent to cooked, edible deboned portion.

Soft, Low Fiber[3]	Low Cholesterol, Low Fat (40–50 GM)	No Concentrated Sweets (Diabetic)	1200	1500	1800	2000[4] Diabetic/Calorie-Controlled
1/2c STR Cranberry Juice	1/2c Cranberry Juice	1/2c UNSW Cranberry Juice	1/3c	1/3c	1/3c	1/3c
1 sl White Toast	1 sl LF Cherry Coffeecake	1 sl DB Cherry Pecan Coffeecake	1/2 sl	1/2 sl	1/2 sl	1/2 sl
1/2c Cream of Wheat	1/2c LF Cream of Wheat with	1/2c DB Cream of Wheat with	1/2c	1/2c	1/2c	1/2c
NO or	2 Tbsp Raisins or	2 Tbsp Raisins or	0	0	2Tbsp	2Tbsp
3/4c Asst Refined Cereals	3/4c Cold Cereals	3/4c UNSW Cold Cereals	3/4c	3/4c	3/4c	3/4c
1 Egg to Order	1 Egg Substitute	1 Egg to Order	1	1	1	1
1 tsp Margarine	1 tsp Margarine	1 tsp Margarine	0	0	1 tsp	1 tsp
1 tsp Jelly	1 tsp Jam/Jelly	1 tsp DB Jam/Jelly	1 tsp	1 tsp	1 tsp	1 tsp
1c Milk	1c Skim Milk	1c Skim Milk	1/2c	1/2c	1/2c	1c
Coffee/Tea/Decaf	Coffee/Tea/Decaf	Coffee/Tea/Decaf	free	free	free	free
2/3c SLF Crm of Tomato Soup	2/3c LF Cream of Tomato Soup	2/3c LF Cream of Tomato Soup	2/3c	2/3c	2/3c	2/3c
with 1 sl Lime	with 1 sl Lime	with 1 sl Lime	1 sl	1 sl	1 sl	1 sl
1/2c oz STR Juice	1/2c LF Waldorf Salad	1/2c LF Waldorf Salad	1/4c	1/4c	1/2c	1/2c
3 oz SLF Roast Lamb with	2 oz Roast Lamb with	3 oz Roast Lamb with	2 oz	3 oz	3 oz	3 oz
2 tsp Mint Jelly	2 tsp Mint Jelly	1 tsp DB Mint Jelly	1 tsp	1 tsp	1 tsp	1 tsp
4 oz SFT Red Bliss Potatoes	4 oz LF Red Bliss Potatoes	4 oz LF Red Bliss Potatoes	0	3 oz	3 oz	3 oz
1/2c Green Beans	1/2c LF Broccoli+	1/2c LF Broccoli	1/2c	1/2c	1/2c	1/2c
1 SFT Refined Dinner Roll	1 Parker House Roll	1 small Parker House Roll	0	0	0	1
1 tsp Margarine	NO	1 tsp Margarine	0	0	0	0
1/2c Milk (1/4c)[3]	1/2c Skim Milk	1/2c Skim Milk	1/4c	1/4c	1/4c	1/2c
Coffee/Tea/Decaf	Coffee/Tea/Decaf	Coffee/Tea/Decaf	free	free	free	free
1 sl SLF Frozen Christmas Loaf	2.5 oz Frozen Christmas Loaf	2.5 oz Frozen Christmas Loaf	2 oz	2 oz	2.5 oz	2.5 oz
2/3c SLF Broth	2/3c LF Split Pea Soup	2/3c LF Split Pea Soup	Broth	2/3c	2/3c	2/3c
5 oz SLF Stuffed Chicken	4 oz LF Stuffed Chicken	5 oz DB Stuffed Chicken	4 oz	5 oz	5 oz	5 oz
2 oz Chicken Gravy	2 oz LF Chicken Gravy	2 oz LF Chicken Gravy	1 oz	1 oz	2 oz	2 oz
1/2c Parsley Noodles	1/2c LF Parsley Noodles	1/2c LF Parsley Noodles	1/4c	1/4c	1/2c	1/2c
1/2c Glazed Carrots	1/2c LF Glazed Carrots	1/2c DB Glazed Carrots	1/2c	1/2c	1/2c	1/2c
1 SFT Refined Dinner Roll	1 Dinner Roll	1 Dinner Roll	0	0	1 sm	1 sm
1 tsp Margarine	NO	1 tsp Margarine	0	0	0	0
1/2c Milk	1/2c Skim Milk	1/2c Skim Milk	1/4c	1/4c	1/4c	1/2c
Coffee/Tea/Decaf	Coffee/Tea/Decaf	Coffee/Tea/Decaf	free	free	free	free
2 Sprinkled Sugar Cookie	1 LF Sprinkled Sugar Cookie	1 DB Sugar Cookie	0	0	0	0
	1 LF Fruitcake Cookie	1 DB Fruitcake Cookie	1	1	1	1
Milk[3] or STR Juice	Skim Milk or Juice	1/2c Skim Milk	1/2c	1/2c	1/2c	1/2c
Plain Cookies, Gelatin,	LF Cookies, LF Crackers,	1 Starch/Bread Exch	1	1	1	1
Plain Crackers, Banana,	Gelatin, Fresh Fruit	1 Meat Exch	0	0	0	1
Vanilla Ice Cream[3]		1 Fat Exch	0	0	1	1

Dining Abroad

Breakfast in Paris
Chilled Apple Juice
Croissants
Oefs ala Florentine with
Mornay Sauce
Cream of Wheat or
Assorted Cold Cereals with
Fresh Raspberries
Assorted Condiments
Your Choice of Beverage

Lunch in Hong Kong
Egg Drop Soup
Chicken Chow Mein
White Rice
Chow Mein Noodles
Mandarin Oranges
Fortune Cookie
Tea

Dinner in Rome
Insalata Verde with
Italian Dressing
Melanzana Parmigiana
Pasta Primavera
La Bruschetta
Granita Di Limone
Your Choice of Beverage

Recipe	Regular, Liberal Bland[1], No Added Salt[2]	1–2 Gm Na (Low Sodium)	Mechanical Soft	Puree
	Breakfast			
	1/2c Apple Juice	1/2c Apple Juice	1/2c Apple Juice	1/2c STR Apple Juice
B1	1/2c Cream of Wheat or	1/2c Cream of Wheat or	1/2c Cream of Wheat or	1c Cream of Wheat
	3/4c Asst Dry Cereals	3/4c SR Asst Dry Cereals	3/4c Asst Dry Cereals+	NO
	1/2c Raspberries	1/2c Raspberries	1/2c Raspberries	1/2c PUR Banana
B7,4	1 srv Egg Florentine with	1 srv SR Egg Florentine with	1 srv Egg Florentine with	1 srv PUR Egg Florentine with
O24	1 oz Mornay Sauce	1 Tbsp SR Mornay Sauce	1 oz Mornay Sauce	1 oz Mornay Sauce
	1 Croissant or	1 Croissant or	1 Croissant+ or	NO
	1 sl Toast	1 sl Toast	1 sl Toast+	1 sl White Bread+
	1 tsp Margarine	1 tsp SR Margarine	1 tsp Margarine	1 tsp Margarine
	1 tsp Jam/Jelly	1 tsp Jam/Jelly	1 tsp Jelly	1 tsp Jelly
	1c Milk	1c Milk	1c Milk	1c Milk
	Coffee/Tea/Decaf	Coffee/Tea/Decaf	Coffee/Tea/Decaf	Coffee/Tea/Decaf
	Lunch			
C16	2/3c Egg Drop Soup	2/3c Egg Drop Soup	2/3c Egg Drop Soup	2/3c STR Egg Drop Soup
E14	1c Chicken Chow Mein	1c SR Chicken Chow Mein	1c SFT Chicken Chow Mein	1c PUR Chicken Chow Mein
L1	1/2c White Rice	1/2c White Rice	1/2c White Rice	1/2c PUR White Rice
	1/4c Chow Mein Noodles	NO	NO	NO
	1 Dinner Roll	1 Dinner Roll	1 SFT Dinner Roll+	1 sl Bread+
	1 tsp Margarine	1 tsp SR Margarine	1 tsp Margarine	1 tsp Margarine
	1/2c Milk	1/2c Milk	1/2c Milk	1/2c Milk
	Coffee/Tea/Decaf	Coffee/Tea/Decaf	Coffee/Tea/Decaf	Coffee/Tea/Decaf
	1/2c Mandarin Oranges	1/2c Mandarin Oranges	1/2c Mandarin Oranges	1/2c PUR Mandarin Oranges
	with Fortune Cookie	with Fortune Cookie	with Fortune Cookie	with Fortune Cookie
	Dinner			
K30	1c Tossed Green Salad with	1c Tossed Green Salad with	1/2c Grape Juice	1/2c STR Grape Juice
P4	1 oz Italian Dressing	1 oz Italian Dressing	NO	NO
G10,D9	6 oz Eggplant Parmesan	6 oz SR Eggplant Parmesan	6 oz SFT Eggplant Parmesan	6 oz PUR Eggplant Parmesan
O22				
M5	3/4c Pasta Primavera	3/4c Pasta Primavera	3/4c SFT Pasta Primavera	3/4c PUR Pasta Primavera
N8	1 sl Garlic Bread	1 sl SR Garlic Bread	1 sl SFT Garlic Bread	1 sl Bread+
	1 tsp Margarine	1 tsp SR Margarine	1 tsp Margarine	1 tsp Margarine
	1/2c Milk	1/2c Milk	1/2c Milk	1/2c Milk
	Coffee/Tea/Decaf	Coffee/Tea/Decaf	Coffee/Tea/Decaf	Coffee/Tea/Decaf
	1/2c Lemon Sherbet	1/2c Lemon Sherbet	1/2c Lemon Sherbet	1/2c Lemon Sherbet
	Snacks			
	Milk or Juice	Juice	Milk or Juice	Milk or STR Juice
	Cookies, Crackers,	SR Cookies, SR Crackers,	Plain Cookies, Gelatin,	Applesauce, SFT Banana,
	Gelatin, Ice Cream,	Gelatin, Fresh Fruit	Plain Crackers+, Ice Cream,	Gelatin, Ice Cream
	Fresh Fruit		Banana	

TERMS: SFT = Soft; SLF = Soft/Low Fiber; GRD = Ground; CHP = Chopped Finely; PUR = Puree; STR = Strained; SR = Sodium or Salt Restricted; LF = Low Fat; FF = Fat Free; LCH = Low Cholesterol; DB = Diabetic; UNSW = Unsweetened; RC = Reduced Calorie; LC = Low Calorie; EXCH = Diabetic Exchange

SERVING UTENSILS: #6 Scoop = 2/3 cup-6 oz; #8 Scoop = 1/2 cup-4 oz; #10 Scoop = 3/8 cup-3 to 4 oz; #12 Scoop = 1/3 cup-2.5 to 3 oz; #16 Scoop = 1/4 cup-2 oz; #30 Scoop = 2 tbsp-1 oz; #60 Scoop = 1 tbsp-1/2 oz. Ounces will vary, based on food used.

1. *Liberal Bland:* Follow a regular diet. Use decaffeinated products. Omit pepper and chili powder.

2. *No Added Salt (3–4 gm NA):* Follow a regular diet. Use SR soups and SR canned meats. Omit salt packets (and shakers), bacon, sausage, smoked, and cured meats, substitute with SR food choices.

3. *Low Fiber:* Follow a soft diet. Do not exceed 2 cups of milk per day. Soft/Low Fiber—Omit pepper, garlic, and onions from recipes.

4. *2200 Calorie Diet:* Follow 2000 calorie diet with the following additions: Lunch—add 1 bread exchange and 1 fat exchange; Dinner—add 1 bread exchange.

+Consider individual tolerance. Daily Alternatives: Lunch and Dinner—Chicken, Hamburger, Cottage Cheese Fruit Plate, or Assorted Sandwiches. Individual preferences are provided upon request.

Amounts specified for food items that contain bone is equivalent to cooked, edible deboned portion.

Soft, Low Fiber[3]	Low Cholesterol, Low Fat (40–50 GM)	No Concentrated Sweets (Diabetic)	1200	1500	1800	2000[4]
			Diabetic/Calorie-Controlled			
1/2c STR Apple Juice	1/2c Apple Juice	1/2c UNSW Apple Juice	1/2c	1/2c	1/2c	1/2c
1/2c Cream of Wheat or	1/2c LF Cream of Wheat or	1/2c DB Cream of Wheat or	1/2c	1/2c	1/2c	1/2c
3/4c Asst Refined Cereals	3/4c Dry Cereals	3/4c UNSW Dry Cereals	3/4c	3/4c	3/4c	3/4c
1/2c Banana	1/2c Raspberries	1/2c UNSW Raspberries	1/4c	1/2c	1/2c	1/2c
1 Poached Egg	1 srv LF Egg Florentine with	1 srv DB Egg Florentine with	1 srv	1 srv	1 srv	1 srv
NO	1 Tbsp SR Mornay Sauce	1 oz SR Mornay Sauce	1 Tbsp	1 Tbsp	1 Tbsp	1 Tbsp
1 Croissant or	NO	1 small Croissant or	1/2	1	1	1
1 sl White Toast	1 sl Toast	1 sl Toast	1 sl	1 sl	1 sl	1 sl
1 tsp Margarine	1 tsp Margarine	1 tsp Margarine	0	0	1 tsp	1 tsp
1 tsp Jelly	1 tsp Jam/Jelly	1 tsp DB Jam/Jelly	1 tsp	1 tsp	1 tsp	1 tsp
1c Milk	1c Skim Milk	1c Skim Milk	1/2c	1/2c	1/2c	1c
Coffee/Tea/Decaf	Coffee/Tea/Decaf	Coffee/Tea/Decaf	free	free	free	free
2/3c SLF Egg Drop Soup	2/3c LF Egg Drop Soup	2/3c Egg Drop Soup	2/3c	2/3c	2/3c	2/3c
1c SLF Chicken Chow Mein	3/4c Chicken Chow Mein	1c Chicken Chow Mein	3/4c	1c	1c	1c
1/2c White Rice	3/4c White Rice	1/2c White Rice	1/3c	1/2c	1/2c	1/2c
NO	NO	1/4c Chow Mein Noodles	0	0	1/4c	1/4c
1 SFT Refined Dinner Roll	1 Dinner Roll	1 Dinner Roll	0	0	1 sm	1 sm
1 tsp Margarine	NO	1 tsp Margarine	0	0	1 tsp	1 tsp
1/2c Milk	1/2c Skim Milk	1/2c Skim Milk	1/2c	1/2c	1/2c	1/2c
Coffee/Tea/Decaf	Coffee/Tea/Decaf	Coffee/Tea/Decaf	free	free	free	free
1/2c Mandarin Oranges	1/2c Mandarin Oranges	1/2c UNSW Mandarin Oranges	1/2c	1/2c	1/2c	1/2c
with Fortune Cookie	with Fortune Cookie	with Fortune Cookie	fortune	fortune	fortune	fortune
1/2c STR Grape Juice	1c Tossed Green Salad with	1c Tossed Green Salad with	1c	1c	1c	1c
NO	2 tsp Italian Dressing	2 tsp Italian Dressing	1 tsp	1 tsp	1 tsp	1 tsp
3 1/2 oz SLF Beef Patty with	6 oz LF Eggplant Parmesan	6 oz DB Eggplant Parmesan	4.5 oz	6 oz	6 oz	6 oz
2 oz SLF Tomato Sauce						
3/4c SFT Pasta Primavera	3/4c LF Pasta Primavera	3/4c LF Pasta Primavera	1/3c	1/2c	1/2c	3/4c
1 SFT Refined Dinner Roll	1 sl LF Garlic Bread+	1 sl LF Garlic Bread	0	0	1 sl	1 sl
1 tsp Margarine	NO	1 tsp Margarine	0	0	0	0
1/2c Milk	1/2c Skim Milk	1/2c Skim Milk	1/2c	1/2c	1/2c	1/2c
Coffee/Tea/Decaf	Coffee/Tea/Decaf	Coffee/Tea/Decaf	free	free	free	free
1/2c Lemon Sherbet	1/2c LF Lemon Sherbet	1/2c LF Lemon Sherbet	1/3c	1/3c	1/2c	1/2c
Milk[3] or STR Juice	Skim Milk or Juice	1/2c Skim Milk	1/2c	1/2c	1/2c	1/2c
Plain Cookies, Gelatin,	LF Cookies, LF Crackers,	1 Starch/Bread Exch	1	1	1	1
Plain Crackers, Banana,	Gelatin, Fresh Fruit	1 Meat Exch	0	0	0	1
Vanilla Ice Cream[3]		1 Fat Exch	0	0	1	1

Independence Day in Mexico

Breakfast
Chilled Pineapple Juice
Peppered Corn Muffin or
Tortilla
Huevos Rancheros with
Salsa and Guacamole
Grits or
Assorted Cold Cereals
Assorted Condiments
Your Choice of Beverage

Lunch
Gazpacho
Arroz con Pollo
Ejotes con Limón
Warm Flour Tortilla or
Warm Dinner Rolls
Citrus Cup
Your Choice of Beverage

Dinner
Cilantro Cabbage Slaw
Snapper Veracruz
Savory Black Beans
Zucchini Olé
Warm Flour Tortilla or
Warm Dinner Rolls
Jericalla
Your Choice of Beverage

Recipe	Regular, Liberal Bland[1], No Added Salt[2]	1–2 Gm Na (Low Sodium)	Mechanical Soft	Puree
	Breakfast			
	1/2c Pineapple Juice	1/2c Pineapple Juice	1/2c Pineapple Juice	1/2c STR Pineapple Juice
B2,1	1/2c Grits or	1/2c Grits or	1/2c Grits or	1c STR Grits
	3/4c Asst Cold Cereals	3/4c SR Asst Cold Cereals	3/4c Asst Cold Cereals+	NO
N16	1 Peppered Corn Muffin or	1 Peppered Corn Muffin or	1 Peppered Corn Muffin or	1 sl Bread+
	1 Tortilla	1 Tortilla	1 Tortilla	NO
B6,5	2 oz Huevos Rancheros	2 oz Huevos Rancheros	2 oz Huevos Rancheros	2 oz Huevos Rancheros
O23	with 1 oz Salsa	with 1 oz Salsa	with 1 oz STR Salsa	with 1 oz STR Salsa
K43	2 Tbsp Guacamole	2 Tbsp Guacamole	2 Tbsp SFT Guacamole	2 Tbsp SFT Guacamole
	1 tsp Margarine	1 tsp SR Margarine	1 tsp Margarine	1 tsp Margarine
	1 tsp Jam/Jelly	1 tsp Jam/Jelly	1 tsp Jelly	1 tsp Jelly
	1c Milk	1c Milk	1c Milk	1c Milk
	Coffee/Tea/Decaf	Coffee/Tea/Decaf	Coffee/Tea/Decaf	Coffee/Tea/Decaf
	Lunch			
C17	2/3c Gazpacho	2/3c SR Gazpacho	2/3c PUR/STR Gazpacho	2/3c PUR/STR Gazpacho
E11	Arroz con Pollo:	Arroz con Pollo:	Arroz con Pollo:	Arroz con Pollo:
	3 oz Chicken with	3 oz Chicken with	3 oz CHP Chicken with	4 oz PUR Chicken with
	1/2c Rice-Vegetables	1/2c SR Rice-Vegetables	1/2c Rice-Vegetables	4 oz PUR Rice-Vegetables
J5	1/2c Ejotes con Limón	1/2c Ejotes con Limón	1/2c Ejotes con Limón	1/2c PUR Ejotes con Limón
	1 Flour Tortilla or	1 Flour Tortilla or	1 Flour Tortilla or	NO
	1 Dinner Roll	1 Dinner Roll	1 SFT Dinner Roll+	1 sl Bread+
	1 tsp Margarine	1 tsp SR Margarine	1 tsp Margarine	1 tsp Margarine
	1/2c Milk	1/2c Milk	1/2c Milk	1/2c Milk
	Coffee/Tea/Decaf	Coffee/Tea/Decaf	Coffee/Tea/Decaf	Coffee/Tea/Decaf
S3	1/2 Citrus Cup	1/2 Citrus Cup	1/2 Canned Citrus Cup	1/2 PUR Citrus Cup
	Dinner			
K7	1/2c Cilantro Cabbage Slaw	1/2c Cilantro Cabbage Slaw	4 oz Juice	4 oz STR Juice
F8	4 oz Snapper Veracruz	4 oz Snapper Veracruz	4 oz CHP Snapper Veracruz	4 oz PUR Snapper Veracruz
L13,M1	1/2c Savory Black Beans	1/2c Savory Black Beans	1/2c Savory Black Beans	1/2c PUR Savory Black Beans
J53,52	1/2c Zucchini Olé	1/2c Zucchini Olé	1/2c SFT Zucchini	1/2c PUR Zucchini
	1 Flour Tortilla or	1 Flour Tortilla or	1 Flour Tortilla or	NO
	1 Dinner Roll	1 Dinner Roll	1 SFT Dinner Roll+	1 sl Bread+
	1 tsp Margarine	1 tsp SR Margarine	1 tsp Margarine	1 tsp Margarine
	1/2c Milk	1/4c Milk	1/2c Milk	1/2c Milk
	Coffee/Tea/Decaf	Coffee/Tea/Decaf	Coffee/Tea/Decaf	Coffee/Tea/Decaf
S18	4 oz Jericalla	4 oz Jericalla	4 oz Jericalla	4 oz Jericalla
	Snacks			
	Milk or Juice	Juice	Milk or Juice	Milk or STR Juice
	Cookies, Crackers,	SR Cookies, SR Crackers,	Plain Cookies, Gelatin,	Applesauce, SFT Banana,
	Gelatin, Ice Cream,	Gelatin, Fresh Fruit	Plain Crackers+, Ice Cream,	Gelatin, Ice Cream
	Fresh Fruit		Banana	

TERMS: SFT = Soft; SLF = Soft/Low Fiber; GRD = Ground; CHP = Chopped Finely; PUR = Puree; STR = Strained; SR = Sodium or Salt Restricted; LF = Low Fat; FF = Fat Free; LCH = Low Cholesterol; DB = Diabetic; UNSW = Unsweetened; RC = Reduced Calorie; LC = Low Calorie; EXCH = Diabetic Exchange

SERVING UTENSILS: #6 Scoop = 2/3 cup-6 oz; #8 Scoop = 1/2 cup-4 oz; #10 Scoop = 3/8 cup-3 to 4 oz; #12 Scoop = 1/3 cup-2.5 to 3 oz; #16 Scoop = 1/4 cup-2 oz; #30 Scoop = 2 tbsp-1 oz; #60 Scoop = 1 tbsp-1/2 oz. Ounces will vary, based on food used.

1. *Liberal Bland:* Follow a regular diet. Use decaffeinated products. Omit pepper and chili powder.

2. *No Added Salt (3–4 gm NA):* Follow a regular diet. Use SR soups and SR canned meats. Omit salt packets (and shakers), bacon, sausage, smoked, and cured meats, substitute with SR food choices.

3. *Low Fiber:* Follow a soft diet. Do not exceed 2 cups of milk per day. Soft/Low Fiber—Omit pepper, garlic, and onions from recipes.

4. *2200 Calorie Diet:* Follow 2000 calorie diet with the following additions: Lunch—add 1 bread exchange and 1 fat exchange; Dinner—add 1 bread exchange.

+Consider individual tolerance. Daily Alternatives: Lunch and Dinner—Chicken, Hamburger, Cottage Cheese Fruit Plate, or Assorted Sandwiches. Individual preferences are provided upon request.

Amounts specified for food items that contain bone is equivalent to cooked, edible deboned portion.

Soft, Low Fiber[3]	Low Cholesterol, Low Fat (40–50 GM)	No Concentrated Sweets (Diabetic)	1200	1500	1800	2000[4]
			Diabetic/Calorie-Controlled			
1/2c STR Apple Juice	1/2c Pineapple Juice	1/2c UNSW Pineapple Juice	1/3c	1/3c	1/2c	1/2c
1/2c Cream of Wheat or	1/2c LF Grits or	1/2c DB Grits or	1/2c	1/2c	1/2c	1/2c
3/4c Asst Refined Cereals	3/4c Cold Cereals	3/4c UNSW Cold Cereals	3/4c	3/4c	3/4c	3/4c
1 sl White Toast or	1 LF Peppered Corn Muffin or	1 DB Peppered Corn Muffin or	1	1	1	1
1 Tortilla	1 Tortilla	1 Tortilla	1	1	1	1
2 oz Scrambled Egg	2 oz LF Huevos Rancheros	2 oz DB Huevos Rancheros	1 oz	1 oz	1 oz	1 oz
NO	with 1 oz Salsa	with 1 oz Salsa	1 oz	1 oz	1 oz	1 oz
2 SFT Tbsp Guacamole	2 Tbsp Guacamole	2 Tbsp Guacamole	0	1 Tbsp	1 Tbsp	1 Tbsp
1 tsp Margarine	1 tsp Margarine	1 tsp Margarine	1 tsp	1 tsp	1 tsp	2 tsp
1 tsp Jelly	1 tsp Jam/Jelly	1 tsp DB Jam/Jelly	1 tsp	1 tsp	1 tsp	1 tsp
1c Milk	1c Skim Milk	1c Skim Milk	1/2c	1/2c	1/2c	1c
Coffee/Tea/Decaf	Coffee/Tea/Decaf	Coffee/Tea/Decaf	free	free	free	free
1/2c Tomato Juice	2/3c Gazpacho	2/3c Gazpacho	2/3c	2/3c	2/3c	2/3c
Arroz con Pollo:	Arroz con Pollo:	Arroz con Pollo:				
3 oz Chicken with	2 LF Chicken with	3 oz LF Chicken with	2 oz	3 oz	3 oz	3 oz
1/2c SLF Rice-Vegetables	1/2c Rice-Vegetables	1/2c Rice-Vegetables	1/3c	1/3c	1/2c	1/2c
1/2c Ejotes con Limón	1/2c LF Ejotes con Limón	1/2c LF Ejotes con Limón	1/2c	1/2c	1/2c	1/2c
1 Flour Tortilla or	1 Flour Tortilla or	1 Flour Tortilla or	0	1	1	1
1 SFT Refined Dinner Roll	1 Dinner Roll	1 Dinner Roll	0	1 sm	1 sm	1 sm
1 tsp Margarine	NO	1 tsp Margarine	0	0	1 tsp	1 tsp
1/2c Milk	1/2c Skim Milk	1/2c Skim Milk	1/2c	1/2c	1/2c	1/2c
Coffee/Tea/Decaf	Coffee/Tea/Decaf	Coffee/Tea/Decaf	free	free	free	free
1/2 Canned Citrus Cup	1/2 Citrus Cup	1/2 Citrus Cup	1/2c	1/2c	1/2c	1/2c
4 oz STR Juice	1/2c LF Cilantro Cabbage Slaw	1/2c LF Cilantro Cabbage Slaw	1/2c	1/2c	1/2c	1/2c
4 oz SLF Snapper Veracruz	4 oz Snapper Veracruz	4 oz LF Snapper Veracruz	3 oz	4 oz	4 oz	4 oz
1/2c Noodles	1/2c Savory Black Beans+	1/2c Savory Black Beans	1/3c	1/3c	1/3c	1/2c
1/2c SFT Zucchini	1/2c Zucchini Olé	1/2c LF Zucchini Olé	1/2c	1/2c	1/2c	1/2c
1 Flour Tortilla or	1 Flour Tortilla or	1 Flour Tortilla or	0	1	1	1
1 SFT Refined Dinner Roll	1 Dinner Roll	1 Dinner Roll	0	1	1	1
1 tsp Margarine	NO	1 tsp Margarine	0	1 tsp	1 tsp	1 tsp
1/2c Milk (1/4)[3]	1/2c Skim Milk	1/2c Skim Milk	1/4c	1/4c	1/4c	1/2c
Coffee/Tea/Decaf	Coffee/Tea/Decaf	Coffee/Tea/Decaf	free	free	free	free
4 oz Jericalla	4 oz LF Jericalla	4 oz DB Jericalla	4 oz	4 oz	4 oz	4 oz
Milk[3] or STR Juice	Skim Milk or Juice	1/2c Skim Milk	1/2c	1/2c	1/2c	1/2c
Plain Cookies, Gelatin,	LF Cookies, LF Crackers,	1 Starch/Bread Exch	1	1	1	1
Plain Crackers, Banana,	Gelatin, Fresh Fruit	1 Meat Exch	0	0	0	1
Vanilla Ice Cream[3]		1 Fat Exch	0	0	1	1

Southern Hospitality

Breakfast
Fresh Squeezed Orange Juice
Aunt Nelle's
Baking Powder Biscuits
Sizzlin' Sausage Patty
Farm Fresh Egg to Order
Pipin' Hot Grits or
Assorted Cold Cereals
Assorted Condiments
Your Choice of Beverage

Lunch
Poppy Seed Cole Slaw
Crispy Oven Fried Chicken
Mashed Potatoes
Okra and Tomatoes
Warm Dinner Rolls
Spiced Peaches
Your Choice of Beverage

Dinner
Vegetable Chowder
Barbecue Beef Short Ribs
Black-Eyed Peas
Seasoned Collard Greens
Cornbread Muffin
Deep Dish Pecan Pie
Your Choice of Beverage

Recipe	Regular, Liberal Bland[1], No Added Salt[2]	1–2 Gm Na (Low Sodium)	Mechanical Soft	Puree
	Breakfast			
	1/2c Orange Juice	1/2c Orange Juice	1/2c Orange Juice	1/2c STR Orange Juice
B2,1	1/2c Grits or	1/2c SR Grits or	1/2c Grits or	1c STR Grits
	3/4c Asst Cold Cereals	3/4c SR Asst Cold Cereals	3/4c Asst Cold Cereals+	NO
N1	1 Biscuit	1 SR Biscuit	1 Biscuit+	1 sl White Bread+
B4,5	1 Egg to Order	1 Egg to Order	1 Egg to Order	1 PUR Egg to Order
D33	1 oz Sausage Patty	NO	1 oz CHP Sausage Patty	NO
	1 tsp Margarine	1 tsp SR Margarine	1 tsp Margarine	1 tsp Margarine
	1 tsp Jelly/Jam	1 tsp Jelly/Jam	1 tsp Jelly	1 tsp Jelly
	1c Milk	1c Milk	1c Milk	1c Milk
	Coffee/Tea/Decaf	Coffee/Tea/Decaf	Coffee/Tea/Decaf	Coffee/Tea/Decaf
	Lunch			
K6	1/2c Poppy Cole Slaw	1/2c Poppy Cole Slaw	1/2c Juice	1/2c STR Juice
E5	3 oz Oven Crisp Chicken	3 oz Oven Crisp Chicken	3 oz CHP Oven Crisp Chicken	3 oz PUR Oven Crisp Chicken
J37	1/2c Mashed Potatoes with	1/2c Mashed Potatoes with	1/2c Mashed Potatoes with	1/2c Mashed Potatoes with
O5	2 oz Chicken Gravy	2 oz SR Chicken Gravy	2 oz Chicken Gravy	2 oz STR Chicken Gravy
J29,3	1/2c Okra & Tomatoes	1/2c SR Okra & Tomatoes	1/2c Okra & Tomatoes+	1/2c PUR Okra & Tomatoes
	1 Dinner Roll	1 Dinner Roll	1 SFT Dinner Roll+	1 sl Bread+
	1 tsp Margarine	1 tsp SR Margarine	1 tsp Margarine	1 tsp Margarine
	1/2c Milk	1/2c Milk	1/2c Milk	1/2c Milk
	Coffee/Tea/Decaf	Coffee/Tea/Decaf	Coffee/Tea/Decaf	Coffee/Tea/Decaf
S9	1/2c Spiced Peaches	1/2c Spiced Peaches	1/2c Spiced Peaches	1/2c PUR Spiced Peaches
	Dinner			
C30	2/3c Vegetable Chowder	2/3c Vegetable Chowder	2/3c Vegetable Chowder+	2/3c PUR/STR Veg Chowder
D7	3 oz Barbecue Short Ribs	3 oz Barbecue Short Ribs	3 oz CHP Barbecue Short Ribs	3 oz PUR Barbecue Short Ribs
O2,C1	1.5 oz Barbecue Sauce	1.5 oz SR Barbecue Sauce	1.5 oz SFT Barbecue Sauce	1.5 oz SFT Barbecue Sauce
L12,1	1/2c Black-eyed Peas	1/2c Black-eyed Peas	1/2c Black-eyed Peas+	1/2c PUR Black-eyed Peas
J13	1/2c Seasoned Collard Greens	1/2c Seasoned Collard Greens	1/2c CHP Collard Greens	1/2c PUR Collard Greens
N15	1 Corn Muffin	1 SR Corn Muffin	1 Corn Muffin+	1 sl Bread+
	1 tsp Margarine	1 tsp SR Margarine	1 tsp Margarine	1 tsp Margarine
	1/2c Milk	1/2c Milk	1/2c Milk	1/2c Milk
	Coffee/Tea/Decaf	Coffee/Tea/Decaf	Coffee/Tea/Decaf	Coffee/Tea/Decaf
R5,S12	1/8 Pecan Pie	1/8 Pecan Pie	1/2c Gelatin with	1/2c Gelatin with
			1 Tbsp Whipped Topping	1 Tbsp Whipped Topping
	Snacks			
	Milk or Juice	Juice	Milk or Juice	Milk or STR Juice
	Cookies, Crackers,	SR Cookies, SR Crackers,	Plain Cookies, Gelatin,	Applesauce, SFT Banana,
	Gelatin, Ice Cream,	Gelatin, Fresh Fruit	Plain Crackers+, Ice Cream,	Gelatin, Ice Cream
	Fresh Fruit		Banana	

TERMS: SFT = Soft; SLF = Soft/Low Fiber; GRD = Ground; CHP = Chopped Finely; PUR = Puree; STR = Strained; SR = Sodium or Salt Restricted; LF = Low Fat; FF = Fat Free; LCH = Low Cholesterol; DB = Diabetic; UNSW = Unsweetened; RC = Reduced Calorie; LC = Low Calorie; EXCH = Diabetic Exchange

SERVING UTENSILS: #6 Scoop = 2/3 cup-6 oz; #8 Scoop = 1/2 cup-4 oz; #10 Scoop = 3/8 cup-3 to 4 oz; #12 Scoop = 1/3 cup-2.5 to 3 oz; #16 Scoop = 1/4 cup-2 oz; #30 Scoop = 2 tbsp-1 oz; #60 Scoop = 1 tbsp-1/2 oz. Ounces will vary, based on food used.

1. *Liberal Bland:* Follow a regular diet. Use decaffeinated products. Omit pepper and chili powder.

2. *No Added Salt (3–4 gm NA):* Follow a regular diet. Use SR soups and SR canned meats. Omit salt packets (and shakers), bacon, sausage, smoked, and cured meats, substitute with SR food choices.

3. *Low Fiber:* Follow a soft diet. Do not exceed 2 cups of milk per day. Soft/Low Fiber—Omit pepper, garlic, and onions from recipes.

4. *2200 Calorie Diet:* Follow 2000 calorie diet with the following additions: Lunch—add 1 bread exchange and 1 fat exchange; Dinner—add 1 bread exchange.

+Consider individual tolerance. Daily Alternatives: Lunch and Dinner—Chicken, Hamburger, Cottage Cheese Fruit Plate, or Assorted Sandwiches. Individual preferences are provided upon request.

Amounts specified for food items that contain bone is equivalent to cooked, edible deboned portion.

Soft, Low Fiber[3]	Low Cholesterol, Low Fat (40–50 GM)	No Concentrated Sweets (Diabetic)	1200	1500	1800	2000[4]
			Diabetic/Calorie-Controlled			
1/2c STR Orange Juice	1/2c Orange Juice	1/2c UNSW Orange Juice	1/2c	1/2c	1/2c	1/2c
1/2c Oatmeal or	1/2c LF Grits or	1/2c DB Grits or	1/2c	1/2c	1/2c	1/2c
3/4c Asst Refined Cereals	3/4c Cold Cereals	3/4c UNSW Cold Cereals	3/4c	3/4c	3/4c	3/4c
1 Biscuit+	1 Biscuit	1 Biscuit	1	1	1	1
1 Egg to Order	1 Egg Substitute	1 Egg to Order	1	1	1	1
NO	NO	1 oz Sausage Patty	0	0	0	0
1 tsp Margarine	1 tsp Margarine	1 tsp Margarine	0	0	0	1 tsp
1 tsp Jelly	1 tsp Jelly/Jam	1 tsp UNSW Jelly/Jam	1 tsp	1 tsp	1 tsp	1 tsp
1c Milk	1c Skim Milk	1c Skim Milk	1/2c	1/2c	1/2c	1c
Coffee/Tea/Decaf	Coffee/Tea/Decaf	Coffee/Tea/Decaf	free	free	free	free
1/2c STR Juice	1/2c Poppy Cole Slaw+	1/2c DB Poppy Cole Slaw	Lettuce	1/2c	1/2c	1/2c
3 oz SLF Oven Chicken	2 oz LF Oven Crisp Chicken	3 oz LF Oven Crisp Chicken	2 oz	3 oz	3 oz	3 oz
1/2c Mashed Potatoes with	1/2c LF Mashed Potatoes with	1/2c LF Mashed Potatoes with	1/4c	1/4c	3/4c	3/4c
2 oz Chicken Gravy	2 oz LF Chicken Gravy	2 oz LF Chicken Gravy	NO	1 oz	1 oz	1 oz
1/2c Green Beans	1/2c LF Okra & Tomatoes	1/2c DB Okra & Tomatoes	1/2c	1/2c	1/2c	1/2c
1 SFT Refined Dinner Roll	1 Dinner Roll	1 Dinner Roll	0	0	1 sm	1 sm
1 tsp Margarine	NO	1 tsp Margarine	0	0	0	1 tsp
1/2c Milk	1/2c Skim Milk	1/2c Skim Milk	1/4c	1/4c	1/2c	1/2c
Coffee/Tea/Decaf	Coffee/Tea/Decaf	Coffee/Tea/Decaf	free	free	free	free
1/2c Spiced Peaches	1/2c Spiced Peaches	1/2c Spiced Peaches	1/2c	1/2c	1/2c	1/2c
2/3c SLF Veg Chowder+	2/3c LF Vegetable Chowder+	2/3c LF Vegetable Chowder	STR	2/3c	2/3c	2/3c
3 oz Short Ribs	2 oz Barbecue Short Ribs	3 oz Barbecue Short Ribs	2 oz	3 oz	3 oz	3 oz
2 oz SLF Broth	1.5 oz Barbecue Sauce	1.5 oz DB Barbecue Sauce	Broth	1 oz	1.5 oz	1.5 oz
1/2c White Rice	1/2c Black-eyed Peas+	1/2c Black-eyed Peas	1/4c	1/3c	1/2c	1/2c
1/2c CHP Collard Greens	1/2c Seasoned Collard Greens	1/2c Seasoned Collard Greens	1/2c	1/2c	1/2c	1/2c
1 SFT Refined Dinner Roll	1 LF Corn Muffin	1 DB Corn Muffin	1	1	1	1
1 tsp Margarine	NO	1 tsp Margarine	0	0	0	1 tsp
1/2c Milk	1/2c Skim Milk	1/2c Skim Milk	1/2c	1/2c	1/2c	1/2c
Coffee/Tea/Decaf	Coffee/Tea/Decaf	Coffee/Tea/Decaf	free	free	free	free
1/2c Gelatin with	1/2c Gelatin with	1/10 DB Pecan Pie	1/10	1/10	1/8	1/8
1 Tbsp Whipped Topping	1 Tbsp Whipped Topping					
Milk[3] or STR Juice	Skim Milk or Juice	1/2c Skim Milk	1/2c	1/2c	1/2c	1/2c
Plain Cookies, Gelatin,	LF Cookies, LF Crackers,	1 Starch/Bread Exch	1	1	1	1
Plain Crackers, Banana,	Gelatin, Fresh Fruit	1 Meat Exch	0	0	0	1
Vanilla Ice Cream[3]		1 Fat Exch	0	0	1	1

Appendixes

Appendix 1
Abbreviations

AP	as purchased	mL	milliliter
asst	assorted	NA	sodium
c	cup	Nia	niacin
CA	calcium	oz	ounce
CHO	carbohydrate	PFA	polyunsaturated fatty acid
Chol	cholesterol	pkg	package
CHP	chopped	por	portion
cn	canned	pro	protein
DB	diabetic	pt	pint
drsg	dressing	PUR	puree
ea	each	qt	quart
EP	edible portion	RC	reduced calorie
exg	exchange	Rib	riboflavin (vitamin B2)
FE	iron	sce	sauce
FF	fat free	SFA	saturated fatty acid
foz	fluid ounces	SFT	mechanical soft
frz	frozen	sl	slice
gal	gallon	SLF	soft/low fiber
gm	gram	sm	small
GRD	ground	SR	sodium restricted
in	inch	srv	serving
iu	international unit	STR	strained
K+	potassium	Tbsp	tablespoon
kcal	kilocalorie	Thi	thiamin (vitamin B1)
kg	kilogram	tsp	teaspoon
lb	pound	UNSW	unsweetened
LC	low calorie	Vit A	vitamin A
LCH	low cholesterol	Vit C	vitamin C
LF	low fat	xlg	extra large
lg	large	°C	degree celsius
med	medium	°F	degree fahrenheit
mg	milligram		

Appendix 2
Weights and Measures

A. Equivalents in U.S. Measures and Weights

3 tsp =	1 Tbsp =	1/2 foz
1/8 cup =	2 Tbsp =	1 foz
1/4 cup =	4 Tbsp =	2 foz
1/2 cup =	8 Tbsp =	4 foz
3/4 cup =	12 Tbsp =	6 foz
1 cup =	16 Tbsp =	8 foz
2 cups =	1 pint =	16 foz (1 pound)
4 cups =	1 quart =	32 foz
16 cups =	1 gallon =	64 foz
8 quarts =	1 peck	
1 bushel =	4 pecks	

B. Metric Equivalents for U.S. Weights, Measures, and Temperatures

Weight		Measure		Temperature	
U.S.	Metric	U.S.	Metric	°F	°C
0.035 oz	1 gm	1/5 tsp	1 mL	32	0
1 oz	28.35 gm	1 tsp	5 mL	100	38
4 oz (1/4 lb)	114 gm	1 Tbsp	14.8 mL	200	95
8 oz (1/2 lb)	227 gm	1 cup	240 mL	212	100
12 oz (3/4 lb)	340 gm	1 qt	0.95 L	300	150
16 oz (1 lb)	454 gm	1.06 qt	1 L	350	175
2.2 lb	1 kg	1 gal	3.8 L	400	205

Appendix 3
Food Portioning Aids

A. Approximate Ladle Equivalents

Ladle numbers refer to the number of ounces a ladle will hold.

Ladle Size	Approximate Measure		Suggested Uses
12 oz	24 Tbsp	1 1/2 cups	large soups, goulash
8 oz	16 Tbsp	1 cup	soups, chili, stew
6 oz	12 Tbsp	3/4 cup	chili, baked or creamed entrees, stews, soups
4 oz	8 Tbsp	1/2 cup	vegetables
2 oz	4 Tbsp	1/4 cup	gravies, sauces
1 oz	2 Tbsp	1/8 cup	relishes, sauces, salad dressing

B. Approximate Dipper Equivalents

Dipper numbers are based on the number of level dippers in one quart.

Dipper Number	Approximate Measure	Approximate Weight	Suggested Uses
6	10 Tbsp; 2/3–3/4 cup	6 oz	entree salads
8	8 Tbsp; 1/2 cup	4 to 5 oz	entrees
10	6 Tbsp; 3/8 cup	3 to 4 oz	vegetables, meat patties
12	5 Tbsp; 1/3 cup	2 1/2 to 3 oz	salads, vegetables
16	4 Tbsp; 1/4 cup	2 to 2 1/4 oz	muffins, desserts
20	3 1/3 Tbsp	1 3/4 to 2 oz	muffins, cupcakes, sandwich fillings
24	2 2/3 Tbsp	1 1/2 to 1 3/4 oz	desserts, sandwich fillings
30	2 Tbsp; 1/8 cup	1 to 1 1/2 oz	large drop cookies
40	1 1/2 Tbsp	3/4 oz	medium drop cookies
60	1 Tbsp	1/2 oz	small cookies, garnishes
100	scant 2 tsp		tea cookies

C. Pan Sizes and Servings

Pan Size	Cut/Number of Portions	Suggested Uses
18 × 26 × 2"	8 × 12 (92 portions)	cakes
	8 × 8 (64 portions)	
	6 × 10 (60 portions)	
	6 × 8 (48 portions)	
18 × 26 × 1"	6 × 10 (60 portions)	sheet cakes, bar cookies, buns
12 × 18 × 2"	5 × 6 (30 portions)	sheet cakes
13 × 18 × 1"	5 × 6 (30 portions)	sheet cakes, bar cookies
	6 × 8 (48 portions)	

C. Pan Sizes and Servings, continued

Pan Size	Cut/Number of Portions	Suggested Uses
9 × 13 × 2"	3 × 5 (15 portions)	cakes
8 × 8"	3 × 3 (9 portions)	cakes
	2 × 5 (10 portions)	
9 × 9"	4 × 4 (16 portions)	cakes
	4 × 3 (12 portions)	
10-inch tube	1/14 to 1/16 (14–16 portions)	chiffon cakes
9-inch round (cake)	1/16 (16 portions)	layer cakes, cornbread
8-inch round (cake)	1/12 to 1/14 (12–14 portions)	layer cakes
9-inch round (pie)	1/8 to 1/10 (8–10 portions)	pies
8-inch round (pie)	1/6 to 1/8 (6–8 portions)	pies
5 × 6 × 4" (loaf)	1/24 to 1/32 (24–32 portions)	quick breads, yeast breads
5 × 8 × 4" (loaf)	1/12 to 1/16 (12–16 portions)	quick breads, yeast breads, cakes
5 × 9 × 2 3/4" (loaf)	1/16 (16 portions)	quick breads, yeast breads, cakes
20 × 12 × 2"	8 × 6 (48 portions)	baked entrees
	6 × 4 (24 portions)	
20 × 12 × 4"	8 × 6 (48 portions)	baked entrees
	6 × 4 (24 portions)	

Appendix 4
Common Can Sizes

Can Size	Average Net Weight or Fluid Measure per Can	Approximate Cups per Can	Number of Portions	Products
No. 10	6 lb 3 oz to 7 lb 5 oz	12 to 13	24 to 26	institutional size fruits and vegetables
No. 3 Cyl	46 foz or 51 oz	5 3/4	10 to 12	juices, some vegetables, institutional size condensed soups
No. 21/2	27 to 29 oz	3 1/2	5 to 7	fruits, some vegetables
No. 2	18 foz or 20 oz	2 1/2	5	juices, ready to serve soups, some fruits
No. 303	16 to 17 oz	2	4	fruits, vegetables, ready to serve soups, combination foods, some meats
No. 300	14 to 16 oz	1 3/4	3 to 4	some fruits, meat products, baked beans
No. 1 (picnic)	10 1/2 to 12 oz	1 1/4	2 to 3	condensed soups, some fruits, vegetables, meat, and fish
8 oz	8 oz	1	2	ready to serve soups, fruits, and vegetables
6 oz	6 oz	3/4	1 to 5	frozen juice concentrates, single serve juices

Can Substitutions

Can Size	Approximate Number of Cans to Use in Place of 1 No. 10 Can
No. 3 Cyl	2
No. 2 1/2	4
No. 2	5
No. 303	7

Food Equivalents

Food	Weight	Measure	Food Facts
Alfalfa Sprouts	1 lb	6 cups	
Allspice, ground	1 oz	5 Tbsp	
Almonds, slivered, chopped	1 lb	3 1/2 cups	
Almonds, whole	1 lb	3 cups	
Anchovies	1 lb	2 cups	
Anise seeds	1 oz	4 Tbsp	
Apples, canned, pie pack	1 lb	2 cups	
Apples, fresh	1 lb	4 small	1 lb AP = 0.9 lb ready to cook with peel
		3 medium	
		2 large	
Apples, peeled, diced	1 lb	3 1/2 cups	
Apples, peeled, sliced	1 lb	4 cups	
Applesauce	1 lb	2 cups	
Apricots, canned halves, drained	1 lb	2 cups	
Apricots, dried, AP	1 lb	3 cups	
Apricots, fresh	1 lb	14 medium	
		12 large	
		10 jumbo	
		8 extra jumbo	
Apricots, stewed halves	1 lb	2 1/4 cups	
Asparagus, canned, cuts	1 lb	2 1/2 cups	1 lb AP = 0.53 lb ready to cook
Asparagus, fresh, stalks	1 lb	16–20 stalks	
Avocado, diced	1 lb	2 1/2 cups	
Avocado, whole	1 lb	2 medium	1 lb AP = 0.67 lb ready to serve raw
Bacon, raw, diced	1 lb	2 1/4 cups	
Bacon, raw, hotel-sliced	1 lb	18 to 22 slices	1 lb AP = 0.3 lb cooked meat
Bacon bits	1 lb	3 3/4 cups	
Bacon fat	1 lb	2 2/3 cups	
Baking powder	1 oz	2 1/3 Tbsp	
Baking soda	1 oz	2 1/3 Tbsp	
Bananas, diced	1 lb	3 cups	
Bananas, mashed	1 lb	2 cups	
Bananas, whole	1 lb	4 small	
		3 medium	
Barbecue sauce	1 lb	2 cups	
Barley, pearl	1 lb	2 cups	
Basil, sweet	1 oz	3/4 cup	
Bay leaves	1 oz	2 cups	
Beans, baked	1 lb	2 cups	
Beans, garbanzo, canned	1 lb	2 1/2 cups	
Beans, great northern, dried	1 lb	2 1/2 cups	
Beans, kidney, dried	1 lb	2 1/2 cups	
Beans, kidney, dried, 1 lb AP, after cooking	2 3/8 lb	6 1/2 cups	

Food	Weight	Measure	Food Facts
Beans, lima, dried	1 lb	2 1/2 cups	
Beans, lima, dried, 1 lb AP, after cooking	2 2/3 lb	6 cups	
Beans, lima, fresh, canned or frz	1 lb	3 cups	
Beans, navy, dried	1 lb	2 1/4 cups	
Beans, navy, dried, 1 lb AP, after cooking	2 1/4 lb	5 1/2 cups	
Beans, snap, green, wax, canned or frz	1 lb	3 cups	1 lb AP = 0.88 lb ready to cook
Bean sprouts, canned, drained	1 lb	4 cups	
Bean sprouts, fresh	1 lb	8 cups	
Beef base	1 lb	1 1/2 cups	
Beef, cooked, diced	1 lb	3 cups	
Beef, cubed, 1-inch	3 oz EP	1 serving	1 lb AP = 0.56 lb cooked lean meat
Beef, dried, solid pack	1 lb	3 3/4 cups	
Beef, ground	3 oz EP	1 serving	No more than 30% fat: 1 lb AP = 0.7 lb cooked meat Lean: 1 lb AP = 0.8 lb cooked lean meat Extra Lean: 1 lb AP = 0.85 lb cooked lean meat
Beef, liver	3 1/2 oz EP	1 serving	1 lb AP = 0.7 lb cooked meat
Beef, raw, ground	1 lb	2 cups	
Beef, roast, chuck, boneless	3 oz EP	1 serving	1 lb AP = 0.7 lb cooked lean meat
Beef, roast, chuck, with bone	3 oz EP	1 serving	1 lb AP = 0.45 lb cooked lean meat
Beef, roast, ribeye	3 oz EP	1 serving	1 lb AP = 0.75 lb cooked lean meat
Beef, roast, round, bottom, boneless	3 oz EP	1 serving	1 lb AP = 0.78 lb cooked lean meat
Beef, roast, rump, boneless	3 oz EP	1 serving	1 lb AP = 0.62 lb cooked lean meat
Beef, roast, sirloin, boneless	3 oz EP	1 serving	1 lb AP = 0.61 lb cooked lean meat
Beef, roast, short ribs	3 oz EP	1 serving	1 lb AP = 0.25 lb cooked lean meat
Beef, steak, flank	3 oz EP	1 serving	1 lb AP = 0.67 lb cooked lean meat
Beef, steak, round, boneless	3 1/2 oz EP	1 serving	1 lb AP = 0.59 lb cooked lean meat
Beef, steak, sirloin, boneless	3 1/2 oz EP	1 serving	1 lb AP = 0.75 lb cooked lean meat
Beef, steak, tenderloin	4 oz EP	1 serving	1 lb AP = 0.9 lb cooked lean meat
Beef brisket, corned, boneless	3 oz EP	1 serving	1 lb AP = 0.42 lb cooked lean meat
Beef brisket, fresh, boneless	3 oz EP	1 serving	1 lb AP = 0.46 lb cooked lean meat
Beets, diced or sliced, canned	1 lb	2 1/3 cups	
Beets, fresh	1 lb	4 medium	With tops: 1 lb AP = 0.44 lb ready to cook No Tops, peeled: 1 lb AP = 0.77 lb No Tops, cooked, slices: 1 lb AP = 0.73 lb
Blueberries, canned	1 lb	2 1/4 cups	
Blueberries, fresh or frz	1 lb	3 cups	1 lb AP = 0.96 lb ready to serve
Bran (All-bran cereal)	1 lb	8 cups	
Branflakes	1 lb	3 qt	
Bread, sandwich	1 1/2 lb	24 slices	1 slice = 1 oz = 5/8-inch
Bread, soft, broken	1 lb	2 1/2 qt	
Bread crumbs, dry, ground	1 lb	4 cups	
Bread crumbs, soft	1 lb	8 cups	
Broccoli, chopped, fresh	1 lb	4 cups	1 lb AP = 0.81 lb ready to cook
Brussel sprouts, fresh	1 lb	4 cups	1 lb AP = 0.76 lb ready to cook
Butter	1 lb	2 cups	
Buttermilk, dry	1 oz	1/4 cup	
Butterscotch chips	1 lb	2 2/3 cups	
Cabbage, green or red; shredded, raw	1 lb	6 cups	1 lb AP = 0.75 lb ready to cook
Cabbage, green or red; chopped, cooked	1 lb	2 1/2 cups	
Cake crumbs, soft	1 lb	6 cups	
Cake mix	1 lb	4 cups	

Food	Weight	Measure	Food Facts
Caraway seeds	1 oz	4 Tbsp	
Carrots, canned, diced	1 lb	3 cups	1 No. 10 can weighs 72 oz drained
Carrots, frozen, sliced	1 lb	3 1/2 cups	
Carrots, raw	1 lb	4 to 5 medium	No tops: 1 lb AP = 0.7 lb ready to cook
Carrots, raw, shredded	1 lb	4 cups	
Carrots, raw, sliced	1 lb	3 cups	
Cauliflower, florets	1 lb	4 cups	1 lb AP = 0.58 lb ready to cook raw
Cauliflower, frz, cooked	1 lb	2 1/2 cups	
Cauliflower, whole head	2 to 2 1/2 lb	1 head	1 head = 6 cups (60–75 florets)
Celery, EP, diced	1 lb	4 cups	
Celery, raw, chopped	1 lb	3 1/2 cups	1 lb AP = 0.83 lb ready to cook raw
			Cooked: 1 lb AP = 0.74 lb
Celery flakes, dried	1 oz	1 1/3 Tbsp	
Celery salt	1 oz	2 Tbsp	
Celery seeds	1 oz	4 Tbsp	
Cheese, cheddar, shredded	1 lb	4 cups	
Cheese, cottage	1 lb	2 cups	
Cheese, cream	1 lb	2 cups	
Cheese, mozzarella, shredded	1 lb	3 1/2 cups	
Cheese, parmesan or romano, grated	1 lb	3 3/4 cups	
Cherries, maraschino, chopped or whole	1 lb	2 cups (50–60 cherries)	
Cherries, Royal Anne, canned, drained	1 lb	2 1/4 cups	
Chicken, cooked, diced	1 lb	3 cups	
Chicken, breast (without back)	5 oz AP	1/2 breast	1 lb AP = 0.66 lb cooked meat
Chicken, drumstick	3 oz AP	1 drumstick	1 lb AP = 0.49 lb cooked meat
Chicken, thigh	3 1/4 oz AP	1 thigh	1 lb AP = 0.5 lb cooked meat
Chicken, whole	2 1/2 to 3 lb	1 fryer	1 lb AP = 0.36 lb cooked meat (without giblets)
			1 lb AP = 0.41 lb cooked meat (with giblets)
Chicken, wings	2 1/2 oz AP	1 wing	1 lb AP = 0.34 lb cooked meat
Chiles, green, diced	1 lb	2 cups	
Chili powder	1 oz	4 Tbsp	
Chives, snipped	1 oz	1/3 cup	
Chocolate, baking	1 lb	16 squares	
Chocolate, grated	1 lb	4 cups	
Chocolate, melted	1 lb	1 3/4 cups	
Chocolate chips or bits	1 lb	2 2/3 cups	
Chocolate wafers	1 lb	4 cups crumbs	
Cinnamon, ground	1 oz	4 Tbsp	
Cinnamon sticks	1 oz	10 pieces	
Citrons, chopped	1 lb	2 1/2 cups	
Clams, chopped meat	1 lb	2 cups	
Cloves, ground	1 oz	4 Tbsp	
Cloves, whole	1 oz	5 Tbsp	
Cocoa	1 lb	4 cups	
Coconut, flaked, shredded	1 lb	4 3/4 cups	
Coffee, ground coarse	1 lb	5 cups	
Coffee, instant	1 oz	8 Tbsp	
Collard greens, canned or frz	1 lb	2 cups	
Collard greens, fresh, AP	1 lb	1 3/4 cups	1 lb AP = 0.69 lb ready to cook
Corn, cream styled, canned	1 lb	1 3/4 cups	1 No. 10 can weighs 100 oz, drained
Corn, on the cob	9 oz	1 ear (6 inches)	

Food	Weight	Measure	Food Facts
Corn, whole, canned or frz, drained	1 lb	2 1/4 cups	1 No. 10 can weighs 70 oz, drained
Corned beef, canned	1 lb	2 1/2 cups	
Cornflake crumbs	1 lb	1 qt	
Cornflakes	1 lb	4 qt	
Corn meal, coarse	1 lb	3 cups	1 lb after cooking yields 6 lb (3 qt)
Cornstarch	1 oz	3 Tbsp	
Corn syrup	1 lb	1 1/2 cups	
Crab in shell	1 lb	1/2 cup cooked meat	
Crabmeat, canned, flaked	1 lb	3 1/4 cups	
Cracker crumbs	1 lb	6 cups	
Crackers, graham	1 lb	60 crackers	
Crackers, saltines (2 × 2 inch)	1 lb	155 crackers	
Cranberries, fresh	1 lb	1 qt	
Cranberries, pulp	1 lb	2 cups	
Cranberry sauce	1 lb	2 cups	
Cream	1 lb	2 cups	
Cream, sour	1 lb	2 cups	
Cream, whipping	1 lb	2 cups	2 cups = 1 qt whipped
Cream of tartar	1 oz	3 Tbsp	
Cream of wheat, quick, AP	1 lb	2 2/3 cups	
Cream of wheat, 1 lb AP, after cooking	8 lb	1 gal	
Croutons	1 lb	2 1/4 qt	
Cucumber, diced, EP	1 lb	3 1/2 cups	
Cucumber, sliced, with peel (1/8-inch slice)	1 lb	60 slices	
Cucumber, whole	1 lb	2 large	1 lb AP = 0.92 lb pared, raw
			1 lb AP = 0.75 lb peeled with seeds removed
Cumin, ground	1 oz	4 Tbsp	
Currants	1 lb	3 cups	
Curry powder	1 oz	4 1/2 Tbsp	
Dates, chopped	1 lb	3 cups	
Dates, pitted	1 lb	2 1/2 cups	
Dill seed	1 oz	4 1/2 Tbsp	
Dill weed	1 oz	3/4 cup	
Eggs, dried, white	1 lb	5 cups	
Eggs, dried, whole	1 lb	5 1/3 cups	
Eggs, dried, yolks	1 lb	5 2/3 cups	
Eggs, hard-cooked, chopped	1 lb	2 2/3 cups	1 dozen = 3 1/2 cups
Eggs, shelled, fresh/frz, whole	1 sm = 1 1/2 oz	5–6 sm = 1 cup	
	1 med = 1 5/8 oz	4–5 med = 1 cup	
	1 lg = 2 oz	4 lg = 1 cup	
	1 xlg = 2 1/4 oz	3 1/2 xlg = 1 cup	
	1 jumbo = 2 1/2 oz	3 jumbo = 1 cup	
Eggs, shelled, fresh/frz, whites	1 sm = 0.83 oz	9–10 sm = 1 cup	
	1 med = 0.99 oz	8–9 med = 1 cup	
	1 lg = 1.1 oz	7–8 lg = 1 cup	
	1 jumbo = 1.37 oz	6–7 jumbo = 1 cup	
Eggs, shelled, fresh/frz, yolks	1 sm = 0.68 oz	11–12 sm = 1 cup	
	1 med = .81 oz	9–10 med = 1 cup	
	1 lg = .99 oz	8–9 lg = 1 cup	
	1 jumbo = 1.13 oz	7–8 jumbo = 1 cup	
Eggplant, diced	1 lb	3 cups	1 lb AP = 0.81 lb ready to cook
Eggplant, sliced	1 lb	16 slices (1/4-inch)	

Food	Weight	Measure	Food Facts
Endive, escarole, chicory	10–16 oz	1 head	1 lb AP = 0.78 lb ready to serve
Endive, escarole, chicory, chopped	1 lb	8 cups	
Farina, raw	1 lb	2 2/3 cups	
Fennel seed	1 oz	4 Tbsp	
Figs, dried, chopped	1 lb	2 1/2 cups	
Fish, cooked, flaked	1 lb	3 cups	
Fish fillets	3 oz	1 serving	1 lb AP = 0.7 lb cooked fish
Fish, whole, dressed	3 oz	1 serving	1 lb AP = 0.3 lb cooked fish
Flour, all-purpose	1 lb	4 cups	
Flour, bread, sifted	1 lb	4 cups	
Flour, buckwheat, sifted	1 lb	3 1/4 cups	
Flour, cake, sifted	1 lb	4 cups	
Flour, pastry, sifted	1 lb	4 cups	
Flour, potato, sifted	1 lb	4 cups	
Flour, rye, sifted	1 lb	5 cups	
Flour, whole wheat	1 lb	3 3/4 cups	
Garlic, fresh	1 oz	6 large cloves	
Garlic, fresh, minced	1 oz	3 Tbsp	
Garlic powder	1 oz	3 Tbsp	
Garlic salt	1 oz	2 Tbsp	
Gelatin, granulated, flavored	1 lb	2 1/4 cups	
Gelatin, granulated, unflavored	1 oz	3 Tbsp	
Ginger, candied, chopped	1 oz	2 2/3 Tbsp	
Ginger, ground	1 oz	4 Tbsp	
Grapefruit, sections	1 lb	2 cups	
Grapefruit, whole	17 oz	1 medium	1 lb AP = 0.51 lb ready to serve raw
Grapenuts	1 lb	1 qt	
Grapes, seedless, fresh	1 lb	3 cups	
Grapes, on stem	1 lb	1 qt	
Grits, hominy	1 lb	3 cups	1 lb AP, after cooking yields 6 1/2 lb (3 1/4 qt)
Ham, cured, boneless	3 oz EP	1 serving	1 lb AP = 0.63 lb cooked meat
Ham, cured, with bone	3 oz EP	1 serving	1 lb AP = 0.53 lb cooked meat
Ham, diced, cooked	1 lb	3 cups	
Ham, fresh, whole boneless	3 oz EP	1 serving	1 lb AP = 0.53 lb cooked meat
Ham, fresh, whole with bone	3 oz EP	1 serving	1 lb AP = 0.45 lb cooked meat
Ham, ground, cooked	1 lb	2 1/4 cups	
Honey	1 lb	1 1/3 cups	
Horseradish, prepared	1 oz	2 Tbsp	
Ice Cream	1 lb	2 2/3 cups	
Jam or Jelly	1 lb	1 1/2 cups	
Kale, chopped, canned or frozen	1 lb	3 cups	1 No. 10 can weighs 62 oz, drained
Kale, chopped, cooked	1 lb	3 cups	1 lb AP = 0.70 lb ready to serve
Lamb, roast, leg, boneless	3 oz EP	1 serving	1 lb AP = 0.6 lb cooked meat
Lamb, roast, leg, with bone	3 oz EP	1 serving	1 lb AP = 0.45 lb cooked meat
Lamb chops	4 oz	1 chop	1 lb AP = 0.45 lb cooked meat
Lard	1 lb	2 cups	
Lemon, thinly sliced	1 lb	3 cups	
Lemon juice	1 lb	2 cups	4 to 5 lemons yield 3/4 cup juice
Lemon peel, fresh	1 oz	4 Tbsp	1 medium lemon yields 3 Tbsp juice and 1 Tbsp lemon peel.
Lentils, cooked	1 lb	2 cups	
Lentils, raw	1 lb	2 1/2 cups	
Lentils, raw, 1 lb AP, after cooking	2 1/2 lb	1 1/4 quarts	

Food	Weight	Measure	Food Facts
Lettuce, chopped/shredded	1 lb	8 cups	
Lettuce, bibb	5 oz–6 oz	1 head	
Lettuce, iceberg	1 lb–2 lb	1 head	1 lb AP = 0.74 lb ready to serve
Lettuce, leaf	6 oz–8 oz	1 head	1 lb AP = 0.6 lb ready to serve
Lettuce, romaine	1 lb–2 lb	1 head	1 lb AP = 0.64 lb ready to serve
Lettuce leaves	1 lb EP	20 leaves	
Macaroni, dry	1 lb	4 cups	1 lb AP, after cooking yields 3 lb (2 qt)
Macaroni, cooked	1 lb	3 cups	
Mace, ground	1 oz	4 1/2 Tbsp	
Mango	12 oz	1 medium	1 lb AP = 0.69 lb ready to serve raw
Maple syrup	1 lb	1 1/2 cups	
Margarine	1 lb	2 cups	
Marjoram	1 oz	6 Tbsp	
Marshmallows (1 1/4 in)	1 lb	2 qt	1 lb-85 marshmallows
Marshmallows, miniature	1 lb	2 qt	10 miniature=1 regular
Matzo farfel	1 lb	7 cups	
Matzo meal	1 lb	1 qt	
Mayonnaise	1 lb	2 cups	
Melon, cantaloupe	1 1/2 lb	1 small	1 lb AP = 0.55 lb ready to serve raw
Milk, evaporated	1 lb	1 3/4 cups	
Milk, fluid, whole	1 lb	2 cups	
Milk, nonfat, dry	1 lb	6 cups	
Milk, sweetened condensed	1 lb	1 1/2 cups	
Mincemeat	1 lb	2 cups	
Molasses	1 lb	1 1/3 cups	
MSG	1 oz	2 Tbsp	
Mushrooms, canned	1 lb	2 cups	1 No. 303 can weighs 10 oz, drained 1 No. 2 can weighs 12 oz, drained 1 No. 10 can weighs 68 oz, drained
Mushrooms, fresh	1 lb AP	30 to 40 small 18 to 20 medium 12 to 14 large 7 to 10 extra large 1 quart	Dried Mushrooms: 5 oz dried = 2 lb fresh 1 lb AP = 0.98 lb ready to cook raw 1 lb AP = 0.22 lb ready to cook, sliced
Mushrooms, fresh, chopped	1 lb	6 cups	
Mushrooms, fresh, sliced	1 lb	7 cups	
Mustard, ground, dry	1 oz	5 Tbsp	
Mustard, prepared	1 oz	2 Tbsp	
Mustard greens, canned or cooked	1 lb	3 1/4 cups	1 lb AP = .59 lb ready to cook raw 1 No. 10 can weighs 60 oz, drained
Mustard seed	1 oz	2 3/4 Tbsp	
Nectarines, sliced	1 lb	2 cups	
Nectarines, whole	1 lb	3 medium	1 lb AP = 0.9 lb ready to serve raw
Noodles, cooked	1 lb	2 3/4 cups	1 lb AP, after cooking yields 3 lb (2 qt)
Noodles, uncooked	1 lb	5 1/3 cups	
Nutmeg, ground	1 oz	3 3/4 Tbsp	
Oats, rolled, quick, AP	1 lb	6 cups	1 lb AP, after cooking yields 2 1/2 lb (4 qt)
Oil, vegetable	1 lb	2 1/8 cups	
Okra, fresh	1 lb	4 cups	1 lb AP = 0.87 lb ready to cook raw
Okra, canned or frz	1 lb	3 cups	1 No. 2 can weighs 12 oz, drained 1 No. 2 1/2 can weighs 18 oz, drained 1 No. 10 can weighs 60 oz, drained

Food	Weight	Measure	Food Facts
Olives, black, whole, unpitted, canned	1 lb	128 to 140 sm 106 to 121 med 91 to 105 lg 65 to 88 extra lg 41 to 50 colossal 3 1/2 cups (average)	
Olives, black, sliced	1 lb	3 1/2 cups	1 No. 10 can weighs 55 oz, drained
Olives, black, chopped	1 lb	2 1/3 cups	1 No. 10 can weighs 90 oz, drained
Olives, green, whole, unpitted, canned	1 lb	128 to 140 sm 106 to 127 med 91 to 105 lg 76 to 90 extra lg 33 to 41 colossal 2 cups (average)	
Olives, green, stuffed	1 lb	2 1/2 cups	
Onions, dehydrated	1 lb	6 cups dry (or 9c reconstituted)	
Onions, grated	1 oz	1 1/3 Tbsp	
Onions, green (scallions)	1 lb	10 1/2 cups	1 lb AP = 0.83 lb ready to serve with tops 1 lb AP = 0.40 lb ready to serve without tops
Onions, mature, fresh, chopped	1 lb	3 cups	1 lb AP = 0.88 lb ready to serve raw
Onions, mature, fresh, sliced	1 lb	4 cups	
Onions, mature, whole	1 lb	1 colossal (14–18 oz) 2 jumbo (8–10 oz) 4 lg med (3–5 oz) 8 prepack (1.5–3 oz)	
Onion powder	1 oz	3 Tbsp	
Onion salt	1 oz	2 1/2 Tbsp	
Onions, shallots, chopped	1 lb	4 cups	1 lb AP yields 2 1/4 cups chopped.
Onion soup mix	1 oz	2 2/3 Tbsp	
Orange juice	1 lb	2 cups	
Orange peel, fresh	1 oz	4 Tbsp	1 med orange yields 3 Tbsp grated peel.
Oranges, diced	1 lb	2 1/2 cups	
Oranges, whole	1 lb	3 to 4 med, unpeeled or 5 peeled	1 lb oranges yields 1 cup juice.
Oregano, ground	1 oz	5 Tbsp	
Oregano, leaf	1 oz	3/4 cup	
Oyster	3/4 oz	1 large	1 lb AP = 0.38 lb cooked oysters
Oysters	1 lb	2 1/4 cups	
Paprika	1 oz	4 Tbsp	
Parsley, chopped	1 oz	3/4 cup	1 lb AP = 0.9 lb ready to serve raw
Parsley, flakes, dried	1 oz	1 1/3 cups	
Parsnips, cooked, diced	1 lb	2 2/3 cups	
Parsnips, whole	1 lb AP	4 medium	1 lb AP = 0.83 lb ready to cook
Peaches, diced or sliced, frz and canned	1 lb	2 cups	
Peaches, fresh	4 oz	1 medium	1 lb AP = 0.76 lb ready to serve sliced
Peaches, fresh, sliced	1 lb	3 cups	
Peanut butter	1 lb	1 3/4 cups	
Peanuts, shelled	1 lb	3 1/4 cups	
Pears, canned, drained, diced	1 lb	2 1/2 cups	
Pears, canned, large halves, drained	1 lb	2 1/8 cups (5 halves)	
Pears, fresh, diced or sliced	1 lb	3 cups	

Food	Weight	Measure	Food Facts
Pears, fresh, whole	1 lb	4 sm (4 1/2 oz) 3 med (5 1/2 oz) 2 lg (8 oz)	1 lb AP = 0.92 lb ready to serve raw
Peas, black-eyed, canned	1 lb	2 2/3 cups	1 No. 10 can weighs 85 oz, drained
Peas, black-eyed, dried	1 lb	2 1/4 cups	
Peas, black-eyed, dried, 1 lb AP, after cooking	1 3/4 lb	4 1/2 cups	
Peas, black-eyed, frz	1 lb	2 cups	
Peas, green, canned	1 lb	2 1/4 cups	1 No. 10 can weighs 70 oz, drained
Peas, green, frz	1 lb	2 2/3 cups	
Peas, whole and split, dried	1 lb	2 1/4 cups	
Peas, whole, split, dried, 1 lb AP, after cooking	2 1/2 lb	5 1/2 cups	
Pecans, chopped	1 lb	3 1/4 cups	
Pecans, whole	1 lb	4 cups	
Pepper, ground	1 oz	4 Tbsp	
Peppercorns	1 oz	6 Tbsp	
Peppers, sweet, fresh	1 lb	4 lg (4 oz ea) 5–6 med (3 oz ea) 6–7 sm (2 1/2 oz)	1 lb AP = 0.8 lb ready to cook raw strips 1 lb AP = 0.73 lb cooked strips
Peppers, sweet, fresh, chopped	1 lb	3 cups	
Pickle relish	1 lb	2 cups	
Pickles, chopped	1 lb	3 cups	
Pimento, chopped	1 lb	2 cups	
Pineapple, canned, crushed or tidbits	1 lb	2 cups	
Pineapple, canned, sliced	1 lb	8 to 12 slices	
Pineapple, fresh cubed.	4 lb	1 medium	One medium pineapple yields 5 1/2 cups diced pineapple. 1 lb AP = 0.52 lb ready to serve raw
Poppy seeds	1 oz	3 Tbsp	
Pork, roast, loin, boneless	3 oz EP	1 serving	1 lb AP = 0.54 lb cooked meat
Pork, roast, loin, with bone	3 oz EP	1 serving	1 lb AP = 0.4 lb cooked meat
Pork chop, with bone	5 1/3 oz	1 chop	1 lb AP = 0.4 lb cooked meat
Pork cutlets	3 oz EP	1 serving	1 lb AP = 0.75 lb cooked meat
Potato chips	1 lb	4 qt	1 lb = 2 qt crushed
Potatoes, canned, sliced	1 lb	2 1/4 cups	1 No. 10 can weighs 75 oz, drained
Potatoes, dehydrated, flakes	1 lb	5 cups	
Potatoes, hash browns	1 lb	3 cups	
Potatoes, Irish, fresh	1 lb	4 to 5 potatoes	
Potatoes, red bliss, fresh	1 lb	7 to 9 small 5 to 6 medium	
Potatoes, russet, fresh	6 oz or under 5 to 10 oz 10 to 16 oz	sm (1 3/4 to 2 1/2 in) med (2 1/4 to 3 1/4 in) lg (3 to 4 1/4 in) (inches specify diameter)	1 lb AP = 0.7 lb ready to cook without skin
Potatoes, sweet, cooked	1 lb	2 cups	
Potatoes, sweet, fresh	1 lb AP	3 medium	1 lb AP = 0.65 lb baked without skin
Poultry seasoning, ground	1 oz	3 Tbsp	
Prunes, cooked	1 lb	2 1/3 cups	
Prunes, cooked, pitted, chopped	1 lb	2 cups	

Food	Weight	Measure	Food Facts
Prunes, dried, size 30/40, AP	1 lb	3 cups	
Pudding, mix, dry, instant	1 lb	2 1/2 cups	
Pumpkin, canned, mashed or puree	1 lb	2 cups	12.5 lb AP yields 1 qt mashed.
Radishes, red, sliced	1 lb	3 1/2 cups	
Radishes, red, whole	1 lb	30–40 radishes (2 bunches)	
Raisins, seeded	1 lb	2 1/2 cups	
Raisins, seedless	1 lb	3 cups	
Raspberries, fresh	1 lb	3 1/4 cups	1 lb AP = 0.97 lb ready to serve
Rhubarb, raw, cut 1-inch pieces	1 lb	4 cups	1 lb AP = 0.85 lb ready to cook
Rice, brown, AP	1 lb	2 1/2 cups	
Rice, brown, cooked	1 lb	2 cups	
Rice, converted, AP	1 lb	2 1/2 cups	
Rice, cooked	1 lb	2 1/4 cups	1 lb AP, after cooking yields 3 3/4 lb (2 qt)
Rice, wild	1 lb	2 2/3 cups	1 lb AP, after cooking yields 1 lb (5 cups)
Rice Krispies	1 lb	4 qt	
Rosemary leaves	1 oz	9 Tbsp	
Rutabagas, fresh	1 lb	3 1/2 cups	1 lb AP = 0.85 lb ready to cook raw
Sage, finely, ground	1 oz	8 Tbsp	
Salad dressing, cooked	1 lb	2 cups	
Salmon, canned	1 lb	2 cups	
Salmon, fresh, cooked, flaked	1 lb	3 cups	
Salt	1 oz	1 5/8 Tbsp	
Salt pork	1 lb	2 cups	
Sauerkraut	1 lb	2 1/2 cups	1 No. 10 can weighs 80 oz, drained
Sausage, bulk	1 lb	2 cups	1 lb AP = 0.45 lb cooked meat
Sausage, link	1 lb	16 links	1 lb AP = 0.45 lb cooked meat
Sesame seed	1 oz	3 Tbsp	
Sherbet	1 lb	2 2/3 cups	
Shortening, melted	1 lb	2 1/4 cups	
Shortening, solid	1 lb	2 cups	
Shrimp, cleaned, cooked, peeled	1 lb	3 1/4 cups	1 lb AP in shell = 0.54 lb cooked shrimp
Soup base	1 oz	2 Tbsp	
Soybean, dried	1 lb	2 1/8 cups	
Spaghetti, cooked	1 lb	2 2/3 cups	1 lb after cooking yields 3 lb (2 qt)
Spaghetti, uncooked, broken	1 lb	1 qt	
Spinach, chopped, canned or frozen	1 lb	2 cups	1 No. 10 can weighs 60 oz, drained
Spinach, fresh, chopped	1 lb	3 1/4 qt	
Spinach, fresh, leaf	1 lb	5 qt	1 lb AP = 0.85 lb ready to cook or serve raw
Spinach, leaf, frozen	1 lb	2 1/3 cups	
Squash, summer or winter, frz	1 lb	2 cups	
Squash, zucchini, diced, cooked	1 lb	3 cups	1 lb AP = 0.95 lb ready to cook or serve raw
Starch, waxy maize	1 oz	3 Tbsp	
Strawberries, fresh, whole	1 lb	3 cups	
Strawberries, frz, sliced	1 lb	2 1/4 cups	
Sugar, brown, lightly packed	1 lb	3 cups	
Sugar, brown, solid packed	1 lb	2 cups	
Sugar, granulated	1 lb	2 1/4 cups	
Sugar, powdered, unsifted	1 lb	3 1/4 cups	
Tapioca, quick cooking	1 lb	3 cups	
Tarragon leaves	1 oz	1 cup	
Tea, bulk	1 lb	6 cups	
Tea, instant	1 oz	8 Tbsp	

Food	Weight	Measure	Food Facts
Thyme, ground	1 oz	6 Tbsp	
Thyme, leaves	1 oz	8 Tbsp	
Tofu, firm, crumbled	1 lb	2 cups	
Tofu, firm, cubes	1 lb	2 1/2 cups	
Tomato, catsup	1 lb	2 cups	
Tomatoes, fresh, whole	under 3 oz	small	Cherry Tomatoes: 1 pint = 23 to 26 or
	3 to 5 oz	large	35 to 45 tomatoes
	5 to 7 oz	extra large	1 lb AP = 0.9 lb ready to cook raw
	8 to 10 oz	maximum large	
Tomatoes, whole or crushed, canned	1 lb	2 cups	
Tomato paste	1 lb	2 cups	
Tomato puree	1 lb	2 cups	
Tomato sauce	1 lb	2 cups	
Tortillas, corn (8 in)	1 lb	16 tortillas	
Tortillas, flour (8 in)	1 lb	12 tortillas	
Tortillas, flour (10 in)	1 lb	9 tortillas	
Tuna, canned	1 lb	2 1/4 cups	
Turkey, dressed, whole	3 oz EP	1 serving	1 lb AP = 0.53 lb cooked meat with skin
(without neck and giblets)			1 lb AP = 0.47 lb cooked meat without skin
Turkey, ground	3 oz EP	1 serving	1 lb AP = 0.85 lb cooked meat
Turkey, roll, boneless, cooked	3 oz EP	1 serving	1 lb AP = 0.92 lb cooked meat
Turkey, roll, boneless, raw	3 oz EP	1 serving	1 lb AP = 0.65 lb cooked meat
Turmeric, ground	1 oz	4 Tbsp	
Turnip greens, canned or frz	1 lb	2 cups	
Turnip greens, fresh, chopped with stems	1 lb	2 cups	1 lb AP = 0.48 lb ready to cook
Turnips, cooked, diced	1 lb	2 3/4 cups	Tops on: 1 lb AP = 0.75 lb ready to cook
			Tops off: 1 lb AP = 0.6 lb ready to cook
Vanilla extract	1 oz	2 Tbsp	
Veal, cubed, 1-inch	3 oz EP	1 serving	1 lb AP = 0.65 lb cooked meat
Veal, ground	3 oz EP	1 serving	1 lb AP = 0.75 lb cooked meat
Veal, roast, leg, boneless	3 oz EP	1 serving	1 lb AP = 0.6 lb cooked meat
Veal cutlets	3 oz EP	1 serving	1 lb AP = 0.8 lb cooked meat
Vinegar	1 lb	2 cups	
Walnut halves	1 lb	5 1/3 cups	1 oz = 11 halves
Walnuts, English, chopped	1 lb	4 cups	
Watercress, chopped	1 lb	8 cups	1 lb AP = 0.92 lb ready to serve raw
Wheat, bulgar	1 lb	3 cups	
Wheat germ	1 lb	5 1/3 cups	
Whipped topping, frz	4 oz	1 3/4 cups	
Yeast, active dry	1 oz	4 Tbsp	1/4 oz = 1 envelope
Yeast, compressed	1 oz	1 package	

Appendix 6
Ingredient Substitutions

If you run out of an ingredient, you can choose from the following alternatives. However, the end product may be altered, so only make substitutions when necessary.

Recipe Ingredient	Recipe Substitutions
1 tsp Baking powder	1/4 tsp baking soda + 1/2 tsp cream of tartar
1 cup Bread crumbs	2/3 cup all-purpose flour
1 cup Bread crumbs, dry	3/4 cup cracker crumbs
1 cup Butter	1 cup margarine or
	1 cup shortening + 1/2 tsp salt or
	7/8 cup cooking oil + 1/2 tsp salt
1 cup Buttermilk	1 Tbsp vinegar or lemon juice + enough milk (or plain yogurt) to make 1 cup; let stand 5 minutes
1/2 cup Catsup	1/2 cup tomato sauce + 2 Tbsp sugar + 1 Tbsp vinegar
6 oz Chocolate, semisweet	6 Tbsp unsweetened cocoa + 7 Tbsp sugar + 1/2 cup shortening
1 oz Chocolate, unsweetened	3 Tbsp unsweetened cocoa + 1 Tbsp oil
1 Tbsp Cornstarch	1 Tbsp all-purpose flour or
	2 tsp waxy maize starch or
	2 tsp arrowroot
1 cup Corn syrup	3/4 cup sugar + 1/4 cup water
1 cup Cream, half and half	7/8 cup milk + 1 1/2 Tbsp melted butter
1 cup Cream, heavy	3/4 cup milk + 2 1/2 Tbsp fat
1 cup Cream, whipping	2 cup whipped topping
Egg, 1 large whole	4 Tbsp beaten egg or
	2 yolks + 1 Tbsp water
1 cup Flour, all-purpose	1 cup + 2 Tbsp cake flour or
	1/2 cup all-purpose flour + 1/2 cup whole-wheat flour or
	1/2 cup all-purpose flour + 1/2 cup bran or
	5/8 cup potato flour or
	7/8 cup cornmeal or
	1 1/4 cups rye flour or
	1 cup rolled oats or
	1 1/2 cups bread crumbs
1 Tbsp Flour, all-purpose (as thickener)	1/2 Tbsp cornstarch, potato starch, or arrowroot or
	2 tsp quick-cooking tapioca
1 cup Flour, cake	1 cup minus 2 Tbsp all-purpose flour
1 cup Flour, self-rising	1 cup all-purpose flour + 1 1/4 tsp baking powder + 1/4 tsp salt

Recipe Ingredient	Recipe Substitutions
1 medium clove Garlic	1/8 tsp garlic, minced, dry or
	1/8 tsp garlic powder or
	1/2 tsp garlic salt
1 Tbsp Ginger, fresh, minced	1/4 tsp ground ginger
1 Tbsp Herbs, fresh	1 tsp whole dried or
	1/4 tsp ground
1 cup Honey	1 1/4 cups granulated sugar + 1/4 cup liquid
1 Tbsp Horseradish, fresh, grated	2 Tbsp prepared horseradish
1 cup Milk, skim	1/3 cup instant nonfat dry milk + water to make 1 cup or
	1/2 cup evaporated skim milk + 1/2 cup water
1 cup Milk, whole	2 tsp melted butter + enough skim milk to make a cup or
	1/2 cup evaporated milk + 1/2 cup water or
	1 cup soy milk or
	1/3 cup nonfat dry milk + water to make 1 cup + 1 Tbsp fat
1 Tbsp Mustard, prepared	1 tsp dry mustard
1 small Onion	1 tsp onion powder or
	1 Tbsp instant minced onion
1 cup Sour cream	1 cup yogurt or
	1/3 cup butter + 3/4 cup buttermilk
4 Tbsp Soy sauce	3 Tbsp worcestershire sauce + 1 Tbsp water
1 cup Sugar, granulated	1 cup packed brown sugar or
	1 3/4 cups powdered sugar (do not substitute in baking) or
	1 1/2 cups corn syrup (reduce liquid in recipe by 1/2 cup) or
	1 cup honey (reduce liquid in recipe by 1/4 to 1/3 cup)
1 cup Tomatoes, canned	1 1/3 cups chopped fresh tomatoes, simmered
1 cup Tomato juice	1/2 cup tomato sauce + 1/2 cup water + dash salt
1 Tbsp Tomato paste	1 Tbsp catsup
1 cup Tomato puree	1/2 cup tomato paste + 1/2 cup water
1 Tbsp Yeast, dry active	1 package (1/4 oz) active dry yeast or
	1 cake compressed yeast
1 cup Yogurt, plain	1 cup buttermilk or
	1 cup sour milk

Guide to Herbs and Spices

Dried herbs and ground or whole spices should be stored in a cool, dry, dark area in air-tight containers. Fresh herbs should be stored in the refrigerator for a few days, or in the freezer for up to one year. Whole herbs and spices will retain their flavor and aroma for up to one year.

Whole herbs and spices are a better choice for long-cooking dishes and can be added at the beginning of cooking. Ground herbs and spices should be added towards the end of cooking because their flavor does not hold up as well.

Dried herbs and spices are much stronger in flavor than fresh. To substitute use three times the amount of fresh herbs as dried.

Herb or Spice	Description	Suggested Uses
allspice, whole or ground	Dried berry of the pimento tree. It has the flavor of a blend of cinnamon, nutmeg, and cloves.	pickling, spicing meats, pot roast, spiced beef, sausage, lamb, poached fish, soups, sauce, baked beans, oyster stew, fruits, squash, sweet potatoes, pudding, baked products
anise seed, whole or ground	It is a grayish brown, small, oval seed. It has a licorice flavor.	poultry, poached fish, carrots, cookies, cakes
star anise	It has a similar flavor to anise, but more pungent. It is an ingredient of Chinese five-spice powder.	Chinese cooking and Malaysian curries
basil, dried leaf or ground	It is a member of the mint family. The leaf color ranges from bright green to dark purple. Sweet basil is the most common variety used in this country. The flavor is sweet and warm with a pungent overtone.	omelets, cheese spreads, roasted meat and poultry, stews, soups, fish, sauces, pasta, green salads, salad dressings, vegetables
bay leaf, whole or ground	The leaves are a yellow-olive green about 1 to 3 inches in length. The flavor is strong and distinctive and mellows in long cooking dishes. One leaf per liquid gallon is adequate.	meats, poultry, and fish soup, stews, aspics, pickles, marinades, tomato dishes, rice
bouquet garni	A variety of herbs tied together in a piece of cheese cloth or with just a string. Parsley branches, bay leaf and celery stalk top is an example of a bouquet garni.	used to flavor sauces, soups, stews and stocks
caraway seed	It is a brown, hard seed with a pleasant, sweet, and slightly sharp taste.	cheese spreads, pot roast, stews, salads, apples, beets, cabbage, rye bread, biscuits, cookies, cakes, pastry, candy

Herb or Spice	Description	Suggested Uses
cardamom, ground	It is a member of the ginger family. Produces an irregular round seed. The flavor is sweet and highly aromatic.	pickling, coffee cakes, danish pastry, curries, soups
cassia buds (Chinese cinnamon)	It has a pungent cinnamon flavor. It is the ripe or immature fruit of the cassia plant.	pickling, stewed fruits, beverages, baked products, mincemeat
celery seeds, flakes, salt	The seeds are a small, round pellet, light brown or tan in color. The taste is similar to that of celery. Celery salt is ground seed and salt.	pickling, cheese spreads, eggs, meat, poultry, soups, stuffing, salads, salad dressings, potatoes, rice
chervil, dried	An aromatic herb with a delicate flavor, similar to tarragon.	french cooking, soups, salads, sauces, eggs, stuffing
chili powder	It is a blend of ground cumin, chili pepper, red pepper, ground oregano, ground garlic powder, ground cloves, ground allspice, and ground dried onions. Different brands vary in flavor and degree of hotness.	cheese, eggs, pot roast, chili, mexican dishes, meat sauces, dips, rice
chinese five-spice powder	It is a blend of anise pepper, star anise, cassia or cinnamon, cloves, and fennel seeds. It is aromatic with a licorice flavor.	Chinese and Southeast Asian dishes
chives	It has a delicate onion flavor.	garnish, cheese spreads, cream sauces, potato salad
cinnamon, ground or sticks	A sweet and pungent spice.	ham glaze, pork roast, pot roast, apples, peaches, squash, beverages, baked products, puddings
cloves, whole or ground	The aroma is pungent and sweet and the flavor is strong and sweet.	pickling, pork, lamb, beef stew, fish, marinades, squash, sweet potatoes, bread, cookies, fruitcake, gingerbread
coriander, fresh (cilantro), seed, ground	The seeds are small with a color ranging from white through orange to a yellowish brown and a shape that shows alternating straight and wavy edges. The flavor is pleasant, mild, distinctive, and slightly citrus.	curries, baked products mexican dishes, chili, dips, salsa
cumin, seed or ground	The seed is yellow-brown, oval and thin, about 1/8 inch long. The flavor is strong, pungent, and somewhat sweet. It is found in chili powder and curry powder.	meats, sausage, pickles, chili, curries, stews
curry powder	This is a blend of spices including ginger, fenugreek, cayenne, tumeric, coriander, and cumin. It has a sweet mild flavor and is deep yellow in color.	Indian cooking, eggs, cheese spread, beef, pork, lamb, veal, chicken, fish, mulligatawny soup, tomatoes, carrots, rice
dill seed or weed	It is a small, ovular shaped, tan seed. It has a mellow, sweet, weedy flavor.	pickles, cheese spreads, lamb chops, meat, fish, sauces, salads, cabbage, cauliflower, green beans
fennel seed, whole, or ground	It is a small, oval seed with a yellowish brown color. It has an aromatic sweet taste resembling anise.	Italian and Swedish dishes, sweet pickles

Herb or Spice	Description	Suggested Uses
fenugreek, whole or ground	It is a small, oval seed with a yellowish brown color. It has a distinctive, pleasant, slightly bitter flavor.	Indian cookery, salads, salad dressings, stuffing
garlic powder or salt	It is ground dehydrated garlic. Garlic salt is a combination of powder and salt.	meats, poultry, soups, salads, salad dressings, gravy
ginger, ground, whole and fresh, candied, pickled	It has a pungent sweet aroma and spicy flavor.	chutney, meat, fish, poultry, Chinese dishes, apples, pears, figs, carrots, sweet potatoes, baked products, gingerbread
mace, ground	It is the skin of a seed from the nutmeg tree. It has a similar aroma and flavor to nutmeg, but more delicate.	eggnog, pot roast, lamb, sausage, poultry, goulash, carrots, cauliflower, cakes, pies, custard
marjoram, dried or whole	The leaves are gray-green with a distinct aromatic and slightly bitter flavor similar to oregano.	souffles, meats, sausage, poultry, fish, soups, stews, stuffing, tomato dishes, vegetables
mint leaves, whole or crushed	It has a strong, sweet, tangy, cool flavor.	lamb, veal, iced tea, sauces, carrots, peas
mustard, seed or ground	There are two main varieties: yellow and brown or white. It has a hot, sharp, pungent flavor with a bite. Prepared mustard is a paste made from mustard and tumeric.	meat, poultry, eggs, salad dressings, sauces
nutmeg, ground	It has a sweet, warm, spicy flavor.	eggnog, custards, meatballs, veal, chicken, sausage, fish, carrots, spinach, sweet potatoes, baked products
onion powder and salt	Onion powder is ground dried onions. Onion salt is a combination of powder and salt.	meats, poultry, soups, salad dressings, gravy
oregano, ground or leaf (Mexican Sage)	The leaves are light green in color. It is strong and aromatic, with an assertive, pleasantly pungent flavor.	cheese spreads, omelets, meatloaf, pork, veal, lamb, poultry, seafood, stuffing, soups, stews, pizza, pasta sauces, tomatoes, vegetables
paprika	Its flavor ranges from mild, pleasant, delicately sweet to hot with a slight bite. Store in the refrigerator.	poached eggs, veal, chicken, fish, salad dressing, asparagus, spinach, garnish
parsley flakes	There are three main types: curly, Italian, and Chinese. Curly-leaf has a mild flavor and is used as a garnish. Italian is mostly used as a seasoning. Parsley has a sweet, aromatic, delicate flavor with a soft bit of spice.	French cooking, eggs, cheese, meat, poultry, fish, soups, stews, vegetables, rice
pepper, black; whole or cracked peppercorn, or ground	Comes from a small, dark brown, dry berry. Ground pepper shows both the light and dark portions of the berry. Black pepper has a more penetrating odor and a more pungent taste than white pepper.	eggs, meat, poultry, fish, stuffing, vegetables, sauces, dough with meat fillings
pepper, cayenne or red; ground, chopped or whole	It is made from dried, ripe, hot chili peppers. The flavor is hot and pungent.	meats, fish, stews, sauces, mexican dishes, corn, onions

Herb or Spice	Description	Suggested Uses
pepper, white; ground	White pepper is the inner part of the berry. It is milder in flavor and less aromatic than black pepper.	eggs, meat, poultry, fish, stuffing, vegetables, cream sauces
peppercorn, green	They are pepper berries that have not been dried. They are freeze-dried or packed in brine or water. The flavor is fresh and pungent.	roasted meats, poultry, cream sauces
peppercorn, szechwan (anise pepper)	It is a dried reddish-brown berry. It has a slightly anise like flavor and aroma, and a mild peppery taste. It is one of the ingredients of Chinese five-spice powder.	Chinese and Japanese cooking
pickling spice	It is made up of a number of mixed spices, such as bay leaf, cinnamon, cloves, cardamon, and peppers.	pickling, relishes, pot roast
poppy seed	It is round, tiny, and blue-gray in color. It has a nutlike flavor.	cheese and egg dishes, creamed soups, stuffing, fish, baked products, fruit salad dressings, noodles, sweet roll fillings
poultry seasoning	A ground blend of sage, thyme, marjoram, and savory. Some varieties may contain rosemary or other spices.	poultry, meat, fish
pumpkin pie spice	A blend of cinnamon, cloves, ginger, and nutmeg or mace.	baked desserts, custards, mashed root vegetables
rosemary, dried	It has a curved and crescent-shaped leaf. The flavor is fresh, distinctive, and sweet with a tea-like aroma.	omelets, roasted meat, roasted poultry, fish, soups, stews, vegetables, fruit cups, garnish
saffron	It has a pleasantly bitter, mildly distinctive flavor and gives a rich, yellow or orange color to foods.	Spanish and Cuban cooking, veal, poultry, creamed fish, soups, sauces, rice
sage, leaf or ground	It is a grayish-green leaf. It has a mild delicate flavor, somewhat astringent and bitter.	cheeses, meats, sausages, poultry, fish, stuffing, chowders, eggplant, lima beans, tomatoes
savory, whole or ground	The leaves are small, brown-green in color, and have a distinctively warm aroma and slightly resinous flavor.	eggs, meats, poultry, fish, soups, stews, sauces, green vegetable salads, cabbage, carrots, tomatoes, rice
sesame seed (benne)	The seed has a mild, sweet, nut flavor. Should be stored in the refrigerator or freezer.	cheese and egg dishes, creamed soups, stuffing, fish, breads, rolls, salads, Asian cooking
tarragon, whole or ground	It has a delicate flavor resembling anise.	French cooking, eggs, poultry, seafood, asparagus, beans, beets, tomatoes, green salads, salad dressings
thyme, leaf or ground	It is brownish-green with a distinctively warm, aromatic, and pungent flavor.	eggs, cheese, meat, poultry, fish, stuffing, soups, stews, sauces, vegetables
tumeric, whole or ground	It is bright yellow in color. The flavor is distinctive, slightly bitter with a pepper-like aroma.	coloring for condiments and mustard

Garnishing Ideas

Attractive presentation makes all the difference to good food. A dish that looks beautiful will taste even better. A garnish should enhance the appearance of a dish and at the same time complement its color, taste, and texture.

In planning garnishes, consider the color and ease of preparation. Using more than one food item can add interest to a garnish. The key to successful garnishing is simplicity.

Foods	Garnishes
	Fruits
apple	rings, wedges, tidbits, swan, cup, wings, stuffed with cranberries, slices with cinnamon
apricot	halves, dried, rose
avocado	slices, halves, fans
banana	slices, split in half, boat
berries: blueberries, raspberries, strawberries	whole
cherries, maraschino: red or green	whole, half
citrus: orange, grapefruit, lemon, lime	sections, cartwheel
citrus peel	rose, twists, basket, gelatin in peel
cranberries	whole or sauce
dates	whole
grapes	whole, frosted
kiwi fruit	slices, coronet
melon: cantaloupe, honeydew, watermelon	balls, wedges, gelatin in melon wedge
peach	slices, halves, diced, spiced, stuffed
pear	slices, halves, wedges, stuffed
pineapple	slices, chunks, boat
plums, red or green	whole, slices
prunes	whole, spiced
raisins or currants	whole
	Vegetables & Herbs
beets	rose, slices
broccoli	flower
cabbage, red	strips, flower
carrot	blossoms, curls, flower, slices
cauliflower	flower
celery	sticks, flower, stuffed
cucumber	rings, strips, wedges, cups, slices, rose, scored and sliced, stuffed

Foods	Garnishes
dill, fresh	leaves
endive	leaves
lettuce	leaves
mint	leaves
mushrooms	grooved caps, slices, stuffed caps
olives, green or black	whole, slices, stuffed
onions, green or white	slices, flower
parsley	leaves, flakes
pepper (green, red, or yellow)	flower, rings, stuffed, cut out shapes
pickle	slices, cut in half
pimento	slices
potatoes	stuffed, duchess, rose
radish	slices, rose, blossom, butterfly, basket
spinach	leaves
tomato	slices, rose, flower, butterfly, basket
turnip	blossom, flower
zucchini	scored and slices, sticks, half slices, wedges, coronet, balls

Nuts & Seeds	
almonds, cashews, peanuts, pecans, pistachios, walnuts	roasted whole, raw whole, halves, chopped, slivered
seeds: poppy, sesame, sunflower	whole

More Garnishing Ideas

Sweets

candy corn, multicolored gum drops, jelly beans, M & M's candies, red hots

chocolate: chips, shavings, sprinkles, special molds

gelatin: flavored or multicolored cubes, diced, molds

jams and jellies

marshmallows, miniature: multicolored or white

mints, party: colored, flavored

peanut brittle, crushed

sprinkles: singular color or multicolored

sugar, powdered, granulated, brown: multicolored or white

whipped toppings

Miscellaneous

bacon: crumbles, strips

capers

caviar

cheese (hard): grated, strips, balls, cubes, triangles, nut covered

coconut: multicolored, shredded, toasted

cream cheese: balls or molded

croutons

eggs: hard-cooked, halves, sections, stuffed halves, deviled halves, grated yolk

flowers: daisies, dandelion, geranium, marigold, pansies, rose petals, violets

seasonings: cinnamon, paprika, parsley

Resources

Biller, Rudolf. *Garnishing and Decoration.* United Kingdom: Virtue and Co. Ltd., 1992.

Rosen, Harvey. *How to Garnish.* Elberon, N.J.: International Culinary Consultants, 1983.

Stachowiak, Yvette. *The Creative Art of Garnishing.* London: Salamander Books Ltd., 1990.

Nutrient Analysis of Menus

This section provides the nutrient analysis of the menus contained in the book. The analyses included are the following:

1. Four Week Cycle Non-Selective Menu for Health Care Facilities. The analysis of the menus for individuals with special needs was not provided separately, but can be cross referenced with the diets for the Health Care Facilities.
2. Vegetarian menu
3. Senior Citizen Nutrition Program
4. Special Holidays and Themes

The nutrients included in the analysis are the following:

KCAL	kcalories
PROT	protein
CHO	carbohydrates
FAT	fat
CHOL	cholesterol
SFA	saturated fatty acids
PFA	polyunsaturated fatty acids
VITA	vitamin A
VITC	vitamin C
THI*	thiamin
RIB*	riboflavin
NIA*	niacin
B-12*	vitamin B12
Ca	calcium
P	phosphorus
Na	sodium
K+	potassium
Fe	iron

*An analysis of those nutrients starred (*) is not available for all food items listed on the menu. Therefore, the actual total for these nutrients may be higher then what has been calculated.

The diabetic exchange was calculated by the exact nutrition information provided by the computer on protein, carbohydrate and fat content of individual food items. The lean meat exchange is used, therefore the fat exchange may reflect a higher fat value.

Nutrition Analysis Resources

USDA Handbook No. 8

USDA Handbook 456

Pennington & Church. *Food Values of Portions Commonly Used.* 15th Edition, 1989

Manufacturer's Product Information

Exchange Lists For Meal Planning. American Diabetes Association, Inc. and The American Dietetic Association, 1986. ANO 1995.

Practocare Nutriplanner, San Diego, Ca.

NUTRIENT ANALYSIS: Week One, Monday

RDA/ESA: MALE 51+	KCAL	PROT gm range	CHO gm none	FAT gm none	CHOL mg none	SFA gm none	PFA gm none	VITA IU 5000	VITC mg 60	THI* mg 1.2	RIB* mg 1.4	NIA* mg 15	B-12* mcg 2.0	Ca mg 800	P mg 800	Na mg range	K mg range	Fe mg 10
Regular, Liberal Bland, and No Added Salt																		
Totals	2233.2	94.4	258.3	98.5	524.1	29.6	23.8	8999	167.8	2.1	2.1	21.4	5.5	1039	1621	2449	3944	21.0
1–2 gm Na (Low Sodium)																		
Totals	2307.8	95.2	256.2	107.4	539.5	33.0	24.8	9014	149.8	2.0	2.2	20.8	5.5	1036	1583	1391	3903	20.8
Mechanical Soft																		
Totals	2020.2	100.6	239.4	78.5	511.9	24.8	16.8	9875	177.7	2.1	2.1	20.2	6.3	1018	1641	2352	4239	21.4
Puree																		
Totals	2074.2	101.2	255.6	77.0	511.9	25.0	16.9	9848	150.3	2.1	2.2	24.2	6.3	974.4	1661	2227	4514	21.4
Soft, Low Fiber																		
Totals	1970.8	92.9	240.8	74.6	480.2	23.9	15.9	9158	150.9	2.2	2.3	22.4	5.5	1115	1461	2409	4181	21.2
Low Fat, Low Cholesterol																		
Totals	1926.0	104.7	289.9	43.9	145.1	10.1	10.0	8777	171.6	2.3	2.4	22.4	5.6	1293	1814	2599	4696	23.1
No Concentrated Sweets																		
Totals	1857.1	112.3	243.6	52.8	449.9	13.2	11.0	8501	174.1	2.3	2.2	25.1	6.7	1285	1999	2773	4472	23.9

DIET	KCAL	PROT GM	CHO GM	FAT GM	KCAL DISTRIBUTIONS: Pro%	CHO%	Fat%	Milk EXG	Frt EXG	Veg EXG	Brd EXG	Meat EXG	Fat EXG
No Concentrated Sweets													
Totals	1857.1	112.4	243.6	52.8	23.6	51.3	25.1	2.7	3.2	3.6	9.2	7.2	5.9
1200 Calorie													
Totals	1213.6	79.6	152.8	33.7	26.2	50.3	25.0	2.1	2.8	2.7	4.4	5.7	3.5
1500 Calorie													
Totals	1511.8	100.8	188.7	42.4	26.6	49.9	25.2	2.1	2.8	2.7	6.7	7.7	3.8
1800 Calorie													
Totals	1801.9	108.4	224.4	56.6	24.0	49.8	28.3	2.1	3.2	3.2	8.4	8.0	6.2
2000 Calorie													
Totals	1991.0	125.2	245.6	61.1	25.1	49.3	27.6	2.6	3.2	3.2	9.4	9.0	6.4

NUTRIENT ANALYSIS: Week One, Tuesday

RDA/ESA: MALE 51+	KCAL range	PROT gm range	CHO gm none	FAT gm none	CHOL mg none	SFA gm none	PFA gm none	VITA IU 5000	VITC mg 60	THI* mg 1.2	RIB* mg 1.4	NIA* mg 15	B-12* mcg 2.0	Ca mg 800	P mg 800	Na mg range	K mg range	Fe mg 10
Regular, Liberal Bland, and no Added Salt																		
Totals	2292.4	97.7	253.5	101.9	570.2	37.7	14.7	6243	185.8	1.5	2.5	23.0	5.3	1388	1629	2497	3940	21.1
1–2 gm Na (Low Sodium)																		
Totals	2172.9	94.9	239.3	96.2	551.7	33.0	13.6	5974	183.7	1.5	2.4	22.6	5.0	1317	1422	1711	3601	20.8
Mechanical Soft																		
Totals	2211.9	95.2	237.7	100.8	569.6	37.8	14.4	5243	175.8	1.4	2.4	21.8	5.3	1307	1547	2241	3596	20.0
Puree																		
Totals	2372.6	103.4	249.7	109.6	615.0	40.0	16.4	5856	179.3	1.4	2.5	24.8	5.4	1324	1685	2276	3860	21.6
Soft, Low Fiber																		
Totals	2144.7	92.2	224.7	100.3	569.6	37.9	14.5	5112	170.2	1.3	2.4	21.0	5.3	1323	1534	1933	3799	19.9
Low Fat, Low Cholesterol																		
Totals	1935.6	104.9	281.7	46.2	154.8	12.3	8.6	7804	185.8	1.6	2.8	21.8	5.7	1662	1871	2580	4530	21.5
No Concentrated Sweets																		
Totals	1922.7	120.0	228.3	60.0	442.2	17.2	9.6	5934	134.9	1.5	2.7	28.5	6.7	1576	1944	2606	4356	23.4

DIET	KCAL	PROT GM	CHO GM	FAT GM	KCAL DISTRIBUTIONS: Pro%	CHO%	Fat%	Milk EXG	Frt EXG	Veg EXG	Brd EXG	Meat EXG	Fat EXG
No Concentrated Sweets													
Totals	1922.7	120.0	228.4	60.0	24.9	47.5	28.1	3.6	3.0	3.5	8.3	8.0	6.9
1200 Calorie													
Totals	1198.6	75.6	159.6	29.8	25.2	53.2	22.4	2.7	3.0	3.5	4.4	4.4	3.0
1500 Calorie													
Totals	1515.3	96.1	190.7	41.9	25.3	50.3	24.8	2.7	3.0	3.5	6.4	6.4	4.3
1800 Calorie													
Totals	1794.4	108.0	221.6	54.3	24.0	49.4	27.2	3.0	3.0	3.5	8.3	7.0	6.1
2000 Calorie													
Totals	1990.2	123.7	250.6	56.4	24.8	50.3	25.5	3.5	3.0	3.5	9.7	8.0	6.1

NUTRIENT ANALYSIS: Week One, Wednesday

	KCAL	PROT gm	CHO gm	FAT gm	CHOL mg	SFA gm	PFA gm	VITA IU	VITC mg	THI* mg	RIB* mg	NIA* mg	B-12* mcg	Ca mg	P mg	Na mg	K mg	Fe mg
RDA/ESA: MALE 51+	range	range	none	none	none	none	none	5000	60	1.2	1.4	15	2.0	800	800	range	range	10
Regular, Liberal Bland, and no Added Salt																		
Totals	2120.1	96.1	217.2	101.1	353.1	22.1	22.2	6725	76.2	1.4	2.0	20.8	4.2	878.8	1454	2062	3744	14.8
1–2 gm Na (Low Sodium)																		
Totals	2054.6	94.2	209.9	97.8	359.1	21.6	20.6	6617	78.8	1.4	2.0	19.9	3.7	864.1	1413	1542	3711	14.6
Mechanical Soft																		
Totals	2048.0	95.7	229.3	87.6	353.1	20.4	14.2	5259	69.6	1.4	2.1	20.8	4.2	874.8	1449	1978	3793	14.9
Puree																		
Totals	2165.3	96.7	287.7	73.4	349.6	20.4	8.5	5201	72.7	1.2	2.1	21.3	4.2	865.5	1423	1830	4071	14.9
Soft, Low Fiber																		
Totals	2080.6	95.0	256.6	79.1	347.9	19.5	8.4	5172	64.9	1.4	2.1	20.8	4.2	867.5	1438	1915	3792	15.1
Low Fat, Low Cholesterol																		
Totals	1924.3	98.4	293.5	44.2	30.9	9.1	11.9	6336	84.9	1.3	1.9	23.5	4.5	957.7	1582	2588	3577	15.1
No Concentrated Sweets																		
Totals	1920.6	115.1	230.3	63.0	321.8	14.2	12.6	5100	83.0	1.5	2.3	27.5	6.0	1103	1802	2727	3590	14.7

DIET	KCAL	PROT GM	CHO GM	FAT GM	KCAL DISTRIBUTIONS: Pro%	CHO%	Fat%	Milk EXG	Frt EXG	Veg EXG	Brd EXG	Meat EXG	Fat EXG
No Concentrated Sweets													
Totals	1920.6	115.1	230.3	63.0	23.9	47.9	29.5	3.0	3.2	3.8	7.7	7.7	8.4
1200 Calorie													
Totals	1204.3	81.0	149.2	33.2	26.9	49.6	24.8	2.5	2.9	3.8	3.1	5.7	3.7
1500 Calorie													
Totals	1520.7	103.5	184.1	43.4	27.2	48.4	25.7	2.5	2.9	4.8	5.1	7.5	4.6
1800 Calorie													
Totals	1788.5	107.5	204.5	63.2	24.0	45.7	31.7	2.5	2.9	4.8	6.4	7.5	8.3
2000 Calorie													
Totals	1975.1	120.5	222.5	70.0	24.4	45.1	31.9	3.0	3.2	5.8	6.6	8.4	9.1

RDA/ESA: MALE 51+	KCAL range	PROT gm range	CHO gm none	FAT gm none	CHOL mg none	SFA gm none	PFA gm none	VITA IU 5000	VITC mg 60	THI* mg 1.2	RIB* mg 1.4	NIA* mg 15	B-12* mcg 2.0	Ca mg 800	P mg 800	Na mg range	K mg range	Fe mg 10
Regular, Liberal Bland, and no Added Salt																		
Totals	2260.0	91.9	226.6	114.8	346.8	36.9	26.7	13247	78.8	1.4	2.2	17.5	3.5	1488	1751	2741	3673	15.8
1–2 gm Na (Low Sodium)																		
Totals	2152.9	84.8	235.0	102.4	720.4	27.0	27.7	8089	71.9	1.5	3.0	16.7	3.6	1219	1477	1529	3685	16.6
Mechanical Soft																		
Totals	2162.5	91.2	266.6	86.3	334.8	33.1	10.7	10912	67.8	1.4	2.1	17.8	3.5	1466	1763	2580	3860	16.1
Puree																		
Totals	2204.0	102.1	286.1	77.4	323.2	30.3	9.9	10654	71.1	1.4	2.2	17.8	4.1	1335	1811	2969	3955	15.8
Soft, Low Fiber																		
Totals	2108.4	92.1	260.9	81.8	334.0	32.5	9.5	10735	63.3	1.3	2.1	17.9	3.6	1451	1774	3058	3526	15.4
Low Fat, Low Cholesterol																		
Totals	1934.7	89.6	300.7	47.9	193.4	13.0	6.4	16076	124.7	1.5	3.0	16.7	3.0	1546	1652	2223	4483	17.6
No Concentrated Sweets																		
Totals	1951.1	111.9	232.4	69.3	279.1	18.8	11.2	16765	121.4	1.5	3.2	20.5	3.9	1768	1922	2609	4638	17.6

DIET	KCAL	PROT GM	CHO GM	FAT GM	KCAL DISTRIBUTIONS: Pro%	CHO%	Fat%	Milk EXG	Frt EXG	Veg EXG	Brd EXG	Meat EXG	Fat EXG
No Concentrated Sweets													
Totals	1951.1	111.9	232.4	69.3	22.9	47.6	31.9	2.7	3.5	4.0	8.4	7.4	8.5
1200 Calorie													
Totals	1202.3	72.4	148.1	39.0	24.0	49.2	29.2	2.1	2.4	3.0	4.8	4.6	4.1
1500 Calorie													
Totals	1506.1	91.0	171.9	54.7	24.1	45.7	32.6	2.1	2.7	4.0	5.5	6.5	6.3
1800 Calorie													
Totals	1781.2	98.7	222.4	60.3	22.1	49.9	30.5	2.1	2.7	4.0	8.9	6.5	7.1
2000 Calorie													
Totals	1998.4	113.9	242.4	69.1	22.8	48.5	31.1	2.7	2.7	4.0	9.8	7.2	8.5

NUTRIENT ANALYSIS: Week One, Friday

RDA/ESA: MALE 51+	KCAL range	PROT gm range	CHO gm none	FAT gm none	CHOL mg none	SFA gm none	PFA gm none	VITA IU 5000	VITC mg 60	THI* mg 1.2	RIB* mg 1.4	NIA* mg 15	B-12* mcg 2.0	Ca mg 800	P mg 800	Na mg range	K mg range	Fe mg 10
Regular, Liberal Bland, and no Added Salt																		
Totals	2725.9	105.1	305.9	123.7	807.3	33.6	27.7	10477	134.9	1.6	2.2	25.1	5.4	1035	1895	2415	4111	23.5
1–2 gm Na (Low Sodium)																		
Totals	2511.7	116.0	289.4	102.0	731.6	28.2	18.9	12074	135.1	1.5	2.1	28.3	4.6	1127	2067	1541	4259	24.0
Mechanical Soft																		
Totals	2445.2	102.7	279.9	105.0	771.8	29.9	21.8	9719	106.7	1.4	2.1	23.5	5.2	1004	1741	2134	3969	21.9
Puree																		
Totals	2452.1	101.1	285.3	105.4	771.1	29.9	21.9	9825	115.9	1.4	2.1	23.9	5.2	948.9	1718	1941	4402	22.0
Soft, Low Fiber																		
Totals	2432.8	101.4	300.4	95.3	768.2	28.2	20.5	8669	94.4	1.2	2.0	23.1	5.2	989.5	1752	2042	3989	21.6
Low Fat, Low Cholesterol																		
Totals	1926.2	103.0	306.6	34.3	158.6	6.6	7.2	10886	107.6	1.4	1.9	23.7	3.8	1202	1848	1557	4345	22.3
No Concentrated Sweets																		
Totals	1976.9	120.0	263.0	49.4	626.4	10.3	8.6	10084	107.3	1.3	1.9	28.9	5.2	1209	2055	1722	4267	22.4

DIET	KCAL	PROT GM	CHO GM	FAT GM	KCAL DISTRIBUTIONS: Pro%	CHO%	Fat%	Milk EXG	Frt EXG	Veg EXG	Brd EXG	Meat EXG	Fat EXG
No Concentrated Sweets													
Totals	1976.9	120.0	263.0	49.4	24.2	53.2	22.4	2.7	5.4	2.3	9.1	8.4	5.3
1200 Calorie													
Totals	1224.2	78.0	171.2	25.4	25.5	55.9	18.7	2.1	4.0	2.5	4.6	5.3	2.3
1500 Calorie													
Totals	1496.5	101.2	200.2	31.2	27.0	53.5	18.7	2.1	4.0	2.6	6.6	7.3	2.7
1800 Calorie													
Totals	1799.7	108.6	241.9	44.5	24.1	53.7	22.2	2.1	4.5	2.6	9.0	7.3	5.0
2000 Calorie													
Totals	1997.1	123.9	263.7	50.1	24.8	52.8	22.5	2.6	4.5	2.6	10.1	8.5	5.3

APPENDIX 9

NUTRIENT ANALYSIS: Week One, Saturday

RDA/ESA: MALE 51+	KCAL range	PROT gm range	CHO gm none	FAT gm none	CHOL mg none	SFA gm none	PFA gm none	VITA IU 5000	VITC mg 60	THI* mg 1.2	RIB* mg 1.4	NIA* mg 15	B-12* mcg 2.0	Ca mg 800	P mg 800	Na mg range	K mg range	Fe mg 10
Regular, Liberal Bland, and no Added Salt																		
Totals	2289.0	103.7	232.5	108.1	663.7	34.7	16.8	9457	99.5	1.3	2.2	17.0	6.5	1273	1840	1981	3899	17.9
1–2 gm Na (Low Sodium)																		
Totals	2119.4	104.1	231.2	89.2	654.0	27.7	8.2	9060	97.8	1.3	2.2	16.0	6.2	1296	1624	1650	3837	17.6
Mechanical Soft																		
Totals	2339.6	107.5	272.4	93.8	639.8	27.0	16.2	9315	110.2	1.4	2.2	17.9	6.2	1320	1663	2036	4106	18.7
Puree																		
Totals	2403.0	118.9	307.4	81.0	681.8	28.9	9.0	9195	118.0	1.4	2.2	20.8	6.8	1122	1882	1444	4747	20.9
Soft, Low Fiber																		
Totals	2308.7	101.7	270.3	93.7	638.5	27.2	16.2	8130	109.1	1.2	2.1	17.5	6.1	1286	1561	2911	3927	16.9
Low Fat, Low Cholesterol																		
Totals	1982.5	104.2	298.9	44.3	124.5	10.2	7.6	10898	103.2	1.5	2.1	16.8	4.5	1404	1694	1806	4131	18.6
No Concentrated Sweets																		
Totals	1908.4	123.2	218.1	62.1	563.8	14.9	8.6	9788	63.2	1.3	2.2	18.4	6.4	1767	1959	2168	4155	18.7

DIET	KCAL	PROT GM	CHO GM	FAT GM	KCAL DISTRIBUTIONS: Pro%	CHO%	Fat%	Milk EXG	Frt EXG	Veg EXG	Brd EXG	Meat EXG	Fat EXG
No Concentrated Sweets													
Totals	1908.4	123.2	218.1	62.1	25.8	45.7	29.3	2.7	1.5	2.0	10.0	8.5	6.7
1200 Calorie													
Totals	1206.4	78.9	150.8	32.5	26.1	50.0	24.2	1.95	1.5	2.0	6.1	4.9	3.2
1500 Calorie													
Totals	1500.8	99.9	176.6	44.7	26.6	47.0	26.8	1.9	1.5	2.0	7.9	6.9	4.5
1800 Calorie													
Totals	1810.3	110.6	209.3	60.7	24.4	46.2	30.1	2.1	1.5	2.0	9.9	7.3	7.1
2000 Calorie													
Totals	1988.8	124.9	227.6	66.5	25.1	45.7	30.1	2.7	1.5	2.0	10.6	8.5	7.4

NUTRIENT ANALYSIS: Week One, Sunday

RDA/ESA: MALE 51+	KCAL range	PROT gm range	CHO gm none	FAT gm none	CHOL mg none	SFA gm none	PFA gm none	VITA IU 5000	VITC mg 60	THI* mg 1.2	RIB* mg 1.4	NIA* mg 15	B-12* mcg 2.0	Ca mg 800	P mg 800	Na mg range	K mg range	Fe mg 10
Regular, Liberal Bland, and No Added Salt																		
Totals	2305.9	102.3	264.7	94.7	604.4	30.4	19.5	6901	112.1	2.1	2.5	27.9	7.9	1179	1560	3582	4005	17.3
1–2 GM NA (Low Sodium)																		
Totals	2285.2	102.3	261.7	93.9	596.2	28.7	21.4	6839	109.2	2.1	2.4	27.6	7.7	1184	1506	1808	3888	17.4
Mechanical Soft																		
Totals	2220.5	101.0	274.3	81.0	604.2	28.7	11.5	5187	99.2	2.0	2.4	27.5	7.9	1168	1535	3493	3941	17.0
Puree																		
Totals	1990.7	96.6	236.9	74.7	552.8	27.13	11.6	5140	106.6	1.8	2.3	26.6	7.5	1019	1427	3075	4076	15.3
Soft, Low Fiber																		
Totals	2193.1	100.8	268.5	80.7	603.5	28.6	11.4	5771	79.1	2.0	2.4	26.8	7.9	1147	1512	4296	3408	16.5
Low Fat, Low Cholesterol																		
Totals	1974.0	91.3	301.2	46.5	193.2	13.0	8.5	8086	114.2	1.9	2.2	23.0	4.8	1180	1483	3237	4129	16.8
No Concentrated Sweets																		
Totals	2076.0	116.2	230.2	76.9	669.3	21.5	13.6	7250	110.5	2.2	2.5	29.2	6.9	1316	1837	3864	4175	16.7

DIET	KCAL	PROT GM	CHO GM	FAT GM	KCAL DISTRIBUTIONS: Pro%	CHO%	Fat%	Milk EXG	Frt EXG	Veg EXG	Brd EXG	Meat EXG	Fat EXG
No Concentrated Sweets													
Totals	2076.0	116.2	230.2	76.9	22.4	44.3	33.3	3.0	3.4	2.6	8.6	7.9	10.5
1200 Calorie													
Totals	1214.4	73.1	155.4	33.2	24.0	51.2	24.6	2.1	3.3	2.5	4.3	4.7	4.2
1500 Calorie													
Totals	1514.2	91.5	178.2	47.7	24.1	47.1	28.3	2.1	3.4	2.6	5.7	6.5	6.1
1800 Calorie													
Totals	1813.8	99.7	213.5	62.9	21.9	47.1	31.2	2.4	3.4	2.6	8.0	6.5	8.7
2000 Calorie													
Totals	2002.8	114.7	222.2	72.6	22.9	44.3	32.6	3.0	3.4	2.6	8.1	7.9	9.7

APPENDIX 9

NUTRIENT ANALYSIS: Week Two, Monday

RDA/ESA: MALE 51+	KCAL range	PROT gm range	CHO gm none	FAT gm none	CHOL mg none	SFA gm none	PFA gm none	VITA IU 5000	VITC mg 60	THI* mg 1.2	RIB* mg 1.4	NIA* mg 15	B-12* mcg 2.0	Ca mg 800	P mg 800	Na mg range	K mg range	Fe mg 10
Regular, Liberal Bland, and No Added Salt																		
Totals	2393.9	94.7	256.6	113.9	768.7	34.9	25.3	13963	167.9	1.6	2.3	19.6	4.2	1253	1717	2551	4158	18.0
1-2 GM NA (Low Sodium)																		
Totals	2221.2	84.3	239.7	107.2	677.9	33.3	27.3	13945	168.3	1.6	2.2	19.2	3.8	1191	1480	1694	3930	16.6
Mechanical Soft																		
Totals	2186.3	91.6	252.9	92.0	725.6	32.2	13.1	9016	159.5	1.5	2.2	18.3	4.0	1135	1499	2032	3693	16.4
Puree																		
Totals	2277.5	94.0	283.3	90.0	576.1	33.5	14.5	9232	170.3	1.3	2.2	20.3	3.9	1071	1451	1783	4008	15.5
Soft, Low Fiber																		
Totals	2202.8	88.0	277.7	84.8	707.7	32.2	13.1	9016	159.5	1.5	2.2	18.3	4.0	1133	1432	1749	3644	16.0
Low Fat, Low Cholesterol																		
Totals	1907.9	102.1	304.5	34.9	278.4	8.8	7.5	12996	159.8	1.6	2.1	25.3	3.4	1239	1671	2296	4433	18.2
No Concentrated Sweets																		
Totals	1894.5	114.2	233.4	58.1	625.2	16.2	8.5	12637	107.4	1.5	2.3	29.5	4.5	1418	1939	2642	4471	18.1

DIET	KCAL	PROT GM	CHO GM	FAT GM	KCAL DISTRIBUTIONS: Pro%	CHO%	Fat%	Milk EXG	Frt EXG	Veg EXG	Brd EXG	Meat EXG	Fat EXG
No Concentrated Sweets													
Totals	1894.5	114.2	233.4	58.1	24.1	49.2	27.6	2.9	2.7	1.5	10.1	6.7	7.5
1200 Calorie													
Totals	1197.0	72.7	160.0	31.6	24.2	53.4	23.8	2.3	2.7	1.3	5.6	3.9	3.8
1500 Calorie													
Totals	1504.5	98.4	197.6	37.7	26.1	52.5	22.5	2.3	2.7	1.3	8.1	5.9	4.1
1800 Calorie													
Totals	1804.2	105.6	236.9	50.7	23.4	52.5	25.2	2.3	2.7	1.7	10.6	6.0	6.3
2000 Calorie													
Totals	1992.2	122.5	262.8	52.7	24.5	52.7	23.8	2.9	2.8	2.0	11.7	7.0	6.3

NUTRIENT ANALYSIS: Week Two, Tuesday

RDA/ESA: MALE 51+	KCAL range	PROT gm range	CHO gm none	FAT gm none	CHOL mg none	SFA gm none	PFA gm none	VITA IU 5000	VITC mg 60	THI* mg 1.2	RIB* mg 1.4	NIA* mg 15	B-12* mcg 2.0	Ca mg 800	P mg 800	Na mg range	K mg range	Fe mg 10
Regular, Liberal Bland, and No Added Salt																		
Totals	2277.8	97.3	275.8	91.2	438.8	30.1	17.3	10158	110.7	1.5	2.2	23.2	4.3	1018	1559	2038	4140	20.5
1–2 GM NA (Low Sodium)																		
Totals	2200.2	92.9	263.8	89.3	430.1	28.7	17.2	9640	90.7	1.5	2.0	21.5	4.0	930.1	1453	1519	3757	20.2
Mechanical Soft																		
Totals	2262.2	98.3	276.3	89.3	528.0	29.5	16.2	10037	108.6	1.5	2.0	23.3	4.3	950.2	1575	1770	4124	21.3
Puree																		
Totals	2201.9	98.3	279.2	79.1	500.1	29.1	12.2	9597	118.4	1.7	2.3	23.7	4.4	998.6	1421	1584.3	4130	20.7
Soft, Low Fiber																		
Totals	2266.3	97.3	271.2	89.9	528.0	30.1	16.2	11053	129.3	1.6	2.2	23.5	4.3	950.0	1379	1736	3946	20.9
Low Fat, Low Cholesterol																		
Totals	1917.9	92.3	303.1	41.7	148.1	12.6	8.3	11003	107.7	1.5	2.0	20.7	3.7	1011	1559	2199	4275	20.4
No Concentrated Sweets																		
Totals	2036.9	112.7	251.5	67.7	458.5	19.3	12.7	10224	109.9	1.5	2.2	24.9	4.9	1193	1860	2284	4400	21.0

DIET	KCAL	PROT GM	CHO GM	FAT GM	KCAL DISTRIBUTIONS: Pro%	CHO%	Fat%	Milk EXG	Frt EXG	Veg EXG	Brd EXG	Meat EXG	Fat EXG
No Concentrated Sweets													
Totals	2036.9	112.7	251.5	67.7	22.1	49.4	29.9	2.7	3.5	2.7	9.5	8.1	7.8
1200 Calorie													
Totals	1209.8	71.1	155.7	35.8	23.5	51.4	26.6	2.1	3.1	2.2	4.3	5.1	3.6
1500 Calorie													
Totals	1507.5	90.6	190.6	44.8	24.0	50.5	26.8	2.1	3.1	2.3	6.4	7.0	4.0
1800 Calorie													
Totals	1797.2	98.3	228.1	57.7	21.9	50.7	28.9	2.2	3.1	2.6	8.7	7.0	6.5
2000 Calorie													
Totals	2015.5	114.6	256.6	62.6	22.7	50.9	27.9	2.7	3.1	2.6	10.2	8.1	6.7

APPENDIX 9

NUTRIENT ANALYSIS: Week Two, Wednesday

RDA/ESA: MALE 51+	KCAL range	PROT gm range	CHO gm none	FAT gm none	CHOL mg none	SFA gm none	PFA gm none	VITA IU 5000	VITC mg 60	THI* mg 1.2	RIB* mg 1.4	NIA* mg 15	B-12* mcg 2.0	Ca mg 800	P mg 800	Na mg range	K mg range	Fe mg 10
Regular, Liberal Bland, and No Added Salt																		
Totals	2413.3	100.1	275.9	107.5	785.6	32.8	18.5	7972	142.6	1.5	2.5	20.0	7.4	1223	1733	2783	3643	18.5
1-2 GM NA (Low Sodium)																		
Totals	2273.2	102.3	281.1	88.5	691.5	29.4	17.8	8419	143.7	1.6	2.6	20.1	7.2	1177	1762	1540	3790	19.4
Mechanical Soft																		
Totals	2406.8	98.6	290.4	100.9	786.2	32.0	14.4	7357	99.0	1.5	2.5	20.1	7.3	1217	1760	2598	3701	17.8
Puree																		
Totals	2437.7	103.7	302.4	96.4	794.1	32.1	12.3	7350	97.9	1.5	2.5	18.8	7.7	1244	1849	2810	3686	18.2
Soft, Low Fiber																		
Totals	2355	97.6	280.3	100.5	786.1	32.0	14.5	7451	96.2	1.4	2.5	19.2	7.4	1234	1747	2277	3793	17.7
Low Fat, Low Cholesterol																		
Totals	1972.4	104.0	307.5	41.1	95.4	12.1	7.1	6917	144.8	1.5	2.1	24.3	4.3	1229	1729	2254	3796	16.8
No Concentrated Sweets																		
Totals	1979.3	113.7	252.5	61.5	505.2	16.7	11.2	7892.1	140.0	1.6	2.5	21.9	5.9	1371	1976	2208	3988	18.3

DIET	KCAL	PROT GM	CHO GM	FAT GM	KCAL DISTRIBUTIONS: Pro%	CHO%	Fat%	Milk EXG	Frt EXG	Veg EXG	Brd EXG	Meat EXG	Fat EXG
No Concentrated Sweets													
Totals	1979.3	113.7	252.5	61.6	22.9	51.0	28.0	3.5	3.4	3.2	9.1	6.7	8.1
1200 Calorie													
Totals	1208.8	69.9	169.5	30.7	23.1	56.1	22.9	2.2	3.2	1.7	5.1	4.3	3.8
1500 Calorie													
Totals	1508.9	92.2	206.3	38.4	24.4	54.6	22.9	2.7	3.2	3.2	6.7	5.6	4.3
1800 Calorie													
Totals	1814.6	98.2	241.6	55.0	21.6	53.2	27.2	2.7	3.4	3.2	8.9	5.7	7.3
2000 Calorie													
Totals	1995.8	114.1	264.5	58.3	22.8	53.0	26.3	3.2	3.4	3.2	10.1	6.7	7.3

NUTRIENT ANALYSIS: Week Two, Thursday

RDA/ESA: MALE 51+	KCAL range	PROT gm range	CHO gm none	FAT gm none	CHOL mg none	SFA gm none	PFA gm none	VITA IU 5000	VITC mg 60	THI* mg 1.2	RIB* mg 1.4	NIA* mg 15	B-12* mcg 2.0	Ca mg 800	P mg 800	Na mg range	K mg range	Fe mg 10
Regular, Liberal Bland, and No Added Salt																		
Totals	2346.7	105.6	280.0	91.2	1083	29.8	13.0	48422	178.5	1.4	4.9	28.2	73.6	949.7	1804	2008	4197	24.9
1-2 GM NA (Low Sodium)																		
Totals	2336.5	105.6	276.3	91.4	1083	29.3	12.2	49801	179.8	1.5	4.9	28.1	73.6	954.6	1784	1707	3972	25.1
Mechanical Soft																		
Totals	2356.5	108.5	297.2	80.6	922.9	27.3	9.2	48228	187.1	1.7	5.3	29.3	73.5	1209	1980	2093	4333	24.8
Puree																		
Totals	2433.7	112.3	320.9	77.4	1007.1	26.7	8.0	54466	196.1	1.6	6.0	32.3	90.6	1190	2067	1973	4428	27.1
Soft, Low Fiber																		
Totals	2232.5	103.9	288.5	72.5	906.1	24.0	7.8	47914	182.6	1.6	5.1	29.2	73.1	1050	1852	2030	4082	24.6
Low Fat, Low Cholesterol																		
Totals	1969.5	95.2	309.2	42.3	126.3	10.3	9.8	25260	141.7	1.3	2.0	17.8	4.5	1128	1614	1655	4529	15.9
No Concentrated Sweets																		
Totals	1914.9	112.4	241.3	56.6	1025	15.8	10.2	24849	169.1	1.5	5.7	34.5	103.7	1094	2011	1783	4574	24.3

DIET	KCAL	PROT GM	CHO GM	FAT GM	KCAL DISTRIBUTIONS: Pro%	CHO%	Fat%	Milk EXG	Frt EXG	Veg EXG	Brd EXG	Meat EXG	Fat EXG
No Concentrated Sweets													
Totals	1914.9	112.4	241.3	56.6	23.4	50.4	26.6	2.7	4.1	3.8	7.3	8.0	6.9
1200 Calorie													
Totals	1208.1	70.5	175.7	24.4	23.3	58.2	18.2	2.2	3.3	3.0	4.7	4.4	2.5
1500 Calorie													
Totals	1514.2	94.2	196.9	38.7	24.8	52.0	23.0	2.2	3.3	3.3	5.8	6.8	4.2
1800 Calorie													
Totals	1812.6	102.3	229.0	55.2	22.5	50.5	27.4	2.2	3.8	3.8	7.3	7.2	6.9
2000 Calorie													
Totals	2008.5	114.7	255.7	59.5	22.8	50.9	26.6	2.8	4.3	3.8	8.0	8.0	7.5

APPENDIX 9

NUTRIENT ANALYSIS: Week Two, Friday

RDA/ESA: MALE 51+	KCAL range	PROT gm range	CHO gm none	FAT gm none	CHOL mg none	SFA gm none	PFA gm none	VITA IU 5000	VITC mg 60	THI* mg 1.2	RIB* mg 1.4	NIA* mg 15	B-12* mcg 2.0	Ca mg 800	P mg 800	Na mg range	K mg range	Fe mg 10
Regular, Liberal Bland, and No Added Salt																		
Totals	2287.6	98.6	247.2	104.3	609.9	32.3	22.8	16476	131.7	1.5	2.1	20.5	4.4	1096	1680	1729	4816	19.1
1–2 GM NA (Low Sodium)																		
Totals	2288.7	98.5	247.0	104.2	609.9	32.3	22.8	16506	132.1	1.5	2.0	20.4	4.4	1093	1663	1450	4619	19.2
Mechanical Soft																		
Totals	2323.2	103.7	273.4	94.7	626.8	33.1	14.9	14919	119.9	1.6	2.2	21.2	4.8	1254	1865	1832	5034	20.0
Puree																		
Totals	2311.3	105.2	292.7	84.9	574.3	28.0	16.5	14883	117.1	1.6	2.2	20.9	4.8	1278	1941	1809	5091	19.8
Soft, Low Fiber																		
Totals	2064.0	93.1	250.5	80.0	601.7	26.1	13.3	11632	90.5	1.3	1.9	20.1	4.4	1082	1625	2293	3857	17.9
Low Fat, Low Cholesterol																		
Totals	1972.8	110.3	308.5	36.5	178.7	8.7	9.7	17823	146.8	1.6	2.1	23.4	3.8	1106	1808	1949	5646	21.2
No Concentrated Sweets																		
Totals	1967.3	120.2	264.0	50.6	629.1	13.7	11.1	18244	102.4	1.6	2.2	25.6	5.2	1266	2006	2017	5643	20.7

DIET	KCAL	PROT GM	CHO GM	FAT GM	KCAL DISTRIBUTIONS: Pro%	CHO%	Fat%	Milk EXG	Frt EXG	Veg EXG	Brd EXG	Meat EXG	Fat EXG
No Concentrated Sweets													
Totals	1967.3	120.2	264.0	50.6	24.4	53.6	23.1	2.8	3.3	4.4	9.8	7.2	6.7
1200 Calorie													
Totals	1199.0	82.3	168.7	23.8	27.4	56.2	17.9	2.1	2.6	4.3	5.2	4.5	2.6
1500 Calorie													
Totals	1495.5	100.3	206.6	32.0	26.8	55.2	19.2	2.2	2.8	4.4	7.1	6.2	3.6
1800 Calorie													
Totals	1795.2	106.7	238.2	49.2	23.8	53.0	24.6	2.2	2.8	4.4	9.2	6.2	6.8
2000 Calorie													
Totals	2006.8	122.2	271.2	51.5	24.3	54.0	23.1	2.8	3.3	4.4	10.3	7.2	6.7

NUTRIENT ANALYSIS: Week Two, Saturday

RDA/ESA: MALE 51+	KCAL range	PROT gm range	CHO gm none	FAT gm none	CHOL mg none	SFA gm none	PFA gm none	VITA IU 5000	VITC mg 60	THI* mg 1.2	RIB* mg 1.4	NIA* mg 15	B-12* mcg 2.0	Ca mg 800	P mg 800	Na mg range	K mg range	Fe mg 10
Regular, Liberal Bland, and No Added Salt																		
Totals	2421.2	97.0	305.8	95.6	543.3	37.9	12.1	24742	146.1	2.1	2.5	18.5	4.2	1477	1816	1970	4414	16.8
1–2 GM NA (Low Sodium)																		
Totals	2344.6	98.5	305.2	87.1	485.9	26.5	11.6	24943	147.7	2.1	4.3	18.3	3.7	1497	1531	1693	4342	16.2
Mechanical Soft																		
Totals	2308.8	96.7	287.0	91.4	512.1	37.8	11.1	24491	101.6	2.0	2.5	18.5	4.1	1450	1906	1801	4324	17.0
Puree																		
Totals	2420.5	98.6	314.5	91.3	512.1	37.7	11.0	24403	89.6	2.0	2.4	18.9	4.1	1462	1982	1828	4310	18.7
Soft, Low Fiber																		
Totals	2276.4	92.1	284.7	90.1	512.1	37.6	10.7	43509	83.4	1.9	2.3	17.3	4.1	1465	1819	1862	3997	17.0
Low Fat, Low Cholesterol																		
Totals	1967.6	96.8	300.2	47.8	118.0	10.8	9.1	26294	146.0	1.9	2.3	17.4	3.1	1509	1594	2808	4562	17.5
No Concentrated Sweets																		
Totals	2125.7	110.1	270.9	71.6	463.0	19.6	11.3	24908	142.2	2.3	2.5	19.8	4.4	1663	1833	2916	4551	16.5

DIET	KCAL	PROT GM	CHO GM	FAT GM	KCAL DISTRIBUTIONS: Pro%	CHO%	Fat%	Milk EXG	Frt EXG	Veg EXG	Brd EXG	Meat EXG	Fat EXG
No Concentrated Sweets													
Totals	2125.7	110.1	270.9	71.6	20.7	50.9	30.3	3.2	3.4	3.0	10.3	7.4	9.2
1200 Calorie													
Totals	1213.2	65.8	171.9	32.2	21.6	56.6	23.9	2.2	2.9	1.6	5.9	3.9	3.6
1500 Calorie													
Totals	1512.7	84.0	194.7	47.2	22.2	51.4	28.1	2.3	2.9	3.0	6.5	6.1	5.7
1800 Calorie													
Totals	1811.3	95.5	242.3	55.6	21.1	53.5	27.6	2.6	3.4	3.0	8.8	6.4	6.8
2000 Calorie													
Totals	2006.9	108.8	259.5	63.8	21.6	51.7	28.6	3.2	3.4	3.0	9.6	7.4	7.7

NUTRIENT ANALYSIS: Week Two, Sunday

RDA/ESA: MALE 51+	KCAL	PROT gm range	CHO gm none	FAT gm none	CHOL mg none	SFA gm none	PFA gm none	VITA IU 5000	VITC mg 60	THI* mg 1.2	RIB* mg 1.4	NIA* mg 15	B-12* mcg 2.0	Ca mg 800	P mg 800	Na mg range	K mg range	Fe mg 10
Regular, Liberal Bland, and No Added Salt																		
Totals	2309.1	108.3	278.0	93.9	606.8	28.8	17.6	5513	117.1	1.3	2.1	18.6	4.7	1225	1711	1591	4273	16.6
1-2 gm Na (Low Sodium)																		
Totals	2281.7	108.2	277.4	79.7	599.2	27.1	17.2	5677	113.5	1.4	2.3	18.6	4.9	1336	1797	1595	4376	16.8
Mechanical Soft																		
Totals	2374.2	108.5	331.5	76.0	502.6	23.5	8.7	11306	99.5	1.5	2.3	21.8	5.3	1408	1935	2769	4713	21.7
Puree																		
Totals	2239.2	110.7	271.2	84.7	710.5	29.3	9.7	11542	99.8	1.3	2.4	20.7	5.5	1424	2092	2531	4801	20.9
Soft, Low Fiber																		
Totals	2383.2	108.7	335.1	73.2	499.0	23.2	11.4	10213	98.3	1.6	2.4	22.3	5.3	1386	1739	2744	4464	21.2
Low Fat, Low Cholesterol																		
Totals	1912.9	78.2	308.5	45.5	215.2	12.1	8.1	5346	111.4	1.3	1.8	16.3	5.3	1198	1474	1549	4028	13.9
No Concentrated Sweets																		
Totals	1996.3	108.0	230.7	73.7	321.3	19.4	10.9	5803	111.0	1.3	2.1	21.5	7.8	1319	1824	1816	4491	14.8

DIET	KCAL	PROT GM	CHO GM	FAT GM	KCAL DISTRIBUTIONS: Pro%	CHO%	Fat%	Milk EXG	Frt EXG	Veg EXG	Brd EXG	Meat EXG	Fat EXG
No Concentrated Sweets													
Totals	1996.3	108.0	230.7	73.7	21.6	46.2	33.2	3.3	3.9	3.3	7.7	7.3	9.3
1200 Calorie													
Totals	1198.1	75.8	161.7	29.6	25.3	53.9	22.2	2.7	3.0	3.3	4.2	5.0	2.4
1500 Calorie													
Totals	1510.1	91.5	184.8	46.3	24.2	48.9	27.6	2.7	3.0	3.3	6.4	6.3	4.7
1800 Calorie													
Totals	1783.9	96.0	223.0	59.0	21.5	50.0	29.7	2.7	3.7	3.3	7.9	6.3	7.0
2000 Calorie													
Totals	1990.6	113.6	237.2	67.2	22.8	47.6	30.3	3.4	3.3	3.3	8.7	7.7	7.7

APPENDIXES

NUTRIENT ANALYSIS: Week Three, Monday

RDA/ESA: MALE 51+	KCAL range	PROT gm range	CHO gm none	FAT gm none	CHOL mg none	SFA gm none	PFA gm none	VITA IU 5000	VITC mg 60	THI* mg 1.2	RIB* mg 1.4	NIA* mg 15	B-12* mcg 2.0	Ca mg 800	P mg 800	Na mg range	K mg range	Fe mg 10
Regular, Liberal Bland, and No Added Salt																		
Totals	2527.2	92.5	317.2	102.5	701.5	34.1	23.1	8388	123.0	1.4	2.4	16.7	4.6	1112	1565	2064	3224	13.3
1-2 gm Na (Low Sodium)																		
Totals	2407.1	87.2	303.9	97.8	683.9	31.3	22.8	7721	121.0	1.3	2.1	16.2	4.1	948.9	1425	1713	3015	12.8
Mechanical Soft																		
Totals	2572.8	100.3	328.7	98.1	722.7	33.4	15.9	8782	184.6	1.5	2.4	19.7	4.5	1069	1592	2167	3391	13.8
Puree																		
Totals	2497.6	103.3	306.2	98.6	725.0	36.1	16.7	9024	183.7	1.6	2.6	19.8	4.8	1173	1687	1958	3822	13.9
Soft, Low Fiber																		
Totals	2484.4	96.5	313.7	96.5	714.9	33.8	16.0	8841	183.7	1.4	2.3	19.2	4.3	1027	1500	1984	3288	13.1
Low Fat, Low Cholesterol																		
Totals	2085.7	98.7	340.1	40.4	141.4	9.2	14.7	9835	128.9	1.4	2.5	19.8	3.9	1127	1591	2351	3917	16.1
No Concentrated Sweets																		
Totals	1911.2	109.8	256.2	50.2	579.8	12.3	14.5	8875	126.5	1.3	2.5	22.4	5.0	1134	1711	2461	3718	16.4

DIET	KCAL	PROT GM	CHO GM	FAT GM	KCAL DISTRIBUTIONS: Pro%	CHO%	Fat%	Milk EXG	Frt EXG	Veg EXG	Brd EXG	Meat EXG	Fat EXG
No Concentrated Sweets													
Totals	1911.2	109.8	256.2	50.2	22.9	53.6	23.6	3.8	5.1	3.2	7.8	6.0	6.6
1200 Calorie													
Totals	1197.0	73.8	170.7	24.3	24.7	57.0	18.3	2.9	2.8	2.7	5.4	3.4	2.7
1500 Calorie													
Totals	1507.5	94.3	210.9	32.5	25.0	55.9	19.4	3.2	3.8	3.2	6.4	5.0	3.7
1800 Calorie													
Totals	1791.8	97.3	243.9	48.2	21.7	54.4	24.2	3.2	4.8	3.2	7.6	5.0	6.7
2000 Calorie													
Totals	1997.5	111.7	274.6	51.0	22.3	54.9	22.9	3.8	5.2	3.2	8.8	6.0	6.7

APPENDIX 9

NUTRIENT ANALYSIS: Week Three, Tuesday

	KCAL	PROT gm	CHO gm	FAT gm	CHOL mg	SFA gm	PFA gm	VITA IU	VITC mg	THI* mg	RIB* mg	NIA* mg	B-12* mcg	Ca mg	P mg	Na mg	K mg	Fe mg
RDA/ESA: MALE 51+	range	range	none	none	none	none	none	5000	60	1.2	1.4	15	2.0	800	800	range	range	10
Regular, Liberal Bland, and No Added Salt																		
Totals	2316.8	102.1	265.2	100.2	442.2	39.1	19.6	37412	160.5	1.9	2.5	19.1	5.2	1614	1918	2366	3804	14.7
1–2 gm Na (Low Sodium)																		
Totals	2121.4	92.9	258.8	85.9	352.9	24.4	18.7	37115	153.3	1.6	3.9	17.2	4.0	1494	1441	1607	3419	13.9
Mechanical Soft																		
Totals	2223.2	100.9	265.2	89.5	441.6	37.9	12.3	22069	156.2	1.8	2.5	18.6	5.2	1598	1886	2184	3693	14.6
Puree																		
Totals	2335.7	101.7	289.0	90.7	536.9	39.3	11.8	22156	160.2	1.7	2.7	19.3	5.5	1593	1772	1747	3959	15.3
Soft, Low Fiber																		
Totals	2156.2	92.8	263.2	84.6	506.7	36.0	11.4	21931	151.2	1.7	2.4	18.1	4.8	1453	1570	1820	3333	14.6
Low Fat, Low Cholesterol																		
Totals	1909.1	103.5	296.3	40.3	121.6	10.3	7.9	36118	156.0	1.7	2.4	19.2	4.4	1646	1671	2487	4339	17.5
No Concentrated Sweets																		
Totals	1912.2	109.7	264.6	51.5	349.0	14.7	8.5	34455	151.9	1.8	2.3	22.3	5.1	1665	1768	2749	4264	18.1

DIET	KCAL	PROT GM	CHO GM	FAT GM	KCAL DISTRIBUTIONS: Pro%	CHO%	Fat%	Milk EXG	Frt EXG	Veg EXG	Brd EXG	Meat EXG	Fat EXG
No Concentrated Sweets													
Totals	1912.2	109.7	264.6	51.5	22.9	55.3	24.2	3.0	3.8	4.6	9.3	7.4	5.1
1200 Calorie													
Totals	1192.3	71.3	174.0	27.4	23.9	58.3	20.7	2.4	3.2	4.6	4.3	4.4	2.6
1500 Calorie													
Totals	1503.0	90.3	218.8	33.9	24.0	58.2	20.3	2.4	3.8	4.6	6.6	6.2	2.7
1800 Calorie													
Totals	1793.3	97.0	257.9	47.4	21.6	57.5	23.7	2.4	4.0	4.6	9.0	6.2	4.9
2000 Calorie													
Totals	1992.4	112.3	281.8	52.2	22.5	56.5	23.6	3.0	4.0	4.6	10.2	7.4	5.1

NUTRIENT ANALYSIS: Week Three, Wednesday

	KCAL	PROT	CHO	FAT	CHOL	SFA	PFA	VITA	VITC	THI*	RIB*	NIA*	B-12*	Ca	P	Na	K	Fe
		gm	gm	gm	mg	gm	gm	IU	mg	mg	mg	mg	mcg	mg	mg	mg	mg	mg
RDA/ESA: MALE 51+	range	range	none	none	none	none	none	5000	60	1.2	1.4	15	2.0	800	800	range	range	10
Regular, Liberal Bland, and No Added Salt																		
Totals	2261.8	103.3	269.5	88.5	642.7	27.6	22.9	6218	148.9	1.5	2.3	20.5	4.6	1348	1713	3178	3730	12.6
1–2 gm Na (Low Sodium)																		
Totals	2155.2	104.6	246.1	85.8	643.2	25.2	23.6	5687	143.3	1.2	2.1	24.3	4.1	1218	1608	1708	3460	12.4
Mechanical Soft																		
Totals	2194.6	101.3	278.6	76.8	643.5	26.8	15.5	5955	125.2	1.5	2.3	20.7	4.6	1271	1558	2397	3561	13.2
Puree																		
Totals	2230.4	103.0	294.0	73.8	636.7	26.2	15.6	5919	132.7	1.6	2.5	22.2	4.6	1265	1564	2332	3895	14.0
Soft, Low Fiber																		
Totals	2095.6	104.0	265.9	69.5	638.1	23.6	15.4	5179	97.5	1.3	2.1	25.9	4.1	1118	1455	1873	3231	13.4
Low Fat, Low Cholesterol																		
Totals	2000.5	110.1	300.3	41.9	139.3	8.6	14.4	6938	162.3	1.7	2.3	22.7	3.7	1426	1832	2721	4742	17.4
No Concentrated Sweets																		
Totals	1995.9	120.8	263.7	52.8	571.8	11.5	15.4	5775	171.9	1.8	2.3	28.0	4.5	1464	2001	3042	4544	17.8

DIET	KCAL	PROT GM	CHO GM	FAT GM	KCAL DISTRIBUTIONS: Pro%	CHO%	Fat%	Milk EXG	Frt EXG	Veg EXG	Brd EXG	Meat EXG	Fat EXG
No Concentrated Sweets													
Totals	1995.9	120.8	263.7	52.8	24.2	52.8	23.8	3.8	3.3	3.6	9.8	7.37	6.3
1200 Calorie													
Totals	1198.4	75.9	155.9	30.9	25.3	52.0	23.2	3.0	2.5	3.3	4.0	4.6	3.5
1500 Calorie													
Totals	1496.8	97.9	193.9	37.4	26.1	51.8	22.5	3.2	2.7	3.6	6.0	6.4	4.0
1800 Calorie													
Totals	1803.5	105.1	243.7	47.0	23.3	54.0	23.4	3.2	3.3	3.6	8.8	6.4	5.5
2000 Calorie													
Totals	1995.9	120.8	263.7	52.8	24.2	52.8	23.8	3.8	3.3	3.6	9.7	7.2	6.3

NUTRIENT ANALYSIS: Week Three, Thursday

RDA/ESA: MALE 51+	KCAL range	PROT gm range	CHO gm none	FAT gm none	CHOL mg none	SFA gm none	PFA gm none	VITA IU 5000	VITC mg 60	THI* mg 1.2	RIB* mg 1.4	NIA* mg 15	B-12* mcg 2.0	Ca mg 800	P mg 800	Na mg range	K mg range	Fe mg 10
Regular, Liberal Bland, and No Added Salt																		
Totals	2294.4	95.3	243.4	109.5	381.4	43.8	16.0	13065	77.3	1.3	2.5	17.1	6.0	1508	1738	2089	3852	15.7
1–2 gm Na (Low Sodium)																		
Totals	2072.8	87.4	227.9	95.8	597.5	36.2	14.9	14340	123.4	1.3	2.4	17.0	5.7	1144	1515	1712	3702	16.8
Mechanical Soft																		
Totals	2268.5	94.8	251.2	103.3	386.8	43.4	12.2	10744	71.2	1.3	2.5	16.9	6.0	1500	1770	2122	3797	15.8
Puree																		
Totals	2410.1	105.1	264.1	108.9	415.5	45.4	12.4	10703	69.4	1.3	2.6	19.1	6.8	1494	1885	2125	3855	17.1
Soft, Low Fiber																		
Totals	2213.9	93.6	241.9	98.6	384.6	42.9	11.0	10513	65.3	1.3	2.6	18.2	6.1	1423	1550	2471	3121	14.7
Low Fat, Low Cholesterol																		
Totals	1918.0	92.0	285.0	49.8	233.0	19.0	5.6	12381	80.3	1.2	2.3	18.1	6.1	1474	1690	2072	4251	18.1
No Concentrated Sweets																		
Totals	2014.3	103.3	235.2	76.8	301.4	26.4	11.6	13218	74.5	1.2	2.4	19.7	7.1	1538	1798	2081	4308	18.4

DIET	KCAL	PROT GM	CHO GM	FAT GM	KCAL DISTRIBUTIONS: Pro%	CHO%	Fat%	Milk EXG	Frt EXG	Veg EXG	Brd EXG	Meat EXG	Fat EXG
No Concentrated Sweets													
Totals	2014.3	103.3	235.2	76.8	20.5	46.7	34.3	3.3	4.6	2.3	7.7	5.8	11.0
1200 Calorie													
Totals	1215.2	67.4	156.6	38.0	22.2	51.5	28.1	2.4	2.9	2.3	4.9	3.1	5.1
1500 Calorie													
Totals	1514.5	83.4	176.9	54.7	22.0	46.7	32.5	2.5	3.2	2.3	5.8	4.8	7.5
1800 Calorie													
Totals	1803.9	88.1	210.1	71.4	19.5	46.5	35.6	2.5	3.9	2.3	7.4	4.8	10.5
2000 Calorie													
Totals	2013.4	104.1	232.4	77.4	20.6	46.1	34.6	3.3	3.9	2.3	8.3	5.8	11.0

NUTRIENT ANALYSIS: Week Three, Friday

RDA/ESA: MALE 51+	KCAL range	PROT gm range	CHO gm none	FAT gm none	CHOL mg none	SFA gm none	PFA gm none	VITA IU 5000	VITC mg 60	THI* mg 1.2	RIB* mg 1.4	NIA* mg 15	B-12* mcg 2.0	Ca mg 800	P mg 800	Na mg range	K mg range	Fe mg 10
Regular, Liberal Bland, and No Added Salt																		
Totals	2385.0	112.8	283.3	91.2	585.8	31.3	14.5	20377	103.3	1.4	2.0	36.6	4.6	1114	1771	2200	3909	20.4
1–2 gm Na (Low Sodium)																		
Totals	2254.5	108.5	264.4	86.5	561.5	28.6	18.2	20188	104.1	1.3	1.8	36.5	4.2	961.1	1658	1775	3810	20.2
Mechanical Soft																		
Totals	2395.1	113.7	277.9	94.6	586.0	31.9	15.8	20528	88.0	1.5	2.0	36.6	4.8	1164	1830	1962	3899	20.1
Puree																		
Totals	2506.0	133.2	285.9	93.8	618.2	30.7	18.0	20765	114.9	1.6	2.1	45.2	5.2	1176	1968	1901	4225	25.6
Soft, Low Fiber																		
Totals	2274.1	112.8	268.8	84.2	559.9	29.0	18.2	24436	101.6	1.5	2.1	36.9	4.7	1145	1560	2045	3773	19.1
Low Fat, Low Cholesterol																		
Totals	1970.2	111.2	289.0	41.9	163.6	9.0	12.8	22223	103.0	1.4	1.9	33.6	4.1	1086	1709	2086	4102	20.2
No Concentrated Sweets																		
Totals	1920.7	115.7	246.9	52.0	484.2	14.0	12.8	20896	112.5	1.3	1.8	37.2	4.7	1101	1782	1848	4028	19.2

DIET	KCAL	PROT GM	CHO GM	FAT GM	KCAL DISTRIBUTIONS: Pro%	CHO%	Fat%	Milk EXG	Frt EXG	Veg EXG	Brd EXG	Meat EXG	Fat EXG
No Concentrated Sweets													
Totals	1920.7	115.7	246.9	52.0	24.1	51.4	24.4	2.9	3.9	2.4	9.1	7.3	6.1
1200 Calorie													
Totals	1217.9	74.7	177.7	23.3	24.5	58.3	17.2	2.2	2.8	2.2	6.4	4.3	1.9
1500 Calorie													
Totals	1506.9	96.4	204.3	33.0	25.6	54.2	19.7	2.3	3.8	2.4	6.9	6.4	2.9
1800 Calorie													
Totals	1797.7	102.3	235.4	49.8	22.7	52.3	24.9	2.3	3.9	2.4	8.8	6.4	5.9
2000 Calorie													
Totals	1992.4	118.4	261.5	52.8	23.7	52.5	23.8	2.9	3.9	2.4	10.1	7.3	6.1

NUTRIENT ANALYSIS: Week Three, Saturday

RDA/ESA: MALE 51+	KCAL range	PROT gm range	CHO gm none	FAT gm none	CHOL mg none	SFA gm none	PFA gm none	VITA IU 5000	VITC mg 60	THI* mg 1.2	RIB* mg 1.4	NIA* mg 15	B-12* mcg 2.0	Ca mg 800	P mg 800	Na mg range	K mg range	Fe mg 10
Regular, Liberal Bland, and No Added Salt																		
Totals	2301.6	88.8	309.5	83.9	611.4	30.4	14.1	31489	164.3	2.0	2.5	16.1	4.1	1283	1599	3124	4411	15.9
1–2 gm Na (Low Sodium)																		
Totals	2318.8	88.5	297.1	90.9	645.5	33.1	9.6	32932	166.9	1.9	2.6	15.7	4.1	1299	1536	1316	3994	16.5
Mechanical Soft																		
Totals	2304.7	87.0	342.4	68.4	585.6	27.7	9.4	29840	218.1	2.1	2.4	16.3	4.0	1185	1465	2993	4148	16.0
Puree																		
Totals	2422.8	97.2	355.2	71.1	601.2	28.4	10.1	29859	218.6	2.4	2.5	17.9	4.2	1196	1620	3370	4304	17.1
Soft, Low Fiber																		
Totals	2221.8	82.5	329.9	67.0	571.0	26.2	9.3	29684	216.9	2.0	2.2	16.2	3.6	1097	1361	2844	3973	16.0
Low Fat, Low Cholesterol																		
Totals	1920.0	92.7	295.3	45.5	105.2	14.2	10.1	35450	189.3	2.1	2.5	16.6	3.5	1302	1620	3088	4633	16.7
No Concentrated Sweets																		
Totals	1899.5	93.4	259.3	58.7	529.1	19.2	11.0	34085	185.5	2.0	2.4	16.7	4.3	1329	1708	3014	4574	16.6

DIET	KCAL	PROT GM	CHO GM	FAT GM	KCAL DISTRIBUTIONS: Pro%	CHO%	Fat%	Milk EXG	Frt EXG	Veg EXG	Brd EXG	Meat EXG	Fat EXG
No Concentrated Sweets													
Totals	1899.5	93.4	259.3	58.7	19.6	54.6	27.8	2.7	4.7	2.9	8.6	5.7	7.7
1200 Calorie													
Totals	1199.2	63.6	170.0	32.5	21.2	56.7	24.4	2.1	3.2	2.7	4.9	3.5	4.1
1500 Calorie													
Totals	1487.4	79.4	205.7	42.0	21.3	55.3	25.4	2.2	4.1	2.9	6.1	5.2	5.0
1800 Calorie													
Totals	1807.1	86.0	252.5	54.8	19.0	55.8	27.3	2.2	4.7	2.9	8.6	5.2	7.3
2000 Calorie													
Totals	1979.4	96.4	276.5	59.0	19.4	55.8	26.8	2.7	4.7	2.9	9.8	5.7	7.7

NUTRIENT ANALYSIS: Week Three, Sunday

RDA/ESA: MALE 51+	KCAL range	PROT gm range	CHO gm none	FAT gm none	CHOL mg none	SFA gm none	PFA gm none	VITA IU 5000	VITC mg 60	THI* mg 1.2	RIB* mg 1.4	NIA* mg 15	B-12* mcg 2.0	Ca mg 800	P mg 800	Na mg range	K mg range	Fe mg 10
Regular, Liberal Bland, and No Added Salt																		
Totals	2563.5	102.9	323.0	102.2	650.0	32.4	15.9	8727	174.1	1.5	2.2	18.0	6.1	1324	1855	2335	4521	21.6
1-2 GM NA (Low Sodium)																		
Totals	2297.5	94.2	304.9	84.5	484.5	25.9	11.7	8461	182.5	1.6	2.1	18.6	6.3	1143	1725	1610	4172	22.8
Mechanical Soft																		
Totals	2460.5	98.3	314.9	95.3	650.0	31.1	12.2	7962	208.6	1.4	2.1	16.7	6.1	1341	1738	2539	4372	19.8
Puree																		
Totals	2277.0	103.4	253.8	96.8	600.1	32.5	12.4	7888	208.6	1.6	2.3	18.9	7.0	1184	1561	2170	4113	19.8
Soft, Low Fiber																		
Totals	2398.8	93.3	310.2	90.8	630.6	28.4	.12.1	7779	207.4	1.5	2.0	17.1	5.6	1163	1468	2444	4037	19.6
Low Fat, Low Cholesterol																		
Totals	2030.4	107.0	308.2	46.2	252.3	12.5	9.8	10623	186.0	1.7	2.2	21.5	7.6	1268	1849	1904	4714	22.1
No Concentrated Sweets																		
Totals	1918.7	110.2	244.8	59.4	562.7	17.7	10.5	9110	207.1	1.7	2.1	22.6	9.0	1190	1913	1927	4457	22.8

DIET	KCAL	PROT GM	CHO GM	FAT GM	KCAL DISTRIBUTIONS: Pro%	CHO%	Fat%	Milk EXG	Frt EXG	Veg EXG	Brd EXG	Meat EXG	Fat EXG
No Concentrated Sweets													
Totals	1918.7	110.2	244.8	59.4	22.9	51.0	27.8	2.8	4.3	2.5	8.4	6.9	8.1
1200 Calorie													
Totals	1211.9	71.2	166.0	31.7	23.5	54.8	23.5	2.3	4.1	2.7	3.7	4.1	4.3
1500 Calorie													
Totals	1493.5	91.9	203.2	37.7	24.6	54.4	22.7	2.3	4.1	2.5	6.2	5.8	4.8
1800 Calorie													
Totals	1814.8	98.2	242.1	54.8	21.6	53.3	27.1	2.3	4.5	2.5	8.4	5.8	7.8
2000 Calorie													
Totals	1998.9	112.8	262.0	60.1	22.5	52.4	27.1	2.8	4.5	2.5	9.4	6.9	8.1

RDA/ESA: MALE 51+	KCAL gm range	PROT gm range	CHO gm none	FAT gm none	CHOL mg none	SFA gm none	PFA gm none	VITA IU 5000	VITC mg 60	THI* mg 1.2	RIB* mg 1.4	NIA* mg 15	B-12* mcg 2.0	Ca mg 800	P mg 800	Na mg range	K mg range	Fe mg 10
Regular, Liberal Bland, and No Added Salt																		
Totals	2362.6	101.6	281.3	97.8	590.7	33.9	16.1	30910	126.2	1.3	2.2	26.7	4.3	1462	1963	3003	3898	15.1
1–2 GM NA (Low Sodium)																		
Totals	2259.7	97.3	266.8	94.5	538.9	25.5	18.1	30548	124.6	1.2	3.0	26.5	3.6	1356	1558	1803	3576	14.7
Mechanical Soft																		
Totals	2301.4	101.7	287.8	87.9	583.3	32.2	10.5	30605	174.4	1.4	2.2	26.8	4.3	1462	1958	2800	3992	14.8
Puree																		
Totals	2331.7	116.9	298.2	77.6	603.9	30.8	11.1	32223	229.7	1.4	2.4	31.8	4.9	1329	1763	2475	4157	15.2
Soft, Low Fiber																		
Totals	2368.8	100.5	297.1	89.5	586.97	33.2	10.4	30335	169.4	1.4	2.3	27.0	4.3	1492	1716	2459	3844	14.4
Low Fat, Low Cholesterol																		
Totals	1928.9	125.0	269.3	43.4	93.9	6.9	11.4	37775	142.4	1.5	2.6	24.7	3.9	1811	1833	2875	4767	19.0
No Concentrated Sweets																		
Totals	1937.2	116.0	246.1	58.9	858.9	15.2	11.2	33335	139.0	1.5	2.3	29.0	5.2	1619	1953	2838	4384	17.3

DIET	KCAL	PROT GM	CHO GM	FAT GM	KCAL DISTRIBUTIONS: Pro%	CHO%	Fat%	Milk EXG	Frt EXG	Veg EXG	Brd EXG	Meat EXG	Fat EXG
No Concentrated Sweets													
Totals	1937.2	116.0	246.1	58.9	23.9	50.8	27.4	3.2	4.5	4.9	7.3	7.1	7.7
1200 Calorie													
Totals	1214.4	76.2	162.7	31.4	25.1	53.6	23.3	2.6	3.3	4.4	3.5	4.5	3.6
1500 Calorie													
Totals	1502.2	94.1	189.9	43.7	25.0	50.5	26.2	2.6	4.3	4.9	4.0	6.2	5.4
1800 Calorie													
Totals	1796.1	100.4	230.7	57.0	22.3	51.3	28.5	2.6	4.8	4.9	6.3	6.2	7.7
2000 Calorie													
Totals	2005.4	118.6	260.1	59.7	23.6	51.8	26.7	3.2	4.5	4.9	8.2	7.1	7.7

NUTRIENT ANALYSIS: Week Four, Tuesday

	KCAL	PROT gm	CHO gm	FAT gm	CHOL mg	SFA gm	PFA gm	VITA IU	VITC mg	THI* mg	RIB* mg	NIA* mg	B-12* mcg	Ca mg	P mg	Na mg	K mg	Fe mg
RDA/ESA: MALE 51+	range	range	none	none	none	none	none	5000	60	1.2	1.4	15	2.0	800	800	range	range	10
Regular, Liberal Bland, and No Added Salt																		
Totals	2259.7	98.3	273.8	88.6	713.8	31.1	15.3	7735	135.6	1.8	2.3	18.5	5.1	1181	1725	2915	3869	19.8
1–2 GM NA (Low Sodium)																		
Totals	2150.2	104.6	263.5	78.4	649.9	21.8	13.1	6741	123.5	1.7	2.1	14.4	3.4	1138	1518	1858	3586	17.1
Mechanical Soft																		
Totals	2235.0	96.3	266.2	88.9	778.1	31.4	15.2	7915	138.6	1.6	2.1	17.5	5.2	1132	1738	3271	3911	19.4
Puree																		
Totals	2370.5	99.1	291.4	91.9	798.9	32.2	16.1	7737	138.4	1.7	2.1	17.7	5.3	1118	1786	3196	3983	20.0
Soft, Low Fiber																		
Totals	2134.7	97.6	258.2	77.4	772.3	25.7	15.6	6394	124.7	1.6	2.1	21.0	4.4	950.0	1427	3362	3400	18.0
Low Fat, Low Cholesterol																		
Totals	1930.4	107.9	273.9	47.1	243.5	11.7	12.2	9745	130.9	1.9	2.3	19.0	4.2	1218	1792	2559	4202	20.3
No Concentrated Sweets																		
Totals	1956.5	109.1	239.1	64.3	667.5	17.6	13.4	8241	133.3	1.8	2.2	20.0	5.2	1215	1838	2835	4160	20.9

DIET	KCAL	PROT GM	CHO GM	FAT GM	KCAL DISTRIBUTIONS: Pro%	CHO%	Fat%	Milk EXG	Frt EXG	Veg EXG	Brd EXG	Meat EXG	Fat EXG
No Concentrated Sweets													
Totals	1956.5	109.1	239.1	64.3	22.3	48.8	29.5	2.6	3.0	2.8	9.6	6.9	8.1
1200 Calorie													
Totals	1197.1	69.3	148.2	37.8	23.1	49.5	28.4	2.1	1.9	2.1	5.3	3.9	4.7
1500 Calorie													
Totals	1508.8	88.3	175.6	51.9	23.4	46.5	31.0	2.1	2.4	2.3	6.6	5.9	6.4
1800 Calorie													
Totals	1800.6	96.0	218.7	62.5	21.3	48.5	31.2	2.1	2.4	2.8	9.3	5.9	8.1
2000 Calorie													
Totals	1990.6	109.1	239.1	68.1	21.9	48.0	30.8	2.6	3.0	2.8	9.6	6.9	8.9

APPENDIX 9

NUTRIENT ANALYSIS: Week Four, Wednesday

RDA/ESA: MALE 51+	KCAL gm range	PROT gm range	CHO gm none	FAT gm none	CHOL mg none	SFA gm none	PFA gm none	VITA IU 5000	VITC mg 60	THI* mg 1.2	RIB* mg 1.4	NIA* mg 15	B-12* mcg 2.0	Ca mg 800	P mg 800	Na mg range	K mg range	Fe mg 10
Regular, Liberal Bland, and No Added Salt																		
Totals	2166.6	104.4	251.0	87.0	661.1	32.2	12.5	17081	118.8	1.7	2.6	20.3	6.5	1402	1612	2003	4297	24.9
1-2 GM NA (Low Sodium)																		
Totals	2079.1	99.9	233.4	86.1	674.2	32.5	4.5	17046	118.0	1.6	2.6	19.3	6.5	1371	1464	1487	4133	23.6
Mechanical Soft																		
Totals	2143.8	101.3	263.0	79.9	660.2	31.7	6.8	14659	145.9	1.6	2.5	19.3	6.5	1376	1533	1744	4180	24.7
Puree																		
Totals	2283.9	111.0	277.0	84.5	680.6	33.6	6.9	14659	145.9	1.8	2.6	21.3	7.5	1404	1628	1766	4299	30.9
Soft, Low Fiber																		
Totals	2100.1	96.8	258.7	76.4	643.4	29.7	6.6	14503	144.7	1.7	2.5	19.8	6.1	1213	1228	1658	3799	24.4
Low Fat, Low Cholesterol																		
Totals	1883.8	105.6	263.0	48.7	143.0	12.3	7.6	19115	121.4	1.6	2.6	20.0	6.1	1431	1575	1825	4642	25.3
No Concentrated Sweets																		
Totals	1844.8	110.7	216.5	62.0	570.9	16.7	8.5	17504	112.2	1.6	2.5	21.0	7.7	1418	1663	1892	4444	25.3

DIET	KCAL	PROT GM	CHO GM	FAT GM	KCAL DISTRIBUTIONS: Pro%	CHO%	Fat%	Milk EXG	Frt EXG	Veg EXG	Brd EXG	Meat EXG	Fat EXG
No Concentrated Sweets													
Totals	1844.8	110.7	216.5	62.0	24.0	46.9	30.2	3.0	3.7	2.0	7.9	8.2	6.2
1200 Calorie													
Totals	1209.4	73.1	155.7	34.6	24.1	51.5	25.8	2.2	3.1	2.0	5.2	4.7	3.1
1500 Calorie													
Totals	1493.7	92.7	190.4	42.4	24.8	51.0	25.6	2.4	3.7	2.0	6.6	6.6	3.4
1800 Calorie													
Totals	1800.1	99.6	226.9	57.5	22.1	50.4	28.7	2.4	4.0	2.0	8.7	7.1	6.0
2000 Calorie													
Totals	1991.4	114.9	248.0	62.8	23.0	49.8	28.3	3.0	3.9	2.2	9.7	8.2	6.2

NUTRIENT ANALYSIS: Week Four, Thursday

RDA/ESA: MALE 51+	KCAL gm range	PROT gm range	CHO gm none	FAT gm none	CHOL mg none	SFA gm none	PFA gm none	VITA IU 5000	VITC mg 60	THI* mg 1.2	RIB* mg 1.4	NIA* mg 15	B-12* mcg 2.0	Ca mg 800	P mg 800	Na mg range	K mg range	Fe mg 10
Regular, Liberal Bland, and No Added Salt																		
Totals	2423.8	107.2	284.4	102.5	292.5	33.8	19.8	8897	87.2	2.1	2.7	25.5	5.5	1192	1760	1895	4604	17.9
1–2 GM NA (Low Sodium)																		
Totals	2395.1	106.4	278.1	102.6	291.5	33.1	19.0	8952	88.3	2.1	2.7	25.2	5.5	1193	1707	1409	4337	17.0
Mechanical Soft																		
Totals	2341.2	107.1	293.9	88.8	292.4	32.0	11.7	7748	123.2	2.2	2.7	25.6	5.5	1178	1744	1888	4631	17.2
Puree																		
Totals	2303.7	116.3	272.2	87.7	326.0	34.2	10.1	7364	122.4	2.5	2.7	24.6	6.5	1178	1801	1837	4453	16.6
Soft, Low Fiber																		
Totals	2297.6	105.9	278.1	88.7	276.6	29.9	11.7	7177	121.6	2.2	2.6	25.0	5.5	981.6	1899	2117	4449	16.2
Low Fat, Low Cholesterol																		
Totals	1922.3	95.7	292.0	46.9	152.6	13.0	8.0	9307	90.3	1.8	2.4	20.8	5.0	1271	1715	2026	4553	17.4
No Concentrated Sweets																		
Totals	1934.0	115.2	217.2	71.1	232.4	19.6	12.8	8853	84.3	2.4	2.6	27.1	6.0	1223	1868	1888	4780	17.4

DIET	KCAL	PROT GM	CHO GM	FAT GM	KCAL DISTRIBUTIONS: Pro%	CHO%	Fat%	Milk EXG	Frt EXG	Veg EXG	Brd EXG	Meat EXG	Fat EXG
No Concentrated Sweets													
Totals	1934.0	115.2	217.2	71.1	23.8	44.9	33.1	2.6	3.2	3.1	8.0	8.2	8.1
1200 Calorie													
Totals	1219.8	75.9	144.3	40.6	24.8	47.3	30.0	1.8	2.3	2.9	4.8	4.9	4.4
1500 Calorie													
Totals	1504.5	94.6	167.9	53.3	25.1	44.6	31.9	1.8	2.7	3.1	5.7	7.0	5.7
1800 Calorie													
Totals	1806.9	104.1	211.9	64.4	23.0	46.9	32.1	2.1	2.9	3.2	8.3	7.1	7.5
2000 Calorie													
Totals	1997.9	116.8	226.7	73.5	23.3	45.3	33.1	2.6	3.2	3.2	8.6	8.2	8.5

NUTRIENT ANALYSIS: Week Four, Friday

	KCAL	PROT gm range	CHO gm none	FAT gm none	CHOL mg none	SFA gm none	PFA gm none	VITA IU 5000	VITC mg 60	THI* mg 1.2	RIB* mg 1.4	NIA* mg 15	B-12* mcg 2.0	Ca mg 800	P mg 800	Na mg range	K mg range	Fe mg 10
RDA/ESA: MALE 51+ range																		
Regular, Liberal Bland, and No Added Salt																		
Totals	2491.1	121.4	271.9	107.2	661.0	35.6	18.7	8437	139.7	1.2	2.1	36.5	4.7	1254	1908	1924	3960	16.0
1–2 GM NA (Low Sodium)																		
Totals	2362.8	118.1	271.1	94.6	640.4	31.4	18.5	8271	139.5	1.2	2.1	36.5	4.6	1161	1839	1743	3936	15.8
Mechanical Soft																		
Totals	2434.5	120.8	282.6	94.4	620.3	33.1	14.5	8309	136.1	1.4	2.1	36.4	4.6	1211	1761	1929	3853	16.0
Puree																		
Totals	2338.8	130.8	262.7	86.8	607.9	29.5	15.2	8225	136.9	1.3	2.1	41.3	4.7	1174	1827	1725	4005	15.6
Soft, Low Fiber																		
Totals	2166.4	124.1	243.2	78.6	587.6	26.1	17.7	8070	135.5	1.2	1.9	40.5	4.3	1019	1635	1665	3691	14.7
Low Fat, Low Cholesterol																		
Totals	1940.7	113.7	277.2	45.1	206.5	10.0	13.6	10264	147.5	1.2	1.9	33.4	4.2	1181	1757	1492	4294	15.8
No Concentrated Sweets																		
Totals	1870.7	120.7	221.7	58.3	537.5	15.2	14.5	8865	142.2	1.2	1.9	37.6	4.9	1238	1896	1620	4149	15.1

DIET	KCAL	PROT GM	CHO GM	FAT GM	KCAL DISTRIBUTIONS: Pro%	CHO%	Fat%	Milk EXG	Frt EXG	Veg EXG	Brd EXG	Meat EXG	Fat EXG
No Concentrated Sweets													
Totals	1870.7	120.7	221.7	58.3	25.8	47.4	28.0	2.8	3.8	1.9	7.6	8.2	7.6
1200 Calorie													
Totals	1209.0	79.8	163.2	29.4	26.4	54.0	21.9	2.2	3.5	1.9	4.5	5.1	3.2
1500 Calorie													
Totals	1503.0	102.3	184.1	42.3	27.2	49.0	25.3	2.2	3.6	1.9	5.7	7.3	4.7
1800 Calorie													
Totals	1800.7	108.3	219.4	57.4	24.0	48.7	28.7	2.2	3.8	1.9	7.8	7.3	7.7
2000 Calorie													
Totals	2009.2	123.8	239.0	66.0	24.6	47.5	29.6	2.8	3.8	1.9	8.5	8.2	9.1

NUTRIENT ANALYSIS: Week Four, Saturday

RDA/ESA: MALE 51+	KCAL range	PROT gm range	CHO gm none	FAT gm none	CHOL mg none	SFA gm none	PFA gm none	VITA IU 5000	VITC mg 60	THI* mg 1.2	RIB* mg 1.4	NIA* mg 15	B-12* mcg 2.0	Ca mg 800	P mg 800	Na mg range	K mg range	Fe mg 10
Regular, Liberal Bland, and No Added Salt																		
Totals	2285.2	119.8	285.9	77.3	551.0	26.6	16.05	8052	157.2	1.6	2.1	29.8	8.5	1145	1740	2303	4059	19.4
1–2 GM NA (Low Sodium)																		
Totals	2164.6	105.3	271.5	76.6	557.3	25.9	16.0	8033	150.8	1.7	2.0	25.9	6.9	1124	1575	1539	3985	16.1
Mechanical Soft																		
Totals	2256.6	108.6	271.5	85.5	540.3	29.6	15.5	7503	117.6	1.5	2.0	27.8	7.6	1123	1580	2300	3716	16.9
Puree																		
Totals	2430.7	117.2	286.7	91.3	569.0	32.1	15.7	7396	116.5	1.6	2.3	30.5	8.4	1110	1462	2300	3630	17.5
Soft, Low Fiber																		
Totals	2218.9	102.7	273.7	79.5	631.6	27.8	14.3	6956	95.6	1.3	2.0	28.4	7.5	957.9	1291	2355	2894	15.9
Low Fat, Low Cholesterol																		
Totals	1956.2	107.7	295.9	41.4	126.2	11.6	7.6	9568	145.3	1.4	2.0	27.5	7.0	1149	1574	1828	4159	18.5
No Concentrated Sweets																		
Totals	1898.5	113.5	232.6	59.5	527.1	18.1	9.5	8139	137.6	1.4	2.0	29.2	8.4	1173	1654	1917	4160	18.3

DIET	KCAL	PROT GM	CHO GM	FAT GM	KCAL DISTRIBUTIONS: Pro%	CHO%	Fat%	Milk EXG	Frt EXG	Veg EXG	Brd EXG	Meat EXG	Fat EXG
No Concentrated Sweets													
Totals	1898.5	113.5	232.61	59.5	23.9	49.0	28.2	2.7	4.8	3.8	6.9	7.2	8.1
1200 Calorie													
Totals	1195.8	80.8	163.7	25.4	27.0	54.7	19.1	2.2	3.9	3.7	3.9	4.7	2.8
1500 Calorie													
Totals	1505.8	104.7	192.8	36.1	27.8	51.2	21.5	2.2	4.3	3.8	5.2	6.8	4.3
1800 Calorie													
Totals	1793.9	109.7	225.4	52.7	24.4	50.2	26.4	2.2	4.8	3.8	6.9	6.8	7.3
2000 Calorie													
Totals	2002.9	124.1	245.2	60.4	24.7	48.9	27.1	2.7	4.8	3.8	7.8	7.8	8.2

APPENDIX 9

NUTRIENT ANALYSIS: Week Four, Sunday

RDA/ESA: MALE 51+	KCAL range	PROT gm range	CHO gm none	FAT gm none	CHOL mg none	SFA gm none	PFA gm none	VITA IU 5000	VITC mg 60	THI* mg 1.2	RIB* mg 1.4	NIA* mg 15	B-12* mcg 2.0	Ca mg 800	P mg 800	Na mg range	K mg range	Fe mg 10
Regular, Liberal Bland, and No Added Salt																		
Totals	2584.7	96.7	330.6	100.2	373.7	30.9	24.4	37625	78.4	1.6	2.4	19.0	6.5	1299	1561	2134	3956	15.8
1-2 GM NA (Low Sodium)																		
Totals	2558.3	94.7	327.6	99.5	332.9	30.0	24.0	37265	79.7	1.6	2.4	18.5	4.3	1308	1529	1747	3793	16.0
Mechanical Soft																		
Totals	2483.6	98.6	333.0	86.3	396.1	29.4	15.6	22303	127.7	1.7	2.4	19.3	6.5	1309	1563	2058	4012	15.8
Puree																		
Totals	2541.0	114.5	320.5	92.5	730.7	31.8	17.0	17862	135.7	1.9	2.5	21.2	7.2	1238	1691	2130	4042	16.6
Soft, Low Fiber																		
Totals	2362.4	90.4	335.0	76.6	282.0	25.4	13.8	17412	128.2	1.8	2.1	19.2	6.1	1168	1302	2019	3346	14.8
Low Fat, Low Cholesterol																		
Totals	2068.0	87.6	323.5	49.6	236.4	13.6	10.5	35901	89.0	1.5	2.1	16.7	4.4	1303	1507	1917	3828	14.2
No Concentrated Sweets																		
Totals	1915.3	101.7	236.8	62.3	186.6	16.5	13.7	35813	68.4	1.5	2.0	20.6	5.4	1221	1562	1944	3827	15.4

DIET	KCAL	PROT GM	CHO GM	FAT GM	KCAL DISTRIBUTIONS: Pro%	CHO%	Fat%	Milk EXG	Frt EXG	Veg EXG	Brd EXG	Meat EXG	Fat EXG
No Concentrated Sweets													
Totals	1915.3	101.7	236.8	62.3	21.2	49.4	29.2	2.8	4.2	4.3	7.4	6.2	8.7
1200 Calorie													
Totals	1206.6	68.0	170.6	28.2	22.5	56.5	21.0	2.2	2.8	4.1	5.0	3.6	3.4
1500 Calorie													
Totals	1494.5	85.0	197.3	40.5	22.7	52.8	24.4	2.2	3.4	4.1	6.1	5.2	5.2
1800 Calorie													
Totals	1799.1	90.6	235.9	54.9	20.1	52.4	27.4	2.2	4.2	4.3	7.7	5.2	7.7
2000 Calorie													
Totals	2005.6	106.0	255.2	62.1	21.1	50.9	27.8	2.8	4.2	4.3	8.6	6.3	8.6

NUTRIENT ANALYSIS: Senior Citizen Nutrition Program

Week One

	KCAL range	PROT gm range	CHO gm none	FAT gm none	CHOL mg none	SFA gm none	PFA gm none	VITA IU 5000	VITC mg 60	THI* mg 1.2	RIB* mg 1.4	NIA* mg 15	B-12* mcg 2.0	Ca mg 800	P mg 800	Na mg range	K mg range	Fe mg 10
RDA/ESA: MALE 51+																		
Monday Totals	944.0	42.4	95.1	46.2	172.0	13.9	10.1	2850	70.1	0.5	1.0	10.5	1.7	532.9	715.1	550.1	1437	5.4
Tuesday Totals	1031.5	44.2	81.2	59.1	152.2	17.5	18.4	3409	37.7	0.5	0.9	9.0	2.3	513.1	593.2	739.0	1209	6.6
Wednesday Totals	818.9	43.2	81.2	36.8	164.9	13.5	4.6	7105	30.1	0.5	0.9	9.1	3.4	436.4	608.2	501.3	1614	5.2
Thursday Totals	773.0	39.6	75.2	36.1	125.3	9.5	12.8	5202	56.5	0.5	0.7	5.7	2.6	497.7	653.2	698.0	1519	4.3
Friday Totals	857.1	37.2	102.5	36.0	102.7	9.6	12.6	7647	89.8	1.3	0.8	8.0	1.6	439.7	669.1	1638	1489	5.2

Week Two

	KCAL range	PROT gm range	CHO gm none	FAT gm none	CHOL mg none	SFA gm none	PFA gm none	VITA IU 5000	VITC mg 60	THI* mg 1.2	RIB* mg 1.4	NIA* mg 15	B-12* mcg 2.0	Ca mg 800	P mg 800	Na mg range	K mg range	Fe mg 10
RDA/ESA: MALE 51+																		
Monday Totals	1022.2	38.5	83.1	60.1	148.5	16.0	15.3	11471	34.5	0.4	0.8	5.7	3.3	428.6	735.8	875.7	1328	5.4
Tuesday Totals	931.0	44.3	84.1	47.5	169.2	16.5	7.5	2949	84.8	1.1	1.1	8.9	1.5	447.5	634.4	481.4	1275	5.1
Wednesday Totals	831.0	40.3	94.3	33.2	121.4	13.1	5.49	20635	87.7	0.5	0.7	11.4	1.2	455.5	605.5	395.6	1736	4.8
Thursday Totals	1038.1	41.5	108.4	49.1	159.9	14.5	15.5	5480	56.0	0.6	1.0	9.4	2.8	454.7	609.0	1053	1691	7.2
Friday Totals	757.3	41.5	72.6	31.4	105.4	9.7	6.8	1899	26.0	0.2	0.4	8.8	1.3	451.4	626.7	568.2	1430	4.6

Week Three

RDA/ESA: MALE 51+	KCAL range	PROT gm range	CHO gm none	FAT gm none	CHOL mg none	SFA gm none	PFA gm none	VITA IU 5000	VITC mg 60	THI* mg 1.2	RIB* mg 1.4	NIA* mg 15	B-12* mcg 2.0	Ca mg 800	P mg 800	Na mg range	K mg range	Fe mg 10
Monday Totals	843.0	42.8	80.1	38.8	107.8	8.9	12.7	5274	32.4	1.1	1.0	5.9	0.9	584.1	326.2	1356	1284	3.6
Tuesday Totals	890.3	46.4	84.3	42.7	75.4	10.9	17.7	3294	36.1	0.4	0.7	14.5	3.1	455.7	682.9	1042	1418	6.6
Wednesday Totals	826.2	43.8	95.8	31.8	142.6	11.9	4.9	2176	73.5	0.4	0.9	7.8	2.3	440.2	643.5	496.6	1213	7.0
Thursday Totals	926.3	45.2	87.1	44.6	268.5	13.1	10.0	1831	24.7	0.5	0.8	11.0	1.8	501.2	706.4	501.4	1406	4.1
Friday Totals	1141.6	44.1	100.6	65.5	145.0	27.0	16.1	4235	32.0	0.7	1.1	5.5	1.9	1071	976.0	1067	1333	4.6

Week Four

RDA/ESA: MALE 51+	KCAL range	PROT gm range	CHO gm none	FAT gm none	CHOL mg none	SFA gm none	PFA gm none	VITA IU 5000	VITC mg 60	THI* mg 1.2	RIB* mg 1.4	NIA* mg 15	B-12* mcg 2.0	Ca mg 800	P mg 800	Na mg range	K mg range	Fe mg 10
Monday Totals	899.4	46.1	102.9	35.3	164.7	13.6	5.4	8402	35.5	0.6	1.1	8.6	3.2	523.6	669.8	627.8	1941	8.3
Tuesday Totals	774.8	40.3	104.5	24.4	105.8	8.0	5.1	1865	58.8	0.5	0.7	14.2	1.2	419.4	695.1	1115	1388	3.7
Wednesday Totals	991.6	36.5	126.5	39.5	155.4	13.3	6.9	16300	37.1	0.9	1.0	7.5	1.6	425.3	631.3	1517	1264	5.0
Thursday Totals	715.0	46.1	89.5	20.7	107.9	7.4	4.5	1754	79.2	0.8	0.9	17.1	1.2	447.4	669.7	862.9	1289	5.5
Friday Totals	742.9	40.7	76.3	31.1	143.9	13.9	1.8	1705	83.2	0.6	0.8	8.9	3.2	415.2	531.3	635.5	1418	4.9

NUTRIENT ANALYSIS: Vegetarian Menu

	KCAL	PROT	CHO	FAT	CHOL	SFA	PFA	VITA	VITC	THI*	RIB*	NIA*	B-12*	Ca	P	Na	K	Fe
RDA/ESA: MALE 51+	range	gm range	gm none	gm none	mg none	gm none	gm none	IU 5000	mg 60	mg 1.2	mg 1.4	mg 15	mcg 2.0	mg 800	mg 800	mg range	mg range	mg 10
Monday Totals	2586	91.0	347.9	102.5	13.7	11.6	41.8	6021	198.8	2.8	1.9	18.5	1.1	897.3	1596	1882	4197	40.9
Tuesday Totals	2422	60.9	371.4	83.8	2.5	8.6	23.3	31891	178.3	2.1	1.9	16.9	1.0	836.7	1342	1955	3336	25.4
Wednesday Totals	2144	71.3	290.4	86.8	13.3	9.6	34.1	12400	181.2	2.1	1.7	15.8	1.1	810.4	1327	1351	3733	33.7
Thursday Totals	2108	65.9	294.2	81.5	173.5	17.0	13.2	13926	205.3	2.0	2.1	15.1	2.9	1271	1446	1656	3637	21.8
Friday Totals	2221	78.8	301.4	86.0	29.7	13.7	27.1	19821	207.5	2.0	1.9	17.0	1.7	1191	1447	1972	3308	32.1
Saturday Totals	2666	83.3	376.6	99.4	107.1	26.2	17.4	10098	146.0	2.4	2.2	19.5	2.1	1473	1973	2503	3487	26.1
Sunday Totals	2152	71.3	351.5	61.5	20.7	9.1	15.9	26391	157.1	2.4	2.0	19.6	1.4	968.7	1681	2042	4427	31.8

APPENDIX 9

NUTRIENT ANALYSIS: New Year's Eve

RDA/ESA: MALE 51+	KCAL range	PROT gm range	CHO gm none	FAT gm none	CHOL mg none	SFA gm none	PFA gm none	VITA IU 5000	VITC mg 60	THI* mg 1.2	RIB* mg 1.4	NIA* mg 15	B-12* mcg 2.0	Ca mg 800	P mg 800	Na mg range	K mg range	Fe mg 10
Regular, Liberal Bland, and No Added Salt																		
Totals	2548.7	96.5	288.8	115.0	506.4	34.8	29.3	16695	95.5	1.4	2.3	17.2	5.1	1086	1561	1724	3520	21.4
1-2 GM NA (Low Sodium)																		
Totals	2445.5	96.5	288.9	103.3	500.5	34.0	16.9	16648	94.8	1.4	2.3	17.2	5.0	1120	1616	1409	3544	21.3
Mechanical Soft																		
Totals	2525.4	99.0	287.4	111.6	526.7	34.2	30.7	16961	94.6	1.3	2.2	24.2	5.2	1064	1536	1721	3515	21.7
Puree																		
Totals	2612.2	108.6	282.0	119.2	587.4	40.1	33.1	16635	94.2	1.5	2.4	27.8	5.8	1124	1537	1535	3662	22.1
Soft, Low Fiber																		
Totals	2562.1	101.2	282.6	116.8	564.4	39.7	31.5	16931	93.9	1.5	2.3	25.0	5.4	1121	1459	1530	3506	22.1
Low Fat, Low Cholesterol																		
Totals	1838.1	82.4	284.4	43.3	120.5	12.4	8.2	17111	94.0	1.3	2.0	14.7	3.9	1076	1471	1556	3464	20.4
No Concentrated Sweets																		
Totals	1915.9	108.6	220.1	67.2	532.3	21.0	10.6	16410	61.7	1.3	2.2	18.0	6.1	1259	1771	1646	3644	21.9

DIET	KCAL	PROT GM	CHO GM	FAT GM	KCAL DISTRIBUTIONS: Pro%	CHO%	Fat%	Milk EXG	Frt EXG	Veg EXG	Brd EXG	Meat EXG	Fat EXG
No Concentrated Sweets													
Totals	1915.4	108.6	220.1	67.2	22.7	45.9	31.5	2.7	3.0	3.3	8.6	8.00	7.9
1200 Calorie													
Totals	1210.3	69.9	152.5	36.5	23.1	50.4	27.1	1.6	2.5	3.3	5.6	5.0	3.4
1500 Calorie													
Totals	1510.5	89.6	180.0	48.7	23.7	47.7	29.0	1.9	2.6	3.3	7.0	7.0	4.6
1800 Calorie													
Totals	1803.7	96.2	220.3	60.1	21.3	48.8	30.0	2.1	2.8	3.3	9.2	7.0	6.8
2000 Calorie													
Totals	1995.9	109.6	230.0	71.1	21.9	46.1	32.1	2.6	3.0	3.3	9.2	8.0	8.6

NUTRIENT ANALYSIS: St. Valentine's Day

RDA/ESA: MALE 51+	KCAL range	PROT gm range	CHO gm none	FAT gm none	CHOL mg none	SFA gm none	PFA gm none	VITA IU 5000	VITC mg 60	THI* mg 1.2	RIB* mg 1.4	NIA* mg 15	B-12* mcg 2.0	Ca mg 800	P mg 800	Na mg range	K mg range	Fe mg 10
Regular, Liberal Bland, and No Added Salt																		
Totals	2975.8	114.6	344.9	130.3	679.8	41.3	27.6	1436.5	303.5	2.0	3.0	35.1	11.6	1644.4	1952.5	3161.6	4462.9	20.1
1–2 GM NA (Low Sodium)																		
Totals	2610.9	110.7	311.8	105.9	673.5	33.1	15.6	1346.2	298.0	2.0	2.8	22.6	10.9	1556.5	1796.1	1083.5	4144.6	20.0
Mechanical Soft																		
Totals	2870.9	113.6	354.5	113.5	686.4	40.1	18.6	1054.4	199.1	1.9	2.9	22.5	11.5	1646.7	1924.7	3105.2	4227.4	18.6
Puree																		
Totals	2555.6	114.9	289.2	107.5	648.8	39.5	19.3	1021.7	206.6	1.7	2.8	30.8	12.1	1479.8	1896.7	2497.2	4444.3	17.7
Soft, Low Fiber																		
Totals	2770.7	107.3	348.6	107.9	667.9	37.1	18.5	1016.1	199.1	1.8	2.7	22.3	11.1	1487.3	1794.2	2906.6	4163.3	18.8
Low Fat, Low Cholesterol																		
Totals	1988.6	93.4	302.9	48.0	114.1	14.3	5.6	1373.0	284.9	1.7	2.4	28.7	9.3	1368.2	1601.4	1979.4	4122.9	17.0
No Concentrated Sweets																		
Totals	2098.3	118.0	245.0	72.6	483.6	20.8	12.0	1387.1	291.4	1.9	2.7	38.1	11.8	1520.2	1919.1	2787.0	4332.0	18.9

DIET	KCAL	PROT GM	CHO GM	FAT GM	KCAL DISTRIBUTIONS: Pro%	CHO%	Fat%	Milk EXG	Frt EXG	Veg EXG	Brd EXG	Meat EXG	Fat EXG
No Concentrated Sweets													
Totals	2098.3	118.0	244.9	72.6	22.5	46.7	31.1	3.4	3.0	5.5	8.6	7.3	10.1
1200 Calorie													
Totals	1202.4	75.8	148.8	35.1	25.2	49.5	26.2	2.4	2.4	4.9	3.9	4.7	3.9
1500 Calorie													
Totals	1492.7	92.4	168.3	51.1	24.8	45.1	30.8	2.6	2.3	4.9	5.1	6.6	5.7
1800 Calorie													
Totals	1798.1	100.6	220.3	58.1	22.4	49.0	29.1	2.6	3.0	5.0	7.7	6.6	7.4
2000 Calorie													
Totals	2001.4	117.5	241.9	63.2	23.5	48.3	28.4	3.4	3.0	5.0	8.6	7.3	8.3

APPENDIX 9

NUTRIENT ANALYSIS: St. Patrick's Day

RDA/ESA: MALE 51+	KCAL range	PROT gm range	CHO gm none	FAT gm none	CHOL mg none	SFA gm none	PFA gm none	VITA IU 5000	VITC mg 60	THI* mg 1.2	RIB* mg 1.4	NIA* mg 15	B-12* mcg 2.0	Ca mg 800	P mg 800	Na mg range	K mg range	Fe mg 10
Regular, Liberal Bland, and No Added Salt																		
Totals	2342.9	92.6	300.1	90.5	470.7	31.5	13.5	9839	175.3	1.7	2.7	21.3	7.0	1278	1673	3102	3338	18.7
1-2 GM NA (Low Sodium)																		
Totals	2171.6	99.9	293.0	70.9	448.8	25.4	9.7	9828	161.9	1.7	2.6	23.4	5.6	1306	1647	1647	3475	18.5
Mechanical Soft																		
Totals	2219.3	90.0	290.1	81.0	464.3	30.0	8.8	18440	102.2	1.7	2.5	20.6	6.9	1206	1625	2915	2906	16.9
Puree																		
Totals	2268.4	93.7	292.1	83.3	491.5	31.1	8.5	19578	108.7	1.9	2.6	23.8	7.3	1268	1461	2783	2917	20.7
Soft, Low Fiber																		
Totals	2233.4	99.8	307.5	69.8	447.1	26.1	9.5	19666	91.6	2.0	2.6	25.8	5.8	1332	1729	2008	3079	20.6
Low Fat, Low Cholesterol																		
Totals	1930.2	82.9	306.6	45.8	140.2	13.5	5.1	10801	168.2	1.7	2.4	18.5	5.7	1296	1600	2591	3358	18.0
No Concentrated Sweets																		
Totals	1967.5	105.0	214.2	78.8	488.4	21.3	9.6	10303	125.8	1.7	2.7	22.8	8.0	1461	1893	3064	3522	19.2

DIET	KCAL	PROT GM	CHO GM	FAT GM	KCAL DISTRIBUTIONS: Pro%	CHO%	Fat%	Milk EXG	Frt EXG	Veg EXG	Brd EXG	Meat EXG	Fat EXG
No Concentrated Sweets													
Totals	1967.5	105.0	214.2	78.8	21.3	43.5	36.0	3.2	2.6	3.4	7.4	7.2	11.5
1200 Calorie													
Totals	1211.6	71.0	133.1	45.7	23.4	43.9	33.9	2.4	1.4	3.1	4.1	4.8	6.2
1500 Calorie													
Totals	1500.3	86.3	161.7	58.2	23.0	43.1	34.9	2.4	1.4	3.3	5.8	6.3	7.8
1800 Calorie													
Totals	1802.8	91.8	200.8	72.4	20.3	44.5	36.1	2.7	2.4	3.3	7.2	6.3	10.4
2000 Calorie													
Totals	2001.8	105.0	214.3	82.6	20.9	42.8	37.1	3.2	2.6	3.4	7.4	7.1	12.3

NUTRIENT ANALYSIS: Passover

	KCAL	PROT gm	CHO gm	FAT gm	CHOL mg	SFA gm	PFA gm	VITA IU	VITC mg	THI* mg	RIB* mg	NIA* mg	B-12* mcg	Ca mg	P mg	Na mg	K mg	Fe mg
RDA/ESA: MALE 51+	range	range	none	none	none	none	none	5000	60	1.2	1.4	15	2.0	800	800	range	range	10
Regular, Liberal Bland, and No Added Salt																		
Totals	2813.9	148.9	333.4	102.8	1109.9	38.2	17.7	1371.6	119.4	1.4	2.4	49.1	6.8	1209.3	1855.7	1603.9	5044.9	13.9
1–2 GM NA (Low Sodium)																		
Totals	2822.3	149.1	334.6	102.7	1109.9	38.2	17.6	1315.5	126.4	1.5	2.3	29.5	6.8	1205.1	1864.2	1075.8	4947.4	14.1
Mechanical Soft																		
Totals	2484.9	145.4	294.0	87.2	1184.9	32.8	16.1	1363.9	114.8	1.4	2.5	49.8	7.2	1278.8	1928.9	1748.7	5453.3	14.8
Puree																		
Totals	2479.7	143.9	299.1	85.9	1119.3	32.4	15.9	1389.7	117.8	1.4	2.5	50.2	6.9	1275.8	1921.2	1736.9	5500.1	14.9
Soft, Low Fiber																		
Totals	2559.4	141.2	325.3	79.4	952.4	27.7	15.4	1165.1	103.7	1.18	2.0	47.1	6.1	1023.4	1649.6	1500.9	4528.0	12.8
Low Fat, Low Cholesterol																		
Totals	2094.6	126.7	325.9	34.9	294.9	6.7	9.9	1170.6	118.9	1.17	1.8	21.9	5.3	1123.4	1548.2	1572.3	4271.2	10.7
No Concentrated Sweets																		
Totals	2115.2	138.3	275.1	53.3	945.9	15.5	10.9	1411.1	118.8	1.4	2.1	25.0	7.3	1212.7	1788.3	1655.5	4895.4	13.3

DIET	KCAL	PROT GM	CHO GM	FAT GM	KCAL DISTRIBUTIONS: Pro%	CHO%	Fat%	Milk EXG	Frt EXG	Veg EXG	Brd EXG	Meat EXG	Fat EXG
No Concentrated Sweets													
Totals	2115.2	138.3	275.1	53.3	25.3	52.0	22.7	3.3	3.3	4.8	11.8	6.6	6.4
1200 Calorie													
Totals	1204.4	84.9	159.8	26.8	26.9	53.1	20.0	2.2	2.0	4.4	6.1	4.4	2.4
1500 Calorie													
Totals	1490.5	111.3	193.0	31.3	29.4	51.7	18.9	2.2	2.5	4.7	8.1	6.0	2.6
1800 Calorie													
Totals	1798.7	118.3	231.2	45.1	26.1	51.4	22.5	2.3	2.5	4.7	10.7	6.0	5.1
2000 Calorie													
Totals	1999.4	134.9	247.5	52.9	26.7	49.5	23.8	3.1	2.3	4.8	11.2	6.6	6.4

APPENDIX 9

NUTRIENT ANALYSIS: Easter

RDA/ESA: MALE 51+	KCAL range	PROT gm range	CHO gm none	FAT gm none	CHOL mg none	SFA gm none	PFA gm none	VITA IU 5000	VITC mg 60	THI* mg 1.2	RIB* mg 1.4	NIA* mg 15	B-12* mcg 2.0	Ca mg 800	P mg 800	Na mg range	K mg range	Fe mg 10
Regular, Liberal Bland, and No Added Salt																		
Totals	2759.6	98.3	352.8	109.2	577.2	31.2	26.7	44481	120.1	1.7	2.4	22.3	3.8	971.1	1407	2450	3504	16.4
1-2 GM NA (Low Sodium)																		
Totals	2799.3	98.7	344.9	116.8	606.0	34.0	27.6	44494	120.1	1.6	2.4	21.9	3.9	1003	1452	1183	3540	15.5
Mechanical Soft																		
Totals	2593.1	96.8	346.0	93.9	577.2	29.3	17.8	39559	104.0	1.5	2.3	21.8	3.8	940.8	1369	2423	3289	14.6
Puree																		
Totals	2383.8	93.5	315.0	85.1	495.1	26.9	14.6	38872	104.3	1.6	2.2	22.6	3.5	1054	1596	2330	3410	14.8
Soft, Low Fiber																		
Totals	2608.2	97.1	336.7	99.4	592.6	31.8	17.9	39404	103.8	1.5	2.3	21.7	3.8	912.0	1915	1419	3247	14.9
Low Fat, Low Cholesterol																		
Totals	2076.5	99.1	327.8	42.5	124.1	10.1	10.3	45539	117.1	1.5	2.4	21.2	2.9	1074	1520	2277	3839	15.1
No Concentrated Sweets																		
Totals	2031.9	114.7	245.4	66.0	526.3	17.7	14.9	44821	118.1	1.7	2.6	23.9	4.5	1255	1738	2573	3876	14.7

DIET	KCAL	PROT GM	CHO GM	FAT GM	KCAL DISTRIBUTIONS: Pro%	CHO%	Fat%	Milk EXG	Frt EXG	Veg EXG	Brd EXG	Meat EXG	Fat EXG
No Concentrated Sweets													
Totals	2031.9	114.7	245.4	66.0	22.5	48.3	29.2	3.1	3.3	4.2	8.8	8.7	7.4
1200 Calorie													
Totals	1221.2	74.4	153.0	35.6	24.3	50.1	26.3	2.4	2.0	4.1	4.7	5.6	2.9
1500 Calorie													
Totals	1497.0	91.7	176.8	47.5	24.5	47.2	28.5	2.4	2.6	4.1	5.6	7.6	4.3
1800 Calorie													
Totals	1790.2	98.1	219.6	58.5	21.9	49.0	29.4	2.6	3.4	4.1	7.5	7.6	6.4
2000 Calorie													
Totals	2006.9	114.2	239.7	66.1	22.7	47.7	29.6	3.1	3.6	4.2	8.2	8.7	7.4

NUTRIENT ANALYSIS: Mother's Day

RDA/ESA: MALE 51+	KCAL gm range	PROT gm range	CHO gm none	FAT gm none	CHOL mg none	SFA gm none	PFA gm none	VITA IU 5000	VITC mg 60	THI* mg 1.2	RIB* mg 1.4	NIA* mg 15	B-12* mcg 2.0	Ca mg 800	P mg 800	Na mg range	K mg range	Fe mg 10
Regular, Liberal Bland, and No Added Salt																		
Totals	2887.1	94.0	346.0	130.6	365.9	33.9	39.2	13628	112.8	1.4	2.2	21.1	4.8	1352	1562	2110	3873	18.4
1-2 GM NA (Low Sodium)																		
Totals	2796.4	95.5	341.8	121.5	359.5	32.6	30.0	15602	112.5	1.4	2.2	24.2	7.5	1315	1537	1261	3932	19.2
Mechanical Soft																		
Totals	2786.4	93.3	357.5	114.1	365.9	31.8	29.6	13273	88.4	1.4	2.2	20.1	4.8	1356	1546	2298	3661	18.5
Puree																		
Totals	2497.2	92.2	332.1	93.7	359.5	28.7	23.8	12520	93.8	1.4	2.1	20.5	4.7	1324	1483	2073	3759	18.3
Soft, Low Fiber																		
Totals	2855.0	105.5	358.5	114.9	520.6	35.3	31.5	15793	98.4	1.7	2.4	22.1	5.4	1604	1710	2270	3943	20.8
Low Fat, Low Cholesterol																		
Totals	2069.7	86.7	344.9	41.7	182.7	8.0	10.7	13993	111.5	1.4	1.9	17.7	4.2	1296	1479	2428	3441	18.0
No Concentrated Sweets																		
Totals	2001.7	102.8	244.3	70.7	296.2	13.6	18.1	13928	108.9	1.4	2.2	20.8	5.1	1432	1624	2457	3567	18.0

DIET	KCAL	PROT GM	CHO GM	FAT GM	KCAL DISTRIBUTIONS: Pro%	CHO%	Fat%	Milk EXG	Frt EXG	Veg EXG	Brd EXG	Meat EXG	Fat EXG
No Concentrated Sweets													
Totals	2001.7	102.8	244.3	70.7	20.5	48.8	31.8	3.1	4.5	3.7	7.0	8.3	9.6
1200 Calorie													
Totals	1207.7	68.9	161.3	33.3	22.8	53.4	24.8	2.0	3.0	2.3	4.6	7.3	2.5
1500 Calorie													
Totals	1511.3	89.3	193.5	44.0	23.6	51.2	26.2	2.4	3.9	3.4	4.9	9.0	4.4
1800 Calorie													
Totals	1808.8	95.5	228.2	59.0	21.1	50.4	29.3	2.6	4.4	3.4	6.4	9.0	7.3
2000 Calorie													
Totals	1995.4	108.9	237.0	70.3	21.8	47.5	31.7	3.1	4.4	3.7	6.4	9.8	9.3

NUTRIENT ANALYSIS: Father's Day

RDA/ESA: MALE 51+	KCAL gm range	PROT gm range	CHO gm none	FAT gm none	CHOL mg none	SFA gm none	PFA gm none	VITA IU 5000	VITC mg 60	THI* mg 1.2	RIB* mg 1.4	NIA* mg 15	B-12* mcg 2.0	Ca mg 800	P mg 800	Na mg range	K mg range	Fe mg 10
Regular, Liberal Bland, and No Added Salt																		
Totals	2594.9	110.9	324.9	97.7	517.3	35.0	15.9	25857	153.4	1.9	2.5	20.3	6.8	1385	1721	2379	4401	20.5
1-2 GM NA (Low Sodium)																		
Totals	2442.2	104.4	325.5	83.5	490.9	28.0	12.6	25594	157.2	1.6	2.6	19.2	5.9	1242	1518	1270	4323	20.4
Mechanical Soft																		
Totals	2533.6	109.9	326.2	90.0	508.3	33.9	13.1	30716	168.2	1.9	2.5	20.0	6.8	1367	1689	2370	4111	20.3
Puree																		
Totals	2575.1	109.9	338.3	89.2	718.6	36.9	11.4	30955	209.4	1.8	2.6	19.5	7.2	1431	1682	2182	4182	21.0
Soft, Low Fiber																		
Totals	2210.0	93.0	316.2	65.5	395.3	24.7	8.5	28728	186.8	1.2	2.2	18.6	5.7	1061	1212	1529	3893	18.0
Low Fat, Low Cholesterol																		
Totals	1993.3	93.7	323.5	38.7	136.9	11.2	6.0	25968	157.3	1.6	2.5	17.0	5.2	1363	1445	1524	4307	18.2
No Concentrated Sweets																		
Totals	2014.8	118.9	252.5	59.4	372.1	17.7	8.1	25753	164.8	1.8	2.6	21.3	6.6	1302	1661	2113	4369	19.1

DIET	KCAL	PROT GM	CHO GM	FAT GM	KCAL DISTRIBUTIONS: Pro%	CHO%	Fat%	Milk EXG	Frt EXG	Veg EXG	Brd EXG	Meat EXG	Fat EXG
No Concentrated Sweets													
Totals	2014.8	118.9	252.5	59.4	23.6	50.1	26.5	2.7	5.2	2.9	8.9	7.8	6.9
1200 Calorie													
Totals	1199.9	75.2	160.3	29.2	25.0	53.4	21.9	2.2	3.5	2.2	4.8	5.0	2.4
1500 Calorie													
Totals	1494.0	95.9	196.2	36.6	25.6	52.5	22.0	2.2	3.5	2.5	7.3	6.3	3.3
1800 Calorie													
Totals	1802.2	103.9	227.8	53.5	23.0	50.5	26.7	2.2	4.3	2.5	8.8	6.5	6.3
2000 Calorie													
Totals	2004.6	121.5	248.1	58.6	24.2	49.5	26.3	2.8	4.3	2.5	9.8	8.0	6.3

NUTRIENT ANALYSIS: Independence Day

RDA/ESA: MALE 51+	KCAL range	PROT gm range	CHO gm none	FAT gm none	CHOL mg none	SFA gm none	PFA gm none	VITA IU 5000	VITC mg 60	THI* mg 1.2	RIB* mg 1.4	NIA* mg 15	B-12* mcg 2.0	Ca mg 800	P mg 800	Na mg range	K mg range	Fe mg 10
Regular, Liberal Bland, and No Added Salt																		
Totals	2839.0	122.6	319.3	123.6	793.0	41.1	17.1	17305	188.3	1.9	2.9	29.4	8.2	1480	1989	2788	4894	24.5
1-2 GM NA (Low Sodium)																		
Totals	2516.6	111.5	323.5	91.3	658.9	30.2	14.3	16963	205.3	1.8	2.7	28.4	7.2	1346	1761	1671	4929	22.8
Mechanical Soft																		
Totals	2669.0	117.6	317.7	106.3	762.9	36.0	12.3	29172	105.3	1.8	2.8	29.0	8.0	1388	1782	2706	4435	23.6
Puree																		
Totals	2733.3	126.9	330.2	103.6	779.1	34.8	12.2	29706	103.2	1.8	2.8	32.6	8.6	1447	1893	2496	4780	25.7
Soft, Low Fiber																		
Totals	2426.3	109.4	327.9	79.1	720.6	28.0	11.5	28961	121.6	1.6	2.5	28.2	7.3	1255	1624	2177	4346	23.5
Low Fat, Low Cholesterol																		
Totals	2030.1	110.2	302.7	46.3	132.8	12.2	8.7	18302.0	204.2	1.8	2.7	26.9	6.4	1459	1813	2264	4918	22.8
NO CONCENTRATED SWEETS																		
Totals	2036.6	125.3	248.3	63.3	600.4	17.7	10.1	16765	207.7	1.8	2.8	32.3	8.5	1453	1955	2509	4866	23.7

DIET	KCAL	PROT GM	CHO GM	FAT GM	KCAL DISTRIBUTIONS: Pro%	CHO%	Fat%	Milk EXG	Frt EXG	Veg EXG	Brd EXG	Meat EXG	Fat EXG
No Concentrated Sweets													
Totals	2036.6	125.3	248.3	63.3	24.6	48.7	27.9	3.0	3.7	5.1	9.1	8.3	6.6
1200 Calorie													
Totals	1204.7	76.8	156.1	33.1	25.5	51.8	24.7	2.0	2.4	4.5	5.2	5.0	2.3
1500 Calorie													
Totals	1502.7	101.5	176.0	45.8	27.0	46.8	27.4	2.2	2.4	4.7	6.4	7.3	3.5
1800 Calorie													
Totals	1810.0	108.2	210.5	62.0	23.9	46.5	30.8	2.2	2.4	4.9	8.5	7.6	6.5
2000 Calorie													
Totals	1996.0	124.0	240.4	62.9	24.8	48.1	28.3	3.0	3.7	4.9	8.6	8.2	6.6

NUTRIENT ANALYSIS: Labor Day

RDA/ESA: MALE 51+	KCAL range	PROT gm range	CHO gm none	FAT gm none	CHOL mg none	SFA gm none	PFA gm none	VITA IU 5000	VITC mg 60	THI* mg 1.2	RIB* mg 1.4	NIA* mg 15	B-12* mcg 2.0	Ca mg 800	P mg 800	Na mg range	K mg range	Fe mg 10
Regular, Liberal Bland, and No Added Salt																		
Totals	2674.7	119.9	289.9	119.4	604.4	34.0	31.0	31094	119.2	1.7	2.8	32.0	5.9	1519	2168	3302	4253	19.2
1–2 GM NA (Low Sodium)																		
Totals	2499.8	117.1	294.3	98.8	564.8	27.0	24.8	29752	114.1	1.6	2.5	27.2	5.2	1398	2043	1341	4255	16.5
Mechanical Soft																		
Totals	2638.0	117.4	294.1	114.0	604.0	33.5	29.5	22035	110.1	1.7	2.7	31.8	5.9	1485	2134	2923	4264	19.2
Puree																		
Totals	2630.6	131.9	310.9	98.9	652.9	34.5	20.7	22202	106.6	2.0	2.9	38.4	6.3	1563	2025	2473	4445	21.7
Soft, Low Fiber																		
Totals	2157.1	106.2	283.0	70.3	535.7	23.0	12.6	19984	117.8	1.7	2.5	31.0	4.9	1276	1638	1536	4108	19.2
Low Fat, Low Cholesterol																		
Totals	1972.9	113.3	289.3	44.1	175.1	8.2	11.3	32881	135.2	1.7	2.6	28.3	5.2	1542	2066	3065	4460	19.3
No Concentrated Sweets																		
Totals	1986.3	119.8	252.8	58.1	523.7	13.2	12.1	31545	138.4	1.7	2.6	32.5	5.9	1544	2153	3248	4305	18.3

DIET	KCAL	PROT GM	CHO GM	FAT GM	KCAL DISTRIBUTIONS: Pro%	CHO%	Fat%	Milk EXG	Frt EXG	Veg EXG	Brd EXG	Meat EXG	Fat EXG
No Concentrated Sweets													
Totals	1986.3	119.8	252.8	58.1	24.1	50.9	26.3	2.9	3.8	4.3	8.1	7.5	8.4
1200 Calorie													
Totals	1211.1	77.2	170.2	27.5	25.5	56.2	20.4	2.1	2.5	3.7	5.2	4.3	3.6
1500 Calorie													
Totals	1498.4	96.8	207.0	33.6	25.8	55.2	20.2	2.1	3.2	4.2	6.6	6.1	4.0
1800 Calorie													
Totals	1803.1	104.0	238.3	50.4	23.0	52.8	25.1	2.3	3.4	4.3	8.1	6.4	7.2
2000 Calorie													
Totals	2012.4	120.3	258.6	58.5	23.9	51.4	26.1	2.9	4.2	4.3	8.1	7.5	8.4

NUTRIENT ANALYSIS: Halloween

RDA/ESA: MALE 51+	KCAL range	PROT gm range	CHO gm none	FAT gm none	CHOL mg none	SFA gm none	PFA gm none	VITA IU 5000	VITC mg 60	THI* mg 1.2	RIB* mg 1.4	NIA* mg 15	B-12* mcg 2.0	Ca mg 800	P mg 800	Na mg range	K mg range	Fe mg 10
Regular, Liberal Bland, and No Added Salt																		
Totals	2638.4	108.09	290.5	119.5	652.0	37.4	25.2	22354	72.3	2.3	3.0	24.0	9.4	1501	1971	3032	4050	16.2
1–2 GM NA (Low Sodium)																		
Totals	2369.4	102.7	291.6	92.6	587.9	29.1	15.4	22627	79.8	2.1	2.8	22.6	10.4	1534	1924	1574	3987	15.8
Mechanical Soft																		
Totals	2627.6	108.6	282.8	121.5	653.6	37.6	26.6	24034	71.6	2.3	3.0	23.9	9.4	1498	1963	3036	3983	16.0
Puree																		
Totals	2439.8	108.8	289.2	97.2	586.3	30.9	22.2	17757	70.1	2.6	2.9	25.5	8.6	1473	1847	2453	4083	15.7
Soft, Low Fiber																		
Totals	2220.9	92.5	255.1	93.9	549.5	29.4	20.8	19783	62.7	2.2	2.3	21.1	7.5	1317	1541	2333	3443	14.1
Low Fat, Low Cholesterol																		
Totals	1967.0	105.4	291.9	45.9	132.5	10.8	11.1	24236	82.1	1.9	2.8	22.4	8.9	1598	1972	2599	4320	16.5
No Concentrated Sweets																		
Totals	2087.7	113.3	242.1	75.8	587.3	21.2	13.3	22303	64.7	2.1	2.8	24.6	9.8	1516	2024	2725	4157	15.7

DIET	KCAL	PROT GM	CHO GM	FAT GM	KCAL DISTRIBUTIONS: Pro%	CHO%	Fat%	Milk EXG	Frt EXG	Veg EXG	Brd EXG	Meat EXG	Fat EXG
No Concentrated Sweets													
Totals	2087.7	113.3	242.1	75.8	21.7	46.3	32.6	3.1	3.7	3.1	8.7	8.3	9.2
1200 Calorie													
Totals	1201.4	72.4	156.1	34.2	24.1	51.9	25.6	2.4	2.7	2.9	4.4	5.3	2.9
1500 Calorie													
Totals	1498.2	89.5	194.9	42.8	23.9	52.0	25.7	2.4	3.2	3.1	6.7	6.8	3.4
1800 Calorie													
Totals	1801.5	96.8	227.3	58.1	21.4	50.4	29.0	2.6	3.3	3.1	8.6	6.8	6.5
2000 Calorie													
Totals	1992.4	109.5	241.7	67.2	21.9	48.5	30.3	3.1	3.7	3.1	8.7	7.8	7.8

APPENDIX 9

733

NUTRIENT ANALYSIS: Thanksgiving

	KCAL	PROT gm	CHO gm	FAT gm	CHOL mg	SFA gm	PFA gm	VITA IU	VITC mg	THI* mg	RIB* mg	NIA* mg	B-12* mcg	Ca mg	P mg	Na mg	K mg	Fe mg
RDA/ESA: MALE 51+	range	range	none	none	none	none	none	5000	60	1.2	1.4	15	2.0	800	800	range	range	10
Regular, Liberal Bland, and No Added Salt																		
Totals	2908.9	122.6	342.8	121.3	574.3	30.6	34.8	16687	181.6	1.8	2.9	33.1	7.4	1232	1788	3097	5274	22.9
1–2 GM NA (Low Sodium)																		
Totals	2876.6	118.4	348.3	117.6	579.6	28.0	38.6	17072	179.1	1.9	3.0	31.4	7.1	1235	1691	1313	4950	23.9
Mechanical Soft																		
Totals	2989.7	121.8	359.5	122.9	553.9	35.7	28.2	15662	142.3	1.7	2.9	32.2	7.3	1238	1806	3411	4948	22.3
Puree																		
Totals	2748.8	131.8	338.8	101.1	534.1	30.9	21.0	14519	147.9	1.6	2.7	34.7	7.4	1225	1896	2865	5417	22.0
Soft, Low Fiber																		
Totals	2691.3	117.2	342.2	98.8	481.1	30.3	21.4	14639	137.0	1.6	2.8	31.6	6.9	1224	1710	3117	4800	21.7
Low Fat, Low Cholesterol																		
Totals	2135.4	102.6	329.1	49.2	135.8	12.2	13.8	15954	174.5	1.6	2.4	29.5	4.2	1071	1528	2858	4979	21.0
No Concentrated Sweets																		
Totals	2104.0	105.6	270.8	66.4	421.9	18.3	18.3	15873	172.4	1.7	2.6	31.4	5.2	1239	1742	3017	5226	21.0

DIET	KCAL	PROT GM	CHO GM	FAT GM	KCAL DISTRIBUTIONS: Pro%	CHO%	Fat%	Milk EXG	Frt EXG	Veg EXG	Brd EXG	Meat EXG	Fat EXG
No Concentrated Sweets													
Totals	2104.0	105.6	270.8	66.4	20.0	51.5	28.4	2.6	5.2	2.9	9.7	7.0	9.0
1200 Calorie													
Totals	1217.8	77.6	154.4	33.6	25.4	50.7	24.8	2.1	2.2	2.4	5.0	5.5	3.8
1500 Calorie													
Totals	1505.1	90.5	190.0	42.5	24.0	50.5	25.4	2.1	3.3	2.9	6.6	6.8	4.4
1800 Calorie													
Totals	1811.4	99.4	232.4	53.7	21.9	51.3	26.7	2.1	4.2	2.9	8.5	7.2	6.4
2000 Calorie													
Totals	1997.2	112.1	253.0	59.6	22.4	50.6	26.8	2.6	4.2	2.9	9.4	8.0	7.0

NUTRIENT ANALYSIS: Christmas

RDA/ESA: MALE 51+	KCAL gm range	PROT gm range	CHO gm none	FAT gm none	CHOL mg none	SFA gm none	PFA gm none	VITA IU 5000	VITC mg 60	THI* mg 1.2	RIB* mg 1.4	NIA* mg 15	B-12* mcg 2.0	Ca mg 800	P mg 800	Na mg range	K mg range	Fe mg 10
Regular, Liberal Bland, and No Added Salt																		
Totals	2817.4	119.4	334.8	115.7	542.8	32.7	27.0	15537	194.4	1.7	2.6	30.7	6.5	1505.8	2001.7	2708.8	4614.2	27.4
1-2 GM NA (Low Sodium)																		
Totals	2778.6	110.2	337.1	114.5	532.5	31.3	26.7	15445	239.4	1.8	2.4	29.6	5.8	1408.9	1826.5	1103.6	4399.7	28.9
Mechanical Soft																		
Totals	2710.2	114.4	342.2	100.9	536.6	30.9	19.9	15064	240.5	1.8	2.5	31.1	6.0	1338.8	1816.2	2556.1	4365.5	27.1
Puree																		
Totals	2756.5	128.6	303.2	115.3	630.1	47.5	14.8	15061	243.6	1.9	2.7	34.7	6.9	1487.1	1953.1	2665.4	4547.1	32.4
Soft, Low Fiber																		
Totals	2328.7	110.2	282.8	85.8	506.3	29.9	13.7	14431	239.9	1.7	2.3	29.8	5.8	1302.7	1714.0	2446.1	4222.3	26.8
Low Fat, Low Cholesterol																		
Totals	1992.8	98.6	301.3	45.6	163.8	17.6	6.4	14046	133.8	1.5	2.2	25.8	4.5	1304.2	1606.6	2380.2	3805.9	25.7
No Concentrated Sweets																		
Totals	2164.9	120.9	261.0	72.9	472.0	25.2	11.5	14680	128.5	1.6	2.3	33.7	6.6	1429.6	1867.7	2852.0	4265.2	26.7

DIET	KCAL	PROT GM	CHO GM	FAT GM	KCAL DISTRIBUTIONS: Pro%	CHO%	Fat%	Milk EXG	Frt EXG	Veg EXG	Brd EXG	Meat EXG	Fat EXG
No Concentrated Sweets													
Totals	2164.9	120.3	261.0	72.9	21.6	48.4	30.0	3.3	4.9	3.4	8.9	7.2	9.1
1200 Calorie													
Totals	1204.4	84.3	156.0	27.4	27.6	51.8	20.5	2.3	3.0	3.3	4.4	6.4	1.5
1500 Calorie													
Totals	1510.2	93.9	174.5	49.3	24.3	46.2	29.4	2.3	3.0	3.4	5.7	7.2	5.1
1800 Calorie													
Totals	1802.6	99.2	220.6	59.9	21.1	48.9	29.9	2.3	4.5	3.4	7.1	7.2	7.2
2000 Calorie													
Totals	1991.7	117.7	245.0	61.3	23.0	49.2	27.7	3.4	4.5	3.4	8.0	7.8	7.4

APPENDIX 9

NUTRIENT ANALYSIS: Dining Abroad

RDA/ESA: MALE 51+	KCAL range	PROT gm range	CHO gm none	FAT gm none	CHOL mg none	SFA gm none	PFA gm none	VITA IU 5000	VITC mg 60	THI* mg 1.2	RIB* mg 1.4	NIA* mg 15	B-12* mcg 2.0	Ca mg 800	P mg 800	Na mg range	K mg range	Fe mg 10
Regular, Liberal Bland, and No Added Salt																		
Totals	2648.2	110.1	271.4	127.5	720.7	38.3	29.4	14881	140.1	1.9	2.8	28.9	4.5	1722	1801	2876	3426	22.9
1–2 GM NA (Low Sodium)																		
Totals	2389.2	89.5	273.1	107.9	540.0	28.5	28.0	13805	139.1	1.9	2.5	28.7	3.2	1195	1356	1692	3307	22.5
Mechanical Soft																		
Totals	2429.9	107.7	278.1	100.4	710.7	32.8	18.3	14368	122.6	1.9	2.8	29.2	4.5	1717.4	1771	2726	3407	22.9
Puree																		
Totals	2385.3	107.1	301.0	85.9	711.4	31.6	15.8	14375	143.5	1.9	2.8	29.7	4.5	1720	1754	2615	3753	23.9
Soft, Low Fiber																		
Totals	2279.1	104.3	289.1	79.8	679.2	25.4	10.6	7589	97.2	1.8	2.5	33.0	5.4	955.0	1390	2095	3527	22.3
Low Fat, Low Cholesterol																		
Totals	1907.3	101.4	278.5	44.9	103.9	6.9	9.3	15140	144.9	1.9	2.5	29.2	2.8	1630	1374	3234	3549	21.9
No Concentrated Sweets																		
Totals	2128.7	112.3	267.5	69.4	501.6	12.6	15.3	14439	145.1	1.9	2.6	31.1	4.0	1647	1501	3557	3536	23.5

DIET	KCAL	PROT GM	CHO GM	FAT GM	KCAL DISTRIBUTIONS: Pro%	CHO%	Fat%	Milk EXG	Frt EXG	Veg EXG	Brd EXG	Meat EXG	Fat EXG
No Concentrated Sweets													
Totals	2128.7	112.3	267.5	69.4	21.1	50.2	29.3	2.6	4.6	4.1	8.5	7.2	11.1
1200 Calorie													
Totals	1205.3	74.5	167.7	27.7	24.7	55.6	20.6	2.1	3.6	3.1	4.0	5.0	3.6
1500 Calorie													
Totals	1496.0	90.8	203.3	37.0	24.2	54.3	22.2	2.1	3.8	3.9	5.6	6.2	5.1
1800 Calorie													
Totals	1801.7	94.3	232.4	56.9	20.9	51.6	28.4	2.1	4.6	3.9	6.8	6.2	8.8
2000 Calorie													
Totals	1997.4	109.8	253.0	62.4	22.0	50.6	28.1	2.6	4.6	4.1	7.6	7.2	9.8

RDA/ESA: MALE 51+	KCAL range	PROT gm range	CHO gm none	FAT gm none	CHOL mg none	SFA gm none	PFA gm none	VITA IU 5000	VITC mg 60	THI* mg 1.2	RIB* mg 1.4	NIA* mg 15	B-12* mcg 2.0	Ca mg 800	P mg 800	Na mg range	K mg range	Fe mg 10
Regular, Liberal Bland, and No Added Salt																		
Totals	2183.2	124.4	233.5	85.8	737.9	25.7	18.0	6039	245.5	1.4	2.2	18.1	10.1	1357	1909	1402	4629	16.0
1–2 GM NA (Low Sodium)																		
Totals	2082.9	123.6	230.3	82.7	737.9	25.2	17.6	5345	233.3	1.4	2.2	17.5	10.1	1085	1898	1072	4479	15.8
Mechanical Soft																		
Totals	2135.5	124.4	239.8	77.3	737.9	24.6	13.2	6171	247.9	1.5	2.2	18.1	10.1	1338	1905	1389	4724	15.9
Puree																		
Totals	2265.1	131.0	270.6	75.2	736.9	25.6	12.8	6125	252.6	1.8	2.3	20.0	10.0	1284	1878	1595	5139	16.2
Soft, Low Fiber																		
Totals	2083.7	120.3	233.2	75.0	751.4	24.7	11.9	5739	173.9	1.6	2.2	18.9	10.0	1250	1720	1770	4264	14.5
Low Fat, Low Cholesterol																		
Totals	1931.4	131.4	256.8	43.2	162.6	7.5	11.8	8803	242.3	1.5	2.3	18.6	9.2	1437	1961	1552	4895	18.3
No Concentrated Sweets																		
Totals	2101.5	136.8	245.6	64.8	935.9	12.9	14.0	6921	248.1	1.5	2.4	20.4	11.1	1513	2116	1579	4868	19.0

DIET	KCAL	PROT GM	CHO GM	FAT GM	KCAL DISTRIBUTIONS: Pro%	CHO%	Fat%	VITA Milk EXG	VITC Frt EXG	THI* Veg EXG	RIB* Brd EXG	NIA* Meat EXG	B-12* Fat EXG
No Concentrated Sweets													
Totals	2101.5	136.8	245.6	64.8	26.0	46.7	27.7	3.4	3.1	5.5	9.0	9.2	6.9
1200 Calorie													
Totals	1198.1	90.2	144.8	29.6	30.1	48.3	22.2	2.5	2.2	4.9	4.2	5.9	2.5
1500 Calorie													
Totals	1498.0	110.1	177.4	39.3	29.4	47.3	23.6	2.5	2.2	5.2	6.6	7.3	3.4
1800 Calorie													
Totals	1802.7	117.3	218.7	52.3	26.0	48.5	26.1	2.5	2.7	5.2	8.3	7.7	5.4
2000 Calorie													
Totals	1997.6	129.7	242.9	57.7	25.9	48.6	26.0	3.3	3.1	5.3	9.0	8.2	6.2

NUTRIENT ANALYSIS: Southern Hospitality

RDA/ESA: MALE 51+	KCAL range	PROT gm range	CHO gm none	FAT gm none	CHOL mg none	SFA gm none	PFA gm none	VITA IU 5000	VITC mg 60	THI* mg 1.2	RIB* mg 1.4	NIA* mg 15	B-12* mcg 2.0	Ca mg 800	P mg 800	Na mg range	K mg range	Fe mg 10
Regular, Liberal Bland, and No Added Salt																		
Totals	2740.9	105.7	304.5	125.2	657.8	38.3	22.0	7668	149.7	1.9	2.3	25.0	6.4	1166	1619	2711	4269	18.5
1–2 GM NA (Low Sodium)																		
Totals	2721.9	103.7	302.3	125.1	657.5	38.1	21.8	7320	142.5	1.8	2.2	22.7	6.3	1247	1711	1215	4142	18.5
Mechanical Soft																		
Totals	2394.6	100.8	263.3	106.6	530.0	35.7	16.8	8153	116.2	1.8	2.2	24.9	6.1	1108	1534	2586	4437	17.4
Puree																		
Totals	2302.1	98.1	282.1	90.0	490.0	31.5	13.8	7890	118.4	1.9	2.2	25.5	5.5	1051	1422	2096	4671	18.0
Soft, Low Fiber																		
Totals	2139.1	89.6	239.4	92.6	496.7	32.1	13.5	5791	101.3	1.4	2.0	22.9	5.5	995.3	1282	2082	3643	14.2
Low Fat, Low Cholesterol																		
Totals	1769.3	85.5	269.9	45.5	178.4	12.4	6.6	7304	143.4	1.7	2.0	19.3	4.7	1143	1417	2240	4155	15.7
No Concentrated Sweets																		
Totals	2006.5	113.2	232.6	70.3	579.1	20.4	11.4	8306	149.0	1.9	2.4	27.2	7.1	1307	1757	2661	4507	17.4

DIET	KCAL	PROT GM	CHO GM	FAT GM	KCAL DISTRIBUTIONS: Pro%	CHO%	Fat%	Milk EXG	Frt EXG	Veg EXG	Brd EXG	Meat EXG	Fat EXG
No Concentrated Sweets													
Totals	2006.5	113.2	232.6	70.3	22.6	46.4	31.6	3.0	3.4	3.5	9.0	7.2	9.2
1200 Calorie													
Totals	1214.5	71.5	142.1	40.0	23.5	46.8	29.6	1.9	2.1	1.5	5.9	4.9	4.4
1500 Calorie													
Totals	1513.5	90.1	172.2	52.5	23.8	45.5	31.2	2.1	2.4	3.3	6.9	6.2	5.9
1800 Calorie													
Totals	1796.1	101.1	219.1	59.0	22.5	48.8	29.6	2.4	2.8	3.5	9.5	6.3	6.9
2000 Calorie													
Totals	1995.7	117.2	225.2	71.1	23.5	45.1	32.1	2.9	2.8	3.5	9.5	7.2	9.1

Glossary

Absorption. The intake and transport of nutrients to the bloodstream.

Acid-Forming Foods. Foods that leave an acid residue. Examples: cereals, legumes, meats, cranberries, plums, prunes, and vinegar.

Agar. A clear, tasteless vegetable gelatin or thickening agent used in ice creams, jams, jellies, mayonnaise, and soups. It is made from algae or seaweed and comes flaked, granulated, or in bar form.

Alkaline-Forming Foods. Foods that leave an alkaline residue. Examples: fruits, milk, vegetables and baking soda.

American Diabetes Association. A voluntary organization to help improve the condition of diabetes, offering services and education to diabetic members.

American Dietetic Association. A professional organization that sets the educational and professional standards for dietitians and dietetic technicians. The objectives are to improve nutritional status, promote education, and conduct research and development in dietetics and nutrition.

Amino Acids. The chemical compounds, including nitrogen, that makes up protein and referred to as "building blocks." Amino acid and protein terminology includes "essential" and "non-essential," "complete" and "incomplete proteins."

Analog. Make or fabricate a food that resembles or simulates another food. Often, substances made to imitate meat. Examples: Textured vegetable protein (soybean origin), used by vegetarians to resemble bacon, hamburgers, or sausage (called meat analogs).

Anorexia. Loss of appetite, as a result of disease.

AP Weight. The "as purchased" weight of a food item before trimming or cutting.

Appetite. Natural desire or craving for a specific food.

Artificial Sweetener. An alternative to granulated sugar or a concentrated sweet (example: honey, brown sugar). There are many artificial sweeteners on the market, such as saccharin and aspartame.

Arteriosclerosis. A variety of conditions causing the artery walls to become thicker, harder, and to lose elasticity. Treated by a diet low in saturated fats and low in cholesterol diets; avoiding tobacco, alcohol, and stress, and increasing exercise.

Aspartame. An artificial sweetener made from protein. May be used by diabetics.

Atherosclerosis. A form of arteriosclerosis. A chronic and often progressive vascular disease, indicated by hardening, thickening, and loss of elasticity of the inner arterial walls, followed by secondary degenerative changes to the heart, kidneys, lungs, brain, or extremities. Blood flows slower through the narrowed arteries. Risk factors include: increased blood cholesterol and triglycerides, obesity, smoking, hypertension, diabetes mellitus, stress, genetics, and inactivity.

Au Gratin. Broiled food dishes having a lightly browned crust, made with bread crumbs, grated cheese, and/or white sauce. Example: Potatoes au Gratin.

Bake. Cooking foods in the oven with dry, hot air. Examples: breads, fish, pastries, or vegetables.

Basal Metabolism Rate (BMR). The rate at which energy is needed for maintenance of body tissue, for growth and for physical and mental activity. It is measured as the energy or heat production of a person at rest and after a 12-hour fast.

Basic Four Food Groups. A food guide developed by the USDA, to simplify the method of making food selections. Foods are divided into four groups: dairy; fruits and vegetables; breads and cereals; and meats, poultry, and fish. Modification of the Basic Four have been developed in a dietary guide emphasizing lowered fats, cholesterol, salt, and meat and increased dietary fiber and starches.

Baste. Brushing or pouring fat or food drippings on cooking foods. Example: roast turkey.

Batter. A thin mixture of starch (flour) and liquid (milk) used to make breads, cakes, or coatings for deep-fried products.

Beat. Mix, by combining with air, the act of stirring, stroking, or whipping vigorously, with a utensil. Examples: eggs and cream.

Bile. Liquid secretions of the liver, discharged into the duodenum and stored in the gallbladder. It aids in the digestion and absorption of fats.

Blanch. Briefly or partially cooking a food item by immersing into boiling water or hot fat and then sometimes into cold water.

Blend. Combine thoroughly, often in a blender, two or more food items. Examples: cake and cookies.

Blood Sugar. Refers to the glucose circulating in the blood and its adequate supply; which is crucial to the normal functioning of all body cells. The blood sugar level or amount present varies from 70 to 100 mg per 100 ml and is partly controlled by the dietary intake and primarily by the hormones insulin and glycogen, and the pituitary and adrenal glands. In dietary treatment for altered blood sugar levels, the principal problem is usually related to an imbalance between supply and demand for insulin and controlling low insulin levels or hyperglycemia (high blood sugar) or high insulin levels or hypoglycemia (low blood sugar).

Boil. Cooking in liquid that is bubbling rapidly, at 212°F (100°C), at sea level.

Bouillon. A clear soup broth, usually beef, chicken, or vegetable.

Braise. Cooking in a covered container in a small amount of liquid.

Bran. Obtained during flour processing, from the outer layers of food grains. It has a laxative effect and gives bulk to the diet. It is used as a breakfast food and baking ingredient and contains carbohydrates, minerals, and vitamins.

Broil. Cooking with dry heat or radiant heat from above, using electric, gas, or charcoal.

Broth. The flavorful, thin liquid part of soup extracted from the boiling, then simmering of meats, vegetables, and sometimes cereals.

Brown. Cooking with heat to attain a brown color.

Brush. Using a thin amount of egg, oil, or sauce to cover food.

Bulk. Undigestible and nonabsorbable fiber from fruits, vegetables, and bran cereals. May help to maintain normal bowel habits.

Caffeine. A stimulant found most frequently in carbonated cola beverages, coffee, tea, and chocolate.

Calorie. (Also known as kilocalories). The unit used to measure the fuel or energy value of food. It is expressed often as the Kcal and is the amount of heat required to raise the temperature of 1 kg of water 1°C.

Calorie Controlled Diets. Used to assist individuals with diabetes mellitus or glucose intolerance, with weight loss or weight gain.

Calorie Requirement. The number of calories (Kcal) needed by a person in a 24 hour period, determined by one's age, sex, size and physical activity. The specific caloric requirement is obtained by using a person's basal metabolism rate (BMR) and factoring in the metabolic action of food, body growth and repair and physical activity.

Cancer. A term for over 100 varieties of malignant cellular growth. The abnormal cancerous cells grow without control, crowding out healthy cells, and using up needed cell nutrients. Contributing carcinogenic factors are known to be alcoholism, smoking, environmental hazards, and dietary factors. Obesity and high-fat diets are linked to cancer, as is stress.

Canola Oil. A mono-unsaturated vegetable oil.

Carbohydrates. A group of sugars and starches, rapidly oxidized, providing the body with abundant fuel, energy, and heat. Found principally in plants and foods such as bread, cereals, potatoes, rice, vegetables (beans, corn, and peas), fruits (apples, banana, oranges, pears), and sugars. Indigestible forms, such as cellulose, provide bulk for the intestine, and greatly aid digestion and elimination and are considered highly desirable in combating the overconsumption of processed and refined foods.

Carcinogen. Any of over 400 different substances that have been identified to cause the development of cancer cells. Dietary components thought to be carcinogenic are nitrite, nitrate compounds, cyclamates, various food colors, saccharin, sassafras tea, and smoked products.

Cardiovascular Disease. Heart or arterial diseases resulting from blood flow obstructions, weakened blood vessels, and the formation of plaque or fatty deposits along arterial walls. The latter, atherosclerosis, is closely associated with high blood "cholesterol" levels.

Casserole. A meal served completely in one (casserole) dish containing a variety or combination of foods.

Cellulose. A fibrous form of indigestible and insoluble carbohydrate, often called roughage, and occurring widely in plants. It has no energy value but provides vital bulk or fiber to the diet, facilitating digestion and elimination, and preventing constipation and other problems. Sources include bran, whole grain cereals, and fibrous fruits and vegetables.

Cereal (See Grains). Normally, a breakfast entree containing one or more grains. Whole grain cereals have a substantially higher nutritive content than do "refined cereals," which remove the germ and bran. Refined or fortified cereals that add certain nutritional components do not nutritionally replace whole grain cereals. Grain is at the base of the new food nutritional pyramid.

Cholesterol. A fatty substance found in saturated fats and body cells. Lower levels are essential to health, while excess levels can get stored in the arteries, causing damage and narrowing of the arteries, possibly leading to heart disease (arteriosclerosis). Lower blood cholesterol levels can be obtained by decreasing saturated fats, such as butter, lard, and hard margarine in the diet. Conversely, a low-fat diet is recommended using starches and carbohydrates as energy sources (grains, fruits, and vegetables).

Cholesterol-Modified Diet. A low-cholesterol diet in combination with a low-fat diet and low-saturated fats is used in the treatment of coronary heart disease.

Chop. Cutting into small irregularly shaped pieces. Example: celery, hard cooked eggs, and onions.

Chronic. Refers to a disease or condition of long duration, example: chronic pancreatitis.

Clarify. To make clear by removing impurities from stock or jelly, or from fat, usually by skimming or adding egg white and straining. Example: chicken stock (consomme).

Clear Liquid Diet. Utilized before surgery, during severe gastrointestinal upset, or before gastrointestinal tests as an intermediate step between intravenous feeding and a full-liquid or solid diet. Diet consists of liquid foods, mainly water and carbohydrates, that are non-irritating and pass through the body easily. Used for short periods (24–36 hours) and is considered nutritionally inadequate.

Coagulate. Thicken, solidify, congeal, or curdle. Changing a liquid (protein) to a soft, semi-solid mass, often by heat acid/alkali reactions, organic solvents, or manual mechanical agitation. Protein internal structure alterations occur, while protein quality is normally retained. Examples: egg white, milk, puffed wheat/rice cereals.

Coat. Covering food with a thinner top layer of another spreadable food. Examples: butter, topping, frosting, or sauce.

Coenzyme. Organic substances, particularly most of the water soluble B-Complex vitamins, that work with or bind to the protein part of an enzyme, enabling that enzyme to catalyze or start a metabolic reaction.

Colitis. An inflammatory bowel disease of the colon with the mucous membranes forming small pouch-like areas. Symptoms include abdominal cramps, diarrhea and the continuous need to eliminate. Severe ulcerative colitis has the colon inflamed and ulcer lined. Causes are poor eating habits, stress, and food allergies. Eat a high vegetable protein and low carbohydrate diet, high in fiber and low in fats. Drink liquids, while eliminating fried foods, dairy products, fats, oils, nuts, spices, seeds, and coffee.

Combine. Mixing together of foods to unite.

Complementary Protein. Incomplete proteins eaten together or combined to supply all the essential amino acids necessary in the diet.

Complete Protein. A protein that contains and supplies all nine essential amino acids, necessary to the diet to build and repair tissue. Examples: egg, cheese, meat, and milk.

Compote. The fruit in syrup and/or long-stemmed serving dish.

Complex Carbohydrate (Polysaccharides). Include starch and fiber, while simple carbohydrates include all types of sugars, such as mono and disaccharides.

Condiment. A spice seasoning or mixture, serving as a topping or spread to food items such as meat, bread, and vegetables. Often high in sugar, salt, and additives. Examples: catsup, relish, mustard, pepper, and pickles.

Consistency Modified Diets. Consistency or texture food modified diets include clear liquid, full liquid, pureed, mechanical soft, soft, low fiber and high fiber.

Constipation. Difficulty in excreting waste matter, characterized by dry, hard stools. Possible relief remedies include eating high roughage or natural laxative foods (prunes), drinking plenty of fluids, and increasing physical activity.

Convenient Foods. Completely or partially prepared foods, processed commercially by a manufacturer. As packaged, it is easily and quickly prepared for home meal use. Nutritional content many vary significantly, dependent upon additives, preservatives, and other factors necessary for packaging, distribution, and storage.

Cornstarch. Finely milled white corn flour, used as a thickening agent in fruit fillings, gravies, puddings, sauces, and also for baking. Extensively used in both Chinese cooking or converted into high-fructose corn syrup, replacing sugar in beverages.

Coronary Heart Disease. Initiated by reduced blood circulation to heart muscle tissue, caused by clots or fatty deposits that block or narrow the arteries. Risk increasing abnormalities include hyperlipemia, diabetes mellitus, hypertension, obesity, and gout. Dietary prevention measures include lowering the intake of saturated fats, cholesterol, salt, and sugar.

Cream. Mixing food with a beater or spoon (back) until creating a smooth and creamy consistency. Examples: normally mixing shortening and sugar for cakes and cookies.

Crohn's Disease. A chronic and long-term inflammatory bowel disease in the digestive tract, common to children and young adults. Foods to avoid are fried, spicy, mucous-forming (processed) foods, animal products, alcohol, caffeine, carbonated beverages, margarine, meat, and wheat.

Crude Fiber. Describes the fiber content of food, made up primarily of cellulose and lignin. That portion of a food sample resisting solution when boiled in dilute acid and alkali.

Cube. Cutting or dicing into small pieces or shapes. Examples: Cheese, vegetables.

Cycle Menu. A menu designed for a specific period of time (example 7 days, 4 weeks) and then repeated.

Cystitis. A common bladder infection and inflammation. It usually is a symptom of other urinary or genital tract disturbances. It is usually more prevalent in women and caused by bacteria. Typically, urination is frequent and painful, necessitating an urgent desire to empty the bladder. It is recommended to drink plenty of liquids, except avoid caffeine, carbonated beverages, coffee, chocolate, and alcohol.

Dairy Substitute. Vegetarians or those with allergies to dairy products or lactose intolerance may substitute soy products, such as soy milk or tofu and/or nuts such as almonds and cashews, for dairy products such as butter, cream, cream cheese, ricotta cheese, and sour cream.

Decaffeinated. Removal of the stimulant caffeine from coffee, tea, or carbonated cola beverages.

Dehydration. Condition resulting from undue loss of water or removal of water from food or tissue, without replacement. Diarrhea, vomiting, and not drinking enough liquids are common causes.

Dextrose. See Glucose.

Diabetes Mellitus. Chronic group of diseases in which the body cannot oxidize or metabolize glucose properly because it lacks or cannot produce insulin. The blood sugar (glucose) level becomes abnormally high with no insulin secretion after carbohydrate food intake. Hypoglycemia can be an indicator of it. The diabetes condition alters the glucose and fat metabolism. Suitable dietary remedies include reducing caloric intake and dietary fat, increasing complex carbohydrates and dietary fiber, setting a goal of weight loss, and adherence to consistency in meal times, size, and composition.

IDDM. Insulin dependent diabetes mellitus effects 5% of the diagnosed cases and is the most severe form, having a dramatic or sudden onset. The classic signs of it include extreme thirst, excessive hunger, greatly increased urination, and sugar in the urine and result in the inability to control and use blood sugar. If untreated, a life-threatening diabetic condition occurs. Insulin, exercise and diet control are often necessary for life and will control it.

NIDDM. Non-insulin dependent diabetes mellitus is the most common form of diabetes mellitus, whereby increased blood sugar levels are not life threatening and may not require insulin use. For the majority with this type of diabetes, blood sugar levels can be controlled by diet management, weight loss, and exercise. Some diabetics use small insulin doses or oral medication.

Diarrhea. Loose or liquid stools caused primarily from viral infections of the intestines and stomach, resulting in decreased ability to absorb food and liquids. Use a clear liquid diet when treating diarrhea.

Dice. Cutting or cubing into uniform pieces or shapes, about 1/2-inch square.

Diet. Any food combinations that constitute regular portions of basic food and beverages over a specific time period. The ratio of the basic foods should not vary over time.

Dietary Goals. Predecessor of Dietary Guidelines which more specifically itemizes steps to improve health by food selection and preparation changes.

Dietary Guidelines. Seven government recommendations for promoting health through proper diet including: eating a variety of foods; maintaining ideal weight; avoid too much fat, saturated fat, cholesterol, sugar, and sodium; eat foods adequate in starch and fiber; and drink alcohol in moderation.

Dietary Laws. Religious group guidelines or regulations for food selection and preparation in meal planning. Examples: Jews, Muslims.

Diet Manuals. Resources available in institutional health care facilities containing practical, specified and approved information and procedures to follow in modified diets. Emphasis is directed to assisting health care professionals to implement modified (therapeutic) diets.

Diet Order. The kind of diet prescribed for each patient, by a physician, in the health care setting. It has specific content for kinds and amounts of foods, route and frequency of feeding, and patient dietary instruction to assist dietitians, nurses and patients, and other health care practitioners.

Dietitian. A registered health care member. The individual has met the educational requirements set forth by the American Dietetic Association. Nutrition expert in meal planning, health, disease, and diet therapy. Educates patients about modified diets and helps them to select the amount and kinds of foods, to assist both recovery and long-term diet maintenance.

Diet Therapy. Modifying or changing a patient's regular diet, often by adding or omitting certain nutrients and foods in specified amounts to or from a diet to meet requirements caused by disease or injury.

Digestion. The breakdown and changes, physical and chemical, that food undergoes in the body, in preparation for its absorption.

Disaster Menu. A policy requiring supplies of non-perishable goods at all times in many hospitals, nursing homes and government-regulated facilities, in the event of internal or external disasters such as a hurricane, flood, or power outage. The menu would consist of pre-selected, non-perishable and non-rancid foods, having a shelf life in excess of 6–12 months. Other items would include water, utensils, supplies, and heating apparatus.

Diuretic. A chemical substance used to increase urine output. Used in sodium-restricted diets for treatment of edema.

Diverticulitis. Severe intestine and colon inflammation of the tiny sacs (diverticula) causing abdominal pain and fever. The condition is treated by the use of a low-fiber diet in the beginning, with later progression to a high-fiber diet.

Diverticulosis. Intestinal disorder with tiny pockets forming on the weak sides of the muscular wall, forming sacs. A high-fiber diet is used to treat it, only if no acute abdominal symptoms are present and temperature is normal. Other symptoms include flatus, constipation, and diarrhea. Severe conditions progress to diverticulitis.

Dredge. Immerse and coat food item in flour mixture before cooking or baking. Examples: Dipping egg-covered chicken in seasoned flour.

Drop Batter. Batter that will drop from a spoon in lumps but too thick to pour. Examples: drop biscuits.

Dysphagia. Difficulty in swallowing.

Edema. Observable body swelling, caused by sodium and water fluid retention. Often puffiness of fingers, ankles, or the entire body. It is a common condition of many nutritional diseases.

Emulsion. A stable liquid mixture, having small drops of one liquid dispersed into a second liquid, with which it's incapable of mixing or blending without the use of an emulsifier (such as with egg yolks in mayonnaise or oil in butter).

Enriched Foods. Improving the nutritional value of foods by adding B vitamins and iron. Particularly necessary for refined grains, where the nutritious germ and bran have been lost. Normally, enrichment does not completely replace trace minerals and fiber lost in refined or processed foods.

Enzymes. Protein organic catalysts that speed up the rate of body chemical reactions. Most require a coenzyme, usually vitamins, to become active. They are primarily responsible for chemical reactions such as hydrolysis, oxidation, and reduction, and are instrumental in the digestion system.

E.P. Weight. "Edible portion." A food item's weight after all trimming and preparation is completed. The part of the food that is most commonly eaten.

Essential Amino Acids. Nine of the 22 amino acids cannot be made by the human body and must be obtained from foods. The nine essential ones are: leucine, lysine, methionine, isoleucine, phenylalanine, threonine, tryptophan, valine, and histidine.

Exchange Lists. Meal planning lists developed by the American Diabetes Association and used by individuals with diabetes who need to regulate what and how much they eat. The six exchange lists are also used in weight- and calorie-control diets. Each food on a list has the same amount of calories, carbohydrates, fat, and protein in the portions listed and can be exchanged for any other food on the same list. The lists are: starch/bread; meat; vegetable; fruit; milk; and fat.

Fast Foods. Commercially prepared food for franchised food outlets, restaurants, or a variety of other food-service facilities, which offer convenient, economical, and time-saving options.

Fats. The highest calorie energy nutrient having 9 calories per gram. Fats are found in butter, margarine, cream, eggs, meats, milk, cheese, and lard. It is recommended that fats be limited to no more than 30% of your daily calories and individuals should limit their intake of saturated fats.

Fettuccine. Dry, flat egg noodles. Example: cheese fettuccine.

Fiber. Known as "roughage" or "bulk." The indigestible but edible plant tissue. Dietary fiber is the portion of food resistant to human digestive enzymes and passes through the intestine undigested. Different fibers (cellulose, gum, pectins, and legumes) lessen constipation; helps control food intake, body weight, and bowel functions; increases the laxative effect; and lowers serum cholesterol levels. Good sources are fruits, vegetables, whole grain cereals and breads, bran, nuts, and seeds.

Fillet. Thin strips of the boneless side of fish or tenderloin meat. Example: Baked or oven-fried fish and sole almandine.

Flake. Fish that has been separated gently with a fork, just after cooking to prepared state.

Flatus. Distention or enlarging of the intestines or stomach with gas or air, caused by bacterial fermentation of undigested food or by swallowing air. Remedial action includes decreasing intakes of fat, carbohydrate, or fiber; avoiding legumes and strongly flavored vegetables, including beans, brussels sprouts, cabbage, cauliflower, corn, peppers, peas, radishes, condiments, carbonated beverages, dried fruits (raisins). Usually associated with gastrointestinal diseases such as diverticulosis, Crohn's disease, etc.

Fold. Retaining air in food mixtures by gently blending (circular, horizontal or vertical) with a utensil. Combining heavy mixtures with lightly whipped ingredients. Example: fruit whip.

Food Additives. Literally hundreds of additives are intentionally used, such as salts, herbs, spices and vitamins, to improve or enhance food products. Many, less familiar non-nutritive additives, are used to improve food appearance, texture, and shelf-storage life, including flavorings, colorings, irradiation, preservatives, sweeteners, and stabilizers. In particular, they are essential to convenience food availability. Health risks have been shown in using nitrites, saccharin, animal drugs, agricultural chemicals, and growth retardants. The use of some additives has raised very serious health questions about their effect on food nutritional value and the cumulative, long-term, and combined effects. Additionally, undesirable incidental additives, such as pesticide sprays for vegetables and radioactive airborne materials, are present in the air and soil and are carried by food and water to users, posing long-standing and somewhat unresolved controversies.

Food Allergy. Negative reactions to specific foods, resulting in asthma, colitis, constipation, dermatitis, diarrhea, edema, eye reddening, headache, hives, itching, nausea, or vomiting. Primarily protein related, and digestion or cooking will assist proteins to lose their allergenic tendencies. Commonly attributed to wheat, dairy products, egg, seafood, chocolate, corn, chicken, pork, and strawberries.

Food and Drug Administration (FDA). Federal government agency enforcing food and drug legislation. Its objective is to safeguard the food supply for human consumption, monitor food and nutrition labeling, food additives, and food-drug interactions.

Food Labeling. Federal food labeling laws provide consumers with highly useful information regarding product content, nutritional value, RDA percentage, sodium content, and additives.

Food Pyramid. Replaces the Basic Four food group. The U.S.D.A. developed the Food Pyramid to assist the American people in making healthier food choices. Six food groups are represented with suggested number of servings.

Food Residue. The indigestible portion of the food, called fiber, bulk, or roughage.

Food Service Director. Commonly the director of nutritional services, this person is responsible for all

department personnel who purchase, plan, fulfill, prepare, or serve modified diet or other meals to institutionalized health care users or patients.

Fortified. Adding nutrients (vitamins or minerals) not normally found in foods or above the levels of the food in its natural or pre-processed state. Examples: Vitamin A (margarine), Vitamin D (milk), also cereal products.

Fricassee. Browning poultry or veal in a small amount of fat to make a light brown stew, followed by steaming or stewing in a small amount of liquid. Example: chicken fricassee.

Fructose. A simple carbohydrate sugar (monosaccharide), found in fruits, honey, and plant juices. A natural fruit sugar, sweeter than sucrose sugars by 1.7 to 1, but with only half as many calories. Often called "fruit sugar" or "levulose."

Fry. Cooking in hot fat. Examples: chicken, fish, potatoes.

Fruits. The edible reproductive part of a seed plant and the sweet pulp of the seed. The carbohydrates contained in fruit are the monosaccharides glucose and fructose. Generally, fruits are low in calories; contain little or no fat; are free of cholesterol; good sources of fiber; low in sodium and excellent sources of vitamins and minerals.

Full Liquid Diet. Consists of foods that are or become liquid at body temperature. A milk-based diet is often a transition between a clear liquid and solid-food diet. The diet provides a texture and consistency for those unable to chew or handle solid foods and is more complete nutritionally than a clear liquid diet. Vitamin or mineral supplementation may be prescribed to provide nutritional adequacy.

Gallstones. The buildup of various-sized stones with high cholesterol or calcium concentration, combined with bile in the gallbladder. They can present no symptoms and the bile supply may be normal. When cholesterol is concentrated in the gallbladder and forms crystals, gallstones occur. If they obstruct passage of the bile, it may cause severe pain. A low-fat diet may be used to treat gallstones.

Garnish. Creating visual attractiveness for the meal served, by adding decorative foods or items to enhance the eye appeal of the primary food served, keeping in mind the color, flavor, or dish shape it decorates. Examples: carrot, egg slices, parsley, pickles, and flower.

Gastritis. Chronic inflammation of the stomach, may be associated with belching, bloating, or heartburn. Chronic conditions follow intake of alcohol; caffeine stimulants; coffee (decaffeinated included); and spices such as chili powder or pepper. Decreasing the secretions of gastric acid is desirable and use of a liberal bland, low-fiber, or soft diet may initially be beneficial.

Gastrointestinal Distress. Disorders of appetite, diet, and excessive eating that affect the digestive and eliminative processes. Other causes include infections, metabolic disorders, long-term poor diets, glandular malfunction, or structural defects. Examples: gastritis, peptic ulcer, chronic constipation, or chronic diarrhea (colitis).

Gelatin. A gelling substance used for preparing jellies or cold desserts. An incomplete protein that can not by itself support life. It swells on contact with liquids, dissolves in hot water, and forms a jelly when cooled. It is used as a thickening agent. Examples: fruited and Boo Berry gelatin.

Glaze. Giving a shiny appearance to hot and cold preparations in various ways, such as reducing stock or gravy to jelly consistency to cover meats or coating hot vegetables with a sugary butter sauce. Examples: glazed ham or cornish game hen; and glazed carrots.

Glucose. Called dextrose or corn sugar in food preparations. It is one of three simple carbohydrates (sugars) called monosaccharides. All carbohydrates, after digestion and absorption, become stored in the body as glucose for later energy use. These carbohydrates are absorbed from the intestinal tract into the bloodstream and circulate as glucose. While it is a significant building block for starches (complex carbohydrates) and animal glycogen, the oxidation of glucose provides 20% of the body's total fuel or energy needs. As the primary energy source for brain and nerve cells, the maintenance of normal blood sugar (glucose) levels (70 to 100 milligrams per 100 milliters of blood) is vital.

Glucose Tolerance Test. A blood test used in the identification or ruling out of hypo or hyperglycemia or diabetes mellitus. It determines how well a person removes high levels of glucose from the blood. A person, after fasting, drinks a concentrated glucose solution (75–100 grams) and the blood glucose levels are determined at certain hourly intervals.

Grains. Currently, grains are at the base of the food groups "pyramid," and their nutritional importance in the construction of the daily meal plan is stressed. This group makes up the bulk of the diet and is an indispensable source of nutrients (vitamins, minerals, high-quality protein) for most of the world's population. When combined with legumes or milk products the amount of usable protein greatly increases.

Gram. The small basic unit of weight measurement in the metric system, equal to 1/28 of an ounce. Abbreviated g. or gm.

Grate. Rubbing a food item over a rough surface utensil, with different sized or shaped holes, to make very small pieces. Examples: cheese, carrots, onions, lemon peel, and orange peel.

Herbs. Aromatic plants used in flavoring and seasoning foods. May have beneficial healing properties. Some are very effective replacements for salt in low-sodium diets. Examples: Parsley, basil, oregano, thyme, and tarragon; chamomile tea.

High-Fiber Diet. Used in the treatment of constipation, diverticulosis, hemorrhoids, irritable bowel syndrome, cancer of the colon, and gallstones.

Honey. A syrupy, sticky, and sweet liquid that is almost totally carbohydrate. It is made by honey bees from plant nectar, deposited in hives, and becomes honey.

Hydrogenation. A chemical process that converts oils, normally vegetable, to solid fats such as shortening or margarine. It makes a unsaturated oil more saturated. It is used for commercial baking purposes; extends shelf life, and prevents rancidity.

Hyperglycemia. A condition, such as uncontrolled diabetes, with a high blood sugar (glucose) level.

Hyperlipidemia. High amounts of fat in the blood or elevated blood serum levels of cholesterol and/or triglyceride. A major contributor and risk factor in arteriosclerosis, coronary heart disease and blood lipid disorders. Causes include diets high in saturated fat, excessive calorie or alcohol intake, excess weight; related conditions including diabetes mellitus. Dietary remedies include lowering cholesterol, total fat, and saturated fat and increasing the intake of complex carbohydrates and fiber. Major aspects of a cholesterol- and fat-modified diet are decreasing eggs, lard, butter, organ meat, cheese, and sugar and substituting vegetable oils, high-grade margarines, skim milk, egg white, whole grains, beans, legumes, fruits, and vegetables.

Hypertension. Commonly known as high blood pressure. A condition with few symptoms that accompanies many renal and cardiovascular disorders, adrenal tumors, and emotional disturbances. High blood pressure sufferers should implement long-term diet modifications, including: sodium restriction, weight reduction, and elimination of alcohol and caffeine.

Hypoglycemia. Low blood sugar (glucose) levels in the circulating blood. Persons with this condition rapidly utilize their glucose within hours of a meal or after exercise. Identification of the condition is obtained by a glucose tolerance test.

Immune System. Protects the body against disease-producing organisms and foreign bodies, such as tumor cells and toxins, by utilizing a biochemical complex of cell structures and processes producing cellular and antibody responses to antigens. Food allergies or immunologic reactions to food are examples of the diet-immune system relationship.

Incomplete Protein. Protein that does not contain all of the essential amino acids and cannot support life and are low in biological value. Example: corn or gelatin.

Insulin. A protein and hormone secreted into the blood from the islets of langerhans in the pancreas, which is critical to the proper metabolism of glucose. Insulin secretion is stimulated by carbohydrate intake. It functions in lowering blood sugar and directs the body's distribution of glucose while maintaining a constant level of glucose in the blood.

Insulin Reaction/Shock. Condition of hypoglycemia (low level of blood sugar), that leads to insulin coma, caused by too much insulin (by intravenous injection) or too little food.

International Units (IU). A unit of measurement, used primarily for vitamins A, D, and E.

Invisible Fats. Those fats disguised in food items and not easily noticed. Examples: meat, milk, nuts, pastries, french fries, and potato chips.

Irradiation. Recently approved FDA food-processing method, which treats food with x-rays, ultraviolet light or radiation from radioactive materials. This process controls microorganism growth in meat products. It inhibits the growth of sprouts on potatoes and onions and delays ripening in some fruits. Foods must be labeled "treated by irradiation."

Irritable Bowel Syndrome. Condition of the large intestine (colon), characterized by cramps, abdominal pain, diarrhea, or constipation. Causes include emotional stress and food intolerance. Constipation may be relieved by a high-fiber diet; diarrhea by avoiding carbonated beverages, coffee, and cold liquids; food intolerance, by testing and reviewing foods not tolerated. Recommended diet is a liberal bland, adapted to an individual's food tolerance.

Julienne. Cutting foods into small, thin strips for garnishing. Examples: meat or cheese for salads or vegetables.

Junk Food. Common term for food containing empty calories, with a low nutrient value but high in fats and simple sugars.

Kilocalorie. The unit of measurement, used in nutrition, for heat or food energy, equal to 1,000 calories. Often expressed as "Kcal", "calorie," or "large calorie".

Kosher. Jewish dietary laws, providing regulations designating the selection and preparation of foods that are deemed fit for consumption.

Knead. A pre-baking method of using the fingers and heel of the hand to fold and work dough into a mass;

distribute ingredients evenly; develop gluten and prepare the dough for rising.

Lactase. The enzyme secreted by the small intestine, that digests lactose (milk sugar), yielding the monosaccharides glucose and galactose.

Lacto-ovo Vegetarian. Consumes primarily plant food and dairy products and eggs, but no meat, fish, or poultry.

Lacto Vegetarian Diet. Vegetarian diet that allows milk and milk products, but excludes meat, poultry, fish, and eggs.

Lactose. The sugar in milk. A disaccharide composed of glucose and galactose, the form of carbohydrate in milk.

Lactose Intolerance. A person's inability to digest lactose or milk products. Symptoms are often mild and include cramps, gas, nausea, diarrhea, and distention. It is prominent among American Indians, African-Americans, Jews, and Asians.

Lard. The rendered fat of hogs, with high concentrations of saturated fat, used in margarine and cooking fats and for baking when edible fats are required.

Lasagna. A baked, layered, cheese and tomato based casserole, made with broad, flat egg noodles.

Leafy Vegetables. Valuable primarily for their vitamin and mineral content. Generally, the greener, the better nutrient value, particularly if lightly cooked or steamed. Roughage is also abundant as are smaller amounts of high quality protein. Examples: kale, spinach.

Lecithin. A group of fatty substances found in soybeans, corn, egg yolk, legumes, liver, meat organs, and milk. Partly composed of choline, which transports lipids through the body. Lecithin is used as an emulsifier in chocolate, baked goods, and ice cream, and in the mixing of oil or fat and water. It is widely used by health food followers, on the assumption its presence may dissolve cholesterol deposits.

Legumes. Legumes are seeds and nuts such as soybeans, peanuts, peas, chick-peas, beans, lima beans, and lentils. All have pods opening along two seams. When the seeds are ripe they have twice the protein of grains and are the most important food plant, other than grains. Called "meat substitutes," they provide B-complex, phosphorus, iron, and calcium to the diet. The protein quality of soybeans (and peanuts), while less than meat, is particularly high and is a staple of vegetarian diets.

Liberal Bland Diet. Diet used to treat peptic ulcers.

Lignin. Indigestible carbohydrate found in plant food and part of crude fiber.

Lipids. Fats that are organic fat substances, insoluble in water. The lipid group includes simple lipids (fats and waxes) and compound lipids and derived lipids (fatty acids and cholesterol). The chemical name for fat is triglyceride. Fatty acids are said to be either saturated, unsaturated, or polyunsaturated.

Liquid Diets. A modified consistency and texture diet, using foods that will pour or are liquid at room temperature. They have a low nutritive value and are used for very limited time periods. Examples are clear and full liquid diets.

Liver. The body organ that secretes bile for fat digestion; the storehouse for body sugar (glycogen) and vitamins A, B, and D, and iron; detoxifies chemical poisons and medicines and excretes others; partly makes blood plasma protein and carries nutrients to other tissues of the body. The liver of animals has a high food value.

Low Fat. This diet may be used in treatment of diseases of the biliary tract, pancreas, and malabsorption syndromes, where fat is not tolerated (celiac disease, short bowel, tropical sprue).

Low-Fiber Diet. Dietary treatment used for Chrohn's disease, ulcerative colitis, acute diverticular disease, and before and after lower bowel surgery.

Lyonnaise. Food dishes garnished with or containing onions. Example: lyonnaise noodles.

Macaroni. Part of the pasta family. A food paste made from flour (hard wheat semolina) and water and dried into fancy shapes or tubes such as shells or macaroni elbows. A carbohydrate source. Example: beef, macaroni casserole; macaroni.

Malnutrition. A general term indicating a seriously impaired condition caused by nutrient or calorie deficiency, excess, or imbalance.

Margarine. A smooth-textured fat for spreading or cooking. The nutritional value is dependent upon type of fat used, combination with foods, hydrogenated process, and any optional ingredients used such as butter, coloring, emulsifiers, flavoring, preservatives, salt, or vitamins.

Marinate. Soaking a food in a seasoned liquid or sauce for a specified time to alter their flavor. Examples: marinated cucumbers, marinated green beans, and cucumber and onion salad.

Mash. Changing a solid food into a soft or uniform mass by mixing, beating, or crushing. Example: mashed potatoes.

Matzo. A flat, unleavened, no-yeast bread or cracker eaten during the Jewish Passover. Matzo meal is used in breading food and other dishes. Examples: matzo cereal; chicken soup with matzo ball; matzo meal muf-

fin, Passover rolls, honeyed latka, Passover sponge cake.

Mayonnaise. A semisolid spread, cold sauce, or salad dressing made with oil, vinegar, and seasoning, and emulsified with egg yolk. Often high in calories, saturated fat, and cholesterol.

Meat. The flesh of animals used as food. The meat group includes beef, veal, pork, fish, and poultry. Generally, the group is nutritionally high in protein, B-complex, and vitamin C. Fat and cholesterol content varies, dependent upon trimming and the leanness of the meat or fish. Organ meats are considered higher in nutritive value.

Meat Analog. High-protein meat substitutes, similar in appearance, protein content, and taste. Usually made of soybean and/or wheat protein, they are referred to as textured vegetable protein (TVP). A vegetarian alternative. Examples: imitation bacon bits or substitute bacon strips, patties, or hot dogs.

Mechanical Soft Diet. Consists of foods and beverages requiring little chewing. It is used for head and neck surgical patients, people with dental problems, or those acutely ill with problems chewing or swallowing but able to utilize more variety and texture than a puree diet. Commonly, all meats are chopped or ground and fruits and vegetables may be pureed. The diet is individualized to the degree of each persons tolerance and limitations.

Metabolism. A general term for all the chemical changes that go on only in the body tissues, after the digestion process. The use of food nutrients by the body, for energy, excretion, or synthesizing new materials for cell growth, maintenance, or repair.

Menu. A detailed list of specific foods and amounts to be served at a meal. It may utilize or recommend modifications, omissions, or substitutes dependent upon the diet followed, cooking techniques, shape of food, etc.

Meringue. A foam, made of egg whites beaten stiff, mixed with sugar, and used as a covering for pies or cakes, or sometimes browned in an oven. Example: meringue.

Milk. Milk and milk products are normally obtained from cow's milk. It is high in protein quality and calcium, phosphorus, riboflavin, and vitamin A, but is a poor source of iron, copper, and vitamins D and C. Good nutritional substitutes are available with evaporated, powder, skim, or soy milk.

Mince. Chopping food into very fine pieces with a knife or by quickly turning a food processor on and off. Examples: celery, onions, or parsley.

Minerals. Inorganic elements or substances that are essential to life. Essential minerals include calcium, phosphorus, magnesium, sodium, potassium, chloride, iron, zinc, iodine, copper, chromium, selenium, manganese, molybdenum, fluorine, silicon, sulfur, cobalt, and several more trace minerals. They function as a constituent of bone and teeth, giving permanence and rigidity to tissue; constitute the primary part of soft tissues, such as muscles, blood cells, and enzymes; and are soluble salts in body fluids, influencing muscle and nerve elasticity and irritability and supply the material for the acidity alkalinity of the digestive juices.

Major Minerals. The largest mineral presence in the body, mostly in bone and teeth.

Calcium. Functions include building and hardening bones, and teeth; blood clotting; muscle contraction; transmitting nerve impulses; sustains normal blood pressure and aids B12 absorption. Good food sources are cottage cheese, hard cheese, and other mild products; broccoli, collards, kale, mustard, or turnip greens; legumes; clams, oysters, salmon, sardines, and shrimp; and whole grains. Absorption is moderate, about 40%, and is aided by vitamin D. RDAs are 800 mg for adults and 1,200 mg for teenagers and pregnancy. Calcium and phosphorus are usually associated in bodily functions.

Chloride. A negatively charged ion or electrolyte that maintains water balance and acid-base balance in the body by moving fluids through the cells and blood vessels. Chloride is a critical part of hydrogen chloride in the stomach and helps break down and digest food, particularly protein. It also helps calcium and iron absorption. Its primary source is salt.

Magnesium. Essential for muscle contraction, transmitting nerve impulses; bone and teeth growth; body temperature maintenance; metabolism of carbohydrate, fat, and protein, and cellular respiration. Concentrated in bones (60%) and soft cell tissue, where its mineral concentration is exceeded only by potassium. Good dietary sources are nuts, whole grains, raw green leafy vegetables, legumes, dried beans and fruits, shellfish, blackstrap molasses, chocolate, table salt, meat, and eggs.

Phosphorus. Essential to bone and teeth growth and maintenance; energy metabolism of fats and carbohydrates; buffer salts in acid-base balance and are part of the genetic linkage in DNA and RNA. Absorption is aided by Vitamin D and its intake is considered adequate if calcium intake is adequate. Dietary sources are organ and other meats; fish; poultry; wheat germ and all other grain foods; nuts; legumes; eggs; milk; dried fruits and vegetables.

Potassium. Potassium ions are in fluids circulating in the cells. Functions to transmit nerve impulses; assists muscle and cardiac contraction; helps correct water and acid-base body imbalances; makes protein and helps the release of energy from nutrients. It's easily depleted by increased excretion by the kidneys or gastrointestinal tract. The daily requirement of 2–4 grams is easily supplied by a variety of dried or fresh fruits, vegetables, nuts, whole grains, meat, poultry, milk, dried beans, seeds, and seafood. Potassium is needed particularly for those on diuretic medication to control blood pressure. Certain other diuretics cause its loss and it needs to be replenished.

Sodium. Sodium ions are primarily in fluids circulating outside the cells. Similarly and together with sodium, potassium functions in keeping a water balance between cells and fluids; for nerves to respond to stimuli; and for nerve impulse transmission to all muscles for contraction. They both act to keep a proper balance of acid and alkali in the blood. Excess sweating can cause high sodium losses and cause muscle cramps. The major dietary source is table salt. Animal food sources contain more than plant sources, except for beets, carrots, celery, kale, and spinach. Other sources are processed foods, where salt has been directly added, or from brine, curing, or pickling. The National Research Council has established estimated minimum requirements for healthy persons over 18 years of age at 500 mg per day.

Sulfur. It is found in most food proteins (1%) and is a constituent of cartilage, hair, and nails. It is intimately linked to protein metabolism and adequate protein intake will preclude its deficiency. Occurs also as a component of thiamine, biotin, and the hormone insulin. Good food sources are chicken, dried beans, liver, nuts, eggs, meat, milk, and cheese.

Trace Minerals. Vital nutrients minutely required.

Chromium. Assists insulin to do its work and stimulates the synthesis of fatty acids and cholesterol in the liver. Only a very small amount of the daily food intake is absorbed. Food sources include beef liver, meat, dark poultry meat, brewer's yeast, whole grains, black pepper, mushrooms, and corn oil.

Cobalt. A constituent of Vitamin B12 (cobalamin). It helps stimulate and maintain red blood cells and a healthy nervous system. It is obtained through animal food sources only, such as meat, poultry, fish, and eggs, and is stored in the liver and the bone marrow.

Copper. It functions as a component of many enzymes; helps make hemoglobin that transports oxygen around the body, and protects blood vessels, bones and nerves. Copper is abundantly available in all body tissues and stored primarily in the liver and other organs. The richest food sources are organ and other meats, cocoa, crustaceans, dried legumes, mushrooms, nuts, shellfish, and whole grains. Only 30% of it is absorbed bodily. Deficiency is rare.

Fluoride. Located primarily in the skeleton and teeth. It increases resistance to tooth decay and may reduce osteoporosis. Added as sodium fluoride in drinking water; animal food sources are gelatin, meat organs, and seafood.

Iron. A constituent of hemoglobin in red blood cells, essential to transporting oxygen to the cells and utilizing it upon arrival. Lowered oxygen capacity creates "iron deficiency anemia" or fatigue and apathy signs in young children. Losses also occur during female menstruation. Food absorption rates vary greatly but are increased with ascorbic acid and decreased by spinach consumption. Dietary sources are liver, meats, blackstrap molasses, shellfish, egg yolk, dark green leafy vegetables, legumes, poultry, dried fruit, and whole grain and enriched breads and cereals.

Manganese. An important trace element with essential functions in all body cells. Functions in assisting enzyme blood formation and building bone structure. Highly concentrated in bones, organs, and glands. Absorption is poor and adversely affected by high levels of dietary calcium and phosphorus. High dietary sources are wheat germ, raw oatmeal, whole wheat, rice, other whole grains, nuts, legumes, leafy vegetables, (turnip greens, spinach, brussel sprouts), bananas, and seeds.

Molybdenum. Functions as a component and assists certain enzymes; involved with the metabolism of fat. Food sources are beef, kidney, legumes, cereal grains, yeast, and dark green leafy vegetables.

Selenium. An antioxidant that works with Vitamin E to prevent oxidation; it's vital for normal heart function. Stored in the liver and kidney, its food sources are: seafood, meat, liver, and whole grains.

Zinc. A vital component in over 70 enzymes involved in making protein; using Vitamin A; faster healing of wounds; immune response; ability to taste; sexual development and is a component of insulin. Functions also in night vision and in the overall growth and maintenance of all tissues. Rich food sources are oysters, seafood, organ meats, wheat germ, wheat bran, whole oatmeal and whole grains, nuts, yeast, lima beans, dried green split peas, milk, and eggs.

Miso. A paste made from fermented soybeans, high in protein, natural enzymes, and B vitamins. It contains about 12% salt (1 tbsp miso = 1/2 tsp salt). Used as a seasoning for soups, sauces, dips, and salad dressings.

Modified Diet. A variation of the regular diet. Its purpose is to lessen possible health problems and their associated risks; give additional nutrients when needed; and relieve or eliminate symptoms or problems. The type of modification provided may change the specific kind and amount of food eaten; and the method and frequency of feeding. It should resemble a person's regular diet, to the extent possible and it should provide all the essential nutrient and calorie requirements, particularly if used for more than a few days.

Monosaccharide. The simplest carbohydrate (sugars), called glucose (dextrose), fructose, or galactose, which provide the units from which all the other more complex sugars and starches are made. They are soluble and the only type of carbohydrate that is absorbed from the intestinal tract into the bloodstream, without change. They are nutritionally important as an energy source. The richest sources are fruits and some fresh vegetables.

Mono-unsaturated Fats. While many health studies link them to lower blood cholesterol levels, they should not be substituted for polyunsaturated fats in most diets. Examples: avocados, olives, olive oil, peanuts, peanut oil, peanut butter, and hydrogenated oil margarine.

Monosodium Glutamate (MSG). A flavor enhancer or spice additive, widely used in fish and meat products, and commercially prepared soups and sauces. A highly controversial substance, containing large amounts of sodium and known to cause some people to develop symptoms such as burning sensations, facial pressure, heaviness of the chest, and some allergic reactions. Sometimes associated with food at Chinese restaurants and often, customer requests to omit it from their food.

Mornay. A white sauce made of cheese.

Natural Foods. Laws currently do not adequately protect its accurate use in food labeling. Commonly perceived as foods that are or should be unrefined; contain no additives or preservatives; grown without chemical fertilizers, hormones, or pesticides (organically grown); highly nutritious and low in calories. In fact, by law, none of these characteristics may be true.

Natural Vitamins. Obtained from natural plant or animal food, as opposed to chemically derived or synthetic vitamins.

Nephritis (Bright's Disease). A non-infectious disease, causing inflammation and malfunction of the kidney, often with blood/protein in the urine with associated hypertension and edema (salt and water retention).

Nephrosclerosis. A kidney disease, caused by long-term atherosclerosis and hypertension, afflicting older people.

Nitrites (Nitrates). Food additives, such as sodium nitrite, used to prevent bacterial growth. Nitrosamine results from high temperature nitrite combinations, sometimes producing tumors in experimental animals. Thus, nitrite/nitrate use is very controversial, but widely used in salt-cured or smoked meats such as bacon, ham, and hot dogs.

No Concentrated Sweets. Omits all sweets and sugars. May be used by diabetics.

Non-Nutritive Sweeteners. Generally speaking the controversial nature of saccharin and aspartame have discouraged diet counselors and physicians from recommending them, particularly for diabetics and pregnant or lactating females. They have no known effect upon blood sugar levels.

No Salt Added Diet. Commonly refers to the 3,000 to 4,000 mg salt modified or sodium-restricted diet, where no salt is added to the food at the table and certain high-sodium foods are restricted.

Nutrient. A general term used for over 50 nourishing chemical substances obtained from food that can be digested, absorbed, and metabolized by the body. These substances are combined into major "nutrient" categories: proteins, carbohydrates, fats, water, minerals, and vitamins. They provide energy or heat, build and repair tissues, and regulate life processes.

Nutrient Additives. A type of food additive to maintain or improve the value of food. Common examples are vitamin A and D to dairy products; B-complex "enriched" substances to refined grains; iodine to salt; and nutrients added to "fortified" breakfast cereals. Vitamin C and E are added to food to retard spoilage, and vitamin E in bacon prevents nitrosamine forming from nitrites.

Nutrition. Essentially the food you eat and how your body uses it. The sum of the process involved in nourishment, by the taking in, assimilation of, and use of nutrients for proper body functioning and maintenance of health. These include ingestion, digestion, absorption, assimilation, and excretion.

Nutritional Labeling. Mandated by the FDA, it serves as a comprehensive nutritional guide for the consumer. Information normally available includes ingredients; food additives; U.S. RDA's number and size of servings; nutrients; fat; cholesterol; sodium; sugar; and calorie content.

Nuts. A variety of normally dry fruits, usually with one edible kernel inside a woody shell. Closely akin to the legume family, they are a highly concentrated food, rich in protein and unsaturated fat, and a good source of niacin, riboflavin, thiamine, iron, and phosphorus. They are more easily digested when chewed well and eaten fresh and raw, due to their compact physical state. Almonds, cashews, and peanuts are easily ground and diluted to make nut butters, milks, and creams. Other popular, healthful nuts are black walnuts, brazil nuts, chestnuts, coconuts, macadamias, pecans, pine nuts, and pistachios.

Oats. A cereal grain containing good sources of fat, minerals, and protein. Used to make oatmeal or rolled oats and shredded, puffed, flaked, and other oat cereals.

Obesity. The condition of accumulating excessive weight, 15% to 25% more than the standard tables indicate for ideal body weight. The excess is fat rather than water, muscle, or bones. It arises often, (excluding genetic, heredity and some glandular disorders), when the intake of food or calories is in excess of the physiological calorie need. Accompanying medical complications include high cholesterol levels; diabetes; heart disease; kidney trouble; high blood pressure; pregnancy complications and decreased life expectancy.

Occupational Therapist. Health care team member who assists clients and convalescing patients to use devices for cooking and eating.

Oils. Two types of oils are commercially available. Saturated oils (fats), that are commonly used such as butter, soy margarine, and vegetable shortening, remain solid at room temperature. Unrefined oils are preferred and obtained from seeds, grains, or nuts that are cold pressed or lightly heated to release the oils, without using chemicals. Unrefined oils stay liquid at room temperature and have higher nutritional values, particularly when combined. Unrefined safflower or peanut oil may be heated for cooking. Others include corn, olive, sesame, soy, and sunflower. Canola oil, a refined highly unsaturated cooking oil, has recently become popular.

Olive Oil. An important basic Italian cooking oil, of many grades. Commonly used as a no- or low-cholesterol oil in low-temperature cooking or as a room temperature dressing.

Organic Foods. Pertains generally to foods grown with "organic gardening" methods, excluding chemical fertilizers or pesticides. Connected with the term "natural foods," which includes minimum refining, and no additives or preservatives.

Osteoporosis. A lack of calcium from the gradual loss or thinning of bone mass, occurring primarily in women after middle age. Causes include estrogen deficiency in menopausal females, inability to absorb calcium, imbalance of calcium-phosphors, lack of exercise, jaundice, gastrectomy, and lactose intolerance. Prevention and treatment includes a diet adequate in protein, calcium, magnesium, phosphorus, and vitamin D.

Palatability. The quality of a food: color, flavor, and texture that impresses the senses of sight, smell, taste, and touch and largely determines its acceptance by the food-consuming person. Particularly relevant when attempting to influence that person to accept unfamiliar modified diet recommendations.

Pancreas. A gland that secretes a digestive juice that acts on all types of food. Amylase digests starches to sugars, lipase digests fat, and protease digests proteins. The pancreas also produces the hormones insulin and glucagon to control blood sugar and digestive enzymes.

Pan-broil. Cooking in an uncovered sauté pan, without fat; to fry, pouring out fat as it arises. Example: bacon.

Pancreatitis. An inflammation of the pancreas, caused by gallstones, bile back flow, or obstruction of the pancreatic duct. Increased risk of developing it are attributed to alcoholism, abdominal injury, drugs, obesity, poor nutrition, and viral infection. Acute or chronic, its symptoms include abdominal pain/swelling; gallbladder infection, gallstones, excessive gas, fever, hypertension, muscle aches, and abnormal fatty stools.

Pan-fry. Cooking in an uncovered pan, with a medium amount of fat.

Parboil. Cooking partially by boiling or simmering liquid. Examples: cooking julienne potatoes before frying.

Parfait. Dessert using a tall narrow parfait glass and/or consisting of alternate layers of ice cream, fruit, or syrup. Example: fruit parfait.

Pasta. General term describing a "paste" usually made from refined semolina hard wheat and water, producing over 100 varieties, shaped as egg noodles, lasagna, macaroni, spaghetti, etc. Whole or processed flours are increasingly being used and ground into flour to make pastas, frequently in combination with bean or vegetable flours. Example: pasta primavera.

Pectin. Non-digestible dietary fiber and a jelly-like substance common to certain fruits and plants, such as citrus, apples, and currants. It causes fruits or jellies to set or solidify when cooked with sugar and fruit juice acid.

Pilaf. Usually a well-seasoned long grain rice or other grain product dish, cooked or sautéed in oil or butter, then boiled in bouillon or broth, often with onions or seasonings. It may contain fish, meat, seafood or other vegetables. Example: rice pilaf.

Poach. Cooking food gently, partially or fully submerged in liquid or water that is hot but not bubbling, at just below the boiling point (160° to 180°F). Examples: eggs, fish, and chicken.

Polysaccharide. Complex carbohydrates containing combinations of monosaccharide (simple sugar building blocks). Starches, glycogen, and cellulose are examples. They are insoluble in water and are major components of cell membranes.

Polyunsaturated Fatty Acids (PUFA). The essential fatty acids, liquid at room temperature, needed for healthy cell membranes include the PUFA: linoleic, arachidonic, and linolenic. Fats high in PUFA include the liquid vegetable oils: safflower, sunflower seed, corn, and soybean. They are also found in fish oils, margarine containing high amounts of these liquid oils, wheat germ, and nuts and legumes such as almonds, peanuts, pecans, walnuts, and peanut butter.

Portion Control. Measurement of the utilized food item to exactly calculate the correct amount needed.

Potato. An edible starchy plant tuber. Includes long white, round white, round red, and russet. They are a nutritious food for fulfilling energy (calorie) requirements, with important minerals such as potassium; B complex and C (ascorbic acid) vitamins, and contain small amounts of protein.

Pot Roasting. A method of cooking large cuts of meat slowly in a tightly covered pot. Food browning is achieved by using a little fat and cooking with stock or liquid and vegetables over low heat until tender. Commonly called braising. Example: brisket of beef.

Poultry. Domesticated fowl or birds, excluding game birds, that are raised for human food. Commonly utilized are chickens, ducks, rock cornish hens, and turkeys. A member of the meat group and nutritionally high in protein, calcium, iron, phosphorus, and vitamins niacin, riboflavin, and thiamine.

Preservative. Chemicals used by manufacturers to increase a food's palatability, safety, or shelf life by preventing rancidity, discoloration, or microorganism growth. While proven to be useful, controversy remains high about the use of some, in regards to potential long-term consumer health hazards.

Process Cheese. Products made by grinding and melting and blending varieties of natural cheese. Emulsifiers, acid, coloring, preservatives, salt, spices, water, and other additives are often used.

Protease. Groups of enzymes secreted by the pancreas that are essential to digest protein. Examples: pepsin, trypsin, chymotrypsin, and dipeptidases.

Protein. Made up of 22 different amino acids (nine essential), which are required for the building and repair of all body cells. Protein is also sometimes used for fuel and excess protein is stored as fat. Good sources include animal proteins: milk, eggs, meat, cheese, fish and vegetable proteins: oatmeal, rice, potato, spinach, soybeans, wheat germ, sunflower seeds, and nuts. Individual protein requirements may vary greatly.

Protein Efficiency Ration (PER). Protein food sources differ in their ability to support growth, maintenance, and repair of body tissues. The PER indicates protein quality for each individual food. Generally, animal PERs are higher than some, but not all vegetable sources. However, combining two or more vegetable food sources can also achieve optimum protein results. High PERs over 2 1/2 are attributed to eggs, soybeans, milk, fish, and meat and intermediate PERs between 1/2–2 1/2 are found in legumes, lentils, nuts, and cereals. Some overlapping of protein quality occurs between plant and animal foods. Proteins low in PER, such as gelatin, cannot support life and are called incomplete proteins.

Puree. Processing food in a food processor or blender, or having it mashed, chopped, strained, or often pushed through a strainer or sieve to obtain a smooth pulp or consistency. The process increases digestibility by removing cellulose.

Puree Diet. A type of modified consistency diet, used to provide soft and smooth foods that are blenderized or strained, for those individuals having difficulty chewing or swallowing. Chewing or swallowing ability will dictate the use of additional thinning liquids such as broth, gravies, milk, or sauces, and cooked cereals; or honey and sugar to provide extra calories. It is important for the diet to have color, flavor, and temperature variety.

Progressive Diet. A transitional diet progressing from clear liquid to full liquid, soft, and finally regular diet. Used for clients having gastrointestinal problems, such as nausea or vomiting.

Quiche. Usually an open savory custard tart, using a base of egg custard, cheese, and many variations, baked in a pastry shell. Examples: quiche lorraine, spinach or broccoli quiche.

Rancid. Having a disagreeable odor or flavor. Usually applied to essential fats that have undergone decomposition, liberating fatty acids. A rancid fat loses nutritive value by destroying vitamins A and E and changes its baking properties.

Recommended Dietary Allowances (RDA). The level of essential daily nutrient intake, from a varied diet, according to a specific age and sex group, that is considered adequate to meet the nutritional needs of all healthy persons. These recommendations serve as a guide only and not as an exact or complete individual nutritional plan for all people.

Recipe. A set of organized instructions to prepare a specified item or dish.

Refined. Foods that have been processed to remove most of the naturally occurring fiber.

Regular Diet. A diet based upon the Food Pyramid and the U.S. Dietary guidelines. The latter specifies eating a variety of foods with adequate starch and fiber and avoiding too much fat, cholesterol, sugar, sodium, and alcohol.

Renal. Refers or pertains to the kidneys.

Rice. The staple cereal grain for over half the world's population. It is very low in fat and high in B complex vitamins, calcium, iron, gluten and a very good source of quality protein. When combined at meals with milk products or legumes, the amount of usable protein greatly increases. Milling, polishing, washing, or boiling decreases its nutrient value. Brown rice (husked but not polished like white rice) is higher in nutrient quality than enriched, parboiled, or other processed rice.

Roast. Cooking uncovered foods by surrounding or exposing to hot, dry heat in an oven; or a spit; or near an open fire of hot embers or stones.

Roughage. Plant fiber such as found in grain bran or apple or vegetable skins. It cannot be broken down by human digestive enzymes or absorbed by the gastrointestinal tract.

Roux. A cooked mixture of equal parts flour and butter or fat, cooked slowly and used to thicken sources or soups.

Saccharin. A food additive and non-calorie sugar substitute. An artificial sweetener, 400 times sweeter than sucrose, widely suspected to be a possible carcinogenic agent. It has no nutritive value.

Salad Dressing. A cooked or uncooked liquid mixture, usually containing vinegar or mayonnaise and seasonings.

Salsa. Seasoned sauce, used for dipping or as a condiment. General name for hot sauces in Mexican-American cooking. Examples: Salsa; Huevos Rancheros.

Salt. Commonly table salt or sodium chloride, used for seasoning or preserving food. Abundantly available in foods. Also called coarse, cooking, flake, iodized, kosher, pickling, rock, or sea salt. Other metal-like salts in foods include calcium, potassium, sodium magnesium, sulfur, manganese, iron, cobalt, and zinc. They occur as chlorides, sulfates, phosphates, and citrates.

Saturated Fats. Normally a fat that is solid or hard at room temperature, containing a large number of saturated fatty acids in the fat molecule. They occur in most animal fat products such as meat, eggs, whole milk, cheese, lard, butter, and ice cream. In plant animals they occur in palm and coconut oil, chocolate and hydrogenated vegetable oils. Common sources of "invisible" fat may also include cookies, french fries, mayonnaise, muffins, pastries, potato chips, and salad dressings. Known to be a contributing factor in atherosclerosis.

Sauce. A flavorful liquid dressing or food topping that is usually thickened, and used to enhance, flavor or season other foods.

Sauté. To cook or fry food in an open pan or skillet, in a small amount of fat, over direct heat, to tenderize and sear in flavor. Examples: onions, peppers, celery, meat, and eggs.

Season. To enhance the flavor of food by adding salt, spices, and other ingredients.

Scald. Heat a liquid, such as milk, to just below the boiling point of 185°F. Immediately removing it from the heat, it can be poured over food or used to dip food into. Also used to loosen the skins of fruits.

Scone. A white flour cake or quick bread, often mixed with barley, oatmeal, or whole wheat flour and combined with buttermilk and baking powder and often containing currants. Example: buttermilk scone.

Scoop or Dipper. A kitchen utensil used to take up flour, sugar, liquid, or ice cream. To take up or out, as with a scoop.

Sea Salt. Unrefined sea salt has been solar evaporated, then dried. Chemical and sugar free, it is high in trace minerals.

Semolina. A high protein flour, often used for the best quality macaroni, spaghetti or other pastas and obtained by milling durum wheat.

Shred. To cut or tear into thin or narrow pieces or irregular strips, using the large, coarse holes of a grater or with a knife. Examples: cabbage or lettuce.

Shortening. A solid tasteless fat, high in saturated fat, and usually butter, lard, or vegetable fat, that is used for baking or deep frying.

Sift. To remove lumps from dry ingredients, such as flour, by shaking them through a sieve.

Simmer. To cook at low heat, in water or liquid, just below the boiling point, when bubbles begin to form and slowly break, just below the surface, at about 185°–200°F.

Skim. Removing the top layer from hot or cold liquids. Examples: scum from soup stock; cream from milk.

Skim Milk. Cows milk containing less than one-half percent milk fat.

Slice. Cutting food into wide but thin pieces.

Smoothies. Normally a healthful, thick breakfast, lunch, or snack beverage, made of fruit, fruit pulp, juice, and ice that is blenderized until smooth.

Sodium Chloride (Table Salt). The usual dietary consumption is 7–15 grams daily, which includes sodium chloride already in foods, plus table salt. Excessive hot weather, sweating, and dehydration or salt depletion can be treated with extra food salt or salt tablets. For severe hypertension, restricting salt intake (sodium chloride) is often recommended.

Sodium Nitrate. Used as an additive in curing meat and fish such as bacon, bologna, corned beef, ham, hot dogs, and smoked fish. In certain conditions, nitrates in food can become toxic nitrites.

Sodium Nitrite. Both sodium nitrate and nitrite are used in cured meats as coloring, flavoring, and preservatives. Nitrites can react with heat and other conditions to form nitrosamine, sometimes cited as causing cancer in animals and therefore their use in foods has been questioned.

Sodium Restricted. Control of hypertension and prevention, control and elimination of edema, congestive heart failure, cirrhosis of the liver, cortisone therapy, kidney disease, or other fluid- or sodium-retaining conditions.

Soft Diet. A diet with a consistency between a liquid and a regular diet. It is appropriate for postoperative patients, and for those with chewing problems, gastrointestinal conditions, or severe infections. Typically, the diet allows liquids or soft texture foods that are easy to digest, containing little indigestible cellulose or tough connective tissue. Normally avoided foods include raw fruits and vegetables, coarse breads and cereals, fried and highly seasoned foods, nuts, and meats.

Sorbitol. A nutritive sweetener with the same caloric value as glucose but only half as sweet as sucrose. It is used in gums, dietetic candies, and ice cream. Overuse has been known to cause diarrhea and gastrointestinal distress.

Soybean. A highly nutritious, vegetable legume, increasingly utilized in North America by vegetarians and many mainstream health adherents. It contains large amounts of assimilable protein, low carbohydrates, high unsaturated fat, and B complex vitamins. Used widely in cereals, biscuits, artificial meat, soy milk, soybean oil, tofu, tamari, and miso.

Spaghetti. The famous cord-like Italian pasta, commonly but not exclusively, made from enriched or refined wheat grain. Other sources ground into flour are whole wheat, buckwheat, corn, rice, and Jerusalem artichoke.

Spices. The oldest food additive, of no nutritional value and part of the aromatic plant, usually not the leaves or seeds. Used as flavoring agent or preservative. Common tropically grown spice products include allspice; cinnamon; cloves; cayenne, chili, and red pepper; mace; paprika; pepper; and saffron.

Sprinkle. To scatter small food particles or drops of liquid on other foods or kitchen containers. Examples: bacon, cheese, herbs, salt, spices, and water.

Standard Recipe. Logical, sequenced instructions, utilized by food service institutions or individuals, to prepare a food item. Ideally contains ingredients; portions; method of preparation and yield.

Starch. The major form in which energy is stored in plants. Found in roots, seeds, tubers, and less in plant stems and leaves. It is over 50% of the solid matter in cereal grains and potatoes. It is important as a component of natural foods, with digestive processes ultimately converting it into dextrin, maltose, and glucose. High starch foods are rice, wheat, rye, barley, oatmeal, cornmeal, buckwheat, beans, peas, and to a lesser extent bananas and potatoes.

Steam. Cooking food in a covered container above a boiling or simmering liquid, often in a perforated container, giving off heat or vapor. Sometimes done by wrapping it in foil, leaves, or other protective covering. Steaming helps the food retain nutrients often lost when submerging the food in the liquid, such as happens in boiling or poaching.

Stew. To cook or simmer slowly in a closed container, at low heat, small cut-up pieces of mixed meat and vegetables, in a small amount of liquid which is usually served as a sauce with the food. It tenderizes food and allows the flavors to combine. Example: beef stew.

Stir. To cause food to move slightly, usually with a circular motion of a kitchen utensil, to mix, or combine solid or liquid foods.

Stock. A clear, thin, un-thickened, white or brown liquid broth, in which meats, vegetables, fish, poultry, bones, or seasonings have been cooked to extract their soluble substance, nutrients, and flavors. Stock is usually seasoned, strained, de-greased and concentrated before used as a soup, sauce, or gravy foundation. See beef, chicken or vegetable stock; sauces; gravies.

Strain. Using a cheese cloth or strainer to pass through and separate liquids and solids, such as from beef stock (bouillon) and chicken stock (consomme) and strawberry sauce. Used in puree modified diet preparation.

Sucrose. Sugar derived from the juice of sugar cane or sugar beets, commonly called table sugar or granulated, powdered, or brown sugar. The average North American dietary intake is about 100 pounds of sugar per year or 125 grams per day. The large consumption of sugar (sucrose) over long periods of time is thought to be a cause of dental problems, heart disease, and diabetes. It is sweeter than glucose and other sugars, except for fructose.

Sugar. Normally refers to cane sugar or sucrose but also to other simple carbohydrates or natural sugars such as dextrose or grape sugar; levulose or fruit sugar; lactose or milk sugar or maltose or malt sugar. A sweet, colorless, white when pure, or brown substance, used as a sweetener or food preservative. Sugar cane and sugar beets are the chief sources of sugar. It is almost 100% carbohydrate and the most efficient source of energy used by the human body. Its use is often linked to high blood sugar levels, diabetes, heart disease, and dental cavities. In food labeling, sugar is often referred to, or disguised as, dextrose, glucose, sucrose, invert sugar, brown sugar, corn syrup, molasses, or honey.

Sugar-free/Sugarless. Food labeling permits using the term sugar-free for certain calorie-containing sugar substances such as mannitol, sorbitol and xylitol. The non-nutritive sweetener saccharin, has no calories. Aspartame equals sugar in calories, but much smaller amounts yield equal sweetening capability and therefore fewer calories. While these substances are permitted with proper food labeling, all are controversial in dietary health.

Sulfites. A preservative, widely used, until recently, in the restaurant and food industry. Used on fruits, vegetables, seafood, and salad bars to keep a fresh look and to prevent discoloration and spoilage; to stop wine and beef fermentation; and as sanitizing agents for food containers and equipment. Reactions to its use have prompted the FDA to limit its use and require labeling. Sulfites are used in fruit drinks, jams, pickles, and relishes.

Sweeteners. Normally refers to non-nutritive artificial sweetening ingredients of sugar substitutes, added to foods such as coffee and colas. These are calcium, potassium, or sodium cyclamates, saccharin and sodium saccharin. Certain foods fulfill the sweetening function without unbalancing blood sugar levels. Fresh and dried fruit, maple syrup, fruit juice concentrates, and rice or barley syrup break down into glucose more slowly and are absorbed into the blood and therefore not as disturbing as most sugars.

Table Salt. A finely ground, free-flowing salt or cooking salt, used in food preparation.

Tahini. A Middle East dish, made of hulled sesame seeds ground into a butter. It is mild in flavor, nutritious, and easily digestible. Used in salad dressings, loaves, burgers, casseroles, and as a thickening agent. Examples: miso dressing; falafel, humus.

Tamari. A naturally fermented, dark, thick soy sauce from soybeans, sea salt, water, and wheat, used in place of salt but still high in sodium. Used for extra flavor in sauces, gravies, soups, and grains.

Texture Vegetable Protein (TVP). Imitation meat products, normally made by extracting the protein from soybean plants. Called meat analogs. They can be used as a filler in foods such as ground meat or as its complete substitute.

Therapeutic Diet. Modifying or changing a person's normal diet to meet necessities created by disease or injury. Usually the adding or subtracting of certain foods and nutrients, in specified amounts, to or from a diet.

Thickening Agents. These additives give body, improved texture, and consistency or coagulating properties to gravies, ice cream, baby food, pies, puddings, salad dressing, sauces, soft drinks, or salad dressings. Included are natural carbohydrate agents such as agar, arrowroot, carrageenan, corn or potato starch, flour, pectin, or tapioca. Others are chemically modified carbohydrates such as cellulose gum and modified starch. They make food thicken by absorbing part of the water present in it.

Tofu. A cheese-like gelatinous soybean curd which is white, soft, bland tasting and absorbs the flavors of the ingredients with which it is cooked. Often referred to as the "food of a thousand tastes," it is an inexpensive protein source containing all the essential amino acids. Because of its nutritional value and versatility, it can be served at any course in a meal, from appetizer to dessert.

Toxicity. All chemical substances have the ability to harm living organisms if consumed in excess quantity. Food additives are allowed at levels 100 times below where harmful effects are known to be zero. Even nutrients, such as iodine, involve a deadly risk, at high dosage levels. Metal toxicity and poisoning is common with aluminum, arsenic, cadmium, copper, lead, mercury, and nickel. Environmental and chemical poisoning is also common, as is food poisoning from microorganisms like bacteria, fungi, viruses, and worms found in milk, meat, fish, and in animal and human droppings or feces.

Trace Elements. Minerals that are essential to the diet, in small amounts, in varying quantities, less than 100 gm per day in humans. The ones found naturally or in food are iron, iodine, copper, manganese, zinc, fluorine, cobalt, molybdenum, selenium, chromium, nickel, tin, vanadium, and silicon. Trace elements are often a part of, or associated with, enzymes and function with the body at the cell level.

Triglyceride. A fatty acid and glycerol compound. They constitute most animal and vegetable fats and are the main lipids in the blood. They circulate with a protein, forming either high- or low-density lipoproteins. The combination and total amount of triglycerides and lipoproteins are key factors in the diagnosis and treatment of diabetes, heart disease, and hypertension.

Ulcerative Colitis. A chronic inflammatory and digestive disease, centered in the large intestine and rectum, producing substantial watery diarrhea that contains blood and mucous, with related fever, abdominal pain and weight loss. It is similar to Crohn's disease. Treatment involves sedatives, sulfa drugs for bowel bacteria, drugs to reduce diarrhea, and the use of a liberal bland or soft diet.

Ulcers. They occur in the gastrointestinal tract. A gastric ulcer is located in the stomach; a peptic ulcer is an open lesion on the mucosa of the stomach or small intestine; a duodenal ulcer arises in the upper third of the small intestine. Recent studies link bacteria, rather than stress, to ulcer development. Avoid alcohol, aspirin, animal fats, caffeine, carbonated drinks, fried foods, salt, smoking, and strong spices. Treatment involves using a liberal bland or soft diet.

Underweight. Less than normal body weight, usually 10 percent or more, after adjusting for age, body build, and height. Severe underweight occurs from poor appetites; with woman associating thinness with beauty; the mentally handicapped; the elderly in prolonged care nursing homes; those undergoing repeated surgical operations; and with those having long-term illnesses.

Unsaturated Fatty Acid. Fatty acids that have at least one double bond between the two carbon atoms, such as oleic, linoleic, and arachidonic acid. Saturated fats have no double bonds. A unsaturated fat is one that contains an unsaturated fatty acid. Mono-unsaturated fatty acids are found in almonds, cashews, fowl, nuts, peanuts, pecans, and olive oil. Polyunsaturated fatty acids are found in corn, cottonseeds, fish, safflower oil, soybeans, and sunflower oil. Low serum cholesterol levels are associated with diets high in polyunsaturated and low in saturated fatty acids.

Uremia. The toxic or excessive buildup of protein waste or urea in the blood and the condition in which it circulates there. The abnormal condition of having these excessive wastes in the blood, as occurs in kidney failure problems such as Bright's disease and nephritis.

Urinary Tract Infections. Normally associated with bacterial infections as cystitis (bladder infection), kidney and bladder problems, and vaginitis. The conditions are usually more common with women, characterized by urinary frequency, burning, painful voiding, blood in the urine, chills, fever, back and abdominal pain, loss of appetite, or nausea and vomiting.

Nephritis, pyelonephritis, or Bright's disease are kidney problems that are potentially serious.

USDA (U.S. Department of Agriculture). Governmental agency involved with the inspection, grading, and labeling of food products. Instrumental in promoting better nutrition by publication of the "Daily Food Guide" and subsequently the "Dietary Guidelines for Americans" in 1980.

USPHS (U.S. Public Health Service). A federal government agency responsible for controlling the arrival of substances, goods, or people from abroad, that could affect U.S. citizen health. It also sets standards for the domestic handling and processing of foods.

Vegan. A strict or total vegetarian who excludes all proteins of animal origin and uses only plant foods.

Vegan Diet. A vegetarian diet that excludes meat, poultry, fish, eggs, and dairy products.

Vegetables. All parts of the plant, cultivated and utilized for food including leaves (cabbage, lettuce, spinach); flowers (broccoli, cauliflower); roots and tubers (beets, carrots, potatoes, turnips); stems (asparagus, celery); and seeds (beans; peas, cereals). Their nutritional value is principally in vitamin and mineral content: ascorbic acid (leaves), carotene (green leafy), calcium, iron, and riboflavin. They are important in providing good roughage for diets.

Vitamins. Organic compounds required for life in small quantities in the diet to maintain good health and growth. They do not provide energy. For the most part, they cannot be synthesized by the body and must be acquired from the diet or dietary supplements. Importantly, no one food contains all the vitamins. Generally, vitamins are classified as either fat or water soluble. The fat-soluble vitamins are A, D, E, and K and are often stored in the body for long-term use; their daily requirements are lower. The water-soluble vitamins are the B complex and C and must be acquired daily because their solubility permits their excretion in urine. Vitamins are normally designated by letters or more recently by specific name.

Vitamin A. Fat soluble, derived from carotene in plants and retinol in fish and meats. The digestive tract converts carotene to retinol in animals. Beta carotene, the most common form of carotene, is found in chard, kale, and spinach (green, leafy vegetables); beans, broccoli, carrots, and yellow squash; apricots and sweet potatoes. Other good sources of vitamin A are cod and fish oils, butter, cheese, egg yolk, and milk. Toxic levels of retinol (not carotene) can occur in doses over 20,000 IUs per day. Vitamin A is necessary for visual sharpness, skeletal growth, and maintenance of mucous membranes, which combat infections.

Vitamin B Complex. Water-soluble vitamin group, differing structurally and in their biologic effect and occurring in large quantities in liver, meats, whole-grain cereals, and yeast. In some foods they appear separately or in combination. Prolonged cooking, particularly with water and heat, destroys the B vitamins.

Vitamin B1. (Thiamine) Essential in the diet for normal metabolism (energy release), especially carbohydrates; growth, and for the health of the cardiovascular and nervous systems. Storage or heating in neutral or alkaline solutions may destroy it. The body does not store it and it needs to be resupplied daily. Deficiencies affect the nervous system, circulation, and the gastrointestinal tract. The best thiamine food sources are brewer's yeast, legumes, organ meats, peanuts, pork, soybeans, wheat germ, and sesame and sunflower seeds. Other sources are whole grain bread and cereals, eggs, fish, fruits, meats, milk, nuts, pasta, poultry, rice, and vegetables.

Vitamin B2. (Riboflavin) Heat stable but destroyed by light exposure. Functions as a coenzyme in the metabolism (energy release) of carbohydrates, fats, and proteins and is essential for successful reproduction and for the health of skin, eyes, and nerve tissues. It is not widely stored in the body, requiring daily intake. The bodily amounts needed vary according to body size, metabolic rate, and growth rate. Widely available in plant and animal tissues. The richest riboflavin food sources are dried yeast, wheat germ and bran, enriched bread, cheese, eggs, leafy vegetables, lean meats, legumes, liver and kidneys, and milk.

Vitamin B6. (Pyridoxine) Functions as a coenzyme, essential to producing and breaking down proteins; makes red blood cells to transport oxygen; glycogen to glucose; antibody production; vitamin B12 absorption; hydrochloric acid and magnesium production; and maintains sodium and potassium balance, which regulates body fluids and proper functioning of the central nervous and muscle/skeletal systems. Pyridoxine is heat stable but sensitive to light and alkalies. Deficiencies are rare but may be seen in chronic alcoholics and from the use of drugs as penicillamine. Increased needs are warranted during aging, cardiac failure, lactation, oral contraceptive use, pregnancy, and radiation exposure. Rich dietary food sources include brewer's yeast, molasses, organ meats, peanuts, rice, salmon, soybeans, wheat germ, and whole grain cereals.

Vitamin B12. (Cobalamin) Cyanocobalamin is an active form of cobalamin, a generic name for various B12 forms. It is essential for the metabolism of carbohydrates, fats, and proteins, for normal blood cell formation, and nerve functions. A lack of cobalamin can result in pernicious anemic. Its deficiency often results in other vitamin deficiencies, particularly folacin. It occurs in animal sources and strict vegetarians can develop deficiencies. It is heat stable but inactivated by acids or alkalies. Rich sources are dairy products, fish, kidney, liver, and muscle meats.

Biotin. Acts as a coenzyme in the synthesis and oxidation of saturated fatty acids and carbohydrates. It's closely linked to the utilization of protein, folic acid, pantothenic acid and cobalamin (vitamin B12). Excellent food sources are widespread and include beef liver, brewer's yeast, cauliflower, dried peas, egg yolk, kidney and liver, mushrooms, roasted peanuts, and unpolished rice.

Choline. Essential for fat metabolism in the body; the normal functioning of nerves; and is a component, along with inositol, of lecithin. Rich food sources include beef liver, egg yolk, green beans, legumes, meats, peas, soybeans, spinach, and wheat germ. Milk and vegetables are moderately good sources.

Folacin. (Folic Acid) Essential for red blood cell growth and reproduction. With Vitamin B12 and C, it acts as a coenzyme in the use and breakdown of proteins and nucleic acid formation (DNA and RNA). It stimulates hydrochloric acid production for digestion and increases the appetite. Deficiencies produce anemia, diarrhea, poor growth, grey hair, and stomach and gastrointestinal problems. It is unstable under conditions of heat, light, and lengthy storage. Increased needs are normal during infancy, pregnancy, and stress. The best food sources are asparagus, dry beans, broccoli, collards, lentils, liver, and spinach. Other good sources are green leafy vegetables, nuts, kidney, and whole wheat products.

Inositol. Its role as a vitamin is not clear, although it occurs widely in plant and animal cells and may be an essential cell constituent. Good food sources are the bran of cereal grains, heart, liver, peanuts, and yeast.

Niacin. Functions as a coenzyme required for the metabolism and use of all major nutrients. Essential for healthy skin, gastrointestinal functioning, nervous system maintenance, and synthesis of the sex hormones. It likely is useful in circulation improvement and reducing high blood cholesterol levels. Deficiencies may result in pellagra, a nerve disease. It is not stored in the body and any excess is excreted, requiring daily replenishment. Rich sources of niacin and its precursor tryptophan include most foods high in thiamine and riboflavin, such as brewer's yeast, fish, lean meats, legumes, liver, nuts, and whole grains. Other good sources are peanut butter, rice, and wheat germ.

Pantothenic Acid. A part of coenzyme A, necessary for the intermediate metabolism of carbohydrates, fats, and proteins, including synthesis, breakdown, and food energy release. It is a component also involved in fatty acid synthesis. It exists in all cells and all natural foods, especially eggs, heart, liver, peanuts, peas, salmon, wheat and rice germ and bran and yeast. Good sources also include broccoli, milk, mushrooms, poultry, sweet potatoes, and whole grains. It is destroyed by acid, alkali, and long-term dry heat. Many canned foods and frozen vegetables and meats lose up to 50% of it.

Vitamin C. (Ascorbic Acid) Essential for forming collagen that holds together cells and tissues in bone, cartilage, skin, teeth, and connective tissue. It strengthens blood vessels; resists bacterial infections; helps wounds heal; aids in iron absorption; prevents oxidation; may help prevent cancer; and lowers the blood cholesterol of people with atherosclerosis. It is water soluble and readily absorbed into the bloodstream but is destroyed by the oxidation that heating accelerates in cooking vegetables. Canning, freezing, or dehydration also causes loss. The best sources of Vitamin C are citrus fruits; rose hips; broccoli, brussel sprouts, cabbage, and leafy green or yellow vegetables; liver, potatoes, and tomatoes.

Vitamin D. A fat-soluble vitamin necessary for normal bone and teeth growth and for helping absorb calcium and phosphorus from food into the body. The natural accumulation of it in normal foods is small and requirements are often met by the enrichment or fortification of milk and dairy products or exposure to sunlight. Fish liver oils, egg yolk, saltwater fish, salmon, sardines, or organ meats are animal sources. A deficiency in infants may cause rickets, and is corrected by using vitamin D fortified milk; while in adults, osteomalacia or osteoporosis may occur.

Vitamin E. A group of fat-soluble vitamins, consisting of tocopherol, and sensitive to ultraviolet light and oxidation. They prevent oxidation (destruction) of polyunsaturated and other fatty acids, Vitamin A, blood cells, and hormones of the pituitary, adrenal, and sex glands. They are essential for normal reproduction, muscle development, health of the cells, and proper functioning of the immune system. The richest dietary sources are wheat germ, vegetable oils (soybean, corn, cottonseed and peanut), butter, eggs, liver, margarine, nuts, soybeans, sweet potatoes, whole grain cereals, whole raw seeds, and vegetable leaves, such as turnip greens. It can be stored in the body for long periods, preventing severe deficiencies.

Vitamin K. A group of fat-soluble, light-sensitive vitamins vital to blood clotting. It occurs widely in foods, especially leafy green vegetables and it can be produced by intestinal bacteria. Rich sources are alfalfa, cabbage, cauliflower, egg yolk, fish liver oils, kelp, molasses, pork liver, soybeans, spinach, vegetable oils, and yogurt.

Water. Nothing survives without water and nothing takes place in the body without it playing a vital role. The body requires and uses it for almost all its primary functions including transporting nutrients; building tissue; maintaining temperature; digestion; absorption; circulation; and excretion. It's needed in all processes of converting food into energy and tissue. It cushions the joints and internal organs against shock; lubricates and moistens tissues such as air passages, eyes, and lungs; and protects the fetus during pregnancy. Water is a major component of most foods, except for fats, dry cereals, and pure sugar. Human weight is over 50% water.

Water-Soluble Vitamins. A group consisting of Vitamin C and six B-complex vitamins: thiamine (B1), riboflavin (B2), pyridoxine (B6), cobalamin (B12), folacin, and niacin. Water-soluble vitamins serve as coenzymes and convert the carbohydrate, fat, and protein digestion end products into body energy.

Whip. Rapidly beating a food product to create air. Examples: egg whites, fruit whip or heavy cream.

Yeast. Naturally occurring one-celled fungi that promotes fermentation and begins chemical processes that make beer, bread, butter, cheese, and wine. The many varieties of yeast, brewer's, dry, and fresh, are rich in protein and the B-complex vitamins.

Bibliography

Adams, Catherine F. *Handbook of the Nutritional Value of Foods in Common Units.* Prepared by Catherine F. Adams for the United States Department of Agriculture. New York: Dover Publications, Inc., 1986.

American Dietetic Association. Position of the American Dietetic Association: Appropriate use of nutritive and non-nutritive sweeteners. *J Am Diet Assoc* (1987) 87(12): 1689.

American Heart Association. *Recommendations for Treatment of Hyperlipidemia in Adults.* Publication No. 72-204-A. Dallas: American Heart Association, 1986.

Addes, P. "Coronary Heart Disease, An Update with Emphasis on Dietary Lipid Oxidation Products," *Food and Nutrition News,* 62 (2), Chicago: National Livestock and Meat Board, 1990.

American Diabetes Association. Nutritional recommendations and principles for individuals with diabetes mellitus: 1986. *Diabetes Care* 10:126, 1987.

American Diabetes Association and American Dietetic Association. *Family Cookbook, Vol. III.* Simon and Schuster, 1987.

American Diabetes Association and American Dietetic Association, The Exchange Lists for Meal Planning, 1995.

The American Heart Association. *American Heart Association Cookbook, Fifth Edition.* New York: Random House, Inc., 1991.

Anderson, J. W. Fiber and health: An overview. *American Journal Gastroenterol* 81(892) 1986.

Barkie, Karen E. *Sweet and Sugarfree.* New York: St. Martin Press, 1982.

Baskette, Michael, C.W.C., C.C.E. and Mainella, Eleanor, R.D. *The Art of Nutritional Cooking.* New York: Van Nostrand Reinhold, 1992.

Balch, James F., M.D. and Balch, Phyllis A., C.N.C. *Prescription for Nutritional Healing.* Avery Publishing Group, Inc. 1990.

Beebe, C. A. Obesity management in people with diabetes. *Diabetes Spectrum* 1:17, 1988.

Brody, Jane E. *Jane Brody's Nutrition Book.* revised edition New York: W. W. Norton & Co., 1987.

Brody, Jane A. *Jane Brody's Good Food Book.* New York: Bantam Books, 1985.

Brody, Jane A. Jane Brody's Good Food Gourmet, New York: W. W. Norton and Co., 1990.

Claudio, Virginia S., Ph.D., M.N.S., R.D. and Lagua, Rosalinda T., M.P.S., M.N.S., R.D. *Nutrition and Diet Therapy Dictionary.* 3rd ed. New York: Van Nostrand Reinhold, 1991.

Connell, A. The role of fiber in the gastrointestinal tract. In *The Clinical Role of Fibre.* Toronto: Medical Education Services, Inc., 1985.

Conner, Sonja L., M.S., R.D. and Conner, William E., M.D. *The New American Diet.* New York: Simon and Schuster, 1986.

De Bakey, Michael E., M.D., Gotto, Antonio M., Jr., M.D., Ph.D., Scott, Lynn W., M.A., R.D., Foreyt, John P., Ph.D. *The Living Heart Diet.* New York: Simon and Schuster, 1984.

Donovan, Mary Deirdre. *The Professional Chef's Techniques of Healthy Cooking.* New York: Van Nostrand Reinhold, 1993.

Drummond, Karen Eich, M.S., R.D. *Nutrition for the Foodservice Professional.* New York: Van Nostrand Reinhold, 1989.

Drummond, K. E., R.D., Vastano, J. F., R.D., Vastano, J. C. *Cook's Healthy Handbook.* New York: John Wiley & Sons, Inc., 1993.

Fettman, John ed. *Prevention Magazine, Food and Nutrition,* Emmaus, PA Rodale Press, 1993.

Florida Dietetic Association. *Diet Manual, Manual of Clinical Dietetics.* Revised 1992. Gainesville, Fla.: Florida Dietetic Assn., 1992.

Gisslen, Wayne. *Advanced Professional Cooking.* New York: John Wiley & Sons, 1992.

Gisslen, Wayne: Professional Cooking. 2d ed. New York: John Wiley & Sons, 1989.

Hartbarger, Janie Coulter and Hartbarger, Neil J. *Eating for the Eighties, A Complete Guide to Vegetarian Nutrition.* New York: Berkley Publication Group, 1983.

Hodges, Carol A. *Culinary Nutrition for Foodservices Professionals.* New York: Van Nostrand Reinhold, 1989.

Hoeg, J. M. Managing the Patient with Hypercholesterolemia. *Nutrition and the M.D.,* 13(9), 1987.

Holt, K. M., and Isenberg, J. I. Peptic ulcer disease: Physiology and pathophysiology. *Hosp Pract* 20(1): 89, 1985.

Howard, R., Herbold, N. *Nutrition in Clinical Care.* New York: McGraw-Hill Book Company, 1978.

Kruppa, Carole. *The Love Your Heart, Low Cholesterol Cookbook.* New York: Surrey Books, 1990.

Lappe, F. M.: *Diet for a Small Plant.* New York: Ballantine Books, 1982.

MacGregor, G. A.: Dietary sodium and potassium intake and blood pressure. *Lancet* 1:750, 1983.

The American Dietetic Association. *Manual of Clinical Dietetics.* Chicago: The Chicago Dietetic Association and The South Suburban Dietetic Association, 1988.

McCormick and Co. *Spices of the World Cookbook.* New York: McGraw-Hill Book Co., 1984.

Green, J. and Haller, H. eds. *Meal Planning Approaches in the Nutrition Management of the Person with Diabetes.* Chicago: Diabetes Care and Education Practice Group, ADA, 1987.

Mosby. *Mosby's Medical and Nursing Dictionary.* St. Louis: C. V. Mosby Company, 1983.

National Academy of Sciences. *Recommended Dietary Allowances.* 10th Edition. Washington, D.C.: Food and Nutrition Board Commission on Life Sciences National Research Council, National Academy Press, 1989.

National Institutes of Health. *Cholesterol Counts,* NIH Publication. No. 85-2699. U.S. Department of Health and Human Services, October, 1985.

Null, Gary. *The Vegetarian Handbook.* New York: St. Martin's Press, 1987.

Nunnelley Hamilton, Eva M., M.S., Whitney, Eleanor N., Ph.D., R.D., Sizer, Frances S., M.S.: *Nutrition Concepts and Controversies.* 5th ed. St. Paul, MN. West Publishing Company, 1991.

Powers, M. A., ed. *Nutrition Guide for Professionals: Diabetes Education and Meal Planning.* Alexandria, Va: American Diabetes Association and The American Dietetic Association, 1988.

Parry, J. W. *The Story of Spices.* New York: Chemical Publishing Co., 1953.

Pennington, A. T., Ph.D. ed. *Bowes and Church's Food Values of Portions Commonly Used.* 15th ed. Revised by Jean A. T. Pennington, Ph.D., R.D. New York: Harper Collins, 1989.

Prevention Magazine. *The Complete Book of Vitamins and Minerals.* pub. city: Emmaus, PA Rodale Press and Wings Books, 1992.

Riely, Elizabeth. *The Chef's Companion.* New York: Van Nostrand Reinhold, 1986.

Rubash, Joyce, R.D. *Master Dictionary of Food and Wine.* New York: Van Nostrand Reinhold, 1990.

Schneider, Sally, Stewart, Tabori & Chang. *The Art of Low-Calorie Cooking.* New York: publisher, 1990.

Shils, M. E., and Young, V. R. *Modern Nutrition in Health and Disease.* 7th ed. Philadelphia: Lea & Febiger, 1988.

Shugart, Grace and Molt, Mary. *Food for Fifty.* New York: Macmillan Publishing Company, 1993.

Slavin, J. L. Dietary fiber: Classification, chemical analyses, and food sources. *J Am Diet Assoc,* 1987, 87:1164.

Stobart, Tom. Herbs, *Spices and Flavorings.* New York: The Overlook Press, 1982.

Suitor, Carol West. *Nutrition: Principles and Applications in Health Promotion.* 2d ed. Philadelphia: J. B. Lippincott, 1984.

Turner, Stephanie, M.P.H., R.D. and Aronowitz, Vivien, M.P.H., R.D. *Healthwise Quantity Cookbook: Area Agency on Aging San Mateo County,* Ca. Washington, D.C.: Center for Science in the Public Interest 1990.

Tver, David. The Nutrition and Health Encyclopedia, 2d ed. New York: Van Nostrand Reinhold, 1989.

United States Department of Agriculture. *Human Nutrition Information Service Dietary Guidelines for Americans: Avoid Too Much Fat, Saturated Fat and Cholesterol.* Home and Garden Bulletin, Number 232-3, April, 1986.

Warshaw, Hope. *The Restaurant Companion.* Chicago, IL: Surrey, 1990.

Watson, Gail C. *Cooking Naturally for Pleasure and Health.* Davie, FL: Falkynor Books, 1982.

Wilson, Randy J. *Non-Chew Cookbook.* 4th ed. Denver, CO: Wilson Publishing, Inc. 1985.

About the Authors

Sandra J. Frank, Ed.D., L.D., R.D., is the President of Nutrition by Design, specializing in customized and computerized menu, recipe, and nutrition services. As a consultant to the health care industry and commercial food service, she produces and develops recipes and menus. Dr. Frank consults on operations, menu planning, food preparation, food delivery, and quality assurance. Well over 200 facilities and organizations in the United States and Canada have utilized her computer assessments and menus. Dr. Frank's menus currently feed over 25,000 people a day.

Dr. Frank provides recipe analysis and nutritional consulting services for weekly food sections in newspapers such as the Atlanta Constitution, the Detroit Free Press, the Fort Lauderdale Sun-Sentinel, and the Fort Worth Star. In addition, she provides recipe analysis and nutrition consultation to national publications, such as Bon Appétit Magazine.

Her 15 years of experience in the area of dietetics includes operational positions as food service and purchasing director in skilled nursing facilities; administrative and clinical dietitian; Dietetic Technician Program Director at Broward Community College and community-based nutritional services for senior citizen, handicapped and AIDS nutrition programs.

Her associations have included the National Retirement Corporation, Reinhart Foods, PYA/Monarch, GA Food Service, Mid-America Food Service, Jewish Vocational Services, Colonnade Medical Center, and Cure AIDS NOW.

Her active memberships include the American Dietetic Association, Florida Dietetic Association, Broward County Dietetic Association, Society for Nutrition Education, and the International Food Services Executive Association (IFSEA). She has been appointed by the Governor of Florida to the Long-Term Care Ombudsman Council and has served on the Dietetic Association Legislative Committee and on the advisory councils for Florida International University and Broward Community College.

Dr. Frank holds an undergraduate degree from Brooklyn College, majoring in foods and nutrition; a masters degree from Long Island University in medical biology, and a Doctorate Degree in Education from Florida Atlantic University.

Robert E. Baker, CFE, is currently the Vice-President of Marketing and Programs for the International Food Service Executives Association (IFSEA) and is editor and feature writer for their HOT-LINE and INSIDE SCOOP publications.

He directly oversees IFSEA Publications, a major distributor of culinary, nutrition, and foodservice management books to industry professionals.

He has been a nutritional and personal health care advocate for over 25 years. Bob was heavily influenced by his father, an early 1950s nutritional pioneer, who converted his own nationally known restaurant to one of the nation's first health-food oriented restaurants. For ten years, Bob's father operated a health-food store, hosted a local radio show, and spoke on nutrition subjects to schools and universities. Bob later co-founded a company distributing food supplements and health-food products to the retail sector.

Bob is a graduate of the Cornell School of Hotel Restaurant Management and has a widely diversified food service and hospitality background. His food service career has spanned restaurants (fast food to theme), hotels, resorts, clubs, airlines, and bar/lounges. He has held positions from busboy to owner and has opened over 15 different facilities in three states and seven countries.

Bob is a Certified Food Executive (CFE) and has been a member of the Cornell Society of Hotelmen, Hawaii Restaurant Association, Jamaica Hotel Association, Philadelphia Convention and Tourist Bureau, and IFSEA.

Index

American cuisine
  breakfast and brunch, 18–19
  cafeterias, 19
  delicatessen, 19
  family style, 19–20
  fast food, 19–20
  mall or food courts, 20–21
  pizza parlors, 21
  salad bars, 22
  sandwich shops, 22–23
  submarine shops, 22–23
American Diabetes Association, 55
American Dietetic Association, 55
Anorexia, 30
Atherosclerosis, 52

Basic Four Food Groups, 3, 5
Blood glucose, 55–56
Blood pressure, 55

Calcium, 74
Calories
  and food labeling, 7–9
  and USDA Food Guide Pyramid, 3–6
  in vegetarian diets, 73
Calorie banking, 16
Cancer, 3, 6, 32
Carbohydrates, 3–9
Cardiovascular disease, 32–36
Cholesterol
  in diabetic and calorie-controlled diets, 55
  and food labeling, 7–9
  restricted foods, 52
  and shopping, 11–12
  and USDA Food Guide Pyramid, 3
Cirrhosis, 11–12
Colitis
  peptic, 34
  ulcerative, 49
Consistency- and texture-modified diets
  high fiber, 47–49
  low fiber, 50–51
  mechanical soft, 43–45
  puree, 46
  soft or surgical soft, 41–43

Constipation, 47
Cortisone therapy, 36
Crohn's disease, 49

Dehydration, 30
Diabetes
  and fatty diets, 6
  and food labeling, 6
  management, 55–56
  and the regular diet, 32
Diabetic and calorie-
    controlled diets
  Calculated calorie diets, 56–58
  No concentrated sweets diet, 56–57
Diarrhea, 30, 34, 47
Dietary Goals For the United States, 3
Dietary Guidelines for Americans, 3
Dietitian, 29, 56
Diet planning
  diet modification, 29
  diet therapy, 29
  implementation problems, 29–31
  implementation process, 31
Dining out
  changing food intake patterns, 17
  developing a plan, 16
  eating environment, 17
  food portions, 15
  frequency, 14
  fullness, 17
  ground rules, 14
  high fat buzzwords, 17
  high sodium buzzwords, 17
  menu choices, 15
  menu warning words, 17
  mindset, 16
  minimizing fat intake, 15
  preplanning strategies, 16
  restaurant eating skills, 14
  selecting restaurants, 14
  special requests, 15
  what to eat, 17–18
  where to stop, 17–27
Diverticulosis, 34, 47, 49
Dysphagia, 45

DATE DUE

GAYLORD			PRINTED IN U.S.A.